The
CANON LAW
LETTER & SPIRIT

In accordance with n.3 of the Norms issued by the Cardinal Secretary of State on 28 January 1983, the translation into English of the text of the Code of Canon Law which appears in this volume has received the approval of the Bishops' Conferences of Australia, Canada, England and Wales, India, Ireland, New Zealand, Scotland and Southern Africa

THE CANON LAW

LETTER & SPIRIT

A PRACTICAL GUIDE TO THE CODE OF CANON LAW

Prepared by
**The Canon Law Society
of Great Britain and Ireland**

in association with
The Canadian Canon
Law Society

Editorial Board:
Rt Rev. Mgr Gerard Sheehy, JCD (Dublin), Chairman
Rt Rev. Mgr Ralph Brown, JCD (Westminster)
Rev. Donal Kelly, JCL (Ossory)
Rev. Aidan McGrath OFM, JCD

Consultant Editor:
Rev. Francis G. Morrisey OMI, JCD (Ottawa)

VERITAS

VERITAS PUBLICATIONS
7–8 Lower Abbey Street, Dublin 1

© The Canon Law Society Trust 1995

All rights reserved. No part of this publication may be reproduced or transmitted in any form or by any means, electronic or mechanical including photocopying, recording or any information storage or retrieval system, without prior permission in writing from the publishers.

First published 1995

ISBN 1–85390–290–X

Nihil obstat: Jerome Curtin JCD
Censor deputatus

Imprimatur: Desmond Connell
Archbishop of Dublin
Dublin, 4 November 1995

The *Nihil obstat* and *imprimatur* are a declaration that a book or pamphlet is considered to be free from doctrinal or moral error. It is not implied that those who have granted the *Nihil obstat* and *Imprimatur* agree with the contents, opinions or statements expressed.

The arms on the cover are those of St Pius X, patron of the Canon Law Society of Great Britain and Ireland.

Typeset by Pantek Arts, Maidstone, Kent.
Printed and bound in Great Britain by Redwood Books, Trowbridge, Wiltshire.

Contents

General Introduction	vii
Apostolic Constitution	xi
Address by Pope John Paul II to CLSGBI, Rome 1992	xvii
Abbreviations	xx
Some Standard Authors and Commentaries	xxiv

THE CODE OF CANON LAW

Book I	General Norms	1
Book II	The People of God	115
Book III	The Teaching Office of the Church	415
Book IV	The Sanctifing Office of the Church	455
Book V	The Temporal Goods of the Church	707
Book VI	Sanctions in the Church	749
Book VII	Judicial Procedures	811

Table of Canons	972
Concordance 1983 Code – 1917 Code	981
Contributors	996
Glossary	998
Index	999

General Introduction

When the revised Code of Canon Law was promulgated in January 1983, a first reaction of the Canon Law Society of Great Britain and Ireland was to consider publishing, for the assistance of those concerned, a commentary on the canons of the new Code. However, a more pressing need quickly presented itself: that namely of making publicly available an official translation into the English language of the text of the Code itself. This was undertaken at once, and its first edition was published (Collins, London) in September 1983, some two months before the promulgated Code itself was to come into effect on 27 November of that year.

In the twelve years intervening since then, work on the present commentary and guide has been proceeding consistently. Expert contributors were invited to participate in the endeavour, from Great Britain, from Ireland, and from Canada. This interval of years has not been without its distinct advantages: indeed it has provided the very positive benefit of enabling this Society to estimate the public reaction to the Code throughout the Church, to consider the intervening contributions of many learned commentators, and in general to evaluate the place of this new law in the life of the Church, particularly in the light of the Second Vatican Council.

As is to be expected at every stage of world development, modern culture, particularly perhaps in the so-called developed world, has produced many new trends, some obviously good and advantageous to society, others of at least dubious if not threatening quality.

The latter half of the twentieth century has had no small measure of such trends.

Among these has been a clear, if not always explicitly expressed, misrepresentation of the role of law in society. The resurgence of democracy – as opposed to the totalitarianism which in so many countries marked the middle years of the outgoing millennium – has tended to implant in the minds of some the idea that law is little more than a constraint upon individual freedom.

This trend has not left the Church untouched. Those who were brought up under the 1917 Code – still a majority, albeit inevitably a dwindling one – have been faced not so much with a resurgence of democracy as with the feeling in the late 1960s that the Second Vatican Council was aimed at a liberation from the constraints of legal regulation: a 'new Church', an 'open Church', a Church which would be quite other than its so-called 'institutional' predecessor.

General Introduction

That the Second Vatican Council introduced a new and enlightening development of thinking into the Church is beyond dispute – as indeed did its preceding Ecumenical Councils, each in its own way and in respect of the particular problems facing the Church at the respective times. The suggestion that the Second Vatican Council introduced the concept of a fundamentally 'new Church' is manifestly false, as will be apparent to anyone who reads carefully through its official documents.

It is against this background that the current Code of Canon Law has to be measured. It was not without purpose that in 1977, while the revision process was still at its early stages, Pope Paul VI required that 'the new Code must prove to be an instrument most finely adapted to the life of the Church'. Nor was it without point that, on the occasion of its promulgation in 1983, Pope John Paul II described the Code as 'the final document of the Second Vatican Council'.

It was clearly this very same point which the Pope had in mind when, in Rome in May 1992, he graciously addressed the 35th annual Conference of this Canon Law Society. The full text of the Holy Father's address (see pp. xvii–xix below) merits a careful reading, not least because of its clear presentation of the place of Canon Law in the life of the Church. A special note must be made of the admonition that:

> **'canonical theory and practice always need to be informed by a sound ecclesiological understanding, and *efforts must always be made to avoid any undue accommodation of ecclesial norms and structures to the prevailing ethos of civil society.*'**

Two points, in particular, may be highlighted from the Pope's address, both of which have from the beginning been central to the aspiration of this commentary.

It is designed to be of its nature pastoral: 'what do I do in this or that practical situation?' – in my parish, in my school, in my religious institute, in my relationship with the State, and so on. The Pope has spelled out the principle:

> **'You are engaged in a service which is ultimately pastoral in nature, for it seeks to strengthen the bonds of communion in the Church through fidelity to the Gospel and the promotion of justice. How often in this delicate and important task are you called upon ... to bring healing and hope in fragile situations of human weakness and sin! ... always keep in mind the eminently pastoral nature of all church law which, while never derogating from the demands of truth, has as its final aim the salvation of souls.'**

At the same time, there is the other, equally important, side of the coin, equally recognised by the Pope. Canon Law, established as it is among the major world systems of law, can make sense only to the extent that its philosophy, its history and its precedents are taken into account – all of which

General Introduction

elements are, in the context of the nature of the Church, acutely noted by the Pope in the same address to this Society:

> '... the letter and spirit of canonical legislation should reflect ever more fully the distinct nature of the Church as the sacrament of union with God and the unity of the whole human race (see Vat. II LG 1). The (Second Vatican) Council ... insisted that the reality of this earthly society, endowed with hierarchical structures, may not be separated from her reality as a spiritual and heavenly community of faith, hope and love, the mystical body of Christ (see ibid. 8). Because the Church's social structure stands at the service of a deeper mystery and communion, Canon Law – precisely as the law of the Church – must be acknowledged as unique in its means and in its ends. ... Only in the light of a sound appreciation of the mystery of the Church will Canon Law become, as it must be, an effective instrument for the continual renewal of ecclesial life.'

Any commentary such as this must, therefore, be not only pastoral but also scholarly in its approach. Apart from those who will rightly seek answers to their practical problems of the here and now, there are clearly many others who would wish to enquire further and to research the reasons why. It is the aim of this commentary – not least in its footnotes – to attempt to assist these too. In the course of its compilation, a vast amount of research and of academic endeavour has been employed by so many accomplished and dedicated canonists. It is our hope that their labours will contribute to further fruitful research in the name of the Church.

In a very real sense, therefore, this volume is presented as a new venture into commentaries on the Code of Canon Law. It is aimed at the simultaneous combination of a practical guide and an academic investigation: not perhaps an easy amalgam to achieve, but one which would appear to be required by the overall pastoral need of the moment.

One particular corollary ought to be mentioned. Canon Law is, as has been noted, one of the instruments which enables the members of the Church to achieve that which, to them, their membership means: part of the path to the salvation earned by Christ on Calvary. It is not of course the only path – no more than is dogmatic theology, moral theology, sacred scripture, church history, etc.: all of which are, each in its own way, necessary. The specific point is that Canon Law does remain *an integral part* of this path. Without an appropriate law, the basic structure would inevitably collapse.

Two further points may be briefly made.

In the first place, even at an immediate glance the very structure of this new Code will be seen to be substantially different from its 1917 predecessor. Gone, for example, are the archaic Roman-law divisions into such as *Persons*, *Things*, etc.: instead, we have *The People of God* and then a clear definition of the various functions of the Church in the current world: a manifestly sensible adjustment of expression to the changed conditions so perceptively recognised by the Second Vatican Council.

Secondly, there is a clear decentralisation which, in various ways, had been called for before and during and since the Vatican Council. One of the problems of making laws for a universal Church, embracing as it does the whole world, is that of accommodating those laws to the ethos of the various and often differing local, cultural, historical, pastoral and other such circumstances of each country or region. Many will have thought that the 1917 Code was over-centralised in this regard. The Second Vatican Council opened the door to a moderate and measured decentralisation which, in so many areas of Church life, permitted local Bishops' Conferences to make their own laws for the areas under their control – subject to the overall supervision of the Holy See, the bastion of unity in the Church. This is a significantly distinctive aspect of the new Code. It remains an aspect to which Bishops' Conferences have yet much room within which to make a serious contribution to the true place of Canon Law in the life of the Church.

A further point must be made in respect of the English-language translation of the text of the Code itself. This volume carries a new and substantially revised version of that which was authorised and published in 1983. Thanks in large measure to a widespread consultation and to many helpful suggestions from our colleagues and friends in canonical circles worldwide, the text in this volume represents the up-to-date version approved by the eight Bishops' Conferences concerned, each of which has been specifically consulted in this regard. As such, it supersedes the version published in 1983.

Those who must first be thanked are clearly all of the contributors who by their generous industry, energy and scholarship have made this commentary possible. Primary among these are of course the members of our own Canon Law Society of Great Britain and Ireland, whose input into the work has amounted to substantially more than half of the whole. A special word of gratitude is due to the Canadian Canon Law Society, so many of whose members generously agreed to cooperate with us in this venture: to each and all go our deeply appreciative and abiding thanks. They will, I know, understand if we single out for particular mention three of their number: Father Robert Harris, the then-President who in 1990 had the vision to see and approve the merit of this combined project; Dr Michel Thériault of Saint Paul University in Ottawa, who has so helpfully and understandingly coordinated our link with all the contributors from Canada; Father Frank Morrisey OMI, a former Dean of the Faculty of Canon Law at Saint Paul University, who at an early stage became our Consultant Editor and has remained ever since a greatly valued guide and support.

To those detailed on our List of Contributors (pp. 996–997) must gratefully be added the names of Father Lawrence Bordonaro CR, JCD (Toronto) and

General Introduction

of Father William Woestman OMI, JCD (Ottawa), each of whom devoted their expertise to a very substantial contribution, by way of source material, to the commentary on, respectively, Cann. 96–196 and 1656–1716, but generously preferred to leave others the credit for the ultimately edited text.

Our thanks must go to Father Gregory McGrane OFMConv. who, under the guidance of Mgr Ralph Brown, is the architect of the Index to this volume.

We remain greatly indebted to Father Austin Flannery OP, the general editor of the invaluable two-volume collection of the conciliar and post-conciliar documents of Vatican II: very generously he gave us permission to cite at will from these volumes.

Finally, but by no means in last place, must be mentioned the other three members of this Editorial Board: Mgr Ralph Brown, Father Donal Kelly and Father Aidan McGrath OFM. Without their indefatigable help, their unrelenting devotedness and their perceptive scholarship, this work simply could not have seen the light of day.

To Miss Ann Lee who from the beginning so generously and assiduously helped to guide this work to its hopefully successful conclusion, and to Mrs Maeve Monahan who so efficiently bore the brunt of all the typing and computerisation involved, must go the abiding gratitude of every member of our Society.

The volume itself is devotedly offered *in bonum Ecclesiae Christi*.

MGR GERARD SHEEHY
CHAIRMAN: EDITORIAL BOARD
DUBLIN, 1 NOVEMBER 1995, THE SOLEMNITY OF ALL SAINTS

APOSTOLIC CONSTITUTION

*To Our Venerable Brothers
the Cardinals, Archbishops, Bishops, Priests, Deacons
and to the other members of the People of God*

JOHN PAUL, BISHOP

SERVANT OF THE SERVANTS OF GOD

For an Everlasting Memorial

OVER the course of time, the Catholic Church has been wont to revise and renew the laws of its sacred discipline so that, maintaining always fidelity to the Divine Founder, these laws may be truly in accord with the salvific mission entrusted to the Church. With this sole aim in view, we today, 25 January 1983, bring to fulfilment the anticipation of the whole Catholic world, and decree the publication of the revised Code of Canon Law. In doing so, our thoughts turn back to this same date in 1959, when our predecessor, John XXIII of happy memory, first publicly announced his personal decision to reform the current body of canonical laws which had been promulgated on the feast of Pentecost 1917.

This decision to renew the Code was taken with two others, of which that Pontiff spoke on the same day: they concerned his desire to hold a synod of the diocese of Rome and to convoke an Ecumenical Council. Even if the former does not have much bearing on the reform of the Code, the latter on the other hand, namely the Council, is of the greatest importance for our theme and is closely linked with its substance.

If one asks why John XXIII had clearly perceived the need to reform the current Code, perhaps the answer is found in the 1917 Code itself. There is however another reason, the principal one, namely that the reform of the Code of Canon Law was seen to be directly sought and requested by the Council itself, which had particularly concentrated its attention upon the Church.

As is quite clear, when the first announcement of the revision of the Code was made, the Council was something totally in the future. Moreover, the acts of its teaching authority, and particularly its teaching on the Church, were to be developed over the years 1962–65. Nevertheless, one cannot fail to see that John XXIII's insight was most accurate, and his proposal must rightly be acknowledged as one which looked well ahead to the good of the Church.

Apostolic Constitution

Therefore, the new Code which appears today necessarily required the prior work of the Council and, although it was announced together with that ecumenical gathering, it follows it in order of time, since the tasks needed for its preparation could not begin until the Council had ended.

Turning our thoughts today to the beginning of that long journey, that is to 25 January 1959 and to John XXIII himself, the originator of the review of the Code, we must acknowledge that this Code drew its origin from one and the same intention, namely the renewal of christian life. All the work of the Council drew its norms and its shape principally from that same intention.

If we now turn our attention to the nature of the labours which preceded the promulgation of the Code and to the manner in which they were performed, especially during the Pontificates of Paul VI, John Paul I and then up to this present day, it is vital to make quite clear that these labours were brought to their conclusion in an eminently collegial spirit. This not only relates to the external composition of the work, but it affects also the very substance of the laws which have been drawn up.

This mark of collegiality by which the process of this Code's origin was prominently characterised, is entirely in harmony with the teaching authority and the nature of the Second Vatican Council. The Code therefore, not only because of its content but because also of its origin, demonstrates the spirit of this Council in whose documents the Church, the universal sacrament of salvation (cf. Const. *Lumen Gentium* n.9, 48), is presented as the People of God, and its hierarchical constitution is shown as founded on the College of Bishops together with its Head.

For this reason therefore, the Bishops and Bishops' Conferences were invited to associate themselves with the work of preparing the new Code, so that through a task of such length, in as collegial a manner as possible, little by little the juridical formulae would come to maturity and would then serve the whole Church. During the whole period of this task, experts also took part, people endowed with particular academic standing in the areas of theology, history and especially canon law, drawn from all parts of the world.

To each and every one of them we express our deepest gratitude today.

We recall, first of all, those Cardinals, now deceased, who headed the preparatory Commission, Cardinal Pietro Ciriaci who began the work, and Cardinal Pericles Felici who over a period of several years guided the labours almost to their goal. We think then of the Secretaries of this Commission, Monsignor, later Cardinal, Giacomo Violardo and Father Raimondo Bidagor SJ, both of whom lavished their talents of learning and wisdom on their role. Together with them, we recall the Cardinals, Archbishops and Bishops, and all who were members of this Commission, as well as the Consultors of the individual study groups engaged over these years in that strenuous task. God has called these to their eternal reward in the meantime. For all of them our suppliant prayer is raised to God.

Apostolic Constitution

With pleasure we also refer to the living: in the first place, to the present Pro-President of the Commission, our venerable brother Rosalio Castillo Lara, who has worked so outstandingly for so long in a role of such responsibility. Next, we refer to our beloved son, Monsignor William Onclin, who has contributed to the successful outcome of the task with assiduous and diligent care. Then there are others who played an inestimable part in this Commission, in developing and completing a task of such volume and complexity, whether as Cardinal members, or as officials, consultors and collaborators in the various study groups or in other roles.

In promulgating this Code today, therefore, we are fully conscious that this act stems from our pontifical authority itself, and so assumes a primatial nature. Yet we are no less aware that in its content this Code reflects the collegial solicitude for the Church of all our brothers in the episcopate. Indeed, by a certain analogy with the Council itself, the Code must be viewed as the fruit of collegial cooperation, which derives from the combined energies of experienced people and institutions throughout the whole Church.

A second question arises: what is the Code? For an accurate answer to this question, it is necessary to remind ourselves of that distant heritage of law contained in the books of the Old and New Testaments. It is from this, as from its first source, that the whole juridical and legislative tradition of the Church derives.

For Christ the Lord in no way abolished the bountiful heritage of the law and the prophets which grew little by little from the history and experience of the People of God in the Old Testament. Rather he fulfilled it (cf. Matt 5:17), so that it could, in a new and more sublime way, lead to the heritage of the New Testament. Accordingly, although St Paul in expounding the mystery of salvation teaches that justification is not obtained through the works of the law but through faith (cf. Rom 3:28; Gal 2:16), nonetheless he does not exclude the binding force of the Decalogue (cf. Rom 13:8–10; Gal 5:13–25; 6:2), nor does he deny the importance of discipline in the Church (cf. 1 Cor 5 and 6). Thus the writings of the New Testament allow us to perceive more clearly the great importance of this discipline and to understand better the bonds which link it ever more closely with the salvific character of the Gospel message.

Granted this, it is sufficiently clear that the purpose of the Code is not in any way to replace faith, grace, charisms and above all charity in the life of the Church or of Christ's faithful. On the contrary, the Code rather looks towards the achievement of order in the ecclesial society, such that while attributing a primacy to love, grace and the charisms, it facilitates at the same time an orderly development in the life both of the ecclesial society and of the individual persons who belong to it.

As the Church's fundamental legislative document, and because it is based on the juridical and legislative heritage of revelation and tradition, the Code must be regarded as the essential instrument for the preservation of right order, both in individual and social life and in the Church's zeal. Therefore, over and above the fundamental elements of the hierarchical and organic structure of the Church established by the Divine Founder, based on apostolic or other no less ancient tradition, and besides the principal norms which concern the exercise of the threefold office entrusted to the Church, it is necessary for the Code to define also certain rules and norms of action.

The instrument, such as the Code is, fully accords with the nature of the Church, particularly as presented in the authentic teaching of the Second Vatican Council seen as a whole, and especially in its ecclesiological doctrine. In fact, in a certain sense, this new Code can be viewed as a great effort to translate the conciliar ecclesiological teaching into canonical terms. If it is impossible perfectly to transpose the image of the Church described by conciliar doctrine into canonical language, nevertheless, the Code must always be related to that image as to its primary pattern, whose outlines, given its nature, the Code must express as far as is possible.

Hence flow certain fundamental principles by which the whole of the new Code is governed, within the limits of its proper subject and of its expression, which must reflect that subject. Indeed it is possible to assert that from this derives that characteristic whereby the Code is regarded as a complement to the authentic teaching proposed by the Second Vatican Council and particularly to its Dogmatic and Pastoral Constitutions.

From this it follows that the fundamental basis of the 'newness' which, while never straying from the Church's legislative tradition, is found in the Second Vatican Council and especially in its ecclesiological teaching, generates also the mark of 'newness' in the new Code.

Foremost among the elements which express the true and authentic image of the Church are: the teaching whereby the Church is presented as the People of God (cf. Const. *Lumen Gentium* n.2) and its hierarchical authority as service (ibid. n.3); the further teaching which portrays the Church as a communion and then spells out the mutual relationships which must intervene between the particular and the universal Church, and between collegiality and primacy; likewise, the teaching by which all members of the People of God share, each in their own measure, in the threefold priestly, prophetic and kingly office of Christ, with which teaching is associated also that which looks to the duties and rights of Christ's faithful and specifically the laity; and lastly the assiduity which the Church must devote to ecumenism.

If, therefore, the Second Vatican Council drew old and new from the treasury of tradition, and if its newness is contained in these and other elements, it is abundantly clear that the Code receives into itself the same mark of fidelity in newness and newness in fidelity, and that its specific content and corresponding form of expression is in conformity with this aim.

The new Code of Canon Law is published precisely at a time when the Bishops of the whole Church are not only asking for its promulgation but indeed are insistently and vehemently demanding it.

Apostolic Constitution

And in fact a Code of Canon Law is absolutely necessary for the Church. Since the Church is established in the form of a social and visible unit, it needs rules, so that its hierarchical and organic structure may be visible; that its exercise of the functions divinely entrusted to it, particularly of sacred power and of the administration of the sacraments, is properly ordered; that the mutual relationships of Christ's faithful are reconciled in justice based on charity, with the rights of each safeguarded and defined; and lastly, that the common initiatives which are undertaken so that christian life may be ever more perfectly carried out, are supported, strengthened and promoted by canonical laws.

Finally, canonical laws by their very nature demand observance. For this reason, the greatest care has been taken that during the long preparation of the Code there should be an accurate expression of the norms and that they should depend upon a sound juridical, canonical and theological foundation.

In view of all this, it is very much to be hoped that the new canonical legislation will be an effective instrument by the help of which the Church will be able to perfect itself in the spirit of the Second Vatican Council, and show itself ever more equal to carry out its salvific role in the world.

It is pleasing to set out these reflections of ours in a trusting spirit as we promulgate this principal body of ecclesiastical laws for the latin Church.

May God grant that joy and peace, with justice and obedience, may commend this Code, and that what is bidden by the head will be obeyed in the body.

Relying, therefore, on the help of divine grace, supported by the authority of the Blessed Apostles Peter and Paul, with certain knowledge and assenting to the pleas of the Bishops of the whole world who have laboured with us in collegial good will, by the supreme authority which is ours, and by means of this Constitution of ours which is to have effect for the future, we promulgate this present Code as it has been compiled and reviewed. We order that henceforth it is to have the force of law for the whole latin Church, and we commit its observance to the care and vigilance of all who are responsible. In order, however, that all may properly investigate these prescriptions and intelligently come to know them before they take effect, we decree and command that they shall come into force from the first day of Advent of the year 1983, all ordinances, constitutions and privileges, even those meriting special and individual mention, as well as contrary customs, notwithstanding.

We therefore, exhort all our beloved children to observe, with sincere mind and ready will, the precepts laid down, buoyed up by the hope that a zealous Church discipline will flourish anew, and that from it the salvation of souls also will be ever more fervently promoted, with the assistance of the Blessed Virgin Mary, Mother of the Church.

Given at Rome, in the Vatican, on the 25th day of January 1983, in the fifth year of our Pontificate.

JOHN PAUL II

Address by
His Holiness Pope John Paul II

22 May 1992

TO THE CANON LAW SOCIETY OF GREAT BRITAIN AND IRELAND
on the occasion of its 35th Annual Conference
held, for the first time, in Rome

Dear Friends,

1. I am pleased to welcome to the Vatican the members of the Canon Law Society of Great Britain and Ireland on the occasion of your 35th Annual Conference. You have wished to hold your meeting this year in Rome in order to express your closeness to the See of Peter, aware as you are of the fundamentally ecclesial nature of the various services which you provide in your work as canonists. I greet you all with affection in the Lord and I thank you for your committed and enlightened efforts to serve the Church through the study and application of her law.

In the 35 years since its foundation, your Society has sought to promote the study of canon law in both its theoretical aspects and its practical applications. By placing your scholarship and pastoral experience at the service of God's People, you have contributed notably to the renewal of ecclesial life mandated by the Second Vatican Council, and in particular to the revision of the Code of canon law. You have also been concerned to make the Church's law more accessible through the publication of a translation of the 1983 Code and the preparation of a commentary for the use of students, parish ministers, members of religious institutes and interested laity.

2. Among the most significant aspects of the renewal of canon law in the period since the Council has been a growing concern that the letter and spirit of canonical legislation should reflect ever more fully the distinct nature of the Church as the sacrament of union with God and the unity of the whole human race (cf. *Lumen Gentium* n.1). The Council, which recalling Christ's establishment of the Church as a visible society, insisted that the reality of this earthly society, endowed with hierarchical structures, may not be separated from her reality as a spiritual and heavenly community of faith, hope and love, the Mystical Body of Christ (cf. op cit n.8). Because the Church's social structure stands at the service of a deeper mystery of grace and communion, canon law – precisely as the law of the Church (*ius Ecclesiae*) – must be acknowledged as unique in its means and in its ends. The

canonical tradition was of course quite aware of the peculiar nature of the Church's legal discipline, as is evident from the history of such institutions as dispensation and canonical custom and the development of the concept of 'canonical equity'. Nevertheless, as the history of your science demonstrates, canonical theory and practice always need to be informed by a sound ecclesiological understanding and efforts must always be made to avoid any undue accommodation of ecclesial norms and structures to the prevailing ethos of civil society. Today, as in the past, canonists are challenged never to lose sight of the mystery of grace and truth which their work is meant to serve and foster.

Only in the light of a sound appreciation of the mystery of the Church will canon law become, as it must be, an effective instrument for the continuing renewal of ecclesial life. Fruitful periods of renewal in the Church have often been accompanied by a desire to recover the authentic discipline of the Catholic tradition, as that tradition has been preserved and handed down in the 'sacred canons'. Familiarity with the results of the Church's long experience in adapting her laws to the changing needs of the People of God is in fact an indispensable reference point for her efforts to meet the challenges of the present time with wisdom and prudence. Today in particular, there is a need for a balanced appreciation of the constant dialectic in the Church's life between the unfailing guidance of the Holy Spirit and the demands of fidelity to the Law of the New Covenant, and for a deeper insight into the social purpose of that 'diversity of gifts both hierarchical and charismatic' (*Lumen Gentium* n.4) which the Spirit has bestowed upon the Church. As canonists, your insights into these creative tensions within the Body of Christ can contribute not only to the development of sound ecclesiological reflection, but also, in a very practical way, to the good working of the various structures which enable the faithful to respond with fidelity to their supernatural calling and to share fully in the Church's mission.

3. In recent years, much of the work of your Society has been devoted to the correct interpretation and implementation of the norms contained in the 1983 Code of canon law. As I observed at the time of its promulgation, the new Code in a sense represents a great effort to translate the ecclesiological teaching of the Second Vatican Council into canonical terms, and consequently its norms must always be seen in relation to the image of the Church which the Council described (cf. Apostolic Constitution *Sacrae Disciplinae Leges*, 25 January 1983). The challenging task of correctly interpreting the legislation contained in the Code demands a readiness to return frequently to the documents in which the teaching of the Council is authoritatively set forth, so as to understand that teaching more deeply and to eliminate whatever false or unilateral interpretations may have arisen. The work of interpretation must always be governed by the principles set down in the Code itself, in harmony with the canonical tradition (cf. CIC Can. 6 §2), which attributes decisive importance to the 'proper meaning of the words considered in their text and context' (CIC c.17), understood in view of the *ratio legis* and in relation to the mind of the legislator. In the end, your concern

for the faithful interpretation of the Code serves the Church by contributing to a better understanding of the Council itself, and thus to a more effective implementation of its teaching.

The work of interpretation demands by its very nature a solid acquaintance with the history of canonical doctrine, especially with regard to the evolution of the corresponding jurisprudence. Those who have been entrusted with the application of the Church's law will certainly need to be familiar with the various prescriptions of positive law, but they must also be able to appreciate the rich tradition from which the present law has developed. It is furthermore essential that they should clearly understand the object and methods proper to canon law, so as to be able to evaluate the relevance, as well as the limitations, of insights drawn from other, related sciences. I am grateful for the concern which your Society has shown for the proper training of future canonists and for the promotion of scholarly interest in the law; these concerns are an important aspect of your service to the Church.

4. Dear friends, we are engaged in a service which is ultimately pastoral in nature for it seeks to strengthen the bonds of communion in the Church through fidelity to the Gospel and the promotion of justice. How often in this delicate and important task are you called upon to be heralds of the 'message of reconciliation' (2 Cor 5:19) and to bring healing and hope in fragile situations of human weakness and sin! Wherever you carry out your work – in classrooms, offices and tribunals – always keep in mind the eminently pastoral nature of all Church law, which, while never derogating from the demands of truth, has as its final aim the salvation of souls (cf. CIC Can. 1752). I pray that your work on behalf of God's People through the faithful application of canon law will always help to build up the communion of Christ's Body in faith, hope and love, and will contribute ever more effectively to the proclamation of the Gospel and its saving truth to the men and women of our time.

With these sentiments, I commend all of you to the loving intercession of Mary, Mirror of Justice, and I cordially impart my Apostolic Blessing as a pledge of lasting joy and peace in Jesus Christ her Son.

ABBREVIATIONS

AA	Vat. II decr *Apostolicam Actuositatem* 18.XI.1965: AAS 59(1966) 837–864
AAS	*Acta Apostolicae Sedis Commentarium officiale* Rome 1909–
AGD	Vat. II decr *Ad Gentes Divinitus* 7.XII.1965: AAS 58(1966) 947–990
AkK	*Archiv für katholisches Kirchenrecht* Mainz 1862–
AP	Pope Paul VI mp *Ad Pascendum* 15.VIII.1972: AAS 64(1972) 947–990
ap con	apostolic constitution
ap exhort	apostolic exhortation
Apol	*Apollinaris* Rome 1928–
Ap Sig	Apostolic Signatura
ASS	*Acta Sanctae Sedis* Rome 1865–1908
ATE	SPCU directory *Ad Totam Ecclesiam* 14.V.1967: AAS 59(1967) 574–592
c(c)	canon(s) in 1917 Code
Can(n)	canon(s) in 1983 Code
CCC	*Catechism of the Catholic Church* Dublin (Veritas) and London (Geoffrey Chapman) 1994
CCEO	*Codex Canonum Ecclesiarum Orientalium* Vatican Press 1990
CCLA	*Code of Canon Law Annotated* Montreal 1993
CCLS	Canadian Canon Law Society
CCom	(Code Commission) Pontifical Commission for the Authentic Interpretation of the Code of Canon Law (1917 Code and 1983 Code up to *Pastor Bonus* in 1988)
CD	Vat. II decr *Christus Dominus*
CLA	*Canon Law Abstracts* CLSGBI 1958–
CLD	Canon Law Digest
CLSA	Canon Law Society of America
CLSANZ	Canon Law Society of Australia and New Zealand
CLSGBI	Canon Law Society of Great Britain and Ireland
CLSNGBI	Newsletter of the Canon Law Society of Great Britain and Ireland
CM	Pope Paul VI mp *Causas Matrimoniales* 28.III.1971: AAS 63(1971) 441–446
CN(USA)	*Complementary Norms* (implementing the 1983 Code) National Conference of Catholic Bishops Washington DC 1991
Comm	*Communicationes* Vatican City 1969–
con	constitution
CT	Pope John Paul II ap con *Catechesi Tradendae* 16.X.1979: AAS 71(1979) 1277–1340
DE	PCPCU *Directory on Ecumenism* 25.III.1993: AAS 85 (1993) 1039ff: Catholic Truth Society London 1993
decl	declaration
decr	decree
DEM	SPCU *Directory concerning Ecumenical Matters*

Abbreviations

DH	Vat. II decr *Dignitatis Humanae* 7.XII.1965: AAS 58(1966) 929–946
DIP	*Dizionario degli Istituti di Perfezione* (ed. Pellicia 1962–1968, Rocca 1969–) 8 vols Rome (Edizioni Paoline)
DOL	Documents on the Liturgy 1963–1979 Collegeville 1982
DPME	Directory on the Pastoral Ministry of Bishops *Ecclesiae imago*, SCB 22.II.1973: LE V coll 6462–6539.
DR	*Documenta Recertiora circa Rem Matrimonialem et Processualem* ed. (Gordon)–Grocholewski 2 vols 1977, 1980
DS	Denzinger & Schönmetzer *Enchiridion Symbolorum* etc.
DV	Vat. II Dogmatic Constitution *Dei Verbum* 18.XI.1965: AAS 58(1966) 817–835
DVCom	Commission for the Interpretation of the Decrees of Vatican II
ECE	Pope John Paul II ap con *Ex corde Ecclesiae* 15.VIII.1990: AAS 82 (1990) 1475–1509: Origins 20(1990) 265–276
EIC	*Ephemerides Iuris Canonici* Rome 1945–
EM	Pope Paul VI mp *De Episcoporum Muneribus* 15.VI.1966: AAS 58(1966) 467–472
encl	encyclical
ES	Pope Paul VI mp *Ecclesiae Sanctae* 6.VIII.1966: AAS 58(1966) 757–787
ET	Pope Paul VI ap exhort *Evangelica Testificatio* 29.VI.1971: AAS 63(1971) 497–526
EuM	SCRit instr *Eucharisticum Mysterium* 25.V.1967: AAS 59(1967) 529–573
FC	Pope John Paul II ap exhort *Familiaris Consortio* 22.XI.1981: AAS 74(1982) 81–191
Fl	*Vatican Council II: The Conciliar and Post Conciliar Documents* ed. Flannery 2 vols Dublin 1975(1992) 1982
GCD	SCC General Catechetical Directory *Ad Normam Decreti* 11.IV.1971: AAS 64 (1972) 97–196
GE	Vat. II decl *Gravissimum Educationis* 28.X.1965: AAS 58(1966) 728–729
GICI	SCDW General Introduction to Christian Initiation Vatican Press 1973
GIRM	SCDW General Instruction on the Roman Missal 4 ed Vatican Press 1975
GS	Vat. II pastoral con *Gaudium et Spes* 7.XII.1966: AAS 58(1966) 1025–1115
IC	*Ius Canonicum* Pamplona 1961–
ID	Pope Paul VI ap con *Indulgentiarum Doctrina* 1.I.1967: AAS 59(1967) 5–24
IIB	SCDF Instruction on Infant Baptism 20.X.1980: AAS 72(1980) 1137–1138
IM	Vat. II decr *Inter Mirifica* 4.XII.1963: AAS 56(1964) 145–157
ImC	SCDW instr *Immensae Caritatis* 25.I.1973: AAS 65(1973) 264–271
instr	instruction
IRIB	Introduction to the Rite of Infant Baptism 2 ed 1973
Jur	*The Jurist* Washington 1940–
LCE	*Legislazione delle Conferenze Episcopali complementare al CIC* Milan 1990
LE	*Leges Ecclesiae post Codicem iuris canonici editae* ed. Ochoa 6 vols Rome 1966–1987
LEF	*Lex Ecclesiae Fundamentalis*
LG	Vat. II dogmatic con *Lumen Gentium* 21.XI.1964: AAS 57(1965) 5–75
lit circ	Circular letter
lit ap	Apostolic letter

Abbreviations

ME	*Monitor Ecclesiasticus* Rome 1948–
mp	motu proprio
MQ	Pope Paul VI mp *Ministeria Quaedam* 15.VIII.1972: AAS 64(1972) 529–534
MR	SCB and SCRIS Directive *Mutuae Relationes* 14.V.1978: AAS 70(1978) 473–506
MS	SCDW Introduction to the New Order of Penance *Misericordiam Suam* 1974
ND	Ed. Neuner & Dupuis *The Christian Faith* London & Sydney 1983
NEP	*Preliminary Explanatory Note* to LG: Fl I 424–426
Not	*Notitiae* Vatican City 1965–
NP	SCDW Introduction to the Rite of Infant Baptism *Nomine Parvulorum*
Nun	*Nuntia* Vatican City 1975–
OE	Vat. II decr *Orientalium Ecclesiarum* 21.XI.1964: AAS 57(1965) 76–89
OR	*L'Osservatore Romano*
Origins	Catholic News Service *Origins* Washington DC
OT	Vatican II decr *Optatam Totius* 28.X.1965: AAS 58(1966) 713–727
OUI	SCDW *Ordo Unctionis Infirmorum Eorumque Pastoralis Curae* 7.XII.1972: AAS 65(1973) 275–276
PB	Pope John Paul II ap con *Pastor Bonus* 28.VI.1988: AAS 80(1988) 841–924
PC	Vat. II decr *Perfectae Caritatis* 28.X.1965: AAS 58(1966) 702–712
PCI	Pontifical Council for the Interpretation of Legislative Texts (since *Pastor Bonus* 1988)
PCPCU	Pontifical Council for Promoting Christian Unity
Per	*Periodica de re Morali Canonica Liturgica* Rome 1905–
PIC	SCDW General Introduction to Christian Initiation *Per Initiationis Christianae*
PM	Pope Paul VI mp *Pastorale Munus* 30.XI.1963: AAS 56(1964) 5–12
PME	Pope Pius XII ap con *Provida Mater Ecclesia* 15.VIII.1936: AAS 28(1936) 313–361
PO	Vat. II decr *Presbyterorum Ordinis* 7.XII.1965: AAS 58(1966) 991–1024
RC	SCRIS instr *Renovationis Causam* 6.I.1969: AAS 61(1969) 103–120
RCom	(Revision Commission) Pontifical Commission for the Revision of the Code of Canon Law
RDCA	SCSDW 29.V.1977 *Rite of Dedication of a Church and an Altar*: DOL nn.4361–4445
rep	reply
rescr	rescript
resol	resolution
REU	Pope Paul VI ap con *Regimini Ecclesiae Universae* 15.VIII.1967: AAS 59(1967) 885–928
RF	SCCE *Ratio Fundamentalis Institutionis Sacerdotalis* 6.I.1970: AAS 62(1970) 321–384
RFR	SCCE *Ratio fundamentalis institutionis sacerdotalis ad normam novi Codicis iuris canonici recognita* Vatican Press 19.III.1985
RM	Pope John Paul II encl *Redemptoris Missio* 7.XII.1990: AAS 83 (1991) 249–340
RPE	Pope Paul VI ap con *Romano Pontifici eligendo* 1.X.1975: AAS 67 (1975) 609–645: CLD 8 133–169: Fl I 423–426

Abbreviations

RR	CLSA *Roman Replies and CLSA Advisory Opinions*
Sac Cael	Pope Paul VI encl *Sacerdotalis Caelibatus* 24.VI.1967: AAS 59(1967) 657–697
Sap Chris	Pope John Paul II ap con *Sapientia Christiana* 15.IV.1979: AAS 71(1979) 469–499: Origins 9(1979–80) 33–45
SC	Vat. II con *Sacrosanctum Concilium* 4.XII.1963: AAS 56(1964) 97–138
SCB	Sacred Congregation for Bishops
SCC	Sacred Congregation for the Clergy
SCCE	Sacred Congregation for Catholic Education
SCCo	Sacred Congregation of the Council
SCCon	Sacred Consistorial Congregation
SCCS	Sacred Congregation for the Causes of Saints
SCDF	Sacred Congregation for the Doctrine of the Faith
SCDW	Sacred Congregation for Divine Worship
SCEP	Sacred Congregation for the Evangelisation of Peoples
Sch	Schema
SCHO	Sacred Congregation of the Holy Office
SCOC	Sacred Congregation for the Oriental Churches
SCPF	Sacred Congregation for the Propagation of the Faith
SCR	Sacred Congregation for Religious
SCRIS	Sacred Congregation for Religious and Secular Institutes
SCRit	Sacred Congregation of Rites
SCSac	Sacred Congregation for the Discipline of the Sacraments
SCSDW	Sacred Congregation for Sacraments and Divine Worship
SCSU	Sacred Congregation for Seminaries and Universities
SDO	Pope Paul VI mp *Sacrum Diaconatus Ordinem* 18.VI.1967: AAS 59(1967) 697–704
SMD	*Schema Canonum Libri III de Ecclesiae Munere Docendi* Rome 1977
SMS	*Schema Canonum Libri IV de Ecclesiae Munere Sanctificandi Pars II de Locis et Temporibus Sacris deque Cultu Divino* Rome 1977
SNG	*Schema Canonum Libri I De Normis Generalibus* Rome 1977
SOE	Pope Paul VI mp *Solicitudo omnium Ecclesiarum* 24.VI.1969: AAS 61 (1969) 473–484
SP	*Schema Canonum de Modo Procedendi pro Tutela Iurium seu de Processibus* Rome 1976
SPCU	Secretariat for Promoting Christian Unity
SPD	*Schema Canonum Libri II De Populo Dei* Rome 1977
SPE	*Schema Canonum Libri V de Iure Patrimoniali Ecclesiae* Rome 1977
SRRDec	Decisions of the Roman Rota Rome 1909–
SS	*Schema Documenti Pontificii Quo Disciplina Canonica de Sacramentis Recogniscitur* Rome 1975
Stud Can	*Studia Canonica* Ottawa 1969–
SVC	*Schema Canonum de Institutis Vitae Consecratae per Professionem Consiliorum Evangelicorum* Rome 1977
UR	Vatican II decr *Unitatis Redintegratio* 21.XI.1964: AAS 57(1965) 90–112
Vorgrimler	*Commentary on the Documents of Vatican II* ed. Vorgrimler 5 vols New York 1966–1969

Abbreviations of Some Standard Authors and Commentaries

Abbo–Hannan	*The Sacred Canons: A Concise Presentation of the Norms of the Church* Abbo–Hannan, St Louis 1957
Beste	*Introductio in Codicem* Beste, Naples 1956
Bouscaren–Ellis	*Canon Law: A Text and Commentary* Bouscaren–Ellis–Korth, Milwaukee 1966
Cappello	*Tractatus canonico-moralis: De Sacramentis* Capello Vols I–V Rome 1942–1947
Chelodi(Matr)	*Jus canonicum de Matrimonio* Chelodi, Vicenza 1947
Chelodi(DP)	*Jus canonicum de Delictis et Poenis et de Judiciis Criminalibus* Chelodi, Vicenza 1943
Chiappetta	*Il Codice di Diritto Canonico: Commento Giuridico-Pastorale* Chiappetta 2 vols Naples 1988
Chiappetta (Il Matr)	*Il Matrimonio nella Nuova Legislazione Canonica e Concordataria* (Manuale giuridico-pastorale) Chiappetta, Rome 1990
Cicognani	*Canon Law* Cicognani (trans. O'Hara–Brennan), Philadelphia 1935
Commentary (CLSA)	*The Code of Canon Law: A Text and Commentary* ed. Coriden – Green–Heintschel, New York Mahwah 1985
Commentary (St Paul's)	*Code of Canon Law Annotated* ed. Caparros–Thériault–Thorn, Montreal 1993
Commentary (Urbanianum)	*Commento al Codice di Diritto Canonico* ed. Pinto, Rome 1985
Coronata	*Institutiones Juris Canonici* Conte a Coronata, 5 vols Turin 1946–1947
Gasparri	*Tractatus Canonicus de Matrimonio* Gasparri, 2 vols Rome 1932
Iorio	*Theologia Moralis* Iorio, 3 vols Naples 1946–1947
Lega–Bartoccetti	*Commentarius in Judicia Ecclesiastica* Lega–Bartoccetti, 2 vols Rome 1950
Maroto	*Institutiones Juris Canonici ad normam novi Codicis* Maroto, 2 vols Rome 1919–1921
Michiels(DP)	*De Delictis et Poenis* Michiels, Lublin 1934
Michiels(NG)	*Normae Generales Juris Canonici* Michiels, 2 vols Tournai 1946

Standard Authors and Commentaries

Pospishil	*Eastern Catholic Marriage Law According to the Code of Canons of the Eastern Church* Pospishil, Brooklyn NY 1991
Regatillo	*Institutiones Juris Canonici* Regatillo, 2 vols Santander 1951
Roberti(DP)	*De Delictis et Poenis* Roberti, 2 vols Rome 1941
Roberti(Proc)	*De Processibus* Roberti, 2 vols Rome 1941
Torre	*Processus Matrimonialis* Torre, Naples 1956
Urrutia	*Les Normes Générales* in *Le Nouveau Droit Ecclésial* Urrutia, Paris 1994
Van Hove	*Commentarium Lovaniense in Codicem Juris Canonici* Van Hove, 1 Vol Tom 1–5 Malines 1933–1945
Vermeersch–Creusen	*Epitome Juris Canonici* Vermeersch–Creusen, 3 vols Malines 1937, 1940
Vorgrimler	*Commentary on the Documents of Vat. II* ed. Vorgrimler, 5 vols New York 1966–1969
Vromant	*De Bonis Ecclesiae Temporalibus* Vromant, Bruges–Paris 1953
Wernz–Vidal	*Jus Canonicum* Wernz–Vidal, 7 vols Rome 1933–1946
Woywood	*A Practical Commentary on the Code of Canon Law* Woywood, 2 vols New York 1962
Wrenn (Interpret)	*Authentic Interpretations on the 1983 Code* Wrenn, CLSA Washington DC 1993
Wrenn (Annul)	*Annulments* Wrenn 4 ed, CLSA Washington DC 1983

BOOK I

GENERAL NORMS

Can. 1 The canons of this Code concern only the latin Church.

Implicit in this very first canon is a profoundly theological and canonical statement concerning the nature of the catholic Church. It implies that the catholic Church, in which subsists the Church of Christ,[1] is not a monolithic institution but a *communion* of different autonomous Churches of the East and of the West. The 'latin Church' expressly mentioned in this canon is one among many such autonomous Churches competent to legislate for their own subjects. Vat. II states that 'the holy catholic Church ... is made up of the faithful who are organically united in the Holy Spirit by the same faith, the same sacraments and the same government. They combine into different groups, which are held together by their hierarchy, and so form particular churches or rites.'[2] Even though these groups or churches differ somewhat among themselves in liturgy, in ecclesiastical discipline and in spiritual tradition, they are nonetheless all equally entrusted to the pastoral guidance of the Roman Pontiff, in whom Christ established a 'lasting and visible source and foundation of the unity both of faith and of communion'.[3]

All of the Oriental Churches at various times separated themselves from the catholic Church by heresy or schism.[4] Some of them have remained separated from Rome and now are known as Eastern Orthodox Churches or simply Orthodox Churches. Several however have reunited with Rome and acknowledge the supremacy of the Roman Pontiff, and are therefore catholic in the full sense of the word.[5] Today, besides the latin Church, there are in the catholic Church some twenty-one autonomous churches, presided over by a Patriarch or a major Archbishop or a Metropolitan. These autonomous churches of the East arise from the Alexandrian, Antiochene, Armenian, Chaldean and Constantinopolitan traditions.[6]

The specific point of this canon is to determine that only those are directly obliged by this Code who are members of the latin Church. Indirectly, however, some members of Oriental Churches may come within its ambit, e.g. if they are expressly (or even implicitly) referred to (see Cann. 350 §§1 and 3, 1015 §2), or if the subject-matter of a canon applies of its very nature to all catholics of whatever rite – such as those

---

[1] Cf. Can. 204 §2; LG 8: Fl I 357.

[2] OE 2: Fl I 441.

[3] LG 18: Fl I 370.

[4] 'The first divisions occurred in the East, either because of the dispute over the dogmatic formulae of the Councils of Ephesus and Chalcedon, or later by the dissolving of ecclesiastical communion between the eastern Patriarchates and the Roman See': UR 13: Fl I 463.

[5] On 18.X.1990 Pope John Paul II promulgated the first-ever common *Code of Canons of the Eastern Churches*, which came into effect on 1.X.1991: AAS 82(1990) 1032–1363, 1702. Official edition: *Codex Canonum Ecclesiarum Orientalium* Libreria Editrice Vaticana 1990. A Latin–English edition: *Code of Canons of the Eastern Churches* CLSA Washington DC 1992.

[6] For a brief description of these Churches, cf. Pospishil *Eastern Catholic Marriage Law According to the Code of Canons of the Eastern Churches* Brooklyn NY 1991 96–113.

canons which proclaim a matter of belief and doctrine, or declare or interpret divine (positive or natural) law.[1]

Can. 2 For the most part the Code does not determine the rites to be observed in the celebration of liturgical actions. Accordingly, liturgical laws which have been in effect hitherto retain their force, except those which may be contrary to the canons of the Code.

4 In the introductory canons (2–6), the legislator acknowledges the fact that ecclesial life is not governed solely by the canons of the Code. There are prescriptions outside the Code which have their own effect: these concern liturgical actions, concordats, acquired rights and privileges, customs, universal laws not abrogated by this Code and particular laws enacted by local authorities. This Can. 2 deals specifically with those liturgical laws which were still in force when the Code came into effect on 27 November 1983.

5 All such liturgical laws contained in the 'liturgical books' (such as the Roman Missal, Roman Pontifical, Ceremonial of Bishops, Divine Office or Liturgy of the Hours, Book of Blessings, etc.), and all documents emanating from the Holy See on liturgical matters, remain in force – save only where there may be conflict between a liturgical law and a canon of this Code, in which case the Code prevails.

6 Vat. II and several post-conciliar documents have modified the then-existing liturgical books. One conciliar document in particular has been the source of intense renewal in liturgy i.e. the Constitution on the Sacred Liturgy.[2] The Congregation for Divine Worship and the Discipline of the Sacraments is responsible for preparing and approving all liturgical books and texts. Liturgical documents from that Congregation usually appear in the periodical *Notitiae*.[3]

Can. 3 The canons of the Code do not abrogate, nor do they derogate from, agreements entered into by the Apostolic See with nations or other civil entities. For this reason, these agreements continue in force as hitherto, notwithstanding any contrary provisions of this Code.

7 Vat. II clearly proclaimed the principle that the political community and the Church are autonomous and independent entities, but it called at the same time for 'mutual cooperation' in favour of the welfare of all human beings. The Council claimed the Church's right to 'true freedom to preach the faith, to proclaim its teaching about society, to carry out its task among people without hindrance, and to pass moral judgements even in matters relating to politics, whenever the fundamental rights of man or the salvation of souls requires it'.[4] According to this principle, therefore, the mission of the Church in the world determines the basis of its relationship with any political community and, consequently, the basis for entering into mutual 'agreements' (*conventiones*) in view of fulfilling that mission.[5] This canon determines the

---

[1] Cf. 1917 Code c.1.

[2] Cf. Fl I 1-36.

[3] For liturgical variations promulgated in the light of the revised Code, cf. Not 19(1983) 540–555.

[4] GS 76: Fl I 985.

[5] Generally, a concordat or agreement (*conventio*) is understood as 'a Church–State agreement or public treaty, having the force of international law, between the Holy See and some sovereign civil government, by which the Church communicates or delegates some of her powers to the State in order that her more important rights may be respected': Abbo–Hannan I 6–7.

status of such agreements as had been entered into before the coming into effect of the Code.[1]

In effect, it states that all such agreements will continue to be integrally honoured – a cornerstone of international law – despite the fact that some of their details may possibly be in conflict with the prescriptions of the Code. These agreements may take different forms, ranging from concordats strictly so called (which govern all matters of a Church–State relationship) to simple partial agreements concerning such matters as protocols, schools, hospitals, military ordinariates, etc. Moreover, these agreements comprise those entered into by the Apostolic See not only 'with nations', but also with 'other civil entities' such as the United Nations, OAS, UNESCO, etc. In all such cases the Pope acts not as the sovereign of Vatican City, rather specifically as the head of the catholic Church as a juridical entity in its own right (see Can. 113 §1).

Can. 4 Acquired rights, and likewise privileges hitherto granted by the Apostolic See to either physical or juridical persons, which are still in use and have not been revoked, remain intact, unless they are expressly revoked by the canons of this Code.

This canon determines the status of two further legal entities vis-à-vis the Code itself, namely *acquired rights* and a specific class of *privileges*. In effect, it grants them both a measure of protection against such prescriptions of the Code as might otherwise modify or even withdraw them.[2]

The term *acquired right* is a technical one. The right in question differs e.g. from an innate right, such as the right to life; it differs also from a legal right i.e. one which is simply granted by positive law, such as the right of a cleric to take a reasonable annual vacation (see Can. 283 §2). It may be simply defined as a right to which one is entitled by reason precisely of the fact that he or she has fulfilled each and all of the then–prevailing law's requirements for the acquisition of that right.[3] Thus e.g. when a priest is appointed by the diocesan Bishop to the office of parish priest (see Cann. 157, 515 §1) he thereby obviously acquires a certain 'right' to that parish, but this becomes an *acquired* right only when he will have formally taken possession of the parish in accordance with the terms of Can. 527; in like manner, one who is, not appointed but rather, elected to an ecclesiastical office will be seen thereby to have a certain 'right' to the office, but this too becomes an *acquired* right only when the further steps required by law – such as the person's acceptance of the election and, in certain situations, its confirmation by a superior authority (see Cann. 176–179) – will have been fulfilled.

The significance of acquired rights is that they have a certain inviolability which the law is very reluctant to infringe. The precise point of this Can. 4 is to prescribe that any such acquired right remains undisturbed ('intact') *even if the legal requirements for its*

---

[1] Cf. Chiappetta I nn.24–32; Regatillo I nn.36–43; Beste 55–56. In the decree on the Pastoral Office of Bishops (CD 20: Fl I 575) Vat. II invited the relevant civil authorities freely to waive the rights and privileges which, by agreement or custom, they may have enjoyed in the matter of the appointment of Bishops (cf. also ES 18: Fl I 602). Pending the response to this invitation – which in each case would hopefully lead to a discussion with the Holy See – this canon affirms the resolution of the Holy See to adhere, in accordance with international law, to such agreements as it had previously made.

[2] In its c.4 the 1917 Code did precisely the same thing. Allowing for minor changes in the text (and for the omission of indults), the recognised commentators on the previous law remain a valuable guide.

[3] For a thorough exposition of this matter, cf. Michiels (NG) I 67ff, especially 77–89; Chiappetta I nn.34–39. For a convenient and clear summary, cf. Conway *Problems in Canon Law* Dublin 1956 11–13.

acquisition might subsequently have been altered. The reason is clear: were the rule to be otherwise, it would manifestly lead to such continual changes as would be destructive of the common good and of the security which the law itself is designed to achieve. It is to be noted that nowhere in the Code itself is any acquired right revoked; on the contrary, there are many instances in which such a right is expressly safeguarded (see e.g. Cann. 36 §1, 38, 121–123, 192, 326 §2, 562, 616 §1, 1196).

12 A *privilege* is defined in Can. 76 §1. It is in effect the Church's response to a particular situation not specifically foreseen by the law, which of its nature is designed for the community in general. It is always, however, in the nature of a favour, even if it had been requested by the recipient. This canon provides that all such, already granted to whomsoever, remain untouched by any contrary prescription of the Code, provided however that:

(a) they will have been granted by the Apostolic See – not therefore by any lesser authority: thus e.g. a privilege granted by a diocesan Bishop would be automatically abolished if it were contrary to a prescription of this Code;

(b) they 'are still in use and have not been revoked': clearly, if they have been revoked, the question of their continued effectiveness does not arise; their being 'still in use' means either that they are being actively availed of, or that nothing has occurred in the meantime which would prevent their being availed of,[1] as e.g. the privilege of a formal oratory in a private house which itself had been destroyed or which had passed into the hands of someone quite other than the original recipient;

(c) they are not 'expressly revoked by the canons of this Code', as e.g. by Cann. 396 §2, 509 §1, 526 §2.

Can. 5 §1 Universal or particular customs which have been in effect up to now but are contrary to the provisions of these canons and are reprobated in the canons of this Code, are completely suppressed, and they may not be allowed to revive in the future. Other contrary customs are also to be considered suppressed, unless the Code expressly provides otherwise, or unless they are centennial or immemorial: these latter may be tolerated if the Ordinary judges that, in the circumstances of place and person, they cannot be removed.

§2 Customs apart from the law, whether universal or particular, which have been in effect hitherto, are retained.

13 The important concept of custom and its various divisions are dealt with in Cann. 23–28. This canon deals solely with the status of such customs as were in existence when the Code came into effect on 27 November 1983. It divides them into three categories, and spells out in each case their respective status in respect of the now-current Code.

14 Customs, whether universal or particular (even centennial or immemorial), which are in fact *contrary* to the provisions of the Code *and are reprobated* by it (a) are completely suppressed and (b) may not be allowed to revive in the future (§1). The effect of such a 'reprobation' is to remove any juridical force whatever from the custom in question, to declare a halt to whatever time may have been running in its favour, to declare it 'unreasonable' (see Can. 24 §2); in fact to direct that the practice involved be corrected. Examples of such reprobation may be seen in Cann. 396 §2, 423 §1, 526 §2, 1076, 1287 §1, 1425 §1.

---

[1] Cf. Regatillo I n.44; Urrutia *De Normis Generalibus* Romae 1983 12.

Book I General Norms

Even if they are not expressly reprobated in the Code, other contrary customs are also suppressed, save only in two situations (§1): 15
(a) if 'the Code expressly provides otherwise', as it does e.g. in Cann. 1263, 1279 §1;
(b) if 'they are centennial or immemorial', in which case they may be tolerated, provided however that the Ordinary (see Can. 134 §1) judges that by reason of the actual circumstances within his jurisdiction, be they of place or of persons, such customs cannot reasonably or prudently be removed.[1] It follows of course that if the Ordinary were positively to judge otherwise, the custom in question would thereby be suppressed.

Customs which are 'apart from the law' (see Can. 24 §2), be they universal or particular, are specifically retained, provided only that they 'have been in effect hitherto' (§2) i.e. in actual practice availed of in the ordinary course of events – not e.g. allowed to fall into desuetude many years ago. This is a new provision, not found in the 1917 Code, which effectively resolves a substantial divergence of opinion among the commentators on that Code. 16

Can. 6 §1 When this Code comes into force, the following are abrogated:

1° the Code of Canon Law promulgated in 1917;
2° other laws, whether universal or particular, which are contrary to the provisions of this Code, unless it is otherwise expressly provided in respect of particular laws;
3° all penal laws enacted by the Apostolic See, whether universal or particular, unless they are resumed in this Code itself;
4° any other universal disciplinary laws concerning matters which are integrally reordered by this Code.

§2 To the extent that the canons of this Code reproduce the former law, they are to be assessed in the light also of canonical tradition.

The Code, which represents stability and the good of the ecclesial community, generally retains existing legislation: in law, change for its own sake is not a virtue. Such was the mind of the legislator when the first general systematic codification of ecclesiastical legislation was carried out in 1917. The purpose of that codification was to order the existing legislation in a systematic way and to present it clearly, in a contemporary style accommodated to the then-current needs. The systematic revision of the present Code had the same purpose, i.e. to provide the Church with a legislation which would preserve what remained relevant in its predecessor, which would reflect and represent the spirit and deliberations of Vat. II and which would meet the exigencies of modern times. Accordingly, this Can. 6 lays down the norms according to which this Code is to be interpreted in relation to all previous legislation. It does this in two ways: (a) by specifying (§1) what previous legislation is formally abrogated or withdrawn; (b) by prescribing (§2) how one is to interpret those 'canons of this Code (which) reproduce the former law' – which, as one would expect, they do in considerable measure. 17

Specifically abrogated are the following: 18

---

[1] Cf. Chiappetta I n.45. It is the view of this commentary that a formal decree of the Ordinary declaring such toleration is not required, that a mere factual toleration suffices. An interesting example under the legislation of the 1917 Code c. 1249 (which has now been replaced by Can. 1248 §1) was the custom in Ireland, arising from the penal times, whereby one could lawfully fulfil one's obligation to assist at Mass 'wherever Mass is celebrated in a catholic rite' (Can. 1248 §1), despite the restrictions then in force under the 1917 Code c. 1249.

(a) *The 1917 Code*, in its entirety (§1 1°) – obviously, since this Code is its revised successor.

(b) All other laws, universal or particular, 'which are *contrary* to the provisions of this Code' (§1 2°). What is in mind here is the vast bulk of legislation (not least, but not only, because of Vat. II) which – as one would expect from a living organism such as the Church – has been promulgated since 1917, both by the Holy See and at local or particular level e.g. in a diocese, by the constitutions of a religious institute, etc. There is one significant exception to this rule i.e. if 'in respect of *particular* laws', 'it is otherwise expressly provided' in the Code itself.[1]

(c) All *penal laws* enacted by the Apostolic See, 'unless they are expressly resumed in this Code itself' (§1 3°). This reflects the very major change in the attitude to penal law which, at the instigation of Vat. II, has been introduced into the Code (see Bk VI). It is to be noted that penal laws promulgated earlier by particular legislators, e.g. at diocesan, provincial or national level, remain in force, provided of course that they or any of them are not contrary to a prescription of the Code (see §1 2° above).

(d) All other *universal disciplinary* laws which have been *integrally reordered* by the Code (§1 4°), i.e. substantially changed in the matter of discipline, not merely altered in minor detail: compare e.g. 1917 Code c.1385 with Cann. 824ff.[2] Note that the reference is solely to universal (not particular) laws, which are of a disciplinary nature, not therefore to those which declare or interpret divine law, positive or natural.

19 A clear consequence of §1 of this canon, as outlined above, is that all laws not coming within its ambit retain their juridical force.[3]

20 In its §2 this canon states a norm of interpretation of those canons which 'reproduce the former law' – which in fact so many of them do. Clearly, the rules of interpretation, as declared in Cann. 16–21, apply. The point of this paragraph – as distinct from its counterpart in the 1917 Code (c.6 nn.2–4), which enjoined quite a complex formula – is to give the simple directive that, in any such interpretation, 'canonical tradition' must be taken into account, i.e. the opinions of recognised commentators, the documents of Vat. II, the general thrust of the Holy See, etc. In all such situations, and in the absence of any official decision by the Council for the Interpretation of Legislative Texts, it will be a matter for informed and prudent judgement to determine the precise meaning of the canon or canons in question. This paragraph gives notice that history and tradition are important factors in any such estimation.

---

[1] There are in fact numerous such provisions, e.g. Cann. 119, 127 §1, 165, 167 §1, 174 §1, 176, 191 §1, 266 §2, 553 §2, etc.

[2] The same has occurred in the approach concerning e.g. associations of the faithful (Cann. 298ff), procedural matters in Bk VII and, as already mentioned, penal legislation. The recognised commentators will be a guide as to whether or not, in any given case, the earlier law has been 'integrally reordered'.

[3] Concerning instructions and, if any, laws, issued by the Roman Congregations before the coming into effect of this Code, cf. Comm 14(1982) 131, where it is expressly stated that such instructions or laws are certainly abrogated by this new Code and that they must be either re-written or again promulgated – 'quod, etsi laboriosum, optimum est pro certitudine iuridica'!

Title I
Ecclesiastical Laws

Can. 7 A law comes into being when it is promulgated.

It is not the purpose of this commentary to enter into a philosophical analysis of the precise definition of what constitutes a 'law'. In the Church, that which is most commonly accepted is from St Thomas: 'an ordination of reason for the common good, promulgated by the one who has care of the community'.[1] Any such investigation into the nature of law is obviously an important one. It does however belong rather to theory than to practice. The ordinary catholic understands 'law' in the sense of a general directive, on whatever matter, from the Holy See, from the local Bishop, from his or her religious institute, etc. It may, however, be added that the basic purpose of law, in any grouping or community, is not to restrict individual freedom, but rather so to order the exercise of that freedom that it will contribute to the well-being of the entire community – even if that may, on occasion, mean a certain restriction on the freedom of this or that individual.

The practical purpose of this canon is to point out that any such law in the Church has effect only 'when it is promulgated,' i.e. when it is made known to those whom it is meant to oblige, in whatever manner is officially determined by law for this purpose. The precise manner is specified in Can. 8. The specific purpose is to ensure that those who are to be obliged by a law will, in so far as is reasonably possible, have adequate advance notice of this fact.

Can. 8 §1 Universal ecclesiastical laws are promulgated by publication in the 'Acta Apostolicae Sedis', unless in particular cases another manner of promulgation has been prescribed. They come into force only on the expiry of three months from the date appearing on the particular issue of the 'Acta', unless because of the nature of the case they bind at once, or unless a shorter or a longer interval has been specifically and expressly prescribed in the law itself.

§2 Particular laws are promulgated in the manner determined by the legislator; they begin to oblige one month from the date of promulgation, unless a different period is prescribed in the law itself.

The manner of the promulgation of 'universal ecclesiastical laws', i.e. those directed to the whole Church, is determined by §1. It is to be 'by publication in the *Acta Apostolicae Sedis*', a document which issues officially from the Holy See, and is circulated worldwide, on average about once each month. The only exception to this rule is where 'in particular cases another manner of promulgation has been prescribed'. This happens on occasion, though not frequently, e.g. it has happened that such laws have been expressly promulgated through their publication in 'L'Osservatore Romano', the official daily newspaper of the Vatican. In such instances, the specific directions given in the text would have to be considered on their own merits.

Assuming the normal promulgation via the *Acta Apostolicae Sedis*, the laws in question would 'come into force only on the expiry of three months', not from the date on the document itself, but rather 'from the date appearing on the particular

---
[1] *Summa Theologica* Ia-IIae q.90 art. 4 ad 1.

issue of the "Acta" which could be, and sometimes is, a matter of weeks or even months after the date on the text of the document. The three-month interval is to be calculated in accordance with Cann. 202 §2 – 203. There are but two exceptions to this rule:

(a) when, 'because of the nature of the case', the law in question would 'bind at once': the obvious example would be a law involving a substantial matter of faith or declaring the divine law;

(b) when the law itself 'specifically and expressly' prescribes either a shorter or a longer interval: the Code itself is a typical, but not the only, example of the latter.

25 As far as 'particular laws' are concerned (§2), i.e. those promulgated by any legislator below the Roman Pontiff, their precise manner of promulgation must be determined by the legislator himself – a point always to be noted. They begin to oblige one month from the date of promulgation – not at once, as under the 1917 Code – unless a different period is, for whatever good reason, prescribed in the law itself. The important practical point here is that whenever a particular law is issued – whether by a diocesan Bishop, by a particular Council, by a Bishops' Conference (in virtue of Can. 455), by a religious institute, etc. – it is essential that care be taken to ensure that such law is effectively communicated to those who are to be obliged by it, with an accurate specification of the date on which the law is to come into effect.

Can. 9 Laws concern matters of the future, not those of the past, unless provision is made in them for the latter by name.

26 The legal principle of this canon has long been recognised in both civil and ecclesiastical legal systems.[1] Because law of its nature is a regulator of human conduct – precisely as an instrument of justice – common sense alone dictates the *general rule* that a law must be concerned with conduct which will occur, and with arrangements which will be made, subsequent to the law itself being made and promulgated: 'laws concern matters of the future'. Any general rule to the contrary would clearly be an absurdity.

27 By way of *exception*, however, a specific law may be made to concern '(matters) of the past' and thus become what is technically known as a 'retroactive' law. The exceptional nature of such an enactment is stressed by this canon's demand that no law can have retroactive effect unless those matters 'of the past' to which it purports to apply, are specifically mentioned 'by name' (*nominatim*). Even then, retroactivity may be applied only to the extent that the matter in question lies within the jurisdiction of the legislator: thus e.g. no legislator may attempt to give retroactive effect to a law which would thereby violate divine or natural law, e.g. by rendering null a marriage which had earlier been validly contracted. In general terms, the following conditions apply:

(a) that a retroactive effect be compatible with the very nature of the case, as would be the situation in e.g. a merely declaratory law (see Can. 16 §2), a penal law which favours the offender (see Can. 1313);

(b) that a retroactive effect be required by the common good, or by the necessity to ensure that the intended beneficial effects of a new law are not negated, as could be the situation in certain invalidating or incapacitating laws (see Can. 10);

---

[1] The principle had its origin in Roman law, was found in medieval civil laws and still finds a place, to a greater or lesser extent, in modern civil jurisdictions. Its explicit canonical origin derives from the 13th century Decretals of Pope Gregory IX (c. 13, X, 1, 2); the 1917 Code c. 10 stated it in precisely the same terms as in the current text: the recognised commentators on that Code remain, accordingly, a valuable guide to interpretation.

(c) that a retroactive effect be never presumed and, in a case of doubt, be not admitted.[1]

Can. 10 Only those laws are to be considered invalidating or incapacitating which expressly prescribe that an act is null or that a person is incapable.

This again is a technical canon, which however determines an important practical matter. It lays down a principle according to which a law may properly be considered either invalidating or incapacitating – with the consequence that an act performed contrary to either such law would be null and void. An *invalidating* law is one which determines that for a person to act in a particular way or in certain circumstances would result in the act itself being invalid and accordingly of no legal effect. There are many such laws in the Code, e.g. Cann. 127 §§1–2, 153 §1, 172, 1108 §1, 1598 §1. An *incapacitating* law is one which determines that a particular *person*, or type of person, is excluded from validly carrying out the specific act which he or she purports to do. Again there are many such in the Code, e.g. 623, 996 §1, 1191 §2, 1322, 1674; in pastoral practice, the most obvious instances are those which determine the diriment impediments to marriage, Cann. 1083–1094.

The specific point of this canon is to prescribe that no law can fit into either of these two categories unless it 'expressly prescribe(s) that an act is null or that a person is incapable'. The term *expressly* is a specifically canonical one and must be understood as such. If a matter is stated *explicitly*, then it is manifestly stated in an 'express' manner: Can. 126 is a clear example among many in the Code. Equally 'express', however, is a matter which is stated *implicitly*, as is exemplified in the following Can. 127: it is explicitly stated that 'for the validity of the act, it is required that the consent be obtained of an absolute majority of those present...', thereby implicitly stating that without such a majority the act would be invalid.[2]

Can. 11 Merely ecclesiastical laws bind those who were baptised in the catholic Church or received into it, and who have a sufficient use of reason and, unless the law expressly provides otherwise, who have completed their seventh year of age.

This canon is a major innovation, in respect not only of the 1917 Code (c.12) but also of the thinking behind the draft of the Revision Commission as late as 1980. It represents in fact a particularly significant appreciation of the theological and ecumenical reflections of Vat. II.[3] It deals with those who are obliged by what are technically called *merely ecclesiastical laws*, i.e. laws whose sole source is the legislative authority of the catholic Church. These are distinguished not only from the divine law, be it natural or positive, but also from ecclesiastical laws which themselves are but declarations or interpretations of the divine law. It is this canon which has given the distinction a particularly practical significance: merely ecclesiastical laws bind those only 'who were baptised *in the catholic Church or received into it*';[4] the other laws mentioned above bind also the unbaptised. Thus e.g. Can. 1057 §1 prescribes that a

---

[1] Cf. Commentary (Urbanianum) 9–10. In pastoral practice, probably the best-known law with retroactive effect is that of Can. 1161 concerning the retroactive validation of a marriage (*sanatio in radice*).

[2] For a thorough exposition of this point, cf. Michiels I 335–340. The 1917 Code c.11 had said 'expressly *or equivalently*'; the latter was omitted in the current Code precisely because of the uncertainty which it generated: cf. Comm 16(1984) 146 at Can. 11.

[3] Cf. Comm 14(1982) 132–133.

[4] The 1917 Code c. 12 included all the baptised, whether in the catholic Church or otherwise.

marriage comes into being by the consent of the parties, which consent, based as it is on the divine-natural law, 'cannot be supplied by any human power': this clearly obliges everyone whether baptised or not; on the other hand, the Church itself, in what is a merely ecclesiastical law (Can. 1108 §1), prescribes certain formalities to be observed in the giving of that consent.

31 The canon stipulates three conditions to be fulfilled for a person to be bound by merely ecclesiastical laws:

(a) *Valid baptism* in the catholic Church, or reception into the catholic Church following valid baptism in some other christian community. What is required is baptism of water, with the approved trinitarian form. Thus the unbaptised, including catechumens (see Can. 206), are not directly bound by purely ecclesiastical laws. They may however be subject to those laws *indirectly*, e.g. when one such contracts marriage with a baptised Catholic who is bound by an impediment created by a merely ecclesiastical law. What if there is a doubt about the other person's baptism? While not all commentators are agreed on the point, an acceptable practical guideline could be as follows: if the doubt concerns the *fact* of baptism, i.e. whether or not a baptism was conferred, the person is not to be obliged by a merely ecclesiastical law; if, on the other hand, the doubt concerns the *validity* of a baptism which was certainly conferred, then the person is obliged. It must be said of course that this guideline is applicable only if every reasonable effort will already have been made, unavailingly, to dispel the doubt, whether of fact or of validity.

(b) *Sufficient use of reason:* This requirement reflects an obvious principle of natural law. A 'sufficient' use of reason is one which enables the person to have an understanding, not merely in the abstract but in a concrete fashion, of the obligation imposed by a law. Thus, those who habitually lack the use of reason, e.g. the mentally handicapped, are clearly not obliged; this is so even in the course of what are called lucid intervals (see Cann. 99, 97 §2). Equally exempt are those who, though habitually of sound mind, are for one reason or another temporarily deprived of the use of reason at the material time; in a doubtful situation, the obligation should not be imposed.

(c) *Completed seventh year of age:* baptised persons who have not completed the age of seven years, even though they may have attained the use of reason, are not subject. The seventh year of age will have been 'completed' on the day after one's seventh birthday (see Cann. 202–203). Unlike the other two conditions, this one allows of exceptions: 'unless the law expressly provides otherwise'. There are indeed situations for which the law so provides, e.g. (a lower age than seven) Cann. 913 §2, 920 §1; (a higher age than seven) Cann. 1252, 1323 1°.

Can. 12 §1 Universal laws are binding everywhere on all those for whom they were enacted.

§2 All those actually present in a particular territory in which certain universal laws are not in force, are exempt from those laws;

§3 Without prejudice to the provisions of Can. 13, laws enacted for a particular territory bind those for whom they were enacted and who have a domicile or quasi-domicile in that territory and are actually residing in it.

32 A *universal* ecclesiastical law is one enacted for the entire Church, or for certain categories of people in the entire Church, e.g. laity, clerics, religious. A *particular* law is one enacted for a specific territory e.g. a diocese, a region, a particular country, or for a specific and limited category of persons e.g. the members of an individual religious institute.

Title I Ecclesiastical Laws

The principle of §1, dealing with *universal* laws, speaks for itself. A situation is considered in §2 which may on occasion modify the application of that principle. It can happen that in a particular territory, e.g. a country or even a diocese, the universal law on a specific matter may not in fact be in force, whether by reason of a contrary custom or of a special exemption or the like. Obviously those who belong to that particular territory are exempt. The specific point of §2 is that even those who do *not* belong to that territory – those e.g. who happen to be visiting there – are equally exempt. A typical example would be that of a country or of a diocese in which the universal law of fasting or of abstinence (see Cann. 1249–1253) is not in fact – for whatever good reason – in force.

In interpreting §3 it must be borne in mind that its directives are 'without prejudice to (i.e. they must take into account) the provisions of Can. 13': the relevant points are dealt with below in the commentary on that canon. This paragraph deals only with those *particular* laws which are 'enacted for a particular territory', such as a diocese or a region or a country; it is not concerned with 'particular' laws which are enacted e.g. for the members of a specific religious institute. The point of the paragraph is to lay down the following three conditions which must *all* be simultaneously fulfilled if a person is to be bound by the particular laws in question:

(a) the person is one of 'those for whom (the laws) were enacted', be they the generality of the faithful, priests, religious, laity, administrators, etc.;

(b) the person has a domicile or a quasi-domicile (see Cann. 102–106) in the territory in question;

(c) the person is at the material time actually residing in the territory – not therefore outside the territory, even for a transient visit.

This however is not the whole story: it is at this point that account must also be taken of Can. 13 and particularly of its §§2–3.

Can. 13 §1 Particular laws are not presumed to be personal, but rather territorial, unless it is established otherwise.

This canon refines the treatment of *particular* laws, begun in Can. 12 §3. It opens in this §1 with a general statement, by way of a legal presumption, on the nature of such laws, i.e. whether they are personal or territorial. A law is *personal* when it is of such a nature that it obliges its subject everywhere, not merely in the territory (the diocese, the region, the country) to which he or she habitually belongs.[1] A law, on the other hand, is *territorial* when it is designed not directly for persons as such but rather for a specific territory, such as a diocese or a country.[2]

The legal presumption is that particular laws – of whatever kind, be they designed for a particular territory or for a particular category of persons – are territorial, not personal, *unless it is established otherwise*. Thus e.g. if a Bishop promulgates a law – say for the priests or for the parents or for the teachers or for those to be married, etc. of his diocese – such a law will oblige only if the person is within the boundaries of that

---

[1] Perhaps the most typical example is a universal law: cf. Can. 12 §1; equally however would be e.g. the particular law contained in the constitutions of a religious institute.

[2] The philosophical discussion as to the nature of law – whether it be personal or territorial – has had a long and varied history in both canonical and civil tradition. The recognised commentators on the 1917 Code (particularly at c.8 §2) deal with the matter extensively. It is to be noted that that c. 8 §2, dealing with *all* law, has been substituted by this Can. 13 §1, which in effect acknowledges that the question of whether law is of its nature personal or territorial arises only in the context of particular law: cf. Comm 3(1971) 85; 16(1984) 145 at Can. 8.

Bishop's diocese. To have it otherwise, the Bishop would require to make this clear in promulgating the law itself – and in doing so he would have to take account also of this Can. 13 §§2–3. Equally however it may be 'established otherwise' by the very nature of the particular law itself. The typical example is that of a law promulgated in the approved constitutions of a religious institute: such a law cannot be other than personal, since it concerns only the individual members of that particular institute, wherever they may be.

Can. 13 §2 *Peregrini* are not bound:

1° **by the particular laws of their own territory while they are absent from it, unless the transgression of those laws causes harm in their own territory, or unless the laws are personal;**

2° **by the laws of the territory in which they are present, except for those laws which take care of public order, or determine the formalities of legal acts, or concern immovable property located in the territory.**

§3 *Vagi* are bound by both the universal and the particular laws which are in force in the place in which they are present.

37 These two paragraphs, which hearken back principally to Can. 12 §3, provide for two categories of person for whom particular laws have a special relevance: *peregrini* and *vagi* (for both see Can. 100, and Glossary). Thus:

(a) *Peregrini*, being absent from their own territory, are not bound by the particular laws of that territory, save in the following two situations:

(i) if 'the transgression of those laws causes harm in their own territory', e.g. a law prohibiting the incitement or support of a disruptive organisation based in the home territory, a law for clerics concerning residence (see Can. 283) or concerning behaviour unbecoming to their state (see Can. 285 §1), and the like.

(ii) if 'the laws are (in fact) personal', e.g. if a Bishop forbids his priests to engage in what are considered unbecoming recreational activities even outside the diocese. It is essential that the competent legislator make quite clear that such a law is intended to be personal (see Can. 13 §1); if there be any real doubt on this point, it will not oblige outside the diocese.

(b) *Peregrini* are not bound 'by the laws of the territory in which they are present', save in the following three situations:

(i) if the laws in question 'take care of public order', i.e. are such that their violation *by anyone* would tend to disrupt the common good of the local community – a concept to be determined more often by common sense than by specific legal definition.[1]

(ii) if the laws 'determine the formalities of legal acts', such as e.g. contracts (in regard to which, in virtue of Can. 1290, the canon law generally adopts the local civil legislation), wills, the conduct of trials, etc.

(iii) if the laws 'concern immovable property located in the territory', e.g. a diocesan law which makes specific regulations about the sale or lease of land or buildings in ecclesiastical ownership.[2]

---

[1] For an insight into the mind of the legislator in this regard, cf. Comm 17(1985) 33 n.5.

[2] This requirement is an addition to those required by the 1917 Code at c.14 §1 2°. For the others, the recognised commentators remain a reliable guide.

(c) *Vagi* are bound 'by both the universal and the particular laws which are in force in the place in which they are present': in other words, as far as *vagi* are concerned the simple principle of territoriality obtains; in effect, they are regarded as if they had a domicile in the place where they find themselves. This regulation, adopted from the 1917 Code (c.14 §2) which corrected some anomalies in the previous legislation, is designed to protect the position of *vagi*, lest otherwise they be left without any specific point of legislative guidance (see e.g. Can. 107 §2).[1]

In any treatment of law and its application, a number of what one might call personal factors necessarily arise: is this law certain? – does it oblige me? – even if I do not know about it, or am wrong in thinking what it means? The next two canons deal with and give clear directions on just these questions: situations of doubt (Can. 14), situations of ignorance or error (Can. 15).

Can. 14 Laws, even invalidating and incapacitating ones, do not oblige when there is a doubt of law. When there is a doubt of fact, however, Ordinaries can dispense from them provided, if there is question of a reserved dispensation, it is one which the authority to whom it is reserved is accustomed to grant.

Doubt is a common feature of human experience. This canon is the guide when there is doubt about a law. The doubt with which the canon is concerned is a *positive* doubt, i.e. when to the ordinary observer (guided obviously by the recognised commentators) there are good reasons both in favour and against what the decision ought to be. It is also an *objective* doubt, i.e. one based on the real situation, not merely on the inability of the person in doubt to appreciate what the situation is. It is against this background that the canon distinguishes between a doubt of law and a doubt of fact.

A *doubt of law* arises when there is a positive and an objective doubt as to whether the law exists, as to what precisely it means, as to whom it intends to oblige, as to whether it may have been superseded, etc. The canon lays down the clear rule that in such a situation the law simply does not oblige, and in consequence that the conscientious person may act accordingly. It is important to note that this rule applies 'even (to) invalidating and incapacitating (laws)' (see Can. 10).

A *doubt of fact* – which assumes that the law itself is not doubtful, but certain – arises when there is a positive and an objective doubt as to whether a given fact or set of facts falls within the compass or scope clearly envisaged by the law, e.g. is this person eighteen years of age and so obliged by the law of fasting (see Cann. 1252, 97 §1)? – has this oil, required for the administration of a sacrament, been blessed by the appropriate minister? – are this couple, wishing to marry, related within the prohibited degrees of consanguinity (see Can. 1091)? etc. Unlike a doubt of law, a doubt of fact does not remove the obligation of the law. The remedy, in an appropriate case,[2] is to apply to the relevant Ordinary (see Can. 134 §1) who is empowered by this canon to grant a dispensation, provided of course that the prescribed conditions for dispensation are verified (see Cann. 85–93). The only restriction on this dispensing power concerns 'a reserved dispensation', i.e. one

---

[1] The so-called 'itinerants' or 'travelling people' are a specific case in point – a group for whom the Church must have a special care.
[2] This will principally be when there is a danger that otherwise the person may act sinfully or even in a manner whereby the act itself may be invalid.

whose dispensation is reserved by law, whether general or particular, to a specific authority, e.g. the Holy See, the Metropolitan, the Bishops' Conference.[1] In such a situation, the criterion (for validity) is whether or not the authority in question 'is accustomed to grant' that dispensation – not, obviously, on the basis of any mere personal whim, but rather by reason of what the general law prescribes (see e.g. Cann. 1078 §3, 1091 §4) or by reason of a particular local or cultural etc. situation in a given territory or jurisdiction.

Can. 15 §1 Ignorance or error concerning invalidating or incapacitating laws does not prevent the effect of those laws, unless it is expressly provided otherwise.

42 Every law of its very nature imposes on its subjects an obligation of knowing it; this indeed is the very point of Can. 7. *Ignorance* is the lack of such due knowledge or information.[2] *Error*, on the other hand, is simply a false or inaccurate judgement – in this context about a law (its meaning, its extent, its continuing force etc.) which is in fact known to the person in question. The sole point of this §1 is to deal with ignorance and error in the context of invalidating or incapacitating laws (see Can. 10).[3] The simple rule is that ignorance, of whatever kind even inculpable, or error however unexplainable, 'does not prevent the effect of those laws'. The reason is equally simple: such laws are designed specifically to guide and protect the common good of the Church, and so cannot be made dependent upon the subjective judgement of individuals. Thus e.g. if a couple marry who are in fact first cousins but simply do not know that (ignorance), or who, perhaps suspecting it, wrongly decide that they are not (error), their marriage is nonetheless invalid. The rule is not, however, absolute: the text excepts the situation where 'it is expressly provided otherwise', the most notable example of which is in a situation of 'common error' (Can. 144; see also Can. 142 §2).

Can. 15 §2 Ignorance or error is not presumed about a law, a penalty, a fact concerning oneself, or a notorious fact concerning another. It is presumed about a fact concerning another which is not notorious, until the contrary is proved.

43 This §2 lays down a general procedural rule as to what may or may not be presumed in the context of ignorance and error. The rule is manifestly for the guidance of those with executive authority such as Ordinaries (see Can. 134), or with judicial authority such as judges in ecclesiastical tribunals.[4] Ignorance or error is *not* presumed:

(a) *about a law or a penalty:* everyone is presumed to know a law which has been properly promulgated (see Can. 7). Accordingly, one who alleges ignorance or error is obliged to prove that this was in fact the case: such proof may more easily be admitted in respect of minors or of the less educated, or when it relates to a matter far removed from the common understanding.[5]

---

[1] For dispensations reserved to the Holy See (or Roman Pontiff) cf. e.g. Cann. 291, 1047 §§1–3, 1078 §2, 1698 §2; for those to other authorities cf. the relevant particular law.

[2] For the various divisions of the concept of ignorance and their consequences, cf. Regatillo I n.83; Vermeersch–Creusen I n.115; Commentary (Urbanianum) 16.

[3] Ignorance and error are obviously factors which have to be taken into account in respect of many other areas of law e.g. laws regarding discipline in general, laws regarding the Sacraments, laws regarding penalties, etc. These are explained in their respective contexts in this commentary.

[4] There are many specific applications of the rule in Book VII. For the definition of a 'presumption' cf. Can. 1584.

[5] Cf. Regatillo I n.83.

(b) *about a fact concerning oneself:* clearly no one can be supposed to be ignorant or in error about what he or she is or has done; contrary proof might however be possible regarding events of the remote past or of minor importance and the like.

(c) *about a notorious fact concerning another person:* in this context 'notorious' means that which is, for whatever reason, a matter of open and public knowledge in the community in question – be that a country, a city, even a small rural area; that which is thus publicly known is, in the absence of contrary proof, presumed to be known by everyone in the area.

The opposite is the situation in respect of *a fact concerning another person which is not notorious* or publicly known: 'until the contrary is proved' such a fact must be presumed not to be accurately known.

Law of its nature, being an attempt to express, normally in writing, that which a competent legislator has in mind, is clearly subject to the possibility of diverse or even divergent opinions as to its true meaning. In every system of law there are established rules – sometimes written, sometimes conventional, sometimes a mixture of both – for its proper interpretation, i.e. rules to enable everyone concerned in so far as possible to discern and to understand precisely what the relevant legislator intended in making this or that law. The Canon Law is no exception. The following Canons 16–21 deal with the principles involved here and with various aspects of the matter in the context of ecclesiastical law.[1]

Can. 16 §1 Laws are authentically interpreted by the legislator and by that person to whom the legislator entrusts the power of authentic interpretation.

The written text of a law can be read and understood in a variety of ways. It is essential that a law be understood correctly. This canon contains basic norms concerning the authoritative interpretation of ecclesiastical laws, i.e. an interpretation which binds others in an objective manner.

The most important form of authoritative interpretation is *authentic* interpretation. Strictly speaking, it is only the legislator – or, clearly his successor in office, e.g. the Pope, a diocesan Bishop or his equivalent (see Can. 381 §2) – who may issue what is referred to in this canon as an *authentic* interpretation,[2] i.e. one which is incontrovertible and binding. This arises from the fact that the essential notion of interpretation has to do with understanding the mind and intention of the legislator.

According to the canon, the legislator can entrust the power of authentic interpretation to others. In practice, this is often what happens. The Pontifical Council for the Interpretation of Legislative Texts was established precisely 'to publish authentic interpretations of universal laws of the Church'.[3] This Council also examines general

---

[1] For the technical terms to distinguish the various types of interpretation, cf. Vermeersch–Creusen I n.120; Commentary (Urbanianum) 17–18; Chiappetta I nn. 155–166.

[2] Besides the Pope and diocesan Bishops there are, of course, other legislators in the Church e.g. particular Councils (Cann. 439–446), Bishops' Conferences (Can. 455), General Chapters of religious institutes (Can. 631 §1). They too are competent to issue authentic interpretations of their laws, but these will have effect only after their review and approval by the appropriate ecclesiastical authority (cf. Cann. 446, 455 §2, 587, 595).

[3] PB 155. This Council was established on 2.I.1984 to interpret the Code of Canon Law promulgated on 25.I.1983 and all other universal laws of the Latin church. The title of the Council and its scope was broadened in PB. It is now competent to issue authentic interpretations of the Code of Canon Law and of the Code of Canons of the Eastern Churches, and all universal legislation of the catholic Church. It is the direct successor of the Pontifical Commission established on 15.IX.1917 for the authentic interpretation of the 1917 Code, the Pontifical Commission for the Revision of the Code of Canon Law established on 28.III.1963, and the Pontifical Commission for the interpretation of the Decrees of Vat. II established on 11.VII.1967.

decrees and instructions of the Roman Curia, the general decrees of Bishops' Conferences and other particular legislation, to make sure that they are in conformity with universal legislation.[1]

Can. 16 §2 An authentic interpretation which is presented by way of a law has the same force as the law itself, and must be promulgated. If it simply declares the sense of words which are certain in themselves, it has retroactive force. If it restricts or extends a law or explains a doubtful one, it is not retroactive.

48   An authoritative interpretation of a law can be issued in three ways:
(a) 'by way of a law' (§2)
(b) 'by way of a court judgment' (§3)
(c) 'by way of an administrative act' (§3)

Only the first of these can be described as an 'authentic interpretation' i.e. an understanding of the mind and intention of the legislator. An interpretation 'by way of a law' is a general statement concerning the law made to the whole community to whom the law is addressed. Such an interpretation is issued by the legislator or the one to whom this power has been entrusted by the legislator e.g. the Pontifical Council for the Interpretation of Legislative Texts.

49   According to the canon, this kind of interpretation requires promulgation (see Cann. 7–8). It has the very same force as the law itself since it expresses the legislator's mind and intention. It is *binding* on all for whom the law was made e.g. the whole Church in the case of a universal law; all those in a particular territory, in the case of a particular law, etc. It cannot be contradicted or *controverted* by a lower authority.

50   Four kinds of authentic interpretation are mentioned in the canon:
– *simple declarative*: where the meaning of the words is clear in itself;[2]
– *restrictive*: where the meaning of the words is narrowed down within their proper meaning;[3]
– *extensive*: where the meaning of the words is expanded beyond their proper meaning;[4]
– *explanatory*: where the law is explained in such a way that an objective doubt is resolved.[5]

51   Only in the case of a simple declarative interpretation can the effects of an authentic interpretation 'by way of a law' be understood as retroactive. Since the purpose of such an interpretation is to clarify the meaning of words which is already objectively certain, no change is made to the status of the law. On the other hand, if the authentic interpretation is restrictive, or extensive, or explanatory, the effects are not retroactive since some innovation has occurred, which accordingly has effect only from the date on which the interpretation itself is promulgated.

---

[1] Cf. PB 156–158.

[2] E.g. CCom rep 14.V.1985: AAS 77(1985) 771. This made clear that a Superior does not have the right to vote with those whose advice or consent he must obtain in accordance with Can. 127 §1.

[3] E.g. CCom rep 26.VI.1984: AAS 76(1984) 746. This made clear the norm of receiving Eucharistic Communion no more than twice on the same day.

[4] E.g. CCom rep 19.I.1988: AAS 80(1988) 1818. This expanded the definition of abortion to include the killing of the foetus at any time after conception.

[5] E.g. CCom rep 29.IV.1987: AAS 79(1987) 1249. This made clear the point that Can. 648 §3 referred to religious in temporary vows as well as those in perpetual vows.

Can. 16 §3 On the other hand, an interpretation by way of a court judgement or of an administrative act in a particular case, does not have the force of law. It binds only those persons and affects only those matters for which it was given.

An authoritative interpretation of law given in a judicial sentence or in an administrative act is also binding. However, it affects only those persons and circumstances for which the decision was made, e.g. in a case of the nullity of a marriage. Unlike an authentic interpretation, a judicial sentence or an administrative may be contradicted following an appeal (see Cann. 1628–1640) or a recourse (see Cann. 1732–1739). Any interpretation of law given in a specific case cannot be established as a binding general norm for others.

Can. 17 Ecclesiastical laws are to be understood according to the proper meaning of the words considered in their text and context. If the meaning remains doubtful or obscure, there must be recourse to parallel places, if there be any, to the purpose and circumstances of the law, and to the mind of the legislator.

In Can. 17 and the two following canons, the legislator supplies some rules of interpretation which must be applied if the law is to be correctly and accurately understood. These rules are helpful in preparing so-called *doctrinal interpretations* of the canons i.e. interpretations of the law given by serious and established commentators or authors. Such interpretations are not of themselves binding. Yet, according to the weight to be attached to the reasons on which they are founded and to the concordance of authors in their regard, they are to be taken seriously into account.

The first rule stated in Can. 17 is that the ecclesiastical law must be understood according to the proper meaning of the words considered in their text and context. The 'proper meaning' of words is that which is commonly attributed to them – normally the dictionary meaning, though in certain circumstances there may be an accepted technical legal meaning. Moreover, all the words must be analysed within their text and context. The text refers to the verbal exposition of the law, i.e. its sentence structure; the *context* is the logical arrangement of the sentence, within an immediately broader perspective e.g. the whole canon, the title, the chapter etc. A textual interpretation may be literally correct, but it may have to be adjusted in accordance with the context in which it is used.

If, after considering their text and context, the meaning of the words of a law still remain obscure or doubtful, then – but only then – recourse must be had to certain subsidiary criteria of interpretation:

(a) *Parallel places* (passages): Unlike c.18 of the 1917 Code, the present canon does not limit parallel passages to those found in the Code; thus a guide to interpreting the law may be found in documents outside the Code, e.g., the decrees of Vat. II, documents coming from offices of the Roman Curia, the Eastern Code, etc.

(b) *The purpose and circumstances of the law*: The purpose of the law is the reason or motive for its existence. Laws are the response to some concrete historic facts, or to religious or social conditions. A consideration of the extrinsic factors surrounding the origin of a law may provide a useful key to understanding it correctly.

(c) *Recourse to the mind of the legislator:* The term 'mind of the legislator' may be understood as the general disposition by which the legislator was inspired and directed to formulate the law in question. This will require a consideration of the legislator's general mentality, attitudes and whole manner of exercising authority. At best, this can only be a subjective assessment of what is implicit in the actions of the legislator. An explicit manifestation of the mind of the legislator is an *authentic* interpretation (see Can. 16 §1).

Can. 18 Laws which prescribe a penalty, or restrict the free exercise of rights, or contain an exception to the law, are to be interpreted strictly.

56 Generally speaking, those laws which impose a burden require strict interpretation; those laws granting favours or faculties enjoy broad interpretation.[1] To interpret law strictly means to give to the words of the law a minimum of extension, while still respecting the meaning of the words and not attributing to them a meaning contrary to the intention of the legislator.

57 Three kinds of laws are to be strictly interpreted:
 (i) those which *establish penalties* of any kind, determined or undetermined, vindictive or medicinal, even penal remedies. This includes penal precepts (see Can. 1319) which are not strictly laws.
 (ii) those which *restrict the free exercise of rights*: i.e. both human rights (e.g. to nurture, to education, to choice of state in life, etc.) and ecclesial rights (e.g. of the baptised to celebrate the sacraments, to hear the word of God, etc.) According to the canon, any law which restricts or limits the free exercise of such rights, e.g. laws on matrimonial impediments (see Cann. 1083–1094), are to be interpreted strictly so as to leave maximum latitude for the exercise of the underlying right.
 (iii) those which *contain an exception* to the law: the Code explicitly provides in several canons exceptions to the general law in order to respond to certain abnormal or extraordinary situations e.g. the use of the extraordinary form of marriage (see Can. 1127, §2). In such cases, strict interpretation prevents the exception from becoming the norm.

Can. 19 If on a particular matter there is not an express provision of either universal or particular law, nor a custom, then, provided it is not a penal matter, the question is to be decided by taking into account laws enacted in similar matters, the general principles of law observed with canonical equity, the jurisprudence and practice of the Roman Curia, and the common and constant opinion of learned authors.

58 Of their very nature laws are intended to provide for the general situation. Yet some situations require a remedy which cannot be found in existing legislation. Can. 19 supplies four objective sources to remedy the absence of norms not only in general but also in particular law:

59 (a) *Laws enacted in similar matters:* A supplementary source of law may be obtained by the analogy of law i.e. by examining laws enacted in similar matters, e.g. Cann. 486–491 provides a supplementary source of law for religious institutes in the matter of archives.

60 (b) *The general principles of law observed with canonical equity:* Many authors regard these 'general principles of law' as referring both to *General Norms* of the Code (Book I), as well as to the universal and fundamental principles evolved from the law of nature, e.g. the principles contained in '*Regulae Iuris*' found in Roman Law and in

---

[1] This is based on the ancient rule of law found in the *Liber Sextus* of Pope Boniface VIII: 'Odia restringi, et favores convenit ampliari' (Reg. 15, RJ in VI°).

authentic collections of canon law.[1] These rules of law facilitate the interpretation and application of canon law. They must be used with caution since they are broad principles. Before applying a rule of law, one should determine whether the case is identical with that covered by the rule, or may possibly be an exception to the rule. According to the canon, these general principles of law are to be applied with 'canonical equity'. Speaking to the Roman Rota in 1973, Pope Paul VI defined this in the words of the great medieval canonist Hostiensis: 'justice tempered with the sweetness of mercy'.[2] The Pope went on to point out that 'in canon law, equity ... is a characteristic of its precepts and the norm of their application; an attitude of mind and spirit that tempers the rigour of the law'.[3]

(c) *The jurisprudence and practice of the Roman Curia:* A good guide to the interpretation of law and a helpful criterion in resolving a problem which does not have an express provision in law is the application of the law in practical matters. The canon makes it clear that the jurisprudence of the Apostolic Signatura and the Roman Rota, as well as the practice of the departments of the Roman Curia, constitute a source of supplementary norms.[4] The 1917 Code e.g. contained no canon similar to the current Can. 1095, yet that lacuna was filled by the jurisprudence of the Roman Rota which had evolved and developed in the meantime.

(d) *Common and constant opinion of learned authors:* Legal experts do not have any power to formulate new laws or to make authentic interpretations. However, their opinion is acknowledged as a legitimate norm for supplementing positive law provided that it is *common and constant*. To be considered a 'common opinion', it must be accepted by several authors of wise repute. An opinion is called 'constant' if it perseveres among authors for several years after it has become a 'common' opinion.

The four supplementary sources mentioned in this canon may not be used to resolve what might be regarded as a *lacuna* in a penal matter. If the law is silent, no penalty exists (see Can. 6 §1 3°). In this way the Code upholds the ancient axiom 'nulla poena sine lege'.

Can. 20 A later law abrogates or derogates from an earlier law, if it expressly so states, or if it is directly contrary to that law, or if it integrally reorders the whole subject matter of the earlier law. A universal law, however, does not derogate from a particular or from a special law, unless the law expressly provides otherwise.

In order to serve the good of souls, ecclesiastical laws must have a certain stability, i.e. they must retain their normative force without constant change. Nevertheless, times and circumstances do change and affect the stability of laws. A law may lose its force either intrinsically or extrinsically. Intrinsically, this occurs when changed circum-

---

[1] E.g. the *Digest* of Justinian (533), the *Liber Extra* of Pope Gregory IX (1234), the *Liber Sextus* of Pope Boniface VIII (1298), etc.

[2] Pope Paul VI Address to the Roman Rota 8.II.1973: in *Papal Allocutions to the Roman Rota 1939–1994* ed. Woestman Ottawa 1994 118.

[3] Ibid.

[4] Cf. una Birminghamien coram Egan 9.XII.1982: SRR Dec 74, 612–618, nn.2–7. This decision stresses the normative value of the jurisprudence of the Roman Rota, a value which cannot be attributed to the jurisprudence of local tribunals. Pope John Paul II emphasised the point: 'Moreover, the influence of the Roman Rota on the activity of regional and diocesan ecclesiastical tribunals should be valued in particular. The jurisprudence of the Rota has always been and must continue to be a sure point of reference for them' (Address 30.I.1986: *Papal Allocutions* ed. Woestman 190).

stances make a law contrary to the demands of the Gospel, to canonical equity etc., or when the fundamental purpose of a law is wholly lost. Such a cessation of law is rare. Much more common is the cessation of law by *extrinsic* means, i.e. by the intervention of the legislator. Since the legislator is the author of the law, it is only right that any alteration to that law should emanate from the same source.

65 The canon draws a distinction between *abrogation*, i.e. the complete revocation of a law, and *derogation*, i.e. the partial revocation of a law. The legislator may abrogate or derogate from an existing law in three ways:

(a) by express revocation, e.g. by virtue of Can. 6 §1 1° the 1917 Code has been abrogated; by virtue of Can. 6 §1 3° all penal laws issued by the Holy See are abrogated *unless* resumed in the Code;

(b) by making a law directly contrary to the original, e.g. by virtue of Can. 6 §1 2° all existing laws *contrary* to the provisions of the current Code were abrogated; the essential incompatibility between the old and the new robs the old law of its force;

(c) by the subsequent total reordering of the subject matter of the law, e.g. by virtue of Can. 6 §1 4° any universal disciplinary norms which are wholly reordered in the Code are abrogated; in this case, while the subject matter may be the same, the new juridical structure replaces the old. A particularly illustrative example may be seen in the context of the so-called 'mixed marriages': one need merely compare the 1917 Code at cc.1060–1064 and 1071 with the current Code at Cann. 1124–1129.

66 In keeping with an ancient legal axiom,[1] the canon points out that universal law in itself does not abrogate or derogate from particular laws or special laws. Thus, laws affecting a specified territory (particular laws) and those affecting a specified category of person (special laws e.g. religious constitutions) are not automatically repealed by a subsequent universal law which is contrary. To have such an effect, the universal law must address the issue expressly, e.g. by the use of a formula such as 'all other things to the contrary, even in particular or special law, notwithstanding'.

Can. 21 In doubt, the revocation of a previous law is not presumed; rather, later laws are to be related to earlier ones and, as far as possible, harmonised with them.

67 If a law is expressly abrogated or derogated from by a subsequent intervention of the legislator, there can be little doubt concerning its status: it is deprived of all force. However, if the revocation takes the form of a subsequent contrary law, or of an integral reordering of the subject matter of a law, the precise status of an earlier law might not always be so clear. Whenever such a doubt arises, the present canon makes it clear that no presumption may be made in favour of the revocation of the earlier law. Indeed, by implication the canon maintains the opposite, namely that the earlier law is presumed still to be in force and of use to the community for which it was made. Thus the earlier law and the subsequent law or laws are understood to be obligatory at the same time. There can be no contradiction between such laws since this would constitute tacit revocation in one of the forms mentioned in Can. 20. However, it may prove difficult to see how both can be observed: in such a dilemma the canon stipulates that the newer law or laws are to be applied in the light of practice based on the earlier law. In this way, they may be seen as complementary rather than contrary. It is to be noted of course that this arises *only* if there is a positive doubt about the revocation.

---

[1] 'In toto iure, generi per speciem derogatur, et illud potissimum habetur quod ad speciem directum est' (l. 80 D. de RJ 50, 17); cf. also Reg. 34, RJ in VI°.

Can. 22 When the law of the Church remits some issue to the civil law, the latter is to be observed with the same effects in canon law, in so far as it is not contrary to divine law, and provided it is not otherwise stipulated in canon law.

Some situations in the life of the People of God are best regulated in accordance with the law of the State in which they live. The Code refers many of these matters to the particular civil legislation (e.g. Cann. 98 §2, 110, 197, 1059, 1062 §1, 1284 §2 3°, 1290 etc.) This canon, not found as such in the 1917 Code, makes it clear that, in these situations, the civil law is considered as a supplementary or subsidiary source of law. Where it applies, the civil laws are to be observed with the very same effects in canon law: the canon may be said to 'canonise' civil law in those situations. However, matters cannot be left to civil law if its prescriptions are contrary to divine law, or if canon law has made other provisions.

Title II
Custom

Can. 23 A custom introduced by a community of the faithful has the force of law only if it has been approved by the legislator, in accordance with the following canons.

The concept of *custom* as explained in this Title is very specific to canon law, and indeed has often been the envy of many civil jurisdictions. A custom may be defined as a common or constant mode of action adopted by a community. Behaviour of this kind by a group is a matter of *fact*. However, canon law acknowledges that such activity can become normative within the group or community. In fact, custom or the practice of the faithful has been a valuable source of law in the Church since its beginnings. The earliest councils and synods often did little besides confirming and endorsing certain customs, giving them the force of law, e.g. the Council of Elvira sanctioned clerical celibacy as an already existing practice;[1] many of the early collections of canon law did the same. There are many arguments in favour of a law based on custom: e.g. it is more adaptable, it is more in keeping with the concept of the Church as a pilgrim People of God guided by the Holy Spirit, etc. Of course, there are some arguments against it: e.g. it undermines unity, it favours disintegration of the community, it is uncertain, etc. Conscious of such arguments, the authorities of the Church have long sought to recognise the value of custom while attempting to harmonise it with other legal structures and institutions. These six canons are part of that ongoing process.[2]

---

[1] Council of Elvira Can. 33, DS 119.

[2] During the preparation of the text, it was argued that the norms governing custom were too restrictive and did not take account of the great importance in the life of the younger Churches. However, this observation was considered to be too general and lacking in solid foundation: cf. Comm 14(1982) 135 at Titulum II.

70 This opening canon makes a clear distinction between the origin of a custom *as fact* and its origin *as law*. As a fact, a custom is introduced by the behaviour and practice of members of a given community. As a fact, however, this custom in itself has no force as a norm. The force of law is given to a custom *only* by the approval of the legislator. The 'legislator' is understood as referring to the one who has power to make laws for the community in question, e.g. the Pope, a plenary or a provincial Council, a diocesan Bishop, a General Chapter of a religious institute, etc. Approval may be given to a custom in a variety of forms: it may be *express*, e.g. a decree sanctioning a certain practice of the community; it may be *tacit*, e.g. if the legislator makes no effort to prohibit or remove the custom even though aware of it. Whatever form it takes, the approval must conform to the norms found in Cann. 24–28.

Can. 24 §1 No custom which is contrary to divine law can acquire the force of law.

71 The juridical foundation of a custom having the force of law lies in the approval of the legislator. This canon makes clear that the legislator's power to approve customs can only be exercised within clearly defined limits. First of all, a legislator has no authority to approve of or tolerate any practice which contravenes the divine law, even if it has been the custom of a community for a long time. Thus, e.g. an ecclesiastical legislator cannot sanction a custom which promotes either euthanasia or abortion, since both are contrary to the right to life (divine natural law); nor can he permit baptism to take place using a liquid other than water (divine positive law), etc.

Can. 24 §2 A custom which is contrary to or apart from canon law, cannot acquire the force of law unless it is reasonable; a custom which is expressly reprobated in the law is not reasonable.

72 Customs may be distinguished according to their relation to other provisions of law. They may be:

(a) *according to the law*, if they involve a particular manner of observing the contents of the law;

(b) *apart from the law*, if they create a new obligation not contained in the law, but not contrary to it;

(c) *contrary to the law*, if they purport to establish a right or obligation which is in opposition to the law.

73 As well as conformity to divine law (§1), the canon understands, as a rule, that customs conform to the prescriptions of canon law, as in (a) above. At the same time, provision is made for the admissibility of some customs which are either apart from or contrary to the law (b and c above). The minimum criterion for their admissibility is that they be *reasonable*, i.e. in conformity with right reason. No positive guidelines are provided for assessing this quality. It is in fact easier to identify what is *unreasonable*, e.g. that which is harmful to the common good, contrary to the constitution of the Church or to the fundamental principles of canon law, etc. The simple fact that a custom is contrary to the law does not thereby make it 'unreasonable' in the sense of this canon. In the last analysis, the judgment on the reasonableness or otherwise of any custom will depend upon the appropriate legislator in accordance with Can. 23 – whose approval, however, may well remain tacit, i.e. by allowing to persist a custom of which he is aware. The only absolute bar on such a legislator's approval arises if the custom in question has been 'expressly reprobated in the law', as e.g. in Cann. 396 §2, 423 §1, 1076, etc.: in accordance with Can. 5 §1 such a custom has now been 'completely suppressed and ... may not be allowed to revive in the future'.

Title II Custom

Can. 25 No custom acquires the force of law unless it has been observed, with the intention of introducing a law, by a community capable at least of receiving a law.

The mere fact of constant behaviour by a group of people does not constitute what canon law understands by a custom having the force of law. Two conditions must be verified by the group concerned:

(a) Firstly, it must be 'a community capable at least of receiving a law'. Commentators on the 1917 Code suggested that this referred only to those groups whose Superior could make laws, or to those who were part of a larger community also capable of making laws, or a community established in some stable fashion.[1] They included among these communities the universal Church, the diocese and its equivalents in law, religious institutes and their constituent parts subject to a major Superior, autonomous monasteries, chapters of canons, etc. They excluded from this kind of community parishes, individual religious houses, families etc. Yet the canon speaks of 'a community capable at least of *receiving* a law', not a community capable of making law. Bearing this in mind, it would appear that any group within the Church which needs laws for its government is capable of introducing a custom, e.g. a parish, a university, a public association of the faithful.[2]

(b) Secondly, the community in question must have observed this custom 'with the intention of introducing a law'. Mere repetition of something does not create a custom, still less a custom with the force of law. The community must adopt this behaviour *intentionally*, i.e. intending to bind itself. Only in this way can the community be said to 'introduce' a custom: it cannot happen by accident. If the custom is either according to or apart from the law, the community can be seen to be acting in good faith. However, if the custom is contrary to the law, it is clear that the community – at least initially – was acting in at least a suspicion of bad faith. If such a custom is in due time approved by the legislator, that which is approved is not the bad faith (to whatever degree) of the originating group but the inherent reasonableness of the practice involved, taking account of all the local circumstances.

Can. 26 Unless it has been specifically approved by the competent legislator, a custom which is contrary to the canon law currently in force, or is apart from the canon law, acquires the force of law only when it has been lawfully observed for a period of thirty continuous and complete years. Only a centennial or immemorial custom can prevail over a canonical law which carries a clause forbidding future customs.

This canon prescribes the length of time within which, generally speaking, a custom either contrary to or apart from the law must have been 'lawfully observed' before it acquires the force of law. Before doing so, however, it lays down one overriding regulation: to the effect that any such custom may acquire the force of law – after whatever, even shorter, interval of its existence – if in the meantime '*it has been specifically approved by the competent legislator*'. Such 'specific approval' may be given:

---

[1] Cf. Van Hove *De consuetudine – De temporis supputatione* Mechliniae–Romae 1933 77; Michiels (NG) 64–65; Vermeersch–Creusen I 159; Capello *Summa Iuris Canonici* I n.112.

[2] Cf. Urrutia n.286.

(a) *expressly*, i.e. by explicit words or deeds sanctioning the practice involved;
(b) *tacitly*, i.e. by acting in such a way that consent is unequivocally implied;
(c) *legally*, i.e. by establishing laws or other norms so that customs which fulfil these conditions are regarded as legally binding.

76 In the absence, however, of such prior specific approval, a custom of this kind may still acquire the force of law by the mere passage of time, namely if it has been observed *lawfully* 'for a period of thirty continuous and complete years'. The word 'lawfully' implies that neither the legislator nor the community shall have done anything to revoke or prohibit the custom: after any intervention of that kind, the observance of the custom cannot be regarded as 'lawful'. The period of thirty years observance must be counted in accordance with Cann. 201–203.[1] An intervention by the legislator or a change in the practice of the community constitutes an interruption; if the custom is to have force, it must be resumed after the interruption and persist unbroken for thirty whole years. While it is necessary to lay down detailed rules of this kind, it must also be remembered that, especially in the matter of local custom, the parameters are not always so clinically clear cut – in which case the situation must be judged in accordance not with the computer but rather with the principle of common-sense (call it, *in casu*, canonical equity).

77 This canon also addresses the matter of customs which are contrary to laws containing clauses which prohibit the introduction of future contrary customs. These laws are not to be confused with those in which contrary customs are 'expressly reprobated' (Can. 24 §2). If the clause is simply prohibitive, e.g. 'excluding all future customs', it is still possible for a contrary custom to develop. Such a custom, however, can prevail over the law only if it shall have been observed for more than one hundred years or for as long as history has recorded.

Can. 27 Custom is the best interpreter of laws.

78 The text of this canon (also in c.29 of the 1917 Code) is derived *verbatim* from Roman Law.[2] The principle enunciated is an acknowledgement that laws are not to be understood as dead texts, void of life: it is the living community to whom a law is given which demonstrates the true meaning of a law by the way in which that law is observed. Any obscurity or doubt concerning such a law can be dispelled by a consideration of the actual practice of the community. It is not, of course, equal in authority to an *authentic* interpretation (see Can. 16), but such custom does provide the preferable solution to doubts concerning the law. There can be no doubt that the 'custom' referred to in the text refers to actual practice, i.e. to the custom of *fact*. This may restrict or expand the actual meaning of the law. However, such a custom can never be apart from or contrary to the law; if it were such, it would constitute not an interpretation of law but rather the establishment of a new norm (see Cann. 24 §2, 26).

Can. 28 Without prejudice to the provisions of Can. 5, a custom, whether contrary to or apart from the law, is revoked by a contrary custom or law. But unless the law makes express mention of them, it does not revoke centennial or immemorial customs, nor does a universal law revoke particular customs.

---

[1] In cc.27 §1 and 28 of the 1917 Code a period of forty years was prescribed. During the revision process, a shorter period of twenty years was proposed. However, the Commission established thirty years as a happy medium: cf. Comm 14(1982) 135 at Can. 26.

[2] Cf. l.37 D. de legg. 1, 3. It is also found in the *Liber Extra* (c.8, X, de consuetudine, I, 4) and in the *Liber Sextus* (Reg. 45, RJ in VI°).

Can. 5 deals with the revocation of customs contrary to or apart from the prescriptions of the current Code which existed at the time when this Code came into effect in 1983. The present canon concerns other customs, whether they existed prior to or after the Code came into effect; it deals only with the causes which lead to the cessation of such customs. Just as a law can be revoked by a contrary law or a contrary custom, so a custom can legally cease to exist because of a contrary custom or a contrary law. A new custom revokes the former custom only when the new has gained the force of law in accordance with Can. 26. A new law revokes an existing custom either explicitly through clauses of revocation or implicitly through provisions which render the custom unlawful or impracticable. However, as a rule, such provisions of law do not affect customs which are more than a hundred years old or immemorial; nor can a universal law revoke contrary particular customs. In both cases, the custom may be revoked only if it is mentioned expressly in the new law.

Thus, this canon establishes the following practical principles:

(a) a particular law may revoke either explicitly or implicitly particular customs which are contrary to it:

(b) a particular custom may revoke a particular contrary custom;

(c) a universal law cannot revoke a particular contrary custom, unless the law contains an express provision to that effect, e.g. the clause: 'notwithstanding any contrary custom';

(d) a law – either universal or particular – cannot revoke a centennial or immemorial custom unless the revocation is contained expressly in that law.

Title III
General Decrees and Instructions

Can. 29 General decrees, by which common provisions for a community capable of receiving a law are made by a competent legislator, are true laws and are regulated by the provisions of the canons on laws.

As well as laws properly so-called, the life of the Church is regulated by other norms. Among these are general decrees and instructions. Broadly speaking, both of these kinds of norms are largely disciplinary or administrative in character. They may be said to supplement or to implement legislation.

This canon – which, like the Title itself, has no parallel in the 1917 Code – describes one kind of general decree: an act by which common provisions are given by a competent authority having legislative power to a community 'capable of receiving a law' (see Can. 25). Thus, the Bishops of a particular Conference are competent legislators and may issue common norms to be observed in all the local Churches within the territory of the Conference (see Can. 455), a community which is capable of receiving a law.[1] General decrees issued in this fashion are, according to the canon, truly laws.

---

[1] Examples of such *general legislative decrees* include the decrees of an Ecumenical Council e.g. IM, CD, PC, PO of Vat. II; the decrees of Bishops' Conferences (cf. LCE); the decrees of a plenary council (Can. 439 §1) or a provincial council (Can. 440 §1).

Hence the provisions of Cann. 7–22 apply to them in the matter of promulgation, interpretation, revocation, etc.

Can. 30 One who has only executive power cannot make a general decree, as in Can. 29, unless in particular cases this has been expressly authorised by the competent legislator in accordance with the law, and provided the conditions prescribed in the act of authorisation are observed.

83 This canon is a corollary of Can. 29. It makes clear that the 'competent legislator' does not include those who exercise only executive power. Thus, excluded from the ability to issue general legislative decrees are Roman Congregations, Vicars general, episcopal Vicars, diocesan Administrators etc. While they may issue general executory decrees (see Can. 31), these authorities cannot make laws.

84 However, the canon contains an exception. Such purely executive authorities *can* issue general legislative decrees if this faculty has been granted to them *expressly* by the Superior legislator; even then, the decrees can be issued only in accordance with the conditions attached to the grant. Some commentators understand this to mean that a Vicar general can issue general legislative decrees if he has been authorised to do so by the diocesan Bishop.[1] Others take the opposite view, arguing that the exception contained in the canon refers only to departments of the Roman Curia expressly authorised to issue general decrees by the Pope; they support this position by recalling the status of these general decrees as laws and the fact that legislative power cannot be delegated (see Can. 135 §2).[2]

85 This latter interpretation – which appears the preferable one – is reinforced by the way in which this authorisation has been regulated in legislation affecting the Roman Curia.[3] The comparative rarity with which the departments of the Roman Curia can issue general legislative decrees supports the view that the only 'competent legislator' envisaged by Can. 30 is the Supreme Pontiff.

Can. 31 §1 Within the limits of their competence, those who have executive power can issue general executory decrees, that is, decrees which define more precisely the manner of applying a law, or which urge the observance of laws.

§2 The provisions of Can. 8 are to be observed in regard to the promulgation, and to the interval before the coming into effect, of the decrees mentioned in §1.

86 General executory decrees are *not* laws. Rather, as defined in the canon, they constitute a means of applying a law more precisely or urging the observance of a law by those for whom it was intended. They are of an *administrative*, not a legislative nature. All those who exercise executive power (see Cann. 136–144) – whether alone or in conjunction with legislative or judicial power – can issue general executory decrees. However, they may do so only within their own sphere of competence, e.g. within the territory of their jurisdiction or within the terms of their delegation. A typical example of general executory decrees may be found in the decrees issued by Bishops' Conferences in which they seek to implement the broad principles of Can. 1126 concerning the declarations and promises involved in mixed marriages.[4]

---

[1] E.g. Chiappetta I n.274.
[2] E.g. Urrutia n.320.
[3] Cf. PB 18; *Regolamento Generale della Curia Romana* n.109 §2 4.II.1992: AAS 84(1992) 244.
[4] Cf. LCE Tavola per Paesi e Canoni at Can. 1126.

Title III General Decrees and Instructions

Even though they are not laws, general executory decrees constitute binding norms (see Can. 32). Hence, the law requires that these be promulgated in the same way as laws (see Can. 8), whether they are of universal or of particular application.

Can. 32 General executory decrees which define the manner of application or urge the observance of laws, bind those who are bound by the laws.

Since they are supplementary or complementary to laws, general executory decrees oblige all those who are bound by those laws whose manner of application they determine or whose observance they urge. Thus e.g. a general executory decree issued by a Roman Congregation in respect of a universal law binds the whole Church; such a decree issued by a diocesan Bishop or his Vicar in respect of a diocesan law binds those subject to the same law; a general executory decree issued by the Supreme Moderator of a clerical religious institute of pontifical right (see Can. 134 §1) in respect of a law proper to the institute binds all members of that institute.

Can. 33 §1 General executory decrees, even if published in directories or other such documents, do not derogate from the law, and any of their provisions which are contrary to the law have no force.

Of their nature, general executory decrees are administrative, not legislative (see Can. 31). They have no effect on the status of laws, i.e. they cannot revoke laws either partially or wholly. Moreover, since their purpose is to provide guidelines for the application or observance of laws, they must conform to the law. Any provision contained in one of these decrees which contradicts the law has no force whatever. The canon makes it clear that this principle applies to all general executory decrees regardless of their author or the form of their publication, e.g. in the Directory for the Application of Principles and Norms on Ecumenism.[1]

Can. 33 §2 These decrees cease to have force by explicit or implicit revocation by the competent authority, and by the cessation of the law for whose execution they were issued. They do not cease on the expiry of the authority of the person who issued them, unless the contrary is expressly provided.

General executory decrees cease to have effect in three ways:
(a) through their *explicit revocation* by the competent authority, i.e. by the issuing of a decree to that effect;
(b) through their *implicit revocation* by the competent authority, i.e. the issuing of norms which run counter to those in the decree;
(c) by the *cessation of the law* (see Can. 20) for the execution of which the decrees were issued: without a law to apply, a general executory decree loses its *raison d'être*.

The canon makes it clear that, unless express provision is made, general executory decrees retain their force even if the authority of their author ceases. This principle is encountered throughout the Code (e.g. Cann. 46, 81, 132 §2, 142 §1, etc.).

Can. 34 §1 Instructions, namely, which set out the provisions of a law and develop the manner in which it is to be put into effect, are given for the benefit of those whose duty it is to execute the law, and they bind them in executing the law. Those who have executive power may, within the limits of their competence, lawfully publish such instructions.

---

[1] Issued by PCPCU 25.III.1993: Origins 23 n.9 129–160.

§2 The regulations of an instruction do not derogate from the law, and if there are any which cannot be reconciled with the provisions of the law, they have no force.

§3 Instructions cease to have force not only by explicit or implicit revocation by the competent authority who published them or by that authority's superior, but also by the cessation of the law which they were designed to set out and execute.

91 Closely related to general executory decrees are documents referred to as *Instructions*. Before the promulgation of the 1917 Code, Roman Congregations issued General Instructions which had the force of law.[1] Pope Benedict XV permitted Congregations to continue to issue Instructions but only so that the canons of the Code might be more fully explained and enforced.[2] In the decades which followed, many Instructions were issued.[3] The Revision Commission made it clear that such Instructions are not to be viewed as laws.[4] Indeed, the canon defines them as documents in which the provisions of a law are set out and explained, and in which the manner of implementing the law is set forth.

92 Instructions bear some clear resemblances to general executory decrees e.g.:
- they may be issued by those with executive authority (see Cann. 136–144) within the limits of their competence (see Can. 31 §1);
- they must conform to the law and cannot derogate from the law (see Can. 33 §1);
- they cease to have effect by implicit or explicit revocation, or by the cessation of the law which they were intended to explain and execute (see Can. 33 §2).

They are also distinctly different from general executory decrees:
- they are not given directly to the community bound by the law they explain, but to those whose responsibility it is to execute the law for the community (see Can. 32);
- they do not require promulgation, nor is there any *vacatio legis* (see Can. 31 §2).

Title IV
Singular Administrative Acts

Chapter I
COMMON NORMS

Can. 35 Within the limits of his or her competence, one who has executive power can issue a singular administrative act, either by decree or precept, or by rescript, without prejudice to Can. 76 §1.

---

[1] E.g. SCHO instr *Matrimonii vinculo* 1868: *Fontes CIC* ed. Gasparri 4 306–309, which established the process for investigating the presumed death of a spouse.

[2] Pope Benedict XV mp *Cum iuris Canonici* 15.IX.1917: CLD 1 56.

[3] E.g. SCSac instr *Provida Mater Ecclesia* 15.VIII.1936: CLD 2, 471–530; SCRit instr. *Inter oecumenici* 26.IX.1964: Fl I 45–56; SCDW instr. *Immensae caritatis* 25.I.1973: Fl I 225–232.

[4] Cf. Comm 14(1982) 136 at Can. 34.

Title IV Singular Administrative Acts

A singular administrative act is not in any sense a law. It is not defined in the Code but may be understood to be an act of executive power towards an individual physical or juridical person concerning the application or observance of laws in particular situations. Such an act may be issued in a decree (see Can. 48) or precept (see Can. 49), or it may take the form of a rescript (see Can. 59 §1). Its author may be anyone having executive authority (see Cann. 136–144). However, if the object of the act is a privilege, the author of the act must be the legislator or 'an executive authority to whom the legislator has given this power' (see Can. 76 §1).

Can. 36 §1 An administrative act is to be understood according to the proper meaning of the words and the common manner of speaking. In doubt, a strict interpretation is to be given to those administrative acts which concern litigation or threaten or inflict penalties, or restrict the rights of persons, or harm the acquired rights of others, or run counter to a law in favour of private persons; all other administrative acts are to be widely interpreted.

The sole criterion established for the interpretation of administrative acts is 'the proper meaning of the words and the common manner of speaking'. This is similar to the criterion supplied in Can. 17 for the interpretation of laws. However, no mention is made of the context of the act, since such acts are made only for a specific set of circumstances. Generally speaking, the meaning of such an act will be clear. However, should a doubt arise, the canon provides a norm for interpretation: there are six situations listed when the terms of the act must be interpreted strictly:

- acts concerning litigation
- acts threatening penalties
- acts imposing penalties
- acts restricting the rights of persons
- acts harmful to the acquired rights of others
- acts which contradict a law in favour of private persons.

Strict interpretation in these cases of doubt provides a good protection to the free exercise of rights. In *all* other cases of doubt, a *broad* interpretation is to be used. This norm is repeated in Cann. 77 and 92.

Can. 36 §2 Administrative acts must not be extended to cases other than those expressly stated.

In keeping with the principle established in Can. 16 §3, a singular administrative act refers only to those persons and those matters for which it was made. Thus, the provisions or decision contained in such an act cannot be extended to cover other persons or situations – no matter how similar – unless this is expressly stated. The analogy of law found in Can. 19 has no place in the interpretation of these acts.

Can. 37 An administrative act which concerns the external forum is to be effected in writing; likewise, if it requires an executor, the act of execution is to be in writing.

Any act which takes place in the external forum (see Can. 130) admits of public proof and has discernible juridical effects. The canon requires that administrative acts for the external forum should be drawn up in writing, e.g. decrees, precepts, rescripts. This is also required if the execution of an act is to be entrusted to another: the act of execution must be in writing (see Can. 40). Unless this requirement is expressly stipulated for validity (e.g. in Cann. 186, 190 §3, 638 §3 etc.), failure to comply in a particular case affects only the lawfulness of the act (see Can. 10).

Can. 38 An administrative act, even if there is question of a rescript given *Motu proprio*, has no effect in so far as it harms the acquired right of another, or is contrary to a law or approved custom, unless the competent authority has expressly added a derogatory clause.

97 All singular administrative acts must be issued in conformity with the law. Thus, they are deprived of juridical force if they infringe the acquired rights of others, or if they are contrary to an existing law, universal or particular, or to an approved custom. The canon foresees the possibility that such an act may contain a clause derogating from those rights or from the law or custom. However, this means that such an act must emanate from the competent *legislator* or someone duly designated (see Can. 76 §1). A derogatory clause must be added to these acts if they are to have any effect; this includes rescripts given *motu proprio*, i.e. at the initiative of the competent authority.

Can. 39 Conditions attached to an administrative act are considered to concern validity only when they are expressed by the particles 'if', 'unless', 'provided that'.

98 The validity of an administrative act may be made contingent on the fulfilment of a particular condition, i.e. a circumstance so united with an act that the act itself depends on it. Here the law restricts the invalidating effect of these conditions. Only those expressed by means of 'if', 'unless' or 'provided that' affect validity. Conditions attached to an act in this manner are regarded as *essential*. There is no mention in this Code of the equivalent forms of expressing these conditions mentioned in c.39 of the 1917 Code.

Can. 40 The executor of any administrative act cannot validly carry out this office before receiving the relevant document and establishing its authenticity and integrity, unless prior notice of this document has been conveyed to the executor on the authority of the person who issued the administrative act.

99 An administrative act may be made effective directly by the authority which issued it, e.g. a local Ordinary dispensing someone in his territory from a matrimonial impediment (see Can. 1078 §1) and communicating that directly to the person concerned. Such an act may also be made effective through the agency of a third party, an 'executor'. In entrusting this task to another, the competent authority may require the executor simply to inform the person concerned that the act has been issued; or the authority may grant to the executor a certain discretion, e.g. leaving it to a parish priest to issue a dispensation provided he is satisfied that the reasons given are true.[1]

100 In whichever form the execution is entrusted to another, no *valid* action can be taken by the executor until and unless he or she shall have first received the administrative act itself and the 'act of execution' (see Can. 37), established that the document is *authentic* i.e. has been issued by the competent authority in the correct form, bearing the requisite signature, date and seal, and ascertained its *integrity* i.e. that it is free from interpolatives, additions, subtractions etc. However, the law permits an executor to act even before the actual document is delivered but only in a

---

[1] Commentators on c.54 of the 1917 Code drew a distinction between the 'exsecutor merus or necessarius' whose task was the simple execution of a rescript, and the 'exsecutor voluntarius' to whom was entrusted the task of determining whether or not the rescript should be executed: cf. Coronata I n.73; Michiels (NG) II 448–452.

case where there has been prior notice of the contents and requirements of the document. It is essential that such information, whether conveyed by telephone or fax, be given either personally by the authority issuing the act or by someone formally appointed by that authority. An effort to eliminate this exception was rejected by the Revision Commission which argued that it was more in keeping with the practice of the Church, especially given the possibilities offered by modern means of communication.[1]

Can. 41 The executor of an administrative act to whom the task of execution only is entrusted, cannot refuse to execute it, unless it is quite clear that the act itself is null, or that it cannot for some other grave reason be sustained, or that the conditions attached to the administrative act itself have not been fulfilled. If, however, the execution of the administrative act would appear to be inopportune, by reason of the circumstances of person or place, the executor is to desist from the execution, and immediately inform the person who issued the act.

Since he or she is only an agent of the authority which issued the act, anyone appointed for the sole task of executing an administrative act *must* ordinarily carry out that task. Only in three specific cases can he or she refuse to act:

(a) if it is clear that the act is invalid, e.g. if its author did not have executive power (see Can. 35);

(b) if the act cannot be upheld for some other grave reason, e.g. if it is against the law or prevailing custom;

(c) if conditions attached to the act, whether for validity (see Can. 39) or not, have not been fulfilled.

Although ordinarily obliged to carry out the task given to him or her, an executor may suspend action in certain circumstances. The canon speaks of a situation where 'the execution of an administrative act would appear to be inopportune, by reason of the circumstances of person or place', e.g. where granting a dispensation might cause adverse comment or scandal. It is for the executor to weigh up the situation and make a decision on whether or not to desist from executing the act. However, the person who issued the act must be informed at once. It is for that authority to determine when and if the act is eventually to be executed.

Can. 42 The executor of an administrative act must proceed in accordance with the mandate. If, however, the executor has not fulfilled the essential conditions attached to the document, or has not observed the substantial form of procedure, the execution is invalid.

Since an executor cannot act in his or her own name, the one entrusted with the task must adhere very carefully to the terms of the mandate or the 'act of execution' (see Can. 37). Failure to observe these terms can invalidate the act of execution. This will occur if essential conditions attached to the mandate are not fulfilled; since the mandate is itself an administrative act, these conditions must be expressed in accordance with Can. 39. Invalidity of execution also occurs when there is a failure to observe the required procedure, e.g. executing in the external forum an act given in the internal forum, or neglect of the proper norms of law concerning the provision of ecclesiastical offices (see Cann. 146–156), etc.

---

[1] Cf. Comm 14(1982) 137 at Can. 40.

Can. 43 The executor of an administrative act may in his prudent judgement substitute another for himself, unless substitution has been forbidden, or he has been deliberately chosen as the only person to be executor, or a specific person has been designated as substitute; however, in these cases the executor may commit the preparatory acts to another.

104 By law, anyone appointed as an executor may freely appoint a substitute for the task. This principle affects those whose role is the simple execution and those who are granted a certain discretion in the matter. There are three exceptions to this norm:

(a) if substitution has been forbidden, e.g. in the act of execution;

(b) if the executor has been specially chosen because of his or her official position or personal talents;

(c) if the authority which issues the act has designated a named individual as the substitute.

Even in these situations, however, an executor may entrust the 'preparatory acts' to someone else, e.g. the establishment of the act's authenticity and integrity (see Can. 40). If the execution of the act requires the power of orders, the substitute must be a cleric; if it does not, the substitute may be a layperson.

Can. 44 An administrative act can also be executed by the executor's successor in office, unless the first had been chosen deliberately as the only person to be executor.

105 The juridical stability of an ecclesiastical office (see Can. 145 §1) means that successive holders of an office have all the rights and faculties proper to that office. According to this canon, a successor inherits not only the rights and faculties for the office, but also the execution of any administrative acts entrusted to his or her immediate predecessor. This principle does not apply where the original execution was entrusted specifically to an individual, e.g. because of his or her personal skills or expertise.

Can. 45 If there has been any error in the execution of an administrative act, the executor may execute it again.

106 In executing an administrative act, an executor may make a mistake. If the error is substantial, i.e. against the requirements of Can. 42, the execution must be repeated since the original act of execution was invalid; if the error is serious, but does not affect the validity of the execution, the executor has the discretion to decide whether or not the execution ought to be repeated; if the error concerns something purely marginal, there is clearly no need to repeat the execution.

Can. 46 An administrative act does not cease on the expiry of the authority of the person issuing it, unless the law expressly provides otherwise.

107 The juridical stability of an ecclesiastical office (see Can. 145 §1) ensures that, in general, whatever is done by the holder of that office continues to have juridical force and value when he or she ceases to hold office. The principle enunciated in this canon is repeated elsewhere (see Cann. 33 §2, 81, 132 §2, etc.). However, the author of an administrative act can restrict the life-span of that act, e.g. by determining in the act that it has effect only 'during my term of office'.

Can. 47 The revocation of an administrative act by another administrative act of the competent authority takes effect only from the moment at which the person to whom it was issued is lawfully notified.

108 A singular administrative act can be revoked by another act of the person who issued it, or an act of his or her successor in office or superior. However, this revocation has

effect only when the person to whom the act was issued has been lawfully notified, i.e. when the appropriate authority has informed him or her of its subsequent action. If the act concerns the external forum, its revocation must be in writing (see Can. 37). Such an act also ceases to have effect if the time for which it was granted has elapsed, or the person for whom it was granted has died.

Chapter II
SINGULAR DECREES AND PRECEPTS

Can. 48 A singular decree is an administrative act issued by a competent executive authority, whereby in accordance with the norms of law a decision is given or a provision made for a particular case; of its nature this decision or provision does not presuppose that a petition has been made by anyone.

The most common form of administrative act in the life of the Church is the singular decree. Such decrees are issued every day by executive authorities in the Church (e.g. Bishops, religious Superiors, etc.); they contain either a *decision* concerning a particular situation, e.g. the decision by a Bishop to remove a *vetitum* imposed after a declaration of the nullity of a marriage, or a *provision* for a particular situation, e.g. the appointment of a parish priest, the establishment of a new religious house, etc (in this general context see also Can. 1732 and our commentary thereon). Singular decrees are not *laws*; they have binding force but only for those persons and matters for which they were given (see Cann. 16 §3, 52). They can be issued only in conformity with existing laws (see Cann. 50–58 §1) and prevailing lawful customs. The canon ends by pointing out that a decree, *of its nature*, comes from the initiative of the executive authority, i.e. it is not the response to a petition. In this way, a decree differs from a rescript. Yet, in some cases a person can request a decree (see Can. 57 §1). 109

Can. 49 A singular precept is a decree by which an obligation is directly and lawfully imposed on a specific person or persons to do or to omit something, especially in order to urge the observance of a law.

A singular precept is defined as a particular type of singular decree. It emanates from a competent executive authority in the Church and its fundamental purpose is to urge the observance of a law. It is addressed to a specific individual person or specific persons and it contains either an *obligation to do something*, e.g. to return to one's religious house, or a *prohibition from doing something*, e.g. celebrating Mass in an unlawful manner. Like all administrative acts, it is normative only for those persons and situations to which it is directed. A singular precept must be issued *directly* by the competent authority. This cannot be done by an executor. 110

Can. 50 Before issuing a singular decree, the person in authority is to seek the necessary information and proof and, as far as possible, is to consult those whose rights could be harmed.

Although issued on the initiative of the competent authority, a singular decree is not to be understood as an arbitrary exercise of power. The prescriptions of this canon constitute a wise and prudent safeguard against abuse of authority. Responsibility is placed on the author of such decrees to seek all the necessary information in advance concerning the situation to be addressed in the decree. Moreover, where possible, there must also be consultation with those persons (physical or juridical) whose rights might be adversely affected by the decision. The norm of the canon upholds the fun- 111 damental principles of equity and the defence of rights. If observed properly, this norm will reduce the necessity to seek recourse against administrative acts (see Cann. 1732–1739).

Can. 51 A decree is to be issued in writing. When it is a decision, it should express, at least in summary form, the reasons for the decision.

112 In accordance with Can. 37, a singular administrative decree (or precept) must be in written form, i.e. at least in the form of a letter, e.g. the decree appointing a parish priest will refer to the parish in which he is to minister, the date on which he is to take up the appointment, etc. Thus, an oral decree is illegal; yet it remains a valid decree. Where the decree contains a decision, e.g. in a matter which is uncertain or disputed, the law requires that the document *must* contain at least a summary exposition of the reasons on which the decision is based. In this way, all danger of arbitrariness on the part of the authority can be avoided and the rights of the individuals can be protected and upheld; thus e.g. a statement of reasons may provide a sound basis for an eventual recourse against the act.

Can. 52 A singular decree has effect in respect only of those matters it determines and of those persons to whom it was issued; it obliges such persons everywhere, unless it is established otherwise.

113 Unlike laws and general decrees, a singular decree does not have a broad application. In keeping with Can. 36 §2, the decision or provision contained in a decree must not be extended beyond the particular case in which it was issued; indeed, the canon, echoing the words of Can. 16 §3, makes it clear that a singular decree binds only those persons and regulates only those matters for which it was issued. The persons to whom or for whom the decree was issued are bound by its decision or provision everywhere; it has a *personal* rather than a territorial foundation. Nevertheless, a singular decree does not oblige outside the territory of competence of the executive authority if the decree says so explicitly or if it deals with something of a purely territorial nature, e.g. a decree or precept enforcing the law of residence for a parish priest (see Can. 533 §1).

Can. 53 If decrees are contrary one to another, where specific matters are expressed, the specific prevails over the general; if both are equally specific or equally general, the one later in time abrogates the earlier in so far as it is contrary to it.

114 Given the frequency of singular administrative decrees, the Code foresees the possibility that more than one might be issued for the same situation. This canon provides a twofold solution if two decrees are contrary to one another. The canon presumes that both decrees emanate from the same authority. First of all, in specific matters, the decree which is more specific prevails; this is an application of the ancient rule of law that the generic is derogated by the specific (see Can. 20).[1] Secondly, if the decision or provision of each decree is equally specific, then the later one is understood to abrogate the earlier decree to the extent that it is contrary. This principle is analogous to that of the succession of laws found in Can. 20.

115 Should it happen that the conflicting decrees were issued by two distinct authorities, the decree issued by that which is hierarchically superior prevails.

Can. 54 §1 A singular decree whose application is entrusted to an executor, has effect from the moment of execution; otherwise, from the moment when it is made known to the person on the authority of the one who issued it.

---

[1] Reg. 34 RJ in VI°.

§2 For a singular decree to be enforceable, it must be made known by a lawful document in accordance with the law.

According to the canon, a singular decree becomes effective either:

(a) *at the moment of execution*, if an executor is appointed to implement the decree; the executor must act in accordance with Cann. 40–45; or

(b) *at the moment of notification*, i.e. when the decision or provision contained in the decree is made known *formally* to the person or persons for whom it was issued. Such notification must originate either directly or indirectly in the person who issued the decree.

As a rule, a singular decree cannot be enforced unless due notification has been given to those for whom it is intended in the form of an authentic document drawn up in accordance with Cann. 37 and 51.

Can. 55 Without prejudice to Cann. 37 and 51, whenever the gravest of reasons prevents the handing over of the written text of a decree, the decree is deemed to have been made known if it is read to the person to whom it is directed, in the presence of a notary or two witnesses; a record of the occasion is to be drawn up and signed by all present.

Sometimes the competent authority might have very serious reasons for not handing over a document, e.g. if there is a risk of action in the civil courts for damages, or if there is no possibility of making an authentic copy in the time available. In these exceptional circumstances, the canon provides an alternative method of notification, viz. a reading of the decree to the person concerned in the presence of a notary or two witnesses. In order to prove the execution of the decree a report of the proceedings should be drawn up and signed by all present, including (if possible) the recipient of the decree.

Can. 56 A decree is deemed to have been made known if the person to whom it is directed has been duly summoned to receive or to hear the decree, and without a just reason has not appeared or has refused to sign.

Ordinarily the process of communicating a decree to the person for whom it was issued consists of sending an invitation to that person to come and receive an authentic copy of the decree. In extraordinary circumstances, the invitation is to hear the decree read and sign a written report (see Can. 55). If the invitation is accepted, the process is completed and the decree is considered by law to have been communicated. However, if the invitation is not accepted, or if the person concerned refuses to sign the report after hearing the decree read and if no just reason is given, then the law considers the communication to have been effected.

Can. 57 §1 Whenever the law orders a decree to be issued, or when a person who is concerned lawfully requests a decree or has recourse to obtain one, the competent authority is to provide for the situation within three months of having received the petition or recourse, unless a different period of time is prescribed by law.

§2 If this period of time has expired and the decree has not yet been given, then as far as proposing a further recourse is concerned, the reply is presumed to be negative.

§3 A presumed negative reply does not relieve the competent authority of the obligation of issuing the decree, and, in accordance with Can. 128, of repairing any harm done.

120 Of its nature, a decree does not presuppose a petition (see Can. 48). Nevertheless, in certain cases a petition or recourse may be presented:
- when the law orders a decree to be issued, e.g. in confirming an election (see Can. 179 §1);
- whenever a legitimately interested person seeks a decree, e.g. a decree granting the permission required for alienation in accordance with Can. 638 §3.

In all these cases, the law obliges the authority to issue a decree within three months of receiving the petition or recourse unless, of course, the law prescribes a different time-limit, e.g. for the admission of a petition in accordance with Can. 1506.

121 If, having received the request, the authority fails to issue the decree a problem clearly arises: what value or juridical force is to be given to such silence? According to the canon, with the lapse of the time-limit, the authority's response is presumed negative. However, unless the law provides otherwise (e.g. Cann. 189 §3, 268 §1, 1506), this presumed negative reply brings with it only the right to hierarchical recourse in accordance with Can. 1737 §1.

122 Even though the time-limit has not been observed, the relevant authority remains *obliged* to issue the decree requested. Since the 'presumed negative reply' only gives the right to further recourse, the issuing of a decree by that authority, albeit belatedly, can resolve the original issue. However, the canon makes it abundantly clear that any authority which fails to act within the prescribed time is obliged to make good any harm caused by the delay (see Can. 128).

Can. 58 §1 A singular decree ceases to have force when it is lawfully revoked by the competent authority, or when the law ceases for whose execution it was issued.

123 A singular decree ceases to have juridical force in two ways:
(a) *extrinsically*, i.e. if the authority explicitly or implicitly *revokes* the decision or provision contained in the decree; explicit revocation occurs when the competent authority declares that the decree no longer has force; implicit revocation occurs when a subsequent decree is issued containing a contrary decision or provision (see Can. 53); it is to be noted that any such revocation has effect only when notified to the person concerned (see Can. 47);
(b) *intrinsically*, i.e. by the cessation of the law (see Can. 20) for whose observance the decree was issued; without a foundation in a law with juridical force, a singular decree has no meaning.

Unless the decree itself states otherwise, it does not cease to have effect when the authority expires of the person who issued it (see Can. 46).

Can. 58 §2 A singular precept, which was not imposed by a lawful document, ceases on the expiry of the authority of the person who issued it.

124 A singular precept is a type of singular decree (see Can. 49). It must be issued in writing (see Cann. 37, 51); exceptionally, that document may be read to the person involved (see Can. 55). In either case, the precept is imposed 'by a lawful document'. As such, it continues to oblige the person for whom it was issued until it ceases in accordance with Can. 58 §1. However, in addition, if a precept is imposed but not by a lawful document, e.g. orally or by a defective document, the force of a precept also ceases upon expiry of the authority of the person who issued it. This constitutes an example of the exception foreseen in Can. 46.

Chapter III
RESCRIPTS

Can. 59 §1 A rescript is an administrative act issued in writing by a competent executive authority, by which of its very nature a privilege, dispensation or other favour is granted at someone's request.

As a singular administrative act, a rescript bears several similarities to a singular decree (see Can. 48): it must be issued in writing (see Cann. 37, 51); it must be issued by an executive authority (see Can. 35); it must be addressed to a particular person (see Cann. 36 §2, 48); it is an administrative matter, i.e. it is not a law, nor it is a judicial decision. Unlike the singular decree, however, a rescript – *of its very nature* – consists of a response to a request; yet as Can. 63 §1 indicates, a rescript may sometimes be issued *motu proprio*, i.e. on the initiative of the competent authority.[1] Finally, whereas a singular decree contains a decision or provision for a particular case (see Can. 48), a rescript is the vehicle by which an authority grants privileges (see Cann. 76–84), dispensations (see Cann. 85–93), and other favours.

Can. 59 §2 Unless it is established otherwise, provisions laid down concerning rescripts apply also to the granting of permission and to the granting of favours by word of mouth.

Executive authority historically has granted favours and given permission by word of mouth alone. Juridically, this activity resulted in a lack of certainty as to the status and force of such acts. In preparing the Code, the Revision Commission insisted on introducing the present norm to provide such certainty.[2] Thus, the norms of Cann. 60–75 apply not only to rescripts in the strict sense (§1) but also to favours and permissions granted by the competent authority by word of mouth alone, unless it is otherwise established, e.g. if the law requires that a favour or permission be given only in writing.

Can. 60 Any rescript can be obtained by all who are not expressly prohibited.

By virtue of this canon, *anyone* may seek and obtain a rescript from any authority in the Church, provided that he or she has not been expressly prohibited from so doing. Thus, non-catholics and non-christians may request and obtain favours from the Church, e.g. a dispensation from a non-consummated marriage (see Can. 1142). All catholics may do likewise, even those under censure, unless the penalty has expressly forbidden such requests. This norm reverses the structures of c.36 §2 of the 1917 Code which excluded specifically from seeking and obtaining rescripts all those who had been excommunicated by a declaratory or condemnatory sentence (c.2265 §2), those under personal interdict (c.2275 3°), and suspended clerics (c.2283).

Can. 61 Unless it is established otherwise, a rescript can be obtained for another, even without that person's consent, and it is valid before its acceptance, without prejudice to contrary clauses.

In addition to seeking a rescript for oneself, the law permits one to request and obtain a rescript for another, even without that person's knowledge or consent, e.g. a diocesan Bishop may seek a privilege from the Holy See for someone in his diocese; a

---

[1] A rescript may be granted *motu proprio* in part or wholly. However, this does not mean that a petition was not presented. It might simply indicate that the response was given *motu proprio* because the reasons contained in the request were insufficient to permit its being granted.

[2] Cf. Comm 3(1971) 87.

dispensation from a non-consummated marriage may be obtained even if one party is unwilling (see Can. 1142); a retroactive validation may be given where one or both parties of the marriage are unaware (see Can. 1164). A favour obtained for someone else is valid, even before the person for whom it was obtained accepts: it is, after all, an act of jurisdiction on the part of the authority. The person to whom the favour is given is not constrained to make use of the favour. In some cases a clause may be added to the rescript making it effective only if it is accepted; sometimes a similar clause is found in the law itself, e.g. the lack of juridical effect of a dispensation from perpetual religious vows if the rescript is rejected in the act of notification (see Can. 692): without the consent of the religious concerned, such a rescript has no juridical force.

Can. 62 A rescript in which there is no executor, has effect from the moment the document was issued; the others have effect from the moment of execution.

129 The canon distinguishes between rescripts not needing an executor and rescripts which need an executor. The former have full juridical effect 'from the moment the document was issued', i.e. from the *date* on which the document was signed and issued. The latter, by contrast, have effect 'from the moment of execution', i.e. from the *date* in which the executor fulfilled his or her task in accordance with Cann. 40–45. As was made clear in Can. 61, unlike singular decrees (see Can. 54) a rescript does not need to be accepted in order to have juridical effect.

Can. 63 §1 Except where there is question of a rescript which grants a favour *Motu proprio*, subreption, that is, the withholding of the truth, renders a rescript invalid if the request does not express that which, according to canonical law, style and practice, must for validity be expressed.

§2 Obreption, that is, the making of a false statement, renders a rescript invalid if not even one of the motivating reasons submitted is true.

§3 In rescripts of which there is no executor, the motivating reason must be true at the time the rescript is issued; in the others, at the time of execution.

130 Since a rescript is essentially a reply to a request (see Can. 59 §1), the law makes the validity of the rescript dependent on the truthfulness of the petition. Two factors can render a rescript invalid in certain circumstances:

(a) *subreption*, i.e. the withholding of the truth or the concealment of facts. The mere fact of subreption in a petition does not have an invalidating effect on a rescript in itself. It does so when it affects what is required for the validity of the act, i.e. those conditions laid down as essential in a law (e.g. the number of abortions must be given for a valid dispensation from the irregularity for the reception of orders according to Can. 1049 §2), or as contained in general guidelines or norms,[1] or as otherwise determined by canonical practice.[2] If it affects something essential, subreption renders the rescript invalid whether the truth was withheld in good faith or in bad faith.

131 However, in the case of a favour granted on the initiative of the competent authority (i.e. *motu proprio*) subreption does not affect the validity of the rescript.

---

[1] E.g. SCDF Procedural Norms regarding a dispensation from priestly celibacy 14.X.1980: CLD 9 96–99.

[2] It is not possible to be more specific on this point since canonical style and practice vary according to the nature of the favour requested, and the current practice of the authority which grants the favour. In any given case, a comparison with similar requests will supply what is necessary.

This is because the wishes of the authority concerned prevail over any defect contained in a petition.

(b) *obreption* i.e. the making of a false statement in the petition. The simple presence of a falsehood in a petition does not of itself render a rescript invalid. It does so only if *not one* of the motivating reasons contained in the request is true. These motivating reasons are the causes which are sufficient for granting the favour, e.g. two principal motives are given for a dispensation from priestly obligations – the regularisation of a situation which has existed for many years, and lack of suitability or ability for ordination *ab initio*.[1] In addition to motivating reasons, there are others which may facilitate the granting of a favour e.g. the serious illness of the petitioner seeking a dispensation from priestly obligations. Obreption affects only the motivating reasons. Even if *only one* of these reasons advanced were true, the rescript would remain valid.

The exception mentioned by law in a case of subreption, i.e. rescripts granted *motu proprio*, does not apply in cases of obreption.

The canon points out clearly that subreption and obreption affect the validity of a rescript only if they pertain to the truth of the motivating reason at the time the rescript is issued or executed in accordance with Can. 62.

Finally, subreption or obreption may be punishable with an ecclesiastical penalty if committed in conformity with Can. 1391.

Can. 64 Without prejudice to the right of the Penitentiary for the internal forum, a favour refused by any department of the Roman Curia cannot validly be granted by another department of the same Curia, or by any other competent authority below the Roman Pontiff, without the approval of the department which was first approached.

The norm established by the canon is clear: no favour already refused by a department of the Roman Curia can be granted validly by another department or by any other authority below the Pope competent to grant the favour.[2] An exception is foreseen: the rescript is valid if the department which was first approached and which issued the refusal, subsequently gives its approval. Thus, in seeking from any authority a rescript which has already been denied by a department of the Roman Curia, mention must be made of the earlier refusal. Without this information, the authority concerned cannot seek and obtain the required approval. Any rescript issued on the basis of such defective information is invalid because of subreption (see Can. 63 §1), since 'the request does not express that which, according to canonical law ... must for validity be expressed'.

This norm does not affect the right of the Penitentiary to issue a favour in the internal forum.[3] Such a favour may be issued validly even though it was refused earlier by another department of the Roman Curia, and even though no mention of the refusal was made in the petition to the Penitentiary. Nor does the norm prevent someone presenting a new request to the same department for the same favour, without mentioning the earlier refusal.

---

[1] Cf. SCDF Reduction to Lay State: Norms 14.X.1980 n.5: CLD 9 94–95.
[2] This is an application of the ancient principle: 'Quum quid una via prohibetur, ad id alia via non debet admitti' (Reg. 84 RJ in VI°).
[3] Cf. PB 118.

Can. 65 §1 Without prejudice to the provisions of §§2 and 3, no one is to seek from another Ordinary a favour which was refused by that person's proper Ordinary, unless mention is made of the refusal. When the refusal is mentioned, the Ordinary is not to grant the favour unless he has learned from the former Ordinary the reasons for the refusal.

138 When a person's proper Ordinary (see Can. 107 §1, 134) refuses a favour, the petitioner is not to approach any other Ordinary, whether proper or not,[1] to seek the same favour unless he or she mentions the earlier refusal. The second Ordinary approached, once he is made aware of the previous refusal, is enjoined not to grant the favour until he has first learned of the reasons for the refusal. This may necessitate direct contact with the proper Ordinary concerned. The second Ordinary is not, however, required to accept the reasons for the first refusal as compelling him also to refuse – the circumstances of place and time, e.g., may now be quite different; what is required is that, in making his own decision, he would take account of the considerations which motivated the earlier refusal. The norm of this canon is a further application of the principle underlying Can. 64. However, failure to comply with the injunctions of this §1 does not render invalid the granting of the favour, save only if the Ordinaries involved are those dealt with in §§2–3.

Can. 65 §2 A favour refused by a Vicar general or an episcopal Vicar cannot be validly granted by another Vicar of the same Bishop, even when he has learned from the Vicar who refused the reasons for the refusal.

139 If the Ordinary who refused the favour and the Ordinary who was subsequently approached is a Vicar of the same diocesan Bishop, then, even if the second Ordinary is in full possession of the reasons for the refusal, he *cannot validly* grant the favour sought. The reason is clear: both men act in the name of the same Bishop and share the same authority; there cannot be a contradiction between them.

Can. 65 §3 A favour refused by a Vicar general or an episcopal Vicar and later, without any mention being made of this refusal, obtained from the diocesan Bishop, is invalid. A favour refused by the diocesan Bishop cannot, without the Bishop's consent, validly be obtained from his Vicar general or episcopal Vicar, even though mention is made of the refusal.

140 If the Ordinary who refused the favour was a Vicar of the diocesan Bishop, the favour cannot be granted validly by that Bishop unless he has been informed of that refusal. Consequently, the Bishop *can* grant the favour validly as soon as he has obtained the requisite information. However, if the Ordinary who refused the favour was the diocesan Bishop, no Vicar can grant the favour even when mention has been made of the refusal, *unless* the Bishop himself gives *express consent*. This provision underscores the unity of authority within a diocese and the role of the Vicar general or episcopal Vicar as an agent of the Bishop.

141 The provisions of Can. 65 §§2–3 refer explicitly to diocesan Ordinaries. These provisions clearly apply to those who are equivalent in law to diocesan Bishops (see Can. 381 §2) and their Vicars. By analogy of law, they are to be understood as applying

---

[1] A person may have more than one proper Ordinary e.g. if he or she has more than one domicile or quasi-domicile (see Cann. 102, 107 §1); the major Superiors of clerical religious institutes of pontifical right at different levels may have cumulative ordinary executive power over the same religious: i.e. the provincial Superior and the supreme Moderator can equally be a 'proper Ordinary' of the same religious.

also to personal Ordinaries and their Vicars e.g. major Superiors in clerical religious institutes and societies of apostolic life of pontifical right.[1]

Can. 66 A rescript is not rendered invalid because of an error in the name of the person to whom it is given or by whom it is issued, or of the place in which such person resides, or of the matter concerned, provided that in the judgement of the Ordinary there is no doubt about the person or the matter in question.

Mistakes in the text of a rescript, as a rule, do not affect the validity of that document provided that:

(a) the mistake has to do with the name or address of the person to whom the rescript is addressed, the name or address of the authority which granted the favour, or the object of the petition, and

(b) there is no doubt in the mind of the competent Ordinary[2] about the person or the matter involved. It belongs to this Ordinary alone to determine whether or not he has any doubt concerning the identity of the person concerned or the details of the matter involved. Should any doubt persist, the rescript is to be held as invalid. In order to obtain the favour requested, recourse must be had to the authority competent to issue the rescript (see Can. 67 §3).

Can. 67 §1 If it should happen that two contrary rescripts are obtained for one and the same thing, where specific matters are expressed, the specific prevails over the general.

§2 If both are equally specific or equally general, the one earlier in time prevails over the later, unless in the later one there is an express mention of the earlier, or unless the person who first obtained the rescript has not used it by reason of deceit or of notable personal negligence.

§3 In doubts as to whether a rescript is invalid or not, recourse is to be made to the issuing authority.

Two rescripts are regarded as contrary if they are granted concerning the same matter in such a way that they cannot be availed of at the same time, e.g. if exactly the same privilege was granted to two persons, a privilege which could be enjoyed by only one, or if two mutually exclusive favours were granted to the same person. Such opposing rescripts must originate in two distinct authorities: if the same authority issued the rescripts then either the latter revokes the earlier, or the individual is free to choose the favour which provides the greater benefit.

The canon supplies two principles for determining which rescript ought to prevail:

(a) in a manner similar to the principle established for singular decrees (see Can. 53), the more specific prevails over the generic;[3]

(b) if the rescripts are equally specific or generic, unlike the principle established for singular decrees (see Can. 53) the earlier rescript as a rule prevails over the later.[4] However, in two sets of circumstances, it is the later rescript which prevails, namely:

---

[1] Cf. Comm 17(1985) 61 at Can. 44.

[2] The Ordinary may be the local Ordinary or a personal Ordinary e.g. a major Superior in a clerical religious institute of pontifical right.

[3] This is yet another application of Reg. 34 RJ in VI°.

[4] 'Qui prior est tempore, potior est iure' (Reg. 54 RJ in VI°).

- if the earlier document is mentioned expressly – this is tantamount to revocation;
- if the favour obtained in the earlier rescript has not been used because of deceit (e.g. deliberate concealment of the favour) or notable personal negligence (e.g. careless failure to submit the rescript to the Ordinary according to Can. 68) on the part of the one who obtained the rescript.[1]

145 In spite of the provisions of Can. 66 and §§1–2 of the present canon, should any doubt remain concerning the invalidity of a given rescript, the law prescribes a recourse to the authority which issued the rescript. That authority alone will be able to give an authoritative response to any queries since ultimately the rescript contains the wishes of that authority for the particular situation in question.

Can. 68 A rescript of the Apostolic See in which there is no executor must be presented to the Ordinary of the person who obtains it only when this is prescribed in the rescript, or when there is question of public affairs, or when it is necessary to have the conditions verified.

146 When a rescript is obtained from the Holy See which does not require an executor, it has effect from the moment it was granted (see Can. 62). The law does not require that such a rescript be presented to the proper Ordinary of the one to whom it was given except in these cases:

(a) if presentation to the Ordinary is prescribed in the rescript itself;
(b) if the object of the rescript involves public matters, e.g. a dispensation in the external forum, a privilege granted to a church, etc.;
(c) if certain conditions must be verified before the favour granted in the rescript can be used.

This norm is identical to that of c.51 of the 1917 Code. The commentators on that canon were in agreement that the requirement of presentation to the Ordinary did not affect the validity of the rescript.[2]

Can. 69 A rescript for whose presentation no time is determined, may be submitted to the executor at any time, provided there is no fraud or deceit.

147 A rescript, even from the Holy See, may be communicated directly to the person who requested it. If its execution is entrusted to another, the rescript has effect from the moment of execution. Unless the competent authority fixes a time limit, the rescript may be given to the executor *at any time*. Thus, a delay in giving a rescript to an executor does not affect the validity of the rescript except if the delay was the result of fraud or deceit; in such a case a later rescript may well prevail over an earlier one (see Can. 67 §2).

Can. 70 If in a rescript the very granting of the favour is entrusted to the executor, it is a matter for the executor's prudent judgement and conscience to grant or to refuse the favour.

148 In a rescript, the competent authority may leave the matter entirely to the discretion of the executor: it will then be for the executor to decide whether or not the favour should be granted. This decision must not be arbitrary: rather it must be the result of prudent judgment on the part of the executor, acting in conscience. The executor must decide on the sufficiency and truthfulness of the reasons presented (see Can. 63), verify that all the conditions have been fulfilled (see Can. 41), etc.

---

[1] The provisions concerning fraud and negligence echo ancient juridical principles: 'Fraus et dolus alicui patrocinari non debent' (c.16, X, I, 3); 'Mora sua cuilibet est nociva' (Reg. 25 RJ in VI°).
[2] Cf. Michiels (NG) II 437.

Title IV Singular Administrative Acts

Can. 71 No one is obliged to use a rescript granted in his or her favour only, unless bound by a canonical obligation from another source to do so.

A person who has received a rescript for his or her personal benefit only, has the right but not an obligation to use it. Nevertheless, its use may become obligatory for some other reason, e.g. out of charity, if failure to use the rescript would be prejudicial to one's neighbour. This canon applies only to rescripts granted to individuals for their own private benefit. It cannot be applied to a rescript granted to a community: in that case all are obliged to make use of the favour granted.

Can. 72 Rescripts granted by the Apostolic See which have expired, can for a just reason be extended by the diocesan Bishop, but once only and not beyond three months.

It can happen that a rescript sought from the Holy See may expire before it is successfully executed or communicated to the beneficiary. To obviate this and other difficulties, the law permits the diocesan Bishop to extend such rescripts.[1] This faculty is given by law to diocesan Bishops only and not to other Ordinaries (see Can. 134 §1), although these latter may be delegated.

The canon attaches three conditions to the use of this faculty:

(a) the rescripts may be extended only for a just reason, e.g. the spiritual welfare of the people (see Can. 87 §1);

(b) they may be extended only for three months; the extension can be given only after the rescript has expired: it cannot be anticipated; the extension dates only from the time it was granted by the Bishop, not from the date of the expiry of the rescript;

(c) they may be extended *only once*, i.e. if the extension expires, it cannot be repeated – in which case a fresh rescript must, if appropriate, be sought from the Holy See.

Can. 73 No rescripts are revoked by a contrary law, unless it is otherwise provided in the law itself.

A rescript, like any singular administrative act, is not revoked by the expiry of the authority of the one who issued it (see Can. 46); nor is it revoked by a subsequent administrative act until that act is lawfully notified to the person for whom the rescript was issued (see Can. 47). According to this canon, a rescript does not cease to have effect even if a contrary law is promulgated subsequently. In this way, the acquired rights of the beneficiary of the rescript are respected. However, such a law could revoke a rescript if it contained a formula such as 'all contrary rescripts are hereby revoked'.

Can. 74 Although one who has been granted a favour orally may use it in the internal forum, that person is obliged to prove the favour for the external forum whenever this is lawfully requested.

While an administrative act concerning the external forum must, as a rule, be effected in writing (see Can. 37), such an act concerning the internal forum may be granted purely by word of mouth. A person who receives such a favour is free to use it lawfully at all times in the internal forum. However, should it be lawfully requested, e.g. by the local Ordinary, the granting of this favour must admit of proof in the external forum. This proof may consist of the testimony of witnesses who

---

[1] This faculty was first given to diocesan Bishops by Pope Paul VI in PM I 1: CLD 6 371.

were present when the favour was granted, or an official written document recording the fact of the grant.

Can. 75 If a rescript contains a privilege or a dispensation, the provisions of the following canons are also to be observed.

154 Rescripts are a general vehicle for the communication of all kinds of favours granted by the competent authority (see Can. 59 §1). As such, they are regulated by the common norms for singular administrative acts (see Cann. 35–47) as well as those expressly given for rescripts (see Cann. 59–74). In addition, whenever they contain privileges or dispensations, they are regulated also by the provisions of Cann. 76–84 and 85–93.

Chapter IV
PRIVILEGES

Can. 76 §1 A privilege is a favour given by a special act for the benefit of certain persons, physical or juridical; it can be granted by the legislator, and by an executive authority to whom the legislator has given this power.

155 A privilege is defined in the canon as 'a favour given by a special act for the benefit of certain persons'. This definition fits in well with canonical tradition which had understood a privilege as a 'favourable private law',[1] i.e. an objective norm which permitted certain persons to act lawfully in a manner different from that of the rest of the community. However, the concept of privilege found in this canon is much more restricted than that contained in the 1917 Code. The basis for the contrast is the manner in which a privilege may be obtained. According to c.63 of the 1917 Code, a privilege could be obtained by direct grant from the competent authority, by communication,[2] by legitimate custom, and by prescription; in addition, other parts of that Code granted certain privileges by law.[3] During the revision process, grave reservations were expressed about this broad concept of privilege, and it was decided to restrict the notion to a purely administrative act.[4]

156 The author of all privileges, directly or indirectly, is the legislator. As the supreme legislator in the Church, the Pope may grant privileges to anyone, even if they are against universal or particular law. Other legislators can grant privileges contrary to law only within the limits of their competence; they may, however, grant privileges which are even apart from universal law. Yet, although the granting of privileges belongs to the legislator, a privilege remains a singular administrative act, not a law. Consequently, the legislator can delegate a purely executive authority to grant privileges (see Can. 137).

---

[1] Cf. Michiels (NG) II 438–488.

[2] Privileges could be acquired through 'communication' when the competent authority extended to others a privilege granted to certain persons. Many privileges were acquired by religious orders in the past by communication. However, c.613 of the 1917 Code prohibited any further communication of this kind and c.64 restricted the use of communication of privileges in general. This institution has been abrogated completely by the current Code.

[3] Cf. cc. 118–123 dealt with the privileges of clerics; cc. 613–625 dealt with the privileges of religious.

[4] Cf. Comm 3(1971) 88–89; 19(1987) 30–33.

Title IV Singular Administrative Acts

The beneficiaries of a privilege can only be specified individual persons, physical or juridical. It cannot be a whole community: otherwise the norm could constitute a law properly speaking. Privileges may be contrary to the law, apart from the law, personal (see Can. 78 §2), or real (see Can. 78 §3); they may impose a burden on or cause inconvenience to others (see Can. 82). They are granted to the beneficiaries by means of a rescript (see Can. 59 §1).

Can. 76 §2 Centennial or immemorial possession of a privilege gives rise to the presumption that it has been granted.

Ordinarily, proof of the fact that a privilege has been granted can be established by the rescript or other administrative act in which it was conceded (see Cann. 37, 59 §1); if the privilege was given orally, this fact may be proved by a document recording the event (see Can. 74). Uninterrupted use of a privilege for more than one hundred years ('centennial') or for as long as can be remembered ('immemorial') does not, in itself, constitute proof that the privilege was in fact granted. However, by virtue of the law, it gives rise to a presumption in favour of the concession. Such a presumption of law can be overturned by facts which establish the contrary but, until then, the onus of proof is taken from those who enjoy the privilege (see Can. 1585).

Can. 77 A privilege is to be interpreted in accordance with Can. 36 §1. The interpretation must, however, always be such that the beneficiaries of the privilege do in fact receive some favour.

The general norm for the interpretation of singular administrative acts (see Can. 36 §1) applies to privileges. Thus, in ordinary circumstances, they are to be understood according to the proper meaning of the words and the common manner of speaking. If there is a doubt, then in the six instances identified in Can. 36 §1, privileges must be strictly interpreted; otherwise, they are to be interpreted broadly. However, even in those cases where strict interpretation is required, a privilege must always be so interpreted that it remains a favour for the person or persons for whom it was granted.

Can. 78 §1 A privilege is presumed to be perpetual, unless the contrary is proved.

Although granted to individual physical or juridical persons, a privilege remains an objective legal norm. As such, it possesses a certain stability. This is expressed in the present canon: unless it is otherwise evident (see Can. 83 §1), a privilege is presumed to be perpetual, i.e. it is not temporary or transitory in nature.[1] Rather, it is presumed to endure as long as the person or thing or place to which it was given continues to exist. Such a presumption can be overturned by contrary proof but, in cases of doubt, the presumption of law must be upheld (see Can. 1585).

Can. 78 §2 A personal privilege, namely one which attaches to a person, is extinguished with the person.

When granted directly to a physical or juridical person, a privilege is described as 'personal'. It thus belongs to that person and can be used anywhere, unless some territorial restriction has been attached to it. A personal privilege cannot be transferred. Thus, it is extinguished with the death of the physical person or the extinction of the juridical person (see Can. 120) to whom it was given.

---

[1] This is in keeping with the principle: 'Decet concessum a principe beneficium esse mansurum' (Reg. 16 RJ in VI°).

Can. 78 §3 A real privilege ceases on the total destruction of the thing or place; a local privilege, however, revives if the place is restored within fifty years.

162 When it is granted directly to a thing or place, e.g. an office or dignity, a church, a shrine etc., a privilege is described as 'real'. Such a privilege lasts as long as the thing or place concerned, i.e. until e.g. the office has been abolished, or the church demolished. In the case of a privilege attached to a place, i.e. a 'local' privilege, the restoration of that place within fifty years of its destruction (whatever the cause) means that the privilege is revived.

Can. 79 Without prejudice to Can. 81, a privilege ceases by revocation on the part of the competent authority in accordance with Can. 47.

163 Although a privilege is of its nature perpetual, it can be revoked in the same way as any other administrative act, i.e. by an act of the competent authority duly and lawfully notified to the beneficiary of the privilege (see Can. 47). The competent authority to issue this revocation is not only the authority which granted the privilege but also its superior or its successor in office. The provision of this canon does not affect that of Can. 81, so that a privilege continues even after the expiry of the authority of the one who granted it. Moreover, unless express provision is made, a privilege is not revoked by a contrary law (see Can. 73).

Can. 80 §1 No privilege ceases by renunciation unless this has been accepted by the competent authority.

164 Since, as a rule, everyone is at liberty to relinquish personal rights, a privilege can be renounced by the beneficiary. However, for the validity of such a renunciation, the law requires that it be made expressly and accepted expressly by the competent authority.[1] *Formal renunciation is not to be confused with non-use or contrary use* which can also have important juridical consequences (see Can. 82).

Can. 80 §2 Any physical person may renounce a privilege granted in his or her favour only.

165 If a privilege was granted to a particular physical person to be used solely and exclusively for his or her benefit, that person is at liberty to renounce the privilege. Of course, in conformity with §1, this renunciation must be made in the proper form and accepted by the competent authority.

Can. 80 §3 Individual persons cannot renounce a privilege granted to a juridical person, or granted by reason of the dignity of a place or thing. Nor can a juridical person renounce a privilege granted to it, if the renunciation would be prejudicial to the Church or to others.

166 A privilege granted to a juridical person (see Cann. 113–116) or one granted by reason of the dignity of a place or thing (see Can. 78 §3) is given for the benefit of many individual physical persons. Consequently, no individual physical person, acting as an individual, can renounce a privilege of this kind – even if the renunciation is made and accepted in the proper form (see §1). However, a juridical person can renounce privileges granted to it, provided that the renunciation does not result in harm or damage to the Church or to other physical or juridical persons. In cases of this kind, the renunciation will be made by individual physical persons acting as legal representatives of the juridical person (see Can. 118). If the juridical person is collegial (see Can. 115 §2), the act of renunciation must conform to the requirements of Can. 119.

---

[1] I.e. the one who granted the privilege, the successor or Superior.

Can. 81 A privilege is not extinguished on the expiry of the authority of the person who granted it, unless it was given with the clause 'at our pleasure' or another equivalent expression.

In accordance with the common norm of all singular administrative acts (see Can. 46) and the perpetual nature of privileges (see Can. 78 §1), a privilege continues to have effect even after the expiry of the authority of the one who granted it. Sometimes, however, the granting of a privilege is qualified with a clause such as 'at our pleasure', 'during my term of office', etc. Such a privilege may be revoked by the competent authority and it ceases when that authority expires. Where the privilege has been obtained from the Holy See, it is essential to note whether such a reservation is made to the person of the Pope or to the Holy See itself: if the former, the privilege ceases with the Pope's death; if the latter, it continues.

Can. 82 A privilege which does not burden others does not lapse through non-use or contrary use; if it does cause an inconvenience for others, it is lost if lawful prescription intervenes.

The canon introduces a further distinction between those privileges which are burdensome to others and those which are not. The basis of this distinction has to do with whether or not the favours or exemptions granted in the privilege have a negative effect on persons other than the beneficiaries. The juridical consequences of the distinction are clear: if the privilege is not burdensome, then, since it is a permanent institution (see Can. 78 §1), it does not cease to exist simply because the beneficiaries fail to use it, or act in a manner contrary to it. On the other hand, if the privilege results in inconvenience for others, the law establishes that it is lost by voluntary non-use or contrary use 'if lawful prescription intervenes', i.e. if the period of time fixed in accordance with Can. 197 passes, the subjective rights acquired by the privilege are lost. However, if the privilege was obtained from the Holy See, prescription has no effect, even if the privilege is burdensome to others (see Can. 199 2°).

Can. 83 §1 Without prejudice to Can. 142 §2, a privilege ceases on the expiry of the time or the completion of the number of cases for which it was granted.

Although of its nature perpetual (see Can. 78 §1), a privilege may be granted for a specified period of time or for a certain number of cases. Such a privilege is lost when the period of time has lapsed or as soon as the number of cases has been completed. To attempt to use the privilege beyond these limits is invalid except in cases of common error in matters of the external forum (see Can. 144 §1), and cases of inadvertence in matters of the internal forum (see Can. 142 §2). If necessary, the diocesan Bishop can extend a privilege granted in a rescript by the Holy See – but only once and for three months (see Can. 72).

Can. 83 §2 It ceases also if in the judgement of the competent authority circumstances are so changed with the passage of time that it has become harmful, or that its use becomes unlawful.

A privilege is intended to be a favour, i.e. an act which confers benefits on someone and is not harmful to others or to the common good. However, the circumstances which occasioned the granting of the privilege may change with the passage of time. If these changes mean that the privilege in itself becomes harmful to the beneficiaries, to the common good or to others, or if its use results in injustice or dishonesty, the privilege ceases. This intrinsic cessation of a privilege follows a judgement by the competent authority[1] concerning the facts of the harmfulness or unlawfulness of the

---

[1] I.e. the one who granted the privilege, the successor or hierarchical superior.

privilege. This decision can be given only if the authority is satisfied that the change in circumstances is certain and permanent. If it is only temporary, the privilege is considered to be merely suspended.[1]

Can. 84 A person who abuses a power given by a privilege deserves to be deprived of the privilege itself. Accordingly, after a warning which has been in vain, the Ordinary, if it was he who granted it, is to deprive the person of the privilege which he or she is gravely abusing; if the privilege has been granted by the Apostolic See, the Ordinary is obliged to make the matter known to it.

171 Generally speaking, the abuse of a power conferred by privilege occurs when that power is used for purposes not intended or approved by the authority which granted the privilege. According to this canon, such abuse does not result in the automatic cessation of the privilege. However, the person who is abusing the privilege may be deprived of that privilege by the competent authority: if the person's Ordinary (see Cann. 107, 134 §1) granted the privilege in the first place, that Ordinary is to issue a warning to the abuser of the privilege; if there is no change in his or her behaviour, the Ordinary may then proceed to deprive him or her of the privilege. The deprivation of privileges may constitute a penalty in itself (see Can. 1336 §1 2°) or may be the result of excommunication (see Can. 1331 §2 3°). If the privilege was granted by the Holy See, the person's Ordinary cannot deprive him or her of that privilege (see Can. 1338 §1); however, the Ordinary is obliged to inform the Holy See of the matter, after a warning has failed to halt the abuse.

Chapter V
DISPENSATIONS

Can. 85 A dispensation, that is, the relaxation of a merely ecclesiastical law in a particular case, can be granted, within the limits of their competence, by those who have executive power, and by those who either explicitly or implicitly have the power of dispensing, whether by virtue of the law itself or by lawful delegation.

172 The concept of *dispensation* is a peculiarly canonical or ecclesiastical one. It is, for the most part, unfamiliar to civil law – though indeed it has had, over the centuries, a not insignificant influence on the development of various civil jurisdictions: the important Common Law area of equity, for example, owes much to it. Its definition in this canon highlights many of its notable features:

(a) it is a purely *administrative* act:[2] it is not legislative in character and it may be granted by anyone who has executive power – within the limits of his or her competence (see e.g. Cann. 87–89) – as well as by anyone to whom the power of dispensing has been granted, explicitly or implicitly, whether this power is granted by virtue of the law (e.g. Can. 1079) or by lawful delegation;

(b) it involves a *relaxation* of the obligation contained in the law but does not affect the juridical stability of the law itself, which retains its force and is not thereby abrogated;

---

[1] Cf. Michiels (NG) II 649.

[2] At an early stage of its work, the Revision Commission rejected the legislative character of the act as expressed in c.80 of the 1917 Code.

(c) it may be granted only in respect of *merely ecclesiastical laws*, i.e. those which emanate purely and solely from a competent ecclesiastical authority; thus divine laws do not admit of dispensation,[1] nor do *all* purely ecclesiastical laws (see Can. 86);

(d) it is granted only *in a particular case*, i.e. for particular individual persons in particular concrete circumstances; while these people are not, as a result, bound by the obligation of the law, all others are;

(e) it is essentially a *temporary* measure, granted to individuals for a particular purpose; it is quite different from a privilege, which of its nature is permanent (see Can. 78 §1) and can always be availed of by the beneficiaries.

Can. 86 In so far as laws define those elements which are essentially constitutive of institutes or of juridical acts, they are not subject to dispensation.

The object of a dispensation can only be a 'merely ecclesiastical law' (Can. 85): effectively, this refers to disciplinary laws only i.e. to those laws which 'command or forbid'.[2] Accordingly the present canon expressly rules out the possibility of dispensation in laws which define which elements are constitutive of juridical institutes or juridical acts.[3] To dispense from such constitutive laws would make no sense: to do so would amount to a derogation from the law in question and the institute or act concerned would be radically and essentially defective.

Can. 87 §1 Whenever he judges that it contributes to their spiritual welfare, the diocesan Bishop can dispense the faithful from disciplinary laws, both universal laws and those particular laws made by the supreme ecclesiastical authority for his territory or his subjects. He cannot dispense from procedural laws or from penal laws, nor from those whose dispensation is specially reserved to the Apostolic See or to some other authority.

According to c.81 of the 1917 Code, Ordinaries subordinate to the Pope could not as a rule dispense their subjects from the general laws of the Church. Under the impetus of Vat. II,[4] Pope Paul VI changed this norm radically: henceforth, diocesan Bishops had the faculty to issue such dispensations, except in certain defined cases.[5] The present canon repeats this norm.

It is the diocesan Bishop or his equivalent (see Can. 381 §2) who alone can grant these dispensations. The faculty is not given to other local Ordinaries or to personal Ordinaries (see Can. 134 §§1–2).[6] The laws from which he may dispense are described as 'disciplinary laws', i.e. those which command or prohibit something.[7] These may be either universal laws, or particular laws issued by the supreme authority of the Church solely for the Bishop's own territory or subjects. Particularly significant

---

[1] It is to be noted that in a small number of the canons (e.g. Cann. 1194, 1196, 1697), the Code uses the term 'dispensation' in an analogous sense.

[2] Pope Paul VI EM IV: CLD 6 396.

[3] Thus e.g. the essential constitutive elements of the institute of 'juridical persons' may be found in Cann. 114–115, those of a 'judicial decision' in Can. 1608, etc.

[4] Cf. LG 27, CD 8: Fl I 382–383, 567.

[5] Cf. EM: CLD 6 395.

[6] The Revision Commission rejected a proposal to describe the author of those dispensations as the 'local Ordinary'. It was decided to retain 'diocesan Bishop' since this was the term used in CD 8: cf. Comm 14(1982) 137 at Can. 87.

[7] Cf. EM IV: CLD 6 396.

is the criterion offered by the Code which allows the diocesan Bishop to grant a dispensation in such a situation, namely 'whenever he (himself) judges that it *contributes to (the) spiritual welfare ... of the faithful*': as often as he so judges he may freely grant a dispensation from these laws, without reference to any other authority. This faculty to dispense is one of ordinary power (see Can. 131 §1) and as such may normally be delegated (see Can. 137 §1).

176 The limits of a diocesan Bishop's power to dispense are clearly established: he is prohibited from granting a dispensation in respect of three types of law:

(a) *procedural laws* (e.g. Can. 1598): these are established to safeguard justice and protect the rights of the faithful; a dispensation from these would not be for the spiritual welfare of the faithful;

(b) *penal laws* (e.g. Can. 1368): to dispense from these would result in grave harm to the faithful and to the common good;

(c) *laws whose dispensation is specially reserved to the Apostolic See or to some other authority*: clearly to grant a dispensation from these laws, a diocesan Bishop would exceed his authority. It is to be noted that the reservation must be made 'specially', i.e. it must be stated either in the law itself (e.g. Can. 1031 §4) or in some other authentic source.[1]

Can. 87 §2 If recourse to the Holy See is difficult, and at the same time there is danger of grave harm in delay, any Ordinary can dispense from these laws, even if the dispensation is reserved to the Holy See, provided the dispensation is one which the Holy See customarily grants in the same circumstances, and without prejudice to Can. 291.

177 While the faculty granted to diocesan Bishops in §1 has to do with ordinary administration, the faculty granted in this paragraph deals explicitly with urgent and extraordinary situations. The law gives the power to dispense from universal and particular disciplinary laws – including those reserved to the Holy See – to *all* Ordinaries (see Can. 134 §1) in situations where the following conditions are simultaneously verified:

(a) *where recourse to the Holy See is difficult*, i.e. whenever particular circumstances (e.g. strike, war, storm) hinder ordinary access to the Holy See by letter (see Can. 1079 §4). Contact with the Holy See by telephone, telegraph or fax is considered extraordinary.

(b) *where there is a danger of grave harm in a delay*, i.e. whenever the Ordinary concerned judges prudently that waiting for the difficulty to be resolved would result in serious harm to the faithful, be that harm physical or spiritual or material: the probability of such harm is sufficient.

(c) *provided that the law is one from which the Holy See is accustomed to grant a dispensation in similar circumstances*: this is something which can only be deduced from the actual practice of the Holy See. However, the canon makes it clear that, no

---

[1] In fact, two authentic interpretations in the context of this canon have hitherto been issued. The first declared that, apart from the case of urgent danger of death, the diocesan Bishop cannot dispense from the canonical form for the marriage of two catholics: cf. PCI rep 14.V.1985: AAS 77(1985) 771; Per 74(1985) 624–628; Wrenn (Interpret) 21–22. The second declared that the diocesan Bishop cannot dispense from the prescription of Can. 767 §1 whereby the homily, particularly at Mass, is reserved to a priest or a deacon: cf. PCI rep 26.V.1987: AAS 79(1987) 1249: Per 77(1988) 613–624; Wrenn (Interpret) 41–43.

matter how grave or urgent the situation, the Ordinary cannot dispense from the law of clerical celibacy (see Cann. 291, 1079 §1).

Although given for extraordinary situations, this faculty is one of ordinary power and, as such, may normally be delegated (see Can. 137 §1), and it is a faculty which is subject to wide, rather than strict, interpretation (see Can. 138).

Can. 88 The local Ordinary can dispense from diocesan laws and, whenever he judges that it contributes to the spiritual welfare of the faithful, from laws made by a plenary or a provincial Council or by the Bishops' Conference.

In normal circumstances, the law attributes to all *local* Ordinaries (see Can. 134 §2) the power to dispense from four categories of law:
- diocesan laws, whether made by the Bishop or by the supreme authority for the diocese;
- laws made by a plenary council (see Can. 439 §1);
- laws made by a provincial council (see Can. 440 §1);
- laws made by the Bishops' Conference (see Can. 447).

In respect of the last three categories of law, the 'just and reasonable cause' (see Can. 90 §1) for the dispensation is constituted by the fact that the dispensation *contributes to the spiritual welfare of the faithful*. The local Ordinary concerned is to make a judgment on the sufficiency of this cause. As an act of ordinary power, this faculty can be delegated (see Can. 137 §1). Local Ordinaries apart from the diocesan Bishop cannot dispense from those matters which the Bishop has reserved to himself (see Can. 479 §§1–2).

No mention is made in the canon of 'personal' Ordinaries such as those religious Ordinaries mentioned in Can. 134 §1. The faculty of these to grant dispensations for their subjects should, rather, be contained in the proper legislation of the institutes concerned, specifically in their constitutions.

Can. 89 Parish priests and other priests or deacons cannot dispense from universal or particular law unless this power is expressly granted to them.

As a general rule of law, no parish priest or other priest or deacon has the power to dispense from ecclesiastical laws, whether universal or particular. Yet, by way of exception, this power may be granted to them either by the law itself (see Cann. 1079 §§2–3, 1080, 1245) or by a special act of delegation. The law requires that the power to dispense must be given 'expressly': this may be either explicit, or implicit as e.g. when a person is appointed to an office to which the power to dispense has been attached.[1]

Can. 90 §1 A dispensation from an ecclesiastical law is not to be given without a just and reasonable cause, taking into account the circumstances of the case and the importance of the law from which the dispensation is given; otherwise the dispensation is unlawful and, unless given by the legislator or his superior, it is also invalid.

§2 A dispensation given in doubt about the sufficiency of its reason is valid and lawful.

---

[1] The possibility of the laity having some power to dispense from an ecclesiastical law was discussed by the Revision Commission but was not found to be canonically admissible: cf. Comm 19(1987) 88–90; Urrutia n.503.

182 A fundamental requirement for any dispensation is a 'just and reasonable cause'. Since law itself is meant to serve the common good, any authorised relaxation must have a sure foundation. The competent authority must make a decision concerning the sufficiency of a cause adduced, by considering the concrete circumstances of the case and the importance of the law from which a dispensation is sought.

183 Those who seek a dispensation are under a serious obligation to make a full and a fully truthful revelation of the facts upon which their request is based. Any attempt at withholding even part of the picture or, worse still, making a false assertion would not merely be wrong in itself but would have very serious consequences in respect of the dispensation which is sought. This canon at §1 spells out these consequences:
- if the one who grants the dispensation is himself the legislator or his superior, the dispensation, while being valid, is unlawful.
- if on the other hand the author is a competent authority at a level lower than the legislator, the dispensation is not only unlawful but in fact invalid and therefore of no effect. At the level of pastoral practice, this point is of particular significance, since the great majority of dispensations in this sphere are those granted by Bishops etc. in respect of the universal laws of the Church.

184 In its §2, however, this canon issues a valuable corrective of any excessive rigidity in regard to the grant of dispensations – again relevant to pastoral practice. If in a given case the dispensing authority should, even after investigation, remain in doubt about the adequacy of the reason or reasons proposed, he may and normally should grant the dispensation, in the assurance that such a dispensation 'is valid and lawful'. This provision underlines the nature of a dispensation as a *favour*; it avoids a rigidity which would be contrary to the very institution of dispensation, and it prevents an excessive scrupulosity on the part of those who might be in doubt.

Can. 91 In respect of their subjects, even if these are outside the territory, those who have the power of dispensing can exercise it even if they themselves are outside their territory; unless the contrary is expressly provided, they can exercise it also in respect of *peregrini* actually present in the territory; they can exercise it too in respect of themselves.

185 Having in Cann. 87–89 identified the limits of the power to dispense possessed by various authorities, the Code proceeds to identify those who may receive such dispensations. This canon is in fact an application of the general principle of Can. 136. The basis of the power to dispense is both territorial and personal. Thus, the competent authorities can dispense their own subjects, i.e. those whose domicile or quasi-domicile is within the appropriate parish or diocese (see Can. 107). It does not matter whether these 'subjects' or even the competent authority is within the confines of the relevant territory. The same authority can grant a dispensation to any *peregrinus* (see Can. 100) who is *actually* within the territory of the authority, unless of course this is expressly prohibited in the law itself. Finally, those with the power to dispense can exercise that power *in their own favour*, i.e. they can dispense themselves from those laws which oblige them and from which they have the power to dispense.[1]

Can. 92 A strict interpretation is to be given not only to a dispensation in accordance with Can. 36 §1, but also to the very power of dispensing granted for a specific case.

---

[1] This point resolves a debate which had existed among commentators on the 1917 Code: cf. Urrutia n.517.

Since it is a relaxation of the law, a dispensation requires careful interpretation. According to this canon, a strict interpretation is to be given to those dispensations which concern litigation, harm or restrict the rights of others, or run counter to a law in favour of private persons (see Can. 36 §1). Other dispensations which do not adversely affect third parties are to be widely interpreted since they constitute a favour. A strict interpretation is also to be given to the faculty of granting a dispensation when this is given for a specific case. This is in fact a direct application of the general principle concerning delegated power found in Can. 138. If the faculty to dispense is given 'for all cases', whether by law or by delegation, that faculty is to be interpreted widely.

Can. 93 A dispensation capable of successive applications ceases in the same way as a privilege. It also ceases by the certain and complete cessation of the motivating reason.

Many dispensations involve a single act, e.g. a dispensation from the canonical form of marriage (see Cann. 1108, 1127 §2). Such dispensations cannot be said to cease since their canonical effects endure in perpetuity. Many other dispensations, however, are capable of successive applications, e.g. a dispensation from the Eucharistic fast (see Can. 919 §1) on the ground of the long distance involved in travelling to Mass: such dispensations may be availed of as long as the situation continues. They cease to be juridically effective in the same way as privileges (see Cann. 79–83):

- they may be revoked by the competent authority;
- they may be renounced by the beneficiary;
- they cease on the expiry of the time or on completion of the number of cases for which they were granted;
- they cease if they become harmful or their use unlawful.

More specifically, dispensations cease when it is certain that the motivating reason (see Can. 90 §1) is no longer applicable and will not be so in the future, e.g. if attendance at Mass becomes available quite near the place where the dispensed person lives.

Title V
Statues and Ordinances

Can. 94 §1 Statutes properly so called are regulations which are established in accordance with the law in aggregates of persons or of things, whereby the purpose, constitution, governance and manner of acting of these bodies are defined.

Throughout the Code, when various juridical bodies are dealt with, mention is made of the 'statutes' of those bodies (e.g. Cann. 304 §1, 451, 505–506, 709 etc.) These statutes are the particular norms by which each of these bodies is governed. They are defined in this canon as 'regulations ... whereby the purpose, constitution, governance and manner of acting of these bodies are defined'. Statutes are purely internal norms. They are to be drawn up in accordance with the law. They govern juridical bodies which are aggregates of persons, e.g. personal prelatures (see Can. 295 §1), or aggregates of things, e.g. shrines (see Can. 1232). These statutes are understood to be the fundamental norms of the bodies concerned; as such, they are not to be easily changed. The most commonly found 'statutes' of this kind are the fundamental norms of institutes of consecrated life; however, these are normally described as 'constitutions' (see Can. 587 §1), while the more particular norms of Can. 587 §4 are often referred to as 'statutes'.

Can. 94 §2 The statutes of an aggregate of persons bind only those persons who are lawfully members of it; the statutes of an aggregate of things bind those who direct it.

189 As purely internal norms, statutes do not bind any person outside the juridical body which they govern. Hence only lawful members of an aggregate of persons (e.g. an association of the faithful, a religious institute, a council of priests) are obliged by the provisions of the statutes. Other persons, even if associated with the juridical body, cannot be bound by these statutes. In the case of aggregates of things, only those who direct them are bound by the statutes, e.g. the rector of a shrine (see Can. 1232 §2).

Can. 94 §3 The provisions of statutes which are established and promulgated by virtue of legislative power, are regulated by the provisions of the canons concerning laws.

190 Of their nature, statutes are purely administrative norms, essential for good management and for the good internal regulations of the body involved. They are not *per se* laws. However, they are considered to be laws if they are established and promulgated by a competent authority with legislative power, e.g. the statutes of personal prelatures (see Can. 295 §1), the constitutions of clerical religious institutes and societies of apostolic life of pontifical right (see Can. 134 §1). The nature of law is not attributed to those statutes which have simply been *approved* by a competent authority, e.g. the statutes of a public association of the faithful (see Can. 314). Those statutes which have the nature of laws are regulated by the principles of Cann. 7–21.

Can. 95 §1 Ordinances are rules or norms to be observed both in assemblies of persons, whether these assemblies are convened by ecclesiastical authority or are freely convoked by Christ's faithful, and in other celebrations: they define those matters which concern their constitution, direction and agenda.

§2 In assemblies or celebrations, those who take part are bound by these rules of ordinance.

191 Meetings of various kinds are an ordinary feature of life in the Church; some of these are formal assemblies at which business is dealt with, e.g. the Synod of Bishops, chapters of religious institutes, council meetings; others are more celebratory in nature and are often liturgical, e.g. the celebration of an important anniversary in a diocese, the celebration of any of the sacraments. The Code makes clear that all such assemblies or celebrations are to be conducted in conformity with their own rules known as 'ordinances'.[1] These norms are to specify how such meetings and celebrations are to be structured, how they are to be directed, and what matters are to be dealt with in the course of the meeting or celebration. All those who participate in such gatherings are bound to observe these rules. Their fundamental purpose is to ensure good order and conduct as well as the full participation of all those involved.

---

[1] The term used in the official latin text is *ordo*, frequently used in ecclesiastical documents in respect of the organisation and the agenda of various assemblies and celebrations, ranging from General Councils of the Church to liturgical celebrations of the sacraments.

Title VI
Physical and Juridical Persons

Chapter I
THE CANONICAL STATUS OF PHYSICAL PERSONS

Can. 96 By baptism one is incorporated into the Church of Christ and constituted a person in it, with the duties and the rights which, in accordance with each one's status, are proper to christians, in so far as they are in ecclesiastical communion and unless a lawfully issued sanction intervenes.

The Code distinguishes two fundamental types of person within the Church: physical persons, i.e. individual human beings, and juridical persons, i.e. aggregates of persons or of things (see Can. 114 §1). The acquisition of personality in the Church means that these persons are capable of exercising certain rights and fulfilling certain obligations *in their own name*.

A physical person attains this canonical personality through baptism. By virtue of this incorporation into the Church, each person acquires those rights and obligations which 'are proper to christians': of itself baptism does not affect a person's fundamental human rights nor his or her rights and obligations as a citizen of the State. While there is 'a genuine equality of dignity and action among all of Christ's faithful' (Can. 208), the rights and obligations of each person are not identical; the differences between individual persons depend on the following factors:

(a) *the status of each person*: each particular category of persons within the Church has its own specific rights and obligations, e.g. the laity (see Cann. 224–231), the clergy (see Cann. 273–289), religious (see Cann. 662–672), married couples and parents (see Cann. 1135–1136) etc.

(b) *ecclesiastical communion*: personality is acquired through valid baptism – the law does not prescribe baptism into the catholic Church; however, all baptised christians do not enjoy the same rights nor are they bound by the same obligations, e.g. those baptised into the catholic Church or received into it are bound to observe the canonical form of marriage (see Can. 1108 §1); those who have not been baptised into the catholic Church or received into it are not bound by merely ecclesiastical laws (see Can. 11).

(c) *lawfully issued sanctions*: even though they have been baptised into the catholic Church or received into it, some persons may be deprived of certain rights or have extra obligations imposed by ecclesiastical penalties imposed according to the law (see Cann. 1341–1352).

Although they do not directly enjoy personality within the church, the unbaptised have the obligation to seek the truth about God and the Church (see Can. 748 §1); moreover, certain concessions are made in their favour, e.g. they may administer valid baptism (see Can. 861 §2) or plead before an ecclesiastical tribunal (see Can. 1476). Other provisions of canon law may also influence their lives, e.g. a dispensation from the matrimonial impediment of disparity of cult (see Can. 1086), or a dissolution of an unconsummated marriage (see Can. 1142).

Can. 97 §1 A person who has completed the eighteenth year of age, has attained majority; below this age, a person is a minor.

§2 A minor who has not completed the seventh year of age is called an

infant and is considered incapable of personal responsibility; on completion of the seventh year, however, the minor is presumed to have the use of reason.

195 The rights and obligations of physical persons are also affected by other factors, i.e. age (see Cann. 97–98), mental capacity (see Cann. 97 §2, 99), place of origin and residence (see Cann. 100–107), relationship to others through consanguinity (see Can. 108), affinity (see Can. 109), or adoption (see Can. 110) and rite (see Cann. 111–112).

196 Three categories of person are distinguished on the basis of age: – those over the age of eighteen who have attained *majority*; – those under eighteen who are considered *minors*; – those under seven years who are called *infants*. This triple distinction is of great importance for the exercise of rights (see Can. 98). Alongside this distinction is a twofold presumption of law:

– those under seven years are presumed not to be capable of personal responsibility;
– those over seven years are presumed to have the use of reason.

Accordingly, all Catholics over the age of seven are bound by merely ecclesiastical laws (see Can. 11).

197 Having established these general norms, the Code often notes a different age for the exercise of specific rights and the assumption of certain obligations, e.g. marriage (see Can. 1083 §1), entry to a novitiate (see Can. 643 §1 1°), ordination to the priesthood (see Can. 1031 §1) etc.

Can. 98 §1 A person who has attained majority has the full exercise of his or her rights.

198 A person acquires the full exercise of his or her rights the day after his or her eighteenth birthday (see Can. 203), provided the presumption of Can. 97 §2 has not been overturned by contrary facts (see Can. 99): thus, e.g. he or she has the right to plead in his or her own name before an ecclesiastical tribunal (see Can. 1476). It should be remembered, however, that the rights involved may also be limited by the factors mentioned in Can. 96.

Can. 98 §2 In the exercise of rights a minor remains subject to parents or guardians, except for those matters in which by divine or by canon law minors are exempt from such authority. In regard to the appointment of guardians and the determination of their powers, the provisions of civil law are to be observed, unless it is otherwise provided in canon law or unless, in specific cases and for a just reason, the diocesan Bishop has decided that the matter is to be catered for by the appointment of another guardian.

199 A baptised minor may have all the rights of one who has attained majority but, as a rule, these rights can be exercised only under the authority of the person's parents or guardians. Yet in certain matters minors are free from this authority, e.g. a fourteen-year-old may be baptised in the ritual Church of his or her choice (see Can. 111 §2); no one (minors included) can be coerced into choosing a state of life (see Can. 219); in spiritual matters, minors over the age of seven 'can plead or respond without the consent of parents or guardians' (see Can. 1478 §3).

200 In the appointment of guardians for a minor and the determination of their powers, the Code leaves the matter to the provisions of civil law (see Can. 22), except in two cases: (a) if canon law has made an alternative provision (see Can. 1479); (b) if in a specific case and for a just reason, the diocesan Bishop (not the local Ordinary) has appointed someone else: such a guardian can act only in that specific case, but the extent of such a person's authority is to be determined in accordance with the prevailing civil law.

Can. 99 Whoever habitually lacks the use of reason is considered as incapable of personal responsibility and is regarded as an infant.

In Can. 97 §2 the law establishes the presumption that a person over the age of seven years has the use of reason and is capable of personal responsibility. Like any other presumption, however, this may admit of proof to the contrary: it could be the case that a person over seven years of age did not in fact have the use of reason – due perhaps to a *transitory* condition such e.g. as drunkenness, the effects of drugs, etc., or even to an *habitual or permanent* condition, such e.g. as a serious mental illness of extended duration. When the cause is transitory, the person affected does not lose the capacity to act except temporarily. However, when the cause is habitual or permanent, the juridical effects are more radical: the persons thus affected are regarded as infants. As such, they are not subject to merely ecclesiastical laws (see Can. 11), nor are they fit to perform a valid juridical act (see Can. 124 §1): they are incapable of contracting marriage (see Can. 1095 §1) and they are technically irregular for the reception of orders (see Can. 1041 1°), they are exempt from ecclesiastical penalties (see Can. 1322), and they cannot stand before a tribunal except through their parents or guardians (see Can. 1478 §1).

Can. 100 A person is said to be: an *incola*, in the place where he or she has a domicile; an *advena*, in the place of quasi-domicile; a *peregrinus*, if away from the domicile or quasi-domicile which is still retained; a *vagus*, if the person has nowhere a domicile or quasi-domicile.

A person's rights and obligations may be affected by territorial considerations. The following seven canons touch on these matters in some detail. This canon identifies four categories of person defined in relation to their place of residence. The words used are technical and do not translate easily into English (see Glossary). The categories are:

(a) *incola*: this may be translated as 'inhabitant'; it refers to a person who is actually located in his or her place of domicile (see Can. 102 §1);

(b) *advena*: this may be rendered as a 'newcomer' or temporary resident; it refers to someone actually located in the place of his or her quasi-domicile (see Can. 102 §2);

(c) *peregrinus*: or 'traveller' or 'pilgrim', refers to a person having a domicile or quasi-domicile but currently located outside that territory;

(d) *vagus*: this is a vagrant, a wanderer who has no domicile or quasi-domicile, a person of no fixed abode.

Can. 101 §1 The place of origin of a child, and even of a neophyte, is that in which the parents had a domicile or, lacking that, a quasi-domicile when the child was born; if the parents did not have the same domicile or quasi-domicile, it is that of the mother.

§2 In the case of a child of *vagi*, the place of origin is the actual place of birth; in the case of a foundling, it is the place where it was found.

The norms for determining a person's place of origin remains more or less the same as those found in c.90 of the 1917 Code: a child – or even a neophyte (i.e. an adult who has just been baptised) – has as place of origin the place of domicile or quasi-domicile of both parents at the time the child was born, i.e. even if the child was born while the parents were away from home, the place of origin is counted as the domicile or quasi-domicile of the parents, not the place of birth. If, for any reason, the parents do not have the same domicile or quasi-domicile, the place of origin is the domicile or quasi-domicile of the mother. Two special cases are catered for:

(a) a child of *vagi* i.e. whose parents have no fixed abode, has as its place of origin the place of birth;

(b) a child who was abandoned has as its place of origin the place where it was found.

204 When the Code was being revised, it was proposed that no canon be included dealing with a person's place of origin. This suggestion was rejected on the basis that the place of origin did help to determine the proper Bishop for the ordination of secular clergy according to c.956 of the 1917 Code.[1] That norm was not, however, retained in the ultimate text of the Code (see Can. 1015 §1). Accordingly, a person's place of origin has now very little canonical significance.

Can. 102 §1 Domicile is acquired by residence in the territory of a parish, or at least of a diocese, which is either linked to the intention of remaining there permanently if nothing should occasion its withdrawal, or in fact protracted for a full five years.

§2 Quasi-domicile is acquired by residence in the territory of a parish, or at least of a diocese, which is either linked to the intention of remaining there for three months if nothing should occasion its withdrawal, or in fact protracted for three months.

§3 Domicile or quasi-domicile in the territory of a parish is called parochial; in the territory of a diocese, even if not in a parish, it is called diocesan.

205 The most important territorial factor affecting physical persons in the Church is their place of residence. Echoing c.92 of the 1917 Code, this canon distinguishes between a person's domicile and quasi-domicile. The root of the distinction lies in the manner in which each is acquired.

206 Domicile or quasi-domicile may be *voluntary* if acquired through the free and deliberate actions of the person concerned, or they may be *necessary* if acquired solely by means of a provision of law (see Cann. 103, 105). Voluntary domicile may be acquired in two ways:

(a) by residing in a particular place with the intention of remaining there permanently; the fact that a person later decides to change residence does not affect the situation, provided that there was originally an intention to remain permanently: the law is wise enough to acknowledge that, for whatever reason, people may wish to change their minds!

(b) by residing in a particular territory for a full five years; in this case a person's intention is irrelevant: the simple fact of residence for the required time is all that is required. The five years are to be calculated as continuous (see Cann. 201 §1, 203).[2]

207 Quasi-domicile is acquired in two similar ways:

(a) by residing in a particular territory with the intention of staying at least three months; a subsequent change of mind does not affect the acquisition of quasi-domicile;

(b) by residing in fact in a place for three months. This period is to be calculated as continuous time (see Cann. 201 §1, 203).[3]

---

[1] Cf. Comm 6(1974) 95 at n.3.

[2] Under the 1917 Code c.92 §1 it was required that there be a residence uninterrupted for *ten years*.

[3] Under the 1917 Code c.92 §2 the required residence was for *the best part of a year*.

The territory of domicile or quasi-domicile is determined by ecclesiastical, not civil or political, boundaries, i.e. it refers to parishes or to dioceses. One who lives within a diocese, without settling in any one parish, e.g. an itinerant, acquires a diocesan domicile or quasi-domicile only. Depending on individual circumstances, a person may have more than one domicile or quasi-domicile.

The possession of a domicile or quasi-domicile is a factor which determines the competent forum for ecclesiastical trials (see Cann. 1408, 1673 2°–3°), the place for marriage (see Can. 1115), and many other important juridical events.

Can. 103 Members of religious institutes and of societies of apostolic life acquire a domicile in the place where the house to which they belong is situated. They acquire a quasi-domicile in the house in which, in accordance with Can. 102 §2, they reside.

Members of religious institutes and societies of apostolic life are required by law to live in a house of their institute or society (see Cann. 665 §1, 740). By virtue of the law, these persons acquire domicile in the place of the house to which they have been lawfully assigned: the actual length of their stay there is not relevant in this context. Since they may, in certain defined circumstances, reside legitimately elsewhere (see Can. 665 §1), the law permits these persons to acquire a quasi-domicile according to Can. 102 §2, i.e. by the intention to reside or by actual residence for three months. This norm was not found in the 1917 Code, although it reflects the actual interpretation and practice based on c.93 of the 1917 Code.[1] The present canon does not affect members of secular institutes, since they are to live in the 'ordinary conditions of the world' (see Can. 714) and are subject to Can. 102 §§1–2. Since they are not yet 'members' of religious institutes or societies of apostolic life, novices and postulants are not affected by the norm of this canon.

Can. 104 Spouses are to have a common domicile or quasi-domicile. By reason of lawful separation or for some other just reason, each may have his or her own domicile or quasi-domicile.

Whereas c. 93 §1 of the 1917 Code declared that a wife could not have a domicile distinct from that of her husband unless they were lawfully separated, this Code adopts a different approach. Based on the obligation of the spouses to maintain a common conjugal life (see Cann. 1134–1135, 1151), the canon directs spouses to have a common domicile or quasi-domicile. By contrast with the earlier norm, the canon recognises that the parties may have separate and distinct domiciles or quasi-domiciles – not only if they are lawfully separated (see Cann. 1152-1153), but if there is 'some other just reason': one could think e.g. of the work-ethic and of the practices resulting from it, especially in the so-called developed countries, in many of which it has become almost an economic necessity that some spouses have to live apart for much of their marital years. The fact that each retains his or her domicile or quasi-domicile does not of course exclude the possibility of a common domicile or quasi-domicile – quite the contrary.

Can. 105 §1 A minor necessarily retains the domicile or quasi-domicile of the person to whose authority the minor is subject. A minor who is no longer an infant can acquire a quasi-domicile of his or her own and, if lawfully emancipated in accordance with the civil law, a domicile also.

---

[1] Cf. Vermeersch–Creusen I n.188.

§2 One who for a reason other than minority is lawfully entrusted to the guardianship or tutelage of another, has the domicile and quasi-domicile of the guardian or curator.

212 The law itself determines more specifically the domicile and quasi-domicile of some categories of person – known as *necessary* or *legal* domicile:

(a) minors (see Can. 97 §1) retain by law the domicile or quasi-domicile of their parents or legal guardians. In addition, after the age of seven (see Can. 97 §2), a person can acquire a quasi-domicile of his or her own, e.g. by attending a boarding school. Moreover, minors can even acquire a proper domicile 'if lawfully emancipated in accordance with the civil law', i.e. if the civil law recognises minors as adults at an age lower than eighteen.

(b) all those others who, for whatever reason, are entrusted to the care of a guardian or curator, e.g. those who habitually lack the use of reason (see Can. 99), have the domicile or quasi-domicile of the person into whose care they are given, even if they have attained their majority.

Can. 106 Domicile or quasi-domicile is lost by departure from the place with the intention of not returning, without prejudice to the provisions of Can. 105.

213 Although *voluntary* domicile and quasi-domicile (see Can. 102 §§1–2) may each be acquired in either of two ways, the law prescribes only *one* way in which each can be lost, i.e. by departure from the place *with the intention of not returning*: the mere fact of departure in itself does not affect the retention of the domicile or quasi-domicile.

214 On the other hand, *necessary* domicile or quasi-domicile (see Cann. 103, 105) is lost when the reason for it ceases, e.g. when a religious is changed to another house; when a minor attains majority; when someone mentally ill recovers the use of reason.

Can. 107 §1 Both through domicile and through quasi-domicile everyone acquires his or her own parish priest and Ordinary.

§2 The proper parish priest or Ordinary of a *vagus* is the parish priest or Ordinary of the place where the *vagus* is actually residing.

§3 The proper parish priest of one who has only a diocesan domicile or quasi-domicile is the parish priest of the place where that person is actually residing.

215 The immediate and principal consequence of considering a person's residence in canon law is that it determines that person's proper or own parish priest and proper or own Ordinary. The canon contains a threefold provision in this regard:

(a) those who have a domicile or quasi-domicile have as their own the parish priest and Ordinary of the place of domicile or quasi-domicile (§1), even if they are not actually resident there; should such persons have more than one domicile or quasi-domicile, they are free to choose their own parish priest and Ordinary;

(b) those who have neither a domicile nor a quasi-domicile anywhere – *vagi* (see Can. 100) – have as their own the parish priest and Ordinary of the place where they actually live (§2);

(c) those who have only a diocesan and not a parochial domicile or quasi-domicile (see Can. 102 §3) have as their own the parish priest of the place where they are actually residing (§3).

Can. 108 §1 Consanguinity is reckoned by lines and degrees.

Consanguinity is the natural relationship between people based on blood, i.e. they share a common ancestry and, to that extent, the same blood: people who are connected in this way are referred to as 'blood relations'. It does not matter whether this relationship arises out of legitimate or illegitimate birth. According to this canon, the relationship is measured in two ways, i.e. by lines and degrees. 216

The *line of consanguinity* refers to the series of persons from whom the persons concerned are descended. If the line is *direct*, it refers to those from whom a person is directly descended, e.g. the relationship of a parent to a child, of a grandparent to a grandchild, etc. If the line is *collateral*, it refers to those persons descended from the same common stock but not descended one from the other, e.g. brothers and sisters, cousins, uncles, aunts, nephews and nieces. *The degree of consanguinity* refers to the closeness or distance of the relationship between two persons in either the direct or the collateral line. 217

Can. 108 §2 In the direct line there are as many degrees as there are generations, that is, as there are persons, not counting the common ancestor.

In order to determine the exact relationship between two persons in the direct line, it is necessary only to count the number of persons or generations involved and eliminate the common ancestor. Thus, a man is related to his mother in the first degree of the direct line; a woman is related to her grandfather in the second degree of the direct line, etc. 218

Can. 108 §3 In the collateral line there are as many degrees as there are persons in both lines together, not counting the common ancestor.

The method of reckoning relationship in the collateral line according to c.96 §3 of the 1917 Code was derived from Germanic law. During the course of revision, it was decided to adopt the simpler and clearer method derived from Roman Law.[1] The new method is to count the number of persons in the direct lines of both persons and omit the common ancestor. The following diagram illustrates the method: 219

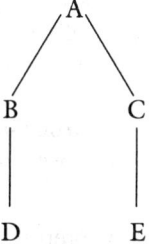

In the diagram the common ancestor is A; B and C are siblings; D and E are first cousins. The relationship between B and C is in the second degree of the collateral line; B and E are related in the third degree of the collateral line; D and E are related in the fourth degree of the collateral line. The correct calculation of the blood relationship between two people has important canonical consequences (see Cann. 478 §2, 492 §3, 1091, 1298, 1448, 1548 §2 2°).

Can. 109 §1 Affinity arises from a valid marriage, even if not consummated, and it exists between the man and the blood relations of the woman, and likewise between the woman and the blood relations of the man.

---

[1] Cf. Comm 6(1974) 97; 14(1982) 141 at Can. 106.

§2 It is reckoned in such a way that the blood relations of the man are related by affinity to the woman in the same line and the same degree, and vice versa.

220 Affinity is a purely *legal* (i.e. not a natural) relationship between people. According to the canon, it arises out of a *valid* marriage between two persons, whether the marriage is sacramental or not, consummated or not. The purely legal basis of this relationship is echoed in the English description of these people as 'in-laws'.

221 The relationship of affinity is contracted only between each party of the marriage and the blood relations of the other party, e.g. between a woman and her husband's parents, brothers and sisters, or between a man and his wife's parents, brothers and sisters etc. The distance or closeness of the relationship of affinity is to be calculated along the same lines and degrees as consanguinity, e.g. a man is related to his mother-in-law in the first degree of the direct line of affinity, etc.

222 The relationship of affinity and the details of the line and degree involved can also have important canonical consequences (see Cann. 492 §3, 1092, 1298, 1448 §1, 1548 §2 2°).

Can. 110 Children who have been adopted in accordance with the civil law are considered the children of that person or those persons who have adopted them.

223 Another purely legal relationship is that which arises from the adoption of a child in accordance with the civil law. Since canon law has no procedure for adoption, this matter is remitted entirely to civil law: to all intents and purposes, therefore, adopted children are regarded by the law of the Church as equivalent to the natural children of those who adopt them. This special relationship *may give rise* to the impediment of legal adoption (see Can. 1094).

Can. 111 §1 Through the reception of baptism a child becomes a member of the latin Church if the parents belong to that Church or, should one of them not belong to it, if they have both by common consent chosen that the child be baptised in the latin Church: if that common consent is lacking, the child becomes a member of the ritual Church to which the father belongs.

§2 Any candidate for baptism who has completed the fourteenth year of age may freely choose to be baptised either in the latin Church or in another autonomous ritual Church; in which case the person belongs to the Church which he or she has chosen.

224 Although it is *one*, the catholic Church comprises within it, in addition to the latin Church, several autonomous Churches each distinguished from the others by proper liturgical rites e.g. Maronites, Melkites, Armenians, Chaldaeans etc.[1] By means of baptism, not only is a person 'incorporated into the Church of Christ' (see Can. 96) but he or she also becomes a member of a specific ritual Church.

225 The membership of autonomous ritual Churches is regulated by law. This canon draws a clear distinction between the membership of someone before the age of fourteen and membership after the age of fourteen:

---

[1] Cf. Can. 1 and our commentary on it. Not included here are particular churches which have simply their own liturgical rites e.g. Milan (Ambrosian) or Toledo (Mozarabic): these are not autonomous churches.

Title VI Physical and Juridicial Persons

(1) Before fourteen years old

The law provides for three sets of circumstances:

(a) if both parents belong to the latin Church, all the children automatically become members of the latin Church at baptism. This principle applies even if a different liturgical rite was used, e.g. a child born of latin Church parents baptised in a Greek Melkite ceremony.

(b) if only one of the parents belongs to the latin Church and both parents are agreed, the child is baptised into the latin Church, irrespective of the actual rite used.

(c) if only one parent belongs to the latin Church and the parents cannot agree, the law decrees that the child concerned becomes a member of whatever ritual Church to which the father belongs; the actual liturgical ceremony involved does not affect this provision.

(2) After fourteen years old

The law permits a candidate for baptism who has completed his or her fourteenth birthday to choose freely the ritual Church into which he or she is to be baptised. This provision of law presumes the person is capable of personal responsibility (see Can. 99). It constitutes one of the exceptions to the general norm of Can. 98 §2, in allowing a minor to exercise a right without being subject to his or her parents.

Can. 112 §1 After the reception of baptism, the following become members of another autonomous ritual Church:

1° those who have obtained permission from the Apostolic See;

2° a spouse who, on entering marriage or during its course, has declared that he or she is transferring to the autonomous ritual Church of the other spouse; on the dissolution of the marriage, however, that person may freely return to the latin Church;

3° the children of those mentioned in nn.1 and 2 who have not completed their fourteenth year, and likewise in a mixed marriage the children of a catholic party who has lawfully transferred to another ritual Church; on completion of their fourteenth year, however, they may return to the latin Church.

Once attained, membership of an autonomous ritual Church is definitive: a person is not at liberty to move from membership of one ritual Church to another, save only in the following restricted circumstances:

1° if a person has received permission from the Holy See to change rite. In accordance with a 1993 decision, this permission can be presumed whenever a member of the faithful of the latin Church requests a transfer to another autonomous ritual Church which has an eparchy *within the same territory, provided that* the diocesan Bishops of both dioceses consent to this in writing;[1] this personal dual consent by the diocesan Bishops concerned is required for the validity of such a transfer.

2° if a husband or wife makes a formal declaration of transferring to the autonomous ritual Church of the other party; such a declaration may be made

---

[1] Secretariat of State rescr ex Audientia Ss.mi 26.XI.1992: AAS 85(1993) 81: CLSNGBI 95 (Sept. 1993) 9.

either at the time the parties enter into marriage or at any stage during it.¹ Any such transfer would not necessarily continue to have effect if the marriage is dissolved, whether by death or by papal dispensation; the party involved may freely return to membership of the latin Church.

3° a child under the age of fourteen also changes whose parents transfer rite in accordance with 1° or 2°. This principle applies also to a person whose parents are in a mixed marriage when the Catholic parent transfers to another autonomous ritual Church. Children over the age of fourteen do not so transfer. Those who have done so under the age of fourteen may on their own initiative later return to membership of the latin Church.

Can. 112 §2 The practice, however long standing, of receiving the sacraments according to the rite of an autonomous ritual Church, does not bring with it membership of that Church.

227 The distinction between *liturgical celebrations of a particular rite* and *actual membership of an autonomous ritual Church* is underlined here. This paragraph makes it clear that the *simple practice* of receiving the sacraments (e.g. baptism, eucharist, penance) in a specific autonomous ritual Church does not result in a change of rite. A person may transfer to another autonomous ritual Church *only* in those circumstances provided for in §1.

Chapter II
JURIDICAL PERSONS

Can. 113 §1 The catholic Church and the Apostolic See have the status of a moral person by divine disposition.

§2 In the Church, besides physical persons, there are also juridical persons, that is, in canon law subjects of obligations and rights which accord with their nature.

228 Individual physical persons become subjects of rights and obligations in the Church by reason of their baptism (see Can. 96). Moreover, canon law has long assigned a particular canonical identity to various groups and entities within the Church: they too are recognised as subjects of rights and obligations, and they form the subject of this Chapter. First and foremost, the canon states that the catholic Church (see Can. 204 §2) and the Apostolic See[2] 'have the status of a *moral person*'. This terminology was common in cc.99–102 of the 1917 Code. In the current Code it is found only in this paragraph; the remainder of this Chapter speaks, as the heading indicates, in terms of '*juridical* person(s)'. This obviously deliberate change of terminology serves to highlight the distinction between, on the one hand, the status of the catholic Church and of the Apostolic See as given them 'by divine disposition' and, on the other, the status given to other juridical persons by virtue of a provision of positive ecclesiastical law (see Can. 114). Some commentators[3] have noted the omission from the canon of any reference to the College of Bishops, which would also appear to enjoy the status of a moral person by divine disposition (see Can. 330, 336).

---

[1] CCEO at its cc.36 and 33 has its own specific regulations in this regard.

[2] Here the term is understood as referring to the totality rather than to any particular department which may function in the name of the whole (cf. Can. 361).

[3] Cf. Chiappetta I n.672; Urrutia n.612.

Can. 114 §1 Aggregates of persons or of things which are directed to a purpose befitting the Church's mission, which transcends the purpose of the individuals, are constituted juridical persons either by a provision of the law itself or by a special concession given in the form of a decree by the competent authority.

Christ's faithful can collaborate in many ways in order to assist the Church's mission, e.g. by setting up associations (see Cann. 215, 298, 299 etc.), pious foundations (see Can. 1303), structures such as parishes, provinces, etc. The goal of these collaborative enterprises often goes beyond that of the individual persons involved. According to this canon, such groups or entities can be established as juridical persons in two ways:

(a) by virtue of the law itself, e.g. seminaries (see Can. 238 §1), public associations of the faithful (see Can. 313), parishes (see Can. 515 §3), religious institutes (see Can. 634 §1), etc. In these cases, juridical personality is bestowed as soon as the entity in question has been lawfully established by the competent authority.

(b) by virtue of a decree of the competent ecclesiastical authority, e.g. in the case of a private association of the faithful (see Can. 322 §1); this may form an integral part of the decree of establishment, or it may constitute a separate, subsequent act.

Can. 114 §2 The purposes indicated in §1 are understood to be those which concern works of piety, of the apostolate or of charity, whether spiritual or temporal.

§3 The competent ecclesiastical authority is not to confer juridical personality except on those aggregates of persons or of things which aim at a genuinely useful purpose and which, all things considered, have the means which are foreseen to be sufficient to achieve the purpose in view.

The law itself confers juridical personality only on those aggregates of persons or things which serve a useful purpose. Whenever an already existing entity seeks juridical personality, the competent authority must investigate the purposes of such a body. According to law (§2), one at least of three purposes is required to warrant such a grant, i.e.

– works of piety, e.g. the promotion of prayer, worship, etc.;
– works of the apostolate, e.g. that of teaching, nursing, etc. in accordance with the doctrine and ethos of the Church;
– works of charity, e.g. feeding the poor, helping the underprivileged and the oppressed, etc.

The works concerned may be of the strictly spiritual order; equally, however, they may belong to the sphere of what some may see as the purely temporal minded, which some might claim to be the exclusive domain of the civil state. In this regard, there should never be overlooked, much less forgotten, the voluntary and often arduous contribution of the Church to the temporal and social endeavours of so many states worldwide.

Having examined the sufficiency of the body's goal, the competent authority must make a prudent judgment concerning juridical personality (§3). In particular, it must be satisfied that the entity has sufficient resources to achieve its purpose: such collaborative efforts within the Church are meant to perpetuate and extend the efforts of individuals. If there is no real expectation that this can be sustained in a reasonable fashion, the competent authority ought not grant juridical personality.

Can. 115 §1 Juridical persons in the Church are either aggregates of persons or aggregates of things.

§2 An aggregate of persons, which must be made up of at least three persons, is collegial if the members decide its conduct by participating together in making its decisions, whether by equal right or not, in accordance with the law and the statutes; otherwise, it is non-collegial.

§3 An aggregate of things, or an autonomous foundation, consists of goods or things, whether spiritual or material, and is directed, in accordance with the law and the statutes, by one or more physical persons or by a college.

232 When considering juridical persons in the Church, certain fundamental concepts and distinctions are to be kept in mind:

(a) juridical persons consist either of aggregates of persons (e.g. a Bishops' Conference) or aggregates of things (e.g. a diocesan trust for holding property). This distinction is already implicit in Can. 114 §1.

(b) juridical persons are *collegial* if their decisions are the result of joint action by the constituent persons. In some cases, all those in a collegial juridical person have *equal rights* (e.g. in a cathedral chapter); in others, some members have restricted rights (e.g. auxiliary Bishops in a Bishops' Conference). To be established validly, a collegial juridical person must comprise at least three persons at the time of establishment; the fact that an already established collegial juridical person subsequently finds itself with less than three persons does not, of itself, affect its canonical status (see Can. 120 §2). Juridical persons are *non-collegial* if they are governed by a person or persons to whom they have been entrusted e.g. the Bishop is entrusted with the juridical person of the diocese and acts in its name (see Can. 393). In both types of juridical person, all decisions must be taken in accordance with the provisions of universal law and particular law, and the statutes of the juridical person itself.

(c) a juridical person consisting of an aggregate of things is known as an 'autonomous foundation' (see Can. 1303 §1 1°). It is made up of goods or things (e.g. property, money, buildings etc.) which are destined for the purposes mentioned in Can. 114 §2. Such a juridical person is directed by one or more physical persons acting singly or collegially according to the statutes.

Can. 116 §1 Public juridical persons are aggregates of persons or of things which are established by the competent ecclesiastical authority so that, within the limits allotted to them, they might in the name of the Church and in accordance with the provisions of law, fulfil the specific task entrusted to them in view of the public good. Other juridical persons are private.

§2 Public juridical persons are given this personality either by the law itself or by a special decree of the competent authority expressly granting it. Private juridical persons are given this personality only by a special decree of the competent authority expressly granting it.

233 In addition to the distinctions encountered in Can. 115, juridical persons may be *public* or *private*.

234 The following features distinguish public juridical persons:

(a) they are established by the competent ecclesiastical authority i.e. by the law itself, e.g. ecclesiastical provinces (see Can. 432 §2), parishes (see Can. 515 §3), religious institutes, provinces, houses etc. (see Can. 634 §1); or alternatively by decree of the appropriate authority, e.g. a Conference of major religious Superiors may be given juridical personality by a decree of the Holy See (see Can. 709).

(b) the task they carry out in accordance with Can. 114 §2 is done *in the name of the Church* i.e. a public juridical person acts formally on behalf of the Church and not simply in its own name;

(c) they are subject not only to their own statutes but also to universal and particular law. Moreover, their property and assets are *ecclesiastical goods* which are governed by the relevant canons of the Code (see Can. 1257 §1);

(d) they are to fulfil the task for which they were established 'for the public good' i.e. for the benefit of the whole community of the faithful.

By contrast, private juridical persons can be established *only* by a special decree of the competent authority. The origin of these bodies lies in the initiative of private individuals. They obtain juridical status only when their statutes have been approved (see Cann. 117, 322). In general, the assets of such persons are regulated only by the statutes; they are *not* ecclesiastical goods (see Can. 1257 §2).

During the preparation of the new Code, it had been argued that the distinction between public and private persons might have to be eliminated. This proposal was rejected on the ground that it was inimical to the conciliar position on freedom of association.[1] A study of Cann. 118–123 reveals the important canonical differences between public and private juridical persons in matters such as cessation, dispositions concerning property etc.

Can. 117 No aggregate of persons or of things seeking juridical personality can acquire it unless its statutes are approved by the competent authority.

All juridical persons, whether they are public or private, must have their statutes (see Can. 94) approved by the competent ecclesiastical authority before they can be established validly. This norm is repeated in Cann. 314 and 322 §2 for public and private associations of the faithful.

Can. 118 Those persons represent, and act in the name of, a public juridical person whose competence to do so is acknowledged by universal or particular law, or by their own statutes; those persons represent a private juridical person who are given this competence by their statutes.

While all juridical persons may have canonical status and identity in their own right, they can act only by means of physical persons who represent them. In the case of public juridical persons, the representatives are appointed or indicated by universal law, e.g. the Bishop for his diocese (see Can. 393), the parish priest for his parish (see Can. 532), by particular law, or by the statutes. In the case of private juridical persons, the representatives are determined solely by the statutes. In both cases, these individuals represent juridical persons in any processes in which they may be involved (see Can. 1480).

Can. 119 In regard to collegial acts, unless the law or the statutes provide otherwise:

    1° in regard to elections, provided a majority of those who must be summoned are present, what is decided by an absolute majority of those present has the force of law. If there have been two inconclusive scrutinies, a vote is to be taken between the two candidates with the greatest number of votes or, if there are more than two, between the two senior by age. After a third inconclusive scrutiny, that person is deemed elected who is senior by age;

---

[1] Cf. Comm 14(1982) 143 at Can. 113.

2° in regard to other matters, provided a majority of those who must be summoned are present, what is decided by an absolute majority of those present has the force of law. If the votes are equal after two scrutinies, the person presiding can break the tie with a casting vote.

3° that which affects all as individuals must be approved by all.

239 Before considering the various principles contained in the canon, it is essential to note that these norms apply to collegial acts *only if* particular law or the statutes of the body in question have made no other provision.

240 The first set of principles given concerns *the conduct of elections* (1°):

(a) not only must all members of the college be summoned for an election (see Can. 166 §1), but a majority of those persons must be actually present i.e. physically present in the designated place, except for the case provided for in Can. 167 §2;

(b) an election is decided whenever one candidate receives an *absolute* majority of the votes *of those present*. An absolute majority consists simply of any number *more than one half* of the votes, and it is to be reckoned on the basis of all those present for the election, whether or not they have all voted or voted validly. This constitutes a major change from the norm of c.101 §1 1° of the 1917 Code whereby the majority was calculated only on the basis of the number of valid votes actually cast;

(c) this absolute majority is essential if someone is to be elected on the first or second scrutiny;

(d) should the first and second scrutinies prove to be inconclusive, i.e. if no candidate obtains an absolute majority of those present, a third ballot is to be held between the two candidates who obtained the greatest number of votes in the preceding ballot. If more than two received the same number of votes, the two candidates for the third ballot are selected on the basis of age;

(e) on the third ballot, even though only two candidates are legitimately involved, a *relative* majority of the votes of those present is sufficient for election;[1] in the event of a tie in the third ballot, 'that person is deemed elected who is senior by age'.

241 The second set of principles regulates *other kinds of collegial acts* (2°) e.g. the dismissal of a religious (see Can. 699 §1):

(a) not only must all be summoned (see Can. 166 §1), but a majority of these must be actually present;

(b) an *absolute* majority of the votes *of those present* obtains the force of law;

(c) in the event of a tie after two scrutinies, the person presiding has the faculty to determine the issue by a casting vote. This presiding person is not obliged to use this casting vote: it is simply a *faculty*. Indeed, the nature of the matter under discussion may suggest that a decision should be deferred until agreement can be reached.

242 The third principle governs those decisions which affect not only the college as such but each and every individual member as well. In these cases, any decision must be *unanimous* i.e. without dissent or abstention, e.g. election by compromise (see Can. 174) which deprives the individual members of the college of their right to vote.

Can. 120 §1 A juridical person is by its nature perpetual. It ceases to exist, however, if it is lawfully suppressed by the competent authority, or if it has been inactive for a hundred years. A private juridical person also ceases to

---

[1] This is not explicitly stated in the canon but was made clear in PCI rep 8.V.1990: AAS 82(1990) 845. Cf. also Wrenn (Interpret) 59–61.

exist if the association itself is dissolved in accordance with the statutes, or if, in the judgement of the competent authority, the foundation itself has, in accordance with the statutes, ceased to exist.

243 The canon opens by stating the fundamental principle that every juridical person is *perpetual* by its nature, i.e. it is not transitory or ephemeral. The thinking behind this rule is that the juridical person can serve the purposes for which it was established in a way that goes beyond the efforts of the individual persons who may at any given time be involved in its functioning. Nevertheless, a juridical person can cease to exist. The canon identifies two ways in which every juridical person, whether public or private, can be extinguished:

(a) *suppression* by the competent ecclesiastical authority. This authority is usually, but not always,[1] the same authority which established the juridical person (see Cann. 312 §1, 320). The act of suppression must be made in the proper form and must be made for just reasons (see Can. 51).

(b) *inactivity* for a continuous period of one hundred years. Any real interruption of this period, no matter how brief, saves the juridical person from extinction. Although it is automatic, the cessation of a juridical person in this way ought to be formally recorded.

244 In addition to the foregoing, *private* juridical persons may cease to exist in two other ways:

(a) in the case of aggregates of persons, if the members decide to dissolve the association in accordance with their own statutes (see Can. 326 §1);

(b) in the case of aggregates of things, if the competent authority decides, in accordance with the statutes, that the foundation which possessed juridical personality has actually ceased to exist.

It is essential that all private juridical persons include in their statutes the exact procedures to be followed in the case of their extinction, not least in respect of their financial or other assets.

Can. 120 §2 If even a single member of a collegial juridical person survives, and the aggregate of persons has not, according to the statutes, ceased to exist, the exercise of all the rights of the aggregate devolves upon that member.

245 A logical consequence of the principles enunciated thus far is that, in collegial juridical persons – both public and private – when only one member remains, the exercise of all the rights of the juridical person devolve upon that single individual: it is this person alone who can act legitimately in the name of the juridical person. However, all its goods and assets continue to belong to the juridical person as such, not to the individual in question.

Can. 121 When aggregates of persons or of things which are public juridical persons are so amalgamated that one aggregate, itself with a juridical personality, is formed, this new juridical person obtains the patrimonial goods and rights which belonged to the previous aggregates; it also accepts the liabilities of the previous aggregates. In what concerns particularly the arrangements for the goods and the discharge of obligations, the wishes of the founders and benefactors, and any acquired rights, must be safeguarded.

---

[1] An obvious exception is the suppression of a diocesan-right religious institute which, although established by the diocesan Bishop, can be suppressed only by the Holy See: cf. Can. 584.

246 When two or more public juridical persons merge to form a new entity which is itself a public juridical person, e.g. the fusion of two dioceses to form a new diocese, the new body acquires both the patrimonial rights and the liabilities of the previous persons. In this way, the existence of the previous aggregates may be said to continue. They are neither suppressed nor extinguished in the sense of Can. 120 §1.

247 Yet the new juridical person must pay careful attention to the wishes of the founders and benefactors of the previous entities and to those persons who may have acquired rights in their regard. This sensitivity to the intentions of donors and acquired rights is echoed elsewhere in the Code (see Cann. 122, 123 etc.).

248 The norm of this canon refers only to public juridical persons. Private juridical persons must provide appropriate norms in their own statutes. The canon also refers only to a *fusion* whereby a new entity is created. It does not apply to various collaborative efforts between public juridical persons in order to achieve their ends more effectively while each retains its own separate identity, e.g. federations or confederations of autonomous monasteries.

Can. 122 When an aggregate which is a public juridical person is divided in such a way that part of it is joined to another juridical person, or a distinct public juridical person is established from one part of it, the first obligation is to observe the wishes of the founders and benefactors, the demands of acquired rights and the requirements of the approved statutes. Then the competent ecclesiastical authority, either personally or through an executor, is to ensure:

> 1° that the divisible common patrimonial goods and rights, the monies owed and the other liabilities, are divided between the juridical persons in question in due proportion, in a fashion which is equitable and right, taking account of all the circumstances and needs of both;
>
> 2° that the use and enjoyment of the common goods which cannot be divided, be given to each juridical person, and also that the liabilities which are proper to each are the responsibility of each, in due proportion, in a fashion which is equitable and right.

249 Public juridical persons may be divided in two distinct ways:

(a) if part of one juridical person is separated from it and united to another public juridical person, e.g. transferring a parish from one diocese to another;

(b) if part of one juridical persons is separated from it and established as a distinct public juridical person e.g. the division of a large diocese in order to form a new diocese.

250 In all cases of division, the competent ecclesiastical authority must provide for the temporal goods of the original juridical person. In doing so, the authority must observe the wishes and intentions of the founders and benefactors, the acquired rights of others, and the statutes of that juridical person. As soon as these demands have been satisfied, the authority may proceed to the distribution of the ownership, use and usufruct of the assets and responsibility for the liabilities.

251 The canon draws a clear distinction between what can be divided and what cannot be divided:

(a) the goods and liabilities which admit of division, e.g. bank accounts, debts etc., are to be shared between the two juridical persons in an equitable and proportionate manner, taking account of the needs and circumstances of each juridical person;

(b) what cannot be divided must also be shared in some way between the two juridical persons: the use and usufruct of assets and responsibility for liabilities are shared equitably and proportionately. In this case, the ownership of a particular property, e.g. a library, may remain vested in the original juridical person, while the use, enjoyment and maintenance of the library is shared by both.

The decision concerning what is equitable and proportionate is to be made by the competent ecclesiastical authority or the executor appointed for the task of dividing the original juridical person. Any such decision presupposes a careful assessment of the needs and circumstances of both juridical persons, and an evaluation of the resources actually available to each.

Can. 123 On the extinction of a public juridical person, the destination of its goods and patrimonial rights as also of its obligations is ruled by law and the statutes. If the statutes do not deal with the matter, the goods and the patrimonial rights go to the next higher juridical person, always with due regard for the wishes of the founders and benefactors and for acquired rights. On the extinction of a private juridical person, the destination of its goods and obligations is governed by its own statutes.

The final canon dealing with the assets and liabilities of public juridical persons concerns the case of extinction (see Can. 120 §1). The primary norm of the Code is that these matters ought to be contained in particular law and in the statutes of each public juridical person. As a subsidiary norm, the canon lays down that, where such particular norms are lacking, responsibility for all goods and liabilities devolves upon the public juridical person which is immediately superior, e.g. the diocese assumes this responsibility whenever a parish is suppressed. Whatever arrangements may be made by this superior juridical person, the canon repeats the injunction to observe the wishes of founders and benefactors and respect the acquired rights of others. This general norm is repeated in more specific form when the Code deals with the suppression of religious houses (see Can. 616 §1).

The property and liabilities of a private juridical person are to be disposed of in accordance with the statutes of the juridical person. No reference is made to these matters in the Code since only the goods of public juridical persons are 'ecclesiastical goods' (see Can. 1257 §1). Nevertheless, the wishes of benefactors and any acquired rights must be respected (see Can. 326 §2).

Title VII
Juridical Acts

Can. 124 §1 For the validity of a juridical act, it is required that it be performed by a person who is legally capable, and it must contain those elements which constitute the essence of the act, as well as the formalities and requirements which the law prescribes for the validity of the act.

As the People of God ordered in this world as a society (see Can. 204), the Church has to be considered from the point of view, among others, of the relationships existing between members of the faithful. These relationships must of course be adjusted to different needs. Of particular importance is that category of event known as a juridical act. It may be defined as 'an externally manifested act of the will by which a certain juridical effect is intended'.[1] A juridical act is thus clearly distinguished from simple juridical *facts* i.e. non-intentional events which have juridical consequences, e.g. age, consanguinity etc.

256 The principal defining feature of the juridical act is its *voluntary* nature: it is a *deliberate* action by a subject; the object of the action is *intended* by the subject; moreover, the intention is in some way externally manifested: otherwise the act will remain purely internal, with no consequences for the social relationships between members of the Church.

257 The opening canon of this Title is concerned with what is required for a *valid* juridical act, namely:

(a) It must be performed by someone who is 'legally capable' i.e. a physical or juridical person (see Can. 96, 113 §2, 114 §1). This person must have the *general* capacity to perform the act, i.e. be possessed of the fundamental requisites, e.g. age, personal responsibility etc., as well as the *specific* capacity so to act in the circumstances, i.e. be free of any impediment rendering the person unable to act. In addition, the subject of the act must be *competent*, i.e. occupy the requisite position or office, e.g. have obtained delegation to assist at a marriage (see Can. 1108), have been appointed as a judge (see Cann. 1421, 1620 1°), etc. Defects in any of these areas may render the individual physical or juridical person incapable of performing a particular act validly, despite having the correct intention.

(b) The act must have within itself all those juridical elements necessary to constitute it. The most fundamental of these is the will of the person acting. Constraints placed on this may affect the validity of the act (see Cann. 125–126). Other such elements vary according to the nature of the act, e.g. water in baptism, perpetuity of the marriage bond, etc. The validity of an act is not, however, contingent upon that which is extrinsic or accidental to the act itself, e.g. the liturgical rite used in administering baptism.

(c) The act must also contain any further formalities required for validity by the law, e.g. the canonical form of marriage as prescribed by Can. 1108.

Can. 124 §2 A juridical act which, as far as its external elements are concerned, is properly performed, is presumed to be valid.

258 As noted above, the external manifestation is necessary if an intentional act is to have the desired juridical effects. This paragraph states a clear and logical consequence of §1, namely, if the external elements of any act have been verified, one must presume the validity of the act. It is this principle which lies behind Can. 1060. This presumption may be overturned, but only by contrary proof.[2]

Can. 125 §1 An act performed as a result of force imposed from outside on a person who was quite unable to resist it, is regarded as not having taken place.

§2 An act performed as a result of fear which is grave and unjustly inflicted, or as a result of deceit, is valid, unless the law provides otherwise.

---

[1] Robleda *De conceptu actus iuridici*: Per 51(1962) 419. An English translation may be found in Hughes *A new Title in the Code: On juridical Acts* Stud Can 14(1980) 392.
[2] Cf. Comm 6(1974) 102.

Title VII Juridical Acts

However, it can be rescinded by a court judgement, either at the instance of the injured party or that party's successors in law, or ex officio.

Since every juridical act is an act of the will, it must be a substantially *free act*. Anything, therefore, which limits the freedom of the subject can affect the validity of a juridical act. This canon deals with external factors which may affect an act's validity:

(a) *force* (§1) may be defined as physical coercion: the canon speaks of force 'imposed from outside' which a person 'was quite unable to resist'. Any act performed as a result of this force is regarded by law as non-existent, e.g. religious profession (see Cann. 656 4°, 658), marriage (see Can. 1103), etc. Clearly, if a person could have resisted the force and chose not to, the act would be valid, since the person's freedom was not effectively removed.

(b) *fear* (§2) may be defined as a disturbance of the mind caused by impending present or future danger. The law, in general, regards any act performed under the influence of fear as valid, even if that fear is grave and inflicted unjustly. By way of exception, however, the law does consider invalid certain acts performed out of fear, e.g. voting (see Can. 172 §1 1°), religious profession (see Can. 656 4°), marriage (see Can. 1103) etc.

(c) *deceit* (the latin term 'dolus') is used in the Code with two distinct meanings: it is either the *deliberate manipulation of another* by telling lies or concealing the truth so that the other is persuaded to perform a juridical act (see Can. 1098), or the *malice* or ill-will by which a person commits an offence (see Can. 1321 §1). Any act performed as a result of deceit *in the former sense* is regarded generally as valid (§2), unless the law provides otherwise (see Cann. 172 §1 1°, 656 4°, 1098).

Even though the law regards as valid those acts performed as a result of fear or deceit, the canon points out that such acts can be rescinded by the judgement of an ecclesiastical court. An action of this kind may be undertaken by the injured party or his or her successors in law; or it may be undertaken *ex officio* by the promoter of justice or the hierarchical superior of the person involved. An act which may thus be rescinded is never to be confused with an act which is invalid or juridically inexistent, e.g. a marriage which is officially declared to have been invalid (null and void *ab initio*) by reason of grave fear, is a substantially different legal entity from a valid act, itself performed under the influence of grave fear, which is subsequently rescinded in accordance with the terms of this canon.[1]

Can. 126 An act is invalid when performed as a result of ignorance or of error which concerns the substance of the act, or which amounts to a condition sine qua non; otherwise it is valid, unless the law provides differently. But an act done as a result of ignorance or error can give rise to a rescinding action in accordance with the law.

This canon deals with intrinsic factors which may affect the validity of a juridical act, namely ignorance and error. These may be defined, respectively, as a lack of due knowledge and a false judgment. According to the canon, these factors may result in the invalidity of a juridical act in only two sets of circumstances:

(a) if the defect of knowledge or the false judgment concerned the substance of the act itself, e.g. the pronouncing of perpetual religious vows thinking or believing that they are purely temporary;

---

[1] It is the failure, or refusal, to appreciate this simple yet fundamental legal distinction which sometimes allows commentators on political and social affairs shamelessly to misrepresent the grant of an ecclesiastical decree of nullity of marriage as 'the Catholic form of divorce'!

(b) if the ignorance or error concerned something which really amounts to a *conditio sine qua non*, even though the object of the lack of knowledge or the error is not the substance of the act, e.g. marrying a person who is sterile believing him or her to be fertile, precisely because the overriding intention in getting married in this case is to have an heir.

262 Apart from these sets of circumstances, the law accepts as valid any act performed as a result of ignorance or error, unless the law provides otherwise e.g. resignation from office (see Can. 188), marriage (see Cann. 1096–1097, 1099), etc. Yet, even where they are accepted as valid, such acts can be rescinded 'in accordance with the law', i.e. in accordance with an ecclesiastical judicial process (see Can. 125 §2 above).

Can. 127 §1 When the law prescribes that, in order to perform a juridical act, a Superior requires the consent or the advice of some college or group of persons, the college or group must be convened in accordance with Can. 166, unless, if there is question of seeking advice only, particular or proper law provides otherwise. For the validity of the act, it is required that the consent be obtained of an absolute majority of those present, or that the advice of all be sought.

263 Before certain juridical acts are performed, the law requires that the Superior obtain the consent or advice of some people. In this context, 'Superior' refers to anyone holding a position of executive authority at any level. Those whose consent or advice must be sought may form a group or college, or may be a number of separate individuals.

264 Where a group of college is involved, all members must be convoked in accordance with Can. 166 §1. A collegial act (see Can. 119 2°) is required. Consequently, an absolute majority of those who must be summoned must be present. However, if the law requires only that advice be given, particular or proper law may determine that a meeting of the group as such is not necessary.

265 When the *consent* of the group is required, an absolute majority of those actually present must agree on the issue in question; a relative majority does not suffice. Moreover, in the event of a tie, consent has not been obtained and the act cannot be performed. In these circumstances, the Superior *cannot* intervene to resolve the tie with a casting vote.[1] The group or college, e.g. the council of a religious Superior (see Can. 627 §1), is an entity in its own right, distinct from the person of the Superior who is *not a member of it*.

266 Whenever *advice* of the group must be sought, the Superior is required to seek the advice of all concerned, i.e. he or she must *ask* for advice on the particular point and then *listen* to what is said. If no response is received, the invitation should be renewed, together with a reminder of the grave obligation involved (see §3 below). If there is still no response, the Superior is free to act. However, if the advice is not actually *asked for*, the act performed would be *invalid*.

Can. 127 §2 When the law prescribes that, in order to perform a juridical act, a Superior requires the consent or advice of certain persons as individuals:

1° if consent is required, the Superior's act is invalid if the Superior does not seek the consent of those persons, or acts against the vote of all or any of them;

2° if advice is required, the Superior's act is invalid if the Superior does not hear those persons. The Superior is not in any way bound to accept their

---

[1] Cf. CCom rep 14.V.1985: AAS 77(1985) 771.

vote, even it if it is unanimous; nevertheless, without what is, in his or her judgement, an overriding reason, the Superior is not to act against their vote, especially if it is a unanimous one.

At times the law prescribes that the consent or advice of one or more persons as *individuals* must be obtained. In these cases:

(a) the Superior is obliged, as an essential requirement, actually to seek the prescribed consent or advice: without this minimum, the act would be invalid;

(b) in cases where consent is required, the Superior cannot validly act contrary to the expressed wishes of any or all of the people concerned, e.g. in an ecclesiastical trial the judge cannot shorten the prescribed time-limits without the consent of the parties (see Can. 1465 §2): should both of them or even only one object, he cannot act validly in this regard (see also Cann. 455 §1, 609 §1, 1602 §1, etc.);

(c) in cases where advice only is required, the Superior is not bound by law to accept this advice, even if it is unanimous. Yet the canon stresses that such advice, especially if unanimous, is not to be set aside lightly: there must be some overriding reason for doing so. This highlights the need to seek advice openly, not as a mere formality which will not affect a decision already made.

Can. 127 §3 All whose consent or advice is required are obliged to give their opinions sincerely. If the seriousness of the matter requires it, they are obliged carefully to maintain secrecy, and the Superior can insist on this obligation.

Not alone is the Superior reminded of his or her obligations in law: so, too, are all those who are bound to give their consent or advice. All such persons, whether acting as part of a group or as individuals, are obliged to express their opinions on the matter in question and to do so sincerely. Such persons are not at liberty to refuse the request of the Superior to give consent or advice. In addition, in more serious matters, they are obliged to maintain secrecy. The Superior can insist on this twofold obligation, even if needs be by means of a precept (see Can. 49).

Can. 128 Whoever unlawfully causes harm to another by a juridical act, or indeed by any other act which is malicious or culpable, is obliged to repair the damage done.

Throughout the Code there are references to the obligations of persons and authorities to make good any damage or harm caused by their acts (e.g. Cann. 57 §3, 982, 1062 etc.). In this canon, the principle is stressed in its broadest possible terms.

Canonically, damage may be caused to another:

(a) by a juridical act performed illegitimately, whether the act was invalid or simply illicit, e.g. when the limits of ordinary administration are exceeded (Can. 1281 §1);

(b) by any other act performed by reason of malice or culpability (see Can. 1321 §1), e.g. damage to another person's good name (see Can. 220) as a result of deliberate lies (malice) or as a result of a culpably excessive indulgence in alcohol (culpability).

Any person, physical or juridical, at any level within the Church, is bound to repair the damage or harm done as a result of such acts. If the offender has not taken the initiative, the injured party has the right to bring an action in this regard (see Can. 1729 §1) .

Title VIII
Power of Governance

Can. 129 §1 Those who are in sacred orders are, in accordance with the provisions of law, capable of the power of governance, which in fact belongs to the Church by divine institution. This power is also called the power of jurisdiction.

272 Vat. II taught that Christ 'established and ever sustains here on earth his holy Church, the community of faith, hope and charity, as a visible organisation'.[1] Within the Church, the Lord set up a variety of ministries to care for God's people and foster their growth.[2] These ministries are exercised in hierarchical order, so that the Bishops are seen to be the primary successors of the apostles, with all others sharing to some degree in the mission given by Christ to the apostles.[3] Within the mission of Christ, three offices or functions (*munera*) may be identified: the office of sanctifying, the office of teaching and the office of governing.[4] The 'power of governance', by which this third office is exercised, belongs to the Church 'by divine institution' i.e. it is derived from the Church's foundation by Christ, not from any purely human source such as the will of the leader or the will of the people.

273 According to this canon, those in sacred orders are 'capable' (*habiles*) of this power of governance, i.e. the various offices related to the exercise of this power may be entrusted to clerics (i.e. deacons, priests, Bishops), within the limits determined by the law. Thus, all clerics do not exercise the same power in the same way or to the same extent. Vat. II made it clear that, even among Bishops, 'a canonical or juridical determination through hierarchical authority is required for such power ordered to action'.[5] For the Council, the reception of episcopal consecration was not in itself enough to be able to carry out a particular function: a further hierarchical act was necessary, e.g. receiving the care of a portion of the People of God, assignment to a specific task within the Church. This determination may be described as a 'canonical mission' (*missio canonica*).

274 The ultimate source of all power within the Church is Christ. While in no way even questioning the unity of that source, a clear distinction must be drawn between the power of governance (see Cann. 130–144) and the power of orders, i.e. the power to perform sacred acts, e.g. to preside at the celebration of the Eucharist, to impart sacramental absolution, etc.; this power, although closely and inextricably connected to the power of governance, belongs properly to the exercise of Christ's office of sanctifying. According to the canon, the power of governance is also known as the 'power of jurisdiction', a term found in cc.196–197, 199–202 of the 1917 Code.

Can. 129 §2 Lay members of Christ's faithful can cooperate in the exercise of this same power in accordance with the law.

275 Although not described as 'capable' of the power of governance, lay members of Christ's faithful 'can cooperate' in the exercise of this power. This is a significantly

---

[1] LG 8: Fl I 357.
[2] Cf. LG 18: Fl I 369.
[3] Cf. LG 20–21: Fl I 371–374.
[4] Cf. LG 21: Fl I 373.
[5] LG NEP n.2: Fl I 424.

new provision of law. It is rooted firmly in Vat. II's teaching on the participation of all the baptised in the one priesthood of Christ and on the roles entrusted specifically to the laity by the hierarchy.[1] The inclusion of this principle was a matter of considerable debate during the process of the Code's revision; some indeed tended to see it as a threat to the proper role of sacred ministers. In the event, an overwhelming majority voted to include it.[2]

This paragraph might at first sight appear to be in opposition to the norm of Can. 274 §1, which reserves to clerics offices involving the exercise of the power of governance. It is to be carefully noted, however, that the present canon speaks of lay people *cooperating* in the exercise of this power. This emphasises the essentially *collaborative* nature of their holding of office and exercise of power. It has been pointed out that both canons are statements of principle, neither of which is absolute or exclusive of the other.[3]

Can. 130 Of itself the power of governance is exercised for the external forum; sometimes however it is exercised for the internal forum only, but in such a way that the effects which its exercise is designed to have in the external forum are not acknowledged in that forum, except in so far as the law prescribes this for determinate cases.

The Church is at once a supernatural mystery: the People of God, and a visible hierarchically-structured human society.[4] The exercise of the power of governance within the Church is ordered to a twofold end: the common good of all and the good of each individual. That which is exercised for the common good has to do principally with the social relations between members of Christ's faithful; this must admit of external proof or verification. Accordingly, this canon speaks of the power of governance of itself being 'exercised for the external forum'. What is exercised solely for the good of a particular individual has to do with that person's relationship with God or with his or her own conscience: in this way, the power of governance may also be exercised 'for the internal forum only'. This internal forum may be *sacramental*, i.e. in the context of the sacrament of penance, or *non-sacramental*, dealing e.g. with consultation or advice on any matter of conscience: it could e.g. concern the like of an occult matrimonial impediment, but it is by no means confined to any such a formal juridical situation.

The consequences of this distinction are that, generally speaking, *any decision for the internal forum* has effect in that forum *alone*. However, in certain exceptional situations, the law may provide otherwise, e.g. a dispensation obtained from the apostolic Penitentiary from an occult impediment is normally effective for the internal forum only, but should that impediment subsequently become a public one (see Can. 1074), the record of the earlier internal forum dispensation would be sufficient for the external forum also (see Can. 1082). Clearly, only an act of the internal *non-sacramental* forum can ever be acknowledged in the external forum in this way.

---

[1] Cf. LG 10, 32–35, AA 24: Fl I 361, 389–393, 790.

[2] Cf. Comm 14(1982) 146–149 at Can. 126. For an in-depth and very profitable study of all the implications of the participation of the laity in the exercise of the power of governance, the interested reader is earnestly recommended to consult the report of the detailed discussion on this matter at the final Plenary Meeting of the Pontifical Commission held in Rome 20–29 October 1981, subsequently issued by PCI: *Congregatio Plenaria 20–29.X.1981* Vatican Press 1991 35–97, 190–229.

[3] Cf. Chiappetta I n.810.

[4] Cf. LG 7–8: Fl I 354–358.

Can. 131 §1 Ordinary power of governance is that which by virtue of the law itself is attached to a given office; delegated power is that which is granted to a person other than through an office.

§2 Ordinary power of governance may be proper or vicarious.

§3 One who claims to have been delegated has the onus of proving the delegation.

279 This canon introduces certain distinctions concerning the power of governance which are encountered in many parts of the Code and which have significant practical consequences.

280 The first distinction is between *ordinary* power and *delegated* power (§1). Power of governance is described as *ordinary* when it is attached to a specific office *by reason of the law itself* e.g. a diocesan Bishop has legislative, executive and judicial power in his diocese (see Can. 391 §1). As soon as a person lawfully takes possession of a particular office, he or she obtains whatever power belongs intrinsically to that office.

281 Power of governance is described as *delegated* when it is conferred upon a person by special concession, either *by the law itself* (e.g. Cann. 976, 1079–1080) or by someone enjoying the ordinary power of governance, e.g. a local Ordinary or a parish priest can delegate a deacon or another priest to assist at a marriage (see Can. 1108 §1). In brief, therefore, while the exercise of ordinary power comes to a person *indirectly* by reason of the office which has by law been assigned to that person, the exercise of delegated power is given *directly* to the person in question.

282 The second distinction is between *proper* ordinary power and *vicarious* ordinary power (§2). The ordinary power of governance is *proper* when it is exercised by the person who holds the particular office, e.g. a diocesan Bishop acting in his own name exercises *proper* ordinary power of governance. That ordinary power is described as *vicarious* when, although attached by law to a particular office, it is exercised by someone who is specifically acting in the name of the office-holder: Vicars general, episcopal Vicars and judicial Vicars are clear instances in point (see Cann. 475, 476, 479, 1420 §§1–2).

283 A practical matter related to the first of the above distinctions is the need for proof that one has in fact been delegated to perform some act. This canon ends with a practical principle in this regard (§3): anyone claiming to have been delegated, whether by law or by another person, whether for one occasion or habitually, must be able to prove the fact of delegation. This highlights the need that all forms of delegation be given in writing.

Can. 132 §1 Habitual faculties are governed by the provisions concerning delegated power.

§2 However, unless the grant has expressly provided otherwise, or the Ordinary was deliberately chosen as the only one to exercise the faculty, an habitual faculty granted to an Ordinary does not lapse on the expiry of the authority of the Ordinary to whom it was given, even if he has already begun to exercise the faculty, but it passes to the Ordinary who succeeds him in governance.

284 'Habitual faculties' may be described as powers granted, not by virtue of the law, but by an act of a higher ecclesiastical authority, e.g. a Bishop may grant a priest the habitual faculty of celebrating three Masses every Sunday (see Can. 905 §2). According to c.66 §1 of the 1917 Code, such concessions were regarded as singular privileges. In the present legislation, however, they are equated with delegated power and are regulated by the relevant provisions of law (see Cann. 131 §2, 133–144).

As a general principle, the law regards an habitual faculty granted to an Ordinary to have been given primarily to the office which he holds. Thus, whenever an individual ceases to hold office, the habitual faculty passes to his successor in office, e.g. the habitual faculties granted to a Vicar general pass to his successor upon the Vicar's retirement. By way of exception, however, the law acknowledges the possibility that such habitual faculties may lapse with the expiry of the authority of the person who received them; this occurs only:

(a) when the act granting them states this expressly; or

(b) when the individual Ordinary was chosen specifically as the *only person* to exercise the faculties, in effect when they were granted directly to the person and not to the office.

Can. 133 §1 A delegate who exceeds the limits of the mandate, with regard either to things or to persons, performs no act at all.

§2 A delegate is not considered to have exceeded the mandate when what was delegated is carried out, but in a manner different to that determined in the mandate, unless the manner was prescribed for validity by the delegating authority.

Any act by which one person delegates another ought to place clear limits on the object and scope of the delegation, e.g. a priest may be delegated to assist at one marriage only, or at all marriages within the parish. If anyone exceeds the mandate and attempts to do something for which no delegation has been received, the act is invalid and has no juridical effect (§1).

However, as a rule, this principle does not extend to the manner in which the act is to be performed (§2); the object of an act of delegation may be attained in more ways than one, all of which are equally lawful and available to the person delegated. The only exception would be if the mandate were to specify that the act, to be valid, is to be performed in a certain way and no other – in which case anything done in contravention of this requirement would render the act itself invalid.

The principles of this canon highlight the need for the delegating authority to make the mandate as clear and unambiguous as possible, as well as the responsibility of the one delegated to know the precise terms of the mandate.

Can. 134 §1 In law the term Ordinary means, apart from the Roman Pontiff, diocesan Bishops and all who, even for a time only, are set over a particular Church or a community equivalent to it in accordance with Can. 368, and those who in these have general ordinary executive power, that is, Vicars general and episcopal Vicars; likewise, for their own members, it means the major Superiors of clerical religious institutes of pontifical right and of clerical societies of apostolic life of pontifical right, who have at least ordinary executive power.

§2 The term local Ordinary means all those enumerated in §1, except Superiors of religious institutes and of societies of apostolic life.

§3 Whatever in the canons, in the context of executive power, is attributed to the diocesan Bishop, is understood to belong only to the diocesan Bishop and to those others in Can. 381 §2 who are equivalent to him, to the exclusion of the Vicar general and the episcopal Vicar except by special mandate.

In its provisions concerning the exercise of ordinary power of governance, the Code speaks of the *Ordinary*, the *local Ordinary*, and the *diocesan Bishop* or his equivalent in

Book I General Norms

law (see Can. 381 §2). To put the matter beyond misunderstanding, the present canon provides an explanation of the identity of these persons.

290 According to the Code, the following are *Ordinaries*:
  (a) the Roman Pontiff;
  (b) diocesan Bishops, territorial prelates, territorial abbots, Vicars apostolic, Prefects apostolic and apostolic Administrators (see Cann. 368, 381 §2);
  (c) those who have the interim government of a local Church while the see is vacant or impeded (see Cann. 413, 419–421);
  (d) Vicars general and episcopal Vicars within a local Church (see Cann. 475–476);
  (e) the major Superiors of clerical religious institutes and societies of apostolic life of pontifical right (see Can. 620); the precise identity of these is to be found in proper legislation of each such institute or society;
  (f) prelates of personal prelatures (see Can. 295 §1); these are not mentioned in the present canon but are clearly to be included.

291 Although they may exercise ordinary power of governance, none of the following are described as Ordinaries: parish priest, judicial Vicars, the major Superiors of lay religious institutes and societies of apostolic life whether of pontifical or diocesan right, the major Superiors of clerical religious institutes and societies of apostolic life of diocesan right, the Moderators of secular institutes whether of pontifical or diocesan right.[1]

292 This canon makes it clear (§2) that only those listed above from (a) to (d) are considered to be *local Ordinaries*. These persons exercise the power of governance in relation to the People of God entrusted to them within a defined territory. The other Ordinaries do so in a purely *personal* basis.

293 Whenever the law speaks of the 'diocesan Bishop', rather than 'local Ordinary', the intention is to restrict the matter to those holding the office of diocesan Bishop or its equivalent in law (see Can. 381 §2). All other local Ordinaries, e.g. temporary administrators (see Cann. 413, 419–421), Vicars general and episcopal Vicars are excluded: they cannot act except by special mandate of the Bishop (see Cann. 462 §1, 524, etc.).

Can. 135 §1 The power of governance is divided into legislative, executive and judicial power.

§2 Legislative power is to be exercised in the manner prescribed by law; that which in the Church a legislator lower than the supreme authority has, cannot validly be delegated, unless the law explicitly provides otherwise. A lower legislator cannot validly make a law which is contrary to that of a higher legislator.

§3 Judicial power, which is possessed by judges and judicial colleges, is to be exercised in the manner prescribed by law, and it cannot be delegated except for the performance of acts preparatory to some decree or judgement.

§4 As far as the exercise of executive power is concerned, the provisions of the following canons are to be observed.

294 Bearing in mind the fundamental unity of the source of power in the Church and the distinction already drawn between the power of orders and the power of governance, further distinctions are here introduced concerning the manner in which the power of governance may be exercised (§1), i.e. *legislative* power, *judicial* power and *executive*

---

[1] During the revision process, it was pointed out that two institutes have the privilege of having their Moderators as Ordinaries: cf. Comm 13(1981) 405 at Can. 21.

power. In all three cases, the power of governance must be exercised in accordance with the norms of universal and particular law.

Legislative power (§2) is concerned with the development, promulgation and interpretation of laws. The following have legislative power: the Roman Pontiff and the College of Bishops for the universal Church; the diocesan Bishop and his equivalents, the Bishops' Conferences and particular councils, for their territories; the major Superiors and Chapters of clerical religious institutes and societies of apostolic life who make laws for their own subjects only.

Legislative power cannot be delegated, unless some other provision is contained in the relevant universal or particular law (§2). This rule refers only to those authorities who are below the Roman Pontiff or an Ecumenical Council. The prohibition against delegation clearly does not affect the delegation of others to issue authentic interpretations (see Can. 16 §1), or to issue general legislative decrees (see Can. 30). The activity of any legislator must be in conformity with that of a higher authority: any law made at a lower level which is in opposition to the provisions of a higher authority is of its nature *invalid*.

Judicial power (§3) is that by which individual judges or colleges of judges resolve controversies and make decisions, based on law and fact, which are binding on the parties involved in the case (see Can. 16 §3). This power cannot be delegated, except for the purpose of certain preliminary acts, e.g. the designation of an auditor to instruct the case (see Can. 1428 §1).

Executive power (§4) is that which is required for ordinary administration or the application of the law. Cann. 136–144 provide the basic norms of law by which executive power must be exercised.

Can. 136 Persons may exercise executive power over their subjects, even when either they themselves or their subjects are outside the territory, unless it is otherwise clear from the nature of things or from the provisions of law. They can exercise this power over *peregrini* who are actually living in the territory, if it is a question of granting favours, or of executing universal or particular laws by which the *peregrini* are bound in accordance with Can. 13 §2 n.2.

The scope of ordinary executive power of governance is principally determined in relation to territory. All those persons who have a domicile or quasi-domicile (see Cann. 102, 107) within a particular territory are regarded as *subjects* of the one exercising therein ordinary executive power. According to this canon, such authorities can exercise this power over their own subjects who are within the prescribed territorial limits or who are actually outside them; this holds good even when the one with executive power is outside the territory. However, the law (both universal and particular) and the nature of the matter concerned may forbid such an exercise of power, e.g. a local Ordinary or parish priest cannot assist validly at a marriage outside his own territory (see Can. 1109) even if it concerns his own subjects; he can validly assist only if delegated in accordance with Can. 1108 §1.

One with ordinary executive power may also exercise it in respect of those persons who have a domicile or quasi-domicile elsewhere (i.e. the *peregrini* of Can. 100) and who are actually present within the territory of the authority in question. But this may be done only in two sets of circumstances:

- granting favours, e.g. a dispensation from an impediment to marriage (see Can. 1078 §1);
- executing universal or particular laws concerning public order, the formalities required for legal acts, and immovable property in the area (see Can. 13 §2 2°).

301 It is to be noted that this canon refers only to the local Ordinary (see Can. 134 §2). The scope of the exercise of ordinary executive power by personal Ordinaries (e.g. Cann. 295 §1, 620) must be determined by proper legislation.

Can. 137 §1 Ordinary executive power can be delegated either for an individual case or for all cases, unless the law expressly provides otherwise.

§2 Executive power delegated by the Apostolic See can be subdelegated, either for an individual case or for all cases, unless the delegation was deliberately given to the individual alone, or unless subdelegation was expressly prohibited.

§3 Executive power delegated by another authority having ordinary power, if delegated for all cases, can be subdelegated only for individual cases; if delegated for a determinate act or acts, it cannot be subdelegated, except by the express grant of the person delegating.

§4 No subdelegated power can again be subdelegated, unless this was expressly granted by the person delegating.

302 Although as a rule neither legislative nor judicial power can be delegated (see Can. 135 §§2–3), executive power can. In this canon and those that follow, fundamental norms are given to regulate delegation and subdelegation:

(a) someone endowed with ordinary executive power can delegate another either *for a single act* e.g. delegation to assist at a particular marriage (see Can. 1108 §1), or *for all cases* i.e. for all acts of a similar nature or for all matters of the same kind (§1). Delegation is not permitted, however, in those cases where it is expressly forbidden by law, as e.g. Can. 508 §1.

(b) someone delegated by the Apostolic See can *subdelegate* another either *for a single act* or *for all cases* (§2). This is not permitted, however, in two sets of circumstances:

– where the delegate was chosen on a purely personal basis i.e. as the only one suited to the task;

– where subdelegation is expressly prohibited.

(c) someone delegated by an authority other than the Apostolic See can also subdelegate another but only for individual cases and only if he or she has been delegated *for all cases*. If the original delegation was for a single act or certain specified acts, then the executive power cannot be subdelegated unless the original delegating authority expressly grants this faculty to the person delegated (§3).

(d) someone subdelegated in accordance with §§2–3 is prohibited from any further subdelegation, unless such a faculty is granted expressly in the mandate of the one who granted delegation in the first place (§4).

Can. 138 Ordinary executive power, and power delegated for all cases, are to be interpreted widely; any other power is to be interpreted strictly. Delegation of power to a person is understood to include everything necessary for the exercise of that power.

303 It is important for the common good and the good of individual members of the faithful that ordinary and delegated executive power be understood correctly by those who must exercise it. The canon provides three useful rules for interpretation in this regard:

(a) ordinary executive power (see Can. 131), as well as executive power delegated *for all cases*, is to be interpreted *widely*, i.e. within the text and context of the law and the mandate, it is to be understood in the broadest meaning attributable to the words (see Can. 17). This rule applies also to habitual faculties (see Can. 132 §1).

(b) all other power is to be interpreted *strictly*, i.e. executive power delegated *for a single act*, judicial power and legislative power. Within the text and context of the relevant law or mandate, this power is to be understood in the narrowest sense of the words (see Can. 18).

(c) the act of delegation contains within it all the faculties needed to exercise the power delegated, whether for a single act or for all cases, e.g. the delegation to preside at a chapter of nuns in an autonomous monastery (see Can. 625 §2) includes the faculties to confirm the elections and other acts of the chapter.

Can. 139 §1 Unless the law prescribes otherwise, the fact that a person approaches some competent authority, even a higher one, does not mean that the executive power of another competent authority is suspended, whether that be ordinary or delegated.

Because of the hierarchical structure of the Church, more than one authority with ordinary or delegated executive power may be competent to act in a particular matter. The law establishes the principle that, simply because one authority has been approached, the competence of the others is in no way suspended or diminished. It does not matter whether the first authority approached was higher or lower. This provision of law stands in marked contrast with the principle governing the activity of two equally competent tribunals (see Can. 1415). Thus e.g. a person is free to seek a dispensation from the Vicar general and also from the diocesan Bishop. However, should the higher authority refuse the favour requested, lower authorities can act only in accordance with Cann. 64–65.

Can. 139 §2 A lower authority, however, is not to interfere in cases referred to higher authority, except for a grave and urgent reason; in which case the higher authority is to be notified immediately.

Although equally competent, as a rule a lower authority is not to become involved in a matter which has been referred already to a higher authority. By way of exception, however, such interventions may be made – but only for a grave and urgent reason, e.g. granting a dispensation in danger of death (see Can. 1079); in such cases the higher authority to which the matter had first been referred must be immediately *informed* of the lower authority's action. Since that authority is competent to act by law, no permission or confirmation is required from the higher authority.

Can. 140 §1 When several people are together delegated to act in the same matter, the person who has begun to deal with it excludes the others from acting, unless that person is subsequently impeded, or does not wish to proceed further with the matter.

§2 When several people are delegated to act as a college in a certain matter, all must proceed in accordance with Can. 119, unless the mandate provides otherwise.

§3 Executive power delegated to several people is presumed to be delegated to them together.

Ordinary executive power may be delegated to another person or to several other persons. In order to eliminate any misunderstandings and avoid possible conflicts, the law provides norms to regulate those situations where more than one individual is delegated:

(a) when delegation is given *in solidum* (i.e. to two or more persons equally) concerning the same matter, the law establishes that the first person to act thereby excludes the others from doing so. If, however, that individual is later prevented from acting or does not wish to proceed further, the delegation may then be exercised by any one of the others involved (§1).

(b) when the delegation is given to a group of people who must act collegially, *all* the persons concerned must act together in accordance with Can. 119. In exceptional circumstances, however, the mandate may make other provisions (§2).

(c) As a general principle, the canon states the presumption that, when two or more persons are delegated, they are delegated *in solidum*. Any claim that they are obliged to act collegially must be *proved*(§3).

Can. 141 If several people are successively delegated, that person is to deal with the matter whose mandate was the earlier and was not subsequently revoked.

307 If two or more individual persons are delegated for the same matter, to act as individuals, the issue is resolved and conflict avoided on the basis of the timing of the individual mandates involved. Unless it has been revoked, either by a separate act or by a subsequent mandate containing a revocation (whether explicit or implicit), the earlier mandate is held as the one to be fulfilled: this is an application of the maxim '*Qui prior est tempore, potior est iure*'.[1]

Can. 142 §1 Delegated power lapses: on the completion of the mandate; on the expiry of the time or the completion of the number of cases for which it was granted; on the cessation of the motivating reason for the delegation; on its revocation by the person delegating, when communicated directly to the person delegated; and on the renunciation by the person delegated, when communicated to and accepted by the person delegating. It does not lapse on the expiry of the authority of the person delegating, unless this appears from clauses attached to it.

308 Delegated power ceases in a number of ways:

(a) upon completion of the mandate, i.e. as soon as the delegated power has been lawfully exercised in the matter concerned;

(b) when the time for which the mandate was given has expired;

(c) when the number of cases for which the mandate was given has been completed;

(d) when the motivating reason for the delegation has ceased, e.g. a delegation to dispense a matrimonial impediment in a particular case ceases if the parties ultimately decide not to marry;

(e) when the delegated power is revoked by the delegating authority and that revocation has been communicated *directly* to the one delegated e.g. in person, or by letter;

(f) when the one delegated resigns, provided that resignation is communicated to and accepted by the delegating authority.

309 As a matter of principle, delegated power does not cease when the authority of the one delegating ceases e.g. when a Bishop resigns or is transferred, a priest remains able to dispense from a matrimonial impediment for which he was earlier delegated. By way of exception, the law foresees that delegated power may cease with the expiry of the authority of the one delegating, but only if this is stated expressly in clauses attached to the mandate itself.

Can. 142 §2 An act of delegated power exercised for the internal forum only, which is inadvertently performed after the time-limit of the delegation, is valid.

---

[1] RJ 54 in VI°.

Title VIII Power of Governance

The exercise of the power of governance for the *internal forum* (see Can. 130) pertains to the welfare of individual persons in the Church. In the light of this purpose, the law establishes a principle of flexibility concerning the cessation of that delegated power: if an act of delegated power is exercised in the internal forum after the time-limit specified in the mandate, the act is recognised as *valid*, provided the act was performed *unintentionally* after the expiry of the time-limit.

Can. 143 §1 Ordinary power ceases on the loss of the office to which it is attached.

Since it is bestowed on a person only by reason of the office to which it is attached (see Can. 131 §1), ordinary executive power ceases when that office is lost (see Can. 184 §1). This principle has particular importance in the situation where Vicars general and episcopal Vicars lose office when the diocese becomes vacant (see Cann. 409 §2, 418 §2 1°, 481).

Can. 143 §2 Unless the law provides otherwise, ordinary power is suspended if an appeal or a recourse is lawfully made against a deprivation of, or removal from, office.

If an office is lost through deprivation (see Can. 196) or removal (see Cann. 192–195), the one who held the office has the right to lodge an appeal or a recourse against the act of deprivation or removal (see Cann. 1353, 1733–1739). Such an appeal or recourse suspends the force of the original act so that the person deprived or removed retains the office pending the outcome of the appeal or recourse. Nevertheless, the power attached to that office is *suspended*, i.e. the office-holder is not permitted to exercise power until the matter has been settled. In the meantime, the competent authority must make the appropriate provision (e.g. Can. 1747 §3).

Can. 144 §1 In common error, whether of fact or of law, and in positive and probable doubt, whether of law or of fact, the Church supplies executive power of governance for both the external and the internal forum.

Good government within the Church depends in good measure on the validity of acts of executive power. In order to protect the faithful from the ill effects of invalid acts of this kind, the canon law developed the concept of 'supplying' the necessary power.[1] It was specifically formulated in c.209 of the 1917 Code. This supplying of power must not be understood as a convalidation of an invalid act; rather it is a concession of the necessary executive power for the act or acts involved granted *by the law itself*: it may be regarded as a kind of *extraordinary* delegation by law, in the interests of the common good of the Church and of the faithful. In this way, a person acting is supplied with the executive power without which the act would otherwise be invalid. This principle applies both to the internal forum and to the external forum.

Executive power may thus be supplied in only the following two sets of circumstances:

(a) In cases of *common error*. Error may be defined as a false judgement concerning some matter. It is not to be confused with ignorance or inadvertence, although either of these may lead a person into error. Commentators on the 1917 Code drew a distinction between, on the one hand, error which was common *de facto* (i.e. held in fact by the majority of persons in a community, e.g. a diocese, a parish, a religious house, etc.) and, on the other hand, error which was common *de iure* (i.e. when a public fact occurs which of its nature is such that it *might well*

---

[1] A detailed history of the sources of this practice in Roman Law and Canon Law may be found in Wilches *De errore communi in iure romano et canonico* Romae 1940.

induce error into the majority of the community, even if in fact very few, if any, are in error in its regard: [1] this distinction is retained in the interpretation of the present canon. A typical (though by no means the only example) would be that of a priest who, having by his own or someone else's inadvertence failed to secure the delegation required by Can. 1108 §1, assists at a marriage of two catholics. The likelihood is that most, if not all, of those present – not least the couple whose marriage it is – would assume the marriage to be normal and valid. In this, they would in fact be 'in common error'. It is precisely for this kind of situation that this canon is applicable: the Church itself 'supplies' the delegation without which the marriage would otherwise be invalid – to the detriment of the common good of the faithful.

(b) in cases of *positive and probable doubt*. Doubt may be defined as a suspension of assent or a state of indecision between assent and denial. It is *positive* when there is a sound reason for believing something but not to the exclusion of a prudent fear of the contrary; it is *probable* when the reason in question is serious and well-founded, even if it co-exists with equally serious and well-founded reasons. The doubt in question may concern either the fact of the situation or the law: a parish priest may e.g. be in doubt as to the extent of the faculties for dispensation he has received (a doubt of law), or in doubt as to the factual situation e.g. whether or not a particular individual is in danger of death (a doubt of fact). In either such situation the Church supplies the necessary executive power.

Can. 144 §2 The same norm applies to the faculties mentioned in Cann. 882, 883, 966, and 1111 §1.

315 Lest there be any confusion, the Code makes explicit the fact that the principles outlined in §1 have a specific application with regard to the administration of the sacrament of confirmation (see Cann. 882–883), the faculty to absolve sins (see Can. 966), and the faculty to assist at marriages (see Can. 1111 §1).

Title IX
Ecclesiastical Offices

Can. 145 §1 An ecclesiastical office is any post which by divine or ecclesiastical disposition is established in a stable manner to further a spiritual purpose.

316 Whereas c.145 of the 1917 Code drew a distinction between a strict and a broad sense of an ecclesiastical office, the present Code, following the teaching of Vat. II,[2] contains a single concept of an ecclesiastical office.

---

[1] Cf. Vermeersch–Creusen I n.284; Wernz–Vidal II n.381; Cappello V nn.670–671; Bouscaren–Ellis 141–143.

[2] 'This (i.e. ecclesiastical office) should in future be understood as any office conferred in a permanent fashion and to be exercised for a spiritual purpose' (PO 20: Fl I 899). 'They (i.e. the laity) have, moreover, the capacity of being appointed by the hierarchy to some ecclesiastical offices with a view to a spiritual end' (LG 33: Fl I 391).

Four distinguishing features are contained in §1:

(a) it is a *post*, i.e. a position of responsibility involving defined rights and obligations;
(b) it is *established in a stable manner*, i.e. the continuity of the post is guaranteed so that it survives indefinitely if the holder of the post changes, or if the post becomes vacant;
(c) it is established *by divine or ecclesiastical disposition*, i.e. some offices are of divine institution, e.g. the Roman Pontiff, the College of Bishops; others are of purely ecclesiastical institution, e.g. the College of Cardinals, parish priests, Vicars general etc.;
(d) it must be to *further a spiritual purpose*, i.e. the post must have, at least as its fundamental good, the welfare of the faithful and the salvation of souls.

The implication of c.145 §1 of the 1917 Code could well be that *the concept of an ecclesiastical office* – at least in its then so-called 'strict sense' – was of one reserved to clerics. There is none such in the present canon. Provided the distinguishing features detailed in the foregoing section are fulfilled, it is clear that an ecclesiastical office, as such, may be given not only to clerics but also to the laity, including obviously to a Superior of a lay religious institute. In saying this, it must equally be recognised that there remain some ecclesiastical offices which are in fact reserved to clerics: Can. 150 is a good example.

Can. 145 §2 The duties and rights proper to each ecclesiastical office are defined either by the law whereby the office is established, or by a decree of the competent authority whereby it is at one and at the same time established and conferred.

The precise scope and content of each ecclesiastical office are determined by positive ecclesiastical law. In the case of an already existing office, this specification is contained in the law which already established the office, e.g. Can. 484. In the case of an office not yet established in law, this specification is contained in the decree by which it is constituted and conferred for the first time.

Chapter I
THE PROVISION OF ECCLESIASTICAL OFFICE

Can. 146 An ecclesiastical office cannot be validly obtained without canonical provision.

No one can validly obtain an ecclesiastical office unless it is granted to him or her by the competent authority in accordance with the law: this is the meaning of 'canonical provision'. Traditionally, this acquisition of office has been understood to consist of three distinct acts:

(a) the designation of the one who is to hold office;
(b) the conferral of the office;
(c) the entry of the office-holder into possession of the office.[1]

This third element is required only in respect of certain offices, e.g. a Bishop (see Can. 382 §2), a parish priest (see Can. 527), etc.

---

[1] Cf. Vermeersch–Creusen I n.230; Wernz–Vidal II n.182; Bouscaren–Ellis 123–124.

Can. 147 The provision of an ecclesiastical office is effected: by its being freely conferred by the competent ecclesiastical authority; by appointment made by the same authority, where there has been a prior presentation; by confirmation or admission by the same authority, where there has been a prior election or postulation; finally, by a simple election and acceptance of the election, if the election does not require confirmation.

321 The law identifies four ways of providing for an ecclesiastical office:

(a) *free conferral* by the competent authority (see Can. 157);

(b) *appointment* by the competent authority of someone who has been *presented* in accordance with the law (see Cann. 158–163);

(c) *confirmation* by the competent authority (see Can. 179) or admission following a valid election (see Cann. 164–177) or postulation (see Cann. 180–183);

(d) simple *election and acceptance* (see Can. 178) if the law does not require confirmation.

The identity of the competent authority is determined in accordance with Can. 148.

Can. 148 Unless the law provides otherwise, the provision of an office is the prerogative of the authority which is competent to establish, change or suppress the office.

322 As a general norm, the provision of an ecclesiastical office in accordance with Can. 147 belongs exclusively to that authority which is competent by law to establish, alter or suppress the office, e.g. it is the diocesan Bishop who appoints parish priests (see Can. 523) since it is he who establishes, alters and suppresses parishes (see Can. 515 §2). By way of exception, the law establishing an office may, for a particular reason, entrust the canonical provision of that office to a different authority.

Can. 149 §1 In order to be promoted to an ecclesiastical office, one must be in communion with the Church, and be suitable, that is, possessed of those qualities which are required for that office by universal or particular law or by the law of the foundation.

§2 The provision of an ecclesiastical office to a person who lacks the requisite qualities is invalid only if the qualities are expressly required for validity by universal or particular law or by the law of the foundation; otherwise it is valid, but it can be rescinded by a decree of the competent authority or by a judgement of an administrative tribunal.

323 Of its nature each ecclesiastical office is established to further a spiritual purpose. Accordingly, 'communion with the Church' is an obvious requirement in a candidate for ecclesiastical office. The 'communion' referred to would appear to be that of Can. 205, i.e. that of those who, having been baptised, are joined to the Church 'through the bonds of profession of faith, the sacraments and ecclesiastical governance'.[1]

324 In addition to the general requirement of 'communion with the Church', each candidate to be promoted to ecclesiastical office must have the specific qualities required by law e.g. Cann. 378 §1, 1420 §4 etc., which themselves are obviously tailored to the office in question. If the relevant law demands these qualities for validity, the provision of anyone lacking them will be *ipso iure* invalid; if they are not expressly required for validity, the provision of someone without these qualities remains valid; it may,

---

[1] Cf. Urrutia n.809. Some authors, e.g. Chiappetta I nn.924–925, take another, more nuanced, view, which however is not substantially different from that favoured here.

however, be rescinded, either by a decree of the competent authority or by a judgement of an administrative tribunal.[1] For the moment, and pending the possible future introduction of administrative tribunals into the law, the power of rescinding envisaged in §2 is effectively limited to 'the competent authority'.

Can. 149 §3 The provision of an office made as a result of simony, is invalid by virtue of the law itself.

Simony is the deliberate act of buying or selling a spiritual good. Since the ultimate purpose of any ecclesiastical office is spiritual, simony at any stage of canonical provision (see Can. 146) renders the act automatically invalid. It does not matter whether the simony occurred with the knowledge of the competent authority or of the person designated to hold the office. Simony, however, is not to be confused with the payment of moderate administrative expenses connected with the provision of an office.

Can. 150 An office which carries with it the full care of souls, for which the exercise of the order of priesthood is required, cannot validly be conferred upon a person who is not yet a priest.

This canon is a clear application of the principle contained in Can. 149 §2: without the essential quality of priestly ordination no one can *validly* receive an ecclesiastical office which involves the full care of souls, e.g. that of parish priest. While Can. 129 §2 points out that lay people may cooperate in the exercise of the power of governance, and Can. 517 §2 permits a Bishop, in the case of necessity, to appoint a deacon or another who is not a priest *to share* in the practical care of a parish, the actual *office* of parish priest cannot validly be conferred on such persons.

Can. 151 The provision of an office which carries with it the care of souls is not to be deferred without grave reason.

Any office involving the care of souls (e.g. Bishop, parish priest, chaplain) has a direct bearing on the welfare of the faithful. Such offices obviously should be filled with a minimum of necessary delay. Although c.155 of the 1917 Code stipulated six months as the maximum delay permitted, no such time limit is included in the present canon.[2] The principle is here stated negatively, but it is clear that the provision of an office should take place as soon as possible unless a grave reason, e.g. scarcity of priests, intervenes: in which case some practical alternative – perhaps along the lines of Can. 517 §2 or the like? – should be put in place at once, so that the good of souls will be catered for in the best way possible.

Can. 152 Two or more offices which are incompatible, that is, which cannot be exercised at the same time by the same person, are not to be conferred upon anyone.

---

[1] The possibility of establishing in the Church – in addition to judicial tribunals – a structure of administrative tribunals was a matter of serious concern to the Revision Commission. Initially, there was positive support for this proposal: cf. Comm 1(1969) 83; 4(1972) 236–237. In the course of its discussions over subsequent years, however, various difficulties and problems were raised, a number of which were voiced as late as the final Plenary Session in October 1981. In the event, a specific section in this regard was included in the final draft of 1982 (cc.1736–1763) but, save for some few important references to it, the section was eliminated from the text of the Code ultimately promulgated in 1983. There is scope here for the serious and well-informed student of ecclesiology.

[2] In the revision process an attempt was made to introduce a time limit. This was rejected as not possible, simply because the circumstances of each case will inevitably be different: cf. Comm 14(1982) 152 at Can. 148.

328 Two offices may be incompatible either because (a) *in fact* they cannot be exercised by the same person at the same time, e.g. parish priest and rector of a seminary a long distance away, or because (b) *according to law* they cannot be combined, e.g. diocesan Administrator and diocesan financial Administrator (see Can. 423 §2), Vicar general or Vicar episcopal and canon penitentiary (see Can. 478 §2), etc. While the canon does not state that the conferral of two such offices renders one or the other provision invalid, it is impossible to see – given the nature of the situation – how invalidity can be avoided: the canon is explicit that the context is 'two or more offices ... which cannot be exercised (*adimpleri nequeunt*) at the same time by the same person'.

Can. 153 §1 The provision of an office which in law is not vacant is by that very fact invalid, nor does it become valid by subsequent vacancy.

329 A prerequisite for the valid conferral of any ecclesiastical office is that the office be vacant at the time of the provision; otherwise any attempt to make provision for it would be automatically *invalid*. The fact that the office becomes vacant later, even shortly later, does not alter this fundamental principle. At a diocesan level this provision can have a very practical application when there is question of transferring a parish priest – more particularly perhaps, a series of parish priests – from one parish to another. The basic principle here is that the first parish becomes vacant *only* when its incumbent takes canonical possession of the parish to which he is being transferred (see Can. 191 §1): it is only *after* that event has taken place that his nominated successor – whatever be the administrative arrangements in the meantime – can validly become 'the new parish priest' who himself achieves that status only when he too takes possession in accordance with Can. 527.

Can. 153 §2 If, however, there is question of an office which by law is conferred for a determinate time, provision can be made within six months before the expiry of this time, and it takes effect from the day the office falls vacant.

330 A modification of the foregoing principle is made where the office is conferred by law for a fixed term, e.g. an episcopal Vicar (see Can. 477 §1), a religious Superior (see Can. 624 §1), even a parish priest as envisaged in the terms of the latter part of Can. 522. In these cases, provision for the office can be made before it becomes vacant in law, but only within six months of the end of the term of office. In keeping with the general principle of §1, however, this provision has no effect until the day the office becomes vacant.

Can. 153 §3 The promise of any office, by whomsoever it is made, has no juridical effect.

331 The canon concludes by repeating the principle of c.150 §2 of the 1917 Code: no mere promise of office has any juridical effect – thereby excluding any element of favouritism.

Can. 154 An office which in law is vacant, but which someone unlawfully still holds, may be conferred, provided that it has been properly declared that such possession is not lawful, and that mention is made of this declaration in the letter of conferral.

332 This canon caters for the situation in which an office which has in fact become vacant, for whatever reason, continues to be occupied, unlawfully, whether by the previous incumbent or by someone else. Since the office is vacant, the competent authority may technically confer it upon a candidate of his own choice. In the interest, however, of the common good and of public order, the canon makes one further

stipulation, namely that the authority in question must first issue a formal declaration – obviously in writing – that the current possession is unlawful, and then include in the letter appointing the lawful successor a specific reference to that declaration.[1]

Can. 155 One who confers an office in the place of another who is negligent or impeded, does not thereby acquire any power over the person on whom the office is conferred; the juridical condition of the latter is the same as if the provision of the office has been carried out in accordance with the ordinary norm of law.

This canon addresses the exceptional situation when another authority has to step in to appoint someone to an office, for the reason that the proper appointing body has for some reason not fulfilled the law, e.g. if a diocesan Administrator has not been elected within the stipulated time of eight days, the Metropolitan must step in to deal with the matter (see Can. 421 §2). The canon goes on to state that in such a situation the intervening authority acquires no special authority over the person appointed. His or her juridical situation is determined as though the provision had been made according to the ordinary norms of law.

Can. 156 The provision of any office is to be made in writing.

Without a written document, provision to an office will not easily be proved in the external forum. This is an application in specific terms of the general norm for all administrative acts in the external forum (see Can. 37).

Article 1
Free Conferral

Can. 157 Unless the law expressly states otherwise, it is the prerogative of the diocesan Bishop to make appointments to ecclesiastical offices in his own particular Church by free conferral.

The most common form of canonical provision is *free conferral*, i.e. the competent authority not only designates the candidate for office but also confers that office. Free conferral is also the means for making provision when the form prescribed by law fails to designate a suitable candidate (see Cann. 162, 165). According to Vat. II, 'the Bishop must have the requisite liberty in making appointments'.[2] Consequently, the rights of others to elect, nominate or present to office within the diocese were to be abolished.[3] In keeping with this principle the Code states that, within the particular Church, it is the right of the *diocesan Bishop* (see Can. 134 §3) and his equivalents (see Cann. 368, 381 §2), but not the local Ordinary, freely to confer ecclesiastical offices. This principle is not in opposition to the need for the Bishop to obtain in some cases the prior advice (see Can. 494 §1) or consent (see Can. 520 §1) of others. There are some, very few, exceptional situations in which 'the law expressly states otherwise' than in accordance with the principle of this canon: an example – which for historical reasons refers in the main to some countries in continental Europe – may be noted at Can. 523.

---

[1] Though some would tend to dissent (cf. e.g. Urrutia n.819), the more solid opinion, based principally upon Cann. 39 and 154, would appear to be that the stipulation of this canon is required for the validity of the ultimate appointment: cf. e.g. Chiappetta I n.940.

[2] CD 28, 31: Fl I 580, 583.

[3] Cf. ES I 18: Fl I 602.

Article II
Presentation

Can. 158 §1 Presentation to an ecclesiastical office by a person having the right of presentation must be made to the authority who is competent to make an appointment to the office in question; unless it is otherwise lawfully provided, presentation is to be made within three months of receiving notification of the vacancy of the office.

§2 If the right of presentation belongs to a college or group of persons, the person to be presented is to be designated according to the provisions of Cann. 165-179.

336 Presentation is the designation of a candidate for ecclesiastical office made by a person or persons distinct from the authority which makes the appointment, e.g. a family may have the right to present a priest for the office of chaplain in their private chapel (see Can. 565). The one making the presentation must have the *right* to do so: it is to be noted that these rights have been reduced greatly as a result of Vat. II.[1] The presentor may be an individual physical person, a juridical person, or a group of people; in all cases, the presentation must take place in accordance with the norms of the Code.

337 Principally, the one designated for office must be presented to the authority which is competent to make the appointment (see Can. 148). Moreover, this must take place within three months of the reception of notification of the vacancy by the one making the presentation (§1). This time limit is to be calculated in accordance with Can. 201 §2 (see Can. 162).

338 While no norm or criterion is provided to help a single person designate a candidate for presentation, the law requires an election (see Cann. 165-179) if the presentation is to be made by a college or group of persons (§2).

Can. 159 No one is to be presented who is unwilling. Accordingly, one who is proposed for presentation must be consulted, and may be presented if within eight canonical days a refusal is not entered.

339 The consent of the person to be presented for appointment to an office is required by law. This consent is presumed if, within eight canonical days (see Can. 201 §2) of being consulted about the matter, the individual concerned has not registered a refusal. However, if the candidate was in fact unwilling, he or she is free to resign the position either before or after appointment (see Cann. 161 §2, 187-189).

Can. 160 §1 One who has the right of presentation may present one or more persons, either simultaneously or successively.

§2 No person may present himself or herself. However a college or a group of persons may present one of its members.

340 Since presentation has to do with putting forward a candidate for office, the law permits the one presenting to put forward one or more persons for the one office (§1). This may be done *simultaneously* thus providing the competent authority with a panel from which to choose the office-holder, or *successively* if the appointing authority fails to appoint the person or persons initially presented (see Can. 161 §1).

341 No one can validly present himself or herself as a candidate for a particular office. Yet the law permits a group or college with the right of presentation to put forward one of its own members (§2).

---

[1] Cf. CD 28, 31: Fl I 580, 583.

Title IX Ecclesiastical Offices

Can. 161 §1 Unless the law prescribes otherwise, one who has presented a person who is judged unsuitable, may within one month present another candidate, but once only.

It belongs to the appointing authority to determine the suitability for office of candidates presented in accordance with the law. Should a particular candidate prove unsuitable and, if no other has been presented simultaneously (see Can. 160 §1), the person with the right of presentation can put forward another candidate. This must be done within a month of being notified of the appointing authority's negative decision. It can be done only *once*: the successive presentations mentioned in Can. 160 §1 cannot be interminable.

Can. 161 §2 If before the appointment is made the person presented has withdrawn or has died, the one with the right of presentation may exercise this right again within one month of receiving notice of the withdrawal or of the death.

Should the person presented resign or die before the appointment is made, the one who made the presentation can exercise that right once more. This also must take place within one month of notification of the resignation or the death. If the person then presented proves to be unsuitable, one last presentation may be made in accordance with §1.

Can. 162 A person who has not presented anyone within the canonical time prescribed by Can. 158 §1 and Can. 161, or who has twice presented a candidate judged to be unsuitable, loses the right of presentation for that case. The authority who is competent to appoint may then freely provide for the vacant office, but with the consent of the proper Ordinary of the person appointed.

In a particular case, the right of presentation is lost:

(a) if no one is presented within three months of being notified that the office is vacant (see Can. 158 §1);
(b) if a second candidate is not presented within one month of being notified of the unsuitability of the first candidate presented (see Can. 161 §1);
(c) if the second person presented also proves to be unsuitable.

Canonical provision in this case reverts to the authority competent to make the appointment: the position is filled by free conferral. In this case, the consent of the proper Ordinary of the candidate is required for the lawfulness of the appointment.

Can. 163 The authority to whom, in accordance with the law, it belongs to appoint one who is presented, is to appoint the person lawfully presented whom he has judged suitable, and who has accepted. If a number lawfully presented are judged suitable, he is to appoint one of them.

When a person has been presented in accordance with the law, has been judged suitable for the office and has indicated acceptance, the competent authority is obliged to appoint him or her to the office in question. If more than one duly presented candidate was judged suitable and indicated acceptance, the authority is free to choose any one of them for the appointment. In keeping with the general principle of Can. 57 §1, such an appointment must be made within three months of the presentation.

Book I General Norms

Article 3
Election

Can. 164 Unless it has been otherwise provided in the law, the provisions of the following canons are to be observed in canonical elections.

346 Election may be defined as the designation of a person as a candidate for ecclesiastical office made in collegial form (see Can. 119 1°) by a group or college having the right to elect. In some cases, designation by election is sufficient to obtain the office as soon as the one elected has accepted (see Can. 178); in others, the election requires confirmation (see Can. 179); finally, election may also be the manner of selecting a candidate or candidates for presentation (see Can. 158 §2).

347 The norms governing elections which are contained in the Code (see Cann. 165–179) are, as a rule, to be observed in all canonical elections. Other provisions, however, even contrary to the norms of the Code, may be contained in special laws[1] or in the particular law of institutes, societies, associations, etc.

Can. 165 Unless it is otherwise provided in the law or in the statutes of the college or group, if a college or a group of persons enjoys the right to elect to an office, the election is not to be deferred beyond three canonical months, to be reckoned from the receipt of notification of the vacancy of the office. If the election does not take place within that time, the ecclesiastical authority who has the right of confirming the election or the right to make provision otherwise, is freely to provide for the vacant office.

348 When an office is to be filled by election, that election must take place within three months of notification of the vacancy. This period must be reckoned according to Can. 201 §1. Should this allotted time elapse without an election, the group or college concerned loses the right to provide for the office for that occasion. Responsibility for this then devolves upon the authority which has the right to confirm the election or which has the right to provide for the office in some other way. That authority is to provide for the vacancy by *free conferral*. It is important to note that such an intervention follows only if the three canonical months have elapsed *without an election having taking place* ('inutiliter'): this would include an invalid election, or the election of someone who for whatever lawful reason cannot be confirmed in office.

349 The law, both universal and particular, can establish a different period within which the election must take place (see e.g. Can. 421 §1).

Can. 166 §1 The one who presides over the college or group is to summon all those who belong to the college or group. When it has to be personal, the summons is valid if it is made in the place of domicile or quasi-domicile or in the place of residence.

350 In order to exercise their right to elect, all members of a college or a group must by law be summoned to take part in an election. The canon gives no indication of the possible methods of issuing this summons: it simply places the responsibility for summoning upon the one who presides over the college or group. Whenever the law – whether universal or particular – prescribes that the summons must be *personal*, it must be communicated to each individual member's address, i.e. domicile, quasi-domicile or actual place of residence. Such a summons may be delivered by post

---

[1] E.g. ap con *Romano Pontifici Eligendo* 1.X.1975: AAS 67(1975) 609 ss: CLD 8 133–169.

(preferably registered) or by hand delivery or by personal contact. Even if the person is not actually present at his or her place of domicile or quasi-domicile, the summons is regarded as lawful and valid if it has been delivered to that address. Where the summons is not required to be personal, notification by the display of a notice in an appropriately public place or even, if needs be, in a relevant journal or other such publication or in the public press is sufficient for a valid summons.

Can. 166 §2 If someone who should have been summoned was overlooked and was therefore absent, the election is valid. However, if that person insists and gives proof of being overlooked and of absence, the election, even if confirmed, must be rescinded by the competent authority, provided it is juridically established that the recourse was submitted within no more than three days of having received notification of the election.

§3 If more than one third of the voters were overlooked, the election is invalid by virtue of the law itself, unless all those overlooked were in fact present.

Care must be taken in summoning electors to an election since an oversight may have serious canonical consequences. If an individual (or a small number of individuals) is overlooked in the summons, any election held in their absence is *valid*. However, that election *must* be rescinded if:

(a) the person pursues the matter;
(b) produces proof that he or she was overlooked (it does not matter whether this was intentional or not);
(c) produces proof that he or she was actually absent from the election;
(d) submits this recourse to the competent authority within three days of having received notification of the election.

In these cases, the burden of proof rests entirely with the individual concerned. There are no presumptions of law in his or her favour.

On the other hand if, in fact, more than a third of the electors were neither summoned nor present at the election, that election is thereby invalid and accordingly of no juridical effect.

Can. 167 §1 When the summons has been lawfully made, those who are present on the day and in the place specified in the summons have the right to vote. Unless it is otherwise lawfully provided in the statutes, votes cast by letter or by proxy cannot be admitted.

The right to vote, according to universal law, belongs only to those who have been lawfully summoned (or ought to have been so summoned) and who are *actually present* at the time and place designated for the election. In principle, all others are excluded from voting, unless the statutes of the group or college permit votes cast by letter or by proxy.

Can. 167 §2 If an elector is present in the building in which the election is being held, but because of infirmity is unable to be present at the election, a written vote is to be sought from that person by the scrutineers.

An exception is made for the sick and elderly who are actually present in the same building in which the election is to take place. As long as they are in the general proximity of where the election is taking place, and the election is not unduly interrupted, the scrutineers must receive their written votes and bring it to the place of the elec-

Book I General Norms

tion, e.g. a sick or elderly nun confined to bed can vote in the election of the superior of the monastery provided she is actually in the same building at the time.

Can. 168 Even if someone has a right to vote in his or her own name by reason of a number of titles, that person may cast only one vote.

355 A person may be entitled to vote in an election on a number of grounds, e.g. because he or she holds a number of offices to which the right of election is attached. The canon makes it clear that, no matter how many titles to vote a person may have, he or she may cast only a single valid vote. Of course, if the statutes permit voting by proxy (see Can. 167 §1), a second (or further) vote may be cast but *in the name of another*, not in his or her own name.

Can. 169 In order that an election be valid, no one may be allowed to vote who does not belong to the college or group.

356 The right of election belongs *exclusively* to members of the group or college designated by law. No outsider is permitted to cast a vote in these elections, no matter how influential; not even a unanimous vote of the other electors can change this. Should such an outsider cast a vote, then the election itself, not just the individual vote, is invalid. This norm protects the legitimate right of electors from unwarranted interference by outsiders.

Can. 170 If the freedom of an election has in any way been in fact impeded, the election is invalid by virtue of the law itself.

357 Not only does the law require that each individual vote must be free; the actual election itself must also be free. Any infringement of the liberty of the group or college of electors renders the election invalid by virtue of the law itself. Moreover, anyone guilty of such an offence may be punished with a just penalty (see Can. 1375). The origins of this canon lie in the Church's resistance to interference in its affairs by the secular authorities. This, with a long history of the Church behind it, was already explicit in c.166 of the 1917 Code.

Can. 171 §1 The following are legally incapable of casting a vote:

1° one incapable of a human act;

2° one lacking active voice;

3° one who is excommunicated, whether by judgement of a court or by a decree whereby this penalty is imposed or declared;

4° one who notoriously defected from communion with the Church.

358 Although genuine members of a group or college, some individuals may be *legally incapable* of voting in any election undertaken by the same group or college. The canon lists four categories of such persons:

(a) anyone incapable of a human act, e.g. anyone afflicted by severe mental illness, semi-consciousness, extreme intoxication, etc. (1°);

(b) anyone lacking active voice, e.g. an exclaustrated religious (see Can. 687), a religious who has become a Bishop,[1] or someone from whom it has been removed as a penalty (see Can. 1336 §1 2°) (2°);

---

[1] Cf. CCom rep 29.IV.1986: AAS 78(1986) 1324.

(c) anyone who has been excommunicated, provided this penalty has been imposed or declared by a court judgement or a decree of the competent authority. Anyone who has been excommunicated *latae sententiae* is not technically 'legally incapable' of voting; however, he or she is forbidden to do so (see Can. 1331 §1 3°) (3°);

(d) anyone who has defected from communion with the Church (see Can. 205), whether by heresy, apostasy or schism (see Can. 751): such a defection must be *notorious*, i.e. known to many people (*de facto*) or capable of being known to many people (*de iure*) (4°).

Can. 171 §2 If any of the above persons is admitted, the vote cast is invalid. The election, however, is valid, unless it is established that, without this vote, the person elected would not have gained the requisite number of votes.

Should any of these persons actually take part in an election, the vote which they cast is invalid. Nevertheless, the fact of their participation does not render the actual election invalid unless it is certain that the outcome of the election depended on their vote, e.g. an election where the outcome was decided by a bare absolute majority is invalid if one of the votes in that election was cast by someone who was not legally capable in accordance with §1.

Can. 172 §1 For a vote to be valid, it must be:

1° free; a vote is therefore invalid if, through grave fear or deceit, someone was directly or indirectly made to choose a certain person or several persons separately;

2° secret, certain, absolute and determinate.

The Code demands five qualities for a *valid vote*:

(a) it must be *free*. Although in general a juridical act performed as a result of grave fear or deceit remains valid (see Can. 125 §2), in the case of a vote, the law determines otherwise. The direct or indirect restriction of a voter's freedom renders the vote invalid.

(b) it must be *secret*, i.e. at the moment of election, no one is permitted to know how any other individual has voted. This is a further guarantee of the secrecy of the vote. While the validity of the practice of having voters sign their voting papers is debated by some,[1] it is clear that at least the spirit, if not the letter, of the law would certainly discourage any such practice.

(c) it must be *certain*, i.e. the expression of the vote cannot contain any ambiguity or doubt: it must be stated with an unambiguous *certainty*, e.g. 'I elect...'

(d) it must be *absolute*, i.e. no conditions may be attached to the vote, such e.g. as 'I elect X but only if ...';

(e) it must be *determinate*, i.e. the identity of the person for whom the vote is cast must be clear beyond question: in practice this means the use of the name and surname of the person, and the exclusion of any alternatives such e.g. as 'I elect X or Y'.

There is nothing in the universal law to prevent someone voting for himself or herself. Particular law, however, may declare that such is invalid.

Can. 172 §2 Conditions attached to a vote before an election are to be considered non-existent.

---

[1] Cf. Chiappetta I n.1024; Urrutia nn.854–855.

361 Any conditions attached to a vote before an election have no juridical standing whatsoever, e.g. if someone were to say 'I will vote for X provided he does so and so', the vote cast would be valid but the conditions attached do not bind in any way: they are 'considered non-existent'.

Can. 173 §1 Before an election begins, at least two scrutineers are to be appointed from among the college or group.

§2 The scrutineers are to collect the votes and, in the presence of the one who presides at the election, to check whether the number of votes corresponds to the number of electors; they are then to examine the votes and to announce how many each person has received.

§3 If the number of votes exceeds the number of electors, the act is null.

§4 All the proceedings of an election are to be accurately recorded by the one who acts as notary. They are to be signed at least by that notary, by the person who presides and by the scrutineers, and they are to be carefully preserved in the archive of the college.

362 The actual procedure of an election consists of several stages which are presented in sequence:

(a) the *appointment of scrutineers* or tellers. There must be *at least two* of these, chosen from among the group or college of electors: the use of outsiders is not permitted. Although no mention is made of it, the tellers are obliged to maintain secrecy about what they learn in the course of their duties. The appointment of tellers must take place *before the election*; so too, must the appointment of the notary (§4).

(b) the *collection of the votes*. As soon as the electors have voted, the tellers are to collect all the votes cast.

(c) the *checking of the number of votes* cast. In the presence of the president of the election, the tellers are to make sure that the number of votes corresponds to the number of electors. It is important when assessing the number of electors to remember the principle of Can. 168 – one person, one vote. Should the tellers discover that they have collected more votes than there are electors, the ballot just taken is null and must be repeated.

(d) the *counting of the votes*. This, too, must take place in the presence of the president, but not necessarily in the presence of the electors. The tellers are to examine the votes and make public the number of votes received by each person. While this may be done as the count proceeds, it is normally done at the end of the count.

(e) the *recording of the election*. At the end of the counting of the votes, a record is to be made of the entire proceedings, i.e a list of the candidates, the number of votes received by each in the various ballots and the final outcome. This document is to be signed by the notary, the president of the election, and the scrutineers; particular law may require others to sign as well. Once completed, these acts are to be stored in the archive of the electoral group or college; they are to be 'carefully preserved' since they prove a person's title to the office in question.

Can. 174 §1 Unless the law or the statutes provide otherwise, an election can be made by compromise, that is the electors by unanimous and written consent transfer the right of election for this occasion to one or more suitable persons, whether they belong to the college or are outside it, who in virtue of this authority are to elect in the name of all.

§2 If the college or group consists solely of clerics, the persons to whom the power of election is transferred must be in sacred orders; otherwise the election is invalid.

§3 Those to whom the power of election is transferred must observe the provisions of law concerning an election and, for the validity of the election, they must observe the conditions attached to the compromise, unless these conditions are contrary to the law. Conditions which are contrary to the law are to be regarded as non-existent.

Election by ballots (see Can. 173) is the *ordinary* means of conducting an election. The law does, however, provide an extraordinary means, to be used in cases where the group or college cannot reach a consensus. This consists of the group or college transferring its right to elect for this occasion to one or more suitable persons. These may be members of the college or group, or complete outsiders, or a mixture. It is for the group or college to designate these people, bearing in mind that they must be suitable; in the case of an electoral group or college of clerics, they must also be in sacred orders: otherwise, any election made by them is invalid (§3). 363

This extraordinary manner of election, known as a *compromise*, can take place only if two conditions are fulfilled: 364

(a) if its use is not expressly prohibited by law (universal or particular) or the statutes of the group or college;

(b) if the members of the group or college *unanimously* transfer the right of election by a written vote. Unanimity in this matter is essential (see Can. 119 3°).

The persons designated to elect by means of this compromise are obliged to observe the provisions of law concerning elections i.e. Cann. 166–173, and any other norms in universal or particular law. In addition, they are obliged to fulfil any conditions attached to the compromise by the group or college. These conditions must be consistent with the law, i.e. not contrary to the provisions of universal and particular law. Conditions which are contrary to law are regarded as non-existent and are to be ignored. 365

Can. 175 A compromise ceases, and the right to vote reverts to those who transferred it, when:

1° it is revoked by the college or group before it has been put into effect.

2° a condition attached to the compromise has not been fulfilled.

3° the election has been held, but invalidly.

The extraordinary manner of election ceases and the group or college resumes its right to elect in three situations: 366

(a) when an absolute majority (see Can. 119 2°) of the group or college revokes the compromise before the persons so designated have had the opportunity to act;

(b) when any one of the conditions mentioned in Can. 174 §3 has not been fulfilled by those designated to make the election;

(c) when those designated have held an election which is then discovered to have been invalid for whatever reason, e.g. because an intruder voted (see Can. 169), because the election was not free (see Can. 170), etc.

Can. 176 Unless it is otherwise provided in the law or the statutes, the person who has received the requisite number of votes in accordance with Can. 119 n.1, is deemed elected and is to be proclaimed by the person who presides over the college or group.

A maximum of three ballots is permitted in elections according to Can. 119 1°. An absolute majority of the votes of those present is required for election. As soon as some- 367 one attains the required number of votes, the president of the electoral college or group is to declare that he or she has been duly elected. In the event of a tie at the end of a third ballot, the senior by age of the two candidates is declared to be elected. As in the case of Can. 119, and elections generally (see Can. 164), particular law or the statutes of the group or college may make other provision, such e.g. as requiring a qualified majority in some ballots and the like. These are obviously exceptional situations.

Can. 177 §1 The election is to be notified immediately to the person elected who must, within eight canonical days from the receipt of notification of the election, intimate to the person who presides over the college or group whether or not he or she accepts the election; otherwise, the election has no effect.

§2 The person elected who has not accepted loses every right deriving from the election, nor is any right revived by subsequent acceptance; the person may, however, be elected again. The college or group must proceed to a new election within one month of being notified of non-acceptance.

368 *Immediately* an election is concluded, the person elected must be notified of what has taken place. If he or she is one of the electors, no special act is required apart from the declaration mentioned in Can. 176. On the other hand, if he or she is not one of the electors or was not present at the election, the president of the election is to make sure that he or she is informed by whatever means are most immediately available.

369 Once a person has been notified of his or her election, the law provides for three eventualities:

(a) if the person *accepts* election, this must be communicated to the president of the election within eight *canonical* days (see Can. 201 §2) of having received notification;

(b) if the person *refuses* election, this decision must also be communicated to the president within eight canonical days of receipt of notification;

(c) if the person *neither refuses nor accepts* within the eight canonical days required, the election is deemed by law to have had no effect and must be repeated.

370 Anyone who refuses election or fails to accept it within the required time loses all claim on the office and all rights derived from the election: a subsequent change of heart cannot remedy the matter. Within one month of receipt of a refusal or the expiry of the eight canonical days without a response, the group or college must proceed to a new election. However, a person who refused or failed to accept an election does remain eligible for election on this subsequent occasion.

Can. 178 If the election does not require confirmation, by accepting the election the person elected immediately obtains the office with all its rights; otherwise, he or she acquires only a right to the office.

371 The law draws a distinction between those elections which require confirmation and those which do not. The canonical consequences of the distinction are considerable. Where no confirmation is required (by either universal or particular law), the one duly elected (see Can. 176) enters immediately into the office concerned and acquires all the rights attached thereto. On the other hand, if the law requires that an election be confirmed, the one elected acquires only a *right* to the office – a right which however cannot be denied except in accordance with the law (see Can. 179 §2).

Can. 179 §1 If the election requires confirmation, the person elected must, either personally or through another, ask for confirmation by the competent authority within eight canonical days of acceptance of the office; otherwise that person is deprived of every right, unless he or she has established that there was just reason which prevented confirmation being sought.

In those cases where confirmation of an election is required, responsibility for seeking confirmation rests with the person elected. From the time of acceptance (see Can. 177 §1), he or she has eight days in which to petition the competent authority for confirmation: these days are to be counted in accordance with Can. 201 §2. Failure to act within that time means that the right (*ius ad rem*) acquired at the acceptance of the election (see Can. 178) would be lost unless the person elected can prove that his or her inaction was due to a genuine impediment e.g. illness, a storm, a strike, civil disturbance, etc. which prevented communication with the competent authority.

Can. 179 §2 The competent authority cannot refuse confirmation if it has found the person elected suitable in accordance with Can. 149 §1, and the election has been carried out in accordance with the law.

§3 Confirmation must be given in writing.

The confirmation of an election is no mere formality: the competent authority must examine the suitability of the one elected (see Can. 149 §1) as well as the legality and validity of the election itself. Once satisfied that all is as it ought to be, the authority is obliged to confirm the election: as already noted the one elected has a right to the office (*ius ad rem*). No time limit is given within which confirmation must be given. However, if no response is given to a lawfully made petition within three months, or if the confirmation is refused, the one elected has the right to have recourse (see Can. 57). When it is given, confirmation of an election, like any other administrative act concerning the external forum (see Can. 37), must be given in writing.

Can. 179 §4 Before receiving notice of the confirmation, the person elected may not become involved in the administration of the office, neither in spiritual nor in material affairs; any acts possibly performed by that person are invalid.

While he or she may have obtained a right to the office (*ius ad rem*) by virtue of election, until that election is confirmed the one elected is forbidden to become involved in any way, spiritually or materially, in the administration of the office. Indeed, should any such intervention be made, the ensuing acts would be *invalid*. Confirmation must have been *obtained*, not merely presumed.

Can. 179 §5 When confirmation has been notified, the person elected obtains full right to the office, unless the law provides otherwise.

Once confirmation has been notified to the one elected, he or she as a rule acquires all the rights pertaining to the office. By way of exception, however, universal or particular law may add certain other preliminary requirements, e.g. formal induction into office, making the profession of faith (see Can. 833), etc.

Article 4
Postulation

Can. 180 §1 If a canonical impediment, from which a dispensation can be and usually is given, stands in the way of the election of a person whom the electors judge more suitable and prefer, they can, unless the law provides otherwise, postulate that person from the competent authority.

§2 Those to whom the power of electing has been transferred by compromise may not make a postulation, unless this is expressly stated in the terms of the compromise.

376 Occasionally in the course of an election, it may emerge that a candidate judged the more suitable by the electors cannot be elected because of the existence of a canonical impediment, say, e.g. the impediment of age, of an excluded third term of office, etc. Provided this be an impediment 'from which a dispensation can be and usually is given' (§1), the electors may in such circumstances *postulate* their preferred candidate, i.e. present him or her to the competent authority so that a dispensation may be obtained from the impediment. The use of postulation is circumscribed by certain conditions:

(a) it must be permitted by law (universal or particular) for that office;

(b) the impediment must be one of purely ecclesiastical law, e.g. lack of professional qualifications, age, ineligibility after a certain number of terms of office, etc.;

(c) it must be an impediment from which the dispensation is customarily given;

(d) there must be 'a just and reasonable cause' (see Can. 90 §1) for the dispensation, e.g. the manifest suitability and advisability of the candidate for the office in question.

377 Should the electors have already transferred their right to elect by a compromise (see Can. 174), postulation is *not permitted*, unless it has been included expressly in the terms of the compromise (§2).

Can. 181 §1 For a postulation to have effect, at least two thirds of the votes are required.

§2 A vote for postulation must be expressed by the term 'I postulate', or an equivalent. The formula 'I elect or postulate', or its equivalent, is valid for election if there is no impediment; otherwise, it is valid for postulation.

378 The extraordinary nature of postulation as a procedure is highlighted by two special provisions:

(a) a qualified majority;

(b) a special formula to be used;

Both provisions serve as a reminder to the electors that a canonical impediment exists.

379 While an absolute majority suffices for an election (see Can. 119 1°), a candidate requires *two-thirds of the votes of those present* to be validly postulated. This qualified majority is required at all ballots. As a result, it can occur that, after two inconclusive ballots, the third ballot is between the one being postulated and the candidate who received the next highest number of votes. Unless the one being postulated obtains at least two-thirds of the votes of those present, then provided the candidate had received at least a *relative majority*, it is he or she who is the person validly elected, 'to the exclusion ... of the postulate'.[1] To avoid this kind of anomaly, particular law may limit the possibility of postulation to the first and second ballots only.

380 The formula to be used in postulation means that electors are left in no state of uncertainty about what they are doing. If an elector is making a postulation only, the formula 'I postulate X' is required. However, the more generic formula 'I elect or postulate X' is sufficient for a valid election or a valid postulation. The latter formula is safer if there is any doubt concerning the existence or the force of the impediment.

Can. 182 §1 The postulation must be sent, within eight canonical days, by the person who presides to the authority competent to confirm the election, to whom it belongs to grant the dispensation from the impediment or, if the person has not this authority, to seek the dispensation from a superior

---

[1] CCom rep 1.VII.1922: AAS 14(1922) 406: CLD 1 142–143: Per II 127.

authority. If confirmation is not required, the postulation must be sent to the authority competent to grant the dispensation.

The responsibility for communicating a postulation rests with the president of the electoral group. He or she must submit the postulation, i.e. seek the necessary dispensation, from the competent authority within eight canonical days (see Can. 201 §2) of the postulation. If confirmation is required, the competent authority to receive the postulation is the one competent to confirm the election; if this authority has the power to grant the required dispensation, the matter ends there. However, if the authority competent to confirm does not have the power to dispense, the request must be forwarded to the appropriate superior authority, e.g. a diocesan Bishop presiding at the election of a Superior of an autonomous monastery (see Can. 625 §2) may be able to confirm an election duly made, but cannot admit a postulation; this must be communicated *at once* to the competent Congregation of the Holy See. If confirmation is not required for the office, the president must forward the postulation directly to the authority competent to grant the dispensation.

Can. 182 §2 If the postulation is not forwarded within the prescribed time, it is by that very fact invalid, and the college or group is for that occasion deprived of the right of election or of postulation, unless it is proved that the person presiding was prevented by a just impediment from forwarding the postulation, or did not do so in due time because of malice or negligence.

In the case of postulation, it is imperative that the necessary request be transmitted within the eight canonical days permitted. If, in fact, this is not done, the postulation is automatically invalid and the right of the college or group to elect is lost for that occasion. Nevertheless, the validity of the postulation may be upheld if it can be established that the failure to communicate was due to a genuine impediment preventing the president from acting, or due to malice or neglect of responsibility on his or her part: such latter behaviour would injure the legitimate rights of the electors and accordingly should not result in the invalidity of the postulation.

Can. 182 §3 The person postulated does not acquire any right from the postulation; the competent authority is not obliged to admit the postulation.

Postulation, like any dispensation (see Can. 85), is a favour: it is not the object of a *right*. By contrast with a person whose election requires confirmation (see Can. 178), a person who is postulated acquires no right to the office: at most, he or she obtains a legitimate expectation. There is therefore no legal obligation on the competent authority to admit the postulation: it remains a gratuitous matter, one for the discretion of the competent authority.

Can. 182 §4 The electors may not revoke a postulation made to the competent authority, except with the consent of that authority.

Once it has been made and communicated, a postulation may not be revoked by the college or group, except with the consent of the authority to which it has been sent.

Can. 183 §1 If a postulation is not admitted by the competent authority, the right of election reverts to the college or group.

§2 If the postulation has been admitted, this is to be notified to the person postulated, who must reply in accordance with Can. 177 §1.

§3 The person who accepts a postulation which has been admitted, immediately obtains full right to the office.

385 If the postulation is rejected by the competent authority, the college or group must meet again to elect someone; the fact of a postulation properly made does not deprive the college of its right to elect. If the postulation is admitted, the person postulated must be notified *immediately*; he or she then has eight canonical days in which to indicate acceptance of the office. Refusal or failure to respond within the prescribed time renders the postulation ineffective (see Can. 177 §1). A person who has been postulated and who accepts the postulation when it has been admitted, thereby obtains full rights to the office concerned, provided any additional requirements of universal and particular law have been observed, e.g. the profession of faith (see Can. 833).

Chapter II
LOSS OF ECCLESIASTICAL OFFICE

Can. 184 §1 An ecclesiastical office is lost on the expiry of a pre-determined time; on reaching the age limit defined by law; by resignation; by transfer; by removal; by deprivation.

§2 An ecclesiastical office is not lost on the expiry, in whatever way, of the authority of the one by whom it was conferred, unless the law provides otherwise.

§3 The loss of an office, once it has taken effect, is to be notified as soon as possible to those who have any right in regard to the provision of the office.

386 Ecclesiastical office duly conferred may be lost in any of the following ways (§1):

(a) through expiry of the term fixed by law (see Can. 153 §2);

(b) through reaching the age beyond which the law does not permit the office to be exercised; such limits may be set by universal or particular law;

(c) through resignation (see Cann. 187–189);

(d) through transfer (see Cann. 190–191);

(e) through removal (see Cann. 192–195);

(f) through deprivation (see Can. 196).

When, during the revision process, it was asked why death was not included, it was pointed out that the canon deals with the *loss* of office, not its *vacancy*![1]

387 As a rule, ecclesiastical office is not lost when the conferring authority loses power. This principle upholds the stable nature of ecclesiastical office (see Can. 145 §1). However, by way of exception, the law (both universal and particular) can make tenure of office contingent upon the continuity of the one who conferred it, e.g. the loss of the office of Vicar general or episcopal Vicar which occurs when a diocese falls vacant (see Can. 481 §1).

388 The effective loss of ecclesiastical office is to be notified at once to all parties with a legitimate right concerning the provision of a successor. Responsibility for this communication rests with the authority who conferred the office. Those to whom the news ought to be communicated include those with the right to present or elect a candidate. Failure to make such a notification does not however affect the loss of office.

---

[1] Cf. Comm 14(1982) 153 at Can. 181.

Can. 185 The title 'emeritus' may be conferred on one who loses office by reason of age, or of resignation which has been accepted.

As a means of honouring someone for services rendered in the exercise of a particular office, the law enables the competent authority to confer the title of 'emeritus' on certain people who have lost office. Such a loss must have taken place either through reaching the designated age limit or through resignation duly accepted. The use of the title 'emeritus' is facultative; a Bishop who resigns obtains the title by law (see Can. 402 §1).

Can. 186 Loss of office by reason of the expiry of a predetermined time or of reaching the age limit, has effect only from the moment that this is communicated in writing by the competent authority.

The loss of office through expiry of the fixed term or reaching the determined age is not automatic. It is effective only from the moment that it is communicated in writing to the person concerned by the competent authority.

Article 1
Resignation

Can. 187 Anyone who is capable of personal responsibility can resign from an ecclesiastical office for a just reason.

An office is lost by *resignation* whenever the office-holder *freely renounces* the office and all rights attached to it. To be lawful, a resignation requires a *just* reason: this must be considered in the light of the importance of the office concerned. Resignation is necessarily a *free* act on the part of the office-holder. Consequently, to be valid, it must be the act of someone capable of personal responsibility i.e. endowed with sufficient use of reason (see Can. 99). Thus, e.g. persons who are severely mentally ill, excessively inebriated, etc. cannot validly resign from office, even though they may be unfit to exercise it. It is important to note that the double principle of personal responsibility and freedom on the part of the one who resigns is as applicable to the person who chooses to resign entirely on his or her own initiative, as it is to the person who accepts the law's invitation to resign (as occurs in respect of a number of office-holders: see e.g. Cann. 354, 401 §1, 411, 538 §3). In both situations, assuming the requisite personal responsibility, the freedom of the individual must be integrally respected.

Can. 188 A resignation which is made as a result of grave fear unjustly inflicted, or of deceit, or of substantial error, or of simony, is invalid by virtue of the law itself.

Since it is essentially a free act, a resignation is invalid by virtue of the law itself if the individual's freedom is in any way infringed. Thus, by way of exception to Cann. 125 §2 and 126, a resignation is rendered invalid by grave fear unjustly inflicted, by deceit and by substantial error.

Can. 189 §1 For a resignation to be valid, whether it requires acceptance or not, it must be made to the authority which is competent to provide for the office in question, and it must be made either in writing, or orally before two witnesses.

§2 The authority is not to accept a resignation which is not based on a just and proportionate reason.

§3 A resignation which requires acceptance has no force unless it is accepted within three months. One which does not require acceptance takes effect when the person resigning communicates it in accordance with the law.

§4 Until a resignation takes effect, it can be revoked by the person resigning. Once it has taken effect, it cannot be revoked, but the person who resigned can obtain the office on the basis of another title.

393 In order to be valid, a resignation must be submitted to the authority competent to provide for the office. Since it is an act which must be proved in the external forum, resignation must be made either in writing or orally before two witnesses. The structure of §1 shows clearly that this external form is required for validity.

394 When such a resignation has been received, what happens next depends on whether or not the law requires the acceptance of the resignation. If no acceptance is required, the resignation is effective immediately it is submitted in accordance with §1 (§3). On the other hand, if acceptance is required (e.g. Cann. 416, 538 §1), the competent authority must examine the reason presented and determine whether or not it is just and proportionate, i.e. depending on the importance of the office, the reasons advanced, etc. (§2). If the reason presented is not found to be adequate, the resignation may be refused, and so the office-holder remains in possession.

395 It is at this point that another important principle is introduced by the law: 'a resignation which requires acceptance has no force unless it is accepted within three months' (§3). Thus, e.g. if a parish priest were to submit his resignation in accordance with the request of Can. 538 §3, this would have effect *only* if it were accepted by the diocesan Bishop within a period of three months from its receipt: thereafter it would cease to have any effect whatever and could not validly be acted upon by the Bishop – thereby excluding any practice of putting such offers of resignation on what might be called 'indeterminate hold'. A person who wishes to resign is at liberty to withdraw the resignation before it takes effect in accordance with §3. However, once communicated to the competent authority or, where required, accepted by that authority, the resignation cannot be withdrawn.

Article 2
Transfer

Can. 190 §1 A transfer can be made only by the person who has the right to provide both for the office which is lost and at the same time for the office which is being conferred.

§2 A grave reason is required if a transfer is made against the will of the holder of an office and, always without prejudice to the right to present reasons against the transfer, the procedure prescribed by law is to be observed.

§3 For a transfer to have effect, it must be notified in writing.

396 A transfer of office involves an individual changing or being changed from one office already lawfully occupied to another which is currently vacant. It is thus, at one and the same time, a means of both losing an office and of being conferred with another. A transfer can be effected only by the authority which is competent simultaneously to provide for both offices involved (§1). It may take place with the consent of the office-holder or even against his or her wishes. In the latter case, the authority must have a serious reason for the transfer; the person concerned must be free and able to exercise his or her right to submit arguments against the transfer; finally, the procedure

required for transfer by universal or particular law must be followed, e.g. Cann. 1748–1752 concerning the transfer of parish priests. Whether the person being transferred is willing or not, the transfer must be notified in writing, since it is an administrative act concerning the external forum (see Can. 37).

Can. 191 §1 In the process of transfer, the first office is vacated by the taking of canonical possession of the other office, unless the law or the competent authority has prescribed otherwise.

§2 The person transferred receives the remuneration attached to the previous office until the moment of obtaining canonical possession of the other office.

Neither the act of the competent authority transferring someone from one office to another, nor the act of notifying the person concerned, has any juridical effect on either of the offices involved. Instead, the person transferred continues to hold the original office, exercise it and receive the attached remuneration until the moment he or she takes canonical possession of the new office. From that moment, and from that only, all rights attached to the first office cease and all those pertaining to the new office begin. By way of exception, universal or particular law may make other provisions.

Article 3
Removal

Can. 192 One is removed from office either by a decree of the competent authority lawfully issued, observing of course the rights possibly acquired from a contract, or by virtue of the law in accordance with Can. 194.

Canonically, removal from office entails the revoking of all rights, privileges and authority associated with that office in such a way that the office becomes vacant. Removal is a very grave matter. It is primarily disciplinary in character; it may exceptionally take the form of a penalty. Removal takes place either by a decree of the competent authority, or automatically by virtue of the law (see Can. 194). When removal is decreed by the competent authority, Cann. 193 and 195 are to be observed carefully, lest the rights of the one removed be harmed unjustly. Moreover, care must also be taken not to harm the rights of others which were acquired on the basis of a contract concerning the ecclesiastical office in question.

Can. 193 §1 No one may be removed from an office which is conferred on a person for an indeterminate time, except for grave reasons and in accordance with the procedure defined by law.

§2 This also applies to the removal from office before time of a person on whom an office is conferred for a determinate time, without prejudice to Can. 624 §3.

§3 When in accordance with the provisions of law an office is conferred upon someone at the prudent discretion of the competent authority, that person, may upon the judgement of the same authority, be removed from the office for a just reason.

§4 For a decree of removal to be effective, it must be notified in writing.

This canon deals with three situations in which removal from office may be decreed by the competent authority. If an office was conferred for an indefinite period of time (e.g. a parish priest according to Can. 522), the office holder can be removed from that office only for *grave* reasons, e.g. mental or physical illness, irreformable incompetence despite strenuous efforts by the appropriate authority, etc. In weighing up the gravity of the causes, the competent authority must take full account of the circumstances involved, the effect on the office holder and, above all, the effect on the common good and the salvation of souls. In the case of parish priests, the provisions of Cann. 1740–1747 must be followed.

400 The same norms apply to the case of a person appointed to office for a fixed term if he or she is to be removed before that term expires. If the office holder is a religious Superior, the reasons for removal will be contained in the institute's own legislation (see Can. 624 §3).

401 However, if the office was conferred purely at the discretion of the competent authority, e.g. a Vicar general or an episcopal Vicar (see Can. 477 §1), the office holder may be removed from office entirely at the judgement of that same authority. A *just* cause suffices for such a removal.

402 Like any administrative act concerning the external forum (see Can. 37), notification of removal must be written.

Can. 194 §1 The following are removed from ecclesiastical office by virtue of the law itself:

1° one who has lost the clerical state;

2° one who has publicly defected from the catholic faith or from communion with the Church;

3° a cleric who has attempted marriage, even a civil one.

§2 The removal mentioned in nn.2 and 3 can be insisted upon only if it is established by a declaration of the competent authority.

403 Three situations are identified where removal from office is automatic:
(a) loss of the clerical state – whether this follows a decree of invalidity, a penalty lawfully imposed, or a rescript of the Holy See (see Can. 290);
(b) public defection from the catholic faith or from communion with the Church, i.e. by heresy, apostasy or schism (see Can. 751), or by excommunication (see Can. 1331 §1 3°). It is essential that the defection admit of external proof: internal rebellion, while perhaps sinful, does not result in the loss of office;
(c) attempted marriage – even a civil marriage – on the part of a cleric.

404 While removal from office is automatic in all three cases, actual removal in the last two can be insisted on only if the competent authority has first issued a formal declaration of the fact (§2). Without such a declaration, the office may indeed be vacant in law but not in fact – a situation which requires a special procedure before the office can be filled again (see Can. 154).

Can. 195 If by a decree of the competent authority, and not by the law itself, someone is removed from an office on which that person's livelihood depends, the same authority is to ensure that the person's livelihood is secure for an appropriate time, unless this has been provided for in some other way.

405 Where a person's livelihood depend on the ecclesiastical office he or she has held, the authority (not 'the law itself') which decreed the removal is obliged to make sure that this person's livelihood is secure 'for an appropriate time' after the removal. Such a provision of law is rooted in natural justice and reflects the essentially administrative

nature of removal. It is for the competent authority to decide what is an appropriate time, e.g. depending on the circumstances, until the person finds a new position or becomes eligible for some kind of employment benefit. No such obligation arises in cases of automatic removal, although the principles of natural justice and, more practically, those of Christian charity may never be overlooked.

Article 4
Deprivation

Can. 196 §1 Deprivation of office, that is, as a punishment for an offence, may be effected only in accordance with the law.

§2 Deprivation takes effect in accordance with the provisions of the canons concerning penal law.

Deprivation of office, canonically, refers to the removal from office as the result of an offence: it is a penalty in the strict sense. Automatic removal (see Can. 194 §1) is tantamount to deprivation. Where it is not automatic, deprivation can take place only in accordance with the law, i.e. only in those cases where it is foreseen as a penalty (e.g. Cann. 1364 §1, 1389 §1, 1396, 1397); a person cannot be deprived of office by an authority which has no competence over that office (see Can. 1338 §1). It may be imposed by decree or judicial sentence, provided that the relevant norms of penal law have been observed (see Cann. 1341–1353, 1717–1728).

Title X
Prescription

Can. 197 Prescription, as a means of acquiring or of losing a subjective right, or as a means of freeing oneself from obligations, is, apart from the exceptions prescribed in the canons of this Code, accepted by the Church in the manner in which it is adopted in the civil legislation of each country.

Prescription is defined as a means by which persons can acquire or lose subjective rights or free themselves from certain obligations. In order for prescription to be effective, certain conditions must be verified:
- the right or obligation must admit of prescription e.g. the right of ownership (see Cann. 1268–1270);
- the person concerned must be in possession of the right or obligation in question and have some rightful claim to it;
- the person must be acting in *good faith* (see Can. 198);
- a specified period of time must have elapsed, e.g. 100 years and 30 years in Can. 1270.

In c.1508 of the 1917 Code, prescription appeared to affect only rights and obligations connected with temporal goods. The Revision Commission believed that these canons should form part of the General Norms of the whole Code since other rights and obligations are also affected by prescription (see Comm 9(1977) 236).

408 In the majority of circumstances and in the interest of good order, the Code refers issues related to prescription to the civil law prevailing in each country. This is an example of the 'canonisation' of civil law alluded to in Can. 22. It is for the laws of each country to determine what rights or obligations may be acquired or lost by prescription, who may so acquire or lose them, what period of time is necessary, etc: by virtue of this canon, those laws become also the laws of the Church in this regard – subject only to the following.

409 There are certain matters in which the Code retains to itself its own specific laws in relation to prescription, whatever the local civil law may prescribe. Thus e.g. Can. 199 specifies issues which are simply not affected by prescription; Cann. 1362–1363 set certain periods of time for the extinction of criminal actions or actions to execute a penalty.

Can. 198 No prescription is valid unless it is based on good faith, not only in its beginning, but throughout the whole time required for the prescription, without prejudice to Can. 1362.

410 In the context of this canon, good faith may be defined as a conviction in conscience that one possesses a particular right as one's own without detriment to the rights of others, or that one is free of particular obligations without prejudice or harm to the rights of others. This conviction must be *certain*, although it may be erroneous. If anyone has a doubt in this regard, then he or she begins to act in bad faith.

411 The law requires that, for the validity of prescription, one must act in good faith not only at the beginning, i.e. when first laying claim to the right or asserting freedom from the obligation, but also throughout the entire period of time demanded by law, whether civil law or canon law as the case may be. During that time, if any doubt emerges, prescription ceases to run.

412 The only exception to this principle is found in Can. 1362: whether the individual concerned acts in good faith or bad, all the criminal actions indicated are extinguished by the lapse of the specified period of time.

Can. 199 The following are not affected by prescription:

1° rights and obligations which are of divine law, whether natural or positive;

2° rights which can be obtained only by apostolic privilege;

3° rights and obligations which bear directly on the spiritual life of Christ's faithful;

4° the certain and undisputed boundaries of ecclesiastical territories;

5° Mass offerings and obligations;

6° the provision of an ecclesiastical office which, in accordance with the law, requires the exercise of a sacred order;

7° the right of visitation and the obligation of obedience, so that Christ's faithful could not be visited by an ecclesiastical authority and would no longer be subject to any authority.

413 Unless excluded by their very nature or by force of law, in principle all subjective rights and obligations can be acquired or lost by means of prescription. This canon, repeating in essence c.1509 of the 1917 Code, identifies seven categories of rights and obligations which are never affected by prescription.

1° Clearly no merely human authority can change matters regulated by divine law, e.g. the rights of spouses cannot be acquired or lost by prescription;

2° An apostolic privilege can be conferred only by the Roman Pontiff. Therefore any favour which can be granted by him alone cannot be acquired or lost by prescription, e.g. the habitual faculty given to a priest to absolve all censures reserved to the Holy See;

3° The Church identifies specific rights and obligations directly related to its people's spiritual life, e.g. Cann. 213–214, 1247, 1249. Such rights cannot be affected by prescription;

4° When ecclesiastical territories, e.g. parishes, dioceses, provinces etc. have boundaries which are accepted as clear and are not disputed, those same boundaries cannot be affected by prescription. It follows of course that, if the boundaries are not certain or are disputed, all other things being equal, prescription can affect them;

5° The rights and obligations acquired through Mass offerings (see Cann. 945–958) are not affected by prescription. As a matter of justice, these obligations must be satisfied by the priest who accepted the offering or who transferred it to another in accordance with the law (see Can. 955 §1);

6° Although many ministries in the Church may be conferred on lay members of the faithful (see Can. 230), they are not ecclesiastical offices (see Can. 145). Offices are acquired by legitimate provision in accordance with Cann. 146–183. In the light of Cann. 197–198, some offices may be acquired by prescription. However, if the office requires the exercise of a sacred order (e.g. Can. 150), prescription does not apply;

7° Obedience is a fundamental obligation of all the faithful (see Can. 212 §1); the right of visitation is a fundamental right of those in ecclesiastical authority (e.g. Cann. 396–398). Such basic rights and obligations cannot be lost completely through prescription. The canon implies that some particular rights and obligations may be affected by prescription, e.g. obedience to a particular authority, or visitation by a specific dignitary. However, each authority must retain the basic right to carry out a visitation and each member of the faithful must remain subject to some ecclesiastical authority.

TITLE XI
The Reckoning of Time

Can. 200 Unless the law provides otherwise, time is to be reckoned in accordance with the following canons.

In the Code almost two hundred canons mention time. Often they refer to the validity of a juridical act which must take place within or at a specified time e.g. Cann. 643 §1 1°, 656 1°, etc. Clearly it is important that all who are to observe these laws understand what is meant by the temporal requirements. As a general norm, all references to time are to be computed according to the prescriptions of Cann. 201–203. These constitute a considerable simplification of the detailed and often confusing norms of cc.31–35 of the 1917 Code. No longer is there any need in universal law to have regard to the distinctions found in c.33 of the 1917 Code, i.e. usual time, mean time, local time, regional time. Unless the law prescribes otherwise, time is understood to be calculated on the basis of the locally accepted standard time, e.g. Greenwich Mean Time.

Can. 201 §1 Continuous time means unbroken time.

§2 Canonical time is time which a person can so use to exercise or to pursue a right that it does not run when one is unaware, or when one is unable to act.

415 An important legal distinction is drawn between 'continuous time' and 'canonical time'. Since, of its nature, time runs from moment to moment without interruption, any period of time mentioned in the law is presumed to be continuous or unbroken unless otherwise stated, i.e. it is not interrupted by ignorance, error, impediment or any other cause. Continuous time is to be reckoned in accordance with Can. 202 §2. On the other hand, if the period of time prescribed in the law is called 'canonical time' then it must be understood as admitting of interruption. This kind of time is that within which a person is free to exercise or pursue a subjective right, e.g. the right to appeal against a contrary judgment (see Can. 1630 §1): the period of fifteen days does not begin to run until the person is made aware of his or her right to lodge an appeal; moreover, the period is interrupted whenever the person is prevented from exercising the right to appeal, e.g. if a postal strike prevented notice of appeal being sent; the period of canonical time begins to run again as soon as the impediment ceases. Since the law gives no further specification, an impediment of any kind suffices to interrupt time provided it effectively prevents the exercise or prosecution of rights, e.g. physical illness, absence from home, etc.

416 Canonical time is not to be presumed. Since it constitutes an exception to the natural norm of continuous time, it must be prescribed either explicitly or implicitly in the law (e.g. Cann. 159, 165, 177 §1, 1630 §1, 1734 §2).

Can. 202 §1 In law, a day is understood to be a space of twenty-four hours, to be reckoned continuously and, unless expressly provided otherwise, it begins at midnight; a week is a space of seven days; a month is a space of thirty days, and a year a space of three hundred and sixty-five days, unless it is stated that the month and the year are to be taken as in the calendar.

§2 If time is continuous, the month and the year are always to be taken as in the calender.

417 In order to provide clarity and to avoid ambiguities, misunderstandings and possible injustices, the Code provides a *legal* definition of some of the principal units of time:

(a) *a day* is defined as a period of twenty-four hours which are to be counted continuously, i.e. without interruption; unless some other provision is made expressly in the law, this period of twenty-four hours is reckoned to begin at midnight;

(b) *a week* is defined as a period of seven days; there is no requirement that they be continuous, but there must be seven complete periods of twenty-four hours; where time is understood to be 'canonical', a week does not include days where the required action cannot be taken.

(c) *a month* is defined as a period of thirty days; these may be continuous or, where necessary, calculated in accordance with Can. 201 §2;

(d) *a year* is defined as a period of three hundred and sixty-five days; this period may be continuous or, depending on the circumstances, it may admit of interruption (see Can. 201 §2).

Notwithstanding the general principles of definition just provided, the law may prescribe that, in a given case, the month and year are to be calculated according to the norms of the calendar: i.e. the month may have twenty-eight, twenty-nine, thirty or thirty-one days; the year may have three hundred and sixty-five or three hundred and sixty-six days. In keeping with the principle of Can. 201 §1, when time is continuous, the month and year are to be calculated according to the calendar, e.g. the five full years of actual residence required for the acquisition of domicile (see Can. 102 §1) or the three months actual residence required for the acquisition of quasi-domicile (see Can. 102 §2). 418

The Code does not offer a definition of any period of time shorter than a day, e.g. an hour (see Can. 919). Such times are to be calculated according to common sense and common practice. 419

Can. 203 §1 The first day is not to be counted in the total, unless its beginning coincides with the beginning of the day, or unless the law expressly provides otherwise.

§2 Unless the contrary is prescribed, the final day is to be reckoned within the total; if the total time is one or more months, one or more years, one or more weeks, it finishes on completion of the last day bearing the same number or, if the month does not have the same number, on the completion of the last day of that month.

Having set forth what is understood in law by the various units of time, the Code addresses the issues of when these periods of time are reckoned to begin and when they are reckoned to end. 420

As a general norm, the first day of any period of time is not to be included in the total e.g. a man may not be ordained a priest earlier than the day following his twenty-fifth birthday (see Can. 1031 §1) since the actual day of his birth is not included in the total. By way of exception, however, the first day may be included, but only if 421

(a) the beginning of the total time coincides exactly with the beginning of the first day i.e. midnight; or

(b) the law has expressly provided otherwise.

By contrast, as a rule the last day of any period is to be counted within the total i.e. a week, month or year ends with the last day of the particular period. To avoid ambiguities, the Code explains how the last day is to be reckoned if the period of time consists of one or more weeks, months or years: such a period ends at midnight on the day bearing the same number as the first e.g. a week beginning on Wednesday ends at midnight the following Wednesday; a month from January 16th ends at midnight on February 16th; a year from January 16th ends at midnight the following January 16th. However, if the month in which the period of time ends has no day bearing the same number as the first day, the period ends at midnight on the last day of that month e.g. a month from January 30th ends at midnight on February 28th or 29th, depending on the year. 422

In all cases, the law can determine, by way of exception, that the last day is not included in the total period of time. This, if it be done, must be done expressly. 423

BOOK II

THE PEOPLE OF GOD

PART I

CHRIST'S FAITHFUL

Can. 204 §1 Christ's faithful are those who, since they are incorporated into Christ through baptism, are constituted the people of God. For this reason they participate in their own way in the priestly, prophetic and kingly office of Christ. They are called, each according to his or her particular condition, to exercise the mission which God entrusted to the Church to fulfil in the world.

This is the first of four introductory canons which are doctrinal in nature, reflecting the Church's theological vision of the kind of Church which Christ intended to establish.[1] Here the Church is spoken of as the 'People of God'. Two important points are made. Firstly, within the People of God there is a fundamental equality among all the members; this arises from their incorporation into Christ and the Church through baptism.[2] All of Christ's faithful, therefore, participate in the priestly, prophetic and kingly mission of Christ. Secondly, however, alongside this basic equality there is a certain functional inequality within the Church. All participate 'in their own way', each 'according to his or her particular condition'. Clerics and laity (see Can. 207) have different functions to fulfil; within each category, functions also differ: e.g. that of the priest is different from that of the Bishop, that of the married person different from that of the religious sister, and so on. But they *each and all* have an essential part in the overall mission of the Church to the world: a point always to be emphasised, not least to and among the laity. — 424

The term 'Christ's faithful' was a matter of some debate in the course of the revision of the Code: did it refer to all baptised persons, or only to catholics?[3] Eventually it was decided that while *theologically* the term includes all the baptised, even those not in full communion with the catholic Church, *in this canon and in the Code* it refers only to those in full communion.[4] The expression 'Christ's faithful' applies to each and every one of these, without distinction of age, office, status or sex. — 425

By speaking of the threefold office of Christ in relation to the mission of the Church, the canon sketches, as it were, a plan for the Code: — 426

(a) the mission of sanctifying (i.e. the priestly office) is the topic of Book IV;

(b) the mission of teaching the Word (i.e. the prophetic office) is covered in Book III;

---

[1] Cf. LG 10: Fl I 359–361.

[2] Cf. LG 11: Fl I 361. Cf. also Cann. 225, 759.

[3] Cf. Comm 12(1980) 60–61.

[4] Cf. Comm 14(1982) 157 at Can. 201.

Book II The People of God

(c) the mission of serving and governing (i.e. the kingly office) is treated in Books II, V, VI and VII.

Can. 204 §2 This Church, established and ordered in this world as a society, subsists in the catholic Church, governed by the successor of Peter and the Bishops in communion with him.

427 This paragraph, taken directly from Vat. II,[1] is not found in any of the drafts prepared by the Revision Commission but was added at the very last stage.

428 While §1 of this canon deals with some of the spiritual and theological elements of the Church, this §2 treats of the visible, human and social elements. The Church is not to be understood solely as an invisible, spiritual reality but also as an organised human society. This society is said to 'subsist' in the catholic Church. Vat. II deliberately chose to use this term, not wishing to identify the Church of Christ with the catholic Church in a way which excluded other churches and christian communities. It recognised that some ecclesial elements of sanctification and truth are found outside the catholic Church. The use of the word 'subsists' is thus a positive statement of identity without being exclusive.[2]

Can. 205 Those baptised are in full communion with the catholic Church here on earth who are joined with Christ in his visible body, through the bonds of profession of faith, the sacraments and ecclesiastical governance.

429 In an effort to distinguish clearly between catholic and non-catholic Christianity, St Robert Bellarmine defined the Church as 'the community of men who are united by the bond of profession of faith and participation of the same sacraments, under the authority of the legitimate pastors and in particular of the one vicar of Christ on earth, the Roman Pontiff'.[3] He was clearly concerned with visible membership of the Church, i.e. the signs by which a catholic can be identified. This canon mentions the same three external bonds. However, no reference is made to *membership* of the Church. Instead, the central point of the canon is 'full communion with the catholic Church'. The concept of communion is deeper and richer than that of membership: it includes and transcends the purely legal and external.

430 The source of the canon lies in Vat. II,[4] where the whole concept of degrees or levels of communion is expounded. Originally, this canon was meant to be part of the *Lex Ecclesiae Fundamentalis*, but subsequently the Commission decided to incorporate it into the Code.[5] The notion of a real but imperfect union with the catholic Church is

---

[1] Cf. LG 8: Fl I 357.

[2] For a fuller treatment of this question cf. Grillmeier *The Mystery of the Church* in Vorgrimler I 149-151.

[3] Bellarmine *De Conciliis* III cap II: Fèvre II (1870) 316–318 – cited by Grillmeier *The People of God* in Vorgrimler I 172.

[4] Cf. LG 14–15: Fl I 365–367.

[5] Cf. Comm 12(1980) 33–34. Parallel to the work of the revision of the Code of Canon Law was the work of an independent commission charged with the task of producing a *Lex Ecclesiae Fundamentalis* or Fundamental Law of the Church. This was intended to be a statement of what could be regarded as the constitutional law of the Church, containing the basic principles and rules governing all its law. The numerous drafts produced reflected the varied reactions and debate raised in the process. There was a fear that such a fundamental statement might impede the legitimate evolution of thought in the area of ecclesiology. Difficulties were also seen in the relationship between the law of the Code, particular local legislation and this constitutional law. (Cf. Gauthier *The progress of the 'Lex Ecclesiae Fundamentalis* Stud Can 12(1978) 377–388.) The work did however proceed, and in 1981 a final draft was submitted to the Pope for approval. This approval was not granted. Instead, approximately half of the canons of the projected text were incorporated into the Code, particularly, though not exclusively, in Book II Title I which deals with the obligations and rights of all Christ's faithful.

given practical expression in Cann. 844, 915 and 916 (admission to holy communion), Cann. 1124–1129 (mixed marriages) and Can. 1183 (church funerals).

Can. 206 §1 Catechumens are linked with the Church in a special way since, moved by the Holy Spirit, they are expressing an explicit desire to be incorporated in the Church. By this very desire, as well as by the life of faith, hope and charity which they lead, they are joined to the Church which already cherishes them as its own.

The text of this canon was inspired by two documents of Vat. II.[1] Catechumens are those persons who have expressed the desire to be incorporated in the Church through baptism. As such they are distinguished from baptised non-catholics who express the desire to belong to the catholic Church. The canon points out the two features by which catechumens are linked with the Church, though not yet joined to it by baptism: 431

(a) their expressed desire to become Christian;

(b) their life of faith, hope and charity.

Can. 206 §2 The Church has a special care for catechumens. While it invites them to lead an evangelical life, and introduces them to the celebration of the sacred rites, it already accords them various prerogatives which are proper to Christians.

Catechumens are distinguished from other non-baptised persons by their desire to belong to the Church and are the object of 'special care'. Already, before baptism, the Church invites them to live according to the Gospel. This is done formally by their admission to the catechumenate in the appropriate liturgical rite (see Can. 788 §1). One of the consequences of this special relationship to the Church is that they may enjoy certain prerogatives which are proper to christians, e.g. they may receive blessings (see Can. 1170) and are to be given christian burial (see Can. 1183 §1). Due to differences in culture and in religious influence on society, it has been left to Bishops' Conferences to make further specifications concerning the activity and prerogatives of catechumens (see Can. 788 §3). 432

Can. 207 §1 By divine institution, among Christ's faithful there are in the Church sacred ministers, who in law are also called clerics; the others are called lay people.

Fundamentally, there are two categories of person in the Church: clerics and lay people. *Clerics* are those who have been ordained as deacon, priest, or Bishop. *All* the others are *lay people*. This distinction, which is 'by divine institution', is an essential element in the hierarchical structure of the Church. It emerges clearly in several areas of the Code, e. g. lay people, admitted to the *ministries* of acolyte or lector, are not thereby entitled to remuneration (Can. 230 §1), whereas clerics, since they give themselves wholly to the ministry of the Church, are so entitled (see Can. 281 §1); in the exercise of *authority*, clerics are 'capable of the power of governance' (Can. 129 §1), whereas the laity can merely 'cooperate in the exercise of this same power' (Can. 129 §2); the *obligations and rights* of lay members of Christ's faithful (see Cann. 224–231) are manifestly distinct from those of clerics (see Cann. 273–289). 433

Can. 207 §2 Drawn from both groups are those of Christ's faithful who, professing the evangelical counsels through vows or other sacred bonds

---

[1] Cf. LG 14, AG 14: Fl I 366, 828–829.

recognised and approved by the Church, are consecrated to God in their own special way and promote the salvific mission of the Church. Their state, although it does not belong to the hierarchical structure of the Church, does pertain to its life and holiness.

434 Another category of persons within the Church is mentioned here. The 1917 Code would simply have referred to these as 'religious'. The current Code gives no label; it simply provides a description of these persons. The canon therefore refers to members of religious institutes, secular institutes, and societies of apostolic life, as well as to men and women who live a consecrated life in the Church in some other approved form. The text of the canon, inspired by Vat. II,[1] makes it clear that this category of persons is not to be added to the basic cleric–lay distinction. Though not of divine institution, it does however belong to the life and holiness of the Church, and as such it has a distinct juridical status (see Cann. 662–672). As a category of persons, it is made up of both clerics and lay; thus, 'in itself, the state of consecrated life is neither clerical nor lay' (Can. 588 §1).

Title I
The Obligations and Rights of all Christ's Faithful

435 This Title (Cann. 208–223) and the next (Cann. 224–231) introduce a major innovation into the Church's law and constitute a particularly significant part of the Code. Here, for the first time in legislative form, is spelled out what might be called a *Charter* of the obligations and of the rights which obtain throughout the Church. The present Title provides such a charter in respect of *all* Christ's faithful, both clerics and lay (see Can. 207), while the following Title gives an additional charter in respect of *lay* members. In Cann. 273–289 and Cann. 662–672, equivalent, additional charters in respect of *clerics* and of *religious* are set out.

436 Note that, whereas in civil society the tendency is to refer to a 'Charter' or a 'Bill' as one of rights only, the Code explicitly recognises that rights and obligations are of their very nature correlative. This is of particular significance in the understanding and in the application of this Code: even a stated right may not lawfully be pursued unless the corresponding obligation is acknowledged, nor may a particular obligation be imposed without due recognition of the correlative right.

Can. 208 Flowing from their rebirth in Christ, there is a genuine equality of dignity and action among all of Christ's faithful. Because of this equality they all contribute, each according to his or her own condition and office, to the building up of the Body of Christ.

437 This canon contains an explicit statement of the radical equality of all the faithful, rooted as it is in their common baptism. This is the basis for the sharing by all the faithful in the mission of Church. The canon is based on the view of the Church as the communion of all the baptised and the text puts into canonical language the

---
[1] Cf. LG 43–44: Fl 1 403–405.

teaching of Vat. II: 'Although by Christ's will some are established teachers, dispensers of the mysteries and pastors for the others, there remains, nevertheless, a true equality between all with regard to the dignity and to the activity which is common to all the faithful in the building up of the Body of Christ'.[1] All forms of discrimination in the basic rights of the person are thus to be rejected.[2]

Can. 209 §1 Christ's faithful are bound to preserve their communion with the Church at all times, even in their external actions.

The theme of ecclesial communion is one which runs through the whole Code. It is found at various levels and in various guises, e.g. hierarchical communion, the communion of Churches, the communion of saints, full communion. According to this canon, a prime obligation of Christ's faithful is to preserve this ecclesial communion at all times. In practice, this will mean making sure that the three bonds of communion mentioned in Can. 205 – profession of faith, the sacraments, and ecclesiastical governance – remain unbroken. The effort to maintain this communion is not to be restricted to any particular activity, e.g. purely religious activity, but is to be an integral part of the Christian's whole pattern of behaviour.

438

Can. 209 §2 They are to carry out with great diligence their responsibilities towards both the universal Church and the particular Church to which they belong.

Communion with and within the particular Church is the basis for communion with and within the universal Church.[3] It is within the particular Church that the individual members of Christ's faithful are to live the Christian life and carry out their duties. According to Can. 368, 'particular Churches ... are principally dioceses ...' or some equivalent entity.[4] Since each particular Church is for the most part divided into parishes or quasi-parishes (see Cann. 515–518), it is clearly at parochial level and within the context of the parish that the majority of the faithful will find the appropriate outlet for the fulfilment of this obligation.

439

No list is given of the responsibilities which the faithful must carry out 'with great diligence'. Clearly they must include the basic duties laid down by the Lord, i.e., love of God and love of neighbour. In addition, each will have the obligations specific to his or her particular way of life. Others will suggest themselves from among the needs of particular circumstances, especially within the individual's parish. However the fulfilment of these duties must always be kept in harmony with the communion which all the faithful are to have with the universal Church.

440

Can. 210 All Christ's faithful, each according to his or her own condition, must make a wholehearted effort to lead a holy life, and to promote the growth of the Church and its continual sanctification.

This canon is a crystallisation of the teaching of Vat. II on the 'call to holiness',[5] a call to all Christ's faithful, irrespective of their juridical status in the Church. Examples of this call, which is another theme running through the whole Code, may be found: for all the faithful in Can. 217; for clerics in Can. 277; for the Bishop in Can. 387; for religious in Can. 673; for children in Can. 795; for parents in Can. 835 §4.

441

---

[1] LG 32: Fl I 389.
[2] Cf. GS 29: Fl I 929.
[3] Cf. Can. 368; LG 23: Fl I 376.
[4] This definition of 'particular Church' concerns only the latin Church. The expression has a different significance within the eastern Churches.
[5] Cf. LG 39–42: Fl I 396–402.

Book II The People of God

Can. 211 All Christ's faithful have the obligation and right to strive so that the divine message of salvation may more and more reach all people of all times and all places.

442 This short canon has its source in two texts of Vat. II which concern the apostolic activity of the laity within the Church.[1] The canon has expanded their scope to apply to all members of Christ's faithful. In essence, it states that the task of evangelisation belongs to all the faithful and is not restricted to any one section, such e.g. as the hierarchy. It echoes and summarises the renewed theology of mission and evangelisation which emerged from Vat. II,[2] and which was developed further by Pope Paul VI after the 1974 Synod of Bishops.[3] The faithful not only have the obligation to spread 'the divine message of salvation', they have the right to do so. The exercise of this right, however, is always subject to the supervision of the competent ecclesiastical authority (see Cann. 754, 756).

Can. 212 §1 Christ's faithful, conscious of their own responsibility, are bound to show christian obedience to what the sacred Pastors, who represent Christ, declare as teachers of the faith and prescribe as rulers of the Church.

443 Once more, the teaching of Vat. II on the laity[4] is made to include all of Christ's faithful without distinction. The whole canon concerns the relationship between the faithful and their pastors. These latter are primarily the Bishops (Can. 375 §1) and parish priests under their authority (see Can. 515 §1). This paragraph focuses particularly on obedience to the pastors which is presented as an obligation binding on all the faithful. The obedience required is quite clearly defined: it must be christian, i.e. based on the example of Christ's obedience;[5] it must be obedience to the pastors as representatives of Christ; it must be obedience to what they declare as teachers of the faith (see Cann. 752–754); it must be obedience to what they determine as rulers of the Church. In giving this obedience, the faithful are to be conscious of their own responsibility, according to their particular status or position within the Church.

Can. 212 §2 Christ's faithful are at liberty to make known their needs, especially their spiritual needs, and their wishes to the Pastors of the Church.

444 The relationship between Christ's faithful and the pastors is not simply one of obedience: it is also one of trust. The faithful, both lay and clerical, have the right to make their needs and wishes known to their pastors. This is the first time that such a right has been explicitly recognised in canonical legislation. Pastors have a corresponding grave responsibility to respect this right of the faithful: it may not be ignored or dismissed. If the attitude of the faithful towards their pastors is to be one of trust, then the attitude of pastors towards the faithful ought to be one of discerning listening.[6] The text of the canon makes it clear that more than spiritual needs may be made known: others would e.g. include material, emotional and intellectual needs.

---

[1] Cf. LG 33, AA 25: Fl I 391, 790.

[2] Cf. AG 2: Fl I 814.

[3] Cf. EN 15–24: Fl II 716–722.

[4] Cf. LG 37: Fl I 395.

[5] Cf. LG 37: Fl I 395.

[6] Cf. PO 9: Fl I 880–881 which, on the relations between priests and lay people, is very profitable reading.

Part I Christ's Faithful

Can. 212 §3 They have the right, indeed at times the duty, in keeping with their knowledge, competence and position, to manifest to the sacred Pastors their views on matters which concern the good of the Church. They have the right also to make their views known to others of Christ's faithful, but in doing so they must always respect the integrity of faith and morals, show due reverence to the Pastors and take into account both the common good and the dignity of individuals.

445 The right to express personal opinions concerning the good of the Church involves something much wider than merely voicing complaint. Above all, it includes true consultation and the proper relationship between the laity and their clergy. Vat. II provides an excellent commentary: 'Priests are to be sincere in their appreciation and promotion of lay people's dignity and of the special role the laity have to play in the Church's mission. They should also have an unfailing respect for the just liberty which belongs to everybody in civil society. They should be willing to listen to lay people, give brotherly consideration to their wishes, and recognise their experience and competence in different fields of human activity'.[1]

446 It is this same attitude which must lie behind the various structured forms of consultation set out in the Code, e.g. the Council of Priests (see Cann. 495–502); the diocesan Pastoral Council (see Cann. 511–514); the diocesan Finance Council (see Cann. 492–494); the Parish Council (see Can. 536); the Parish Finance Council (see Can. 537). Moreover, it is the same attitude which ought to mark the relationship between a Bishop and his priests at all times (see Can. 384).

447 The canon speaks not just of the faithful's right to manifest their views, but also of their duty to do so at times. However, such expression of opinions is not to be random or capricious. Instead, it must be done in accordance with the knowledge, competence and position of the individual concerned. As well as making known their views directly to the Pastors, the faithful have the right also to express their opinions to other members of the faithful. The canon qualifies the exercise of this right: the faithful 'must always respect the integrity of faith and morals, show due reverence to the Pastors and take into account both the common good and the dignity of individuals'. Indulging in carping criticism almost for its own sake, especially if (as so often happens) it is ill-informed, is not an exercise of this right, but an abuse which violates the virtue of charity and can seriously harm the Church to which the critic professes allegiance.

Can. 213 Christ's faithful have the right to be assisted by their Pastors from the spiritual riches of the Church, especially by the word of God and the sacraments.

448 This fundamental right of all the faithful brings with it a serious obligation on the part of their Pastors (see Cann. 386–387). Specific examples of how they can fulfil this obligation and so respond to this right are contained in the Code: e.g. by preaching and catechetical formation (Cann. 756–780); by ensuring that theology is taught in catholic universities (see Can. 811); by ensuring proper preparation for the sacraments (see Can. 843 §2); by care of the sick (see Can. 911 §1); by providing for the hearing of confessions (see Can. 986).

449 A similar right was recognised in c.682 of the 1917 Code but the language used was quite different: no mention was made of 'the word of God and the sacraments';

---

[1] PO 9: Fl I 880. Cf. also Can. 529 §2.

instead, the laity (not *all the faithful*) had the right to receive from the clergy (not their Pastors) 'spiritual goods and especially the aids necessary for salvation'. The present canon, based on Vat. II,[1] brings to the fore another of the major themes running through the Code: word and sacrament. This flows from Vat. II's teaching that Christ is present in the word of God as well as in the sacraments.[2] At the time of the Reformation, catholics began to insist less on the word (which was taken up by other Christians) and concentrated more on the sacraments. The Council restored the balance by re-emphasising the significance of the word in the life of the Church.

Can. 214 Christ's faithful have the right to worship God according to the provisions of their own rite approved by the lawful Pastors of the Church; they also have the right to follow their own form of spiritual life, provided it is in accord with Church teaching.

450 This canon recognises two rights of the faithful: the right to worship God according to the provisions of their own rite, and the right to follow their own form of spiritual life. This recognition is firmly rooted in Vat. II's teaching on the respect due to the human person and on religious liberty.[3]

451 The word 'rite' here may refer to a particular ritual Church, e.g. the Ukrainian Church, or to a liturgical rite within the latin Church, e.g. the Ambrosian rite. What is clear is that the faithful are entitled to worship God according to the approved prescriptions of their own Church. This right of the faithful is closely related to the obligation on sacred ministers 'to celebrate the sacraments according to their own rite' (Can. 846 §2).

452 The Code recognises the individual's right to live the spirituality of christian life in his own or her own way. The only constraint, but an important one, is that the person's behaviour in this regard must be consonant with the Church's teaching. In consequence, no one may insist on uniformity for its own sake. Thus, e.g. a parish or a local religious community cannot be forced to accept a particular spirituality, e.g. charismatic, contemplative, etc. simply because the parish priest or the Superior considers this to be the most appropriate form of spirituality.

Can. 215 Christ's faithful may freely establish and direct associations which serve charitable or pious purposes or which foster the Christian vocation in the world, and they may hold meetings to pursue these purposes by common effort.

453 Vat. II acknowledged the right of the faithful, laity and clergy, to form associations; indeed, it recommended that such associations be established.[4] This canon gives juridical expression to that recognition. Three purposes for which the faithful might establish groups are listed: charitable purposes, pious i.e. religious purposes, and the purpose of fostering the Christian vocation in the world. For details of such associations and their purposes, see Cann. 298–329.

Can. 216 Since they share the Church's mission, all Christ's faithful have the right to promote and support apostolic action, by their own initiative, undertaken according to their state and condition. No initiative, however, can lay claim to the title 'catholic' without the consent of the competent ecclesiastical authority.

---

[1] Cf. LG 37: Fl I 394.
[2] Cf. SC 7: Fl I 4–5.
[3] Cf. GS 26, DH 2: Fl I 927–928, 800–801.
[4] Cf. AA 19, PO 8: Fl I 786, 879.

According to Can. 211 all the faithful have the obligation and right to engage in evangelisation. This canon further specifies this right. It clearly affirms the right of all to use their own initiative in the promotion of apostolic action. No distinction is made here between laity and clergy. This right has its foundation in baptism and in the mission of the whole Church.[1]

The use of the name 'catholic' is considered as indicating that the initiative is in some way representative of the catholic Church. Hence the competent authority must examine the initiative concerned and, if appropriate, give approval. This is a principle which runs through the Code, e.g. Cann. 216, 300, 803, 806, 808.

Can. 217 Since Christ's faithful are called by baptism to lead a life in harmony with the gospel teaching, they have the right to a christian education, which genuinely teaches them to strive for the maturity of the human person and at the same time to know and live the mystery of salvation.

This canon refers to christian education in its widest sense. This is a much broader concept than the education of children or even than catholic education as legislated for in Cann. 793–821. The goal of this education is twofold: the maturity of the human person, and the knowledge and living of the mystery of salvation. Neither can be separated from the other. The precise nature and form of this education will vary according to the needs of each individual and the level of growth which he or she has attained. The text is firmly rooted in conciliar teaching.[2]

Can. 218 Those who are engaged in fields of sacred study have a just freedom to research matters in which they are expert and to express themselves prudently concerning them, with due submission to the magisterium of the Church.

In the matter of theological and allied studies Vat. II clearly established the principle of academic freedom of research and of expression; equally, it pointed to the limitations on that freedom.[3] In effect, the Council drew attention to the fact that the Church itself has, by the will of Christ, a direct mandate to teach and to give mandatory expression to that teaching. This canon puts that conciliar doctrine into legal form: while emphasising that the freedom is a positive one, it makes the point that an unfettered freedom inevitably becomes an abuse.

The freedom in question is for those, and those only – be they cleric or lay (see Can. 229 §2) – 'who are engaged in fields of sacred study ... in which they are expert', i.e. academically qualified and experienced. It is a 'just', or lawful, freedom in that it must avoid unfounded or excessive pronouncements. It is a freedom which in its expression must be exercised 'prudently', whether in writing (theological and allied journals, conferences etc. should be the preferred vehicles), or in teaching, bearing particularly in mind the level of student understanding. Above all, it is a freedom which may be exercised only 'with due submission to the magisterium of the Church'.[4]

Can. 219 All Christ's faithful have the right to immunity from any kind of coercion in choosing a state of life.

---

[1] Cf. LG 33, AA 3, 15–22, 24, PO 9: Fl I 390–391, 768–769, 783–788, 789–790, 800–881; cf. also Cann. 756–759.
[2] Cf. GE 1–2, AA 30: Fl I 726–728, 794–796.
[3] Cf. GS 62: Fl I 968.
[4] Cf. Cann. 747–755; also SCDF instr *Donum veritatis* 24.V.1990: AAS 82(1990) 1550–1570: Origins 20(1990) 118–126.

459 While the right to immunity from this kind of coercion did figure in cc.214, 971, 1087, 2352 of the 1917 Code in respect of specific situations, it is now, thanks to Vat. II's insistence on the essential dignity and freedom of the human person,[1] the subject of a universal principle for every member of the Church.

460 The principle is *not* that each has a right to choose whatever state in life he or she might wish: thus e.g. a seminarian as such does not have a right to be ordained, nor does a novice as such have a right to be admitted to religious profession; not every person has the right to marry, e.g. an impotent person or an undispensed priest. The principle, rather, is that everyone of Christ's faithful has the positive right not to be subjected to 'any kind' of coercion or pressure in making his or her choice of a state in life. This is so whether or not such coercion would result in the invalidity of the choice. So e.g. Can. 1103 prescribes very specific conditions for the kind of force or fear which would render a marriage null and void; while a lesser coercion might not result in invalidity, it would nevertheless be a violation of the person's right to a totally free choice, and could therefore become the subject of a judicial enquiry in the Church, if only for some form of christian adjustment or compensation (see Can. 221 §1).

461 It is a right to immunity from coercion, not in entering but rather in 'choosing', a state of life. It would therefore equally be a violation of this right if one were to be coerced into *not* choosing a preferred state, e.g. prevented from choosing a single life, rather than choosing a religious or a priestly life. This is clearly a matter of which parents and other advisors should prudently take notice.

Can. 220 No one may unlawfully harm the good reputation which a person enjoys, or violate the right of every person to protect his or her privacy.

462 Two rights are recognised and protected here: the right to one's good name or reputation, and the right to one's privacy – this latter having been inserted only after the final draft was submitted to the Pope.[2] No one may 'unlawfully' infringe either right. The right to one's good reputation is manifestly based on the natural law, rooted in the dignity of the human person and acknowledged as such by Vat. II,[3] but a person may by his or her own conduct obviously forfeit this right.

463 The right to one's privacy is equally given protection against unlawful invasion. This right certainly includes, but extends beyond, the protection of one's personal correspondence. Just how far it extends will depend upon that delicate balance which must be maintained between the inherent rights of the individual and the demands of the common good. This could well become a critical issue in the matter of candidates for the priesthood or for the religious life (see Cann. 241, 642). The canon carries an implied warning to Superiors and others that, while observing the criteria laid down by the Church, they must seriously take into account these basic rights of the individual (see Cann. 483 §2, 1352 §2, 1361 §3, 1390 §2, 1455 §3, 1598 §1).

Can. 221 §1 Christ's faithful may lawfully vindicate and defend the rights they enjoy in the Church before the competent ecclesiastical forum in accordance with the law.

464 Reference was made earlier to the major innovation introduced into the Church's law by this particular series of canons concerning the obligations and the rights of Christ's

---

[1] Cf. GS 26, 29, 52: Fl I 927, 929–930, 956.

[2] For the history of the drafting of this canon, cf. RCom SPD 30 at Cann. 32, 33; Sch 1982 36 at Can. 220.

[3] Cf. GS 26–27: Fl I 927–928.

faithful (see the commentary at the start of this Title). The effectiveness of this innovation will be measured in great part by the extent to which the rights themselves are recognised in practice and are officially vindicated when threatened or abused. The application of this canon is pivotal in this regard. It is a formal statement that all may lawfully *vindicate* and *defend* the rights they enjoy in the Church – and precisely 'before the competent ecclesiastical forum' i.e. the appropriate tribunal (see Cann. 1404–1416, 1671–1673), or organ of administrative recourse (see Cann. 1732–1739). True, the Code stresses that recourse to such a forum should never be the first step (see Cann. 1446, 1733 §1); yet, it insists that everyone in the Church has the right to which this canon refers. Tribunals in the Church have hitherto for the most part been concerned with cases of alleged nullity of marriage. This canon clearly signals the need for a wider vision of judicial or quasi-judicial service to all the people of God.

Can. 221 §2 If any members of Christ's faithful are summoned to trial by the competent authority, they have the right to be judged according to the provisions of law, to be applied with equity.

If summoned before an ecclesiastical tribunal, any member of the faithful has the right to the 'due process of law', i.e. no one can be judged in a manner which is unjust or arbitrary. Every case must be judged 'according to the provisions of law', which are to be found in detail in Book VII. And those provisions must be applied with canonical equity (see Can. 19): true justice must always be tempered by compassion and administered in a humane fashion in accordance with the spirit of the Gospel. 465

Can. 221 §3 Christ's faithful have the right that no canonical penalties be inflicted upon them except in accordance with the law.

With this paragraph the protection of the rights of the faithful is extended into the domain of penal law. The 1917 Code, in its c.2222, gave to ecclesiastical authorities quite extensive powers to impose penalties. The current Code is more restricted in this sphere: if no penalty is stated in the law, then none can be imposed – except as permitted by the limited provisions of Can. 1399. 466

Can. 222 §1 Christ's faithful have the obligation to provide for the needs of the Church, so that the Church has available to it those things which are necessary for divine worship, for works of the apostolate and of charity and for the worthy support of its ministers.

This obligation corresponds to the right of the Church, 'in pursuit of its proper objectives' (Can. 1254). If the Church has the right to 'acquire, retain, administer and alienate temporal goods', the members of the Church have the obligation of providing what is necessary. This obligation has a threefold implication, namely the provision of time, of talent and of financial support. Even among those whose financial resources are restricted a generous wealth of talent or of time is rarely absent. 467

The canon speaks of 'Christ's faithful', without distinction: all are therefore obliged, be they lay, clerical or religious – each obviously in accordance with his or her personal and financial means. True, the clergy are urged, not obliged, to give to the Church and to charity any surplus in the income from their respective offices (see Can. 282 §2), but the obligation of this canon certainly applies to what might be other personal income. Professed religious do not enjoy the administration of personal property; however, the obligation of this canon is relevant to the disposition which they are obliged to make before first profession (see Can. 668 §§1–5). 468

Can. 222 §2 They are also obliged to promote social justice and, mindful of the Lord's precept, to help the poor from their own resources.

469 This is a brief statement of one of the major preoccupations of the Church today: social justice and helping the poor. There probably has been no single topic so much explored in papal writings in the last 100 years, from *Rerum Novarum* of Pope Leo XIII in 1891[1] to *Centesimus Annus* of Pope John Paul II in 1991.[2] The question of social justice as a central feature of Christianity emerged also at Vat. II,[3] and later in the message from the Synod of Bishops *Convenientes Ex Universo* of 30 November 1971.[4] The text of this paragraph was not contained in the earlier drafts of the Code: it was added at the time of the formal consultation with Pope John Paul in 1982.

Can. 223 §1 In exercising their rights, Christ's faithful, both individually and in associations, must take account of the common good of the Church, as well as the rights of others and their own duties to others.

470 'In availing of any freedom men must respect the moral principle of personal and social responsibility; in exercising their rights individual men and social groups are bound by the moral law to have regard for the rights of others, their own duties to others and the common good of all.'[5] This excerpt from Vat. II, the immediate source of this paragraph, makes it clear that there are limits to the exercise of the rights of Christ's faithful, and it spells out what these limitations are: (a) the common good of the Church, not the broader 'common good of all'; (b) the rights of others, thus avoiding unnecessary conflicts; (c) the duties of Christ's faithful towards others, a reminder of the responsibilities each person has towards others.

Can. 223 §2 Ecclesiastical authority is entitled to regulate, in view of the common good, the exercise of rights which are proper to Christ's faithful.

471 This provision is not intended as a basis for the arbitrary use of authority and it should not be understood as such. It is, rather, a limitation upon the exercise of the rights of the faithful intended as a protection against possible abuses arising from the exercise of alleged rights by individuals or groups. Like the previous paragraph, this one should be understood in the light of the Council's teaching: 'man's freedom should be given the fullest possible recognition and should not be curtailed except when and insofar as is necessary'.[6]

---

[1] Cf. ASS 23(1891) 641–670.
[2] Cf. AAS 83(1991) 793–867: Origins 21(1991) 1–24.
[3] Cf. GS 29, 69: Fl I 929–930, 975–976.
[4] Cf. Fl II 695–710.
[5] DH 7: Fl I 805.
[6] DH 7: Fl I 805.

Title II
The Obligations and Rights of the Lay Members of Christ's Faithful

Can. 224 Lay members of Christ's faithful have the obligations and rights enumerated in the canons of this title, in addition to those obligations and rights which are common to all Christ's faithful and those stated in other canons.

Having outlined the fundamental obligations and rights of all Christ's faithful, the Code now focuses on those which belong specifically to lay people (see Can. 207 §1). In addition to the rights and obligations contained in Cann. 208–223, lay people have those mentioned in Cann. 225–231 and elsewhere in the Code, e.g. Can. 759 dealing with the rights and obligations of lay people as witnesses to the good news of the Gospel, Cann. 1282 and 1287 §1 dealing with their obligations as administrators of ecclesiastical goods.

Can. 225 §1 Since lay people, like all Christ's faithful, are deputed to the apostolate by baptism and confirmation, they are bound by the general obligation and they have the right, whether as individuals or in associations, to strive so that the divine message of salvation may be known and accepted by all people throughout the world. This obligation is all the more insistent in circumstances in which only through them are people able to hear the Gospel and to know Christ.

The canon deals with the obligation and the right of all the faithful, by reason of their baptism and confirmation, to engage in the apostolate.[1] They may do so individually or in groups. By referring specifically to the laity, this canon removes two possible misunderstandings: (a) the error of thinking that spiritual tasks within the Church belong only to the clergy; and (b) that of thinking that the renewed role of the laity is simply to undertake tasks which hitherto were done by the clergy. Instead, it states in a general way the form of apostolate which is proper to the laity as such, wherever they may be throughout the world. Moreover, the canon concludes with the further illuminating prescription that this obligation of the laity actively to engage in the Church's apostolate 'is all the more insistent in *circumstances* in which *only through them* are people able to hear the Gospel and to know Christ'. It is significant to note that it speaks of 'circumstances', not countries or regions (such as missionary territories, where the help of lay people is so often widely recognised as indispensable). In fact, the canon highlights not only the obligation but the prerogative of the laity to engage in their privileged position, arising from their baptism and confirmation, of promoting the Gospel and the knowledge of Christ in their ordinary daily avocations – as parents, teachers, factory workers, farmers, academics, doctors, lawyers, politicians, etc. etc.

Can. 225 §2 They have also, according to the condition of each, the special obligation to permeate and perfect the temporal order of things with the spirit of the Gospel. In this way, particularly in conducting secular business and exercising secular functions, they are to give witness to Christ.

---

[1] Cf. LG 33, AG 21: Fl I 390–391, 838–839; Cann. 204, 211, 216.

Book II The People of God

474 A special domain of lay apostolic activity is the order of temporal affairs. Their role in this domain, according to Vat. II, is to renew it and make it increasingly more perfect. The laity 'ought to take on themselves as their distinctive task this renewal of the temporal order. Guided by the light of the Gospel and the mind of the Church, prompted by Christian love, they should act in this domain in a direct way and in their own specific manner ... The temporal order is to be renewed in such a way that, while its own principles are fully respected, it is harmonised with the principles of the Christian life and adapted to the various conditions of times, places and peoples'.[1] The temporal order has not been left to the laity, as if it were in some way a second best, as the Council makes abundantly clear: 'By reason of their *special vocation* it belongs to the laity to seek the kingdom of God by engaging in temporal affairs and directing them according to God's will'.[2]

Can. 226 §1 Those who are married are bound by the special obligation, in accordance with their own vocation, to strive for the building up of the people of God through their marriage and family.

475 Within the broader vocation of the laity lies the more specific vocation of marriage. This canon acknowledges the special duty of married people to work for the building up of the People of God through their marriages and their families. They also have a vital role to play in the structure of civil society in today's world.[3] It is through their marriages that many lay people live out their apostolate in the Church. Vat. II says that the fundamental duty of married people is 'to give clear proof in their lives of the indissolubility and holiness of the marriage bond, to assert with vigour the right and duty of parents and guardians to give their children a christian upbringing, to defend the dignity and legitimate autonomy of the family: this has always been the duty of married persons; today, however, it has become the most important aspect of their apostolate'.[4]

Can. 226 §2 Because they gave life to their children, parents have the most serious obligation and the right to educate them. It is therefore primarily the responsibility of christian parents to ensure the christian education of their children in accordance with the teaching of the Church.

476 This paragraph speaks for itself. Further specific details of this right and obligation are found elsewhere in the Code, e.g., education of children by good example (see Can. 774 §2), choice of the means to promote the catholic education of their children (see Can. 793 §1), sending children to catholic schools (see Can. 798), the duties of parents with regard to baptism (see Cann. 851 §2, 855, 867, 868), to confirmation (see Can. 890), to the Eucharist (see Can. 914). This canon is the foundation on which all the other specific rights and duties rest. The responsibility mentioned here is primarily that of the parents. But it is not exclusive to them. Where necessary, the Church also has the right and duty to provide for the christian education of children.[5] The role of the Church in this regard is detailed in Book III.

Can. 227 To lay members of Christ's faithful belongs the right to have acknowledged as theirs that freedom in secular affairs which is common to all citizens. In using this freedom, however, they are to ensure that their

---

[1] AA 7: Fl I 774.
[2] LG 31: Fl I 389.
[3] Cf. AA 11, GS 47: Fl I 778–780, 949.
[4] AA 11: Fl I 778–779.
[5] Cf. GE 3: Fl I 728–730.

actions are permeated with the spirit of the Gospel, and they are to heed the teaching of the Church proposed by the magisterium, but they must be on guard, in questions of opinion, against proposing their own view as the teaching of the Church.

Lay members of the Church have the same civil rights and freedoms as all citizens. According to this canon, they have the right to have this fact acknowledged by the competent civil authority. Parallel however is an obligation on the part of the laity to exercise their civil liberty in a manner which is in keeping with the Gospel and the official teaching of the Church.

Can. 228 §1 Lay people who are found to be suitable are capable of being admitted by the sacred Pastors to those ecclesiastical offices and functions which, in accordance with the provisions of law, they can discharge.

The question of lay persons exercising ecclesiastical offices is a complex one, which is considered more closely in the context of Cann. 129 and 274 §1. It is sufficient to note here that, so far as the law is concerned, lay persons may be given – or may 'cooperate in' (Can. 129 §2) – certain ecclesiastical offices – with the proviso of course that they 'are found to be suitable', i.e. appropriately qualified for the office in question (see e.g. Cann. 483 §2, 517 §2, 1421 §2, 1428 §2, 1435).

Can. 228 §2 Lay people who are outstanding in the requisite knowledge, prudence and integrity are capable of being experts or advisors, even in councils in accordance with the law, in order to provide assistance to the Pastors of the Church.

The pastors of the Church have much need of the assistance of its lay members as experts or advisors, in a variety of spheres. To carry out this role, the lay people must obviously be 'outstanding in the requisite knowledge, prudence and integrity'. The canon foresees the possibility of such lay experts and advisors assisting the pastors not just as individuals but 'even in councils'. Since no further specification is made in the text, this may be understood as referring to councils or synods at all levels, from the parish finance committee (see Can. 537) to an ecumenical council (see Can. 339 §2).[1]

Both paragraphs of this canon use the technical term 'capable of' (*habiles sunt*) to indicate that the reference is to the capacity, not the strict right, of the laity to participate in the functions in question here. That capacity is activated when they are selected, in accordance with the requirements of the canon: thereafter however they have the same right to be heard as any other lawful participant.

Can. 229 §1 Lay people have the duty and the right to acquire the knowledge of Christian teaching which is appropriate to each one's capacity and condition, so that they may be able to live according to this teaching, to proclaim it and if necessary to defend it, and may be capable of playing their part in the exercise of the apostolate.

If lay people are to exercise the role proper to them in the Church, they must be adequately prepared. The canon encapsulates the teaching of Vat. II in this regard.[2] The

---

[1] Particularly as far as the so-called traditional councils are concerned (diocesan synods, provincial and plenary synods, ecumenical councils), this is a significant change from the position which existed under the 1917 Code in its cc.223, 282, 286, 358, where participation in the work of these bodies was for the most part seen as a solely clerical concern.

[2] Cf. AA 29–30: Fl I 793–796. Cf. also Cann. 793–821 on catholic education.

knowledge to be imparted must be adapted 'to each one's capacity and condition'. It cannot be purely theoretical; it must also be of a practical nature and rooted in experience, since the goals towards which it is directed are practical, i.e. living according to Christian teaching, proclaiming and defending it, and exercising the apostolate.

482 Not only have the laity a right to play this part in the exercise of the apostolate: they equally have a duty to do so. Clearly, the first imperative of that obligation is to conduct their personal life, in all its aspects, in accordance with this Christian teaching; and they should not – whatever the claims for a 'pluralist' society – be afraid or ashamed 'to proclaim it'. Even more, it may at times be necessary that it be the laity who will positively 'defend it', whether in private or even in public. Current society has thrown up an urgent need for an educated and articulate laity who will play a full part in this regard, particularly through the media of newspapers, magazines, radio and television (see also Can. 747 §1).

Can. 229 §2 They also have the right to acquire that fuller knowledge of the sacred sciences which is taught in ecclesiastical universities or faculties or in institutes of religious sciences, attending lectures there and acquiring academic degrees.

483 This paragraph takes the educational rights of the laity a step further: no longer are the sacred sciences to be the domain of clerics alone. Directly related to this right of lay people to study in this field is the responsibility of ecclesiastical authorities to provide the opportunities for them to exercise that right (see Can. 811 §1).

Can. 229 §3 Likewise, assuming that the provisions concerning the requisite suitability have been observed, they are capable of receiving from the lawful ecclesiastical authority a mandate to teach the sacred sciences.

484 The logical conclusion of the admission of lay people to the study of the sacred sciences is that they may also teach them in theological schools and faculties. Two conditions are prescribed: (a) those concerned must have the 'requisite suitability', i.e., they must have obtained the required academic qualifications etc.; (b) they must be given a 'mandate to teach' by the lawful ecclesiastical authority. The significance of this *mandate* will be explored later in Book III (see Can. 812). It is clear that a lay person with the appropriate academic degrees does not thereby have the *right* to teach the sacred sciences: just as for clerics, they may do so *only if* they are duly authorised by the ecclesiastical authority concerned.

Can. 230 §1 Lay men whose age and talents meet the requirements prescribed by decree of the Bishops' Conference, can be given the stable ministry of lector and of acolyte, through the prescribed liturgical rite. This conferral of ministry does not, however, give them a right to sustenance or remuneration from the Church.

§2 Lay people can receive a temporary assignment to the role of lector in liturgical actions. Likewise, all lay people can exercise the roles of commentator, cantor or other such, in accordance with the law.

§3 Where the needs of the Church require and ministers are not available, lay people, even though they are not lectors or acolytes, can supply certain of their functions, that is, exercise the ministry of the word, preside over liturgical prayers, confer baptism and distribute holy communion, in accordance with the provisions of the law.

Part I Christ's Faithful

485 Three different types of lay ministry are dealt with in this canon:
(a) ministries conferred on a stable basis (§1);
(b) ministries where the assignment is temporary (§2);
(c) ministries exercised on a supply basis where ministers are not available (§3).

486 The stable ministries of lector and acolyte are reserved to men, 'in keeping with the venerable tradition of the Church'.[1] This is one of the few canons which makes a distinction between men and women, and it is the only one in this title of the Code. These two stable ministries are not confined solely to liturgical celebrations. It is part of the ministry of the lector to proclaim the word of God, to provide catechetical instruction and to prepare the faithful for the reception of the sacraments.[2] As an extraordinary minister of the Eucharist, the acolyte can be called on to distribute holy communion or to expose the Blessed Sacrament (see Cann. 910 §2, 943). He is also instructed to have a special care for the sick.[3] These ministries are conferred by the Ordinary, i.e., the Bishop and, in clerical religious institutes and clerical societies of apostolic life, of pontifical right, the competent major Superior.[4] Moreover, Bishops' Conferences may request the Holy See to establish other stable ministries for their territories, if they judge these to be necessary or helpful.[5] On 27 October 1977, the Holy See gave permission to Bishops' Conferences to establish such new ministries in their own regions.[6] The present canon makes it clear that, while lector and acolyte are stable ministries, they are exercised on a voluntary basis and do not involve any right to financial support.

487 The stable ministry of lector is conferred in a liturgical rite; the temporary assignment of some person to exercise the role of lector is much less formal. Both men and women may be so assigned. The person concerned may be asked to carry out specific functions on specific occasions, e.g., he or she will be asked to read at Masses on a particular Sunday. The other roles mentioned in this paragraph – 'commentator, cantor or other such' – are also conferred and exercised in this informal manner.[7] However, if the Bishops' Conference considers it useful or necessary, these could be established as stable ministries.

488 This canon's §3 speaks of extraordinary ministries which can be exercised by lay people, either men or women. Two prerequisites are mentioned: the needs of the Church, and the non-availability of ministers. In such circumstances, lay people can be authorised to supply some of the functions of the absent or impeded ministers. The canon does not allow the lay people in question to act solely on their own initiative: since the responsibility for the pastoral welfare of his people falls on the Bishop, it is he

---

[1] MQ n.7: Fl I 431.

[2] Cf. MQ n.5: Fl I 430.

[3] Cf. MQ n.6: Fl I 430–431.

[4] Cf. MQ n.9: Fl I 431.

[5] Cf. MQ: Fl I 428–429. Cf. also AG 15, 17: Fl I 831, 833–834.

[6] Cf. SCSDW letter *Novit profecto* 27.X.1977: DOL n.2966. Cf. LCE Tavola per Paesi e Canoni at Can. 230.

[7] For a number of years after the promulgation of this Code in 1983 there was a divergence both of canonical opinion and of pastoral practice concerning the admissibility or otherwise of female 'altar servers' at Mass. In the context of this Can. 230 §2, the matter was resolved by the reply of PCI 30.VI.1992 (AAS 86(1994) 541), a reply which was followed, at the Pope's request, by a circular letter from SCDW 15.III.1994 (AAS loc. cit. 542): Origins 23(1993-1994) 777–779. In effect, a general permission for the use of female altar servers is granted, subject only to the judgement of an individual Bishop in view of the special circumstances of his diocese.

Book II The People of God

who must decide whether the circumstances warrant such extraordinary ministries. The list of functions mentioned here is not exhaustive; the Code foresees other cases where lay people may act as extraordinary ministers (see e.g. Cann. 517 §2, 1112).

Can. 231 §1 Lay people who are pledged to the special service of the Church, whether permanently or for a time, have a duty to acquire the appropriate formation which their role demands, so that they may conscientiously, earnestly and diligently fulfil this role.

489   The duty mentioned in this paragraph – 'to acquire the appropriate formation which their role demands' – echoes the rights and duties concerning Christian education and theological formation found in Cann. 217 and 229 §1. This underlines the need for those lay people who are engaged in the service of the Church to acquire the necessary knowledge and training so that they may carry out their services in a fitting manner.

Can. 231 §2 Without prejudice to the provisions of Can. 230 §1, they have the right to a worthy remuneration befitting their condition, whereby, with due regard also to the provisions of the civil law, they can becomingly provide for their own needs and the needs of their families. Likewise, they have the right to have their insurance, social security and medical benefits duly safeguarded.

490   Since all Christ's faithful are 'obliged to promote social justice' (Can. 222 §2), it is only right that this concern should be reflected in the Church's legislation. The focus of concern in this paragraph is those lay people who work, full-time or part-time, for the Church. Their right to appropriate remuneration and welfare benefits is fundamental. It is a clear echo of recent papal teaching.[1] Can. 281 provides a similar norm for clerics, and Can. 1274 §3 states that a special fund may be set up in each diocese to provide for such needs.

Title III
Sacred Ministers or Clerics

Chapter I
THE FORMATION OF CLERICS

Can. 232 It is the duty and the proper and exclusive right of the Church to train those who are deputed to sacred ministries.

491   While the 1917 Code in its c.1352 indicated that the Church had the right to train persons for ecclesiastical ministries, the current law adds that it has also the duty to do so. This duty, its spirit and its motivation are spelled out in detail by Vat. II.[2]

---

[1] Cf. Pope John Paul II encl *Laborem exercens* 19: AAS 73(1981) 625–629.

[2] Cf. OT 2–4: Fl I 708–711.

Part I Christ's Faithful

Can. 233 §1 It is the duty of the whole christian community to foster vocations so that the needs of the sacred ministry are sufficiently met in the entire Church. In particular, this duty binds christian families, educators and, in a special way, priests, especially parish priests. Diocesan Bishops, who must show the greatest concern to promote vocations, are to instruct the people entrusted to them on the importance of the sacred ministry and the need for ministers in the Church. They are to encourage and support initiatives to promote vocations, especially movements established for this purpose.

492 The stress laid by this canon on the duty of the whole community to foster vocations represents a significant shift of emphasis from the previous Code. Every community ought to have an interest in and a concern for the fostering of priestly vocations. Particular responsibility for this is placed not just upon the clergy, but upon the wide variety of people mentioned here. The Bishop's duty in this regard is repeated in Can. 385.

Can. 233 §2 Moreover, priests and especially diocesan Bishops are to be solicitous that men of more mature years who believe they are called to the sacred ministries are prudently assisted by word and deed and are duly prepared.

493 A recent feature in the life of the Church is the significant increase in the number of 'men of more mature years' who feel called to a priestly or diaconal ministry. This paragraph, clearly inspired by Vat. II[1] and by a subsequent letter from the Holy See on Vocations of Adults,[2] urges that such later vocations be encouraged, helped and directed by Bishops and by priests; it is clear from the preceding paragraph that 'the whole Christian community' has a distinct role to play in this endeavour.

Can. 234 §1 Minor seminaries and other institutions of a similar nature promote vocations by providing a special religious formation, allied to human and scientific education; where they exist, they are to be retained and fostered. Indeed, where the diocesan Bishop considers it expedient, he is to provide for the establishment of a minor seminary or similar institution.

494 While commending the concept of the minor seminary, Vat. II indicated that these institutions stood in need of renewal. It pointed out e.g. that the way of life in the minor seminary should be suitably adapted to the mentality and development of young people; that there should be close and regular contact between the boys and their families; that courses of studies should be so arranged that pupils might be able to continue them elsewhere should they leave the minor seminary.[3] The canon does not make the minor seminary obligatory; its tone is explanatory rather than prescriptive. Recognising that the effectiveness of a traditional minor seminary (see 1917 Code c.1354 §2) will greatly depend upon local circumstances, the Code commits the matter in great measure to the judgement of the diocesan Bishop.[4]

Can. 234 §2 Unless the circumstances of certain situations suggest otherwise, young men who aspire to the priesthood are to receive that same human and scientific formation which prepares their peers in their region for higher studies.

---

[1] Cf. OT 3: Fl I 710.
[2] SCCE 14.VII.1976: CLD 8 946–955.
[3] Cf. OT 3: Fl I 710.
[4] For an instructive record of the genesis of this canon through the process of revision, cf. RCom SPD 48 at Can. 85 §2; Comm 14(1982) 36 at Can. 85 §2; Comm 14(1982) 160 at Can. 205.

495 This can be seen as an application of the broad principle of Can. 806 §2 (see our commentary) which prescribes that academic standards in catholic schools should be at least as high as those in other schools in the same area. It underlines the need for proper academic and professional standards in the priesthood.

Can. 235 §1 Young men who intend to become priests are to receive the appropriate religious formation and instruction in the duties proper to the priesthood in a major seminary, for the whole of the time of formation or, if in the judgement of the diocesan Bishop, circumstances require it, for at least four years.

496 The obligation of residing in a major seminary is for the precise purpose of the aspirant's spiritual formation: 'the appropriate religious formation and instruction in the duties proper to the priesthood' – whether the concomitant intellectual formation in philosophy and theology takes place within the seminary itself, or elsewhere as e.g. in an approved university. The clear norm of this first paragraph is that aspirants to the priesthood must spend 'the whole of the time of formation', i.e. not fewer than six full years, in a major seminary (see Can. 250). It is only by way of exception that this duration may be reduced, and then only to not fewer than four years. The decision as to whether 'circumstances require it' is to be made by the diocesan Bishop. The canon does *not* say that even in such exceptional circumstances, e.g. in the case of a 'late vocation', four years will always be sufficient.

Can. 235 §2 Those who lawfully reside outside the seminary are to be entrusted by the diocesan Bishop to a devout and suitable priest, who shall ensure that they are carefully formed in the spiritual life and in discipline.

497 Where circumstances, such as health, in the Bishop's judgement exceptionally justify the residence of a candidate for the priesthood outside the seminary, the Bishop is to entrust him to the care of 'a devout and suitable priest' who will oversee his spiritual and disciplinary formation. This is quite a different situation from the laudable practice in some places of assigning candidates, especially towards the latter end of their seminary formation, to a parish in order to perfect their practical pastoral skills. However, even in such a situation the parish priest must bear in mind that the spiritual formation of the candidate is not yet completed and if necessary he should convey his observations in this regard to the diocesan Bishop, either directly or, in an appropriate situation, through the rector or other authority in the seminary.

498 In all of this canon there is a clear implication that the relevant diocesan Bishop must have his hand very much 'on the pulse' of the major seminary under his control. He must make himself personally aware of the spiritual formation which is given there, of the disciplinary regulations which exist to ensure the appropriate formation of the students, of the curriculum and content of each and every one of the teaching courses of the relevant sciences, philosophical and theological. In so far as needs may be, he is obliged to intervene to ensure the necessary standards.

Can. 236 Those who aspire to the permanent diaconate are to be formed in the spiritual life and appropriately instructed in the fulfilment of the duties proper to that order, in accordance with the provisions made by the Bishops' Conference:

   1° young men are to reside for at least three years in a special house, unless the diocesan Bishop for grave reasons decides otherwise;

   2° men of more mature years, whether celibate or married, are to prepare for three years in a manner determined by the same Bishops' Conference.

Vat. II sanctioned the reintroduction of the permanent diaconate in the latin Church,[1] and Pope Paul VI promulgated norms for its restoration in the mp *Sacrum Diaconatus Ordinem* of 18 June 1967.[2] This institution is not however made obligatory for the entire latin Church. The decision as to whether it be formally reintroduced is left to each local Bishops' Conference – to which also is committed the task of prescribing (subject to review by the Holy See: see Can. 455) the appropriate programme of formation.[3]

Within this general ambit, the canon lays down two specific regulations:

(a) 'Young men', i.e. those who are under thirty-five years of age and, it would seem, unmarried, 'are to reside for at least three years in a special house', in which the prescribed programme will be followed. For *grave* reasons the diocesan Bishop may make other arrangements.

(b) Men of more mature years, i.e. thirty-five and more, whether married or not, are to follow such formation programme as may be determined by the Bishops' Conference, not necessarily in a specific house or institute (see Cann. 1031 §2, 1037).

Can. 237 §1 Where it is possible and advisable, each diocese is to have a major seminary; otherwise, students preparing for the sacred ministries are to be sent to the seminary of another diocese, or an inter-diocesan seminary is to be established.

§2 An inter-diocesan seminary may not be established unless the prior approval of the Apostolic See has been obtained, both for the establishment of the seminary and for its statutes. Approval is also required from the Bishops' Conference if the seminary is for the whole of its territory; otherwise, from the Bishops concerned.

Vat. II clearly states that 'major seminaries are necessary for priestly training'.[4] The norm established here is that, 'where it is possible and advisable', each diocese should have its own such seminary.[5] Recognising that local circumstances may make this difficult or even impossible, the canon allows two, but only two, other possibilities: either that the aspirants be sent to the seminary of some other diocese, or that an inter-diocesan seminary be established (unless, of course, one such already exists).

The second paragraph of this canon confines itself to the conditions which must be fulfilled if a new inter-diocesan seminary, be it regional or national, is to be established. The text speaks for itself.

Can. 238 §1 Seminaries which are lawfully established have juridical personality in the Church by virtue of the law itself.

§2 In the conduct of all its affairs, the rector acts in the person of the seminary, unless for certain matters the competent authority has prescribed otherwise.

---

[1] Cf. LG 29, AG 16: Fl I 387, 832–833.

[2] Cf. CLD 6 577–584. This was further developed in the mp *Ad Pascendum* 15.VIII.72: CLD 7 695–698.

[3] For details of those Bishops' Conferences which have so far undertaken this task, cf. LCE Tavola per Paesi e Canoni at Can. 236.

[4] OT 4: Fl I 710.

[5] Cf. RCom SPD 48 at Can. 87; Sch 1980 46 at Can. 208 §1; Comm 14(1982) 160 at Can. 208.

503 For the concept and the implications of 'juridical personality' see Cann. 113–123. No distinction is made here between minor and major seminaries. It is the rector, and he alone, who is the legal representative of the seminary 'in the conduct of all its affairs'. He may of course share some of his responsibility with others (see Can. 239 §3), but it is he who is ultimately responsible. Normally speaking, it would be exceptional for the competent authority to remove certain matters from the rector's competence and reserve them to a higher authority or assign them to someone else. The authority would of course always require that he be kept personally informed.

Can. 239 §1 In all seminaries there is to be a rector who presides over it, a vice-rector, if circumstances warrant this, and a financial administrator. Moreover, if the students follow their studies in the seminary, there are to be professors who teach the various subjects in a manner suitably coordinated between them.

504 The current law has dropped the concept of the two separate boards of government found in c.1359 §1 of the 1917 Code: one for discipline and the other for temporal administration. Although the rector is the one ultimately responsible for the administration of the seminary, the other staff members have their roles to play in assisting him. In addition to the financial administrator or bursar mentioned in §1 the seminary should have its own finance committee, or at least two counsellors, who are to assist in the performance of the administrator's (i.e. the rector's) duties.

505 If the academic training, as well as the spiritual formation, is carried out within the seminary itself, the teaching is to be done in a coordinated fashion. This requires that the professors, under the direction of the rector, should together draw up a programme which would harmonise the various disciplines – a programme which should be submitted to the appropriate diocesan Bishop for his approval.

Can. 239 §2 In every seminary there is to be at least one spiritual director, though the students are also free to approach other priests who have been deputed to this work by the Bishop.

506 This paragraph deals *solely with spiritual direction*, not necessarily with the sacrament of Penance. In each seminary there is to be at least one spiritual director, who will normally be a full-time member of the staff, upon whom falls the responsibility of directing the spiritual programme of the seminary and of being available to those students who may wish to consult him. There may be more than one such who, whether members of the seminary staff or not, are to be specifically 'deputed to this work by the Bishop'. There is no reason of course why a student should not choose any of these directors as his confessor (see Can. 246 §4), but this is a matter which is governed, rather, by the norm of Can. 240 §1. While, in the context of spiritual direction, this §2 refers to 'priests', other possibilities would not appear to be excluded, such as competent and experienced women religious, duly deputed by the Bishop.

Can. 239 §3 The seminary statutes are to determine the manner in which the other moderators, the professors and indeed the students themselves, are to participate in the rector's responsibility, especially in regard to the maintenance of discipline.

507 It is the seminary statutes (see Can. 243) which are to determine the harmonious running of the many aspects necessarily involved in the overall formation of priests, under the direction of the rector. Discipline is highlighted, as is the acquisition of an essential personal sense of responsibility by the students themselves.

Can. 240 §1 Besides ordinary confessors, other confessors are to come regularly to the seminary; while maintaining seminary discipline, the students are always free to approach any confessor, whether inside or outside the seminary.

The law upholds the freedom of the individual in the very important and delicate area of the sacrament of Penance. Confessors, whether designated as 'ordinary' or not, are to come to the seminary *regularly*, so that a choice of confessors is always available within the seminary itself to the students. Moreover, subject only to the necessary requirements of internal discipline, every student is at all times free to approach any confessor of his choice, even outside the seminary. (For a parallel norm in respect of members of religious institutes, see Can. 630.)

Can. 240 §2 In deciding about the admission of students to orders, or their dismissal from the seminary, the vote of the spiritual director and the confessors may never be sought.

The distinction between the internal forum and the external forum is fundamental and must be safeguarded. Anything communicated in the internal forum, whether sacramental (to confessors) or non-sacramental may not be revealed; neither may any knowledge or opinion gained or formed in the course of spiritual direction, even if it does not strictly come within the internal forum.

Can. 241 §1 The diocesan Bishop is to admit to the major seminary only those whose human, moral, spiritual and intellectual gifts, as well as physical and psychological health and right intention, show that they are capable of dedicating themselves permanently to the sacred ministries.

The diocesan Bishop – not the rector – is responsible for admissions to the major seminary. In the case of one who is sent to the major seminary of another diocese, the student's own diocesan Bishop will obviously share this responsibility. In the case of an inter-diocesan seminary, the responsibility is that of the group of Bishops concerned or of the one of their number deputed for this purpose. In all cases, the competent Bishop will of course be guided by those to whom he commits this task, e.g. the rector, the diocesan director of vocations, etc. The advice of the *candidate's own parish priest* should never be omitted or disregarded. The ultimate responsibility, however, remains that of the Bishop.

The criteria for the evaluation of the candidates are listed in the canon, which draws much of its inspiration from Vat. II.[1] It is to be noted that *only* those who meet these requirements are to be admitted. 'Notwithstanding the regrettable shortage of priests, due strictness should always be brought to bear on the *choice* and *testing* of students. God will not allow his Church to lack ministers if the worthy are promoted, and those who are not suited to the ministry are guided with fatherly kindness and in due time to adopt another calling.'[2] A careful balance has to be struck here: while maintaining a strict standard for admission, it must also be borne in mind that one of the main functions of a seminary is to test and foster incipient vocations. An over-exacting standard for admission could be as unproductive as one which, for the sake of increasing numbers, would fall short of that required by the Code.

---

[1] Cf. OT 6: Fl I 712.
[2] OT 6: Fl I 712.

512 The 1917 Code requirement (c.1363 §1) of legitimate birth for those entering a seminary is no longer operative.[1] Among the criteria, the canon refers to the 'psychological health' of the candidate. It does not refer to, though it does not exclude, clinical psychological testing as one of the means to making a judgement on the candidate's psychological health. Experience has proved that an over-reliance on such testing can be perilous; it should never be the sole determinant (see our commentary on Can. 1029). Here again the right to a good reputation and the right to privacy must be respected (see Can. 220).

Can. 241 §2 Before they are accepted, they must submit documentation of their baptism and confirmation, and whatever else is required by the provisions of the Programme of priestly formation.

513 The national programme for priestly formation (see Can. 242 §1) should specify what other documentation is required of candidates. In this, the general guidelines of the *Ratio Fundamentalis Institutionis Sacerdotalis* issued by the Sacred Congregation for Catholic Education should be followed.[2]

Can. 241 §3 If there is question of admitting those who have been dismissed from another seminary or religious institute, there is also required the testimony of the respective superior, especially concerning the reason for their dismissal or departure.

514 Great care must be taken when someone seeks admission to the seminary after having previously been in another seminary or a religious institute. Only his former Superior is in a position to give a full report on the reasons for his departure or dismissal. This report should be communicated directly to the Bishop concerned and obviously must be kept confidential. The obligation of Bishops with regard to this investigation is spelled out in the revised version of the *Ratio fundamentalis*.[3] A similar report is required in the case of such a person seeking admission to religious life (see Can. 645 §2).

515 Of particular concern today is the admission to the seminary of candidates who have received a declaration of the nullity of their marriage, especially if a *vetitum* has been imposed on the man concerned. Even though a civil divorce has been granted in those countries where it is available, a letter from the former spouse stating that she has no objection should be obtained. Furthermore, it should be determined that the candidate was not the cause of the breakup of the marriage and that there is little or no danger of scandal. Finally, before admitting such a person, the Bishop should consider carefully the situation of any children born of the marriage who are still minors.[4] The foregoing observations are made in the light of an experience which would suggest that not infrequently the breakdown of the earlier marriage was attributable to a defect – even if personally faultless – in the husband which would render him, to say the least, an unlikely candidate for the commitment required for the priesthood.

Can. 242 §1 In each country there is to be a Programme of priestly formation. It is to be drawn up by the Bishops' Conference, taking account of the norms issued by the supreme ecclesiastical authority, and it is to be approved

---

[1] In PM Pope Paul VI removed this impediment, provided only that the candidates were not the offspring of adulterous or sacrilegious unions: even this latter restriction no longer operates.

[2] Cf. RF 39: LE IV 5716; RFR 39: LE VI 9086.

[3] Cf. LE VI 9086–9087 n.39.

[4] Many of the main issues raised in this matter are to be found in the exchange of correspondence about a particular case published in CLD 9 611–621.

by the Holy See; moreover, it is to be adapted to new circumstances, likewise with the approval of the Holy See. This Programme is to define the overall principles governing formation in the seminary and the general norms which take account of the pastoral needs of each region or province.

§2 The norms of the Programme mentioned in §1 are to be observed in all seminaries, whether diocesan or inter-diocesan.

In 1970 the Sacred Congregation for Catholic Education issued the *Ratio Fundamentalis Institutionis Sacerdotalis*. This was prepared as a result of a proposal put to the Synod of Bishops in 1967. It contains the fundamental principles and materials to be incorporated into the local programmes which were prescribed by the Council[1] and was thus intended as a kind of blueprint for these programmes. The *Ratio fundamentalis* was updated in the light of the 1983 Code. The revised version was promulgated by the Congregation for Catholic Education on the 19th March 1985. Between 1970 and 1985 several other documents were issued by the Congregation touching on various aspects of priestly formation.[2] Bishops' Conferences are to take account of all these documents in drawing up their own programme. Programmes drawn up before 1985 may well need revision and updating in the light of these documents and of the revised *Ratio fundamentalis*. 516

The norms contained in any such programme apply to all the seminaries within the territory of the respective Bishops' Conference. Each religious institute is also to have its own particular programme of studies for those who are to be ordained (see Can. 659 §3). 517

Can. 243 In addition, each seminary is to have its own rule, approved by the diocesan Bishop or, in the case of an inter-diocesan seminary, by the Bishops concerned. In this, the norms of the Programme of priestly formation are to be adapted to the particular circumstances and developed in greater detail, especially on points of discipline affecting the daily life of the students and the good order of the entire seminary.

This seminary rule consists of specific regulations designed to implement the broader general principles of the *Ratio fundamentalis* and the national programme of priestly formation. It will obviously vary from seminary to seminary, depending on particular local circumstances, but an unchangeable element must always be a clear and firm insistence on the fundamental requirement of '*discipline* affecting the daily life of the students and the good order of the entire seminary'. 518

Can. 244 The spiritual formation and the doctrinal instruction of the students in a seminary are to be harmoniously blended. They are to be so planned that the students, each according to his talents, simultaneously develop the requisite human maturity and acquire the spirit of the Gospel and a close relationship with Christ.

---

[1] Cf. OT 1: Fl I 708.

[2] Cf. e.g. lit circ on the teaching of philosophy in seminaries 20.I.1972: LE IV 6214–6219; *Orientamenti educativi per la formazione al celibato sacerdotale* 11.IV.1974: LE VI 7563–7599; lit circ on the teaching of Canon Law to candidates for the priesthood 2.IV.1975: LE V 7012–7016: CLD 8 955–963; *La formazione teologica di futuri sacerdoti* 22.II.1976: LE V 7155–7175: Origins 6(1976–1977) 173–190; instr on liturgical formation in seminaries 3.VI.1979: LE VI 7764–7785: CLD 9 821–871; lit circ on spiritual formation in seminaries 6.I.1980: LE 7857–7867: CLD 9 871–894.

519 The integration of the spiritual formation and doctrinal instruction of candidates for the priesthood was called for by Vat. II.[1] Underlying this canon is the notion that education in the seminary must lead to growth not only in the spheres of the spiritual and intellectual life but also in ordinary human development or maturity. Even more fundamentally underlying it is the aim that each student would 'acquire the spirit of the Gospel and *a close relationship with Christ*' – a relationship which, in the last analysis, can be established only through personal prayer.

Can. 245 §1 Through their spiritual formation students are to be fitted for the fruitful exercise of the pastoral ministry, and are to be inculcated with a sense of mission. They are to learn that a ministry which is always exercised with lively faith and charity contributes effectively to their personal sanctification. They are to learn to cultivate those virtues which are highly valued in human relationships, in such a way that they can arrive at an appropriate harmony between human and supernatural values.

520 This canon outlines the principal thrusts of spiritual formation. In effect, it is a summary of the thinking of Vat. II about the spiritual formation of future priests[2] – a thinking which is very helpfully developed by the Congregation for Catholic Education in its circular letter on this topic of the 6th January 1980, already cited above.

Can. 245 §2 Students are to be so trained that, filled with love for Christ's Church, they are linked to the Roman Pontiff, the successor of Peter, in humble and filial charity, to their own Bishop as his faithful co-workers, and to their brethren in friendly cooperation. Through the common life in the seminary, and by developing relationships of friendship and of association with others, they are to be prepared for the fraternal unity of the diocesan *presbyterium*, in whose service of the Church they will share.

521 The priest is not someone who stands alone: on the contrary – candidates in seminaries are to be educated to develop and respect the bonds which will unite them to others in the Church. Love of the Church, respect for the Pope and the diocesan Bishop ought to be actively fostered during the period of formation. At the same time, the law positively encourages friendship as a sound preparation for the apostolate. Development of mature human relationships is of the utmost importance if the fraternal unity of the *presbyterium* is to become a living reality.

Can. 246 §1 The celebration of the Eucharist is to be the centre of the whole life of the seminary, so that the students, participating in the very charity of Christ, may daily draw strength of soul for their apostolic labour and for their spiritual life particularly from this richest of sources.

§2 They are to be formed in the celebration of the liturgy of the hours, by which the ministers of God, in the name of the Church, intercede with Him for all the people entrusted to them, and indeed for the whole world.

§3 Devotion to the Blessed Virgin Mary, including the rosary, mental prayer and other exercises of piety are to be fostered, so that the students may acquire the spirit of prayer and be strengthened in their vocation.

§4 The students are to become accustomed to approach the sacrament of penance frequently. It is recommended that each should have a director

---

[1] Cf. OT 4, 12: Fl I 711, 717.
[2] Cf. OT 8–9, 11: Fl I 713–715, 716; PO 3, 8–9: Fl I 866–868, 878–881.

of his spiritual life, freely chosen, to whom he can trustfully reveal his conscience.

§5 Each year the students are to make a spiritual retreat.

This canon may very well be considered as a convenient *vade mecum* for those seminarians – and their Superiors – who are seriously concerned with what should be no less than the minimum necessary for their development into that spiritual life upon which their future as priests will depend:

- the celebration of the Eucharist must be the centre of their lives – a theme found throughout the Code (see e.g. Cann. 528 §2, 608, 719 §2, 899, 904, 909, etc.). An inevitable consequence follows: the daily attendance at Mass must – apart from exceptional circumstances, such as illness, a necessary absence or the like – be an essential feature of every seminarian's formation (§1).
- closely related to the seminarian's understanding of the Eucharistic sacrifice must be his understanding of the consequent need, on his part, officially to pray 'in the name of the Church', so that the fruits of the Incarnation may become available to all the people entrusted to him in his future ministry – 'and indeed for the whole world'. It is here that 'the liturgy of the hours' becomes a pivotal part of the prayer-life of a cleric (§2; see Can. 276 §2 3°), for which accordingly every seminarian must be appropriately formed.[1]
- the traditional forms of prayer and devotion mentioned in §3 were deliberately inserted by the Revision Commission, to highlight their enduring importance in that formation which is designed to ensure that the students will 'acquire *the spirit of prayer* and (thereby) be strengthened in their vocation'.[2]
- frequent approach to the sacrament of Penance (§4) is another theme which runs through the Code in the context of priestly and religious training (see e.g. Cann. 276 §2 5°, 528 §2, 664, 719 §3; in the matter of a student having free recourse to a spiritual director, who need not be his confessor, see our commentary on Can. 239 §2).
- in its §5 this canon echoes the *Ratio fundamentalis* in prescribing an annual retreat for all seminarians;[3] the details – duration, content, etc. – are not determined: those are left to be specified in the national programme or in the rule of the seminary itself, but what is manifestly required is that any such retreat be a total withdrawal from the ordinary day-to-day concerns and preoccupations, and be devoted, in a conducive environment, to prayer, to contemplation and to reflection.

Can. 247 §1 By appropriate instruction they are to be prepared to observe celibacy and learn to hold it in honour as a special gift of God.

Can. 277 §1 affirms the cleric's obligation to perfect and perpetual continence. The present canon stresses the need for preparation for this commitment during the period of formation and education. This instruction must be one of the major concerns of those charged with this formation.[4] This paragraph is based on the teaching of Vat. II which points out that celibacy is not just a legal obligation but also a 'precious gift of God which they should ask for humbly and to which they should hasten to respond freely and generously, under the inspiration and with the assistance of the Holy Spirit'.[5]

---

[1] Cf. RF n.53: LE IV 5721; RFR n.53: LE VI 9092.
[2] Cf. Comm 14(1982) 48 at Can. 98 §3.
[3] Cf. RF n.56: LE IV 5722.
[4] Detailed guidelines for this education and preparation can be found in the instr from SCCE 11.IV.1974 *Orientamenti educativi per la formazione al celibato sacerdotale*: LE IV 7563–7599.
[5] OT 10: Fl I 715; cf. also PO 16: Fl I 892–894, and Can. 277 §1.

Can. 247 §2 The students are to be given all the requisite knowledge concerning the duties and burdens which are proper to the sacred ministers of the Church, concealing none of the difficulties of the priestly life.

524 Careful thought must be given by those in charge of seminaries as to how an appropriate education in all the duties and responsibilities of the clerical state should be given. There must be a clear and unambiguous exposition of the various difficulties that have to be faced in clerical life, with particular reference to difficulties that are likely to be encountered in the students' own social and cultural milieu. Relevant in this context are two well-known occasions recorded in the Gospels. The rich man who, having professed to Jesus that he had kept all the commandments since he was a boy, was faced with the request that there was one thing further he must do: 'sell all you have and give to the poor ... (and) then come and follow me'; he was not prepared to make that commitment, and so he walked sadly away (see Lk 18:18–22). By contrast, following the multiplication of the few loaves which thereby were able to feed some five thousand people, Jesus took occasion at Capernaum to speak to the crowds who had sought him out and to the apostles, in what has become the renowned eucharistic discourse: in this he insisted that, to have eternal life, his followers must 'eat the flesh of the Son of Man and drink his blood' – a proposition which many of those present found it impossible to accept and accordingly 'many of his disciples broke away and would not remain in his company any longer'. Turning to his twelve apostles Jesus asked: 'Do you too want to leave me'? Faced with that challenge, the apostles, through Simon Peter, made their own very deliberate decision: they decided to stay (see Jn 6:59–69). It is such a decision which every seminarian must be made to face, in whatever area of his life may be relevant.

Can. 248 The doctrinal formation given is to be so directed that the students may acquire a wide and solid teaching in the sacred sciences, together with a general culture which is appropriate to the needs of place and time. As a result, with their own faith founded on and nourished by this teaching, they ought to be able properly to proclaim the Gospel to the people of their own time, in a fashion suited to the manner of the people's thinking.

525 The text of this canon is based on the *Ratio fundamentalis*.[1] The doctrinal formation of the student has a twofold objective: to nourish and strengthen his own faith, and to enable him to proclaim the Gospel to the people of his own time. In all of this, attention is to be given to the question of culture. The student should be educated not only in the culture of the place where he trains, but also in that of the place where he is going to minister. This will enable him to speak 'in a fashion suited to the manner of the people's thinking'.[2]

Can. 249 The Programme of priestly formation is to provide that the students are not only taught their native language accurately, but are also well versed in latin, and have a suitable knowledge of other languages which would appear to be necessary or useful for their formation or for the exercise of their pastoral ministry.

526 The requirement that a student know both his own language and latin was part of the 1917 Code's c.1364 2°. Since then, the actual use and knowledge of latin in the Church has significantly declined, in spite of many efforts on the part of Popes and

---

[1] Cf. LE IV 5723. This is repeated in RFR: LE VI 9094.
[2] Cf. OT 13–17, GS 58, 62, AG 16: Fl I 717–721, 962–963, 966–968, 831–833.

Part I Christ's Faithful

Vat. II to promote it.[1] This canon still requires that students for the sacred ministries should be 'well versed in latin' – a matter which should seriously be taken in hand by every Bishop involved in seminary training. Experience has proved that devoted students are willing and able to take up this challenge. Without a knowledge of latin, many of the sources used in theological research remain beyond the access of students. A knowledge of other languages is also required: their own language and others which appear 'to be necessary or useful for their formation or for the exercise of their pastoral ministry'. Much will depend here on the particular ministry to which the seminarian appears to be destined. The overall thrust of this canon clearly requires that a training in the appropriate language or languages be an integral part of seminary formation. The *Ratio fundamentalis* states that these language studies should precede or be combined with philosophical studies.[2]

Can. 250 The philosophical and theological studies which are organised in the seminary itself may be conducted either in succession or conjointly, in accordance with the Programme of priestly formation. These studies are to take at least six full years, in such a way that the time given to philosophical studies amounts to two full years and that allotted to theological studies to four full years.

At least six full years of studies are required for education to the priesthood. The canon shows that these studies can be arranged in two ways: either by keeping philosophy and theology apart or by integrating the philosophy with theology. Whichever manner of teaching is chosen in a seminary, care must be taken to ensure that the proportion of time allotted to philosophical and theological studies is in accord with the prescriptions of this canon. Formerly dispensation from this six-year programme was reserved to the Holy See.[3] Although this reservation does not appear in the Code, it is difficult to see how, apart from very exceptional circumstances, it could be of service either to the student or to those to whom he is to minister to reduce the time of his preparation to less than the minimum required by this canon. 527

Can. 251 Philosophical formation must be based on the philosophical heritage that is perennially valid, and it is also to take account of philosophical investigations over the course of time. It is to be so given that it furthers the human formation of the students, sharpens their mental edge and makes them more fitted to engage in theological studies.

This canon summarises Vat. II's approach to the study of philosophy.[4] Details of the contents and method are set out in the *Ratio fundamentalis*[5] and in the circular letter from the Congregation for Catholic Education of 20 Jan. 1972 dealing with the teaching of philosophy in seminaries.[6] 528

The phrase 'the philosophical heritage that is perennially valid' comes from Vat. II.[7] In response to a query about the meaning of the phrase, issued on 20.XII.1965, the 529

---

[1] Cf. Pope John XXIII ap con *Veterum Sapientia* 22.II.1962: CLD 5 642–681; Pope Paul VI mp *Studia latinitatis* 22.II.1964: AAS 56(1964) 225–231; OT 13: Fl I 717.
[2] Cf. RF n.66: LE VI 9096.
[3] EM IX 7: LE III 4992: AAS 58 (1966) 470.
[4] Cf. OT 13: Fl I 718–719.
[5] Nn.70–75: LE VI 9097–9098.
[6] Cf. LE IV 6214–6219.
[7] OT 15: Fl I 718.

Congregation for Seminaries and Universities stated that it refers to 'the principles of St Thomas'.[1] This was the understanding of the words when Pope Pius XII used them in his encyclical *Humani Generis*.[2] The Revision Commission decided not to mention Thomistic philosophy explicitly, since it regarded it as included in the phrase itself.[3] For all that, philosophical formation must not be taken up exclusively with this heritage: it must also take into account 'philosophical investigations over the course of time'.

Can. 252 §1 Theological formation, given in the light of faith and under the guidance of the magisterium, is to be imparted in such a way that the students learn the whole of catholic teaching, based on divine Revelation, that they make it a nourishment of their own spiritual lives, and that in the exercise of the ministry they may be able properly to proclaim and defend it.

§2 Students are to be instructed with special care in sacred Scripture, so that they may acquire an insight into the whole of sacred Scripture.

§3 Lectures are to be given in dogmatic theology, based always on the written word of God and on sacred Tradition; through them the students are to learn to penetrate more deeply into the mysteries of salvation, with St Thomas in particular as their teacher. Lectures are also to be given in moral and pastoral theology, canon law, liturgy, ecclesiastical history, and other auxiliary and special disciplines, in accordance with the provision of the Programme of priestly formation.

530 This canon sketches out the method and contents of theological formation in a seminary. The method and scope are outlined in §1, which paraphrases Vat. II.[4] The second paragraph highlights the special position of sacred Scripture in this formation, while the third is a compendium of the various subjects to be covered in a seminary's theology course. These parts of the course are explained further in the 1976 Instruction on the theological formation of candidates for the priesthood.[5] Details of the exact content and method are left to each Programme for Priestly Formation. The explicit mention of St Thomas in §3 was made at the request of several consulting bodies.[6]

Can. 253 §1 The Bishops concerned are to appoint as teachers in philosophical, theological and juridical subjects only those who are of outstanding virtue and have a doctorate or a licentiate from a university or faculty recognised by the Holy See.

531 Those only may be appointed to teach in seminaries who: (a) are of outstanding virtue, i.e. well-developed as human beings and as christians; (b) have the requisite academic qualification, namely either 'a doctorate or a licentiate from a university or faculty recognised by the Holy See' i.e. one governed by the norms of Cann. 816–817. While the first of those two conditions speaks for itself, the second represents a distinctly more exacting requirement in respect of academic qualification than did that of the 1917 Code in its c.1366 §1. Despite some suggestions to the contrary,

---

[1] Cf. CLD 6 252.

[2] Cf. AAS 42(1950) 561.

[3] Cf. Comm 14(1982) 52 at Can. 104.

[4] Cf. OT 16: Fl I 719.

[5] SCCE instr 22.II.1976 especially nn.78–115: LE V 7167–7173.

[6] Cf. Comm 14(1982) 165 at Can. 223 §3.

the Revision Commission took a firm stance on this matter, allowing only that exceptional cases could be dealt with by way of dispensation and accordingly judged on their merits in each situation.[1] Nothing in the text of this §1 would exclude the appointment of qualified lay people as teachers in seminaries.

Can. 253 §2 Care is to be taken that different professors are appointed for sacred Scripture, dogmatic theology, moral theology, liturgy, philosophy, canon law and church history, and for other disciplines which are to be taught by their own distinctive methods.

The 1917 Code in its c.1366 §3 listed four subjects which each required a separate professor: sacred Scripture, dogmatic theology, moral theology and church history. The present canon explicitly adds three further such subjects – liturgy, philosophy and canon law – and provides also for those other disciplines 'which are to be taught by their own distinctive methods'. The reasoning behind this norm is clear: teachers should not be overburdened but should be able to maintain the highest possible standards in their proper subject. It must be acknowledged that, while this is a goal to which ecclesiastical authority is positively obliged to strive (*'curetur'*), it may not always in practice be possible of immediate achievement. In some situations the solution may well be through the use or establishment of an inter-diocesan seminary (see Cann. 237, 242 §2, 243).

Can. 253 §3 A professor who seriously fails in his or her duty is to be removed by the authority mentioned in §1.

In giving the reason for the removal of a professor in the broadest of terms – serious failure in his or her duty – the law leaves a wide margin of discretion to the Bishop or Bishops concerned. This authority will determine in a particular case if the professor has seriously failed. The Revision Commission made it abundantly clear that a professor who is dismissed in this way has the right of recourse against the decree of removal:[2] the procedure for recourse is contained in Cann. 1732–1739. Before issuing a decree of removal (see Cann. 192–193), the competent authority should always have due regard to the provisions of the relevant civil law.

Can. 254 §1 In their lectures, the professors are to be continuously attentive to the intimate unity and harmony of the entire doctrine of faith, so that the students are aware that they are learning one science. To ensure this, there is to be someone in the seminary who is in charge of the overall organisation of studies.

§2 The students are to be taught in such a way that they themselves are enabled to research various questions by their own appropriate investigations and in a scientific manner. There are, therefore, to be assignments in which, under the guidance of the professors, the students learn to work out certain subjects by their own efforts.

This canon, which is so rich in its own terms, is specifically aimed at providing an effective and integrated education for the seminarians. To this end:

(a) there is in each seminary to be a director/prefect/dean of studies in charge of the overall coordination of teaching;

---

[1] Cf. Comm 14(1982) 166 at Can. 244.
[2] Cf. Comm 14(1982) 55 at Can. 106 §3.

Book II The People of God

(b) the students themselves are to be trained to acquire a truly scientific approach to their sacred studies – the object being that they would approach these studies with interested and enquiring minds so that they would 'learn to work out *certain* subjects by their own efforts'.

The canon makes it clear that this approach, proposed by Vat. II and incorporated in the *Ratio fundamentalis*,[1] is to be governed by two basic principles, namely (i) that both professors and students 'are to be continuously attentive to the intimate unity and harmony of the entire doctrine of faith', and (ii) that the research by the seminarians must always remain 'under the guidance of the professors'. These principles place as much an obligation on the professors as they do on the students.

Can. 255 Although the whole formation of students in the seminary has a pastoral purpose, a specifically pastoral formation is also to be provided there; in this the students are to learn the principles and the techniques which, according to the needs of place and time, are relevant to the ministry of teaching, sanctifying and ruling the people of God.

535 This is a significant addition to the law. It provides explicitly for pastoral training, one of the major thrusts of Vat. II.[2] The provision for 'pastoral training' in c.1365 §3 of the 1917 Code was both theoretical and limited. The present norm prescribes practical training on a much broader scale. The *Ratio fundamentalis* spells out in more detail what is to be done in this sphere (in the national programmes and in seminary rules).[3] In a note to the *Ratio* the Congregation explains that students should by degrees acquire a pastoral attitude of mind and develop in themselves, along with a theoretical knowledge of the subject, those practical abilities which will enable them to bring Christ's grace and teaching to people of every state and condition.[4]

Can. 256 §1 Students are to be carefully instructed in whatever especially pertains to the sacred ministry, particularly in catechetics and homiletics, in divine worship and in a special way in the celebration of the sacraments, in dealing with people, including non-catholics and unbelievers, in parish administration and in the fulfilment of other tasks.

§2 The students are to be instructed about the needs of the universal Church, so that they may have a solicitude for encouraging vocations, for missionary and ecumenical questions, and for other pressing matters, including social problems.

536 This canon spells out the areas of *ministry* in which seminarians are to be particularly trained (§1). These areas were identified by Vat. II and repeated in the *Ratio fundamentalis*.[5] Moreover, the students' view of ministry is to extend beyond their immediate environment, so that it will include 'the needs of the universal Church', with the consequences detailed in §2. In this way 'they will be imbued with a truly catholic spirit'[6] and be prepared to instil a similar concern for the whole Church in the hearts of the faithful (see Can. 529 §2).

---

[1] Cf. OT 5, 17: Fl I 711–712, 721; RF nn.90–91: LE VI 9105–9106.
[2] Cf. OT 19–21: Fl I 721–723.
[3] Cf. RF nn.94–99: LE VI 9106–9108.
[4] Cf. RF note 217: LE VI 9106.
[5] Cf. OT 19: Fl I 721–722; RF nn.94–95: LE VI 9106–9107.
[6] RF n.96: LE VI 9107.

Can. 257 §1 The formation of students is to ensure that they are concerned not only for the particular Church in which they are incardinated, but also for the universal Church, and that they are ready to devote themselves to particular Churches which are beset by grave needs.

§2 The diocesan Bishop is to ensure that clerics who intend to move from their own particular Church to a particular church in another region, are suitably prepared to exercise the sacred ministry there, that is, that they learn the language of the region, and have an understanding of its institutions, social conditions, usages and customs.

537 The text of both paragraphs of this canon is taken almost word-for-word from the renowned mp *Ecclesiae Sanctae* of Pope Paul VI in 1966,[1] a document which was issued to give effect to four decrees of Vat. II.[2] In speaking of the 'particular Church' (rather than the 'diocese', as the mp does) the canon reflects the influence of the ecclesiology of Vat. II.

538 The first paragraph describes one of the basic goals of the whole seminary formation programme: to make students so aware of the needs both of the local and of the universal Church that they are motivated, each according to his own inclination and capacity, to serve those needs. The second paragraph, a consequence of the first, points to a phenomenon which has become a feature of apostolic ministry in recent years – itself reflecting an age-old tradition in the Church: namely the practice whereby some priests, ordained for and incardinated into their own particular Church, would wish to offer themselves to serve, at least for a period of years, the needs of other dioceses or regions 'which are beset by grave needs': the experience in respect of various regions of South America is a current example. In so far as a priest may wish to offer himself for this ministry, and provided he is considered suitable for the task, he is to be facilitated by his diocesan Bishop, primarily by being 'suitably prepared to exercise the sacred ministry there', in accordance with the terms set out in this §2.

Can. 258 In order that the students may also by practice learn the art of exercising the apostolate, they are in the course of their studies, and especially during holiday time, to be initiated into pastoral practice by suitable assignments, always under the supervision of an experienced priest. These assignments, appropriate to the age of the student and the conditions of the place, are to be determined by the Ordinary.

539 Can. 255 enunciates the principle that in the course of seminary formation there should be specific and practical training for pastoral ministry. The present canon lays down as a norm that students are not only to *learn about* pastoral practice but are actually to *learn it*, by means of suitable assignments. These are to take place during the course of studies and especially during holiday time. The *Ratio fundamentalis* gives some examples of what the work might be: teaching catechism, taking an active part in liturgical celebrations in the parish, visiting the sick, the poor and the imprisoned, helping priests engaged in ministry to young people and workers, etc.[3] The Code and the *Ratio* insist that these apostolic exercises must be properly supervised, by 'an experienced priest' who will obviously be required to inform the diocesan Bishop accordingly.

---

[1] Cf. ES I 3 (1–3): Fl I 593–594.
[2] I.e. CD, PO, AGD, PC.
[3] Cf. RF n.98: LE VI 9108.

Book II The People of God

Can. 259 §1 It belongs to the diocesan Bishop or, in the case of an inter-diocesan seminary, to the Bishops concerned to determine those matters which concern the overall control and administration of the seminary.

§2 The diocesan Bishop or, in the case of an inter-diocesan seminary, the Bishops concerned, are frequently to visit the seminary in person. They are to oversee the formation of their students, and the philosophical and theological instruction given in the seminary. They are to inform themselves about the vocation, character, piety and progress of the students, with a view particularly to the conferring of sacred orders.

540 While the day-to-day life of a seminary will be supervised by its rector, this canon makes it clear that the ultimate responsibility for its overall control and administration rests with the Bishop or Bishops concerned: §2 is particularly significant in this regard. It is simply not sufficient for any Bishop, or number of Bishops, to appoint to the seminary a rector and other staff and, by that fact alone, wholly to entrust to them the formation of the students. On the contrary, the Bishop is seriously obliged '*frequently* to visit the seminary in person', thus (and otherwise) to inform himself, at first hand, of:

(a) the spiritual formation given to the students;
(b) the level of discipline exercised in their regard;
(c) the precise philosophical and theological curriculum employed, including details of the number of lectures given in each discipline, the text-books used, etc.
(d) 'the vocation, character, piety and progress' of each student, knowing that it is he alone who will ultimately be responsible for 'the conferring of sacred orders' on these students.

This canon clearly places a very grave personal obligation on the Bishop, or Bishops, involved.

Can. 260 In the fulfilment of their duties, all must obey the rector, who is responsible for the day-to-day direction of the seminary, in accordance with the norms of the Programme of priestly formation and the rule of the seminary.

541 Besides taking care of the day-to-day running of the seminary, it is the rector's responsibility to implement the various prescriptions of the law, i.e. the national programme for priestly formation and the local seminary rules. The *Ratio fundamentalis* sees him as the coordinator of the other staff members and the one who is charged with maintaining a close cooperation between them.[1] Obedience to the rector is a major factor in the smooth running of the seminary: hence the necessity for great care and sensitivity in the selection and appointment of a seminary rector.

Can. 261 §1 The rector of the seminary is to ensure that the students faithfully observe the norms of the Programme of priestly formation and the rule of the seminary; under his authority, and according to their different positions, the moderators and professors have the same responsibility.

§2 The rector of the seminary and the director of studies are to see to it that the professors discharge their duties properly, in accordance with the provisions of the Programme of priestly formation and the rule of the seminary.

---

[1] Cf. RF n.29: LE VI 9084.

The rector is given a twofold responsibility: (a) supervision of the students' observance of the legal norms (§1); (b) supervision of the professors' discharge of their duties (§2). Each of these responsibilities is shared: the first is shared in a subordinate fashion, with the rest of the staff members and professors each according to his or her position; the second is shared with the director of studies who is in charge of the overall organisation of studies in the seminary (see Can. 254 §1).

Can. 262 The seminary is to be exempt from parochial governance. For all those in the seminary, the function of the parish priest is to be discharged by the rector of the seminary or his delegate, with the exception of matters concerning marriage and without prejudice to the provisions of Can. 985.

This canon repeats the substance of c.1368 of the 1917 Code. The seminary rector has the basic rights and duties of a parish priest, as outlined in Can. 530 and elsewhere in the Code: he may e.g. dispense from the obligation of a holy day or a day of penance (see Can. 1245), dispense from an oath or a vow (see Cann. 1196, 1203), celebrate a funeral in the church or oratory attached to the seminary (see Can. 1177 §2), etc. However, two exceptions are mentioned: (a) the seminary rector does not have the functions or powers of a parish priest insofar as marriage is concerned: in effect, the prescribed preparation for marriage (see Cann. 1063–1072) and the requisite formal assistance at a marriage with its consequent implications (see Cann. 1108–1123); (b) the seminary rector may not hear the confessions of the students resident in the same house 'unless in individual instances the students of their own accord request it' (Can. 985).

Can. 263 The diocesan Bishop must ensure that the building and maintenance of the seminary, the support of the students, the remuneration of the teachers and the other needs of the seminary are provided for. In an interdiocesan seminary this responsibility devolves upon the Bishops concerned, each to the extent allotted by their common agreement.

Part of the responsibility entrusted to Bishops by Can. 259 §1 is that of providing sufficient finances to the seminary. The present canon indicates in broad terms where such money should be directed. In its discussions on the text, the Revision Commission pointed out that, in the case of an inter-diocesan seminary, the criterion for determining each Bishop's contribution should not simply be the number of students from his diocese in the seminary. Since there can be financially secure dioceses which may have few seminarians, and poor dioceses with many, account must be taken of the actual financial resources available to each diocese.[1]

Can. 264 §1 To provide for the needs of the seminary, the Bishop can, apart from the collection mentioned in Can. 1266, impose a levy in the diocese.

§2 Every ecclesiastical juridical person is subject to the levy for the seminary, including even private juridical persons, which have an establishment in the diocese. Exception is made for those whole sole support comes from alms, or in which there is actually present a college of students or of teachers for furthering the common good of the Church. This levy should be general, proportionate to the revenues of those who are subject to it, and calculated according to the needs of the seminary.

To meet the financial needs of the seminary for which he is, solely or jointly, responsible the Bishop has a twofold source of revenue:

---

[1] Cf. Comm 14(1982) 60 at Can. 116 a.

(a) He may order a special collection to be taken up throughout the diocese, in accordance with Can. 1266;

(b) He may impose a levy in the diocese. The subjects of this levy are all public and private juridical persons which have an establishment in the diocese.[1] Exempt from this levy are juridical persons whose entire support depends on alms (e.g. a contemplative monastery), and juridical persons which have attached a college of students or of teachers whose aim is to further the common good of the Church (e.g. a house, be it of formation or of higher studies, run by religious).

546 This seminary levy should be:

(a) *general*, i.e. imposed upon *all* the juridical persons mentioned, subject only to the exceptions mentioned above;

(b) *proportionate*, i.e. based on a percentage of the revenue of each individual juridical person;

(c) *determined*, i.e. 'calculated according to the needs of the seminary': if there is no real need, no such levy would be permissible.

This levy is not imposed on physical persons, and it is to be distinguished from the levy mentioned in Can. 1263.

Chapter II
THE ENROLMENT OR INCARDINATION OF CLERICS

Can. 265 Every cleric must be incardinated in a particular Church or in a personal prelature, or in an institute of consecrated life or a society which has this faculty: accordingly, acephalous or 'wandering' clergy are by no means to be allowed.

547 Incardination is one of the oldest juridical institutions in the Church. Its roots lie in the principle of not ordaining any cleric except for the service of a determined church. The Councils of Nicaea and Chalcedon outlawed the practice of 'absolute ordinations'; the Council of Trent confirmed this condemnation. The purpose of incardination is threefold:

(a) it is *pastoral*, i.e. a cleric is ordained for the service of the particular church to which he thereby belongs;

(b) it constitutes an effective structure within the Church for maintaining *discipline*, establishing a bond between the cleric and the competent ecclesiastical authority;

(c) it provides the cleric with a *guarantee* that his rights will be safeguarded, particularly his right to employment and adequate sustenance.

548 A cleric may be incardinated into one of the juridical entities mentioned in the canon:

(a) a particular Church, as defined in Can. 368 (see Can. 381 §2);

(b) a personal prelature, as set out in Can. 294;

(c) an institute of consecrated life, which will mean either a religious institute (see Can. 266 §2) or, under special circumstances, a secular institute (see Can. 266 §3).

(d) a clerical society of apostolic life (see Cann. 266 §2, 736 §1).

---

[1] Cf. Cann. 115–116 on the nature of public and private juridical persons.

Can. 266 §1 By the reception of the diaconate a person becomes a cleric, and is incardinated in the particular Church or personal Prelature for whose service he is ordained.

§2 A member who is perpetually professed in a religious institute, or who is definitively incorporated into a clerical society of apostolic life, is by the reception of the diaconate incardinated as a cleric in that institute or society unless, in the case of a society, the constitutions determine otherwise.

§3 A member of a secular institute is by the reception of the diaconate incardinated into the particular Church for whose service he was ordained, unless by virtue of a concession of the Apostolic See he is incardinated into the institute itself.

According to c.111 §2 of the 1917 Code, a person became a cleric and was incardinated by the reception of first tonsure. In 1972 Pope Paul VI suppressed the tonsure and joined entrance into the clerical state to the diaconate.[1] This was further elaborated in his other document of the same day.[2] The present canon simply codifies the new norm: by reception of the diaconate (a) a person becomes a cleric; (b) the cleric is incardinated.

The three paragraphs of the canon make explicit where individual clerics will be incardinated:

(a) a secular or diocesan cleric is incardinated in the particular Church for whose service he is ordained;

(b) a cleric belonging to a personal Prelature is incardinated in that Prelature;

(c) a perpetually professed member of a religious institute is incardinated as a cleric in that institute; he is thus bound to the institute by a twofold bond – by virtue of his vows and by incardination;

(d) a definitively incorporated member of a clerical society of apostolic life is incardinated as a cleric in that society; again he has a twofold bond to the society: the canon, however, foresees that the constitutions of the society might determine otherwise;

(e) by contrast, a member of a secular institute is incardinated into the particular Church for whose service he is ordained, unless the Apostolic See has authorised incardination into the institute.

Wherever the cleric is incardinated, the incardination is definitive. Unless he loses the clerical state (see Can. 290), a cleric remains always subject to the ecclesiastical authority of his place or institute of incardination.

Can. 267 §1 To be validly incardinated in another particular Church, a cleric who is already incardinated must obtain a letter of excardination signed by the diocesan Bishop, and in the same way a letter of incardination signed by the diocesan Bishop of the particular Church in which he wishes to be incardinated.

§2 Excardination granted in this way does not take effect until incardination is obtained in the other particular Church.

A cleric incardinated in one particular Church can seek to be incardinated in another. This canon details the requirements for the *validity* of such a transfer:

---

[1] MQ 1: Fl I 429.
[2] AP: Fl I 437–440.

- there must be a letter of excardination from the Bishop of the Church where he is incardinated;
- there must be a letter of incardination from the Bishop of the Church where he wishes to be incardinated;
- these letters must both be signed by the respective Bishops and addressed to the cleric in question.

It is only the diocesan Bishop who can act in this matter, not the Vicar General or other episcopal Vicar.[1]

552 This canon applies only to clerics incardinated in a particular Church, i.e. secular or diocesan clerics; special arrangements are made for incardination in institutes of consecrated life and societies of apostolic life.[2] The procedure outlined in §1 clearly presupposes communication between the Bishops concerned before the formal transfer takes place. In keeping with the principle of Can. 265, it is clear from §2 that there can be no period of time when the cleric is not incardinated.

Can. 268 §1 A cleric who has lawfully moved from his own particular Church to another is, by virtue of the law itself, incardinated in that latter Church after five years, if he has declared this intention in writing to both the diocesan Bishop of the host diocese and his own diocesan Bishop, and neither of the two Bishops has indicated opposition in writing within four months of receiving the cleric's written request.

§2 By perpetual or definitive admission into an institute of consecrated life or a society of apostolic life, a cleric who in accordance with Can. 266 §2 is incardinated in that institute or society, is excardinated from his own particular Church.

553 This canon is a substantial innovation in the Church's law: it introduces the concept of an *automatic* process of excardination – incardination. Precisely because of that, its terms must be strictly adhered to and rigorously applied. In fact, the Code allows for three forms of this automatic procedure, two of which are dealt with in this canon; the third will be mentioned later.

554 The first is that envisaged by §1, which concerns a cleric incardinated in one particular Church but lawfully resident in another. Such a cleric will, 'by virtue of the law itself', become incardinated in the diocese in which he is resident, subject to the following exigent conditions:

(a) he must manifest his wish to transfer his incardination to the diocese in which he now resides;

(b) he must, in writing, notify this wish to the two Bishops concerned;

(c) he must have completed a five-year stay in the diocese of his current residence – a stay which must be both legitimate (i.e. having the consent of the two Bishops) and uninterrupted (i.e. neither Bishop having at any stage during that period withdrawn his consent);

(d) he must establish that, within a period of four months from the receipt by the two Bishops concerned of his written submission, neither of them has, in writing, 'indicated opposition' to his proposal.[3]

---

[1] Cf. Comm 14(1982) 167 at Can. 238.

[2] Cf. Can. 268 §2.

[3] The text of the canon is based upon lit ap ES n.3(5): Fl I 594. This matter was the subject of an illuminating decision by Ap Sig of 27.VI.1978, reported in CLD 9 52–60.

The second form of automatic excardination–incardination is dealt with in §2. It involves a cleric who enters an institute of consecrated life or a society of apostolic life. A cleric who is thus incardinated into the institute or society in accordance with Can. 266 §2 is, by virtue of his perpetual profession or definitive incorporation (not before then), automatically excardinated from his own particular Church.

The third form of automatic transfer of incardination is not dealt with in this canon. It concerns the incardination into a particular Church of a cleric who has legitimately left or been dismissed from an institute of consecrated life or a society of apostolic life. The norms, which are similar to those in §1 of this canon, are contained in Cann. 693, 701, 727 §2, 743.

Can. 269 A diocesan Bishop is not to incardinate a cleric unless:

1° the need or the advantage of his particular Church requires it, and the provisions of law concerning the worthy support of the cleric are observed;

2° he knows by a lawful document that excardination has been granted, and has also obtained from the excardinating Bishop, under secrecy if need be, appropriate testimonials concerning the cleric's life, behaviour and studies;

3° the cleric declares in writing to the same Bishop that he wishes to enter the service of the new particular Church in accordance with the norms of law.

Certain conditions, which speak for themselves, are to be fulfilled before a diocesan Bishop proceeds to incardinate a cleric. These conditions are more or less the same as those required by the 1917 Code. Some details have been omitted, such e.g. as the obligation to investigate the cleric's family background as well as his life and behaviour, or the need to take even greater care if the cleric was from another country; a written declaration replaces the oath to be sworn before the Ordinary. The reference to seeking information even under secrecy finds parallels in other canons.[1] The conditions set out here are only for the *lawfulness* of incardination; they do not affect the validity of the act.

Can. 270 Excardination can be lawfully granted only for a just reason, such as the advantage of the Church or the good of the cleric. It may not, however, be refused unless grave reasons exist; it is lawful for a cleric who considers himself to be unfairly treated and who has found a Bishop to receive him, to have recourse against the decision.

This canon balances the preceding one. It contains the conditions for lawful excardination. The law states quite simply that excardination can be granted 'only for a just reason'. Two examples of just reasons are given: 'the advantage of the Church' and 'the good of the cleric'. By contrast, a request for excardination cannot be refused 'unless grave reasons exist'. The Bishop's decision should not be arbitrary but should be made only after a careful consideration of all the factors involved. Should the cleric who made the request feel aggrieved, the law gives him the right of recourse.[2]

---

[1] Cf. e.g. Cann. 127 §3, 645 §4, 1455.

[2] The procedures to follow are contained in Cann. 1732 ff: cf. Comm 14(1982) at Can. 241.

Can. 271 §1 Except for a grave need of his own particular Church, a Bishop is not to refuse clerics seeking permission to move whom he knows to be prepared and considers suitable to exercise the ministry in regions which suffer from a grave shortage of clergy. He is to ensure, however, that the rights and duties of these clerics are determined by written agreement with the diocesan Bishop of the place to which they wish to move.

559 'Priests ... should recall that the solicitude of all the Churches ought to be their intimate concern. For this reason priests of those dioceses which are blessed with greater abundance of vocations should be prepared gladly to offer themselves – with the permission and encouragement of their own Ordinary – for the exercise of their ministry in countries or missions or tasks that are hampered by shortage of clergy.'[1] The canon is seeking to give practical effect to this teaching of Vat. II. More detailed directives in this regard were issued by the Sacred Congregation for the Clergy in March 1980.[2] In that document, the Congregation sought to address the problem of an unbalanced distribution of clergy throughout the world. Since the Council, many dioceses have established links with parts of the Church in need of clergy and many clerics have gone to serve in these places. A cleric seeking permission to go to such a region is not to be refused, 'except for a grave need of his own particular Church'.

560 The rights and duties of a cleric who moves to another Church are to be determined in a *written* agreement drawn up by the two Bishops concerned. This reflects the general policy found in the Code which calls for written proof in case of any subsequent misunderstanding.

Can. 271 §2 A Bishop can give permission to his clerics to move to another particular Church for a specified time. Such permission can be renewed several times, but in such a way that the clerics remain incardinated in their own particular Church, and on returning there enjoy all the rights which they would have had if they had ministered there.

561 This provision amounts to a safeguard for those clerics who work in another Church for a specified time. In granting permission and in renewing it, the Bishop must make sure that the cleric's rights are intact on his return to his own Church. Such rights include salary, pension fund, seniority, health insurance etc. Although not explicitly stated, it would be wise to have all this in a written document drawn up between the cleric and his own Bishop.

Can. 271 §3 A cleric who lawfully moves to another particular Church while remaining incardinated in his own, may for a just reason be recalled by his own Bishop, provided the agreements entered into with the other Bishop are honoured and natural equity is observed. Under the same conditions, the Bishop of the other particular Church can for a just reason refuse the cleric permission to reside further in his territory.

562 Since there has been no change in incardination, the cleric remains subject to the Bishop of his own particular Church, even while ministering elsewhere. In order to preserve natural equity and to avoid any arbitrary decisions, the written agreements mentioned in §1 should contain some indication of the kind of reason for which a

---

[1] PO 10: Fl I 882.

[2] SCC Directive norms for co-operation among local churches and for a better distribution of the clergy *Postquam apostoli* 22.III.1980: CLD 9 760–787.

cleric can be recalled or asked to leave, the length of the period of notice, etc. It should be noted that either Bishop requires a *just* cause to act, not necessarily a grave one.

Can. 272 The diocesan administrator cannot grant excardination nor incardination, nor permission to move to another particular Church, unless the episcopal see has been vacant for a year, and he has the consent of the college of consultors.

This canon, which corresponds in part to c.113 of the 1917 Code, gives practical effect in one area to the principle of Can. 428 §1: 'While the see is vacant, no innovation is to be made'. The Revision Commission made it clear that excardination-incardination belonged to the diocesan Bishop alone.[1] The diocesan Administrator can grant excardination and incardination, and give permission to move to another particular Church, only if two conditions are fulfilled: i.e. that the see has been vacant for a year, and that the college of consultors has given its consent.

Chapter III
THE OBLIGATIONS AND RIGHTS OF CLERICS

Having dealt with the rights and obligations of all Christ's faithful (Cann. 208–223) and then with the same in respect of lay members of the Church (Cann. 224–231), the Code now turns to the obligations and rights of clerics.[2] It is important to recognise that any canons such as these, which deal with obligations and rights relating to a particular part of the Church, must be understood in the light of the fundamental obligations and rights of all Christ's faithful.[3]

Can. 273 Clerics have a special obligation to show reverence and obedience to the Supreme Pontiff and to their own Ordinary.

This first canon deals with the obligation of obedience. In its draft form, it was criticised as appearing to be based on a theological opinion which saw the Pope as Bishop of the universal Church. The Revision Commission rejected the criticism and stated that a cleric is bound by a special reverence and obedience, not merely towards his own Ordinary, but also towards the Supreme Pontiff, the successor of Peter, who is indeed the Ordinary for the entire Church.[4] The relationship which should exist between clerics and their Bishop was described in more detail by Vat. II.[5] Unlike members of institutes of consecrated life (see Can. 590 §2), clerics as such do not have a vow of obedience to the Roman Pontiff, but they are obliged to show reverence and obedience to him, as also to their Ordinary to whom they promise the same in the rite of ordination to priesthood and diaconate.

Can. 274 §1 Only clerics can obtain offices the exercise of which requires the power of order or the power of ecclesiastical governance.

---
[1] Cf. Comm 14(1982) 168 at Can. 238.
[2] The obligations and rights of religious are dealt with in Cann. 662–672.
[3] Cf. Comm 14(1982) 168 at Cann. 244–264.
[4] Cf. Comm 14(1982) 169 at Can. 247; cf. also Can. 134 §1 where the Pope is described as an 'Ordinary'.
[5] Cf. PO 7: Fl I 875–878.

566 Substantially, this paragraph repeats the contents of c.118 of the 1917 Code. However, matters are complicated by the assertions found in other canons of the present Code. Thus, e.g. Can. 129 §1 states that 'those who are in sacred orders are ... capable of the power of governance ...', while Can. 228 §1 states that 'lay people who are found to be suitable are capable of being admitted ... to those ecclesiastical offices and functions which ... they can discharge'. There would appear to be an element of conflict between these canons. The problem is rooted in a theological question relating to various theories of the source of power in the Church.[1] No easy resolution can be found to the problem and the issue was intensely debated by the Revision Commission.[2] Since the matter is still one of doctrinal discussion, and accordingly not one to be determined in a Code of law, the present texts restrict themselves to reflecting what would appear to be the current state of theology and practice in this matter.

Can. 274 §2 Unless excused by a lawful impediment, clerics are obliged to accept and faithfully fulfil the office committed to them by their Ordinary.

567 A practical consequence of obedience to his Ordinary is the acceptance and fulfilment by a cleric of whatever duty is committed to him by his Ordinary. This is a serious matter: persistent disobedience can be punished with a just penalty (see Can. 1371 2°). There can of course be excusing causes, as recognised by this canon: it is for the Ordinary to decide whether or not a particular 'lawful impediment' – such as age, illness or any other particular consideration – is sufficient to excuse a cleric from the non-acceptance or non-fulfilment of a particular duty.

Can. 275 §1 Since all clerics are working for the same purpose, namely the building up of the body of Christ, they are to be united with one another in the bond of brotherhood and prayer. They are to seek to cooperate with one another, in accordance with the provisions of particular law.

568 'All priests, who are constituted in the order of priesthood by the sacrament of Order, are bound together by an intimate sacramental brotherhood ...'.[3] This conciliar teaching has been expanded in this canon, which speaks of 'clerics', thereby including deacons. Three means of building up the body of Christ are given particular prominence:

– brotherhood among clerics;
– bonds of prayer between clerics;
– a spirit of cooperation between clerics.

Each of these is developed in subsequent canons (see Cann. 276, 278, 280).

Can. 275 §2 Clerics are to acknowledge and promote the mission which the laity, each for his or her own part, exercises in the Church and in the world.

569 The principle of lay involvement in the mission of the Church is set out in Can. 225; in fact, it is a principle which pervades the whole of the Code. Following the teaching of Vat. II[4] the Code here obliges clerics not only to acknowledge the mission of the laity, but actively to promote it – a point which is made, even more explicitly, in regard to the obligations of a parish priest (see Can. 529 §3).

---

[1] Cf. LG 24, NEP 2: Fl I 378, 424–425.
[2] Cf. Comm 14(1982) 146–149 at Can. 126.
[3] PO 8: Fl I 878.
[4] Cf. PO 9: Fl I 880.

Can. 276 §1 Clerics have a special obligation to seek holiness in their lives, because they are consecrated to God by a new title through the reception of orders, and are stewards of the mysteries of God in the service of His people.

The obligation of clerics to strive for *holiness in their (own) lives* is central to the concept of a clerical vocation. The text of this canon is taken directly from Vat. II.[1] And this same theme of holiness runs throughout the Code:

- Can. 210 calls on all the faithful to make a wholehearted effort to lead a holy life;
- Can. 245 §1 speaks of the personal sanctification of seminarians;
- Can. 278 §2 points out that the holiness of clerics is promoted through associations;
- Can. 387 calls on the Bishop to be an example of holiness;
- Can. 673 requires that the first apostolate of religious consists in the witness of their life consecrated to God;
- Can. 835 §4 calls on parents to share in a special way in the sanctifying office of the Church.

Can. 276 §2 In order that they can pursue this perfection:

1° **they are in the first place faithfully and untiringly to fulfil the obligations of their pastoral ministry;**

2° **they are to nourish their spiritual life at the twofold table of the sacred Scripture and the Eucharist; priests are therefore earnestly invited to offer the eucharistic Sacrifice daily, and deacons to participate daily in the offering;**

3° **priests, and deacons aspiring to the priesthood, are obliged to carry out the liturgy of the hours daily, in accordance with their own approved liturgical books; permanent deacons are to recite that part of it determined by the Bishops' Conference;**

4° **they are also obliged to make spiritual retreats, in accordance with the provision of particular law;**

5° **they are exhorted to engage regularly in mental prayer, to approach the sacrament of penance frequently, to honour the Virgin Mother of God with particular veneration, and to use other general and special means to holiness.**

The means of pursuing holiness listed here are clearly reminiscent of the means of the spiritual formation of seminarians contained in Can. 246. They speak for themselves, and are necessarily to be pondered with diligence by every cleric. Their immediate source, itself consecrated by tradition, may be found in Vat. II.[2]

Can. 277 §1 Clerics are obliged to observe perfect and perpetual continence for the sake of the Kingdom of heaven, and are therefore bound to celibacy. Celibacy is a special gift of God by which sacred ministers can more easily remain close to Christ with an undivided heart, and can dedicate themselves more freely to the service of God and their neighbour.

---

[1] PO 12–13: Fl I 885–889.
[2] In particular PO: Fl I 863–902.

572 The first known law about clerical celibacy appears to have been Can. 33 of the Council of Elvira in approximately the year AD 300.[1] The Second Lateran Council in 1139 declared the marriages of those in Holy Orders to be invalid. This legislation was repeated at the Council of Trent[2] and was incorporated in the 1917 Code in its cc.132 and 1072. More recently, Pope Paul VI reiterated the Church's teaching in his 1967 encyclical[3] in which he takes up and develops the major themes contained in the teaching of Vat. II in this area:[4] both the conciliar decree and the papal encyclical are necessary source-material for a proper understanding of this canon – a canon which describes celibacy as 'a special gift of God' which enables clerics to remain close to Christ 'with an undivided heart', and serve God and his people 'more freely'.

573 This paragraph underwent many changes during the revision process. In the 1977 draft, married deacons were explicitly exempted from the obligation of celibacy but were stated to be bound by it if they became widowed.[5] After much debate and consultation and several drafts, the existing text emerged. In effect, this reverts to the original position, even though it does not contain an explicit exemption of married deacons. A widowed deacon is not exempt and, by virtue of Can. 1087, is impeded from remarriage. This does not, however, absolutely exclude the possibility of a dispensation from the Holy See in particularly serious circumstances of an individual case.

Can. 277 §2 Clerics are to behave with due prudence in relation to persons whose company can be a danger to their obligation of preserving continence or can lead to scandal of the faithful.

574 This exhortation to prudence is a natural and practical consequence of the preceding paragraph. In earlier drafts, this had formed part of a separate canon.[6] Its present position reinforces the link with the gift of celibacy. Although the present norm is much less detailed than c.133 of the 1917 Code, note that it speaks of 'persons' (i.e. male and female) – not only of women, as did the previous canon – who could be an obstacle to continence.

Can. 277 §3 The diocesan Bishop has authority to establish more detailed rules concerning this matter, and to pass judgment on the observance of the obligation in particular cases.

575 More detailed provisions about the whole matter of the observance of the law of celibacy and the safeguards mentioned in the preceding paragraph are – if such are deemed necessary – for the diocesan Bishop to establish at local level, not for the Bishops' Conference. Two earlier drafts had included a reference to the Bishop consulting his council of priests before establishing or issuing such norms.[7] However, this requirement was removed because of the delicacy of the matter and also because the Bishop may have relevant information which is not known to the council of priests and which, by reason of a necessary confidentiality, cannot be revealed to its members.[8]

---

[1] Cf. DS 119.
[2] Cf. DS 1809–1810.
[3] Sac Cael: Fl II 285–317.
[4] Cf. PO 16: Fl I 892–894.
[5] Cf. Sch 1977 at Can. 135.
[6] E.g. Sch 1977 at Can. 136.
[7] Sch 1977 at Can. 136, Sch 1980 at Can. 251 §2.
[8] Cf. Comm 14(1982) 170 at Can. 251 §2.

Can. 278 §1 Secular clerics have the right of association with others for the achievement of purposes befitting the clerical state.

Can. 215 acknowledges the right of all Christ's faithful to 'establish and direct associations which serve charitable or pious purposes or which foster the christian vocation in the world'. That norm clearly includes clerics.[1] However, specific mention of the right of clerics to do so is made here because of the particular importance of that right.[2] In so far as limitations have to be placed on this right, these are adequately catered for in §3 of this canon.[3]

The term 'secular clergy' (rather than 'diocesan clergy') is used deliberately to distinguish them from clerics belonging to an institute of consecrated life or a society of apostolic life who may be working in a parochial ministry in a diocese.[4]

Can. 278 §2 Secular clerics are to hold in high esteem those associations especially whose statutes are recognised by the competent authority and which, by a suitable and well-tried rule of life and by fraternal support, promote holiness in the exercise of their ministry and foster the unity of the clergy with one another and with their Bishop.

The text of this paragraph, which derives from Vat. II,[5] outlines the purposes of associations of clergy:
- to offer a well-tried rule of life;
- to provide fraternal support;
- to promote holiness in the exercise of ministry;
- to foster the unity of the clergy among themselves and with their Bishop.

This recommendation stands alongside the right of clerics, already recognised in §1, to form their own associations. There is no obligation or compulsion to belong even to 'approved' diocesan, national or international associations.

Can. 278 §3 Clerics are to refrain from establishing or joining associations whose purpose or activity cannot be reconciled with the obligations proper to the clerical state, or which can hinder the diligent fulfilment of the office entrusted to them by the competent ecclesiastical authority.

This paragraph places appropriate limits on the right enunciated in §1. The text is a juridical summary of a document issued on 8 March 1982 by the Sacred Congregation for the Clergy. This document describes as 'undoubtedly irreconcilable with the clerical state ... those associations of clerics, even if elected or constituted only civilly, which directly or indirectly, in a manifest or clandestine manner, pursue aims relating to politics, even if presented under the external aspect of wanting to favour humanitarian ideals, peace and social progress ... (and) those associations which intend to unite deacons or presbyters in a type of "union", thus reducing their sacred ministry to a profession or career comparable to functions of a profane character ...'.[6] Membership of such associations is thus expressly forbidden to clerics. While this declaration would appear to have been specifically directed against such associations in some eastern European countries, its effective incorporation into the Code makes it applicable to all clerics throughout the Church.

---

[1] Cf. PO 8: Fl I 878–880.
[2] Cf. Comm 9(1977) 245.
[3] Cf. Comm 14(1982) 171 at Can. 252.
[4] Ibid.
[5] PO 8: Fl I 879.
[6] SCC 8. III. 1982: AAS 74(1982) 642–645: Origins 11(1982) 647 III–IV.

Can. 279 §1 Clerics are to continue their sacred studies even after ordination to the priesthood. They are to hold to that solid doctrine based on sacred Scripture which has been handed down by our forebears and which is generally received in the Church, as set out especially in the documents of the Councils and of the Roman Pontiffs. They are to avoid profane novelties and pseudo-science.

§2 Priests are to attend pastoral courses to be arranged for them after their ordination, in accordance with the provisions of particular law. At times determined by the same law, they are to attend other courses, theological meetings or conferences, which offer them an occasion to acquire further knowledge of the sacred sciences and of pastoral methods.

§3 They are also to seek a knowledge of other sciences, especially those linked to the sacred sciences, particularly in so far as they benefit the exercise of the pastoral ministry.

580 Vat. II clearly recognised the importance of the ongoing training of clergy.[1] It stressed the necessary relationship between seminary training and post-ordination studies, the responsibility of the Bishops to set up appropriate structures and programmes, and the fundamental sources of such ongoing education: Scripture, the Fathers, and the Church's magisterium.

581 After the Council, various directives were issued in an attempt to implement the conciliar teaching. These were eventually incorporated into the *Ratio fundamentalis*, both in its original and in its revised version.[2] This document made several specific suggestions, e.g. pastoral training of younger priests over a number of years; triennial examinations; a month's course after five years of ordination, comprising a week's retreat and three weeks of refresher courses. However, it is clearly pointed out that all these suggestions will come to nothing unless there is proper coordination between the seminary and this post-ordination training, and unless they are organised by a priest who is genuinely outstanding in intellectual ability, virtue and experience.[3] Benefit to the exercise of the pastoral ministry is the principal, though not the sole, reason for the recommended study of other sciences, sacred and profane.

Can. 280 Some manner of common life is highly recommended to clerics; where it exists, it is as far as possible to be maintained.

582 The 'common life' recommended to clerics by this canon must not be confused with the 'common life' which religious are obliged to observe (see Can. 665 §1). No matter what form it may take, no juridical bond is established between clerics by the sharing of a 'common life'. Vat. II gives the rationale behind this canon and some examples of the form of 'common life' envisaged: 'In order to enable priests to find mutual help in cultivating the intellectual and spiritual life, to promote better cooperation amongst them in the ministry, to safeguard them from possible dangers arising from loneliness, it is necessary to foster some kind of community life or social relations with them. This however can take different forms according to varying personal and pastoral needs: by priests living together where this is possible, or by their sharing a common table, or at least meeting at frequent intervals'.[4] While the Council

---

[1] Cf. OT 22, PO 19: Fl I 723–724, 897–898.
[2] Cf. RF 100–101: LE IV 5734–5735; LE VI 9108–9109.
[3] Cf. RF 101: LE VI 9109.
[4] PO 8: Fl I 879.

mentioned only priests, the canon refers to all clerics, and thus provision should be made at local level for some form of common life which will include permanent deacons, whether married or celibate.

Can. 281 §1 Since clerics dedicate themselves to the ecclesiastical ministry, they deserve the remuneration that befits their condition, taking into account both the nature of their office and the conditions of time and place. It is to be such that it provides for the necessities of their life and for the just remuneration of those whose services they need.

§2 Suitable provision is likewise to be made for such social welfare as they may need in infirmity, sickness or old age.

Appropriate remuneration for the clergy is obviously a basic right. This is stated at some length in the Council's decree on the Ministry and Life of priests, where the joint responsibility of Bishops and the faithful in this regard is highlighted: '... insofar as provision is not made from some other source for the just remuneration of priests, the faithful are bound by a real obligation of seeing to it that the necessary provision for a decent and fitting livelihood for the priests is available. This obligation arises from the fact that it is for the benefit of the faithful that priests are working. Bishops are bound to warn the faithful of their obligation in this connection'.[1] The Revision Commission made it clear that such remuneration should be viewed in the light of the special vocation of the priesthood – a sacred ministry which cannot be reduced to something of a purely economic nature.[2] This §1 makes it equally clear that this remuneration must be such as to cater 'for the remuneration of those whose services they need': e.g. the modest requirement of a housekeeper, even part-time; the requirement of a competent person who would see to the necessary maintenance and care of a parochial house; etc. There is here a clear obligation on the part of the diocesan Bishop to be sensitive to the reasonable needs of his priests. 583

The purpose of the remuneration referred to above is to provide for the necessities of life of those who are active in the ministry. In its §2 the canon points to the need to make provision for those who have, at whatever age, become ill, or who simply have become too old to be able to continue. Where an adequate social welfare system is not organised by the State, the competent Bishops' Conference – or, in the absence of a directive from that source, the diocesan Bishop – should make due provision in keeping with canon and civil law.[3] In this way, the necessities of a reasonable way of life will be provided for, even after a wholly active ministry has ceased to be possible. 584

Can. 281 §3 Married deacons who dedicate themselves full-time to the ecclesiastical ministry deserve remuneration sufficient to provide for themselves and their families. Those, however, who receive a remuneration by reason of a secular profession which they exercise or have exercised, are to see to their own and to their families' needs from that income.

The final paragraph of this canon deals with married deacons. Celibate deacons, insofar as they require adequate support, are included in the provisions of the first paragraph. This third paragraph is substantially a repetition of the norms contained in the 1967 mp of Pope Paul VI.[4] There is one significant change from the original papal 585

---

[1] PO 20: Fl I 899.
[2] Cf. Comm 14(1982) 172 at Can. 255 §2.
[3] Cf. PO 21: Fl I 900; Can. 1274 §2.
[4] Cf. SDO 20–21: CLD 6 581.

document: there is no longer any reference to the Bishops' Conference in this regard. It would seem clear, therefore, that it is up to the appropriate diocesan Bishop to provide for the appropriate remuneration – bearing in mind that 'those ... who receive a remuneration by reason of a secular profession, which they exercise or have exercised (a pension could be relevant in this context) are to see to their own and to their families' needs from that income'.

Can. 282 §1 Clerics are to follow a simple way of life and avoid anything which smacks of worldliness.

586 The Code here seeks to give juridical expression to the recommendation made by Vat. II: '... priests are invited to embrace voluntary poverty ... priests and Bishops alike are to avoid everything that might in any way antagonize the poor. More than the rest of Christ's disciples they are to put aside all appearance of vanity in their surroundings ...'.[1] The simplicity of life for which this canon calls will have to be evaluated carefully in accordance with the circumstances of time and place.

Can. 282 §2 Goods which they receive on the occasion of the exercise of an ecclesiastical office, and which are over and above what is necessary for their worthy upkeep and the fulfilment of all the duties of their state, they may well wish to use for the good of the Church and for charitable works.

587 Having stated the desirability of a simple way of life, the canon goes on to point out what clerics might wish to do with any surplus income received through their ministry. This is a specification of the general principle stated in Can. 222 §2 which obliges *all* the faithful to help the poor from their own resources. The fact that this paragraph is framed in the manner of an exhortation in no way diminishes this obligation of Christian charity.

Can. 283 §1 Clerics, even if they do not have a residential office, are not to be absent from their diocese for a considerable time, to be determined by particular law, without the at least presumed permission of their proper Ordinary.

588 This paragraph deals with *absences* of clerics from the diocese other than the permitted holidays (see §2). They may not be absent 'for a considerable time'. Taking account of the divergence of opinions which attended this same phrase in the 1917 Code (c.143), the current law simply states that 'a considerable time' is 'to be determined by particular law', i.e. by the law or approved custom of the diocese, by a competent provincial or plenary council or by a decree of the Bishops' Conference in accordance with Can. 455. Any such absence from the diocese must be with the permission of the Ordinary: the Code speaks of 'the at least presumed permission', i.e. that permission which it is prudently considered would be given if asked for. This canon applies also to permanent deacons.[2]

Can. 283 §2 They may, however, take a rightful and sufficient holiday every year, for the length of time determined by general or by particular law.

589 According to Vat. II, 'priests' remuneration should be such as to allow the priest a proper holiday each year. The Bishop should see to it that priests are able to have this holiday'.[3] Taking this injunction as its guideline, the present paragraph states the

---

[1] PO 17: Fl I 895, 896.
[2] Cf. Comm 14(1982) 169 at Can. 246.
[3] PO 20: Fl I 899.

principle for all clerics. The Code does stipulate the maximum length of holiday for some clerics (see Cann. 395 §2, 410, 427 §1 and 429, 533 §2, 550 §2). The maximum holiday period for other clerics is to be determined by particular law. The Bishop is to establish norms to provide for the proper care of a parish during the parish priest's absence on holidays (see Can. 533 §3).

Can. 284 Clerics are to wear suitable ecclesiastical dress, in accordance with the norms established by the Bishops' Conference and legitimate local custom.

Pope John Paul II has stated that ecclesiastical dress for clerics, like the habit for religious, has a value as a sign and public witness to the world of their identity and special relationship with God.[1] This canon, using the same language as c.136 §1 of the 1917 Code, does not enter into details concerning the form of this 'suitable ecclesiastical dress'. It is for Bishops' Conferences to legislate on these details, bearing in mind the local customs and traditions.[2] The canon does not bind permanent deacons (see Can. 288).

Can. 285 §1 Clerics are to shun completely everything that is unbecoming to their state, in accordance with particular law.

While retaining the general principles of the 1917 Code, the present law does not give details of what might be unbecoming to the clerical state. Since this can vary with time and place, it is left to local legislation to specify what such activities might be. Even without such legislation, any form of criminal or immoral activity is obviously forbidden. Also clearly unbecoming for a cleric would be such occupations as executioner, bodyguard etc.

Can. 285 §2 Clerics are to avoid whatever is foreign to their state, even when it is not unseemly.

The present law retains the distinction of the 1917 Code between what is 'unbecoming' to the clerical state and what is merely 'foreign'. Again, the Code does not specify what might be considered foreign, except for those activities listed in §§3 and 4. Thus, e.g., by general law at least, a cleric is no longer forbidden to practise medicine or surgery as he was under the previous law (c.139 §2).

Can. 285 §3 Clerics are forbidden to assume public office whenever it means sharing in the exercise of civil power.

The earlier drafts of this paragraph, which replaces c.139 §4 of the 1917 Code, were much more complex than the present simply-stated principle; they had foreseen the possibility of clerics assuming public office, provided only that the permission of the competent authority had been obtained. The promulgated text does not explicitly cater for such exceptions. However, if a Bishop judged that it would serve a spiritual purpose, he could, in virtue of Can. 87 §1, dispense from the norm of this canon in a particular case. In view of the Church's well-publicised stance on this matter he would have to pay special attention to the 'just and reasonable cause' demanded by Can. 90. The canon is not against running for election as such, e.g. in the case of Catholic School Boards, but it is against operating under the banner of one political party as distinct from others.

---

[1] Cf. Comm 14(1982) 114–115.

[2] For those Bishops' Conferences which have legislated on this matter, cf. LCE Tavola per Paesi e Canoni at Can. 284.

Can. 285 §4 Without the permission of their Ordinary, they may not undertake the administration of goods belonging to lay people, or secular offices which involve the obligation to render an account. They are forbidden to act as surety, even with their own goods, without consulting their proper Ordinary. They are not to sign promissory notes which involve the payment of money but do not state the reason for the payment.

594 Two norms of the 1917 Code in its cc.137 and 139 §2 are substantially encompassed in this paragraph:

(a) clerics are not to take charge of the financial affairs of lay people or to accept any secular (i.e. non-ecclesiastical) office which involves having 'to render an account', *without the permission of their Ordinary*. Thus, e.g. permission is required if a cleric is to be the executor of a lay person's will, the director of a credit union, etc. In normal circumstances this permission is readily given, as e.g. in the case of a priest being the executor of the last will of his parent or of a close family friend; in fact, there is in some dioceses a general regulation to the effect that one at least of the executors of a priest's last will be another priest.

(b) clerics are not to act as surety or sign promissory notes involving the payment of money, *without first consulting their Ordinary*: permission is not required – consultation is; yet it is assumed that the prudent advice of the Ordinary would normally be accepted. The mention of promissory notes is an addition to c.137 of the 1917 Code but this simply makes explicit something already contained in the principle.

The reasoning behind these norms is to safeguard the position of the cleric and make sure that he is able to carry out his life and ministry without unnecessary distractions.

595 Can. 288 exempts permanent deacons from the provisions of §§3 and 4 of this canon. Can. 672, on the other hand, states that religious are bound by all its provisions.

Can. 286 Clerics are forbidden to practise commerce or trade, either personally or through another, for their own or another's benefit, except with the permission of the lawful ecclesiastical authority.

596 This canon repeats the norm of c.142 of the 1917 Code except that the lawful ecclesiastical authority may now permit trading or commerce, but only, of course, in special circumstances. Insofar as the main details are the same as the previous law, the commentators on the 1917 Code remain a valuable guide.[1] In general, what is forbidden is habitual, not isolated, transactions. The sort of transactions which are forbidden are profit-seeking ones, e.g. buying merchandise with the intention of selling it unchanged at profit, or strictly industrial transactions, e.g. buying merchandise, changing it by means of hired labour and then selling it at a profit. Accordingly, e.g. holding stocks and shares would not be prohibited; speculation in them would be; whereas e.g. buying an old car and refurbishing it oneself would not be prohibited. The 'lawful ecclesiastical authority' is the diocesan Bishop for secular clerics and the major Superior for religious.

597 Clerics who violate this prescription of law 'are to be punished according to the gravity of the offence' (Can. 1392). The very strict penalty imposed by the Sacred Congregation for the Council on 22.III.1950, whereby a cleric violating this prescription incurred a *latae sententiae* excommunication specially reserved to the Holy See,[2] has been abrogated.

---

[1] For an informative summary, cf. Commentary (CLSA) 226–227.
[2] Cf. AAS 42(1950) 330: CLD 3 68–69.

Can. 287 §1 Clerics are always to do their utmost to foster among people peace and harmony based on justice.

The present canon states strongly and positively what a cleric must consider to be one of his main concerns: to strive in every reasonable way to foster peace and harmony, based on justice. The 1917 Code, in its c.141 §1, spoke in a negative fashion, forbidding clerics to take part in internal strife and public order disturbances. The active and positive promotion of peace and justice has been one of the major concerns of the Church, particularly in recent years. It has been the subject of many initiatives and interventions by the Popes over the years.[1] It is impossible to justify clerics and religious indulging in acts of violence or major civil disobedience, even for what purports to be a good purpose.[2]

Can. 287 §2 They are not to play an active role in political parties or in directing trade unions unless, in the judgement of the competent ecclesiastical authority, this is required for the defence of the rights of the Church or to promote the common good.

Clerics are forbidden to play an active role in political parties or in directing trade unions. This is because their ministry is to all the faithful, whether of a political party, a trade union, or otherwise. The canon does, however, envisage the possibility of their having to play an active role in certain situations to protect the rights of the Church or to promote or safeguard the common good. The competent ecclesiastical authority will have to judge whether or not such action ought to be taken. This paragraph has obvious connections with Can. 285 §3 and should be read also in the light of Can. 285 §§1–2.

Can. 288 Permanent deacons are not bound by the provisions of Cann. 284, 285 §§3 and 4, 286, 287 §2, unless particular law states otherwise.

Unless particular local legislation provides otherwise, the permanent deacon is *not*:
(a) obliged to wear ecclesiastical dress (see Can. 284);
(b) forbidden to assume public office (see Can. 285 §3);
(c) forbidden to undertake the administration of goods belonging to lay people etc. (see Can. 285 §4);
(d) forbidden to practise trade or commerce (see Can. 286);
(e) forbidden to play an active role in political parties etc. (see Can. 287 §2).

Can. 289 §1 As military service ill befits the clerical state, clerics and candidates for sacred orders are not to volunteer for the armed services without the permission of their Ordinary.

The 1917 law in its c.121 stated that clerics were immune from military service, but, in the absence of an agreement between the Church and the civil power, such canonical legislation cannot be enforced. Hence, in the present formulation the embargo is on 'volunteering' to serve in the armed forces without permission – an embargo which applies also to permanent deacons.[3] The canon does not refer to a chaplaincy

---

[1] A sample of these can be found in lists of papal addresses and other documents contained in CLD 5 236, 6 219–220, 7 129, 8 187, 9 114, 10 24. A significant array is contained in the collection *Proclaiming justice and peace: documents from John XXIII to John Paul II* ed. Walsh & Davies London 1984.
[2] Cf. the letter sent in the Pope's name to the Archbishop of Prague 14.II.1983 regarding priests belonging to the peace movement in the then Czechoslovakia: AAS 75(1983) 516–522.
[3] Cf. Comm 14(1982) 174 at Can. 264.

service but rather to the regular armed forces where it may be necessary to engage in actual warfare where lives may be taken. The Church's position on *the pastoral care of military personnel* is an entirely different matter, which is comprehensively treated and encouraged in the ap con (21.IV.1986) of Pope John Paul II *Spirituali militum curae*.[1]

Can. 289 §2 Clerics are to take advantage of exemptions from exercising functions and public civil offices foreign to the clerical state, which are granted in their favour by law, agreements or customs, unless their proper Ordinary has in particular cases decreed otherwise.

602 Certain civic duties which oblige all citizens are regarded as foreign to the clerical state, e.g. in some places, jury service. Where the civil law of an area grants an exemption or excuse from such duties or functions, clerics are to avail themselves of these – save only where, in a particular case, their proper Ordinary has decided otherwise.

Chapter IV
LOSS OF THE CLERICAL STATE

Can. 290 Sacred ordination once validly received never becomes invalid. A cleric, however, loses the clerical state:

1° by a judgement of a court or an administrative decree, declaring the ordination invalid;

2° by the penalty of dismissal lawfully imposed;

3° by a rescript of the Apostolic See; this rescript, however, is granted by the Apostolic See to deacons for only grave reasons and to priests for only the gravest of reasons.

603 The canon clearly distinguishes between being ordained and the juridical status of a cleric. While one cannot enjoy clerical status unless one is ordained, it is possible to lose that status after ordination. The canon specifies three cases of loss of the clerical state:

(a) when the ordination is declared invalid by a judgement or an administrative decree: such a declaration removes the very basis for enjoying clerical status;

(b) when the person ordained, having committed an external violation of a law or precept, is lawfully dismissed from the clerical state. This is an expiatory penalty (see Can. 1336 §1 5°), which may be imposed only for the limited number of offences mentioned as such in the general law of the Church (see Cann. 1364 §2, 1367, 1370 §1, 1387, 1395 §§1–2; see also Can. 1317).

(c) when the cleric has been granted a rescript from the Holy See. This rescript may be sought either by the cleric himself or, even without the cleric's consent, by his

---

[1] Cf. AAS 78(1986) 481–486; Comm 18(1986) 12–17. Cf. also Beyer *Commentary on the Apostolic Constitution 'Spirituali militum curae'* CLSNGBI 76 (December 1988) 48–99; Vallini *L'Ordinariato Militare: Natura Teologica e Giuridica alla luce della cost. apost. 'Spirituali militum curae'* Fulda 7.IX.1992.

Ordinary, i.e. Bishop or major religious Superior.[1] The use of the phrase 'the gravest of reasons' in respect of priests (as distinct from 'grave reasons' in relation to deacons) is significant: the rare use of this phrase elsewhere in the Code always points to truly exceptional circumstances (see e.g. Cann. 55, 679, 703).

Can. 291 Apart from the cases mentioned in Can. 290 n.1, the loss of the clerical state does not carry with it a dispensation from the obligation of celibacy, which is granted solely by the Roman Pontiff.

If an ordination is proved to have been invalid (1°), then the person is obviously not bound by any of the obligations attached to the clerical state, even celibacy. Dismissal from the clerical state (2°) is a very different matter; it clearly does not carry with it a dispensation from the obligation of celibacy. In this context it is important to distinguish accurately between, on the one hand, the invalidity of orders or a dismissal from the clerical state and, on the other, a dispensation from the obligation of celibacy, itself a necessary attendant on sacred orders: hence the thrust of this canon.

The current procedure in this matter of a dispensation from the obligations of priestly ordination, including celibacy, is laid down by the Sacred Congregation for the Doctrine of the Faith in a letter of 1980, with accompanying norms, to all Ordinaries and Moderators General of clerical religious institutes.[2] By a letter (unpublished) from the Secretariat of State in 1989 competence for handling all cases of dispensation from clerical celibacy was transferred to the Congregation for Divine Worship and the Discipline of the Sacraments.[3]

The norms issued in 1980 introduced a more restricted regime for the issue of such rescripts. In general, there are two types of case which will be given consideration: (a) those of priests who have been out of the active ministry for many years, who have since contracted irregular unions and who wish to return to the Sacraments, and (b) those of priests who should never have been ordained 'because they lacked a due sense of freedom and responsibility, or because the competent Superiors were not able, at the proper time, to judge in a prudent and sufficiently suitable manner whether the candidate was really fit to live his life perpetually in celibacy dedicated to God'.[4] It would, however, appear unreliable to assume that these two are the *only* categories which will be admitted for consideration.

Can. 292 A cleric who loses the clerical state in accordance with the law, loses thereby the rights that are proper to the clerical state and is no longer bound by any obligations of the clerical state, without prejudice to Can. 291. He is prohibited from exercising the power of order, without prejudice to Can. 976. He is automatically deprived of all offices and roles and of any delegated power.

The cleric who loses the clerical state also loses the *rights* belonging to that state. Thus, to take a significant example, he loses the right to the appropriate remuneration

---

[1] In the first draft of this canon (Sch 1977 at Can. 150) the reference to a rescript was qualified by the phrase 'granted at the request of the cleric'. This qualification was subsequently removed when it was pointed out that a rescript is governed by the universal prescriptions of law and, in particular, by Cann. 60–61. Accordingly, there can be no doubt that the rescript in question here may be sought by the Ordinary even without the cleric's consent. Whether or not it will then be granted depends obviously on the Holy See's evaluation of the merits of the case as presented.

[2] Letter of Cardinal Seper 14.X.1980: AAS 72(1980) 1132–1137: CLD 9 92–96.

[3] Letter of Secretariat of State 8.II.1989 n.230.139.

[4] Letter of Cardinal Seper cit: CLD 9 94–95.

detailed in Can. 281 §§1–2; on the other hand – in accordance with the spirit of equity which pervades the Code – 'if he is truly in need' the Ordinary is obliged 'to provide (for him) in the best way possible' (Can. 1350 §2): this is a matter in which charity, not confrontation, is the appropriate motivation. Correspondingly, the loss of the clerical state frees the person from all the *obligations* of that state, except that of clerical celibacy, as Can. 291 makes clear. Thus, e.g. he is no longer obliged to continue his sacred studies (see Can. 279) or to wear suitable ecclesiastical dress (see Can. 284); similarly, certain prohibitions on clerics no longer apply: e.g. he may assume public office (see Can. 285 §3), or practise commerce or trade (see Can. 286), etc.

608 A validly ordained cleric who has lost the clerical state obviously retains the power of orders (see Can. 290), but he is forbidden to exercise that power – with the sole exception foreseen by the Code in Can. 976, i.e. absolution of a penitent in danger of death.

609 A dismissed cleric automatically loses all offices, positions and functions linked to the clerical state. It is clear from the deliberations of the Revision Commission that a dismissed cleric would thereby lose the 'canonical mission' – subsequently renamed the 'mandate' – which would entitle him to teach theology in the name of the Church.[1]

610 The canon adds that the cleric also loses 'any delegated power' – a point not mentioned on some earlier drafts. Delegated power is not an office nor is it, as such, attached to the clerical state: it may in its exercise be, on occasion, shared by lay people. A significant consequence of its mention here would appear to be that a cleric who has lost the clerical state not only loses whatever delegated power (even by general delegation) he may up to then have had, but thereby loses also the *capacity to receive delegated power*, save only that which the law permits to lay people. A practical pastoral consequence would concern the requisite delegation to assist at a marriage: a priest or deacon in this situation would not qualify under the terms of Can. 1108 §1; he could *perhaps* qualify *only* under the exacting terms of Can. 1112.

611 Apart from these requirements of the universal law, further restrictions on someone who has lost the clerical state may be imposed either in the document imposing the penalty of dismissal (Can. 290 2°) or in the rescript of the Apostolic See (Can. 290 3°). In each individual case, therefore, careful attention must be paid to the terms of these documents, all of which must, where possible, be explained in detail and with charity to the ex-cleric in question.

Can. 293 A cleric who has lost the clerical state cannot be enrolled as a cleric again save by rescript of the Apostolic See.

612 Apart from some alterations in the terminology, this canon repeats the norm of c.212 §2 of the 1917 Code. No one, having lost the clerical state (by whatever of the three measures mentioned in Can. 290), can be readmitted to that state unless the Holy See will have acceded to a request for readmission. A rescript to that effect will contain detailed instructions as to what must be done by the laicised cleric, by the Ordinary who is willing to accept him, and by the cleric's previous Ordinary.[2]

---

[1] Cf. Comm 14(1982) 175 at Can. 267; 15(1983) 104–105 at Can. 767. Cf. also Can. 812.
[2] Cf. RR 1981 8.

Title IV
Personal Prelatures

Can. 294 Personal prelatures may be established by the Apostolic See after consultation with the Bishops' Conferences concerned. They are composed of deacons and priests of the secular clergy. Their purpose is to promote an appropriate distribution of priests, or to carry out special pastoral or missionary enterprises in different regions or for different social groups.

The *personal prelature* is a new concept. Prior to Vat. II some provisions had been made for various groups of people on the basis that, within these groups, jurisdiction was personal rather than territorial. Thus, e.g. military vicariates were established for military personnel, separate hierarchies for several different ritual Churches were set up in the same territory to cater for the needs of the faithful of each rite, etc. In August 1954 the parish of Pontigny was established as a prelacy *nullius*, with its own prelate and special norms:[1] this gave a solid juridical structure to the so-called 'Mission de France', an association of secular priests dedicated to missionary activity within France; the purpose of the prelacy was to provide a pool of priests who could be sent wherever they were needed in France.

Vat. II, while upholding the traditional structure of dioceses in the Church,[2] recognised that this did not meet the needs of all[3] and made some concrete proposals, including the establishment of personal prelatures, to deal with this situation.[4] Further details on these were set out in Pope Paul VI's mp *Ecclesiae Sanctae*.[5] All of the foregoing forms the basis for the current legislation of the Code on this matter.

The only body competent to establish a personal prelature is the Apostolic See. No local Bishop or group of Bishops may presume to set up a structure similar to this to meet certain regional needs. Before any prelature is established, however, the Bishops' Conferences concerned (i.e. those in whose territory the proposed prelature will be operative) must be consulted, though their consent is not required. Membership of a prelature is confined to 'deacons and priests of the secular clergy'; religious are excluded. The purpose for which a prelature can be established may vary widely within the terms of this canon: it may be 'to promote an appropriate distribution of priests', or it may be 'to carry out special pastoral or missionary enterprises in different regions or for different social groups'.

Hitherto only one personal prelature has been established, that of *the Holy Cross and Opus Dei*. Although that association had been founded in 1938, it had long sought a distinct juridical structure. The results of many years of study were presented to the Congregation for Bishops in 1979. In 1982 that Congregation judged that the structure of the personal prelature as envisioned by Vat. II best suited the needs of Opus Dei.[6] Pope John Paul II formally established the prelature in the same year.[7]

---

[1] Cf. AAS 46(1954) 567–574.
[2] Cf. LG 23: Fl I 376.
[3] Cf. CD 18: Fl I 574.
[4] Cf. PO 10: Fl I 882.
[5] Cf. ES I 4: Fl I 594–595.
[6] Cf. SCB *Declaration on the Prelature of the Holy Cross and Opus Dei* 23.III.1982: AAS 75(1983) 464–468.
[7] Cf. ap con *Ut sit validum* 28.XI.1982: AAS 75(1983) 423–425.

Can. 295 §1 A personal prelature is governed by statutes laid down by the Apostolic See. It is presided over by a Prelate as its proper Ordinary. He has the right to establish a national or an international seminary, and to incardinate students and promote them to orders with the title of service of the prelature.

§2 The Prelate must provide both for the spiritual formation of those whom he has promoted with the above title, and for their becoming support.

617 The internal government of a personal prelature is regulated by its statutes. These are drawn up and approved by the Holy See. There is a clear analogy with the particular legislation of institutes of consecrated life and societies of apostolic life. The Prelature of *Opus Dei* is governed by its own 'particular code'.[1]

618 This canon sets out in summary form the rights and obligations of the Prelate:
 – he has the right to establish a seminary, either a national one or an international one;
 – he has the right to incardinate students;
 – he has the right to promote them to orders;
 – he, therefore, has the obligation to provide for the proper formation of these persons;
 – he is obliged to provide for the spiritual welfare of clerics incardinated into the prelature;
 – he is obliged to provide for their fitting support.

It will be for the statutes of each prelature to spell out these rights and obligations in greater depth and detail.

619 The Prelate is the proper Ordinary for the clergy of the prelature. The laity are not, however, removed from the jurisdiction of the local Ordinary, except for what is regarded as their purely internal formation and apostolic work in the context of the prelature (see Can. 296). Incardination of clerics into the prelature takes place at ordination to the diaconate (see Cann. 265–266 §1). Nothing in the canon suggests that the Prelate will be a Bishop. Hence, unlike Prelates of territorial prelatures, it would appear that he would not have the right to attend meetings of the local Bishops' Conference – unless the approved statutes were expressly to prescribe otherwise.

Can. 296 Lay people can dedicate themselves to the apostolic work of a personal prelature by way of agreements made with the prelature. The manner of this organic cooperation and the principal obligations and rights associated with it, are to be duly defined in the statutes.

620 The laity within a personal prelature are not subjects as such. They are associated with it by individual agreement. Their role is to dedicate themselves in some measure to the apostolic mission of the prelature. Details of the nature of their contribution and the consequent rights and obligations within the prelature are left for the statutes of each prelature to define. 'There is no reason why laymen, whether celibate or married, should not dedicate their professional service, through contacts with the prelature, to its works and enterprises.'[2]

---

[1] Cf. *Ut sit validum* II loc cit. 424. The full text of this particular code is published in LE VI 8504–8531.
[2] ES I 4: Fl I 595.

Can. 297 The statutes are likewise to define the relationships of the prelature with the local Ordinaries in whose particular Churches the prelature, with the prior consent of the diocesan Bishop, exercises or wishes to exercise its pastoral or missionary activity.

The relationship which must exist between the prelature and the local Ordinary is not unlike that which ought to exist between local Ordinaries and religious communities established in their territory. Given the Bishop's primary role in the sanctifying, governing and teaching offices of the Church, great pains were taken in the drafting of the canons concerning the apostolate of religious institutes (see especially Cann. 678, 680–683). The statutes of a personal prelature should take into account the various issues addressed in those canons when it comes to define its own relationship with local Church.[1] Note that the canon speaks of the *diocesan Bishop* – not the local Ordinary – as the competent authority whose consent must be obtained for the exercise of the prelature's activity; again there are distinct echoes of the relationship between religious institutes and particular Churches (see e.g. Cann. 609 §1, 611, 612, 616 §1).

Title V
Associations of Christ's Faithful

Chapter I
COMMON NORMS

Can. 298 §1 In the church there are associations which are distinct from institutes of consecrated life and societies of apostolic life. In these associations, Christ's faithful, whether clerics or laity, or clerics and laity together, strive with a common effort to foster a more perfect life, or to promote public worship or christian teaching. They may also devote themselves to other works of the apostolate, such as initiatives for evangelisation, works of piety or charity, and those which animate the temporal order with the christian spirit.

This Title, divided into four chapters, replaces the much more detailed provisions of cc.684–725 of the 1917 Code. It is logically structured, dealing first with norms common to all associations, then successively with public and with private associations, and finally with special norms for exclusively lay associations. The influence of Vat. II, particularly its decree on the Apostolate of Lay People,[2] is significantly noticeable throughout.

This opening canon begins by distinguishing these associations from institutes of consecrated life and societies of apostolic life. Members of Christ's faithful who gather in

---

[1] Cf. e.g. the particular code of *Opus Dei* nn.171–180: LE VI 8527–8528.
[2] Cf. Fl I 766–798.

such associations are not necessarily bound by the profession of the evangelical counsels. These groups are open to both men and women, lay and cleric, not excluding religious (see Can. 307 §3). The possible purposes of any such association are clearly stated: (a) to foster a more perfect life; (b) to promote public worship; (c) to promote Christian teaching; (d) to launch initiatives for evangelisation; (e) to encourage works of piety or charity; (f) to animate the temporal order with the Christian spirit.

Can. 298 §2 Christ's faithful are to join especially those associations which have been established, praised or recommended by the competent ecclesiastical authority.

624 While the faithful are free to join other societies or associations, they are encouraged to join those 'especially' which have received some measure of recognition or endorsement from the Church. These are of two basic kinds: those which have been established by the competent ecclesiastical authority, which are called public associations (see Can. 301 §3), and those simply praised or recommended by that authority and known as private associations (see Can. 299 §2).

Can. 299 §1 By private agreement among themselves, Christ's faithful have the right to constitute associations for the purposes mentioned in Can. 298 §1, without prejudice to the provisions of Can. 301 §1.

625 The right to form associations is acknowledged in general terms in Can. 215, which itself gives juridical expression to the right already acknowledged by Vat. II.[1] No such right was explicitly recognised in the 1917 Code, though it was perhaps implied in the prescription (c.686 §§1–2) which required that associations be established or approved by the competent authority. The present canon acknowledges the right of the faithful to form associations for the purposes listed in Can. 298 §1. These are established 'by private agreement among themselves'. However, if the purpose is to teach in the name of the Church, or to promote public worship, then the law requires that the association be established not by the members themselves but by the competent ecclesiastical authority (see Can. 301 §1).

626 The associations envisaged by this canon can be of different kinds:
 – voluntary associations of the faithful which as yet have no recognition by Church authorities;
 – private associations without juridical personality (see Can. 310);
 – public associations which have been formally established (see Can. 301 §3).

If any of these associations develop, it is possible, though not necessary, that they may, in time, become institutes of consecrated life or societies of apostolic life.

Can. 299 §2 Associations of this kind, even though they may be praised or commended by ecclesiastical authority, are called private associations.

627 Associations of the faithful established by the private agreement of the faithful may indeed receive praise or commendation from the Church authorities. This paragraph states clearly that such recognition in no way alters their juridical status: they remain private associations.

Can. 299 §3 No private association of Christ's faithful is recognised in the Church unless its statutes have been reviewed by the competent authority.

---

[1] Cf. AA 19: Fl I 786.

Part I Christ's Faithful

This paragraph, not contained in the earlier drafts of the Code, was added at a late stage by the Revision Commission.[1] It does not deprive the faithful of their natural right to form an association without seeking any recognition, but such an association would operate outside the structure of Church law and as such would have no canonical rights (see Cann. 310, 322). The purpose of the review of the statutes is to ensure that they contain nothing contrary to Church teaching: it is not for the Bishop or whatever other competent authority is involved to rewrite the statutes.

Can. 300 No association may call itself 'catholic' except with the consent of the competent ecclesiastical authority, in accordance with Can. 312.

The use of the term 'catholic' would indicate that the association will be considered as being in some way representative of the catholic Church. As such, the requirement of the canon that the consent of the competent authority must be obtained is nothing less than a corollary of the prescription of Can. 216. Both canons give juridical expression to the injunction of Vat. II: '... no enterprise must lay claim to the name "Catholic" if it has not the approval of legitimate ecclesiastical authority'.[2] Similar specific expressions of this principle are found in respect of schools and universities (see Cann. 803 §3, 808).

Can. 301 §1 It is for the competent ecclesiastical authority alone to establish associations of Christ's faithful which intend to impart Christian teaching in the name of the Church, or to promote public worship, or which are directed to other ends whose pursuit is of its nature reserved to the same ecclesiastical authority.

The law here reserves to ecclesiastical authority the right to establish certain associations of the faithful. The private agreement of the faithful is not sufficient if the association is to serve certain specific purposes. Three types of such association are indicated:

- those which intend to impart Christian teaching in the name of the Church;
- those which intend to promote public worship;
- those which intend to pursue other ends which of their nature are reserved to the ecclesiastical authority concerned.

The expression 'in the name of the Church' occurs frequently in the Code (see e.g. Cann. 313, 675 §3, 1108 §2, 1192, 1282). It implies that the particular activity is in a formal way representative of the activity of the Church.

Can. 301 §2 The competent ecclesiastical authority, if it judges it expedient, can also establish associations of Christ's faithful to pursue, directly or indirectly, other spiritual ends whose attainment is not adequately provided for by private initiatives.

This paragraph is an example of the principle of subsidiarity. Where certain needs have not been met by existing public and private associations, the competent authority has the power to establish other associations to serve these needs. The role of the competent authority is not simply to step in and form associations in a vacuum, but

---

[1] The Commission explained the addition by stating that, while the right of association is a natural right needing no act from authority, in order to give legal recognition to an association it is necessary to be able to establish its existence. Associations in the Church – as indeed in the State – must therefore make authority aware of their existence. In addition, the same authority will then testify to the christian authenticity of the association: cf. Comm 15(1983) 82–83 at Can. 674.

[2] AA 24: Fl I 789–790.

also to encourage other members of the faithful to take the initiative and form the appropriate associations.

Can. 301 §3 Associations of Christ's faithful which are established by the competent ecclesiastical authorities are called public associations.

632 This paragraph, together with Can. 299 §2, makes explicit the distinction between those associations *established* by the competent authority (public) and those which have been praised or commended (private). Until they have been formally established by decree, associations of the faithful remain private. Once established, they are governed by the norms of Cann. 312–320.

Can. 302 Associations of Christ's faithful are called clerical when they are under the direction of clerics, imply the exercise of sacred orders, and are acknowledged as such by the competent authority.

633 Can. 298 §1 envisages associations composed of clerics, or of lay people, or of clerics and lay people together. This canon sets down the criteria by which an association may be designated as *clerical*. These are:
– that it must be under the direction of clerics;
– that it presupposes the exercise of sacred orders;
– that it is acknowledged as clerical by the competent authority.

634 These three general criteria are repeated verbatim in Can. 588 §2 which describes what is meant by a clerical institute of consecrated life. It is to be noted that clerics, and not just priests, are specified: the canon applies equally to an association of deacons. Any association in which all three of the criteria contained in this canon are not verified is not to be considered clerical. In effect, this means that, unless the association is clerical in accordance with this canon, a lay person may be its moderator (see Can. 317 §3).

Can. 303 Associations whose members live in the world but share in the spirit of some religious institute, under the overall direction of the same institute, and who lead an apostolic life and strive for Christian perfection, are known as third orders, or are called by some other suitable title.

635 In its c.700 the 1917 Code made a basic threefold distinction of associations: third orders, confraternities and pious unions; detailed prescriptions governing each category were contained in cc.702–725. The only one of these categories mentioned by name in the present Code is that of 'third orders'. These are associations joined to a particular religious institute, e.g. Franciscans (all branches), Dominicans, Carmelites, etc. Can. 677 §2 speaks of the obligation of these institutes to make sure that the members of such associations are imbued with the genuine spirit of the religious family.

636 The final clause of the canon recognises that not all such associations are actually called 'third orders'. Those linked with the Benedictines, e.g. are known as Oblates of St Benedict, and what was hitherto known as the Third Order of St Francis is now known as the Secular Franciscan Order.

Can. 304 §1 All associations of Christ's faithful, whether public or private, by whatever title or name they are called, are to have their own statutes. These are to define the purpose or social objective of the association, its centre, its governance and the conditions of membership. They are also to specify the manner of action of the association, paying due regard to what is necessary or useful in the circumstances of the time and place.

In contrast with cc.689 §1 and 697 of the 1917 Code, this canon contains detailed indications of the contents of the statutes of these associations. They must specify the purpose or social objective of the association; they must specify its headquarters, its form of government, its conditions for membership, and finally the manner in which its activities are conducted – this last element is to reflect the socio-cultural circumstances in which the association finds itself.

Although not mentioned as required by law, other elements which should be included in these statutes are: an outline of the basic spirituality of the association; an indication of those to whom (or for whose benefit) the association is aimed; a list of the officials, e.g. the Moderator, the chaplain, the administrators of temporal goods, the finance committee or two counsellors. It would also be useful to name the senior officials who are to be consulted when the need arises (see Cann. 317 §1, 318 §2, 320 §3); the procedure for admission to membership and for dismissal; procedures for the election of officials and their removal from office; mechanisms for changing the statutes; norms for carrying out the purpose of the association, for visitation by the competent authority, and for financial administration.

Can. 304 §2 Associations are to select for themselves a title or name which is in keeping with the practices of the time and place, especially one derived from the purpose they intend.

The 1917 Code in its c.688 prescribed that associations must not select a title for themselves which smacked of levity or unbecoming novelty or which expressed a form of devotion not approved by the Holy See. This rather negative prescription has been replaced by the present canon which states its principle in a more positive manner: the name of the association is to be as descriptive as possible of its work or function, according to local and historical circumstances.

Can. 305 §1 All associations of Christ's faithful are subject to the supervision of the competent ecclesiastical authority. This authority is to ensure that integrity of faith and morals is maintained in them and that abuses in ecclesiastical discipline do not creep in. The competent authority has therefore the duty and the right to visit these associations, in accordance with the law and the statutes. Associations are also subject to the governance of the same authority in accordance with the provisions of the canons which follow.

Every association of the faithful, whether private or public, must operate within a relationship with ecclesiastical authority. This canon contains the principal elements of that relationship. A clear distinction is drawn in the text between 'supervision' and 'governance'. *Supervision* refers to the overall responsibility which any Bishop or other competent authority has to safeguard faith and morals and to uphold ecclesiastical discipline, whether relating to individuals or to associations. *Governance* refers to a direct and positive intervention of the competent authority within the life and activity of the association.

In order to carry out this responsibility, the authority is given 'the duty and the right' to visit these associations. The areas within which the authority may comment or take action are to be described more specifically in the statutes of each association. A recent example of this type of intervention is to be found in a letter of the Congregation for the Doctrine of the Faith to the Archbishop of Cologne concerning certain practices of the association known as 'Opus Angelorum'.[1]

---

[1] Cf. AAS 76(1984) 175–176.

Can. 305 §2 Associations of every kind are subject to the supervision of the Holy See. Diocesan associations are subject to the supervision of the local Ordinary, as are other associations to the extent that they work in the diocese.

642 This paragraph indicates the identity of the 'competent ecclesiastical authority' mentioned in the preceding paragraph. Initially, the role of supervision had been entrusted to the Bishops' Conference for regional associations.[1] This was removed in a subsequent draft text, and an attempt to restore it was firmly rejected by the Revision Commission, not least because this would have created a 'national curia' which was judged not to be opportune.[2] The practical effect is therefore that associations, whether strictly diocesan or inter-diocesan, are subject to the supervision of the local Ordinary to the extent to which they operate in the diocese. All associations, local, national, international and universal, are subject to supervision by the Holy See.

Can. 306 To enjoy the rights and privileges, indulgences and other spiritual favours granted to an association, it is necessary and sufficient that a person be validly received into the association in accordance with the provisions of the law and with the association's own statutes, and be not lawfully dismissed from it.

643 This canon repeats unchanged the substance of c.692 of the 1917 Code. It indicates the need for the statutes of an association to spell out the conditions for membership, the procedure for admission, and the circumstances and reasons in and by which a person ceases to be a member. The benefits of an association accrue to all those who have validly entered the association and have not left it. The law makes no distinction between the benefits accruing to active members and those accruing to dormant members. However, the indulgences mentioned are governed by the norms contained in Cann. 992–997. In particular, in order to obtain the indulgence, a person 'must fulfil the prescribed works at the time and in the manner determined by the terms of the grant' (Can. 996 §2): membership of an association alone is not sufficient.

Can. 307 §1 The admission of members is to take place in accordance with the law and with the statutes of each association.

§2 The same person can be enrolled in several associations.

§3 In accordance with their own law, members of religious institutes may, with the consent of their Superior, join associations.

644 Gone from the present legislation is the former requirement (c.694 §2) that valid entry into an association with 'moral personality' necessitated the inscription of one's name on the membership list. The first paragraph simply repeats the initial prescription of the 1917 Code's c.694 §1, leaving details concerning valid admission to the statutes of each association.

645 Gone, too, is the former restriction (c.705) forbidding a person to belong to more than one third order: the current Code omits any reference to this, while repeating the text of c.693 §2 of the previous Code (§2). Thus there is nothing in universal law prohibiting a person from belonging to several associations. Of course, the statutes of an individual association may exclude from membership individuals who have already assumed obligations elsewhere which are not in harmony with those of the association.

---

[1] Cf. SPD 34 at Can. 44.
[2] Cf. Comm 15(1983) 84 at Can. 679.

Part I Christ's Faithful

Two conditions circumscribe the ability of religious to join associations of the faithful (§3): **646**

(a) doing so must be in accordance with the proper law of the institute;

(b) they must have received the consent of their Superior.

No specific reference is made to third orders, as was done in c.704 §1 of the 1917 Code. It is clear, however, that religious may not enter any association which would involve obligations in conflict with those proper to their own institute.

Missing entirely from this canon is any reference to the prohibition against non-catholics joining these associations. They had been explicitly excluded by c.693 §1 of the 1917 Code, along with members of condemned societies, persons notoriously under censure, and public sinners. In the preparation of the present canon, there was much discussion on this matter.[1] The final draft which was presented to Pope John Paul contained a fourth paragraph explicitly excluding non-catholics from membership, except where the local Ordinary judged there was no danger.[2] But that paragraph was removed, obviously at the direction of the Pope. Hence, unless the statutes of a particular association forbid it, it seems clear that baptised non-catholics may join private and public associations of the faithful; apart from those excluded by Can. 316 §1 from joining public associations, there is no general prohibition. **647**

Can. 308 No one who was lawfully admitted is to be dismissed from an association except for a just reason, in accordance with the law and the statutes.

Dismissal from any association can take place only for a just cause. The statutes should define these causes more closely and they should indicate who has the authority to dismiss and what procedure should be followed. Universal law foresees dismissal for those who have publicly rejected the catholic faith, or have defected from ecclesiastical communion, or upon whom an excommunication has been imposed or declared (see Can. 316 §§1–2). **648**

Can. 309 Associations that are lawfully constituted have the right, in accordance with the law and the statutes, to make particular norms concerning the association, to hold meetings, to appoint moderators, officials, ministers and administrators of goods.

A much greater degree of autonomy is envisaged here than was the case in c.697 of the 1917 Code. According to the present canon, all associations which have been lawfully constituted (either by commendation or formal establishment) have the rights indicated in this canon. The local Ordinary, therefore, no longer has by law the right to a specific role in the inner workings of an association, as he had under cc.698 §1 and 715 of the previous Code. The statutes of an association may, of course, provide otherwise, but it is considered that this would occur only in a very exceptional situation. **649**

As in the law for institutes of consecrated life, the Code uses the general term 'moderator' to denote the person in charge. An association is thus free to use its own preferred vocabulary, e.g. president, director, leader, minister, etc. **650**

Can. 310 A private association which has not been constituted a juridical person cannot, as such, be the subject of duties and rights. However, Christ's faithful who are joined together in it can jointly contract obliga-

---

[1] Cf. SPD 34 at Can. 46 §3; Comm 12(1980) 101 at Can. 46; Comm 15(1983) 84 at Can. 681.
[2] Cf. Sch 1982 at Can. 307 §4.

tions. As joint owners and joint possessors they can acquire and possess rights and goods. They can exercise these rights and obligations through a delegate or a proxy.

651 Public associations of the faithful automatically become juridical persons upon their establishment (see Can. 313). Private associations, while per se not juridical persons, can become such by decree of the appropriate competent ecclesiastical authority (see Can. 322 §1). The present canon gives a certain recognition to the private associations which are not juridical persons. It acknowledges that members of these associations can be joint owners and joint possessors. Their rights are thus individual rather than belonging to the association as such. From the point of view of canon law, those who administer the goods of such an association are considered to be proxies or delegates of the individual members gathered as a group. From the point of view of the association, they may be seen to be acting on its behalf. This canon exempts private associations from many of the prescriptions of the Code – such e.g. as Cann. 113–123 concerning juridical persons – thereby giving them greater freedom, but without the protection of the law. The temporal goods of such private associations are not ecclesiastical goods (see Can. 1257).

Can. 311 Members of institutes of consecrated life who preside over or assist associations which are joined in some way to their institute, are to ensure that these associations help the apostolic works existing in the diocese. They are especially to cooperate, under the direction of the local Ordinary, with associations which are directed to the exercise of the apostolate in the diocese.

652 In its decree on the apostolate of lay people, Vat. II urged that 'dissipation of forces must be avoided'.[1] Such dissipation can occur when there are too many groups attempting to do the same work in the same area. The Code seeks to give heed to these cautionary words by emphasising here the need for cooperation in the apostolate with local associations and institutes. While this is entrusted to the overall direction of the local Ordinary, the responsibility for effecting this cooperation rests on the members of the institutes of consecrated life who care for the association. The basic thrust of this canon is identical to that of Can. 680 which speaks of cooperation in the apostolate between religious and the secular clergy.

Chapter II
PUBLIC ASSOCIATIONS OF CHRIST'S FAITHFUL

Can. 312 §1 The authority which is competent to establish public associations is:

   1° the Holy See, for universal and international associations;

   2° the Bishops' Conference in its own territory, for national associations which by their very establishment are intended for work throughout the whole nation;

---
[1] AA 19: Fl I 786.

3° the diocesan Bishop, each in his own territory, but not the diocesan Administrator, for diocesan associations, with the exception, however, of associations the right to whose establishment is reserved to others by apostolic privilege.

Depending on the geographical extension of the association (universal, international, national, diocesan) the authority competent to establish it is, in turn, the Holy See, the Bishops' Conference or the diocesan Bishop. The inclusion of the Bishops' Conference is an innovation. The Code provides no criteria which a Bishops' Conference might use in establishing national associations, but the following could serve as useful guidelines:

- the usefulness for the Church;
- a truly national or regional programme;
- doctrinal orthodoxy, avoiding extreme positions;
- approval at the diocesan level by one or more diocesan Bishops;
- a certain period of time during which the association has functioned satisfactorily at diocesan level.

If a national association is established, it would appear advisable that one Bishop should be named to act on behalf of the others.

At the diocesan level, it is only the diocesan Bishop who can establish public associations; the diocesan administrator is explicitly excluded: so too, implicitly, are other Ordinaries. The exception mentioned in 3° clearly refers to third orders and other associations joined in some way to an institute of consecrated life: by apostolic privilege, the actual establishment of such associations belongs to members of the institute concerned; yet, as the next paragraph shows, the diocesan Bishop has a distinct say in the establishment of these associations in his diocese.

Can. 312 §2 The written consent of the diocesan Bishop is required for the valid establishment of an association or branch of an association in the diocese, even though it is done in virtue of an apostolic privilege. Permission, however, which is given by the diocesan Bishop for the establishment of a house of a religious institute, is valid also for the establishment in the same house, or in a church attached to it, of an association which is proper to that institute.

By reason of this paragraph, the power of a Bishop concerning the establishment of associations of the faithful or branches of associations in his diocese is quite substantial. Nothing can be done validly without his written consent. He can, therefore, effectively prevent a national or international association from operating in his diocese. It is understood of course that the canon refers only to public associations; the people of the diocese are still free to establish private associations or join public associations based in another diocese.

This paragraph indicates one limitation on the Bishops' power in this area, namely that consent for a religious foundation automatically brings with it consent for the establishment of any association of the faithful proper to the religious institute concerned. Diocesan Bishops should be aware of this when giving consent for a religious foundation. Once consent is given, the establishment in the house or church of an association proper to the institute cannot be prevented by the Bishop, even though such an event might not occur for many years after the religious foundation.

Can. 313 A public association or a confederation of public associations is constituted a juridical person by the very decree by which it is established by the authority competent in accordance with Can. 312. Moreover, in so far as is required, it thereby receives its mission to pursue, in the name of the Church, those ends which it proposes for itself.

657 The valid establishment of a public association or a confederation of public associations brings with it the status of a public juridical person. Hence, these associations are governed by the prescriptions of Cann. 113–123 as well as the norms of this part of the Code. Furthermore, in keeping with the description of public juridical persons found in Can. 116 §1, the association receives in its decree of establishment the ecclesial mission which it is to carry out 'in the name of the Church'. Specific details of this mission depend on the actual nature and purpose of each association or confederation.

Can. 314 The statutes of any public association require the approval of the authority which, in accordance with Can. 312 §1, is competent to establish the association; this approval is also required for a revision of, or a change in, the statutes.

658 Until they have been approved by the authority which established the association, its statutes have no force. According to Can. 117, no group can obtain juridical personality unless its statutes are approved by the competent authority. It seems logical to conclude that approval of the statutes must take place prior to, if not simultaneously with, the decree of establishment mentioned in the preceding canon. However, if a Bishop were to sanction the establishment of a branch of a national association already established by the Conference of Bishops, he would have no say in the approval or revision of statutes, except as a member of the Conference. His powers in this regard would be even less were he to permit the establishment of a branch of an international or universal public association established by the Holy See.

Can. 315 Public associations can, on their own initiative, undertake projects which are appropriate to their character, and they are governed by the statutes, but under the higher direction of the ecclesiastical authority mentioned in Can. 312 §1.

659 This is a further example of the principle of subsidiarity. The associations may take the initiative in undertaking projects. But the competent authority is to ensure that overall policy and particular activity corresponds to the purposes of the association as expressed in the statutes. This is one specific area where the authority is charged with supervision of associations (see Can. 305 §1). To make sure that the initiative is not stifled while discipline is maintained, there is need for dialogue and a sense of balance between associations and the competent authority.

Can. 316 §1 A person who has publicly rejected the catholic faith, or has defected from ecclesiastical communion, or upon whom an excommunication has been imposed or declared, cannot validly be received into public associations.

660 Because it represents a restriction on the free exercise of rights, in accordance with Can. 18 this canon is to be interpreted strictly. Therefore, it applies only to public associations, not to private ones. Moreover, as has already been seen, it does not apply to non-catholics as such (see above at Can. 307). The only persons who are barred from valid membership of any public association by virtue of this canon are catholics who:

(a) have publicly rejected the catholic faith; or

(b) have publicly defected from ecclesiastical communion; or

(c) have had an excommunication publicly imposed or declared on them.

This constitutes a departure from the provisions of c.693 §1 of the 1917 Code which was sweeping in its exclusion of non-catholics, those belonging to condemned societies, those notoriously under censure and public sinners. The Revision Commission wanted a clearer, more limited statement.[1] In the 1980 draft the term 'notorious' was retained,[2] but this was changed subsequently to 'publicly'. Thus, the rejection of the faith, the defection from ecclesiastical communion, or the imposition or declaration of an excommunication need not be notorious: it is sufficient that it be provable in the external forum (see Can. 1074).

Can. 316 §2 Those who have been lawfully enrolled but who fall into one of the categories mentioned in §1, having been previously warned, are to be dismissed, in accordance with the statutes of the association, without prejudice to their right of recourse to the ecclesiastical authority mentioned in Can. 312 §1.

While the first paragraph of this canon deals with the exclusion of a person from valid membership, the second concerns the dismissal of someone who is already a legitimate member of a public association of the faithful. According to this canon, echoing the provisions of Can. 308, the statutes of each association ought to contain an outline of the procedure for dismissal. The statutes should also state at which level of the association the decision to dismiss is taken and a more detailed indication of other causes for dismissal. A warning must always be given before dismissal and the law gives the person the right to have recourse to the competent ecclesiastical authority against dismissal.

Can. 317 §1 Unless the statutes provide otherwise, it belongs to the ecclesiastical authority mentioned in Can. 312 §1 to confirm the moderator of a public association on election, or to appoint the moderator on presentation, or by its own right to appoint the moderator. The same authority appoints the chaplain or ecclesiastical assistant, after consulting the senior officials of the association, wherever this is expedient.

This canon reflects a further change in the law. Whereas c.698 §1 of the 1917 Code required that the local Ordinary appoint the moderator of a public association, the present law indicates a variety of ways in which an association may receive a moderator; in each case, the statutes of the association are to determine the issue in detail. The canon makes it clear that, unless some other provision is made in the statutes, the authority competent to make the appointment or confirm the election of the moderator is the same authority which established it in the first place, i.e. the Holy See, the Bishops' Conference, or the diocesan Bishop.

The appointment of a chaplain or ecclesiastical assistant for a public association belongs to the competent authority already mentioned: it would appear that the statutes of the association are not free to decide otherwise. However, the canon does oblige the authority to consult the 'senior officials of the association' before making such an appointment.

---

[1] Cf. Comm 15(1983) 86 at Can. 692.

[2] Cf. Sch 1980 at Can. 692 §1.

Can. 317 §2 The norm of §1 is also valid for associations which members of religious institutes, by apostolic privilege, establish outside their own churches or houses. In associations which members of religious institutes establish in their own church or house, the appointment or confirmation of the moderator and chaplain belongs to the Superior of the institute, in accordance with the statutes.

665 This paragraph makes an important distinction between associations established by religious outside their own houses and those which are established within their own houses. The former are governed by the norm of the first paragraph of this canon in the appointment of a moderator and chaplain, unless of course the statutes provide otherwise; the latter are governed by the norm of the second half of this paragraph: the appointment to both offices belongs to the Superior of the institute. Although it is not expressly stated, the statutes of these associations should also determine whether the religious Superior is to confirm the election of the moderator, appoint a moderator on presentation, or appoint one by his or her own right. Moreover, there ought to be consultation of the senior officials before a chaplain or ecclesiastical assistant is appointed.

Can. 317 §3 The laity can be moderators of associations which are not clerical. The chaplain or ecclesiastical assistant is not to be the moderator, unless the statutes provide otherwise.

666 The clear implication of c.698 §2 of the 1917 Code was that the moderator of each association should be a priest. Now, lay men and women may be moderators in lay associations and in others which include clerics but which are not acknowledged by law as clerical associations (see Can. 302). Another change is that, unless the statutes provide otherwise, the moderator and the chaplain or ecclesiastical assistant should not be the same person, something which c.698 §4 of the 1917 Code certainly permitted.

Can. 317 §4 Those who hold an office of direction in political parties are not to be moderators in public associations of Christ's faithful which are directly ordered to the exercise of the apostolate.

667 Because public associations of the faithful act in the name of the Church (see Can. 313), they should not be closely identified with any particular political party. The term 'office of direction' appears to refer to any position of responsibility within a political party and not just to that of leader. It must be stressed that it is the office of moderator of a public association of the faithful which may not be combined with a leadership role in a political party. There is nothing to prevent such a political leader becoming a member, or being active as a member, of a public association. Moreover, the public associations mentioned in this paragraph are only those 'which are directly ordered to the exercise of the apostolate'.

Can. 318 §1 In special circumstances, when serious reasons so require, the ecclesiastical authority mentioned in Can. 312 §1 can appoint a commissioner to direct the association in its name for the time being.

668 In this provision of law, we have an example of the supervision of all associations of the faithful mentioned in Can. 305 §1. Thus, e.g. if an association appears to be in or heading towards some serious difficulty, the competent authority can intervene by appointing a commissioner who will take over the direction of the association in the name of the authority. An intervention of this kind must be understood to be extraor-

Can. 318 §2 The moderator of a public association may be removed for a just reason, by the person who made the appointment or the confirmation, but the moderator himself or herself and the senior officials of the association must be consulted, in accordance with the statutes. The chaplain can, however, be removed by the person who appointed him, in accordance with Cann. 192-195.

The removal of the moderator of a public association requires a just, though not necessarily a grave, reason. It is for the competent authority to decide if the reason is sufficient. However, before any removal can take place, the moderator and other officials who are to be identified in the statutes of the association, must be consulted. Nothing is said in the canon about recourse against such removal, but the procedure to be followed is that of recourse against administrative decrees found in Cann. 1732-1739. 669

The law does not prescribe any consultation before the removal of the chaplain. However, the reference to Cann. 192-195 on removal from ecclesiastical office is a distinct warning against any arbitrary removal. 670

Can. 319 §1 Unless otherwise provided, a lawfully established public association administers the goods it possesses, in accordance with the statutes, and under the overall direction of the ecclesiastical authority mentioned in Can. 312 §1. It must give a yearly account to this authority.

§2 The association must also faithfully account to the same authority for the disbursement of contributions and alms which it has collected.

Since a lawfully established public association of the faithful is a public juridical person (see Can. 313), its temporal goods are subject to the provisions of Book V of the Code, and accordingly the statutes of each association should conform to those provisions. While the direct supervision of all temporal goods belongs to the internal authorities of each association, everything must be done under the overall supervision of the authority which established the association. This is reflected in the twofold requirement of the canon: 671

(a) an account of the administration must be given to the competent authority each year;
(b) a further account of what was collected and disbursed must also be given to the same authority.

The first requirement appears to refer to all the assets of an association, the second to annual income and expenditure.

Can. 320 §1 Associations established by the Holy See can be suppressed only by the Holy See.

This paragraph speaks for itself: if the authority competent to establish the association in accordance with Can. 312 §1 is the Holy See, no other authority can suppress it. 672

Can. 320 §2 For grave reasons, associations established by the Bishops' Conference can be suppressed by it. The diocesan Bishop can suppress those he has established, and also those which, by apostolic indult, members of religious institutes have established with the consent of the diocesan Bishop.

673 If the competent authority is either the Bishops' Conference or the diocesan Bishop, then that same authority has the right to suppress the association if there are serious reasons. In essence, this norm of law is the same as that contained in c.699 §1 of the 1917 Code, except for the inclusion of the Bishops' Conference as a competent authority. Note that the diocesan Bishop may not suppress public associations of the faithful established in the houses or churches of religious institutes; only those established outside their houses by apostolic indult may be so suppressed.

674 The present canon omits any reference to recourse against suppression, something mentioned explicitly in c.699 §1 of the 1917 Code. Nevertheless, Cann. 1732–1739 concerning recourse against an administrative act do apply in this case.

Can. 320 §3 A public association of the faithful is not to be suppressed by the competent authority unless the moderator and other senior officials have been consulted.

675 This is an example of a situation where a Superior must consult with others before acting (see Can. 127 §1). Should this consultation not take place, any suppression which followed would be invalid. Although it is not stated explicitly, the senior officials who must be consulted would appear to be the same as those who are to be consulted in the case of the removal of the moderator (see Can. 318 §2). The statutes of each association should specify who these senior officials are.

Chapter III
PRIVATE ASSOCIATIONS OF CHRIST'S FAITHFUL

Can. 321 Christ's faithful direct and moderate private associations according to the provision of the statutes.

676 The freedom which the faithful enjoy in forming associations for various purposes is reinforced by this canon. While public associations of the faithful are governed by the norms of Cann. 312–320 as well as by their own statutes, private associations are governed simply by the statutes of each association. This means that they are able to conduct their own affairs with a greater degree of autonomy, allowing of course that this autonomy is not absolute since all associations of the faithful remain under the supervision of the appropriate ecclesiastical authority (see Can. 305 §1).

Can. 322 §1 A private association of Christ's faithful can acquire juridical personality by a formal decree of the competent ecclesiastical authority mentioned in Can. 312.

§2 No private association of Christ's faithful can acquire juridical personality unless its statutes are approved by the ecclesiastical authority mentioned in Can. 312 §1. The approval of the statutes does not, however, change the private nature of the association.

677 The possibility of a private association acquiring juridical personality is something new to the law. Formerly, only an association which was formally established by an ecclesiastical authority, and not one which was simply praised or commended, could obtain juridical personality. Acquiring juridical personality means that the association becomes, as such, the subject of rights and duties. Juridical personality is acquired by a decree of the competent ecclesiastical authority; this decree is very different from that by which a public association is established by the same authority. In itself, the acquisition of juridical personality does not alter the private status of an association.

In order to be recognised, each private association of the faithful must have its statutes reviewed by the competent authority (see Can. 299 §3). Before such an association can acquire juridical personality, the statutes must be approved by the same authority. Although they are capable of acquiring and administering temporal goods, these goods are not considered 'ecclesiastical goods', nor are such associations directly subject to the norms of Book V (see Can. 1257). Nevertheless, their statutes ought to be consistent with the principles contained there and they must conform to those canons which speak specifically of private juridical persons (see e.g. Cann. 1257 §2, 1263, 1265 §1, 1267 §1, 1269, 1279 §1, 1280).

Can. 323 §1 Although private associations of Christ's faithful enjoy their own autonomy in accordance with Can. 321, they are subject to the supervision of ecclesiastical authority, in accordance with Can. 305, and also to the governance of the same authority.

Here we find a balance being struck between the autonomy of such associations set forth in Can. 321 and the principle of supervision by the competent ecclesiastical authority established in Can. 305. In spite of the difference of language, the norm stated here is essentially the same as that contained in cc.336 §2 and 690 §1 of the 1917 Code. Among the sources listed for this canon is a lengthy response from the Sacred Congregation of the Council, dated 13 November 1920, concerning the status of the Society of St Vincent de Paul.[1] The Congregation concluded that, while the Society was not to be considered either a pious union or a confraternity (and, therefore, not subject to the canons concerning such associations), 'the Ordinary has the right and duty of watching that nothing against faith or morals occurs and, if any abuses occur, to correct and repress them'.

Can. 323 §2 It is also the responsibility of ecclesiastical authority, with due respect for the autonomy of private associations, to oversee and ensure that there is no dissipation of their forces, and that the exercise of their apostolate is directed to the common good.

The origins of this paragraph lie in the decrees of Vat. II on the pastoral office of Bishops in the Church and on the apostolate of the laity.[2] This function of the ecclesiastical authority is not to be understood as interference in the internal affairs of the association, but as a concrete example of its responsibility to coordinate the apostolate. The canon stresses that the autonomy of these associations must be respected, but this autonomy does not exempt them from being part of a coordinated approach to the apostolate which seeks to avoid unnecessary and unhelpful duplication and dissipation of forces. Similar norms are found in Cann. 311 and 680.

Can. 324 §1 A private association of Christ's faithful can freely designate for itself a moderator and officers, in accordance with the statutes.

§2 If a private association of Christ's faithful wishes to have a spiritual counsellor, it can freely choose one for itself from among the priests who lawfully exercise a ministry in the diocese, but the priest requires the confirmation of the local Ordinary.

---

[1] Cf. SCCon resol 13.XI.1920: AAS 13(1921) 135–144; an English summary of the decision is to be found in CLD 1 714–715.
[2] Cf. CD 17, AA 19, 24: Fl I 573–574, 786, 789–90.

681 The autonomy of private associations is demonstrated clearly in this canon: each association has the right to designate its own moderator without any need of confirmation by ecclesiastical authority. This contrasts sharply with the procedures for public associations stated in Can. 317 §1. It is for the statutes of each association to specify how the designation of the moderator is to be done, i.e. by election or by some other method. If there is to be an election, the association is not bound to observe the norms of Cann. 164–179, since this is not strictly an ecclesiastical office. Nevertheless, the statutes may well refer to these norms or may even be modelled on them.

682 The autonomy is further reinforced in the second paragraph where it is made clear that the decision to have or not to have a 'spiritual counsellor' belongs to the association itself. Moreover, the association can freely choose whatever priest it wishes, provided only he is among those 'who lawfully exercise a ministry in the diocese'. Ordinarily, this will mean that priests who live outside the diocese or who are no longer actively engaged in the ministry within the diocese are excluded. However, the local Ordinary, to whom confirmation of the appointment belongs, may decide to consider this activity in itself as a form of legitimate ministry and confirm as spiritual counsellor a priest from an adjacent diocese or a priest in his own diocese who is otherwise retired from the active ministry.

683 There was discussion during the preparation of the text as to whether the appointment of such a counsellor or chaplain by a private association needs confirmation by the local Ordinary. The text as promulgated reflects the decision that such a confirmation concerns the relationship between the priest and the Bishop; it is not the association which needs approval for the appointment of such a counsellor, but the priest himself.[1]

Can. 325 §1 A private association of Christ's faithful is free to administer any goods it possesses, according to the provisions of the statutes, but the competent ecclesiastical authority has the right to ensure that the goods are applied to the purposes of the association.

684 A private association of the faithful is free to administer its own goods according to the terms of its statutes and the norms of law. If the association has not been granted juridical personality, then any goods belong, canonically, not to the association as such but to the members of the association as joint owners (see Can. 310). The first part of this paragraph again vindicates the autonomy of private associations. The second part was added only in the final draft,[2] reflecting the desire of Vat. II that, even in temporal affairs, the Church should ensure that moral principles are observed.[3]

Can. 325 §2 In accordance with Can. 1301, the association is subject to the authority of the local Ordinary in whatever concerns the administration and distribution of goods which are donated or left to it for pious purposes.

685 Since, according to Can. 1301 §1, 'the Ordinary is the executor of all pious dispositions', he has authority over private associations in the matter of the administration and distribution of goods donated to those associations. This implies a duty on the part of the private association to advise the Ordinary of such gifts or bequests. It is for the Ordinary to decide about the disposal of such goods or funds, respecting in the first place the intentions of the donor.

---

[1] Cf. Comm 12(1980) 120 at Can. 67 §2.
[2] Sch 1982 at Can. 325 §1.
[3] Cf. AA 24: Fl I 790.

Can. 326 §1 A private association of Christ's faithful is extinguished in accordance with the norms of the statutes. It can also be suppressed by the competent authority if its activity gives rise to grave harm to ecclesiastical teaching or discipline, or is a scandal to the faithful.

A private association of the faithful can come to an end in two different ways: it can become extinct, or it can be suppressed. The statutes should make provision for the possible extinction of the association, foreseeing a variety of circumstances when this step may need to be taken. The canon itself gives three reasons for the suppression of an association: activity which causes harm to ecclesiastical teaching, or to ecclesiastical discipline, or which is a cause of scandal to the faithful. It is interesting to note that the Code is relatively specific here with regard to private associations, while Can. 320, dealing with the suppression of public associations, refers only to 'grave reasons'.

This norm of law clearly applies to those associations whose statutes have been recognised or approved by the competent authority. However, if a private association has never actually sought recognition, the competent authority cannot suppress something whose existence it has never acknowledged. Nonetheless, the authority could, for sound pastoral reasons, prohibit such an association from operating in or from churches within his territory.

Can. 326 §2 The fate of the goods of a private association which ceases to exist is to be determined in accordance with the statutes, without prejudice to acquired rights and to the wishes of the donors.

One issue which ought always to be dealt with in the statutes concerning the extinction or suppression of a private association is the fate of its temporal goods. Can. 123 states that if a public juridical person becomes extinct without appropriate provisions in its statutes, arrangements concerning its goods are to be made by the immediately superior juridical person. No similar provision of law covers private associations, although this lacuna was noted by the Revision Commission.[1] Since the goods of a private association are not regarded as ecclesiastical goods, a parallel cannot be drawn with the law on public associations, e.g. the local Ordinary cannot claim any right to, nor has he any responsibility for, the property of such associations. This highlights once again the need for statutes which cover all eventualities. Indeed, the competent authority which reviews or approves these statutes should ensure that this issue is addressed in them. Moreover, it is for the same authority to make sure, by reason of its role of supervision, that acquired rights and donors' intentions are especially respected in the disposal of the property of any private association.

Chapter IV
SPECIAL NORMS FOR LAY ASSOCIATIONS

Can. 327 Lay members of Christ's faithful are to hold in high esteem associations constituted for the spiritual purposes mentioned in Can. 298. They should especially esteem those associations whose aim is to animate the temporal order with the christian spirit, and thus greatly foster an intimate union between faith and life.

---

[1] Cf. Comm 12(1980) 122 at Can. 69.

689 The three canons of this chapter are essentially exhortatory in character. They are directed explicitly and specifically only to lay members of Christ's faithful. The juridical structure and scope of all lay associations are governed by the norms of Cann. 298–326. Can. 327, reflecting the expressed wishes of Vat. II,[1] commends to the attention of the lay faithful those associations which are founded to animate the temporal order with a christian spirit. This is specifically mentioned in Can. 225 §2 as the special obligation of the lay faithful.

Can. 328 Those who head lay associations, even those established by apostolic privilege, are to ensure that their associations cooperate with other associations of Christ's faithful, where this is expedient. They are to give their help freely to various christian works, especially those in the same territory.

690 This canon repeats the principle found in Cann. 311 and 323 §2. Those in charge of lay associations are to make sure that proper collaboration and cooperation exist between all such associations, particularly those in the same territory. In this way useless rivalries between groups of the faithful and a dissipation of forces are to be avoided.

Can. 329 Moderators of lay associations are to ensure that the members receive due formation, so that they may carry out the apostolate which is proper to the laity.

691 According to Can. 231 §1, those lay people who exercise a special apostolate in the Church are obliged to receive the appropriate formation for their role. The present canon lays the responsibility for this formation on the moderators of lay associations, thus fulfilling the wish of Vat. II.[2]

---

[1] Cf. AA 21–22: Fl I 788.
[2] Cf. AA 28–32: Fl I 793–797.

PART II

THE HIERARCHICAL CONSTITUTION OF THE CHURCH

Section I
THE SUPREME AUTHORITY OF THE CHURCH

Chapter I
THE ROMAN PONTIFF AND THE COLLEGE OF BISHOPS

Can. 330 Just as, by the decree of the Lord, Saint Peter and the rest of the Apostles form one College, so for a like reason the Roman Pontiff, the Successor of Peter, and the Bishops, the successors of the Apostles, are united together in one.

In Vat. II the Church undertook the difficult task of reflecting on the very nature of the Church itself. The outcome of these reflections was the Dogmatic Constitution on the Church, *Lumen Gentium*. Chapter III of that document dealt with the hierarchical constitution of the Church, and the text of the present canon repeats what is found there. This is a doctrinal canon, originally intended for inclusion in the *Lex Ecclesiae Fundamentalis*. It sets forth the basic relationship between the Roman Pontiff and the College of Bishops: just as Peter and the Apostles formed a College, so the Pope and the Bishops also form a College. It is important that the concept of 'College' be properly understood.

In the *Nota Explicativa Praevia* attached by Vat. II to *Lumen Gentium*, it is clearly stated: 'The word "College" is not taken in the *strictly juridical* sense, that is as a group of equals who transfer their powers to their chairman, but as a permanent body whose form and authority is to be ascertained from revelation... The parallel between Peter and the apostles on the one hand and the Pope and the Bishops on the other does not imply the transmission of the extraordinary power of the apostles to their successors, nor obviously does it imply *equality* between the head and the members of the college, but only a *proportion* between the two relationships: Peter–apostles and Pope–Bishops.'[1] The canon must be understood in the light of this explanatory note. The Pope and the Bishops continue in the Church the ministry and role of Peter and the Apostles which was given to them by the Lord himself.

---

[1] LG NEP I: Fl I 424.

Article 1
The Roman Pontiff

Can. 331 The office uniquely committed by the Lord to Peter, the first of the Apostles, and to be transmitted to his successors, abides in the Bishop of the Church of Rome. He is the head of the College of Bishops, the Vicar of Christ, and the Pastor of the universal Church here on earth. Consequently, by virtue of his office, he has supreme, full, immediate and universal ordinary power in the Church, and he can always freely exercise this power.

694 Down through the centuries, the Church has sought to express accurately the nature of the role and ministry of the Pope. For this reason, it is not easy to identify any single source for the present canon. Its present expression is heavily indebted to Vat. II,[1] but traces of doctrinal statements many hundreds of years old can be found in it.[2]

695 The canon speaks of the Pope first as the Bishop of the Church of Rome and identifies him as the successor of Peter to whom the role and authority of Peter, given by the Lord himself, has been transmitted. An indication of the nature of this role and authority is provided in the three titles which the canon then attributes to the Pope: head of the College of Bishops, Vicar of Christ, and Pastor of the whole Church. Not all the Pope's titles are included in the canon. For example, he is also Patriarch of the West, Primate of Italy, and Archbishop and Metropolitan of the Province of Rome. These titles specify his role on a more local level, while those contained in the canon refer to his mission within the entire Church throughout the world.

696 The canon ends with a description of the extent and nature of the Pope's power. That power is *supreme*, i.e. there is no other power above it in the Church; it is *full*, i.e. it lacks nothing in its exercise; it is *immediate*, i.e. it can be exercised without any intermediary; it is *universal*, i.e. it is exercised over the whole Church; it is *ordinary*, i.e. it belongs to the office; it is *freely exercised*, i.e. it is independent of any other power, ecclesiastical or civil. This power of the Pope, moreover, is to be exercised *in the Church*; the medieval claims to a papal authority over and above that of political rulers have long since been set aside. The unique status and power of the Pope in the Church has practical implications which can be seen throughout the entire Code.

Can. 332 §1 The Roman Pontiff acquires full and supreme power in the Church when, together with episcopal consecration, he has been lawfully elected and has accepted the election. Accordingly, if he already has the episcopal character, he receives this power from the moment he accepts election to the supreme pontificate. If he does not have the episcopal character, he is immediately to be ordained Bishop.

697 The 1917 Code (c.219) spoke of the legitimately elected Pope obtaining full power immediately on accepting election. The present canon takes matters a step further: the full power is acquired by the one who has been lawfully elected and who has received episcopal consecration. This reflects the age-old and still unresolved doctrinal ques-

---

[1] E.g. LG 18, 20, 22, 23; LG NEP 3, 4; OE 3; UR 2; CD Fl I 370, 372, 374–375, 376, 425–426, 442, 454, 564.

[2] E.g. the Council of Sofia (343–344): DS 133; the Council of Lyons (1274): DS 861; the Letter of Pope Clement VI to the Armenians (1351): DS 1052–1057; the Council of Florence (1439) *Laetentur caeli*: DS 1307; Vat. I *Pastor Aeternus* (1870): DS 3056–3064.

tion of the origin of power in the Church: does power come only from sacred orders or are there other sources? The present canon does not attempt to solve this problem. Instead it takes up the ap con of Pope Paul VI[1] and simply asserts the necessity of episcopal consecration. As the canon states, if the person elected is already a Bishop, he obtains full and supreme power immediately on acceptance of the election; if he is not yet a Bishop, he is to be consecrated at once. According to Pope Paul VI's norms, the election of someone not yet a Bishop is not to be communicated until he has been consecrated.[2]

698 The Code of Canon Law does not contain any norms for the election of the Pope. These are to be found in the Apostolic Constitution already mentioned. Cardinals under the age of 80 have the right to vote in a papal election. The maximum number of such Cardinals taking part in a conclave has been fixed at 120. Election may take place by acclamation, by compromise or, as is usual, by ballot. In theory, any male Catholic is eligible to be elected, but since 1378 only Cardinals have been elected. This means that, in the light of Can. 351 §1, the person elected will almost certainly already be a Bishop. The Middle Ages saw the election of some deacons, e.g. Pope Gregory VII and Pope Innocent III; these governed the Church for a few months after their elections and before consecration,[3] but the Church does not foresee such a situation in practice today. Since the Pope is the highest authority in the Church, the election needs no confirmation.

Can. 332 §2 Should it happen that the Roman Pontiff resigns from his office, it is required for validity that the resignation be freely made and properly manifested, but it is not necessary that it be accepted by anyone.

699 Like its predecessor (c.221), this Code foresees the possibility that a Pope may resign his office. In line with the previous norm, the canon points out that such a resignation does not need to be accepted by anyone. It does specify that, for its validity, it must be 'freely made and properly manifested'. This provision is clearly inspired by the general norms on resignation found in Cann. 188 and 189 §1. Thus e.g. a resignation obtained by force would be invalid; the proper manifestation of the resignation would appear to require that it be made to the College of Cardinals who must elect a successor, and it must be made either in writing or before two witnesses. Apart from the confusion at the time of the Great Western Schism, no Pope has resigned since 13 December 1294 when Pope Celestine V renounced his office after just five months. There is no procedure to indicate what should be done in a situation where a Pope is so incapacitated that he is unable to manifest his intention to resign.

Can. 333 §1 By virtue of his office, the Roman Pontiff not only has power over the universal Church, but also has pre-eminent ordinary power over all particular Churches and their groupings. This reinforces and defends the proper, ordinary and immediate power which the Bishops have in the particular Churches entrusted to their care.

700 The authority of the Pope outlined in Can. 331 is here seen in relation to the local Churches and their Bishops. The Pope's authority in the whole Church is matched by his ordinary power in all the particular Churches (e.g. dioceses) and their groupings (e.g. Patriarchates, Provinces, etc.). The canon makes it clear that the Pope has this

---

[1] Cf. RPE: CLD 8 133–169.

[2] Cf. RPE 89: CLD 8 168.

[3] Comm 9(1977) 115–116.

power by virtue of his office. It is a concrete expression of the Roman Pontiff's primacy in the Church, of his continuing the role of Peter. The power which this canon ascribes to him at local level must not be understood as competing with that of the local Bishops, nor must it be seen as undermining their authority. Instead, the canon states that it 'reinforces and defends' the power of the local Bishops, a concept which is firmly rooted in the teaching of Vat. I[1] and Vat. II.

Can. 333 §2 The Roman Pontiff, in fulfilling his office as supreme Pastor of the Church, is always joined in full communion with the other Bishops, and indeed with the universal Church. He has the right, however, to determine, according to the needs of the Church, whether this office is to be exercised in a personal or in a collegial manner.

701 The Church as 'communion' is a basic concept in the ecclesiology of Vat. II.[2] It has found its juridical expression in Cann. 204–205 of the Code. The Pope, in fulfilling his office as supreme Pastor, is described as being always in full communion with the other Bishops and with the whole Church. This is reminiscent of the teaching both of Vat. I and of Vat. II which spoke of St Peter as the lasting and visible source and foundation of the unity both of faith and of communion.[3] In exercising this role and strengthening the bonds of communion between the People of God, between the particular Churches, and between the Bishops and himself, the Pope is free to determine whether to act personally or collegially. In other words, it belongs to the Pope as head of the College of Bishops, rather than to its members, to determine the manner in which he will exercise his office.[4]

Can. 333 §3 There is neither appeal nor recourse against a judgement or a decree of the Roman Pontiff.

702 Because of the Pope's primacy of authority and power, meaning that there is no higher authority in the Church, no decision made by him can be appealed against. The 1917 Code stated (c.228 §2) specifically that there was no appeal from a decision of the Pope to an Ecumenical Council. While the text of the present canon is much broader, the Code still counts as an offence an appeal against an act of the Pope to an Ecumenical Council or to the College of Bishops (see Can. 1372).

Can. 334 The Bishops are available to the Roman Pontiff in the exercise of his office, to cooperate with him in various ways, among which is the synod of Bishops. Cardinals also assist him, as do other persons and, according to the needs of the time, various institutes; all these persons and institutes fulfil their offices in his name and by his authority, for the good of all the Churches, in accordance with the norms determined by law.

703 In the exercise of his ministry to the whole Church, the Pope has the assistance of various people and bodies. They are listed in outline in this canon which has clearly been inspired both by the 1917 Code (c.230) and by the decree of Vat. II on the pastoral office of Bishops.[5] The remaining canons of this section deal in some detail with these people and institutions: the Bishops, the Synod of Bishops, the Cardinals, the Roman

---

[1] Cf.Vat. I *Pastor Aeternus* 3: DS 3061; LG 27: Fl I 383.
[2] Cf. LG 1, 4, 7, 13; UR 2, 3, 7, 14, 15: Fl I 350, 352, 355–356, 364–365, 453–456, 460, 464–465.
[3] Cf. Vat. I *Pastor Aeternus*: DS 3051; LG 18: Fl I 370.
[4] Cf. Comm 13(1981) 48 at Can. 31 §2.
[5] Cf. CD 9: Fl I 568.

Can. 335 When the Roman See is vacant, or completely impeded, no innovation is to be made in the governance of the universal Church. The special laws enacted for these circumstances are to be observed.

The general principle of Can. 428 §1 governing a vacant diocese is here applied to the See of Rome. While it is vacant or completely impeded, no changes may be made to the government of the whole Church. The See becomes vacant if the Pope dies or resigns. It is impeded if a situation arises such as is envisaged in Can. 412, i.e. imprisonment, banishment, exile or incapacity. In such circumstances, the 'special laws' referred to are to be observed. At the time of the promulgation of the Code, these special laws, in the event of the See of Rome becoming vacant, were contained in the ap con *Romano Pontifici Eligendo* of Pope Paul VI. No such special laws have been promulgated to cover the eventuality of the See being impeded. 704

Article 2
The College of Bishops

Can. 336 The head of the College of Bishops is the Supreme Pontiff, and its members are the Bishops by virtue of their sacramental consecration and hierarchical communion with the head of the College and its members. This College of Bishops, in which the apostolic body abides in an unbroken manner, is, in union with its head and never without its head, also the subject of supreme and full power over the universal Church.

The text of this canon, drawn from the teaching of Vat. II,[1] contains a further explanation of the relationship between the Pope and the College of Bishops outlined in Can. 330. The fundamental assertion of this canon is that the College of Bishops is also the subject of supreme power in the Church. However, to offset any traces of medieval conciliarism, the canon makes it clear that the College is the subject of supreme power only 'in union with its head and never without its head'. Thus, in the Church there are two subjects of supreme power: the Roman Pontiff alone, and the Roman Pontiff together with the College of Bishops. 705

The two criteria for membership of the College of Bishops are contained in this canon: sacramental consecration and hierarchical communion. In line with a centuries-old tradition, the sacramentality of episcopal consecration was clearly taught by Vat. II.[2] The concept of hierarchical communion proved to be a more complex issue. In order to avoid erroneous interpretations of the principles set out by the Council, it issued an explanatory note as an appendix to the Constitution *Lumen Gentium*. This note explains how various concepts used in the Constitution are to be understood, e.g. *college, communion, collegiality*. Among other points, the Note says: '...it is expressly stated that *hierarchical* communion with the head and members is required. The idea of *communion* was highly valued in the early Church, as indeed it is today 706

---

[1] Cf. e.g. LG 20, 22–23, NEP; CD 4; AGD 38: Fl I 371–372, 374–378, 424–426, 565–566, 851.
[2] Cf. LG 21: Fl I 373–374.

especially in the East. It is not to be understood as some vague sort of *goodwill*, but as *something organic* which calls for a juridical structure as well as being enkindled by charity'.[1] A consequence of this is that membership of the College of Bishops is confined to those who are consecrated Bishops (and so e.g. not apostolic Administrators or even Bishops-elect) and who are in communion with Rome (and so e.g. not in schism).

707 A further echo of Can. 330 can be found in the assertion that in the College of Bishops abides 'the apostolic body'. From this it is clear that the members of the College of Bishops are the successors of the apostles. However, the succession is not from individual apostles to individual Bishops, rather it is a corporate succession. In other words, the relationship which existed between the apostles and Peter is now to be found in the relationship between the College of Bishops and the Pope.

Can. 337 §1 The College of Bishops exercises its power over the universal Church in solemn form in an Ecumenical Council.

708 Three ways in which the College of Bishops acts are described in the three paragraphs of this canon. First and foremost, the College acts in a solemn manner in an Ecumenical Council. This is an exercise of the College's supreme power over the whole Church. As Can. 336 indicates in principle, and Cann. 338–341 set forth in detail, an Ecumenical council cannot be separated from the Roman Pontiff.

Can. 337 §2 It exercises this same power by the united action of the Bishops dispersed throughout the world, when this action is as such proclaimed or freely accepted by the Roman Pontiff, so that it becomes a truly collegial act.

709 This paragraph describes a less solemn but no less real way in which the College of Bishops exercises supreme power. Two conditions must be verified in order that an act of the Bishops be recognised in this way. Firstly, it must be the united action of Bishops around the world; local action taken by a group of Bishops does not suffice. Secondly, it must be proclaimed or freely accepted by the Pope as an exercise of supreme power: an example of this type of activity was the work of the Bishops in the revision of the Code of Canon Law.[2]

Can. 337 §3 It belongs to the Roman Pontiff to select and promote, according to the needs of the Church, ways in which the College of Bishops can exercise its office in respect of the universal Church in a collegial manner.

710 The third type of action by the College of Bishops is less solemn and formal than are the other two. It is the Roman Pontiff rather than the College itself who determines the manner in which this form of collegiality is realised and exercised. A clear post-Conciliar example of this kind of activity is the Synod of Bishops.[3] Other initiatives by groups of Bishops throughout the Church, such as joint pastoral letters or joint declarations on certain current problems, are an expression of their common membership of the College of Bishops; in themselves, however, they are not expressions of collegiality in the strict sense as understood in this canon.

---

[1] LG NEP 2: Fl I 425.

[2] Pope John Paul II made this point in the ap con *Sacrae disciplinae leges* promulgating the New Code on 25.I.1983.

[3] Cf. Cann. 342–348.

Can. 338 §1 It is the prerogative of the Roman Pontiff alone to summon an Ecumenical Council, to preside over it personally or through others, to transfer, suspend or dissolve the Council, and to approve its decrees.

In the aftermath of the Great Western schism, a theory had developed within the Church which proposed that the Pope was accountable to an Ecumenical Council. By the time of the Council of Trent, such a theory no longer had any widespread support. The Code, in this canon, spells out clearly the role of the Pope in relation to an Ecumenical Council. It is he who has the right to convoke such a Council, to preside over it (alone or through others), to transfer it, suspend it, or dissolve it; and it is he who approves its decrees.

Can. 338 §2 It is also the prerogative of the Roman Pontiff to determine the matters to be dealt with in the Council, and to establish the order to be observed. The Fathers of the Council may add other matters to those proposed by the Roman Pontiff, but these must be approved by the Roman Pontiff.

In addition to the fundamental rights stated in the preceding paragraph, the Pope also has the right to set the agenda for the Ecumenical Council, to establish the order to be followed in it, and to approve of other matters which the conciliar fathers propose to be included in the agenda. This whole canon is a clear statement of the role of the Pope within the College of Bishops.

Can. 339 §1 All Bishops, but only Bishops, who are members of the College of Bishops, have the right and the obligation to be present at an Ecumenical Council with a deliberative vote.

This canon represents an important change from the 1917 Code in its c.223 §§1-2. There the invitation to participate in an Ecumenical Council was made on the basis of *jurisdiction*. Thus residential Bishops, even if not yet consecrated, Abbots Primate, Abbots of monastic Congregations, the supreme Moderators of exempt clerical religious institutes, and Cardinals, even if not Bishops, had the right to attend with a deliberative vote; if invited, titular Bishops had a deliberative vote, unless it was otherwise stated in the invitation. Under the present law those not yet consecrated as Bishops, even Cardinals, do not have a right to be present with a deliberative vote, whereas titular Bishops and retired Bishops have this right. This statement of principle is in keeping with the teaching of Vat. II,[1] and with the criteria for membership of the College of Bishops set forth in Can. 336.

Can. 339 §2 Some others besides, who do not have the episcopal dignity, can be summoned to an Ecumenical Council by the supreme authority in the Church, to whom it belongs to determine what part they take in the Council.

The invitation of others who are not Bishops to an Ecumenical Council and their participation in it are matters which the law leaves to the discretion of the supreme authority. These 'others' would include those who are equivalent in law to Bishops, Bishops not yet consecrated, probably some representatives of the major institutes of consecrated life and societies of apostolic life, and whatever experts are considered to be necessary or helpful. Given the increasing appreciation of the role of the laity in the life of the Church, it is to be expected that the supreme authority would include some laypeople.

---

[1] Cf. CD 4: Fl I 565–566.

Book II The People of God

Can. 340 If the Apostolic See should become vacant during the celebration of the Council, it is by virtue of the law itself suspended until the new Supreme Pontiff either orders it to continue or dissolves it.

715 In c.229 of the 1917 Code, it was presumed that a newly elected Pope would continue an Ecumenical Council convoked by his predecessor and interrupted by the vacancy of the Holy See. The present norm envisages that he may either continue or dissolve it. A parallel norm can be found in Can. 347 concerning the Synod of Bishops, and a similar norm for a diocesan synod is to be found in Can. 468 §2. The suspension of an Ecumenical Council during the vacancy of the Roman See is one way of ensuring that the principle of Can. 335 is observed. When Pope John XXIII died in 1963, Vat. II was suspended; one of the first acts of the newly-elected Pope Paul VI was to convoke the second period of the Council.

Can. 341 §1 The decrees of an Ecumenical Council do not oblige unless they are approved by the Roman Pontiff as well as by the Fathers of the Council, confirmed by the Roman Pontiff and promulgated by his direction.

716 This paragraph, which is in substantial accord with c.227 of the 1917 Code, speaks for itself.

Can. 341 §2 If they are to have binding force, the same confirmation and promulgation is required for decrees which the College of Bishops issues by truly collegial actions in another manner introduced or freely accepted by the Roman Pontiff.

717 Since, apart from an Ecumenical Council, other ways of collegial action are possible (see Can. 337 §§2–3), there must a legal criterion whereby to know which of them has binding force. Such actions also require the confirmation and promulgation of the Pope. Examples of this could include a universal petition for the proclamation of a dogma of the faith (as was clearly the case when in 1950 Pope Pius XII declared as an article of faith the Assumption of the Blessed Virgin Mary) or the canonisation of a saint.

Chapter II
THE SYNOD OF BISHOPS

Can. 342 The synod of Bishops is a group of Bishops selected from different parts of the world, who meet together at specified times to promote the close relationship between the Roman Pontiff and the Bishops. These Bishops, by their counsel, assist the Roman Pontiff in the defence and development of faith and morals and in the preservation and strengthening of ecclesiastical discipline. They also consider questions concerning the mission of the Church in the world.

718 The synod of Bishops is a new concept and practice in the life of the Church. Its origins lie in the deliberations of Vat. II and it was established before the end of the Council.[1] Between 1967 and 1994, there were eleven general assemblies of the synod of Bishops. These dealt with topics such as justice, the role of the laity in the Church,

---

[1] Cf. Pope Paul VI ap con *Apostolica Solicitudo* 15.IX.1965: AAS 57(1965) 775–780.

Part II The Hierarchical Constitution of the Church

the family, priestly formation, etc. In addition to these sessions, there have been special synods involving Bishops from particular parts of the world, e.g. for the Netherlands, for the Ukraine, for Europe and for Africa.

The description of the synod of Bishops in the canon comes from the cited Apostolic Constitution.[1] It is a group of Bishops from different parts of the world who meet at specified times. Although it meets only occasionally, the synod itself (as distinct from its membership) is a permanent institution in the Church. It is an instrument of the collegial action of the Bishops spoken of in Can. 337 §2, and is a concrete means of assisting the Pope in the exercise of his office as required by Can. 334. 719

The Synod has a fourfold purpose: 720

(a) to promote the close relationship between the Roman Pontiff and the Bishops;

(b) to assist the Pope in the defence and development of faith and morals;

(c) to assist the Pope in the preservation and strengthening of ecclesiastical discipline;

(d) to consider questions concerning the mission of the Church in the world.

Can. 343 The function of the synod of Bishops is to discuss the matters proposed to it and set forth recommendations. It is not its function to settle matters or to draw up decrees, unless the Roman Pontiff has given it deliberative power in certain cases; in this event, it rests with the Roman Pontiff to ratify the decisions of the synod.

This canon sets out the limits of competence of the synod of Bishops. Its function is clearly consultative: its activity is defined as 'discussing' and 'setting forth recommendations', not 'settling matters' or even 'drawing up decrees'. However, the canon does foresee the possibility that the Pope might wish to use the synod as a deliberative body. In such a case, the decisions of the synod will require ratification by the Pope in accordance with the principle established in Can. 341 §2. 721

Can. 344 The synod of Bishops is directly under the authority of the Roman Pontiff, whose prerogative it is:

1° to convene the synod, as often as this seems opportune to him, and to designate the place where the meetings are to be held;

2° to ratify the election of those who, in accordance with the special law of the synod, are to be elected, and to designate and appoint other members;

3° at a suitable time before the celebration of the synod, to prescribe the outlines of the questions to be discussed, in accordance with the special law;

4° to determine the agenda;

5° to preside over the synod personally or through others;

6° to conclude, transfer, suspend or dissolve the synod.

The auxiliary role of the synod is again reflected in the rights of the Pope listed in this canon. It is he who has the right to convene the synod when and where he sees fit; he ratifies the election of those to be elected, and designates and appoints others; he 722

---

[1] ap con cit: AAS vol cit 776–777.

Book II The People of God

prescribes the outlines of the questions to be discussed; he sets the agenda; he presides, either personally or through others; he decides on the conclusion, transfer, suspension or dissolution of the synod. These prerogatives are parallel to his rights in respect of the Ecumenical Council contained in Can. 338. The 'special law of the synod' mentioned in 2° is the ap con already cited.[1] This contains the general guidelines for the election of synod members, the procedures to prepare for a synod, and the manner in which the business is to be conducted.

Can. 345 The synod of Bishops can meet in general assembly, in which matters are dealt with which directly concern the good of the universal Church; such an assembly is either ordinary or extraordinary. It can also meet in special assembly, to deal with matters directly affecting a determined region or regions.

723 The Code envisages three types of assembly of the Synod of Bishops:

(a) a general assembly which is classed as *ordinary*;

(b) a general assembly which is classed as *extraordinary*;

(c) a *special* assembly which focuses on matters which affect a specific territory.

724 The general *ordinary* assembly deals with matters affecting the whole Church. It meets regularly every few years. These assemblies have dealt with major questions in the life of the Church: the implementation of Vat. II (1967), priestly ministry and justice in the world (1971), evangelisation (1974), catechesis (1977), the Christian family (1980), reconciliation and penance (1983), the vocation and mission of the laity (1987), priestly formation (1990). The general *extraordinary* assembly deals with matters of particular importance at the time. So far there have been two such assemblies: the first, in 1969, dealt with the question of the relationship between the Pope and the Bishops' Conferences; the second, in 1985, dealt with the life of the Church in the twenty years since the end of Vat. II. *Special* assemblies deal with more restricted local matters, e.g. the assemblies of the Bishops of the Netherlands and the Ukrainian Bishops which took place in 1980; a Synod for Africa and Madagascar was convoked in 1990 to discuss the theme of the Church in Africa and her evangelising mission towards the year 2000; a Synod for Europe was announced in 1990 to discuss how the Church can respond to the changing circumstances in Europe. In 1986, the Pope held a special meeting with the Bishops of Brazil, but this was not classified as a synod. Similarly, during his many journeys throughout the world, the Pope has made a point of meeting with the Bishops of the region, but these encounters do not qualify as synods.

Can. 346 §1 The synod of Bishops meeting in ordinary general assembly is comprised, for the most part, of Bishops elected for each assembly by the Bishops' Conferences, in accordance with the norms of the special law of the synod. Other members are designated according to the same law; others are directly appointed by the Roman Pontiff. Added to these are some members of clerical religious institutes, elected in accordance with the same special law.

---

[1] The practical details of organising an assembly of the Synod of Bishops are set forth in the *Ordo Synodi Episcoporum Celebrandae* based on the provisions of *Apostolica Solicitudo*. It was first published on 8.XII.1966: CLD 6 401–411, and later updated and published on 24.VI.1969: CLD 7 322–338. A further amendment of this *Ordo* was published on 20.VIII.1971: CLD 7 338–341.

This canon outlines the membership of each type of assembly of the synod of Bishops. An ordinary general assembly consists mainly of Bishops elected by their respective Conferences in accordance with the special law which determines a quota depending on the number of Bishops in each Conference. The same special law also involves others, e.g. Oriental Patriarchs, Major Metropolitans, Oriental Metropolitans not subject to a Patriarch, the Cardinals in charge of the various Roman dicasteries. The Pope also has the prerogative of appointing others as members. Some members of clerical religious institutes are also to be elected in accordance with the special law of the synod. The choice of the term 'clerical religious institutes' is deliberate; the expression 'institutes of consecrated life' would have included clerical secular institutes. The Revision Commission noted that these were not provided for in the Apostolic Constitution, but that that was not a reason why such persons might not be invited.[1]

Can. 346 §2 The synod of Bishops meeting in extraordinary general assembly for the purpose of dealing with matters which require speedy resolution, is comprised, for the most part, of Bishops who, by reason of the office they hold, are designated by the special law of the synod; others are appointed directly by the Roman Pontiff. Added to these are some members of clerical religious institutes, elected in accordance with the same law.

Because of the nature of the business dealt with in an extraordinary general assembly, there is often not time for the lengthy process of the election of representatives from the various Conferences. The criterion for attendance at such an assembly is the office held by the individual Bishop; thus, e.g. it is the Presidents of the Bishops' Conferences who take part in these assemblies, in addition to Oriental Patriarchs, etc. and the Cardinals in charge of the Roman Curia. The number of religious who attend such a meeting is reduced from ten to three.[2] As always, the Pope may appoint others as members.

Can. 346 §3 The synod of Bishops which meets in special assembly is comprised of members chosen principally from those regions for which the synod was convened, in accordance with the special law by which the synod is governed.

Special assemblies of the synod are made up for the most part of members of the Bishops' Conference or Conferences concerned. The fundamental qualification of the others who take part is some knowledge of the region for which the synod was convened, or some expertise in the problems being addressed. Thus, only the Cardinals whose dicasteries have some particular interest attend by virtue of the law, and the religious who are chosen must be similarly well acquainted with the problems of the region, if not actually from the region.[3] The Pope may also select others to attend.

Can. 347 §1 When the meeting of the synod of Bishops is concluded by the Roman Pontiff, the function entrusted in it to the Bishops and other members ceases.

Membership of the synod of Bishops is essentially transitory. As soon as the assembly is concluded, whatever function was entrusted to the members of the synod ceases.

---

[1] Cf. Comm 14(1982) 182 at Can. 282.
[2] Cf. *Ordo Synodi Episcoporum Celebrandae* art. 5 §2 1–2.
[3] Cf. *Ordo Synodi Episcoporum Celebrandae* art. 5 §3 1–2; art. 6 §2 4.

Only the Secretariat is permanent; when the synod concludes its business, it ceases to exist as an assembly.

Can. 347 §2 If the Apostolic See becomes vacant after the synod has been convened or during its celebration, the meeting of the synod, and the function entrusted in it to the members, is by virtue of the law itself suspended, until the new Pontiff decrees either that the assembly is to be dissolved or that it is to continue.

729 The provision of Can. 340 concerning an Ecumenical Council finds its parallel in this paragraph. Should the Apostolic See fall vacant during an assembly of the synod, everything is suspended pending the election of a new Pope. This is another example of the principle of Can. 335 which directs that no innovation is to be made during the vacancy of the Holy See.

Can. 348 §1 There is to be a permanent general secretariat of the synod, presided over by a Secretary general appointed by the Roman Pontiff. The Secretary is to have the assistance of a council of the secretariat, composed of Bishops, some elected by the synod of Bishops itself in accordance with the special law, others appointed by the Roman Pontiff. The function of all these persons ceases with the beginning of a new general assembly.

730 Originally, *Apostolica Solicitudo* had provided simply for a permanent secretary with suitable help; in addition, there was to be a special secretary who would remain in office solely for the period of the synod meeting. Both these officials were to be named by the Pope. The structure in the Code is much more elaborate. There is now not only a permanent secretariat, but also a council of Bishops, some elected by the synod, some appointed by the Pope. All the persons mentioned in this canon remain in office until the beginning of the next assembly of the synod. In this way, continuity is provided for without there being permanent appointments. The involvement of Bishops in the Council to assist the Secretary is a further sign of the collegial nature of the synod's activity.

Can. 348 §2 For each assembly of the synod of Bishops there are one or more special secretaries, who are appointed by the Roman Pontiff. They remain in office only until the end of the synod assembly.

731 In addition to the more stable institutions outlined in the preceding paragraph, there are to be one or more special secretaries who have a role only for the duration of the synod assembly.

Chapter III
THE CARDINALS OF THE HOLY ROMAN CHURCH

Can. 349 The Cardinals of the Holy Roman Church constitute a special College, whose prerogative it is to elect the Roman Pontiff in accordance with the norms of a special law. The Cardinals are also available to the Roman Pontiff, either acting collegially, when they are summoned together to deal with questions of major importance, or acting individually, that is, in the offices which they hold in assisting the Roman Pontiff especially in the daily care of the universal Church.

The College of Cardinals can be traced to a group of clergy who, in the early centuries, gathered around the Pope as his collaborators and councillors. By the twelfth century, they consisted of seven Bishops of dioceses close to Rome, twenty-eight priests attached to Roman churches, and twenty deacons.[1] Since 1059, the principal function of this group was to elect the new Pope. The size of the College has varied down through history: Pope Sixtus V established a maximum number of seventy, a figure that was enshrined in c.231 §1 of the 1917 Code. The pontificates of Pope John XXIII and Pope Paul VI saw a dramatic increase in the number of Cardinals, although the number eligible to vote in a Conclave was fixed at one hundred and twenty.[2] By 29 June 1991, the number of Cardinals had risen to the unprecedented figure of one hundred and sixty-two, although only one hundred and twenty of these, being under eighty years of age, were eligible to take part in a conclave.

The canon describes the three roles of the College of Cardinals:

(a) the election of the Pope; this is governed by the special norms contained in the ap con *Romano Pontifici Eligendo*.

(b) giving assistance to the Pope in a collegial fashion; this role was extensively exercised during the pontificate of Pope John Paul II by regular meetings of the entire College to discuss such matters as finances, restructuring the Roman Curia, etc.

(c) giving assistance to the Pope as individuals and by reason of their particular office, e.g. those Cardinals who are Prefects of Congregations in the Roman Curia.

Can. 350 §1 The College of Cardinals is divided into three orders: the episcopal order, to which belong those Cardinals to whom the Roman Pontiff assigns the title of a suburbicarian Church, and eastern-rite Patriarchs who are made members of the College of Cardinals; the presbyteral order, and the diaconal order.

§2 Cardinal priests and Cardinal deacons are each assigned a title or a deaconry in Rome by the Roman Pontiff.

§3 Eastern Patriarchs within the College of Cardinals have their patriarchal see as a title.

§4 The Cardinal Dean has the title of the diocese of Ostia, together with that of any other Church to which he already has a title.

§5 By a choice made in Consistory and approved by the Supreme Pontiff, Cardinal priests may transfer to another title; Cardinal deacons may transfer to another deaconry and, if they have been a full ten years in the diaconal order, to the presbyteral order: priority of order and of promotion is to be observed.

§6 A Cardinal who by choice transfers from the diaconal to the presbyteral order, takes precedence over all Cardinal priests who were promoted to the Cardinalate after him.

Traditionally, the College of Cardinals has been divided into three orders: Bishops, priests, and deacons. A proposal was made to the Revision Commission that this threefold distinction ought to be abolished. However, the Pope made it clear that the three orders should remain.[3]

---

[1] Cf. Morrison *Cardinal, I (History of)* New Catholic Encyclopedia 3 104–105.

[2] Cf. RPE 33: CLD 8 167.

[3] Cf. Comm 14(1982) 182 at Can. 286.

Book II The People of God

735 Originally, the Cardinal Bishops were Bishops of dioceses neighbouring Rome. Pope John XXIII restricted the relationship of Cardinal Bishops to their suburbicarian sees to the purely titular.[1] There are seven such sees: Ostia, Albano, Frascati, Palestrina, Porto–Santa Rufina, Sabina–Poggio Mirteto, Velletri–Segni. However, the Dean of the College adds the diocese of Ostia to whatever other suburbicarian title he has. Following the desire expressed by Vat. II[2] for a greater recognition of the significance of the Eastern Patriarchs, Pope Paul VI included them in the episcopal order of Cardinals.[3] This move was not greeted enthusiastically by all the Patriarchs, since they regard the College of Cardinals as something belonging to the Patriarchate of the West alone. However, some Patriarchs have indeed been named as Cardinals. Although Cardinal Bishops, they do not belong to the clergy of Rome, even by the legal fiction of a title,[4] nor do they have a vote in the election of the Dean of the College.

736 At the time of their creation, Cardinal priests and deacons are assigned the title of a church in Rome. These are divided into 'presbyteral titles' and 'deaconries'. The law (§§5–6) permits each Cardinal to select a new title or deaconry if certain conditions are fulfilled.

Can. 351 §1 Those to be promoted Cardinals are men freely selected by the Roman Pontiff, who are at least in the order of priesthood and are truly outstanding in doctrine, virtue, piety and prudence in practical matters; those who are not already Bishops must receive episcopal consecration.

737 The qualifications for appointment as Cardinal are set out, but without the numerous restrictions of c.232 of the 1917 Code, arising e.g. from illegitimacy, blood relationship with another Cardinal, irregularity, etc. The choice of these men by the Pope is now a free one. In former times, he accepted nominees put forward by secular rulers. The insistence that the candidates be at least in the order of priesthood came only with the 1917 Code; previously deacons were admitted. Now, in keeping with a change in the law introduced by Pope John XXIII,[5] upon nomination they must be consecrated Bishops unless they are dispensed from this obligation, as occurred in recent times in the cases of Henri de Lubac, Pietro Pavan and Paolo Dezza.

Can. 351 §2 Cardinals are created by decree of the Roman Pontiff, which in fact is published in the presence of the College of Cardinals. From the moment of publication, they are bound by the obligations and they enjoy the rights defined in the law.

738 The creation of Cardinals takes place at the moment of the publication of the Pope's decree in consistory. From this moment, those named have the rights and obligations of Cardinals. The 1917 Code (cc.238–239) contained a very detailed list of the rights, privileges and obligations of Cardinals. No such list was included in the present Code, since the Commission felt that the privileges of Cardinals were more or less the same as those of Bishops.[6] They are now to be found in the appropriate places throughout the Code.[7]

---

[1] Cf. Pope John XXIII mp *Suburbicariis sedibus* 11.IV.1962: CLD 5 270–272.
[2] Cf. OE 9: Fl I 445.
[3] Cf. Pope Paul VI mp *Ad purpuratorum patrum* 11.II.1965: CLD 6 310–311.
[4] mp cit. 2: CLD 6 310.
[5] Pope John XXIII mp *Cum gravissima* 15.IV.1962: CLD 5 273–274.
[6] Cf. Comm 14(1982) 184 at Can. 290.
[7] E.g. Cann. 967, 1242, 1405 1§ 1°, etc.

Can. 351 §3 A person promoted to the dignity of Cardinal, whose creation the Roman Pontiff announces, but whose name he reserves *in petto*, is not at that time bound by the obligations nor does he enjoy the rights of a Cardinal. When his name is published by the Roman Pontiff, however, he is bound by these obligations and enjoys these rights, but his right of precedence dates from the day of the reservation *in petto*.

Cardinals created *in petto*, i.e. those whose creation is kept secret, are not announced, usually for political reasons. If their names are not published during the lifetime of the Pope, they can never claim their status. However, if their names are published, they acquire precedence from the day of their reservation.   739

Can. 352 §1 The Dean presides over the College of Cardinals. When he is unable to do so, the sub-Dean takes his place. The Dean, or the sub-Dean, has no power of governance over the other Cardinals, but is considered as first among equals.

§2 When the office of Dean is vacant, those Cardinals who have a suburbicarian title, and only those, under the presidency of the sub-Dean if he is present, or of the oldest member, elect one of their number to act as Dean of the College. They are to submit his name to the Roman Pontiff, to whom it belongs to approve the person elected.

§3 In the same way as set out in §2, the sub-Dean is elected, with the Dean presiding. It belongs to the Roman Pontiff to approve also the election of the sub-Dean.

§4 If the Dean and sub-Dean do not already have a domicile in Rome, they are to acquire it there.

The College of Cardinals is a college in the strict sense of the word. It has a president from among its own ranks: the Dean (not the Pope), and the sub-Dean as his substitute. The College has its own particular law, only part of which is incorporated in the Code. Formerly, it was the most senior Cardinal Bishop who became Dean (1917 Code c.237 §1). Pope Paul VI changed this by introducing an election for both offices within the College.[1] This change is the basis of the present canon. The Dean is now elected by the Cardinals who hold suburbicarian sees from among the same Cardinals. Thus the Eastern Patriarchs who are Cardinals, even though they are Cardinal Bishops, have neither active or passive voice in the election.   740

Can. 353 §1 Cardinals assist the Supreme Pastor of the Church in collegial fashion particularly in Consistories, in which they are gathered by order of the Roman Pontiff and under his presidency. Consistories are either ordinary or extraordinary.

§2 In an ordinary Consistory all Cardinals, or least those who are in Rome, are summoned for consultation on certain grave matters of more frequent occurrence, or for the performance of especially solemn acts.

§3 All Cardinals are summoned to an extraordinary Consistory, which takes place when the special needs of the Church and more serious matters suggest it.

§4 Only an ordinary Consistory in which certain solemnities are celebrated, can be public, that is when, in addition to the Cardinals, Prelates, representatives of civil states and other invited persons are admitted.

---

[1] Cf. Pope Paul VI mp *Sacro Cardinalium Consilio* 26.II.1965: AAS 57(1965) 296–297: CLD 6 312–313.

741 The collegial assistance given by the College of Cardinals to the Pope is ordinarily done in consistories. Ordinary consistories take place several times a year, though not at regular intervals. At such meetings, the agenda will include filling vacant dioceses, hearing the Pope's mind on important matters, and discussing business relating to different departments of the Curia. An ordinary consistory at which e.g. newly created Cardinals are to receive the ceremonial red biretta is open to non-Cardinals. Extraordinary consistories take place much less frequently. All Cardinals throughout the world are summoned to such meetings. In this way, the Pope has available to him a wide variety of experience when considering the special needs of the Church and other more serious matters: e.g. the extraordinary consistory which took place in April 1991 dealt with threats to human life and the danger of sects.

Can. 354 Cardinals who head the departments and other permanent sections of the Roman Curia and of Vatican City, who have completed their seventy-fifth year, are requested to offer their resignation from office to the Roman Pontiff, who will consider all the circumstances and make provision accordingly.

742 Under the 1917 Code, there was no provision for the retirement of Cardinals. The present norm was introduced by Pope Paul VI in 1970:[1] it is a *request* that (as in the case of diocesan Bishops: see Can 410 §1) Cardinals would, on completion of their seventy-fifth year, offer their resignation to the Pope. Thereafter it is a matter for the Pope to decide whether or not to accept such an offer or to make any other appropriate arrangement.

Can. 355 §1 It belongs to the Cardinal Dean to ordain the elected Roman Pontiff a Bishop, if he is not already ordained. If the Dean is prevented from doing so, the same right belongs to the sub-Dean or, if he is prevented, to the senior Cardinal of the episcopal order.

§2 The senior Cardinal Deacon announces the name of the newly elected Supreme Pontiff to the people. Acting in place of the Roman Pontiff, he also confers the pallium on metropolitan Bishops or gives the pallium to their proxies.

743 This canon contains details of the role of the Cardinals following the election of a new Pope. If he is not yet a Bishop, the Dean, the sub-Dean, or the senior Cardinal Bishop, is to ordain him. It is the right of the senior Cardinal Deacon to announce the name of the newly elected Pope to the people. The other prerogative assigned to the senior Cardinal Deacon concerns the conferral of the pallium; in this instance, he is acting on behalf of the Pope.

Can. 356 Cardinals have the obligation of cooperating closely with the Roman Pontiff. For this reason, Cardinals who have any office in the Curia and are not diocesan Bishops, are obliged to reside in Rome. Cardinals who are in charge of a diocese as diocesan Bishops, are to go to Rome whenever summoned by the Roman Pontiff.

744 Only those Cardinals who have an official appointment in the Roman Curia are obliged to live in Rome. During the preparation of the present Code, the Revision Commission made it clear that mere membership of one of the Roman congregations did not constitute such an official appointment.[2] Cardinals who have retired from

---

[1] Cf. Pope Paul VI mp *Ingravescentem aetatem* 21.XI.1970: CLD 7 143–144.
[2] Cf. Comm 14(1982) 101 at Can. 171.

being diocesan Bishops are not required to live in Rome, nor are those who have retired from office in the Roman Curia. Those who are diocesan Bishops are obliged to go to Rome whenever summoned by the Pope, e.g. to take part in an extraordinary consistory.

Can. 357 §1 When a Cardinal has taken possession of a suburbicarian Church or of a titular Church in Rome, he is to further the good of the diocese or church by counsel and patronage. However, he has no power of governance over it, and he should not for any reason interfere in matters concerning the administration of its goods, or its discipline, or the service of the Church.

§2 Cardinals living outside Rome and outside their own diocese, are exempt in what concerns their person from the power of governance of the Bishop of the diocese in which they are residing.

Because of their special status within the Church, it is necessary to spell out quite clearly the relationship between Cardinals and the local Church. The first paragraph of this canon points out that the Cardinals retain only a moral authority and the obligations of patronage in the suburbicarian sees or Roman churches assigned to them. They are not to intervene in any way in the administration of these. The second paragraph refers to Cardinals who are not resident either in Rome or in their own diocese. Such Cardinals are personally exempt from the jurisdiction of the local Bishop. This exemption does not extend to others in their company.

Can. 358 A Cardinal may be deputed by the Roman Pontiff to represent him in some solemn celebration or assembly of persons as a *Legatus a latere*, that is, as his alter ego; or he may, as a special emissary, be entrusted with a particular pastoral task. A Cardinal thus nominated is entitled to deal only with those affairs which have been entrusted to him by the Roman Pontiff himself.

A Cardinal who is commissioned by the Pope to carry out some special pastoral task will have the extent of his authority defined in his letter of appointment. This canon is placed here rather than in the section on papal legates (see Cann. 362–367), because the function of a *Legatus a latere* is entrusted only to Cardinals, who exercise this function when e.g. they are deputed to represent the Pope at Eucharistic Congresses or other special pastoral assemblies of the faithful throughout the world.

Can. 359 When the Apostolic See is vacant, the College of Cardinals has only that power in the Church which is granted to it by special law.

The special law referred to in this canon is contained in the cited ap con *Romano Pontifici Eligendo*. During the vacancy of the See of Rome, the government of the Church is in the hands of the College of Cardinals, but 'only in regard to ordinary business and those matters which cannot be deferred, and with regard to the preparation of all those matters which are necessary for the election of the new Pope'.[1] Power is given to the College to interpret anything which is doubtful or obscure. Finally, when business is conducted by the College, it must act in a collegial fashion and according to the decision of the majority.[2]

---

[1] Cf. RPE 1: CLD 8 136.
[2] Cf. RPE 3–6: CLD 8 136–137.

Book II The People of God

Chapter IV
THE ROMAN CURIA

Can. 360 The Supreme Pontiff usually conducts the business of the universal Church through the Roman Curia, which acts in his name and with his authority for the good and for the service of the Churches. The Curia is composed of the Secretariat of State or Papal Secretariat, the Council for the public affairs of the Church, the Congregations, the Tribunals and other Institutes. The constitution and competence of all these is defined by special law.

748 The Curia is an instrument used by the Pope in his role as universal pastor rather than as Bishop of Rome. It acts in his name and with his authority, for the good of the Churches and in their service. It is to be noted that the canon uses the word 'usually': the Pope is not *bound* to operate within this framework, and is free to set up alternative means and structures for achieving the same ends.

749 No detailed description of the various departments of the Roman Curia, their internal structure and their competence is to be found in the Code. All such information is now to be found in the ap con *Pastor Bonus* of 28 June 1988.[1]

Can. 361 In this Code the terms Apostolic See or Holy See mean not only the Roman Pontiff, but also, unless the contrary is clear from the nature of things or from the context, the Secretariat of State, the Council for the public affairs of the Church, and the other Institutes of the Roman Curia.

750 This norm is virtually identical with that of c.7 of the 1917 Code. The Code uses the terms 'Apostolic See' and 'Holy See' interchangeably. The law makes a major distinction between the following:

(a) the Roman Pontiff, i.e. the person of the Pope;

(b) the supreme authority of the Church, i.e. the Roman Pontiff alone, and the Roman Pontiff with the College of Bishops;

(c) the Apostolic See or the Holy See, i.e. the Roman Pontiff, and the Roman Curia.

In the light of this distinction, the canon speaks for itself.

Chapter V
PAPAL LEGATES

Can. 362 The Roman Pontiff has an inherent and independent right to appoint Legates and to send them either to particular Churches in various countries or regions, or at the same time to States and to public Authorities. He also has the right to transfer or recall them, in accordance with the norms of international law concerning the mission and recall of representatives accredited to States.

751 From the earliest times, the Pope has sent Legates to represent him at Church Councils and among local Churches. In the fifteenth century came the development

---

[1] Cf. AAS 80(1988) 841–924, 1867. For a version in English, cf. CCLA 1166–1279.

of the papal representative sent to States in a stable manner; these became the Nuncios of the present day. The canons of this chapter are inspired by the mp of Pope Paul VI, *Solicitudo omnium ecclesiarum*.[1] This document saw a more precise determination of the role of papal legates and a significant shift in emphasis. The principal thrust now is the function of the papal representative towards the particular Churches rather than towards the civil authorities.[2] An example of the ecclesial, as distinct from the political, thrust of this institution is shown in the present canon where the legate is described first of all as having been sent to particular Churches, 'or at the same time' to governments and civil authorities, indicating that the diplomatic role is to be understood as somewhat secondary. The principle point of this canon is to state unambiguously the right of the Pope to appoint such representatives.

Can. 363 §1 To Legates of the Roman Pontiff is entrusted the office of representing in a stable manner the person of the Roman Pontiff in the particular Churches, or also in the States and public Authorities, to whom they are sent.

According to the papal document, the legates are ecclesiastics, for the most part in the episcopal order.[3] Their task is to represent in a stable manner the person of the Pope in the particular Churches and civil authorities to whom they are sent. The Code contains no details of the different types of legate; these distinctions remain part of the special law concerning legates.[4] The authority of such a representative is limited to the territory to which he is sent.

Can. 363 §2 Those also represent the Apostolic See who are appointed to pontifical Missions as Delegates or Observers at international Councils or at Conferences and Meetings.

While the previous paragraph dealt with the appointment of a representative of a stable nature, e.g. a Papal Nuncio or an Apostolic Delegate, this paragraph provides for special appointments for particular occasions. Such persons, although not necessarily holding an ecclesiastical office, act on behalf of the Apostolic See. Representatives of this type have proved to be a useful source of information to the Holy See about the major concerns of today's world.

Can. 364 The principal task of a Papal Legate is continually to make more firm and effective the bonds of unity which exist between the Apostolic See and the particular Churches. Within the territory assigned to him, it is therefore the responsibility of a Legate:

1° to inform the Apostolic See about the conditions in which the particular Churches find themselves, as well as about all matters which affect the life of the Church and the good of souls;

2° to assist the Bishops by action and advice, while leaving intact the exercise of their lawful power;

3° to foster close relations with the Bishops' Conference, offering it every assistance;

---

[1] Cf. CLD 7 277–284.
[2] Cf. Comm 12(1980) 237–241 at Cann. 176 bis–184.
[3] Cf. SOE I 1: CLD 7 277.
[4] Cf. SOE I 2–3: CLD 7 277–278.

4° in connection with the appointment of Bishops, to send or propose names of candidates to the Apostolic See, as well as to prepare the informative process about those who may be promoted, in accordance with the norms issued by the Apostolic See;

5° to take pains to promote whatever may contribute to peace, progress and the united efforts of peoples;

6° to work with the Bishops to foster appropriate exchanges between the Catholic Church and other Churches or ecclesial communities, and indeed with non-christian religions;

7° to work with the Bishops to safeguard, so far as the rulers of the State are concerned, those things which relate to the mission of the Church and of the Apostolic See;

8° to exercise the faculties and carry out the other instructions which are given to him by the Apostolic See.

754 The most important responsibilities of the papal legates are set forth in this canon in summary form. Although it is quite a full list, it is by no means exhaustive. What is abundantly clear from this canon is the primacy of the ecclesial role of the legate: his principal contact at local level is to be with the Bishops.

Can. 365 §1 A papal Legate who at the same time acts as envoy to the State according to international law, has in addition the special role:

1° of promoting and fostering relationships between the Apostolic See and the Authorities of the State;

2° of dealing with questions concerning relations between Church and State; especially, of drawing up concordats and other similar agreements, and giving effect to them.

§2 As circumstances suggest, in the matters mentioned in §1, the papal Legate is not to omit to seek the opinion and counsel of the Bishops of the ecclesiastical jurisdiction and to keep them informed of the course of events.

755 When a papal legate is also accredited diplomatically, his function is governed not only by canon law but also by international law. His role, however, is not confined to the relationship between the Holy See and the State; the legate also represents the local Church to the State, especially where formal agreements such as concordats are involved. The local Bishops' knowledge of the situation and their views must always be taken seriously into account. For this reason the canon imposes on the legate the twofold obligation of seeking the opinion and counsel of the local Bishops and of keeping them informed of the course of events.

Can. 366 Given the special nature of a Legate's role:

1° the papal Legation is exempt from the power of governance of the local Ordinary, except for the celebration of marriages;

2° the papal Legate has the right to perform liturgical celebrations, even in pontificalia, in all churches of the territory of his legation; as far as it is possible, he is to give prior notice to the local Ordinary.

Because of the special dignity of his office, the papal legate is accorded two particular privileges by the law:

(a) exemption from the local Ordinary. Thus he can give faculties to priests to hear confessions in the chapel of the legation, he can exercise his own faculties there, and he can celebrate other sacred functions. The sole exception is marriage: delegation from the appropriate authority is always required;

(b) he has the right to carry out liturgical functions in any church of the territory to which he has been appointed, even in *pontificalia*. This privilege is similar to that given in Can. 436 §3 to a Metropolitan within his Province.

Can. 367 The office of papal Legate does not cease when the Apostolic See is vacant, unless otherwise specified in the pontifical letter; it does cease, however, on the expiry of the mandate, on receipt by him of notification of recall, and on acceptance of his resignation by the Roman Pontiff.

In keeping with Can. 184 §1 which outlines the ways of losing ecclesiastical office, this canon indicates the three ways in which the office of legate ceases:

(a) the expiry of his mandate;

(b) his recall from the place to which he was sent;

(c) his resignation from office, if and when accepted by the Pope.

In keeping with the principle of Can. 184 §2, the vacancy of the Apostolic See does not have any effect on the office of a legate, unless this was mentioned specifically in the letters of appointment.

Section II
PARTICULAR CHURCHES AND THEIR GROUPINGS

Title I
Particular Churches and the Authority Constituted within them

Chapter I
PARTICULAR CHURCHES

Can. 368 Particular Churches, in which and from which the one and only catholic Church exists, are principally dioceses. Unless it is established otherwise, the following are equivalent to a diocese: a territorial prelature, a territorial abbacy, a vicariate apostolic, a prefecture apostolic and a permanently established apostolic administration.

758 From a theological point of view a particular Church is constituted by three elements: the People of God, the Pastor, the *presbyterium*. Historically, particular Churches have been defined juridically on a territorial basis.

759 The diocese (see Can. 369) is described as the principal form of particular Church because it is the most common. The other forms of particular Church (see Cann. 370–372) are equivalent in law to a diocese. They represent stages in the growth of the particular Church towards its establishment as a diocese. The pastor of each of these may be and often is a Bishop, but this is not required by law; be he a Bishop or not, he is equivalent in law to a diocesan Bishop (see Can. 381 §2), and is also a local Ordinary (see Can. 134). In each particular Church and in the unity of all particular Churches is found the one and only catholic Church.

Can. 369 A diocese is a portion of the people of God, which is entrusted to a Bishop to be nurtured by him, with the cooperation of the *presbyterium*, in such a way that, remaining close to its pastor and gathered by him through the Gospel and the Eucharist in the Holy Spirit, it constitutes a particular Church. In this Church, the one, holy, catholic and apostolic Church of Christ truly exists and functions.

760 The text of this canon is taken word for word from Vat. II.[1] The emphasis is on the community and the *presbyterium* gathered around the Bishop, rather than on the geographical area assigned to a Bishop. This reflects better the understanding of the early Church, where territorial boundaries were not rigidly fixed and the influence of the Bishop extended only gradually from the city to the countryside as Christianity spread.

761 The relationship between the Bishop, *presbyterium* and people is described in fundamentally dynamic terms: it is the Bishop's responsibility to gather the people in the Holy Spirit; the means proposed for this are the proclamation of the Gospel and the celebration of the Eucharist. The Bishop's authority in these areas is not simply a responsibility entrusted to him, but a fundamental part of his role as diocesan Bishop. When the People of God are so gathered and animated, the one Church founded by Christ is truly present and active.

Can. 370 A territorial prelature or abbacy is a certain portion of the people of God, territorially defined, the care of which is for special reasons entrusted to a Prelate or an Abbot, who governs it, in the manner of a diocesan Bishop, as its proper pastor.

762 Territorial prelatures originated in the special privileges granted to certain Chapters in the Middle Ages; these governed adjacent territory free from the jurisdiction of the local diocesan Bishop.[2] Their rights were somewhat curtailed by the Council of Trent,[3] but the institution itself continued to be accepted. All of the present prelatures were established in the twentieth century. While some are found in Europe e.g. Loreto, Pompeii, Klaipeda in Lithuania, Tromso and Trondheim in Norway, the great majority are in Latin America or the Philippines. They are seen as a provisional arrangement in territories not dependent on the Congregation for the Evangelisation of Peoples, where there are as yet insufficient ecclesial structures for a diocese to be constituted. There is one anomalous inclusion which has only one parish, the *Mission*

---

[1] CD 11: Fl I 569.

[2] Hence their original title of prelatures *nullius dioeceseos* i.e. of no diocese.

[3] Sess. XXIII c. 10; XXIV c. 9 *De Ref.*

de France, based at Pontigny, established on 15 August 1954 as a means of supplying the dioceses of France with greater manpower flexibility. This is governed by a special statute rather than the general norms of the Code for a diocese.[1]

Territorial abbacies have undergone a similar development. Gradually the exemption from diocesan jurisdiction enjoyed by the monastic community was extended to the communities outside which depended on the monastery for their pastoral care. In recent years one or two new ones were created to deal with situations similar to those mentioned above (e.g. Claraval in Brazil and St Peter's, Muenster in Canada), but most are ancient monasteries e.g. Monte Cassino, Subiaco, Pannonhalma. In 1976 Pope Paul VI decided that no more territorial abbacies should be created, save in most exceptional circumstances.[2]

In the context of this canon, the term 'prelate' means someone entrusted with hierarchical authority though not necessarily a Bishop. In practice, however, it is customary for territorial prelates to be ordained Bishop, whereas territorial abbots are not. Both a prelate and an abbot are described as the 'proper pastor' because they are given their power by the law itself, and are not exercising it in the name of the Supreme Pontiff or the local Bishop, even if their territory is an enclave within a diocese. Even if not ordained Bishop, they have the right of membership in the Bishops' Conference (see Can. 454 §1).

Can. 371 §1 A vicariate apostolic or a prefecture apostolic is a certain portion of the people of God, which for special reasons is not yet constituted a diocese, and which is entrusted to the pastoral care of a Vicar apostolic or a Prefect apostolic, who governs it in the name of the Supreme Pontiff.

§2 An apostolic administration is a certain portion of the people of God which, for special and particularly serious reasons, is not yet established by the Supreme Pontiff as a diocese, and whose pastoral care is entrusted to an apostolic Administrator, who governs it in the name of the Supreme Pontiff.

Vicars, Prefects and Administrators apostolic differ from territorial prelates and abbots in that their power is not proper but vicarious: it is exercised in the name of the Supreme Pontiff. However, in other respects they have the same power and rights, and are equally regarded as equivalent to diocesan Bishops (see Can. 381 §2). Vicars apostolic are normally in episcopal orders but prefects apostolic are not. Vicariates and prefectures are understood to be stages towards the establishment of a diocese. The first stage in this process, not mentioned in the Code, is the establishment of a Mission *sui iuris*.[3] This is followed by the erection of a Prefecture. The final stage before erection as a diocese is that of Apostolic Vicariate.

Apostolic Administrations are distinct and extraordinary arrangements. From the 13th century onwards the Pope occasionally appointed an apostolic Administrator to a vacant see. Currently they are erected by the Congregation for Bishops in consultation with the Secretariat of State.[4] Several have been established in recent years to cater for Catholics living in the states of the former Soviet Union. The criteria for the

---

[1] For the current status of the *Mission de France*, cf. Le Tourneau *La Mission de France: passé, présent et avenir de son statut juridique* Stud Can 24(1990) 357–382.

[2] Cf. Pope Paul VI mp *Catholica Ecclesia* 23.X.1976 n.2: CLD 8 237.

[3] Missions *sui iuris* began with the decr *Excelsum* of 12.IX.1896.

[4] Cf. PB 47 §1, 76, 78.

Book II The People of God

establishment of an Apostolic Administration appear to be delicate political situations preventing a more stable arrangement.

Can. 372 §1 As a rule, that portion of the people of God which constitutes a diocese or other particular Church is to have a defined territory, so that it comprises all the faithful who live in that territory.

767 Theologically, a particular Church is defined first and foremost in terms of 'a portion of the people of God'. However, juridically, each particular Church has clearly defined territorial boundaries. By baptism one is constituted a person not only in the universal Church (see Can. 96) but also in a particular Church as is clear from the norms concerning domicile (see Cann. 100–107) and rite (Cann. 111–112). Within the territory assigned to the particular Church, the diocesan Bishop or his equivalent has responsibility for all members of Christ's faithful.

Can. 372 §2 If however, in the judgement of the supreme authority in the Church, after consultation with the Bishop's Conferences concerned, it is thought to be helpful, there may be established in a given territory particular Churches distinguished by the rite of the faithful or by some other similar quality.

768 Bearing in mind the general principle of §1, the Code acknowledges that it is sometimes necessary to provide special pastoral care and attention for groups living within the territory of dioceses or other particular Churches. These people are distinct from other members of Christ's faithful because of their membership of another autonomous ritual Church or for some other reason e.g. belonging to the armed forces of a country, belonging to an ethnic or linguistic minority. If the Holy See considers it helpful, particular Churches may be established for these people in the same territory as already existing dioceses or particular Churches. Where the numbers merit it, separate dioceses are established for faithful of differing rites; in other cases, where numbers are smaller, apostolic exarchates or ordinariates are established on a national or international basis. The establishment and organisation of a military ordinariate are governed by special norms issued after the promulgation of the Code.[1] Whatever the form of particular Church to be established, the law requires that the Bishops' Conferences concerned must be consulted beforehand. Although membership of such a particular Church depends on some personal quality, each will have its own clearly defined territorial limits.

Can. 373 It is within the competence of the supreme authority alone to establish particular Churches; once they are lawfully established, the law itself gives them juridical personality.

769 In the first millennium new dioceses were generally established by a mother diocese without reference to the Holy See, but by the 11th century the erection of a diocese had been reserved to the Holy See.[2] The text of this canon is based on c.215 of the 1917 Code. Vat. II decided that the local Bishops' Conference was to be involved in

---

[1] Cf. AAS 78(1986) 481–486: English trans. in CLSNGBI 69(March 1987) 8–14. For a detailed commentary cf. Beyer *Commentary on the Apostolic Constitution 'Spirituali Militum Curae'* CLSNGBI (December 1988) 48–89; also Gutierrez *De Ordinariatus militaris nova constitutione* Per 76(1987) 189–218; Ghirlanda *De differentia Praelaturam personalem inter et Ordinariatum militarem seu castrensem* Per 76(1987) 219–251; Le Tourneau *La nouvelle organisation de l'Ordinariat aux Armées* Stud Can 21(1987) 37–66. The text of the statutes of the Ordinariate for the UK may be found in Ius Ecclesiae 1(1989) 786–792.

[2] Cf. Decretum Gratiani C.I. Dist. XXII.

any revision of diocesan boundaries.[1] However, the Code makes no reference to such prior consultation. It is the Congregation for Bishops which is competent to establish a new particular Church.[2]

A particular Church gains juridical personality automatically by its decree of erection. It is a non-collegial body, and in all juridical transactions the Bishop (or his equivalent) acts in the name of the particular Church (see Can. 393) There is no explicit reference to division, union or suppression of particular Churches: these matters are dealt with in the general provisions of the Code for juridical persons (see Cann. 120–123).

Can. 374 §1 Each diocese or other particular Church is to be divided into distinct parts or parishes.

Although not stated, this canon is an application of the principle of subsidiarity to the life of the Church. In order to provide properly for the pastoral care of the faithful, the Bishop or prelate is under an obligation to divide up the diocese or particular Church. This division is usually territorial; however, the Bishop may also establish ritual parishes, or national parishes for those of a different rite or nationality.

Can. 374 §2 To foster pastoral care by means of common action, several neighbouring parishes can be joined together in special groups, such as vicariates forane.

The groupings of neighbouring parishes for pastoral purposes has been a widespread practice in the Church for many centuries. According to c.217 of the 1917 Code, these groupings were mandatory unless the Bishop referred the matter to the Holy See. However, the Revision Commission preferred to leave any decision concerning joint action by parishes entirely to the Bishop.[3] The criterion for grouping parishes is whatever will best foster pastoral care.

Chapter II
BISHOPS

Article 1
Bishops in General

Can. 375 §1 By divine institution, Bishops succeed the Apostles through the Holy Spirit who is given to them. They are constituted Pastors in the Church, to be the teachers of doctrine, the priests of sacred worship and the ministers of governance.

The office of Bishop is not simply an administrative convenience established by the Church, and therefore something which could be abandoned; rather, in keeping with the teaching of Vat. II, it is part of Christ's will for his Church. As a body, the college of Bishops is understood to be the successors of the Apostles. This succession is not a merely human affair; it is of divine institution, although no indication is given of the

---

[1] Cf. CD 22–24: Fl I 576–578; ES Ia 12: Fl I 598.
[2] Cf. PB 76.
[3] Cf. Comm 17(1985) 97; 18(1986) 71–74; 12(1980) 283–285; 14(1982) 204.

nature of this institution.[1] The basic threefold ministry spelt out in the canon is a gift and a responsibility entrusted to the Bishop by the Holy Spirit: i.e. to be a teacher of doctrine, a priest of sacred worship and a minister of governance. As a theological scheme, this threefold ministry is a comparatively recent concept; it was the preferred model of ministry of Vat. II and is reflected in the structure of the Code: Books III and IV deal with the teaching and sanctifying offices, while the pastoral role of governance is spread throughout the Code.

Can. 375 §2 By their episcopal consecration, Bishops receive, together with the office of sanctifying, the offices also of teaching and of ruling, which however, by their nature, can be exercised only in hierarchical communion with the head of the College and its members.

774 The offices of sanctifying, teaching and ruling are conferred on all Bishops in their episcopal consecration. However, the canon makes clear that the exercise of this ministry is dependent upon the Bishop's connection with the Pope as head of the college of Bishops and with the rest of the members of the college.[2] Practical expressions of this hierarchical communion are contained in the apostolic letters by which a Bishop is appointed (see Cann. 379; 382 §§2–3), membership of the Bishops' Conference etc.

Can. 376 Bishops to whom the care of a given diocese is entrusted are called diocesan Bishops; the others are called titular Bishops.

775 Normally a Bishop is appointed for the pastoral care of a portion of the people of God in a determined territory which is constituted as a diocese (see Can. 369). Such a Bishop is referred to in the Code as a 'diocesan Bishop'. In the early centuries the concept of the depth of bond between Bishop and his people was such that a Bishop without responsibility for a particular flock was inconceivable. The first breach in this principle was made by the Council of Nicaea,[3] which allowed converted schismatic Bishops to retain their titles but without any pastoral responsibility for their sees. Later, the number of such Bishops increased with the expulsion of the Church from North Africa and parts of Spain. Many of these offered their services to Bishops in the West as auxiliaries and, after their deaths, others were consecrated to succeed them, a practice regulated by the Councils of Vienne and Trent.[4] Since the end of the nineteenth century, such Bishops have been known as titular Bishops.[5]

776 The term 'titular' in the Code includes all those who are not diocesan Bishops, i.e. all coadjutors, auxiliaries, those in the service of the Holy See, and also retired diocesan Bishops who are no longer given a titular see but are styled 'Bishop emeritus' of the diocese from which they have retired (see Can. 402 §1).

Can. 377 §1 The Supreme Pontiff freely appoints Bishops or confirms those lawfully elected.

777 In the early centuries, a Bishop was elected by popular vote. Gradually, however, the election came to be restricted to members of the clergy of the diocese. As a result of the growth of interference in these elections by civil authorities, the Holy See came to reserve to itself the right to appoint Bishops. Today, in fact, the majority of Bishops

---

[1] Cf. LG 20: Fl I 372.
[2] Cf. LG 21: Fl I 373; NEP 2: Fl I 424–425.
[3] Nicaea Can. 8.
[4] Cf. C. 5 in Clem. 1, 3; Sess. XIV c. 2, De Ref.
[5] Cf. lit ap *In Suprema* 10.VI.1882; note also Pope Gregory XV decr *Inscrutabilis* 5.II.1622.

in the Catholic Church are freely appointed by the Pope. In addition to the right of the Synod of Bishops of Eastern Rite Patriarchal Churches (see CCEO Can. 110), a few European dioceses have retained the right to elect their own Bishop, subject to confirmation by the Pope e.g. some dioceses in Germany, Salzburg in Austria, Chur, St Gallen, and Basel in Switzerland.

Can. 377 §2 At least every three years, the Bishops of an ecclesiastical province or, if circumstances suggest it, of a Bishops' Conference, are to draw up, by common accord and in secret, a list of priests, even of members of institutes of consecrated life, who are suitable for the episcopate; they are to send this list to the Apostolic See. This is without prejudice to the right of every Bishop individually to make known to the Apostolic See the names of priests whom he thinks are worthy and suitable for the episcopal office.

In order to supply the Apostolic See with the relevant information on possible candidates for episcopal office, the law obliges local Bishops to forward a list of the names of suitable priests. This is to be done by the Bishops of a province or a Bishops' Conference at least every three years. The list is to be drawn up in secret and by the common agreement of the Bishops assembled. It may include the names of priests from institutes of consecrated life. Meetings to prepare such a list are conducted in accordance with norms issued by the Holy See.[1] The joint process does not restrict the right of an individual Bishop to forward directly to the Holy See the names of priests whom he considers to be worthy and suitable candidates for episcopal office.

Can. 377 §3 Unless it has been lawfully prescribed otherwise, for the appointment of a diocesan Bishop or a coadjutor Bishop, a *ternus*, as it is called, is to be proposed to the Apostolic See. In the preparation of this list, it is the responsibility of the papal Legate to seek individually the suggestions of the Metropolitan and of the Suffragans of the province to which the diocese in question belongs or with which it is joined in some grouping, as well as the suggestions of the president of the Bishops' Conference. The papal Legate is, moreover, to hear the views of some members of the college of consultors and of the cathedral chapter. If he judges it expedient, he is also to seek individually, and in secret, the opinions of other clerics, both secular and religious, and of lay persons of outstanding wisdom. He is then to send these suggestions, together with his own opinion, to the Apostolic See.

When provision must be made for a new diocesan Bishop or a coadjutor, the law envisages a further process. This involves the preparation of a short-list of names of candidates for the office. Responsibility for drawing up this list – known as a 'ternus' – rests with the papal Legate (either the Apostolic Nuncio or the apostolic Delegate). He must consult individually the Bishops of the ecclesiastical province concerned and the president of the Bishops' Conference, asking for suggestions; he is also required to seek the views of *some* of the diocesan consultors and members of the cathedral chapter. Furthermore, if he considers it to be appropriate he is to consult other individuals, clerics, religious and laity. Such a consultation must be secret. As well as the results of his consultation, the Legate must forward his own opinion to the Holy See.

---

[1] Cf. Council for the Public Affairs of the Church: Norms *Episcoporum delectum*, on promotion to the episcopate in the latin Church 25.III.1972: AAS 64(1972) 386–391: CLD 7 366–372.

This procedure is to be followed in all cases for the provision of a diocesan Bishop or a coadjutor, except where particular law or custom has established otherwise, e.g. in those dioceses where the Bishop is elected by the cathedral chapter, as mentioned above under §1.

Can 377 §4 Unless it has been lawfully provided otherwise, the diocesan Bishop who judges that his diocese requires an auxiliary Bishop, is to propose to the Apostolic See a list of the names of at least three priests suitable for this office.

780 The procedure for the selection of suitable candidates for the office of auxiliary Bishop is much less formal. The diocesan Bishop is obliged to draw up a list of at least three names of priests whom he believes to be worthy and suitable. This list is to be submitted to the Holy See by the Bishop. It had been suggested that the Bishop should seek the opinion of the other Bishops of the province if the names were not on the list prepared in accordance with §2, but this proposal was rejected by the Revision Commission.[1]

Can. 377 §5 For the future, no rights or privileges of election, appointment, presentation or designation of Bishops are conceded to civil authorities.

781 Vat. II sought to reclaim for the competent ecclesiastical authority the exclusive right to appoint Bishops.[2] In the past, various rights and privileges (e.g. nomination, presentation) were granted to civil authorities. The Council asked that such authorities 'initiate discussions with the Holy See with the object of freely waiving the aforesaid rights and privileges which they at present enjoy by agreement or custom'.[3] Some countries have already accepted this invitation and renounced their rights and privileges concerning the appointment of Bishops, e.g. Peru, Monaco, Haiti. The Code makes it clear that further rights and privileges of this kind will not be granted.

Can. 378 §1 To be a suitable candidate for the episcopate, a person must:

1° **be outstanding in strong faith, good morals, piety, zeal for souls, wisdom, prudence and human virtues, and possess those other gifts which equip him to fulfil the office in question;**

2° **be held in good esteem;**

3° **be at least 35 years of age;**

4° **be a priest ordained for at least five years;**

5° **hold a doctorate or at least a licentiate in sacred Scripture, theology or canon law, from an institute of higher studies approved by the Apostolic See, or at least be well versed in these disciplines.**

§2 The definitive judgement on the suitability of the person to be promoted rests with the Apostolic See.

782 This list of qualities is not intended to be exhaustive. Other desirable qualities in a candidate for the episcopate include: good judgement, an equable temperament, strong character, devotion to the Apostolic See, fidelity to the magisterium, a spirit of

---

[1] Cf. Comm 14(1982) 205 at Can. 344 §4.
[2] Cf. CD 20: Fl I 575.
[3] Ibid.

sacrifice, management skills, a social sense, spirit of dialogue and cooperation, an understanding of the signs of the times, and impartiality.[1]

It is to be noted that reference is made to 'the office in question'; this means not only the episcopate in general, but also the particular office to be filled; consequently, local and national considerations must be taken into account.

The canon makes clear that, whatever the outcome of any consultation, the definitive judgement on the suitability of a candidate rests with the Holy See. Thus certain requirements, e.g. that of age or length of ordination, could be dispensed. This definitive judgement might be delegated to others as is the case provided for in Can. 184 of the Eastern Code: provided that the Roman Pontiff has given his assent to the inclusion of a candidate's name on the list of potential Bishops, then his election can be announced by the Patriarch without further approval from the Holy See.

Can. 379 Unless prevented by a lawful reason, one who is promoted to the episcopate must receive episcopal consecration within three months of receiving the apostolic letter, and in fact before he takes possession of his office.

The law requires those appointed as Bishops to receive episcopal consecration within three months of their appointments. Such a norm prevents undue delays in caring for the people who have been deprived of a pastor. Perhaps more significantly, the canon demands that those appointed as Bishops must receive episcopal consecration *before* they take possession of their office. This is in keeping with the principle enunciated in Can. 375 §2 concerning the source of the threefold ministry of the Bishop and that contained in Can. 332 §1 pointing out that the Pope acquires full and supreme power 'when, together with episcopal consecration, he has been lawfully elected and has accepted the election'.

Can. 380 Before taking canonical possession of his office, he who has been promoted is to make the profession of faith and take the oath of fidelity to the Apostolic See, in accordance with the formula approved by the same Apostolic See.

All those promoted to the episcopate, or to an office equivalent to that of diocesan Bishop, are required to take the oath before a delegate appointed by the Apostolic See (Can. 833 3°). This will normally be the Apostolic Nuncio or Delegate.

The formula to be used is *not* that issued by the Congregation for the Doctrine of the Faith which took effect on 1.III.1989, but a similar one specifically for Bishops issued earlier which came into effect on 1.VII.1987.[2] The new formula consists of the Profession of the Faith, i.e. the Nicene Creed with some short additions, and a separate oath of fidelity to the Holy See and to the carrying out of the office of Bishop.

Article 2
Diocesan Bishops

Can. 381 §1 In the diocese entrusted to his care, the diocesan Bishop has all the ordinary, proper and immediate power required for the exercise of his

---

[1] Cf. Norms *Episcoporum delectum* 25.III.1972 VI 2: CLD 7 369.

[2] For the text of the general formula, cf. Comm 21(1989) 32–34: AAS 81(1989) 104–106. The specific text for Bishops does not seem to have been published, but is referred to by Betti *Professione di fede e giuramento di fedeltà* Not 25(1989) 321–325.

pastoral office, except in those matters which the law or a decree of the Supreme Pontiff reserves to the supreme or to some other ecclesiastical authority.

788 Whereas c.334 §1 of the 1917 Code spoke of Bishops as the 'ordinary and immediate pastors in the dioceses entrusted to them', the present canon, inspired by Vat. II,[1] refers to their power as ordinary, *proper* and immediate. The description 'proper' means that each diocesan Bishop has power to act in his own name; within the diocese entrusted to him, he acts as vicar of Christ[2] – not as vicar of the Pope. Within his diocese, his power is *ordinary*, i.e. it is attached to his office as a diocesan Bishop; he does not act as a delegate of a higher authority; he loses this power when he retires from office. Finally, his power is *immediate*, i.e. he can exercise that power personally and directly for the benefit of the people entrusted to his care. In practice, however, it is normal for a diocesan Bishop to exercise many of his jurisdictional powers through the agency of appointed delegates (see Cann. 134–142; 475–476; 1419–1421).

789 The canon speaks of some limitations on the power of a diocesan Bishop. Some of these come from the law itself, e.g. the internal autonomy of institutes of consecrated life (see Can. 586); the power to dispense from certain laws and impediments (see Cann. 87, 1078). Other restrictions may come as the result of a direct intervention of the Supreme Pontiff in particular circumstances.

Can. 381 §2 Those who are at the head of the other communities of the faithful mentioned in Can. 368, are equivalent in law to the diocesan Bishop, unless the contrary is clear from the nature of things or from a provision of the law.

790 Can. 368 lists particular Churches which are equivalent to a diocese. This paragraph points out that those who are at the head of such communities are equivalent to the diocesan Bishop, unless it is otherwise clear or provided for. Thus, a territorial prelate or abbot (see Can. 370) has 'ordinary, proper and immediate power' in the prelature or abbacy entrusted to him. On the other hand, Vicars and Prefects apostolic (see Can. 371 §1) as well as apostolic Administrators (see Can. 371 §2) have ordinary power in their territories, but this power is *vicarious*, not proper, i.e. they exercise their power not in their own name but in that of the Supreme Pontiff.

Can. 382 §1 One who is promoted a Bishop cannot become involved in the exercise of the office entrusted to him before he has taken canonical possession of the diocese. However, he is able to exercise offices which he already held in the same diocese at the time of his promotion, without prejudice to Can. 409 §2.

791 There are three stages in the appointment of a Bishop: appointment (see Can. 377 §1), consecration (see Can. 375 §2) and canonical possession of the diocese. The first two stages are prerequisites for the third. Thus a Bishop-elect is forbidden from becoming involved in the exercise of his office until he has taken canonical possession of the diocese. However, the Code permits a Bishop-elect who already held office in the diocese, e.g. as chancellor or judicial vicar, to continue in that office until the canonical possession. If the Bishop-elect was previously an auxiliary Bishop, he is to continue to function in whatever office he may have held, e.g. Vicar General or Vicar

---

[1] Cf. LG 27: Fl I 383; CD 11: Fl I 569.
[2] Cf. LG 27: Fl I 382.

episcopal (see Cann. 406; 409 §2). He may not, however, exercise any authority reserved to a diocesan Bishop, e.g. the appointment of parish priests, until he has taken canonical possession.

Can. 382 §2 Unless he is lawfully impeded, one who is not already consecrated a Bishop and is now promoted to the office of diocesan Bishop, must take canonical possession of his diocese within four months of receiving the apostolic letter. If he is already consecrated, he must take possession within two months of receiving the apostolic letter.

The period of time within which a newly appointed Bishop is to take canonical possession of his diocese is dependent on whether or not the Bishop-elect has already received episcopal consecration. Thus, if he is not already a Bishop, he must receive consecration within three months of the reception of the apostolic letters (see Can. 379) and take possession within four months of that same date; if he is already in episcopal orders, the law gives him two months from the reception of the apostolic letters to take possession of the diocese.

Can. 382 §3 A Bishop takes canonical possession of his diocese when, personally or by proxy, he shows the apostolic letter to the college of consultors, in the presence of the chancellor of the curia, who makes a record of the fact. This must take place within the diocese. In dioceses which are newly established he takes possession when he communicates the same letter to the clergy and the people in the cathedral Church, with the senior of the priests present making a record of the fact.

The procedure of taking canonical possession of a diocese consists in the presentation of the apostolic letters to the college of consultors of the diocese or to the cathedral chapter if that body exercises the functions of the consultors (see Can. 502 §3). The presentation must be made by the Bishop himself or by his duly appointed proxy. It must be done in the diocese, and the chancellor of the curia must be present to record the fact.

In a diocese which has been newly created, special arrangements have to be made since, as yet, there will be no consultors or chapter or chancellor. The Bishop-elect is required to communicate his letters of appointment to the clergy and people of the diocese. He is to do this in the cathedral and the senior priest present is to record the fact.[1]

Can. 382 §4 It is strongly recommended that the taking of canonical possession be performed with a liturgical act in the cathedral Church, in the presence of the clergy and the people.

It is only right that such a solemn juridical act with momentous consequences for the faithful of a particular Church should take place within a liturgical celebration, preferably the Eucharist. Of course, if the canonical possession has to be by proxy, a less formal setting is probably preferable.

Can. 383 §1 In exercising his pastoral office, the diocesan Bishop is to be solicitous for all Christ's faithful entrusted to his care, whatever their age, condition or nationality, whether they live in the territory or are visiting

---

[1] Conversely, where two or more dioceses have been united, as happened for many Italian dioceses in 1986, even if there are several co-cathedrals, there is only to be one canonical possession and liturgical reception: *Caerimoniale Episcoporum* 1135, 1141–1148; cf. Not 22(1986) 948–950.

there. He is to show an apostolic spirit also to those who, because of their condition of life, are not sufficiently able to benefit from ordinary pastoral care, and to those who have lapsed from religious practice.

§2 If he has faithful of a different rite in his diocese, he is to provide for their spiritual needs either by means of priests or parishes of the same rite, or by an episcopal Vicar.

§3 He is to act with humanity and charity to those who are not in full communion with the catholic Church; he should also foster ecumenism as it is understood by the Church.

§4 He is to consider the non-baptised as commended to him in the Lord, so that the charity of Christ, of which the Bishop must be a witness to all, may shine also on them.

796 The role of a diocesan Bishop has to do with the pastoral welfare of the people entrusted to his care. The four paragraphs of this canon identify groups of people who have a claim on the Bishop's concern. First and foremost, all of Christ's faithful in the diocese are entrusted to him, i.e. all those who have been baptised or received into the Catholic Church. In his ministry, the Bishop is to manifest no distinction of persons on the basis of age, social status or nationality. Moreover, he is to give special attention to those who need particular pastoral care, e.g. those in irregular marital unions, and those who, for whatever reason, have lapsed from religious practice.

797 The second group mentioned in the canon consists of those who belong to a different ritual Church. The diocesan Bishop is obliged to care for these by providing them with proper parishes or priests or by placing them under the direct care of an episcopal Vicar.

798 Finally, the Bishop is reminded of his duty to encourage links with the faithful of other Churches, to promote ecumenism in conformity with the universal law of the Church, and to give good example to those not yet baptised, showing special care for the welfare and formation of catechumens (see Can. 206).

Can. 384 He is to have special concern for the priests, to whom he is to listen as his helpers and counsellors. He is to defend their rights and ensure that they fulfil the obligations proper to their state. He is to see that they have the means and the institutions needed for the development of their spiritual and intellectual life. He is to ensure that they are provided with adequate means of livelihood and social welfare, in accordance with the law.

799 Since the cooperation of the *presbyterium* is essential to the pastoral care of the faithful in the particular Church (see Can. 369), the law obliges the diocesan Bishop to demonstrate special care and attention towards his priests.[1] He is required to seek their advice *informally* as 'sons and friends',[2] and *formally* through structures such as the council of priests (see Can. 495) and the college of consultors (see Can. 502). In particular, the Bishop takes on certain obligations towards his priests:

(a) he must *defend all their rights,* those accruing both from natural justice and from the law of the Church;

(b) he must make sure they have what they need to carry out their obligations;

---

[1] A particularly valuable guide in this regard is the Directory on the pastoral ministry of Bishops: DPME; in respect of this and the following canon, cf. nn.107–117, 118–119, 197 of that Directory.
[2] CD 16: Fl I 573.

(c) he must provide whatever is necessary for their ongoing spiritual and intellectual formation (see Can. 279), in whatever way this can best be done in the local circumstances;

(d) he must make sure that all his priests have 'remuneration that befits their condition' (Can. 281 §1); this provision is to be regulated by particular law (see Can. 1274) as is that for whatever the priests need by way of social welfare for 'infirmity, sickness or old age' (Can. 281 §2).

Can. 385 He must in a very special way foster vocations to the various ministries and to consecrated life, having a special care for priestly and missionary vocations.

A particular expression of the Bishop's pastoral care is to be found in his fostering of vocations, a task that belongs to the whole Church (see Can. 233) – a task which has become even more urgent in view of the recent significant decline in vocations to the priesthood and to religious life – particularly, let it be said, in the so-called 'developed' western world. Could it be that those countries and dioceses which are witnessing this decline are in fact seeing a repetition of the conduct of that *rich young man who walked sadly away* from the invitation of Christ (see Mk 10:17–22; Matt 19: 16–22; Lk 18:18–25)? – and whom Christ did not pursue to offer anything less than 'come and follow me'. In this canon, the law speaks of vocations 'to the various ministries'. Clearly, this refers primarily to priesthood and diaconate; however, it also includes the lay ministries mentioned in Can. 230. By implication, Bishops are reminded that their concern for vocations must transcend the immediate needs of their own diocese: each Bishop is to be solicitous of those who are called to institutes of consecrated life, both men and women, and to those who receive a 'missionary' vocation, both laity and clergy.

Can. 386 §1 The diocesan Bishop is bound to teach and illustrate to the faithful the truths of faith which are to be believed and applied to behaviour. He is himself to preach frequently. He is also to ensure that the provisions of the canons on the ministry of the word, especially on the homily and catechetical instruction, are faithfully observed, so that the whole of christian teaching is transmitted to all.

Bishops are authentic teachers, endowed with the authority of Christ. They are to preach to the people assigned to them the faith which is destined to inform their thinking and direct their conduct. As 'moderators of the entire ministry of the word in their Churches' (Can. 756 §2), Bishops have also a supervisory role, but with a positive purpose, i.e. 'so that the whole of Christian teaching is transmitted to all'. This is not simply a question of ensuring that teaching is correct, but also that it is balanced and that the more challenging aspects of the Gospel are not omitted. They are given a particular responsibility for upholding and enforcing the universal law of the Church on the ministry of the word, i.e. preaching and catechetical instruction (see Cann. 756–780).

Can. 386 §2 By whatever means seem most appropriate, he is firmly to defend the integrity and unity of the faith to be believed. However, he is to acknowledge a just freedom in the further investigation of truths.

In addition to their responsibility to supervise the teaching of the faith, Bishops are charged with protecting its integrity and unity. They are to do so 'by whatever means seem most appropriate'. These will vary according to the circumstances e.g. an informal dialogue with individuals or groups or more formal procedures by which teachers or writers may be sanctioned (see Cann. 805; 812; 823; 1364–1369; 1371). However, any action taken by the Bishop must respect the legitimate 'just freedom' granted by the law to experts in the sacred sciences in the area of research and expression of views (see Can. 218).

Can. 387 Mindful that he is bound to give an example of holiness in charity, humility and simplicity of life, the diocesan Bishop is to seek in every way to promote the holiness of Christ's faithful according to the proper vocation of each. Since he is the principal dispenser of the mysteries of God, he is to strive constantly that Christ's faithful entrusted to his care may grow in grace through the celebration of the sacraments, and may know and live the paschal mystery.

803 The sanctifying office of the Church 'is exercised principally by Bishops' (Can. 835 §1). Inspired by the teaching of Vat. II,[1] this canon stresses that the personal holiness of the Bishop is an essential prerequisite for the effective exercise of that office. A life distinguished by charity, humility and simplicity will help the Bishop lead the faithful to fulfil their own particular vocation (see Cann. 210, 225–226). Moreover, in their quest for holiness, the faithful have the right to be assisted through the word of God and the sacraments (see Can. 213): the primary responsibility for providing these sources of holiness rests with the diocesan Bishop.

Can. 388 §1 After he has taken possession of the diocese, the diocesan Bishop must apply the Mass for the people entrusted to him on each Sunday and on each holy day of obligation in his region.

§2 The Bishop must himself celebrate and apply the Mass for the people on the days mentioned in §1; if, however, he is lawfully impeded from so doing, he is to have someone else do so on those days, or do so himself on other days.

§3 A Bishop who, in addition to his own, is given another diocese, even as administrator, satisfies the obligation by applying one Mass for all the people entrusted to him.

§4 A Bishop who has not satisfied the obligation mentioned in §§1–3, is to apply as soon as possible as many Masses for the people as he has omitted.

804 One of the first obligations incumbent on a Bishop after taking canonical possession of his diocese is that of applying Mass for the people entrusted to him, whether he has charge of one diocese or more than one. He is bound to do this every Sunday and on every holy day of obligation in his region (see Can. 1246). The obligation is *personal*, i.e. he himself must discharge this duty unless legitimately impeded, e.g. by illness or other serious reason, in which case he is obliged to have another priest apply the Mass on the day in question or apply the Mass himself on another day. So grave an obligation is this that a Bishop who has not applied the required Masses must, as soon as possible, offer as many Masses for that intention as he has omitted. A corresponding obligation binds every parish priest (see Can. 534).

Can. 389 He is frequently to preside at the celebration of the most holy Eucharist in the cathedral Church or in some other Church of his diocese, especially on holy days of obligation and on other solemnities.

---

[1] Cf. CD 15: Fl I 571–572; 1 Cor 4:1; Comm 18(1986) 143.

Part II The Hierarchical Constitution of the Church

Vat. II emphasised the symbolic importance of the Bishop as the centre of the liturgical life of the diocese, particularly when celebrating the Eucharist in the cathedral surrounded by the college of priests, ministers, and with the people taking an active part.[1] The obligation to celebrate frequently in this way is not new, and is closely connected with the obligation of residence stated in Can. 395; apart from what is prescribed in §3 of that canon, the Code does not attempt to specify the days on which the Bishop is to preside in the cathedral or elsewhere in the diocese. It uses the word 'frequently' to indicate that such celebrations are to be the norm rather than the exception. At other times a Bishop is free to celebrate in his private chapel (see Can. 1227) or elsewhere.

Can. 390 The diocesan Bishop may carry out pontifical functions throughout his diocese. He may not do so outside his diocese without the consent of the local Ordinary, either expressly given or at least reasonably presumed.

Pontifical functions are those for which the liturgical books prescribe the use of pontifical insignia, i.e. the crosier and mitre, as e.g. at confirmation, ordination, dedication of a Church. A diocesan Bishop may celebrate such ceremonies anywhere in his diocese. However, since they imply jurisdiction, a Bishop may not so act in another diocese without the consent of the competent local Ordinary – a consent which is normally requested and normally granted; it may, in exceptional circumstances, be 'reasonably presumed'. In the case of a Metropolitan, see Can. 436 §3.

Can. 391 §1 The diocesan Bishop governs the particular Church entrusted to him with legislative, executive and judicial power, in accordance with the law.

§2 The Bishop exercises legislative power himself. He exercises executive power either personally or through Vicars general or episcopal Vicars, in accordance with the law. He exercises judicial power either personally or through a judicial Vicar and judges, in accordance with the law.

The threefold distinction of ecclesiastical power found in Can. 135 is applied here to the Bishop's governance of a particular Church. A Bishop receives this power in episcopal consecration and exercises it in hierarchical communion (see Can. 375 §2). The canon distinguishes the manner in which each type of power is exercised:

(a) *legislative* power is exercised *personally* by the Bishop and cannot be delegated (see Can. 135 §2). Whatever laws are made by a diocesan Bishop may not be contrary to those made by a higher authority, such as the Holy See itself or the Bishops' Conference as approved by the Holy See. In some cases, while legislating alone, the Bishop is required to consult beforehand with an advisory body such as the council of priests, e.g. when regulating the destination of stole fees (see Can. 531).

(b) *executive power*, by which the diocese is governed on a day-to-day basis, may of course be exercised personally by the Bishop and to a great extent generally is. In view however of the complexity of administration in so many modern dioceses, there are clearly areas which the Bishop has to delegate to others, such as a Vicar general (see Can. 475) or an episcopal Vicar (see Can. 476). It should always be borne in mind that the delegation of executive power must conform to the prescriptions of Cann. 136–144. There is the further fact that there are situations in which the diocesan Bishop simply may not delegate his executive power, principally in those situations where the law reserves a particular function to the *diocesan Bishop* rather than to the local Ordinary (see e.g. Cann. 524, 609 §1).

---

[1] Cf. SC 41: Fl I 14–15.

Book II The People of God

(c) judicial power may also be exercised by the Bishop personally (see Cann. 1419 §1, 1420 §2). This however is, and should be, extremely rare. The normal practice is that judicial power is exercised by the judicial Vicar whom the Bishop is obliged to appoint (see Can. 1420 §1), and by the other judges contemplated in the law (see Cann. 1421–1422). All judicial activity must be conducted in accordance with the norms of Book VII of the Code.

Can. 392 §1 Since the Bishop must defend the unity of the universal Church, he is bound to foster the discipline which is common to the whole Church, and so press for the observance of all ecclesiastical laws.

§2 He is to ensure that abuses do not creep into ecclesiastical discipline, especially concerning the ministry of the word, the celebration of the sacraments and sacramentals, the worship of God and the cult of the saints, and the administration of goods.

808 Although he has 'all the ordinary, proper and immediate power' required for his pastoral office (Can. 381 §1), each diocesan Bishop does not govern his diocese in isolation from the universal Church. He is charged with the responsibility of defending and preserving the unity of the whole Church. This canon identifies two ways in which the Bishop can do this:

(a) firstly, by promoting the common discipline of the universal Church and ensuring that all ecclesiastical laws are observed in his diocese. In effect, this also means using his power to dispense in exceptional situations (see Cann. 87–88).

(b) secondly, by seeking to prevent abuses in those matters which are central to the episcopal ministry, such as the ministry of the word (see Cann. 756–780), the celebration of the sacraments and sacramentals (see Cann. 840–1172), divine worship and veneration of the saints (see Cann. 834–839; 1186–1190), the administration of ecclesiastical property (see Cann. 1254–1310), etc.

Can. 393 In all juridical transactions of the diocese, the diocesan Bishop acts in the person of the diocese.

809 In juridical transactions on the part of the diocese the Bishop does not act in his own name as an individual, but as the legal representative of the diocese. As such, he must ensure that all canonical formalities are observed in these transactions e.g. obtaining the consent of those required by Can. 1292 §1 in alienating ecclesiastical goods.

810 No one else can act in the person of the diocese without a special mandate.

811 Clearly there may be a divergence between the requirements of canon and civil law, as the Code itself recognises (e.g. Cann. 1290 and 1296). It may not always be possible to give this canon full effect in civil law; nevertheless, the Bishop retains the responsibility in canon law to protect the interests of the diocese by whatever means are feasible (see Can. 1284 §2 2°).

Can. 394 §1 The Bishop is to foster various forms of the apostolate in his diocese and is to ensure that throughout the entire diocese, or in its particular districts, all works of the apostolate are coordinated under his direction, with due regard for the character of each apostolate.

§2 He is to insist on the faithful's obligation to exercise the apostolate according to the condition and talents of each. He is to urge them to take part in or assist various works of the apostolate, according to the needs of place and time.

By reason of their incorporation into the Church at baptism, all Christ's faithful have the right to promote and engage in apostolic activity, on their own initiative (see Can. 216). This right belongs to lay people, clergy and members of institutes of consecrated life. No permission is required to undertake apostolic activity. However, common sense demands that there ought to be some coordination of these efforts. As the one to whom care for the people of a particular Church is entrusted, the Bishop is obliged to foster and coordinate apostolic activity in his diocese and within its constituent parts in order to demonstrate the unity of the particular Church.[1] His exhortation to the faithful to participate in the apostolate is a reminder that, for all Christ's faithful, apostolic action is an *obligation* as well as a right.

Can. 395 §1 The diocesan Bishop is bound by the law of personal residence in his diocese, even if he has a coadjutor or auxiliary Bishop.

§2 Apart from the visit *ad limina*, attendance at councils or at the synod of Bishops or at the Bishop's Conference, at which he must be present, or by reason of another office lawfully entrusted to him, he may be absent from the diocese, for a just reason, for not longer than one month, continuously or otherwise, provided he ensures that the diocese is not harmed by this absence.

§3 He is not to be absent from his diocese on Christmas Day, during Holy Week, or on Easter Sunday, Pentecost and Corpus Christi, except for a grave and urgent reason.

§4 If the Bishop is unlawfully absent from the diocese for more than six months, the Metropolitan is to notify the Apostolic See. If it is the Metropolitan who is absent, the senior suffragan is to do the same.

The various obligations incumbent on a diocesan Bishop require his residence within the diocese. Even if he is assisted by an auxiliary or coadjutor Bishop, a diocesan Bishop must ordinarily reside *personally* in his diocese. The canon makes clear the practical implications of the law of residence:

- he may be absent from the diocese for no longer than one month in the year, e.g. for personal holidays; this includes vacations in the territory of the diocese since 'presence' in this case refers to *active* presence;
- he may be absent from the diocese for purposes such as those mentioned in the canon; these legitimate absences are in addition to the month already mentioned;
- he must be present in the diocese on the days specified in §3; only for 'a grave and urgent reason' can this obligation be neglected e.g. serious illness, war, national disaster; the days mentioned are of immense significance to a Bishop's role of pastor of the particular Church.

In order to prevent possible abuses in this matter, the law charges the Metropolitan (or senior suffragan Bishop on the case of an absent Metropolitan) with the responsibility of reporting absences exceeding six months on the part of a Bishop within the ecclesiastical province. This forms part of the supervisory role of a Metropolitan (see Can. 436 §1 1°). The report must be sent to the Holy See which will then decide what action, if any, is to be taken. If the circumstances warrant it, a just penalty may be imposed (see Can. 1396) – including, if need be, deprivation of office.

Can. 396 §1 The Bishop is bound to visit his diocese in whole or in part each year, so that at least every five years he will have visited the whole

---

[1] Cf. CD 17: Fl I 574.

diocese, either personally or, if he is lawfully impeded, through a coadjutor or auxiliary Bishop, a Vicar general, an episcopal Vicar or some other priest.

§2 The Bishop has a right to select any clerics he wishes as his companions and helpers in a visitation, any contrary privilege or custom being reprobated.

814 The pastoral visit is clearly the pre-eminent way in which the Bishop can be present to his diocese. Provided circumstances permit, it should be carried out personally by him. Nevertheless, the use of the auxiliary Bishop, the Vicar general, episcopal Vicar, dean or other priest can also be a valuable supplement as a substitute. The law obliges the Bishop to conduct at least partial visitation *every* year, so that the whole diocese is visited at least every five years. While direct pastoral contact with the priests and the people ought to be done by the Bishop himself, some elements of visitation, e.g. inspection of the physical fabric, registers, financial matters, etc., can be delegated to specialists or to others who are specifically delegated for the purpose.

815 While the Bishop's choice of companions for visitation might appear to have been restricted by c. 343 §2 of the 1917 Code, he now clearly has a completely free hand: he may choose any number of clerics he likes, deacons as well as priests; moreover, they need not even be priests from his own *presbyterium*. The Code does not expressly give the Bishop a right to be accompanied by lay people or religious who are not clerics, but this is not excluded. Any customs contrary to the current norm, even local and immemorial ones (e.g. having the Dean by right accompany the Bishop) are suppressed and cannot be revived (see Can. 5 §1).

Can. 397 §1 Persons, catholic institutes, sacred things and places within the boundaries of the diocese, are subject to ordinary episcopal visitation.

§2 The Bishop may visit the members of religious institutes of pontifical right and their houses only in the cases stated in the law.

816 Ordinary episcopal visitation entails the right of the diocesan Bishop to visit and inspect the following:
- physical persons living in the diocese, e.g. lay people, secular clergy, etc.
- juridical persons located within the diocese, e.g. parishes, associations of the faithful etc.
- catholic institutes within the diocese i.e. those bodies calling themselves 'catholic' (see Can. 300), e.g. schools, charitable organisations etc. It is to be noted that *private* schools, while subject to the supervision of the Bishop, are *not* subject to ordinary episcopal visitation.[1]
- sacred places within the diocese (see Cann. 1205–1243), e.g. churches, oratories, cemeteries.
- sacred things (see Can. 1171) located or used within the diocese, e.g. sacred vessels, relics etc.
- the autonomous monasteries mentioned in Can. 615 and individual houses of religious institutes of diocesan right (see Can. 628 §2).
- the houses of religious institutes of pontifical right but only in respect of the care of souls, public worship and other external apostolates (see Cann. 678 §1, 681 §1, 683).
- the papal Legation, but only in respect of the celebration of marriages (see Can. 366 1°).

---

[1] Cf. Comm 18(1986) 153.

The law does not require the Bishop to inspect each and every one of those listed above. However, within the limits mentioned, he has the *right* to do so, either personally or through a delegate.

Can. 398 The Bishop is to endeavour to make his pastoral visitation with due diligence. He is to ensure that he is not a burden to anyone on the ground of undue expense.

The visitation of a diocese is not simply a matter of bureaucracy. It is an opportunity for the Bishop to meet with the people of God entrusted to his care. Visitation must be undertaken diligently, always bearing in mind the pastoral nature of episcopal office. While it is only right that the Bishop should be refunded for any expenses incurred as a result of visitation, the law reminds him not to be a burden to anyone in this regard.

Can. 399 §1 Every five years the diocesan Bishop is bound to submit to the Supreme Pontiff a report on the state of the diocese entrusted to him, in the form and at the time determined by the Apostolic See.

§2 If the year assigned for submitting this report coincides in whole or in part with the first two years of his governance of the diocese, for that occasion the Bishop need not draw up and submit the report.

In an act of hierarchical communion, each diocesan Bishop is obliged to submit a report on his diocese to the Holy See every five years. The five-year periods are fixed; thus each year Bishops from specified regions of the world are required to send in their reports.[1] The whole Church is covered in this way every five years. The Apostolic See has also determined the form of this report:[2] it deals with every aspect of the pastoral life and administration of a diocese, such as the general religious situation, finance, liturgy, clergy, institutes of consecrated life, education, laity, ecumenism. A Bishop is excused from preparing this report only if the year assigned by the Holy See coincides with his first two years in office.

Can. 400 §1 Unless the Apostolic See has decided otherwise, in the year in which he is bound to submit the report to the Supreme Pontiff, the diocesan Bishop is to go to Rome to venerate the tombs of the Blessed Apostles Peter and Paul, and to present himself to the Roman Pontiff.

§2 The Bishop is to satisfy this obligation personally, unless he is lawfully impeded; in which case he is to satisfy the obligation through the coadjutor, if he has one, or the auxiliary, or a suitable priest of his *presbyterium* who resides in his diocese.

§3 A Vicar apostolic can satisfy this obligation through a proxy, even through one residing in Rome. A Prefect apostolic is not bound by this obligation.

The visit *ad limina Apostolorum* has a very long history. Its roots can be traced to the fourth century. By the late middle ages, the visit was an obligation for all Bishops unless dispensed. The discipline was revised by Pope Sixtus V, later by Pope Pius X,

---

[1] Cf. SCB decr *Ad Romanam Ecclesiam* 29.VI.1975 n.2: CLD 8 249.

[2] Cf. SCB, SCOC, SCEP: Quinquennial Report by Residential Bishops 1975 (Private): CLD 9 214–238.

and most recently by Pope John Paul II.[1] This visit is obligatory for all diocesan Bishops, territorial prelates and military ordinaries.[2] Because their territory is not yet ready to be formed into a diocese, Vicars apostolic are permitted to make their visit, expressing union with the Holy See, through a proxy, even one living in Rome; neither Prefects apostolic nor Administrators apostolic, however, are bound by this canon since they exercise their pastoral office in the name of the Supreme Pontiff (see Can. 371).

820 The visit involves visiting the Basilicas of St Peter and of St Paul in Rome: as proof they are required to sign a register in the sacristies. They must also visit the Congregation for Bishops, and present themselves for an audience with the Pope; frequently this latter is done as a group for all those from a particular region, and the arrangements will be coordinated in advance. The obligation is to be carried out in person, but the Code provides a list of proxies in order of preference, if health or other lawful reasons make this difficult or impossible. From the fact that any priest may be chosen, it is clear that the obligation of this expression of hierarchical communion is given great importance, and may not be omitted simply because the Bishop cannot go personally. Auxiliary and coadjutor Bishops are not themselves obliged to make the visit.

Can. 401 §1 A diocesan Bishop who has completed his seventy-fifth year of age is requested to offer his resignation from office to the Supreme Pontiff, who, taking all the circumstances into account, will make provision accordingly.

§2 A diocesan Bishop who, because of illness or some other grave reason, has become unsuited for the fulfilment of his office, is earnestly requested to offer his resignation from office.

821 Earlier drafts of this canon had spoken of the resignation of a Bishop at seventy-five as obligatory.[3] However, the final text reflects more accurately the principle established by Vat. II:[4] a Bishop who attains his seventy-fifth birthday is requested to offer his resignation to the Pope. Those Bishops under the age of seventy-five who, for some serious reason, are no longer suited to the episcopal office, similarly are invited to submit their resignation. In all cases, the Apostolic See will decide whether the resignation should be accepted and what provision should be made for the diocese.

822 In order the better to care for the increasing number of retired Bishops, the Holy See issued in 1988 special norms for Bishops leaving office.[5] These make more detailed provision for retired Bishops to receive documents of the Holy See in the same way as Bishops in office, the use of retired Bishops as coopted members or consultors by Roman Dicasteries, eligibility to represent a Bishops' Conference at a Synod of Bishops,[6] and relationships with the Bishops' Conference of the place where they

---

[1] A new Directory for the *ad limina* visit was issued by the Congregation for Bishops on 29.VI.1988. This spells out the purpose, the long and short term preparation, and the format of the visit itself; it is accompanied by theological, pastoral and canonico–historical notes: English trans. CLSNGBI 75(Sept. 1988) 89–133.

[2] Cf. Pope John Paul II ap con *Spirituali militum curae* 21.IV.1986: AAS 78(1986) 481–486: Comm 18(1986) 12–17. Cf. Beyer *Commentary on the ap con 'Spirituali militum curae'* CLSNGBI 76(Dec. 1988) 48–89.

[3] Cf. Comm 18(1986) 155–156, 12(1980) 308, 14(1982) 208.

[4] Cf. CD 21: Fl I 575–576; ES 11: Fl I 597.

[5] Cf. SCB Norms for Bishops leaving office 31.X.1988: Comm 20(1988) 167–168: CLSNGBI 79(Sept. 1989) 17–22.

[6] Cf. PCI rep 2.VII.1991: AAS 83(1991) 1093.

reside. Retired Bishops are to receive the principal documents of the Conference, and use is to be made of their talents, even if the statutes do not provide for them to attend plenary sessions with a consultative vote.

Can. 402 §1 A Bishop whose resignation from office has been accepted, acquires the title 'emeritus' of his diocese. If he so wishes, he may have a residence in the diocese unless, because of special circumstances in certain cases, the Apostolic See provides otherwise.

§2 The Bishops' Conference must ensure that suitable and worthy provision is made for the upkeep of a Bishop who has resigned, bearing in mind the primary obligation which falls on the diocese which he served.

It was determined after Vat. II that the diocese must provide for the retirement of its Bishop, and that the Bishops' Conference should lay down general norms as to how this was to be done.[1] In the light of consultation, the Revision Commission decided that a poor diocese might be unable to carry the whole cost of this, and so a further responsibility was entrusted to the Bishops' Conference.[2] The recent norms for retired Bishops are more specific: 'Zealous and careful provision is to be made for his financial well-being and, within the limitations of diocesan resources, to be generously afforded'.[3] These norms make clear that the responsibility of the diocese does not end with financial provision; there is a positive duty to supply him with diocesan documents and generally keep him informed; moreover, the Bishops' Conference must keep him in touch with their activities.[4] The link with his former diocese is maintained by his title: a retired Bishop is no longer given a titular See; rather he retains his own title to which 'emeritus' is added. Such a Bishop can also choose to continue living in his diocese, unless the Holy See may for a particular reason decide otherwise.

Article 3
Coadjutor and Auxiliary Bishops

Can. 403 §1 When the pastoral needs of the diocese require it, one or more auxiliary Bishops are to be appointed at the request of the diocesan Bishop. An auxiliary Bishop does not have the right of succession.

§2 In more serious circumstances, even of a personal nature, the diocesan Bishop may be given an auxiliary Bishop with special faculties.

§3 If the Holy See considers it more opportune, it can ex officio appoint a coadjutor Bishop, who also has special faculties. A coadjutor Bishop has the right of succession.

'In governing their dioceses, Bishops must take the good of the Lord's flock as their highest objective. This will often demand the appointment of auxiliary Bishops, the Bishop of the diocese being unable to perform his duty sufficiently well for the good of souls on his own, either because of the great size of the diocese, the number of inhabitants, some special pastoral problem or for some other reasons.'[5] The Code foresees three categories of *auxiliary Bishop*:

---

[1] Cf. ES 11: Fl I 597.
[2] Cf. Comm 18(1986) 156–157.
[3] SCB Norms 21.X.1988: Comm 20(1988) 168: CLSNGBI 79(Sept. 1989) 19.
[4] Ibid.
[5] CD 25: Fl I 578.

- the ordinary auxiliary appointed at the request of the diocesan Bishop who has made a prudent judgement concerning the needs of the diocese; his duties are determined in the letters of appointment and by the diocesan Bishop in accordance with Cann. 406 §2 – 408 §1;
- the auxiliary with special faculties appointed at the request of the diocesan Bishop or by the Holy See on its own initiative. Such an appointment takes place where the ordinary reasons are pressing and very serious, or where they are aggravated e.g. by the illness or other personal difficulties of the diocesan Bishop. The special faculties of such an auxiliary Bishop are to be specified in his letters of appointment; since they limit in some way the rights of the diocesan Bishop, these faculties are to be interpreted strictly (see Can. 18);
- if the Holy See judges that the welfare of the people of God is best served by a certain continuity, it can appoint a coadjutor Bishop with the right of succession. While his duties will be similar to those of the ordinary auxiliary (§1), unlike that auxiliary the coadjutor will succeed to the diocese when the diocesan Bishop leaves office. In effect, this means that there will be no vacant see. The appointment of a coadjutor with the right of succession is an exceptional occurrence. It may take place in response to a request by the diocesan Bishop, or on the initiative of the Holy See as a result of reliable information given to it.

825 An auxiliary Bishop is assigned the title of an ancient and now extinct diocese; a coadjutor Bishop, on the other hand, is now assigned the title of the particular Church for which he is destined.[1] Such a provision does not mean that the coadjutor cannot be transferred to another particular Church or even be deprived of his right of succession.[2] However, what the present Code highlights is that auxiliary Bishops and coadjutor Bishops, even when appointed for personal reasons, are appointed primarily to the particular Church rather than to the person of the diocesan Bishop.

Can. 404 §1 The coadjutor Bishop takes possession of his office when, either personally or by proxy, he shows the apostolic letter of appointment to the diocesan Bishop and the college of consultors, in the presence of the chancellor of the curia, who makes a record of the fact.

§2 An auxiliary Bishop takes possession of his office when he shows his apostolic letter of appointment to the diocesan Bishop, in the presence of the chancellor of the curia, who makes a record of the fact.

§3 If the diocesan Bishop is wholly impeded, it is sufficient that either the coadjutor Bishop or the auxiliary Bishop show their apostolic letter of appointment to the college of consultors, in the presence of the chancellor of the curia.

826 As is the case for a diocesan Bishop, a newly appointed auxiliary or coadjutor Bishop must take canonical possession of his office before becoming involved in its exercise (see Can. 382 §1). The act of taking canonical possession for a coadjutor Bishop consists of presenting his apostolic letters of appointment to the diocesan Bishop and the college of consultors in the presence of the chancellor of the curia (§1); since the circumstances which warranted his appointment might be urgent, a coadjutor Bishop

---

[1] Cf. SCB letter 31.VIII.1976 (private): CLD 8 252–253: Comm 9(1977) 223.

[2] An interesting example was the case of Bishop Errington, given to Cardinal Wiseman as coadjutor with right of succession to the See of Westminster. Wiseman could not get on with him, and persuaded Pope Pius IX to deprive him of his coadjutorship in 1860. On Wiseman's death Errington was the choice of the Chapter, but Manning was appointed.

may present these letters personally, or through a proxy. By contrast, an auxiliary Bishop is obliged to present these letters to the diocesan Bishop in the presence of the chancellor (§2); no mention is made of the college of consultors.

In both cases, the chancellor is required to make a written record of the fact of canonical possession of the office, and to ensure the preservation of that record in the curial archives.

The law makes provision for the canonical possession of office where the diocesan Bishop is wholly impeded, i.e. unable to communicate with his diocese even by letter (see Can. 412). In such a situation, the newly appointed coadjutor or auxiliary Bishop need only show their letters of appointment to the college of consultors. This is to be done in the presence of the chancellor of the curia; although no explicit mention is made of it, the chancellor must make a written record of the fact.

Can. 405 §1 The coadjutor Bishop and the auxiliary Bishop have the obligations and the rights which are determined by the provisions of the following canons and defined in their letters of appointment.

Vat. II asked that 'suitable faculties should be conferred on ... coadjutors and auxiliary Bishops so that without prejudice to the unity of the diocesan administration or to the authority of the diocesan Bishop, their labours may be more effective, and the dignity of the episcopal office clearly safeguarded'.[1] This aspiration is fulfilled by this canon which indicates in general terms the rights and obligations of coadjutor and auxiliary Bishops.

Can. 405 §2 The coadjutor Bishop, or the auxiliary Bishop mentioned in Can. 403 §2, assists the diocesan Bishop in the entire governance of the diocese, and takes his place when he is absent or impeded.

From this canon it appears that, with the exception of the right of succession, the offices of coadjutor Bishop and auxiliary with special faculties are almost identical. Such a Bishop is required to assist the diocesan Bishop in the government of the whole diocese; if the diocesan Bishop is absent or impeded, his place is taken by the coadjutor or the special auxiliary.

Can. 406 §1 The coadjutor Bishop, and likewise the auxiliary Bishop mentioned in Can. 403 §2, is to be appointed a Vicar general by the diocesan Bishop. The diocesan Bishop is to entrust to him, in preference to others, those matters which by law require a special mandate.

As a consequence of the special position in a diocese of the coadjutor Bishop or auxiliary Bishop with special faculties (see Can. 405 §2), the law insists that the diocesan Bishop appoint such an assistant as a Vicar general. It is to be noted that the appointment is not by law; rather the appointment comes from the diocesan Bishop. In this way it is clearly demonstrated that the coadjutor or special auxiliary share in the ministry of the diocesan Bishop. The central role of the coadjutor or special auxiliary is further underlined by the law's stated preference that he should be appointed to any position involving the exercise of executive power which requires a special mandate for the diocesan Bishop (see Can. 134 §3).

Can. 406 §2 Unless the apostolic letter provides otherwise and without prejudice to the provision of §1, the diocesan Bishop is to appoint his auxiliary or auxiliaries as Vicar general or at least episcopal Vicar, in dependence solely on his authority, or on that of the coadjutor Bishop or of the auxiliary Bishop mentioned in Can. 403 §2.

---

[1] CD 25: Fl I 578.

832 In similar fashion, the law recommends that the simple auxiliary Bishop mentioned in Can. 403 §1 should be appointed as Vicar general or least episcopal Vicar. Of course, the papal letters of appointment may provide otherwise, e.g. by requiring that the auxiliary be appointed to a specific office in the diocese. In order to preserve the unity of the episcopal ministry in the diocese, auxiliaries are to act only in dependence on the diocesan Bishop or, should the situation arise, the coadjutor or special auxiliary.

Can. 407 §1 For the greatest present and future good of the diocese, the diocesan Bishop, the coadjutor and the auxiliary Bishop mentioned in Can. 403 §2, are to consult with each other on matters of greater importance.

§2 In assessing matters of greater importance, particularly those of a pastoral nature, the diocesan Bishop ought to consult the auxiliary Bishops before all others.

§3 The coadjutor Bishop and the auxiliary Bishop, since they are called to share in the cares of the diocesan Bishop, should so exercise their office that they act and think in accord with him.

833 This canon seeks to safeguard the unity of diocesan administration and respect for episcopal dignity. The general principle of the coadjutor and auxiliaries working as one with the diocesan Bishop stated in §3 is derived from Vat. II.[1] The first two paragraphs specify the obligations that accompany this, particularly with regard to the diocesan Bishop. Because of the particular responsibility of an auxiliary with special faculties and because the coadjutor is intended to be the successor of the diocesan Bishop, it is essential that they are fully informed about major decisions; the requirement of consultation is distinctly more imperative than for other auxiliaries.[2] In the case of the simple auxiliary, the domain of consultation is described as concerning matters of greater importance, mainly of a pastoral nature. In the case of the coadjutor or auxiliary with special faculties, the specifically pastoral reference is omitted, since all matters of greater importance, e.g. matters of legal or of financial import, must be the object of mutual consultation. The coadjutor or auxiliary should also consult the diocesan Bishop, not least in those areas where he has a special responsibility. Unless otherwise stated in the apostolic letters, the grant of special faculties to an auxiliary does not imply that the diocesan Bishop is to be ignored: on the contrary.

834 The precise meaning of 'matters of greater importance' is not defined. However the same criteria apply as in the consultation of the Council of Priests (see Can. 500 §2), where the same term is used. The clear implication is that the diocesan Bishop should not raise an important matter with the Council of Priests before he has consulted the auxiliaries or coadjutor. This includes the financial consultation mentioned in Can. 1277 even though the auxiliary or coadjutor is not referred to in that canon.

Can. 408 §1 As often as they are requested to do so by the diocesan Bishop, a coadjutor Bishop and an auxiliary Bishop who are not lawfully impeded, are obliged to perform those pontifical and other functions to which the diocesan Bishop is bound.

835 The diocesan Bishop may fulfil some of the liturgical or pastoral obligations arising out of his office, e.g. presiding at the Eucharist in the cathedral (see Can. 389), visitation (see Can. 396 §1) etc., by entrusting the task to his coadjutor or auxiliary. The

---

[1] Cf. ibid.

[2] The Code uses 'are to consult' (*consulant*) in §1, as against the considerably milder 'ought to consult' (*consulere velit*) of §2.

law makes it clear that such a request cannot be refused unless the coadjutor or auxiliary is equally impeded, e.g. by reason of another official engagement. There is no obligation to accede to a request to fulfil some duty freely accepted by the diocesan Bishop outside of his official responsibilities, e.g. a retreat for priests of another diocese. Nevertheless, the coadjutor or auxiliary would normally choose to respond to such a request as a demonstration of fraternal cooperation.

Can. 408 §2 Those episcopal rights and functions which the coadjutor or the auxiliary Bishop can exercise are not habitually to be entrusted to another by the diocesan Bishop.

While the diocesan Bishop is always free to delegate anyone of his choice for a particular function, he is reminded by the canon that he should not do so habitually if the function is one which can be discharged by the coadjutor or auxiliary Bishop. This provision reinforces the special position in the diocese occupied by a coadjutor or auxiliary.

Can. 409 §1 When the episcopal see falls vacant, the coadjutor immediately becomes the Bishop of the diocese for which he was appointed, provided he has lawfully taken possession.

A See becomes vacant not only on the death of the diocesan Bishop, but also upon his resignation when accepted, transfer or deprivation (see Can. 416). Where a coadjutor has been appointed, he succeeds 'immediately', i.e. when, but only when, he takes canonical possession of his office (see Cann. 404 §1, 382 §§2–3).

Can. 409 §2 Unless the competent authority has provided otherwise, when the episcopal see is vacant and until the new Bishop takes possession of the see, the auxiliary Bishop retains all and only those powers and faculties which he had as Vicar general or as episcopal Vicar when the see was occupied. If he is not appointed to the office of diocesan administrator, he is to exercise this same power of his, conferred by the law, under the authority of the diocesan administrator, who governs the diocese.

Can. 481 prescribes that the offices of Vicar general and episcopal Vicar are so linked to that of the diocesan Bishop that, when the see falls vacant or the office of diocesan Bishop is suspended, they also cease from office or are suspended. In accordance with the wishes of Vat. II, auxiliary Bishops are exempted from this provision (see also Can. 481 §2). They continue to enjoy the powers of episcopal or general Vicar – and this by virtue of the law itself rather than by appointment of the diocesan Bishop.

When the see is vacant, the auxiliary Bishop may be subject to the authority of a non-episcopal diocesan administrator chosen in accordance with Can. 421. Vat. II desired that, unless there were grave reasons to the contrary, the office of diocesan administrator should be entrusted to one of the auxiliary Bishops.[1] However, concern was also expressed for the complete freedom of choice of the college of consultors in choosing a diocesan administrator. The Revision Commission rejected suggestions that it was inappropriate to elect a non-episcopal diocesan administrator if there was an auxiliary Bishop in the diocese. Three reasons were given: (a) it is not incongruous for a priest to be nominated diocesan administrator; (b) there can be circumstances rendering it inexpedient for the auxiliary to become administrator immediately; (c) the imposition of the auxiliary or senior auxiliary would itself be contrary to the freedom that Vat. II wished to preserve.[2]

---

[1] Cf. CD 26: Fl I 579.
[2] Cf. Comm 14(1982) 209.

Can. 410 The coadjutor Bishop and the auxiliary Bishop are bound, like the diocesan Bishop, to reside in the diocese. Other than for the fulfilment of some duty outside the diocese, or for holidays, which are not to be longer than one month, they may not be away from the diocese except for a brief period.

840 The obligation of residence in the diocese binds the coadjutor and the auxiliary just as it does the diocesan Bishop. However, the reason for which absence from the diocese is permitted is stated more broadly than for the diocesan Bishop (see Can. 395 §§2–3), i.e. 'the fulfilment of some duty outside the diocese'. Apart from these duties, and from holidays not exceeding one month, the coadjutor and auxiliary may not be absent except for a 'brief period', a phrase which generally speaking is to be understood as 'about one week', thus allowing for a reasonable flexibility depending on the circumstances while at the same time excluding unreasonable excesses.

Can. 411 The provisions of Cann. 401 and 402 §2, concerning resignation from office, apply also to a coadjutor and an auxiliary Bishop.

841 This canon speaks for itself. Although it does not make express mention of the requirements – as for diocesan Bishops – concerning residence and support, it is certain that these requirements apply equally to coadjutor and auxiliary Bishops.

Chapter III
THE IMPEDED OR VACANT SEE

Article 1
The Impeded See

Can. 412 The episcopal see is understood to be impeded if the diocesan Bishop is completely prevented from exercising the pastoral office in the diocese by reason of imprisonment, banishment, exile or incapacity, so that he is unable to communicate, even by letter, with the people of his diocese.

842 This contains one of the few definitions found in the Code. The essence of the impeded episcopal see lies in the Bishop's inability to communicate effectively with his diocese. If this cannot be done, even by letter, the minimum administration of the diocese is rendered impossible. The canon identifies four possible causes of an impeded see: three have to do with the physical absence of the Bishop due to imprisonment, banishment or exile; the fourth has to do with the Bishop's personal incapacity due to physical or mental ill-health.

Can. 413 §1 Unless the Holy See has provided otherwise, when the see is impeded, the governance of the diocese devolves on the coadjutor Bishop, if there is one. If there is no coadjutor or if he is impeded, it devolves upon an auxiliary Bishop, or a Vicar general, or an episcopal Vicar, or another priest: the order of persons to be followed is to be that determined in the list which the diocesan Bishop is to draw up as soon as possible after taking possession of his diocese. This list, which is to be communicated to the

Metropolitan, is to be revised at least every three years, and kept under secrecy by the chancellor.

§2 If there is no coadjutor Bishop or if he is impeded, and the list mentioned in §1 is not at hand, it is the responsibility of the college of consultors to elect a priest who will govern the diocese.

§3 The person who undertakes the governance of the diocese according to the norms of §§1 or 2, is to notify the Holy See as soon as possible that the see is impeded and that he has undertaken the office.

843 Should a see become impeded for any of the reasons mentioned in Can. 412, the law provides for the interim government of the diocese in three ways:

(a) if a coadjutor has been appointed, he takes over the government of the diocese immediately, provided he has taken canonical possession of his office (see Can. 404 §§1, 3).

(b) if no coadjutor has been appointed, or if he too is impeded, the government of the diocese devolves upon the one indicated in a list drawn up by the Bishop. According to this canon, each diocesan Bishop is obliged to prepare such a list as soon as possible after taking canonical possession of the diocese; the list is to be guarded in secret by the chancellor and communicated to the Metropolitan (or, presumably, to the senior suffragan if the diocese is a Metropolitan see). The Code suggests one possible order of preference i.e. auxiliary Bishop, Vicar general, Vicar episcopal etc. Nevertheless, the Bishop is free to determine whatever order he prefers.

(c) if no coadjutor has been appointed, or if he too is impeded and if the list is not available, responsibility for choosing someone to govern the diocese falls on the college of consultors (see Can. 502): it must elect a priest to govern the diocese for the period the see is impeded.

Once appointed, the person in charge of the diocese must inform the Holy See of the situation, indicating that the see is impeded, giving the reason why and pointing out that he has taken up office in accordance with Can. 413 §1 or §2. The Holy See will determine what other steps, if any, are to be taken.[1]

Can. 414 Whoever is called, in accordance with Can. 413, to exercise the pastoral care of the diocese for the time being, that is, only for the period during which the see is impeded, is in his pastoral care of the diocese bound by the obligations, and has the power, which by law belong to the diocesan administrator.

844 Juridically speaking, the one chosen to succeed to the government of a diocese when it is impeded is the equivalent to a diocesan administrator. He is bound to the same obligations (see Cann. 427–428) and has the same power, limited by a similar principle i.e. while the see is impeded no innovation is to be made (see Can. 428 §1). His authority lasts only while the see is actually impeded.

Can. 415 If the diocesan Bishop is prohibited from exercising his office by reason of an ecclesiastical penalty, the Metropolitan is to refer the matter at

---

[1] It would seem that this canon – which makes no reference to an auxiliary Bishop with special faculties (cf. Can. 403 §2) – must be interpreted in the light of Can. 405 §2, which expressly states that, in the absence of a coadjutor, 'the auxiliary Bishop mentioned in Can. 403 §2' takes the place of the diocesan Bishop 'when he is . . . impeded'.

once to the Holy See, so that it may make provision; if there is no Metropolitan, or if he is the one affected by the penalty, it is the suffragan senior by promotion who is to refer the matter.

845 Similar to the case of the impeded see is that of a Bishop who incurs an ecclesiastical penalty involving the prohibition of his exercise of office (see Cann. 1331–1336). In such a situation, the provisions of Can. 413 are not effective. Rather, the Metropolitan has the duty of referring the matter to the Holy See. Since the Holy See is competent to judge Bishops in penal cases (see Can. 1405 §1 3°), it is likely that *ferendae sententiae* penalties would be accompanied by provisions for the government of the diocese. The responsibility of the Metropolitan appears to be limited to those cases where the Bishop incurs a *latae sententiae* penalty. If there is no Metropolitan, or if he is impeded, or if he is the one who incurred the penalty, the senior suffragan Bishop is to act. It should be noted that when the see is impeded in this way, the Vicars general and Vicars episcopal lose their authority, unless they themselves are also Bishops (see Can. 481 §2).

Article 2
The Vacant See

Can. 416 The episcopal see becomes vacant by the death of the diocesan Bishop, by his resignation accepted by the Roman Pontiff, by transfer, and by deprivation notified to the Bishop.

846 Four causes for the vacancy of an episcopal see are identified:
(a) the *death* of the Bishop *ipso facto* leaves the diocese vacant;
(b) the Bishop's *resignation* as soon as it is *accepted* by the Pope also leaves the see vacant;
(c) so too does the *transfer* of the Bishop but only as soon as he takes canonical possession of the new diocese (see Can. 418 §1);
(d) finally, a diocese is left vacant as soon as the Bishop has been informed that he has been *deprived* of the see.

Can. 417 Until they have received certain notification of the Bishop's death, all actions taken by the Vicar general or the episcopal Vicar have effect. Until they have received certain notification of the aforementioned pontifical acts, the same is true of actions taken by the diocesan Bishop, the Vicar general or the episcopal Vicar.

847 Although a diocese is automatically vacant after the death of its Bishop, the law provides that the Vicars general and Vicars episcopal can continue to exercise their office until they have received certain news of the death. Thus rumours or second-hand reports are not enough; the offices in question must be objectively certain before ceasing to act. Similarly, the diocesan Bishop, the Vicars general and Vicars episcopal can continue to act until they have received certain information of the accepted resignation or have been notified of the transfer or deprivation. This provision of law means that the people of God continue to be cared for.

Can. 418 §1 Within two months of receiving certain notification of transfer, the Bishop must proceed to the diocese to which he has been transferred and take canonical possession of it. On the day on which he takes

possession of the new diocese, the diocese from which he has been transferred becomes vacant.

§2 In the period between receiving certain notification of the transfer and taking possession of the new diocese, in the diocese from which he is being transferred the Bishop:

> 1° has the power, and is bound by the obligations, of a diocesan Administrator; all powers of the Vicar general and of the episcopal Vicar cease, without prejudice to Can. 409 §2;
>
> 2° receives the full remuneration proper to the office.

A Bishop who has been transferred to another diocese is given two months from the time he receives certain news of the event to take canonical possession of his new diocese (see Can. 382 §2). By the act of taking canonical possession, the first diocese becomes vacant (see Can. 191 §1). Yet, in a sense, the diocese has already become vacant: after he receives certain news of his transfer, the diocesan Bishop governs the original diocese as a diocesan Administrator, and Vicars general and Vicars episcopal cease to function unless they are also auxiliary Bishops (see Can. 409 §2). During the period between notification of the transfer and taking canonical possession of the new diocese, the Bishop can make no changes (see Can. 428 §1). In accordance with Can. 191 §2, he is entitled to draw his salary as Bishop until his actual departure. With the canonical possession of the new diocese, all rights in the former diocese cease.

Can. 419 While the see is vacant and until the appointment of a diocesan Administrator, the governance of the diocese devolves upon the auxiliary Bishop. If there are a number of auxiliary Bishops, it devolves upon the senior by promotion. If there is no auxiliary Bishop, it devolves upon the college of consultors, unless the Holy See has provided otherwise. The one who thus assumes the governance of the diocese must without delay convene the college which is competent to appoint a diocesan Administrator.

Before the appointment of a diocesan Administrator, the law provides for the interim government of a diocese by entrusting that responsibility to the auxiliary Bishop if there is one or to the senior auxiliary if there is more than one. Should there be no auxiliary Bishop, the law entrusts the immediate government of the diocese to the college of consultors – unless, of course, the Holy See has determined otherwise, e.g. by appointing an apostolic Administrator. The primary duty of whoever takes over the diocese at this point is to convoke the body whose role it is to appoint a diocesan Administrator i.e. the college of consultors (see Can. 421 §1) or the cathedral chapter (see Can. 502 §3). This responsibility must be discharged immediately so that the election may take place within the required time.

Can. 420 Unless the Holy See has prescribed otherwise, when the see is vacant in a vicariate or a prefecture apostolic, the governance is assumed by the Pro-Vicar or Pro-Prefect who was designated for this sole purpose by the Vicar or Prefect immediately upon taking possession.

The interim government of an apostolic vicariate or prefecture (see Can. 371 §1) is entrusted by law to a pro-Vicar or pro-Prefect. He is a priest who must be designated as such by the Vicar or Prefect apostolic as soon as possible after taking canonical possession of his office. Thus, there is no need for the council of the vicariate or prefecture (see Can. 495 §2) to meet. Since the Vicar and Prefect apostolic act in the name of the Pope, the Holy See may well provide otherwise during a vacancy.

Can. 421 §1 Within eight days of receiving notification of the vacancy of an episcopal see, a diocesan Administrator is to be elected by the college of consultors, to govern the diocese for the time being, without prejudice to the provisions of Can. 502 §3.

§2 If, for any reason, the diocesan Administrator is not lawfully elected within the prescribed time, his appointment devolves upon the Metropolitan. If the Metropolitan see is itself vacant, or if both the metropolitan see and a suffragan see are vacant, the appointment devolves on the suffragan who is senior by promotion.

851 The election of a diocesan Administrator belongs to the college of consultors or, if the Bishops' Conference has so decided, to the cathedral chapter (see Can. 502 §3). The election must take place within eight days of the receipt by the college of notification that the see is vacant. If the election does not take place within the specified time or if it is carried out in contravention of the norms of law (see Cann. 424–425), the right to provide devolves upon the Metropolitan or senior suffragan Bishop (see Can. 425 §3).

852 In such a case, the Metropolitan is not bound to consult the college of consultors, since it has lost its right to be involved. However, he must inform the college so that there is juridical certainty as to when interim governance (see Can. 419) of the diocese ceases.

Can. 422 The auxiliary Bishop or, if there is none, the college of consultors, must as soon as possible notify the Apostolic See of the death of the Bishop. The person elected as diocesan Administrator must as soon as possible notify the Apostolic See of his election.

853 The task of informing the Holy See of the death of the Bishop, and the consequent vacancy falls to whoever has interim charge of the diocese, i.e. the auxiliary Bishop or the college of consultors (see Can. 419). The information must be communicated *at once*. The term used in the canon implies a shorter timescale than that for convening the college of consultors (see Can. 419), and certainly much less than eight days, since two separate notifications are envisaged, i.e. of the death of the Bishop and of the election of the Administrator. In practice this means that notification will be given to the Apostolic Nuncio or Delegate (see Can. 363 §1).

Can. 423 §1 Only one diocesan Administrator is to be appointed, contrary customs being reprobated; otherwise the election is invalid.

854 In some places, under the 1917 Code, a custom had prevailed of the chapter electing several vicars capitular to administer together the affairs of a diocese during a vacancy. The Code now makes it abundantly clear that such a custom is prohibited. Only *one* diocesan Administrator is to be elected. Any other provision renders the election invalid.

Can. 423 §2 The diocesan Administrator is not to be at the same time the financial administrator. Accordingly, if the financial administrator of the diocese is elected Administrator, the finance committee is to elect another temporary financial administrator.

855 According to this Code, the office of diocesan Administrator is incompatible with that of financial administrator (see Can. 494). The establishment of this principle removes any possibility of allegations of misconduct during a vacancy. Indeed, should the financial administrator find himself elected as diocesan Administrator, the law obliges the diocesan finance council to choose a temporary replacement. As soon as a

new Bishop is appointed, the financial administrator is free to resume his office – provided, of course, that he himself has not been made the diocesan Bishop.

Can. 424 The diocesan Administrator is to be elected according to the norms of Cann. 165-178.

An *election* of a diocesan Administrator is required. It is not open to the diocesan Bishop to designate the administrator by some other means prior to death, transfer, etc. The person who presides over the election will be the one upon whom the government of the diocese has devolved in accordance with Can. 419. He may vote in the election only if he is already a member of the college of consultors; if he is not a member and attempts to vote, the election will be rendered invalid (see Can. 169). The law obliges the college of consultors to follow Cann. 165-178 in electing a diocesan Administrator. Thus, in the college's own statutes, the following modifications to the norm of the law might be made:

– a vote by letter or by proxy may be permitted (see Can. 167 §1);
– election by compromise may be forbidden (see Can. 174 §1);
– a qualified majority different from that mentioned in Can. 119 §1° may be prescribed (see Can. 176).

In all other matters, the norm of the Code is prescriptive.

Can. 425 §1 Only a priest who has completed his thirty-fifth year of age, and has not already been elected, nominated or presented for the same see, can validly be deputed to the office of diocesan Administrator.

Three requirements are listed for the valid appointment of a diocesan Administrator:
– he must be a priest; it is not necessary that he be a priest of the diocese;
– he must be at least thirty-five years of age;
– he must not have been elected, nominated or presented for the same episcopal see.

The first two conditions are required in all cases. In practice, the third has relevance only in those places where the cathedral chapter elects the Bishop or where the civil authorities submit a candidate for appointment.

Can. 425 §2 As diocesan Administrator a priest is to be elected who is outstanding for doctrine and prudence.

In addition to the requirements for validity, the law demands that the candidate for diocesan Administrator must be distinguished for his 'doctrine and prudence'. This requirement is reminiscent of what is demanded in a Bishop (see Can. 378 §1 1°). However, such qualities affect only the lawfulness of the election, not its validity.

Can. 425 §3 If the conditions prescribed in §1 have not been observed, the Metropolitan or, if the Metropolitan see itself is vacant, the suffragan senior by promotion, having verified the truth of the matter, is to appoint an Administrator for that occasion. The acts of a person elected contrary to the provisions of §1 are by virtue of the law itself invalid.

If someone is elected to the office of diocesan Administrator by the college of consultors in defiance of the prescriptions of §1, the canonical consequences are most serious. The election is invalid and the college has lost the right to select an Administrator. That task falls to the Metropolitan or the senior suffragan who must first be sure of the facts. In such circumstances the one who had been elected has no authority whatever: his acts are not only illicit but also invalid.

Can. 426 Whoever governs the diocese before the appointment of the diocesan Administrator, has the power which the law gives to a Vicar general.

860 The powers given to a Vicar general are indicated in Can. 479: he has the executive, but not judicial or legislative powers which belong by law to the diocesan Bishop, and can perform the same administrative acts, within the limits of that same canon. It is in this way that a diocese is governed in the short period between the vacancy and the appointment of a diocesan Administrator.

Can. 427 §1 The diocesan Administrator is bound by the obligations and enjoys the power of a diocesan Bishop, excluding those matters which are excepted by the nature of things or by the law itself.

§2 The diocesan Administrator obtains his power on his acceptance of the election, without the need of confirmation from anyone, but without prejudice to the provision of Can. 833 n.4.

861 There is no requirement for a diocesan Administrator to take canonical possession of his office or seek confirmation of his election. It suffices for the person elected to signify to the college his acceptance of the office. The new Administrator must, however, make the requisite profession of faith in the presence of the college of consultors (see Can. 833 4°). In general, the diocesan Administrator has the same power and obligations as a diocesan Bishop, but with some exceptions arising from the nature of things: e.g. if he is not a Bishop, then he cannot carry out pontifical functions within the diocese (see Can. 390); he cannot grant incardination or excardination, except in certain circumstances (see Can. 272); he cannot establish a public association of the faithful (see Can. 312 §1 3°), etc.

Can. 428 §1 While the see is vacant, no innovation is to be made.

§2 Those who have the interim governance of the diocese are forbidden to do anything which could in any way prejudice the diocese or the rights of the Bishop. Both they, and in like manner any other persons, are specifically forbidden to remove, destroy or in any way alter documents of the diocesan curia, either personally or through another.

862 Essentially those who govern a diocese during a vacancy, whether it is the interim government of Can. 419 or the diocesan Administrator, exercise a function best described as that of a *caretaker*. The law establishes a clear general principle: during the vacancy, nothing new is to be done. Thus, e.g. parish priests cannot be appointed unless the see has been vacant for a year (see Can. 525 2°). From that broad general principle, the law derives a more particular norm: those in charge of the diocese are to do nothing which might harm or restrict the rights of the diocese or the incoming Bishop. They are free to act for the benefit of the diocese provided this does not offend the general principle of §1. More specifically, those to whose care a vacant diocese has been entrusted are strictly forbidden to abuse their responsibility by removing, destroying or altering documents stored in the diocesan offices. The incoming Bishop must find everything just as it was.

Can. 429 The diocesan Administrator is bound by the obligations of residing in the diocese, and of applying the Mass for the people in accordance with Can. 388.

863 During his term of office, the diocesan Administrator is bound fully by the requirements of a diocesan Bishop concerning residence in the diocese (see Can. 395), and the celebration of Mass for the intention of the people of the diocese (see Can. 388).

Can. 430 §1 The office of the diocesan Administrator ceases when the new Bishop takes possession of the diocese.

§2 Removal of the diocesan Administrator is reserved to the Holy See. Should he perchance resign, the resignation is to be submitted in authentic form to the college which is competent to elect, but it does not require acceptance by the college. If the diocesan Administrator is removed, resigns or dies, another diocesan Administrator is to be elected in accordance with Can. 421.

The office of Administrator can cease in four ways: by death, removal, resignation, and by the taking of canonical possession by the new Bishop. In the first three cases, a replacement diocesan Administrator is needed, and the procedure will be followed as when the see first became vacant, viz., a period of interim rule, the convening of the consultors within eight days, and an election. This applies even if he has been removed by the Holy See. Just as the Administrator's acceptance did not need confirmation, so his resignation does not need acceptance by the college. It must, however, be submitted in the appropriate legal form, i.e. in writing, or before two witnesses (Can. 189 §1). Although he is elected by the college of consultors (or nominated by the Metropolitan or senior suffragan in accordance with Can. 421 §2 or 425 §3), the Administrator is in no sense answerable to them; hence, his removal is reserved to the Holy See. 864

By virtue of Can. 19, it would seem that the provisions for a vacant parish in Can. 540 §3 ought to be applied to a vacant see, so that the new Bishop is entitled to receive an account of what had been done during the vacancy. 865

Title II
Groupings of Particular Churches

Chapter I
ECCLESIASTICAL PROVINCES AND ECCLESIASTICAL REGIONS

Can. 431 §1 Neighbouring particular Churches are to be grouped into ecclesiastical provinces, with a certain defined territory. The purpose of this grouping is to promote, according to the circumstances of persons and place, a common pastoral action of various neighbouring dioceses, and the more closely to foster relations between diocesan Bishops.

An ecclesiastical province is quite simply the grouping of a number of neighbouring dioceses within a defined geographical territory. The purpose of such a grouping is twofold:
(a) to promote common pastoral action within the dioceses concerned;
(b) to strengthen the relationship between the diocesan Bishops. 866

An institution of this kind is a concrete expression of the principle that the universal Church exists and functions within the particular Churches (see Can. 369), and an example of the practical implications of hierarchical communion (see Can. 375 §2).

Can. 431 §2 From now onwards, as a rule, there are to be no exempt dioceses. Accordingly, individual dioceses and other particular Churches which exist within the territory of an ecclesiastical province, must be included in that ecclesiastical province.

867 According to the norm of law, every diocese and particular Church is to belong to an ecclesiastical province. In the past it was not uncommon to find dioceses and other particular Churches being exempted from this, i.e. being subject immediately to the Holy See. The canon makes it clear that such a practice is exceptional and will be discontinued. However, a number of particular Churches do remain immediately subject to the Holy See, e.g. the dioceses of Switzerland in which there are no provinces.

Can. 431 §3 It is the exclusive prerogative of the supreme authority in the Church, after consulting the Bishops concerned, to establish, suppress or alter ecclesiastical provinces.

868 Even if they consider it desirable or useful, individual Bishops cannot establish, suppress or alter an ecclesiastical province. This is reserved to the Apostolic See. However, the law requires that the Holy See consult the Bishops concerned before establishing, suppressing or altering a province. Competence in this area belongs to the Congregation for Bishops.

Can. 432 §1 The provincial council and the Metropolitan have authority over the ecclesiastical province, in accordance with the law.

869 The Metropolitan does not have any legislative power outside his own diocese, and his executive power is limited to one of vigilance towards his suffragans (see Can. 436 §1). Otherwise his rights are purely liturgical (see Can. 436 §3). However through the provincial council, the province as whole is subject to the collective legislative and executive authority of its respective Bishops (see Can. 445).

Can. 432 §2 By virtue of the law, an ecclesiastical province has juridical personality.

870 The province enjoys juridical personality by reason of the law itself; it can therefore own property and defend its rights in the ecclesiastical courts. Based on an analogy of law (see Cann. 19, 118, 435), the Metropolitan represents the province in juridical matters in the same way as the diocesan Bishop represents the diocese (see Can. 393).

Can. 433 §1 If it seems advantageous, especially in countries where there are very many particular Churches, the Holy See can, on the proposal of the Bishops' Conference, join together neighbouring provinces into ecclesiastical regions.

§2 An ecclesiastical region can be constituted a juridical person.

871 The initiative for establishing an ecclesiastical region must come from the Bishops' Conference. However the actual creation of such a grouping is a matter for the Holy See, i.e. the Congregation for Bishops. Neither the Bishops of the provinces concerned nor the Bishops' Conference has the authority to establish such a grouping. The establishment of a region will assist the ecclesiastical provinces in fulfilling their twofold purpose (see Can. 431 §1). An ecclesiastical region does not enjoy juridical personality unless this is explicitly granted, either in the decree of erection or subse-

quently. Much will depend on the scope and purpose that the Bishops have in mind for the region.

Can. 434 It is for a meeting of the Bishops of an ecclesiastical region to foster cooperation and common pastoral action in the region. However, the powers given to Bishops' Conferences in the canons of this Code do not belong to such a meeting, unless some of these powers have been specially granted to it by the Holy See.

It is clear that the Bishops at a regional meeting cannot do more than reach joint decisions to be implemented on the basis of their individual episcopal authority within their own dioceses. The Bishops' Conference cannot delegate its own legislative or executive authority to a regional body, nor can the individual Bishops do this (see Can. 135 §2). The Holy See, of course, could grant such power to an ecclesiastical region. The practical consequence of this canon is that an individual Bishop is not bound by the decisions of an ecclesiastical region in the same way as he is by the decisions of the Bishops' Conference or of a provincial council.

Although a regional meeting of Bishops may not enjoy the same powers as the Bishops' Conference, it is subject to the same limitation with regard to who may preside. An authentic interpretation by the Holy See in 1988 states that an auxiliary Bishop cannot hold the post of president or vice-president.[1]

Chapter II
METROPOLITANS

Can. 435 An ecclesiastical province is presided over by a Metropolitan, who is Archbishop in his own diocese. The office of Metropolitan is linked to an episcopal see, determined or approved by the Roman Pontiff.

The office of presidency within the ecclesiastical province is enjoyed automatically by the Bishop of the Metropolitan see, and not as the result of an election among the Bishops who comprise the province. The Metropolitan carries the title 'Archbishop' within his own diocese, but this does not give him any greater authority within his diocese than any other diocesan Bishop. The prefix 'arch-' indicates his authority with regard to the province as a whole, to the extent defined by law, and not to a preeminence on the part of the diocese of which he is Bishop. Within the ecclesiastical province, the Metropolitan is *primus inter pares*.

Can. 436 §1 Within the suffragan dioceses, the Metropolitan is competent:

1° **to see that faith and ecclesiastical discipline are carefully observed and to notify the Roman Pontiff if there be any abuses;**

2° **for a reason approved beforehand by the Apostolic See, to conduct a canonical visitation if the suffragan Bishop has neglected it;**

3° **to appoint a diocesan Administrator in accordance with Cann. 421 §2 and 425 §3.**

---

[1] CCom rep 19.I.1988: AAS 81(1989) 388.

§2 Where circumstances require it, the Apostolic See can give the Metropolitan special functions and power, to be determined in particular law.

§3 The Metropolitan has no other power of governance over suffragan dioceses. He can, however, celebrate sacred functions in all Churches as if he were a Bishop in his own diocese, provided, if it is the cathedral Church, the diocesan Bishop has been previously notified.

875 In this canon (§1), three areas of the Metropolitan's responsibility in his province are indicated:

(a) a vigilance on matters of faith and the observance of ecclesiastical discipline: if he should become aware of any abuses in that domain, he is to notify the Holy See; this includes the obligation to inform the Holy See of the unlawful absence of a suffragan Bishop from his diocese in accordance with Can. 395 §4. This responsibility of vigilance does not however imply any authority on the part of the Metropolitan to intervene in the internal governance of the suffragan diocese.

(b) in particular circumstances, to be approved beforehand by the Apostolic See, the Metropolitan can conduct visitation (see Can. 396) in the diocese of a suffragan Bishop who has neglected this duty. This provision is clearly designed for an exceptional situation, such as when the suffragan Bishop will have been remiss in this regard over a long period of time: hence the reason for the requirement of prior approval from the Holy See.

(c) where the appropriate college has failed within the prescribed time to choose a diocesan administrator during a vacancy, or has chosen one invalidly (see Cann. 421 §2, 425 §3), the obligation to make provision devolves automatically upon the Metropolitan. In addition, the Metropolitan is to refer the matter to the Holy See if one of the suffragan Bishops is prohibited from the exercise of his office by reason of an ecclesiastical penalty (see Can. 415).

876 The law foresees the possibility (§2) that the Metropolitan might be granted special powers and functions by the Holy See. The scope and purpose of this power is to be determined in particular law. This is a new regulation, for use 'where circumstances require it'. It was introduced principally to cater for the conditions in very large city or conurbation Sees which are divided not into 'areas' but rather into suffragan dioceses (Paris is a recent case in point). The Revision Commission considered that it could well be appropriate in such circumstances that the Metropolitan be given 'special functions and power', lest otherwise there might result 'a destruction of the unity of governance' in the locality.[1]

877 Although he has no power of jurisdiction within the other dioceses of his province, the Metropolitan has certain liturgical rights (§3). Thus, he may celebrate sacred rites in any Church within his province. However, if he wishes to celebrate in the cathedral of one of the suffragan Bishops, he must notify him beforehand.

Can. 437 §1 The Metropolitan is obliged to request the pallium from the Roman Pontiff, either personally or by proxy, within three months of his episcopal consecration or, if he has already been consecrated, of his canonical appointment. The pallium signifies the power which, in communion with the Roman Church, the Metropolitan possesses by law in his own province.

---

[1] Comm 18(1986) 74. The concept is an interesting one, which could profitably bear research into the theological issues involved.

§2 The Metropolitan can wear the pallium, in accordance with the liturgical laws, in any Church of the ecclesiastical province over which he presides, but not outside the province, not even with the assent of the diocesan Bishop.

§3 If the Metropolitan is transferred to another metropolitan see, he requires a new pallium.

The pallium consists of a band of white wool, with two pendants, one at the front and one at the back, marked with six black silk crosses. It is made from the wool of a lamb presented to the Pope on the feast of St Agnes, and is blessed by him on the solemnity of SS Peter and Paul, before being placed in a container over the tomb of Peter. The pallium represents the personal grant of authority to the Metropolitan within the province; consequently, it cannot be worn outside of it, nor can it be used again by the same Bishop if he has been transferred to another Metropolitan see. The occasions when the pallium is to be worn are indicated in the liturgical books, particularly the *Caerimoniale Episcoporum*. 878

Can. 438 The title of Patriarch or Primate, apart from conferring a prerogative of honour, does not in the latin Church carry with it any power of governance, except in certain instances where an apostolic privilege or approved custom establishes otherwise.

Initially, there was just one patriarchate in the West, that of Rome. Subsequent centuries saw the appointment of Latin patriarchs to Oriental sees and the granting of the title of Patriarch to the Archbishops of Venice and Lisbon. In the West the title of primate was more widespread; it is still in use in some places, e.g. the Archbishop of Armagh is the primate of all Ireland. From the time of Pope Nicholas I (864), those with patriarchal or primatial titles in the West have been denied any additional authority to that exercised by other metropolitans. By special apostolic privilege or custom some such sees do enjoy a degree of the power of governance, e.g. the Latin Patriarch of Jerusalem and the Patriarch of Lisbon may wear the pallium outside of their provinces (within Portugal in the case of Lisbon);[1] the Primate of Poland was granted certain faculties with regard to marriage cases involving non-consummation.[2] 879

Chapter III
PARTICULAR COUNCILS

The Code legislates for two kinds of particular councils: 880

(a) a *plenary* council, i.e. a council for all the particular Churches within the territory of the same Bishops' Conference;

(b) a *provincial* council, i.e. a council for all the particular Churches within the territory of the same ecclesiastical province.

Can. 439 §1 A plenary council for all the particular Churches of the same Bishops' Conference is to be celebrated as often as the Bishops' Conference, with the approval of the Apostolic See, considers it necessary or advantageous.

---

[1] Cf. Comm 14(1982) 1990.
[2] SCSac indult *Extraordinaria adiuncta* granted to Primate of Poland 1.III.1950: DR II 5501–5511.

§2 The norm laid down in §1 is valid also for a provincial council to be celebrated in an ecclesiastical province whose boundaries coincide with the boundaries of the country.

881 The initiative in calling a plenary council rests with the Bishops' Conference: one is to be held as often as the Conference considers it to be useful or necessary. However, the approval of the Holy See is required. In this way the unity of the Church is safeguarded and the freedom of Bishops is protected.[1] The permission of the Holy See is also required in the case of a provincial council where the *territorial limits of the ecclesiastical province coincide with those of the country* – not otherwise.

Can. 440 §1 A provincial council, for the various particular Churches of the same ecclesiastical province, is celebrated as often as, in the judgement of the majority of the diocesan Bishops of the province, it is considered opportune, without prejudice to Can. 439 §2.

§2 A provincial council may not be called while the Metropolitan see is vacant.

882 The celebration of a provincial council is permitted whenever it is considered appropriate. Permission is not required from the Holy See within the terms of Can. 439 §2. But such a council may not be called while the Metropolitan see is vacant. If however that See should become vacant during the course of the council, or even after it had been properly and formally summoned, it need not for that reason alone be suspended.[2] The suffragan Bishops may elect one of their number to preside (as in the situation referred to in Can. 442 §2), and thus allow the work of the council to continue. Moreover, a provincial council can be called only with the consent of the *majority* of the *diocesan* Bishops of the province. They must therefore be consulted beforehand.

Can. 441 It is the responsibility of the Bishops' Conference:

1° to convene a plenary council;

2° to choose a place within the territory of the Bishops' Conference for the celebration of the council;

3° to elect from among the diocesan Bishops a president of the plenary council, who is to be approved by the Apostolic See;

4° to determine the order of business and the matters to be considered, to announce when the plenary council is to begin and how long it is to last, and to transfer, prorogue and dissolve it.

883 The decisions of a plenary council are expressions of the Bishops' power of governance and of legislation. The Bishops' Conference has a completely free hand to choose the location, and determine the timing and agenda. The Conference can also elect the president but, as with the decision to convoke a plenary council, this election must receive approval from the Holy See. Although this is not stated in so many words, it may be presumed that the presidency of such a council, as with that of the Bishops' Conference, is restricted to those who are diocesan Bishops.[3]

---

[1] Cf. Comm 12(1980) 256 at Can. 189.
[2] Cf. Chiappetta I n.1954.
[3] Cf. PCI rep 19.I.1989: AAS 81(1989) 388.

The choice of a location within the Conference's own territory may seem obvious, **884** but in the past plenary councils have been held in Rome, e.g. the Latin-American Plenary Council of 1899.

Can. 442 §1 It is the responsibility of the Metropolitan, with the consent of the majority of the suffragan Bishops:

1° to convene a provincial council;

2° to choose a place within the territory of the province for the celebration of the provincial council;

3° to determine the order of business and the matters to be considered, to announce when the provincial council is to begin and how long it is to last, and to transfer, prorogue and dissolve it.

§2 It is the prerogative of the Metropolitan to preside over the provincial council. If he is lawfully impeded from doing so, it is the prerogative of a suffragan Bishop elected by the other suffragan Bishops.

Making the arrangements for a provincial council is the responsibility of the **885** Metropolitan. The Code also gives the suffragan Bishops some say in the matter: the Metropolitan needs the consent of the majority of his suffragans in drawing up the agenda and timetable, and in choosing a venue for the council; he cannot transfer, prorogue or dissolve the council without their agreement.

Should the Metropolitan be impeded from carrying out his duties, the presidency of a **886** provincial council passes to a suffragan Bishop chosen by the other suffragans. The Metropolitan is impeded if the circumstances envisaged in Cann. 412–415 exist, though other kinds of lawful impediment may also arise e.g. ill health. However, if he is both willing and able to preside, then the suffragans cannot prevent him from exercising this role.

The title 'suffragan' derives from the right of 'suffrage' at a provincial council. It is **887** clear that the diocesan Bishops of dioceses pertaining to a province are suffragan Bishops, and have a right to vote on these preliminary matters. However there are others equivalent in law to diocesan Bishops who also have a deliberative vote at provincial councils, i.e. exempt Bishops (who despite Can. 431 §2 still exist), territorial prelates and abbots, Vicars and Prefects apostolic, and diocesan Administrators (see Can. 427 §1).[1] The term suffragan Bishop must be understood as a corollary of the 'suffragan dioceses' of Can. 436. Territorial prelatures, vicariates and prefectures are not suffragan dioceses, even though they are linked to a province; thus, it would appear that the prelate, even if in fact a Bishop, does not have a voting right at this preliminary stage.

Can. 443 §1 The following have the right to be summoned to particular councils and have the right to a deliberative vote:

1° diocesan Bishops;

2° coadjutor and auxiliary Bishops;

3° other titular Bishops who have been given a special function in the territory, either by the Apostolic See or by the Bishops' Conference.

---

[1] Cf. Comm 14(1982) 193 at Can. 318.

§2 Other titular Bishops who are living in the territory, even if they are retired, may be called to particular councils; they have the right to a deliberative vote.

§3 The following are to be called to particular councils, but with only a consultative vote:

1° Vicars general and episcopal Vicars of all the particular Churches in the territory;

2° the major Superiors of religious institutes and societies of apostolic life. Their number, for both men and women, is to be determined by the Bishops' Conference or the Bishops of the province, and they are to be elected respectively by all the major Superiors of institutes and societies which have an establishment in the territory;

3° the rectors of ecclesiastical and catholic universities which have an establishment in the territory, together with the deans of their faculties of theology and canon law;

4° some rectors of major seminaries, their number being determined as in n.2; they are to be elected by the rectors of seminaries situated in the territory.

§4 Priests and others of Christ's faithful may also be called to particular councils, but have only a consultative vote; their number is not to exceed half of those mentioned in §§1-3.

§5 The cathedral chapter, the council of priests and the pastoral council of each particular Church are to be invited to provincial councils, but in such a way that each is to send two members, designated in a collegial manner. They have only a consultative vote.

§6 Others may be invited to particular councils as guests, if this is judged expedient by the Bishops' Conference for a plenary council, or by the Metropolitan with the suffragan Bishops for a provincial council.

888 This canon contains the norms for membership of particular councils. Some must be invited, others may be invited; some have deliberative voice, others have a consultative voice only.

889 In the revision of the Code every effort was made to ensure the greatest practicable degree of representation. Those categories in which there are potentially many participants may send only a limited number of representatives, e.g. the representative bodies of a diocese, institutes of consecrated life, societies of apostolic life, etc. The cathedral chapter, the Council of Priests and the Pastoral Council are limited to two representatives, who must be designated in a collegial manner (see Cann. 164–179). In the case of the major Superiors and seminary rectors, the number of representatives is to be established by the Bishops' Conference or respectively the Bishops of the province. Other participants are limited by law according to the number of those in Can. 443 §3 1°–3°. The extent of the number of observers, if any, is to be established by the Bishops' Conference or respectively by the Bishops of the province.

From the clear distinction that is made between the terms 'deliberative' and 'consultative' on the one hand, and 'guests' on the other, it is clear that the latter do not have a *vote*, as such, of any kind. This does not, however, mean that they might not be invited to speak to the assembly if they would wish to do so; on the contrary, at least courtesy would require that they ought to be so invited and, if they accept, that their expressions of opinion or advice be given careful consideration.

Can. 444 §1 All who are summoned to particular councils must attend, unless they are prevented by a just impediment, of whose existence they are obliged to notify the president of the council.

The obligation to attend a particular council is not simply a moral one: it is also a legal one; the president of the council is entitled to an explanation of the reason for non-attendance, not simply an apology. However, 'a just impediment' suffices to excuse, e.g. illness, a serious commitment which cannot without harm be abandoned or postponed, an urgent personal or familial situation, etc. It is for the president to determine if the 'just impediment' submitted is an adequate reason for excusation; in the normal reasonable case, it will be. This prescription of law covers all who are actually summoned to a particular council, whether they have a deliberative or a consultative vote.

Can. 444 §2 Those who are summoned to a particular council in which they have a deliberative vote, but who are prevented from attending because of a just impediment, can send a proxy. The proxy, however, has only a consultative vote.

In general, canon law does not favour the use of a proxy (see e.g. Can. 167 §1). However, it may be permitted in certain circumstances by particular legislation or, as in this case, by universal law. Only those with a deliberative vote in the council (see Can. 443 §§1–2) may send a proxy if they are lawfully impeded from attending and have notified the president in accordance with §1. The proxy, however, enjoys only a consultative vote.

Can. 445 A particular council is to ensure that the pastoral needs of the people of God in its territory are provided for. While it must always respect the universal law of the Church, it has power of governance, especially legislative power. It can, therefore, determine whatever seems opportune for an increase of faith, for the ordering of common pastoral action, for the direction of morals and for the preservation, introduction and defence of a common ecclesiastical discipline.

The attention of every particular council is to be focused on the pastoral needs of the People of God in its own territory. This kind of assembly is not the appropriate forum for the discussion of issues which affect the universal Church. In the same way, the council's capacity to make law is limited by the requirement that decisions do not run counter to the universal law of the Church (see Can. 135 §2). Within that limit, however, it can make laws binding on all those who reside within that territory (see Can. 13) and can issue general decrees (see Can. 29).

Can. 446 When a particular council has concluded, the president is to ensure that all the acts of the council are sent to the Apostolic See. The decrees drawn up by the council are not to be promulgated until they have been reviewed by the Apostolic See. The council has the responsibility of defining the manner in which the decrees will be promulgated and the time when the promulgated decrees will begin to oblige.

894 Laws take effect only when promulgated; unless otherwise specified, particular laws take effect one month after promulgation (see Can. 8 §2). In the case of any particular council, plenary or provincial, this cannot happen until *all the acts*, not simply the text of any proposed laws, have been reviewed by the Holy See. Once the review has been completed and suggested amendments (if any) made, the laws are to be promulgated, and they take effect on the expiry of the prescribed time.[1]

Chapter IV
BISHOPS' CONFERENCES

Can. 447 The Bishops' Conference, a permanent institution, is the assembly of the Bishops of a country or of a certain territory, exercising together certain pastoral offices for Christ's faithful of that territory. By forms and means of apostolate suited to the circumstances of time and place, it is to promote, in accordance with the law, that greater good which the Church offers to mankind.

895 'From the earliest ages of the Church, Bishops in charge of particular Churches, inspired by a spirit of fraternal charity and by zeal for the universal mission entrusted to the apostles, have pooled their resources and their aspirations in order to promote both the common good and the good of individual Churches.'[2] According to c.292 of the 1917 Code, the Bishops of an ecclesiastical province were required to meet at least every five years. Gradually, such meetings become more frequent and more broadly based. Soon they were set up in a stable fashion as Conferences of Bishops. Vat. II declared – 'it is often impossible ... for Bishops to exercise their office suitably and fruitfully unless they establish closer understanding and cooperation with other Bishops'.[3] The conciliar and post-conciliar decrees on Bishops' Conferences are the immediate source of the current legislation.[4]

896 The opening canon of this chapter presents in summary form the essential features of the Bishops' Conference:
  – it is a stable institution, meeting regularly, with permanent structures to assist its work (see Cann. 451–453);

---

[1] For those matters explicitly entrusted by the Code to particular councils, cf. Cann. 753, 823 §2, 952 §1.
[2] CD 36: Fl I 386.
[3] CD 37: Fl I 587.
[4] Cf. CD 38: Fl I 587–588; ES 41: Fl I 609–610.

- it is made up of those in charge of particular Churches within a specified geographical limit, i.e. a country or some other defined territory (see Can. 448);
- its purpose is to assist common action on the part of the Bishops for the greater good of the people of God (see Can. 455).

Can. 448 §1 As a general rule, the Bishops' Conference includes those who preside over all the particular Churches of the same country, in accordance with Can. 450.

§2 A Bishops' Conference can, however, be established for a territory of greater or less extent if the Apostolic See, after consultation with the diocesan Bishops concerned, judges that circumstances suggest this. Such a Conference would include only the Bishops of some particular Churches in a certain territory, or those who preside over particular Churches in different countries. It is for the Apostolic See to lay down special norms for each case.

According to the canon, the normal territory within which a Bishops' Conference is established is to be defined by the political boundaries of a particular country (§1). Nevertheless, circumstances may suggest that other arrangements should be made (§2), i.e. establishing a Conference which includes more than one country, e.g. Gambia, Liberia and Sierra Leone, or establishing more than one Conference within the confines of the one political entity, e.g. the Conferences of Scotland and of England and Wales. In these cases, the Bishops concerned are to be consulted before the Conference is set up. The precise details of the composition and operation of these exceptional Bishops' Conferences are to be set forth in norms provided by the Holy See.

Can. 449 §1 It is for the supreme authority of the Church alone, after consultation with the Bishops concerned, to establish, suppress, or alter Bishops' Conferences.

Although the origins of the Bishops' Conference lie in the spontaneous collaboration and communication between neighbouring Bishops, the authority to establish, suppress or alter the composition of these Conferences is reserved exclusively to the Holy See, i.e. respectively to the Congregation for Bishops and to the Congregation for the Evangelisation of Peoples. Before a Conference is established, the Bishops concerned must be consulted.

Can. 449 §2 A Bishops' Conference lawfully established has juridical personality by virtue of the law itself.

As a public juridical person, the Conference enjoys the same rights and responsibilities as any other juridical person (see Cann. 113–123). The president acts in its name (see Can. 118), but his power to do so is limited by Can. 455 §4.

Can. 450 §1 By virtue of the law, the following persons in the territory belong to the Bishops' Conference: all diocesan Bishops and those equivalent to them in law; all coadjutor Bishops, auxiliary Bishops and other titular Bishops who exercise in the territory a special office assigned to them by the Apostolic See or by the Bishops' Conference. Ordinaries of another rite may be invited, but have only a consultative vote, unless the statutes of the Bishops' Conference decree otherwise.

§2 The other titular Bishops and the Legate of the Roman Pontiff are not by law members of the Bishops' Conference.

900 The criterion for membership of the Bishops' Conference is not a simple one: it involves two elements, namely episcopal governance and episcopal orders. Either element is a basis for entitlement to membership, but neither by itself suffices for automatic membership with full voting rights. Of the two, the more significant element is that of pastoral office; some titular Bishops, although obviously in episcopal orders, need not be invited, and even auxiliary Bishops do not in all matters have a deliberative vote (see Can. 454 §2), whereas a non-episcopal, territorial prelate or abbot has a right to attend and to a deliberative vote. Retired Bishops are not mentioned as members of the Bishops' Conference. However, the Holy See has recently encouraged Conferences to invite them to participate and keep them fully informed.[1] Although the universal law does not grant membership to 'other titular Bishops' e.g. those working for an international agency of the Holy See or to the Apostolic Legate, the statutes of a particular Conference may choose to make them members.

901 The law indicates that Bishops of other Rites may be invited; the Conference can give them a deliberative vote if it wishes. Nothing is said about inviting auxiliaries or titular Bishops of another Rite, but there seems no reason why they should not be invited under §2, especially since the other Rites are to be treated equally. However it needs to be borne in mind that the Conference is essentially an institution for cooperation among Bishops belonging to the latin Rite.

Can. 451 Each Bishops' Conference is to draw up its own statutes, to be reviewed by the Apostolic See. In these, among other things, arrangements for the plenary meetings of the Conference are to be set out, and provision is to be made for a permanent committee of Bishops, and a general secretariat of the Conference, and for other offices and commissions by which, in the judgement of the Conference, its purpose can more effectively be achieved.

902 The statutes of each Bishops' Conference must cover the frequency and other arrangements for plenary meetings, whether ordinary or extraordinary (see Can. 453); the manner of electing the President, Vice-president and Secretary (see Can. 452); the composition and meetings of the permanent committee, its relationship with the Plenary Meeting (see Can. 457), and the composition and roles of other commissions or offices. The statutes must indicate whether auxiliary and other titular Bishops have a deliberative or consultative vote (see Can. 454); they must also determine the size of the majority required when not determined by law, and the manner of the promulgation of Conference decisions (see Can. 455 §§2–3).

903 The requirement of such statutes reflects the permanent nature of the Conference, and its character as a juridical person (see Can. 117). Although the statutes must be reviewed and approved by the Holy See, their authority derives from that of the Bishops who constitute the Conference.

---

[1] Cf. SCB Norms for Bishops leaving office 31.X.1988: Comm 20(1988) 167–168: CLSNGBI 79 (Sept. 1989) 18–19.

Can. 452 §1 Each Bishops' Conference is, in accordance with the statutes, to elect its president, and to determine who, in the lawful absence of the president, will exercise the function of the pro-president, and to designate a general secretary.

§2 The president of the Conference or, when he is lawfully impeded, the pro-president, presides not only over the general meetings of the Bishops' Conference but also over the permanent committee.

The question of the presidency of the Conference of Bishops is one closely connected with its theological basis. In 1989 the Pontifical Council for the authentic interpretation of the Church's laws was asked two related questions, namely whether an auxiliary Bishop could be president or pro-president (a) of a Bishops' Conference, or (b) of the regional meeting of Bishops referred to in Can. 434. The reply was that he could not, in either situation: this remains the authoritative ruling.[1]   904

According to the canon, the role of the president is to preside over both plenary meetings and those of the permanent or standing committee of Bishops. He also acts in the name of the Conference in those situations where the Conference is empowered by general law or special mandate to make general decrees, or where he has the unanimous consent of the diocesan Bishops (see Can. 455). He is also required to send the acts to the Holy See for information and review (see Can. 456).   905

The role of the Pro-president is to stand in for the president when he is impeded. The Code does not preclude the designation of a permanent Pro-president. The role of the General Secretariat is spelt out in Can. 458.   906

Can. 453 Plenary meetings of the Bishops' Conference are to be held at least once a year, and moreover as often as special circumstances require, in accordance with the provisions of the statutes.

A plenary meeting of the Bishops' Conference is made up of all those who have a right to attend, either by virtue of Can. 450 §1 or by virtue of the statutes. The statutes are to provide for the frequency of ordinary meetings, which must take place at least once a year; in addition, they must set out the procedure to be followed in convening an extraordinary meeting.   907

Can. 454 §1 By virtue of the law diocesan Bishops, those equivalent to them in law and coadjutor Bishops have a deliberative vote in plenary meetings of the Bishops' Conference.

§2 Auxiliary Bishops and other titular Bishops who belong to the Bishops' Conference have a deliberative or consultative vote according to the provisions of the statutes of the Conference. Only those mentioned in §1, however, have a deliberative vote in the making or changing of the statutes.

---

[1] Cf. PCI rep 19.I.1988: AAS 81(1989) 388: Per 80(1991) 107. The reasoning behind this interpretation, based as it is on the very nature of the institutions concerned, is set out in detail by the then-President of the Pontifical Council: cf. Comm 21(1989) 94–98, a useful summary of which in English may be found in Wrenn (Interpret) 52–54. It is the view of this commentary that the interpretation in question was simply declarative, in the sense of Can. 16 §2. Be that as it may, it is certain that the reasoning which motivated the interpretation merits careful theological and juridical research.

908 According to universal law, only diocesan Bishops, their equivalent in law (see Cann. 368, 381 §2) and coadjutors have the right to a deliberative vote in Bishops' Conferences. It is for the statutes to determine the degree of participation in the Conference of auxiliary and other titular Bishops: they may be given a deliberative vote on some or all matters; or they may be given a consultative vote only on all matters. Notwithstanding any provision of the statutes, only those who have a deliberative vote by virtue of the universal law can vote validly in the making and alteration of the statutes.

Can. 455 §1 The Bishops' Conference can make general decrees only in cases where the universal law has so prescribed, or by special mandate of the Apostolic See, either on its own initiative or at the request of the Conference itself.

§2 For the decrees mentioned in §1 validly to be enacted at a plenary meeting, they must receive at least two thirds of the votes of those who belong to the Conference with a deliberative vote. These decrees do not oblige until they have been reviewed by the Apostolic See and lawfully promulgated.

§3 The manner of promulgation and the time they come into force are determined by the Bishops' Conference.

§4 In cases where neither the universal law nor a special mandate of the Apostolic See gives the Bishops' Conference the power mentioned in §1, the competence of each diocesan Bishop remains intact. In such cases, neither the Conference nor its president can act in the name of all the Bishops unless each and every Bishop has given his consent.

909 Of the canons on the Bishops' Conference, this one has the greatest number of practical applications. It also has serious theological ramifications, precisely because it touches intimately the autonomy of individual Bishops and the relationship of diocesan Bishops with each other and with the Holy See. Its basic provisions reflect the clear wishes of Vat. II.[1] In drafting the text, the Revision Commission sought to safeguard the authority both of the Pope and of the Bishops in their own dioceses.[2]

910 The Bishop's Conference is truly a legislative body. It exercises legislative power through general legislative decrees (see Can. 29) and general executive decrees (see Cann. 31–33).[3] The limits of this power are established clearly: the Conference can issue decrees only in those cases prescribed by universal law (see e.g. Cann. 230, 236, 538 §3, 1126 etc.),[4] or where the Holy See has granted the Conference a special mandate to do so.

---

[1] Cf. CD 38 (4): Fl I 587–588.

[2] Cf. Comm 14(1982) 199.

[3] Cf. CCom rep 14.V.1985: AAS 77(1985) 771.

[4] An extensive list of references to canons where the Bishops' Conference has a legislative role is given in Commentary (CLSA) 370–372. A particularly significant document in this regard is the letter sent 8.XI.1983 by the Cardinal Secretary of State to each Bishops' Conference, indicating where the Conference (a) *may* and (b) *must* issue local norms: cf. Comm 15(1983) 135–139. A study of that letter, in conjunction e.g. with LCE and other such publications, would suggest that not a few Bishops' Conferences have even yet a substantial volume of unfinished business!

For validity, these decrees must be discussed and approved at a plenary session of the Conference. Drafts may be prepared by the permanent committee or the general secretariat, but the final text must emanate from the plenary meeting. Two thirds of the votes of Conference members with a deliberative vote (see Can. 454) are required. It is important to note that the votes required refer to *all members* with a deliberative vote, not just to all those present with such a vote. Having been approved in this way, the decrees are to be sent for review to the Holy See (see Can. 456). Only when this process has been completed can the decrees be promulgated in the manner determined by the Conference in accordance with Can. 8 §2, indicating when the decrees come into force.

A general decree lawfully issued by the Bishops' Conference obliges all the members of that Conference. In the absence of any such decree, 'the competence of each diocesan Bishop remains intact' ... and 'neither the Conference nor its president can act in the name of all the Bishops unless each and every Bishop has given his consent' (§4), i.e. each and every *diocesan Bishop and his equivalent* (see Cann. 368, 381 §1).

Can. 456 When a plenary meeting of the Bishops' Conference has been concluded, its minutes are to be sent by the president to the Apostolic See for information, and its decrees, if any, for review.

At the end of the plenary meeting, the president of the Conference has the duty to forward to the Holy See a brief report of the proceedings, i.e. the names of those present, a summary of the discussions, and the outcome of voting on any decrees. In addition, he must send the text of the proposed decrees to the Holy See for review. The minutes of the plenary meeting keep the Holy See informed of what is taking place within the Conference and permit a thorough examination of the decrees submitted for review.

Can. 457 The permanent committee of Bishops is to prepare the agenda for the plenary meetings of the Conference, and it is to ensure that the decisions taken at those meetings are duly executed. It is also to conduct whatever other business is entrusted to it in accordance with the statutes.

One of the principal differences between a plenary Council and the Bishops' Conference is that the latter is a permanent institution (see Can. 447). Since it meets in plenary session at least once a year (see Can. 453), there must be an executive body to prepare the sessions and ensure that its decisions are implemented. Such a committee is mandatory (see Can. 451): its form, role and composition are to be spelled out in the Statutes. The Code entrusts to the committee as a whole, not just to the President or Secretary, the task of preparing the agenda for the plenary meetings, and of ensuring the implementation of decisions. The latter task is one of overseeing rather than direct intervention; failures should be reported back to the plenary meeting. The term 'decisions' rather than 'decrees' was deliberately chosen to embrace a wider range of matters, including decisions in doctrinal and financial affairs.[1] The permanent committee can conduct other business on behalf of the Conference, either by explicit reference back from the plenary meeting, or on its own initiative, but subject to the norms laid down in the statutes, and the restriction of Can. 455 §4.

---

[1] Cf. Comm 12(1980) 269-270.

Book II The People of God

Can. 458 The general secretariat is to:

1° prepare an account of the acts and decrees of the plenary meetings of the Conference, as well as the acts of the permanent committee of Bishops, and to communicate these to all members of the Conference and likewise to record whatever other acts are entrusted to it by the president or the permanent committee;

2° to communicate to neighbouring Bishops' Conferences such acts and documents as the Conference at a plenary meeting or the permanent committee of Bishops decides to send to them.

915 In addition to a permanent committee of Bishops, a general Secretariat is also needed to deal with correspondence and with all the organisational and paperwork engendered by the Conference. The appointment of a person as secretary to the Conference is to be specified in the statutes. It might be one of the Bishops, or a priest, deacon or lay-person, since the role is strictly secretarial and not executive. When on occasion the role is not simply secretarial, but one of transmitting the minutes and decisions to the Holy See (rather than just to Conference members or to other Conferences for information) this task is entrusted not to the Secretariat, but to the President of the Conference (see Can. 456).

916 The 1988 norms on Bishops leaving office[1] impose an additional responsibility on the Secretariat. If retired Bishops living within the territory of the Conference are not members, they too are to be sent copies of the main documents of the Conference.

Can. 459 §1 Relations are to be fostered between Bishops' Conferences, especially neighbouring ones, in order to promote and defend whatever is for the greater good.

§2 However, the Apostolic See must be consulted whenever actions or matters undertaken by Conferences have an international character.

917 The conciliar and post-conciliar decrees on Bishops' Conferences encouraged contacts between Conferences.[2] In practice, contacts between Conferences can take place at three levels: (a) the first has to do with pastoral concerns which cross national boundaries e.g. migration, refugee problems etc; this may require cooperation of agencies at local level without involving the whole Conference; (b) a second level is that of bilateral contacts between the Conferences of two or more neighbouring countries, e.g. those of Ireland, Scotland, England and Wales, concerning pastoral matters of their common concern; (c) a third level is the establishment of formal international links with the approval of the Holy See, of which the most highly developed is CELAM for Latin America.[3] As a general principle, the law requires that the Holy See must be consulted if the contacts between Bishops' Conferences lead to joint action of an international nature.

---

[1] SCB Norms 31.X.1983 loc cit: norm 4.

[2] Cf. CD 38: Fl I 588; ES I 41: Fl I 609–610.

[3] Cf. Hortal *Relationships among Episcopates* Jur 48(1988) 175–180. For a detailed history of the development of such relationships, cf. Fürer *Bishops' Conferences in their Mutual Relations* Jur 48(1988) 153–174.

Such consultation is not necessary if the contacts are restricted to a sharing of information and expertise, such as took place in Dublin (1977) and in Ottawa (1978) during the course of the consideration of the then-drafts of the current Code.

Title III
The Internal Ordering of Particular Churches

Chapter I
THE DIOCESAN SYNOD

Can. 460 The diocesan synod is an assembly of selected priests and other members of Christ's faithful of a particular Church which, for the good of the whole diocesan community, assists the diocesan Bishop, in accordance with the following canons.

The origins of the diocesan synod can be traced back to the fourth century. According to Lateran IV and Trent, synods were to be celebrated in each diocese annually. In c.356 of the 1917 code, however, the obligation was reduced to at least every ten years. No norm is provided in the present Code for the regularity of meetings. **918**

The canons on the diocesan synod must be read in conjunction with those concerning the rights and obligations of all Christ's faithful (see Cann. 211, 212 and 216). The faithful as a whole, both clergy and laity, have a right and duty to make their needs known to their Bishop, and to take an active part in the apostolic work of the Church. Participation in a diocesan synod is one way of fulfilling those duties. **919**

The Directory on the Pastoral Ministry of Bishops mentions several ways in which a synod may help the Bishop in carrying out his ministry: 'by adapting the laws and norms of the universal Church to local conditions, by indicating the policy and programme of apostolic work in the diocese, by resolving difficulties encountered in the apostolate and administration, by giving impetus to general projects and undertakings and by correcting errors in doctrine and morals if any have crept in'.[1] **920**

Can. 461 §1 The diocesan synod is to be held in each particular Church when the diocesan Bishop, after consulting the council of priests, judges that the circumstances suggest it.

The calling of a synod belongs to the diocesan Bishop. All those particular Churches described in Can. 368 are bound by this canon; so, too, is a military ordinariate. Before calling a synod, even if he judges it useful or necessary, the Bishop must consult the council of priests. He is not bound to follow the council's advice, but he should not act against it in so serious a matter without an overriding reason (see Can. 127 §2 2°). **921**

---

[1] DPME 163: LE V 6514–6515.

Can. 461 §2 If a Bishop is responsible for a number of dioceses, or has charge of one as his own and of another as Administrator, he may convene one diocesan synod for all the dioceses entrusted to him.

922 Sometimes, a diocesan Bishop has several responsibilities, e.g. in Italy a number of very small dioceses have been amalgamated in recent years, under one Bishop; formerly in such circumstances the Bishop was expected to hold a separate synod for each diocese; now one synod for all the dioceses involved suffices. The situation where a Bishop has the permanent administration of another diocese is anomalous and rare, arising usually from political exigencies. Here, too, a single synod suffices since both dioceses are effectively governed as one.

Can. 462 §1 Only the diocesan Bishop can convene a diocesan synod. A person who has interim charge of a diocese cannot do so.

§2 The diocesan Bishop presides over the diocesan synod. He may, however, delegate a Vicar general or an episcopal Vicar to fulfil this office at individual sessions of the synod.

923 The Code makes a clear distinction between the roles of convening, and presiding over, a synod. This canon makes it clear that the diocesan Bishop cannot delegate any other person to convoke a synod. This does not of course exclude him from delegating others to conduct the necessary preparatory work: in fact, such delegating will almost always be necessary.[1]

924 According to c.361 of the 1917 Code, any priest could be delegated to preside over sessions of the synod. The present law is much more restrictive: only a Vicar general or episcopal Vicar can be so delegated. Indeed there is a strong presumption that the Bishop will preside in person, since he can delegate only for individual sessions, not in a general way.

Can. 463 §1 The following are to be summoned to the diocesan synod as members and they are obliged to participate in it:

1° **the coadjutor Bishop and the auxiliary Bishops;**

2° **the Vicars general and episcopal Vicars, and the judicial Vicar;**

3° **the canons of the cathedral church;**

4° **the members of the council of priests;**

5° **lay members of Christ's faithful, not excluding members of institutes of consecrated life, to be elected by the pastoral council in the manner and the number to be determined by the diocesan Bishop or, where this council does not exist, on a basis determined by the diocesan Bishop;**

6° **the rector of the major seminary of the diocese;**

7° **the vicars forane;**

8° **at least one priest from each vicariate forane to be elected by all those who have the care of souls there; another priest is also to be elected, to take the place of the first if he is prevented from attending;**

---

[1] For the details of the necessary preparatory work – preparatory commissions, dissemination of information, call to prayer, etc. – cf. DPME 164: LE V 6515.

Part II The Hierarchical Constitution of the Church

9° some Superiors of religious institutes and of societies of apostolic life which have a house in the diocese: these are to be elected in the number and the manner determined by the diocesan Bishop.

§2 The diocesan Bishop may also invite others to be members of the diocesan synod, whether clerics or members of institutes of consecrated life or lay members of Christ's faithful.

§3 If the diocesan Bishop considers it opportune, he may invite to the diocesan synod as observers some ministers or members of Churches or ecclesial communities which are not in full communion with the catholic Church.

Under c.358 of the 1917 Code the diocesan synod was a purely clerical affair. Now lay participation is obligatory. The canon lists all those who must be summoned to the diocesan synod:

- the coadjutor Bishop, auxiliary Bishops, Vicars general, episcopal Vicars, the judicial Vicar, the canons of the cathedral chapter, the members of the council of priests, the rector of the major seminary, and the Vicars forane are all *ex officio* members;
- the laity are to be chosen by the pastoral council or by the Bishop himself in a manner determined beforehand; these include members of institutes of consecrated life;
- at least one priest and a substitute are to be elected by all 'who have the care of souls' in each vicariate forane;
- superiors of religious institutes and societies of apostolic life with a house in the diocese are to be chosen in the manner determined by the Bishop.

This system ensures a wide representation of the faithful within the diocese.

In addition to those who must be represented or present, the Bishop may supplement the representation with others, clerics, religious or lay (§2). This appears a useful device when some groups might otherwise be under- or unrepresented, e.g. deacons, young people, ethnic minorities, etc. However the implication of the second and third paragraphs taken together is that the synod cannot be a completely open assembly to which all who wish may be admitted. A synod is not the same as an open ended pastoral congress. Should members of other Churches be invited by the Bishop, their status will be that of observers (§3), but this would not seem to exclude their being invited on occasion to speak to the assembly.

925

926

Can. 464 A member of the synod who is lawfully impeded from attending, cannot send a proxy to attend in his or her place, but is to notify the diocesan Bishop of the reason for not attending.

A proxy is someone chosen and given a mandate to represent a named individual for a particular purpose. The Code prohibits an individual member of the synod from nominating such a proxy to attend in his or her stead. The law itself allows for a system of substitution in the case of the priest representative where a substitute is elected for this purpose (see Can. 463 §1 8°). There is nothing to prevent a Bishop making a similar arrangement for lay members or religious (see Can. 463 §1 5° and 9°), or for those to be chosen by virtue of Can. 463 §2. This canon does not apply to observers (see Can. 463 §3) since they are not under any obligation to attend, and so are free to send proxies.

927

Attendance at a synod is not a mere honour but a responsibility of great importance. Only a lawful impediment suffices to excuse, and the Bishop is to be notified of the

928

reason. This is not simply a matter of courtesy, but rather so that the Bishop may judge whether he considers the reason sufficient.

Can. 465 All questions proposed are to be subject to the free discussion of the members in the sessions of the synod.

929 Although it is not stated, it is taken for granted and the Revision Commission so intended, that the agenda of a synod is a matter for the Bishop to decide.[1] However, it would defeat the object of the exercise if the Bishop were not willing to accept on the agenda matters of general concern. He must bear in mind the members' right to make their needs and views known to him in matters concerning the good of the Church (see Can. 212 §§2 and 3).

930 Once an item has been placed on the agenda, free, albeit not unlimited, discussion must be allowed. Opportunity must be given to all those who wish to speak on a particular issue, not just to those who represent a particular point of view. How this can be given effect must be dealt with in the standing orders of the assembly.

Can. 466 The diocesan Bishop is the sole legislator in the diocesan synod. Other members of the synod have only a consultative vote. The diocesan Bishop alone signs the synodal declarations and decrees, and only by his authority may these be published.

931 The Bishop cannot delegate his legislative power (see Can. 135 §2). He cannot, therefore, allow the synod members a deliberative vote, nor appear to do so by asking them to add their signatures to his; the only signature to be added will be that of an approved notary. Any legislation is his own, but arrived at as a result of the consultation process, and clearly, having reflected on Can. 127, he will not lightly depart from the consensus in reaching his decisions. He is not obliged to issue the decrees at the final session of the synod, as was formerly supposed in the liturgical books, but may issue them later on. The presumption is that they will be promulgated in the manner usual in the diocese, and take effect one month later unless otherwise provided (see Can. 8 §2). The subject matter need not be confined to legislation, but legislation must be drafted in conformity with Cann. 7–22 and 29–34.

Can. 467 The diocesan Bishop is to communicate the text of the declarations and decrees of the synod to the Metropolitan and to the Bishops' Conference.

932 The particular church does not exist in isolation, and relationships between dioceses of the same province (see Can. 431 §1) and Bishops' Conference (see Can. 447) are to be fostered. Informing the Metropolitan and Bishops' Conference of the decisions of a synod is an expression of the wider communion to which the particular Church belongs.

Can. 468 §1 If he judges it prudent, the diocesan Bishop can suspend or dissolve the diocesan synod.

933 The matter of the suspension or dissolution of the diocesan synod rests with the diocesan Bishop alone. He is not required to consult anyone. However, his decision ought to be communicated individually and in writing to each of the synod members, indicating at least briefly the reasons for the decision (see Cann. 51, 54 §2, 55).

---

[1] Cf. Comm 14(1982) 211 at Can. 384.

Can. 468 §2 Should the episcopal see become vacant or impeded, the diocesan synod is by virtue of the law itself suspended, until such time as the diocesan Bishop who succeeds to the see decrees that it be continued or declares it terminated.

When a see is vacant or impeded the principle of 'no innovation' applies, and so it would be inappropriate for the synod to meet in such circumstances. It follows, therefore that those who are in interim charge of a diocese not only cannot convene a synod, but cannot preside over one already convoked. The Bishop who succeeds, on taking possession, must issue a decree continuing or terminating the synod. This is to be communicated to all the members of the synod. If the incoming Bishop decides to continue the synod, its membership may well undergo some changes: those whose offices cease when the see becomes vacant may not be reappointed to their previous position, e.g. Vicars general or episcopal Vicars. Their place in the resumed synod will be taken by the new incumbents of the offices concerned.

Chapter II
THE DIOCESAN CURIA

Can. 469 The diocesan curia is composed of those institutes and persons who assist the Bishop in governing the entire diocese, especially in directing pastoral action, in providing for the administration of the diocese, and in exercising judicial power.

The term 'diocesan curia' is used to refer to a collection of organisations, councils, committees and individual offices which contribute to the practical running of a diocese. According to Vat. II, 'the diocesan curia should be so organised that it may be a useful medium for the Bishop not only for diocesan administration but also for pastoral activity'.[1] The canon identifies three areas where the curia ought to be of assistance to the Bishop: directing pastoral action, administration, and the exercise of judicial power.

The size of the various bodies and number of individual offices will vary from diocese to diocese. Generally speaking, however, the curia is made up of the Vicar(s) general and episcopal Vicars with their ancillary staff (see Cann. 475–481); the Chancellor, possibly a vice-Chancellor, other notaries and their support staff, as well as the diocesan archives (see Cann. 482–491); the financial committee and financial administrator (see Cann. 492–494); the judicial Vicar, other judges, and the personnel of the tribunal (see Cann. 1420–1423, 1428–1437). In addition to these, the Bishop may establish other offices, councils or commissions as he thinks fit.

Can. 470 The appointment of those who fulfil an office in the diocesan curia belongs to the diocesan Bishop.

Within his own diocese, the diocesan Bishop is free to make appointments to ecclesiastical office by free conferral (see Can. 157). This prerogative includes the appointment of all who hold office in the diocesan curia. Although free to appoint whomever he chooses, the Bishop must do so in conformity with the general norms of canon law (see Cann. 146–156), the civil laws governing employment in the case of the

---
[1] CD 27: Fl I 579–580.

Book II The People of God

laity, and specific provisions of law for certain offices e.g. the need to consult the college of consultors and the finance committee before appointing a financial administrator (see Can. 494 §1).

Can. 471 All who are admitted to an office in the curia must:

1° promise to fulfil their office faithfully, as determined by law or by the Bishop.

2° observe secrecy within the limits and according to the manner determined by law or by the Bishop.

938 All those who are appointed to offices within the diocesan curia assume a twofold obligation:

(a) before taking up their office, they are required to promise to fulfil that office faithfully; details of the scope of each particular office are contained in the law itself or are determined by the Bishop. There is no universal regulation concerning the manner in which the promise is to be made, though it is frequently incorporated in a written formula of oath whereby the obligation in (b) below is undertaken.

(b) they are obliged by virtue of the law itself to observe secrecy concerning the discharge of their office; the limits of that secrecy are determined either by the law e.g. access to the archives (see Cann. 487–490), or by the Bishop in guidelines for all curial offices or for a particular office. Any breach of this obligation can be punished according to the gravity of the offence (see Can. 1389).

Can. 472 The provisions of Book VII on 'Processes' are to be observed concerning cases and persons involved in the exercise of judicial power in the curia. The following canons are to be observed in what concerns the administration of the diocese.

939 Although the diocesan curia is regarded as a single entity, the activity of those who work in it is regulated according to two separate sets of norms. Those who are engaged in judicial activity are obliged by the norms governing processes found in Book VII of the Code. Those whose work is administrative or pastoral are subject to the norms of the following canons (Cann. 473–494).

Can. 473 §1 The diocesan Bishop must ensure that everything concerning the administration of the whole diocese is properly coordinated and is directed in the way that will best achieve the good of that portion of the people of God entrusted to his care.

§2 The diocesan Bishop has the responsibility of coordinating the pastoral action of the Vicars general and episcopal Vicars. Where it is useful, he may appoint a Moderator of the curia, who must be a priest. Under the Bishop's authority, the Moderator is to coordinate activities concerning administrative matters and to ensure that the others who belong to the curia properly fulfil the offices entrusted to them.

§3 Unless in the Bishop's judgement local conditions suggest otherwise, the Vicar general is to be appointed Moderator of the curia or, if there are several Vicars general, one of them.

§4 Where the Bishop judges it useful for the better promotion of pastoral action, he can establish an episcopal council, comprising the Vicars general and episcopal Vicars.

The general principle of law is that responsibility for the government of the diocese rests ultimately with the Bishop. Through his coordination and direction of pastoral activity and ordinary administration, the Bishop serves the people of God entrusted to him. This canon provides norms to assist the Bishop in attaining this goal; some are obligatory, others are facultative.

Thus, he is obliged to coordinate the pastoral activity of the Vicar(s) general and the episcopal Vicars; he is to ensure that there is no unnecessary duplication in their activities and that the whole diocese is well served by them. As Vicars of the Bishop, they are accountable to him alone. The Bishop *may* decide that it is useful to appoint a Moderator of the Curia, who must be a priest. His function is to direct the smooth and efficient administration of the curia and to ensure that all the officials carry out their designated duties. As a general rule – but not if 'in the Bishop's judgement local conditions suggest otherwise' – this Moderator ought to be a Vicar general of the diocese.[1] The Bishop may also decide to set up an 'episcopal council': its function is the promotion of pastoral activity in the diocese; its membership is limited to the Vicars general and the episcopal Vicars. Of course, the Bishop may decide to establish other auxiliary bodies whose membership is broader and more flexible than that of the episcopal council.

Can. 474 Acts of the curia which of their nature are designed to have a juridical effect must, as a requirement for validity, be signed by the Ordinary from whom they emanate. They must also be signed by the chancellor of the curia or a notary. The chancellor is bound to notify the Moderator of the curia about these acts.

The term 'acts of the curia' in this canon refers to written documents which record or effect a juridical act, whether or not such a written form is required for the validity of the juridical act, e.g. decrees, rescripts, privileges and dispensations. The document is invalid if it is not signed by the person performing the act; it must also be signed by the chancellor or a notary. If the law itself requires for validity that an act be done in writing, and if the curial act is invalidated by the lack of a signature, the juridical act also will be invalid: e.g. Can. 156 states that the provision of any office is to be made in writing; for lawfulness, this must be signed by the Bishop and chancellor or notary; however this is not required for validity: an oral appointment is valid, and the failure of the Bishop to sign a letter of appointment does not invalidate it; it simply means that the document itself lacks validity as a proof of appointment. On the other hand, the transfer from one office to another must for validity be notified in writing (see Can. 190 §3).

If some other notary has been used, the Ordinary concerned must give the chancellor a copy of the acts, because of his overall responsibility for the curial archives (see Can. 482 §1), which is not confined to filing, but includes ensuring that copies are sent to those entitled to them. It is for the Moderator, if one exists, to ensure that other interested departments of the curia are informed.

---

[1] The institution of a Moderator of the curia is a new one, introduced by the current Code. It is one which should seriously be considered. In the maelstrom of modern life, particularly perhaps in the western world, the ever-growing burden of day-to-day administration in some dioceses is such that it can make it extremely difficult for the Bishop to attend adequately to other and even more vital tasks of his episcopal office, such as detailed in Cann. 375, 383–387, 396–397, etc. It is in circumstances of this kind that the assistance of a Moderator – who must of course himself reflect the mind of the Bishop – can be invaluable.

Book II The People of God

Article 1
Vicars General and Episcopal Vicars

Can. 475 §1 In each diocese the diocesan Bishop is to appoint a Vicar general to assist him in the governance of the whole diocese. The Vicar general has ordinary power, in accordance with the following canons.

§2 As a general rule, one Vicar general is to be appointed, unless the size of the diocese, the number of inhabitants, or other pastoral reasons suggest otherwise.

944 The appointment of a Vicar general is obligatory no matter how small the diocese. His power is exercised throughout the whole diocese. According to the canon, there should be only one Vicar general in each particular Church, unless pastoral reasons suggest otherwise. However, when there are auxiliary Bishops, they must all be appointed Vicars general, or at least episcopal Vicars (see Can. 406), out of respect for their episcopal office. In practice, many large dioceses appoint a number of Vicars general, whether or not auxiliary Bishops. Any difficulties arising from over-lapping jurisdiction are best resolved by the diocesan Bishop with the help of his episcopal council (see Can. 473 §4).

945 The Vicar general is listed among those referred to as Ordinaries (see Can. 134 §1). According to Can. 131 §1 'ordinary power of governance is that which by virtue of the law itself is attached to a given office'. This power may be proper or vicarious (see Can. 131 §2). The power of a diocesan Bishop is ordinary and proper (see Can. 381 §1); that of a Vicar general is ordinary but *vicarious*, i.e. his power belongs to the office itself but is exercised in the name of the diocesan Bishop. His authority, within the limits set by law, is the same as that of the Bishop (see Can. 479 §3) and cannot be exercised contrary to the will or mind of the Bishop (see Can. 480). On occasion, a Vicar general may enjoy additional authority by virtue of a special mandate to deal with matters reserved by law to the 'diocesan Bishop' rather than the 'local Ordinary'; in such circumstances, the Vicar general's power is *delegated* not ordinary (see Cann. 137–142).

Can. 476 As often as the good governance of the diocese requires it, the diocesan Bishop can also appoint one or more episcopal Vicars. These have the same ordinary power as the universal law gives to a Vicar general, in accordance with the following canons. The competence of an episcopal Vicar, however, is limited to a determined part of the diocese, or to a specific type of activity, or to the faithful of a particular rite, or to certain groups of people.

946 As an institution the office of episcopal Vicar is new, and the legislation in the Code derives from Vat. II and post-conciliar norms.[1] The canon envisages four possible criteria for the appointment of episcopal Vicars: (a) the diocese may be divided up territorially, with a Vicar for each area; in this case his functions will be all those of a Vicar general, but only for that specific area of the diocese; (b) in the same way he may be given responsibility for catholics of another rite, when they have no hierarch of their own; (c) he may be given responsibility for a particular language or cultural group within the diocese; (d) he may also be appointed for specific activities e.g. financial affairs, or the general pastoral care of marriage and families. The episcopal Vicar cannot act validly outside the area of his competence. In all cases, the limits of the Vicar's responsibility must be defined in his decree of appointment.

---

[1] Cf. CD 23(3), 27: Fl I 577, 579: ES I 14(1–2): Fl I 599.

Can. 477 §1 The Vicar general and the episcopal Vicar are freely appointed by the diocesan Bishop, and can be freely removed by him, without prejudice to Can. 406. An episcopal Vicar who is not an auxiliary Bishop, is to be appointed for a period of time, which is to be specified in the act of appointment.

§2 If the Vicar general is absent or lawfully impeded, the diocesan Bishop can appoint another to take his place. The same norm applies in the case of an episcopal Vicar.

Unless otherwise stated, ecclesiastical offices within the diocese are freely conferred by the Bishop (see Can. 157). In some cases, e.g. the financial administrator, the Bishop's freedom is qualified by a requirement of consultation before appointment or removal (see Can. 494). In the case of a Vicar general or an episcopal Vicar the diocesan Bishop has a completely free hand in making the appointment when the candidate is simply a priest; he may also freely remove him; the requirements of grave reasons and proper procedure in the norms laid down in Can. 193 §§1 & 2 do not seem to apply, although there is the implication that at least a just cause is needed and that the decree of removal must be notified in writing (see Can. 193 §§3 & 4). The Bishop does not have the same freedom with regard to his auxiliary Bishops; by virtue of the law, he *must* appoint them at least episcopal Vicars, if not Vicars general (see Can. 406), and for the same reason cannot freely remove them from office. 947

Generally, it is presumed that any office is conferred for an indefinite period of time, unless otherwise stated: a parish priest e.g. can be appointed for a specified period of time only if this has been sanctioned – and to the extent that it has been thus sanctioned – by the Conference of Bishops (see Can. 522). In the case of an auxiliary Bishop, the appointment, whether as Vicar general or episcopal Vicar, must be indefinite; in the case of a priest, his appointment as episcopal Vicar must be for a specified period of time and not indefinitely; however, that of Vicar general may be indefinite or for a specified period; unless the latter is expressly included in the letter of appointment it is presumed that the appointment is for an indefinite period. 948

Only a diocesan Bishop in the strict sense of the word, a territorial prelate and an abbot can appoint a Vicar general or episcopal Vicars (see Can. 370). The power of Vicars and Prefects apostolic, while indeed being *ordinary power of governance* in the terms of Can. 131 §1, is not *proper* but rather *vicarious* power (see Can. 131 §2) since it is exercised 'in the name of the Supreme Pontiff' (Can. 371). Such Vicars or Prefects may, however, appoint delegates to carry out similar functions (see Can. 137). The same applies to the temporary diocesan Administrator when a see is vacant. In this situation the Vicars general and episcopal lose their ordinary power (see Can. 481); to appoint a Vicar general or an episcopal Vicar would be an excluded innovation (see Can. 428 §1). But there is nothing to hinder the administrator appointing delegates to help him, and it would seem desirable that he should take account of the experience of those who previously held office as Vicars general or episcopal. 949

If the Vicar general or an episcopal Vicar is absent, or impeded, e.g. for health reasons, then the Bishop can appoint a replacement, whether on a temporary or on a permanent basis (§2). 950

Can. 478 §1 The Vicar general and the episcopal Vicar are to be priests of not less than thirty years of age, with a doctorate or licentiate in canon law or theology, or at least well versed in these disciplines. They are to be known for their sound doctrine, integrity, prudence and practical experience.

951 Only a priest or Bishop can be appointed as Vicar general or episcopal Vicar. Many dioceses appoint a 'Vicar for religious'; there is no difficulty about appointing a male religious to this role if he is a priest. However if a religious sister or brother is designated to assist the Bishop in matters pertaining to religious life, they cannot be appointed as episcopal Vicars in the technical sense. In addition to the requirement of priesthood, the person appointed as Vicar general or episcopal Vicar must be over thirty years of age and have the requisite academic and personal qualifications.

Can. 478 §2 The office of Vicar general or episcopal Vicar may not be united with the office of canon penitentiary, nor may the office be given to blood relations of the Bishop up to the fourth degree.

952 Since their role relates to the *external forum*, it would be grossly improper to combine the office of Vicar general or episcopal Vicar with that of the canon penitentiary (see Can. 508). In general, it is desirable that the Vicar general not be appointed as judicial Vicar as well (see Can. 1420 §1). Excluded from appointment to either office are those related by blood to the diocesan Bishop up to the level of first cousin.

Can. 479 §1 In virtue of his office, the Vicar general has the same executive power throughout the whole diocese as that which belongs by law to the diocesan Bishop: that is, he can perform all administrative acts, with the exception however of those which the Bishop has reserved to himself, or which by law require a special mandate of the Bishop.

§2 By virtue of the law itself, the episcopal Vicar has the same power as that mentioned in §1, but only for the determined part of the territory or type of activity, or for the faithful of the determined rite or group, for which he was appointed; matters which the Bishop reserves to himself or to the Vicar general, or which by law require a special mandate of the Bishop, are excepted.

§3 Within the limits of their competence, the Vicar general and the episcopal Vicar have also those habitual faculties which the Apostolic See has granted to the Bishop. They may also execute rescripts, unless it is expressly provided otherwise, or unless the execution was entrusted to the Bishop on a personal basis.

953 The power of governance exercised by the Vicar general and episcopal Vicar is essentially one with that of the Bishop: they have the same power given by the law, and the same habitual faculties which the Holy See has granted to the diocesan Bishop (§§1–3).

954 There are, however, some limitations. Where the law speaks of the 'diocesan Bishop' rather than the 'local Ordinary', a Vicar can act only if he has a special mandate from the Bishop, either for a specific case or in a more general way: it is possible for him to give a general mandate for all those actions where the law requires one, subject to any *ad hoc* reservation he may choose to make (§1). Equally the Bishop may withdraw some particular area or case for his own consideration, but such a reservation must be made in an explicit manner, and is not presumed.

955 The episcopal Vicar has identical power and status to the Vicar general; what is limited is his remit (§2). The exercise of his authority is limited to the area indicated in his letter of appointment. For this reason, any extension of his remit, even in a temporary way (e.g. during the absence of the Vicar general), ought to be recorded in writing to avoid disputes over the validity of his actions.

Can. 480 The Vicar general and episcopal Vicar must give a report to the diocesan Bishop concerning more important matters, both those yet to be attended to and those already dealt with. They are never to act against the will and mind of the diocesan Bishop.

Since the authority of the Vicar is one with that of the Bishop, it must be exercised in unity with and dependency on him. The law itself provides for the invalidity of rescripts granted without the Bishop's consent, if he has already refused them (see Can. 65 §3). If he has not refused but the request is known to be against his wishes, the rescript is unlawful but not invalid. The Bishop cannot retroactively reserve a matter to himself; consequently, advance consultation with the Vicars is necessary, as is a report on major actions taken by the Vicar. Without adequate mutual communication the office of Vicar general or episcopal Vicar could well become ineffectual or counter-productive. 956

Can. 481 §1 The power of the Vicar general or episcopal Vicar ceases when the period of their mandate expires, or by resignation. In addition, but without prejudice to Cann. 406 and 409, it ceases when they are notified of their removal by the diocesan Bishop, or when the episcopal see falls vacant.

§2 When the office of the diocesan Bishop is suspended, the power of the Vicar general and of the episcopal Vicar is suspended, unless they are themselves Bishops.

The law itself requires an auxiliary Bishop to be appointed Vicar general or episcopal Vicar (see Cann. 406 and 409); consequently, while his power as Vicar is closely linked with that of the diocesan Bishop, it is retained when the see becomes vacant, or if the power of the diocesan Bishop is suspended. The power of an auxiliary Bishop as Vicar ceases only by resignation, death or transfer, or by his removal from office as auxiliary. In addition, a Vicar general or episcopal Vicar who is not an auxiliary Bishop loses his power also when his period of appointment expires (see Can. 477 §1), or when he is notified by the Bishop of his removal (see Cann. 192–195), or when the see falls vacant (see Cann. 416–417). The Vicar general or episcopal Vicar loses his power temporarily if the diocesan Bishop is himself suspended from office, and to the extent that he is suspended from the exercise of his power of governance (see Cann. 1333–1335), e.g. if the Bishop were found guilty of simony (see Cann. 1380) or attempted marriage (see Can. 1394 §1): this suspension affects only those Vicars general and episcopal Vicars who are not Bishops. 957

Article 2
The Chancellor, other Notaries and the Archives

Can. 482 §1 In each curia a chancellor is to be appointed, whose principal office, unless particular law states otherwise, is to ensure that the acts of the curia are drawn up and dispatched, and that they are kept safe in the archive of the curia.

§2 If it is considered necessary, the chancellor may be given an assistant, who is to be called the vice-chancellor.

§3 The chancellor and vice-chancellor are automatically notaries and secretaries of the curia.

958 The term chancellor comes from an official at the Roman court, who sat at the entrance (*ad cancellos*) to check access. He became distinguished from other notaries by his role of overall supervision of the issuing of documents, and their preservation. Because of his learning he often also developed a teaching role, giving rise to the office of chancellor in fledgling universities. The importance of the office is indicated by the fact that it is mandatory, and by the provision that he may, if necessary, be given an assistant. In fact the Revision Commission took it for granted that he would be given a professional archivist to help him look after the historical material, and so thought it unnecessary to write this into the text.[1] The Chancellor may, but need not, be a cleric: in principle a lay man or woman may be, and nowadays not infrequently is appointed. If, however, the office is amalgamated with that of the Moderator of the Curia, or entrusted with delegated power of governance by the Bishop, then only a priest may be appointed.[2]

959 The law requires the personal intervention of the chancellor in a number of cases: e.g. he must witness and record the showing of the apostolic letters to the college of consultors by a new diocesan Bishop (see Can. 382 §3), coadjutor Bishop or auxiliary (see Can. 404); he must report to its Moderator (if he exists) all acts with juridical effect emanating from the curia (see Can. 474), etc.

Can. 483 §1 Besides the chancellor, other notaries may be appointed, whose writing or signature authenticates public documents, whether in respect of all acts, or of judicial acts alone, or only for acts concerning a particular issue or business.

§2 The chancellor and notaries must be of unblemished reputation and above suspicion. In cases which could involve the reputation of a priest, the notary must be a priest.

960 It is essential that important actions and decisions are recorded on adequately authenticated documents. Before acting on the basis of any document, the executor is required to check its authenticity and integrity (see Can. 40). For any document to be 'authentic' in this sense the original signature or the making of a copy must be witnessed and signed by a duly authorised notary. The role of the notary is then to give public testimony, by his or her signature, to the fact that the document has been signed by the person alleged, and that copies are accurate, whether made in manuscript form or photostatically. In the case of an official copy, the formula '*cum originali concordat*' is normally used. Without such a signature the document may be correct but it is not authentic. In some cases the signature of a notary is required for validity, e.g. the judicial depositions of witnesses (see Can. 1569); in others it is required for lawfulness only.

961 Because of the importance attached to official documents, there must be no suspicion that the chancellor or the notaries are doubtful in moral character, or capable of falsifying documents. Moreover, such documents will frequently be confidential in nature, requiring a total discretion of the part of every notary: hence the emphasis placed here on the unblemished character required for the chancellor and other notaries. As a further safeguard, cases involving the reputation of a priest require that the notary be himself a priest (§2) – an important prescription especially when dealing with a penal process involving a priest.

---

[1] 'Additio proposita non videtur necessaria, quia subintelligitur': Comm 14(1982) 214 at Can. 401.
[2] Cf. Comm 13(1981) 121–122 at Can. 296.

Notaries are freely appointed by the Bishop, (see Can. 470), in writing (see Can. 156) and are subject to the promise required in Can. 471. The letter of appointment should clearly indicate whether they are authorised to authenticate all documents or only in specified areas, e.g. judicial or financial: indeed one may be appointed only for a particular case. The notary may be lay, male or female, but must be catholic (see Can. 149 §1).

Can. 484 The office of notary involves:

1° writing acts and documents concerning decrees, arrangements, obligations, and other matters which require their intervention;

2° faithfully recording in writing what is done, and signing the document, with a note of the place, the day, the month and the year;

3° while observing all that must be observed, showing acts or documents from the archives to those who lawfully request them, and verifying that copies conform to the original.

The responsibility of a notary is not simply clerical. Under the overall responsibility of the Chancellor, the notary must ensure that documents are drawn up in the correct form. This may involve a familiarity with the civil as well as the canonical requirements. Notaries must be prepared to draft such documents on request; they are also expected to refuse to sign or prepare documents which do not correspond with the law. Failure to do so could render them liable to an ecclesiastical penalty (see Can. 1391).

Can. 485 The chancellor and the other notaries can be freely removed by the diocesan Bishop. They can be removed by a diocesan Administrator only with the consent of the college of consultors.

Although the Bishop can freely remove the Chancellor and other notaries, a just reason is required (see Can. 193 §3), and this must be stated at least in summary form in the decree (see Cann. 51, 193 §4). Furthermore, any rights arising from a contract of employment must be observed (see Can. 192). The Revision Commission commented that for this reason an appropriate clause allowing dismissal must be written into such contracts.[1] This is a matter of no small importance when lay people are appointed to such offices, since their contracts may be enforceable at civil law.

During the vacancy of the see the diocesan Administrator is not permitted to make any innovation, and is explicitly forbidden to interfere with the archives (see Can. 428). He is not permitted to remove the chancellor or notaries, both as a statement of general principle and as a safeguard. In order to take such a step, he would require the consent of the college of consultors. Since he is not allowed to remove them from office at his prudent discretion (see Can. 193 §3), he can do so only for grave reasons and in accordance with the procedure defined by law (see Can. 193 §1). If a chancellor should be removed in this way, it would be necessary that a temporary appointment be made until the diocesan See is filled – not least for the purpose of witnessing and recording the presentation of the Apostolic letters by the incoming Bishop (see Can. 382 §3).

Can. 486 §1 All documents concerning the diocese or parishes must be kept with the greatest of care.

---

[1] Comm 14(1982) 214 at Can. 405: 'In huiusmodi contractibus prudentes clausulae revocatoriae poni semper debent'.

§2 In each curia there is to be established in a safe place a diocesan archive where documents and writings concerning both the spiritual and the temporal affairs of the diocese are to be properly filed and carefully kept under lock and key.

§3 An inventory or catalogue is to be made of documents kept in the archive, with a short synopsis of each document.

966 Certain documents must be preserved in the diocesan archives:
  (i) documents and writings concerning both the spiritual and temporal affairs of the diocese (see Can. 486 §2);
  (ii) duplicate copies of the inventories or catalogues of parochial and similar archives within the diocese (see Can. 491 §1);
  (iii) a register of the conferring of the sacrament of Confirmation, unless by decree of the Bishops' Conference one such is to be kept in each parish;[1]
  (iv) a register of the conferring of the sacrament of Orders (see Can. 1053);
  (v) documents recording the dedication or blessing of churches or cemeteries (see Can. 1208);
  (vi) copies of inventories of temporal goods which qualify as ecclesiastical (see Cann. 1257 §1, 1283 3°);
  (vii) where conveniently possible, copies of title deeds and other documents establishing the rights of the Church or a juridical person to its goods (see Can. 1284 §2 9°);
  (viii) copies of the documents whereby pious foundations are established (see Can. 1306 §2).

967 In the narrow sense, the archive refers to a locked room (see Can. 487) in which are stored those files which are closed, or at least not in day-to-day use. In a wider sense, it embraces all the paperwork in the curial offices which may eventually find its way there. Each department will have its own criteria concerning what needs to be kept and for how long; as well as criteria about levels of confidentiality and the length of time before material is transferred from active files to archives, and from the general to historical archives.

968 A catalogue of the contents of each archive is to be kept and updated. Access to the contents of the archive may be facilitated by the use of modern technology for cataloguing and indexing, e.g. on microfilm or computer disk.

969 The archive room itself must be in a safe place. The concern here is not with unauthorised access, since this is covered in the canons that follow, but with protection from natural hazards such as damp, flooding or fire, earthquakes, insect infestation etc.

Can. 487 §1 The archive must be locked, and only the Bishop and the chancellor are to have the key; no one may be allowed to enter unless with the permission of the Bishop, or with the permission of both the Moderator of the curia and the chancellor.

970 The archive where files are stored must be kept locked. Only the Bishop and the chancellor are to have the key – either each having access to the one key or each possessing an identical key. Access to the archive may be granted by the Bishop alone without the consent of the chancellor, or by the mutual agreement of both the chancellor and the Moderator of the curia. The chancellor alone cannot grant access. The

---

[1] Cf. LCE Tavola per Paesi e Canoni at Cann. 535, 895.

permission may be for a specific occasion or in general terms, e.g. in the case of a professional archivist who works as assistant.

Access to the archive room is distinct from access to the material contained therein. Researchers and other interested persons are not at liberty to inspect whatever material they like; rather, they may be given access to the catalogue and to those materials which, if approved, they request.

Can. 487 §2 Persons concerned have the right to receive, personally or by proxy, an authentic written or photostat copy of documents which are of their nature public and which concern their own personal status.

Persons have a right to inspect or receive an authentic copy of those documents which are of their nature public and concern their own personal status, e.g. baptismal and marriage records. They do not have a right to documents which do not relate to their own status. Equally there is no right of access to other documents, e.g. letters attached to marriage dispensation forms. Provision must be made for the issuing of authenticated copies either in manuscript or photostatic form.

In all likelihood, the bulk of documents in the archive will be private in nature, and not concern matters of personal status. Access to these is at the discretion of the Bishop or that jointly of the chancellor and Moderator of the curia.

Can. 488 It is not permitted to remove documents from the archive, except for a short time and with the permission of the Bishop or of both the Moderator of the curia and the chancellor.

Unfortunately, it is the experience of many archives that people do not respect the trust placed in them, and that documents are stolen or mutilated, or loaned and then not recovered. It is the responsibility of the chancellor to ensure that this does not happen. For this reason, direct access to the filing cabinets or cupboards should not be allowed; rather items should be taken on request to a working space in a supervised area, preferably within the general area of the archive. Removal from this area requires the explicit permission of the Bishop or of the Moderator and chancellor. This permission is to be given only for a short period of time and is to be carefully supervised.

Can. 489 §1 In the diocesan curia there is also to be a secret archive, or at least in the ordinary archive there is to be a safe or cabinet, which is securely closed and bolted and which cannot be removed. In this archive documents which are to be kept under secrecy are to be most carefully guarded.

§2 Each year documents of criminal cases concerning moral matters are to be destroyed whenever the guilty parties have died, or ten years have elapsed since a condemnatory sentence concluded the affair. A short summary of the facts is to be kept, together with the text of the definitive judgement.

Documents which are of great sensitivity need to be kept in conditions of maximum security. Among the documents which must be kept in this particular archive are the following:

(i) documents of criminal cases concerning matters of a moral nature (§2);
(ii) the register of dispensations granted from occult marriage impediments in the internal but non-sacramental forum (see Can. 1082);
(iii) the register of marriages celebrated secretly (see Can. 1133);

(iv) documentary proof of canonical warnings or corrections when someone has been about to commit an offence, or is suspected of having committed one, or has been guilty of scandalous behaviour (see Can. 1339);

(v) the acts of a preliminary investigation for a penal process that was closed without a formal trial (see Can. 1719);

(vi) any other matters the Bishop considers secret.

976 Provision is made for the routine destruction of certain documents which are of a highly sensitive and potentially defamatory nature, once their usefulness has ceased. Thus, because a plaint of nullity can be alleged against a condemnatory judgement up to ten years from the date of publication (see Can. 1621), the full acts of a criminal case concerning moral matters must be kept until the ten years have elapsed. After that time only a summary must be kept, not the complete acta. In cases where the party involved has died, *all* the material must be destroyed; not even the brief summary of the facts is to be retained.[1]

Can. 490 §1 Only the Bishop is to have the key of the secret archive.

§2 When the see is vacant, the secret archive or safe is not to be opened except in a case of real necessity, and then by the diocesan Administrator personally.

§3 Documents are not to be removed from the secret archive or safe.

977 The confidentiality of the material stored in the secret archive is to be preserved as strictly as possible. Thus, the Code prescribes that only the Bishop is permitted to have the key to that archive (§1). In practical terms, it might be advisable that he make the key's whereabouts known, e.g. to the Vicar general, to the Moderator of the curia or to the Chancellor, on the explicit understanding of course that only the Bishop himself may have access to that archive.

978 When the diocese is vacant, as a general rule the secret archive must remain closed. Only in a case of true necessity may it be opened and then only by the diocesan Administrator personally (§2).

979 Even when the archive is opened by the Bishop or Administrator, the law forbids the removal of any documents from it (§3). The only exception foreseen by law is the removal of those documents needed to complete a penal process (see Can. 1719).

Can. 491 §1 The diocesan Bishop is to ensure that the acts and documents of the archives of cathedral, collegiate, parochial and other churches in his territory are carefully kept and that two copies are made of inventories or catalogues. One of these copies is to remain in its own archive, the other is to be kept in the diocesan archive.

§2 The diocesan Bishop is to ensure that there is an historical archive in the diocese, and that documents which have an historical value are carefully kept in it and systematically filed.

§3 In order that the acts and documents mentioned in §§1 and 2 may be inspected or removed, the norms laid down by the diocesan Bishop are to be observed.

980 The Bishop is responsible only for archives attaching to churches within his diocese. He must ensure that a copy of their inventory or catalogue is kept in the curial archive and regularly updated. He must inspect the care of parish archives during his

---

[1] Cf. CCom rep 5.VIII.1941: CLD 2 132.

visitation, or in some other way (see Can. 535 §4). Where there is a high security risk or where registers of great age and fragility are concerned, the Bishop may stipulate that these be kept in the historical archive of the diocese, or be deposited elsewhere, e.g. the local public records office (see Can. 535 §5). Archives have a considerable value to historians, and the Bishop is not just encouraged but required to establish a properly ordered historical archive, and to provide appropriate means to this end, including the services of a trained archivist.

The actual inspection of archive material is left to the discretion of the Bishop. He is to lay down norms for access to and the copying of items in the historical archive and in the archives of the churches of the diocese. 981

Article 3
The Finance Committee and the Financial Administrator

Can. 492 §1 In each diocese a finance committee is to be established, presided over by the diocesan Bishop or his delegate. It is to be composed of at least three of Christ's faithful, expert in financial affairs and civil law, of outstanding integrity, and appointed by the Bishop.

§2 The members of the finance committee are appointed for five years, but when this period has expired they may be appointed for further terms of five years.

§3 Persons related to the Bishop up to the fourth degree of consanguinity or affinity are excluded from the finance committee.

The establishment of a finance committee is a requirement of the law, not an option. Like the college of consultors, it continues in existence when the see is vacant. The specific criteria for appointment to the finance committee in addition to the general norms of Can. 149 §1, are primarily those of expertise in the field of finance and of civil law. In order to preclude any suspicion of corruption, they are to be of outstanding integrity, and may not be related to the Bishop either by blood or by marriage, within the fourth degree (see Cann. 108–109). Appointment is open to lay people, religious or clergy, male or female. There must be at least three members on the committee. They are appointed for a fixed term, but may be reappointed. As with all curial appointments they must promise to fulfil their office faithfully, and to observe secrecy (see Can. 471). The appointment must be made in writing (see Can. 156). 982

The finance committee is presided over by the Bishop in person, or by his delegate who may not, however, be the financial administrator of Can. 494: the latter is a servant of the finance committee, not a member of it. Subject to the debate on Can. 129, the Bishop's delegate ought to be at least in deacon's orders; but it would seem appropriate that the delegate be the Vicar general or at least an episcopal Vicar. The Code does not preclude the possibility of someone else being asked to chair the meeting of the committee. 983

Can. 493 Besides the functions entrusted to it in Book V on 'The Temporal Goods of the Church', it is the responsibility of the finance committee to prepare each year a budget of income and expenditure over the coming year for the governance of the whole diocese, in accordance with the direction of

the diocesan Bishop. It is also the responsibility of the committee to account at the end of the year for income and expenditure.

984 All the temporal goods belonging to a diocese must be regulated in accordance with the provisions of Book V (Can. 1257 §1), and also by any diocesan statutes. Specific mention is made of the finance committee within Book V, e.g.: the Bishop is required to obtain the consent, not merely the advice, of the finance committee if he wishes to carry out an extraordinary act of administration (see Can. 1277) or to alienate property, or otherwise adversely affect the financial state of the diocese (see Can. 1292, 1295); he must obtain their advice for other matters of greater moment (see Can. 1277), before levying a tax (see Can. 1263), when deciding what counts as extraordinary administration for juridical persons subject to him (see Can. 1281 §2), when investing funds assigned to an endowment (see Can. 1305), and when reducing the obligations attached to a gift, will or other pious foundation (see Can. 1310 §2).

985 In day-to-day terms, the most basic task of the finance committee is the preparation of an annual diocesan budget (income and expenditure account, balance sheet, etc.). In general, the finance committee is to give advice about overall diocesan financial strategy and planning.[1]

Can. 494 §1 In each diocese a financial administrator is to be appointed by the Bishop, after consulting the college of consultors and the finance committee. The financial administrator is to be expert in financial matters and of truly outstanding integrity.

§2 The financial administrator is to be appointed for five years, but when this period has expired, may be appointed for further terms of five years. While in office he or she is not to be removed except for a grave reason, to be estimated by the Bishop after consulting the college of consultors and the finance committee.

§3 It is the responsibility of the financial administrator, under the authority of the Bishop, to administer the goods of the diocese in accordance with the plan of the finance committee, and to make those payments from diocesan funds which the Bishop or his delegates have lawfully authorised.

§4 At the end of the year the financial administrator must give the finance committee an account of income and expenditure.

986 The Bishop must appoint a financial administrator. Both the finance committee and the college of consultors must be consulted before making the appointment. Legal expertise is not required, because that will be available in the committee itself, but financial expertise is a *sine qua non*. As well as fulfilling the general criteria for ecclesiastical office (see Can. 149 §1), the administrator may be clerical or lay, male or female. His or her appointment must be for fixed terms of five years. The administrator enjoys a greater security of tenure than many other office holders, since in addition to the procedures required by Cann. 192–195, the Bishop must also first consult the college of consultors and the finance committee if it is proposed to remove him or her. There are, however, certain circumstances in which the office may be lost other than by resignation or deprivation, e.g. if he is elected diocesan

---

[1] Cf. Farrelly *The Diocesan Finance Council: Functions and Duties According to the Code of Canon Law* Stud Can 23(1989) 149–166.

Administrator during the vacancy of the see, he must relinquish the office of financial administrator, and the finance committee must elect a temporary replacement (see Can. 423 §2).

As an administrator, the task is not to make policy decisions – a function which belongs to the Bishop with the finance committee – but to carry out the policy they have established, to make payments in accordance with the budget policy, and administer the funds on a day-to-day basis. It is the administrator's responsibility to ensure that proper accounts are kept and laid before the committee at the end of the financial year. Civil legislation may also lay down guidelines which must be followed. The basic responsibility of the administrator is to manage the diocesan funds in accordance with canon law. In addition to the functions given him by universal law, the Code permits the Bishop to entrust certain other functions to the administrator (see Can. 1278).

Chapter III
THE COUNCIL OF PRIESTS AND THE COLLEGE OF CONSULTORS

Can. 495 §1 In each diocese there is to be established a council of priests, that is, a group of priests who represent the *presbyterium* and who are to be, as it were, the Bishop's senate. The council's role is to assist the Bishop, in accordance with the law, in the governance of the diocese, so that the pastoral welfare of that portion of the people of God entrusted to the Bishop may be most effectively promoted.

Vat. II recognised the need for Bishops to listen to the views of their presbyterate and to consult them about matters that concern the needs of the pastoral work and the good of the diocese.[1] The text of this and the following canons is derived from the postconciliar legislation that sought to give effect to this wish.[2] The law requires the establishment of a Council of priests in every diocese. This council is to represent all the members of the *presbyterium* of the diocese. Therefore, its membership is restricted to priests alone, i.e. it cannot include deacons or lay-people.[3] It is described as the 'senate of the Bishop', a title reserved to the cathedral chapter by c.391 §1 of the 1917 Code. Its function is to assist the Bishop in governing the whole diocese: it does this by encouraging unity among the priests in the diocese and by providing helpful advice and information to the Bishop when requested to do so by the Bishop or when required to do so by the law (see Cann. 461 §1, 1215 §2, 1222 §2 etc.).

Can. 495 §2 In vicariates and prefectures apostolic, the Vicar or Prefect is to appoint a council composed of at least three missionary priests, whose opinion, even by letter, he is to hear in the more serious affairs.

Vicars and Prefects apostolic are not obliged to have a council of priests. Instead they must have a smaller council of at least three priests. The Vicar or Prefect is required

---
[1] Cf. PO 7: Fl I 876.
[2] Cf. ESI 15–17: Fl I 600–602; SCC lit circ *De Consiliis Presbyteralibus* 11.IV.1970: AAS 62(1970) 459–465.
[3] Cf. Comm 13(1981) 129 at Can. 309 §2.

to seek their advice when more serious matters arise in the particular Church. They may be consulted even by post instead of personally when the circumstances so warrant.

Can. 496 The council of priests is to have its own statutes. These are to be approved by the diocesan Bishop, having taken account of the norms laid down by the Bishops' Conference.

990 In order to ensure its proper functioning and to maintain the correct relationship with the diocesan Bishop, the council of priests is obliged to draw up its own statutes. These do not have force until they are approved by the Bishop. In preparing these particular norms, each council of priests is to take account of the norms issued by the Bishop's Conference: thus a degree of uniformity will be found throughout the individual dioceses of a country or region.

Can. 497 As far as the designation of the members of the council of priests is concerned:

   1° about half are to be freely elected by the priests themselves in accordance with the canons which follow and with the statutes;

   2° some priests must, in accordance with the statutes, be members ex officio, that is belong to the council by reason of the office they hold;

   3° the diocesan Bishop may freely appoint some others.

991 Among the principal functions of the statutes of the council of priests is to provide norms for the size and membership of the council. According to the Code, there are three categories of members:

   – those freely elected by the priests (see Can. 498); the statutes must determine the method of election (see Can. 499);

   – those who, by virtue of their office, are automatically members; these *ex officio* members must be listed in the statutes;

   – those freely appointed by the Bishop.

Of the total membership, 'about half' is to be elected: in this way, the council can be seen to function as a body able to provide independent advice and assistance to the Bishop.

Can. 498 §1 The following have the right to both an active and a passive voice in an election to the council of priests:

   1° all secular priests incardinated in the diocese;

   2° priests who are living in the diocese and exercise any office for the benefit of the diocese, whether they be secular priests not incardinated in the diocese, or priest members of religious institutes or of societies of apostolic life.

§2 In so far as the statutes so provide, the same right of election may be given to other priests who have a domicile or quasi-domicile in the diocese.

992 By virtue of this canon, all those who have a right to vote in elections for the council of priests are also eligible for election. The Code distinguishes between those who have this right by virtue of universal law, and those who do not, but may have it conferred upon them by the statutes of the council. All secular priests incardinated in

the diocese have the right, regardless of whether they are living in the diocese or elsewhere, both to vote and to be elected. The second category, i.e. priests of another diocese or priests of a religious institute or society of apostolic life, earns its right to take part in the election by virtue of exercising some office for the good of the diocese, and provided that they live within the diocese. The office in question might be exercised outside the diocese, but for its good, e.g. representing the diocese on some national body. However, such a priest who exercises an office within the diocese does not gain the right to participate in the election if he resides outside the diocese (§1). The statutes of the council could, but are not obliged to, grant the right to active and passive voice to other priests who live within the diocese, e.g. priests from another diocese who are living in retirement (§2).

Can. 499 The manner of electing the members of the council of priests is to be determined by the statutes, and in such a way that as far as possible the priests of the *presbyterium* are represented, with special regard to the diversity of ministries and to the various regions of the diocese.

If it is to fulfil its function as the Bishop's senate, the council of priests is to count among its members the widest possible representation of the diocesan *presbyterium*. Thus, care should be taken to ensure the participation of priests from every age-group, from the major priestly ministries within the diocese e.g. parochial ministry, education including seminary education and formation, youth work, on-going spiritual formation of priests etc., and from each of the major territorial divisions within the diocese, e.g. the deaneries.

Can. 500 §1 It is the prerogative of the diocesan Bishop to convene the council of priests, to preside over it, and to determine the matters to be discussed in it or to accept items proposed by the members.

§2 The council of priests has only a consultative vote. The diocesan Bishop is to consult it in matters of more serious moment, but he requires its consent only in the cases expressly defined in the law.

§3 The council of priests can never act without the diocesan Bishop. He alone can make public those things which have been decided in accordance with §2.

The council of priests cannot act apart from the Bishop, and it is he who is to decide the agenda of its meetings, whether on his own initiative or at the suggestion of the members. It is also his right to preside at these meetings, either personally or through a delegate (whether a member of the council or not); some Bishops have adopted the often-helpful practice of simply attending the meetings but not presiding.

The council of priests is of its very nature a consultative body: as such, it has no decision-making authority. The canon does, however, foresee the possibility that, by way of exception, the law might require the Bishop to seek the *consent* of the council of priests before acting. At present there are no situations in the general law where the Bishop is required to secure this consent.[1] On pain of acting invalidly however

---

[1] The possibility of the diocesan Bishop giving a deliberative vote to his council of priests was discussed by the Revision Commission and rejected (Comm 13(1981) 131–133 at Can. 314; Comm 14(1982) 217 at Can. 420). However, since the text of the canon speaks only of 'the cases expressly defined in *the law*', making no reference to whether the law in question is universal only or also particular, the possibility would appear to remain that, in given circumstances, the Bishop might voluntarily bind himself to seeking the *consent* of his council of priests.

(see Can. 127 §2), he is obliged to *consult* the council in each of those circumstances thus prescribed in the Code.

Can. 501 §1 The members of the council of priests are to be designated for a period specified in the statutes, subject however to the condition that over a five year period the council is renewed in whole or in part.

996 The term of office of the council of priests is left to the discretion of the statutes. The law requires that membership of the council must be renewed, in whole or in part, over a five-year period, but the council itself does not have a five-year life span. This renewal may be achieved by having phased elections. This provision strikes a balance between a necessary continuity and a helpful freshness in the advice and assistance given by the council.

Can. 501 §2 When the see is vacant, the council of priests lapses and its functions are fulfilled by the college of consultors. The Bishop must reconstitute the council of priests within a year of taking possession.

997 Because the council is an expression of the *presbyterium* of which the Bishop is an integral part and functions as the Bishop's senate, it is not appropriate for it to continue in existence when there is no diocesan Bishop. Moreover, no changes can be made during the vacancy of the see (see Can. 428 §1), and so the matters which the council might be discussing must be left until the new Bishop arrives. This provision does not apply to the missionary council mentioned in Can. 495 §2 (see Can. 502 §4).

Can. 501 §3 If the council of priests does not fulfil the office entrusted to it for the welfare of the diocese, or if it gravely abuses that office, it can be dissolved by the diocesan Bishop, after consultation with the Metropolitan; in the case of a metropolitan see, the Bishop must first consult with the suffragan Bishop who is senior by promotion. Within a year, however, the diocesan Bishop must reconstitute the council.

998 The Bishop may suppress the council of priests only if either of two conditions is fulfilled: either the council must have neglected its duty of service to the well-being of the diocese, or it must have positively abused its position, e.g. by interfering in matters which are not its concern or discussing matters the Bishop has not allowed to be placed on the agenda. Before taking this step, the Bishop must first consult his Metropolitan (or, respectively, the senior suffragan). He must then issue a duly notarised decree, indicating the reasons in at least summary form (see Can. 51). The significance of the council in the life of a diocese is underlined by the requirements that a new council be appointed within a year of the dissolution of its predecessor. It is obviously the mind of the law that this kind of situation would rarely, if ever, occur.

Can. 502 §1 From among the members of the council of priests, the diocesan Bishop freely appoints not fewer than six and not more than twelve priests, who are for five years to constitute the college of consultors. To it belong the functions determined by law; on the expiry of the five year period, however, it continues to exercise its functions until the new college is constituted.

999 It is for the Bishop to designate the members of the college of consultors, a necessary institution in every diocese. His choice is limited to those priests who are members of the council of priests. The term of office of each is for five years. Should a period of time elapse after the end of this without the Bishop having made the required new appointments, the term of office of the college is prorogued by the law itself.

Although membership of the council of priests is the *criterion for appointment*, if membership of that body is lost, e.g. by the setting up of a new council of priests, those appointed continue to serve out their five-year term as consultors.[1] If a consultor leaves office, for whatever reason, prior to the expiry of his five-year term, the Bishop may, but need not, replace him; he is obliged to replace him only if the number would fall below the minimum level of six.[2] The replacement shall complete only the unexpired term; it is the college, not necessarily its individual members, whose term is five years.

There are certain matters concerning which the diocesan Bishop is obliged to *consult* the college of consultors, others concerning which he is obliged to have the *consent* of the college before he may act. These are stated in their respective contexts throughout the Code. These obligations have serious consequences, which must be understood in the light of the clear prescriptions of Can. 127.[3]

Can. 502 §2 The diocesan Bishop presides over the college of consultors. If, however, the see is impeded or vacant, that person presides who in the interim takes the Bishop's place or, if he has not yet been appointed, then the priest in the college of consultors who is senior by ordination.

The college of consultors is a diocesan body whose role is to assist in the governance of the diocese. As such, its president is the diocesan Bishop. If the see is impeded or vacant, the college is presided over by the one taking the Bishop's place in accordance with Cann. 413, 419 and 421. Until the appointment of an interim administrator, the senior among the consultors presides at their meetings.

When the see is vacant, additional duties devolve upon the college of consultors; unless there is an auxiliary Bishop, the senior member of the college by ordination must convoke the college to elect a diocesan Administrator (see Can. 419), until which time he enjoys the power of Vicar general (see Can. 426); within eight days, the college must meet to elect the Administrator (on pain of forfeiting its right: see Can. 421); when elected, he must make his profession of faith in the presence of the college (see Can. 833 4°); the consultors also take on the role otherwise exercised by the council of priests (see Can. 501 §2).

Can. 502 §3 The Bishops' Conference can determine that the functions of the college of consultors be entrusted to the cathedral chapter.

The universal law permits each Bishops' Conference to entrust the functions of the college of consultors to the cathedral chapter. In some countries, the Conference has left this choice to the discretion of the diocesan Bishop, while in others it has been ruled out as unnecessary.[4]

Can. 502 §4 Unless the law provides otherwise, in a vicariate or prefecture apostolic the functions of the college of consultors belong to the council of the mission mentioned in Can. 495 §2.

In apostolic vicariates and prefectures the same body which fulfils the role of the council of priests also carries out the function of the consultors, namely the council of

---

[1] Cf. CCom rep 26.VI.1984: AAS 76(1984) 747.

[2] Cf. ibid: loc cit.

[3] It is to be noted that, during the vacancy of a diocesan see, there are additional situations in which the diocesan Administrator – precisely because of the transitory nature of his office – is required, before acting, to have the consent of the college of consultors, e.g. Cann. 272, 485, 1018 §1 2°.

[4] Cf. LCE Tavola per Paesi e Canoni at Can. 502.

at least three priests mentioned in Can. 495 §2 – subject to the possibility of particular local law making another appropriate regulation.

Chapter IV
THE CHAPTER OF CANONS

Can. 503 A chapter of canons, whether cathedral or collegiate, is a college of priests, whose role is to celebrate the more solemn liturgical functions in the cathedral or the collegiate church. It is for the cathedral chapter, besides, to fulfil those roles entrusted to it by law or by the diocesan Bishop.

1005 This canon introduces a major change into the legislation concerning chapters of canons, particularly in respect of cathedral chapters. Under the 1917 Code (c. 391 §1) every cathedral chapter had two main functions: (a) to participate in the more solemn liturgical worship of the cathedral; (b) to assist the diocesan Bishop as 'his senate and counsel' (*senatus et consilium*) – with the corollary of supplying a limited measure of authority when the diocesan see might become vacant: in effect, taking over immediately and, within eight days, electing a Vicar-Capitular who would govern the diocese during the interregnum. This current canon has *specifically limited* such a chapter's function to the former of its two functions, namely 'to celebrate the more solemn liturgical functions in the cathedral...'. Its second function under the 1917 Code has effectively been transferred to the council of priests (see Can. 495 §1), a selected number of whose members – to be known as the 'college of consultors' (see Can. 421 §1) – will henceforth supply the limited measure of authority when the see becomes vacant; the only exception to this latter regulation will occur when the faculty granted in Can. 502 §3 has been invoked by the Bishops' Conference.

Can. 504 The establishment, alteration or suppression of a cathedral chapter is reserved to the Apostolic See.

1006 This reservation to the Holy See arises from the fact that all such decrees of erection in recent centuries have been granted by the Holy See, and cannot therefore be changed by a lower legislator. The reservation refers only to cathedral chapters, not to chapters of collegiate churches: these may be established, altered and suppressed by the diocesan Bishop. As a public juridical person, a chapter is in principle perpetual (see Can. 120).

Can. 505 Every chapter, whether cathedral or collegiate, is to have its own statutes, established by lawful capitular act and approved by the diocesan Bishop. These statutes are not to be changed or abrogated except with the approval of the diocesan Bishop.

1007 It is solely for the chapter to enact its own statutes, although these and any changes in them require the Bishop's approval. The statutes are not established on the authority of the Bishop as diocesan legislation, but by the authority of the chapter itself as a public juridical person. The Bishop does, however, have the authority to dispense from them in appropriate circumstances in accordance with the norms governing dispensations (see Can. 85ff).

Can. 506 §1 The statutes of a chapter, while preserving always the laws of the foundation, are to determine the nature of the chapter and the number

of canons. They are to define what the chapter and the individual canons are to do in carrying out divine worship and their ministry. They are to decide the meetings at which chapter business is conducted and, while observing the provisions of the universal law, they are to prescribe the conditions required for the validity and for the lawfulness of the proceedings.

§2 In the statutes the remuneration is also to be defined, both the fixed salary and the amounts to be paid on the occasion of discharging the office; so too, having taken account of the norms laid down by the Holy See, the insignia of the canons.

The statutes of a chapter are to contain norms which regulate or determine the following:
- the nature and structure of the chapter i.e. whether it is a cathedral chapter or a collegiate chapter;
- the number of canons in the chapter;
- the role of the chapter as a body and of the individual canons in what pertains to their participation in divine worship and their ministry in the Church;
- the frequency and manner of chapter meetings as well as what is required for valid and lawful proceedings;
- the remuneration, if any, to be given to the individual canons;
- the insignia to be won by the members of the chapter in the discharge of their liturgical functions.[1]

Can. 507 §1 Among the canons there is to be one who presides over the chapter. In accordance with the statutes other offices are also to be established, account having been taken of the practice prevailing in the region.

§2 Other offices may be allotted to clerics not belonging to the chapter, so that, in accordance with the statutes, they may provide assistance to the canons.

In addition to those matters dealt with in Can. 506, the statutes of the chapter must determine the particular offices to be carried out by members of the chapter, e.g. Secretary, Treasurer, etc. Where necessary, the statutes may assign other offices to be fulfilled by clerics who are not members of the chapter. The only office mentioned in this canon and required by law is that of the one who presides over the chapter (§1): traditionally, he is referred to as the 'provost' or the 'dean'. He is appointed in accordance with Can. 509 §1. The other offices are to be conferred according to the statutes.

Can. 508 §1 The canon penitentiary both of a cathedral church and of a collegiate church has by law ordinary faculties, which he cannot however delegate to others, to absolve in the sacramental forum from *latae sententiae* censures which have not been declared and are not reserved to the Apostolic See. Within the diocese he can absolve not only diocesans but outsiders also, whereas he can absolve diocesans even outside the diocese.

---

[1] Cf. SCC lit circ 30.X.1970: CLD 7 382–383; SCC lit circ 18.III.1987: AAS 79(1987) 603–604.

§2 Where there is no chapter, the diocesan Bishop is to appoint a priest to fulfil this office.

1010 One of the most important roles entrusted to a member of the chapter is that of penitentiary. He is the canon who, by virtue of his office, can absolve from many ecclesiastical penalties without the need for recourse to higher authority. So important is this role in the life of the particular Church that the Bishop is obliged to appoint some priest as penitentiary if there is no chapter in the diocese. The function of the canon penitentiary is clearly defined: he has the *ordinary* faculty of absolving from *latae sententiae* censures (see Cann. 1331–1335) which have not been declared by administrative decree or judicial sentence (see Cann. 1341–1342) and which are not reserved to the Holy See (e.g. Cann. 1367; 1370 §1; 1378 §1; 1382; 1388 §1). Therefore he cannot absolve any *ferendae sententiae* penalties or expiatory penalties (see Cann. 1336–1338). He cannot delegate this faculty to anyone else. He can exercise this faculty *only* within the internal sacramental forum. Within the territory of the diocese he may absolve those who have a domicile or quasi-domicile (see Can. 102 §§1–2) in the diocese, as well as anyone else who happens to be in the diocese; outside of the diocese, he may absolve *only* those who have a domicile or quasi-domicile in the diocese.

Can. 509 §1 It belongs to the diocesan Bishop, after consultation with the chapter, but not to the diocesan Administrator, to bestow each and every canonry both in the cathedral church and in a collegiate church; any privilege to the contrary is revoked. It is also for the diocesan Bishop to confirm the person elected by the chapter to preside over it.

§2 The diocesan Bishop is to appoint to canonries only priests who are of sound doctrine and life and who have exercised a praiseworthy ministry.

1011 The law gives the Bishop the right of appointment to all vacancies both in cathedral and in collegiate chapters, without exception. This follows Vat. II's wish that all restrictions upon Bishops concerning this matter should be abolished.[1] The Code permits the chapter to elect its president or dean, but his election requires the confirmation of the Bishop (see Can. 179).

1012 Only priests can be appointed canons, although the offices mentioned in Can. 507 §2 could be conferred on deacons. The Code clearly envisages that ordinarily only men of mature years will be appointed as canons.

Can. 510 §1 Parishes are no longer to be united with chapters of canons. Those which are united to a chapter are to be separated from it by the diocesan Bishop.

§2 In a church which is at the same time a parochial and a capitular church, a parish priest is to be appointed, whether chosen from the chapter or not. He is bound by all the obligations and he enjoys all the rights and faculties which by law belong to a parish priest.

---

[1] Cf. ES 18 §1: Fl I 602. The only restriction – if it can be called such – placed by the canon is that an appointment to the chapter should be preceded by 'consultation with the chapter'. In view of the tenor of the papal document cited in this note, it would appear that the diocesan Bishop may himself determine the manner of consultation: whether e.g. with the entire chapter as a body or with a representative number of its members, whether for each individual appointment or rather only on occasion to determine or to vary a principle according to which such appointments shall be made, etc.

§3 The diocesan Bishop is to establish certain norms whereby the pastoral duties of the parish priest and the roles proper to the chapter are duly harmonised, so that the parish priest is not a hindrance to capitular functions, nor the chapter to those of the parish. Any conflicts which may arise are to be settled by the diocesan Bishop, who is to ensure above all that the pastoral needs of the faithful are suitably provided for.

§4 Alms given to a church which is at the same time a parochial and a capitular church, are presumed to be given to the parish, unless it is established otherwise.

The Code lays down the very clear principle that one priest must have personal responsibility for the pastoral care of a parish (see Can. 515 §1), even if it is the cathedral parish or a parish attached to a collegiate Church. In the past, it was not unusual, especially perhaps in continental Europe, to have parishes 'united with' – in effect, run and administered by – a chapter of canons. The current Code rules against any such arrangement for the future; accordingly, where this has been the case hitherto, the diocesan Bishop is specifically required to ensure the separation of all parishes from their administration by a chapter of canons (§1). The principal means of implementing this is to appoint a parish priest (§2). He may be a member of the chapter or any other priest working in the diocese: the choice rests solely with the Bishop. That parish priest has all the rights and obligations of other parish priests (see Cann. 528–535); there can be no question of the chapter exercising a supervisory role. It is for the diocesan Bishop to lay down appropriate norms to regulate the mutual use of the church building and facilities, and to avoid friction (§3). The Code makes it clear that any alms received are *presumed* to be given for the benefit of the parish; this presumption is reversed *only* if it becomes certain, from authentic documents or other such statements, that the specific intention of the donor was to benefit *solely* the capitular Church.

1013

Chapter V
THE PASTORAL COUNCIL

Can. 511 In each diocese, in so far as pastoral circumstances suggest, a pastoral council is to be established. Its function, under the authority of the Bishop, is to study and weigh those matters which concern the pastoral works in the diocese, and to propose practical conclusions concerning them.

Among the consultative bodies recommended by Vat. II to assist the Bishop in his role as pastor is the diocesan pastoral council.[1] If, in the judgement of the diocesan Bishop – 'in so far as pastoral circumstances suggest' – he is required to establish such a body. The Bishop's obligation is therefore made dependent upon his estimate of the pastoral circumstances of his own diocese – a condition which will obviously vary from diocese to diocese even within a given Bishops' Conference. It is understood of course that the sole concern of Vat. II is positively to make available to each diocese such legal structures – the pastoral council is clearly a new entity – as may be helpful to the People of God in their pilgrim journey. This council's role is purely consultative (see Can. 514 §1) and its attention is directed towards any matters

1014

---

[1] Cf. CD 27: Fl I 580.

concerning pastoral works in the diocese. After studying these under the authority of the Bishop, the council may propose *practical* conclusions. The Bishop is not obliged to consult the pastoral council, still less is he bound to abide by its conclusions; nevertheless, a prudent Bishop will attentatively listen to and seriously consider proposals made by the council.

Can. 512 §1 A pastoral council is composed of members of Christ's faithful who are in full communion with the catholic Church: clerics, members of institutes of consecrated life, and especially lay people. They are designated in the manner determined by the diocesan Bishop.

§2 The members of Christ's faithful assigned to the pastoral council are to be selected in such a way that the council truly reflects the entire portion of the people of God which constitutes the diocese, taking account of the different regions of the diocese, of social conditions and professions, and of the part played in the apostolate by the members, whether individually or in association with others.

§3 Only those members of Christ's faithful who are outstanding in firm faith, high moral standards and prudence are to be assigned to the pastoral council.

1015 The diocesan pastoral council is an expression of the multi-faceted life of a particular Church. Its membership is to be drawn from all categories of Christ's faithful who are in full communion with the catholic Church; this includes clergy, members of institutes of consecrated life and *especially* lay people. While the manner of selecting the members of the pastoral council is left to the Bishop, the criteria of §3 are to be noted. Membership of the diocesan pastoral council involves a serious responsibility towards the life of the diocese. Although not to be understood as representatives of particular 'constituencies', the members of the diocesan pastoral council are to reflect the various geographical regions of the diocese, as well as the different social groups, professions and apostolates in the diocese. Out of this richness and diversity, truly valuable advice can be given to the Bishop.

Can. 513 §1 The pastoral council is appointed for a determinate period, in accordance with the provisions of the statutes drawn up by the Bishop.

§2 When the see is vacant, the pastoral council lapses.

1016 The membership of the pastoral council is designated for a determined period. During a vacancy in the See, the membership lapses. There is no obligation on the new Bishop to reconstitute the pastoral council. It is the responsibility of the Bishop, not of the pastoral council itself, to draw up the statutes. These must contain norms for the appointment of members.

1017 The Council does not enjoy juridical personality unless specifically given this by the Bishop (see Can. 114 §1). It must be brought into existence by a properly drawn up decree signed by the Bishop, and duly notarised (see Cann. 51, 474). Likewise appointment as a member is an official act by the Bishop, and must be made in writing (see Can. 156), duly notarised (see Can. 474).

Can. 514 §1 The pastoral council has only a consultative vote. It is for the diocesan Bishop alone to convene it, according to the needs of the apostolate, and to preside over it. He alone has the right to make public the matters dealt with in the council.

§2 It is to be convened at least once a year.

The role of the council is to give the Bishop practical advice relating to pastoral work. As already stated, its vote is purely consultative, and there are no matters in law which must be referred to it. If it has been established in a diocese, it must be convened in a plenary session at least once a year; the frequency of other meetings is to be indicated in the statutes. The fact that the Bishop must preside does not preclude the appointment of a chairperson to conduct the meeting. Subsidiary committees do not need to be convened by the Bishop: details of this sort must be determined in the statutes, which ought also to indicate the kind of confidentiality to be observed, the appropriate way in which different kinds of documents or decisions may be made public, etc.

Chapter VI
PARISHES, PARISH PRIESTS AND ASSISTANT PRIESTS

Can. 515 §1 A parish is a certain community of Christ's faithful stably established within a particular Church, whose pastoral care, under the authority of the diocesan Bishop, is entrusted to a parish priest as its proper pastor.

Vat. II shifted the overall juridical emphasis from the previous purely territorial basis of a parish *to the people who constitute the parish community*, especially centred around the Eucharist[1] – thus more accurately reflecting the variety of local situations throughout the universal church and, at the same time, enabling the law to cater, as occasion may demand, in a practical and pastoral manner for this variety. A parish exists within the wider community of the particular Church under the authority of the Bishop.

The Bishop is the proper pastor of the diocese as a whole (see Cann. 369–370); the parish priest is the proper pastor of the parish, but under the authority of the Bishop. The Code, by using the term 'pastor', makes reference to the theological link between the ministry of the priest and that of the Bishop, as one of participation (see Can. 519). The parish priest assists the Bishop in caring for these people, and is answerable to him. However, he is not simply the Bishop's delegate; having been appointed by him, the parish priest enjoys ordinary authority within the parish.

Can. 515 §2 The diocesan Bishop alone can establish, suppress or alter parishes. He is not to establish, suppress or notably alter them unless he has consulted the council of priests.

The establishment of new parishes, the suppression or alteration of existing parishes belong exclusively to the diocesan Bishop: no other local Ordinary, e.g. a Vicar general, has the authority to make any changes to the parish structure within a particular Church. For the Bishop, the principal criterion for any such modification is the salvation of souls.[2] However, before acting, the law obliges the Bishop to consult the council of priests. Any such action taken without its advice would be invalid (see Can. 127 §2 2°).

Can. 515 §3 A lawfully established parish has juridical personality by virtue of the law itself.

---

[1] Cf. SC 42: Fl I 15; CD 29–30: Fl I 580–582.
[2] Cf. CD 32: Fl I 583; ES I 21 3: Fl I 604.

1022 By virtue of the law, any parish which has been established according to law enjoys automatic juridical personality. Consequently, it may acquire, administer and alienate property in its own name. As a juridical person, the term 'parish' refers solely to the juridical entity created by the decree of the Bishop; it does not refer to the totality of the people living in the parish. The sole juridical representative of the parish is the parish priest (see Can. 532).

Can. 516 §1 Unless the law provides otherwise, a quasi-parish is equivalent to a parish. A quasi-parish is a certain community of Christ's faithful within a particular Church, entrusted to a priest as its proper pastor, but because of special circumstances not yet established as a parish.

§2 Where some communities cannot be established as parishes or quasi-parishes, the diocesan Bishop is to provide for their spiritual care in some other way.

1023 The term 'quasi-parish' is used to describe a community which in most respects is a parish, but for some specific reason cannot yet formally be erected as one, regardless of its location. Juridically, it is regarded as equivalent to a lawfully established parish (see Can. 515 §3).

1024 In some instances not even a quasi-parish is the appropriate means of providing for particular communities (§2). What the Code has in mind would seem to be groups within a particular church, e.g. the sick and the staff in a hospital community, the staff and travellers at a major airport, seamen in a port, members of distinct ethnic or linguistic groups, etc. all of whom have clearly identifiable needs which however cannot adequately be met by the formal distribution of tasks within a parish. It is the Bishop's duty to provide for the spiritual welfare of these people.

Can. 517 §1 Where circumstances so require, the pastoral care of a parish, or of a number of parishes together, can be entrusted to several priests jointly, but with the stipulation that one of the priests is to be the moderator of the pastoral care to be exercised. This moderator is to direct the joint action and to be responsible for it to the Bishop.

1025 This canon proposes an entirely new concept, that of 'team-ministry'. It is obviously an attempt by the Code to provide for the growing problem of a shortage of priests in the Church: this provision would not have even been thought of when the 1917 Code was being framed! In itself, it is clearly a laudable endeavour. Being such a new concept, however, its operation and effects must be carefully thought out in pastoral practice. It has its manifest inherent problems, e.g. each of the priests assigned to such a ministry would appear to have the responsibility which would normally be that ultimately of a parish priest – yet there is to be a 'moderator of the pastoral care to be exercised', who is 'to direct the joint action' and, most importantly, is 'to be responsible for it to the Bishop' (Can. 517 §1); responsibilities are to be shared 'by common counsel' (Can. 543 §2) – yet it is only the moderator who formally 'takes possession' of the parish or parishes involved, while for the other priests 'the profession of faith lawfully made replaces the taking of possession' (Can. 542 3°); 'the faculty to assist at marriages, and all the faculties to dispense which are given to a parish priest by virtue of the law itself, belong to all' 'yet all of these faculties are to be exercised under the direction of the moderator' (Can. 543 §1). It is clear that there are delicate and sensitive canonical issues yet to be determined in this matter. Certain it is that no prudent Bishop would embark on the establishment of a 'team-ministry' without having first been clear on its canonical implications, and then having determined precisely how he intended such a ministry to operate in his diocese.

Can. 517 §2 If, because of a shortage of priests, the diocesan Bishop has judged that a deacon, or some other person who is not a priest, or a community of persons, should be entrusted with a share in the exercise of the pastoral care of a parish, he is to appoint some priest who, with the powers and faculties of a parish priest, will direct the pastoral care.

A very different way of coping with the pastoral problems arising from a shortage of priests is when a parish is entrusted to an individual, or to a group of persons who lack priestly orders, e.g. a deacon, catechist or religious community. The possibility of such participation arises from the basic fact of the sacrament of baptism (see Cann. 129 §2, 204 §1, 230). Those who are not priests cannot be entrusted with the full care of souls (see Can. 150). Some priest in the particular Church must be assigned to take care of those aspects which call for priestly orders, e.g. the parish priest of a neighbouring parish, the dean, or a diocesan official. The others may be given various liturgical and pastoral responsibilities within the parish. It is not uncommon to refer to such people as 'pastoral administrators' or 'parish ministers'. The law has made provision for Sunday celebrations in the absence of a priest (see Can. 1248 §2) during which those entrusted with their pastoral care may exercise their ministry. 1026

Can. 518 As a general rule, a parish is to be territorial, that is, it is to embrace all Christ's faithful of a given territory. Where it is useful, however, personal parishes are to be established, determined by reason of the rite, language or nationality of Christ's faithful of a certain territory, or on some other basis.

While keeping in mind the change of emphasis referred to under Can. 515 §1 above and the purpose of that change, this canon retains the *general rule* – from which, as occasion demands, exceptions may be made – that 'a parish is to be territorial, that is, it is to embrace all Christ's faithful of a given territory'. Thus, *all the faithful* living in that territory belong to that parish. Among the exceptions envisaged by Vat. II was the need, on occasion, to make special provision for those who belong to different rites and nationalities.[1] Where there are long-term established groups of immigrants, the setting up of personal parishes is to be encouraged, in preference to chaplaincies.[2] The same is to be said for members of Oriental rites who have no hierarch of their own, and are entrusted to the pastoral care of the local latin rite Bishop. Generally, membership of a personal parish is cumulative with that of a territorial parish, unless otherwise indicated in the decree of erection. 1027

Can. 519 The parish priest is the proper pastor of the parish entrusted to him. He exercises the pastoral care of the community entrusted to him under the authority of the diocesan Bishop, whose ministry of Christ he is called to share, so that for this community he may carry out the offices of teaching, sanctifying and ruling with the cooperation of other priests or deacons and with the assistance of lay members of Christ's faithful, in accordance with the law.

Taken by itself, this chapter of the Code does not give an adequate picture of the relationship between the parish priest and the community entrusted to him, since it concentrates on the rights and duties of the parish priest. These canons must be read in conjunction with Cann. 208–231 where the rights and responsibilities of the 1028

---

[1] Cf. CD 23: Fl I 577.
[2] Cf. mp *De Pastorali Migratorum Cura* 33 §1, 22.VIII.1969: CLD 7 207–208.

faithful are set out. The relationship is one of mutual support in building the community of the parish and drawing in those who are outside. Cooperation with deacons and other priests and collaboration with lay people are positive obligations.

1029 The parish priest is described as the 'proper pastor' and a sharer in the Bishop's ministry. Vat. II taught that 'all priests, whether diocesan or religious, share and exercise with the Bishop the one priesthood of Christ'.[1] The diocesan clergy have a common concern with the Bishop for the whole diocese. There must be unity of purpose and a bond of supernatural charity. The Bishop is proper pastor of the diocese as a whole, and has authority over the whole diocese, including the parishes that constitute it (see Cann. 391 §1; 394 §1). However, he exercises that pastoral role largely in an indirect manner, entrusting the people in parishes to a parish priest as their proper pastor. As such, the parish priest makes his own decisions but always in the spirit of the Bishop's concerns and policies.

Can. 520 §1 A juridical person may not be a parish priest. However, the diocesan Bishop, but not the diocesan Administrator, can, with the consent of the competent Superior, entrust a parish to a clerical religious institute or to a clerical society of apostolic life, even by establishing it in the church of the institute or society, subject however to the rule that one priest be the parish priest or, if the pastoral care is entrusted to several priests jointly, that there be a moderator as mentioned in Can. 517 §1.

§2 The entrustment of a parish, as in §1, may be either in perpetuity or for a specified time. In either case this is to be done by means of a written agreement made between the diocesan Bishop and the competent Superior of the institute or society. This agreement must expressly and accurately define, among other things, the work to be done, the persons to be assigned to it and the financial arrangements.

1030 This canon echoes the provision of Can. 510 forbidding the union of a parish to a chapter of canons. A single individual priest must be appointed as parish priest or moderator of joint pastoral action (see Can. 517 §1), even when the parish has been entrusted, in perpetuity or for a determined time, to a religious institute or a society of apostolic life. The practice of entrusting parishes to such institutes and societies has a long history. It is the sole prerogative of the diocesan Bishop to make such arrangements. During a vacancy in the diocese, the diocesan Administrator is expressly forbidden to undertake anything of the kind, a further illustration of the principle of no innovation (see Can. 428 §1).

1031 To avoid possible disagreements, it is essential that a detailed contract be made between the Bishop and appropriate Superior. This must set out the principles governing the ownership and administration of property; it should also contain norms governing the notice to be given and the arrangements to be made if a decision is taken by the institute or society to withdraw from the parish. The pastoral care of the parish and the use of the church for public worship remain under the authority of the Bishop, but are subject also to the supervision of the appropriate Superior (see Can. 678). However, the Bishop cannot interfere in the internal life of the community (see Can. 586).

Can. 521 §1 To be validly appointed a parish priest, one must be in the sacred order of priesthood.

§2 He is also to be outstanding in sound doctrine and uprightness of character, endowed with zeal for souls and other virtues, and possessed of

---

[1] CD 28: Fl I 580.

those qualities which by universal or particular law are required for the care of the parish in question.

§3 In order that one be appointed to the office of parish priest, his suitability must be clearly established, in a manner determined by the diocesan Bishop, even by examination.

The only requirement mentioned by the canon for the valid appointment of a parish priest is priestly ordination. Thus, a deacon cannot be appointed as parish priest; nor can the title be used by a deacon or lay person entrusted with pastoral care in accordance with Can. 517 §2. 1032

The other qualities listed demonstrate the significance of the role of parish priest in the life of the Church. Since he is to 'carry out the offices of teaching, sanctifying and ruling' (see Can. 519), he must have what is needed to be a teacher, a leader and a sanctifier. Particular law, e.g. norms of the Bishops' Conference, may add further qualities to be required, e.g. age or number of years as a priest. It is for the Bishop to decide the method by which the suitability of a candidate for the office of parish priest is assessed, e.g. he may set up a selection committee, or even on occasion specify an examination such as was required by c.459 §3 3° of the 1917 Code – though it is to be noted that any form of competitive examination is no longer permitted. 1033

Can. 522 It is necessary that a parish priest have the benefit of stability, and therefore he is to be appointed for an indeterminate period of time. The diocesan Bishop may appoint him for a specified period of time only if the Bishops' Conference has by decree allowed this.

In the light of Vat. II, the law bases the stability of the office of parish priest on the good of souls.[1] The erstwhile distinction found in c.454 §2 of the 1917 Code between irremovable and removable parish priests has been abolished. A parish priest is now appointed for an indefinite period rather than in perpetuity. A Bishop cannot move a priest to another parish or office unless the good of souls, necessity or the advantage of the Church demand it, and then only with his agreement, unless the procedure determined in Cann. 1740–1752 is adhered to. Although his appointment may be for an indefinite period, the parish priest must be left in the parish long enough to carry out his ministry effectively. 1034

A fixed term of office for a parish priest is possible but only when this has been decreed by the Bishops' Conference. In this regard, it is essential that diocesan Bishops act in strict accord with the precise terms laid down by the decree of their respective Bishops' Conferences, as approved by the Holy See. A study of this matter will reveal that some Bishops' Conferences, a distinct minority, have opted for a fixed term of parochial office as the norm. The vast majority have, rather, maintained the principle that appointment for 'an indeterminate period of time' must remain the norm, and accordingly that such appointments 'for a specified period of time' may be only by way of exception: a typical example, shared by the majority of Bishops' Conferences, is that of the Irish Bishops' Conference which permits a fixed term of office 'to cater for *special situations* which may *on occasion* call for an appointment other than for an indeterminate period of time'.[2] 1035

Can. 523 Without prejudice to Can. 682 §1 appointment to the office of parish priest belongs to the diocesan Bishop, who is free to confer it on

---

[1] CD 31: Fl I 583.

[2] Cf. LCE Tavola per Paesi e Canoni at Can. 522.

whomsoever he wishes, unless someone else has a right of presentation or election.

1036 The provision of the office of parish priest is governed by the norms laid down in Cann. 146–156, and must therefore be made in writing. A distinction can be made between the appointment to the office, which is restricted for validity to the diocesan Bishop, and the selection of the person to be appointed. In the case of a religious, or member of a society of apostolic life, the candidate for the office of parish priest is designated by the Superior and appointed by the Bishop, or the Bishop may suggest a candidate to the Superior and appoint him with the Superior's consent (see Can. 682 §1). Vat. II wished that the rights of others to present or nominate a parish priest be eliminated so that the Bishop would have a free hand.[1] However, the wording of the canon suggests that such rights and privileges continue in some places, perhaps as the result of historical circumstances or of a concordat between the Holy See and the respective civil authorities.

Can. 524 The diocesan Bishop is to confer a vacant parish on the one whom, after consideration of all the circumstances, he judges suitable for the parochial care of that parish, without any preference of persons. In order to assess suitability, he is to consult the Vicar forane, conduct suitable enquiries and, if it is appropriate, seek the view of some priests and lay members of Christ's faithful.

1037 The Bishop must appoint a parish priest to a vacant parish as soon as reasonably possible. He must not defer the appointment without grave cause (see Can. 151). In making provision for the vacancy, the Bishop is to avoid all prejudice and bias. The canon speaks of what is necessary before a judgement is made concerning a candidate's suitability.

1038 The Bishop is required to consult the Vicar forane (or 'dean') in whose vicariate (or 'deanery') the vacant parish is located; such a consultation is necessary if the appointment is to be valid (see Can. 127 §2 2°). Other enquiries about the candidate are encouraged, including seeking the opinion of some priests as well as lay members of the faithful.

Can. 525 When a see is vacant or impeded, it is for the diocesan Administrator or whoever governs the diocese in the interim:

    1° to institute priests lawfully presented for a parish or to confirm those lawfully elected to one;

    2° to appoint parish priests if the see has been vacant or impeded for a year.

1039 While a diocese is vacant (see Can. 416) or impeded (see Can. 412), no innovation is to take place (see Can. 428 §1). The appointment of someone to a stable office amounts to an innovation. Yet the pastoral care of the faithful must be provided for. So the diocesan Administrator or the one entrusted with the governance of a diocese in accordance with Can. 413 may proceed to institute as parish priests those who had been lawfully provided for the offices before the diocese became vacant or impeded. If the situation in the diocese remains unchanged for more than a year, then the diocesan Administrator, or the one who governs in accordance with Can. 413, can validly appoint and institute new parish priests.

---

[1] Cf. CD 31: Fl I 583.

Can. 526 §1 A parish priest is to have the parochial care of one parish only. However, because of a shortage of priests or other circumstances, the care of a number of neighbouring parishes can be entrusted to the one parish priest.

§2 In any one parish there is to be only one parish priest, or one moderator in accordance with Can. 517 §1; any contrary custom is reprobated and any contrary privilege revoked.

No parish priest may have charge of more than one parish. This rests on the principle that no one may hold two incompatible offices simultaneously (see Cann. 152, 533 §1). However, the canon does provide for an exception to this norm: the care of a number of contiguous parishes may be entrusted to a single parish priest if there is a shortage of priests or if other circumstances warrant it. In such a case, the ordinary pastoral care of such parishes might be given to a deacon, or to members of the laity or to a religious community in accordance with Can. 517 §2. But the duties of parish priests in respect of the faithful of all the parishes are given to the one priest appointed. 1040

Whatever internal arrangements might be made among a number of priests living and working in the same parish, the law requires – without exception – that *one* of them fulfils the role of parish priest or moderator (see Can. 517 §1). 1041

Can. 527 §1 One who is promoted to exercise the pastoral care of a parish obtains this care and is bound to exercise it from the moment he takes possession.

The institution of a new parish priest involves a number of elements: 1042

(a) the act of appointment by the Bishop (see Can. 524);

(b) the profession of faith before the local Ordinary or his delegate (see Can. 833 6°);

(c) the act of taking possession of his office.

It is with this last element that this canon is concerned. It lays down the clear principle that, whatever the preceding elements, a newly-appointed parish priest takes on the rights and obligations of that office *only* 'from the moment he takes possession' of his designated parish. The manner of this taking possession is determined in §2 of this canon – it can vary from place to place – but a not infrequent current assertion must be corrected, to the effect namely that the ceremony of 'taking possession', whatever form it may take, is no more than a ceremony: it is in fact *the sole event* which installs the incoming incumbent as the parish priest of that parish. The appointment by the diocesan Bishop becomes effective *only* on that occasion.

Can. 527 §2 The local Ordinary or a priest delegated by him puts the parish priest into possession, in accordance with the procedure approved by particular law or by lawful custom. For a just reason, however, the same Ordinary can dispense from this procedure, in which case the notification of the dispensation to the parish replaces the taking of possession.

The Code does not specify any procedure to be followed in taking possession; this is left to particular law and local custom. Because of the nature of the office, it is appropriate that the act of taking possession should be public, involving the participation of the faithful. It is for the local Ordinary i.e. the diocesan Bishop, the Vicar general, or a priest delegated by the Ordinary, to install the parish priest in office. Whatever form this takes in the local Church, the Code provides for the 1043 possibility of circumstances – to be determined by the local Ordinary – in which it would be reasonable to him to grant a dispensation from the normal procedure. Should this be the case (and it is clearly envisaged that this would be an exceptional situation), the grant of this dispensation – as publicly announced, e.g. at Mass on Sunday, by promulgation in a parish newsletter, etc. – would have precisely the same effect as the normally-prescribed manner of taking parochial possession.

Can. 527 §3 The local Ordinary is to determine the time within which the parish priest must take possession of the parish. If, in the absence of a lawful impediment, he has not taken possession within this time, the local Ordinary can declare the parish vacant.

1044   In making an appointment to a parish, the Bishop must determine a period of time within which the parish priest is to take possession of his office. Failure to take possession, or to obtain a dispensation, within that time means that the Bishop may act, declare the parish vacant and make an alternative provision for the parish.

Can. 528 §1 The parish priest has the obligation of ensuring that the word of God is proclaimed in its entirety to those living in the parish. He is therefore to see to it that the lay members of Christ's faithful are instructed in the truths of faith, especially by means of the homily on Sundays and holydays of obligation and by catechetical formation. He is to foster works which promote the spirit of the Gospel, including its relevance to social justice. He is to have a special care for the catholic education of children and young people. With the collaboration of Christ's faithful, he is to make every effort to bring the gospel message to those also who have given up religious practice or who do not profess the true faith.

1045   The parish priest exercises the role of teacher in his parish, with the primary obligation of ensuring that the word of God is preached in its entirety i.e. that the mystery of Christ is faithfully and fully presented (see Can. 760).

1046   The Gospel message must be brought to all those living in the parish, not simply to those who come to Mass or are otherwise involved in the life of the Church. There is a positive obligation for the parish priest to reach out to those who may appear to have given up the practice of their faith, and also to those who are not members of the Church. Special mention is made of the need to foster awareness of the Church's teaching on matters of social justice.

1047   Particular reference is made to the two forms of proclaiming God's word which he can carry out directly, i.e. preaching and catechesis (see Cann. 756–780). However, the parish priest is not expected to carry out these obligations by himself. He is to ensure that a homily is preached on all occasions foreseen by law (see Can. 767 §4). But he is to enlist the support of other clerics, religious and lay people for the work of catechesis (see Can. 776), and to encourage parents in their role as educators (see Can. 774). He also has a positive duty to facilitate the provision of catholic schools, and to ensure, so far as he can, that they are in fact available for all the people of the parish (see Can. 794 §2).

Can. 528 §2 The parish priest is to take care that the blessed Eucharist is the centre of the parish assembly of the faithful. He is to strive to ensure that Christ's faithful are nourished by the devout celebration of the sacraments, and in particular that they frequently approach the sacraments of the blessed Eucharist and penance. He is to strive to lead them to prayer,

including prayer in their families, and to take a live and active part in the sacred liturgy. Under the authority of the diocesan Bishop, the parish priest must direct this liturgy in his own parish, and he is bound to be on guard against abuses.

The parish priest carries out the office of *sanctifying* through his role as the leader of the liturgy and prayer in his parish. The celebration of the Eucharist is to be the *principal act of worship of the parish as a whole*, and of the individuals who constitute it (see Can. 899). However, he is to ensure that the centrality of the Eucharist in the life of the Church extends beyond the liturgical celebration into the worship of the Eucharist outside Mass (see Can. 934–944). The Eucharist must be reserved in every parish church, and every parish church must for that reason be open for prayer for at least some hours every day (see Can. 937). The faithful have a right to pray before the Blessed Sacrament, and this is to be denied them only for a grave reason. Exposition of the Blessed Sacrament is to be encouraged, and annually the longer and more solemn exposition, formerly called the 'Forty Hours' (see Cann. 941-942). He is encouraged to foster the frequent reception of Holy Communion, and of course himself to celebrate Mass daily, even if the congregation is small, or altogether absent (see Can. 904). 1048

The parish priest has a responsibility for the proper formation of the people so that they can participate in the liturgy in a living and active way. This touches not only liturgical catechesis but the shaping of the liturgical life of the parish. Ultimately, he is responsible for how the liturgy is celebrated in his parish, not only in the Church and by himself, but also by other priests or leaders, and in chapels, schools or other places where liturgy may be celebrated (other than the internal life of religious communities). 1049

Can. 529 §1 So that he may fulfil his office of pastor diligently, the parish priest is to strive to know the faithful entrusted to his care. He is therefore to visit their families, sharing especially in their cares, anxieties and sorrows, comforting them in the Lord. If in certain matters they are found wanting, he is prudently to correct them. He is to help the sick and especially the dying in great charity, solicitously restoring them with the sacraments and commending their souls to God. He is to be especially diligent in seeking out the poor, the suffering, the lonely, those who are exiled from their homeland, and those burdened with special difficulties. He is to strive also to ensure that spouses and parents are sustained in the fulfilment of their proper duties, and to foster the growth of christian life in the family.

§2 The parish priest is to recognise and promote the specific role which the lay members of Christ's faithful have in the mission of the Church, fostering their associations which have religious purposes. He is to cooperate with his proper Bishop and with the *presbyterium* of the diocese. Moreover, he is to endeavour to ensure that the faithful are concerned for the community of the parish, that they feel themselves to be members both of the diocese and of the universal Church, and that they take part in and sustain works which promote this community.

The parish priest must also exercise the office of *governance*. To be an effective pastor, the parish priest must know his flock. Experience has proved that this simply cannot be done without systematic and personal visitation; it may valuably be supplemented by visitation through assistant priests or by others, e.g. religious and lay people. In 1050 addition to systematic visitation, there is a special obligation to visit and comfort those who are bereaved or sick. The parish priest has a positive duty to seek out those in need, the suffering, poor, lonely, exiles and refugees. The Code exhorts the parish priest to seek out and assist those with special difficulties, e.g. the disabled, the infirm, the mentally ill, the housebound and aged, young people. Among his special duties is care and concern for the welfare of the Christian family.

1051 Particular mention is made of associations of lay people and their initiatives. Lay people do not require the parish priest's permission to hold meetings, form associations, or exercise an apostolate. This is their right flowing from baptism and guaranteed by the Code (see Cann. 211, 215, 216). The role of the parish priest is to encourage these and to coordinate them so that there is no friction and that effort is not wasted (see Can. 223). In governing his parish, the parish priest is obliged to work closely along with the Bishop and the others of the diocesan *presbyterium*. He is to do all he can to create and sustain an awareness among his parishioners that they belong to a true community, not just at local level in the parish, but also at diocesan level and the level of the universal Church.

Can. 530 The functions especially entrusted to the parish priest are as follows:

1° the administration of baptism;

2° the administration of the sacrament of confirmation to those in danger of death, in accordance with Can. 883 n.3;

3° the administration of Viaticum and of the anointing of the sick, without prejudice to Can. 1003 §§2 and 3, and the imparting of the apostolic blessing;

4° the assistance at marriages and the nuptial blessing;

5° the conducting of funerals;

6° the blessing of the baptismal font at paschal time, the conduct of processions outside the church, and the giving of solemn blessings outside the church;

7° the more solemn celebration of the Eucharist on Sundays and holydays of obligation.

1052 The functions listed in the canon are *not reserved* to the parish priest; they are 'especially entrusted' to him: in other words, it is he who has the major responsibility to ensure that they are fulfilled. This does not in any way preclude the possibility – so often the case in practice – that he would share the fulfilment of these functions with others involved in the parochial ministry, such as his assistant priests or other duly appointed ministers. Rectors of churches may not lawfully exercise any of the functions here mentioned without the consent or delegation of the parish priest (see Can. 558).

Can. 531 Even though another person has performed some parochial function, he is to give the offering he receives from Christ's faithful on that occasion to the parish fund unless, in respect of voluntary offerings, there is a clear contrary intention on the donor's part; it is for the diocesan Bishop, after consulting the council of priests, to prescribe regulations concerning the destination of these offerings and to provide for the remuneration of clerics who fulfil such a parochial function.

According to Can. 1264, it is for the Bishops of each ecclesiastical province to determine what offerings are to be made by the faithful on the occasion of the administration of the sacraments or sacramentals. Such offerings, where they exist, are not to be confused with the offerings made for the celebration of Mass (see Cann. 945-958), nor ought they be confused with personal gifts made by the faithful to an individual cleric. The offerings mentioned in this canon, often referred to as 'stole fees', must be paid into parish funds, whether the person performing the function belongs to the parish or not. These offerings are the property of the parish (see Can. 1267 §1), and not that of the parish priest as c.463 §3 of the 1917 Code had (subject to one exception) determined.

The diocesan Bishop, after consultation with the council of priests, must decide how these funds are to be administered and applied, as well as how non-parochial clergy who fulfil a parochial function are to be remunerated.

Can. 532 In all juridical matters, the parish priest acts in the person of the parish, in accordance with the law. He is to ensure that the parish goods are administered in accordance with Cann. 1281-1288.

The present concept of the parish is one of a community which forms a juridical person, and to whom the material goods of the parish belong. Can. 1279 §1 establishes the general principle that the one with the direct power of governance over the person to whom the goods belong is entrusted with their administration, with the assistance of a finance committee (see Can. 1280). Hence parish priests are bound by the obligations of Cann. 1281-1288 in the manner in which they administer parish property and funds.

The Code does indeed describe the parish as a community. Juridically, however, the members of that community cannot act in its name or on its behalf. This issue has been clarified by a judgement of the Signatura Apostolica,[1] and a response issued by the Commission for the Interpretation of the Code.[2]

Can. 533 §1 The parish priest is obliged to reside in the parochial house, near the church. In particular cases, however, where there is a just reason, the local Ordinary may permit him to reside elsewhere, especially in a house common to several priests, provided the carrying out of the parochial duties is properly and suitably catered for.

§2 Unless there is a grave reason to the contrary, the parish priest may each year be absent on holiday from his parish for a period not exceeding one month, continuous or otherwise. The days which the parish priest spends on the annual spiritual retreat are not reckoned in this period of vacation. For an absence from the parish of more than a week, however, the parish priest is bound to advise the local Ordinary.

§3 It is for the diocesan Bishop to establish norms by which, during the parish priest's absence, the care of the parish is provided for by a priest with the requisite faculties.

---

[1] Cf. Ap Sig 21.XI.1987, Prot N 17447/85 CA: Comm 20(1988) 88-94.
[2] Cf. CCom rep 29.IV.1987: AAS 80(1988) 1818.

1057 The parish priest is obliged to live within the parish, near the Church, and in the parochial house (§1). In consequence, there is an obligation on the parish to provide a suitable house for him to live in. Even if he has a house of his own or a family residence nearby, he may not live there without the Ordinary's permission. The Code acknowledges that there may have to be exceptions, due to particular local circumstances: it may not, e.g. be possible to acquire or to build a house within the parish boundary, in which case a house within a neighbouring parish may be the only realistic option. The canon expresses in this regard a certain preference for 'a house common to several priests': this could especially be the case where a number of priests, living in common, are commissioned to look after a number of parishes. But the canon in no way suggests that, even when it is possible to have the parochial house within the parish, the parish priest must live there alone; on the contrary, it is the established practice in many dioceses – not all – that the parish priest and his assistant priests occupy the same parochial house.

1058 The canon specifically mentions only two just reasons for a parish priest's temporary absence from his parochial house: an annual 'holiday not exceeding one month, continuous or otherwise'; the 'annual spiritual retreat', which is normally spent elsewhere than in the parish (§2). It makes no mention of absence by reason of illness, assigned study courses, or other such: these, clearly, must be made the subject of a special arrangement with the diocesan Bishop in each case. For absences of longer than one week, for whatever reasonable purpose, the parish priest does not require the permission of either the Bishop or other local Ordinary, but he is obliged to inform one or other, so that care may be taken to ensure the needs of the parish.

1059 In stating (§3) that 'it is for the diocesan Bishop to establish norms by which, during the parish priest's absence, the care of the parish is provided for by a priest with the requisite faculties', this does not necessarily mean that it is the Bishop's responsibility to provide a substitute priest in each individual case; frequently, this is a matter long determined by established diocesan custom and practice.[1]

Can. 534 §1 When he has taken possession of his parish, the parish priest is bound on each Sunday and holyday of obligation in his diocese to apply the Mass for the people entrusted to him. If he is lawfully impeded from this celebration, he is to have someone else apply the Mass on these days or apply it himself on other days.

§2 A parish priest who has the care of several parishes is bound to apply only one Mass on the days mentioned in §1, for all the people entrusted to him.

§3 A parish priest who has not discharged the obligation mentioned in §§1 and 2, is as soon as possible to apply for the people as many Masses as he has omitted.

1160 This canon applies to the parish priest as pastor; it is the same obligation which binds the diocesan Bishop in relation to the diocese as a whole (see Can. 388). The obligation to offer the Mass for the people binds the parish priest only after he has

---

[1] For the arrangements to be made in the case of longer-term absences, cf. Cann. 539, 541 §1, 549.

taken possession of the parish (see Can. 527). He must carry out this obligation *personally*; he may do so while in the parish or even outside it, e.g. on holidays. If, for a legitimate reason, he is unable to fulfil the obligation on a particular day, he must make sure either that another priest celebrates the Mass on that day or that he celebrate it himself on another day (§1). Each parish priest is required to celebrate only *one* Mass *pro populo*, even if he has the care of several parishes (§2). If, however, any of the Masses prescribed by §§1–2 has been omitted, inadvertently or otherwise, the parish priest is strictly bound to apply each and all 'as soon as possible' (§3).

Can. 535 §1 In each parish there are to be parochial registers, that is, of baptisms, of marriages and of deaths, and any other registers prescribed by the Bishops' Conference or by the diocesan Bishop. The parish priest is to ensure that entries are accurately made and that the registers are carefully preserved.

§2 In the register of baptisms, a note is to be made of confirmation and of matters pertaining to the canonical status of Christ's faithful by reason of marriage, without prejudice to the provision of Can. 1133, and by reason of adoption, the reception of sacred order, the making of perpetual profession in a religious institute, or a change of rite. These annotations are always to be reproduced on a baptismal certificate.

§3 Each parish is to have its own seal. Certificates concerning the canonical status of Christ's faithful, and all acts which can have juridical significance, are to be signed by the parish priest or his delegate and secured with the parochial seal.

§4 In each parish there is to be an archive, in which the parochial books are to be kept, together with episcopal letters and other documents which it may be necessary or useful to preserve. On the occasion of visitation or at some other opportune time, the diocesan Bishop or his delegate is to inspect all of these matters. The parish priest is to take care that they do not fall into unauthorised hands.

§5 Older parochial registers are also to be carefully safeguarded, in accordance with the provisions of particular law.

The canon requires every parish to have a register of baptisms, marriages and deaths. Among other books not mentioned – but which might be required by particular legislation of the Bishops' Conference or the diocesan Bishop – are registers of the reception of baptised Christians, or of First Communicants.[1] Elsewhere in the Code the following are also mentioned as books to be kept in the parish: the register of foundation Masses or other obligations (see Can. 1307 §2); the parish accounts (see Can. 1284 §2 7°); the register of catechumens (see Can. 788 §1). Other documents which must be kept include title deeds and similar documentation relating to temporal goods, insurance policies etc. (see Can. 1284 §2 9°); the dossier of papers collected as part of marriage preparation (see Cann. 1066–1070), etc. All of this

1061

---

[1] For an overall view of the matters involved here, cf. LCE Tavola per Paesi e Canoni at Cann. 535, 877, 895, 1053–1054.

Book II The People of God

emphasises the necessity that in each diocese, according to its needs, there be established a clear programme – worked out in detail and, in so far as necessary, with the help of canonical expertise – which will guide and assist the diocesan Bishop or his delegate on the occasion of the parochial visitation prescribed by Can. 396. A simple check-list would appear to meet the need.

1062   All matters concerning the status of a person must be entered on the baptismal register: e.g. the fact of adoption (unless there are special regulations for this); the reception of sacred orders; the making of perpetual profession in a religious institute; change of rite; defection from the faith by a formal act; marriage (see Can. 1122); a declaration of the nullity of a marriage; the dispensation from religious vows or from the obligations of sacred ordination. Any certificates issued – and this must be controlled by the parish priest or his authorised delegate – must produce these annotations in their entirety; there is a danger that, otherwise, the certificates might be used fraudulently, e.g. to attempt to establish freedom to marry, eligibility for sacred orders, etc.

1063   The Code is explicit on the need for and use of a parish seal. The purpose of this is to act as a security precaution to prevent the issuing of fraudulent documents. It follows that the parochial seal itself must be stored in a secure place, and that access to it must be controlled by the parish priest or his delegate.

1064   The last two paragraphs of the canon deal with the safe custody of registers and documents, those currently in use and those which are older. It is for the Bishop to provide detailed norms concerning the transfer of such documents and access to them.

Can. 536 §1 If, after consulting the council of priests, the diocesan Bishop considers it opportune, a pastoral council is to be established in each parish. In this council, which is presided over by the parish priest, Christ's faithful, together with those who by virtue of their office are engaged in pastoral care in the parish, give their help in fostering pastoral action.

§2 The pastoral council has only a consultative vote, and it is regulated by the norms laid down by the diocesan Bishop.

1065   The Code is quite clear that the faithful have the right and duty to do what they can to spread the message of salvation (see Can. 211), and to make known to their pastors their views on matters pertaining to the good of the Church (see Can. 212 §3). At the diocesan level, the faithful may exercise that right and fulfil their obligation through participation in the diocesan pastoral council (see Cann. 511–514). If the Bishop considers it opportune – and this is a matter exclusively for the diocesan Bishop to determine, after consultation with his council of priests – a *parish pastoral council* may also be established in each parish. This could provide an even more immediate opportunity for the faithful to fulfil their obligation and to exercise their right.

1066   The role of the pastoral council is to consider those matters concerning pastoral work in the parish, and to propose practical measures. It is obviously only a consultative body, but yet with a distinct brief to help the parish priest coordinate the different pastoral ventures which the clergy, religious and lay people of the parish are undertaking or proposing to undertake. The membership of any such parish pastoral council, and its manner of operation, is to be determined by the Bishop – again underlining the fact that it is the Bishop to whom is entrusted the overall pastoral care of the diocese (see Cann. 375, 381). It is clear that, in this context – as in so many others – the most sensitive care must be exercised to accommodate, and to develop a genuine ecclesial understanding of, on the one hand the indisputable authority of the diocesan Bishop and, on the other, the right of his flock to express their views precisely in order to assist him in fulfilling his apostolic office. This was very much the theme of Vat. II.

Can. 537 In each parish there is to be a finance committee to help the parish priest in the administration of the goods of the parish, without prejudice to Can. 532. It is ruled by the universal law and by the norms laid down by the diocesan Bishop, and it is comprised of members of Christ's faithful selected according to these norms.

The provision of this canon follows the general principle laid down in Can. 1280, requiring that every juridical person must have a finance committee. The existence of this committee does not detract from the parish priest's standing as the one who acts in the name of the parish (see Can. 532). However, such a committee provides the parish priest with valuable insight and advice, so that he may act more effectively in the interests of the parish. **1067**

The diocesan Bishop is to lay down norms for the appointment of the committee and the conduct of its affairs. The parish priest is to remember that he must consult his committee when the law so requires (see Can. 127 §2 2°); otherwise he may leave himself liable to an action for damages in canon law, even if his actions are valid in civil law (see Can. 1296). **1068**

Can. 538 §1 A parish priest ceases to hold office by removal or transfer effected by the diocesan Bishop in accordance with the law; by his personal resignation, for a just reason, which for validity requires that it be accepted by the diocesan Bishop; and by the lapse of time if, in accordance with the particular law mentioned in Can. 522, he was appointed for a specified period of time.

§2 A parish priest who is a member of a religious institute or is incardinated in a society of apostolic life, is removed in accordance with Can. 682 §2.

§3 A parish priest who has completed his seventy-fifth year of age is requested to offer his resignation from office to the diocesan Bishop who, after considering all the circumstances of person and place, is to decide whether to accept or defer it. Having taken account of the norms laid down by the Bishops' Conference, the diocesan Bishop must make provision for the appropriate maintenance and residence of the priest who has resigned.

When it comes to leaving the office of parish priest, the Code makes a clear distinction between religious and secular clergy. For religious, the Bishop and the Superior each have the right to remove a parish priest, provided prior notice has been given to the other; the consent of the other authority to this removal is not required (see Can. 682 §2). **1069**

For secular clergy, the following causes of cessation from the office of parish priest are (apart, obviously, from death) envisaged: removal, transfer, resignation, completion of term of office, retirement. In the case of enforced removal, the process prescribed by Cann. 1740–1747 must be followed. **1070**

The normal procedure of the transfer of a parish priest from one parish to another is accomplished by a discussion (orally or in writing) between the priest and his **1071** diocesan Bishop, and the normal outcome is the priest's acceptance of the Bishop's proposal, specific circumstances having been mutually agreed. Very rarely is this a matter of contention: when, exceptionally, it becomes such, the prescriptions of Cann. 1748–1752 are to be applied.

1072 An innovation in this Code (§3) is the *request* that parish priests who have completed their seventy-fifth year submit their resignation. The law *asks* them to do so; it does not *require* it. If the parish priest does not in fact offer his resignation, the Bishop has no automatic right to remove him, still less simply to declare him retired. If he feels it necessary, he must follow the procedure set down for the removal of a parish priest (see Cann. 1740–1747). Age by itself does not constitute an adequate cause for removal, particularly if the man's mental and physical health are up to the discharge of his duties. When the resignation of such a priest is accepted, the Bishop must provide for his pension and accommodation.

1073 The offer of the parish priest's resignation must be made to the Bishop of the diocese where he is ministering, not necessarily (though it will usually be) that of his incardination.[1] Once the resignation has been made, it is effective *only* if it is *accepted by the diocesan Bishop within three months* (see Can. 189 §3). Until the Bishop has accepted the resignation, it may be withdrawn by the parish priest, but not afterwards (see Can. 189 §4). The resignation must be submitted to the Bishop in writing or orally before two witnesses (see Can. 189 §1). The acceptance should also be given in writing. A parish priest who has been appointed for a fixed term, where particular law has permitted this (see Can. 522), ceases to hold office upon the expiry of that period (see Can. 184 §1). He is not required to submit a resignation, nor is any acceptance of this necessary: his office ceases *de iure*.

Can. 539 When a parish is vacant, or when the parish priest is prevented from exercising his pastoral office in the parish by reason of imprisonment, exile or banishment, or by reason of incapacity or ill health or some other cause, the diocesan Bishop is as soon as possible to appoint a parochial administrator, that is, a priest who will take the place of the parish priest in accordance with Can. 540.

1074 If the parish priest is unable to carry out his ministry, properly or at all, due to any of the reasons listed in the canon, or if the parish is actually vacant, the Bishop is required to provide for the parish. Vacancy is clearly a temporary thing, pending the appointment of a permanent successor; the other situations foreseen may be temporary or permanent, and the incapacity of the parish priest may be partial or complete. If a priest is permanently incapable of carrying out his functions, then, if he will not resign, steps must be taken for his removal or transfer. In the meantime, an administrator should be appointed. If the incapacity is partial, then an administrator is to be appointed to replace the parish priest until he is able to return to full duties or until a substitute is appointed definitively. An administrator may be appointed only by the diocesan Bishop.

Can. 540 §1 The parochial administrator is bound by the same obligations and has the same rights as a parish priest, unless the diocesan Bishop prescribes otherwise.

§2 The parochial administrator may not do anything which could prejudice the rights of the parish priest or could do harm to parochial property.

---

[1] Cf. Comm 14(1982) 227 at Can. 477.

§3 When he has discharged his office, the parochial administrator is to give an account to the parish priest.

Usually, when a case of this kind occurs, the administrator will be a temporary figure, pending the appointment of a new parish priest or until the existing priest is able to reassume his responsibilities. For this reason, the general principle applied to a diocese applies here too – no innovation while the office is vacant or impeded. Consequently, the parochial administrator, while he legally represents the parish in the meantime, may not take decisions which might prejudice the finances of the parish, nor make major innovations such as might prejudice the rights of a future parish priest or the existing one on his return. It is to the parish priest, rather than to the Bishop, that the administrator is to give an account of his stewardship.

Can. 541 §1 When a parish is vacant, or when the parish priest is impeded from exercising his pastoral office, pending the appointment of a parochial administrator the interim governance of the parish is to be undertaken by the assistant priest; if there are a number of assistants, by the senior by appointment; if there are none, by the parish priest determined by particular law.

§2 The one who has undertaken the governance of the parish in accordance with §1, is at once to inform the local Ordinary of the parish vacancy.

When a parish becomes vacant or the parish priest impeded, it may not be possible to arrange a substitute immediately. Until such action is taken, the care of the parish is entrusted to the assistant priest, if there is one; if there is more than one, to the assistant priest senior by appointment (not by ordination); in the absence of any such appropriate arrangement, another parish priest to be specified by the law of the diocese or of the region. The first duty of such a priest is to inform the local Ordinary of the situation, explaining e.g. the cause of the vacancy or the reason why the parish priest is impeded.

Can. 542 The priests to whom, in accordance with Can. 517 §1, is jointly entrusted the pastoral care of a parish or of a number of parishes together:

1° **must possess the qualities mentioned in Can. 521;**

2° **are to be appointed in accordance with Cann. 522 and 524.**

3° **obtain the pastoral care only from the moment of taking possession: their moderator is put into possession in accordance with Can. 527 §2; for the other priests, the profession of faith lawfully made replaces the taking of possession.**

Having detailed the responsibilities and requirements of individual parish priests, the Code now applies the same to those priests to whom a parish or group of parishes is entrusted jointly by virtue of Can. 517 §1. Thus, they must all be ordained priests (see Can. 521 §1) and possessed of the personal qualities required by universal and particular law (see Can. 521 §2); they are appointed either for an indeterminate time or, if the Bishops' Conference has so permitted, for a fixed term of office (see Can. 522); the choice of such priests belongs to the Bishop but he must consult the Vicar forane and conduct any other enquiries he sees appropriate (see Can. 524). The Code requires that the moderator be put in possession of the parish or parishes in the manner laid down by particular law (see Can. 527 §2). A profession of faith must be made personally by all the others in the team (see Can. 833 6°); this replaces any ceremony of induction for them.

Can. 543 §1 Each of the priests to whom the care of a parish or of a number of parishes together is jointly entrusted, is bound to fulfil the duties and functions of a parish priest mentioned in Cann. 528, 529 and 530. They are to do this according to a plan determined among themselves. The faculty to assist at marriages, and all the faculties to dispense which are given to a parish priest by virtue of the law itself, belong to all, but are to be exercised under the direction of the moderator.

§2 All the priests who belong to the group:

1° are bound by the obligation of residence;

2° are by common counsel to establish an arrangement by which one of them celebrates the Mass for the people, in accordance with Can. 534.

3° in juridical affairs, only the moderator acts in the person of the parish or parishes entrusted to the group.

1078 The pastoral responsibilities, juridical obligations and rights of a parish priest belong equally to all members of the team entrusted with parochial care according to Can. 517 §1. The sole exception in the Code is that of representing the parish in juridical affairs, which includes implicitly the care of the parochial registers. This is reserved to the one appointed as moderator. Any special faculties which are reserved personally to the moderator by the diocesan Bishop, e.g. to grant permission for mixed marriages, do not belong to other members of the team; they share only those faculties given to a parish priest by law. It is essential that any such group of priests must, as a priority, draw up a plan so that the pastoral care of the parish or parishes is carried out in a properly coordinated fashion.

Can. 544 When one of the priests, or the moderator, of the group mentioned in Can. 517 §1 ceases to hold office, or when any member of it becomes incapable of exercising his pastoral office, the parish or parishes whose care is entrusted to the group do not become vacant. It is for the diocesan Bishop to appoint another moderator; until he is appointed by the Bishop, the priest of the group who is senior by appointment is to fulfil this office.

1079 The principle of joint pastoral action foreseen in Can. 517 §1 is that each member is equally and fully responsible. Consequently, as long as one member of the group continues in office the parish or group of parishes is not vacant. If one of the group ceases from office or is impeded, the Bishop may freely appoint a successor or replacement; similarly, if the moderator ceases from office or is impeded, it is for the Bishop to appoint a successor or a replacement. Where a moderator has ceased to hold office or has become impeded, until other arrangements are made the senior member of the group by appointment assumes the responsibilities of moderator. In the case of parity of appointment, seniority may be determined by ordination or by age.

Can. 545 §1 Whenever it is necessary or opportune for the due pastoral care of the parish, one or more assistant priests can be joined with the parish priest. As cooperators with the parish priest and sharers in his concern, they are, by common counsel and effort with the parish priest and under his authority, to labour in the pastoral ministry.

§2 An assistant priest may be appointed either to help in exercising the entire pastoral ministry, whether in the whole parish or in a part of it or for a particular group of the faithful within it, or even to help in carrying out a specific ministry in a number of parishes at the same time.

While there is no requirement in law to appoint an assistant priest in a parish, it would be the normal wish of the diocesan Bishop to do so, save only when he recognises that such an appointment is either unnecessary or, in the circumstances, impossible. In appropriate situations he may appoint one or a number, depending on the needs of the parish. Every assistant priest is to work under the authority of the parish priest, but they are all understood to be his 'cooperators and sharers in his concern': it is 'by common counsel and effort with the parish priest ... (that they are) to labour in the pastoral ministry'. 1080

Unless otherwise stated in the letter of appointment, the ministry of the priest appointed to assist the parish priest is presumed to be to the whole parish; of course, the parish priest may ask him to concentrate on certain areas or aspects of parish life. However, the Bishop may require such an assistant to concentrate his activities on certain kinds of ministry, or to certain groups of people, such as migrants within the parish. He may also wish to appoint an assistant to carry out a ministry which covers a number of parishes, e.g. coordinator of youth ministry within a particular group of parishes. It is important that any such specifications be clearly detailed in the letter of appointment, so that both parish priest and assistant are fully aware of what the Bishop wishes them to do. In keeping with changed conditions, this canon clearly gives scope for a wider variety of assignments than did c.476 of the 1917 Code. 1081

Can. 546 To be validly appointed an assistant priest, one must be in the sacred order of priesthood.

No one may be appointed an assistant priest until he has first been ordained to the presbyterate. Thus, even if a parish has been entrusted to the care of a deacon in accordance with Can. 517 §2, he may not assume the role assigned by the Code to the 'assistant priest'. However, the Holy See has indicated that a deacon entrusted with such pastoral care may be regarded as equivalent to an assistant priest and, in particular, given *general* delegation to assist at marriages.[1] 1082

Can. 547 The diocesan Bishop freely appoints an assistant priest; if he has judged it opportune, he will have consulted the parish priest or parish priests of the parishes to which the assistant is appointed, and the Vicar forane, without prejudice to Can. 682 §1.

The appointment of an assistant to a parish priest rests solely with the Bishop. Neither the parish priest to whom the assistant priest is given, nor the Vicar forane, has any *right* to be consulted over the appointment. However, a Bishop may certainly make such consultations; indeed it is difficult to see how, in normal circumstances, he can judge the appropriateness of the appointment without doing so. 1083

Can. 548 §1 The obligations and rights of assistant priests are defined not only by the canons of this chapter, but also by the diocesan statutes, and by the letter of the diocesan Bishop; they are more specifically determined by the direction of the parish priest.

---

[1] Cf. DVCom rep 19.VII.1970: CLD 7 752. For the rights entrusted to *permanent deacons*, subject to the judgement of the diocesan Bishop, cf. SDO 16: CLD 6 581–582.

§2 Unless it is otherwise expressly provided in the letter of the diocesan Bishop, the assistant priest is by virtue of his office bound to help the parish priest in the entire parochial ministry, with the exception of the application of the Mass for the people. Likewise, if the matter should arise in accordance with the law, he is bound to take the place of the parish priest.

§3 The assistant priest is to report regularly to the parish priest on pastoral initiatives, both those planned and those already undertaken. In this way the parish priest and the assistant or assistants can by their joint efforts provide a pastoral care of the parish for which they are together answerable.

1084 An assistant priest in a parish enjoys the rights and obligations given to all clerics by universal law (see Cann. 273–289). His rights and obligations *within the parish to which he is assigned* are determined by four sources:
– the canons of this chapter of the Code, e.g. Cann. 545–552;
– the diocesan statutes, in so far as they may deal with this matter;
– the letter of appointment by the Bishop, which may contain an indication of special responsibilities;
– the decisions of the parish priest, after consultation with the assistant priest.

1085 The ministry of such an assistant encompasses all aspects of parish life, unless some specific work has been given to him (see Can. 545 §2). However, he is not responsible for celebrating the Mass *pro populo*: that obligation belongs *personally* to the parish priest.

1086 The cooperation and joint pastoral action of the parish priest and his assistants is regulated by the requirement that they report to him regularly on all pastoral initiatives in the parish. In this way, they can truly work together, 'by common counsel and effort', for the good of the people entrusted to their care. In many parishes the laudable practice has been established whereby the parish priest and his assistant(s) meet together on a regular basis – on occasion perhaps over a meal – to discuss the pastoral concerns of the parish.

Can. 549 When the parish priest is absent, the norms of Can. 541 §1 are to be observed, unless the diocesan Bishop has provided otherwise in accordance with Can. 533 §3, or unless a parochial administrator has been appointed. If Can. 541 §1 is applied, the assistant priest is bound by all the obligations of the parish priest, with the exception of the obligation to apply the Mass for the people.

1087 Can. 541 deals with the situation of a parish which is vacant or where the parish priest is impeded from carrying out his duties. In the long term an administrator is to be appointed, but in the short term that role is carried out by the assistant priest senior by appointment. The present canon applies the same provision to temporary absences, e.g. vacations, retreats, etc. Unless the Bishop makes other arrangements, the senior assistant (if there is more than one) automatically substitutes for the parish priest, without any need of a formal appointment either by the Bishop or by the parish priest.

Can. 550 §1 The assistant priest is bound to reside in the parish or, if he is appointed for a number of parishes at the same time, in one of them. For a

just reason, however, the local Ordinary may permit him to reside elsewhere, especially in a house common to several priests, provided the carrying out of the pastoral duties does not in any way suffer thereby.

§2 The local Ordinary is to see to it that, where it is possible, some manner of common life in the parochial house be encouraged between the parish priest and the assistants.

§3 As far as holidays are concerned, the assistant priest has the same rights as the parish priest.

The obligation of residing in the parish, except for the situation foreseen in §1, is of universal law. The practice varies according to local custom. It is common in some countries for the clergy to live together in a parochial house, while in others the clergy live alone but in the same neighbourhood. Vat. II strongly encouraged a common form of life for clergy because of the mutual support thus provided;[1] the Code facilitates this even to the extent of permitting a common residence outside of the parish. The local Ordinary is charged with the responsibility of encouraging the priests living in the same parish to share some form of common life; this is to be encouraged particularly between the parish priest and the assistants. The equality of rights of holidays given to assistant priests means not only the same length (see Can. 533 §2), but also that the timing must be a matter of mutual agreement between the parish priest and the assistants. **1088**

Can. 551 The provisions of Can. 531 are to be observed in respect of offerings which Christ's faithful make to the assistant priest on the occasion of his exercise of the pastoral ministry.

The assistant priest in a parish is subject to the principle enunciated in Can. 531, namely that any offerings made by the faithful on the occasion of a priest's exercise of parochial duties are regarded as belonging to the parish. These funds are to be distributed in accordance with local custom and practice. However, if it is clear that the offering is made *personally* to the priest – and this should never be presumed – it becomes his property, not that of the parish. **1089**

Can. 552 Without prejudice to Can. 682 §2, an assistant priest may for a just reason be removed by the diocesan Bishop or the diocesan Administrator.

Assistant priests have always had a lesser security of tenure than parish priests. No formal procedure is required for their removal, and a just cause, rather than a grave cause, suffices (see Can. 193 §3). Nevertheless, a reason is required, and that reason should be given, since such a decision must be given in writing (see Can. 193 §§4 & 5). In the case of a religious priest occupying this office, the diocesan Bishop or the religious Superior can remove him without the consent of the other, but prior notice must be given by the authority who is seeking his removal (see Can. 682 §2). **1090**

---

[1] Cf. CD 30: Fl I 581.

Book II The People of God

Chapter VII
VICARS FORANE

Can. 553 §1 The Vicar forane, known also as the dean or the archpriest or by some other title, is the priest who is placed in charge of a vicariate forane.

§2 Unless it is otherwise prescribed by particular law, the Vicar forane is appointed by the diocesan Bishop; if he has considered it prudent to do so, he will have consulted the priests who are exercising the ministry in the vicariate.

1091 Every diocese must be divided into parishes (see Can. 374 §1); according to Can. 374 §2, these may be linked together into groups such as vicariates forane or deaneries. If such a grouping of parishes is established, it is presided over by a priest known in law as the Vicar forane. In different countries, the Vicar forane is known by a specific title e.g. Dean, Archpriest, etc.

1092 It is the diocesan Bishop, not the Vicar general or episcopal Vicar, who appoints the Vicar forane. In some places, he is chosen by the priests of the area through an election. Such a selection process in particular law is not contrary to the Code provided it is understood that *appointment to* the office belongs solely to the Bishop. Before making any appointment, the Bishop may decide to consult the priests who minister within the territory of the vicariate. The authority exercised by the Vicar forane is *ordinary*, since it belongs to the office by law, and *vicarious*, since it is exercised *in the name of* the diocesan Bishop.

Can. 554 §1 For the office of Vicar forane, which is not tied to the office of parish priest of any given parish, the Bishop is to choose a priest whom, in view of the circumstances of place and time, he has judged to be suitable.

§2 The Vicar forane is to be appointed for a certain period of time, determined by particular law.

§3 For a just reason, the diocesan Bishop may in accordance with his prudent judgement freely remove the Vicar forane from office.

1093 The only criterion mentioned in the canon for choosing a priest as Vicar forane is the judgement of suitability made by the Bishop. There is no necessity that a parish priest be appointed; it is clear that an assistant priest or a retired parish priest may be appointed; indeed, the priest may even be a member of a religious institute or society of apostolic life, provided the appropriate Superior either proposes him or at least consents to the appointment (see Can. 682 §1). The term of office must be decided by particular law. However, the Bishop is free to remove the Vicar forane at his own discretion, although he ought to communicate this in writing (see Can. 193 §4).

Can. 555 §1 Apart from the faculties lawfully given to him by particular law, the Vicar forane has the duty and the right:

1° to promote and coordinate common pastoral action in the vicariate;

2° to see that the clerics of his district lead a life befitting their state, and discharge their obligations carefully;

3° to ensure that religious functions are celebrated according to the provisions of the sacred liturgy; that the elegance and neatness of the churches and sacred furnishings are properly maintained, particularly in regard to the celebration of the Eucharist and the custody of the blessed Sacrament; that the parish registers are correctly entered and duly safeguarded; that ecclesiastical goods are carefully administered; finally, that the parochial house is looked after with care.

§2 In the vicariate entrusted to him, the Vicar forane:

1° is to encourage the clergy, in accordance with the provisions of particular law, to attend at the prescribed time lectures and theological meetings or conferences, in accordance with Can. 279 §2.

2° is to see to it that spiritual assistance is available to the priests of his district, and he is to show a particular solicitude for those who are in difficult circumstances or are troubled by problems.

§3 When he has come to know that parish priests of his district are seriously ill, the Vicar forane is to ensure that they do not lack spiritual and material help. When they die, he is to ensure that their funerals are worthily celebrated. Moreover, should any of them fall ill or die, he is to see to it that books, documents, sacred furnishings and other items belonging to the Church are not lost or removed.

§4 The Vicar forane is obliged to visit the parishes of his district in accordance with the arrangement made by the diocesan Bishop.

Detailed local responsibilities entrusted to the Vicar forane need to be defined by particular law and diocesan policy. The first priority in universal law is given to his role of fostering common pastoral action within his district. He is required to visit the parishes; the degree of formality and the frequency of such visits will be determined by the local diocesan policy. Only by having a thorough knowledge of the priests and the nature of the parishes can he carry out his responsibilities. He has a positive role of leadership and responsibility for the clergy within the district. He must make sure that they are properly looked after when ill, making arrangements, if necessary, for nursing and spiritual care, contacting diocesan funds for sick clergy, etc. It is the Vicar forane's special responsibility to keep an eye on and arrange help for priests with problems. Spiritual assistance should be understood in the broad terms of building up a spirit of fraternity through social gatherings. It is for the Vicar forane to encourage the clergy in their spiritual and intellectual growth. The Code requires clergy to continue their studies and in Can. 279 offers a framework in which this is to be pursued. 1094

The Vicar forane also has a duty of vigilance, on behalf of the Bishop, to ensure proper administration in the parishes and that liturgical and other abuses and negligence are remedied promptly, more by a private word of encouragement or reproof than by a formal report to the Bishop. A final but occasionally important duty arises when a priest dies. The family and executors of a deceased priest may be unaware of what belongs to the parish and what to the priest, and may attempt to remove papers or other items which belong to the Church; the Vicar forane is to do what is necessary to retain what belongs rightfully to the parish or the diocese. 1095

Chapter VIII
RECTORS OF CHURCHES AND CHAPLAINS

Article 1
Rectors of Churches

Can. 556 Rectors of churches are here understood to be priests to whom is entrusted the care of some church which is neither a parochial nor a capitular church, nor a church attached to the house of a religious community or a society of apostolic life which holds services in it.

1096 The office of rector in itself carries with it no direct pastoral responsibility or care of souls, but simply the care of a church building.

1097 Parochial churches and parish chapels-of-ease are not included among those churches given to the care of a rector; neither are those belonging to chapters of canons. churches belonging to religious communities or to societies of apostolic life which are actually used by these communities are also excluded. However, churches which belong to such institutes, but are used e.g. as public oratories and not by the community, must have a rector appointed.

Can. 557 §1 The rector of a church is freely appointed by the diocesan Bishop, without prejudice to a right of election or presentation to which someone may lawfully have claim: in which case the diocesan Bishop has the right to confirm or to appoint the rector.

§2 Even if the church belongs to some clerical religious institute of pontifical right, it is for the diocesan Bishop to appoint the rector presented by the Superior.

§3 The rector of a church which is attached to a seminary or to a college governed by clerics, is the rector of the seminary or college, unless the diocesan Bishop has determined otherwise.

1098 The right to appoint a rector generally belongs to the diocesan Bishop. If some other person or persons have the right to elect or present a rector to the church, e.g. the family or confraternity which runs the building, it is for the Bishop to appoint the priest presented or confirm the priest elected. In the case of a church belonging to a religious institute of pontifical right, the Bishop appoints the priests presented by the appropriate Superior. The Vicar general or episcopal Vicar of the diocese would require a special mandate to make or confirm such an appointment. Unless the Bishop has decided otherwise, the act of appointment as rector of the seminary or a college governed by clerics, e.g. a school, carries with it, by virtue of the law itself, the appointment as rector of the church attached to it.

Can. 558 Without prejudice to Can. 262, the rector of a church may not perform in his church the parochial functions mentioned in Can. 530 nn.1-6, without the consent or, where the matter requires it, the delegation of the parish priest.

1099 Generally speaking, in the churches mentioned in Can. 556, there is a right to the celebration of all liturgical functions (see Cann. 559, 1219, 1225), subject to the proviso that these do not affect adversely the rights of the parish. The Code does not now *reserve* any functions to the parish priest, but certain functions (see Can. 530 1°–6°) are *entrusted* to him especially. Consequently, the rector of a church needs the parish priest's consent to celebrate these in his church. In addition, he requires delegation to assist at marriages. Any offerings given on the occasion of such celebrations are to be applied in accordance with Can. 531.

Can. 559 The rector can conduct liturgical celebrations, even solemn ones, in the church entrusted to him, without prejudice to the legitimate laws of a foundation, and on condition that in the judgement of the local Ordinary these celebrations do not in any way harm the parochial ministry.

The rector has a right to celebrate in his church liturgical functions, other than those mentioned in Can. 530 1°–6°, without the permission of the parish priest. In arranging liturgical celebrations he is to exercise a particular care to ensure that no harm is done to the parochial ministry. 1100

Can. 560 Where he considers it opportune, the local Ordinary may direct the rector to celebrate in his church certain functions for the people, even parochial functions, and also to open the church to certain groups of the faithful so that they may hold liturgical celebrations there.

The rector is not under any obligation from universal law to celebrate Mass or conduct other liturgical functions at a time convenient to the faithful. The local Ordinary, if he considers it opportune, however, can require such duties of him. Clearly, if so directed by the Bishop the rector gains the right to carry out those functions independently of the parish priest, even if they are those mentioned in Can. 530 1°–6°. Delegation to assist at marriages would still be required, but in this situation it might be appropriate for the Ordinary to give the rector general delegation. The rector might also be instructed by the local Ordinary to allow access to his church for particular groups, so that they can hold liturgical celebrations, etc., e.g. a linguistic or ethnic group. 1101

Can. 561 Without the permission of the rector or some other lawful Superior, no one may celebrate the Eucharist, administer the sacraments, or perform other sacred functions in the church. This permission is to be given or refused in accordance with the law.

If the church is to be used for any sacred celebration, the permission of the rector is required. In some cases, e.g. where the church belongs to a religious institute, the permission of the appropriate Superior is sufficient. 1102

Permission cannot be given or refused at the whim of the rector or Superior, but only 'in accordance with the law'. A priest wishing to celebrate Mass must be permitted to do so in accordance with Cann. 901, 903; in the case of confessions, the rector or Superior must be satisfied that the priest has the requisite faculties (see Can. 966); for preaching, the general requirements are laid down in Can. 764, although permission can and should be withheld if the rector has reason to believe that the content will be at variance with the doctrine of the Church (see Can. 760). 1103

Can. 562 Under the authority of the local Ordinary, having observed the lawful statutes and respected acquired rights, the rector of a church is obliged to see that sacred functions are worthily celebrated in the church, in accordance with liturgical and canon law, that obligations are faithfully fulfilled, that the property is carefully administered, and that the

maintenance and adornment of the furnishings and buildings are assured. He must also ensure that nothing is done which is in any way unbecoming to the holiness of the place and to the reverence due to the house of God.

1104 The principal duties of a rector are sketched out in this canon. They are to be discharged in accordance with any lawful statutes or acquired rights which affect the church. The first duty mentioned concerns the worthy celebration of liturgical functions: it is the responsibility of the rector to make sure these are celebrated according to the correct liturgical books and the appropriate canonical norms. The rector is required to see that any particular obligations associated with the church are fulfilled, e.g. prayers for donors or benefactors. In accordance with Can. 1279, he must administer the goods of the church with care and attention. Finally, it is his responsibility to see to the maintenance and adornment of the church and to do all that is necessary to prevent anything from happening which is in any way 'discordant with the sacred character of the place' (Can. 1220 §1).

Can. 563 For a just reason, the local Ordinary may in accordance with his prudent judgement remove the rector of a church from office, even if he had been elected or presented by others, but without prejudice to Can. 682 §2.

1105 As always, a religious can be removed from office in the diocese without the consent of the Superior, but with prior notice (see Can. 682 §2); equally the Superior can also remove the religious from office without the consent of the local Ordinary. It is to be noted that while only the diocesan Bishop can appoint a rector or confirm his appointment, a Vicar general or episcopal Vicar (as local Ordinary) can remove him. A just cause suffices, and this must be indicated in summary form in the written notification of removal (see Cann. 193 §§3 & 4, 51). Hierarchical recourse is possible within the terms of Cann. 1732–39.

Article 2
Chaplains

Can. 564 A chaplain is a priest to whom is entrusted in a stable manner the pastoral care, at least in part, of some community or special group of Christ's faithful, to be exercised in accordance with universal and particular law.

1106 Canonically, a chaplain is defined as a priest to whom the pastoral care of a community or group of the faithful is entrusted, e.g. a community not yet ready for establishment as a parish (see Can. 516 §2), a community of immigrants, a school, a hospital, etc. The nature and extent of the pastoral care is to be specified in particular law or in the letter of appointment. In current usage, the word 'chaplain' is used in a broad sense to refer to all those engaged in pastoral activity, e.g. in schools, hospitals, prisons. Many of these pastoral workers are lay or religious. Lest there by any confusion, the canons of this part of the Code refer exclusively to the canonical office of chaplain, an office which can be conferred only on a priest. The responsibilities and role of other 'chaplains' ought to be defined clearly in particular legislation.

Can. 565 Unless the law provides otherwise or unless special rights lawfully belong to someone, a chaplain is appointed by the local Ordinary, to whom also it belongs to appoint one who has been presented or to confirm one elected.

A chaplain may be appointed in one of three ways:

(a) he may be freely appointed by the local Ordinary if there is no special provision in particular law and if no rights of presentation or election exist;
(b) he may be presented by another authority e.g. the principal of the school if this is specified in law, and appointed by the local Ordinary;
(c) he may be elected by the group e.g. a confraternity and have his election confirmed by the local Bishop.

Can. 566 §1 A chaplain must be given all the faculties which due pastoral care demands. Besides those which are given by particular law or by special delegation, a chaplain has by virtue of his office the faculty to hear the confessions of the faithful entrusted to his care, to preach to them the word of God, to administer Viaticum and the anointing of the sick, and to confer the sacrament of confirmation when they are in danger of death.

§2 In hospitals and prisons and on sea voyages, a chaplain has the further faculty to be exercised only in those places, to absolve from *latae sententiae* censures which are neither reserved nor declared, without prejudice to Can. 976.

By universal law (§1), a chaplain can administer the sacraments of the sick and confirmation in the case of the dying, which are the special responsibility of parish priests (see Can. 530 2°–3°). He also has the right to preach and hear the confessions of those entrusted to his care. For the other functions mentioned in Can. 530, he is dependent on the parish priest, unless particular law or his letter of appointment give him more extensive faculties.

Because of the difficulty of recourse, chaplains to hospitals, prisons and on board ship have faculties to absolve from *latae sententiae* censures which are not reserved or declared (§2). They may absolve from these penalties even outside the danger of death (see Can. 976). The chaplain's faculty in these situations is even more extensive than that of the canon penitentiary, insofar as it is not restricted to the sacramental forum (see Can. 508 §1).

Can. 567 §1 The local Ordinary is not to proceed to the appointment of a chaplain to a house of a lay religious institute without consulting the Superior. The Superior has the right, after consulting the community, to propose a particular priest.

§2 It is the responsibility of the chaplain to celebrate or to direct liturgical functions; he may not, however, involve himself in the internal governance of the institute.

The Code guarantees to each religious institute a true autonomy of life, and it is the responsibility of the diocesan Bishop to uphold this, even in diocesan institutes (see Cann. 586, 593, 594). The chaplain is provided to houses of lay religious institutes exclusively for liturgical purposes, and not for the internal formation of the religious. The Ordinary must consult the Superior, and the latter is to consult the community before proposing a chaplain. Having made the necessary consultation, the Bishop is free to appoint anyone whom he considers suitable. Obviously he should not ignore the advice given, except for an overriding reason (see Can. 127 §2 2°).

Can. 568 As far as possible, chaplains are to be appointed for those who, because of their condition of life, are not able to avail themselves of the

ordinary care of parish priests, as for example, migrants, exiles, refugees, nomads and sea-farers.

1111 The ordinary pastoral care of the faithful is exercised by parish priests. However, due to particular circumstances of life, many people are unable to avail themselves of this care. The law makes the local Ordinary responsible for providing due pastoral care for these people. Some groups are listed here: migrants, exiles, refugees, nomads and sea-farers. Other can be added e.g. prisoners, students, those confined to hospital, etc.

Can. 569 Chaplains to the armed forces are governed by special laws.

1112 The armed forces in any country constitute a community with very special needs and problems. The 'special laws' mentioned in the canon are contained in ap con *Spirituali militum curae* of 21 April 1986[1] and in the statutes approved by the Holy See for each country or region.

1113 Where a military ordinariate is created, it is equivalent to a diocese (see Cann. 368–369). The powers of the military Ordinary are proper, and he is equivalent to a diocesan Bishop wherever this is mentioned in the Code. In some countries, for practical reasons, the office is combined with that of a diocesan Bishop. Whether this be so or not, the military Ordinary belongs to the Bishops' Conference of the country whose armed forces are entrusted to his care. The extent of the responsibilities of the Ordinary and of the chaplains is specified in the norms for each country. Jurisdiction is personal, and so it applies outside national boundaries to those who pertain to the ordinariate. The jurisdiction of the military Ordinary and of the chaplains is cumulative with that of the diocesan Bishop and clergy. Thus, e.g. military personnel may have recourse to either, subject only to military discipline. A full-time military chaplain is, in effect, the parish priest of a personal parish (see Can. 518), belonging to the military ordinariate and possessing all the rights and obligations of a parish priest. The local parochial clergy also have a pastoral responsibility for the military personnel in their parish, especially if there is no permanent chaplain to minister to their needs. In some cases, they may act as 'auxiliary' chaplains: each country's statutes will specify the role and responsibilities of these 'auxiliary' chaplains and their connection with the Ordinariate.

Can. 570 If a non-parochial church is attached to an establishment of a community or group, the rector of the church is to be the chaplain, unless the care of the community or of the church requires otherwise.

1114 The kind of church mentioned in this canon is one of those referred to in Can. 556. Misunderstandings and possible disputes can be avoided if the same person fulfils the offices of rector of the church and chaplain to the community or group. However, this may not always be advisable or practicable, e.g. if the group attached to the church is not really connected with it but simply makes use of its facilities at the request of the Bishop (see Can. 560), or if the rector lacks the qualities required for the chaplaincy of this group, or if the chaplain has to operate in a number of different centres, etc.

---

[1] Cf. AAS 78(1986) 481–486. For a short study, cf. Ombres *The Pastoral Care of the Armed Forces in Canon Law* Priests and People 2(1988) 234–239. For more detailed studies, cf. Beyer *Commentary on the Apostolic Const. 'Spirituali Militum Curae'* CLSNGBI 76(Dec. 1988) 48–89; Le Tourneau *La nouvelle organisation de l'Ordinariat aux Armées* Stud Can 21(1987) 37–66; Gutierrez *De Ordinariatus militaris nova constitutione* Per 76(1987) 189–218; Ghirlanda *De differentia Praelaturam personalem inter et Ordinariatum militarem seu castrensem* Per 76(1987) 219–251.

Can. 571 In the exercise of his pastoral office a chaplain is to maintain the due relationship with the parish priest.

The provision of a chaplain is intended to care for the particular needs of some of the faithful. It must never be understood as a challenge to the rightful authority or role of the parish priest. The law places the onus on the chaplain to coordinate his ministry in such a way that it does not interfere with the responsibilities of the parish priest. At all times, the chaplain is to understand his role as supplementary or complementary to that of the parish priest: in no sense is he to be seen as a rival.

Can. 572 In regard to the removal of a chaplain, the provisions of Can. 563 are to be observed.

A chaplain appointed according to Can. 565 may be removed by the local Ordinary (not only the diocesan Bishop) for a just reason. This provision of law affects those freely appointed by the Ordinary, those presented by others and appointed by the Ordinary, and those whose election was confirmed by the Ordinary. As always, a religious holding the office may be removed either by the Ordinary or his own Superior, provided that prior notice will have been given (see Can. 682 §2).

PART III

INSTITUTES OF CONSECRATED LIFE AND SOCIETIES OF APOSTOLIC LIFE

INTRODUCTION

1117   The call to a life consecrated to God through profession of the evangelical counsels has been a feature of the Church from the earliest times. Individuals such as St Anthony and St Benedict felt called to live a life of solitude and penance. Gradually, they attracted a number of disciples who began to live the same style of life. Eventually, this led to the evolution of various groups of men and women living a consecrated life together. Down through the centuries, the authorities of the Church have sought for an appropriate form of juridical recognition for such people and institutes. At first, they were known as 'regulars' since they professed to follow a particular 'rule' or approved way of life. Later, they were referred to by the generic term of 'religious'.

1118   The 1917 Code in c.487 offered a definition of the *religious life* as a stable manner of living in common, in which the faithful, besides observing the common precepts of the Gospel, also profess by means of vows to observe the evangelical counsels of obedience, chastity and poverty. Alongside those who lived such a life were so-called societies of the *common life*, in which groupings of men and of women lived in community without the vows (1917 Code cc. 673–681). Later still came the approval of *secular institutes*, in which the members made profession of the vows but lived 'in the world', i.e. normally in their own homes and at their own avocations.

1119   Vatican II constituted a major watershed in the understanding of this consecrated way of life. In its documents one finds a new understanding of the place of consecrated life within the Church, as well as the principles for a renewal of that life based on respect for and fidelity to the spirit, intentions and example of the founders and foundresses. The Code has sought to express this insight in juridical terms. It no longer contains the detailed distinctions of the types of institute found in c.488 of the 1917 Code. Instead, generic terms e.g. institute, Moderator, member, are used; it is for each institute to find the appropriate expression within its own proper legislation.

1120   Nevertheless, the Code does make some important distinctions. Whereas the Code of 1917 had spoken of 'religious', this Code speaks of 'institutes of consecrated life', of which there are two varieties: *religious institutes* and *secular institutes*. In addition, where the 1917 Code had mentioned 'societies of men and women living in common without vows', the present Code speaks of 'societies of apostolic life'. The overall treatment is divided into two sections. Section I concerns *Institutes of Consecrated Life*; in this section, after the *Norms common to all Institutes of Consecrated Life* (Title I), there is a lengthy treatment of the various aspects of life in *Religious Institutes* (Title II), followed by norms specific to *Secular Institutes* (Title III). The smaller Section II concerns *Societies of Apostolic Life*, whose members live in community but do not necessarily make formal profession of life according to the evangelical counsels.

Part III Institutes of Consecrated Life and Societies of Apostolic Life

Section I
INSTITUTES OF CONSECRATED LIFE

Title I
Norms Common to All Institutes of Consecrated Life

Can. 573 §1 Life consecrated through profession of the evangelical counsels is a stable form of living, in which the faithful follow Christ more closely under the action of the Holy Spirit, and are totally dedicated to God, who is supremely loved. By a new and special title they are dedicated to seek the perfection of charity in the service of God's Kingdom, for the honour of God, the building up of the Church and the salvation of the world. They are a splendid sign in the Church, as they foretell the heavenly glory.

This introductory canon finds its inspiration and its thrust in Vat. II,[1] from which it draws its rich spiritual content. The concluding sentence signals in particular the prophetic role of consecrated life: 'witnessing to the new and eternal life which we have acquired through the redemptive work of Christ and preluding our future resurrection and the glory of the heavenly Kingdom'.[2]   1121

The description of consecrated life is to be understood also in the context of Can. 207 §2, concerning the place or state in the Church of those who are so consecrated. There, again reflecting Vat. II, the point is made that institutes of consecrated life do not form 'a kind of middle way between the clerical and lay conditions of life'.[3] It is, rather, a state to which anyone, cleric or lay person, may be called, according to the personal vocation of each (see Can. 588).   1122

The 'new and special title' refers to the consequences of taking on the obligations of the consecrated life, the profession of the evangelical counsels as a mode of life. These words link this consecration to baptismal consecration and indicate an obligation additional to those assumed by all the faithful (see Cann. 204, 208). In speaking of 'a stable form of living', the canon implies that the aim is to assume the obligations for life.   1123

In order to take account of secular institutes – to which also this canon applies – there is no reference here to 'public' profession; neither is there reference to living 'in common'. These two ideas are introduced in Can. 607 §2, in the context both of the vows of religious and of their way of life.   1124

Can. 573 §2 Christ's faithful freely assume this manner of life in institutes of consecrated life which are canonically established by the competent ecclesiastical authority. By vows or by other sacred bonds, in accordance with

---

[1] Cf. LG 43–44: Fl I 402–405; PC 1: Fl I 611–612.
[2] LG 44: Fl I 404.
[3] LG 43: Fl I 403.

the laws of their own institutes, they profess the evangelical counsels of chastity, poverty and obedience. Because of the charity to which these counsels lead, they are linked in a special way to the Church and its mystery.

1125 The precise import of the more juridical elements which distinguish consecrated life, is examined in more detail later: the free assumption of the manner of life; the ecclesiastical approbation of the institute; the vows or other sacred bonds (see Cann. 643 §1 4°, 578–579, 599–602).

1126 The 'vows or other sacred bonds' are to be specified in the proper law (*ius proprium*) of the institute. The canon does not here indicate in which text of the institute's law this is to be done. The question of vow or sacred bond is so crucial to the nature of the institute and its membership, and is so closely linked with the time-honoured customs of the institute, that one expects to find this basic choice specified in the constitutions themselves; the precise expression and formulae could of course be further determined in other official documents such as directories, manuals etc.

Can. 574 §1 The state of persons who profess the evangelical counsels in these institutes belongs to the life and holiness of the Church. It is therefore to be fostered and promoted by everyone in the Church.

1127 The first sentence, mirroring Vat. II,[1] is a further statement of the point made in Can. 207 §2. The second sentence goes further than, and has a somewhat different motivation from, the Council's general injunction to priests, educators and parents to foster and protect religious vocations in young people.[2] It is precisely because consecrated life is so linked with the holiness and the prophetic role of the Church, and is seen as a gift from God (see Can. 575), that it becomes the duty of all the faithful to protect and promote it. This duty springs in part from the fact that all the laity have the 'vocation of applying to the building up of the Church and to its continual sanctification all the powers which they have received from the goodness of the Creator and the grace of the Redeemer'.[3]

Can. 574 §2 Some of Christ's faithful are specially called by God to this state, so that they may benefit from a special gift in the life of the Church and contribute to its saving mission according to the purpose and spirit of each institute.

1128 The stress here is that the initiative in vocation lies with God who calls, not with the person who responds.[4] The purpose of the call is 'to contribute to its (the Church's) saving mission *according to the spirit and purpose of each institute*'. This formulation stresses that the call of God is to service *through an institute*. In this way the approved nature and vocation of the institute is protected against abuse in the name of personal vocation. Moreover, the canon goes back, if only by implication, to the primitive inspiration of each institute, suitably adapted 'under the impulse of the Holy Spirit and with the guidance of the Church' to the needs of the modern world.[5] This concept of the spirit and purpose of an institute is one which permeates the entire law on religious life.

---

[1] Cf. LG 44: Fl I 405.
[2] Cf. PC 24: Fl I 622–623.
[3] LG 33: Fl I 390.
[4] Cf. LG 43: Fl I 403; PC 1: Fl I 611.
[5] PC 2: Fl I 612.

Can. 575 The evangelical counsels, based on the teaching and example of Christ the Master, are a divine gift which the Church received from the Lord and which by His grace it preserves always.

'The teaching and example of Christ provide the foundation of the counsels of chaste self-dedication to God, of poverty and of obedience'[1] – the mediated will of God. It was only gradually over the centuries, however, that the three evangelical counsels, as such and together, had become explicit in the formulae of consecration, as the epitome of total consecration to God. The ascetics of the desert had adopted celibacy, monastic orders added a particular form of obedience, mendicant orders stressed poverty. The three counsels, recognised by the seventh century, seem to have become an explicit part of profession formulae under Pope Innocent IV in the middle of the thirteenth century, although, since together they express the totality of consecration, all three had long been implicit in the life-style adopted.[2]

Can. 576 It is the prerogative of the competent authority in the Church to interpret the evangelical counsels, to legislate for their practice and, by canonical approval, to constitute the stable forms of living which arise from them. The same authority has the responsibility to do what is in its power to ensure that institutes grow and flourish according to the spirit of their founders and to their sound traditions.

The basic right of the Church to interpret, to legislate for and to order the living of the evangelical counsels is asserted expressly in Vat. II.[3] Prior to the Council, while the more detailed expression of the content and spirit of the vows was to be found in the approved constitutions of institutes, many of these took their wording practically verbatim from the examples provided by the Holy See. The conciliar decree *Perfectae Caritatis* then provided a detailed interpretation of the counsels. The theme was again taken up and developed by Pope Paul VI in *Evangelica Testificatio*, which considers the counsels and their importance in consecrated life from the point of view of their global witness and eschatological significance.[4] Later canons of the present Code (Cann. 599–601) also show the Church at its work of interpreting and regulating the practice of the counsels, as do countless private replies of the Holy See commenting on constitutions submitted for approval.

This canon refers to the 'spirit of the founders' and the 'sound traditions' of the institute, themes to be taken up again in subsequent canons (see Cann. 578, 587). The two are not necessarily identical. In some institutes, especially when the community has come into existence as a result of divisions arising from historical, geographical or cultural factors, it may be difficult to determine a precise 'founder'. But the history of religious life does provide examples of institutes where 'sound traditions' (as opposed to casual accretions with the passage of time or at the whim of some Superiors) show a development and evolution from the original inspiration.

Can. 577 In the Church there are very many institutes of consecrated life, with gifts that differ according to the grace which has been given them: they more closely follow Christ praying, or Christ proclaiming the Kingdom of God, or Christ doing good to people, or Christ in dialogue with the people of this world, but always Christ doing the will of the Father.

---

[1] LG 43: Fl I 402; cf. PC 12–14: Fl I 617–619.

[2] Cf. St Thomas, *Summa Theologica* IIa-IIae q. 186 2.

[3] Cf. LG 43: Fl I 402.

[4] Cf. ET 13–18: Fl I 686–694; AAS 63(1971) 497ff.

1132 This canon, theological in tone, encapsulates the teaching of Vat. II.[1] It relates the activities of all those consecrated to the one saving action of Christ. In this way and at its deepest level, the essential unity of vocation is explained as a conformation to Christ in one aspect or other of his salvific mission, 'always doing the will of the Father'. At the same time, the call expresses itself in different forms of activity (including the activity of prayer), and hence the diversity of the institutes. Within the one canon, all forms of consecrated life find themselves depicted: contemplatives, those with a general apostolic purpose, those founded to address a particular work of the apostolate (schools, hospitals, missions, etc.), and secular institutes.

Can. 578 The mind of the founders and their dispositions concerning the nature, purpose, spirit and character of the institute which have been approved by the competent ecclesiastical authority, together with its sound traditions, all of which comprise the patrimony of the institute itself, are to be faithfully observed by all.

1133 In the past, in approving new institutes of simple vows and later alterations to constitutions, the Holy See would appear to have used the same yardstick for all. In marked contrast, this new Code here explicitly 'canonises' the variety of life within institutes. It demands only that they be approved, and it lists those elements which competent ecclesiastical authority must examine, namely

- the intention of the founders;
- the nature of the institute (clerical, lay, secular);
- the purpose or mission (general or specific);
- the spirit of the institute (its basic spirituality);
- its character (conventual, integrally apostolic, mixed);
- its sound traditions.

In order to be able to make its distinctive contribution to the life and mission of the Church, an institute must be able to identify all these points. In practice, many apostolic institutes find it difficult to identify clearly their character. Having obtained their initial approbation at a time when the general thrust of the Church was towards conformity and uniformity, for the sake of what was then considered the greater good, they adopted practices which were not always in keeping with the service and the way of life initially envisaged. In particular, many institutes of women had enjoined upon them a greater degree of enclosure than was planned, while others accepted its necessity unthinkingly, thus developing traditions which were not necessarily sound (see Can. 667 §1).

1134 The general phrase 'competent ecclesiastical authority' is here used, since the canon applies to all institutes of consecrated life. Subsequent canons define who has such competence and the degree of that competence (see Cann. 579, 582, 589, 591).

1135 It is noted that the injunction of this canon is to be observed by all (*omnibus*). It applies to the members, obviously, by virtue of their vow of obedience; it is of obligation that they respect the patrimony.[2] Members of the Church's hierarchy are to 'ensure that religious institutes established all over the world for building up the Body of Christ may develop and flourish in accordance with the spirit of their founders',[3] and 'Bishops and their immediate collaborators have the duty to try and form an exact

---

[1] Cf. LG 46: Fl I 406.
[2] Cf. ET 11: Fl I 685.
[3] LG 45: Fl I 405.

Part III Institutes of Consecrated Life and Societies of Apostolic Life

idea of the distinctive nature of each institute'.[1] Clergy and people are to respect its forms and take example from the life-style, while collaborating in building up the Body of Christ and promoting vocations.[2]

Can. 579 Provided the Apostolic See has been consulted, diocesan Bishops can, by formal decree, establish institutes of consecrated life in their own territories.

This canon derives almost directly from the 1917 Code c.492 §1. Following the establishment of Bishops' Conferences,[3] it was originally felt that the foundation of a new institute of consecrated life should perhaps involve a wider consideration than was possible within any one diocese, so that the necessity and viability of the new group could be better discerned.[4] After consultation, however, the idea of an intervention by the local Bishops' Conference was abandoned, and the matter was left to the diocesan Bishop. The Bishop, in his discernment, is helped by the guide-lines provided in the directive *Mutuae Relationes*.[5] In this way a balance is achieved between the needless multiplication of similar institutes and the individual Bishop's duty to discern new gifts of consecrated life and to assist their promoters (see Can. 605).

1136

There still remains the necessity to consult the Holy See, which obviously is required for the validity of the act. The term approbation is not here used, but is reserved for a later stage in the development of the institute. But the reference to Rome is no mere formality; it requires the production of statutes and other relevant documents, on the successful completion of which a *nihil obstat* may be granted. The group in question will, however, have had an independent existence for some time before that request is made. It will have started as a voluntary group within the diocese, coming together to test the validity of the life-style and the viability of the project. From there it will progress to become first a private association of the faithful (see Can. 321), and then a public association of the faithful with approved statutes (see Can. 312). Only when it is ready to progress beyond that stage is the intervention of the Holy See required. The appropriate Roman Congregation will examine statutes, prayer manuals, other writings, the works and the history of the group, etc.; as late as 1981, it was requiring that the group consist of 25–30 fully trained members before granting the *nihil obstat*.

1137

Can. 580 The aggregation of one institute of consecrated life to another is reserved to the competent authority of the aggregating institute, always safeguarding the canonical autonomy of the other institute.

The history of religious life has shown many examples of Orders (First Orders) aggregating to themselves Congregations, usually of sisters, who share the same spirit and to a degree share the life-style, the while preserving their own individuality which came to them from the different circumstances of their foundation, their different founders, and traditions. Aggregation implies not only the communication of spiritual gifts, but also the development of a similar spirituality and the recognition of a certain (non-juridical) bond between the institutes. The link is tenuous but real; it belongs more to the spiritual than to the juridical field.[6]

1138

---

[1] MR 47: Fl II 235.
[2] Cf. PC 24: Fl I 622–623.
[3] Cf. CD 38: Fl I 587; ES I 41: Fl 1 609.
[4] SVC 3, 7 §2.
[5] Cf. MR 51: Fl II 237.
[6] Cf. LE II 3770–3771.

1139 In so far, however, as it has a juridical ingredient, this must be regulated: hence the purpose of this canon,[1] which prescribes (a) that the 'canonical autonomy' of *both* institutes must be safeguarded, and (b) that the right to aggregate is invested not in the supreme Moderator (1917 Code c.292 §1) but rather in 'the competent authority of the aggregating institute': this is to be defined by the proper law (*ius proprium*) of the institute where, since it concerns a public act, one would expect to find it in the constitutions and with provision that the Superior would require the appropriate intervention by the relevant council.

1140 A question remains: apart from the reservation to the competent authority of the aggregating institute, is any further step required before any such aggregation may be lawful? Of its nature, aggregation involves an agreement between two institutes of consecrated life, both of which will, in accordance with Can. 573 §2, necessarily have received recognition by the appropriate ecclesiastical authority. Even though both institutes remain autonomous after aggregation, it would appear that – apart from those institutes in which the right to aggregate has long been exercised and recognised – specific reference should be made to the authority responsible for the original recognition of each institute.[2]

Can. 581 It is for the competent authority of the institute to divide the institute into parts, by whatever name these may be called, to establish new parts, or to unite or otherwise modify those in existence, in accordance with the constitutions.

1141 In c.494 §1 of the 1917 Code all structural changes within an institute of pontifical right were reserved to the Holy See, as were any changes of allegiance of monastic houses from one monastic congregation to another. In 1970 this was modified, to allow the creation and alteration of provinces to be organised within the institute itself, 'but with the continuing obligation to have recourse to the Holy See for the initial division into provinces or for their total suppression'. The General Chapter was to establish norms concerning alterations in provinces, and these norms were to be inserted into the constitutions.[3] The present canon removes the obligation of recourse to the Holy See in order to divide into provinces or to suppress all provincial development, leaving the entire interior organisation of an institute in its own hands. In effect, this grants to all institutes a faculty that had been granted to some before 1917. The canon sets no minimum level to the size of provinces.[4]

1142 It is for each institute to makes its own provision, but the relevant norms are to be built into the constitutions, thus allowing for their scrutiny and approval by the Holy See. Since the existence of provinces affects the structure of an institute in a basic way, it is a matter exclusively for the highest level of authority within the institute. While some institutes prefer to leave this in the hands of a General Chapter, where a wider consultation can be seen to be taking place, others have thought it better to leave the competence with the Superior General and his or her council. The very complexity of the modern world, with rapidly changing political, geographic and social situations, does have to be taken into account in this regard. This will in

---

[1] The canon reforms the relevant section of c.492 §1 of the 1917 Code.

[2] This would certainly appear to be so in respect of institutes approved by the Holy See: cf. Can. 583. As for other institutes, cf. Cann. 576, 578.

[3] SCRIS decr 6.VI.1970: AAS 62(1970) 549–550.

[4] Earlier the Holy See had set limits to the number of provinces and to the number of houses and personnel within each province: cf. Schaeffer *De Religiosis* Roma 1947 133. Already, however, that practice had been modified under the conditions of the post-war world.

considerable measure depend upon local circumstances, in some at least of which it may well be considered advisable to entrust the matter to the more expeditious competence of the Superior General and council.

Can. 582 Fusions and unions of institutes of consecrated life are reserved to the Apostolic See alone. To it are likewise reserved confederations or federations.

These changes in the structure of institutes, since they involve more than one institute of consecrated life, are specifically reserved to the Holy See. Though fusions and unions were not unknown before Vat. II, the need to make specific provision for them in the Code became urgent following the decrees of the Council, which spoke of the need for small institutes and monasteries 'to be amalgamated with more flourishing institutes whose aims and spirit differ little from their own'; warning had also been given that such unions required very careful preparation at all levels.[1]

1143

The terms 'fusion' and 'union', though not always used precisely, both imply the suppression of one or more juridical person. A *fusion* or merger takes place when a small institute merges with a larger one of similar spirituality and apostolic thrust, taking on its name, its life-style, customs, and identity. Hence the original small institute ceases to exist. All members of the merging institute have to express in writing their agreement to the fusion and its consequences; alternatively, they are free to make other arrangements e.g. transfer to another institute or apply for secularisation. Legal dispositions are made with regard to property and commitments.[2] In the case of *unions*, several smaller groups cease to exist and a new group, a new juridical person comes into existence. This involves new constitutions, new elections and a new, agreed life-style. It is a quasi-organic coming together of the parts, to be undertaken after a review of the foundation and sound traditions of such institutes as acknowledge the same general founder, share the same spirit and rule, but came into existence in different places through separate foundations, and in different political or geographical conditions.

1144

'Federations' or 'confederations' imply a somewhat looser form of coming together, in which the individual groups keep their own canonical status, but cede some rights in order to give structure and stability to the new body, the *Federation* or the *Confederation*. The fuller body may, therefore, undertake some services towards the whole group, e.g. formation in an agreed spirituality, novitiate training, etc. Such federations are common among autonomous monasteries belonging to the one institute.

1145

Can. 583 Changes in institutes of consecrated life which affect elements previously approved by the Apostolic See, cannot be made without the permission of the same See.

This canon follows the principle that the approving authority is the one to authorise changes. While it applies particularly to constitutions approved by the Holy See, it also applies to any other disposition which the Holy See makes in respect of an institute. Not only institutes of pontifical right are affected; even though the diocesan Bishop establishes and approves constitutions for institutes of diocesan right, dispositions which might have been made by the Holy See in the course of the consultation prior to the erection also come under this ruling.

1146

---

[1] PC 21: Fl I 622; cf. ES II 39–41: Fl I 632.
[2] Cf. SCRIS deccr 2.XII.1970, 28.V.1971: *Commentarium pro Religiosis* 59 (1978) 236–237.

Can. 584 Only the Apostolic See can suppress an institute and dispose of its temporal goods.

1147 In c.493 of the 1917 Code, it was stated explicitly that the suppression of diocesan right institutes, even where only a single house remained, was reserved to the Apostolic See. This exclusive right is secured by the broader expression of this canon, although the more specific principle is repeated in Can. 616 §2. Since all goods of institutes of consecrated life are ecclesiastical property, it is appropriate that the disposal of the property of a suppressed institute should pass to the Holy See by whose permission, even if the institute were of diocesan right, it had originally been founded.

1148 Suppression of an institute can follow a recognition that it is no longer viable, e.g. where over a long period no new members had been received. It can also be a penal measure, where an institute has seriously and incorrigibly deviated from the original purpose of its foundation.

Can. 585 The competent authority of an institute can suppress parts of the same institute.

1149 In the light of the new principle governing the internal division of an institute (see Can. 581), this canon modifies the provisions of c.494 of the 1917 Code which reserved the suppression of such internal divisions to the Apostolic See. The 'parts of the same institute' refer to those divisions called provinces, regions, districts, etc. in the proper law of the institutes. Can. 616 deals with the suppression of individual religious houses, while Cann. 120–123 regulate the disposal of the property of extinct juridical persons.

Can. 586 §1 A true autonomy of life, especially of governance, is recognised for each institute. This autonomy means that each institute has its own discipline in the Church and can preserve whole and entire the patrimony described in Can. 578.

§2 Local Ordinaries have the responsibility of preserving and safeguarding this autonomy.

1150 Can. 578 enjoins on members of an institute of consecrated life the preservation of the patrimony of the institute. The present canon provides the fundamental juridical structure by which this injunction can be fulfilled, i.e. 'a true autonomy of life'. This means, above all, the right of each institute to have its own proper law and internal structures of government. Although not taken from any one source, the canon is clearly inspired by conciliar and post-conciliar teaching concerning the relationship between the local Ordinary and institutes of consecrated life.[1] By reason of this canon, any undue involvement of the local Ordinary in the internal life and government of an institute is strictly prohibited. Indeed, local Ordinaries are obliged by reason of §2 to do what they can to preserve and protect the autonomy of each institute. While the institution of exemption (see Can. 591) is one means of ensuring this autonomy of life, all those in consecrated life remain subject to the authority of the Bishop in those matters which pertain to the care of souls, public worship and other works of the apostolate (see Can. 678 §1).

Can. 587 §1 To protect more faithfully the vocation and identity of each institute, the fundamental code or constitutions of the institute are to contain, in addition to those elements which are to be preserved in accordance

---

[1] Cf. CD 35 3–4: Fl I 585; MR 13c, 34: Fl II 219, 231.

with Can. 578, basic norms about the governance of the institute, the discipline of the members, the admission and formation of members, and the proper object of their sacred bonds.

Following the call of Vat. II, institutes of consecrated life undertook a radical review of their manner of life, of prayer and of work;[1] this resulted in an overhaul of the basic legislation of each institute. This process was going on at the same time as the preparation of the 1983 Code, and it has continued since then as institutes update their legislation in the light of the new Code. This canon identifies what each institute requires by way of proper legislation. First and foremost, there should be a fundamental book of rules or constitutions which must contain all that is essential to the charism, the particular way of life, and the stability of each institute. These elements are listed in §1: 1151

- anything already mentioned in Can. 578;
- the basic governmental structures at all levels;
- the basic life-style;
- principles governing admission and basic formation;
- the content of the sacred bonds.

Particularly in the last element, the Code recognises the individuality of institutes because, although the basic requirements of the vows are common to all, are legally binding and afford a complete self-dedication to God, the practices by which this is secured differ according to the spirituality of the foundation and the customs of the institute. 1152

Can. 587 §2 This code is approved by the competent ecclesiastical authority, and can be changed only with the consent of the same.

The canon does not itself specify the 'competent ecclesiastical authority'; in effect, this is defined in Can. 589, which identifies the competent ecclesiastical authority in this context: for institutes of pontifical right, it is the Holy See, acting through its appropriate Roman Congregation; for an institute of diocesan right, it is the Bishop of the diocese in which the principal house of the institute is situated, after consultation with other Bishops in whose diocese the institute may have houses (see Can. 595 §1). In either case, the principle remains that the approving authority is the one to authorise changes. Thus those matters contained in the constitutions are not entirely within the complete control of the institute. 1153

Can. 587 §3 In the constitutions, the spiritual and juridical elements are to be aptly harmonised. Norms, however, are not to be multiplied without necessity.

Two important principles are enunciated in this paragraph: 1154

(a) the spiritual foundation of an institute's legislation must be articulated and then harmonised with the more juridical elements; this allows quotations from Scripture and from the works of the founder or foundress to be incorporated into the text of the constitutions;

(b) within this fundamental code, norms are not to be multiplied; the constitutions are to contain only what is *essential*; other norms can be included in other, secondary collections.

---

[1] Cf. PC 3: Fl I 613.

Can. 587 §4 Other norms which are established by the competent authority of the institute are to be properly collected in other codes, but these can be conveniently reviewed and adapted according to the needs of time and place.

1155 The other 'codes' here referred to belong equally to the 'proper law' of the institutes. Their titles and their contents will vary from institute to institute, but they gain their place and force of law from their relationship to the constitutions. These will include a directory or 'book of rules' or 'statutes' concerning the ordinary details of daily living, applicable to all members, but subject to review, and therefore liable to change, at a General Chapter of the institute. There may also be Manuals, into which are gathered the present regulations concerning practices of prayer, financial administration, formation, etc. In institutes divided into provinces, there may well be also provincial or regional statutes or directives which allow for variations in culture and life-style. Normally, these require the approval of the supreme Moderator with the consent of his or her council.

Can. 588 §1 In itself, the state of consecrated life is neither clerical nor lay.

1156 This canon is a natural complement to Can. 207: in the Church there are clerics and lay people; from both groups are drawn those who live a life consecrated to God by profession of the evangelical counsels. 'This form of life has its own place in relation to the divine and hierarchical structure of the Church. Not, however, as though it were a kind of middle way between the clerical and lay conditions of life.'[1] The principle therefore is that the *state itself of consecrated life* cannot be defined in terms of being either clerical or lay. However, as the following paragraphs of this canon make clear, each individual institute of this life must be defined as either clerical or lay.

Can. 588 §2 A clerical institute is one which, by reason of the end or purpose intended by the founder, or by reason of lawful tradition, is under the governance of clerics, implies the exercise of sacred orders, and is recognised as such by the authority of the Church.

1157 In the spirit of Can. 578, the description of a clerical institute is based not simply on numerical considerations, as had been the case in c.488 4° of the 1917 Code, but rather on the intentions of the founder, on its apostolate and on its recognition by ecclesiastical authority. At any given time, a large number of the members of a clerical institute may be lay, either definitively if they have made final profession as 'brothers', or temporarily if they have been professed as candidates for major orders.

1158 The canon states explicitly that a clerical institute is 'under the governance of clerics', a natural consequence of the powers assigned to Superiors of clerical institutes in Can. 596 §2. In the wake of Vat. II, several institutes requested that *all* members (clerics and lay) should be eligible for the office of Superior. The Holy See clarified the matter in 1969: non-clerical members of clerical institutes could be councillors at all levels if the constitutions so permitted, or they could be employed in administrative work, but the offices of Superior and vicar were to be reserved to clerical members.[2] Exceptions in individual cases have been granted both before and after the promulgation of the Code, at both local and provincial level.[3] In each case, however, there has been a special stipulation with regard to those matters which require the exercise of sacred orders.

---

[1] LG 43: Fl I 403.

[2] Cf. SCRIS decr 27.XI.1969: CLD 7 469–470.

[3] SCRIS private rep 12.XI.1974; CLD 8 342; SCRIS private rep 7.XI.1978; CLD 9 346; SCRIS private rep 30.VII.1983: LE VI 8661.

Part III Institutes of Consecrated Life and Societies of Apostolic Life

Can. 588 §3 A lay institute is one which is recognised as such by ecclesiastical authority because, by its nature, character and purpose, its proper role defined by its founder or by lawful tradition, does not include the exercise of sacred orders.

Although ecclesiastical recognition is mentioned first, a lay institute is also defined primarily according to the intention of the founder: 'its proper role ... does not include the exercise of sacred orders'. All institutes of women are, therefore, lay institutes, as are many institutes of men founded for a particular apostolic purpose e.g. education, nursing. A lay institute of men may well have priests or deacons among its members, but only to serve the needs of the institute.[1] When members of such institutes are presented for sacred orders, the dimissorial letters are given by the diocesan Bishop, who is also responsible for checking the formation of the proposed candidate (see Cann. 1019 §2, 1050, 1051).

1159

Can. 589 An institute of consecrated life is of pontifical right if it has been established by the Apostolic See, or approved by it by means of a formal decree. An institute is of diocesan right if it has been established by the diocesan Bishop and has not obtained a decree of approval from the Apostolic See.

The new law makes a simple distinction between institutes of consecrated life:

1160

(a) they are *of pontifical right* if they have been established directly by the Apostolic See, or if they have received a decree of approval from the same supreme authority; this latter would be the case even when the institute had, as it were, begun its life as one of diocesan right but had subsequently been granted a formal decree of approval by the Apostolic See: it is to be noted that the 'consultation' with the Apostolic See required, even for validity, by Can. 579 is not, nor does it supply, the 'approval' referred to in this Can. 589.

(b) they are *of diocesan right* if they have been established by the diocesan Bishop in accordance with Can. 579, but have not at any stage received a formal decree of approval by the Apostolic See, either because such approval was not sought or because though sought it was not granted.

The origins of this distinction lie in Pope Leo XIII's ap con *Conditae a Christo*, which recognised as true religious communities those of women who professed simple vows and did not observe strict enclosure.[2] The present simpler and clearer law supersedes the provisions of cc.488 3° and 492 of the 1917 Code.

1161

Can. 590 §1 Institutes of consecrated life, since they are dedicated in a special way to the service of God and of the whole Church, are in a particular manner subject to its supreme authority.

A life consecrated to God by profession of the evangelical counsels is dedicated to God's service in the Church.[3] Juridically, therefore, it follows that *institutes* of consecrated life are subject in a special manner to the Pope and the College of Bishops, in whom is found the supreme authority of the Church (see Cann. 330–331, 336). In practice, this means that such institutes have particular ties to the Roman Curia through whom the Pope usually conducts the business of the universal Church (see Can. 360).

1162

---

[1] Cf. PC 10: Fl I 616.

[2] Cf. ap con *Conditae a Christo* 8.XII.1900: Fontes Codicis Iuris Canonici (1917) III 562–566.

[3] Cf. LG 44: Fl I 404; PC 5: Fl I 614.

Can. 590 §2 The individual members are bound to obey the Supreme Pontiff as their highest Superior, by reason also of their sacred bond of obedience.

1163 In addition to the respect and obedience required of all the faithful (see Cann. 204 §2; 209; 212 §1), *individual members* of institutes of consecrated life are bound in a special way, by virtue of their vow, to obey the Pope in his own person. This particular obedience, in so far as it is the object of a vow, does not extend to any official or department of the Roman Curia, except by special mandate of the Pope himself.

Can. 591 The better to ensure the welfare of institutes and the needs of the apostolate, the Supreme Pontiff, by virtue of his primacy in the universal Church, and with a view to the common good, can withdraw institutes of consecrated life from the governance of local Ordinaries, and subject them to himself alone, or to some other ecclesiastical authority.

1164 Historically, the Popes sometimes withdrew certain religious orders from the jurisdiction of the local Ordinaries. This practice, known as *exemption*, allowed the Pope to act freely in certain places at times of special difficulty, e.g. to combat heresy or to reform the life of the clergy. However, it was often viewed with suspicion by local Bishops who saw it as an infringement of their own authority in the local Church. Under c.488 2° of the 1917 Code, all religious in solemn vows were 'exempt' by law; so, too, were others to whom this had been granted by way of privilege. For all that, no consistent explanation was given for this exemption.

1165 The present canon, rooted in Vat. II,[1] supplies the rationale for exemption: the Pope can exempt an institute:

(a) for the welfare of the institute itself, i.e. the better to safeguard its patrimony (see Cann. 578; 586);

(b) the better to care for the apostolates undertaken by the institute, especially if these have been undertaken at the request of the Holy See.

The withdrawal from local jurisdiction is to be done 'with a view to the common good'. This is a more satisfactory approach than the older one which saw exemption rather in terms of a privilege for the institute.

Can. 592 §1 To promote closer union between institutes and the Apostolic See, each supreme Moderator is to send a brief account of the state and life of the institute to the same Apostolic See, in the manner and at the time it lays down.

1166 This ruling marks a departure from that of the 1917 Code and of subsequent legislation, whereby reports to the Holy See had to be submitted at fixed five-year intervals and in accordance with a detailed predetermined questionnaire. The present canon leaves the Holy See free to ask for a detailed report whenever it may wish, e.g. if a particular situation or problem were to arise in an institute. Otherwise the report is to be 'brief', suggesting a departure from the more stereotyped and very detailed reporting in the past. Obviously this will be a matter for determination from time to time by the Holy See.

Can. 592 §2 Moderators of each institute are to promote a knowledge of the documents issued by the Holy See which affect the members entrusted to them, and are to ensure that these documents are observed.

---

[1] Cf. LG 45: Fl I 405; CD 35 §3: Fl I 585; ES II 24–25: Fl I 604–605; MR 8, 22: Fl II 215, 224–225.

All members of institutes of consecrated life have the duty to be familiar with those documents issued by the Holy See which affect them. Such knowledge will assist them in living their consecrated life and in the exercise of their ministry in conjunction with the Bishops.[1] The canon speaks of 'documents issued by the Holy See'; this refers both to documents published to the whole Church and to specific communications addressed to the particular institute. There is a clear obligation on the Superiors of each institute to ensure that all of this information is officially disseminated among the members; it would not suffice that it be left to chance discovery by individuals.

Can. 593 In their internal governance and discipline, institutes of pontifical right are subject directly and exclusively to the authority of the Apostolic See, without prejudice to Can. 586.

In effect, this canon establishes the principal means of safeguarding the 'true autonomy of life' of each institute (see Can. 586). If an institute has been established or approved by the Holy See, the local Bishop has no rights in *the internal structures* of the institute. This canon may not, however, be read in isolation: by virtue of other canons, the local Bishop has serious responsibilities in respect of all such institutes in his diocese (see Cann. 616 §1; 678; 683).

Can. 594 An institute of diocesan right remains under the special care of the diocesan Bishop, without prejudice to Can. 586.

A much more immediate responsibility is incurred by the diocesan Bishop in respect of institutes of diocesan right. In preparing the text of this canon, the Revision Commission made it clear that the 'special care' is to be exercised by the Bishop not as an internal Superior, but as an ecclesiastical Superior; indeed, the Commission described as abuses the efforts of some Bishops to change the official dress of such institutes or to alter their internal structures of government.[2] Yet the diocesan Bishop has the responsibility of making sure that, in the internal government of the institute, the norm of law is followed and abuses are prevented.

Can. 595 §1 It is the Bishop of the principal house who approves the constitutions, and confirms any changes lawfully introduced into them, except for those matters which the Apostolic See has taken in hand. He also deals with major affairs which exceed the power of the internal authority of the institute. If the institute had spread to other dioceses, he is in all these matters to consult with the other diocesan Bishops concerned.

This canon follows on from the previous one and refers exclusively to diocesan institutes, whose relationship with the diocesan Bishop parallels that of pontifical institutes with the Holy See. Diocesan institutes can spread into other dioceses: the canon indicates the relative responsibilities of the diocesan Bishops involved. The main responsibility rests with the Bishop of the 'principal house': in effect, this is the mother-house or, if it is different, the one in which the general government is located. He is to approve the constitutions and lawful changes in them, and deal also with 'major affairs which exceed the power of the internal authority of the institute'.

The nature of these 'major affairs' will depend in part upon the constitutions of the institute. They will include, e.g. any matter arising from *lacunae* in the norms of the institute; the transfer of the principal house from one diocese to another; in cases of

---

[1] MR 29, 33: Fl II 228, 230.

[2] Cf. Comm 18(1986) 199 at Can. 4 §1.

departure and dismissal, to grant or to confirm the relevant decree (see Cann. 686, 688, 691, 700). The canon also lays on this Bishop the duty of consulting with other diocesan Bishops who may be concerned. His duties do not preclude the intervention of the Holy See, either in general matters involving all institutes of consecrated life, or in matters beyond his powers e.g. financial matters involving sums in excess of that established for the region (see Can. 638 §3).

Can. 595 §2 The diocesan Bishop can grant a dispensation from the constitutions in particular cases.

1172   Though based on the principle that the lawgiver has the right to dispense from his own laws, and therefore naturally applicable to the Bishop of the principal house who approves the constitutions, the power appears also to belong to other diocesan Bishops in whose dioceses the members of these institutes live. The authority is limited to 'particular cases', and does not therefore extend to granting general dispensations which would in effect amount to a change in the constitutions.

Can. 596 §1 Superiors and Chapters of institutes have that authority over the members which is defined in the universal law and in the constitutions.

1173   This canon establishes the broad principle which is elaborated for religious institutes in Cann. 617–620, 631–633 and, for secular institutes, in Can. 717. The precise scope of the authority of these Superiors and chapters (at all levels within the institute) is to be specified in the fundamental code or constitutions of each institute (see Can. 587).

Can. 596 §2 In clerical religious institutes of pontifical right, they have in addition the ecclesiastical power of governance, for both the external and the internal forum.

1174   Whereas c.501 §1 of the 1917 Code had restricted ecclesiastical jurisdiction to Superiors of exempt clerical institutes, the present canon acknowledges that this ecclesiastical power of governance belongs by right to Superiors in all clerical religious institutes of pontifical right. By virtue of Can. 732, Superiors of clerical societies of apostolic life of pontifical right also have this power of governance. Excluded from this provision of law are secular institutes of pontifical and diocesan right, lay religious institutes of pontifical and diocesan right, and clerical religious institutes of diocesan right. This 'ecclesiastical power of governance' is to be understood in the light of the general norms of law (see Cann. 129–144). The Superiors mentioned may, therefore, according to their status, grant dimissorial letters for the ordination of their subjects (see Can. 1019 §1), or grant faculties to hear, in houses of their institutes, the confessions of members of the institute and of those who normally reside there (see Cann. 967 §3, 968 §1, 969 §2).

Can. 596 §3 The provisions of Cann. 131, 133 and 137–144 apply to the authority mentioned in §1.

1175   This paragraph clarifies the nature of that power by which religious Superiors govern within their institutes. Although it is not to be confused with 'ecclesiastical power of governance' (see Can. 596 §2),[1] it bears many similarities to it. Thus this power may be ordinary or delegated (see Can. 131 §1), proper or vicarious (see Can. 131 §2). All matters related to the delegation of this power are regulated by the general provisions of Cann. 133, 137–144.

---

[1] Cf. Comm 15(1983) 64 at Can. 523 3.

Can. 597 §1 Every catholic with a right intention and the qualities required by universal law and the institute's own law, and who is without impediment, may be admitted to an institute of consecrated life.

At the very foundation of a life consecrated to God by the profession of the evangelical counsels lies a divine vocation (see Can. 573 §1). Discernment of such a vocation is not always an easy task. This canon presents in broad principle what is required in an individual before he or she is admitted to an institute of consecrated life:

- the candidate must be catholic, i.e. in full communion with the catholic Church (see Can. 205);
- he or she must have the right intention: this must be discerned by those responsible within the institute; purely human motives are not sufficient, e.g. education or accommodation;
- the candidate must have the qualities demanded by universal law (see Cann. 642–645, 720–721) and by the proper law of the institute.

While indicating that a person with these qualities may be admitted to the institute, the canon does not give rise to a right to be admitted (with subsequent recourse) nor does Can. 1491 apply: there is a right to admit but not a right to be admitted.

Can. 597 §2 No one may be admitted without suitable preparation.

This paragraph marks a change in practice following the deliberations of Vat. II and subsequent consideration of initial formation. Gone are the detailed prescriptions for postulancy with regard to time, place and purpose demanded by cc.539–541 of the 1917 Code. Instead, the onus is placed upon the institute to work out its own prenovitiate preparation, having due regard to its own nature, the needs of the candidate and documents emanating from the Holy See.[1] The preparation required will, therefore, vary both in duration and in content, and it will include also some awareness of the need for stability and emotional maturity.

Can. 598 §1 Each institute, taking account of its own special character and purposes, is to define in its constitutions the manner in which the evangelical counsels of chastity, poverty and obedience are to be observed in its way of life.

This paragraph, which stresses the observance of the evangelical counsels as the essence of consecrated life, derives from the thinking of Vat. II[2] and had no counterpart in the 1917 Code. It introduces a set of three canons, devoted in turn to each of the three counsels. The whole section was the subject of much discussion before the final promulgated text was agreed, both as to its content and its precise expression.[3] There were some who felt that more detail was required, lest the individual institutes produce texts with too little detail. However, the Holy See laid down the essentials which it would expect to find on each counsel when approving the text of constitutions.[4] Regulations in this regard are to appear in the constitutions or fundamental code of each institute.

Can. 598 §2 All members must not only observe the evangelical counsels faithfully and fully, but also direct their lives according to the institute's own law, and so strive for the perfection of their state.

---

[1] Cf. RC 4, 11–12: Fl I 639–645.
[2] Cf. PC 12–14: Fl I 617–620; LG 44: Fl I 403–405; ET 7: Fl I 683–684.
[3] Cf. Comm 11(1979) 309–310.
[4] Cf. SCRIS letter 10.VII.1972: Fl II 200–202.

1180 This paragraph, inspired by c.593 of the 1917 Code, makes it clear that the observance of the three evangelical counsels in the abstract does not constitute consecrated life. Rather, all who belong to an institute must live in obedience, chastity and poverty according to the proper law of that institute. In this way, each charism, the patrimony of each institute (see Can. 578) as a gift to the Church, is expressed in a particular way, even though they are all fundamentally similar through the profession of the evangelical counsels.

Can. 599 The evangelical counsel of chastity embraced for the sake of the Kingdom of heaven, is a sign of the world to come, and a source of greater fruitfulness in an undivided heart. It involves the obligation of perfect continence observed in celibacy.

1181 This is a theological description of the object of the vow of chastity, as well as a brief statement of the juridical consequences of professing this counsel. As described here, chastity is something fundamentally positive and firmly based on the teaching of Vat. II:[1] it is embraced for the Kingdom of God, a sign of the world to come, and helps the individual to serve God with an undivided heart. A similar description underlies the obligation of celibacy for clerics (see Can. 277 §1). The juridical statement makes matters clearer from a practical point of view: profession of chastity in this way means adopting a celibate way of life, i.e. a life of perfect continence in which legitimate sexual relationships are deliberately but freely renounced.

Can. 600 The evangelical counsel of poverty in imitation of Christ, who for our sake was made poor when he was rich, entails a life which is poor in reality and in spirit, sober and industrious, and a stranger to earthly riches. It also involves dependence and limitation in the use and the disposition of goods, in accordance with each institute's own law.

1182 The theological exposition of the evangelical counsel of poverty, again rooted in Vat. II,[2] focuses on the imitation of Christ and involves a particular style of life, one that is actually poor, without the observable trappings of the rich. Having thus spelled out the spiritual dimensions of poverty, the canon outlines its canonical consequences, developed in more detail for religious in Can. 668, i.e. dependence, which is a reliance on the institute to provide what is necessary; and limitation, in that even though many members of institutes of consecrated life can retain their personal patrimony, they are unable freely to dispose of these goods during their lifetime. According to the character of each institute, more detailed dispositions concerning poverty are to be contained in the institute's own law.

Can. 601 The evangelical counsel of obedience, undertaken in the spirit of faith and love in the following of Christ, who was obedient even unto death, obliges submission of one's will to lawful Superiors, who act in the place of God when they give commands that are in accordance with each institute's own constitutions.

1183 Once again the doctrinal part of this canon comes from conciliar and post-conciliar documents, the wording being revised in the course of compilation to reflect the different documents. While earlier drafts had spoken of 'the example of Christ' and 'dedication of the will'[3] the preferred text mentions 'the following of Christ' and 'submis-

---

[1] Cf. PC 12: Fl I 617–618; ET 13–15: Fl I 686–688.
[2] Cf. PC 13: Fl I 618; ES II 23–24: Fl I 629; ET 20–21: Fl I 690.
[3] PC 14: Fl I 619.

sion of one's will'. The description of Superiors as those 'who act in the place of God', traditional in religious life from the time of St Benedict – discussed in depth by the Revision Commission, especially with regard to its relevance to secular institutes[1] – has been retained.

The consequent canonical effects involve submission of the will to 'lawful Superiors ... when they give commands that are in accordance with each institute's own constitutions'. While the basic rights and obligations of Superiors are set out in subsequent canons (see Cann. 617–630), the constitutions of each institute are to indicate which Superiors – major Superiors only, or all Superiors – may invoke obedience by virtue of the vow. The Code itself provides norms concerning the member's freedom of conscience (see Can. 630).

Can. 602 The fraternal life proper to each institute unites all the members into, as it were, a special family in Christ. It is to be so defined that it proves of mutual assistance for all to fulfil their vocation. By their fraternal union, rooted and based in charity, the members are to be an example of universal reconciliation in Christ.

By definition, an individual who has made profession of the evangelical counsels within an approved institute of consecrated life cannot live in isolation from other members of the same institute. By virtue of their common profession, all members share in the fraternal life of the institute and are united as 'a special family in Christ'. The Code leaves it to each institute to determine the specific form of this fraternal life, so that the members might be assisted in living their response to God's call. Whatever the exact details, this fraternal life is intended to give witness to the Church and to the world of the reconciliation which has been won in Christ. As it stands, the canon is very general; more precise norms are to be found elsewhere (see Cann. 607 §2, 665, 714, 731). But even its very generality unquestionably rules out of order the practice, observable since Vat. II in some mainly western-style institutes, whereby for what are little more than trivial, personal and not infrequently selfish reasons some individual members choose – and are permitted – to live alone, apart from their community.[2]

Can. 603 §1 Besides institutes of consecrated life, the Church recognises the life of hermits or anchorites, in which Christ's faithful withdraw further from the world and devote their lives to the praise of God and the salvation of the world through the silence of solitude and through constant prayer and penance.

While most of the canons of this section of the Code are addressed to those who live a consecrated life in religious or secular institutes, this canon speaks of a type of consecrated life lived by an individual outside an institute. Hermits or anchorites represent one of the oldest forms of consecrated life in the history of the Church. In this canon, the terms are used synonymously, although custom acknowledges a difference: the term *hermit* implies one who lives apart, in a place far from human habitation, while the term *anchorite* suggests one who lives a solitary life in a cell near to a community.

---

[1] Cf. Comm 11(1979) 317–318 at Can. 34.

[2] A most significant document in this regard, which should be carefully studied by all concerned, was issued by SCRIS 2.II.1994 *Congregavit nos in unum Christi amor*: for the official translation in English cf. Origins 23 693–712.

1187 As recognised in the Code, this way of life is characterised by the following features:
- withdrawal from the world, i.e. the individual goes to live apart from others and does not engage in an external apostolate towards others;
- solitude, i.e. the hermit or anchorite lives alone and in silence;
- constant prayer and penance, i.e. it is not a way of life to be undertaken by the idle; these people devote their lives completely to the praise of God.

Can. 603 §2 Hermits are recognised by law as dedicated to God in consecrated life if, in the hands of the diocesan Bishop, they publicly profess, by a vow or some other sacred bond, the three evangelical counsels, and then lead their particular form of life under the guidance of the diocesan Bishop.

1188 Any Christian may choose to live an eremitical style of life such as that described in §1. However, canonical recognition of that way of life depends upon the verification of the conditions mentioned in this paragraph:
- there must be a rule or way of life drawn up under the guidance of the local Bishop and approved by him;
- the individual must make a public profession of the three evangelical counsels by means of vows or other sacred bonds;
- this must be done into the hands of the local diocesan Bishop in order to highlight the special relationship of dependence between the hermit and the local bishop.

While it is not explicitly prescribed by universal law, such a choice of lifestyle should be preceded by careful discernment and preparation. Since the rule of life in this case has the form of a particular law, the Bishop has the power to dispense from it (see Can. 88).

Can. 604 §1 The order of virgins approximates to these forms of consecrated life. Through their pledge to follow Christ more closely, virgins are consecrated to God, mystically espoused to Christ and dedicated to the service of the Church, when the diocesan Bishop consecrates them according to the approved liturgical rite.

1189 Another form of individual consecrated life mentioned here is that of consecrated virginity. This is also one of the oldest forms of consecrated life within the Church. Yet, in more recent centuries, the practice had fallen into desuetude, except among a few monastic institutes. Requests from Bishops to be able to bless and consecrate virgins living in the world were refused by the Holy See earlier this century.[1] However, at the very beginning of Vat. II, the Fathers of the Council had indicated their intention of revising the ancient rite of consecration of virgins,[2] and this was eventually promulgated in 1970.[3]

1190 This canon itself was not found in the first drafts. It was introduced after much debate within the Revision Commission.[4] The text makes it clear that this way of life is to be approximated to other forms of consecrated life. The Code uses the traditional term 'order' rather than 'state'; however, this does not imply some kind of organisation. The essence of this kind of life is presented briefly: they are to pledge

---

[1] Cf. SCR letter 25.III.1927: AAS 19 (1927) 38–39.

[2] Cf. SC 80: Fl I 23.

[3] Cf. SCDW decr 31.V.1970 *Mos virgines Consecrandi*: Not 1970 114 ff: CLD 7 421–425; cf. also Fl II 193–194.

[4] Cf. Comm 11(1979) 331–334 at Can. 39.

Part III Institutes of Consecrated Life and Societies of Apostolic Life

themselves to following Christ more closely by observing a life of virginity; this consecration is for the service of the Church, not for the gratification of the individual. This service is spelled out in the 1970 Norms attached to the rite of consecration: these women must spend their time in works of penance and mercy, in apostolic activity and devout prayer.[1]

According to the rite, such a consecration may be made by nuns and by women leading a life in the world; in fact, the canon refers solely to the latter. These women must never have been married or have lived openly in a manner contrary to chastity; they must also provide evidence that they will persevere in their life of service; they must be admitted to this consecration by their local Bishop who will stipulate how they are to lead their consecrated lives.[2]

Can. 604 §2 Virgins can be associated together to fulfil their pledge more faithfully, and to assist each other to serve the Church in a way that befits their state.

While virgins may, and often do, live on their own, they *may* also in virtue of this paragraph live together in groups, constituting small communities with a plan or way of life which is more or less determined in accordance with their own agreed wishes. There is no obligation on them so to live – this paragraph is purely permissive – nor do such communities thereby acquire juridical or moral personality in the Church (see Cann. 113 §2, 115 §1). On the other hand, should they wish to acquire this status, they may apply to the diocesan Bishop having first submitted their statutes for approval (see Cann. 114, 117): should the appropriate decree be issued, each such community would be a *public juridical person* in the sense of Can. 116.

Can. 605 The approval of new forms of consecrated life is reserved to the Apostolic See. Diocesan Bishops, however, are to endeavour to discern new gifts of consecrated life which the Holy Spirit entrusts to the Church. They are also to assist promoters to express their purposes in the best possible way, and to protect these purposes with suitable statutes, especially by the application of the general norms contained in this part of the Code.

Four forms of consecrated life are recognised formally by the Code: religious institutes, secular institutes, hermits, and consecrated virgins; alongside these are societies of apostolic life. The Church, conscious that these do not exhaust or express fully the variety of the gifts of the Spirit to the Church,[3] makes provision in this canon for other forms of consecrated life. Final approval of such forms belongs to the Holy See, but it is for the local diocesan Bishops to encourage such experiments, to test them and offer a preliminary approval based on the norms of the Code. It is to be noted that this canon deals with new *forms* of consecrated life, not new institutes.

Can. 606 Provisions concerning institutes of consecrated life and their members are equally valid in law for both sexes, unless it is established otherwise from the context or from the nature of things.

Among the principles which guided the revision of the Code was the avoidance of any kind of discrimination in drawing up norms concerning men and women who lived a consecrated life.[4] This was inspired by c.490 of the 1917 Code, which is the

---

[1] SCDW op cit 2: CLD 7 423.
[2] Ibid 5: CLD 7 423.
[3] Cf. PC 1: Fl I 611–612; LG 45: Fl I 405–406; AG 18: Fl I 834–835.
[4] Cf. Comm 2(1970) 176 at 7.

fundamental source of the present text. The canon states the principle of the equality of the sexes before the law, while it acknowledges that there may be occasions to establish specific norms for individuals or institutes of either sex, e.g. Can. 611 3° gives a new foundation of clerical religious the right to a church; Can. 667 §3 prescribes a particular type of enclosure for monasteries of nuns.

Title II
Religious Institutes

Can. 607 §1 Religious life, as a consecration of the whole person, manifests in the Church the marvellous marriage established by God as a sign of the world to come. Religious thus consummate a full gift of themselves as a sacrifice offered to God, so that their whole existence becomes a continuous worship of God in charity.

1195 This opening canon is an attempt to define religious life and so distinguish it from other approved forms of consecrated life. This first paragraph, based on conciliar and post-conciliar teaching, is a theological statement identifying four essential elements of religious life:

– the consecration of the whole person;
– the marriage established by God as a sign of the world to come;
– the full gift of self as a sacrifice;
– the continuous worship of God in charity.[1]

According to Pope Paul VI, 'without in any way undervaluing human love and marriage', it is the consecrated chastity of the religious which 'evokes this union (of Christ and the Church) in a more immediate way'.[2] By profession of the three evangelical counsels, the total giving of oneself to God, 'who alone is worthy of such a sweeping gift', constitutes one's whole life as a continuing act of religion.

Can. 607 §2 A religious institute is a society in which, in accordance with their own law, the members pronounce public vows and live a fraternal life in common. The vows are either perpetual or temporary; if the latter, they are to be renewed when the time elapses.

1196 The distinguishing canonical factors of a religious institute are that its members take public vows and share a fraternal life in common.

1197 A vow is a deliberate and free promise made to God, which the virtue of religion requires that it be fulfilled (see Can. 1191). It is *public* 'if it is accepted in the name of the Church by a lawful Superior' (see Can. 1192 §1). A distinction had been drawn in the 1917 Code between solemn vows and simple vows: the former were made by members of Orders, the latter by members of Congregations (see c.488 2°); any act

---

[1] Cf. LG 44: Fl I 403; PC 12: Fl I 617; ET 13: Fl I 686–687; PC 5: Fl I 614; RC 2: Fl I 637.
[2] ET 13: Fl I 687.

contrary to a solemn vow was invalid, while an act contrary to a simple vow was illicit but not necessarily invalid (see c.579). Under the 1917 Code, the nature of the vows had serious consequences for ownership of property (cc.580; 582) and for capacity for marriage (c.1073). The present Code, in Can. 1192 §2, retains the terms but the distinction no longer has any juridical significance.[1] The evangelical counsels (see Cann. 599–601) constitute the content of the vows.

A fraternal life in common has always been considered an intrinsic element of religious life. Vat. II spoke of life in common in terms of prayer, sharing the same spirit, mutual sharing and support, being a 'true family'.[2] It is for each institute to determine the precise implications of this in accordance with Can. 655. In view of a growing trend in some quarters towards manifest abuses in this regard – arising in the main from a misunderstanding of the spirit of Vat. II – the Holy See has on numerous occasions in recent years stressed the necessity of this 'family life in common' as an integral part of religious life. The phenomenon of members of religious institutes living alone on a permanent basis must be regarded as wholly exceptional (see Can. 665 §1) and a matter of very serious concern to those in charge within the institute.[3]

Can. 607 §3 The public witness which religious are to give to Christ and the Church involves that separation from the world which is proper to the character and purpose of each institute.

A further distinguishing feature of religious life is 'separation from the world'. The physical dimension of this is specified in Can. 667. However, the life of religious is to be regulated so that this separation is to be visible on other levels, e.g. a horarium setting aside time for prayer together, particular prescriptions concerning the life of poverty and chastity, etc. Life in a religious institute is to be marked in a clear manner as a life of penance and renunciation, a strong countersign against the values prevalent and advocated in certain contemporary elements of a materially-oriented society. In its own legislation, each institute is to determine more precisely how this is to be implemented.

Chapter I
RELIGIOUS HOUSES AND THEIR ESTABLISHMENT AND SUPPRESSION

Can. 608 A religious community is to live in a lawfully constituted house, under the authority of a Superior designated according to the norms of law. Each house is to have at least an oratory, in which the Eucharist is celebrated and reserved, so that it may truly be the centre of the community.

The description of a religious house reflects again the essential importance of fraternal life in common. The canon prescribes that a community of religious is to live together in a 'house'; yet that 'house' is not to be identified necessarily with a particular building, e.g. several 'houses' may exist in one large edifice; several small residences may be united as one 'house' provided that their proximity permits the fulfilment of the other requirements of the canon, i.e. access to the Superior, celebration and reservation of the Eucharist.

---

[1] Cf. Comm 17(1985) 120–132.

[2] PC 15: Fl I 620.

[3] Cf. in particular SCRIS private rep 1977 *Religious living alone in apartments*: CLD 9 446–452; SCRIS 2.II.1994 *Congregavit nos in unum Christi amor*: Origins 23 693–712.

1201 Whatever the material details, each religious house must be set up by the appropriate authority in accordance with the universal law of the Church and the proper law of the institute. Moreover, each house must have a properly designated Superior, who is to take responsibility for the rest of the community; he or she is obliged by Can. 629 to reside in the house. In recent years there has been a certain experimentation in some quarters which would purport to have the religious house governed by *all the members* belonging to it, working together as it were a 'governing team'. Any such practice would be contrary to the law. Whereas the greatest possible cooperation and harmony is always to be encouraged and promoted between the Superior and the other members of the house, the law is unambiguous that there is to be *one person* designated as Superior and authorised to act as such, and accordingly that the other members of the house, while being collaborators with the Superior in communal charity, are his or her subjects in accordance with the constitutions (see also Cann. 617–619).

1202 Whereas c.1265 §1 2° of the 1917 Code required the Bishop's permission for the reservation of the blessed Eucharist, now all duly constituted religious houses must have at least an oratory in which Mass is to be celebrated and the Blessed Sacrament reserved. These oratories are subject to the provisions of Cann. 934–943, 1229, 1239. The very purpose of this regulation is that the Eucharist may truly be the centre of the community life; it is precisely that which differentiates a religious community from other groups of people living together.[1]

Can. 609 §1 Houses of a religious institute are established, with the prior written consent of the diocesan Bishop, by the authority competent according to the constitutions.

§2 For the establishment of a monastery of nuns, the permission of the Apostolic See is also required.

1203 The valid canonical establishment of religious houses requires two separate elements:

(a) the written consent of the diocesan Bishop;
(b) the decree of the Superior of the institute who, according to the proper law of the institute, is responsible for constituting a house.

By canonical establishment, the house acquires juridical personality and is subject to the laws concerning juridical persons (see Cann. 113–123). A third element is required for the establishment of a monastery of nuns (see Can. 614), namely the permission of the Holy See obtained from the Congregation for Institutes of Consecrated Life and Societies of Apostolic Life.

Can. 610 §1 In establishing religious houses, the welfare of the Church and of the institute are to be kept in mind, and care must be taken to safeguard everything that is necessary for the members to lead their religious life in accordance with the purposes and spirit proper to the institute.

1204 This paragraph calls for a strict discernment on the part of both authorities engaged in the process of establishing a religious house. It is for the Bishop, as head of the local Church, to assess how the proposed foundation will benefit the diocese, taking into account also the numbers of other religious houses within the diocese, their work and their means of support. It is for the relevant Superior of the institute to judge whether the institute has sufficient members to give the proposed foundation an adequate degree of stability.

---

[1] Cf. ET 47–48: Fl I 701–702.

In addition, everything must be done to ensure that the new community will be able to live according to the spirit and purpose of the institute. Thus the apostolic works entrusted to the community must be in harmony with the patrimony of the institute (see Can. 578). The members must also be assured of what is necessary for the internal life of the community and the public witness they are expected to give. The canon makes no mention of the minimum number of members for such a community, but a canonically established religious house must have at least three members (see Can. 115 §2).

Can. 610 §2 No house is to be established unless it is prudently foreseen that the needs of the members can be suitably provided for.

Whereas c.496 of the 1917 Code was concerned principally with the question of financial support, this paragraph states a more general principle: before a new religious house is set up, the Bishop and the relevant religious Superior should consider the needs of the projected new community, i.e. economic needs, needs related to accommodation, spiritual support and services. Only if both authorities are satisfied that adequate provision can be made should the new foundation proceed.

Can. 611 The consent of the diocesan Bishop for the establishment of a religious house carries with it the right:

1° **to lead a life according to the character and purposes proper to the institute;**

2° **to engage in the works which are proper to the institute, in accordance with the law, and subject to any conditions attached to the consent;**

3° **for clerical religious institutes to have a church, subject to the provisions of Can. 1215 §3, and to conduct the sacred ministries, with due observance of the law.**

When the diocesan Bishop gives the permission mentioned in Can. 609 §1, the law confers certain rights on the new religious community. Two of these rights refer to all religious; the third refers only to clerical institutes; all three are closely related to the patrimony of the institute (see Can. 578). Only the first right is unqualified, i.e. the members have a right to live according to the spirit and character of their institute; the Bishop cannot be involved in this since it belongs to the internal discipline of the institute (see Can. 586 §2). The right to carry out the proper works of the institute may be subject to conditions set by the Bishop in virtue of his responsibility to coordinate the apostolate (see Can. 394 §1); however, he cannot require religious to undertake works alien to their charism. Although the law gives clerical institutes the right to a church in which they may exercise the sacred ministries, no such church may be constructed without the specific permission of the Bishop (see Can. 1215 §3). In order to avoid confusion and possible conflict, all details concerning the apostolate (including the question of a church) should be the object of careful prior negotiations and of an agreed document, *before the permission is granted*.

Can. 612 The consent of the diocesan Bishop is required if a religious house is to be used for apostolic works other than those for which it was constituted. This permission is not required for a change which, while observing the laws of the foundation, concerns only internal governance and discipline.

The Bishop is charged with the coordination of the apostolate in the diocese (see Can. 394 §1) and in all such matters religious are subject to the authority of the diocesan Bishop (see Can. 678 §1). The present canon is a natural consequence of these principles. If permission was obtained from the Bishop for the establishment of a house for specified apostolic works, these works may not be changed without the express consent of the Bishop. However, the canon refers only to external works of the apostolate. Changes of a purely internal nature which do not affect the apostolate e.g. establishment of a novitiate or an infirmary, do not require further episcopal permission, though it would obviously be normal to pay the Bishop the courtesy of informing him of such developments.

Can. 613 §1 A religious house of canons regular or of monks under the governance and care of their own Moderator is autonomous, unless the constitutions decree otherwise.

1209 Canons regular (e.g. Premonstratensians) and monks (e.g. Benedictines) are among the oldest forms of religious life. Historically, they lived in communities subject to a local Superior or Abbot. Each house with an abbot was autonomous or *sui iuris*. The present canon recognises this tradition and makes it part of universal law. In addition, the canon acknowledges the possibility that the fundamental legislation of such an institute may contain provisions regulating the relationship between an autonomous house and other houses of the institute (e.g. filial houses).

Can. 613 §2 The Moderator of an autonomous house is by law a major Superior.

1210 The principle enunciated in this paragraph is identical to that found in Can. 620. In the context of §1, this serves to underline the autonomy of each house of canons regular and monks. Moreover, if the institutes are of pontifical right, these Superiors are also Ordinaries (see Can. 134 §1).

Can. 614 Monasteries of nuns which are associated with an institute of men, have their own rule of life and governance, in accordance with the constitutions. The mutual rights and obligations are to be defined in such a way that spiritual good may come from the association.

1211 Many monasteries of nuns have close historical ties with religious institutes of men, e.g. Benedictines, Cistercians, Carmelites, Poor Clares. In some cases, this association involves a degree of dependence on the major Superior of the men's institute. This association does not deprive the individual monasteries of a true autonomy of life: each monastery is to regulate its internal life and discipline in accordance with the constitutions. Any rights or obligations arising out of this association are to be defined carefully in the fundamental legislation of both institutes. This is the most secure way of guaranteeing the spiritual benefits of the historical link while safeguarding the nuns' autonomy.

Can. 615 If an autonomous monastery has no major Superior other than its own Moderator, and is not associated with any institute of religious in such a way that the Superior of that institute has over the monastery a real authority determined by the constitutions, it is entrusted, in accordance with the norms of law, to the special vigilance of the diocesan Bishop.

1212 Other monasteries exist which do not belong to a religious institute with a supreme Moderator and which do not have any association with another institute to which they are in some way subordinated juridically (e.g. monasteries of the Visitation). Monasteries of this kind are committed by this canon to the special care of the diocesan Bishop. His duties towards these monasteries are found in Cann. 625 §2; 628 §2

1°; 637; 638 §4; 688 §2; 699 §2. Although in theory this canon could refer to monasteries of men or women, in practice it applies more to monasteries of nuns.

Can. 616 §1 After consultation with the diocesan Bishop, a supreme Moderator can suppress a lawfully established religious house, in accordance with the constitutions. The institute's own law is to make provision for the disposal of the goods of the suppressed house, with due regard for the wishes of founders or benefactors and for lawfully acquired rights.

Within this one canon is contained all the general legislation about the closure of houses, together with directives about the disposal of the goods of the house in question.

The first paragraph deals with the closure of a religious house established in accordance with Can. 609 §1. What is involved is the total suppression of the house, not a change in personnel. The process foreseen in the canon is much simpler than that contained in c.498 of the 1917 Code: the supreme Moderator of the institute suppresses the house after having consulted the diocesan Bishop. This *consultation* is required for validity (see Can. 127 §2 2°). The *consent* of the Bishop is not necessary, nor is there to be any recourse to the Holy See as the 1917 Code had required for exempt religious. The proper law of the institute may indicate further persons or bodies whose consent or advice is needed.

This same proper law of the institute must also provide for the disposal of the property pertaining to the religious house (see Can. 123). The canon makes reference to the wishes of founders or benefactors (see Can. 1300). Before any definitive decision is taken, where possible the relevant authority should consult with these people or their successors. Should certain rights have been acquired through a person's association with a particular house (e.g. right of burial), these must be considered and attended to before the house is closed. In all cases, the appropriate prescriptions of civil law must also be observed.

Can. 616 §2 The Holy See alone can suppress the sole house of an institute, in which case it is also reserved to the Holy See to prescribe concerning the property of the house.

In conformity with Can. 584, the law reserves the closure of the sole house of an institute to the Apostolic See since, in effect, this amounts to the total suppression of the institute. It does not matter whether the institute has dwindled in size until it occupies only one house or whether it was only ever established in one house. The Holy See alone has authority to suppress such a house and dispose of its property; those goods which belong to such a house are ecclesiastical goods (see Can. 1257 §1) and accordingly not the property of the members of the institute.

Can. 616 §3 Unless the constitutions enact otherwise, the suppression of the autonomous houses mentioned in Can. 613 belongs to the general chapter.

Where the house to be closed is an autonomous house of canons regular or monks (see Can. 613), the Code attributes to the general chapter (see Can. 631 §1) of the institute the authority given to the supreme Moderator of other institutes (see Can. 616 §1). While it is not mentioned explicitly, by analogy of law the general chapter must also provide for the disposal of property (see Can. 123). This paragraph does however foresee the possibility that the constitutions of the institute might have made alternative provisions in this regard.

Can. 616 §4 The suppression of an autonomous monastery of nuns pertains to the Apostolic See; the provisions of the constitutions are to be observed concerning the property of the monastery.

1218 Since the erection of an autonomous monastery of nuns requires the specific intervention of the Holy See (see Can. 609 §2), it is only to be expected that its closure also requires the same intervention. Property is to be disposed of in accordance with the constitutions; should they fail to have made provision, the disposal is to be determined by the Holy See (see Can. 123).

Chapter II
THE GOVERNANCE OF INSTITUTES

Article 1
Superiors and Councils

Can. 617 Superiors are to fulfil their office and exercise their authority in accordance with the norms of the universal law and of their own law.

1219 This introductory canon places the legal source of the authority of the Superior in the provisions of universal Church law and that of the institute. The Church's law itself enjoins certain responsibilities on Superiors, while others are left to be spelt out in the institute's own law, e.g. those occasions when either the advice or the consent of the Superior's council is required for the validity of the Superior's action (see Can. 627). The provisions of this canon, as with those of the next two, apply to Superiors at all levels within religious institutes.

Can. 618 The authority which Superiors receive from God through the ministry of the Church is to be exercised by them in a spirit of service. In fulfilling their office they are to be docile to the will of God, and are to govern those subject to them as children of God. By their reverence for the human person, they are to promote voluntary obedience. They are to listen willingly to their subjects and foster their cooperation for the good of the institute and the Church, without prejudice however to their authority to decide and to command what is to be done.

1220 This canon first states the theological basis for the authority of the Superior: it derives from God through the ministry of the Church. This reflects the constant teaching of the Church, brought out even more pointedly by Vat. II and later documents, where the virtue of obedience and the nature of religious authority are clearly set out.[1]

1221 From this theological understanding of obedience derive the instructions about the manner in which Superiors are to exercise their authority – in a spirit of humility and in the search for the will of God and the good of the Church. Voluntary obedience is seen as something to be encouraged through appropriate dialogue and consultation. Throughout, Superiors are to consider those in their charge as children of God – not in a mere adult–child relationship, rather as fellow children of the same Father.

1222 Finally, the canon gives a clear statement of the right of the Superior to govern and to command. Without that right, it would be unjust to place upon Superiors the respon-

---
[1] Cf. LG 43, 45: Fl I 403, 405; PC 14: Fl I 619; ET 25: Fl I 692; MR 13: Fl II 218.

sibilities that are consequent upon their office. It recognises that the Superior is no mere executive of the consensus or majority opinion, but has the authority to govern, an authority which is not diminished by the manner in which it is to be exercised, i.e. through discussion and with respect for those in their charge.

Can. 619 Superiors are to devote themselves to their office with diligence. Together with the members entrusted to them, they are to strive to build in Christ a fraternal community, in which God is sought and loved above all. They are therefore frequently to nourish their members with the food of God's word and lead them to the celebration of the liturgy. They are to be an example to the members in cultivating virtue and in observing the laws and traditions proper to the institute. They are to give the members opportune assistance in their personal needs. They are to be solicitous in caring for and visiting the sick; they are to chide the restless, console the fainthearted and be patient with all.

This canon contains a description of the qualities desirable in a religious Superior. Rooted firmly in the teaching of Vat. II,[1] the canon stresses the need for the Superior to have a sound spiritual and religious life, to give example and encouragement to others, to provide proper leadership, and to show care and concern for all those in any kind of need. None of the qualities listed is prescriptive in the strict sense. However, the canon provides an objective yardstick for those who must elect or appoint such Superiors. 1223

Can. 620 Major Superiors are those who govern an entire institute, or a province or a part equivalent to a province, or an autonomous house; the vicars of the above are also major Superiors. To these are added the Abbot Primate and the Superior of a monastic congregation, though these do not have all the authority which the universal law gives to major Superiors.

The canon lists those who hold the office of major Superior: 1224

- those who govern an entire institute (referred to in the Code as the supreme Moderator);
- those who govern a province or quasi-province (i.e. a stably constituted internal territorial division of the institute (see Can. 621));
- those who govern an autonomous house;
- the Vicars of the above.

The Abbot Primate and Superior of a monastic congregation (e.g. Benedictines and Cistercians) are also considered major Superiors. However, these offices may not involve any real jurisdiction over the constituent monasteries of such an institute. The exact nature and scope of their authority is to be found in the proper law of the institute. The canon uses the generic term 'congregation'; this includes those groupings called 'Confederations' or 'Federations'.

The proper law of a religious institute must distinguish clearly the nature and scope of the offices of major Superior. In particular, it must define the relationship between the supreme moderator and the other major Superiors. 1225

The Code also recognises as major Superiors the vicars of those who govern an institute, or a part of it, or an autonomous house i.e. those duly designated by the proper 1226

---

[1] Cf. LG 44: Fl I 404; PC 6, 15: Fl I 614–615, 620; DV 25: Fl I 764; ES II 16: Fl I 627; CD 15–16: Fl I 571–573; PO 7: Fl I 875–876.

law of the institute to take the place of the relevant Superior if he or she is absent or impeded. The canon does not apply to those who substitute for a major Superior in an *ad hoc* manner.

1227 Since it is the policy of the Code to use general terms, leaving institutes to translate these into the familiar terms of their own legislation, it is essential that institutes define clearly the status they attach to internal divisions of a stable nature. In some institutes, these divisions have a status 'equivalent to a province', with a Major Superior at its head; in others, they have a lesser status, and their Superiors exercise an authority delegated to them by their immediate major Superior.

Can. 621 The union of several houses which constitutes an immediate part of the same institute under the same Superior and has been canonically established by lawful authority, is called a province.

1228 This canon contains one of the few definitions found in the Code. A 'province' is understood to be the primary internal division of an institute. It consists of a number of houses united under one overall Superior, without prejudice to the authority of the supreme Moderator of the institute. Whereas c. 494 §1 of the 1917 Code reserved the matter to the Apostolic See, it is for the proper law of each institute to determine when and how a province is to be established or suppressed.

Can. 622 The supreme Moderator has authority over all provinces, houses and members of the institute, to be exercised in accordance with the institute's own law. Other Superiors have authority within the limits of their office.

1229 The generic term 'supreme Moderator' is used to designate the one who exercises supreme authority in a religious institute, regardless of the particular title he or she holds. Whatever the nature of internal divisions and their government, this supreme Moderator has authority over the whole institute and all its constituent parts. This authority must be exercised in accordance with the proper law of the institute, e.g. in some cases, that authority may be highly centralised; in others, more authority may be devolved upon major Superiors at a lower level, or even to local Superiors. In all cases, the proper law must establish the limits of the authority exercised by Superiors at all levels within the institute.

Can. 623 To be validly appointed or elected to the office of Superior, members must have been perpetually or definitively professed for an appropriate period of time, to be determined by their own law or, for major Superiors, by the constitutions.

1230 A prerequisite for the valid election or appointment of a Superior within a religious institute is perpetual or definitive profession within that institute. The appointment or election of a member in temporary vows is invalid. Moreover, the proper law of each institute is to complement this requirement of universal law by determining how long after final profession a person becomes eligible for the office of Superior. In the case of a major Superior, this specification must be part of the constitutions or fundamental code of the institute; in the case of Superiors at other levels, this determination may be remitted to a secondary code or collection of norms, e.g. statutes, directories.

Can. 624 §1 Superiors are to be constituted for a certain and appropriate period of time, according to the nature and needs of the institute, unless the constitutions establish otherwise for the supreme Moderator and for Superiors of an autonomous house.

The principle of universal law is that all religious Superiors are to be elected or appointed for *a fixed term of office*. While c.505 of the 1917 Code sought to prescribe limits for the local Superior, this canon leaves the determination of all periods of office to the proper legislation of each institute. In this way, the nature and needs of each institute can be catered for. Should the tradition of an institute or autonomous house be to have the supreme Moderator elected or appointed for life, this must be stated clearly in the constitutions which are submitted for approval by the Holy See. 1231

Can. 624 §2 An institute's own law is to make suitable provisions so that Superiors constituted for a defined time do not continue in offices of governance for too long a period of time without an interval.

This paragraph, applicable at all levels of government, places an added responsibility upon institutes to ensure a change of leadership. In their renewed constitutions, institutes have been conscious of this need to make provision so that the same person does not hold the same (or similar) office for too long a time. The canon does not prohibit the taking up of office again, after an appropriate lapse of time. 1232

Can. 624 §3 During their period in office, however, Superiors may be removed or transferred to another office, for reasons prescribed in the institute's own law.

The temporary nature of the office of Superior at all levels is emphasised by this paragraph which indicates two ways in which a term of office may be curtailed: 1233
(a) by removal from office; this may be necessary because of the serious and prolonged ill-health of a Superior or because of serious malpractice or incompetence;
(b) by transfer to another office, e.g. because of a new undertaking, a serious and unforeseen need elsewhere in the institute, or service at a different level of government.

The institute's own law is to indicate the specific reasons for which a Superior may be thus transferred or removed from office, bearing in mind the general norms concerning transfer and removal from office (see Cann. 190–195).

Can. 625 §1 The supreme Moderator of the institute is to be designated by a canonical election, in accordance with the constitutions.

The only method of making valid provision for the office of supreme Moderator of a religious institute is by *canonical election*. This takes place in accordance with Cann. 164–179 and with whatever complementary or supplementary norms are found in the institute's own legislation, e.g. concerning previous consultations of the members. Normally this election takes place in the General Chapter of the institute, although the Holy See has granted the faculty of direct and universal suffrage in some cases.[1] 1234

Can. 625 §2 The Bishop of the principal house of the institute presides at the election of the Superior of the autonomous monastery mentioned in Can. 615, and at the election of the supreme Moderator of an institute of diocesan right.

The presence of the local Bishop is not required at the election of the supreme Moderator of institutes of religious women of pontifical right; this had been required in c.506 §4 of the 1917 Code. The local Bishop, however, is to preside at the election of the Superior of the autonomous monasteries mentioned in Can. 615, i.e. those 1235

---

[1] Cf. e.g. SCRIS private rep 24.X.1972: CLD 8 357.

with no other major Superior and with no jurisdictional link with another institute. Similarly, he is to preside at the election of the supreme Moderator of an institute of diocesan right. In this case, it is the Bishop of the principal house who is involved. The Code no longer speaks of this Bishop's right under c.506 §4 of the 1917 Code to confirm or even rescind these elections.

Can. 625 §3 Other Superiors are to be constituted in accordance with the constitutions, but in such a way that if they are elected, they require the confirmation of the competent major Superior; if they are appointed by the Superior, the appointment is to be preceded by suitable consultation.

1236 The wording of this canon is deliberately chosen to cover both the elected and the appointed Superior. The proper law of each institute is to determine the most appropriate manner of selecting and constituting Superiors. Members of the institute are to have some part in this process, either by voting in elections or otherwise expressing their views during consultation. No one elected acquires the rights to office unless that election has been confirmed in accordance with Can. 179.

Can. 626 Superiors in conferring offices, and members in electing to office, are to observe the norms of the universal law and the institute's own law, avoiding any abuse or preference of persons. They are to have nothing but God and the good of the institute before their eyes, and appoint or elect those whom, in the Lord, they know to be worthy and fitting. In elections, besides, they are to avoid directly or indirectly lobbying for votes, either for themselves or for others.

1237 The canon considers the dispositions necessary both in those who appoint and in those who elect. Setting aside personal favouritisms, they are to seek the will of God and choose the most suitable person. Abolished is the requirement of c.506 §1 of the 1917 Code that in certain cases an oath to this effect be taken beforehand by the electors. While the canon forbids any form of lobbying or canvassing, for oneself or for others, it does not exclude the duty of informing oneself about the qualities of the candidates and their approach to the office. What is excluded is any form, however subtle, of manipulation of the electoral body. Those who make provision for an office, whether through election or appointment, must do so on the basis of objective criteria expressed in the universal law of the Church and the proper law of the institute.

Can. 627 §1 Superiors are to have their own council, in accordance with the constitutions, and they must make use of it in the exercise of their office.

1238 While on one hand stressing the close connection between Superior and council in the matter of advising and discerning, on the other hand the canon emphasises in its wording the *distinct roles* involved. The Superior *has* a council, and hence is not part of it. The council exists only in relation to the Superior. When the council votes, the Superior takes note of that in the way prescribed, but *does not* vote with the council – a point specifically made in an authentic interpretation by the Holy See.[1]

1239 The canon leaves to institutes themselves to determine in the constitutions the details of the establishment and structure of such councils. While the size of these councils will vary, the Code requires a minimum of four members in a general council for a valid vote to dismiss a religious (see Can. 699 §1). If the permanently established council is smaller, proper legislation must provide the means to increase the number.

---

[1] Cf. CCom rep 14.V.1985: AAS 77(1985) 771 ad II.

Can. 627 §2 Apart from the cases prescribed in the universal law, an institute's own law is to determine the cases in which the validity of an act depends upon consent or advice being sought in accordance with Can. 127.

A council participates in the decision making process in three ways:

(a) If a *collegial vote* is required (see Can. 699 §1) the Superior is obliged to carry out the decision;

(b) If the *consent* of the council is called for, the Superior cannot act validly without that consent (i.e. a majority decision of the council: see Cann. 647 §§1–2, 684 §1, 690); however, having obtained that consent, the Superior is not obliged to execute the decision;

(c) If *advice only* is demanded for validity (see Cann. 689 §1, 697), the Superior must consult the council before acting. He or she is not bound by the result of the consultation, although it ought not be set aside lightly (see Can. 127 §2 2°).

In addition to these interventions of the council demanded by the Code, the institute itself may specify those other occasions when and how the council must intervene in a decision.

Can. 628 §1 Superiors who are designated for this office by the institute's own law are at stated times to visit the houses and the members entrusted to them, in accordance with the norms of the same law.

The visitation of religious communities is a long-established method of ensuring a high quality of religious life among the members of an institute. It provides the relevant Superior with an opportunity to assess the life and ministry of individuals and communities. It provides the members with an opportunity to discuss matters of importance with the Superior. The Code leaves it to the proper law of each institute to designate the Superior for this role and to determine all details concerning the manner and frequency of visitation.

Can. 628 §2 The diocesan Bishop has the right and the duty to visit the following, even in respect of religious discipline:

   1° the autonomous monasteries mentioned in Can. 615;

   2° the individual houses of an institute of diocesan right situated in his territory.

The diocesan Bishop's right and duty of visitation is exercised only in respect of the two types of institute indicated in the canon. He does not have the right or duty to make a visitation of houses of institutes of pontifical right, except as provided for by Can. 683. Such visitations as are envisaged here provide access to ecclesiastical authority for members of autonomous communities. For institutes of diocesan right, the power of visitation is given to the diocesan Bishop in whose territory each individual house is located; the Bishop of the principal house is to visitate only that house and such others of the institute as are located in his diocese. The diocesan Bishop who makes the visitation is competent to grant dispensations from the constitutions in particular cases (see Can. 595 §2). No specific intervals are determined in the Code for these episcopal visitations.

Can. 628 §3 The members are to act trustingly with the visitor and are bound to reply to his lawful questions truthfully in charity. It is not lawful for anyone in any way to divert members from this obligation or otherwise to hinder the scope of the visitation.

1243 In this paragraph is repeated the substance of c.513 §1 of the 1917 Code. However, the tone is more positive and more pastoral. While it is difficult to legislate for mutual trust, the opening phrase indicates the spirit in which the visitation is to take place: members are obliged to reply to legitimate questioning but truthfully and in charity. Moreover, they are obliged to respect the purpose of the visitation and not in any way impede its progress.

Can. 629 Superiors are to reside each in his or her own house, and they are not to leave it except in accordance with the institute's own law.

1244 The law does not countenance 'absentee Superiors'. It imposes the primary duty on all Superiors to live in the house for which they are responsible, and so to be available to those whom they are called upon to serve. At the same time, by referring to 'the institute's own law', it makes provision for necessary absence for purposes of apostolate, recreation, retreat or other designated service. This obligation of residence must be understood in the context of the current concept of 'religious house' (see Can. 608).

Can. 630 §1 While safeguarding the discipline of the institute, Superiors are to acknowledge the freedom due to the members concerning the sacrament of penance and the direction of conscience.

1245 This single canon, concerning the Sacrament of Penance, replaces cc.518–530 of the 1917 Code. It may seem strange to find a canon so closely allied to the internal spiritual life located in a section concerning the government of institutes, but this canon deals with the duty of Superiors to make proper provision for the availability of the sacrament. In framing this particular canon, the Revision Commission kept in mind a number of factors, e.g. the difficulty of finding confessors in every place where a religious house is established, the obligation placed on religious to approach the sacrament frequently, etc.[1]

1246 This first paragraph establishes the freedom of the individual members of an institute to choose their own confessor and spiritual director. Superiors at all levels within the institute are required to acknowledge this liberty. Of course, the exercise of this freedom must not be permitted to undermine the basic discipline of the institute: in selecting a confessor or spiritual director, the members are to act within the limits of a reasonable conduct within their religious family.

Can. 630 §2 Superiors are to take care, in accordance with the institute's own law, that the members have suitable confessors available, to whom they may confess frequently.

1247 While the fundamental choice of a confessor rests with the individual, every Superior has the duty of making sure that a real choice of confessor can be made, i.e. that a sufficient number of suitable priests is available. In many places, it will not be possible to offer a wide selection on a frequent basis. Nevertheless, the Superior must do what is possible to provide this choice.

Can. 630 §3 In monasteries of nuns, in houses of formation and in more numerous lay communities, there are to be ordinary confessors, approved by the local Ordinary after consultation with the community. There is, however, no obligation to approach these confessors.

1248 The broad principle enunciated in the preceding paragraph is made more specific in respect of certain categories of religious houses, i.e. monasteries of nuns, formation

---

[1] Cf. Comm 12(1980) 161–170 at Can. 15.

houses, large lay communities. In these cases, provision must be made for more than one confessor. An innovation is that the community must first be consulted about the suitability of the confessors in question before the approval of the local Bishop is sought; clearly, however, not every individual preference need be met. Moreover, while the Superior has the responsibility of making this provision, the members are under no obligation to avail themselves of it.

Can. 630 §4 Superiors are not to hear the confessions of their subjects unless the members spontaneously request them to do so.

This regulation parallels that applying to rectors of seminaries (see Can. 985). It provides a double protection: for the subject, preventing any undue pressure in a matter concerning the internal forum; for the Superior, preventing any suggestion that he has, in his role as Superior, used information which came to him through the sacrament.

Can. 630 §5 The members are to approach their Superiors with trust and be able to open their minds freely and spontaneously to them. Superiors, however, are forbidden in any way to induce the members to make a manifestation of conscience to themselves.

The final paragraph encourages a relationship of deep mutual trust in which a member can, if he or she so wishes, reveal matters of conscience to a Superior. Where this occurs spontaneously, the Superior is bound never to reveal this confidence without the individual's express permission. However, as with c.530 §1 of the 1917 Code, Superiors are strictly forbidden to put members in a situation where they feel obliged to make revelations of this kind. To do such would be a grave abuse of the office of Superior, for which a just penalty may be imposed (see Can. 1389 §1).

Article 2
Chapters

Can. 631 §1 The general chapter which possesses supreme authority in an institute according to the constitutions, is to be composed in such a way that, representing the whole institute, it becomes a true sign of its unity in charity. Its principal functions are to protect the patrimony of the institute mentioned in Can. 578, to foster appropriate renewal in accordance with that patrimony, to elect the supreme Moderator, to deal with more important matters, and to issue norms which all are bound to obey.

The term 'chapter' has its origins in the daily meeting of a community of monks to listen to the reading of a chapter from the Rule of St Benedict. Gradually, this meeting developed to include an interpretation of the text given by the abbot, as well as discussions and decisions related to the Rule. As religious life evolved, the 'chapter' acquired a distinct juridical structure within each institute. It was found on various levels – local, provincial, general – each with its own sphere of competence. Curiously, the 1917 Code made only one passing reference to this institution in its c.501 §1. After Vat. II, however, the General Chapter was entrusted with the task of implementing the renewal of each institute.[1]

---

[1] Cf. ES II 1–3: Fl I 624–625; Pope Paul VI alloc *Magno gaudio* 23.V.1964: CLD 6 429–431.

Book II The People of God

1252 The General Chapter is described as having 'supreme authority' within an institute. This authority lasts only while the chapter is in session. It does not undermine the authority of the supreme Moderator, who continues, even while the chapter is in session, to deal with the day-to-day administrative and governmental affairs of the institute. However, the General Chapter provides a forum within which the supreme Moderator can give an account of the exercise of his or her authority, since this body represents the whole institute. While it is in session, the General Chapter provides an opportunity for the members to give a corporate witness of their 'unity in charity'.

1253 Without going into details, the canon identifies five major functions of a General Chapter. The first two are a continuation of the role assigned to it after Vat. II, namely to protect the patrimony of the institute and promote the ongoing renewal of the institute based on that patrimony. The third function is to elect the supreme Moderator, a clear expression of the General Chapter's 'supreme authority'. Some smaller institutes have, however, been granted the faculty of electing their supreme Moderator by direct universal suffrage.[1] The General Chapter also handles matters of major moment for the whole institute, e.g. the preparation of a programme of studies (see Can. 659 §3). Finally, it belongs to the General Chapter to promulgate laws affecting all the members of an institute.

Can. 631 §2 The composition of the general chapter and the limits of its powers are to be defined in the constitutions. The institute's own law is to determine in further detail the order to be observed in the celebration of the chapter, especially regarding elections and the matters to be treated.

1254 The Code wisely does not enter into details about how the General Chapter is to be the representative body described in §1. The actual composition of the chapter varies enormously in different institutes, depending on their size, location, tradition and apostolates. All such details must be set forth in the constitutions of the institute, which must also define the limits of the General Chapter's power: although it is the supreme authority in an institute, it cannot act in a purely arbitrary fashion, nor can it do anything which would be harmful to the patrimony of the institute. All other matters concerning the frequency and manner of celebrating General Chapters, as well as the regulations governing elections and the preparation of the chapter agenda, are to be dealt with in the institute's own legislation. Since many of these matters will need to be modified from time to time, it is best that they be contained not in the constitutions but rather in one of the more flexible codes of the institute.

Can. 631 §3 According to the norms determined in the institute's own law, not only provinces and local communities, but also any individual member may freely submit their wishes and suggestions to the general chapter.

1255 As a body representing the whole institute, a General Chapter must deal with matters of concern to the members. This paragraph establishes in broad terms a basic mechanism by which the members of an institute can bring matters to the attention of a General Chapter. Each province (or its equivalent) and each house has the right to send submissions on behalf of its constituent members. Not only that: each individual member, in his or her own right, has the freedom to make such submissions. The institute's own law must determine when and how these submissions are to be made. Of course, as the highest authority in the institute, the General Chapter can set its own agenda once in session.[2] Nevertheless, this canon does guarantee the participation of all members in a General Chapter as desired by Vat. II.[3]

---

[1] SCRIS rep 26.III.1980, 8.XI.1980, 24.VIII.1981, 29.VII.1982: CLD 10 102–106.
[2] Cf. SCRIS private rep 5.V.1977: CLD 9 344.
[3] Cf. PC 4 §1: Fl I 613; ES II 4: Fl I 625.

Can. 632 The institute's own law is to determine in greater detail matters concerning other chapters and other similar assemblies of the institute, that is, concerning their nature, authority, composition, procedure and time of celebration.

In addition to the General Chapter, many institutions also have chapters at lower levels, e.g. some institutes have provincial chapters which parallel the General Chapter; in others, the provincial chapter is simply a preparation for a General Chapter; some institutes also have had chapters in which the business of a particular house is determined, while in autonomous monasteries the local chapter is often the only effective assembly in the institute. The Code, respecting the specific traditions and practices of each institute, does not make any prescription for these. Rather, the proper law of each institute must determine all that is required for such assemblies.

Can. 633 §1 Participatory and consultative bodies are faithfully to carry out the task entrusted to them, in accordance with the universal law and the institute's own law. In their own way they are to express the care and participation of all the members for the good of the whole institute or community.

§2 In establishing and utilising these means of participation and consultation, a wise discernment is to be observed, and the way in which they operate is to be in conformity with the character and purpose of the institute.

This canon provides sound principles for participatory and consultative bodies, *other than chapters and councils*, which an institute may from time to time set up in an advisory capacity, in respect e.g. of a current problem, of a proposed new initiative, etc. Not only does the canon recognise the value of such bodies; it also stresses the responsibility undertaken by those who are appointed to them (§1). There is at the same time (§2) an implied warning that such groups should not be established rashly, lest a multiplicity of them might simply produce a stultifying effect on good and clear government. When bodies of this kind are established, their terms of reference should be laid down accurately in writing, and it should always be made clear that they do not enjoy any decision-making status. At all times, they are to operate in accordance with 'the character and purpose of the institute', and for 'the good of the whole institute or community'.

Article 3
Temporal goods and their administration

Can. 634 §1 Since they are by virtue of the law juridical persons, institutes, provinces and houses have the capacity to acquire, possess, administer and alienate temporal goods, unless this capacity is excluded or limited in the constitutions.

The canon acknowledges the right of all religious houses, their various stable groupings (provinces etc.) and each institute itself, as juridical persons, to acquire, possess, administer and alienate property in their own name. The last phrase of this paragraph indicates that, in some institutes, this fundamental right may be limited; however any such limitation can be effective only if it is expressed in the constitutions of the institute. This restriction of patrimonial capacity may refer to a whole institute, e.g. a mendicant religious order (see Can. 1265 §1), or it may refer only to a house or some internal division of the institute which is financially wholly dependent on a more centralised higher authority.

Can. 634 §2 They are, however, to avoid all appearance of luxury, excessive gain and the accumulation of goods.

1259 While it is the members of the institute, not the institute itself, which is vowed to poverty, the institute's administration must respect the reasons for which the Church claims a right to possession and administration of goods (see Can. 1254 §2). Moreover, each religious institute, in accordance with its own character and purpose, is called to give a corporate witness to the evangelical poverty professed by its members (see Can. 600). In keeping with the spirit of Vat. II, that which is not being used for the purposes provided in law, should be distributed to the poor.[1]

Can. 635 §1 Since the temporal goods of religious institutes are ecclesiastical goods, they are governed by the provisions of Book V on 'The Temporal Goods of the Church', unless there is express provision to the contrary.

1260 The reason why the temporal goods of religious institutes are to be administered in accordance with the provisions of Cann. 1254–1310 is specifically because the goods of an institute are 'ecclesiastical goods'. As such, they are subject to the general authority of the Roman Pontiff (see Can. 1256), who is the supreme administrator and steward of all ecclesiastical goods. Thus, in a case of urgent necessity, the Roman Pontiff could order the goods of one institute to be used to cover the debts and necessities of another juridical person in the Church. Among the temporal goods included in this provision are funds which have been set aside in accordance with the civil law in order to facilitate the administration of a particular apostolic work.

Can. 635 §2 Each institute, however, is to establish suitable norms for the use and administration of goods, so that the poverty proper to the institute may be fostered, defended and expressed.

1261 In addition to the norms of universal law, the use and administration of temporal goods by a religious institute is to be governed by norms proper to the institute. Since economic and financial affairs can differ widely from time to time and from place to place, it is best that, except for a few broad principles, these norms be part of a secondary code. This allows more easily for adaptation and updating. The purpose of such proper legislation is to help preserve the identity of each institute, i.e. to express, foster and defend the particular manner in which the evangelical counsel of poverty is lived (see Can. 598 §1).

Can. 636 §1 In each institute, and in each province ruled by a major Superior, there is to be a financial administrator, distinct from the major Superior and constituted in accordance with the institute's own law. The financial administrator is to administer the goods under the direction of the respective Superior. Even in local communities a financial administrator is to be constituted, in so far as possible distinct from the local Superior.

1262 The law draws a clear distinction between the roles of Superior and financial administrator. While the Superior has overall responsibility for administration, it is the financial administrator who takes care of the immediate day-to-day direction of financial matters. The office of financial administrator is not compatible with that of major Superior. Thus, in a more succinct manner, the present canon re-states the principle of c.516 §§2–3 of the 1917 Code. The canon goes further: as a norm, the financial administrator even at local level should also be distinct from the local Superior; although the law does acknowledge that this may not in individual circumstances be possible, it regards such an arrangement as distinctly exceptional.

---

[1] Cf. PC 13: Fl I 618–619; GS 69: Fl I 975; ET 17–18: Fl I 688–689.

Can. 636 §2 At the time and in the manner determined in the institute's own law, the financial administrator and others with financial responsibilities are to render an account of their administration to the competent authority.

Since the financial administrator and all others with similar responsibilities (see Can. 1280) are required to carry out their duties 'under the direction of the respective Superior' (§1), the law demands that they give an account of their office on a regular basis. It is for the institute's own law to determine precisely the identity of the authority to whom this account is to be given, as well as the frequency and manner of such reports. Useful criteria for this internal accountability may be found in Can. 1284 §2.

Can. 637 Once a year, the autonomous monasteries mentioned in Can. 615 are to render an account of their administration to the local Ordinary. The local Ordinary also has the right to be informed about the financial affairs of a religious house of diocesan right.

The local Ordinary is given a twofold role in respect of the financial affairs of religious in his diocese:

(a) Autonomous monasteries with no other external Superior or constitutional link with another institute (see Can. 615) are bound to render an account of all their financial affairs to the local Ordinary on an annual basis. The local Ordinary and the monastic Superior should determine the details of this account.

(b) The local Ordinary also has the right to be *informed* of the financial affairs of a religious house of diocesan right. The law gives no indication of how this information is to be supplied or how often. Moreover, this right to information concerns the affairs of a *house*, not those of the whole institute. Whatever arrangements are made in this regard must respect the true internal autonomy of the institute (Can. 586) and the responsibilities of the Bishop of the principal house of a diocesan institute (Can. 595 §1).

Can. 638 §1 It is for an institute's own law, within the limits of the universal law, to define the acts which exceed the purpose and the manner of ordinary administration, and to establish what is needed for the validity of an act of extraordinary administration.

Ordinary administration involves expenditure and other financial dealings which are necessary for the day-to-day life of members of a house, province or institute and for the ordinary maintenance of the property concerned. Anything which exceeds this is referred to as 'extraordinary administration'. This canon is closely related to Can. 1281 §2. However, it does not enter into specifics concerning the distinction between ordinary and extraordinary administration. Rather, the determination of this is left to the proper law of individual institutes. This must take into account the nature of the institute, the apostolates exercised, and the requirements of universal law (see Cann. 638 §3, 639, 1291–1294). Moreover, the institute's own law must set forth clearly what is required for a valid act of extraordinary administration, e.g. that the Superiors at various levels cannot spend more than a fixed amount of money without the consent of their respective council or local chapter.

Can. 638 §2 Besides Superiors, other officials designated for this task in the institute's own law may, within the limits of their office, validly make payments and perform juridical acts of ordinary administration.

1266 Ordinary administration is conducted by the respective Superiors by virtue of their office and by 'other officials' who are appointed for this purpose in accordance with the institute's own law e.g. bursars, financial councils, etc. The precise scope of each office is to be specified in the proper law. All such officials can carry out what is needed for ordinary administration without express permission from higher authority.

Can. 638 §3 For the validity of alienation, and of any transaction by which the patrimonial condition of the juridical person could be adversely affected, there is required the written permission of the competent Superior, given with the consent of his or her council. Moreover, the permission of the Holy See is required if the transaction involves a sum exceeding that which the Holy See has determined for each region, or if it concerns things donated to the Church as a result of a vow, or objects which are precious by reason of their artistic or historical significance.

1267 Alienation is an act by which the ownership of property is transferred definitively to another person (see Cann. 1291–1296). The contracting of large debts and undertaking large mortgages are understood to be transactions 'by which the patrimonial condition of the juridical person could be adversely affected'. The law lays down that all such acts are valid only if, in each case and at the appropriate level or levels, the competent Superior – having obtained the consent of his or her council – has given prior written permission. In addition, where the sum of money involved exceeds the maximum determined by the Holy See 'for each region',[1] the permission of the same Holy See is required for the validity of the act. This permission is also required in two other cases:

(a) where the object involved was given to the Church as a result of a vow; in this case, it has become a sacred object (see Can. 1171);

(b) where the object is 'precious' precisely by reason of its artistic or historical significance (see Can. 1292 §2); having to seek permission from the Holy See is a safeguard for the cultural and artistic heritage of the Church.

Can. 638 §4 For the autonomous monasteries mentioned in Can. 615, and for institutes of diocesan right, the written consent of the local Ordinary is necessary.

1268 The prior written consent of the local Ordinary is required for the validity of an act of extraordinary administration undertaken by an autonomous monastery of the kind mentioned in Can. 615 or by an institute of diocesan right. In the latter case, it is the diocesan Bishop of the principal house who is competent to give consent (see Can. 595 §1). Should the sum involved exceed that set by the Holy See for the region, the request for permission from Rome must be accompanied by the written consent of the diocesan Bishop.

Can. 639 §1 If a juridical person has contracted debts and obligations, even with the permission of the Superior, it is responsible for them.

1269 Since any juridical person can carry out financial transactions in its own name, that juridical person remains responsible for any debts or obligations incurred, even if it has received permission for the transaction from the relevant Superior. This does not preclude the possibility of other juridical persons within the institute – e.g. another

---

[1] This sum will often, though not necessarily, be the same as that which, with the approval of the Holy See, is determined by the relevant Bishops' Conference for its region, in accordance with Can. 1292.

house or another province – coming to the assistance of the one concerned, as an earnest of familial support. However, the responsibility at law for debts and other obligations remains with the contracting body, and not with the Superior who gave the necessary permission.

Can. 639 §2 If individual members have, with the permission of the Superior, entered into contracts concerning their own property, they are responsible. If, however, they have conducted business for the institute on the mandate of a Superior, the institute is responsible.

When, with the permission of the Superior, *individual members* of religious institutes are dealing with *their own property*, they are themselves responsible for any loss or obligation which accrues. If, however, they act on the specific instruction of the Superior and as an agent of the institute *in its business*, the institute bears responsibility for any loss or obligation.

This regulation applies not only to matters concerning the personal patrimony of the religious; it also applies to contracts in which an individual religious is placed under some kind of obligation. In such cases, it should be agreed in the individual contract whether the religious is acting as an agent of the institute or on his or her own responsibility. Whereas in some respects it may be to the advantage of the institute to consider the religious as its agent (e.g. in matters of taxation), in other respects it could be financially disadvantageous if the whole institute (or a large part of it) were to be considered liable in civil law for damages arising from the action of one of its members.

Can. 639 §3 If a religious has entered into a contract without any permission of Superiors, the religious is responsible, not the juridical person.

Any contract entered into by an individual religious without the required permission remains the responsibility of the religious concerned, not of the institute or any part of it. If the religious, therefore, had any personal patrimony, that could be distrained upon to fulfil any financial obligation involved. The juridical person concerned is not obliged by law to assist a member in such circumstances. Nevertheless, it may, on the basis of charity, assist him or her.

Can. 639 §4 However, an action can always be brought against a person who has gained from a contract entered into.

This norm is closely related to Can. 1281 §3 which acknowledges the right of a juridical person to bring an action against administrators who have caused damage. In this case, the appropriate Superior within an institute can initiate action against someone who has profited from an illegal contract. While the canon refers primarily to an action before an ecclesiastical tribunal, the redress could be sought in the civil forum, provided the necessary permission would have been granted (see Can. 1288).

Can. 639 §5 Religious Superiors are to be careful not to allow debts to be contracted unless they are certain that normal income can service the interest on the debt, and by lawful amortization repay the capital over a period which is not unduly extended.

The canon deals with the criteria for granting permission to contract debts. While no direct limit is set on the duration of debts, the norm is that payment of the interest must be within the capacity of the normal income of the juridical person concerned, and there should be a prospect of repaying the capital within a period acceptable in civil law. It is important that, before sanctioning such debts, Superiors should take into account any already existing debts, as well as the number of members involved and the work concerned.

Can. 640 Taking into account the circumstances of the individual places, institutes are to make a special effort to give, as it were, a collective testimony of charity and poverty. They are to do all in their power to donate something from their own resources to help the needs of the Church and the support of the poor.

1275 Vat. II urged religious to give a corporate witness to poverty in their manner of life.[1] This exhortation is repeated almost verbatim in the canon. In seeking to relieve the needs of the Church and the poor, religious Superiors, bursars etc. should be generous and be seen to be such. They may not however exceed the limits of ordinary administration (see Can. 1285), nor should they forget the obligations they have towards their own members (see Can. 670) and employees (see Can. 1286 2°).

Chapter III
THE ADMISSION OF CANDIDATES AND THE FORMATION OF MEMBERS

Article 1
Admission to the Novitiate

Can. 641 The right to admit candidates to the novitiate belongs to the major Superiors, in accordance with the norms of the institute's own law.

1276 'Religious life begins with the novitiate',[2] a period of intense preparation for first profession of the evangelical counsels. Admission to the novitiate is a major step and it is appropriate that this is reserved to major Superiors (see Can. 620). The Code makes no mention of the intervention by the Superior's council which had been required by c.543 of the 1917 Code or of a probationary period prior to novitiate known as postulancy (see cc.539–541 of the 1917 Code). The Revision Commission believed that such references were unnecessary in universal law.[3] Accordingly, it is for the proper law of each institute to determine more in detail, to the extent which may be considered necessary or advantageous, the procedure and requirements for admission.

Can. 642 Superiors are to exercise a vigilant care to admit only those who, besides being of required age, are healthy, have a suitable disposition, and have sufficient maturity to undertake the life which is proper to the institute. This health, disposition and maturity are to be established, if necessary even by the use of experts, without prejudice to Can. 220.

1277 In this canon, Superiors are reminded of their responsibility to admit worthy candidates to the institute. They are provided with useful criteria in their assessment of the suitability of these candidates: besides age, health, a suitable disposition and sufficient maturity are required. These qualities are to be weighed up in relation to the kind of life into which the candidate seeks admission. The requirements should not be too severe, since the candidate is entering what is, by definition, a period specifically designed *to form* the person for religious life; the candidate is not at that stage making

---

[1] Cf. PC 13: Fl I 618.
[2] RC 13(1): Fl I 646.
[3] Cf. Comm. 12(1980) 185 at Can. 25.

any definitive commitment: on the contrary, the novitiate is inter alia the time when the person's 'resolution and suitability are to be tested' (see Can. 646). Neither, on the other hand, should the requirements be too lax, since the novitiate is in fact the beginning of religious life. In order to assist the Superior in making this assessment, the law permits the use of experts, e.g. medical doctors, psychologists, etc. However, the use of such people is qualified:

(a) they are to be used only 'if necessary', i.e. if the candidate's suitability cannot be established by other means, e.g. long-term contact, interview, pre-novitiate training or postulancy;

(b) they must never be used in such a way that the candidate's right to privacy is violated (see Can. 220), i.e. he or she must willingly agree to undergo whatever tests are proposed. (In this regard, see commentary on Can. 241 §1).

Can. 643 §1 The following are invalidly admitted to the novitiate:

1° one who has not yet completed the seventeenth year of age;

2° a spouse, while the marriage lasts;

3° one who is currently bound by a sacred bond to some institute of consecrated life, or is incorporated in some society of apostolic life, without prejudice to Can. 684;

4° one who enters the institute through force, grave fear or deceit, or whom the Superior accepts under the same influences;

5° one who has concealed his or her incorporation in an institute of consecrated life or society of apostolic life.

Can. 597 §1 permits admission into an institute of consecrated life to catholics who have the right intention and the required qualities, and who are not impeded by law. This canon presents five impediments of universal law. The presence of any one of these renders a novitiate invalid:

1° *age*: only after his or her seventeenth birthday can someone be admitted to a novitiate;

2° *marriage*: no one who is currently bound by the ties of marriage can enter the institute. This impediment is constituted by an existing valid or putative canonical marriage. It does not exist in the case of a marriage which has been declared invalid, or in the case of one whose spouse has died. However, in both of these cases, the Superior should be sure that the candidate has no outstanding obligations, e.g. support of former spouse or children; in the case where a marriage has been declared invalid, the Superior may, subject to the normal conditions, seek relevant information from the competent matrimonial tribunal: this may be all the more advisable where the invalidity of the marriage has been declared by reason of serious psychological factors in one or other partner. Where a marriage has broken down but has not been declared null, a dispensation must be sought from the Holy See before requesting admission to the novitiate;[1]

3° *sacred bond*: no one can be admitted validly to a novitiate who is already bound by profession in another institute of consecrated life or incorporation into a society of apostolic life. Such a transfer may only be made in accordance with Can. 684;

---

[1] Cf. SCRIS private rep 21.VIII.1975: CLD 10 112–113; summary of a case, CLD 11 86–90.

4° *force, grave fear or deceit*: a person entering religious life must do so freely, not constrained by physical force, or grave fear, nor inveigled by deceit. The ecclesiastical jurisprudence concerning Cann. 1098 and 1103 is a useful guide in understanding this impediment. The Superior who admits a candidate must also be free from constraint. The candidate must be honest in revealing information about himself or herself, e.g. serious illnesses, previous history, qualifications, etc.; otherwise, the novitiate will be invalid;

5° *dishonesty*: i.e. deliberately concealing one's previous incorporation in an institute of consecrated life or society of apostolic life. In the light of Can. 18, 'incorporation' must be understood as profession (see Can. 654) or its equivalent. Failure to disclose one's time in a postulancy or novitiate does not constitute the impediment; neither does (the unlikely) inadvertent omission of the fact of incorporation.

Can. 643 §2 An institute's own law can constitute other impediments even for the validity of admission, or attach other conditions.

1279 The number of invalidating impediments in universal law has been reduced to five (see §1). However, the law leaves it to each institute to determine any further obstacles to admission to the novitiate. These may be:

(a) impediments which, unless dispensed, would invalidate admission, e.g. illegitimacy;

(b) impediments which, unless dispensed, render the admission illicit, e.g. membership of a political party;

(c) situations or conditions which may result in refusal or deferral of admission, e.g. obligations to care for elderly parents.

Dispensations from such impediments can be granted by the major Superior (see Can. 85).

Can. 644 Superiors are not to admit secular clerics to the novitiate without consulting their proper Ordinary; nor those who have debts which they are unable to meet.

1280 Superiors are prohibited by law from accepting into the novitiate:

(a) a secular cleric (priest or deacon) without first consulting with the Ordinary of the diocese in which he is incardinated (see Cann. 265, 266 §1);

(b) insolvent debtors, for the obvious reason of scandal, and to avoid the danger of adverse repercussions in civil law notwithstanding the provision of Can. 639 §3.

An admission of either category of person in violation of this canon, is unlawful but valid.

Can. 645 §1 Before candidates are admitted to the novitiate they must produce proof of baptism and confirmation, and of their free status.

§2 The admission of clerics or others who had been admitted to another institute of consecrated life, to a society of apostolic life, or to a seminary, requires in addition the testimony of, respectively, the local Ordinary, or the major Superior of the institute or society, or the rector of the seminary.

§3 An institute's own law can demand further proofs concerning the suitability of candidates and their freedom from any impediment.

§4 The Superiors can seek other information, even under secrecy, if this seems necessary to them.

Part III Institutes of Consecrated Life and Societies of Apostolic Life

The documents and enquiries required before a candidate may be accepted into the novitiate, may be summarised as follows: 1281

(i) an authentic certificate of baptism drawn from the baptismal register (see Can. 877 §1) or based on other information (see Can. 876);

(ii) an authentic certificate of confirmation drawn from the confirmation register (see Can. 895) or based on other information (see Can. 894); an official note on the baptismal certificate would suffice;

(iii) an authentic official statement of 'free status', i.e. that the applicant is not now married: e.g. an authentic official note on a baptismal certificate of recent date, a decree of nullity of marriage;

(iv) in an appropriate case, an official statement, signed by the respective authority mentioned, testifying that the applicant had earlier been admitted to the novitiate of another institute or society or to a seminary; this report may also usefully give a brief history of the individual's time in the other institute, society or seminary and provide some information concerning his or her departure;

(v) in so far as the institute's own law may require this, an official letter from some other person (e.g. the competent parish priest, another priest, an employer, or any other responsible person), concerning the applicant's suitability and freedom;

(vi) at the discretion of the Superior, 'other information, even under secrecy' may be sought. Information received 'under secrecy' differs from that which is contained in a 'confidential' report. Where the civil law prescribes a 'right of information', such information should not be kept in the applicant's personal file for longer than necessary; this applies to psychological reports or other documents which are not for public scrutiny. In all enquiries of this nature, the requirement of Can. 220 must be scrupulously observed.

Article 2
The Novitiate and the Formation of Novices

Can. 646 The novitiate, by which life in an institute begins, is ordered to these ends: that the novices come to a better awareness of their divine vocation, particularly the vocation proper to the institute, that they experience the institute's manner of life and form their minds and hearts in its spirit, and that their resolution and suitability are tested.

With valid admission to the novitiate, a person begins life within a religious institute. This particular period of formation has a fourfold purpose: 1282

(a) to assist the novices to understand better the nature of a divine vocation; more specifically to help them discern their vocation within this particular institute;

(b) to give the novices a firsthand experience of the life of the institute;

(c) to provide them with what is necessary for their formation in the spirit of the institute;

(d) to provide those in charge with an opportunity to discern the vocation of the novices and their suitability for a life of commitment within the institute.

How these aims are to be achieved is determined more specifically in Cann. 650, 652 and in the proper law of each institute.

Can. 647 §1 The establishment, transfer and suppression of a novitiate house are to take place by a written decree of the supreme Moderator of the institute, given with the consent of his or her council.

1283 The period of novitiate is carefully delineated in terms of time (see Cann. 648–649) and place (see Can. 647 §§2–3). The location of such a house is of the utmost importance. The law reserves to the supreme Moderator the authority to establish, transfer or suppress a novitiate house. This must be done in writing and only after the supreme Moderator's council has given its consent. The norm of c.554 §1 of the 1917 Code, which required institutes of pontifical right to obtain the permission of the Holy See in order to establish a novitiate house, no longer applies.

Can. 647 §2 To be valid, a novitiate must take place in a house which is duly designated for this purpose. In particular cases and by way of exception, and with the permission of the supreme Moderator, given with the consent of his or her council, a candidate can make the novitiate in another house of the institute, under the direction of an approved religious who takes the place of the director of novices.

1284 In normal circumstances, the novitiate is to be conducted only in a house of the institute designated specifically for that purpose in accordance with §1. There may be exceptions to this norm, but only 'in particular cases'. Normally formation is to take place in the group (*coetus*) of novices. However, the canon allows a novice who, e.g. by reason of language, age or culture, could not easily share training with the main group, to follow the novitiate in another house of the institute. For this, the permission of the supreme Moderator given with the consent of the council, must be obtained. The religious who is in charge of this one individual represents the director of novices. The other house chosen for this purpose must provide the experience of life required by law (see Can. 646), as well as the opportunity for the novice to discuss his or her vocation. Similarly, the religious chosen to act in place of the director of novices must be properly prepared for the task (see Can. 651 §3).

Can. 647 §3 A major Superior can allow the group of novices to reside, for a certain period of time, in another specified house of the institute.

1285 This provision of law permits the removal of the whole novitiate group to another house of the institute, provided that there is a good reason for doing so, in keeping with the general aim of the novitiate, e.g. if major building reconstruction were taking place in the novitiate house, if it were customary in the area to move elsewhere for an annual vacation, etc. The period of time away from the novitiate house must, however, be fixed, generally brief and certainly no longer than necessary. Permission can be given by the relevant major Superior, without need to approach the supreme Moderator.

Can. 648 §1 For validity, the novitiate must comprise twelve months spent in the novitiate community, without prejudice to the provision of Can. 647 §3.

1286 For validity, according to c.555 §1 2° of the 1917 Code, a novitiate had to last for 'a complete and unbroken year' i.e. no less than 365 consecutive days. By contrast, the present canon requires a duration of 'twelve months', i.e. at least 360 days (see Can. 202 §1). This period of time must be spent in the designated novitiate house, except for the temporary residence of the group of novices permitted in accordance with Can. 647 §3.

Can. 648 §2 To complete the formation of the novices, the constitutions can prescribe, in addition to the time mentioned in §1, one or more periods of apostolic activity, to be performed outside the novitiate community.

Here the Code safeguards the fruits of the experimentation which followed Vat. II.[1] 1287
It is envisaged that the apostolic activity, if prescribed by the constitutions, be undertaken to benefit the formation of the novice, not least by enabling him or her to experience life in communities of the institute beyond the novitiate community. These periods of apostolic activity are to be added to the twelve months required for the validity of the novitiate.

Where an institute has legislated for a two-year novitiate, such apostolic training can 1288
easily be accommodated (see §3 below).

Can. 648 §3 The novitiate is not to extend beyond two years.

The maximum period of the novitiate has been constant since it was introduced after 1289
Vat. II.[2] Thus an institute's proper law may prescribe a novitiate which lasts anywhere between twelve months and two years. This will permit the institute a sufficient flexibility so that the purpose of the novitiate can be fulfilled, while at the same time ensuring that the period before commitment is not prolonged unduly.

Can. 649 §1 Without prejudice to the provision of Cann. 647 §3 and 648 §2, a novitiate is invalidated by an absence from the novitiate house of more than three months, continuous or broken. Any absence of more than fifteen days must be made good.

If a novice is absent from the novitiate for more than three months (i.e. 90 days), the 1290
novitiate is considered invalid; this period of three months may be continuous or made up of a number of absences. An absence of less than fifteen days has no effect on the validity of the novitiate. However, an absence of more than fifteen days and less than three months must be made good, i.e. the appropriate number of days must be added so that the novice's time in the novitiate community comprises twelve months (see Can. 648 §1). The provisions of this canon refer to unforeseen absences, not to those periods covered by Cann. 647 §3 and 648 §2.

Can. 649 §2 With the permission of the competent major Superior, first profession may be anticipated, though not by more than fifteen days.

This paragraph makes possible a suitable flexibility in choosing the date of first profession, by allowing it to be anticipated by up to fifteen days, e.g. to coincide with a 1291
feast, to allow for journeys, etc. This anticipation requires the permission of the appropriate major Superior.

Can. 650 §1 The object of the novitiate demands that novices be formed under the supervision of the director of novices, according to a programme of formation to be defined by the institute's own law.

§2 The governance of the novices is reserved to the director of novices alone, under the authority of the major Superiors.

In order to achieve the aims of the novitiate (see Can. 646), the law requires that the 1292
novices must be trained in the life of the institute under the guidance of a director of novices (see Can. 651), who is to follow a programme of training and education prepared in accordance with the proper law of the institute. An indication of the content of the programme is to be found in Can. 652 §2.

During the novitiate, the director of novices is the person *solely responsible* for the welfare of the novices. Others may have an auxiliary role (see Can. 651 §2), but the 1293

---

[1] Cf. RC 23–34: Fl I 649.
[2] Cf. RC 24 (1): Fl I 649.

director has the responsibility, under the overall direction and supervision of the major Superior. In exercising this office, those novice directors and their assistants who are priests are not to hear the confessions of their novices, unless they are spontaneously requested to do so (see Can. 985).

Can. 651 §1 The director of novices is to be a member of the institute who has taken perpetual vows and has been lawfully designated.

1294 The present Code simplifies the requirements for the director of novices. While c.559 §1 of the 1917 Code specified the age, length of time in final vows and other qualities, this canon demands only two things: that the director be a perpetually professed member of the institute, and that he or she be properly designated by the competent authority. An institute's own law may seek additional requirements.

Can. 651 §2 If need be, directors of novices may be given assistants, who are subject to them in regard to the governance of the novitiate and the programme of formation.

1295 Those who may be appointed to assist the director of novices are subject to the director's authority in all that concerns the administration of the novitiate, as well as in the implementation of the programme of formation. They must obviously work in unison with the director, forming a single team. In all matters pertaining to their own religious life, such assistants are of course subject to their own local Superior.

Can. 651 §3 Those in charge of the formation of novices are to be members who have been carefully prepared, and who are not burdened with other tasks, so that they may discharge their office fruitfully and in a stable fashion.

1296 Only those who have been prepared for the task are to be placed in charge of the formation of novices. Moreover, those responsible for the government of an institute are to make sure that these persons are not given other responsibilities which are incompatible with their primary task. The law expects the directors of novices to be free in order to devote their time and energy to the work of formation 'in a stable fashion'.

Can. 652 §1 It is the responsibility of the directors of novices and their assistants to discern and test the vocation of the novices, and gradually to form them to lead the life of perfection which is proper to the institute.

1297 The fundamental responsibility of a novice-director and his or her assistants is twofold: (a) to discern and test the vocation of the individual novices; (b) to form them into the way of perfection proper to the institute. The former involves a developing judgement as to the existence or otherwise of a genuine religious vocation in this particular institute; the latter involves following a carefully prepared spiritual programme, inspired not least by the life and example of the director (and assistants). In these ways, the director of novices helps to achieve the fundamental aims of the novitiate (see Can. 646). The proper law of each institute may specify further how the director and the assistants are to accomplish the task thus entrusted to them.

Can. 652 §2 Novices are to be led to develop human and christian virtues. Through prayer and self-denial they are to be introduced to a fuller way of perfection. They are to be instructed in contemplating the mystery of salvation, and in reading and meditating on the sacred Scriptures. Their preparation is to enable them to develop their worship of God in the sacred liturgy. They are to learn how to lead a life consecrated to God and their neighbour in Christ through the evangelical counsels. They are to learn about the

character and spirit of the institute, its purpose and discipline, its history and life, and be imbued with a love for the Church and its sacred Pastors.

This paragraph constitutes a summary of the programme of formation which is to guide the education and training of novices. It looks for the integration of various areas of study so as to contribute to the fuller human and religious development of the candidate. The areas to be included are both practical and theoretical: prayer and self-denial; contemplation of the mystery of salvation; meditation on sacred Scripture; a practice and study of sacred liturgy; practice of living a consecrated life; a study of the institute itself; a reverence for the Church and its Pastors. Each institute can make further specifications concerning the content of this programme of formation and the methods employed to assist the novices in their development.

Can. 652 §3 Novices, conscious of their own responsibility, are to cooperate actively with the director of novices, so that they may faithfully respond to the grace of their divine vocation.

Since one of the aims of the novitiate is to provide the novices with the opportunity to come to a deeper awareness of their own vocation in the Church and in the institute (see Can. 646), their role during the period of novitiate is not to be purely passive. The formation programme of each institute should specify the manner in which novices are to 'cooperate actively' with their director in the discernment of their vocation.

Can. 652 §4 By the example of their lives and by prayer, the members of the institute are to ensure that they do their part in assisting the work of formation of the novices.

Without prejudice to the prescriptions of Cann. 650–651, concerning the specific responsibilities of the director of novices and the assistants, this canon is a more dynamic statement of the responsibility of every member to make the life of the institute vital and attractive.[1] Whereas c.564 §1 of the 1917 Code favoured segregation between novices and professed members of the institute, contact between them is now encouraged so that the novice might make an assessment in the light of what he or she sees in the community. The institute, through its members, is called upon to create 'the atmosphere of generosity provided by a fervent and united community, in the midst of which young religious will be enabled to learn by experience the value of mutual fraternal assistance as an element of readier progress and perseverance in their vocation'.[2]

Can. 652 §5 The period of novitiate mentioned in Can. 648 §1, is to be set aside exclusively for the work of formation. The novices are therefore not to be engaged in studies or duties which do not directly serve this formation.

The specific purpose of the novitiate is the formation of novices in the life and spirit of the institute. They must not, therefore, be engaged in studies or apostolic activities which do not directly contribute to this end. While some study of Scripture, Church history and other theological, moral or canonical questions will form a valid part of novitiate study, the manner of their treatment should contribute directly to novitiate training and formation, and not as part of a later academic study. Similarly, purely secular studies, either to prepare for a future apostolic work or to finish off uncompleted academic qualifications, are forbidden during this time. The same is true of the

---

[1] Cf. PC 24: Fl I 623.
[2] Cf. RC 5: Fl I 642.

pastoral activities of novices. These are designed to contribute to the formation of the novice and, while obviously linked to works of the apostolate in keeping with the character of the institute, they must be undertaken with the needs of the novice in view, rather than those of the work itself or of the institute.

Can. 653 §1 A novice may freely leave the institute. The competent authority of the institute may also dismiss a novice.

1302 This paragraph establishes the complete freedom of the novice to leave the institute at any time during the novitiate, and the equal freedom of the institute, through its competent authority, to dismiss a novice.

1303 While it is obviously desirable that the novice should take and weigh advice before taking such a step and so avoid precipitate action, the Code gives the novice a total freedom in this delicate matter. Indeed, the Revision Commission deliberately removed from an earlier draft a phrase saying that prudent advice should be taken before any decision to leave.[1]

1304 It is for the institute's own legislation to specify who is the competent Superior to dismiss a novice and the procedure to be adopted: it is usually reserved to the same Superior who is competent to admit to the novitiate. Whenever a dismissal occurs, it should be carried out in accordance with the principles of natural justice, and it should always be made clear that a candidate has no personal right to enter the novitiate, nor a novice to remain in the novitiate or to make profession in the institute. This is a very delicate matter, which should always be conducted with the sensitivity of great charity: in so far as is humanly possible, a dismissed novice should never be made to feel lessened by the event – in fact, the contrary.

Can. 653 §2 On the completion of the novitiate, a novice, if judged suitable, is to be admitted to temporary profession; otherwise the novice is to be dismissed. If a doubt exists concerning suitability, the time of probation may be prolonged by the major Superior, in accordance with the institute's own law, but for a period not exceeding six months.

1305 By the end of the period of novitiate, the aims set forth in Can. 646 ought to have been achieved: if the novice has been judged suitable in accordance with the formation programme and freely requests it, he or she is to be admitted to temporary profession; on the other hand, if he or she was found to be unsuitable, the novice is to be dismissed. In both cases, the formation programme will have fulfilled its purpose, i.e. to assist the novice in discerning his or her particular vocation, and to help those in charge of formation to make a proper judgement concerning the candidate's suitability for life in the institute.

1306 A third option is open to the major Superior at the end of the novitiate: if a doubt about a novice's suitability should persist, the time of probation may be extended to allow further reflection and discernment. Any such extension may not however exceed six months. The institute's own law is to determine whether or not such a deferral is permissible or desirable.

---

[1] Cf. Comm 13(1981) 168 at Can. 36 §1.

Article 3
Religious Profession

Can. 654 By religious profession members make a public vow to observe the three evangelical counsels. Through the ministry of the Church, they are consecrated to God and are incorporated into the institute with the rights and duties defined by law.

Observance of the three evangelical counsels of chastity, poverty and obedience (see Cann. 599–601) lies at the very essence of consecrated life in the Church (see Can. 573 §1). This way of life is taken on freely by those who make profession of the counsels in an institute of consecrated life (see Can. 573 §2). In religious institutes, this profession is made by means of a *public vow*, i.e. 'a deliberate and free promise made to God' (Can. 1191 §1), 'accepted in the name of the Church by a lawful Superior' (Can. 1192 §1). This applies to both temporary profession and perpetual profession. In the immediate aftermath of Vat. II, it had been possible for a number of years in some institutes to prepare for perpetual profession by profession of a sacred bond other than a vow.[1] This is not however any longer permissible.

The effect of religious profession is twofold:

(a) the person is consecrated to God through the ministry of the Church, i.e. the person is dedicated to God's service in a particular way: the Church's role is central, since it is the Church which receives the gift of the evangelical counsels (see Can. 575) and within which they are lived by members of approved institutes (see Cann. 574, 576–577);

(b) the person is incorporated into the institute (temporarily, in the case of temporary profession; definitively, in the case of perpetual profession) and acquires the rights and obligations set out in universal law (see Cann. 662–672) and the proper law of the institute.

Can. 655 Temporary profession is to be made for the period defined by the institute's own law. This period may not be less than three years nor longer than six years.

Each institute, in its own legislation, must determine the length of time to be spent in temporary profession. That period must not last less than three years nor more than six. After Vat. II the universal law had established a minimum period of three years and a maximum of nine.[2] However, in the preparation of the Code, it was felt that nine years was too long as a norm, and the Revision Commission reduced the maximum period to six years.[3] In exceptional circumstances, according to Can. 657 §2, the period of temporary profession may indeed be extended, but this may not exceed a total of nine years.

Can. 656 The validity of temporary profession requires:

1° that the person making it has completed at least the eighteenth year of age;

2° that the novitiate has been made validly;

---

[1] Cf. RC 7, 34: Fl I 643, 653.
[2] Cf. RC 37: Fl I 654.
[3] Cf. Comm 13(1981) 170 at Can. 38 §1.

3° that the admission has been granted freely by the competent Superior, after a vote of his or her council;

4° that the profession be explicit and made without force, grave fear or deceit;

5° that the profession be received by the lawful Superior, personally or through another.

1310 This canon sets out the five conditions for the validity of temporary profession. Failure to observe any one of them renders the profession invalid:

1° *age*: since a person must be at least seventeen years old for valid admission to the novitiate, the minimum age for valid temporary profession is over eighteen years; the institute's own law could determine a higher age.

2° *valid novitiate*: the one making temporary profession must have passed at least twelve months in the duly designated novitiate community in accordance with Can. 648 §1 and the institute's own law.

3° *lawful admission*: not alone must the one wishing to make profession submit a formal request to do so: he or she must also be admitted to profession by the competent Superior, i.e. the one specified by the institute's own law; in admitting someone to profession, the Superior must be free of all undue influences, must follow the norms of universal and proper law, and have obtained the vote of his or her council, consultative or deliberative according to the institute's own law.

4° *free expression*: the one making profession must do so in full freedom, in a clear and unambiguous manner; moreover, he or she must be free of the influence of force, grave fear or deceit (see Can. 643 §1 4°).

5° *lawful reception*: this is a matter for the internal governance of an institute: for validity, the profession must be received by a Superior designated by the institute's own law or duly delegated; this norm applies also in institutes of diocesan right and in the autonomous monasteries mentioned in Can. 615.

Can. 657 §1 When the period of time for which the profession was made has been completed, a religious who freely asks and is judged suitable is to be admitted to a renewal of profession or to perpetual profession. Otherwise the religious is to leave.

1311 While temporary profession in religious life is made with a view to ultimate perpetual profession, the process is not automatic. The period of temporary commitment is a time for further formation and of adjustment within the institute; accordingly, at the end of that time a further assessment of suitability is required. The religious must freely ask to continue in the institute. Those in charge of the formation of the religious must then determine whether or not he or she is suitable. Each institute's own legislation must include regulations for making that assessment, so that the decision is made with the maximum objectivity. If the religious does not ask for further profession, or is judged unsuitable, he or she must leave the institute. The major Superior responsible for admitting to further profession (temporary or perpetual) must *consult* his or her council before excluding a religious from profession (see Can. 689 §1).

Can. 657 §2 If it seems opportune, the period of temporary profession can be extended by the competent Superior in accordance with the institute's own law. The total time during which the member is bound by temporary vows may not, however, extend beyond nine years.

This canon gives to the competent Superior the right to extend, *by way of exception*, the period of temporary profession (see Can. 655) up to a total of nine years. The phrase 'in accordance with the institute's own law' refers, not to the basic right conferred by the canon, but rather to the manner in which the Superior may exercise it, i.e. either on his or her own initiative, or with the consultative or deliberative vote of the council. Superiors, in choosing to avail themselves of this opportunity, must remember that this is an exception to the norm. Serious damage can be done, both to the individual and to the institute, if perpetual profession is denied after a prolonged period of temporary profession.

Can. 657 §3 Perpetual profession can, for a just reason, be anticipated, but not by more than three months.

There are many good reasons why perpetual profession might be anticipated, e.g. in order to permit a full community celebration of the event, to coincide with a major liturgical feast, to facilitate the beginning of new apostolic work by the newly professed, etc. While c.577 §2 of the 1917 Code permitted the anticipation by one month of the renewal of temporary profession, it contained no such norm in respect of perpetual profession. The possibility of anticipating it now by up to three months provides ample opportunity for all concerned to find a suitable day.

Can. 658 Besides the conditions mentioned in Can. 656, nn.3, 4 and 5, and others attached by the institute's own law, the validity of perpetual profession requires:

1° **that the person has completed at least the twenty-first year of age;**

2° **that there has been previous temporary profession for at least three years, without prejudice to the provision of Can. 657 §3.**

The minimum age for perpetual profession – completion of the twenty-first year – is the same as that given in c.573 of the 1917 Code. It is now virtually impossible for this norm to be infringed, given the minimum age for valid novitiate (see Can. 643 §1 1°) and temporary profession (see Can. 656 1°), the duration of the novitiate (see Can. 648) and the period of temporary profession (see Can. 655). The only difficulty which might arise is in the case of anticipation of perpetual profession in accordance with Can. 657 §3. If the institute's own law has added further conditions for validity, these must be fulfilled before perpetual profession.

Article 4
The Formation of Religious

Can. 659 §1 After first profession, the formation of all members in each institute is to be completed so that they may lead the life proper to the institute more fully, and fulfil its mission more effectively.

§2 The institute's own law is, therefore, to define the programme for this formation and its duration. In this, the needs of the Church and the conditions of people and times are to be kept in mind, in so far as this is required by the purpose and character of the institute.

Initial formation of religious does not end with the novitiate. Universal law requires that, during the time of temporary profession, this initial formation should be completed. The purpose of such formation is twofold:

- to assist the religious to lead the life of the institute more fully;
- to help the religious carry out the proper mission of the institute.

Consequently, if academic or professional studies are undertaken during this period, they must be so arranged and adapted that the primary focus of post-novitiate formation is not in any way obscured.

1316 Each institute must prepare an adequate programme of formation for this period. An outline of the general content of such a programme is contained in Can. 660. The matter is, however, developed in detail in the indispensable 'Directives on Formation in Religious Institutes', issued in 1990 by the Holy See.[1] Every programme must take account of the needs of the Church, must be adapted to local circumstances and updated regularly, always in keeping with the purpose and character of each institute.[2] While the duration of this post-novitiate formation is to be determined by each institute's own legislation, it must last at least three years.[3]

Can. 659 §3 The formation of members who are being prepared for sacred orders is governed by the universal law of the Church and the institute's own programme of studies.

1317 In those institutes which include clerics among their members, additional attention is to be given to the preparation of candidates for sacred orders. The programme of formation and studies must conform to Cann. 232–264, other provisions of the universal law,[4] similar provisions of a local nature,[5] and the purpose and character of the institute itself.[6]

Can. 660 §1 Formation is to be systematic, adapted to the capacity of the members, spiritual and apostolic, both doctrinal and practical. Suitable ecclesiastical and civil degrees are to be obtained as opportunity offers.

1318 The description of religious formation provides a basic guide-line for the preparation of an institute's programme. Above all, the formation must be *systematic* i.e. it must be planned and well-structured, educating the religious in the various aspects of the institute's life and mission. This programme must also be adapted to the capacity of the members, so that each can benefit from it to the maximum. Finally, the programme of formation must be balanced, combining elements which are spiritual and apostolic, doctrinal and practical. In addition, where appropriate, religious are encouraged to pursue relevant academic degrees at ecclesiastical or civil universities or institutes.

Can. 660 §2 During the period of formation, members are not to be given offices and undertakings which hinder their formation.

1319 This paragraph is closely related to Can. 652 §5. If they are to benefit properly from this period of formation after novitiate, religious in temporary profession are to be left free from offices or responsibilities which are not compatible with the demands of the particular formation programme. This rule is all the more apposite in respect of

---

[1] Cf. SCRIS 2.II.1990 *Potissimum institutioni*: AAS 82(1990) 470–532; official translation in English in Origins 19(1990) 677–699. In the current context, cf. in particular nn.58–65, 86–100: Origins 690–691, 694–697.

[2] In respect e.g. of institutes dedicated to contemplation, cf. op cit nn.72–85: Origins 693–694.

[3] Cf. op cit n.60: Origins 691.

[4] *Potissimum institutioni* nn.101–107: Origins 697.

[5] e.g. the *Programme of priestly formation* drawn up in accordance with prescription of Can. 242 §1.

[6] The preparation of candidates for sacred orders will differ according to whether the institute itself is 'clerical' (cf. Can. 588 §2), or the sacred ministers are ordained solely for ministry within the institute.

temporarily-professed members who will already have shown a particular potential for certain responsibilities or offices: it must never be overlooked that they are each and all still *in formation*.

Can. 661 Religious are to be diligent in continuing their spiritual, doctrinal and practical formation throughout their lives. Superiors are to ensure that they have the assistance and the time to do this.

In addition to a programme of initial formation, each institute is to organise a programme for the *ongoing formation of the perpetually professed members*. Responsibility for this ongoing formation is twofold:
- the religious themselves must do what is necessary to renew and update themselves in spiritual, doctrinal and practical matters;
- the Superiors within each institute are obliged to provide whatever the members need for this ongoing formation.[1]

Such continual renewal is to be seen as a normal part of religious life, not as something extraordinary or unusual. It enables religious to deepen the commitment they made at profession to the life and mission of the institute.

Chapter IV
THE OBLIGATIONS AND RIGHTS OF INSTITUTES AND OF THEIR MEMBERS

Can. 662 Religious are to find their supreme rule of life in the following of Christ as proposed in the Gospel and as expressed in the constitutions of their own institutes.

The fundamental principle which inspires all religious is to follow Christ. Discipleship lies at the heart of every truly christian life.[2] A life consecrated through profession of the evangelical counsels is a particular way of following Christ more closely (see Can. 573 §1). In order to achieve this, religious must be thoroughly conversant with the person of Christ as revealed in the Scriptures, especially in the Gospels. Moreover, they must be familiar with the particular expression of discipleship expressed in their own constitutions. Thus, according to the spirit and purpose of each institute, religious are to be found following Christ in a life dedicated to prayer, or to preaching the Kingdom of God, or to apostolic works of charity, or to entering into dialogue with contemporary society, etc. (see Can. 577).

Can. 663 §1 The first and principal duty of all religious is to be the contemplation of things divine and constant union with God in prayer.

No matter what kind of apostolic activity they are engaged in, religious are obliged to consider their way of life at all times in terms of their relationship to God. Without a deep spiritual life, it is simply not possible to 'follow Christ more closely' (Can. 573 §1). Thus the canon presents a series of exhortations, presenting to religious the means by which they may attain the good of 'contemplation of things divine and con-

---

[1] Both responsibilities are spelled out in more detail in *Potissimum institutioni* nn.67–71: Origins loc cit 692–693.
[2] Cf. LG 40: Fl I 397.

stant union with God in prayer'. Particularly to be noted in this regard is the detailed instruction issued by the Holy See on the many aspects of this contemplative dimension of religious life.[1]

Can. 663 §2 Each day the members are to make every effort to participate in the Eucharistic Sacrifice, receive the most holy Body of Christ and adore the Lord himself present in this sacrament.

1323 Since it is 'the summit and the source of all worship and christian life' (see Can. 897), the Eucharist must have a central place in the spiritual life of all religious. They are urged to participate in the Mass daily, to receive Holy Communion, and to spend some time in adoration of the Blessed Sacrament. This is no simple exhortation: it is a spiritual imperative, for the achievement of which *every effort*, even at the cost of personal sacrifice, must be made.

Can. 663 §3 They are to devote themselves to reading the sacred Scriptures and to mental prayer. In accordance with the provisions of their own law, they are to celebrate the liturgy of the hours worthily, without prejudice to the obligations of clerics mentioned in Can. 276 §2 n.3. They are also to perform other exercises of piety.

1324 Other means of fostering a life of continuous intimacy with God include the reading of sacred Scripture, the practice of mental prayer and the celebration of the liturgy of the hours. Each institute is to determine the extent of the celebration of the liturgy of the hours, taking into account the nature of the institute and the particular obligations incumbent upon clerical members of the institute (see Can. 276 §2 3°). Its own legislation should also indicate other suitable 'exercises of piety' by which the members' spiritual life is to be nourished and sustained.

Can. 663 §4 They are to have a special devotion, including the marian rosary, to the Virgin Mother of God, the example and protectress of all consecrated life.

1325 Devotion to the Blessed Virgin Mary has been a feature of life in religious institutes from their first appearance in the Church. She is understood to be a model to be imitated and someone to whom religious can have recourse. Members of religious institutes are encouraged to deepen their personal and communal devotion to Mary, the Mother of God. This is to be expressed in a manner appropriate to each institute. The explicit mention of the rosary is a significant addition in the current Code (see also Can. 246 §3).

Can. 663 §5 They are faithfully to observe the period of annual retreat.

1326 As Jesus withdrew from time to time to spend time alone with his Father (see Luke 6:12), so those who follow him must put aside some time each year for more intense spiritual exercises. The duration and manner of the annual retreat is a matter for each institute's own legislation. 'The contemplative dimension is the real secret of renewal for every religious life. It vitally renews the following of Christ because it leads to an experiential knowledge of him.'[2]

Can. 664 Religious are earnestly to strive for the conversion of soul to God. They are to examine their consciences daily and to approach the sacrament of penance frequently.

---

[1] Cf. SCRIS *La plenaria* January 1981, *The Contemplative Dimension of Religious Life*: Fl II 244–259.
[2] SCRIS op cit 30: Fl II 258.

The phrase 'conversion of soul' used in this canon is redolent of the *conversio morum* 1327 which was a traditional description of monastic life. To attain this end, the canon demands daily examination of conscience – a long-standing practice of religious life – and frequent approach to the sacrament of penance. Weekly confession was encouraged by c.595 §1 3° of the 1917 Code. A decree of the Holy See in 1970 altered this slightly, urging religious 'to receive the sacrament of penance frequently, that is twice a month', and urging their Superiors to 'encourage them in this effort and (to) make it possible for (them) to go to confession at least every two weeks, and even oftener if they wish to do so'.[1] The Revision commission confirmed that this was to be the meaning given to 'frequently' in this canon.[2]

Can. 665 §1 Religious are to reside in their own religious house and observe the common life and they are not to leave it, except with the permission of the Superior. For a lengthy absence from the religious house, the major Superior, for a just reason, and with the consent of his or her council, can authorise a member to live outside a house of the institute; such an absence is not to exceed one year, unless it be for reasons of health, studies or an apostolate to be exercised in the name of the institute.

Fraternal life in common is an essential element of religious life (see Can. 607 §2). In 1328 order to observe this better, the law requires that religious must reside in their own houses. Of course, the manner of that fraternal life will vary, depending on the nature of the institute, e.g. a monastic institute will have a more structured form of fraternal life while an apostolic institute will have a more flexible programme. Whatever the nature of the institute, any absence from one's own religious house requires the permission of the competent Superior. This permission may be *tacit* i.e. if someone is appointed to a ministry which involves absences; it may be *presumed* i.e. if permission is always given in similar circumstances, e.g. to attend a funeral; or it may be *explicit* i.e. if a formal request is made. Proper law must determine the competence of the local Superior in this matter.

Permission for 'lengthy' absences is the domain of the major Superior.[3] Before grant- 1329 ing such permission, the major Superior must have the consent of his or her council and must be satisfied that there is 'a just cause' for the absence, e.g. to care for a sick or aged relative. Ordinarily, the major Superior can permit such absences for no more than a year. Should it be necessary to extend the absence beyond a year, the Holy See must be approached. In practice, cases of real need are dealt with very sympathetically.[4]

No approach to the Holy See is necessary, however, if the cause of the prolonged 1330 absence is one of those mentioned explicitly in the canon, i.e. health, studies or apostolate exercised in the name of the institute. In these cases, the major Superior, with the consent of his or her council, can grant extended absence from a house of the institute. Religious to whom this is granted remain full members of the institute, enjoying all the rights and privileges, including active and passive voice in elections.

Can. 665 §2 Members who unlawfully absent themselves from a religious house with the intention of withdrawing from the authority of Superiors, are to be carefully sought out and helped to return and to persevere in their vocation.

---

[1] SCRIS *Dum canonicarum* 8.XII.1970 (3): AAS 63(1971) 318–319: Fl I 677.

[2] Cf. Comm 13(1981) 181.

[3] Each institute should specify what is meant by a 'lengthy' absence. A week may be a long time to be absent from a monastery, while a month may not be an unusual length to be absent from another kind of house.

[4] Cf. SCRIS *Quitte ton pays* 1976: Fl II 205–208.

1331 The 1917 Code had strong words for religious who absented themselves unlawfully from their houses, describing them as 'apostates' or 'fugitives' (c.644, §§1 and 3) and imposing severe *latae sententiae* penalties (cc.2385–2386). By contrast, the tone of the present Code is much more pastoral: the law requires the Superior to seek out such religious; the obligation of the competent Superior is to do all that is possible to facilitate the return of the religious to the life of the institute. Nevertheless, should such an unlawful absence exceed six months, despite the efforts of the Superior, the member may be dismissed from the institute (see Can. 696 §1).

Can. 666 In using the means of social communication, a necessary discretion is to be observed. Members are to avoid whatever is harmful to their vocation and dangerous to the chastity of a consecrated person.

1332 The twentieth century has witnessed a revolution in means of communication: the written word, in all its forms, has been joined by the spoken word (telephone, radio) and the moving image (cinema, television, video). Because of the particular demands of their way of life (see Cann. 607, 663, etc.), religious are urged to exercise discretion in their use of such means. While 'they can be of considerable benefit' if properly used, and 'contribute greatly to the enlargement and enrichment' of the human mind, they can be used in ways that are harmful and damaging.[1] The canon identifies some particular negative consequences for religious life of the indiscriminate use of the communications media. If care is not exercised, community life can be disrupted and undermined, e.g. if recreation is reduced to the passive watching of television, or if the atmosphere of a house is so invaded by radio etc. that the 'first and principal duty of all religious' (see Can. 662) cannot be observed. Moreover, religious have no control over the content of what is transmitted through the means of social communication; without great care and attention, indiscriminate use of these media can be harmful to a life of consecrated chastity. Each institute, according to its own character and purpose, should in its own legislation make more detailed provisions in this regard.

Can. 667 §1 In accordance with the institute's own law, there is to be in all houses an enclosure appropriate to the character and mission of the institute. Some part of the house is always to be reserved to the members alone.

1333 A life in which prayer is to be central (see Can. 662) and which is shared fraternally with others is greatly assisted by the principle by which part of each religious house is reserved to the members alone, i.e. all outsiders (of either sex) are excluded as a rule from that part of the house. Such a principle guarantees the minimum requirements for privacy and silence. Since this 'enclosure' must reflect the character and mission of each institute, appropriate norms should be included in the institute's own law.

Can. 667 §2 A stricter discipline of enclosure is to be observed in monasteries which are devoted to the contemplative life.

1334 The purpose of 'enclosure' is to safeguard the essential features and values of religious life and to facilitate the observance of its fundamental obligations. Naturally, therefore, a community of monks leading a contemplative form of life requires a greater degree of silence, tranquillity and freedom from disturbance. Detailed prescriptions of this 'stricter discipline of enclosure' should be contained in the institute's own legislation.

Can. 667 §3 Monasteries of nuns who are wholly devoted to the contemplative life must observe Papal enclosure, that is, in accordance with the norms

---

[1] IM 2: Fl I 284.

Part III Institutes of Consecrated Life and Societies of Apostolic Life

given by the Apostolic See. Other monasteries of nuns are to observe an enclosure which is appropriate to their nature and is defined in the constitutions.

Two types of enclosed nuns are mentioned in this paragraph: those who are 'wholly devoted to the contemplative life', i.e. who have no other apostolic activity (e.g. Carmelites, Poor Clares, Cistercians); and those who combine a contemplative life with a limited form of apostolic work within the immediate environs of the monastery (e.g. Benedictine nuns who have schools). The former are obliged to observe a very strict form of enclosure known as 'papal enclosure'. This is governed by particular norms issued by the Apostolic See to regulate life within the enclosure as well as entry into it and exits from it.[1] Nuns of the other category are obliged to observe a form of enclosure that is specified in the constitutions of the institute.

Can. 667 §4 The diocesan Bishop has the faculty of entering, for a just reason, the enclosure of nuns, whose monasteries are situated in his diocese. For a grave reason and with the assent of the Abbess, he can permit others to be admitted to the enclosure and permit the nuns to leave the enclosure for whatever time is necessary.

This paragraph affirms the threefold competence and responsibility of the diocesan Bishop in the matter of the enclosure of nuns. First of all, he can enter the enclosure of any such monastery located in his diocese; he may do so 'for a just reason' e.g. to conduct the visitation mentioned in Can. 628 §2 1°, or even to make a purely pastoral visit. Secondly, he can permit others to enter the enclosure 'for a grave reason', e.g. doctors or nurses who must care for a sick nun, a workman who must do some repairs; however, he cannot give this permission without the agreement of the Abbess. Thirdly, he may permit the nuns to leave the enclosure, e.g. to consult a doctor, to exercise their civil rights; such permission refers only to 'whatever time is truly needed' for the business at hand. These facilities refer to monasteries of nuns with papal enclosure, as well as to others.[2]

Can. 668 §1 Before their first profession, members are to cede the administration of their goods to whomsoever they wish and, unless the constitutions provide otherwise, they are freely to make dispositions concerning the use and enjoyment of their goods. At least before perpetual profession they are to make a will which is valid also in civil law.

Profession of the evangelical counsel of poverty 'entails a life which is poor in reality and in spirit ... It also involves dependence and limitation in the use and the disposition of goods ...' (Can. 600). The present canon provides universal norms to regulate the disposition of goods by those who make religious profession.

Three distinct juridical acts are involved, at least the first two of which must be carried out before first profession, i.e. towards the completion of the novitiate:

(a) *cession of administration*, i.e. the religious is required to hand over the management of any *fixed* property he or she actually owns at the time, whatever the nature of that property, e.g. house, land, stocks, shares, money on deposit, etc. The day-to-day management of such property is to be handed over to a person or persons of the member's own choice: this may be an individual e.g. one of the member's own family, or a recognisable group of individuals, or an institute such

---

[1] Cf. SCRIS instr *Venite Seorsum* 15.VIII.1969: AAS 61(1969) 674–690 VII: Fl I 671–675.

[2] Cf. op cit VII 7–8: Fl I 672–673.

as a bank or a firm of lawyers. It may even be – but it certainly need not be – an authorised representative of the institute into which the member is to be professed. In making the choice the member should be prudently advised, but any form of coercion or pressure must be sedulously avoided.

(b) *transfer of use and enjoyment*, i.e. the religious is also required to make whatever arrangements are necessary and appropriate concerning the free transfer to another of the use and enjoyment (usufruct) of his or her property. While its management will, in virtue of (a) above, have been handed over to someone else, this property itself remains that of the member (but see §3 of this canon). What is required here is that he or she assigns to a specified person or persons the benefit which may accrue from the property, by way e.g. of rent on a house or land, dividends from shares, interest on money on deposit, etc. The assignee may be the member himself or herself (thus to increase the personal patrimony); equally it may be a member of the family or the institute itself or a reliable third party. This particular disposition is, however, subject to there being no contrary provision in the institute's constitutions.

(c) *a will*, i.e. all religious are required to make a will concerning the disposal of any property in their possession at the time of their death. In preparing such a will, it will normally be necessary to consult a civil lawyer, to ensure that it can be executed in civil law. While a will may be made before first profession, it must have been made prior to perpetual profession. Once again the complete freedom of the testator must be ensured, subject only to serious considerations of prudence and of charity.

1339 Care must be taken to ensure that the documents pertaining to the above-mentioned three juridical acts be officially recorded in the archives of the institute and stored in secure and safe custody.

Can. 668 §2 To change these dispositions for a just reason, and to take any action concerning temporal goods, there is required the permission of the Superior who is competent in accordance with the institute's own law.

1340 Once the dispositions mentioned in §1 have been made, a religious is not free to alter or adjust them or take any other action related to personal property. Should the need or the occasion arise, he or she must obtain the prior permission of the competent Superior: the identity of this Superior is to be specified in the institute's own law. Such an occasion requires 'a just reason': this will be sensibly interpreted to include such factors as a substantial change in either the condition of the property or the circumstances of one or more of the beneficiaries, the death of one or more of the appointees, etc.

Can. 668 §3 Whatever a religious acquires by personal labour, or on behalf of the institute, belongs to the institute. Whatever comes to a religious in any way through pension, grant or insurance also passes to the institute, unless the institute's own law decrees otherwise.

1341 One important practical consequence of the dispositions mentioned in §1 concerns the ownership of property acquired by a religious *after even first profession*: by law it becomes the property of the institute when acquired in any one of the following three ways:
– by the *personal labour* of the religious, e.g. remuneration either for ministry (including Mass stipends), or for professional work such as lecturing, consultations, publications, etc.;

- when property is received *on behalf of the institute*, e.g. when a house, to be used by the institute, is purchased in the name of one or a number of the members;
- by receipt of money from sources such as pensions, grants and insurance, e.g. the receipt of the old age pension or the like. In the case of this third source of income, the institute's own law may determine otherwise, by decreeing e.g. that the money be devoted to a particular charity or even, in exceptional cases, that it be retained and put to good use by the individual member.

If, at any time after first profession, a member of a religious institute lawfully acquires property, of whatever kind, in a manner other than the three specified above, the general principle is that, unless the contrary is clearly expressed, this property accrues to the member him or her self, not to the institute. This is particularly relevant in respect of gifts given to religious and, more significantly perhaps, of inheritances of which, often without their advance knowledge, they become the beneficiaries. In this regard, it is to be noted that there are two specific exceptions to the general principle noted above: (a) the regulation stated in §5 of this canon; (b) the possibility that in a given institute the rule of Can. 598 §1 may have determined otherwise. 1342

Even, however, in cases in which the general principle operates, it has always to be borne in mind that the beneficiary of such a gift or inheritance is one who has already taken a vow to observe the evangelical counsel of poverty which, in accordance with Can. 600, 'entails a life which is poor in reality and in spirit ... (and is) a stranger to earthly riches'. There cannot therefore be any question of the personal material aggrandisement of the religious beneficiary, who in fact is obliged to deal with this property, be it money or otherwise, in accordance with the law and the spirit of the vow of poverty. 1343

Can. 668 §4 When the nature of an institute requires members to renounce their goods totally, this renunciation is to be made before perpetual profession and, as far as possible, in a form that is valid also in civil law; it shall come into effect from the day of profession. The same procedure is to be followed by a perpetually professed religious who, in accordance with the norms of the institute's own law and with the permission of the supreme Moderator, wishes to renounce goods in whole or in part.

In some institutes, in addition to the dispositions concerning temporal goods mentioned in §1, members are required to renounce *all ownership* of property. Traditionally, these were institutes in which members professed *solemn* vows. The Code insists that this renunciation must be made before perpetual profession. Moreover, as far as possible, this is to be done in a way which is acceptable and valid in civil law. However, in practice, this latter is not always possible since some civil legislations do not permit a person to renounce ownership of what he or she does not actually possess: competent advice should always be sought in this regard. 1344

It may happen that, although their institute does not demand such a renunciation, individual religious may seek to renounce their ownership, partially or totally. In order to do this, they must ensure that the provisions of their institute's own law allow it and, in addition, obtain the permission of their supreme Moderator. 1345

Can. 668 §5 Professed religious who, because of the nature of their institute, totally renounce their goods, lose the capacity to acquire and possess goods; actions of theirs contrary to the vow of poverty are, therefore, invalid. Whatever they acquire after renunciation belongs to the institute in accordance with the institute's own law.

1346 The complete renunciation of ownership required by certain institutes has one very serious juridical consequence: all perpetually professed members thereby lose their personal capacity to own or acquire property or goods in their own name. The principle of §3 applies to these religious even more forcefully: no matter what an individual religious receives – even by way of gift or inheritance – it necessarily belongs to the institute. The institute's own law must identify the juridical person which acquires the goods in question, i.e. house, province, or institute. Since the individual no longer has any patrimonial capacity, an act contrary to the vow of poverty is not just unlawful but also invalid. The provisions of this paragraph do not apply to those religious who *voluntarily* renounce their ownership (as under §4 above).

Can. 669 §1 As a sign of their consecration and as a witness to poverty, religious are to wear the dress of their institute determined in accordance with the institute's own law.

1347 A distinctive form of dress has always been a feature of religious life. Originally, it expressed the life of prayer and penance embraced by the monks and nuns. Later, in more apostolic institutes, the members adopted the contemporary dress of clerics or of servants. The habit was thus an external witness to the consecrated life of the religious and a sign of their belonging to the one institute. As the number of religious institutes increased, more and more attention was given to those details by which one form of dress was differentiated from others. This was particularly true in the case of institutes of women.

1348 Vat. II called for the adaptation of religious habits to the requirements of health, the demands of different times and places, and the needs of the apostolate.[1] This led many institutes to discard the artificial accretions of centuries, and some even to abandon entirely the concept of a common form of dress. This is an issue which since Vat. II has generated much emotive debate and comment among religious. For all that, the law of the Church still firmly upholds the value of wearing the 'habit of the institute', seeing it as a sign of the consecrated life of the members and as a corporate witness to poverty; it goes further: in this canon it positively prescribes the wearing of the habit as a matter of clear obligation. It does indeed leave the determination of the nature of the habit, as well as all regulations concerning the circumstances of its use, to the proper legislation of each institute. In doing so however, so far from countenancing the abandonment of the concept, the law specifically requires that all religious wear a form of dress which is specific to their own institute and which of itself is recognisable as a witness to the consecrated life espoused by the person in question. The mere appendage of a symbol, such as a cross or even a crucifix, to what is otherwise to all outward appearances a secular attire does not fulfil this requirement of the Church's law. It may not be forgotten that the habit of religious is not only 'a sign of their consecration' but, perhaps more importantly, 'a witness to poverty', itself a challenge to the modern world of materialism.

Can. 669 §2 Clerical religious of an institute which does not have a special habit are to wear clerical dress in accordance with Can. 284.

1349 Some clerical institutes, even from their foundation, did not adopt a habit, choosing instead to dress according to the local and universal requirements for secular clergy. For these clerics, the 'suitable ecclesiastical dress' established by the Bishops' Conference and legitimate custom (see Can. 284) constitutes the sign of consecration and the witness to poverty mentioned in §1.

---

[1] Cf. PC 17: Fl I 621; ET 12: Fl I 691.

Part III Institutes of Consecrated Life and Societies of Apostolic Life

Can. 670 The institute must supply the members with everything that, in accordance with the constitutions, is necessary to fulfil the purpose of their vocation.

Just as Bishops are charged with the welfare of clerics in the service of the diocese (see Cann. 281, 384), so each religious institute must provide the members with whatever they need in order to live their vocation as fully as possible. Clearly, this means provision of food, clothing, accommodation and health care, but it also includes the necessary initial and ongoing formation (see Cann. 659–661), and whatever spiritual, intellectual or professional assistance an individual religious might need. The constitutions of each institute are to determine how this provision is to be made.

Can. 671 Religious are not to undertake tasks and offices outside their own institute without the permission of the lawful Superior.

The purpose of this canon is not to stifle the initiative of religious or to limit their apostolate, but to ensure that all works, whether deriving from the main apostolate of the religious or voluntarily assumed, are passed through the proper channels. In this way, only those works will be undertaken which are in keeping with the nature of the institute and the talents of the individual. It is especially important that all such involvement which necessitates the signing of contracts and the administration of goods should only be undertaken with the permission of the Superior (see Can. 639 §§2–3). The principle of this canon underlies the provisions of Cann. 681–682; it also applies to voluntary activities which may seriously diminish the availability of the religious to the community or present a danger to health by reason of over-work. The canon speaks of the 'lawful Superior' whose permission is required if works or responsibilities are to be undertaken outside the institute: if a stable or long-term apostolate or office is to be given to a member or members of the institute, it would appear that the permission of the major Superior is necessary; if other voluntary works are to be taken by individuals, the permission of the local Superior is required and will normally be given.

Can. 672 Religious are bound by the provisions of Cann. 277, 285, 286, 287 and 289. Clerical religious are bound by the provisions of Can. 279 §2. In lay institutes of pontifical right, the permission mentioned in Can. 285 §4 can be given by the proper major Superior.

In addition to the obligations contained in this part of the Code, religious are required to observe the provisions of certain canons concerning clerics. Thus, they must observe what universal law and particular law has established in the matter of celibacy (see Can. 277). They must not engage in activities alien to the religious life, e.g. public office, the administration of goods belonging to others (see Can. 285); they are forbidden to practise trade or commerce (see Can. 286); they must promote peace and justice but may not be actively involved in political parties or trade unions (see Can. 287); they are not to volunteer for the armed services and they are to avail themselves of any lawful exemptions from public or civil functions (see Can. 289). Since, in some cases, clerics may be permitted to take part in these activities with the permission of their Ordinary, it is the major Superior who can permit religious to do so.

Two provisions of this canon refer specifically to two categories of religious: all religious clerics are required to obey the prescriptions of particular law concerning the theological and pastoral renewal (see Can. 279 §2); members of lay institutes of pontifical right may undertake the responsibilities mentioned in Can. 285 §4 with the permission of their major Superior.

Chapter V
THE APOSTOLATE OF INSTITUTES

Can. 673 The apostolate of all religious consists primarily in the witness of their consecrated life, which they are bound to foster through prayer and penance.

1354 According to Vat. II, 'consecrated life, ... while not entering into the hierarchical structure of the Church, belongs undeniably to her life and holiness'.[1] This means that religious institutes have an essential role to play in the apostolic life of the Church. This opening canon on the apostolate enunciates a vital principle: the first apostolate of all religious lies in the witness of their consecrated life, whether the institute is ordered towards contemplation or apostolic works. All religious, without exception, have the obligation to promote this witness by means of prayer and penance, undertaken by individuals and by communities. This canon recalls the fundamental teaching concerning consecrated life found in Can. 573. The following canons of this chapter make further general determinations in this matter of the religious apostolate.

Can. 674 Institutes which are wholly directed to contemplation always have an outstanding part in the mystical Body of Christ. They offer to God an exceptional sacrifice of praise. They embellish the people of God with very rich fruits of holiness, move them by their example, and give them increase by a hidden apostolic fruitfulness. Because of this, no matter how urgent the needs of the active apostolate, these institutes cannot be called upon to assist in the various pastoral ministries.

1355 The principle contained in Can. 673 is, very significantly, applied first of all to institutes wholly dedicated to contemplation. These exercise no external apostolic action, yet they are regarded as 'an outstanding part' of the Church. The first part of the canon presents a brief description of their way of life by which they give this witness within the Church and thus participate in the apostolate. The second part underlines the intrinsic value of this form of life: no matter how urgent the demands, these religious cannot be pressed to help out in active pastoral ministry. Here we have a striking example of the law itself protecting the patrimony of an institute.

Can. 675 §1 Apostolic action is of the very nature of institutes dedicated to apostolic works. The whole life of the members is to be imbued with an apostolic spirit, and the whole of their apostolic action is to be animated by a religious spirit.

§2 Apostolic action is always to proceed from intimate union with God and is to confirm and foster this union.

§3 Apostolic action exercised in the name of the Church and by its command is to be performed in union with the Church.

1356 The principle of Can. 673 is also applied to those institutes which are dedicated to apostolic works.[2] The canon contains three important doctrinal statements:

---

[1] LG 44: Fl I 405.

[2] This includes institutes founded for specific apostolic works (e.g. teaching, nursing), others which undertake apostolic activity of all kinds, and those in which the contemplative life is combined with a limited form of apostolic activity.

(a) apostolic activity is not some kind of optional extra but is an integral part of the life of these institutes (§1);
(b) a close union with God is to be the source of all apostolic activity; the deepening of that union is to be a primary result of that same activity (§2);
(c) apostolic activity by religious can never take place in isolation from the Church: it is always to be exercised 'in the name of the Church and by its command', whether the mandate is specific i.e. a particular work entrusted by a Bishop, or general i.e. the approval of an institute dedicated to a particular work (§3).

Can. 676 Lay institutes of men and women participate in the pastoral mission of the Church through the spiritual and corporal works of mercy, performing very many different services for people. They are therefore to remain faithful to the grace of their vocation.

Lay religious life was given explicit praise in Vat. II, 'for it is so useful to the Church in the exercise of its pastoral duty of educating the young, caring for the sick, and in its other ministries'.[1] It was not to be understood as any less valuable simply because it did not involve the exercise of sacred orders. This same appreciation is discernible in the text of the canon. The exercise of spiritual and corporal works of mercy is already a participation in the Church's mission: in taking on more 'direct' forms of pastoral work, religious are to be faithful to their calling and not undervalue the more 'traditional' works of the institute.

1357

Can. 677 §1 Superiors and members are faithfully to hold fast to the mission and works which are proper to the institute. According to the needs of time and place, however, they are prudently to adapt them, making use of new and appropriate means.

The apostolic life of a religious institute cannot remain static. As times change and the institute finds itself faced with new conditions and new problems – social, cultural, professional, political, familiar etc. – it becomes necessary from time to time to make adaptations appropriate to the new needs. This adaptation will entail a careful analysis of contemporary conditions, and an equally careful reflection on the origins and development of the institute. This is the key to the proper understanding of this §1. Whatever adaptations may be proposed, 'Superiors and members are to hold fast to the mission and works which are proper to the institute': in other words, while they may involve alterations in methods, approaches, policy, *adaptations do not mean substitutions*. Such adaptations as are envisaged in this canon must always remain in total conformity with the patrimony of the institute (see Can. 578).

1358

Can. 677 §2 Institutes which have associations of Christ's faithful joined to them are to have a special care that these associations are imbued with the genuine spirit of their family.

Among the works proper to a number of religious institutes is the particular pastoral care of any lay association joined to the institute, e.g. a third order (see Can. 303). The specific goal of this pastoral care is the formation and development of the members of these associations in the spirituality proper to the institute, suitably adapted to the lives and conditions of the associates.

1359

Can. 678 §1 In matters concerning the care of souls, the public exercise of divine worship, and other works of the apostolate, religious are subject to

---
[1] PC 10: Fl I 616.

the authority of the Bishops, whom they are bound to treat with sincere submission and reverence.

1360 The direction of all apostolic works in his diocese is the prerogative of the diocesan Bishop (see Can. 394). It is also the Bishop's responsibility to ensure the observance of proper ecclesiastical discipline in matters pertaining to Christian worship (see Can. 392 §2). Religious, therefore, are not completely free agents in their exercise of apostolic works, even those proper to the institute and which they can exercise as of right (see Can. 611 2°). They are subject to the authority of the diocesan Bishop in three specific areas:

(a) *the care of souls*, i.e. those works which involve the pastoral care of people in parishes and the exercise of the sacred priesthood (see Can. 150);

(b) *the public exercise of divine worship*: this includes all liturgical celebrations properly so called, since liturgy is always a *public* act (see Can. 834), and all other paraliturgical and devotional celebrations in which the faithful take part;

(c) *other works of the apostolate*, i.e. those works directed towards people outside the institute e.g. education, nursing, social work etc.

In all these specific matters and at all times religious, like the rest of the faithful, are obliged to show obedience and respect to the Bishops (see Can. 212 §1).

Can. 678 §2 In the exercise of an external apostolate towards persons outside the institute, religious are also subject to their own Superiors and must remain faithful to the discipline of the institute. If the need arises, Bishops themselves are not to fail to insist on this regulation.

1361 Apostolic activity does not exhaust the essence of religious life. Thus, those who are engaged in an external apostolate must never neglect the obligations arising out of their profession of the evangelical counsels. They remain subject to their Superiors – as religious, rather than as apostolic workers, they are obliged to live according to the proper discipline of their institute.[1]

1362 Should religious engaged in an apostolate in his diocese neglect these obligations, the Code urges the Bishop to do what he can to remind them of their duties. This must not be interpreted as an infringement of the internal autonomy of the institute (see Can. 586 §1); rather, it is an example of how the Bishop can fulfil his obligation to preserve and safeguard that autonomy (see Can. 586 §2).

Can. 678 §3 In directing the apostolic works of religious, diocesan Bishops must proceed by way of mutual consultation.

1363 Since religious exercising external apostolates are subject to the dual authority of the Bishop and of their Superiors, the possibility exists of a dispute or conflict of competence. In order to overcome this, Vat. II urged regular consultations between Bishops and Superiors.[2] A document published in 1978 jointly by the Congregations for Bishops and for Religious and Secular Institutes sought to develop the principles of this consultation and provide practical guidelines for its implementation.[3] The 'mutual consultation' of which the canon speaks will include discussions between individual Bishops and religious Superiors, as well as contacts between Bishops' Conferences and Conferences of major Superiors (see Cann. 708–709).

---

[1] This point has been authentically underlined in a reply of the Code Commission concerning religious who are appointed Judges of the Roman Rota: cf. CCom rep 19.I.1988: AAS 80(1988) 1819.
[2] CD 35 §6: Fl I 586.
[3] MR: Fl II 209–243.

Can. 679 For the gravest of reasons, a diocesan Bishop can forbid a member of a religious institute to remain in his diocese, provided the person's major Superior has been informed and has failed to act; the matter must, however, immediately be reported to the Holy See.

The provision of this canon might at first sight appear to be contrary to the principles of Can. 586: it is of the essence of internal autonomy that Superiors be free to appoint members anywhere within the institute. However, the canon must be understood according to its 'text and context' (Can. 17): a Bishop cannot insist on the removal of a religious for a matter of purely internal discipline; rather, 'the gravest of reasons' must be specifically related to one at least of the areas governed by Can. 678 §1. An intervention of this kind by the Bishop is subject to three conditions:

(a) the competent major Superior must have been informed of the problem;

(b) that Superior must have failed to take appropriate action;

(c) the Holy See must be appraised of what has taken place.

In itself, this is not a penalty but rather a norm for the necessary administration of discipline. Should the circumstances warrant it, however, the Bishop could initiate proceedings for the imposition of a penalty (see Cann. 1320, 1337, 1341–1353).

Can. 680 Organised cooperation is to be fostered among different institutes and between them and the secular clergy. Under the direction of the Bishop, there is to be a coordination of all apostolic works and actions, with due respect for the character and purpose of each institute and the laws of its foundation.

Three separate but related issues are addressed in this canon which serves as an introduction to Cann. 681–683.

(a) Religious institutes are themselves to cooperate closely in matters of apostolic activity. This can usefully be done through the Conference of major Superiors. The concept of institutes competing with one another is wholly alien to consecrated life.

(b) Religious institutes and secular clergy are also to cooperate closely in these matters. The work of evangelisation is much too important and serious to be hampered by rivalry, hostility or suspicion.

(c) Within a diocese, all apostolic activity is to be under the direction of the Bishop (see Can. 394), with due regard having been taken to the patrimony and lawful autonomy of each institute (see Cann. 578, 586).

Can. 681 §1 Works which the diocesan Bishop entrusts to religious are under the authority and direction of the Bishop, without prejudice to the rights of religious Superiors in accordance with Can. 678 §§2 and 3.

Three specific areas of apostolic activity are always subject to the sole authority of the Bishop (see Can. 678 §1). Among them are such specific works entrusted by the Bishop to the care of religious, as e.g. a parish, a hospital, a school, a retreat house. In these situations it is only in those matters pertaining to internal religious discipline and mutual consultation with the Bishop that the religious Superior's rights remain unhindered (see Can. 678 §§2–3).

Can. 681 §2 In these cases a written agreement is to be made between the Bishop and the competent Superior of the institute. This agreement must expressly and accurately define, among other things, the work to be done, the members to be assigned to it, and the financial arrangements.

1367 The due autonomy of both authorities involved is to be safeguarded in a written agreement or contract between the Bishop and the competent religious Superior. The canon identifies three essential points to be covered in such a document:
- *the work to be done*: this must be clearly specified e.g. the running of a parish, the administration of a hospital etc.
- *the members to be assigned*: there must be an indication of the number of religious required for the work and the qualifications needed for the particular task.
- *financial arrangements*: provision must be made so that a just and equitable plan is agreed as between the needs of the diocese and those of the institute involved.

1368 A vast experience has proven the value, indeed the necessity, of the advance written agreement required by this paragraph. Before a Bishop entrusts to any religious institute an apostolic work for which he remains responsible, there must be a process of negotiation which, hopefully, will result in a clear agreement on many relevant matters; without such an agreement, there is a real danger of an unedifying and a destructive conflict at some stage in the future. Any such danger can well be avoided by a sensitive approach to the prior negotiation: by the Bishop, to the character, discipline and patrimony of the institute; by the institute, to the central position of the diocesan Bishop in the divinely-constituted structure of the Church.

Can. 682 §1 If an ecclesiastical office in a diocese is to be conferred upon a member of a religious institute, the religious is appointed by the Bishop on presentation by, or at least with the consent of, the competent Superior.

1369 'Unless the law expressly states otherwise, it is the prerogative of the diocesan Bishop to make appointments to ecclesiastical offices in his own particular Church...' (Can. 157). The appointment of a religious to such an office does require either the previous presentation of the member by the competent Superior (as e.g. in the case of a parish priest) or at least the consent of the competent Superior to the appointment. Once appointed, within the limits of the mandate the religious is accountable to the Bishop, but remains subject to the authority of the religious Superior in matters of internal discipline (see Cann. 678 §§1–2, 680 §1).

Can. 682 §2 The religious can be removed from the office at the discretion of the authority who made the appointment, with prior notice given to the religious Superior; or by the religious Superior, with prior notice being given to the appointing authority. Neither requires the other's consent.

1370 In the matter of the removal of a religious from a diocesan office, such e.g. as a parish, the provision of this paragraph safeguards the freedom of action of both the diocesan Bishop and of the religious Superior. Either authority may have good reason to remove the religious concerned: the law does not require the consent of either; nor does it mention the necessity of giving reasons. However, it does stress the need for prior notice to be given by the authority removing the religious. The length of this notice could be specified in a written agreement at the time of the appointment to the office, or it could – as it often is – be mutually agreed on each given occasion.

Can. 683 §1 Either personally, or through a delegate, the diocesan Bishop can visit churches or oratories to which Christ's faithful have habitual access, schools other than those open only to the institute's own members and other works of religion or charity entrusted to religious, whether these be spiritual or temporal. He can do this at the time of the pastoral visitation, or in a case of necessity.

Can 678 §1 identifies three main areas of apostolic activity in which religious are subject to the authority of the Bishop. This canon provides one way in which the Bishop might exercise this authority, namely by visitation. The law gives the Bishop the right to visit churches and oratories open to the faithful: this is related to the care of souls and the public exercise of divine worship; he also has the right to visit schools and other works of religion or charity entrusted to religious in his diocese, e.g. a hospital, retreat house etc.:[1] an expression of his authority over 'other works of the apostolate' (Can. 678 §1).

The Bishop may make this visitation personally or through a delegate. It can occur at the ordinary time of pastoral visitation, or if some crisis or emergency arises. Only one exception to the scope of this visitation is mentioned: the Bishop has no right to visit schools which are reserved exclusively to members of the institute; of course he may, and normally should, be invited to do so.

Can. 683 §2 If the diocesan Bishop becomes aware of abuses, and a warning to the religious Superior having been in vain, he can by his own authority deal with the matter.

If in the course of visitation abuses related to the apostolic works are discovered, the Superior is to be informed. If the Superior does not take adequate action, the Bishop is authorised to deal with the matter himself. Given a proper relationship between the Bishop and the religious institute, this ought to be a very exceptional situation.

Chapter VI
THE SEPARATION OF MEMBERS FROM THE INSTITUTE

Article 1
Transfer to another Institute

Can. 684 §1 Perpetually professed members cannot transfer from their own religious institute to another, except by permission of the supreme Moderators of both institutes given with the consent of their respective councils.

After profession, a religious can be separated legitimately from his or her institute in three ways:
- by transfer to another institute (see Cann. 684–685);
- by departure from the institute, which may be temporary (see Cann. 686–687) or definitive (see Cann. 688–693);
- through dismissal from the institute by the competent authority (see Cann. 694–704).

The transfer of a perpetually professed religious from one institute to another has never been regarded favourably by the Church. Requests for such transfers were discouraged by ecclesiastical authority, although permission was sometimes granted if the transfer was to 'a stricter order', i.e. to an institute of more austere lifestyle. This practice lay behind the norm of c.632 of the 1917 Code: a religious could not transfer even to 'a stricter order' without the permission of the Holy See.

---
[1] Cf. ES I 39 §2: Fl I 608–609.

1376   In preparing the text of this canon, the Revision Commission decided to retain the negative formulation of the 1917 Code, since transfer must be understood as something exceptional.[1] However, the authorisation of the Holy See is no longer required. Instead, the permission of the supreme Moderators of both institutes must be obtained, each having obtained the prior consent of his or her council. The transfer can only be made from one religious institute to another, whether of pontifical or of diocesan right, but not to a secular institute or a society of apostolic life. However, there is no requirement that the new institute be 'stricter'. It is to be noted that this paragraph refers only to perpetually professed religious and not to those in temporary vows.

Can. 684 §2 On completion of a probationary period of at least three years, the member can be admitted to perpetual profession in the new institute. A member who refuses to make this profession, or is not admitted to do so by the competent Superiors, is to return to the original institute unless an indult of secularisation has been obtained.

1377   The process of transfer consists primarily of a probationary period of at least three years in the new institute. This provides the religious with ample opportunity to understand the demands of a new way of life, and the institute with sufficient time to assess the suitability of the individual. There is no requirement of a novitiate as there had been in c. 633 §1 of the 1917 Code. Nevertheless, the canons dealing with the novitiate provide a good summary of what should be accomplished during the three years of probation (see Cann. 646, 652).

1378   At the end of this probation, if he or she freely asks and is judged to be suitable, the religious is admitted to perpetual profession in the new institute. However, should the religious refuse to make profession or should the competent authority refuse to admit him or her to profession, he or she must return to the original institute – save only where the religious in question has sought and obtained an indult of secularisation (see Can. 691).

Can. 684 §3 For a religious to transfer from one autonomous monastery to another monastery of the same institute, federation or confederation, the consent of the Major Superior of both monasteries and of the chapter of the receiving monastery is required and is sufficient unless the institute's own law has established further conditions. A new profession is not required.

1379   This paragraph treats of the transfer of religious within the same institute, federation or confederation, where, though the spirit and purpose is common to all constituent monasteries, the monasteries themselves are autonomous as regards their interior life and discipline. The process of transfer differs from that outlined in §§1–2, in that no new profession is required. Permission to transfer must be received from both the major Superiors concerned; to give that consent validly, the receiving major Superior must have the consent of the chapter of his or her monastery. In addition to what is demanded by universal law, the institute's own legislation can make other requirements binding on a religious seeking to transfer.

1380   It is to be noted that the paragraph speaks only of 'a religious', without making any reference to whether he or she was in temporary vows or perpetually professed. During the preparation of the Code, it did seem that all such transfers involved *only* perpetually professed religious.[2] Nevertheless, in a reply dated 29 April 1987, the

---

[1] Cf. Comm 13(1981) 326.
[2] Cf. Comm 13(1981) 328 at Can. 67 n.6.

Part III Institutes of Consecrated Life and Societies of Apostolic Life

then Code Commission made it clear that the term 'religious' in this paragraph refers to those in temporary vows as well as those who are perpetually professed.[1]

Can. 684 §4 The institute's own law is to determine the time and manner of the probation which must precede the member's profession in the new institute.

All details concerning the length of time to be spent in probation before a religious makes profession in the new institute (see §§1–2) are to be contained in that institute's own law. This must also determine how the transferring religious is to be formed in the life and spirit of the institute. Cann. 659–660 provide general guidelines for preparing such a programme.

Can. 684 §5 To transfer to a secular institute or to a society of apostolic life, or to transfer from these to a religious institute, the permission of the Holy See is required and its instructions are to be followed.

The Code draws a clear distinction between religious institutes (see Can. 607), secular institutes (see Can. 710), and societies of apostolic life (see Can. 731). The initial paragraph of this canon provides for a transfer between two religious institutes. A transfer to a secular institute or a society of apostolic life from a religious institute, and a transfer to a religious institute from either of the other groups, entails a substantial change in the way of life. Consequently, the permission of the Holy See is required. If this is given, the relevant Congregation in Rome will issue instructions to be followed by the individual and by the institute or society involved. This paragraph cannot be invoked if a religious seeks to become incorporated into a pious union or some other association of the faithful.[2]

Can. 685 §1 Until profession is made in the new institute, the rights and obligations of the member in the previous institute are suspended, but the vows remain. From the beginning of probation, the member is bound to observe the laws of the new institute.

This canon determines the juridical status of a religious *during the process of transfer*. The basic obligation to observe the vows remains. However, since he or she is no longer living fully the life of the original institute, the rights and obligations proper to that institute, e.g. active and passive voice in elections, are suspended. Moreover, as soon as the formal period of probation (see Can. 684 §2) begins, that religious is obliged by the internal laws, rules and regulations of the new institute. In this way he or she comes to get a real experience of life within that institute.

Can. 685 §2 By profession in the new institute the member is incorporated into it and the earlier vows, rights and obligations cease.

The process of transfer ends with the perpetual profession of the religious in the new institute. All ties with the original institute thereby cease. Thereafter the religious is bound by the proper laws of the new institute, and can exercise all the rights given to a perpetually professed member in that new institute.

---

[1] CCom rep 29.IV.1987: AAS 79(1987) 1249 ad I.
[2] SCRIS private letter 28.X.1982 Prot. N. 37307/81 in CLD 10 120.

Article 2
Departure from the Institute

Can. 686 §1 With the consent of his or her council, the supreme Moderator can, for a grave reason, grant an indult of exclaustration to a perpetually professed member for a period not exceeding three years. In the case of a cleric, the indult requires the prior consent of the Ordinary of the place where the cleric must reside. To extend this indult or to grant one for more than three years, is reserved to the Holy See, or, in an institute of diocesan right, to the diocesan Bishop.

1385   The term 'exclaustration' refers to a religious living outside a house of his or her institute, i.e. outside the 'cloister'. A religious may make a formal request to do this for personal reasons, e.g. to reflect on his or her vocation, to care for an ailing, possibly dying, parent or other wholly dependent close relative, etc. Exclaustration is to be distinguished from the legitimate absence of a religious permitted for reasons of health, studies or apostolate (see Can. 665 §1). According to c.638 of the 1917 Code, only the Holy See was competent to grant such an indult in institutes of pontifical right; the local Ordinary was similarly competent in institutes of diocesan right. Now, however, exclaustration for up to three years can be granted by the supreme Moderator of each institute, provided his or her council has given its consent (see Can. 127 §2 1°). An extension of that original indult or an indult for a period longer than three years must in institutes of pontifical right be requested from the Holy See, from the local Ordinary in institutes of diocesan right.[1]

1386   If the religious seeking exclaustration is a cleric, the law also requires the consent of the local Ordinary of the place where the cleric is going to live. When approaching an Ordinary in these circumstances, the supreme Moderator is obliged to provide such information concerning the religious concerned and the reasons for seeking exclaustration as will enable the Ordinary to make an informed decision and assume the care of the cleric involved (see Can. 687).

Can. 686 §2 Only the Apostolic See can grant an indult of exclaustration for nuns.

1387   In the case of enclosed nuns, the sole authority competent to grant an indult of exclaustration is the Holy See, i.e. the Congregation for Institutes of Consecrated Life and Societies of Apostolic Life. This reservation to the Holy See does not affect the authority of the diocesan Bishop to permit nuns to leave the enclosure on occasion (see Can. 667 §4). The canon applies to all nuns, whether wholly or only partly dedicated to contemplation.

Can. 686 §3 At the request of the supreme Moderator acting with the consent of his or her council, exclaustration can be imposed by the Holy See on a member of an institute of pontifical right, or by a diocesan Bishop on a member of an institute of diocesan right. In either case a grave reason is required, and equity and charity are to be observed.

1388   Imposed exclaustration is a practice which was developed as a result of the experience of the Congregation for Religious[2] in dealing with some troublesome individuals.

---

[1] The local Ordinary in question is that of the place where the religious is staying (cf. CCom rep 24.VII.1939: CLD 2 173).

[2] It is first mentioned explicitly by A. Gutierrez in *Commentarium pro Religiosis* 32(1953) 336–339.

Although it is imposed, it must not be understood to be a penalty. Rather, it is an administrative act, a precept ordering the religious to remain outside a religious house. The precept implies a suspension of the obligation to observe enclosure and a deprivation of the right to a common life.[1] Imposed exclaustration is used in order to protect the welfare both of the institute and of the individual, in a case where the behaviour of the individual is seriously disruptive of the life of the institute.

When exclaustration is imposed, arrangements must be made by the Superiors within the institute to provide for the needs of a religious; in the case of a cleric, the appropriate local Ordinary must also be informed by the institute, though obviously his consent is not required as in §1 of this canon.

The initiative in such an action rests with the supreme Moderator. Having discussed the matter with the council and having obtained its consent, he or she must make a formal request of the appropriate authority, i.e. the Holy See for institutes of pontifical right, the diocesan Bishop for institutes of diocesan right. While it is not required by law, the procedure outlined in Can. 697 should in general be followed. This will enable the supreme Moderator to present all the relevant information to the competent authority; it also permits the individual religious to offer arguments in his or her defence.[2]

Can. 687 Members who are exclaustrated are considered as dispensed from those obligations which are incompatible with their new condition of life. They remain dependent on and under the care of their Superiors and, particularly in the case of a cleric, of the local Ordinary. They may wear the religious habit, unless the indult specifies otherwise, but they lack active and passive voice.

It is important that the juridical status of an exclaustrated religious be properly understood. He or she remains a member of the religious institute. However, the manner of life is greatly modified: by reason of the indult or precept of exclaustration, such a religious is regarded as having been dispensed from those obligations incompatible with the new condition of life, e.g. obligation to a life in common. The vows retain their binding force, but the manner of living in poverty and obedience must be adjusted to suit the new situation; it may not however be so reduced as to make it in practice negligible or almost non-existent.

The relationship between exclaustrated religious and both their Superiors and the local Ordinary should be defined in the indult or precept. In this way the authorities can fulfil their responsibilities towards these religious, and the religious can give an account of themselves on a regular basis. The definition of this relationship is especially important in the case of a religious cleric.

By contrast with c.639 of the 1917 Code, the law now permits these religious to wear the habit of the institute unless for a specific reason this is expressly prohibited by the indult. On the other hand, this canon reiterates the norm of the 1917 Code concerning active and passive voice: since exclaustrated religious no longer participate fully in the life of the institute, they cannot vote in elections nor are they eligible for office within the institutes.

Can. 688 §1 A person who, on the completion of the time of temporary profession, wishes to leave the institute, is free to do so.

---

[1] Cf. Ap Sig decision 28.XI.1975: CLD 9 458.

[2] Cf. ibid 459.

1394 At the end of the period of temporary profession, unless further profession is freely requested and granted (see Can. 657 §1), all obligations arising from profession cease. Since the onus to request profession lies with the individual, failure to make the request is considered as a decision to leave the institute.

Can. 688 §2 A person who, during the time of temporary profession, for a grave reason asks to leave the institute can obtain an indult to leave. In an institute of pontifical right, this indult can be given by the supreme Moderator with the consent of his or her council. In institutes of diocesan right, and in the monasteries mentioned in Can. 615, the indult must, for validity, be confirmed by the Bishop in whose diocese is located the house to which the person is assigned.

1395 A religious in temporary vows is incorporated into the institute (see Can. 654) but not definitively. By reason of the commitment undertaken in profession, a religious can leave the institute during temporary profession only for a serious reason, e.g. difficulty with the obligations of religious life, family problems etc. The one wishing to leave must submit a petition to the supreme Moderator, indicating briefly the reasons for the request. An indult to leave, or a dispensation from the obligations of temporary profession, can be granted by the same supreme Moderator, having received the consent of his or her council. This indult can be granted in this way by the Supreme Moderator of either a clerical or a lay institute. If the applicant belongs to an institute of diocesan right or one of the autonomous monasteries mentioned in Can. 615, a further element is required for the validity of the indult, namely the indult's confirmation by the local diocesan Bishop of the religious, i.e. the Bishop of the diocese in which is located the religious house to which the religious is assigned.

Can. 689 §1 The competent major Superior, after consulting his or her council, can for just reasons exclude a member from making further profession on the completion of temporary profession.

1396 At the end of the period of temporary profession, the Superiors of the institute are to make a judgement on the suitability of those who ask for further profession, whether a renewal of temporary profession or final profession (see Can. 657 §1). The law gives the right to the competent Superior, i.e. the one designated by proper law, for a just reason to exclude such a religious from further profession. The validity of this refusal requires that the Superior *consult* his or her council: there is no obligation on the Superior to accept what the council may advise (see Can. 127 §2 2°).

Can. 689 §2 Even though contracted after profession, a physical or psychological infirmity which, in the judgement of experts, renders the member mentioned in §1 unsuited to lead a life in the institute, constitutes a reason for not admitting the member to renewal of profession or to perpetual profession, unless the infirmity was contracted through the negligence of the institute or because of work performed in the institute.

1397 Among the reasons for which a person might be refused admission to the renewal of temporary profession or to perpetual profession is an illness which might be physical or psychological. The decision to refuse profession belongs to the Superior mentioned in §1. However, the law requires the assistance of appropriate experts, such e.g. as doctors, psychiatrists, psychologists, in making this judgement. These are to be asked about the history, cause, development and effects of the illness, in particular as to whether it is irreversible. It belongs to the Superior, having carefully taken account of these professional opinions, to decide whether or not the individual should be admitted to further profession. The law does however foresee a twofold exception: (a) if the illness was the result of negligence by the institute, e.g. a negligent failure to obtain proper assistance when the symptoms were first manifest; (b) if the illness was the direct and established consequence of work carried out by the religious or by direction of the institute. In the case of either of these two exceptions, the Superior would not be entitled on that ground to refuse permission either to a renewal of temporary profession or to perpetual profession. More significantly perhaps is to be noted that, while the kind of infirmity referred to in this paragraph could well justify a decision to refuse this permission, the canon *does not positively require* that it be for this reason refused. There remains a distinct obligation on the Superior to take appropriate account of natural justice, of equity and of the demands of Christian charity.

Can. 689 §3 A religious who becomes insane during the period of temporary vows cannot be dismissed from the institute, even though unable to make a new profession.

The person who becomes insane while under temporary profession is incapable of making further profession (see Can. 99), nor can he or she be dismissed from the institute. The current Code follows the practice of the Holy See since 1925 when a similar judgement was given after the problem had been studied by the full Assembly of the relevant Congregation and the decision confirmed by Pope Pius XI.[1] The person, therefore, remains in the state he or she was at the onset of the illness, i.e. a temporarily professed member of the institute. The institute has the obligation to care for that member in the most appropriate way, though not necessarily within a community if the good of the member and the safety of the community should require otherwise (see Cann. 665 §1, 670).

Can 690 §1 A person who lawfully leaves the institute after completing the novitiate or after profession, can be readmitted by the supreme Moderator, with the consent of his or her council, without the obligation of repeating the novitiate. The same Moderator is to determine an appropriate probation prior to temporary profession, and the length of time in vows before making perpetual profession, in accordance with the norms of Cann. 655 and 657.

According to c. 640 §2 of the 1917 Code, a person who left a religious institute could be readmitted only by an indult of the Holy See: a new novitiate was demanded and the religious took his or her place of seniority within the institute from the date of the new profession. This discipline was changed in 1969: readmission of such a religious could be authorised by the supreme Moderator of the institute with the consent of his or her council.[2] These dispositions have been made part of the Code. The general law does not now require a new novitiate. Rather, the supreme Moderator is required to determine the duration and nature of the time of probation prior to new profession. As a rule, this period is not to be less than three years nor more than six years (see Can. 655), although it may be extended to nine years (see Can. 657 §2).

The provisions of this canon refer only to those who left the institute *lawfully*, i.e. those who, upon completion of the novitiate (see Can. 648) or the period of temporary profession, choose not to make profession or renew profession; those who, upon

---

[1] Cf. SCRIS rep 5.II.1925: CLD 1 309–310.

[2] Cf. RC 38 (1): Fl I 654.

completion of either period, are not admitted by the competent Superior to profession or renewal of profession; those who have left the institute during the time of profession (either temporary or perpetual) by obtaining an indult from the competent authority (see Cann. 688 §2, 691). Moreover, the canon deals only with readmission to the *same* institute. The admission of someone who had been a member of another institute is dealt with in Can. 643 §1.

Can. 690 §2 The Superior of an autonomous monastery, acting with the consent of his or her council, has the same faculty.

1401 The Superior of an autonomous monastery is regarded by law as a major Superior (see Can. 620). In the matter of the readmission of someone who had left after completing the novitiate or after profession, the Superior of an autonomous monastery has the same faculty as a supreme Moderator. He or she requires the consent of the council to authorise a readmission. There is no need to have any recourse to the local Bishop.

Can. 691 §1 A perpetually professed religious is not to seek an indult to leave the institute, except for the gravest of reasons, weighed before the Lord. The petition is to be presented to the supreme Moderator of the institute, who will forward it to the competent authority with his or her own opinion and that of the council.

1402 Perpetual profession in a religious institute involves a lifelong commitment of the individual to a particular way of life within the institute. A request to leave the institute after perpetual profession can only be regarded as very exceptional. The law permits such a request to be made but only 'for the gravest of reasons, weighed before the Lord', e.g. a genuine inability to observe the obligations of religious life, a vocation to the priesthood in a lay institute, etc. A purely subjective judgement by an individual is not sufficient: there must be a distinct effort on the part of the competent Superior to discern whether or not the alleged reason has a foundation in objective reality.

1403 Once identified, the reason should be set forth clearly in a petition presented to the supreme Moderator of the institute. Having studied the request personally and with his or her council, the supreme Moderator is to pass the petition to the competent authority (see §2). In doing so, he or she must include a personal opinion on the merits of the application as well as the opinion of the council.

Can. 691 §2 In institutes of pontifical right this indult is reserved to the Apostolic See. In institutes of diocesan right, the indult can be granted by the Bishop in whose diocese is located the house to which the religious is assigned.

1404 This paragraph identifies the authority competent to grant an indult to leave a religious institute: the Holy See, for all institutes of pontifical right; the local Bishop, in the case of an institute of diocesan right. While the 1917 Code did not specify which Bishop could grant such an indult, the Holy See made it clear in 1939 that it was the Bishop of the place in which the petitioner was living.[1] That norm has now been incorporated into the Code: since the canon speaks only of 'Bishop' and not 'Ordinary', the indult cannot be granted by a Vicar general or Vicar episcopal.

Can. 692 An indult to leave the institute which is lawfully granted and notified to the member, by virtue of the law itself carries with it, unless it has been rejected by the member in the act of notification, a dispensation from the vows and from all obligations arising from profession.

---

[1] CCom rep 24.VII.1939: CLD 2 173. It is obvious that, in an exceptional case, the Holy See could also intervene in the case of an institute of diocesan right.

Ordinarily an indult to leave a religious institute is communicated by the competent authority to the petitioner through the competent Superior of the institute. He or she must make sure that the individual understands and appreciates the contents and significance of the indult. It has effect immediately it is notified to the petitioner, *unless he or she rejects it at that time*. Hence, even when presented with such an indult, a religious has the right and the freedom to refuse it. Rejection, however, must be clearly expressed in some public form, whether in writing or in the presence of at least one reliable witness. Failure to make such an explicit rejection is considered as acceptance of the indult. By accepting the indult or, having been properly informed, by failing to reject it, the religious is thereby dispensed from observance of the vows and all other obligations arising from religious profession.

Can. 693 If the member is a cleric, the indult is not granted until he has found a Bishop who will incardinate him in his diocese, or at least receive him there on probation. If he is received on probation, he is by virtue of the law itself incardinated in the diocese after five years, unless the Bishop has rejected him.

Since 'acephalous or "wandering" clergy are in no way allowed' (Can. 265), a religious cleric cannot be permitted to leave the institute until he has found a Bishop willing to accept him as a cleric of his diocese. If the Bishop does this at once, the indult to leave the institute has the effect of a document of exclaustration (see Can. 267 §1) and the cleric is enrolled among the clergy of the diocese. If on the other hand – as more often happens – the Bishop receives him *on probation*, the cleric remains incardinated in his religious institute, even though effectively dispensed from the obligations of profession. However, after five years from the date of the Bishop's acceptance of him on probation, the cleric in question is, by automatic operation of the law itself, incardinated into the diocese – save only if, *before the expiry of that time*, the Bishop has (preferably, though not necessarily, in writing) stated that he does not wish such an incardination to take place.[1]

Article 3
The Dismissal of Members

Dismissal consists in the enforced definitive separation of a religious from his or her institute. It is a penal measure reserved for serious offences. In all matters pertaining to dismissal, the law must be interpreted strictly (see Can. 18). Three types of dismissal are provided for in the Code: automatic (see Can. 694), compulsory (see Can. 695) and facultative (see Can. 696).

Can. 694 §1 A member is to be considered automatically dismissed if he or she:

1° has notoriously defected from the catholic faith;

2° has contracted marriage or attempted to do so, even civilly.

---

[1] There is a significant difference between this regulation (see also Can. 727 §2) and that of Can. 268 §1 where much more detailed requirements are stipulated before automatic incardination can take place (see our commentary on that latter canon). It is to be noted that the current Cann. 693 and 727 §2 are substantially the same as the 1917 Code at its c.641 §2.

1408 If a religious in either temporary or perpetual vows commits either of the offences mentioned in this paragraph, he or she is dismissed from the institute *by that very fact*. It is important that the scope of each offence be understood clearly:

(a) Defection from the Catholic faith is specifically manifested in cases of heresy, apostasy or schism (see Can. 751). *It may, but does not always necessarily*, arise in cases where there is the 'obstinate attachment to, or diffusion of, teachings condemned by the magisterium of the Church' or the 'public adherence to materialistic or atheistic ideologies' mentioned in Can. 696 §1 (see relevant commentary below). Whatever the circumstances, any such defection involves automatic dismissal *only if it is notorious*, i.e. either established by a formal and official ecclesiastical declaration, or is in such a way publicly known that it is in fact not possible to refute or excuse it (see Cann. 171 §1 4°, 1330; 1917 Code c.2197 3°).

(b) The only members of religious institutes who can in fact validly 'contract marriage' are those in temporary profession who are not already clerics (see Cann. 1087–1088); the others can do no more that 'attempt marriage' – therefore invalidly – whether in a religious or a civil ceremony. All of the above, whatever their motivation, incur the automatic dismissal of this canon.

Can. 694 §2 In these cases, the major Superior with his or her council must, after collecting the proofs, without delay make a declaration of the fact, so that the dismissal is juridically established.

1409 Where either offence mentioned in §1 has been committed, the responsibility of the competent major Superior (not necessarily the supreme Moderator) is, in association with the council (its consent is not necessary), to gather the evidence to establish the fact of what has happened, and then make a straightforward declaration (preferably in writing) that the religious in question has been automatically dismissed from the institute. It is important to note that the dismissal does not depend on this declaration: even if the declaration is not made, the religious is and remains dismissed from the institute.[1]

Can. 695 §1 A member must be dismissed for the offences mentioned in Cann. 1397, 1398 and 1395, unless, for the offences mentioned in Can. 1395 §2, the Superior judges that dismissal is not absolutely necessary, and that sufficient provision has been made in some other way for the amendment of the member, the restoration of justice and the reparation of scandal.

1410 The law *obliges* the competent authority of a religious institute to dismiss any member found guilty of various offences against human life and liberty (see Cann. 1397–1398), including homicide, kidnapping, mutilation and procured abortion, and certain offences against the Sixth Commandment (see Can. 1395). It is understood, of course, that before such a religious may be dismissed, there must be proof that the offence did in fact occur and that it was juridically imputable (see Cann. 1321–1324).

1411 Although, as a rule, dismissal must be imposed for those offences against the Sixth Commandment mentioned in Can. 1395 §2, the competent Superior may, in a particular case, decide otherwise. This cannot, however, be a purely arbitrary decision. The Superior must be sure that *effective* arrangements have been made to provide for the correction and amendment of the offender. Moreover, bearing in mind the nature of the offence and the damage caused to another person, especially if it be a juvenile, the Superior must ensure that everything necessary be done to restore justice and to repair the scandal caused.

---

[1] Cf. CCom rep 30.VII.1934: CLD 2 175.

Can. 695 §2 In these cases, the major Superior is to collect the proofs concerning the facts and the imputability of the offence. The accusation and the proofs are then to be presented to the member, who shall be given the opportunity for defence. All the acts, signed by the major Superior and a notary are to be forwarded, together with the written and signed replies of the member, to the supreme Moderator.

The procedure in cases of obligatory dismissal comprises the following steps: 1412
- the major Superior (personally or through a delegate) must gather all available evidence pertaining to the fact and imputability of the alleged offence;
- the allegation and the evidence gathered is to be communicated to the religious accused; this can be done in writing (i.e. sending a copy of the documentation) or by giving it to the religious in the presence of two witnesses;
- having had the opportunity to study the accusation and the evidence, the religious must be invited to respond formally to the allegation; this should be done in writing or, if made orally and transcribed, should be signed by the religious concerned;
- having received the response of the accused (or if none has been received after an appropriate length of time), all the documentation is to be sent to the supreme Moderator. These acts must be signed by the major Superior and a duly designated notary.

Having received all the necessary information, the supreme Moderator or the Bishop (see Cann. 699–700) *must*, if satisfied about the offence and its imputability, issue a decree of dismissal.

Can. 696 §1 A member can be dismissed for other causes, provided they are grave, external, imputable and juridically proven. Among such causes are: habitual neglect of the obligations of consecrated life; repeated violation of the sacred bonds; obstinate disobedience to the lawful orders of Superiors in grave matters; grave scandal arising from the culpable behaviour of the member; obstinate attachment to, or diffusion of, teachings condemned by the magisterium of the Church; public adherence to materialistic or atheistic ideologies; the unlawful absence mentioned in Can. 665 §2, if it extends for a period of six months; other reasons of similar gravity which are perhaps defined in the institute's own law.

Dismissal *may be imposed* on a religious for other grave offences. The canon establishes 1413 the principle that these offences must be 'grave, external, imputable and juridically proven' (see Can. 1321). Those offences listed all constitute serious breaches of religious and ecclesiastical discipline. However, this list is not exhaustive. Dismissal may be determined as the penalty for other causes of a similar nature and gravity. The institute's own law may actually define some of these.

Can. 696 §2 A member in temporary vows can be dismissed even for less grave reasons determined in the institute's own law.

Superiors can decide to dismiss a religious in temporary vows for reasons less 1414 serious than those referred to in §1. However, they must be defined in the institute's own law and they must be 'external, imputable and juridically proven'. Unless there is a matter of injustice or grave scandal, in practice the Superior may decide not to dismiss the person but simply refuse to admit him or her to further profession.

Can. 697 In the cases mentioned in Can. 696, if the major Superior, after consulting his or her council, judges that the process of dismissal should be commenced:

1° the major Superior is to collect or complete the proofs;

2° the major Superior is to warn the member in writing, or before two witnesses, with an explicit caution that dismissal will follow unless the member reforms. The reasons for dismissal are to be clearly expressed and the member is to be given every opportunity for defence. If the warning has no effect, another warning is to be given after an interval of at least fifteen days;

3° if this latter warning is also ineffectual, and the major Superior with his or her council judges that there is sufficient proof of incorrigibility, and that the defence by the member is insufficient, after fifteen days from the last warning have passed in vain, all the acts, signed by the major Superior and a notary, are to be forwarded, together with the signed replies of the member, to the supreme Moderator.

1415 The dismissal of a religious for the reasons mentioned in Can. 696 is a very grave matter. Before initiating any proceedings for dismissal, the major Superior is obliged to consult his or her council; although not constrained by law to follow this advice, the major Superior should have an 'overriding reason' to act against it (see Can. 127 §2 2°).

1416 The procedure for the dismissal of a religious comprises several stages. This canon deals with three essential, initial steps:

(a) *the collection or completion of the evidence* i.e. the major Superior must gather together all the information necessary to establish the facts. He or she may do this personally or through a delegate.

(b) *two canonical warnings* i.e. the major Superior is required to issue a formal warning to the religious on two separate occasions. This may be done in writing or orally in the presence of two witnesses. If it is done orally, care must be taken to draw up a written record of what was said; this should be signed by the major Superior, the witnesses and a notary. If the warning is given in writing, there should be some proof of its delivery to the religious concerned. The canonical warning must contain these elements: a brief statement of the complaint concerning the religious; a clear indication of what specific action is required by way of amendment; an explicit warning that dismissal will follow unless there is due amendment; an invitation to make a response. After the first warning has been given to the religious, the major Superior must allow at least fifteen days for proof of amendment or for a written reply before proceeding to the second warning, which itself shall be a repetition of the first.

(c) *forwarding the acts to the supreme Moderator*: if the second warning produces no results within fifteen days, the major Superior must meet with his or her council to determine whether or not the religious has shown proof of correction or has submitted a sufficient defence. In this case, the Superior is obliged to act in accordance with the consent of his or her council.[1] If the decision is that 'there is sufficient proof of incorrigibility, and that the defence by the member is insufficient', then all the acts of the case are to be sent to the supreme Moderator of the institute. These

---

[1] Cf. CCom rep 14.V.1985: AAS 77(1985) 771.

acts consist of the evidence collected by the major Superior, the warnings issued in accordance with the law, and any written replies from the religious concerned. The law requires that the documents be signed by the major Superior and the notary.

Can. 698 In all the cases mentioned in Cann. 695 and 696, the member always retains the right to communicate with, and send replies directly to the supreme Moderator.

Whether the dismissal is required by law (see Can. 695) or the procedure is instituted by the major Superior in accordance with Cann. 696–697, the law guarantees the right of the individual religious to deal directly with the supreme Moderator. Thus a religious is free to respond to an accusation or canonical warning communicated by the major Superior by replying immediately to the supreme Moderator.

Can. 699 §1 The supreme Moderator with his or her council are to proceed in a collegial fashion in accurately weighing the proofs, the arguments and the defence. For validity, the council must comprise at least four members. If by a secret vote it is decided to dismiss the religious, a decree of dismissal is to be drawn up, which for validity must express at least in summary form the reasons in law and in fact.

The second phase of the dismissal process involves the supreme Moderator and his or her council. By law, the council must have at least four members for such an occasion. If, in fact, the council is smaller, particular law must provide a mechanism by which the required number is made up. Working together as a body, the Moderator and council are to evaluate the acts presented, weighing up the evidence, the arguments and the replies of the accused. Finally, they are to hold a secret vote. If the outcome of that vote is in favour of dismissal, a decree must be drawn up. This decree must contain an outline of the reasons for dismissal, in law and in fact; it must also indicate the right of the religious to have recourse and the effect of that recourse (see Can. 700).

Can. 699 §2 In the autonomous monasteries mentioned in Can. 615, the judgement about dismissal belongs to the diocesan Bishop. The Superior is to submit the acts to him after they have been reviewed by the council.

The procedure for dismissal is somewhat different in monasteries with no major Superior other than their own Moderator, and with no jurisdictional bond with another religious institute (see Can. 615). The Superior of the monastery must follow the procedure contained in Can. 697 1° and 2°. However, the acts of the case and the replies of the religious concerned are to be forwarded to the diocesan Bishop. On the basis of these documents, he is to make a judgement. If it is in favour of dismissal, the decree is to be issued. However, it must be confirmed by the Holy See, since the diocesan Bishop has the power to dismiss only religious of diocesan right.

Can. 700 A decree of dismissal has no effect unless it is confirmed by the Holy See, to whom the decree and all the acts are to be forwarded. If the matter concerns an institute of diocesan right, the confirmation belongs to the Bishop in whose diocese is located the house to which the religious belongs. For validity the decree must indicate the right of the person dismissed to have recourse to the competent authority within ten days of receiving the notification of the decree. The recourse has a suspensive effect.

1420 The final phase of the dismissal process comprises two stages:
   (a) *confirmation*: the supreme Moderator must send the decree of dismissal and all the acts to the competent ecclesiastical authority, i.e. to the Congregation for Institutes of Consecrated Life and Societies of Apostolic Life in the case of pontifical-right institutes, or to the diocesan Bishop of the house to which the religious belongs in the case of an institute of diocesan right. If, after careful examination, the authority is satisfied concerning the merits of the case and the procedures followed, the decree is confirmed and is made effective.
   (b) *notification*: only after the decree has been confirmed can it be notified formally to the religious. In making this notification, attention should be drawn to that part of the decree indicating the right of the religious to have recourse within ten days.

1421 Should he or she so decide, the religious may lodge a recourse with the authority which confirmed the decree of dismissal. In the case of a member of a diocesan right institute, recourse should be made to the appropriate Congregation in Rome. Until such a recourse, if made, is decided, the effects of the decree are simply suspended. If, after recourse, the decree of dismissal is upheld, the religious may have a final recourse to the Apostolic Signatura, *but only* concerning the validity of the procedures, not concerning the merits of the case.

Can. 701 By lawful dismissal both the vows and the rights and duties deriving from profession automatically cease. If the member is a cleric he may not exercise sacred orders until he finds a Bishop who will, after a suitable probation, receive him into his diocese in accordance with Can. 693, or who will at least allow him to exercise his sacred orders.

1422 The lawful dismissal of a religious results in the definitive separation of that person from the institute. All rights and obligations arising out of religious profession cease. In the case of a religious cleric, the law makes a further point: such a man is not permitted to exercise his sacred ministry until he finds a Bishop who is willing to receive him into his diocese or who will permit him to exercise sacred ministry in his diocese while he searches for a Bishop who will receive him definitively. The process for the probation and reception of such a cleric is provided for in Can. 693. Although no longer a religious, such a cleric is still bound by the obligations of the clerical status.

Can. 702 §1 Whoever lawfully leaves a religious institute or is lawfully dismissed from one, cannot claim anything from the institute for any work done in it.

§2 The institute, however, is to show equity and evangelical charity towards the member who is separated from it.

1423 By reason of their profession of evangelical poverty, whatever a religious receives by way of income from the work in the institute, from pensions or from other such sources belongs not to the individual but to the institute. For this reason those who are legitimately separated from the institute, whether by lawful departure or lawful dismissal, have no claim in justice to seek remuneration for work done while in the institute. Nevertheless, the law does exhort the institute to show equity and charity in making provision for those who are lawfully separated. Such arrangements should take account of the individual's age, health, qualifications, ability to take care of himself or herself, and the like. This is an important pastoral consideration, the neglect of which would be an indictment of the institute's 'evangelical charity'.

Can. 703 In a case of grave external scandal, or of extremely grave and imminent harm to the institute, a member can be expelled forthwith from

Part III Institutes of Consecrated Life and Societies of Apostolic Life

the house by the major Superior. If there is danger in delay, this can be done by the local Superior with the consent of his or her council. The major Superior, if need be, is to introduce a process of dismissal in accordance with the norms of law, or refer the matter to the Apostolic See.

In certain cases, the law gives religious Superiors the power to take immediate action against religious. The canon speaks of two sets of circumstances: **1424**

(a) 'a case of grave external scandal', i.e. unlawful or inappropriate activity by the religious which is objectively serious and publicly known;

(b) 'a case of extremely grave and imminent harm to the institute', i.e. where very serious damage to the institute is foreseen as a result of the activity of one of its members.

In these circumstances, the major Superior – or, in an emergency, the local Superior with the consent of his or her council – can expel the religious concerned from the religious house where he or she was living. This course of action is, at best, an interim measure. If the scandal or harm is averted by the expulsion, the Superior need do no more than find an alternative house for the religious. However, if scandal or the risk of harm persists, the major Superior is given two options: to initiate dismissal proceedings in accordance with Can. 697, or to refer the matter to the Holy See. In doubt, the preferable procedure would be a reference to the Holy See. **1425**

Can. 704 In the report to be sent to the Apostolic See in accordance with Can. 592 §1, mention is to be made of members who have been separated in any way from the institute.

At regular intervals, each religious institute is required to present to the Holy See a report on the state and life of the institute (see Can. 592 §1). This is to include an account of all those members who have been separated from the institute in any way, e.g. the number of novices who departed voluntarily or were dismissed; the number of those in temporary vows who departed voluntarily or were dismissed; the number of perpetually professed members who are in exclaustration, those who have been dispensed, and those who have been dismissed. **1426**

Chapter VII
RELIGIOUS RAISED TO THE EPISCOPATE

The provisions of this Chapter VII are more restricted *in scope* than those of the corresponding chapter in the 1917 Code cc.626–631, which concerned not only religious raised to the episcopate but those also raised to any ecclesiastical dignity or given charge of a parish; religious given charge of a parish are now dealt with particularly in Cann. 520 and 682. The current law deals here solely with religious who are appointed Bishops, whether diocesan or titular (see Can. 376), *and* with those who are equivalent in law to a diocesan Bishop (see Cann. 368, 381 §2).[1] It does not apply to those religious who are appointed to an office within a diocese, such e.g. as a Vicar general, an episcopal Vicar, or to any other ecclesiastical office or dignity.[2] **1427**

---

[1] Cf. Chiappetta n.2807; Comm 13(1981) 363 at Can. 82.
[2] Cf. CCom rep 19.I.1988: AAS 80(1988) 1819, which deals specifically with religious who are appointed as Auditors of the Roman Rota.

Can. 705 A religious raised to the episcopate remains a member of his institute, but is subject only to the Roman Pontiff by his vow of obedience. He is not bound by obligations which he prudently judges are not compatible with his condition.

1428 The canon enunciates the fundamental principle: 'a religious raised to the episcopate *remains a member of his institute*'. Accordingly he remains, in general, both subject to the obligations arising from his religious profession, and in possession of those spiritual benefits and orientations which are specific to his own institute.

1429 Recognising however that his new status as Bishop requires some modifications in his way of life, the relevant current law may be summarised as follows:

(a) in the context of his vow of obedience, he no longer remains subject to the authority of his religious Superiors; he becomes instead subject exclusively to the Pope.

(b) he remains bound by the other obligations arising from his religious profession, *save only* by those which he himself prudently judges to be incompatible with his new status: one can think e.g. of certain obligations of the vow of poverty, of the obligation to live a community life, of the obligation in respect of certain devotional practices, etc.

(c) he may no longer vote, or be voted for, in respect of any office or other ballot decision within the institute.[1]

Can. 706 In the case of the religious mentioned above:

1° if he has lost the ownership of his goods through his profession, he now has the use and enjoyment and the administration of the goods he acquires. In the case of a diocesan Bishop and those mentioned in Can. 381 §2, the particular church acquires their ownership; in the case of others, they belong to the institute or the Holy See, depending on whether the institute is or is not capable of possessing goods.

2° if he has not lost the ownership of his goods through profession, he recovers the use and enjoyment and administration of the goods he possessed; what he obtains later he acquires fully.

3° in both cases, however, any goods he receives which are not personal gifts must be disposed of according to the intentions of the donors.

1430 Among the most significant changes in the life of a religious appointed a Bishop is the alteration in his observance of the vow of poverty. The law makes a distinction between those religious who renounce ownership (see Can. 668 §§4–5) and those who do not. The former, when made Bishops, regain the use, enjoyment and administration of temporal goods acquired by them *after* promotion to the episcopate. However, they do not regain the power of ownership, which was itself renounced: on the contrary, if the religious becomes a diocesan Bishop or the equivalent (see Can. 381 §2), the power of ownership is vested in the diocese, or its equivalent, entrusted to him; if the religious becomes a titular Bishop, the power of ownership is vested in the institute or, if the institute itself is incapable of ownership, in the Holy See (see Can. 634 §1). On the other hand, those who do not renounce ownership at profession regain the use, enjoyment and administration of their own property and at the same time gain personal ownership of any goods which they may subsequently

---

[1] Cf. CCom rep 29.IV.1986: AAS 78(1986) 1324: Comm 18(1986) 409 III.

acquire, e.g. by way of family inheritance, of gift, etc. The canon concludes by recalling the obvious and established principle that any goods received other than as personal gifts may be used *only for the purpose for which they were given* (see Cann. 1267 §3, 1300–1310).

Can. 707 §1 A religious Bishop 'emeritus' may choose his own place of residence, even elsewhere than in a house of his institute, unless the Holy See disposes otherwise.

§2 If he has served a diocese, Can. 402 §2 is to be observed concerning his suitable and worthy maintenance, unless his own institute wishes to provide such maintenance. Otherwise, the Apostolic See is to make other provision.

The law provides for the residence and the upkeep of retired religious Bishops. Full freedom is given to the individual to choose his place of residence after retirement: it might be in a house of his institute or elsewhere. In a particular case, the Holy See may make a special provision. Should he have served a diocese or its equivalent, the primary responsibility for his maintenance rests with the diocese or other which he served, in accordance with the norms established by the Bishops' Conference (see Can. 402 §2). However, the religious institute may assume this responsibility, either jointly with the diocese or completely. In a particular case, the Holy See may intervene and make a special provision. 1431

Chapter VIII
CONFERENCES OF MAJOR SUPERIORS

Can. 708 Major Superiors can usefully meet together in conferences and councils, so that by combined effort they may work to achieve more fully the purpose of each institute, while respecting the autonomy, nature and spirit of each. They can also deal with affairs that are common to all and work to establish suitable coordination and cooperation with the Bishops' Conferences and with individual Bishops.

The law recognises the value of some stable form of communication and collaboration between religious institutes. The roots of the conferences and councils of which the canon speaks lie in the experience of religious throughout the world following the First International Congress of the States of Perfection held in Rome in 1950. With the encouragement of Pope Pius XII, religious institutes organised congresses and established committees to foster better relations between the institutes themselves and between the institutes and the Bishops.[1] The usefulness of these institutions was recognised explicitly by Vat. II,[2] and their establishment was fostered in the years following the Council.[3] 1432

The Code does *not require* the establishment of conferences or councils of major Superiors (see Can. 620). Indeed, it is to be noted that, in so far as they exist, they do not in any way constitute or even suggest an institution parallel to that of the Bishops' Conference. They are of a nature and purpose which is completely different; in particu- 1433

---

[1] Cf. Nardin *Conferenze dei Religiosi*: DIP 2 1424–1426.
[2] Cf. CD 35(5): Fl I 585–586; PC 23: Fl I 622; AG 33: Fl I 849.
[3] Cf. ES II 42–43: Fl I 633; III 21: Fl I 862; MR 61–66: Fl II 241–242.

lar, they do not enjoy any part of the power of governance in the Church (see Cann. 129–144, 330–341). In fact, Conferences of Major Religious Superiors are helpfully to be found in almost every country, organised both nationally and internationally. The specific purpose of these entities is threefold: to assist each participating institute to achieve its own purpose; to address those issues which are common to all the participating institutes; to promote ever closer collaboration with individual Bishops and with Bishops' Conferences: in this particular regard they must always be sensitive to issues either determined or under consideration by the Bishops, and act accordingly.

Can. 709 Conferences of major Superiors are to have their own statutes which must be approved by the Holy See. Only the Holy See can establish them or give them juridical personality. They remain under the ultimate direction of the Holy See.

1434 Conferences of major Superiors are wholly dependent juridically on the Holy See, both for their existence and their activity. The Holy See is the only authority competent to establish these Conferences, to grant them juridical personality (see Cann. 113 §2, 114 §1), and to approve the statutes by which they are regulated. Moreover, the Holy See retains an ongoing interest in the activities of these Conferences: they remain under its 'ultimate direction'.

Title III
Secular Institutes

Can. 710 A secular institute is an institute of consecrated life in which Christ's faithful, living in the world, strive for the perfection of charity and endeavour to contribute to the sanctification of the world, especially from within.

1435 While consecrated life in religious institutes is characterised by a distinctive 'separation from the world' (see Can. 607 §3), the distinguishing feature of the second major form of consecrated life, namely secular institutes, is 'insertion into the world'. The origins of these institutes lie in the sixteenth century with the foundation by St Angela Merici of the Company of St Ursula. This was a group of women who sought to dedicate themselves totally to God while continuing to live in their own homes. Under pressure from several Bishops, many of these women came together to form religious congregations. However, in some dioceses groups of these secular women continued with their work, principally of education. Similar groups emerged in the Church during the eighteenth, nineteenth and early twentieth centuries. The 1917 Code gave no canonical recognition to these groups, who did not make public vows and did not live in common. However, in 1947, after an extensive study by the Roman Curia, Pope Pius XII formally recognised these associations as 'secular institutes' and provided legislation for their establishment and internal government.[1]

---

[1] Cf. Pope Pius XII ap con *Provida Mater Ecclesia* 2.II.1947: CLD 3 135–146; mp *Primo feliciter* 12.III.1948: CLD 3 147–151; SCRIS instr *Cum Sanctissimus* 19.III.1948: CLD 3 151–157. A further instructive point of reference is to be found in three significant Addresses by Pope Paul VI – to First International Congress of Secular Institutes 26.IX.1970: AAS 62(1970) 619–624: LE IV 5887–5890; – to Members of Secular Institutes 2.II.1972: AAS 64(1972) 206–212: LE IV 6221–6225; – to International Meeting of Moderators of Secular Institutes 20.IX.1972: AAS 64(1972) 615–620: LE IV 6310–6313.

Part III Institutes of Consecrated Life and Societies of Apostolic Life

Since then, the Church has striven to find an accurate theological and canonical expression for these secular institutes. Vat. II, although addressing the topic in a document devoted to the renewal of *religious life*, stated clearly 'that secular institutes are not religious institutes'.[1] The Code locates them firmly among institutes of consecrated life, and this initial canon highlights the essential elements of such an institute. First and foremost, it is an institute of *consecrated life*, i.e. in which the members dedicate themselves to God through profession of the evangelical counsels (see Can. 573). Unlike members of religious institutes, members of secular institutes continue to live 'in the world', and it is there that they seek to achieve their twofold aim of themselves attaining perfection in charity and achieving the sanctification of the world from within. The precise meaning of this *consecrated secularity* is made explicit in the canons which follow.[2] There are at present some 130 secular institutes in the Church, with approximately 60,000 members.

Can. 711 Without prejudice to the provisions of the law concerning institutes of consecrated life, consecration as a member of a secular institute does not change the member's proper canonical status among the people of God, be it clerical or lay.

There are two fundamental categories of person in the Church: clerics and lay people (see Can. 207 §1). Drawn from both are those who profess the evangelical counsels in an institute of consecrated life (see Can. 207 §2). However, such consecration to God in an institute of consecrated life does not affect the fundamental canonical status of a person, insofar as consecrated life does not belong to the hierarchical structure of the Church and is, in itself, neither clerical nor lay (see Cann. 207 §2, 588 §1). This general principle is applied expressly in this canon to members of secular institutes.

Can. 712 Without prejudice to the provisions of Cann. 598-601, the constitutions are to establish the sacred bonds by which the evangelical counsels are undertaken in the institute. They are to define the obligations which these bonds entail, while always professing in their manner of life the secular character proper to the institute.

Pope Pius XII had required that the members of secular institutes make profession of the three evangelical counsels by means of some kind of stable bond, e.g. private vow, oath or consecration.[3] In accordance with Can. 598, the determination of this bond is left to the particular legislation of each institute. This same legislation is also to identify the practical obligations arising out of consecration, taking care to avoid anything which is not consistent with or adapted to a truly secular way of life. Such care must be exercised especially when dealing with matters related to obedience and poverty.

Can. 713 §1 Members of these institutes express and exercise their special consecration in apostolic activity. Like a leaven, they endeavour to permeate everything with an evangelical spirit for the strengthening and growth of the Body of Christ.

Apostolic activity is understood to be the necessary fruit and expression of life consecrated in a secular institute. The members are to exercise their apostolate in an unos-

---

[1] PC 11: Fl I 616–617.

[2] It is important in this context to note that *'secular'* is not equivalent to *'lay'*. Being an institute of consecrated life, a secular institute is 'in itself ... neither clerical nor lay' (Can. 588 §1): it may be either, or it may even be mixed (see Can. 588 §§2-3); the matter is dealt with expressly in Can. 713 §§2-3.

[3] Cf. ap con *Provida Mater Ecclesia*: CLD 3 143.

tentatious manner; indeed, the canon compares them to leaven '...which, always and everywhere active, mingling with every class of persons from the lowest to the highest, strives by example and in every way to reach and to transfuse them individually and collectively until the whole mass is so permeated that it is all leavened in Christ'.[1]

Can. 713 §2 Lay members participate in the evangelising mission of the Church in the world and from within the world. They do this by their witness of christian life and of fidelity to their consecration, and by the assistance they give in directing temporal affairs to God and in animating the world by the power of the Gospel. They also offer their cooperation to serve the ecclesial community in accordance with the secular manner of life proper to them.

1440   The apostolic activity of lay members of secular institutes constitutes their sharing in the Church's mission of preaching the Gospel. The canon stresses that they must participate in this in a truly *secular* fashion, i.e. not as pseudo-religious. First and foremost, they share in the Church's mission by their witness of Christian living and faithfulness in their consecration. Other elements of their service to the Church include their efforts to direct temporal affairs to God and bring the Gospel into the heart of the world, as well as the specific forms of service which they offer and to which they are assigned in their local ecclesial community, diocese, parish etc. Open to them is a vast apostolate in the fields of social, cultural, political, industrial, educational etc. life.

Can. 713 §3 Clerical members, by the witness of their consecrated lives, especially in the *presbyterium*, support their colleagues by a distinctive apostolic charity, and in the people of God they further the sanctification of the world by their sacred ministry.

1441   Clerical members of secular institutes share the clerical state of their brother clerics and give witness to their consecration in a twofold way: towards fellow clerics they offer the support and example of their lives as clerics; towards the laity, they offer the exercise of their sacred ministry and encouragement in a Gospel way of living. Theirs equally is the task of influencing secular society in the direction of the Gospel of Christ: not by direct action, which is the sphere of the laity, but rather by their pastoral activity in a truly-dedicated fulfilment of their sacred ministry.

Can. 714 Members are to live their lives in the ordinary conditions of the world, either alone, in their families or in fraternal groups, in accordance with the constitutions.

1442   Whereas members of religious institutes are bound to a common life (see Cann. 607 §2, 665 §1), members of secular institutes are not. In fact, in their initial recognition by the Holy See, it was stated that secular institutes 'do not impose community life or domicile in common on all their members' and do not have 'a common life that is externally organised'.[2] The canon expresses this specific character of the vocation, and allows for a variety of lifestyle, in keeping with the constitutions of individual institutes. Members may live alone, with their families, or in groups with other members. However, where they do live together, they are to avoid developing practices of a common life which are not in keeping with their secular vocation.

---

[1] Pope Pius XII mp *Primo feliciter*: CLD 3 148.

[2] Pope Pius XII ap con *Provida mater Ecclesia*: CLD 3 142–143.

Can. 715 §1 Clerical members incardinated in a diocese are subject to the diocesan Bishop, except for whatever concerns the consecrated life of their own institutes.

As a rule, all members of secular institutes who are clerics are incardinated into the diocese for whose service they were ordained (see Can. 266 §3). They are truly *secular* clerics. Like all other *secular* clerics, they are subject to the authority of their Bishop. The *only exception* to this concerns the demands of the consecrated life, e.g. spiritual obligations, personal lifestyle, etc. Although not required by law, such clerics should inform their Bishop of their incorporation into the secular institute. In this way, possible misunderstandings and conflicts may be avoided.

Can. 715 §2 Those who, in accordance with the norm of Can. 266 §3, are incardinated in the institute, and who are appointed to works proper to the institute, or to the governance of the institute, are subject to the Bishop in the same way as religious.

Exceptionally, 'by virtue of a concession of the Apostolic See' (Can. 266 §3), clerical members of a secular institute may be incardinated into the institute itself. Such members may be appointed to certain works belonging to the institute or to positions of governance within the institute. In these cases, the law regards the relationship of these clerics to the Bishop as equivalent to that which exists between religious and the Bishop i.e. they are subject to his authority 'in matters concerning the care of souls, the public exercise of divine worship and other works of the apostolate' (Can. 678 §1; see also Can. 682).

Can. 716 §1 All members are to take an active part in the life of the institute, in accordance with the institute's own law.

§2 Members of the same institute are to preserve a rapport with one another, carefully fostering a unity of spirit and a genuine fraternity.

Canon 602 requires that each institute of consecrated life is to define the fraternal life of the institute in its own legislation so that all its members may benefit from mutual assistance and so give example of universal reconciliation in Christ. In religious institutes, legislation concerning the common life fulfils this requirement. The present canon indicates in brief what this entails for secular institutes:

(a) all members must take an active part in the internal life of the institute; the constitutions of each institute are to determine the nature of that participation;

(b) all members must maintain a real link with other members, recognising that they are brothers and sisters in the institute, sharers in the same vocation by which they seek to follow Christ more closely (see Can. 573 §1).

Can. 717 §1 The constitutions are to determine the institute's own form of governance. They are to define the period of time for which Moderators exercise their office and the manner in which they are to be designated.

§2 No one is to be designated supreme Moderator unless definitively incorporated into the institute.

§3 Those entrusted with the governance of the institute are to ensure that its unity of spirit is maintained, and that the active participation of the members is developed.

While seventeen canons of the Code determine the fundamental structures of government within religious institutes, only one canon is devoted to the government of secular institutes. Universal law leaves such matters entirely to the constitutions of each institute, giving a brief indication of some principles concerning Superiors:

(a) the method of selecting Superiors and their term of office are to be specified in the constitutions;

(b) only a definitively incorporated member of the institute may be chosen as supreme Moderator; this parallels the principle established in Can. 623 for religious;

(c) the fundamental role of those in authority within the secular institute is closely related to the obligations of the members mentioned in Can. 716, i.e. to ensure the unity of spirit among members and their active participation in the life of the institute.

Can. 718 The administration of the goods of the institute must express and foster evangelical poverty. It is governed by the norms of Book V on 'The Temporal Goods of the Church', and by the institute's own law. This same law of the institute is also to define the obligations, especially the financial obligations, of the institute towards the members engaged in its work.

1447 Since they are public juridical persons, secular institutes are subject to the norms of Book V of the Code: their goods are considered to be ecclesiastical goods. In addition, the proper legislation must determine these matters in more detail, e.g. by specifying which internal entities enjoy the juridical personality bestowed by the law on religious institutes, provinces and houses (see Can. 634 §1). The administration of these goods must reflect the evangelical poverty professed by the members of the secular institute. Again, this is something which should be addressed in the institute's own legislation. The canon ends by recalling the responsibility of secular institutes to define their obligations towards members who undertake work for the institute. In general, each member, whether lay or clerical, has charge of his or her own financial situation in accordance with the authentic secular character of the institute, with due regard to the requirements of evangelical poverty. Moreover, justice requires that the institute honour obligations to those who serve it in any capacity, e.g. just wage, health insurance, pension.

Can. 719 §1 In order that they may respond faithfully to their vocation and that their apostolic action may proceed from their union with Christ, the members are to devote themselves assiduously to prayer, to engage in a suitable way in the reading of the sacred Scriptures, to make an annual retreat and to carry out other spiritual exercises in accordance with their own law.

§2 The celebration of the Eucharist, daily where possible, is to be the source and strength of their whole consecrated life.

§3 They are to go freely to the sacrament of penance and receive it frequently.

§4 They are to be free to obtain the necessary spiritual direction. Should they so desire, they may seek such counsel even from their Moderators.

1448 This canon identifies the principal sources from which members of secular institutes are to draw nourishment for their spiritual lives. They include:

(a) personal prayer and the study of Scripture;

(b) an annual retreat and other spiritual exercises which form part of their patrimony;

(c) celebration of the Eucharist; where possible, this is to be a feature of daily life;

(d) free and frequent access to the sacrament of penance: 'frequent' means about every two weeks (see Can. 664);

(e) spiritual direction: the members are free to choose a spiritual director; their choice may include a Moderator of the institute, provided obviously that there is not even a suspicion of compulsion.

The determination of various details concerning these means of sanctification is left to the proper legislation of each institute. It is important that this reflect accurately the secular character of the vocation of the members rather than impose on them obligations more suited to the religious life. Many of the sources of spiritual nourishment mentioned reflect those indicated for religious in Cann. 662–672. However, there is no mention in this canon of the use of the means of social communication (see Can. 666), the liturgy of hours (see Can. 663 §3), or devotion to the Blessed Virgin Mary (see Can. 663 §4). It would seem appropriate that, in framing its own law, the institute should at least consider these matters.

Can. 720 The right of admitting a person to the institute, or to probation, or to the taking of sacred bonds, both temporary and perpetual or definitive, belongs to the major Moderators with their council, in accordance with the constitutions.

When dealing with the issues related to admission into secular institutes, the Code is careful to avoid the use of terms usually associated with religious institutes. In the present canon, the general principle is established that admission into the institute, to probation and to the taking of sacred bonds is reserved to the competent 'major Moderator'. It is for the institute's own law to identify this person more closely and to specify the role of his or her council in these matters, i.e. whether their vote is consultative or deliberative.

Can. 721 §1 The following are invalidly admitted to initial probation:

1° one who has not yet attained majority;

2° one who is currently bound by a sacred bond in any institute of consecrated life, or incorporated in a society of apostolic life;

3° a spouse, while the marriage lasts.

Universal law establishes three invalidating impediments to entry into secular institutes. The first impediment is *age*: only those over eighteen years of age (see Can. 97 §1) can be admitted validly. This is a year older than that required for the valid admission to a religious novitiate (see Can. 643 §1 1°). The second impediment is *current incorporation* into an institute of consecrated life (whether religious or secular) or into a society of apostolic life; the impediment is constituted by either temporary or definitive incorporation and is parallel to the impediment for entry into the novitiate in religious institutes (see Can. 643 §1 3°). The third impediment, that of *an existing bond of marriage*, parallels the norm of Can. 643 §1 2° concerning religious.

Can. 721 §2 The constitutions can establish other impediments to admission, even for validity, or attach conditions to it.

This norm repeats for secular institutes that which Can. 643 §2 establishes for religious institutes. Among the other impediments which a secular institute might profitably add in its constitutions are those contained in Can. 643 §1 4°–5°.

Can. 721 §3 For a person to be received into the institute, that degree of maturity is required which is necessary to live fittingly the life proper to the institute.

Although the Code does not require it, the proper legislation of a secular institute can indicate various means by which a judgement is to be made concerning the maturity of a candidate. Indeed, it may recommend the use of experts as is suggested for religious in Can. 642, taking account however of the conditions specified in that canon and also of the relevant observations in this commentary on Can. 241 §1.

Can. 722 §1 The initial probation is to be so arranged that the candidates can better recognise their divine vocation, in fact that proper to the institute, and be trained in the spirit and manner of life of the institute.

1454 The fundamental purpose of the period of initial probation in a secular institute is identical to that of the novitiate in religious institutes (see Can. 646), i.e. to assist the individual candidates in their discernment of God's call, of their call to that particular institute, and to prepare them for a life to be spent in the institute.

Can. 722 §2 Candidates are to be properly formed to live a life according to the evangelical counsels. They are to be taught how to translate this life completely into their apostolate, applying those forms of evangelisation which best correspond to the purpose, spirit and character of the institute.

1455 A more specific goal of initial probation is to prepare the candidates for what is entailed in a life consecrated by profession of the three evangelical counsels. In keeping with the principles enunciated in Can. 713, they are to learn how to express their consecration in apostolic activity. This paragraph echoes the aims of the novitiate for religious contained in Can. 652 §2.

Can. 722 §3 The constitutions are to define the manner and time of the probation to be made before the first sacred bonds are undertaken in the institute; this time is not to be less than two years.

1456 Apart from the general principles set forth in §§1–2, the canon gives no guide-lines concerning the content or manner of initial probation in a secular institute. Such matters are left to the constitutions of each institute. The duration of this period is also left to the constitutions, save only that it be not less than two years.

Can. 723 §1 When the time of the initial probation has been completed, a candidate who is judged suitable is either to undertake the three evangelical counsels sealed with a sacred bond, or leave the institute.

§2 The first incorporation is to be temporary, in accordance with the constitutions, but is to be for not less than five years.

§3 When this period of incorporation has been completed, a member who is judged suitable is admitted to perpetual or definitive incorporation, that is, by temporary bonds which are always to be renewed.

§4 Definitive incorporation is equivalent to perpetual incorporation in respect of defined juridical effects, which are to be established in the constitutions.

1457 This canon deals with the three forms of incorporation into a secular institute which are envisaged in the law.[1] They are:
- *first incorporation* (§§1–2), i.e. the consecration of one's life through the evangelical counsels of poverty, chastity and obedience, 'sealed with a sacred bond', itself to be determined in accordance with Can. 712. This incorporation is of its nature temporary, for a period to be determined by the institute's constitutions.
- *perpetual incorporation* (§§3–4), i.e. the same consecration which is, however, to be made once only, for life.
- *definitive incorporation* (§§3–4), i.e. the same consecration which, while being for a specified number of years, must always be renewed at the expiry of that specified period: 'it might be said that definitive incorporation is potentially perpetual, and

---

[1] Cf. Beyer *Le Droit de la Vie Consacrée II: Instituts et Sociétés* Paris 1988 258–259.

this is where the difference lies between definitive incorporation and that which is simply temporary'.[1]

1458 Following the period of initial probation, the suitability of each candidate is to be assessed by the competent authority (§1). If found suitable, the candidate is to proceed to the *first incorporation* defined above: the only alternative is to leave the institute; obviously, a candidate judged to be unsuitable must leave in any event. Whereas Can. 653 §2, in the context of a religious institute, allows for the possibility of a short extension of the novitiate in a case where some doubt remains about a candidate's suitability, no such extension is permitted here. While this canon does not specify the conditions for the validity of this first incorporation, there would appear to be no doubt that, with the appropriate adjustments, the requirements of Can. 656 apply.[2]

1459 The overall duration of this first incorporation may not be shorter than five years (§2), though the constitutions may require that the consecration be renewed at intervals during that period, thus to give the candidate an opportunity for even greater reflection and resolve. Equally, the constitutions may determine a period longer than five years; some are known to have extended the time until the attainment of a specified age.[3]

1460 At the close of the period of first incorporation, a further appraisal of the member's suitability is to be made (§3). Should this be favourable, the person must be admitted – at that person's choice, after mature consideration of all the circumstances – to either perpetual or definitive incorporation, as defined above. Should it be unfavourable, the prescription of Can. 726 §1 applies.

1461 Although the sacred bond involved in definitive incorporation is in one sense temporary, it is not in any way provisional: it is, as explained above, potentially perpetual in that it *must be renewed periodically*. Accordingly, it is in fact 'equivalent to perpetual incorporation' (§4) in regard to quite a number of juridical effects, which themselves are to be determined as such in each institute's constitutions: one thinks of such matters as having active or passive voice in elections, admissibility to the post of director of formation, eligibility for the office of major or even supreme Superior, etc. In this regard, it is to be noted – in reverse, as it were – that the prescription of Can. 717 §2, requiring that the supreme Moderator be definitively incorporated into the institute, does not in any way exclude the eligibility of one who is perpetually incorporated.

Can. 724 §1 After the first undertaking of the sacred bonds, formation is to continue without interruption in accordance with the constitutions.

§2 Members are to be formed simultaneously in matters human and divine. The Moderators of the institute are to have a serious concern for the continued spiritual formation of the members.

1462 Formation within the secular institute does not end with the period of first incorporation. Rather, the law requires that it continue until perpetual or definitive incorporation. The guiding principle of this formation is that it ought to combine 'matters human and divine'. Clearly, this formation is related to the life of each particular institute since the secular character of these institutes involves the members living and working 'in the world'. Responsibility for ongoing formation rests with the Moderators, who are to have a particularly 'serious concern' for the *spiritual* formation of the group.

---

[1] CCLA 485; cf. Chiappetta n.2861.
[2] Cf. Chiappetta n.2860.
[3] Cf. Beyer op cit 258.

Book II The People of God

Can. 725 The institute can associate with itself, by some sort of bond determined in the constitutions, other members of Christ's faithful who seek evangelical perfection according to the spirit of the institute.

1463 Lay people, married and single, have been associated in some ways with secular institutes for many years; so, too, have secular clergy. This loose connection was acknowledged implicitly by Pope Pius XII when he referred to the obligations of members 'in the strict sense'.[1] By reason of this canon, secular institutes are given the same rights as religious institutes in the matter of associations of the faithful (see Cann. 303, 677 §2). Details of the links between such associate members and the secular institute, and of the bonds by which they are bound to the life and work of the institute, are to be defined in the constitutions of the institute itself.

Can. 726 §1 When the time of temporary incorporation is completed, the member can freely leave the institute or can, for a just cause, be excluded from renewing the sacred bonds by the major Moderator after consultation with his or her council.

§2 A temporarily incorporated member who freely requests it can, for a grave reason, be granted an indult to leave the institute by the supreme Moderator with the consent of his or her council.

1464 The canon deals with the departure from a secular institute (other than by dismissal) before the time of definitive or perpetual incorporation, and is analogous to the prescriptions concerning religious (see Can. 688). While the major Moderator can exclude someone from renewing bonds, only the supreme Moderator can grant an indult to depart – the former after consultation with, the latter only having had the consent of, the council (see Can. 127). No mention, however, is made of the need to have the indult confirmed by the diocesan Bishop in the case of an institute of diocesan right (see Can. 688 §2).

Can. 727 §1 A perpetually incorporated member who wishes to leave the institute must, after seriously weighing the matter before the Lord, petition the Holy See through the supreme Moderator if the institute is of pontifical right; otherwise the indult can also be obtained from the diocesan Bishop, as determined in the constitutions.

§2 For a cleric who is incardinated in the institute, the provision of Can. 693 is to be observed.

1465 The procedure for seeking a dispensation from the obligations of perpetual incorporation in a secular institute is identical to that laid down for perpetually professed religious (see Can. 691), i.e. the member must address a petition to the Holy See through the supreme Moderator; if the institute is of diocesan right, it may be addressed also to the diocesan Bishop in the manner defined in the constitutions. As in the case of religious, members of secular institutes are to seek such an indult only 'after seriously weighing the matter before the Lord'. In the case of a cleric, such an indult may not be granted until he has found a Bishop willing to accept him definitively or at least on probation (see Can. 693). There is no need to outline a procedure for those definitively incorporated, since failure to renew the sacred bond has the same effect, i.e. departure from the institute.

---

[1] Pope Pius XII ap con *Provida Mater Ecclesia*: CLD 3 143.

Can. 728 When an indult to leave the institute has been lawfully granted, all bonds, rights and obligations deriving from incorporation cease.

The effects of an indult to leave a secular institute after perpetual incorporation are identical to those of an indult to leave a religious institute (see Can. 692); the individual loses all rights and obligations arising out of this incorporation. Whereas Can. 692 makes the efficacy of the indult dependent on its notification to the petitioner, an indult to leave a secular institute is effective immediately it is granted.

1466

Can. 729 A member is dismissed from the institute in accordance with the norms of Cann. 694 and 695. The constitutions are also to determine other reasons for dismissal, provided that they are proportionately grave, external, imputable and juridically proven. The procedure established in Cann. 697–700 is to be observed and the provisions of Can. 701 apply to the person who is dismissed.

The reasons for automatic and compulsory dismissal from a religious institute apply also to dismissal from a secular institute (see Cann. 694–695). Exactly the same procedure (see Cann. 697–700) is to be observed, and the effects are those detailed in Can. 701. The canon requires that the constitutions of each institute determine other reasons for which a member might be dismissed. In the case of religious institutes Can. 696 does indicate the *kind of additional reasons* envisaged. This canon does not, but it can certainly be taken that the list in Can. 696 is, with appropriate adjustments, a good guideline for the constitutions of secular institutes.

1467

Can. 730 For a member to transfer from one secular institute to another, the provisions of Cann. 684 §§1, 2 and 4 and 685 are to be observed. In order, however, that a transfer be made to a religious institute or a society of apostolic life or from those to a secular institute, the permission of the Apostolic See is required, whose instructions are to be followed.

In the matter of transferring from one secular institute to another, the principles and procedure for the transfer between religious institutes is to be followed. Thus, a perpetually incorporated member must obtain the permission of the supreme Moderators of both institutes, given with the consent of their respective councils (see Can. 684 §1); perpetual incorporation must be preceded by at least three years probation in the new institute (see Can. 684 §2); the duration and manner of this probation is to be determined in the constitutions of each secular institute (see Can. 684 §4). During this time, all rights and obligations in the original institute are suspended (see Can. 685 §1); they cease altogether with incorporation into the new institute (see Can. 685 §2).

1468

As a consequence of the different foundation and patrimony of each way of life, a member of a secular institute can transfer to a religious institute or to a society of apostolic life only with the explicit permission of the Holy See (see Can. 684 §5). The same principle applies to members of religious institutes or of societies of apostolic life seeking to transfer to a secular institute.[1]

1469

---

[1] Shortly after the promulgation of the Code, the Holy See issued a corrected version of the official Latin text of this canon (cf. AAS 75(1983): Pt II Appendix, 323 at Can. 730), the translation of which correction is incorporated into our text above. Unfortunately, when the definitive and annotated Latin text was issued in 1989 (Libreria Editrice Vaticana) yet another error had crept in: in that text *694* should read *684*.

SECTION II
SOCIETIES OF APOSTOLIC LIFE

Can. 731 §1 Societies of apostolic life approximate to institutes of consecrated life. Their members, without taking religious vows, pursue the apostolic purpose proper to each society. Living a fraternal life in common in their own special manner, they strive for the perfection of charity through the observance of the constitutions.

§2 Among these societies are some in which the members, through a bond defined in the constitutions, undertake to live the evangelical counsels.

1470 The origins of today's societies of apostolic life lie in the sixteenth and seventeenth centuries which saw the establishment of the Oratorians by St Philip Neri, and the Congregation of the Mission and the Daughters of Charity by St Vincent de Paul. These groups studiously resisted efforts to organise them or recognise them as religious. In the 1917 Code they were described as societies of men and women living in common without vows. After a prolonged debate, the Revision Commission decided to refer to them as 'societies of apostolic life'[1] and to locate the canons concerning them after the Section on *Consecrated Life*, i.e. Cann. 573–730.

1471 The opening canon is doctrinal in nature, attempting to identify what makes these societies similar to, and yet distinct from, institutes of consecrated life. At least superficially, societies of apostolic life are very similar to institutes of consecrated life, e.g. they live a fraternal life in common and strive for the perfection of charity (see Cann. 573 §1, 607 §2). The members – as a rule – do not take religious vows, i.e. do not profess the evangelical counsels by means of public vows (see Can. 1192 §1). Moreover, while for religious the fundamental apostolate lies in the witness of their consecrated life (see Can. 673), the basic aim here is to pursue the particular apostolic activity of the society, e.g. works of charity, of missionary evangelisation, of education, etc.

1472 The second paragraph introduces something of an anomaly: it recognises that some of these societies do, in fact, undertake to live the evangelical counsels. However, these are not undertaken by means of public vows; rather, in those particular societies the nature of the bond involved is determined in the constitutions.

Can. 732 Cann. 578–597 and 606 apply to societies of apostolic life, with due regard, however, for the nature of each society. For the societies mentioned in Can. 731 §2, Cann. 598–602 also apply.

1473 The juridical similarity between these societies and institutes of consecrated life is highlighted by the frequent reference to canons concerning the latter. These canons deal with fundamental questions concerning the identity, autonomy, structures and legislation of the societies of apostolic life as well as their juridical relationship to the local Church and the Holy See. For those societies in which the evangelical counsels are undertaken by some recognised form of bond, the contents of the doctrinal Canons 598–602 apply. In all cases, clearly, what is said of institutes of consecrated life must be appropriately adapted to the nature and circumstances of each society of apostolic life.

Can. 733 §1 A house is established and a local community is constituted by the competent authority of the society, with the prior written consent of the diocesan Bishop. The Bishop must also be consulted when there is a question of its suppression.

---

[1] Cf. Comm 13(1981) 380–389.

Part III Institutes of Consecrated Life and Societies of Apostolic Life

The canon draws a distinction between the establishment of a house and the constitution of a community. Unlike religious (see Can. 665), members of societies of apostolic life can live a fraternal life in common outside their own houses. The constitutions of the society must identify the authority competent to establish a house or constitute a community. In both cases, for validity, the diocesan Bishop must give his prior written consent. The same Bishop must be consulted if a house or community is to be suppressed. These norms echo Cann. 609 §1 and 616 §1. Although no mention is made of the disposal of the goods of a suppressed house or community, by analogy with Can. 616 §1 it would seem that this should be addressed in the society's own law. 1474

Can. 733 §2 Consent to establish a house carries with it the right to have at least an oratory in which the Blessed Eucharist is celebrated and reserved.

In a clear parallel with Can. 608, the canonical establishment of a house for a society of apostolic life confers the right to have an oratory in which Mass can be celebrated and the Blessed Sacrament reserved. 1475

Can. 734 The governance of the society is determined by the constitutions, without prejudice, in accordance with the nature of each society, to Cann. 617-633.

The precise structures of government of each society of apostolic life are to be determined by the constitutions. The Code demands that these must be in accordance with the basic principles established in Cann. 617–633 which deal with Superiors and Councils, chapters and the administration of temporal goods. Such guidelines reinforce the juridical similarities between these societies and religious institutes. 1476

Can. 735 §1 The admission, probation, incorporation and formation of members are determined by each society's own law.

§2 For admission into the society, the conditions prescribed in Cann. 642-645 are to be observed.

§3 The society's own law must determine a programme of doctrinal, spiritual and apostolic probation and formation that is adapted to the purpose and character of the society. In this way members can recognise their divine vocation and be suitably prepared for the mission and way of life they have chosen.

Details concerning the admission, preparation and incorporation of members into societies of apostolic life are left to the proper law of each society. The Code requires that the norms for admission to a religious institute (see Cann. 642–645) be observed, suitably adapted to the character of each society. Moreover, each society, just like religious and secular institutes (see Cann. 659, 722), is to draw up its own particular programme of probation and formation. As with the institutes of consecrated life, the aim of this programme is the discernment of each member's vocation and his or her preparation for the life and mission of the society. 1477

Can. 736 §1 In clerical societies, the clerics are incardinated into the society unless the constitutions determine otherwise.

§2 The norms concerning the secular clergy apply to the programme of studies and reception of Orders, without prejudice to §1.

By reason of the general reference made in Can. 732, societies of apostolic life may be either lay or clerical (see Can. 588 §§2–3). This is the first canon of this section to focus on the distinction. It establishes the norm that members of clerical societies of 1478 apostolic life are incarnated into the society.[1] In this, they are similar to religious institutes (see Can. 266 §2). However, the constitutions of a society can determine that clerical members are incardinated into a particular Church (see Can. 368), an option which is not available to religious institutes. The distinction from religious is heightened by the requirement that members of clerical societies of apostolic life are to be trained in accordance with the universal and particular norms for the formation of secular clergy.[2]

Can. 737 For the members, incorporation carries with it the rights and obligations defined in the constitutions. On the part of the society, it implies a responsibility to lead the members towards the purpose of their vocation in accordance with the constitutions.

1479 In keeping with the general principle enunciated in Can. 735 §1, the Code does not seek to specify anything concerning the nature or manner of incorporation into a society of apostolic life. Rather, in this canon, it highlights the mutual responsibilities involved in the act of incorporation: the member acquires those rights and assumes those obligations defined in the constitutions (these will vary depending on whether the incorporation is temporary or definitive); the society takes up the duty of caring for the welfare of the member and providing what is needed for the fulfilment of his or her vocation.

Can. 738 §1 All members are subject to their own Moderators in matters concerning the internal life and discipline of the society, in accordance with the constitutions.

§2 They are also subject to the diocesan Bishop in matters concerning public worship, the care of souls and other works of the apostolate, with due regard to Cann. 679–683.

§3 The relationship between a member who is incardinated in a diocese and his proper Bishop is to be defined in the constitutions or in particular agreements.

1480 Further similarities between societies of apostolic life and religious institutes emerge when considering the relationship between members of these societies and ecclesiastical authority. First and foremost, as members of a society, they are governed by the Moderators of the society in what concerns the internal life and discipline of the society. The constitutions must determine clearly the structures of internal government and the relationship between those and the individual member. Secondly, in the same way as religious, members of societies of apostolic life are subject to the jurisdiction of the diocesan Bishop in matters of public worship, the care of souls and other works of the apostolate (see Can. 678 §1). The similarity with religious is reinforced by the reference to those canons in which the relationship between the diocesan Bishop and religious institutes is regulated more closely (see Cann. 679–683).

1481 However, the difference between these societies and religious institutes emerges in the provision of the third paragraph. Since some members of these societies may be

---

[1] Initially the faculty of incardination had been limited to societies of pontifical right: cf. Comm 13(1981) 392 at Can. 7. The omission of any reference to the status of the society means that, unless their constitutions make an explicit contrary determination, members of societies of apostolic life of diocesan right are also incardinated into the society.

[2] This means they are subject to the relevant norms of Cann. 232–264, the *Ratio Fundamentalis Institutionis Sacerdotalis* 19.III.1985: LE VI 9069–9109 and the Programme of Priestly Formation of the country in which they reside.

incardinated into the diocese (see Can. 736 §1), special arrangements are necessary if these members are to play an active role in the life of their society. Consequently, the relationship of such a member to his proper Bishop i.e. the Bishop of incardination, must be clearly defined. This can be done either in the society's constitutions or in particular agreements to be drawn up as each case arises.

Can. 739 Apart from the obligations which derive from their constitutions, members are bound by the common obligations of clerics, unless the nature of things or the context establishes otherwise.

Commentators agree that, at least at first sight, the precise sense of this canon is not easy to interpret.[1] The following would appear accurately to state the law:

(a) All members of a society of apostolic life, whether men or women,[2] are bound by two types of obligations: those specified in their own constitutions in accordance with Can. 737 and, *in addition,* those termed in this canon 'the common obligations of clerics' – a phrase which would seem to hearken back to Can. 672 concerning religious.

(b) Accordingly, with the sole exception of Can. 279 §2, the canons specified in Can. 672 are to be enumerated among the common obligations of clerics which bind the members of *each and every* society of apostolic life.

(c) Equally to be included are obligations such e.g. as reverence and obedience to the Pope and to their own Ordinary (see Can. 273); union with one another and with their associates in a familial and prayerful bond (see Can. 275), the diligent pursuit of holiness (see Can. 276), the observance of perfect and perpetual continence (see Can. 277 §§1–2), the avoidance of activities alien to their state and way of life (see Can. 285 §§1–2), etc.

(d) Excluded, as far as lay members are concerned, are obviously those obligations which refer specifically and exclusively to clerics. Moreover, even in what concerns clerical members, such obligations are excluded when it is clear from 'the nature of things or the context' that they are not applicable: thus e.g. in respect of the clerical members who in accordance with Can. 736 §1 are incardinated into the society itself, in respect of any society whose specific apostolic work would render inconsistent the application of this or that 'common obligation', etc.

1482

Can. 740 Members must live in a lawfully constituted house or community and observe a common life, in accordance with their own law. This same law also governs their absence from the house or community.

Like religious (see Can. 665 §1), members of societies of apostolic life are required by law to reside with other members in a house or community of the society constituted in accordance with Can. 733 §1. The proper law of each society must provide norms for the regulation of the common life, and for legitimate absences of a member from the house or community to which he or she has been assigned.

1483

Can. 741 §1 Societies and, unless the constitutions provide otherwise, their constituent parts and their houses are juridical persons. As such, they are capable of acquiring, possessing, administering and alienating temporal goods in accordance with the provisions of Book V on 'The Temporal Goods of the Church', of Cann. 636, 638 and 639, and of their own law.

---

[1] Cf. Commentary (Urbanianum) 465. A particularly valuable point of reference is Beyer op cit 296–298.

[2] Cf. Comm 13(1981) 396 at Can. 10. The observation that 'the canon clearly is addressed only to clerical societies' (Commentary (CLSA) 537) would not appear to be correct.

1484 In those matters concerning the acquisition, possession, administration and alienation of property, societies of apostolic life are almost identical to religious institutes. By universal law, each society is established as a public juridical person; so, too, are the constituent parts of a society and its individual houses – although the constitutions of a society can limit juridical personality at lower levels. The reference to Cann. 636, 638 and 639 means that the society is governed by the norms for religious concerning financial administration, the competence of authority in ordinary and extraordinary administration, and liability in contracting debts.

Can. 741 §2 Members are also capable, in accordance with their own law, of acquiring, possessing, administering and disposing of temporal goods, but whatever comes to them in consideration of the society is acquired for the society.

1485 While members of religious institutes after profession cede the administration of their goods to others (see Can. 668 §1) and sometimes lose their capacity to acquire and possess goods in their own name (see Can. 668 §§4–5), members of societies of apostolic life retain the right and capacity to acquire, own, administer and alienate property in their own name. However, anything which comes to them by reason of their membership of the society is not acquired by them personally but rather by the society.

Can. 742 The departure and dismissal of a member who is not definitively incorporated are governed by the constitutions of each society.

1486 Since no vows are involved, the process of departure and dismissal is less complicated in societies of apostolic life for those who have not yet made a definitive commitment. However, universal law requires that the constitutions of each society provide the norms for these procedures.

Can. 743 A member who is definitively incorporated can obtain an indult to leave the society from the supreme Moderator with the consent of his or her council, unless the constitutions reserve this to the Holy See. This means that the rights and obligations deriving from definitive incorporation cease, without prejudice to Can. 693.

1487 As a rule, the competent authority to grant an indult to leave a society of apostolic life is the supreme Moderator, who must have the consent of his or her council. However, some societies may specify within their constitutions that the only competent authority is the Holy See. This is more likely to be the case in those societies whose members assume the evangelical counsels in accordance with Can. 731 §1. Obtaining the indult means the cessation of all rights and obligations arising out of definitive incorporation in the society, except in the case of a cleric who must first find a Bishop willing to receive him into his diocese at least on probation (see Can. 693).

Can. 744 §1 Permission for a member who is definitively incorporated to transfer to another society of apostolic life is likewise reserved to the supreme Moderator with the consent of his or her council. The rights and obligations of the member's own society are suspended for the time being, but the member has the right to return to it before definitive incorporation into the new society.

1488 The process by which a member can transfer from one society of apostolic life to another is very similar to that required for religious (see Cann. 684–685). It is the supreme Moderator of each society, with the consent of his or her council, who is competent to permit such a transfer. As with members of religious and secular institutes, the rights and obligations of a member during the transfer process are suspended. At any stage prior to definitive incorporation into the new society, the member is free to return to his or her own society. Since no mention is made of them in the Code, each society must legislate for all matters pertaining to the duration and manner of probation in the new society.

Can. 744 §2 To transfer to an institute of consecrated life or from such an institute to a society of apostolic life, the permission of the Holy See is required, and its instructions are to be followed.

This norm is closely related to Cann. 684 §5 and 730. Only the Holy See is competent to permit someone to transfer from a society of apostolic life to an institute of consecrated life and vice versa. Each favourable response to such a request is accompanied by specific instructions which the members and the authorities concerned must observe.

Can. 745 The supreme Moderator, with the consent of his or her council, can grant a definitively incorporated member an indult to live outside the society for a period not exceeding three years. Rights and obligations which are not compatible with the new condition are suspended, but the member remains under the care of the Moderators. Moreover, if the member is a cleric, the consent of the Ordinary of the place where he must reside is required, and the member remains also under the care of the Ordinary and dependent upon him.

One of the few obligations of members of societies of apostolic life mentioned in the Code is that of living in a lawfully constituted house or community of the society (see Can. 740). Only the supreme Moderator, with the consent of his or her council, can permit a definitively incorporated member to live outside the society; in addition, if the member is a cleric, the prior consent of the local Ordinary of his residence must also be obtained. There are striking similarities between this procedure and that required for exclaustration among religious (see Can. 686). In the same way as exclaustrated religious, members of these societies living lawfully outside enjoy only those rights and are bound only by those obligations which are compatible with their new situation; all other rights and obligations arising out of their membership are suspended. Permission to live outside a house or community of the society can be given for a maximum of three years. No mechanism is provided by the Code by which this absence may be extended; nor is there any mention of enforced absence from the society. However, in a particular case, the Holy See should be consulted.

Can. 746 For the dismissal of a member who is definitively incorporated, the provisions of Cann. 694–704 are to be observed, making the appropriate adjustments.

The reasons for dismissal from a society of apostolic life, the procedure to be followed and the effects of such a dismissal are, with appropriate adjustments, identical to those contained in Cann. 694–704 for religious. These norms must be meticulously observed in all cases of dismissal.

BOOK III

THE TEACHING OFFICE OF THE CHURCH

INTRODUCTION

Vat. II identified a triple mission given by Christ to the Church: teaching, sanctifying and governing: this corresponds to the triple office of Christ as priest, prophet and king.[1] The present Code reflects this triple division. Instead of being included as part of the amorphous *De Rebus* of the 1917 Code, the teaching office of the Church is now given a distinct book and title.

This reflects the increased emphasis placed on the word of God which was central to the vision of Vat. II, notably in the Dogmatic Constitution *Dei Verbum* on divine revelation. The responsibility of the Church for the word of God is presented in various ways and under different headings: the role of the magisterium, preaching the word of God, teaching, missionary endeavours, the use of communication media, the profession of faith to be made by those involved in various aspects of the Church's teaching mission. Each of these is the subject of a number of canons in this Book III.

Can. 747 §1 It is the obligation and inherent right of the Church, independent of any human authority, to preach the Gospel to all peoples, using for this purpose even its own means of social communication; for it is to the Church that Christ the Lord entrusted the deposit of faith, so that by the assistance of the Holy Spirit, it might conscientiously guard revealed truth, more intimately penetrate it, and faithfully proclaim and expound it.

This canon is based on several texts of Vat. II;[2] it was in fact originally part of the LEF. With the assistance of the Holy Spirit the Church has the task of guarding revealed truth conscientiously, of searching more profoundly for its meaning and of proclaiming and expounding it faithfully. The Church proclaims its duty and its right to proclaim the Gospel as something inherent in its very nature and deriving from Christ himself.[3] This right is independent of any earthly power, even if it is not recognised by all states. The Church has repeatedly asked in the United Nations, and in similar agencies, for a full implementation of the right to freedom of conscience and freedom of religion enshrined in the UNO charter and elsewhere.

Can. 747 §2 The Church has the right always and everywhere to proclaim moral principles, even in respect of the social order, and to make judgements about any human matter in so far as this is required by fundamental human rights or the salvation of souls.

1492

1493

1494

---

[1] Cf. LG 9–17, 31, 34–36: Fl I 359–369, 388–389, 391–394; Can. 204 §1. Cf. also AA 2, 6–7, 9–10: Fl I 767–768, 772–775, 776–778.

[2] Cf. LG 25, DV 8, GS 76: Fl I 379–381, 754–755, 984–985.

[3] Cf. Arrieta *The Active Subject of the Church's Teaching Office (Cann. 747–748)* Stud Can 23(1989) 243–256.

1495 The obligation and right of the Church is not confined to an abstract proclamation of the truth; it also has the authority to proclaim moral principles, whether for individuals or for society. And when a fundamental human right or the salvation of souls is at stake it can, and must, pronounce on questions of fact. This was clearly affirmed by Vat. II.[1]

Can. 748 §1 All are bound to seek the truth in the matters which concern God and his Church; when they have found it, then by divine law they are bound, and they have the right, to embrace and keep it.

1496 The dual obligation stated here – of seeking the truth and of embracing it when it is found – is based on Vat. II.[2] It is an obligation of divine law, and it is paralleled by the right to embrace and keep the truth. This right is not universally recognised by civil law, despite the freedom of thought, of conscience and of religion affirmed in Article 18 of the Universal Declaration of Human Rights approved and proclaimed by the United Nations in 1948.

Can. 748 §2 It is never lawful for anyone to force others to embrace the catholic faith against their conscience.

1497 This is a repetition of the principle contained in c.1351 of the 1917 Code, and it reflects the teaching of the Church from the earliest centuries,[3] even if Christians have not always respected that true liberty of conscience.

Can. 749 §1 In virtue of his office the Supreme Pontiff is infallible in his teaching when, as chief Shepherd and Teacher of all Christ's faithful, with the duty of strengthening his brethren in the faith, he proclaims by definitive act a doctrine to be held concerning faith or morals.

§2 The College of Bishops also possesses infallibility in its teaching when the Bishops, gathered together in an Ecumenical Council, exercise the magisterium and, as teachers and judges of faith and morals, definitively declare for the universal Church a doctrine to be held concerning faith and morals; likewise, when the Bishops, dispersed throughout the world but maintaining the bond of union among themselves and with the successor of Peter, together with the same Roman Pontiff authentically teach matters of faith or morals, and are agreed that a particular teaching is definitively to be held.

§3 No doctrine is understood to be infallibly defined unless this is manifestly demonstrated.

1498 This canon indicates the two subjects of infallibility in the Church: the Supreme Pontiff (§1), and the College of Bishops together with the Supreme Pontiff (§2). The 'infallibility ... with which the divine redeemer wished to endow his Church in defining doctrine pertaining to faith and morals, is coextensive with the deposit of revelation, which must be religiously guarded and loyally and courageously expounded'.[4] The doctrine contained in this §1 concerning the personal infallibility of the Pope derives from Vat. I *Pastor Aeternus*[5] and is confirmed in the teaching of Vat. II.[6]

---

[1] Cf. DH 14: Fl I 811; GS 76: Fl I 984–985.

[2] Cf. DH 2: Fl I 801–802.

[3] Cf. e.g. St Augustine *Contra Litteras Petiliani*: Patrologia Latina 43 c.315. For more recent documents cf. Pope Leo XIII encl *Immortale Dei* 1.XI.1885; Pope Pius XII address to the Roman Rota 6.X.1946: AAS 38(1946) 391ff: CLD 3 650–659.

[4] LG 25: Fl I 380.

[5] Cf. DS 3050–3075. Cf. also letter to German Bishops DS 3112–3117.

[6] LG 25: Fl I 380.

Introduction

The exercise of the Pope's infallibility is circumscribed by a number of conditions: (1) he must be speaking as chief Shepherd and Teacher of all Christ's faithful and not as a private individual or even as a theologian; (2) he must be speaking on a matter of faith or morals and not e.g. on a question of physical science; (3) he must proclaim definitively a doctrine to be held by all the faithful, i.e. in such a manner that there can be no doubt of his intention. Such definitions of the Supreme Pontiff are of themselves – not from the consent of the Church – irreformable, since they are pronounced with the assistance of the Holy Spirit promised to him in Peter. They need no approval of others nor do they allow of any appeal. 　1499

The second subject of infallibility (§2) is a collective one: the College of Bishops exercising either their solemn or their ordinary magisterium. The solemn magisterium is exercised when the Bishops are legitimately gathered in an Ecumenical Council; the ordinary magisterium is that exercised by them when they are not in a Council but are still united among themselves. In both cases they must be in union with the Pope and they must teach definitively on matters of faith or morals. 　1500

When something is taught infallibly, either by the Pope personally or by the College of Bishops, there can be no question of a new doctrine. What takes place is an unerring definition of what is already contained in divine revelation.[1] 　1501

Before a doctrine is accepted as infallibly defined this must be clearly established (§3). However, even though a doctrine has not been 'manifestly demonstrated' as infallibly defined, it is clearly not the Church's intention that the faithful should have to await a formal, infallible decision before accepting a doctrinal or moral teaching. Indeed the universal ordinary magisterium can be considered as the usual expression of the Church's infallibility.[2] 　1502

Can. 750 Those things are to be believed by divine and catholic faith which are contained in the word of God as it has been written or handed down by tradition, that is, in the single deposit of faith entrusted to the Church, and which are at the same time proposed as divinely revealed either by the solemn magisterium of the Church, or by its ordinary and universal magisterium, which in fact is manifested by the common adherence of Christ's faithful under the guidance of the sacred magisterium. All are therefore bound to shun any contrary doctrines.

The sources of this canon are to be found principally in c.1323 §1 of the 1917 Code and in the documents of Vat. II.[3] It gives the first category of truths to be believed – those namely which must be believed by 'divine and catholic faith'. Such truths must (a) be part of the deposit of faith, i.e. contained in the word of God, either written or handed down by the tradition of the Church; (b) be proposed for belief as divinely revealed either by the solemn magisterium of the Church (by the Pope or by an Ecumenical Council) or by its ordinary and universal magisterium manifested by the common adherence of the faithful under the guidance of the Church's pastors. A truth which is contained only in the word of God, without any definition by the Church, is to be believed simply by 'divine faith'; only those which satisfy both conditions must be believed by divine and catholic faith. 　1503

---

[1] Ibid.: Fl I 380–381.

[2] This, e.g. was clearly the case even before Pope Pius XII, on 1.XI.1950, solemnly defined as infallible the doctrine of the Assumption of the Blessed Virgin Mary. Cf. also Ford and Grisez *Contraception and the Infallibility of the Ordinary Magisterium* Theological Studies 39(1978) 264–269.

[3] Cf. LG 25: Fl I 380; DV 5: Fl I 752; DV 10: Fl I 755.

1504 *Tradition*, i.e. truths divinely revealed and handed down as such, though not formally contained in sacred Scripture, forms an essential part of the deposit of faith. This tradition must be carefully distinguished from 'traditions' (e.g. liturgical or canonical traditions) which vary from age to age, while 'tradition' itself remains constant even if its expression may vary with changing circumstances. Private revelations, even if commemorated by feastdays in the Church (e.g. the feast of the Sacred Heart or of Our Lady of Lourdes), do not form part of the deposit of the faith.

1505 The faithful must not only believe what is formally proposed to them; they must also avoid any doctrine contrary to what is of divine and catholic faith. This does not, of course, preclude legitimate dissent from non-infallible doctrine. In giving assent to the infallible magisterium of the Church the faithful themselves participate in this infallibility.[1]

Can. 751 Heresy is the obstinate denial or doubt, after baptism, of a truth which must be believed by divine and catholic faith. Apostasy is the total repudiation of the christian faith. Schism is the withdrawal of submission to the Supreme Pontiff or from communion with the members of the Church subject to him.

1506 This canon, itself based on c.1325 §2 of the 1917 Code (although changed in emphasis), defines three serious offences against the faith and against the community of the Church. Although the phrase 'after baptism' is textually applied only to heresy, it applies also to the other two offences: without this qualification, these would be meaningless as offences.

1507 There are two elements in *heresy*. The first is 'obstinate denial or doubt': the word 'obstinate' implies a persistence in denial or doubting, even after warnings have been given. The denial must be conscious and wilful. The second element concerns the matter which is denied or doubted: it must be a truth which is to be believed by divine and catholic faith (see Can. 750). Denial of other truths might well be offensive, rash, even sinful, but it would not constitute formal heresy.

1508 *Apostasy* is a total rejection of the christian faith which is received in baptism. It must be a total rejection; if it were merely partial it could constitute heresy but not apostasy. Such a rejection could take place if a person formally joined another sect which e.g. denied the divinity of Christ or totally abandoned any religion. Mere failure to practise one's religion, or even defection from the Church by a formal act (see Cann. 1086 §1, 1117, 1124), would not necessarily constitute apostasy.

1509 *Schism* is the breaking of the bond of unity which Christ prayed for in his Church (see John 17:20–21). It consists in the withdrawal of submission to the Supreme Pontiff or from communion with the members of the Church subject to him, specifically from the Bishops. There must be a real repudiation of this authority, not just a simple act of disobedience. In practice, schism will almost inevitably involve heresy, since it means rejecting papal supremacy and infallibility.

1510 Since the offences defined in this canon carry with them particularly serious penalties and consequences (see Cann. 1364, 194 §1 2°, 1044 §1 2°, 1184 §1 1°), they are to be strictly interpreted in accordance with Can. 18.

Can. 752 While the assent of faith is not required, a religious submission of intellect and will is to be given to any doctrine which either the Supreme Pontiff or the College of Bishops, exercising their authentic magisterium,

---

[1] Cf. LG 12: Fl I 363; DV 10: Fl I 755.

Introduction

declare upon a matter of faith and morals, even though they do not intend to proclaim that doctrine by definitive act. Christ's faithful are therefore to ensure that they avoid whatever does not accord with that doctrine.

The 'authentic' magisterium of the Pope and of the College of Bishops is distinguished from their infallible magisterium, as is the corresponding response of the faithful. When either teaches authentically, but not infallibly, the faithful are required to give 'a religious submission of intellect and will' and an avoidance of whatever is not in keeping with the doctrine proposed. This means a real internal assent,[1] not just an external adherence, but it does not call for 'the assent of faith'. It does not preclude either a development and deeper understanding of the doctrine in question, or the 'just freedom' of research acknowledged in Can. 218 to competent people.[2]

Can. 753 Whether they teach individually, or in Bishops' Conferences, or gathered together in particular councils, Bishops in communion with the head and the members of the College, while not infallible in their teaching, are the authentic instructors and teachers of the faith for Christ's faithful entrusted to their care. Christ's faithful are bound to adhere, with a religious submission of mind, to this authentic magisterium of their Bishops.

A further level of authentic teaching is described here: that of Bishops, whether acting individually, as members of a Bishops' Conference, or in particular councils. Provided that they are in communion with the head and the members of the College of Bishops, they teach authentically those entrusted to their care. The response demanded by this teaching is to be 'a religious submission of mind'.[3] There is still a certain debate in the Church as to whether Bishops' Conferences have an authentic teaching role as such or if they are confined to the authority of the individual Bishops.[4]

Can. 754 All Christ's faithful are obliged to observe the constitutions and decrees which lawful ecclesiastical authority issues for the purpose of proposing doctrine or of proscribing erroneous opinions; this holds particularly for those published by the Roman Pontiff or by the College of Bishops.

This canon covers yet a further level of response to the expression of the Church's authentic teaching. It speaks specifically of 'observing' constitutions and decrees issued in doctrinal matters by lawful ecclesiastical authority, particularly by the Pope or by the College of Bishops (as e.g. in the constitutions of Vat. II). It would also cover disciplinary matters. Other less solemn pronouncements such as circular letters, notifications, instructions should receive proportionate respect. Particular attention and respect should be paid to documents issued by the Congregation for the Doctrine of the Faith and other dicasteries of the Holy See.

---

[1] '... the faithful ... are obliged to submit to their Bishops' decision ... in matters of faith and morals and to adhere to it with a ready and respectful allegiance of mind. This loyal submission of the will and intellect must be given, in a special way, to the authentic teaching authority of the Roman Pontiff, even when he does not speak *ex cathedra* in such wise, indeed, that his supreme teaching authority be acknowledged with respect, and that one sincerely adhere to decisions made by him...': LG 25: Fl I 379. It is the clear view of this commentary that the term *obsequium* of Can. 752 (with its corollary reference in Can. 753) is properly translated as 'submission'.

[2] On this matter, cf. SCDF instr *The Ecclesial Vocation of the Theologian* 24.V.1990: AAS 82(1990) 1550–1570: Origins 20(1990) 117–126.

[3] Cf. Sobanski *Les canons 753 et 754: problèmes choisis* Stud Can 23 (1989)) 285–298.

[4] Cf. e.g. Legrand, Manzanares and Garcia y Garcia *Les Conférences épiscopales, Théologie, Statut Canonique, Avenir* Paris 1988 (Collection 'Cogitatio Fidei' n.149).

Can. 755 §1 It pertains especially to the entire College of Bishops and to the Apostolic See to foster and direct among catholics the ecumenical movement, the purpose of which is the restoration of unity between all christians which, by the will of Christ, the Church is bound to promote.

1514 Because of the danger of indifferentism, the Church has not always been in favour of some of the methods proposed to restore unity among Christians. Since Pope John XXIII and Vat. II, the Church's attitude has changed and the ecumenical movement is now not only laudable but mandatory. However because of the sensitive and complex issues involved, progress towards unity cannot be left to private individuals, no matter how well-intentioned. It is therefore primarily for the entire College of Bishops and the Apostolic See to promote and regulate the ecumenical movement. Vat. II produced its decree.[1] Among the principal documents to have appeared since then are the *Directory concerning Ecumenical Matters*, issued in two parts by the Secretariat for Promoting Christian Unity[2] and the updated Directory issued by the Pontifical Council for promoting Christian Unity.[3]

1515 In addition to ecumenical dealings with other Christians, the Church is also engaged in reaching out to other religions such as Judaism, Islam, Hinduism, Buddhism. Offices within the Roman Curia, such as the Pontifical Council for Inter-Religious Dialogue and the Pontifical Council for Dialogue with Non-Believers, are charged with this task.

Can. 755 §2 It is a matter for the Bishops and, in accordance with the law, for Bishops' Conferences, to promote this same unity and, in line with the various needs and opportunities of the circumstances, to issue practical norms which accord with the provisions laid down by the supreme authority of the church.

1516 In addition to the Directory mentioned above, the Code assigns to Bishops or to Bishops' Conferences various duties in the ecumenical field.[4] A number of Bishops' Conferences have drawn up directories about such matters as mixed marriages.[5]

Title I
The Ministry of the Divine Word

Can. 756 §1 The office of preaching the Gospel to the universal Church has been committed principally to the Roman Pontiff and to the College of Bishops.

---

[1] Cf. UR: Fl I 452 ff.

[2] DEM pt I 14.V.1967: AAS 59 (1967) 574–592: Fl I 483–501; pt II 16.IV.1970: AAS 52 (1970) 705–724: Fl I 515–532.

[3] AAS 85 (1993) 1039–1119: Origins 23(1993) 129–160.

[4] Cf. e.g. Cann. 383 §3, 463 §3, 825 §2, 844, 933, 1124–1129, 1183 §3.

[5] Cf. LCE Tavola per Paesi e Canoni at Cann. 1126–1127; CN(USA) 16, 17, 35–45.

Title I The Ministry of the Divine Word

The first four canons of this section present in hierarchical order those responsible for the ministry of the divine word.[1] For the universal Church the duty of preaching the Gospel falls principally upon the Pope and the College of Bishops. This duty corresponds to the fundamental right of all Christ's faithful 'to be assisted by their Pastors from the spiritual riches of the Church, especially by the word of God and the sacraments' (Can. 213). The role of the Pope and of the Bishops for the whole Church is aptly set out by Vat. II.[2]

1517

Can. 756 §2 For the particular Churches entrusted to them, that office is exercised by the individual Bishops, who are the moderators of the entire ministry of the word in their Churches. Sometimes, however, in accordance with the law, a number of Bishops simultaneously carry out that office in respect of a number of different Churches.

Particular Churches are described in Can. 368: normally these are dioceses entrusted to Bishops, but other types of territory are possible which are equivalent in law to dioceses and whose superiors are equivalent to Bishops. Bishops 'are the Moderators of the entire ministry of the word in their Churches'. They are to preach personally and are also to oversee the teaching of the word of God in their territories (see Can. 386 §1). Usually they exercise this ministry individually, but 'in accordance with the law', i.e. observing the directives of superior authority, they may combine in teaching a number of Churches, e.g. in a nation, a region, a province. This is frequently done by Bishops' Conferences when they address matters of common concern to the individual Churches of their area.

1518

Can. 757 It belongs to priests, as cooperators with the Bishops, to proclaim the Gospel of God. For the people entrusted to their care, this task rests especially on parish priests, and on other priests entrusted with the care of souls. Deacons also are to serve the people of God in the ministry of the word, in union with the Bishop and his *presbyterium*.

The ministry of priests in relation to the word of God is described in Vat. II as being in particular 'an application of the eternal truth of the Gospel to the concrete circumstances of life'.[3] It is the immediate means by which most people hear the message of the Gospel and have it explained and applied to their lives. The duties of the parish priest in this regard are given in Can. 528 §1, those of assistant priests are covered by Can. 548, those of chaplains by Can. 566 §1. The present canon makes special mention of the duty of deacons in the ministry of the Word. Among the functions of the deacon, 'in conjunction with the Bishop and his body of priests', according to Vat. II, are 'to read the sacred scripture to the faithful, to instruct and exhort the people'.[4] The deacon's function in regard to preaching is governed by Cann. 764 and 767 §1.

1519

Can. 758 By reason of their consecration to God, members of institutes of consecrated life bear particular witness to the Gospel, and so are fittingly called upon by the Bishop to help in proclaiming the Gospel.

Religious 'are a splendid sign in the Church' (Can. 573 §1) and 'bear particular witness to the Gospel'; they are in a special manner dedicated 'to the building up of the Church'. As well as the witness that they bear by their very lives they are assigned a

1520

---

[1] Cf. Huels *The Ministry of the Divine Word* (Cann. 756–761) Stud Can 23(1989) 325–344.
[2] CD 2–3: Fl I 564–565.
[3] PO 4: Fl I 869.
[4] LG 29: Fl I 387.

specially active role in the ministry of the word of God. Their function here is subordinate to the Bishop who, however, may not call upon members of institutes totally directed to contemplation to assist in such ministry, 'no matter how urgent the needs of the active apostolate' (Can. 674).

Can. 759 The lay members of Christ's faithful, by reason of their baptism and confirmation, are witness to the good news of the Gospel, by their words and by the example of their christian life. They can also be called upon to cooperate with Bishops and priests in the exercise of the ministry of the word.

1521 Because lay people 'are deputed to the apostolate by baptism and confirmation', they have the obligation and the right 'to strive so that the divine message of salvation may be known and accepted by all people throughout the world' (Can. 225; see also Can. 211). Like religious, they exercise this apostolate by the example of their lives and also by being called upon to cooperate with the Bishops and priests in a more active ministry. Can. 394 §2 obliges the Bishop 'to insist on the faithful's obligation to exercise the apostolate' and Can. 529 §2 lays a similar obligation on the parish priest.

Can. 760 The mystery of Christ is to be faithfully and fully presented in the ministry of the word, which must be founded upon sacred Scripture, Tradition, liturgy and the magisterium and life of the Church.

1522 This canon is concerned with the content of the ministry of the word. Its essential content is to be the mystery of Christ, Son of God and Son of Man, sent by the Father to redeem the human race, who died and rose again, who ascended into heaven and sent the Holy Spirit, who is Head and founder of the Church, who is to come again in judgment on the last day. The instruction given about this mystery 'should be founded upon sacred Scripture, Tradition, liturgy and the magisterium and life of the Church'.[1]

Can. 761 While pride of place must always be given to preaching and catechetical instruction, all the available means of proclaiming christian doctrine are to be used: the exposition of doctrine in schools, in institutes of higher learning, at conferences and meetings of all kinds; public declarations by lawful authority on the occasion of certain events; the printed word and other means of social communication.

1523 The wording of this canon is again closely based on the text of Vat. II.[2] The means of proclaiming christian doctrine are dealt with in a general fashion here; many of these are treated of in more detail in the first four titles of Book III. There is a strong preference for direct oral communication by means of preaching and catechesis. This has a long tradition in the Church and indeed has a sound scriptural foundation: 'So faith comes from what is preached, and what is preached comes from the word of Christ' (Rom 10:17). But, given the need to preach the Gospel to all, other means, including christian education, public declarations and the printed word are mentioned as well as other non-specified means of communication.

---

[1] These words of the canon are taken almost verbatim from CD 14: Fl I 571.
[2] Cf. CD 13: Fl I 571.

Title I The Ministry of the Divine Word

Chapter I
PREACHING THE WORD OF GOD

Can. 762 The people of God are first united through the word of the living God, and are fully entitled to seek this word from their priests. For this reason sacred ministers are to consider the office of preaching as of great importance, since proclaiming the Gospel of God to all is among their principal duties.

Once again based on the teaching of Vat. II,[1] this canon enunciates two important principles: the right of the people of God to receive the word of God from their pastors (see Can. 213), and the corresponding obligation laid on sacred ministers to proclaim the word as one of their principal duties. Can. 904 says that the celebration of the Eucharist is one 'in which priests fulfil their principal role'. The way in which the word of God and the sacraments, particularly the Eucharist, are constantly presented together shows how intimately connected they are in the priest's ministry[2] and gives a very special point to the legislation in Can. 767 concerning the homily.

1524

Can. 763 Bishops have the right to preach the word of God everywhere, even in churches and oratories of religious institutes of pontifical right, unless the local Bishop has expressly forbidden it in particular cases.

Those who may preach are determined by Cann. 763–766. Can. 767 gives special regulations about who may preach the homily. This present Can. 763 derives from the 1963 directive of Pope Paul VI.[3] Although the 1917 Code (c.349 §1 1°) allowed Bishops to preach everywhere, this was only with the at least presumed permission of the local Ordinary and was in fact an extension of one of the privileges granted to Cardinals (c.239 §1 3°). Now a Bishop, residential or titular, is given the right to preach anywhere, even in churches and oratories of religious of pontifical right,[4] without even presumed permission. This right is not extended to Vicars or Prefects apostolic or to apostolic Administrators unless they are in episcopal orders. The diocesan Bishop, but not any other local Ordinary, may forbid the use of the right, but only in a particular case; he may not impose a general prohibition.

1525

Can. 764 Without prejudice to the provisions of Can. 765, priests and deacons, with the at least presumed consent of the rector of a church, have the faculty to preach everywhere, unless this faculty has been restricted or removed by the competent Ordinary, or unless particular law requires express permission.

Under the 1917 Code (cc.1337–1338) priests and deacons required a specific faculty to preach, to be granted by the local Ordinary or by the competent religious Superior. Vat. II recognised the fundamental nature of their mission to preach the word of God[5] and so this faculty is now granted to them by the law itself and may be exercised with the at least presumed permission of the rector of a church.[6] It may be

1526

---

[1] Cf. PO 4: Fl I 868.

[2] Cf. e.g. PO 5: Fl I 871 '... the Eucharist appears as the source and summit of all preaching of the Gospel'.

[3] Cf. PM II 1: AAS 56(1964) 11.

[4] This is an exception to the norm of Can. 765 and reflects the importance of the teaching role of the Bishop.

[5] Cf. LG 28 and 29: Fl I 384, 387.

[6] Obviously the term 'rector of a church' will be understood in a wider sense here than that given in Can. 556 and will include parish priests and superiors of churches of religious.

restricted or removed by the competent Ordinary – the cleric's own Ordinary or the Ordinary of the place; or particular law may require express permission: such particular law could be diocesan, provincial, regional etc. and would be designed to combat a general danger rather than a particular abuse.

Can. 765 To preach to religious in their churches or oratories, permission is required of the Superior who is competent according to their constitutions.

1527   As stated above in Can. 764, this canon imposes one restraint on the generality of the preceding one. In order to preach to religious in their own churches or oratories a priest or deacon needs permission from the Superior designated in the constitutions of the institute. This does not apply to preaching to religious outside their own churches or, with the at least presumed permission of the rector of the church, to preaching to others in religious churches. In virtue of Can. 763 Bishops do not need such permission. Chaplains to religious have this permission automatically in virtue of Can. 566 §1.

Can. 766 The laity may be allowed to preach in a church or oratory if in certain circumstances it is necessary, or in particular cases it would be advantageous, according to the provisions of the Bishops' Conference and without prejudice to Can. 767 §1.

1528   In the 1917 Code at c.1342 §2 all lay people, even religious, were forbidden to preach in church. The present law reflects the renewed appreciation of the prophetic role of the laity in the Church.[1] The term 'laity' means anyone, including religious, who has not been at least ordained a deacon (see Can. 207 §1). Lay men or women may be allowed to preach if this is *necessary*, e.g. if there is a shortage of clergy or if they are impeded, or even if it is *advantageous*, e.g. in celebrations with particular groups such as children, the handicapped, members of a different language group, etc.[2] in accordance with the provisions laid down by the local Bishops' Conference.[3] The homily referred to in Can. 767 §1 has its own very special place, and is accordingly reserved to a priest or deacon. That allowed, the Code permits a distinct flexibility in the regulations to admit the laity to preach in their local churches, subject always to the guidance of the diocesan Bishop.

Can. 767 §1 The most important form of preaching is the homily, which is part of the liturgy itself, and is reserved to a priest or deacon. In the course of the liturgical year, the mysteries of faith and the rules of christian living are to be expounded in the homily from the sacred text.

1529   The Congregation of Rites has described the homily as 'an explanation either of some aspect of the readings from holy scripture or of another text from the Ordinary or Proper of the Mass of the day, taking into account the mystery which is being celebrated and the particular needs of the hearers'.[4] It should expound the mysteries of faith and the duties of christian living as these are reflected by the liturgy during the

---

[1] Cf. e.g. LG 35: Fl I 391–393.

[2] In view of the prohibition against a lay person giving the homily at Mass, it is interesting to note that the Directory on Children's Masses allows a lay person to address the children (*verba ad pueros dirigat*) after the Gospel: SCDW Directory: 1.X.1973 n.24: AAS 66(1974) 37. The translation in Fl I 262 is perhaps misleading, speaking as it does of 'preaching a homily': despite the place in the Mass of such an address, it does not constitute the homily referred to in Can. 767 §1.

[3] Cf. LCE Tavola per Paesi e Canoni at Can. 766.

[4] SCRit instr *Inter oecumenici* 26.IX.1964 n.9: AAS 56(1964) 877ff: CLD 6 88.

course of the year. Because of its ritual nature and its intimate connection with the Eucharist, the homily is reserved to a priest or a deacon. The diocesan Bishop may not dispense from this reservation.[1] However, as has been noted in the preceding Can. 766, a lay person could be given permission to preach even at Mass, albeit that his or her address would not constitute the homily of this canon; indeed some Bishops' Conferences, while allowing this, have specified that it take place not after the Gospel, but at some other stage in the course of the Mass.[2]

Can. 767 §2 At all Masses on Sundays and on holy days of obligation, celebrated with a congregation, there is to be a homily and, except for a grave reason, this may not be omitted.

The basic reason for this prescription is the close connection between the liturgy of the word and the liturgy of the Eucharist, which together 'form but one single act of worship'.[3] A practical reason is that for many of the faithful, this is the only time that they are regularly able to hear the word of God.

1530

Can. 767 §3 It is strongly recommended that if a sufficient number of people are present, there be a homily at weekday Masses also, especially during Advent and Lent, or on a feast day or an occasion of grief.

While a homily on the occasions mentioned here is not obligatory, it is strongly recommended. To the reasons given under the preceding paragraph, one could add the fact that on these occasions those present at Mass might well be considered to be particularly receptive to the word of God.

1531

Can. 767 §4 It is the responsibility of the parish priest or the rector of a church to ensure that these provisions are carefully observed.

Parish priests are assigned particular obligations in proclaiming the word of God (see Can. 528 §1) and, for the churches which they govern, rectors of churches are assigned the same duties with regard to the homily. Both are to see to it that the law on the homily, whether this be given by themselves or by another, is carefully observed.[4]

1532

Can. 768 §1 Those who announce the word of God to Christ's faithful are first and foremost to set out those things which it is necessary to believe and practise for the glory of God and the salvation of all.

§2 They are also to explain to the faithful the teaching of the magisterium of the Church concerning the dignity and freedom of the human person; the unity, stability and duties of the family; people's social obligations and the ordering of temporal affairs according to the plan established by God.

Having determined who may preach the word of God, the Code in this canon goes on to state in a general way the content of preaching. Based on the teaching of Vat. II,[5] the canon lists the primary content of the things which must be believed and carried out for God's glory and the salvation of all. It next lists the principal things in the

1533

---

[1] Cf. CCom rep 26.V.1987: AAS 79(1987) 1249: CCLA 1292–1293: Wrenn (Interpret) 41–43: Per 77(1988) 613–624.

[2] Significant examples are the Conferences of England and Wales and of Nigeria: cf. LCE 355, 485; CCLA 1336, 1377. And there are other examples: cf. LCE Tavola per Paesi e Canoni at Can. 766.

[3] SC 56: Fl I 19.

[4] Can. 386 §1 imposes a corresponding obligation on the Bishop for his diocese.

[5] Cf. CD 12: Fl I 569–570.

natural order which are to be taught. All preaching must be done in accordance with the Church's official teaching; the preacher is not giving his own message but is speaking in the name of God and of the Church.

Can. 769 Christian teaching is to be explained in a manner that is suited to the condition of the hearers and adapted to the circumstances of the times.

1534 Based again on Vat. II,[1] this canon prescribes the method of preaching. It must be adapted 'to the condition of the hearers': in practical terms, this simply means using a language and a style of speaking that can be easily understood by the particular congregation involved. It certainly also demands the avoidance of abstruse and complicated argumentation which – whatever its obvious value in academic or other such circles – has little, if any, contribution to make to the day-to-day preaching of the Gospel of Christ. For all that, it must be 'adapted to the circumstances of the times'. It must, in other words, demonstrate the preacher's accurate appreciation of the modern life which he is addressing, recognising the current issues and the living conditions (whatever these may be, good or bad) of his people. All of this clearly imposes on the preacher – more often than not, the local parish priest or assistant priest – the obligation of a serious and sustained study, based on the Scriptures and on the official teaching of the Church, with an accordingly critical analysis of what is daily portrayed by many newspaper, radio and television outputs.

Can. 770 At certain times, according to the regulations of the diocesan Bishop, parish priests are to arrange for sermons in the form of retreats and missions, as they are called, or in other forms adapted to requirements.

1535 The parish mission or retreat is a more systematic set of sermons, instructions and pious exercises designed for spiritual renewal in a parish. In its c.1349 §1 the 1917 Code required a parish mission at least every ten years; the present law leaves the frequency and indeed the style of such exercises to diocesan regulations. Many forms of spiritual exercise in which instruction can be given are available: missions, retreats, days of recollection, vigils, prayer meetings, Lenten or Advent sermons etc., and these can be adapted to local circumstances.

Can. 771 §1 Pastors of souls, especially Bishops and parish priests, are to be solicitous that the word of God is preached also to those of the faithful who, because of the circumstances of their lives, cannot sufficiently avail themselves of the ordinary pastoral care or are even totally deprived of it.

§2 They are also to take care that the message of the Gospel reaches those living in their territory who are non-believers, since these too, no less than the faithful, must be included in the care of souls.

1536 'Special concern should be shown for those members of the faithful who, on account of their way of life, are not adequately catered for by the ordinary pastoral ministry of the parochial clergy or are entirely deprived of it. These include the many migrants, exiles and refugees, sailors and airmen, itinerants and others of this kind, even those simply abroad on holidays.'[2] The Gospel must be preached to all mankind. Those who are wholly or partly deprived of ordinary pastoral care must have special provision made for them.[3] Can. 528 §1 not only obliges the parish priest to ensure that the

---

[1] Cf. CD 13: Fl I 570.

[2] CD 18: Fl I 574.

[3] This e.g. has been done for members of armed forces (Pope John Paul II ap con *Spirituali militum curae* 21.IV.1986: AAS 78(1986) 481–486: CLSNGBI 76 (Dec. 1988) 48–89); – for migrants and travellers (Pontifical Commission for the Spiritual Care of Migrants and Travellers decr *Pro Materna* 19.III.1982: AAS 74(1982) 742–745: CLD 10 34–38).

word of God is proclaimed to those in his parish, but it specifically mentions those who have given up religious practice or who do not profess the true faith. Non-believers are to have the Gospel message made available to them: the missionary activity of the Church (see Cann. 781–791) is not confined to the so-called 'missionary countries'. Even though it will be to an obviously lesser extent – though not less real for that – it may well be at the doorstep of many a parish, in which of course its activity, undefined in this canon, will be inspired and guided by the missionary and outlooking zeal of the diocesan Bishop.

Can. 772 §1 In the exercise of preaching, everyone is moreover to observe the norms laid down by the Bishop of the diocese.

§2 In expounding christian teaching on radio or television, the provisions of the Bishops' Conference are to be observed.

The diocesan Bishop has the duty to oversee the ministry of the word in his diocese (§1: see Can. 386 §1). It is up to him to determine both the standards whereby a priest or deacon be admitted to the critical office of preaching, and the programme for such preaching – in the setting up of which he must clearly have taken account of the foregoing canons of this Chapter. Where he has set up such norms, all, even religious of pontifical rite, are bound to observe them. Radio and television usually cover a wider area than a single diocese; of themselves they require special training and expertise in their use; accordingly christian teaching on these media is properly subject to norms laid down by the appropriate Bishops' Conference (§2). A number of Conferences have in fact issued such norms.[1] 1537

Chapter II
CATECHETICAL FORMATION

While not attempting a rigorous definition, Pope John Paul II has said that '... it can be taken ... that catechesis is an education of children, young people and adults in the faith, which includes especially the teaching of Christian doctrine imparted, generally speaking, in an organic and systematic way, with a view to initiating the hearers into the fullness of Christian life'.[2] Its purpose is to develop in believers 'a living, explicit and active faith, enlightened by doctrine'.[3] 1538

Can. 773 Pastors of souls especially have the proper and serious duty of seeing to the catechesis of the christian people, so that, through doctrinal formation and the experience of the christian life, the faith of the people may be living, manifest and active.

This canon states in a general way the duties already mentioned in regard to catechesis by Can. 386 §1 for the diocesan Bishop and by Can. 528 §1 for the parish priest. 1539

---

[1] For specific examples of such norms in English-speaking countries, cf. CCLA at Can. 772: 1322–1323, 1347, 1377–1378, 1397, 1412. For a more global view, cf. LCE Tavola per Paesi e Canoni at Can. 772. Distinctly to be noticed are the conditions laid down by the respective Bishops' Conferences throughout the world, each viewing its own local circumstances, all sounding at least a moderate note of caution – not as such a critical one, rather a realistic one – concerning the manner in which those entrusted with the task of 'expounding christian teaching' should avail themselves of the current media of radio and television.

[2] CT 18: Fl II 772.

[3] CD 14: Fl I 571.

These duties are spelled out in more detail by the canons of this chapter. Can. 774 lays the care for catechesis on all members of the Church, but the present canon, repeating the tenor of c.1329 of the 1917 Code, makes this a particular and serious duty for pastors of souls.

Can. 774 §1 The care for catechesis, under the direction of lawful ecclesiastical authority, extends to all members of the Church, to each according to his or her role.

§2 Before all others, parents are bound to form their children, by word and example, in faith and in christian living. The same obligation binds sponsors and those who take the place of parents.

1540   All members of the Church have the responsibility of making the message of salvation known (see Can. 211) and are witnesses to the Gospel by word and example (see Can. 759). They also have a duty, each according to his or her role, to care for catechesis. The roles of various members are specified by the following canons. Pride of place is given to the role of parents in forming their children in the faith and in christian living.[1] The obligation on parents is extended to baptismal sponsors and to those who take the place of parents.

Can. 775 §1 While observing the provisions made by the Apostolic See, it is the responsibility of diocesan Bishops to issue norms concerning catechetical matters; to ensure that appropriate means of catechesis are available, even by preparing a catechism, if this seems opportune; to foster and to coordinate catechetical initiatives.

1541   The duties of the Bishop towards catechetical matters can in general be said to be managerial. Subject to the prescriptions laid down by the Holy See, he is to issue norms for his territory, e.g. concerning the order and manner of teaching; he is to ensure that suitable resources are available, usually through a catechetical office, even by issuing a catechism;[2] he is to foster and coordinate catechetical initiatives.

Can. 775 §2 If it is thought to be useful, the Bishops' Conference may, with the prior approval of the Apostolic See, publish catechisms for its territory.

1542   At the request of the Synod of Bishops in 1977, and after extensive consultation, a new 'Catechism of the Catholic Church' was promulgated by Pope John Paul II in 1992.[3] It is intended to be 'a sure and authentic reference text for teaching catholic doctrine and particularly for preparing local catechisms'.[4] If a Bishops' Conference decides to issue a catechism or catechisms for its territory, it must have the prior approval of its text by the Apostolic See.

Can. 775 §3 The Bishops' Conference may establish a catechetical office, whose principal purpose is to assist individual dioceses in catechetical matters.

1543   The decree *Provido sane*[5] in 1935 and the general catechetical directory *Ad normam decreti*[6] in 1971 prescribed the setting up in each diocese of a catechetical office. The

---

[1] Cf. e.g. GE 3: Fl I 728.

[2] A diocesan catechism does not need the prior approval of the Holy See: cf. Can. 827 §1. Since 1992, however, it will obviously have to have taken serious account of CCC.

[3] English translation for the United Kingdom and Ireland 1994, Chapman (London), Veritas (Dublin).

[4] Pope John Paul II ap con *Fidei Depositum* 11.X.1992: CCC 5.

[5] Cf. AAS 27(1935) 145–154: CLD 2 412–418.

[6] Cf. AAS 64(1972) 97–176: Fl II 529–605 (n.126: Fl 596).

present law returns the matter to the Bishops' Conference, without however making it mandatory that such an office be set up. Accordingly the law does not oblige each diocese to have a catechetical office. On the other hand, given the onerous duties imposed on the Bishop in this matter, it would clearly be very difficult indeed for him to carry them out without such assistance.

Can. 776 By virtue of his office, the parish priest is bound to ensure the catechetical formation of adults, young people and children. To this end, he is to avail himself of the help of clerics attached to the parish, as well as of members of institutes of consecrated life and of societies of apostolic life, being mindful of the character of each institute; and the assistance of lay members of Christ's faithful, especially catechists. All of these, unless they are lawfully impeded, are not to refuse to give their labours willingly. The parish priest is also to promote and to foster the role of parents in the family catechesis mentioned in Can. 774 §2.

One of the most important of the parish priest's duties is to see to the catechetical formation of all his flock (see Can. 528 §1). In fulfilling this duty he is to call liberally upon those who can help him: other clerics attached to the parish, whether assistant priests or deacons; religious and members of societies of apostolic life, taking account of the character of their institute;[1] lay people, especially those trained as catechists. Since the obligation of caring for catechesis 'extends to all members of the Church' (Can. 774 §1), none of those listed here should refuse his or her willing help. Special mention is made of the parish priest's duty to support parents in the catechesis of their children.

1544

Can. 777 In a special way the parish priest is to ensure, in accordance with the norms laid down by the diocesan Bishop that:

1° an adequate catechesis is given for the celebration of the sacraments;

This canon lists a number of special types of catechesis entrusted in a special way to the parish priest. The first is that given for the celebration of the sacraments. Can. 851 deals with the preparation of adult candidates for baptism and that of the parents and sponsors of infant candidates. Cann. 1063–1064 cover preparation for marriage.

1545

2° children are properly prepared for first confession and first holy communion, and for the sacrament of confirmation, by means of catechetical formation over an appropriate period of time;

Can. 914 mentions the function of parents and those who take their place in preparing children for holy communion even before the duty of the parish priest. Can. 890 speaks of preparation for the sacrament of confirmation. An appendix to the General Catechetical Directory deals with the first reception of penance and the Eucharist.[2]

1546

3° children after they have made their first holy communion, are given a richer and deeper catechetical formation;

The catechetical formation of children should not cease or diminish after they have passed the milestone of their first holy communion. Indeed, since this sacrament marks an important stage in their full christian initiation (see Can. 842 §2), it should also signal a fuller instruction in the faith.

1547

---

[1] He may not call upon members of institutes wholly devoted to the contemplative life: Can. 674.
[2] GCD appendix: Fl II 600–603.

4° As far as their condition allows, catechetical formation is given to the mentally and physically handicapped;

1548   Treating of the catechesis of handicapped children and adolescents the General Catechetical Directory says 'This task may not be relegated to a secondary or subsidiary place. ... Catechesis must offer these the possibility of living the life of faith in keeping with their state'.[1] Physically handicapped young people will have special needs in this regard: because they may well be in special schools, a particular and sensitive care must be taken to ensure that they receive adequate formation.

5° the faith of young people and of adults is strengthened, enlightened and developed by various catechetical methods and initiatives.

1549   At various ages and stages of development people will have particular needs in relation to catechetical formation. The parish priest is to be aware of this and is to act accordingly.[2]

Can. 778 Religious Superiors and Superiors of societies of apostolic life are to ensure that catechetical formation is diligently given in their churches and schools, and in other works in any way entrusted to their care.

1550   Cann. 758 and 776 deal with the duty of religious and members of societies of apostolic life to assist the Bishop and the parish priest in proclaiming the word of God and in catechetical formation. The present canon is even wider in scope: it covers their churches, schools and other apostolic works, whether they have been invited to teach by the local Bishop or parish priest, or have undertaken the work on their own initiative. Their Superiors are to be diligent in seeing to it that proper catechetical formation is given in all of these places. In their preaching (see Can. 772 §1) and in their teaching in school (see Can. 806 §1) they are subject to the directives and vigilance of the diocesan Bishop.

Can. 779 Catechetical formation is to be given by employing all those aids, educational resources and means of social communication which seem the more effective in securing that the faithful, according to their character, capability, age and circumstances of life, may be able more fully to learn catholic teaching and more effectively to put it into practice.

1551   In order to be effective, catechetical formation must make use of the most effective means of instructing all of the faithful and of preparing them to put that instruction into practice in their lives.[3] These means may have to be adapted to local conditions and must obviously take into account the circumstances of those being instructed.

Can. 780 Local Ordinaries are to ensure that catechists are duly trained to carry out their office properly, namely, that continuing formation is available to them, that they have an appropriate knowledge of the teaching of the Church, and that they learn both the theory and the practice of the principles of pedagogy.

1552   The role of the catechist is '...at the very least a function of great importance in the Church'.[4] For this reason local Ordinaries (and not just Bishops) are charged with

---

[1] GCD 91: Fl II 581.

[2] Cf. GCD 77–97: Fl II 574–585.

[3] Effective aids are listed in GCD 116–124: Fl II 593–595; cf. also CT 46–50: Fl II 789–793.

[4] CT 71: Fl II 807.

seeing that they are properly trained. They must have continuing training available to them and are to be duly trained in the Church's teaching and in educational theory and practice.[1]

Title II
The Missionary Activity of the Church

Can. 781 Because the whole Church is of its nature missionary and the work of evangelisation is to be considered a fundamental duty of the people of God, all Christ's faithful must be conscious of the responsibility to play their part in missionary activity.

This canon, which is taken almost directly from Vat. II,[2] states the principle of the missionary nature of the whole Church and the consequent duty of all Christ's faithful – and not just 'professional' missionaries – to the work of evangelisation. Each of them has 'the obligation and the right to strive so that the divine message of salvation may more and more reach all people of all times and all places' (Can. 211). This responsibility may be fulfilled in different ways: by spiritual support, financial assistance, even by some form of active participation. In general terms missionary activity means spreading the kingdom of God and preparing the way for his coming;[3] more specifically, the mission *ad gentes* has the objective: 'to found Christian communities and develop churches to their full maturity'.[4]

1553

Can. 782 §1 The Roman Pontiff and the College of Bishops have the responsibility for the overall direction and coordination of the initiatives and activities which concern missionary work and cooperation.

§2 Being charged with responsibility for the universal Church and for all the Churches, all Bishops are to have a special solicitude for missionary activity, especially by arousing, fostering and sustaining missionary initiatives in their own particular Churches.

In exercising the supreme authority in the Church, the Roman Pontiff and the College of Bishops have overall responsibility for the direction and coordination of all missionary activity. The Pope exercises his office in this regard principally through the Congregation for the Evangelisation of Peoples.[5] Bishops are given particular responsibilities for missionary activities by fostering vocations (see Can. 385) and by various other means, spiritual and temporal.[6]

1554

---

[1] On the formation of catechists, cf. GCD 108–115: Fl II 589–593.
[2] Cf. AGD 35: Fl I 849.
[3] Cf. AGD 1: Fl I 813.
[4] RM 48: Origins 20(1990–1991) 555.
[5] Cf. PB 85–92.
[6] Cf. ES III especially 3–11: Fl I 858–859.

Can. 783 Members of institutes of consecrated life, because of the dedication to the service of the Church deriving from their very consecration, have an obligation to play a zealous and special part in missionary activity, in a manner appropriate to their institute.

1555 Members of institutes of consecrated life (see Cann. 573–730) '... are dedicated ... by a special title ... to ... the service of God's Kingdom, for the honour of God, the building up of the Church and the salvation of the world'.[1] Their service in this area must of course always be in accordance with the character of their institute. The fact is that so many institutes and societies have been founded specifically for missionary work in the church: a simple glance, not only over this millennium but going back over the years since the Church's institution by Christ, will establish that a substantial and indispensable part of the mission *ad gentes* has been instituted by, and continues to be staffed by, members of these institutes.

Can. 784 Missionaries, that is, those who have been sent by the competent ecclesiastical authority to engage in missionary activity, may be chosen from the indigenous population or from others, be they secular clergy, or members of institutes of consecrated life or of a society of apostolic life, or other lay members of Christ's faithful.

1556 The term 'missionary' – designating one sent by the competent authority in the Church to undertake missionary work – is no longer restricted to priests or religious or to people from another place. It now includes all 'those people who are endowed with the proper natural temperament, have the necessary qualities and outlook, and are ready to undertake missionary work ... whether they are natives of the place or foreigners, priests, religious or lay people'.[2] There is in this canon, reflecting Vat. II, a certain welcome preference for natives of the place, so that the christian faith may be perceived as belonging to the place itself and its people (as Christ clearly intended) – no longer in any sense a piece of cultural imperialism.

Can. 785 §1 Catechists are to be given a role in missionary work. These are lay members of Christ's faithful who have received proper formation and are outstanding in their living of the christian life. Under the direction of missionaries, they are to present the Gospel teaching and engage in liturgical worship and in works of charity.

1557 *Catechists* are of the highest importance in missionary work, particularly (but not only) where there is a shortage of clergy and of religious.[3] They are to be lay people of exemplary christian life who have received special training. Their function is described here as presenting Gospel teaching and engaging in liturgical worship and in works of charity. They are to work under the direction of the missionaries whom they assist. Full-time catechists should be paid a proper and just wage.[4]

Can. 785 §2 Catechists are to receive their formation in schools founded for this purpose. If there are no such schools, they are to be formed under the direction of the missionaries.

---

[1] Cf. LG 44: Fl I 403–405; CD 33: Fl I 33.
[2] AGD 23: Fl I 841.
[3] Cf. AGD 17: Fl I 833; RM 73: Origins 20(1990–1991) 561.
[4] Cf. AGD 17: loc cit.; RM 73: loc cit.

Since the role of catechists is of such great importance, their training must be very carefully prepared. It should 'be in keeping with cultural progress and such that ... they will be able to perform their task as well as possible'.[1] Where possible it should be given in schools set up for this purpose. In the absence of these, the duty of seeing to their formation falls on the missionaries themselves.

Can. 786 Missionary activity properly so called, through which the Church is implanted among peoples or groups where it has not yet taken root, is carried out by the Church especially by sending heralds of the Gospel, until the new Churches are fully constituted, that is, are equipped with their own resources and sufficient means so that they themselves can carry on the work of evangelisation.

Although the missionary activity of the Church cannot be totally separated from its ordinary duty of pastoral care,[2] it is a specific activity with special aims which are described here in terms taken from Vat. II.[3] It means preaching the Gospel to non-christians and building up the newly founded Churches until they are fully established and can stand on their own.

Can. 787 §1 By the testimony of their words and of their lives, missionaries are to establish a sincere dialogue with those who do not believe in Christ, so that, taking their native character and culture into account, ways may be opened up by which they can be led to know the message of the Gospel.

Not only by their words, but also by their very lives, missionaries are to reach out to those who do not believe in Christ, so that they too may be prepared to receive the Gospel message. They are to take account of the character and culture of those to whom they bear this witness and, above all, the dialogue they initiate must be sincere. Vat. II lists some practical ways in which christians can cooperate with and reach out to non-believers.[4]

Can. 787 §2 Missionaries are to ensure that they teach the truths of the faith to those whom they judge to be ready to receive the message of the Gospel, so that, if they freely request it, they may be admitted to the reception of baptism.

This paragraph takes the process of evangelisation a distinct stage further. When missionaries judge that a person is ready to receive the Gospel message, they are to teach that person the truths of the faith with a view to baptism. It must however be clear that the person freely asks to be baptised; there must not be even a hint of any coercion (see Can. 748 §2).

Can. 788 §1 Those who have expressed the wish to embrace faith in Christ, and who have completed the period of their preliminary catechumenate, are to be admitted to the catechumenate proper in a liturgical ceremony, and their names are to be inscribed in the book which is kept for this purpose.

§2 By formation and their first steps in christian living, catechumens are to be initiated into the mysteries of salvation, and introduced into the life of faith, liturgy and charity of the people of God, as well as into the apostolate.

---

[1] Ibid.
[2] Cf. RM 34: Origins 20(1990–1991) 551.
[3] Cf. AGD 6: Fl I 819.
[4] Cf. AGD 11–12: Fl I 825–827.

§3 It is the responsibility of the Bishops' Conference to establish norms regulating the catechumenate, determining what should be done by catechumens and what should be their prerogatives.

1562 *The restoration of the catechumenate* called for by Vat. II[1] has particular relevance in mission territories, where the initiation and baptism of adults is the norm rather than the exception. The catechumenate is to consist of distinct steps; the present canon directs that it is to be preceded by a preliminary period before candidates are admitted to the catechumenate proper, and this admission is to be marked by a specific liturgical ceremony[2]; moreover the names of the catechumens are to be entered in a special register (§1). This registration is because of the 'various prerogatives' accorded to catechumens (see Can. 206 and also §3 of the present canon). Because of the 'special way' in which catechumens are linked with the Church, they may be given blessings (see Can. 1170) and church funeral rites (see Can. 1183 §1); on the other hand, if they wish to marry catholics, they remain bound by the impediment of disparity of cult and need to be dispensed (see Can. 1086 §1).

1563 Vat. II decreed that 'the juridical status of catechumens should be clearly defined in the new Code of Canon Law'.[3] The manner in which this directive has been implemented (§3) is that Bishops' Conferences have been assigned the responsibility to determine in a practical way the arrangement of the catechumenate and the functions and prerogatives of catechumens.[4] Of particular interest is the permission given in mission territories to adapt suitable elements in local initiation rites to the christian ritual.[5]

1564 The catechumenate 'is not a mere exposition of dogmatic truths and norms of morality, but a period of formation in the whole Christian life' through which 'the catechumens should be properly initiated into the mystery of salvation ... and they should be introduced into the life of faith, liturgy and charity of the People of God by successive sacred rites'.[6] This initiation is not just a matter for clergy and catechists; it is the concern of the whole christian community, particularly the sponsors.[7]

Can. 789 By means of appropriate formation, neophytes are to be led to a deeper knowledge of the Gospel truths, and to the fulfilment of the duties undertaken in baptism. They are also to be imbued with a sincere love of Christ and his Church.

1565 *Neophytes* are those who have been baptised recently. Full initiation into the christian life does not come automatically with baptism and the other sacraments of initiation. These sacraments need to be lived in daily life and brought to fruition. The neophyte will also need further and deeper instruction in the truths of the faith. Accordingly this canon calls for special care and formation of these people.[8]

---

[1] Cf. SC 64: Fl I 21.
[2] Cf. AGD 14: Fl I 828.
[3] AGD 14: Fl I 829.
[4] Some examples of how a number of English-speaking Bishops' Conferences have dealt with this matter may be consulted in CCLA 1323, 1347, 1378, 1419. For a more global view, cf. LCE Tavola per Paesi e Canoni at Can. 788.
[5] Cf. SC 65: Fl I 21.
[6] AGD 14: Fl I 828.
[7] Ibid.
[8] Precisely because neophytes are new to the christian life, Can. 1042 3° imposes a simple impediment, subject to the judgement of the Ordinary, to their receiving sacred orders.

Title II The Missionary Activity of the Church

Can. 790 §1 In mission territories it is the responsibility of the diocesan Bishop :

1° to promote, regulate and coordinate both new initiatives and established works concerning missionary activity;

2° to ensure that there are proper agreements with the Moderators of those institutes which dedicate themselves to missionary activities, and that relationships with them are for the good of the mission.

§2 The provisions made by the diocesan Bishop in accordance with §1 n.1 are binding on all missionaries, including religious and their helpers residing in his territory.

Following the teaching of Vat. II,[1] the law here affirms the authority of the diocesan Bishop with regard to both new and established missionary activity. Since mission territories have for long been staffed largely by religious and other missionary institutes, there is a long history to the relations between them and the diocesan Bishop or his equivalent (see Cann. 368, 381 §2). Numerous questions have arisen concerning, e.g. the ownership of churches and other buildings, the financial support of missionaries, etc. To cater for this situation, the diocesan Bishop is now entrusted with the clear responsibility to ensure that proper written agreements are drawn up with the Moderators of those institutes which are working in his territory.[2] The prime consideration in all relationships between the Bishop and missionary institutes must be 'the good of the mission'. All, including religious and their helpers, are bound to observe whatever provisions the Bishop makes concerning either missionary activity or agreements between him and the various missionary institutes.

1566

Can. 791 In order to foster missionary cooperation, in each diocese:

1° missionary vocations are to be promoted;

2° a priest is to be appointed to promote missionary initiatives, especially the 'Pontifical Missionary Works';

3° a day for the missions is to be celebrated annually;

4° each year an appropriate financial contribution for the missions is to be sent to the Holy See.

This canon lists a number of duties incumbent on each diocese with regard to the missions. Obviously, missionary vocations must be fostered: this is a necessary part of the missionary activity of the Church. In addition to the normal fostering of vocations to the priesthood and religious life, a diocese could have a policy of allowing its priests to go to mission territories or of 'adopting' a parish or parishes in such places. Each diocese is to have a priest with special responsibility for Pontifical Missionary Works:[3] he could be a diocesan or a member of a missionary institute. In each diocese

1567

---

[1] Cf. AGD 30, 32: Fl I 847, 848.

[2] Cf. SCEP instr *Relationes in Territoriis* 24.II.1969: AAS 61(1969) 281–287: CLD 7 845–851.

[3] These works are: The Pontifical Work for the Propagation of the Faith, The Pontifical Work of the Holy Childhood, The Pontifical Work of St Peter the Apostle for Native Clergy; to these could be added The Pontifical Missionary Union of the Clergy. It must be noted, however, that these named works must be accommodated to those which have been set up and are operative in the various countries throughout the catholic world.

'a day for the missions is to be celebrated annually' – clearly a matter of obligation for the diocesan Bishop to arrange, according to the circumstances of his diocese. The primary objective of such a day is to generate in the diocese, however small, an appreciation of the need for a missionary trust on the part of the whole Church. Not only that: each diocese is required, as an integral part of its missionary appreciation, and in accordance with its own means, to contribute to the Holy See – itself in charge of the overall missionary activity of the Church – an appropriate sum from the diocese itself, from the parishes and other diocesan communities.[1]

Can. 792 The Bishops' Conference is to establish and promote means by which those who come to their territory from the missions, for the purpose of work or study, are to be given a fraternal welcome and helped with suitable pastoral care.

1568 Since many mission territories are among the less developed parts of the world, it is not uncommon for various people – priests, religious, laity – to come from them to so-called more developed places – to work, perhaps to study, not infrequently and very sensibly simply to relax after their labours. This canon obliges Bishops' Conferences to make special provision for such people.[2] They are to ensure a fraternal welcome for them and are to see that they are given proper pastoral care, including the provision of at least temporary pastoral work in the diocese in so far as this may be considered appropriate to assist and support these missionaries.

Title III
Catholic Education

Can. 793 §1 Parents, and those who take their place, have both the obligation and the right to educate their children. Catholic parents have also the duty and the right to choose those means and institutes which, in their local circumstances, can best promote the catholic education of their children.

§2 Parents have moreover the right to avail themselves of that assistance from civil society which they need to provide a catholic education for their children.

1569 Among the most important Church documents on catholic education are Pope Pius XI's 1929 encyclical[3] and the declaration in this matter of Vat. II.[4] The fundamental right and duty of parents with regard to the education of their children is stated in the encyclical, and this is repeated in the declaration which itself is the immediate source for the canons on education.[5] As a result of their general rights and duties in this area,

---

[1] ES III 8: Fl I 858.

[2] Cf. LCE Tavola per Paesi e Canoni at Can. 792.

[3] Pope Pius XI encl *Divini Illius Magistri* 31.XII.1929: AAS 22(1930) 49–86.

[4] GE: Fl I 725–737.

[5] Cf. GE 3: Fl I 728–729.

parents have the specific right and duty to choose the schools and other means available to them which will best provide for the catholic education of their children.[1]

To the right of choice acknowledged to parents corresponds a duty on the part of the civil authority so to allocate funds 'that parents are truly free to select schools for their children in accordance with their conscience'.[2] While recognising that this duty is more fully acknowledged in some states than in others, it must be stressed that the issue here is not a denominational, much less a solely catholic, one.

Can. 794 §1 The Church has in a special way the duty and the right of educating, for it has a divine mission of helping all to arrive at the fullness of christian life.

§2 Pastors of souls have the duty of making all possible arrangements so that all the faithful may avail themselves of a catholic education.

The Church's duty and right of educating comes 'not only because the Church must be recognised as a human society capable of imparting education' but particularly because 'it has the duty of proclaiming the way of salvation to all men, of revealing the life of Christ to those who believe, and of assisting them ... so that they may be able to attain to the fulness of that life'.[3] The duty of pastors of souls – whether these be Bishops' Conferences, individual Bishops or clerics in the parochial ministry – to do all in their power to provide for a catholic education, corresponds to the right of the faithful to a christian education 'which genuinely teaches them to strive for the maturity of the human person and at the same time to know and live the mystery of salvation' (Can. 217). They may make such provision in different ways, according to local circumstances: they could, e.g., receive state aid in whole or in part towards the running of Church schools, they could see to the teaching of religion in state schools, they could set up their own Church-funded schools, etc.

Can. 795 Education must pay regard to the formation of the whole person, so that all may attain their eternal destiny and at the same time promote the common good of society. Children and young persons are therefore to be cared for in such a way that their physical, moral and intellectual talents may develop in a harmonious manner, so that they may attain a greater sense of responsibility and a right use of freedom, and be formed to take an active part in social life.

This canon, which states in a general way the content of education, is taken from the teaching of Vat. II.[4] Education must be concerned with the formation of the whole person: the very words of the canon are worth serious reflection; they speak for themselves.

Chapter I
SCHOOLS

Can. 796 §1 Among the means of advancing education, Christ's faithful are to consider schools as of great importance, since they are the principal means of helping parents to fulfil their role in education.

---

[1] The right of parents to choose and to provide for the religious and moral education of their children has been acknowledged in a number of international agreements: cf. CCLA 518 for some examples.
[2] GE 6: Fl I 731.
[3] GE 3: Fl I 729.
[4] Cf. GE 1: Fl I 727.

§2 There must be the closest cooperation between parents and the teachers to whom they entrust their children to be educated. In fulfilling their task, teachers are to collaborate closely with the parents and willingly listen to them; associations and meetings of parents are to be set up and held in high esteem.

1573 As has already been noted, parents have the primary responsibility for the education of their children. Given however the complexity of present-day society, they can rarely carry out this duty unaided. They need schools to provide all the expertise that modern education demands. Schools are therefore not a substitute for the family in the area of education, but are partners with it. For this reason, there is to be close cooperation between parents and teachers, with mutual dialogue and the setting up of parent–teacher associations. Since there is a very real danger that parents, having entrusted the education of their children to experts, may abdicate some or all of their own responsibilities, these associations are not just nominal but should be given a very real value: the words of §2 very much bring home the point.

Can. 797 Parents must have a real freedom in their choice of schools. For this reason Christ's faithful must be watchful that the civil society acknowledges this freedom of parents and, in accordance with the requirements of distributive justice, even provides them with assistance.

1574 While acknowledging a real freedom of choice of schools in this canon, the Code obliges parents to send their children to those schools which will provide for their catholic education (see Can. 798). All of Christ's faithful must do what they can to see that the civil authority acknowledges the parents' rights in this matter and, because this is no more than just, generally gives whatever financial assistance is available.

Can. 798 Parents are to send their children to those schools which will provide for their catholic education. If they cannot do this, they are bound to ensure the proper catholic education of their children outside the school.

1575 Because education must be in religion and morals as well as in the secular sciences, parents are obliged to see that their children are sent to those schools where they will receive a proper catholic education. This usually, but not always, means catholic schools in the sense of Can. 803.[1] There are other possibilities: they might be state schools with permanent religious teachers; they could be state schools which allow clergy or other qualified teachers of religion access; they could be schools of another Christian denomination which allow similar access. In the absence of any suitable school, the duty of providing for catholic education remains primarily on the parents, who must of course be aided by the parish priest to whom it is committed 'to have a special care for the catholic education of children and young people' (Can. 528 §1). This could take various forms, as e.g. Sunday schools, other instruction by clergy, religious or catechists, even if needs be individual instruction in the home.

Can. 799 Christ's faithful are to strive to secure that in the civil society the laws which regulate the formation of the young, also provide a religious and moral education in the schools that is in accord with the conscience of the parents.

1576 There are many organisations, some of them political, some not, which are anxious to influence the content and method of the education of the young. Since the conscience of the parents is paramount in this area, and since the matter is of concern to the

---

[1] Cf. GE 8: Fl I 734.

whole Church, all Christ's faithful should exercise what influence they can to see that educational laws are in accord with the parents' belief and wishes. This is not to take from the state its duty and right to demand certain standards in education, but the faithful must see to it that the Church's voice is heard and heeded.

Can. 800 §1 The Church has the right to establish and to direct schools for any fields of study or of any kind and grade.

Since the Church is not just for the young but for all, it has the right to establish schools for all, for all disciplines and at any grade. This follows both from the Church's divine mission and from its historical involvement in education. It should never be overlooked or left out of account that for many centuries – Europe is only one example – the Church was almost the sole provider of schools; nor should it go unrecognised that, in many countries throughout the world today, the civil authorities would face even greater problems were they not able to rely on the apostolic and pastoral efforts of the Church in the field of education.

Can. 800 §2 Christ's faithful are to promote catholic schools, doing everything possible to help in establishing and maintaining them.

The help to be given to catholic schools by the faithful will obviously range in accordance with the circumstances of the individual: financial contributions, lobbying for state legislation, recognition or financial aid, teaching or serving on school committees, etc.

Can. 801 Religious institutes which have education as their proper mission are to keep faithfully to this mission and earnestly strive to devote themselves to catholic education, providing this also through their own schools which they have established with the consent of the diocesan Bishop.

Religious institutes whose proper mission is education are here instructed to keep faithfully to this demanding but essential task. The sense of the canon is that they may fulfil their function either in local diocesan or parochial schools or in schools of their own. Where religious are working in diocesan or parochial schools, there should be a written agreement between the local Ordinary and the competent religious Superior about the terms of their involvement.[1] Religious need the Bishop's consent to set up their own schools and are subject to diocesan policy and supervision in the running of them.[2]

Can. 802 §1 If there are no schools in which an education is provided that is imbued with a christian spirit, the diocesan Bishop has the responsibility of ensuring that such schools are established.

In the absence of suitable schools it is the diocesan Bishop's duty to see that such are provided. He is accorded a fairly wide discretion in deciding how to do this, taking account of local circumstances: he may do it by setting up catholic schools, by seeing to it that the requisite religious and moral education is provided in other schools, or by whatever other appropriate means may be within his grasp; whatever the circumstances, the Bishop's overall obligation remains.

Can. 802 §2 Where it is suitable, the diocesan Bishop is to provide for the establishment of professional and technical schools, and of other schools catering for special needs.

---

[1] Cf. ES I 30: Fl I 606.
[2] Cf. CD 35 n.4: Fl I 585. Cf. also ES 1 29 n.2, 39 nn.1 & 2: Fl I 606, 608.

1581 In addition to the normal primary and secondary schools, there are other more specialised professional and technical schools. Where in his judgement it is suitable, the diocesan Bishop is to provide, by whatever means may be needed and are within his control, for the setting up of these schools, and for others such as schools for the blind, the deaf or others with special needs, teacher training colleges, etc.[1] Many religious institutes specialise in one or more of these apostolates.

Can. 803 §1 A catholic school is understood to be one which is under the control of the competent ecclesiastical authority or of a public ecclesiastical juridical person, or one which in a written document is acknowledged as catholic by the ecclesiastical authority.

§2 Instruction and education in a catholic school must be based on the principles of catholic doctrine, and the teachers must be outstanding in true doctrine and uprightness of life.

§3 No school, even if it is in fact catholic, may bear the title 'catholic school' except by the consent of the competent ecclesiastical authority.

1582 Juridically, that which constitutes a catholic school depends either on who controls it or on legal acknowledgement by the proper authority. To be 'catholic', the school must be under the control of the competent ecclesiastical authority, or of a public ecclesiastical juridical person (see Cann. 113–123), e.g. a diocese, a parish, a religious institute or, finally, it must be given this status in a written document issued by the competent authority – at the minimum, the Holy See, a diocesan Bishop or other local Ordinary.

1583 Having defined what legally constitutes a catholic school, the Code goes on to state in general terms the qualities which a catholic school ought to have. Its teaching and operation should be based on catholic doctrine and its teachers must be examples in both faith and morals.

1584 Even if a school fulfils the criteria of §2 and is therefore catholic in fact, it may not legally call itself such except by consent of the proper authority, i.e. in accordance with §1.

Can. 804 §1 The formation and education in the catholic religion provided in any school, and through various means of social communication, is subject to the authority of the Church. It is for the Bishops' Conference to issue general norms concerning this field of activity and for the diocesan Bishop to regulate and watch over it.

§2 The local Ordinary is to be careful that those who are appointed as teachers of religion in schools, even non-catholic ones, are outstanding in true doctrine, in the witness of their christian life, and in their teaching ability.

1585 Because it is 'the obligation and inherent right of the Church, independent of any human authority, to preach the Gospel to all peoples' (Can. 747 §1), it has authority in the special field of education in the catholic religion, whether this be in school or in other media of communication. This authority, taken for granted in catholic schools, extends to other schools as well. Bishops' Conferences may issue general norms about religious education,[2] and individual Bishops are to implement these and to oversee this field of activity.

---

[1] Cf. GE 9: Fl I 734–735.

[2] Cf. LCE Tavola per Paesi e Canoni at Can. 804.

The qualities of teachers in catholic schools are described in Can. 803 §2. Here the same requirements, together with the additional one that they be of outstanding teaching ability, are stated for all teachers of religion, whether in catholic schools or not. The local Ordinary, primarily the diocesan Bishop, is given the responsibility of seeing to this.

Can. 805 In his own diocese, the local Ordinary has the right to appoint or to approve teachers of religion and, if religious or moral considerations require it, the right to remove them or to demand that they be removed.

It may not always be possible for the Ordinary to control the appointment or dismissal of teachers of religion in state-run or state-aided schools. Much will depend on the terms of their contracts of employment. In some countries, the civil courts have recognised that the character of a catholic school demands that a teacher's lifestyle be not out of harmony with christian living; in some indeed there has been upheld the dismissal of a teacher living in an irregular marital union. This is clearly a very delicate area, in which all Bishops must tread with great sensitivity and prudence, while always bearing in mind the Church's teaching mission to the world. If there is question of dismissing a teacher, for whatever reason, natural justice will certainly demand that the Ordinary allow him or her a total right of defence.

Can. 806 §1 The diocesan Bishop has the right to watch over and inspect the catholic schools situated in his territory, even those established or directed by members of religious institutes. He has also the right to issue directives concerning the general regulation of catholic schools; these directives apply also to schools conducted by members of a religious institute, although they retain their autonomy in the internal management of their schools.

The diocesan Bishop (not any local Ordinary, unless he is specifically acting as the Bishop's delegate in this matter) has a right to supervise and inspect all catholic schools in his territory. This right extends even to schools set up or run by a religious institute, except those open only to the members of the institute (see Can. 683 §1). He can also issue general directives about the running of catholic schools; these apply even to the schools of religious, allowing that they have autonomy in the internal management of their schools. The directives could cover such areas as ensuring compliance with state regulations about safety, hygiene, insurance and the like, and also such things as catechetical texts, examinations in Christian doctrine, cooperation among schools, etc.

Can. 806 §2 Those who are in charge of catholic schools are to ensure, under the supervision of the local Ordinary, that the instruction given in them is, in its academic standards, at least as distinguished as that in other schools in the region.

Here is established the principle that catholic schools must, at the academic level, be at least up to, if not better than, that of any other school. This is not any facile claim to an unwarranted eminence. Nor is it simply to attract pupils – correct though any such ambition would be. It is primarily to proclaim that the Church views all facets of education as integrally important – not just those (though by no means excluding those) which have to do with the teaching of religion. 'Catholic schools .. are no less zealous than other schools in the promotion of culture and in the human formation of young people.'[1]

---

[1] GE 8: Fl I 732.

Chapter II
CATHOLIC UNIVERSITIES AND OTHER INSTITUTES OF HIGHER STUDIES

Can. 807 The Church has the right to establish and to govern universities, which serve to promote the deeper culture and fuller development of the human person, and to complement the Church's own teaching office.

1590 Can. 800 §1 states the Church's right to establish and direct schools of all kinds and grades. The present canon states this right specifically with regard to universities. Historically, the modern university owes its origin to the medieval catholic universities, such as those of Bologna and Paris, in which both sacred and profane sciences were studied.

1591 The Code does not define what constitutes a catholic university, allowing a great degree of diversity to accord with widely differing circumstances. Basic to the understanding of its nature is the 1990 apostolic constitution of Pope John Paul II *Ex Corde Ecclesiae* which, while not giving a legal definition of the term, gives a description of its function: 'Every Catholic university, as a university, is an academic community which, in a rigorous and critical fashion, assists in the protection and advancement of human dignity and of a cultural heritage through research, teaching and various services offered to the local, national and international communities'.[1] The document goes on to detail a number of essential characteristics which must mark the catholic university. It must have:

(1) 'a Christian inspiration not only of individuals but of the university community as such.

(2) a continuing reflection in the light of the catholic faith upon the growing treasury of human knowledge, to which it seeks to contribute by its own research.

(3) fidelity to the Christian message as it comes to us through the Church.

(4) an institutional commitment to the service of the people of God and of the human family in their pilgrimage to the transcendent goal which gives meaning to life'.[2]

1592 A catholic university, therefore, is one in which the human sciences are studied in the light of faith and of the teaching of the Church. Besides the functions common to all universities it '... brings to its task the inspiration and light of the Christian message'.[3]

Can. 808 No university, even if it is in fact catholic, may bear the title 'catholic university' except by the consent of the competent ecclesiastical authority.

1593 This, like Can. 803 §3, is a specific example of the general principle laid down by Can. 216 that the title 'catholic' may be used by any initiative only with the consent of the competent ecclesiastical authority. The ap con *Ex Corde Ecclesiae* states that catholic universities may be established or approved by the Holy See, a Bishops' Conference or other assembly of catholic hierarchy, or by a diocesan Bishop. The diocesan Bishop may consent to a catholic university being set up by a religious institute or public juridical person and the competent authority may consent to the use of the term

---
[1] ECE 12: Origins 20(1990–1991) 268.
[2] Ibid. 13: op cit 269.
[3] Ibid. 14: loc cit.

'catholic' by a university set up by other persons.[1] Those matters which fall within the competence of the Holy See are dealt with by the Congregation for Catholic Education, which exercises a 'higher supervision' on catholic universities and ratifies their statutes.[2] A list of catholic universities may be found in the *Annuario Pontificio*.[3]

Can. 809 If it is possible and appropriate, Bishops' Conferences are to take care to have within their territories suitably located universities or at least faculties, in which the various disciplines, while retaining their own scientific autonomy, may be researched and taught in the light of catholic doctrine.

Because of the invaluable part they play in the promotion of knowledge and culture and in the harmonisation of these with the faith, Bishops' Conferences are obliged to provide for catholic universities where this is 'possible and appropriate'. They are to draw up general norms in accordance with canon law, taking into account the statutes of each university and, as far as possible and appropriate, the civil law.[4] Academic autonomy is fully recognised: 'Freedom in research and teaching is recognised and respected according to the principles and methods of each individual discipline, so long as the rights of the individual and of the community are preserved within the confines of the truth and the common good'.[5]

Can. 810 §1 In catholic universities it is the duty of the authority which is competent in accordance with the statutes to ensure the appointment of teachers who are suitable both in scientific and pedagogical expertise and in integrity of doctrine and uprightness of life, and if these qualities are lacking, to ensure that they are removed from office, in accordance with the procedure determined in the statutes.

'The identity of a catholic university is essentially linked to the quality of its teachers and to respect for catholic doctrine. It is the responsibility of the competent authority to watch over these two fundamental needs in accordance with what is indicated in canon law.'[6] The acknowledged freedom in research and teaching which was referred to under Can. 809, is not unreservedly absolute: if a catholic university teacher is found lacking in either professional expertise or in doctrine or probity of life, he or she is to be removed in accordance with the statutes of the university. These should be so framed as to preclude any dismissal based merely on personal antipathy or other insufficient cause, and they must always guard the principles of natural justice, not least the right of defence.

Can. 810 §2 The Bishops' Conference and the diocesan Bishops concerned have the duty and the right of seeing to it that, in these universities, the principles of catholic doctrine are faithfully observed.

Bishops, whether individually or together, are the principal preachers and guardians of the word of God in the Churches entrusted to them (see Can. 756). Their rights and duties in this regard must extend to catholic universities in their territories. It is to be noted that, as Bishops, their function is confined to overseeing the observation

---

[1] Ibid. Art 3: op cit 274.
[2] PB Art 116 §§2–3: CCLA 1235.
[3] Cf. *Annuario Pontificio* Vatican City 1994 1649–1659.
[4] ECE Art 1 n.2: op cit 274. For an example of such norms cf. Origins 23(1993–1994) 474, where a proposed draft of ordinances for the USA is published, and Origins 23 605ff where these are discussed.
[5] ECE Art 2 n.5: op cit 274.
[6] Ibid. Art 4 n.1: loc cit: this article refers specifically to the present canon.

of the principles of catholic doctrine; it does not extend to judging the professional expertise of the teachers, which is rather a matter for appropriately competent persons or bodies.

Can. 811 §1 The competent ecclesiastical authority is to ensure that in catholic universities there is established a faculty or an institute or at least a chair of theology, in which lectures are given to lay students also.

§2 In every catholic university there are to be lectures which principally treat of those theological questions connected with the studies of each faculty.

1597 This canon, reflecting the teaching of Vat. II,[1] requires that all catholic universities have, if not an actual faculty, some organised means of giving lectures in theology which are to be open to, among others, lay students. Specifically, there are to be lectures on the theological questions which are connected with the various other disciplines, e.g. the moral questions arising from the practice of medicine, the relationship between religion and the physical sciences, etc.

Can. 812 Those who teach theological subjects in any institute of higher studies must have a mandate from the competent ecclesiastical authority.

1598 The Apostolic Constitution *Sapientia Christiana* spoke of a canonical 'mission' to teach theological subjects.[2] However in view of certain practical and theoretical difficulties, the present law requires a *mandate* rather than a mission.[3] This mandate is required because those who teach these subjects do so, not of their own authority, but in the name of the Church;[4] the mandate may be given to lay-people (see Can. 229 §3). In an appropriate situation it may, for a serious reason, be withdrawn.

Can. 813 The diocesan Bishop is to be zealous in his pastoral care of students, even by the creation of a special parish, or at least by appointing priests with a stable assignment to this care. In all universities, even in those which are not catholic, the diocesan Bishop is to provide catholic university centres, to be of assistance to the young people, especially in spiritual matters.

1599 In order to provide for the pastoral care of students, whether of catholic or other universities, the diocesan Bishop has a special obligation, and a number of options open to him. He may set up a special parish for this purpose, most likely a personal parish (see Can. 518), or he can appoint chaplains (see Can. 564) which is probably the more usual and practical course. All universities, not just catholic ones, are to have *a catholic university centre* which is to give assistance, especially spiritual, to young people.[5]

Can. 814 The provisions which are laid down for universities apply equally to other institutes of higher studies.

1600 The concepts of 'university', 'university college' etc. vary considerably from country to country. Also there are today many third-level educational establishments which in one way or another do not conform to the university model. The present canon extends the law relating to universities to all of these.

---

[1] Cf. GE 10: Fl I 735.
[2] Sap Chris Art 27 §1: Origins 9(1979–1980) 39.
[3] Cf. Comm 15(1983) 104–105 at Can. 767.
[4] Cf. Sap Chris loc cit.
[5] Cf. also ECE Art 6: Origins 20(1990–1991) 275 where pastoral care is directed to be provided to *all members of the university*, not just to the students.

Chapter III
ECCLESIASTICAL UNIVERSITIES AND FACULTIES

Can. 815 By virtue of its mission to proclaim revealed truth, the Church has the right to have its own ecclesiastical universities and faculties to study the sacred sciences and subjects related to them, and to teach these disciplines to students in a scientific manner.

Can. 807 states the Church's right to establish universities, i.e. catholic universities. The present canon states its right to establish ecclesiastical universities and faculties by reason of its mission to proclaim revealed truth. These are institutes in which the sacred sciences – principally theology, sacred Scripture, liturgy, church history and canon law, and ancillary subjects such as philosophy, patristics, archaeology and languages – are studied and taught scientifically. The most significant overall legislation in this area was contained in the 1931 Apostolic Constitution of Pope Pius XI *Deus Scientiarum Dominus*.[1] This was substantially supplemented in 1979 by the aforementioned ap con *Sapientia Christiana* and its accompanying *Ordinationes*.[2] Since the Code deals with this subject only in a general fashion and does not integrally reorder it, these norms remain in force (see Can. 6 §1 4°). 1601

Can. 816 §1 Ecclesiastical universities and faculties may be constituted only by the Apostolic See or with its approval. Their overall direction also belongs to the Apostolic See.

§2 Each ecclesiastical university must have its own statutes and programme of studies approved by the Apostolic See.

Ecclesiastical universities and faculties are generally subject to the Congregation for Catholic Education. This congregation erects them, or approves of those which have been erected by others, and ratifies their statutes.[3] Unless the Holy See has erected or approved a university or faculty it cannot claim ecclesiastical status, even if in fact it teaches and studies the sacred sciences. 1602

Can. 817 Only a university or a faculty established or approved by the Apostolic See may confer academic degrees which have canonical effects in the Church.

Candidates for certain offices in the Church must have canonical academic degrees, e.g. seminary professors (see Can. 253 §1), Bishops (see Can. 378 §1 5°), Vicars general and episcopal Vicars (see Can. 478 §1), ecclesiastical judges (see Can. 1421 §3), promotors of justice and defenders of the bond (see Can. 1435). For some (not all) of these, an equivalent knowledge – i.e. that the candidate be 'well versed in the (relevant) discipline', even without a degree – is accepted. In some countries, by concordat or other agreement, canonical degrees are accorded civil recognition. 1603

Can. 818 The provisions of Cann. 810, 812 and 813 concerning catholic universities apply also to ecclesiastical universities and faculties.

These provisions concern the appointment and removal of teachers, the observance of catholic doctrine, the mandate needed to teach theological subjects, and the pastoral care of the students. 1604

---

[1] Pope Pius XI ap con *Deus Scientiarum Dominus* 24.V.1931: AAS 23(1931) 241–262.
[2] Cf. SCCE *Ordinationes ad Constitutionem Apostolicam 'Sapientia Christiana' rite Exsequendam* 29.IV.1979: AAS 71(1979) 500–521.
[3] Cf. PB Art 116 §2: CCLA 1235.

Can. 819 In so far as the good of a diocese or religious institute or indeed even of the universal Church requires it, young persons, clerics and members of institutes, outstanding in character, intelligence and virtue, must be sent to ecclesiastical universities or faculties by their diocesan Bishops or the Superiors of their institutes.

1605 In contrast to c.1380 of the 1917 Code, which made university-level education merely desirable and spoke of it only in relation to clerics, the present law makes it mandatory on the Bishop or the religious Superior to send people to ecclesiastical universities or faculties in certain circumstances. These are stated in very broad terms: where the good of the diocese, the institute or even the universal Church demands it. Those to be sent are young people, clerics or members of religious institutes; while no specific mention of lay people is made in the canon, it is certainly the mind of the Church that in appropriate circumstances – of which today there are many – the laity also be sent to such universities and faculties.[1]

Can. 820 Moderators and professors of ecclesiastical universities and faculties are to ensure that the various faculties of the university cooperate with each other, to the extent that their aims permit. They are also to ensure that between their own university or faculty and other universities and faculties, even non-ecclesiastical ones, there be a mutual cooperation in which, through conferences, coordinated scientific research and other means, they work together for the greater increase of scientific knowledge.

1606 Cooperation, both within a university and between universities, is encouraged, for the greater increase of scientific knowledge, both religious and secular. This was a distinct theme of Vat. II.[2]

Can. 821 Where it is possible, the Bishops' Conference and the diocesan Bishop are to provide for the establishment of institutes for higher religious studies, in which are taught theological and other subjects pertaining to christian culture.

1607 The institutes envisaged here, while not universities and therefore not strictly subject to the laws binding these, could well be guided by the principles contained in these canons. They would include institutes of religious studies, pastoral, missionary, catechetical institutes, and the like.

Title IV
The Means of Social Communication and Books in Particular

Can. 822 §1 In exercising their office the pastors of the Church, availing themselves of a right proper to the Church, are to make an ample use of the means of social communication.

---

[1] Cf. GE 10: Fl I 735–736.
[2] Cf. GE 12: Fl I 737; GS 62: Fl I 966–968.

Title IV The Means of Social Communication and Books in Particular

§2 Pastors are also to teach the faithful that they have the duty of working together so that the use of the means of social communication may be imbued with a human and christian spirit.

§3 All Christ's faithful, especially those who in any way take part in the management or use of the media, are to be diligent in assisting pastoral action, so that the Church can effectively exercise its mission through these means.

Pastors of the Church are required 'to make an ample use of the means of social communication' (§1), described in Vat. II as 'the press, the cinema, radio, television and others of a like nature'.[1] There is nothing hesitant about this injunction: it is a clear imperative, based on '*a right which belongs to the Church*'. This – the only canon in the Code dealing so specifically with the impact of the current means of social communication in the context of Church's mission to the world – raises two vital issues:

(a) it prescribes that the Church in each country is positively to make use of these means, in accordance with its local possibilities, to preach the Gospel of Christ;

(b) it prescribes, furthermore – and perhaps even more significantly – that all Christ's faithful who are personally involved '*in the management or use of the media*' (§3: see also §2) should strive, in so far as they can, 'that the Church can effectively exercise its mission through these means' (§3).

1608

There is here a clear reminder to those of the faithful who are, in one way or another, closely associated with the media, that they may not divorce their allegiance to the faith from their professional commitments. *They are not being asked* to attempt the impossible – such e.g. as converting a particular medium to being simply a catholic organ: a manifestly unreasonable proposition. They are being asked to do whatever they can, within every reasonable means, to ensure 'that the Church can effectively exercise its mission through these means' (§3). There is a distinct harkening back here to, in particular the prescriptions of Cann. 208, 209 §1, 211, 216, 225, and to the profound ecclesiological implications of membership of the Church of Christ – a fact which those involved in the media (neither more nor less than anyone else) may not in any true conscience avoid. 'It is the Church's birthright to use and own any of these means which are necessary or useful for the formation of Christians and for pastoral activity.'[2] As far as the universal Church is concerned, these aims are overseen by the Pontifical Council for Social Communications.[3]

Can. 823 §1 In order to safeguard the integrity of faith and morals, pastors of the Church have the duty and the right to ensure that in writings or in the use of the means of social communication there should be no ill effect on the faith and morals of Christ's faithful. They also have the duty and the right to demand that where writings of Christ's faithful touch upon matters of faith and morals, these be submitted to their judgement. Moreover, they have the duty and the right to condemn writings which harm true faith or good morals.

§2 For Christ's faithful entrusted to their care, the duty and the right mentioned in §1 belong to the Bishops, both as individuals and in particular councils or Bishops' Conferences; for the whole people of God, they belong to the supreme authority in the Church.

---

[1] IM 1: Fl I 283.

[2] IM 3: Fl I 285.

[3] Cf. PB Artt 169–170: CCLA 1253. This Council is the successor of a lesser commission set up by Pope Pius XII in 1948.

Book III The Teaching Office of the Church

1609 While still keeping the general media of communication in mind, the Code moves from here principally into the area of *writings*: books, pamphlets, documents of various kinds. This canon and those which follow find their inspiration and thrust in a significant decree of the Congregation for the Doctrine of the Faith (Holy Office as it then was named) dating from 1975.[1] The right and duty of the Church to guard and expound revealed truth as regards both faith and morals is firmly affirmed in Can. 747. The present canon applies this to writings and to other media of communication. It states a triple right and duty for pastors of the Church: (i) to exercise vigilance in such a way that neither writings nor other media would adversely affect the faith and morals of the faithful; (ii) to give prior approval to works by members of the faithful which touch on questions of faith and morals; (iii) to condemn writings which are harmful to faith or morals. Bishops, acting individually or together, exercise this right and duty for those in the dioceses, provinces or regions in their care. For the whole Church, the supreme authority performs this function, i.e. the Supreme Pontiff and the College of Bishops. The Pope exercises his authority in this matter principally through the Congregation for the Doctrine of the Faith.[2]

1610 Beginning in the mid-sixteenth century, the *Index librorum prohibitorum* listed those books condemned by the Holy See as injurious to faith or morals. Reading or even possessing books on this Index was forbidden without a special dispensation. In 1966 the Index itself, and the censures associated with it, lost the force of ecclesiastical law, even though it retained its moral force as a warning against writings which could endanger faith or morals.[3]

Can. 824 §1 Unless it is otherwise provided, the local Ordinary whose permission or approval for publishing a book is to be sought according to the canons of this title, is the author's proper local Ordinary, or the Ordinary of the place in which the book is published.

§2 Unless it is established otherwise, what is said in the canons of this title about books, applies also to any writings intended for publication.

1611 Two terms are used here in regard to publishing written material: 'permission' and 'approval'. Permission (*licentia*) is usually expressed by the word *imprimatur*, and it carries with it an implicit declaration that the work contains no doctrinal or moral error. Approval (*approbatio*) seems to involve something more than permission, rather an acknowledgement, at least in general terms, of the positive worth of the work.

1612 When the permission or approval of the local Ordinary is required, this may be either the author's proper Ordinary (as determined by Can. 107 §§1–2), or the Ordinary of the place in which the book is published.[4] The rule of Can. 65 §1 about seeking from another Ordinary a favour which was denied by one's proper Ordinary holds good here:[5] the second Ordinary must be informed of the refusal and of the reasons for it.

---

[1] SCDF decr *Ecclesiae Pastorum* 19.III.1975: AAS 67(1975) 281–284: CLD 7 181–184.

[2] Cf. PB Art 51: CCLA 1214–1217.

[3] Cf. SCDF notification 14.VI.1966: AAS 58(1966) 445: CLD 6 814–815. In November 1966 the SCDF made it clear that c.1399 of the 1917 Code, which forbade certain categories of books and c.2318, which imposed certain penalties in this area, were abrogated: SCDF decr 15.XI.1966: AAS 58(1966) 1186: CLD 6 817–819.

[4] The third option given in c.1385 §2 of the 1917 Code – the Ordinary of the place of printing – has been suppressed, clearly for reasons associated with modern printing practice among publishers.

[5] Cf. Comm 15(1983) 106–107.

Title IV The Means of Social Communication and Books in Particular

This canon (§2) extends to *all writings intended for publication* the norms which are laid down for 'books'. It would not cover private documents, such as class notes or other writings of limited circulation. Neither, it would appear, would it extend to audio or visual recordings.

Can. 825 §1 Books of the sacred Scriptures may not be published unless they are approved by the Apostolic See or the Bishops' Conference. The publication of translations of the sacred Scriptures requires the approval of the same authority, and they must have necessary and sufficient explanatory notes.

Books of the sacred Scriptures, whether in the original language, in latin or in a vernacular translation, need the prior approval either of the Holy See or of the local Bishops' Conference. A suggestion to confine the giving of approval to the Holy See was not admitted by the Revision Commission, on the ground that this would represent an 'excessive centralisation', and moreover that it was not in the 1917 Code.[1] An important point to be noted is that the Church has consistently insisted on the need for explanatory notes in published translations of the Scriptures.

Can. 825 §2 With the permission of the Bishops' Conference, catholic members of Christ's faithful, in cooperation with separated brethren, may prepare and publish versions of the Scriptures, with appropriate explanatory notes.

Vat. II spoke with approval of scriptural translations being made 'in a joint effort with the separated brethren', subject to the agreement of the authorities of the Church.[2] In any such enterprise the guidelines issued jointly by the Secretariat for Christian Unity and the United Bible Society on 2.VI.1968 should be observed.[3]

Can. 826 §1 For liturgical books, the provisions of Can. 838 are to be observed.

Can. 838 states the powers of the Holy See, Bishops' Conferences and individual Bishops to order the liturgy and to publish liturgical books. In particular it subjects vernacular translations and adaptations of these books to the review of the Holy See. Special care is needed in translating the sacramental formulae, so that 'the meaning intended by the Church is aptly expressed by the translation'.[4]

Can. 826 §2 To republish liturgical books or to publish translations of all or part of them, it must be established, by an attestation of the Ordinary of the place in which they are published, that they accord with an approved edition.

Republishing original texts or publishing official translations of them requires a comparison with the approved text (*editio typica*) and an attestation (*concordat cum originali*) by the Ordinary of the place of publication that they are in accord with this. A decree of the Congregation of Rites issued in 1966 gives more detailed regulations.[5]

---

[1] Cf. Comm 15(1983) 107 at Can. 780.

[2] DV 22: Fl I 763.

[3] Secretariat for Christian Unity *Information Service* 5(1968) 22–25: Irish Theological Quarterly 35(1968) 388–394.

[4] SCDF decl 25.I.1974: AAS 66(1974) 661: CLD 8 72. On 30.III.1992 the SCDF issued an instruction entitled *Instruction on some Aspects of the Use of the Instruments of Social Communication in Promoting the Doctrine of the Faith*, which summarises and restates the present law in this area; an official English text is published in Origins 23(1992–1993) 92–96.

[5] SCRit decr *Cum Nostra Aetate* 27.I.1966: AAS 58(1966) 169–171: CLD 6 811–814.

Can. 826 §3 Prayer books, for either the public or the private use of the faithful, are not to be published except by permission of the local Ordinary.

1618 By 'prayer books' here are meant non-liturgical books of prayers, so many of which are of great help to the faithful. In so far as they contain liturgical texts or translations of these, they come under §2 above. The local Ordinary (to be determined in accordance with Can. 824 §1) will obviously take great care before approving any new form of devotion which might lead the faithful in a direction other than that which accords with the Church's magisterium.

Can. 827 §1 Without prejudice to the provisions of Can. 775 §2, the publication of catechisms and other writings pertaining to catechetical formation, as well as their translations, requires the approval of the local Ordinary.

1619 Catechisms and other catechetical texts may be prepared by the local Ordinary or with his approval. It must, however, be borne in mind that Can. 775 §2 does provide for the issuing of a catechism by a Bishops' Conference for its territory, subject to the prior approval by the Holy See: this, very often, may be the preferable option for the pastoral needs of a given country or territory.

Can. 827 §2 Books dealing with matters concerning sacred Scripture, theology, canon law, church history, or religious or moral subjects may not be used as textbooks on which the instruction is based, in elementary, intermediate or higher schools, unless they were published with the approbation of the competent ecclesiastical authority or were subsequently approved by that authority.

§3 It is recommended that books dealing with the subjects mentioned in §2, even though not used as textbooks, and any writing in which there is anything of special concern to religion or good morals, be submitted to the judgement of the local Ordinary.

1620 Textbooks, when they are used, do acquire a certain standing and respect among students. It is for this reason, among others, that it is required that they be approved by the authority competent to guide and control ecclesiastical education – who, more often than not, is the diocesan Bishop, particularly in the case of seminaries. Noticeable in recent years has been the decline in the use of formal textbooks in the teaching of theological and allied disciplines in many seminaries – a decline which this commentary would regard as regrettable and even dangerous. This canon lists the subjects of the texts which need this approval, at all levels of education, from elementary to third level, including seminaries and ecclesiastical faculties. This approval may be given beforehand or subsequently; it need not be given to the works specifically as textbooks: general approval suffices.[1] While the competent authority will normally be the local Ordinary, in the case of scriptural texts it must be either the Holy See or the Bishops' Conference (see Can. 825 §1). The approval of which this canon speaks (§2) is not needed for works which are intended to be used for reference and not as texts. However, although such works do not need the required formal approval, it is recommended that they be submitted to the local Ordinary's judgement (§3). Particular law, or the statutes of a school or institution, might make this mandatory.

Can. 827 §4 Books or other written material dealing with religion or morals may not be displayed, sold or given away in churches or oratories,

---

[1] Cf. Comm 15(1983) 107 n.2 at Can. 782.

Title IV The Means of Social Communication and Books in Particular

unless they were published with the permission of the competent ecclesiastical authority or were subsequently approved by that authority.

The reason for the prohibition stated here is that when written material is made available in churches or oratories, most people will assume that the Church approves of it and so may be misled by certain types of 'pious' literature, tendentious polemics or other sorts of suspect works. Accordingly, before being displayed, sold or even given away in a church or oratory, any works dealing with religion or morals must have received approval from the competent ecclesiastical authority, whether before or after their publication.

Can. 828 Collections of decrees or acts published by any ecclesiastical authority may not be republished without first seeking the permission of the same authority and observing the conditions which it lays down.

This canon is concerned with the republishing of collections of decrees or acts already issued by some ecclesiastical authority, such as the *Enchiridion Indulgentiarum* or the *Acta Apostolicae Sedis*. Such republishing needs the prior permission of the authority in question, and any conditions laid down by that authority must be observed, the clear purpose of this prescription being to ensure the authenticity of the documents reproduced and to protect the rights of the author. Collections made by private persons do not come within the ambit of this canon, nor, it would seem, do historical or critical editions.

Can. 829 Approval of or permission to publish a work is valid for the first edition, but not for new editions or translations of it.

This norm repeats the substance of c.1392 §1 of the 1917 Code and applies only to new editions or translations of the work in question; there is always the possibility that these may contain new material. The norm does not apply to simple reprintings of the work.[1]

Can. 830 §1 While every local Ordinary retains his right to submit the judgement of books to persons approved by him, the Bishops' Conference may draw up a list of censors, outstanding for their knowledge, right doctrine and prudence, who will be available to diocesan curias; it may even establish a commission of censors whom the local Ordinaries can consult.

§2 In carrying out his or her task, a censor must put aside all preference of persons and look only to the teaching of the Church concerning faith and morals, as declared by its magisterium.

§3 The censor must give an opinion in writing. If it is favourable, the Ordinary may, in his prudent judgement, give his permission for the work to be published, adding his own name and the date and place of the permission. If he does not give this permission, the Ordinary must inform the author of the reasons for the refusal.

Censors are those, be they clerics or laity, outstanding for knowledge in the subject concerned, for right doctrine and for prudence, on whose judgement the local Ordinary can rely when he gives or refuses to give permission or approval for the publication of books. He may appoint his own censors, on a permanent or on an ad hoc basis; alternatively, he may have recourse to a list or even a commission of censors approved by the Bishops' Conference. Such a list or commission could well make

---

[1] Cf. SCDF instr on Social Communication etc. 9: Origins 23(1992–1993) 94.

available to the local Ordinary a degree of knowledge on a wider range of subjects than might otherwise be available to him.

1625 The consequences of an unfavourable judgement by the censor could be very serious, involving professional and even financial loss for the author. On the other hand, the consequences of a favourable judgement in the case of a book containing grave errors could be equally serious. For these reasons the censor must put aside all personal considerations and be guided in his decision solely by the Church's official teaching: he should not e.g. condemn a work because it contains a view with which he or she disagrees but which has not been marked with official disapproval.

1626 The Ordinary is not bound by the censor's judgement; the final decision remains his own. The censor is to give his opinion in writing. If this is favourable, the Ordinary may give his permission, adding his own name and the date and place of the permission: these are all to be printed in the work.[1] If permission is refused, the Ordinary must inform the author why this was done. The author may then seek permission from another Ordinary, competent in accordance with Can. 824 §1, having informed him of the refusal, or he has the right of recourse in accordance with the norms of Cann. 1732–1739. In this case the recourse will be to the Congregation for the Doctrine of the Faith.[2]

Can. 831 §1 Unless there is a just and reasonable cause, no member of Christ's faithful may write in newspapers, pamphlets or periodicals which clearly are accustomed to attack the catholic religion or good morals. Clerics and members of religious institutes may write in them only with the permission of the local Ordinary.

§2 It is for the Bishops' Conference to lay down norms determining the requirements for clerics and members of religious institutes to take part in radio and television programmes which concern catholic doctrine or morals.

1627 In interpreting this canon it is important to recognise that its prohibition – such as it is: 'unless there is a just and reasonable cause' to the contrary – concerns only those 'newspapers, pamphlets or periodicals *which clearly are accustomed to attack the catholic religion or good morals*' (§1). That there are such cannot be doubted, and in many circumstances they are readily discernible. It must, however, be recognised that in some circumstances (perhaps in some countries more than others), the criterion for the discernment of the principle laid down in this canon is a matter for prudent judgement in each case. Because of the nature of the publications in question, and because of the danger of even appearing to support them, *no member of the faithful* may write in them without a just and reasonable cause – such e.g. as the writing of a letter to refute some erroneous statement made in the publication. Clerics, religious and members of societies of apostolic life (see Can. 739) may not make their own judgement about the just cause: they are specifically required to have the permission of the *local Ordinary* before writing – a permission which, unless the contrary is clear, may in many cases be reasonably presumed.

1628 Television and radio reach a wider audience than do books, and they do have a more immediate influence. For this reason Bishops' Conferences are given the responsibility to determine the requirements for clerics and religious to take part in programmes

---

[1] Cf. CCom rep 29.IV.1987: AAS 79(1987) 1249: CCLA 1292: Wrenn (Interpret) 39–40.
[2] Cf. SCDF instr cit 10.3: Origins loc cit.

which have a religious content (§2). The requirements could include, besides integrity of faith and doctrine, training in the special techniques needed in these media.[1]

Can. 832 To publish writings on matters of religion or morals, members of religious institutes require also the permission of their major Superior, in accordance with the constitutions.

In addition to the permission or approval required in Can. 831, religious require also the permission of the major Superior who is competent in accordance with the constitutions of their institute, if they are to publish writings concerned with religion or morals. In each case it will be a matter of consulting the precise text of the constitutions in question.

Title V
The Profession of Faith

Can. 833 The following are bound to make a profession of faith personally, according to a formula approved by the Apostolic See:

1° in the presence of the president or his delegate: all who, with a deliberative or a consultative vote, take part in an Ecumenical Council, a particular council, the synod of Bishops, or a diocesan synod; in the presence of the council or synod: the president himself;

2° in accordance with the statutes of the sacred College: those promoted to the dignity of Cardinal;

3° in the presence of a delegate of the Apostolic See: all who are promoted to the episcopate, and all those who are equivalent to a diocesan Bishop;

4° in the presence of the college of consultors: the diocesan Administrator;

5° in the presence of the diocesan Bishop or his delegate: Vicars general, episcopal Vicars and judicial Vicars;

6° in the presence of the local Ordinary or his delegate: parish priests; the rector, professors of theology and philosophy in seminaries, at the beginning of their term of office; and those who are to be promoted to the order of diaconate;

7° in the presence of the Chancellor or, in the absence of the Chancellor, the local Ordinary, or the delegates of either: the rector of an ecclesi-

---

[1] For the manner in which Bishops' Conferences worldwide have dealt with this matter to date, cf. LCE Tavola per Paesi e Canoni at Can. 831. Some examples from English-speaking countries may be consulted in CCLA 1325–1326, 1348, 1380, 1398, 1413, 1420.

astical or catholic university, at the beginning of the term of office; in the presence of the rector if he is a priest, or of the local Ordinary or the delegates of either: those who in any universities teach subjects which deal with faith or morals, at the beginning of their term of office;

1630   8° **in accordance with the constitutions: Superiors in clerical religious institutes and clerical societies of apostolic life.**

The profession of faith in this canon is not that demanded of all the faithful or that which is made in the course of the liturgy. It is a special profession called for by law from those who are assuming certain offices or positions. It is to be made according to a formula approved by the Holy See. Unlike the 1917 Code, the present Code does not include such a formula. Up to 1989 the formula published by the Congregation for the Doctrine of the Faith in 1967 was in force.[1] A new formula was published on 27 February 1989 and was accompanied by the text of an oath of fidelity.[2] Before this, an oath of fidelity was required only from priests who were promoted to the episcopate (see Can. 380). That situation is now changed, in accordance with the terms of this canon. Vernacular translations of the two formulae – to be prepared by the respective Bishops' Conferences – may, subject to the approval of the text by the Holy See,[3] be used, and that in fact is the normal practice at the moment.[4]

---

[1] Cf. AAS 59(1967) 1058.

[2] In OR 27.II.1989. The latin text of both is published in AAS 81(1989) 104–106.

[3] Cf. SCDF rescr 19.IX.1989: AAS 81(1989) 1169.

[4] On the promulgation of the 1989 formulae, a certain measure of canonico-ecclesiological controversy was generated in some quarters. It is the clear opinion of this commentary that the ecclesiological imperative – never more clearly stated than in Vat. II – requires the integral implementation of Can. 833 and of the ensuing directives of the Holy See in its regard. Cf. Cann. 204, 330, 331, 336 – in which context the serious scholar will consult *inter alia* LG 8–9, 14, 18, 20, 22–23, 31, 34, 36, 38; AA 2, 6–7, 9–10; CD 2, 4, 44, 49; OE 3; UR 2; AGD 38; GS 40 – the English version of all of which is available in Fl I.

BOOK IV

THE SANCTIFYING OFFICE OF THE CHURCH

INTRODUCTION

1631 In marked contrast to the 1917 Code which, following Roman Law classification, dealt with the material contained in this book under the heading *De Rebus* ('Things'), the present Code views it from a theological and a pastoral perspective. It places it in the context of the threefold mission of Christ and the threefold office of the Church, the offices of teaching, sanctifying and governing. The title of the Book, 'The Sanctifying Office of the Church', might at a casual glance seem to cover only the means by which the faithful are made holy. In fact the term 'sanctify' (*sanctificare*) in this context has a twofold meaning: to make (people) holy and to glorify the Holy (God).[1] The Code therefore does not create a distinction between the means of sanctification and divine worship; rather, it sees the two as parts of a harmonious whole. This is reflected in the manner in which the book is laid out. In the 1917 Code the Sacraments were first dealt with, next sacred places and times, and only then divine worship. That order of things was retained in the early draft of the present Code.[2] However, as a result of the consultation conducted throughout the Church, which among other things reflected the spirit of Vat. II, the present order emerged, in which there is no longer a separate part for divine worship, precisely because this is seen as integral to the sanctifying office of the Church.

1632 After six introductory canons, the book is divided into three parts: I The Sacraments, II The Other Acts of Divine Worship, III Sacred Places and Times. The introductory canons lay down the basic principles of liturgical law and are in part doctrinal, in part normative. Part I deals with the seven Sacraments, in general and then individually. Part II is concerned with Sacramentals; the Liturgy of the Hours; Church Funerals; the Cult of the Saints, of Sacred Images and of Relics; Vows and Oaths. Part III treats of Sacred Places, including Churches, Oratories and Private Chapels, Shrines, Altars, Cemeteries, and of Sacred Times under the headings of Feast Days and Days of Penance.

INTRODUCTORY CANONS

Can. 834 §1 The Church carries out its office of sanctifying in a special way in the sacred liturgy, which is indeed seen as an exercise of the priestly office of Jesus Christ. In the liturgy, by the use of signs perceptible to the senses, our sanctification is symbolised and, in a manner appropriate to each sign, is brought about. Through the liturgy a complete public worship is offered to God by the head and members of the mystical body of Christ.

---

[1] Comm 15(1983) 171.
[2] Cf. SS and SMS.

1633 This paragraph has its roots in the 1947 encl. *Mediator Dei* of Pope Pius XII and in the constitution SC of Vat. II. The liturgy is not the sole means of sanctification, but it is the pre-eminent one: 'the liturgy by its very nature is far superior to any of (the other forms of devotion)'[1] and is 'the summit toward which the activity of the Church is directed; it is also the fount from which all her power flows'.[2] In the liturgy all Christ's faithful participate in the priesthood of Christ, and so are made holy and offer public worship to God.

Can. 834 §2 This worship takes place when it is offered in the name of the Church, by persons lawfully deputed and through actions approved by ecclesiastical authority.

1634 This paragraph specifies how to recognise acts of worship as liturgical. Firstly, they must be 'offered in the name of the Church by persons lawfully deputed'. This deputation is not confined to a special act deputing an individual, but includes also the deputation that comes from the sacraments, particularly and fundamentally the sacrament of Baptism:[3] ' ... the faithful are appointed by their baptismal character to Christian religious worship'.[4] An example of such deputation, formally recognised, is the exhortation to the laity to participate in the liturgy of the hours.[5] Secondly, the acts must be 'approved by ecclesiastical authority'. This phrase replaces that found in the corresponding norm of the 1917 Code, c.1256, which called for the acts to be 'by institution of the Church'. Approval is normally by way of inclusion of the act in the official liturgical books of the Church, but Can. 838 gives some scope for local adaptation and regulation.

Can. 835 §1 The sanctifying office is exercised principally by Bishops, who are the high priests, the principal dispensers of the mysteries of God and the moderators, promoters and guardians of the entire liturgical life in the Churches entrusted to their care.

1635 This is a doctrinal rather than a normative canon, and it lists in order the roles played by different members of the Church in the office of sanctifying.

1636 First in order come the Bishops: 'The Bishop, invested with the fulness of the sacrament of Orders, is the "steward of the grace of the supreme priesthood", above all in the Eucharist, which he himself offers, or ensures that it is offered, from which the Church ever derives its life and on which it thrives'.[6] The Bishop by virtue of his episcopal ordination is the liturgical president of his diocese and from this comes his role in regulating, promoting and safeguarding the liturgy in the diocesan Church.

Can. 835 §2 This office is also exercised by priests. They, too, share in the priesthood of Christ and, as his ministers under the authority of the Bishop, are consecrated to celebrate divine worship and to sanctify the people.

1637 Priests come next: 'Whilst not having the supreme degree of the pontifical office, and notwithstanding the fact that they depend on the Bishops in the exercise of their own proper power, the priests are for all that associated with them by reason of their sacerdotal dignity; and in virtue of the sacrament of Orders ... they are consecrated in order

---

[1] SC 13: Fl I 7.

[2] SC 10: Fl I 6. Cf. CCC n.1067.

[3] Cf. Comm 15(1983) 172 at Can. 789 §2.

[4] LG 11: Fl I 361.

[5] Cf. SC 100: Fl I 28.

[6] LG 26: Fl I 381; cf. also 382.

Introduction

... to celebrate divine worship as true priests of the New Testament'.[1] The role of the priest in the liturgy is always in union with, and under the authority of, his Bishop.

Can. 835 §3 Deacons have a share in the celebration of divine worship in accordance with the provisions of law.

This paragraph speaks of deacons in general terms only; it leaves their functions to be defined by the law. Vat. II describes these functions: 'It pertains to the office of a deacon, in so far as it may be assigned to him by the competent authority, to administer baptism solemnly, to be custodian and distributor of the Eucharist, in the name of the Church to assist at and to bless marriages, to bring Viaticum to the dying, to read the sacred scripture to the faithful, to instruct and exhort the people, to preside over the worship and the prayer of the faithful, to administer sacramentals, and to officiate at funeral and burial services'.[2] These functions belong equally to permanent deacons and to deacons who are advancing to the priesthood,[3] insofar as they are assigned to them by the local Ordinary.[4]

1638

Can. 835 §4 The other members of Christ's faithful have their own part in this sanctifying office, each in his or her own way actively sharing in liturgical celebrations, particularly in the Eucharist. Parents have a special share in this office when they live their married lives in a christian spirit and provide for the christian education of their children.

This paragraph echoes Vat. II: ' ... liturgical services pertain to the whole Body of the Church. They manifest it, and have effects on it. But they also touch individual members of the Church in different ways, depending on their orders, their role in the liturgical services, and their actual participation in them'.[5] By baptism each member of the faithful is given a fundamental share in the priesthood of Christ and therefore a role in the liturgy. In addition, individuals may be given the stable ministries of lector or acolyte, they may receive temporary assignment to particular roles or they may even supply the functions of ministers in certain circumstances (see Can. 230). Special mention is made of the sanctifying office exercised by parents towards one another and towards their children: a point easily missed but in fact one of valuable significance for pastoral practice, where there is an ideal opportunity to stress to parents that 'when they live their married lives in a christian spirit and provide for the christian education of their children', they truly have a 'special share' in the sanctifying office of the Church.[6]

1639

Can. 836 Since christian worship, in which the common priesthood of Christ's faithful is exercised, must proceed from and rest upon faith, sacred ministers are to strive diligently to arouse and enlighten this faith, especially by the ministry of the word by which faith is born and nourished.

'Before men can come to the liturgy they must be called to faith and to conversion.'[7] 'The baptised, by regeneration and the anointing of the Holy Spirit, are consecrated to be a spiritual house and a holy priesthood ... Though they differ essentially and not only

1640

---

[1] LG 28: Fl I 384.
[2] LG 29: Fl I 387.
[3] Cf. DVCom 26.III.1968, 4.IV.1969: AAS 60 (1968) 363, 61 (1969) 348: CLD 7 133.
[4] Cf. SDO 22: AAS 59(1967) 697–704: DOL n.2536.
[5] SC 26: Fl I 10. Cf. Can. 837 §1.
[6] Cf. LG 41: Fl I 399.
[7] SC 9: Fl I 6.

in degree, the common priesthood of the faithful and the ministerial or hierarchical priesthood are none the less ordered one to another; each in its own proper way shares in the one priesthood of Christ.'[1] This canon illustrates one way in which the ministerial priesthood is 'ordered to' the common priesthood of the faithful. It emphasises the absolute need for faith in Christian worship, and it prescribes that ordained ministers, Bishops, priests and deacons, are to 'arouse and enlighten this faith, especially by the ministry of the word'. A number of canons in Title I of Book III lay down the obligations of the ministerial priesthood towards the word of God (see Cann. 756–757, 760, 762–764, 767–772, 773, 775–777). Those canons have particular application here in regard to the faith which is necessary for participation in the liturgy.

Can. 837 §1 Liturgical actions are not private, but are celebrations of the Church itself as the 'sacrament of unity', that is, the holy people united and ordered under the Bishops. Accordingly, they concern the whole body of the Church, making it known and influencing it. They affect individual members of the Church in ways that vary according to orders, role and actual participation.

§2 Since liturgical actions by their very nature call for a community celebration, they are, as far as possible, to be celebrated in the presence of Christ's faithful and with their active participation.

1641   The first paragraph, a direct quotation from *Sacrosanctum Concilium* n.26, is descriptive rather than normative. It emphasises the essentially public nature of the liturgy, every act of which involves both the whole Church and each of its individual members according to their orders, role and actual degree of participation. The second paragraph is derived from the same conciliar document n.27, and it lays down the rule that, as a consequence of their public and community nature, liturgical actions should, where possible, be carried out with the faithful present and actively participating. This is particularly true of the Mass and the sacraments.[2] While there is not an absolute prohibition on celebrating Mass without a congregation (see Can. 906), the clear preference is for a communal celebration.

Can. 838 §1 The ordering and guidance of the sacred liturgy depends solely upon the authority of the Church, namely, that of the Apostolic See and, as provided by law, that of the diocesan Bishop.

1642   This canon determines who has the power to regulate the Church's liturgy. Its first paragraph is taken from *Sacrosanctum Concilium*, merely adding the clarifying word 'diocesan'.[3] It corresponds to two canons in the 1917 Code, cc. 1260 and 1257, but it makes one important derogation from the latter. It begins by stating the basic principle that regulation of the liturgy is a matter for the Church's authority,[4] thereby excluding civil authority or those outside the Church from any competence in this field; although the wording is different, the purport is the same as that of c.1260 of the 1917 Code. It goes on however to specify which Church authority is competent. C.1257 of the 1917 Code reserved solely to the Holy See the power to order the sacred liturgy and to approve liturgical books. The present canon, while reaffirming the authority of the Apostolic See in this matter, assigns competence also to the diocesan Bishop 'as provided by law' (see this canon §4).

---

[1] LG 10: Fl I 360-361.

[2] Cf. SC 27: Fl I 11; cf. also CCC n.1108.

[3] Cf. SC 22: Fl I 9; Comm 15(1983) 173 at Can. 792 §1.

[4] For the most recent Instruction in this regard cf. SCSDW instr *De Liturgia Romana et Inculturatione* 25.I.1994: AAS 87(1995) 288-314: Comm 27(1995) 10-29.

Introduction

Can. 838 §2 It is the prerogative of the Apostolic See to regulate the sacred liturgy of the universal Church, to publish liturgical books and review their vernacular translations, and to be watchful that liturgical regulations are everywhere faithfully observed.

This paragraph specifies the role of the Apostolic See in terms that closely correspond to c. 1257 of the 1917 Code. While it does not use the exclusive '*unius*' of the previous law, it clearly reserves to the Holy See the power to regulate the liturgy of the universal Church, to publish liturgical books, to review their vernacular translations, to oversee the observance of liturgical regulations. The clear purpose of this rule is to ensure that, while catering for local adaptations, there be throughout the Church a liturgy which is substantially uniform. Liturgical books are officially issued by the Apostolic See in latin, each in a so-called 'typical edition' (*editio typica*). Translation of these into the vernacular is the function of the local Bishops' Conferences (see Can. 838 §3). But the translations must be 'reviewed' by the Apostolic See. The 1980 draft used the term 'approve' (*approbare*)[1] but the change to 'review' (*recognoscere*) was made, not in any way to weaken the authority of the Apostolic See in this matter, but simply in the interests of uniformity with the terminology used in Can. 455 §2 in regard to the review of decrees made by Bishops' Conferences. The review of vernacular translations is no mere formality; it is an act of the power of governance by a superior authority which is necessary before the act of the inferior body can have any force.[2]

1643

Can. 838 §3 It pertains to Bishops' Conferences to prepare vernacular translations of liturgical books, with appropriate adaptations as allowed by the books themselves and, with the prior review of the Holy See, to publish these translations.

This paragraph lists the power of the Bishops' Conference to prepare vernacular translations of liturgical books; to adapt rites as allowed in these books; to publish the translations after they have been reviewed by the Apostolic See as prescribed in §2.[3] The adaptations allowed for in the official liturgical books form one example of such regulation of the liturgy by the Bishops' Conference, but they do not exhaust all the possibilities. Vat. II foresees 'an even more radical adaptation of the liturgy' in certain places and circumstances, and it allows for the introduction of such adaptation with the consent of the Apostolic See.[4]

1644

Can. 838 §4 Within the limits of his competence, it belongs to the diocesan Bishop to lay down in the Church entrusted to his care, liturgical regulations which are binding on all.

This paragraph refers to the power of the diocesan Bishop already touched on in §1. 'The liturgical life of the diocese [is] centred around the bishop ... ':[5] as a consequence he has the power 'within the limits of his competence', i.e. as provided for in the law, to make liturgical regulations for his diocese. The paragraph parallels c.1261 of the 1917 Code but it goes farther. The previous law simply gave Bishops the duty of seeing that the laws on divine worship were followed properly and in a becoming manner, and it empowered him to make laws for this purpose. Now he can act for his

1645

---

[1] Sch 1980 Can. 792 §2.
[2] Cf. Comm 15(1983) 173 R.2 at Can. 792 §2.
[3] Cf. SC 22 (2): Fl I 9.
[4] SC 40: Fl I 14.
[5] SC 41: Fl I 14.

diocese in a manner similar to the way in which the Bishops' Conference acts for the larger territory, e.g. by making allowable local adaptations: such liturgical regulations as are made by the Bishop are binding on all, including religious, even exempt, unless they are of a different rite.[1]

Can. 839 §1 The Church carries out its sanctifying office by other means also, whether by prayer, in which it asks God to make Christ's faithful holy in the truth, or by works of penance and of charity, which play a large part in establishing and strengthening in souls the Kingdom of Christ and contribute to the salvation of the world.

1646 'The sacred liturgy does not exhaust the entire activity of the Church.'[2] Accordingly recognition is given here to the other means by which the Church's sanctifying office is fulfilled, namely prayer and works of penance and charity. By placing them in the present context, the law emphasises that all these means are not independent ways to holiness but are, as it were, subsumed in and inspired by the liturgy: ' ... the liturgy is the summit toward which the activity of the Church is directed; it is also the fount from which all her power flows'.[3] In effect, at the level of pastoral practice, say in a parish, this simply means that there is an essential link between e.g. the Sunday Mass and the sanctifying activity of the faithful, laity and priest alike, during the week – be that by way of prayer, personal or family, of penance or of works of charity: the Mass should lead to these, and they in turn should find their inspiration in the Mass.

Can. 839 §2 Local Ordinaries are to ensure that the prayers and the pious and sacred practices of the christian people are in full harmony with the laws of the Church.

1647 In order to ensure that these other means genuinely accord with the liturgy, this paragraph obliges all local Ordinaries to see that 'the pious and the sacred practices' are in harmony with the Church's laws. *Pious practices* are those non-liturgical celebrations in widespread or of even universal usage, which may have recognition even from the Apostolic See e.g. the Rosary, the Stations of the Cross. *Sacred practices* are more local, with episcopal or customary approbation: ' ... such devotions should be so drawn up that they harmonise with the liturgical seasons (and) accord with the sacred liturgy...'[4] This regulation replaces cc.1259 and 1261 of the 1917 Code, without however repeating the restrictions of c.1259. Hence prayers and pious practices no longer need the review and express permission of the local Ordinary before they can be used in churches or oratories, nor is the local Ordinary forbidden to approve new litanies for public recitation.

---

[1] Cf. 1917 Code c.1261 §2; CD 35 (4): Fl I 585.
[2] SC 9: Fl I 6.
[3] SC 10: Fl I 6. Cf. CCC n.1073.
[4] SC 13: Fl I 7.

PART I

THE SACRAMENTS

Can. 840 The sacraments of the New Testament were instituted by Christ the Lord and entrusted to the Church. As actions of Christ and of the Church, they are signs and means by which faith is expressed and strengthened, worship is offered to God and our sanctification is brought about. Thus they contribute in the most effective manner to establishing, strengthening and manifesting ecclesiastical communion. Accordingly, in the celebration of the sacraments both the sacred ministers and the other members of Christ's faithful must show the greatest reverence and due care.

This canon replaces c.731 §1 of the 1917 Code. Although the normative part of it contained in the last sentence is substantially the same as that in the former law, the theological introduction is much fuller and richer: it reflects in particular the teaching of Vat. II. The sacraments are 'actions of Christ and of the Church': ' ... Christ is always present in his Church, especially in her liturgical celebrations. ... By his power he is present in the sacraments ...'[1] They express the faith of the Church and strengthen the faith of its members. Even where a person's faith is weak or lacking, a valid sacrament always expresses the faith of the Church. The sacraments offer worship to God and bring about the sanctification of Christ's faithful and so serve to establish, strengthen and make manifest the Body of Christ which is the Church. 'The purpose of the sacraments is to sanctify men, to build up the Body of Christ, and finally to give worship to God. Because they are signs, they also instruct. They not only presuppose faith, but by words and objects they also nourish, strengthen, and express it. That is why they are called *sacraments of faith*.'[2]   1648

Because of the central and all-important place of the sacraments in the life of the Church, all of Christ's faithful are obliged to 'show great reverence and due care' in the celebration of the sacraments. In its c.731 §1 the 1917 Code spoke of 'administering and receiving' the sacraments. In keeping with the terminology employed throughout the documents of Vatican II,[3] this Code speaks in terms of 'celebrating' them. A similar change of emphasis appears here in yet another way. The original draft of this canon spoke of 'the sacred ministers and the faithful themselves';[4] the current text pointedly refers to 'the sacred ministers and the other members of Christ's faithful', thereby stressing the fundamental point made in Cann. 204 §1 and 207 §1, and maintaining the notion of communal celebration of the sacraments.   1649

Can. 841 Since the sacraments are the same throughout the universal Church, and belong to the divine deposit of faith, only the supreme authority in the Church can approve or define what is needed for their validity. It belongs to the same authority, or to another competent authority in accordance with Can. 838

---

[1] SC 7: Fl I 4–5.
[2] SC 59: Fl I 20. Cf. CCC nn.1115, 1123, 1210.
[3] Cf. Comm 15(1983) 174–175 at Can. 794.
[4] SS Can. 1.

§§3 and 4, to determine what is required for their lawful celebration, administration and reception and for the order to be observed in their celebration.

1650 This canon distinguishes between those elements necessary for the validity of the sacraments and those needed for their lawful and proper celebration; it determines who the authorities are that are competent to decide on the one and the other. Only the supreme authority in the Church can decide on what is needed for the valid celebration of the sacraments: 'supreme authority' means either the Roman Pontiff or an Ecumenical Council.[1] It is because the sacraments are the same in the whole Church, and because they form part of the divine deposit of faith, that the decision on their essentials is so reserved. Matters pertaining to the lawful celebration, administration and reception of the sacraments, and the order of their celebration, can be decided by the supreme authority or by either Bishops' Conferences or the diocesan Bishop. By referring to Can. 838 §§3 and 4 the text makes it clear that the power of the lesser authorities in this regard is subject to the limitations imposed by that canon. Thus e.g. in Can. 849 the supreme authority determines what is necessary for the valid conferring of baptism; in the succeeding canons it also determines a number of requisites for its lawful conferral. But the local Bishops' Conference or even the local Bishop can determine within those limits the particular adaptation of the rite to be used, and Can. 877 §1 explicitly gives the Bishops' Conference a particular power of decision in the registration of the baptism of adopted children.

Can. 842 §1 A person who has not received baptism cannot validly be admitted to the other sacraments.

1651 The statement in this paragraph is new, although of course the doctrine behind it is not. That doctrine formed the basis for the statement of c.737 §1 of the 1917 Code, which called baptism 'the gateway and foundation of the sacraments'.[2] Valid reception of any of the other sacraments is simply not possible for one who has not received baptism.[3]

Can. 842 §2 The sacraments of baptism, confirmation and the blessed Eucharist so complement one another that all three are required for full christian initiation.

1652 This paragraph is also new and states the need for confirmation and the Eucharist, as well as baptism, for full initiation into the Church. 'Men and women ... are made a new creation through water and the Holy Spirit ... Signed by the giving of the same Spirit in Confirmation, they become more like Our Lord and filled with the Holy Spirit. ... Finally, as part of the eucharistic assembly, they eat the flesh of the Son of Man and drink his blood ...'[4] In the latin Church the order followed in the canon is normally seen in practice only in the initiation of adults. That this precise sequence is not of obligation can be seen from the widespread practice in the latin Church of the sequence: baptism, penance, communion, confirmation. This practice is recognised in regard to confirmation in Can. 891 which allows the deferment of this sacrament to a later age than that of discretion, and in Can. 914 which enjoins the reception of Holy Communion by children who have reached the age of discretion but directs that they should first make their sacramental confession.

---

[1] Cf. Cann. 330, 331, 336, 337; cf. also CCC n.1118.
[2] Cf. Can. 849.
[3] In this context cf. Can. 849 and its implications, especially in respect of baptism by desire.
[4] GICI 1–2: Fl II 22. Cf. CCC nn.1229, 1275.

Part I The Sacraments

Can. 843 §1 Sacred ministers may not deny the sacraments to those who opportunely ask for them, are properly disposed and are not prohibited by law from receiving them.

This paragraph gives practical effect to the rights of all Christ's faithful 'to make known ... their spiritual needs ... to the Pastors of the Church' (Can. 212 §2) and 'to be assisted by their Pastors from the spiritual riches of the Church, especially by the word of God and the sacraments' (Can. 213).[1] It corresponds in part to c.467 §1 of the 1917 Code which obliged parish priests, among their other duties, to administer the sacraments to the faithful whenever they legitimately asked for them. The present law obliges all sacred ministers to administer the sacraments to all who (a) ask for them opportunely, (b) are properly disposed, (c) are not prohibited by law from receiving them: 1653

(a) what can be considered 'opportune' in this context will obviously vary with the sacrament, the person and the circumstances, but the phrase 'may not deny' seems to imply a presumption that the request is opportune unless the contrary is manifestly the case.

(b) the same presumption would seem to operate in regard to proper disposition. The principal disposition, required for all the sacraments, is faith (see Can. 836).

(c) in general, prohibition by law will be clear, e.g. Can. 915, forbidding reception of the Eucharist; Cann. 1040–1041, debarring certain persons from the reception of orders; Can. 1124, forbidding mixed marriages which do not have a special permission.

Can. 843 §2 According to their respective roles in the Church, both pastors of souls and the other members of Christ's faithful have a duty to ensure that those who ask for the sacraments are prepared for their reception. This should be done through proper evangelisation and catechetical instruction, in accordance with the norms laid down by the competent authority.

This paragraph obliges not only pastors of souls but all the faithful, each in his or her own way, to ensure that all those who seek the sacraments are properly prepared by 'evangelisation and catechetical instruction'. This is a putting into practice of Can. 836 and also of the numerous canons in Book III Titles I–III, detailing the rights and duties of all Christ's faithful in regard to the word of God. Parents in particular have a special duty here in preparing their children for the sacraments (see Cann. 774 §2, 776). 1654

Can. 844 §1 Catholic ministers may lawfully administer the sacraments only to catholic members of Christ's faithful, who equally may lawfully receive them only from catholic ministers, except as provided in §§2, 3 and 4 of this canon and in Can. 861 §2.

This canon replaces c.731 §2 of the 1917 Code which simply forbade administering the sacraments to 'heretics or schismatics, even though erring in good faith and asking for them', without prior reconciliation to the Church; it was however accepted that that prohibition did not apply to giving the sacraments of penance and anointing of the sick to non-catholics in danger of death.[2] The present law derives ultimately from the decrees of Vat. II on ecumenism and on the oriental Churches. More immediately, its norms come from the Directory concerning Ecumenical Matters *Ad Totam Ecclesiam* issued in 1967 by the Secretariat for the Promotion of the Unity of 1655

---

[1] Cf. LG 37: Fl I 394.

[2] Cf. e.g. Vermeersch–Creusen II n.16.

Christians. The general principles to be followed are outlined in the decree on ecumenism: 'The expression of unity very generally forbids common worship. Grace to be obtained sometimes commends it'.[1] The canon accordingly begins with a general prohibition against inter-Church sharing of the sacraments, but follows this immediately with important exceptions. The exceptions are graded according to the Churches or Christian communities involved and to the general or particular circumstances of the case. Exceptions are made in this canon for three sacraments only: penance, the Eucharist and anointing of the sick. Baptism is referred to as a special case with its own rules (see Can. 861 §2). Neither is the question of mixed marriages covered here (see Cann. 1124–1127).

1656 Since the sacraments are among the principal means and signs of ecclesiastical communion,[2] 'signifying the oneness in faith, worship and life of the community',[3] and since other christians are divided from the catholic Church in varying degrees in faith, worship and discipline, free and general sharing of the sacraments cannot be allowed; it would purport to be a sign of something which does not in fact exist. For this reason the first paragraph of this canon in general allows catholic ministers to administer the sacraments only to catholics and allows catholics to receive them only from catholic ministers. But because other christians do, in varying degrees, share a common faith with the catholic Church, and because of special spiritual needs, a degree of sharing of the sacraments is allowable.

Can. 844 §2 Whenever necessity requires or a genuine spiritual advantage commends it, and provided the danger of error or indifferentism is avoided, Christ's faithful for whom it is physically or morally impossible to approach a catholic minister, may lawfully receive the sacraments of penance, the Eucharist and anointing of the sick from non-catholic ministers in whose Churches these sacraments are valid.

1657 This paragraph covers the first exception, the case of a catholic seeking the sacraments of penance, the Eucharist and anointing from a non-catholic minister. Four conditions must be met before this can lawfully take place.

(a) There must be a real necessity or a genuine spiritual advantage e.g. the need to receive the sacrament of penance when one is in mortal sin, the need for all three sacraments in danger of death; a genuine spiritual advantage would be realised in the case of a special desire to receive the Eucharist, particularly by one accustomed to doing so regularly.

(b) There must be no danger of error or indifferentism. 'A mutual sharing in sacred things, which runs counter to the unity of the Church, or which involves formal adhesion to error or the danger of aberration in the faith, of scandal and of indifferentism, is forbidden by the law of God.'[4] The error to be avoided is not just that of the person seeking the sacraments; it is also that of other members of the Church, and even that of the members of the other Church whose minister is approached. As far as possible, all those involved should be aware of the reasons for, and the true significance of, the approach.

(c) It must be physically or morally impossible for the catholic to approach a catholic minister. A thing is considered morally impossible if it cannot be done without

---

[1] UR 8: Fl I 461.
[2] Cf. Can. 840.
[3] DEM 55: Fl I 499.
[4] OE 26: Fl I 450.

Part I The Sacraments

extraordinary effort, grave inconvenience or great expense: relevant factors would be imprisonment, personal danger in time of war, illness, serious personal reasons for not wanting to approach the only available catholic minister.

(d) The Church of the minister approached must have valid sacraments. The minister himself must have been validly ordained,[1] but this is not of itself sufficient; his Church must also be one whose sacraments are valid. So there is question not only of the personal validity of the minister's orders – which would be required for the validity, not just the liceity, of the sacrament sought – but of the status of the sacraments in that Church. 'The question of reciprocity arises only with these Churches which have preserved the substance of the Eucharist, the Sacrament of Orders and apostolic succession.'[2] As regards the eastern Orthodox Churches not in communion with Rome, their sacraments are recognised as valid and their priests are validly ordained.[3] The same would be true of some of the 'Old Catholics' in Holland and elsewhere. The question of the status and beliefs of the many different Christian Churches and communions in the western world is a difficult one, as the decree on ecumenism itself observed.[4] In particular, a difficulty arises with Churches in the Anglican communion. Although the Council recognises it as occupying a special place 'among those in which Catholic traditions and institutions in part continue to exist',[5] it has not been formally recognised as having the same standing in the present context as the eastern Churches. So, even if a particular Anglican priest is certainly in valid orders, it would be unlawful for a catholic to seek the sacraments from him, apart from danger of death.

Can. 844 §3 Catholic ministers may lawfully administer the sacraments of penance, the Eucharist and anointing of the sick to members of the eastern Churches not in full communion with the catholic Church, if they spontaneously ask for them and are properly disposed. The same applies to members of other Churches which the Apostolic See judges to be in the same position as the aforesaid eastern Churches so far as the sacraments are concerned.

§§3 and 4 allow catholic ministers to administer the three sacraments already mentioned to non-catholics in certain circumstances. The conditions to be met for doing this lawfully vary in accordance with the degree to which the Church of the individual concerned has retained the catholic tradition regarding the sacraments. The sacraments are more easily shared with those with whom the catholic Church has a closer degree of unity. 1658

This §3, based on the *Directory concerning Ecumenical Matters*,[6] deals with members of the eastern Churches and of Churches judged by the Apostolic See to be in the same position as these as far as the sacraments are concerned. The only requirements for lawful administration of these sacraments to such people are that they spontaneously ask for them and are properly disposed. The first of these requirements evidently forbids any form of suggestion or pressure by a catholic minister to induce an individual to receive a sacrament. The requirement regarding disposition would be the same as for a catholic with whom the individual is presumed to share a common 1659

---

[1] DEM 55: Fl I 499.
[2] SPCU *Dopo la pubblicazione* 9: Fl I 562.
[3] Cf. UR 15: Fl I 465.
[4] Cf. UR 19: Fl I 467.
[5] UR 13: Fl I 463.
[6] Cf. DEM 42–47: Fl I 496–497.

faith in the sacraments. There has been no formal decision as to what Churches are in the same position as the eastern Churches. Hence, unless the conditions of §4 are verified, a catholic minister may not lawfully administer these sacraments to e.g. members of the Anglican communion.

Can. 844 §4 If there is a danger of death or if, in the judgement of the diocesan Bishop or of the Bishops' Conference, there is some other grave and pressing need, catholic ministers may lawfully administer these same sacraments to other christians not in full communion with the catholic Church, who cannot approach a minister of their own community and who spontaneously ask for them, provided that they demonstrate the catholic faith in respect of these sacraments and are properly disposed.

1660 This paragraph turns to members of Churches other than those dealt with in §3.[1] These Churches are further removed from the catholic Church in faith and worship and, specifically, in their belief and practice with regard to the sacraments. Accordingly, *in addition to the two already listed in §3*, three further requirements must be met for lawful administration.

(a) There must be either a danger of death, or another grave or pressing need which is to be estimated by the diocesan Bishop or the Bishops' Conference. Estimation of danger of death will be made by the minister approached in the individual case; other grave and pressing needs require the judgement of higher authority: examples of such need are imprisonment, persecution,[2] distance and expense.[3]

(b) It must be impossible for the person concerned to approach a minister of his own community. The impossibility here can be either physical or moral.

(c) The person must demonstrate the catholic faith in respect of these sacraments. Such faith is presumed in members of the eastern Churches and of those Churches judged to be in the same condition, but it must be shown to exist in the cases of others. Obviously this must be done with great sensitivity and charity, especially if the person is ill.

Can. 844 §5 In respect of the cases dealt with in §§ 2, 3 and 4, the diocesan Bishop or the Bishops' Conference is not to issue general norms except after consultation with the competent authority, at least at the local level, of the non-catholic Church or community concerned.

1661 This is a clear regulation in respect of the cases dealt with in §§ 2–4 of this canon. The 1980 draft of the Code, following the *Directory concerning Ecumenical Matters*,[4] required a favourable outcome to such consultation, but this was eliminated from the final text, because 'the internal legislative activity of the Church cannot be tied to the consent of non-catholic parties without eventual prejudice to pastoral necessities'.[5] The regulation concerns only the issuing of 'general norms'; accordingly, it would not forbid a diocesan Bishop to issue a ruling in a particular case even without the consultation envisaged.

Can. 845 §1 Because they imprint a character, the sacraments of baptism, confirmation and order cannot be repeated.

---

[1] Cf. DEM 55: Fl I 499.
[2] Cf. DEM 55: Fl I 499.
[3] Cf. SPCU *In Quibus Rerum Circumstantiis* VI: Fl I 559.
[4] DEM 42: Fl I 496–497.
[5] Comm 15(1983) 176 at Can. 797 §5.

Part I The Sacraments

This repeats c.732 §1 of the 1917 Code almost word for word; the only change is the insertion of the word 'because', making it even clearer that the imprinting of the character is the precise reason why these sacraments cannot be repeated. The canon does not give any theological exposition on the nature of these sacraments but reiterates the doctrine of the Council of Trent regarding the character,[1] and it states not that they *should* not be repeated but that they *cannot* be repeated.

Can. 845 §2 If after diligent enquiry a prudent doubt remains as to whether the sacraments mentioned in §1 have been conferred at all, or conferred validly, they are to be conferred conditionally.

This paragraph corresponds to c.732 §2 of the 1917 Code but, in instructing that these sacraments be conferred conditionally in case of doubt, it omits, for the sake of clarity and precision, the word 'again'. This itself emphasises the impossibility of repetition. Moreover it demands a 'diligent enquiry' if there is a doubt about either their conferral or their validity; a mere suspicion of invalidity or non-conferral does not warrant the giving of these sacraments conditionally. The commonest situation where the possibility of conditional conferral can arise is in the reception of other Christians into full communion with the catholic Church. 'Indiscriminate conditional baptism of all who desire full communion with the catholic Church cannot be approved.'[2]

Can. 846 §1 The liturgical books, approved by the competent authority, are to be faithfully followed in the celebration of the sacraments. Accordingly, no one may on a personal initiative add to or omit or alter anything in those books.

The directive of c.733 §1 of the 1917 Code is substantially repeated here. Added is an explicit prohibition against any individual additions, omissions or changes to the official texts. Under the previous law only the Apostolic See was the 'competent authority' in regard to liturgical texts. Now, however, Bishops' Conferences and diocesan Bishops have powers in this regard (see Cann. 838, 841). But no matter what authority is responsible, no individual, 'not even a priest',[3] may make his own alterations to the liturgy. While this regulation of course allows for such individual adaptations or variations as are catered for in the official texts themselves, it is a clear statement that no one may lawfully go beyond those texts and, as it were, conduct one's 'personal liturgy'.

Can. 846 §2 The ministers are to celebrate the sacraments according to their own rite.

This paragraph corresponds to c.733 §2 of the 1917 Code, but it contains an important change. The earlier law, with some specific exceptions in regard to the Eucharist, decreed that *everyone* should follow his or her own particular rite (whether it be one of the eastern rites or one of the rites of the latin Church – Roman, Ambrosian, Mozarabic etc.). The present law obliges only the minister, leaving the rest of Christ's faithful free to receive the sacraments under any rite. This freedom should not in any way be seen as weakening the position of the individual rites, all of which the Church regards as being of equal right and dignity, and wishes to be preserved and fostered.[4] In a concelebrated Mass 'any latin-rite priest may concelebrate with other latin-rite priests, even if the Mass is celebrated according to a rite other than his own'.[5] Obviously, a priest who has bi-ritual faculties could celebrate in either rite.

---

[1] Council of Trent Sess. VII *de sacramentis in genere* Can. 9. Cf. CCC n.1121.
[2] DEM 14: Fl I 489. Cf. Can. 869.
[3] Cf. SC 22 (3): Fl I 9–10.
[4] Cf. SC 4: Fl I 2.
[5] SCRit *Rite of Concelebration* Introduction 7: DOL n.1800.

Can. 847 §1 In administering sacraments in which holy oils are to be used, the minister must use oil made from olives or other plants, which, except as provided in Can. 999 n.2, has recently been consecrated or blessed by a Bishop. Older oil is not to be used except in a case of necessity.

1666 Holy oils are used in the sacraments of baptism, confirmation, orders and anointing of the sick. They are: chrism, used in confirmation and orders; oil of catechumens, used in baptism; oil of the sick, used in anointing of the sick. Chrism is consecrated (see Can. 880 §2); the others are blessed. This canon treats of the nature of the oil to be used, its preparation and its custody. It replaces cc. 734 and 735 of the 1917 Code and introduces some modifications. Formerly, olive oil was required; now olive oil or oil made from other plants may be used.[1] The oil must have 'recently been consecrated or blessed by a Bishop', except as provided for in Can. 999 2° which allows a priest in case of necessity to bless the oil for the anointing of the sick in the course of celebrating the sacrament. 'Recently' will usually mean on the preceding Holy Thursday at the Mass of the Chrism, but it may have taken place at another time. The prohibition against using older oils outside of a case of necessity is repeated from the earlier law, but the eking out of diminished stocks of holy oils by adding unblessed oil to them, allowed by c.734 §2 of the 1917 Code, is no longer permitted.

Can. 847 §2 The parish priest is to obtain the holy oils from his own Bishop and keep them carefully in fitting custody.

1667 This requirement is a sign of the communion of the parishes in the diocese with the Bishop and with one another. The paragraph does not repeat the previous rather detailed instructions about the safe and reverent custody of the oils, but states simply that the parish priest should 'keep them carefully in fitting custody'. In carrying out this obligation he should bear in mind that the reverent custody of the *olea sacra* has a very long tradition in the Church – as anyone who has visited the many still-extant medieval churches and monasteries throughout Europe will have witnessed. Can. 1003 §3 specifically allows any priest to carry the oil of the sick on his person, or e.g. in his car, but even then he should be clear that it is not 'just another piece of equipment': it belongs to the realm of the sacred.

Can. 848 For the administration of the sacraments the minister may not ask for anything beyond the offerings which are determined by the competent authority, and he must always ensure that the needy are not deprived of the help of the sacraments by reason of poverty.

1668 This canon replaces c.736 of the 1917 Code. It forbids the minister even to seek, let alone to demand, anything beyond the legally established offerings. The offerings on the occasion of administering the sacraments (and sacramentals) are to be determined by the provincial Bishops' meeting; this includes also offerings made for funerals (see Cann. 1264, 1181). Offerings for the celebration and application of Mass are to be determined by the provincial council, the provincial Bishops' meeting or by diocesan custom (see Can. 952 §§1 and 2). The final clause of the canon is new; it warns against the danger that the needy be deprived of the sacraments because of their poverty. This could well require priests in some cases to seek out and to offer the sacraments to people who are ashamed to ask for them because of their inability to make the customary offering.

---

[1] This change was introduced by the SCDW in the *Rite for the Blessing of Oils* 3.XII.1970: DOL n.3863. The ap con *Sacram Unctionem Infirmorum* 30.XI.1972 confirmed the change: DOL n.3317.

Part I The Sacraments

Title I
Baptism

Can. 849 Baptism, the gateway to the sacraments, is necessary for salvation, either by actual reception or at least by desire. By it people are freed from sins, are born again as children of God and, made like to Christ by an indelible character, are incorporated into the Church. It is validly conferred only by a washing in real water with the proper form of words.

This canon, which replaces and amplifies c.737 §1 of the 1917 Code, provides a brief theological introduction to the legislation on baptism. It deals with the necessity of baptism, its effects and the elements needed for its valid conferral. 1669

Baptism is necessary for salvation 'either by actual reception or at least by desire'. This has been the constant teaching of the Church.[1] It should be noted, however, that baptism of desire, although it suffices for salvation and does produce a special bond with the Church (see Can. 206), does not produce the juridical effects of actual reception of the sacrament. 1670

The effects of baptism are to free people from their sins,[2] to give them rebirth as children of God, by an indelible character to make them like to Christ (see Can. 845), and to incorporate them into the Church. By incorporation into the Church a person becomes the subject of the juridical rights and duties of a member of Christ's faithful. These juridical effects of baptism are not something added to its theological effects but flow directly from them. 1671

Two requirements for the valid conferral of baptism are given in this canon, 'a washing in real water' and 'the proper form of words'. The term 'real water' replaces the expression 'real and natural water' of c.737 §1 of the 1917 Code. The suppression of the word 'natural' serves to remove any doubt about the validity of e.g. distilled water. Any real water, or even a mixture of water and other substances, provided that water predominates and the mixture would be commonly considered as water, suffices for validity.[3] In the latin Church the proper form of words is 'I baptise you in the name of the Father, and of the Son, and of the Holy Spirit'. This canon does not mention the intention of either the minister or the recipient of the sacrament, both of which also affect validity: see Cann. 869 §2, 861 §2. 1672

The distinction in c.737 §2 of the 1917 Code between *solemn* and *non-solemn* or *private* baptism no longer exists. 1673

Chapter I
THE CELEBRATION OF BAPTISM

Can. 850 Baptism is administered according to the rite prescribed in the approved liturgical books, except in a case of urgent necessity when only those elements which are required for the validity of the sacrament must be observed.

---

[1] Cf. Council of Trent Sess. VI *de iustificatione* Can. 4; CCC nn.1213, 1226 and, in respect of infants who die without baptism, n.1261.

[2] Cf. Romans c.6; Nicene Creed: 'We acknowledge one baptism for the forgiveness of sins'.

[3] Cf. Iorio III 29–30.

1674 The approved liturgical books are *The Rite of Baptism for Children* (1973)[1] and *The Rite of Christian Initiation of Adults* (1972)[2] and the adaptations of these made by Bishops' Conferences for their own areas. Both documents give shorter rites for use in danger of death and other circumstances, and these should be used if possible. In cases of 'urgent necessity' when even the shorter forms of the rite cannot be used, only the elements needed for validity, as given in Can. 849, need be observed: thus e.g. in imminent danger of death, in time of persecution or in other circumstances which would make the full celebration of the rite impossible or dangerous.

Can. 851 The celebration of baptism should be properly prepared. Accordingly:

1° an adult who intends to receive baptism is to be admitted to the catechumenate and, as far as possible, brought through the various stages to sacramental initiation, in accordance with the rite of initiation as adapted by the Bishops' Conference and with the particular norms issued by it;

2° the parents of a child who is to be baptised, and those who are to undertake the office of sponsors, are to be suitably instructed on the meaning of this sacrament and the obligations attaching to it. The parish priest is to see to it that either he or others duly prepare the parents, by means of pastoral advice and indeed by communal prayer, bringing a number of families together, and, where possible, visiting them.

1675 This canon, which enjoins proper preparation for baptism, is almost totally new: the 1917 Code in c.752 §1 contented itself with ruling that an adult should be 'properly instructed' before receiving baptism. The present law reflects the restoration of the catechumenate by Vat. II[3] and, in the case of children, a concern for the preparation of those who will have the primary responsibility for the development of the children's faith. This latter has vital pastoral implications in many parts of the Church today, not least in the so-called developed countries. In a number of these – especially if they have had a 'catholic tradition' – the baptism of children can be almost taken for granted, with little active realisation of the profoundly fundamental consequences of this sacrament for the faith and the ensuing Christian life of the children. This canon is a salutary reminder to parents, to sponsors, to priests and to all who may be involved.

1676 The canon summarises the steps to be taken in the preparation of both adults and infants, which are given in detail in *The Rite of Christian Initiation of Adults* and in *The Rite of Baptism for Children*. An adult is to be admitted to the catechumenate and, as far as possible, brought through the various stages of the rite of initiation. Specific provision is made for the Bishops' Conference to adapt this rite to local circumstances. Cann. 788 and 789 also make rules regarding catechumens and describe their formation. In the preparation of parents and sponsors of children who are to be baptised, the primary responsibility falls on the parish priest, though he may fulfil this duty either personally or through others. In addition to assistant priests and religious working in the parish, other members of the community may be entrusted with this task: indeed this would be an obvious opportunity for the laity to exercise the functions mentioned in Cann. 225 §1 and 529 §2.

---

[1] Cf. DOL nn.2285–2315.
[2] Cf. DOL nn.2328–2488.
[3] Cf. SC 64–66, AGD 14: Fl I 21, 828–829.

Can. 852 §1 The provisions of the canons on adult baptism apply to all those who, having ceased to be infants, have reached the use of reason.

§2 One who is incapable of personal responsibility is regarded as an infant even in regard to baptism.

1677 An 'infant' is one who has not yet completed the seventh year of age; on attaining this age the person is presumed to have the use of reason (see Can. 97 §2). Before the age of seven, or even after it if the person has not in fact reached the use of reason, due e.g. to mental handicap, the rite to be observed is that for the baptism of infants. After that age, the rite is that for the baptism of adults. However *The Rite of Christian Initiation of Adults* contains specific directions for the adaptation of the rite for 'children of catechetical age' and allows for appropriate adaptations to particular circumstances.[1] Can. 863 requires that the baptism of those of fourteen years or over should be referred to the diocesan Bishop.

Can. 853 Apart from a case of necessity, the water to be used in conferring baptism is to be blessed, in accordance with the provisions of the liturgical books.

1678 The use of blessed water is for lawfulness only, not for validity, and in a case of necessity unblessed water may lawfully be used. The blessing of the water takes place within the rite of baptism itself, except in paschal time when the water blessed during the Easter Vigil should be used.[2] The water should be natural and clean and, if the weather is particularly cold, it should be slightly heated beforehand.[3]

Can. 854 Baptism is to be conferred either by immersion or by pouring, in accordance with the provisions of the Bishops' Conference.

1679 The 1917 Code in c.758 mentioned the possibility of baptism by immersion, pouring or sprinkling and, while allowing the validity of all three forms, directed that the first or second method or a combination of both should be used. The present canon suppresses any reference to baptism by sprinkling[4] so that baptism by this method would be unlawful though, presumably, valid. It prescribes baptism by immersion or pouring, leaving it to the Bishops' Conference to determine whether one method or the other or both are to be used.

Can. 855 Parents, sponsors and parish priests are to take care that a name is not given which is foreign to christian sentiment.

1680 This canon allows rather greater freedom in the choice of a name than did the corresponding c.761 of the 1917 Code. The previous law obliged the parish priest to see that the person being baptised was given a christian name and, if this were not possible, he was to add a saint's name to that chosen by the parents. The present law allows any name to be given which is not 'foreign to christian sentiment', and it puts the obligation for this successively on the parents, the sponsors and the parish priest. What is acceptable will vary somewhat from one culture to another. So, to call a boy 'Jesus' is quite acceptable in some cultures, while in others it would offend christian sensibilities; a name like 'Satan' would certainly be foreign to any form of christian culture.

Can. 856 Though baptism may be celebrated on any day, it is recommended that normally it be celebrated on a Sunday or, if possible, on the vigil of Easter.

---

[1] Cf. DOL nn.2458–2475.
[2] Cf. SC 70: Fl I 22.
[3] Cf. GICI 18, 20: Fl II 26.
[4] Cf. Comm 13(1981) 216–217.

Book IV The Sanctifying Office of the Church

1681 Baptism may be conferred on any day, but a certain preference is given to Sundays and to the Easter Vigil as both of these are celebrations of the Lord's resurrection.[1] A proposal to give priority to the Easter Vigil over Sundays was rejected, because it is not the customary time at which baptism is administered and because of the prescription of Can. 867 which requires that infants be baptised within the first few weeks of life.[2] On Sundays baptism may be celebrated during Mass, but this should not be done too often.[3] In the case of adult baptism (and the other sacraments of initiation) a definite preference is given in the liturgical text to the Easter Vigil, and other times are seen as exceptional.[4] In all of this matter, however, an always relevant factor must be the established pastoral practice of the place or region, whether this arises from custom or from the regulations of either the Bishops' Conference or the diocesan Bishop.

Can. 857 §1 Apart from a case of necessity, the proper place for baptism is a church or an oratory.

1682 This and the three canons which follow it determine the place of baptism and correspond, with some changes, to cc. 773–776 of the 1917 Code. This paragraph lays down the general principle that baptism is to be conferred in a church or oratory, a sole exception being made for 'a case of necessity', e.g. danger of death, illness, lack of a church or oratory in the place (see Can. 860 §1).

Can. 857 §2 As a rule and unless a just reason suggests otherwise, an adult is to be baptised in his or her proper parish church, and an infant in the proper parish church of the parents.

1683 This paragraph determines what church should be used. For adults it is the person's proper parish church, i.e. the church of the parish where he or she has a domicile or quasi-domicile (see Cann. 102 and 107); for children it is the proper parish church of the parents (see Cann. 101 and 105). The parish church of the individual is prescribed because incorporation into the church is made by incorporation into the local community of which the parish church is the centre. However exceptions to this general rule are allowed for 'a just reason', such as distance from the parish church, grave inconvenience in a particular case or even a well-founded pastoral reason. The case of baptism being conferred by a Bishop in the cathedral church is not a real exception, since he is the pastor for the whole diocese.

Can. 858 §1 Each parish church is to have a baptismal font, without prejudice to the same right already acquired by other churches.

1684 Here is emphasised the primacy of the parish church as the place of baptism, while respecting the rights that other churches within the parish may have 'acquired' (see Can. 4). Such rights cannot, however, exclude the right of the parish church to have its own baptismal font.

Can. 858 §2 The local Ordinary, after consultation with the local parish priest, may for the convenience of the faithful permit or order that a baptismal font be placed also in another church or oratory within the parish.

1685 This permits the local Ordinary to authorise or even to order the placing of a font in another church or oratory within the parish boundaries 'for the convenience of the

---

[1] Cf. IRIB 9: Fl II 32.
[2] Cf. Comm 15(1983) 179 at Can. 810.
[3] Cf. IRIB 9: Fl II 32.
[4] Cf. *Rite of Christian Initiation of Adults* 49–62: DOL nn.2376–2389.

faithful'. He must first consult the local parish priest. 'Normally, it is for the parish priest to celebrate the sacrament in those places too.'[1] Among the possible circumstances which would justify such a step would be the size of the parish in question, or the existence within it of different ethnic groups.

Can. 859 If, because of distance or other circumstances, the person to be baptised cannot without grave inconvenience go or be brought to the parish church or the oratory mentioned in Can. 858 §2, baptism may and must be conferred in some other church or oratory which is nearer, or even in some other fitting place.

If there is grave inconvenience in using the parish church or the alternative church or oratory mentioned in Can. 858 §2, because of the distance involved or other circumstances such as serious illness, then baptism may and must be conferred preferably in another church or oratory which is more convenient, or even in another suitable place. The addition of the last location was made to take account of the needs of mission territories,[2] but corresponding needs elsewhere would also justify the use of such a place. However, it is to be noted that the alternatives allowed in this canon are exceptions to the general rule that baptism is to be conferred in the parish church, and that they can be justified only by 'grave inconvenience'. 1686

Can. 860 §1 Apart from a case of necessity, baptism is not to be conferred in private houses, unless the local Ordinary should for a grave reason permit it.

This explicitly forbids the use of private houses for the conferring of baptism unless in a case of necessity or when the local Ordinary has given permission 'for a grave reason'. A merely social reason would never be a sufficient justification. This prohibition effectively excludes a private house from being automatically regarded as a 'fitting place' under Can. 859. 1687

Can. 860 §2 Unless the diocesan Bishop has decreed otherwise, baptism is not to be conferred in hospital, except in a case of necessity or for some other pressing pastoral reason.

Because in some countries children are usually born in hospitals or nursing homes, the practice had grown up of baptising them there; in some places indeed it was exceptional for a child to be baptised in his or her own parish. This paragraph takes note of that practice and, in order to protect the primacy of the parish church as the place of baptism, prohibits it, except in three cases, namely: where the diocesan Bishop has decreed otherwise, a case of necessity such as danger of death, some other pressing pastoral reason. No particular restrictions are put on the Bishop's powers in this matter, but he must have regard to the general rule of Can. 857 §2. 1688

To summarise:

(a) Apart from a case of necessity, baptism should be conferred in a church or oratory (Can. 857 §1). 1689
(b) Unless there is a just reason to the contrary, the church should be the proper parish church of the person to be baptised (Can. 857 §2).
(c) If there is such a just reason, the church may be the alternative church designated by the local Ordinary (Can. 858 §2), or a church within the the parish which already has an acquired right to a baptismal font (Can. 858 §1).

---

[1] IRIB 11: Fl II 32.
[2] Comm 13(1981) 218 at Can. 34.

(d) If there is grave inconvenience involved in using the churches or oratories mentioned in (b) and (c) above, baptism may and must be conferred in a nearer church or oratory or even in some other fitting place (Can. 859).

(e) In a case of necessity baptism can be conferred anywhere (Cann. 857 §1, 860 §§ 1, 2).

(f) Baptism in private houses or in hospitals is forbidden except in cases of necessity or in the other cases detailed in Can. 860.

Chapter II
THE MINISTER OF BAPTISM

Can. 861 §1 The ordinary minister of baptism is a Bishop, a priest or a deacon, without prejudice to the provision of Can. 530 n.1.

1690 In contrast to the 1917 Code which named only a priest as the ordinary minister of baptism and designated a deacon as an extraordinary minister,[1] the present law names as ordinary minister a Bishop, a priest or a deacon. The reference to Can. 530 1°, which numbers the conferring of baptism among the functions especially entrusted to the parish priest, re-emphasises the importance of the parochial community as the one through which a person is incorporated into the Church. Practical considerations will usually make it impossible for the Bishop to confer baptism on more than a small number of his people. He will normally baptise infants only on special occasions, such as the Easter Vigil or possibly on the occasion of officially visiting a parish. As regards the baptism of those over the age of fourteen, Can. 863 has a special norm.

Can. 861 §2 If the ordinary minister is absent or impeded, a catechist or some other person deputed to this office by the local Ordinary, may lawfully confer baptism; indeed, in a case of necessity, any person who has the requisite intention may do so. Pastors of souls, especially parish priests, are to be diligent in ensuring that Christ's faithful are taught the correct way to baptise.

1691 This paragraph introduces an important innovation in the law. It allows the designation of lay persons as stable extraordinary ministers of baptism when the ordinary minister is absent or impeded. Catechists are mentioned in the canon explicitly but not exclusively. Their appointment to this ministry is particularly appropriate in view of their function in instructing adult catechumens and in preparing the families of infants who are to be baptised. Others who could appropriately be appointed would be those who similarly help in such instruction in accordance with Can. 851, particularly those who, because of a shortage of priests, are given 'a share in the exercise of the pastoral care of a parish' in accordance with Can. 517 §2. In a case of necessity any person, even one who is not baptised, can confer baptism, provided he or she has the requisite intention: the minimum required is the 'intention of doing what the Church does'.[2]

1692 There are special forms of the rite of baptism for adults in danger of death,[3] for the baptism of children by a catechist[4] and for the baptism of children in danger of death in the absence of the ordinary minister.[5] Of at least as much practical importance is

---

[1] 1917 Code cc. 738 §1, 742 §2.
[2] Cf. e.g. Iorio 35.
[3] Cf. DOL nn.2442–2446.
[4] Cf. DOL n.2304.
[5] Cf. DOL n.2305.

Part I The Sacraments

that priests 'be diligent in ensuring that Christ's faithful are taught the correct way to baptise': it would surely help the faithful, especially for occasions of emergency, if this were done, by way of a few words in a homily or otherwise, say once or twice a year.

Can. 862 Except in a case of necessity, it is unlawful for anyone without due permission to confer baptism outside his own territory, not even upon his own subjects.

This canon clearly has in mind an ordinary minister of baptism in accordance with Can. 861 §1. Occasionally a priest, or even a Bishop, is for one good reason or another asked to baptise either a child or an adult in a parish or a diocese other than his own. This regulation is to remind him that, 'apart from a case of necessity', as e.g. an unforeseen emergency, he requires 'due permission', i.e. the permission of whoever would otherwise be the ordinary minister. In effect and in pastoral practice, this will normally mean a courteous consultation in advance with the parochial clergy. *Inter alia* the rule is designed to underline that of Can. 857 §2 and to safeguard the registration of the baptism as required by Cann. 877–878.

1693

Can. 863 The baptism of adults, at least of those who have completed their fourteenth year, is to be referred to the diocesan Bishop, so that he himself may confer it if he judges this appropriate.

Bishops 'are in charge ... of the administration of baptism' and 'the baptism of adults and their preparation for it is especially commended to them'.[1] This canon repeats the substance of c.744 of the 1917 Code, with the addition of the reference to those of fourteen years and over. The obligation to refer baptisms to the diocesan Bishop applies only when the person to be baptised has reached the age of fourteen, but this does not take from the Bishop's responsibility towards those of a lower age, much less does it prevent such baptisms being referred to him (see Can. 861 §1). In practice, a Bishop could, if he considered it appropriate, adopt a general policy regarding the baptism of adults, leaving these to the ordinary ministers at parish level.

1694

Chapter III
THE PERSONS TO BE BAPTISED

Can. 864 Every unbaptised person, and only such a person, can be baptised.

All human beings (including the unborn) can be baptised, but only if they have not already been validly baptised. Christ commanded his apostles to 'make disciples of all the nations; baptise them in the name of the Father and of the Son and of the Holy Spirit'.[2] Baptism cannot be repeated because of the indelible character it imprints (see Can. 845 §1). Can. 869 deals with cases where the baptism or its validity is doubtful.

1695

Can. 865 §1 To be admitted to baptism, an adult must have manifested the intention to receive baptism, must be adequately instructed in the truths of the faith and in the duties of a christian, and tested in the christian life over the course of the catechumenate. The person must moreover be urged to have sorrow for personal sins.

---

[1] GICI 12: Fl II 25.

[2] Matt 28:19.

1696 This canon refers only to the baptism of adults, i.e. in this context, those who have attained the use of reason (see Can. 852). The first paragraph deals with normal circumstances, the second with cases where there is danger of death.

1697 This paragraph expands on the requirements of c.752 §1 of the 1917 Code. Under normal circumstances the person to be baptised must have the intention to be baptised, must be properly instructed, must have undergone probation in the catechumenate (see Can. 851), and is to be urged to sorrow for personal sins. The absence of the proper intention, i.e. the intention to receive and accept this sacrament as it is understood by the Church, would render the baptism invalid – a point to be borne in mind when another motivation, such e.g. as an impending marriage, may also be operative.

Can. 865 §2 An adult in danger of death may be baptised if, with some knowledge of the principal truths of the faith, he or she has in some manner manifested the intention to receive baptism and promises to observe the requirements of the christian religion.

1698 In danger of death the requirements are not so stringent, but the essentials must still be observed. These are:

(a) 'some knowledge of the principal truths of the faith'. The canon does not detail what these are, but it would be sufficient that the person profess at least a general belief in God, in Jesus Christ and in the truths taught by the Church.

(b) the intention, shown explicitly or implicitly, even at some time in the past, of being baptised. A person cannot be lawfully or validly baptised against his or her will.

(c) a promise, which may be implicit, to live the life of a Christian.

The Rite of Christian Initiation of Adults lays down similar requirements, and it adds that 'the person must also make a promise to go through the complete cycle of initiation upon recovering'.[1] The imposition of this last obligation will, of course, depend upon the circumstances of each individual case.

Can. 866 Unless there is a grave reason to the contrary, immediately after receiving baptism an adult is to be confirmed, to participate in the celebration of the Eucharist and to receive holy communion.

1699 This canon, which refers only to *adults*, gives practical effect to the principle enunciated in Can. 842 §2 which requires baptism, confirmation and the Eucharist for full christian initiation. C.753 §2 of the 1917 Code contained a similar rule but did not oblige the reception of confirmation at this time. The three sacraments are conferred within the same rite and the requirement that the person 'participate in the celebration of the Eucharist' emphasises that the rite normally takes place during the Easter Vigil or during a ritual Mass at another time.[2] If it is a priest who confers the baptism, he can also confer confirmation (see Can. 883 2°). That the obligation imposed by this canon is a serious one can be seen from the present text which changed the 'just reason' required in the 1980 draft to 'grave reason'.[3]

Can. 867 §1 Parents are obliged to see that their infants are baptised within the first few weeks. As soon as possible after the birth, indeed even before it, they are to approach the parish priest to ask for the sacrament for their child, and to be themselves duly prepared for it.

---

[1] DOL n.2443. Cf. CCC n.1248.
[2] DOL nn.2423–2424.
[3] Cf. Comm 15(1983) 181 at Can. 820.

Part I The Sacraments

§2 If the infant is in danger of death, it is to be baptised without any delay.

'The Church ... has baptised not only adults but children as well from the earliest times.'[1] The present canon reflects that tradition and lays down the rules governing when an infant is to be baptised under normal circumstances (§1) and in danger of death (§2). Under normal circumstances an infant is to be baptised 'within the first few weeks'. This is a change from the norm of c.770 of the 1917 Code which demanded that infants be baptised 'as soon as possible'. This may reflect the fact that in many countries the rate of infant mortality is much lower than it used to be, but more importantly it enables both parents to be present at the ceremony[2] and it allows time for the parents, the sponsors and the family to be prepared for the baptism in accordance with Can. 851 2°. In order to ensure that there is sufficient time for this preparation, the parents are to approach a priest of the parish as soon as possible after the birth; indeed they are well advised, where possible, to approach him even before the birth. The Bishops' Conference may make regulations determining a longer interval between birth and baptism for special reasons.[3] An infant who is in danger of death is to be baptised without any delay. This is because of the necessity of baptism for supernatural life and for salvation (see Can. 849).

Can. 868 §1 For an infant to be baptised lawfully it is required:

1° **that the parents, or at least one of them, or the person who lawfully holds their place, give their consent;**

2° **that there be a realistic hope that the child will be brought up in the catholic religion. If such hope is truly lacking, the baptism is, in accordance with the provisions of particular law, to be deferred and the parents advised of the reason for this.**

In stating requirements for the lawful baptism of infants, this canon again distinguishes between normal cases and cases of danger of death. Under normal circumstances, the consent of the infant's parents or of those who take the parents' place, e.g. guardians or other such, is strictly required. This absolutely prohibits baptising children without the permission of at least one parent or equivalent, or without his or her knowledge. In addition to this consent, there must also be a 'realistic hope that the child will be brought up in the catholic religion'. Such a hope is easily verified when the parents are practising catholics, or where other family members or the sponsors or other members of the local community can give reliable assurances to this effect.[4]

If these assurances are not forthcoming or are judged to be inadequate, then the baptism is to be deferred 'in accordance with the provisions of particular law' and the parents are to be advised of the reason for this. Particular law here would include a law made by a diocesan Bishop for his diocese or by a particular Council for its territory, and also include a general decree made by the Bishops' Conference in accordance with Can. 455. In the absence of any particular law on the matter, the individual priest must himself take a firm pastoral stand, even in the face of strong opposition, on the basic theological principle which is involved in the conferral of baptism. This will be particularly so if he knows – as can unhappily be the case in some current circumstances – that the request for a child's baptism is little if anything

---

[1] IRIB 2: Fl II 29. Cf. CCC n.1250.
[2] Cf. IRIB 8: Fl II 31.
[3] Cf. IRIB 8: Fl II 31; IRIB 25: DOL n.2309.
[4] Cf. SCDF rep 13.VII.1970: DOL n.2318; IIB 30: Fl II 113.

more than a desire to meet a social convention, or to pacify the sensitivities of others such e.g. as grandparents. This is a task which will always call for a delicate balance between firmness and genuine pastoral concern. On occasion, a particularly intractable case may have to be referred to the diocesan Bishop.

1703 The canon speaks only of deferral of baptism in such cases; it does not speak of refusal. The *Instruction on Infant Baptism* does indeed speak of the possibility of the refusal of the sacrament where assurances about the child's catholic upbringing are 'certainly non-existent'.[1] It makes it clear, however, that such refusal is not a means of bringing pressure to bear on the parents or a form of discrimination, but is really an 'educational delay ... aimed at helping the family to grow in faith or to become more aware of its responsibilities'.[2] If, however, despite the 'educational delay' and the pastoral steps taken during it, it is certain that the child will not be educated as a catholic, then the deferral of baptism may have to be indefinite – while, if at all possible, leaving open the door to a future change of heart.[3]

Can. 868 §2 An infant of catholic parents, indeed even of non-catholic parents, is lawfully baptised in danger of death, even if the parents are opposed to it.

1704 An infant in danger of death is lawfully baptised even if the parents are opposed to this. In danger of death, the will of God that all be baptised and the consequent entitlement of the child to baptism, take precedence over the parents' rights. The 1980 draft of this canon had limited this norm with a clause excluding cases where such a baptism could cause a hatred (*odium*) of religion, but the Commission dropped this clause, deciding that such hatred would be a 'lesser evil'.[4] The Code does not prescribe baptism in such circumstances; it permits it. In some countries or regions it may be wise or even necessary to bear in mind the civil law, or the custom-based, implications of baptising a child against the wishes of its parents.

Can. 869 §1 If there is doubt as to whether a person was baptised or whether a baptism was conferred validly, and after serious enquiry this doubt persists, the person is to be baptised conditionally.

1705 Baptism cannot be received a second time, but in a case of doubt it is celebrated conditionally (see Can. 845). The present canon gives the rules for such conditional celebration. Although the wording of this paragraph positively enjoins conditional baptism in certain circumstances, the remainder of the canon and the statement of Can. 845 make it quite clear that conditional baptism is the exception rather than the rule. 'Indiscriminate conditional baptism of all who desire full communion with the Catholic Church cannot be approved.'[5]

1706 The rule is that if, after a serious enquiry, a doubt remains either about the fact of baptism or the validity of a baptism which was certainly conferred, then the person is to be baptised conditionally. Doubt about the fact of baptism may arise from e.g. the non-availability of baptismal records or even the failure to register a baptism. In that event witnesses such as parents, sponsors or the minister may be able to dispel the doubt (see Can. 876) and, if available, they should be sought out. If the doubt concerns the validity of the baptism, the enquiry should investigate the matters raised in §2 of this canon.

---

[1] IIB 28 (2): Fl II 112.
[2] Ibid. 31: 113.
[3] Ibid. 30, 31: 113–114.
[4] Comm 15(1983) 182 at Can. 822 §2.
[5] DEM 14: Fl 1 489.

Part I The Sacraments

Can. 869 §2 Those baptised in a non-catholic ecclesial community are not to be baptised conditionally unless there is a serious reason for doubting the validity of their baptism, on the ground of the matter or the form of words used in the baptism, or of the intention of the adult being baptised or of that of the baptising minister.

This paragraph deals with those already baptised in 'a non-catholic ecclesial community'. It does not apply to those baptised in the Orthodox Churches;[1] their baptism is recognised as valid.[2] No such general recognition is given to other churches or ecclesial communities, although local recognition may have been given.[3] Of relevance too is a reply of the Holy Office in 1949 which declared that, assuming the necessary matter and form, 'in adjudicating matrimonial cases, baptism given by the Disciples of Christ, the Presbyterians, the Congregationalists, the Baptists, the Methodists ... is to be presumed valid, unless the contrary is proved in a particular case', i.e. unless it is proved that the minister's intention was defective.[4] *A fortiori* the situation would be the same in respect of the Anglican Communion. In the case of other ecclesial communities the position may be less clear and should therefore be investigated in each case.[5]

1707

The rule is that those already baptised are *not* to be baptised conditionally *unless* there is a serious doubt about the validity of their baptism arising from:

1708

(a) the matter (water), or the form of words used: e.g. there have been reports of a form such as ' ... in the name of the Creator, the Redeemer and the Sanctifier' being used, to avoid so-called 'sexist' language: such a formula would be invalid, since it does not expressly refer to the Three Persons of the blessed Trinity.

(b) the intention of the person being baptised, if that person was an adult (see Can. 865 §1).

(c) the intention of the minister.

The reason for this prohibition is two-fold: firstly, valid baptism cannot be repeated; secondly, it helps in 'placing a proper value on the baptism conferred by ministers of the churches and ecclesial communities separated from us'.[6]

The canon does not determine what ceremonies are to be used in receiving baptised adults into the Church. The Appendix to the *Rite of Christian Initiation of Adults* directs that if baptism is to be given conditionally in such cases, it is to be given privately; it also directs that the local Ordinary is to determine in individual cases what rites are to be included or excluded. The local Ordinary and the Bishops' Conference may make appropriate adaptations to the rite to take account of various circumstances.[7]

1709

Can. 869 §3 If in the cases mentioned in §§ 1 and 2 a doubt remains about the conferring of the baptism or its validity, baptism is not to be conferred

---

[1] Cf. Comm 15(1983) 182 at Can. 823 §2.

[2] Cf. DEM 12: Fl 1 488.

[3] Cf. CLD 7 591, which reports mutual recognition between the catholic Church and various reformed Churches in Belgium and in the Philippines.

[4] AAS 41(1949) 650: CLD 3 423.

[5] An official Notification of 9.III.1991 by the Congregation for the Doctrine of the Faith declared to be invalid baptism conferred in the group known as 'Christian Community' (or 'Die Christengemeinschaft') of one Rudolf Steiner: AAS 83(1991) 422. A similar notification was issued on 20.XI.1992 in respect of 'The New Church' of one Emmanuel Swedenborg: AAS 85(1993) 179.

[6] DEM 18: Fl I 490.

[7] Cf. DOL nn.2482 and 2487.

until the doctrine of the sacrament of baptism is explained to the person to be baptised, if that person is an adult. Moreover, the reasons for doubting the validity of the earlier baptism should be given to the person or, where an infant is concerned, to the parents.

1710 In all cases of conditional baptism, the candidate is to be instructed in the doctrine of the sacrament and the reasons for the doubt concerning the validity of the earlier baptism are to be explained, to the candidate if he is an adult, to the parents in the case of children. As well as ensuring proper catechesis, this also promotes a proper respect for the beliefs and practices of other Christians.

Can. 870 An abandoned infant or a foundling is to be baptised unless diligent enquiry establishes that it has already been baptised.

1711 This canon repeats the norm of c.749 of the 1917 Code but suppresses any mention of conditional baptism. If a diligent enquiry – as diligent as can reasonably be made in such circumstances – fails to show that an abandoned infant or a foundling has been baptised, the child is to be presumed as not having been baptised and is therefore to be baptised unconditionally. Outside of danger of death, however, the prescription of Can. 868 §1 2° must be observed, i.e. the child should not be baptised unless there is a realistic hope that it will be brought up in the catholic religion.

Can. 871 Aborted foetuses, if they are alive, are to be baptised, in so far as this is possible.

1712 Like the preceding one this canon repeats a prescription of the 1917 Code (c. 747) and suppresses any mention of conditional baptism. A foetus which is aborted, whether naturally or intentionally, is to be baptised unconditionally if it is alive and if this is possible. Since the matter is a serious one, a minor degree of inconvenience would not eliminate this obligation. If there is a doubt as to whether or not the foetus is alive, it should be baptised. The prescription of Can. 861 §2, which enjoins the instruction of the faithful in the correct way to baptise, receives special point here in reference to parents, doctors, midwives, nurses and others who might be present.

1713 The detailed instructions of cc.746 and 748 of the 1917 Code about baptism *in utero* or during labour, and about the baptism of abnormal foetuses, are not repeated. Baptism in such cases is left to prudent pastoral judgement.

Chapter IV
SPONSORS

Can. 872 In so far as possible, a person being baptised is to be assigned a sponsor. In the case of an adult baptism, the sponsor's role is to assist the person in christian initiation. In the case of an infant baptism, the role is together with the parents to present the child for baptism, and to help it to live a christian life befitting the baptised and faithfully to fulfil the duties inherent in baptism.

1714 From early times it has been the practice in the Church to assign a sponsor or godparent to everyone being baptised. The present Code continues that tradition and describes briefly the function of the sponsor in the case of adult baptism and in the case of infant baptism. The General Introduction to Christian Initiation gives fuller directives on these functions.[1]

1715 This canon and the two which follow represent a simplification of the eight canons (cc.762–769) of the 1917 Code which governed the same matter. Because there is now no direct canonical consequence arising from sponsorship – unlike the previous law (cc.768, 1079) where it induced a spiritual relationship which gave rise to a matrimonial impediment – there are no longer any prescriptions for valid sponsorship. A person who is to be baptised is to be assigned a sponsor 'in so far as possible'. Under normal circumstances this will always be possible, but in danger of death or other similar difficult circumstances it may not be.

Can. 873 One sponsor, male or female, is sufficient; but there may be two, one of each sex.

1716 This canon repeats the substance of c.764 of the 1917 Code and excludes the multiplication of sponsors. One person is sufficient and, if there is only one, that person may be of either sex. If there are two, one should be male, the other female. Any additional persons would be witnesses, not sponsors.

Can. 874 §1 To be admitted to undertake the office of sponsor, a person must:

1° be appointed by the candidate for baptism, or by the parents or whoever stands in their place, or failing these, by the parish priest or the minister; to be appointed the person must be suitable for this role and have the intention of fulfilling it;

1717 Who is to appoint a sponsor? An adult appoints his or her own sponsor. In the case of an infant, the sponsor is chosen by the parents or those who take their place; failing these, the parish priest or the minister makes the appointment. Only those suitable for the role may be chosen: 2°–4° below list the necessary qualifications, some positive, some negative. The *Rite of Christian Initiation* states that the sponsor is to be 'approved by the priest'.[2] The sponsor must accept his or her role with 'the intention of fulfilling it': by accepting this role a sponsor undertakes a serious religious duty; the task should never even appear to be reduced to one of mere social convention.

2° be not less than sixteen years of age, unless a different age has been stipulated by the diocesan Bishop, or unless the parish priest or the minister considers that there is a just reason for an exception to be made.

1718 The general rule about the age of the sponsor is that he or she must be not less than sixteen years of age. However, the diocesan Bishop may by regulation determine a different age, and the parish priest or the minister may make an exception for a good reason in individual cases, e.g. in some situations a younger person, perhaps even one of the family, might be considered an appropriate sponsor; this however should never be done for a merely frivolous or social reason.

3° be a catholic who has been confirmed and has received the blessed Eucharist, and who lives a life of faith which befits the role to be undertaken;

4° not labour under a canonical penalty, whether imposed or declared;

---

[1] GICI 8–10: Fl II 24–25.
[2] DOL n.2370.

1719 The sponsor must be a catholic who has received all three sacraments of christian initiation, and must moreover live 'a life of faith which befits the role to be undertaken'. Obviously, one who has not been fully initiated cannot appropriately testify to a catechumen's faith and goodness of life or, in the case of infant baptism, properly assist the parents in the catholic upbringing of the child. The same is true of one who does not practise his or her faith, and of one under a canonical penalty. Local legislation may determine more specifically the qualities necessary in a sponsor.[1]

5° not be either the father or the mother of the person to be baptised;

1720 Both parents of the person to be baptised are disqualified from being sponsors. This is in accordance with traditional practice, and moreover it emphasises the 'more important ministry and role in the baptism of children' that natural parents have over godparents.[2] The disqualifications in the 1917 Code of spouses of the candidates, of those in sacred orders and of religious, are no longer applicable.

Can. 874 §2 A baptised person who belongs to a non-catholic ecclesial community may be admitted only in company with a catholic sponsor, and then simply as a witness to the baptism.

1721 Because 'a godparent is not merely undertaking his responsibility for the christian education of the person baptised (or confirmed) as a relation or friend' but 'is also, as a representative of a community of faith, standing as sponsor for the faith of the candidate',[3] a member of a non-catholic ecclesial community may not act as a sponsor. However, such a person may be admitted as a christian witness to the baptism, provided that there is a catholic sponsor. This paragraph, speaking as it does of 'ecclesial community', does not apply to the eastern Orthodox Churches. A member of one of these may be admitted as a sponsor together with a catholic, as is explicitly allowed in the *Directory concerning Ecumenical Matters*.[4]

Chapter V
PROOF AND REGISTRATION OF BAPTISM

Can. 875 Whoever administers baptism is to take care that if there is not a sponsor present, there is at least one witness who can prove that the baptism was conferred.

Can. 876 To prove that baptism has been conferred, if there is no conflict of interest, it is sufficient to have either one unexceptionable witness or, if the baptism was conferred upon an adult, the sworn testimony of the baptised person.

1722 Because baptism has serious juridical consequences, its proof is a matter of distinct importance. Ordinarily, proof will be by means of an authentic copy of the entry in

---

[1] Cf. Comm 15(1983) 184 at Can. 830 §1 n.3.

[2] Cf. IRIB 5: Fl II 30.

[3] DEM 57: Fl I 500.

[4] DEM 48: Fl I 497. Cf. Comm 15(1983) 184 at Can. 828, where the suppression of the explicit mention of this in earlier schemata of the Code is explained: 'It does not seem necessary to express this in a Code for the latin Church'.

the baptismal register. These two canons provide for the case where, for whatever reason, this is not available. One of the functions of a sponsor is to witness to the baptism; if there is no sponsor, the minister is to ensure that a suitable witness is present. The testimony of one such unexceptionable witness, or even of the baptised person if he or she was baptised as an adult, is sufficient proof in normal circumstances. Where, however, there is 'a conflict of interest', further proof may in some circumstances be necessary. Such a conflict would arise when the determination as to whether a person was baptised or not is essential to the solution of a problem or of a controverted matter, e.g. in a case of the Pauline privilege (see Can. 1143 §1). Photographs and similar mementoes could provide an element of proof if not even one witness was available.

Can. 877 §1 The parish priest of the place in which the baptism was conferred must carefully and without delay record in the register of baptism the names of the baptised, the minister, the parents, the sponsors and, if there were such, the witnesses, and the place and date of baptism. He must also enter the date and place of birth.

In addition to the entries required by the previous law (c.777 §1 of the 1917 Code) the register must also contain the date and place of birth, and the names of the witnesses mentioned in Can. 875 if there were such. Because the fact of baptism is so crucial and because the baptismal register will contain other important entries concerning the person's status (see Can. 535 §2), the entry must be made 'carefully and without delay'. The individual has a right in justice to have such an important document carefully preserved and kept up to date. The onus of ensuring that this is done falls on the parish priest of the place of baptism, even if he did not himself confer the sacrament; he may of course delegate the execution of the details to another reliable person.

Can. 877 §2 In the case of a child of an unmarried mother, the mother's name is to be entered if her maternity is publicly known or if, either in writing or before two witnesses, she freely asks that this be done. Similarly, the name of the father is to be entered, if his paternity is established either by some public document or by his own declaration in the presence of the parish priest and two witnesses. In all other cases, the name of the baptised person is to be registered, without any indication of the name of the father or of the parents.

This paragraph protects the reputation of the parents where the mother is unmarried. The mother's name is to be entered in the register only if her maternity is publicly known (i.e. by a substantial number of people), or if she freely asks that this be done either in writing or before two witnesses. In the case of the father the requirements are more strict, presumably because of a greater danger of error or deceit about the child's true paternity. His name may be entered only if his paternity is established either by a public document (which may be civil or ecclesiastical) or by his own declaration before the parish priest and two witnesses. If, in the case of either parent, the appropriate conditions are not fulfilled, then the name of the baptised person is to be recorded without any reference to the parents, even if the minister knows who the parents are, or who one of them is. The prescriptions of this paragraph, to which priests should pay a specially careful attention, could well have a serious civil-law relevance, especially in those countries where Church records may be subpoena'd as proof in e.g. a paternity suit.

Can. 877 §3 In the case of an adopted child, the names of the adopting parents are to be registered and, at least if this is done in the local civil registration, the names of the natural parents in accordance with §§ 1 and 2, subject however to the rulings of the Bishops' Conference.

1725 This regulation about adopted children is a new and a very important one. Firstly, the names of the adopting parents are to be entered in the baptismal register. This will involve making a change to the register itself, or at least an addition to it. Whether the names of the natural parents are to be entered will depend (a) on whether they have already been entered, or can be entered, in accordance with §§ 1 and 2; (b) on whether such entries are made in the local civil registration; (c) on the ruling of the local Bishops' Conference. In view of the especial accuracy and delicacy required here, the practical pastoral rule is that every priest faced with this situation should, as a first essential, acquaint himself with the regulation in this regard made by his own Bishops' Conference[1] – a matter on which he may, if needs be, seek the advice of his own diocesan curia.

Can. 878 If the baptism was administered neither by the parish priest nor in his presence, the minister of baptism, whoever that was, must notify the parish priest of the parish in which the baptism was administered, so that he may register the baptism in accordance with Can. 877 §1.

1726 The onus of ensuring the entry is always on the parish priest of the place of baptism. Where he does not confer the sacrament himself or witness it, this canon obliges the minister to notify him so that he can carry out his task. This will be of particular relevance where the baptism takes place somewhere other than in the parish church (see also Can. 862).

Title II
The Sacrament of Confirmation

INTRODUCTION

1727 A proper understanding of the present-day practice with regard to each sacrament must take into account both its original institution and its subsequent historical development. This is particularly true in the case of the sacrament of confirmation, whose separation from baptism is closely bound up with the development of the catechumenate in the Church. In the early Church, as is clear from such texts as the 3rd-century Apostolic Tradition of Hippolytus,[2] there was a close relationship between baptism, confirmation and the Eucharist – a relationship which indeed is recalled in Can. 842 §2. A detailed analysis of the development of the catechumenate is clearly beyond the scope of this work. However, generally speaking, it can be said that the Western Church, in maintaining a necessary link between the Bishop and the minister of confirmation, effectively separated this sacrament from baptism. With the spread of the Church out of the cities and into rural areas, it was no longer physically possible for the Bishop to be at hand to confirm the newly baptised, and so confirmation was deferred until he could visit them.[3] This is the background of what has become a pattern in so many parts of today's Western Church.

---

[1] In fact, almost every Bishops' Conference has already provided specific guidelines, appropriately adapted to its own country or region: cf. LCE Tavola per Paesi e Canoni at Can. 877.
[2] Cf. Whitaker *Documents of the Baptismal Liturgy* London SPCK 1981 6.
[3] Cf. Crichton *Christian Celebration: The Sacraments* London 1973 92.

Can. 879 The sacrament of confirmation confers a character. By it the baptised continue their path of christian initiation. They are enriched with the gift of the Holy Spirit, and are more closely linked to the Church. They are made strong and more firmly obliged by word and deed to witness to Christ and to spread and defend the faith.

This introductory canon provides the theological foundation for the title on confirmation. It, and its sources, could well form the basis for instruction in preparation for the reception of this sacrament and for a homily on its occasion. Its sources are the teaching of Vat. II, the Apostolic Constitution *Divinae Consortium Naturae* approving the new rite of confirmation, and the new *Rite of Confirmation* itself. The 1917 Code made no mention of the character conferred by this sacrament. The present Code, following the general statement already made in Can. 845 §1, simply states that the sacrament confers a character and does not further elucidate the matter. During the revision process there was some discussion about eliminating this statement but the final decision was to retain it.[1] The second sentence stresses once more the link between confirmation and the two other sacraments of initiation. The canon goes on to describe the effects of the sacrament in terms that follow closely those used in Vat. II.[2]

1728

Chapter I
THE CELEBRATION OF CONFIRMATION

Can. 880 §1 The sacrament of confirmation is conferred by anointing with chrism on the forehead which is done by the laying on of the hand, and by the words prescribed in the approved liturgical books.

There are two essential elements in the celebration of the sacrament of confirmation. The first is the 'anointing with chrism on the forehead, which is done by the laying on of the hand'. A reply of the Commission for the Interpretation of the Decrees of Vatican II issued in 1972 makes it clear that the anointing with chrism with the thumb on the forehead 'sufficiently expresses the laying on of hands' which is required for validity.[3] This is not to remove the importance to the rite of the laying on of hands with the prayer 'All-powerful God'. Although not required for validity, this is still an important part of the rite and 'contributes ... to a more thorough understanding of the sacrament' in that it 'represents the biblical gesture by which the gift of the Holy Spirit is invoked and in a manner well suited to the understanding of the Christian people'.[4] The second essential element is the use of the words prescribed in the approved liturgical books. These are 'Be sealed with the gift of the Holy Spirit'. The approved liturgical books governing this sacrament are *The Rite of Confirmation*, *The Rite of Christian Initiation* and the adaptations of these made by Bishops' Conferences for their own areas.

1729

Can. 880 §2 The chrism to be used in the sacrament of confirmation must have been consecrated by a Bishop, even when the sacrament is administered by a priest.

---

[1] Cf. Comm 10(1978) 75.
[2] Cf. LG 11: Fl I 361; CCC nn.1302–1303, 1316.
[3] rep 9.VI.1972: AAS 64 (1972) 526: DOL n.2529.
[4] SCDW Rite of Confirmation: DOL n.2518.

1730 Chrism was formerly required to be made from olive oil and balsam. Now it may be made from any vegetable oil and 'some aromatic substance'.[1] The use of chrism in this sacrament has a very long history and, as early as the first Council of Toledo in 398, it was insisted that only the Bishop should bless it.[2] This insistence, continued in the present canon, reflects the linking of confirmation to the Bishop and hence to the apostolic laying on of hands.

Can. 881 It is desirable that the sacrament of confirmation be celebrated in a church and indeed during Mass. However, for a just and reasonable cause it may be celebrated apart from Mass and in any fitting place.

1731 This canon recommends that confirmation take place within the Mass 'in order that the fundamental connection of this sacrament with all of christian initiation may stand out in clearer light'.[3] Those who have already made their first Holy Communion should also receive the Eucharist at this Mass and it is fitting that the minister of confirmation should celebrate the Mass. If other priests join him in celebrating the sacrament, it is appropriate that they join him in concelebrating the Eucharist.[4] 'For a just and reasonable cause' the celebration of the sacrament may take place outside of Mass. An example of such a cause would be where the candidates are children who have not yet received their first Holy Communion. In such a case there should be a celebration of the word of God.[5] Whether confirmation is celebrated within the Mass or in the context of a celebration of the word of God, 'pains should be taken to give the liturgical service the festive and solemn character that its significance for the local Church requires' and this will be achieved by having 'a community celebration' in which 'all the people of God, represented by the families and friends of the candidates and by members of the local community will take part'.[6]

1732 The canon also allows flexibility as regards the place of celebration, as did c.791 of the 1917 Code. If there is 'a just and reasonable cause', 'any fitting place' may be used. Thus, e.g., there would be no problem about celebrating confirmation in a hospital or in a private house during an illness or other similar emergency.

Chapter II
THE MINISTER OF CONFIRMATION

Can. 882 The ordinary minister of confirmation is a Bishop. A priest can also validly confer this sacrament if he has the faculty to do so, either from the universal law or by way of a special grant from the competent authority.

1733 In declaring the Bishop to be the ordinary minister of confirmation the Code reflects the long-standing discipline and tradition of the Western Church where in normal circumstances the celebration of this sacrament was reserved to the Bishop. However, as c.782 of the 1917 Code acknowledged, it was always admitted that there was no intrinsic reason why a priest could not also be a minister of confirmation, and indeed provision

---

[1] DOL nn.3863–3864.
[2] Cf. Whitaker op cit 223–224.
[3] SCDW *Introduction to the Rite of Confirmation*: DOL n.2522.
[4] Ibid.
[5] Ibid.
[6] DOL n.2513.

was made for him to do this in certain limited circumstances. In order to make the sacrament accessible to those who, because of their circumstances, could not approach a Bishop, there was a gradual relaxation of the reservation of confirmation to the Bishop. *Spiritus Sancti Munera* in 1946 gave parish priests power to confirm in danger of death.[1] In 1963 *Pastorale Munus* allowed Bishops to grant this faculty to hospital chaplains and others.[2] This canon continues the process of adjustment and states in a general way that priests can confer this sacrament if they have the faculty to do so, either from the universal law (see Can. 883) or by way of a special grant (see Can. 884).

Can. 883 The following have, by law, the faculty to administer confirmation:

1° within the confines of their jurisdiction, those who in law are equivalent to a diocesan Bishop;

For 'those who in law are equivalent to a diocesan Bishop', see Cann. 368, 381 §2. In addition, the diocesan Administrator, who governs a diocese while the see is vacant, is also declared by Can. 427 §1 to enjoy the power of a diocesan Bishop. All of the above have by law the faculty to administer confirmation within the territories assigned to them.   1734

2° in respect of the person to be confirmed, the priest who by virtue of his office or by mandate of the diocesan Bishop baptises one who is no longer an infant or admits a person already baptised into full communion with the catholic Church.

The term 'by virtue of his office' limits the category of priests who enjoy the faculty to confirm. Those who qualify include: a parish priest (see Can. 530 2°), a parochial administrator (see Can. 540 §1), each of the priests jointly entrusted with the care of a parish (see Can. 543 §1), an assistant priest who takes the place of the parish priest in his absence or pending the appointment of a parochial administrator (see Cann. 549, 541 §1). Another who would qualify would be an episcopal Vicar for confirmation, if such a priest were appointed for this 'specific type of activity' (see Can. 476).   1735

By virtue of Can. 863 the baptism of all those who have completed their fourteenth year must be referred to the Bishop. In many cases the Bishop will not confer the baptism himself but will remit this to a local priest. In such a case he might well issue a special mandate for confirming the candidate also, if the priest did not already qualify by virtue of his office. He might even include the faculty to confirm in the so-called diocesan faculties issued to assistant priests on their appointment.   1736

A person ceases to be an infant on completing his or her seventh year (see Can. 97 §2). In normal circumstances confirmation will not be conferred before this age (see Can. 891). Since the principal reason for an earlier age will be danger of death, and since in this eventuality any priest can confer the sacrament (see 3° of the present canon), the seeming restriction contained in the present section, i.e. to those over seven years of age, is more apparent than real.   1737

The admission of an adult into full communion with the church includes several different types of case, e.g. a person joining the catholic Church from another Church or ecclesial communion; the readmission of one who, with or without fault of his or her own, after baptism joined another religion or was brought up without any christian formation. In all of these cases, a priest who qualifies under this section may confer confirmation.   1738

---

[1] Cf. SCSac decr 14.IX.1946: AAS 38(1946) 349 ff: CLD 3 303ff.
[2] Cf. Pope Paul VI mp 30.XI.1963: AAS 56(1964) 5ff: CLD 6 370ff.

3° in respect of those in danger of death, the parish priest or indeed any priest.

1739 The Church is anxious lest a person who has not been confirmed should die without this sacrament because the Bishop is not available. *Spiritus Sancti Munera* in 1946 gave parish priests the power to confirm in danger of death and this power was later extended, with some limitations, to other priests (see above under Can. 882). The present canon gives some preference to parish priests, but grants the power to confirm in danger of death to all priests without restriction.

1740 It is to be noted that, although the power of governance is not involved, Can. 144 §2 explicitly extends the norms concerning the supplying of power in cases of common error and positive doubt to this Can. 883.

Can. 884 §1 The diocesan Bishop is himself to administer confirmation or to ensure that it is administered by another Bishop. If necessity so requires, he may grant to one or several specified priests the faculty to administer this sacrament.

1741 As 'principal dispensers of the mysteries of God'[1] diocesan Bishops have an obligation to administer confirmation in their dioceses. If for a good reason a Bishop cannot personally fulfil this obligation, he is to see to it that the sacrament is conferred by another Bishop. 'If necessity so requires' the diocesan Bishop may grant to one or to several priests the faculty to confer. This phrase is vague, but it is implicit in this canon and in the general tenor of the introduction to the *Rite of Confirmation* that priests should not be granted this faculty if a Bishop is available. It is possible that the pastoral need cannot be met by the number of Bishops available and that therefore the assistance of priests will also be required. These priests may be specified either by name or by office, e.g. the Vicar(s) general, episcopal Vicars, the Vicars forane.

1742 During the drafting of this canon it was suggested that the Bishop be required to seek permission from the Apostolic See to grant this faculty to a priest. It was feared that otherwise a trend might arise whereby Bishops would habitually give this faculty to their priests and so lose contact with their people.[2] However the present text was retained as the discipline had already been changed in the *Rite of Confirmation*.

Can. 884 §2 For a grave reason the Bishop, or the priest who by law or by special grant of the competent authority has the faculty to confirm, may in individual cases invite other priests to join with him in administering the sacrament.

1743 The introduction to the *Rite of Confirmation* suggests that such a reason would be verified when there is a large number to be confirmed.[3] Other examples of sufficient reason would be where the Bishop or authorised priest is in poor health and where the number of candidates present would impose a severe strain on him or would unduly prolong the ceremony. The injunction that the authorisation of other priests be done only 'in individual cases' is designed to prevent the concelebration of confirmation becoming standard practice.

Can. 885 §1 The diocesan Bishop is bound to ensure that the sacrament of confirmation is conferred upon his subjects who duly and reasonably request it.

---

[1] CD 15: Fl I 571.
[2] Cf. Comm 15(1983) 186–187.
[3] Cf. DOL n.2517.

This canon is an explicit example of the right of the faithful 'to be assisted by their Pastors from the spiritual riches of the Church, especially by the word of God and the sacraments' (Can. 213); it also makes specific, with regard to confirmation, the general norm of Can. 843 §1 that 'Sacred ministers may not deny the sacraments to those who opportunely ask for them, are properly disposed and are not prohibited by law from receiving them'. The Bishop may fulfil this obligation personally, by another Bishop or by an authorised priest as permitted by Can. 884 §1.

Can. 885 §2 A priest who has this faculty must use it for those in whose favour it was granted.

Since the faculty to confirm is given, either by law or by special mandate, not for the good of the priest but for the good of those in his care, he has an obligation to use it. Thus, e.g. when a priest baptises someone in danger of death, he should also confirm that person on the same occasion.

Can. 886 §1 In his own diocese a Bishop may lawfully administer the sacrament of confirmation even to the faithful who are not his subjects, unless there is an express prohibition by their own Ordinary.

§2 In order lawfully to administer confirmation in another diocese, unless it be to his own subjects, a Bishop needs the permission, at least reasonably presumed, of the diocesan Bishop.

Can. 885 §1 determines the Bishop's duty to confer confirmation; this canon determines his right to do so. It does not affect the validity of his actions, merely their lawfulness. There are no restrictions on his right to confirm his own subjects, i.e. those who have a domicile or quasi-domicile in his diocese. He can confirm them either within his diocese or outside of it. Thus, e.g. a Bishop on pilgrimage, say in Lourdes, could lawfully confirm his own subjects there without any reference to the local Bishop. *Vagi*, who have no domicile or quasi-domicile anywhere, are subject to the Bishop of the place where they are actually resident (see Can. 107 §2), and so he may confirm them within the confines of that territory. Likewise he may confirm any of the faithful within his territory, even if they are not his subjects, unless their own Ordinary has expressly forbidden this. In order lawfully to confirm non-subjects outside of his diocese he must have the permission, at least reasonably presumed, of the local Bishop.

Can. 887 A priest who has the faculty to administer confirmation may, within the territory assigned to him, lawfully administer this sacrament even to those from outside the territory, unless there is a prohibition by their own Ordinary. He cannot, however, validly confirm anyone in another territory, without prejudice to the provision of Can. 883 n.3.

The power of a priest with the faculty to confirm is similar to, but more circumscribed than, the power of a Bishop. Like the Bishop he can, within the territory assigned to him, lawfully confirm anyone, even those from outside the territory, unless their own Ordinary has forbidden this. Confirmation conferred despite such a prohibition would, however, still be valid. The territory concerned could be a parish or, with the special mandate of the Bishop, even a diocese or a part of a diocese. Unlike the Bishop, a priest conferring confirmation outside his territory acts invalidly, except in danger of death (see Can. 883 3°).

Can. 888 Within the territory in which they can confer confirmation, ministers may confirm even in exempt places.

The 1917 Code in its c.792 gave the Bishop the right to confer the sacrament in places in his diocese which were normally exempt from his jurisdiction. The present canon extends this right to all approved ministers of the sacrament.

Book IV The Sanctifying Office of the Church

Chapter III
THE PERSONS TO BE CONFIRMED

Can. 889 §1 Every baptised person who is not confirmed, and only such a person, is capable of receiving confirmation.

1749 The only requirement for the valid reception of confirmation is that the candidate be baptised and not yet confirmed. Baptism is 'the gateway to the sacraments' (Can. 849) and a person who has not been baptised 'cannot validly be admitted to the other sacraments' (Can. 842 §1). It is not necessary that the candidate have the use of reason, and so even the profoundly mentally handicapped can, and should, receive the sacrament.

Can. 889 §2 Apart from the danger of death, to receive confirmation lawfully a person who has the use of reason must be suitably instructed, properly disposed and able to renew the baptismal promises.

1750 Lawful reception of the sacrament requires in candidates who have the use of reason that they be suitably instructed, properly disposed and able to renew the baptismal promises. The inclusion of the phrase 'who have the use of reason' reflects the tradition of the Western Church which for the most part has postponed the conferring of confirmation until around the age of discretion (see Can. 891 below). The requirement that the candidate be 'suitably instructed' reflects the concern which led to the institution of the catechumenate in the early Church and indeed to its restoration in our own time for the initiation of adults into the faith and life of the Church.

1751 In danger of death a person should be baptised if necessary and then confirmed. In the case of an infant who has not yet reached the use of reason, no more need be done. If, however, the person has the use of reason, before he or she is confirmed 'there should as far as possible, be some spiritual preparation ... suited to the individual situation'.[1]

Can. 890 The faithful are bound to receive this sacrament at the proper time. Parents and pastors of souls, especially parish priests, are to see that the faithful are properly instructed to receive the sacrament and come to it at the opportune time.

1752 The proper time for the reception of this sacrament is determined broadly by the canon which follows, Can. 891. The responsibility of preparing the baptised belongs to the People of God,[2] but it falls in a special way on parents, pastors and particularly on parish priests. The duty of parents arises from their own position as baptised and confirmed members of the Church (see Can. 774 §2). Parish priests are given a special responsibility in the preparation and catechetical formation of children preparing for confirmation (see Can. 777 2°). The requirement of Can. 777 4° that mentally and physically handicapped people be given catechetical formation in accordance with their capacity has a particular relevance in regard to preparing them for confirmation.

1753 In places where confirmation is legitimately postponed to a relatively late age, there can be a very real danger that adolescents will not be prepared for the sacrament or receive it. Frequently this omission will be noted only when the person concerned comes to be married in the Church. Can. 1065 §1 states that 'Catholics who have not yet received the sacrament of confirmation are to receive it before being admitted to marriage, if this

---

[1] DOL n.2521.
[2] DOL n.2512.

Part I The Sacraments

can be done without grave inconvenience'. The *Rite of Confirmation* allows the local Ordinary in such cases to defer the sacrament until after the marriage 'if it is foreseen that the conditions for a fruitful reception of confirmation cannot be satisfied'.[1]

Can. 891 The sacrament of confirmation is to be conferred on the faithful at about the age of discretion, unless the Bishops' Conference has decided on a different age, or there is a danger of death or, in the judgement of the minister, a grave reason suggests otherwise.

In deciding the age for the conferring of this sacrament the Code allows considerable flexibility, reflecting the considerable differences in practice which have obtained in the Western Church. The general norm is the same as in c.788 of the 1917 Code and sets the age 'at about the age of discretion', i.e. about seven years of age. However, it immediately allows the Bishops' Conference to decide on a different age, either greater or less. An inspection of the decrees of Bishops' Conferences[2] shows a wide variation in this matter, with some Conferences making no determination at all,[3] others being fairly specific,[4] and still others leaving the determination either to the local Bishop[5] or to the local catechetical programme.[6] Although the general practice seems to favour an age later than the age of discretion, there could be good reason for determining on an earlier age. Such a situation could arise in a place where there are large numbers of Eastern-rite catholics, in order to allow for unity in pastoral approaches and catechetical programmes. — 1754

Whatever the established age, two exceptions to it are allowed. Firstly, if there is danger of death the person should be confirmed immediately, no matter what his or her age (see above under Can. 889 §2). Secondly, the minister of the sacrament is allowed to decide on a different age for 'a grave reason'. This different age could be earlier, e.g. where there would be a danger that waiting for the later age might mean that the sacrament would never be received, or later, e.g. where the candidate is manifestly unprepared for confirmation. — 1755

Chapter IV
SPONSORS

Can. 892 As far as possible the person to be confirmed is to have a sponsor. The sponsor's function is to take care that the person confirmed behaves as a true witness of Christ and faithfully fulfils the duties inherent in this sacrament.

Sponsors 'bring the candidates to receive the sacrament, present them to the minister for the anointing, and will later help them to fulfil their baptismal promises faithfully under the influence of the Holy Spirit whom they have received'.[7] The canon requires a sponsor 'as far as possible', making it clear that this requirement does not affect the — 1756

---

[1] DOL n.2521.
[2] Cf. LCE Tavola per Paesi e Canoni at Can. 891.
[3] E.g. England and Wales, Scotland, USA.
[4] E.g. India twelve–fourteen, Ireland eleven–twelve, Philippines at least seven.
[5] E.g. Gambia, Liberia and Sierra Leone, Nigeria.
[6] E.g. Canada.
[7] *Rite of Confirmation*: DOL n.2514.

validity of the sacrament. However the practice of having a sponsor at confirmation represents an ancient custom in the Church and should not lightly be omitted. The practice which has existed in some places, whereby one person, e.g. the local schoolteacher, would simply 'act' as sponsor to all of those being confirmed, is certainly against the purpose and spirit of the law, and should be discouraged.

Can. 893 §1 A person who would undertake the office of sponsor must fulfil the conditions mentioned in Can. 874.

1757 The qualities required in a sponsor have already been enumerated and discussed under Can. 874; *inter alia* 5° of that canon forbids either parent of the candidate from undertaking the role of sponsor. The *Rite of Confirmation* states that 'even the parents themselves may present their children for confirmation'.[1] During the drafting of the Code there were requests that parents should not be forbidden to act as sponsors, but these were rejected by the Commission as being based on a misunderstanding of the sponsor's role, i.e. to help the parents to carry out their responsibilities and, if necessary, to make up for any failure of the parents in this regard. The Commission added that parents could indeed present their children but that in such a case it would have to be said that there were no sponsors.[2]

1758 Other restrictions which were in the 1917 Code have been abolished. Thus e.g. a spouse may now act as sponsor for his or her partner, and indeed would make a very fitting one. There are no restrictions on clerics or religious acting as sponsors, nor is there any longer a requirement that the sponsor be of the same sex as the candidate.

Can. 893 §2 It is desirable that the sponsor chosen be the one who undertook this role at baptism.

1759 This recommendation is directly contrary to c.796 1° of the 1917 Code which forbade the same person to act as sponsor for both sacraments in normal circumstances. The *Rite of Confirmation* states that 'it is desirable that the godparent at baptism, if available, also be the sponsor at confirmation' and adds 'this change expresses more clearly the link between baptism and confirmation and also makes the function and responsibility of the sponsor more effective'.[3]

Chapter V
PROOF AND REGISTRATION OF CONFIRMATION

Can. 894 To establish that confirmation has been conferred, the provisions of Can. 876 are to be observed.

1760 The provisions for proof of conferral of confirmation are exactly the same as those given for proof of baptism in Can. 876. If there is no conflict of interest it suffices to have the evidence of one reliable witness or, if the sacrament was conferred on an adult, the sworn testimony of the person confirmed.

Can. 895 The names of those confirmed, the minister, the parents, the sponsors and the place and date of the confirmation are to be recorded in the confirmation register of the diocesan curia or, wherever this has been

---

[1] Ibid.
[2] Cf. Comm 15(1983) 189.
[3] DOL n.2514.

Part I The Sacraments

prescribed by the Bishops' Conference or by the diocesan Bishop, in the register to be kept in the parochial archive. The parish priest must notify the parish priest of the place of the baptism that the confirmation was conferred, so that it may be recorded in the baptismal register, in accordance with Can. 535 §2.

This canon prescribes the details to be recorded in the confirmation register: the names of those confirmed, the minister, the parents and the sponsors, the place and date of the confirmation. The register may be a central diocesan one or, if the Bishops' Conference or even the diocesan Bishop so decide, it may be a parochial one. In the English-speaking world the Bishops' Conferences of England and Wales, Gambia, Liberia and Sierra Leone, Ireland and the Philippines have directed that a register be kept in each parish.[1] Notification of confirmation must be sent in accordance with this canon to the place of baptism: the baptismal register is, as it were, the central register relating to the canonical status of a member of Christ's faithful.   1761

Can. 896 If the parish priest of the place was not present, the minister, personally or through someone else, is to notify him as soon as possible that the confirmation was conferred.

If the parish priest of the place of confirmation was not present, the minister is to notify him of the fact so that he may carry out the duty imposed on him by Can. 895. Since confirmation may on occasion now be conferred by priests other than the diocesan Bishop, there is some danger that it may go unrecorded – hence the present canon.   1762

Title III
The Blessed Eucharist

INTRODUCTION

The Eucharist is the final sacrament of initiation. With its reception comes the fullness of participation in the new life given us at baptism and in the life of the Church. 'The Eucharist is ... the sacrament that is the fullest sign of our new life ... '[2] The triple dimension of this sacrament as 'at once sacrament and sacrifice, sacrament and communion, sacrament and presence',[3] is its characteristic; the essential unity of these three elements is well echoed in the layout of this title. This is in contrast to the 1917 Code which treated of the reservation and veneration of the Blessed Sacrament in a totally different part of its Book III. A proposal to cover the question of Mass offerings under Book V, which deals with Church property, was rejected by the Revision Commission and it was decided to deal with the question under the present title 'because of the special connection which (these) questions have with the celebration of Mass'.[4]   1763

---

[1] LCE Tavola per Paesi e Canoni at Can. 895.
[2] Pope Paul VI encl *Redemptor Hominis* 20: DOL n.1329.
[3] Ibid: DOL n.1330.
[4] Cf. Comm 7(1975) 31.

Can. 897 The most august sacrament is the blessed Eucharist, in which Christ the Lord himself is contained, offered and received, and by which the Church continually lives and grows. The eucharistic Sacrifice, the memorial of the death and resurrection of the Lord, in which the Sacrifice of the cross is for ever perpetuated, is the summit and the source of all worship and christian life. By means of it the unity of God's people is signified and brought about, and the building up of the body of Christ is perfected. The other sacraments and all the ecclesiastical works of the apostolate are bound up with, and directed to, the blessed Eucharist.

1764 This introductory canon contains the principal elements of catholic theology on the Eucharist. It takes as its source recent statements of the magisterium and especially the documents of Vat. II. It echoes closely the statement on the Eucharist given in the Constitution on the Sacred Liturgy[1] and together with Cann. 898–899 it sets forth the theological foundation for the canons which follow.

Can. 898 Christ's faithful are to hold the blessed Eucharist in the highest honour. They should take an active part in the celebration of the most august Sacrifice; they should receive the sacrament with great devotion and frequently, and should reverence it with the greatest adoration. In explaining the doctrine of this sacrament, pastors of souls are assiduously to instruct the faithful about their obligation in this regard.

1765 This canon lays down general norms regarding religious behaviour in relation to the Eucharist. These norms arise from the dogmatic principles expressed in Can. 897. They call for the highest honour to be accorded to the sacrament, for active participation by the faithful in the celebration of the eucharistic Sacrifice,[2] for frequent reception of it and for great reverence to be paid to it. Finally it gives pastors of souls the task of instructing the faithful in both doctrine and practice regarding the Eucharist.[3]

Chapter I
THE CELEBRATION OF THE EUCHARIST

Can. 899 §1 The celebration of the Eucharist is an action of Christ himself and of the Church. In it Christ the Lord, through the ministry of the priest, offers himself, substantially present under the appearances of bread and wine, to God the Father, and gives himself as spiritual nourishment to the faithful who are associated with him in his offering.

1766 As the Constitution on the Liturgy explains, 'Christ ... always associates the Church with himself in this great work',[4] and so the celebration of the Eucharist is the action not only of Christ, but also of the Church. In the Eucharist Christ continues to offer himself 'to the Father for the world's salvation through the ministry of priests'.[5] He is 'the spiritual food of the faithful under the appearances of bread and wine'.[6]

---

[1] Cf. SC 47: Fl I 16. Cf. also CCC nn.1358–1359, 1407, 1419.
[2] Cf. SC 48: Fl I 16.
[3] Cf. Cann. 528 §2, 777.
[4] SC 7: Fl I 5.
[5] EuM 3: Fl I 103.
[6] Ibid. quoting from Pope Paul VI encl *Mysterium Fidei*.

Part I The Sacraments

Can. 899 §2 In the eucharistic assembly the people of God are called together under the presidency of the Bishop or of a priest under his authority, who acts in the person of Christ. All the faithful present, whether clerics or lay people, unite to participate in their own way, according to their various orders and liturgical roles.

The celebration of the Eucharist is an action of the Church. When the faithful come together as 'an altar community'[1] they do so under the presidency of the Bishop or a priest in communion with him. In exercising his ministry the Bishop or priest does not act in his own name, but 'in the person of Christ'. Although 'the prayers addressed to God by the priest ... are said in the name of the entire holy people and of all present',[2] the faithful 'should take part in the sacred action, conscious of what they are doing, with devotion and full collaboration'.[3] 1767

Can. 899 §3 The eucharistic celebration is to be so ordered that all the participants derive from it the many fruits for which Christ the Lord instituted the eucharistic Sacrifice.

This paragraph calls for the Eucharist to be organised and celebrated in such a way that all those participating are drawn into the prayer of the Church, listen attentively to the word of God and receive the Body of Christ in holy communion. 1768

Article 1
The Minister of the Blessed Eucharist

Can. 900 §1 The only minister who, in the person of Christ, can bring into being the sacrament of the Eucharist, is a validly ordained priest.

Although the language used is different, this paragraph repeats the norm of c.802 of the 1917 Code in affirming that for validity the minister who celebrates the Eucharist must be a validly ordained priest. Can. 1378 §2 1° determines the penalties for invalidly attempting to celebrate Mass. 1769

Can. 900 §2 Any priest who is not debarred by canon law may lawfully celebrate the Eucharist, provided the provisions of the following canons are observed.

For lawful celebration of the Eucharist, as well as observing the canons which follow, a priest must not have incurred an irregularity or impediment (see Can. 1044), an excommunication (see Can. 1331 §1 1°), interdict (see Can. 1332) or suspension (see Can. 1333 §1 1°). 1770

Can. 901 A priest is entitled to offer Mass for anyone, living or dead.

In its cc.809 and 2262 §2 2° the 1917 Code had placed some restrictions on offering Mass for those who had been excommunicated. The present canon expresses no such restrictions. Cann. 1184–1185 forbid a funeral Mass for certain people, but this would not prevent a priest saying Mass for these people. Prudence might have to be exercised in publicly announcing such Mass intentions. 1771

---

[1] LG 26: Fl I 381.
[2] SC 33: Fl I 12.
[3] SC 48: Fl I 16.

Can. 902 Unless the benefit of Christ's faithful requires or suggests otherwise, priests may concelebrate the Eucharist; they are, however, fully entitled to celebrate the Eucharist individually, but not while a concelebration is taking place in the same Church or oratory.

1772 This canon is a reversal of c.803 of the 1917 Code which forbade concelebration apart from an ordination Mass. It reflects the desire of Vat. II to restore the practice of concelebration as being a means 'whereby the unity of the priesthood is appropriately manifested'.[1] Accordingly it extended the number of occasions on which it was possible to concelebrate Mass.[2] The General Instruction on the Roman Missal added slightly to that list of occasions.[3]

1773 The only restriction placed on concelebration by this canon is a general one: it is permitted 'unless the benefit of Christ's faithful requires or suggests otherwise'. Thus, e.g., a priest should not concelebrate if by so doing he would deprive people of Mass on a Sunday or holyday of obligation or even on other special occasions such as a pilgrimage.

1774 As Bishops 'are the principal dispensers of the mysteries of God' and as 'it is their function to control, promote and protect the entire liturgical life of the Church entrusted to them',[4] they undoubtedly have the power to impose regulations concerning concelebration.[5]

1775 Despite the encouragement of concelebration, each priest retains the right (he is 'fully entitled') to celebrate Mass individually, save only at the same time as a concelebration in the same church or oratory.[6]

Can. 903 A priest is to be permitted to celebrate the Eucharist, even if he is not known to the rector of the church, provided either that he presents commendatory letters, not more than a year old, from his own Ordinary or Superior, or that it can be prudently judged that he is not debarred from celebrating.

1776 This is a simplified and less detailed rule than that contained in the corresponding c. 804 of the 1917 Code. A priest who presents himself at a church should be allowed to celebrate Mass if *either* of two conditions is fulfilled:

(a) that he present a document commending him, not more than a year old and signed by his Ordinary or Superior. Such a document is (or was) commonly called a *celebret*.

(b) that 'it can be prudently judged that he is not debarred from celebrating'. As the law is stated, it is in favour of his being allowed. If in particular circumstances there is a clear danger of impostors or debarred priests turning up, the Bishop can always issue special regulations.[7]

Can. 904 Remembering always that in the mystery of the eucharistic Sacrifice the work of redemption is continually being carried out, priests are to celebrate frequently. Indeed, daily celebration is earnestly recommended, because, even if it should not be possible to have the faithful present, it is an

---

[1] SC 57: Fl I 19.
[2] Ibid.
[3] Cf. GIRM 154–5: Fl I 185.
[4] CD 15: Fl I 571–572.
[5] Cf. SC 57: Fl I 19, and GIRM 155: Fl I 185 where this is stated explicitly.
[6] Cf. e.g. SC 57: Fl I 19.
[7] Cf. Comm 15(1983) 192 at Can. 856.

action of Christ and of the Church in the carrying out of which priests fulfil their principal role.

Under the 1917 Code at c.805 a priest was obliged to say Mass only 'several times a year', although Bishops and religious Superiors were to see to it that they celebrated at least every Sunday and holyday of obligation. The present canon does not lay down a minimum; it recommends daily celebration, as did Vat. II, precisely because in celebrating Mass a priest is fulfilling his principal function.[1] Indeed so earnest is this recommendation that, in order to follow it, a priest is allowed to override the rule of Can. 906 requiring the participation of at least one of the faithful at Mass.

Can. 905 §1 Apart from those cases in which the law allows him to celebrate or concelebrate the Eucharist a number of times on the same day, a priest may not celebrate more than once a day.

The general norm is that a priest can celebrate Mass once a day unless the law allows him to do so more often. The General Instruction on the Roman Missal indicates when the law so allows:

(a) A priest who has concelebrated at the Chrism Mass on Holy Thursday may again celebrate or concelebrate at the evening Mass.

(b) A priest who has celebrated or concelebrated at the Paschal Vigil may again celebrate or concelebrate on Easter Sunday.

(c) At Christmas every priest may celebrate or concelebrate three Masses, provided each Mass takes place at its own proper time.

(d) A priest who has celebrated at a synod, a pastoral visitation or a meeting of priests with their Bishop may also celebrate again if this would be of service to the faithful and provided the Bishop agrees to it. The same applies to a meeting of religious with their own Ordinary or with his delegate.[2]

A reply of the Congregation for Divine Worship in 1973 made it clear that the permission given here for celebrating another Mass was for a second Mass only, not for a third one.[3] Account must also, however, be taken of any special permission given in this regard by the local Bishop (see §2 below).

The 1917 Code at c.806 allowed a priest to say three Masses on All Souls' Day as well as on Christmas Day. Neither the present Code nor the Instruction quoted above repeats the permission for All Souls' Day. But the Roman Missal does give three different sets of text for Mass on that day. There would seem to be a doubt of law here, and so a priest could lawfully say three Masses on 2 November.

Can. 905 §2 If there is a scarcity of priests, the local Ordinary may allow priests, for a good reason, to celebrate twice in one day or even, if pastoral need requires it, three times on Sundays or holydays of obligation.

The local Ordinary may allow priests to binate, i.e. to celebrate Mass twice in one day if priests are scarce and there is a good reason. A good reason would be e.g. serving the needs of a large number of people. He may permit priests to trinate, i.e. to celebrate three times, on Sundays or holydays of obligation. The Ordinary may not give a broader faculty than is permitted in this canon without permission of the Holy See.[4]

---

[1] Cf. PO 13: Fl I 888.

[2] Cf. GIRM 158: Fl I 186.

[3] SCDW rep 31.I.1973: LE 6454.

[4] Cf. Comm 15(1983) 192 at Can. 858 §2.

However, in an individual case and for sufficient reason, a diocesan Bishop could dispense from this canon in virtue of Can. 87 §1. What he cannot do is to give *general* permission for more than two Masses on weekdays and three on Sundays.

Can. 906 A priest may not celebrate the eucharistic Sacrifice without the participation of at least one of the faithful, unless there is a good and reasonable cause for doing so.

1782 In restoring the liturgy the Church wishes to promote 'that full, conscious and active participation in liturgical celebrations which is demanded by the very nature of the liturgy, and to which the christian people ... have a right and obligation by reason of their baptism'.[1] This canon gives concrete expression to that principle in relation to the Eucharist and forbids the celebration of Mass without at least one member of the faithful being present and participating, unless 'there is a good and reasonable cause'. Since Can. 904 allows a priest to celebrate without having the faithful present in order that he may celebrate daily, it can be taken that the priest's sense of devotion and desire to celebrate is sufficient cause. The effect of the present canon is to make such solo celebration the exception rather than the rule. Every reasonable effort should be made to have the faithful present.

1783 Unlike the 1917 Code at c.813 §1, the present law does not forbid a priest to celebrate without an altar server. Neither does it forbid, as did the earlier law at c.813 §2, a woman to serve Mass inside the sanctuary. The removal of the earlier prohibition was no accidental omission. When it was proposed in 1978 that a corresponding rule be part of the new Code, the Revision Commission replied that such a proposal was 'somewhat out of date', seeing that the Supreme Authority in the Church had allowed the possibility of women distributing holy communion, proclaiming the readings and reading intentions in the prayers of the faithful. Accordingly it was decided not to say anything on this matter in the Code.[2] From this alone it did seem that the former prohibition was abrogated by the present Code.

1784 However, before the Code came into effect, two instructions from the Congregation for Divine Worship, one in 1970,[3] the other in 1980,[4] explicitly forbade women to serve at the altar, and the General Instruction on the Roman Missal (1970) merely allowed women to be entrusted with 'those ministries which may be exercised outside the sanctuary'.[5] After the Code came into effect in 1983, it was argued, rightly, that the first two were not law but rather instructions on how the law existing at that time (the 1917 Code) was to be implemented. The third document, however, certainly did constitute liturgical law and so would not be abrogated by the Code;[6] that law did *not*, however, contain an explicit prohibition against female altar servers and, in so far as it implied any prohibition, that did not appear to be consistent with the functions already allowed to women by the Legislator. In the absence, therefore, of a clear and binding prohibition, and given both the deliberate omission of such a prohibition from the Code itself and the contradiction between what is allowed to women and any such prohibition, a common view emerged among responsible canonists that the prohibition against female altar servers no longer obtained. That opinion was in effect

---

[1] SC 14: Fl I 7–8.
[2] Cf. Comm 13(1981) 242 at Can. 67.
[3] SCDW instr *Liturgiae Instaurationes* 5.IX.1970 7: Fl I 217.
[4] SCDW instr *Inaestimabile Donum* 3.IV.1980 18: Fl II 98.
[5] GIRM 70: Fl I 183.
[6] Cf. Can. 2.

endorsed when, by letter of 15 March 1994, the Congregation for Divine Worship and the Discipline of the Sacraments informed the Presidents of all Bishops' Conferences that the Pontifical Council for the Interpretation of Legislative Texts had, with the approval of the Pope, determined that this was indeed the correct interpretation of Can. 230 §2.[1]

Can. 907 In the celebration of the Eucharist, deacons and lay persons are not permitted to say the prayers, especially the eucharistic prayer, nor to perform the actions which are proper to the celebrating priest.

Liturgical actions are celebrations of the Church which manifest her nature and reflect her structure.[2] They reflect both the common dignity of the faithful[3] and their hierarchical differences.[4] For this reason, 'in liturgical celebrations each person, minister or lay man who has an office to perform, should carry out all and only those parts which pertain to his office by the nature of the rite and the norms of the liturgy'.[5] Since the only minister who can bring the Eucharist into being is the priest (see Can. 900 §1), he alone should recite the eucharistic prayer, 'the climax of the entire celebration'.[6] Likewise other prayers and actions designated as 'presidential' are reserved to the priest.[7]

1785

Can. 908 Catholic priests are forbidden to concelebrate the Eucharist with priests or ministers of Churches or ecclesial communities which are not in full communion with the catholic Church.

Although there have been significant changes regarding administering the Eucharist to, and receiving it from, members of other Churches or ecclesial communities (see Can. 844), there is still a prohibition on concelebrating with priests or ministers of such communities. Worship should express the unity of the Church[8] and the Eucharist in particular is 'a sign of unity'.[9] In the absence of such unity, concelebration of the Eucharist would be inappropriate. The 'brotherly bond of the priesthood' which is symbolised and strengthened by concelebration[10] is not yet present between catholic priests and the priests or ministers of other Churches or ecclesial communities. Moreover inter-Church concelebration could lead to confusion in the minds of the faithful. Can. 1365 prescribes 'a just penalty' for anyone guilty of prohibited participation in religious rites.

1786

Can. 909 A priest is not to omit dutifully to prepare himself by prayer before the celebration of the Eucharist, nor afterwards to omit to make thanksgiving to God.

This canon is similar to the corresponding c.810 in the 1917 Code. A priest should prepare for Mass by prayer and should give thanks to God afterwards. While the

1787

---

[1] For a helpful discussion of this issue as it appeared in 1988, cf. Johnson *Who may serve Mass? A Quest for the Ius Vigens* Jur 48(1988) 692–708. For the details of the decision by the Pontifical Council, cf. our commentary on Can. 230 §2.

[2] Cf. SC 26: Fl I 10.

[3] Cf. LG 32: Fl I 389.

[4] Cf. LG 10: Fl I 361.

[5] SC 28: Fl I 11.

[6] GIRM 10: Fl I 164.

[7] Ibid. 10–11: Fl I 164–5.

[8] UR 8: Fl I 461.

[9] SC 47: Fl I 16.

[10] EuM 47: Fl I 128.

priest's prayer-life, which should be part of himself, will certainly foster this preparation and thanksgiving, the canon does at least suggest that some period of prayer be set aside immediately before and immediately after the celebration of Mass.

Can. 910 §1 The ordinary minister of holy communion is a Bishop, a priest or a deacon.

1788 In c.845 §2 of the 1917 Code a deacon was designated an extraordinary minister of the Eucharist. Vat. II declared that 'it pertains to the office of a deacon, in so far as it may be assigned to him by the competent authority ... to be custodian and distributor of the Eucharist...'.[1] The present law confirms this. A special point may be made in respect of the reception of first holy communion. Since this is an integral part of the threefold celebration of christian initiation – baptism, confirmation and the blessed Eucharist – and since the ordinary minister of both baptism and confirmation sacramentally represents Christ in the initiation of new members of his Body, only an ordained minister, as in this §1, should be the minister of first holy communion. The use of an extraordinary minister, as in §2 below, should be countenanced for this occasion only in the most extreme circumstances of urgency or danger, certainly never on the mere ground of familial or social opportunity.

Can. 910 §2 The extraordinary minister of holy communion is an acolyte, or another of Christ's faithful deputed in accordance with Can. 230 §3.

1789 In 1972 the mp *Ministeria Quaedam* described the role of an acolyte in this regard: 'he is also to distribute communion as a special minister when the ministers spoken of in the *Codex Iuris Canonici* (of 1917) at c.845 are not available or are prevented by ill health, age or another pastoral ministry from performing this function, or when the number of communicants is so great that the celebration of Mass would be unduly prolonged'.[2] In the following year the instruction *Immensae Caritatis* allowed Ordinaries to choose suitable persons as extraordinary ministers of the Eucharist, either temporarily or even on a more permanent basis.[3] The criteria for using this faculty were substantially the same as those mentioned above.

1790 Can. 230 §3 allows among other things the appointment of lay people to distribute holy communion. In appointing and utilising them, the criteria given above should be followed. Those appointed must be properly instructed and should distinguish themselves by their christian life, faith and morals, and their selection should not cause scandal among the faithful.[4] The Code Commission has stated that the extraordinary minister 'may not exercise his or her supplementary function ... when ordinary ministers, who are not in any way impeded, are present in the church, though not taking part in the Eucharistic celebration'.[5] The phrase 'not in any way impeded' would leave the extraordinary ministers free to function if e.g. the ordinary ministers were not properly vested, had not been notified or could not easily approach the sanctuary.

Can. 911 §1 The duty and right to bring the blessed Eucharist to the sick as Viaticum belongs to the parish priest, to assistant priests, to chaplains and, in respect of all who are in the house, to the community Superior in clerical religious institutes or societies of apostolic life.

---

[1] LG 29: Fl I 387.
[2] MQ V: DOL n.2931.
[3] Cf. ImC: Fl I 227.
[4] Cf. ImC: Fl I 228.
[5] CCom rep 20.II.1987: AAS 80(1988) 1373: Per 78(1989) 269–277: Wrenn (Interpret) 44–45.

§2 In a case of necessity, or with the permission at least presumed of the parish priest, chaplain or Superior, who must subsequently be notified, any priest or other minister of holy communion must do this.

1791 This paragraph determines who has the duty and right to bring Viaticum to the sick, i.e. holy communion as a sacrament of the dying. It lists parish priests, assistant priests and chaplains. In houses of clerical religious or societies of apostolic life the same function belongs to the community Superior in respect of all those in the house, whether or not they are members of the institute. These ministers have been described as the 'ordinary ministers' of Viaticum.[1]

1792 Where the priests mentioned in §1 are not available, any priest, deacon, acolyte or authorised extraordinary minister not only may, but must, bring Viaticum to the sick. In such a case, the minister is obliged subsequently to inform the appropriate 'ordinary minister'.

Article 2
Participation in the Blessed Eucharist

Can. 912 Any baptised person who is not forbidden by law may and must be admitted to holy communion.

1793 This canon, which is almost identical to its predecessor in the 1917 Code c.853, affirms the juridical entitlement of each baptised person to receive holy communion unless forbidden by law. Can. 844 restricts the cases in which holy communion may be given to those not in full communion with the catholic Church, and imposes lesser restrictions on catholics receiving the Eucharist from non-catholic ministers. There are a number of prohibitions and restrictions expressed in the canons which follow (see Cann. 913, 915–917, 919 §1).

Can. 913 §1 For holy communion to be administered to children, it is required that they have sufficient knowledge and be carefully prepared, so that according to their capacity they understand what the mystery of Christ means, and are able to receive the Body of the Lord with faith and devotion.

1794 Until the 12th century communion was given to infants under the form of wine. The Fourth Lateran Council in 1125 prescribed that all who had reached the age of discretion should receive communion once a year. By the time of the Renaissance the usual age for First Communion was eleven years of age. In 1910 Pope Pius X in the decree *Quam Singulari* laid down that 'children should approach the Holy Table with the devotion that is proper to their age once they reach the use of reason'; he also insisted on adequate prior catechesis.[2]

1795 This canon does not state what level of knowledge or preparation the children should have reached except to say in general terms that they must have, in accordance with their capacity, an adequate understanding of what is involved and be able to receive communion with faith and devotion. The normal age for first communion will be about seven years (see Can. 914). At this age it is presumed that a child can sufficiently understand what is involved in the Eucharist. Careful preparation will engender faith and devotion as well as giving knowledge.

---

[1] SCDW *Hominum Dolores* 7.XII.1972 29: DOL n.3349.
[2] Cf. Crawford *Infant Communion* Theological Studies 31(1970) 523–536.

Can. 913 §2 The blessed Eucharist may, however, be administered to children in danger of death if they can distinguish the Body of Christ from ordinary food and receive communion with reverence.

1796 Communion may be given to children under the age of reason who are in danger of death, provided they can distinguish the Body of Christ from ordinary food and receive it with reverence. The rites and ceremonies of the sacrament, and the attitude and behaviour of the parents and of the minister will often help the child to distinguish and to approach the Eucharist with an adequate reverence, even if he or she is unable to give articulate expression to belief. Similar considerations could be invoked in the case of the mentally handicapped even outside of danger of death.

Can. 914 It is primarily the duty of parents and of those who take their place, as it is the duty of the parish priest, to ensure that children who have reached the use of reason are properly prepared and, having made their sacramental confession, are nourished by this divine food as soon as possible. It is also the duty of the parish priest to see that children who have not reached the use of reason, or whom he has judged to be insufficiently disposed, do not come to holy communion.

1797 Three principal issues are dealt with in this canon:

(a) who should prepare children for holy communion;

(b) when children should receive first communion;

(c) ensuring that children not properly disposed do not receive holy communion.

1798 The primary duty of preparing children for holy communion and of ensuring that they receive it falls on parents or those who take their place and on the parish priest (see Can. 772 3°).[1]

1799 The time for first holy communion is when the child reaches the use of reason. According to Can. 97 §2, this is presumed to occur on completion of the seventh year. First communion should be made as soon as possible after this. The canon requires that children be properly prepared. This preparation will take place within the family and in school, and in special cases – e.g. lack of a catholic school, where there are learning difficulties etc. – it will be done by individual catechesis. In addition to this preparation the canon requires that the children have made their first confession. The 1917 Code did not specify any order in the reception of penance and communion, setting the age of discretion as the age for both sacraments. During the 1960s and 1970s the practice grew up of postponing first confession until some years after first communion. However there was a strong official reaction against this practice,[2] and the phrase 'having made their sacramental confession' was added to the final draft of this Code. This restores and makes obligatory the practice which had become traditional. It should be noted that the requirement of confession before communion in this canon refers only to *first* communion.

1800 Finally, the canon gives the parish priest the duty of ensuring that children who have not reached the use of reason or who, in his judgement, are not properly disposed, do not come to communion. He will have to make prudent, individual judgements here, and he should be guided by all the circumstances of a given case and not just by

---

[1] Cf. EuM 14: Fl I 112.

[2] SCC General Catechetical Directory 11.IV.1971: CTS London addendum 100–104; SCC/SCSac decl *Sanctus Pontifex* 24.V.1973: Fl I 241; SCDW letter *In Quibusdam Ecclesiae Partibus* 31.III.1977: DOL n.3149.

circumstances of age or mental ability. This calls for a special degree of delicate and sensitive pastoral care in dealing both with the child and with its parents. The prescription of c.854 §4 of the 1917 Code remitting this judgement to the children's confessor was abrogated as involving a use of confessional knowledge.[1]

Can. 915 Those upon whom the penalty of excommunication or interdict has been imposed or declared, and others who obstinately persist in manifest grave sin, are not to be admitted to holy communion.

This canon deals with those who are to be excluded from holy communion. 'Of its very nature celebration of the Eucharist signifies the fullness of profession of faith and the fullness of ecclesial communion'.[2] Those upon whom the penalty of excommunication or interdict has been imposed or declared are by definition no longer in full communion with the catholic Church and this is juridically a public fact. Their exclusion from eucharistic communion is a sign and consequence of this (see Can. 1331 §1 2°). Likewise excluded are those 'who obstinately persist in manifest grave sin'. In this third case, unlike the first two, there has been no public imposition or declaration of the person's state and so, before a minister can lawfully refuse the Eucharist, he must be certain that the person obstinately persists in a sinful situation or in sinful behaviour that is manifest (i.e. public) and objectively grave.

1801

Those who are divorced and remarried find themselves in this situation.[3] Apart from 'the fact that their state and condition of life objectively contradict that union of life between Christ and the Church which is signified by the Eucharist', there is also the consideration of possible error and confusion in the minds of the faithful about the Church's teaching on the indissolubility of marriage.[4]

1802

Can. 916 Anyone who is conscious of grave sin may not celebrate Mass or receive the Body of the Lord without previously having been to sacramental confession, unless there is a grave reason and there is no opportunity to confess; in this case the person is to remember the obligation to make an act of perfect contrition, which includes the resolve to go to confession as soon as possible.

The ultimate source of this canon is the doctrine of St. Paul about receiving the Body of the Lord unworthily.[5] *Eucharisticum Mysterium* quotes the Council of Trent and c.856 of the 1917 Code in terms which are substantially the same as the present law.[6] This canon makes explicit what was traditional doctrine, that an act of perfect contrition includes the intention of going to confession as soon as possible. One who is conscious of grave sin must first go to confession before celebrating Mass or receiving holy communion, unless there is a grave reason and there is no opportunity to confess. A grave reason would exist e.g. for a priest who had to say Mass for a congregation, or for a lay person who might lose his or her good name by not receiving communion in certain circumstances. The opportunity to confess might be wanting, not only due to

1803

---

[1] Cf. Comm 15(1983) 193 at Can. 863 §3.
[2] SPUC instr *In Quibus Rerum Circumstantiis* IV 1: AAS 64(1972) 518–525: Fl I 557.
[3] Cf. Comm 15(1983) 194 at Can. 867.
[4] For a clear and practical appreciation of the Church's caring and sensitive attitude in this matter, the reader is earnestly referred to the relevant section of Pope John Paul II's ap exhort *The Christian Family in the Modern World* 22.XI.1981: FC 84: Fl II 888–889.
[5] Cf. 1 Cor 11:28–29.
[6] EuM 35: Fl I 122–123.

the lack of any priest, but also e.g. from not wishing to confess to the only priest available because of a family relationship or a friendship with him etc.

Can. 917 One who has received the blessed Eucharist may receive it again on the same day only within a eucharistic celebration in which that person participates, without prejudice to the provision of Can. 921 §2.

1804 The 1917 Code at cc. 857, 858 §1 allowed the reception of holy communion a second time on the same day only in danger of death or in order to avoid irreverence to the blessed Eucharist. Between the end of Vat. II and the Code this regulation was gradually relaxed.[1] After the promulgation of the Code there was some debate as to whether the word 'again' meant twice only or as often as a person attended Mass. A reply from the Code Commission in 1984 made it clear that it means twice only.[2] Consequently the present law is that a person may receive holy communion a second time on the same day, but only on the occasion of participating in a Mass – unless of course there is danger of death.

Can. 918 It is most strongly recommended that the faithful receive holy communion in the course of a eucharistic celebration. If, however, for good reason they ask for it apart from the Mass, it is to be administered to them, observing the liturgical rites.

1805 'The more perfect form of participation in the Mass' is that 'whereby the faithful after the priest's communion receive the Lord's Body from the same sacrifice'.[3] Nevertheless 'priests ... are not to refuse to give communion to the faithful who ask for it even outside Mass'.[4] This may be done if there is good reason, such e.g. as would exist in the case of those who cannot be present at Mass or who are sick or elderly.[5]

Can. 919 §1 Whoever is to receive the blessed Eucharist is to abstain for at least one hour before holy communion from all food and drink with the sole exception of water and medicine.

1806 The discipline of c.858 §1 of the 1917 Code, which required a natural fast from the midnight preceding the reception of holy communion, was relaxed by Pope Pius XII.[6] In 1964 at a session of Vat. II Pope Paul VI shortened the fast from solid food to one hour for both priests and faithful.[7] The present law is that anyone who is to receive holy communion must abstain for one hour from all food and drink except for water and medicine, whether liquid or solid.

Can. 919 §2 A priest who, on the same day, celebrates the blessed Eucharist twice or three times may consume something before the second or third celebration, even though there is not an hour's interval.

---

[1] Cf. SCRit instr *Inter Oecumenici* 26.IX.1964 60: DOL n.352; SCRit instr *Tres Abhinc Annos* 4.V.1967 14: DOL n.460; ImC: Fl I 229–30.

[2] CCom rep 26.VI.1984: AAS 76(1984) 746: Per 73(1984) 285–287. Cf. Wrenn (Interpret) 11–12, who rightly concludes that this was a *restrictive* interpretation and accordingly not retroactive, cf. Can. 16 §2.

[3] SC 55: Fl I 18.

[4] SCDW *Holy Communion and Worship of the Eucharist outside Mass* 14: DOL n.2092.

[5] Cf. loc cit.

[6] Cf. ap con *Christus Dominus* 6.I.1953: AAS 45(1953) 15–24, CLD 4 269–277; mp *Sacram Communionem* 19.III.1957: AAS 49(1957) 177–8, CLD 4 286–8.

[7] Cf. DOL n.2117.

In 1963 *Pastorale Munus* allowed Bishops 'to permit priests who celebrate two or three Masses to take something to drink even though an interval of one hour does not intervene before the celebration of the next Mass'.[1] Now such a priest does not need the Bishop's permission, and he is not confined to having something to drink, but may 'consume something', i.e. have something to eat.

Can. 919 §3 The elderly and those who are suffering from some illness, as well as those who care for them, may receive the blessed Eucharist even if within the preceding hour they have consumed something.

Special norms for the sick and elderly and for those who care for them had been in place since 1973.[2] The present law represents a further removal of restrictions. There is no longer any specified time of fasting for any of the sick or elderly or (note) for 'those who care for them', including nurses, home-helps, members of the family etc.

Can. 920 §1 Once admitted to the blessed Eucharist, each of the faithful is obliged to receive holy communion at least once a year.

This precept dates from a period in the Church's history when the reception of holy communion was neglected. All the faithful who have been admitted to first holy communion are obliged from then on to receive at least once a year. A proposal to make this a grave obligation in conscience was rejected because 'the law does not determine moral gravity'.[3] This is obviously a minimal expression of law and it in no way takes from the fact that reception of holy communion is the fullest way of participating in the Mass, and that frequent reception should be actively encouraged.

Can. 920 §2 This precept must be fulfilled during paschal time, unless for a good reason it is fulfilled at another time during the year.

The preferred time for the fulfilment of this precept is Paschal time, which was defined in the 1917 Code as being from Palm Sunday to Low Sunday and was capable of being lengthened. From the time laid down for its fulfilment this precept was known as 'Easter duty' and was commonly held to include the obligation of going to confession. In fact there was (and is) *per se* no such obligation, as one is obliged to confess one's sins only if they are grave. For 'a good reason' now the obligation may be satisfied at any time of the year, e.g. the non-availability of a needed confessor, a local custom of receiving holy communion at Christmas, etc.

Can. 921 §1 Christ's faithful who are in danger of death, from whatever cause, are to be strengthened by holy communion as Viaticum.

'Communion given as Viaticum should be considered as a special sign of participation in the mystery celebrated in the Mass, the mystery of the death of the Lord and his passage to the Father. By it, strengthened by the Body of Christ, the Christian is endowed with the pledge of the resurrection in his passage from this life.'[4] Viaticum is the sacrament of those who are in danger of death, whatever the cause. Although the language of this canon is less peremptory than that of its predecessor (see 1917 Code c.864 §1), there is still an obligation on each of the faithful to receive Viaticum and on pastors of souls to see that it is available to them.

---

[1] PM 3: DOL n.714.
[2] Cf. SCDW *Holy Communion and Worship of the Eucharist outside Mass* 24: DOL n.2102.
[3] Comm 15(1983) 195 at Can. 872.
[4] EuM 39: Fl I 124.

Can. 921 §2 Even if they have already received holy communion that same day, it is nevertheless strongly recommended that in danger of death they should communicate again.

1812 This is the exception provided for in Can. 917, which itself allows the faithful to receive holy communion a second time on the same day only during Mass. In danger of death this restriction ceases, and indeed it is earnestly recommended that the person receive a second time, even outside of Mass.

Can. 921 §3 While the danger of death persists, it is recommended that holy communion be administered a number of times, but on separate days.

1813 The law recommends that those in danger of death receive holy communion a number of times, but on separate days. Indeed if at all possible, communion should be brought to them daily if they cannot go to church.[1]

Can. 922 Holy Viaticum for the sick is not to be unduly delayed. Those who have the care of souls are to take assiduous care that the sick are strengthened by it while they are in full possession of their faculties.

1814 This canon is almost identical to c.865 of the 1917 Code. Viaticum should be brought to those in danger of death in good time, i.e. while they are still in possession of their faculties. This obligation falls primarily on those listed in Can. 911, but those who look after the sick – family members, nurses and other carers – would also have an obligation here.

Can. 923 Christ's faithful may participate in the eucharistic Sacrifice and receive holy communion in any catholic rite, without prejudice to the provisions of Can. 844.

1815 Catholics are free to participate in the celebration of the Eucharist and to receive communion in any catholic rite. This emphasises the essential unity of the different Churches. In certain circumstances Can. 844 also allows them to receive communion from non-catholic ministers of Churches in which there is a valid Eucharist.

Article 3
The Rites and Ceremonies of the Eucharistic Celebration

Can. 924 §1 The most holy Sacrifice of the Eucharist must be offered in bread, and in wine to which a small quantity of water is to be added.

1816 'Following the example of Christ, the Church has ever made use of bread and wine with water when celebrating the Lord's Supper.'[2] The practice of the Church in regarding bread and wine as the essential elements of the Eucharist is based on the gospel accounts of the Last Supper.[3] The addition of 'a small quantity of water' is symbolic of the union of divine and human nature in Jesus Christ, and also of the mystical union of the faithful with Christ through his sacrificial death. Wine to which water in a greater or even an equal quantity has been added would be invalid.

---

[1] EuM 40: Fl I 125.
[2] GIRM 281: Fl I 194.
[3] Cf. Matt 26:26–29; Mark 14:22–25; Luke 22:17–20.

Can. 924 §2 That bread must be wheaten only, and recently made, so that there is no danger of corruption.

The bread used for the Eucharist must, in accordance with the tradition of the whole Church, be made solely from wheat and, in accordance with the tradition of the latin Church, it should be unleavened.[1] More detailed requirements concerning its shape and appearance can be found in the liturgical law.[2] In addition, it must be of recent make so that there is no danger of corruption.

1817

A practical problem arises for those who suffer from coeliac disease. Such people are unable to absorb gluten, a normal constituent of wheat, and are made quite ill by even small traces of it in their diet. Since 1967 Bishops could allow those who are unable to receive communion under the species of bread to receive it under the species of wine alone,[3] and there is now general permission for this in Can. 925. In 1982 a reply from the Congregation for the Doctrine of the Faith stated that the local Ordinary could not permit a priest to consecrate special gluten-free hosts for the communion of coeliacs.[4] It did not rule on the validity of using such bread, merely on its lawfulness. An accompanying reply made it clear that coeliacs could of course be permitted to receive under the species of wine only.[5]

1818

Can. 924 §3 The wine must be natural, made from grapes of the vine, and not corrupt.

For validity the wine used at Mass 'must be made from the fruit of the vine (see Lk. 22:18), natural and pure, unmixed with anything else'[6] (see this canon §1). It must not be corrupt, i.e. it must not have turned to vinegar or otherwise begun to decompose.

1819

The use of 'must' (*mustum*), i.e. unfermented grape juice, as material for the Mass has long been considered by theologians and canonists, among whom the common opinion was that, while valid, it is gravely forbidden except perhaps in a case of necessity[7] – a position which would clearly require that 'must' may be used, in whatever situation, only with the permission of the Holy See. In recent years this problem has assumed a new significance, particularly in the context of priests who suffer from the disease of alcoholism or from some other such which prevents them from consuming even a minimal quantity of consecrated wine. The initial response of the Holy See was not only itself to grant personal requests but to authorise a number of Bishops' Conferences and of individual Ordinaries to grant permission to individual priests to use 'must' in the celebration of Mass, subject to certain limitations.[8] Later however the grant of such

1820

---

[1] Cf. SCDW instr *Inaestimabile Donum* 8: Fl II 96.

[2] Cf. e.g. GIRM 283: Fl I 194.

[3] EuM 41: Fl I 125.

[4] AAS 74(1982) 1298: CLD 10 199.

[5] In the context of the blessed Eucharist, the problem arising for those suffering from coeliac disease, be they celebrants of the Mass or recipients of holy communion, remains at the time of this writing under active consideration by the Holy See: for the most recent directive cf. SCDF letter 19.VI.1995 to Presidents of Bishops' Conferences (Prot. N. 89/78, to date unpublished): hosts which are totally gluten-free remain invalid matter for the Eucharist, but low-gluten hosts are valid, subject to specified conditions.

[6] GIRM 284: Fl I 195. A useful summary of the regulations in this regard issued from time to time by the Holy See may be found in Regatillo *Ius Sacramentarium* ed 3 Santander 1960 110–112.

[7] Cf. Cappello I nn.257, 270; Vermeersch–Creusen II n.85; Chiappetta II n.3250; CLD 8 519.

[8] In 1974 e.g. such a faculty was granted by the SCDF to the Ordinaries of the USA: for details cf. CLD 8 517–519; Commentary (CLSA) 657.

general authorisation was withdrawn.[1] The current position is that 'must' may be used in the celebration of Mass only by such individual priests as may be authorised thereto by the Holy See and subject to such conditions as may be prescribed.[2]

Can. 925 Holy communion is to be given under the species of bread alone or, in accordance with the liturgical laws, under both species or, in case of necessity, even under the species of wine alone.

1821 The reception of holy communion under both species, once common in the latin Church, was gradually abandoned[3] and, except for the celebrant of the Mass, the norm became reception under the species of bread alone. This is still the preferred or traditional practice, as the present canon shows. However, Vat. II stated that 'communion under both kinds may be granted when the Bishops think fit, not only to clerics and religious but also to the laity, in cases to be determined by the Apostolic See'.[4] The present canon leaves to liturgical law the determination of when it may be allowed. A detailed list of occasions when communion under both kinds may be given will be found in the General Instruction on the Roman Missal.[5] Communion under the species of wine alone will be rather rare and confined to 'cases of necessity', e.g. for the sick who are unable to receive or to swallow even a tiny host, for coeliacs (as mentioned at Can. 924), etc. In this context it is suggested that there be kept in the tabernacle a small securely-sealed vessel of the Precious Blood, for Viaticum in emergencies outside Mass:[6] this supply must of course be renewed frequently, at intervals of not longer than about two weeks.

Can. 926 In the eucharistic celebration, in accordance with the ancient tradition of the latin Church, the priest is to use unleavened bread wherever he celebrates Mass.

1822 This requirement is for lawfulness only. It reflects the long-standing practice of the latin Church in using unleavened bread as Christ would have done at the Last Supper.[7]

Can. 927 It is absolutely wrong, even in urgent and extreme necessity to consecrate one element without the other, or even to consecrate both outside the eucharistic celebration.

1823 This canon repeats almost exactly c.817 of the 1917 Code. It does not determine the validity of a consecration done in defiance of the law, but from the language used – the latin has the word *nefas* which is used only four times in the Code and which implies something so unlawful as to be almost unthinkable – it is clear that this is a

---

[1] This was done by way of a letter of 12.IX.1983 from the SCDF to the representatives of the Holy See throughout the world: cf. RR 1984 2–3. Cf. also SCDF *Responsa ad proposita dubia* 29.X.1982: AAS 74(1982) 1298. The withdrawal of the authorisation did not however affect those priests to whom permission had earlier been granted in virtue of the general faculty. One discussion of the entire matter may be found in Huels *Select Questions of Eucharistic Discipline* CLSA Proceedings of 47th Annual Convention 1985 (CLSA Washington DC 1986) 56–59.

[2] Individual requests to the Holy See are normally submitted by the appropriate Ordinary. Many such are granted: cf. e.g. LE V 4588 7479; RR 1986 3–4, 1988 1, 1989 4–5; others however have been refused or deferred: cf. RR 1987 1–3.

[3] Cf. SCDW instr *Memoriale Domini* 29.V.1969: AAS 61(1969) 541–547: Fl I 148.

[4] SC 55: Fl I 18.

[5] Cf. GIRM 242: Fl I 187–8.

[6] Cf. *Pastoral Care of the Sick: Rites of Anointing and Viaticum* 181 Liturgical Press Collegeville Minn. 1983.

[7] Cf. e.g. Matt 26:17.

most serious prohibition. No reason will excuse from observing the law, not even 'urgent and extreme necessity'. The canon is not a matter of purely positive law; it is based on the fact that the Mass follows the rite used by Our Lord at the Last Supper.[1]

Can. 928 The eucharistic celebration is to be carried out either in the latin language or in another language, provided the liturgical texts have been lawfully approved.

Although today by far the commonest language for the celebration of Mass will be the local vernacular, latin remains the universal language and the one in which the original text is issued. It may always be used, and in some cases – e.g. gatherings of people of different language – it would be desirable.[2] The latin text is approved by the Apostolic See, and the vernacular texts and allowable adaptations are prepared by local Bishops' Conferences, subject then to review by the Holy See (see Can. 838 §§ 2–3). 　　1824

Can. 929 In celebrating and administering the Eucharist, priests and deacons are to wear the sacred vestments prescribed by the rubrics.

The different ministries performed in the course of the celebration of the Eucharist are distinguished by the different vestments worn.[3] The General Instruction on the Roman Missal lists in detail the proper vestments,[4] and it allows Bishops' Conferences to 'determine and propose to the Holy See any adaptations in the shape or style of vestments which they consider desirable by reason of local custom or needs'.[5] Celebration of the Eucharist in ordinary clothing or in unapproved or inadequate vestments is strictly prohibited. 　　1825

Can. 930 §1 A priest who is ill or elderly, if he is unable to stand, may celebrate the eucharistic Sacrifice sitting but otherwise observing the liturgical laws; he may not, however, do so in public except by permission of the local Ordinary.

This provision had no equivalent in the 1917 Code and, before the issuing of *Pastorale Munus* in 1963,[6] the permission granted here would have needed a special indult. Note that, in order to celebrate a public Mass sitting, such a priest needs the permission of the local Ordinary; in private, he needs no such permission. 　　1826

Can. 930 §2 A priest who is blind or suffering from some other infirmity, may lawfully celebrate the eucharistic Sacrifice by using the text of any approved Mass, with the assistance, if need be, of another priest or deacon or even a properly instructed lay person.

The permission granted here also has its origins in *Pastorale Munus*.[7] The present rule is very flexible and makes wide provision for priests who are blind, have poor eyesight or suffer from some other infirmity. The assistance of another person, cleric or lay person, is optional, depending on the individual priest's needs. 　　1827

---

[1] Cf. Matt 26:26–27; Mark 14:22–24; Luke 22:19–20. Cf. also CCC n.1408.
[2] Cf. SCRit instr *Musicam Sacram* 5.III.1967 48: Fl I 92.
[3] Cf. GIRM 297: Fl I 196.
[4] Ibid. 298–310: Fl I 196–198.
[5] Ibid. 304: Fl I 197.
[6] Cf. PM 10: DOL n.721.
[7] Cf. PM 5–6: DOL nn.716–717.

Article 4
The Time and Place of the Eucharistic Celebration

Can. 931 The celebration and distribution of the Eucharist may take place on any day and at any hour, except those which are excluded by the liturgical laws.

1828 The law on the time of celebration and distribution of the Eucharist has been greatly relaxed since the publication of the 1917 Code. The norm now is that both of these may take place at any time which is not forbidden by liturgical law; the time, therefore, will be determined chiefly by pastoral considerations. The celebration of the vigil Masses of Sundays and holydays of obligation must take place in the evening and not earlier.[1] There are also restrictions governing Masses during Holy Week: the Chrism Mass should normally be celebrated on the morning of Holy Thursday; the Mass of the Lord's Supper should be on the evening of the same day or, by way of exception in a case of necessity, even earlier; the Easter Vigil should not begin before dark and should end before daylight; Mass is not allowed on Good Friday or during daylight on Holy Saturday. As regards the distribution of holy communion, this may of course be done during any Mass and during the Good Friday ceremonies. It may be brought to the sick at any time except on Holy Saturday, when it may be brought only as Viaticum.[2]

Can. 932 §1 The eucharistic celebration is to be carried out in a sacred place, unless in a particular case necessity requires otherwise; in this case the celebration must be in a fitting place.

1829 The norm is that Mass is to be celebrated in a sacred place (see Can. 1205); any other place is to be regarded as exceptional. Sacred places include churches (Can. 1214), oratories (Can. 1223), private chapels (Can. 1226). An obvious case of the 'necessity' envisaged in this canon would be where a church is being rebuilt or refurbished; it is not however limited to that: equivalent or cognate situations can arise not only in missionary territories but elsewhere also, including such e.g. as holiday camps for youth, conferences or conventions of one kind or another, retreats or missions in prisons, etc. Between the end of Vat. II and the promulgation of the present Code Bishops were empowered to allow the celebration of Mass for special groups in other places, including even private houses.[3] It would seem that it is not the intention of the present law to abrogate such permission. Rather it seems reasonable to assume that the 'necessity' in question should be widely interpreted, its principal aim being the pastoral advantage to be gained by such celebrations.

1830 Customary law may also have established that Mass can be celebrated in private houses or other suitable places e.g. where religious persecution or lack of churches in the past gave rise to such practice. A clear example of this would be the so-called 'station Masses' in parts of Ireland where, since the penal times of religious persecution, Mass has been and still is celebrated annually in private houses for certain parishes or areas of a parish.

1831 When Mass is celebrated outside the normal sacred place, it is strictly required that the venue chosen be a fitting one, both as regards its cleanliness and decor and as regards its associations. Obviously a building or a house normally used for some unfitting, disreputable or unlawful purpose, no matter how clean, would not be an

---

[1] For the definition of 'evening' in this context, cf. commentary on Can. 1248 §1.
[2] These restrictions come from the rubrics of the Roman Missal for the Easter Triduum.
[3] Cf. e.g. SCB Directory on the Pastoral Ministry of Bishops 85: DOL n.2655.

Part I The Sacraments

appropriate place for the celebration of Mass. The criterion to be applied can only be the profound reverence due to the blessed Eucharist.

Can. 932 §2 The eucharistic Sacrifice must be carried out at an altar that is dedicated or blessed. Outside a sacred place an appropriate table may be used, but always with an altar cloth and a corporal.

Mass in a sacred place must be celebrated on an altar which is either dedicated or at least blessed (see Cann. 1171, 1235–1239). Detailed rules regarding altars are given in the General Instruction on the Roman Missal.[1] When Mass is celebrated elsewhere than in a sacred place, an appropriate table or other such is to be used, the minimum equipment of which must be a clean white cloth (such as would be on an altar) and a corporal. 　1832

Can. 933 For a good reason, with the express permission of the local Ordinary, and provided scandal has been eliminated, a priest may celebrate the Eucharist in a place of worship of any Church or ecclesial community which is not in full communion with the catholic Church.

There are three requirements before a priest may celebrate Mass in a place of worship belonging to another Church or ecclesial community not in full communion with the catholic Church: 　1833

(a) there must be good reason. This could be the lack of a catholic church in the area, or the lack of one big enough for a particular occasion. The sufficiency of the reason will be estimated by the local Ordinary.

(b) the local Ordinary must give his *express* permission – a permission which therefore may not be presumed.

(c) there must be no scandal. There should be no doubt or confusion in the minds of the faithful regarding what is taking place, namely a catholic celebration of the Eucharist, the reason for which in that place should, if needs be, be explained.

The Directory on Ecumenical Matters recommended 'that with the approval of the local Ordinary separated Eastern priests and communities be allowed the use of catholic churches, buildings and cemeteries and other things necessary for their religious rites, if they ask for this, and have no place in which they can celebrate sacred functions properly and with dignity'.[2] It also stated with regard to other separated brethren that if they 'have no place in which to carry out their religious rites properly and with dignity, the local Ordinary may allow them the use of a catholic building, cemetery or church'.[3] 　1834

Chapter II
THE RESERVATION AND VENERATION OF THE BLESSED EUCHARIST

Can. 934 §1 The blessed Eucharist:

1° must be reserved in the cathedral church or its equivalent, in every parish church, and in the church or oratory attached to the house of a religious institute or society of apostolic life.

---

[1] Cf. GIRM 259–267: Fl I 190–191.

[2] DEM 52: Fl I 498–499.

[3] DEM 61: Fl I 501.

Book IV The Sanctifying Office of the Church

2° may be reserved in a Bishop's chapel and, by permission of the local Ordinary, in other churches, oratories and chapels.

1835   The practice of reserving the Eucharist is an ancient one whose primary purpose was, and is, the administration of Viaticum. Two other purposes are the distribution of communion outside Mass and the adoration of Our Lord Jesus Christ present in this sacrament.[1] The worship shown to the Eucharist outside Mass has its origin and purpose in the celebration of the Eucharist in the sacrifice of the Mass.[2] This receives special point today when in many places, due to a shortage of priests, celebrations of the word of God, followed by distribution of holy communion, take the place of Sunday Mass. Such celebrations involving holy communion and the adoration of the Eucharist are necessarily centred around the Mass, draw their power and meaning from it and lead the faithful towards it.

1836   This first paragraph of the canon determines the places where the blessed Eucharist must be reserved and those where it may be reserved. It *must* be reserved in cathedral churches or their equivalent (see Can. 368), in every parish church and in the church or oratory attached to the house of a religious institute or society of apostolic life.[3] It *may* be reserved in a Bishop's chapel and, with the permission of the local Ordinary, in other churches, oratories and chapels. A proposal to limit somewhat the powers of the Ordinary in this regard was not accepted: the Revision Commission left it to the Ordinary to decide on the sufficiency of the reasons for such permission.[4]

Can. 934 §2 In sacred places where the blessed Eucharist is reserved there must always be someone who is responsible for it, and as far as possible a priest is to celebrate Mass there at least twice a month.

1837   The person who will be responsible for the Eucharist will normally be a local priest or deacon, but a lay person could also have this function. As far as possible a priest is to celebrate Mass in the place where the Eucharist is reserved at least twice a month. This serves to emphasise the connection between the Eucharist reserved and the Mass, and also to ensure that the sacred species are renewed regularly. The phrase 'as far as possible' allows some latitude for areas where priests may be scarce or unable to come twice a month. In cases where such a state of affairs is more than a temporary one, the diocesan Bishop or even the local Bishops' Conference could make particular regulations about the matter.

Can. 935 It is not lawful for anyone to keep the blessed Eucharist in personal custody or to carry it around, unless there is an urgent pastoral need and the prescriptions of the diocesan Bishop are observed.

1838   This canon repeats the prescription c.1265 §3 of the 1917 Code, forbidding the practice of keeping the blessed Eucharist in personal custody or carrying it around, but it

---

[1] Cf. EuM 49: Fl I 129.

[2] Cf. SCDW *Holy Communion and Worship of the Eucharist outside Mass* 2: DOL n.2194; EuM 3: Fl I 103–104.

[3] For the distinction between a church and an oratory, cf. Cann. 1214, 1223.

[4] Cf. Comm 15(1983) 198 at Can. 886 §2 n.2. It has become customary that private chapels (cf. Can. 1226) – often termed 'prayer rooms' – are established in large ecclesiastical institutions, such as religious houses, retreat centres, catholic hospitals etc.; not infrequently more than one such is to be found in any one such particularly large institution. To have reservation of the blessed Sacrament in any or all of these requires the permission of the local Ordinary, who will *inter alia* guard against an undue proliferation and ensure the frequent renewal of the sacred hosts (cf. Can. 939).

adds a qualifying phrase 'unless there is an urgent pastoral need and the prescriptions of the diocesan Bishop are observed'. There would be a genuine pastoral need e.g. if a priest or other eucharistic minister has the pastoral care of a large area and needs to have the Eucharist near at hand in a place other than a designated sacred place. Similarly the carrying of the Eucharist between mission stations would be justified under this heading. While the judgement as to what constitutes an 'urgent pastoral need' may be left to the minister concerned, the canon does indicate that the diocesan Bishop may lay down specific local regulations in this regard.

Can. 936 In a house of a religious institute or other house of piety, the blessed Eucharist is to be reserved only in the church or principal oratory attached to the house. For a just reason, however, the Ordinary can permit it to be reserved also in another oratory of the same house.

It is fitting that, as the principal sign and source of ecclesial unity, the Eucharist should be reserved in one central place rather than in many. Hence this canon prescribes that in a house of a religious institute or in other houses of piety (such as a seminary, a catholic boarding-school, hospital or orphanage), in normal circumstances it should be reserved only in the church or principal oratory attached to the house. Where there are several separate communities in the same building there can be separate oratories, each having reservation.[1] A just reason for allowing reservation in another oratory of the same house would exist e.g. if the church or principal oratory were frequented by the public to such an extent as to prove distracting to those in prayer before the blessed Sacrament, or if it were far away or otherwise difficult of access to members of the community (see also Can. 934 §1 2° above). 1839

Can. 937 Unless there is a grave reason to the contrary, a church in which the blessed Eucharist is reserved is to be open to the faithful for at least some hours every day, so that they can pray before the blessed Sacrament.

As stated under Can. 934 §1, one of the reasons for reservation of the Eucharist is the adoration of Our Divine Lord present in the sacrament. Hence the prescription of the present canon which is designed to ensure for the faithful a reasonable and ready access for this purpose. The canon does recognise that there may on occasion be 'a grave reason to the contrary'; in recent years e.g. considerations of security against theft and vandalism have in certain places, particularly in some large cities, made it more difficult than hitherto to ensure the free access to which the devout faithful are entitled. Even in such conditions, however, those with charge of churches are duty bound to devise means of overcoming the difficulty in so far as possible; in many places e.g. the establishment of, as it were, a duty-roster from among the parishioners or other such persons (and including of course the priests themselves) – each praying before the blessed Sacrament at arranged, say, half-hour periods – has proved not only an effective deterrent to vandals but also a powerful incentive of devotion to the blessed Sacrament: a precious heritage which should never be allowed to diminish, much less to lapse. The facile device of simply locking the doors of a public church each day immediately after the last morning Mass is wholly contrary to both the letter and the spirit of the Church's law. 1840

Can. 938 §1 The blessed Eucharist is to be reserved habitually in only one tabernacle of a church or oratory.

This canon, in its five paragraphs, deals in general terms with various aspects of the tabernacle in which the blessed Eucharist may be reserved.[2] The reason for the pre- 1841

---

[1] Cf. CCom rep 3.VI.1918: AAS 10(1918) 346: CLD 1 601.
[2] For more specific details in this regard, cf. GIRM 276–237.

scription of its §1 is the same as for that of Can. 936 – the unity symbolised and brought about by the Eucharist. In special circumstances, e.g. when very large numbers of people are present and a consequently large number of ciboria required, another tabernacle or suitable place might have to be used. This should however be a temporary measure only.

Can. 938 §2 The tabernacle in which the blessed Eucharist is reserved should be sited in a distinguished place in the church or oratory, a place which is conspicuous, suitably adorned and conducive to prayer.

1842 This paragraph is concerned with the siting of the tabernacle: ' ... it is more in keeping with the nature of the celebration that the eucharistic presence of Christ which is the fruit of the consecration ... should not be on the altar from the very beginning of Mass through the reservation of the sacred species in the tabernacle'.[1] Instead, it is recommended that where possible, especially in churches which have a lot of visitors, there should be a special chapel for reservation of the Eucharist, distinct from the central part of the church.[2] This will not always be possible, and the tabernacle may then be in a central place in the church, e.g. on the former main altar where there is a newer, forward altar.

Can. 938 §3 The tabernacle in which the blessed Eucharist is habitually reserved is to be immovable, made of solid and non-transparent material, and so locked as to give the greatest security against any danger of profanation.

§4 For a grave reason, especially at night, it is permitted to reserve the blessed Eucharist in some other safer place, provided it is fitting.

§5 The person in charge of a church or oratory is to see to it that the key of the tabernacle in which the blessed Eucharist is reserved, is in maximum safe keeping.

1843 The security of the tabernacle which houses the blessed Sacrament must be a primary concern of all those entrusted with its care, so that any danger of profanation is minimised. The tabernacle is to be 'immovable' as opposed to portable, i.e. it is to be securely fixed in position. It is to be made of solid material, not something flimsy like cloth or light wood, and it is to be securely locked. Moreover, the material used is not to be transparent, as this could give the impression of permanent exposition (§3).

1844 'For a grave reason, especially at night' (§4), the law allows the transfer of the Eucharist to a place safer than the tabernacle. This is clearly a matter which will be determined by local circumstances; in very exceptional circumstances it might be considered wise to consult the local Ordinary, but normally this matter is left to the prudent judgement of the custodian of each particular tabernacle. Such a 'safer place' might be e.g. the priest's own dwelling house. A safe in the sacristy has on occasion been considered in this context, but with the advent of modern sophisticated technology for gaining access to 'security safes' (so often the custodians of money and other valuables), this option should be looked at only with reserve. Whatever place is chosen should be 'fitting' to the reverence due to the real Presence of Christ in the Eucharist.

1845 Whoever has charge of a church or oratory, whether cleric or lay person, has a serious responsibility to ensure that the tabernacle key be at all times 'in maximum safe keeping' (§5). This implies (a) that it be clearly known which precise person is responsible for the custody of the key; (b) that, when the key is in use, all reasonable and positive

---

[1] EuM 55: Fl I 131–132.
[2] Cf. ibid.

Part I The Sacraments

steps be taken to ensure against its loss or larceny; (c) that, when it is not in use, the key itself be locked in a secure and unostentatious place.

Can. 939 Consecrated hosts, in a quantity sufficient for the needs of the faithful, are to be kept in a pyx or ciborium, and are to be renewed frequently, the older hosts having been duly consumed.

The quantity of hosts to be reserved will depend on the needs of the faithful for Viaticum and holy communion outside Mass. The hosts are to be kept in a pyx or ciborium which may be made not only from metal, precious or otherwise, but also from any material locally held in esteem as suitable for use in worship e.g. ebony, certain hardwoods.[1] The hosts are to be renewed 'frequently', in order to avoid danger of corruption: a guideline to the desired frequency may be found in the rule of Can. 934 §2 which requires that as far as possible a priest celebrate Mass at least twice a month in places where the Eucharist is reserved. 1846

Can. 940 A special lamp is to burn continuously before the tabernacle in which the blessed Eucharist is reserved, to indicate and to honour the presence of Christ.

This canon refers simply to a 'special lamp', without specifying what kind of lamp this should be. Traditional usage has been that it be an oil lamp or a lamp with a wax candle: this is specified in the 1973 document of the Congregation for Divine Worship on *Holy Communion and Worship of the Eucharist outside Mass*.[2] It is desirable therefore to have that traditional type of lamp; however, since the canon does not specify this, it would seem permissible to use an appropriate electric lamp, at least in cases of necessity. 1847

Can. 941 §1 In churches or oratories which are allowed to reserve the blessed Eucharist, there may be exposition, either with the ciborium or with the monstrance, in accordance with the norms prescribed in the liturgical books.

Exposition of the blessed Eucharist, which 'stimulates the faithful to an awareness of the marvellous presence of Christ, and is an invitation to spiritual communion with him'[3] may be done either with the pyx or with a monstrance. The rules which govern it are principally to be found in the norms laid down by the Congregation of Divine Worship in 1973.[4] 1848

Can. 941 §2 Exposition of the blessed Sacrament may not take place while Mass is being celebrated in the same area of the church or oratory.

The reason for this prohibition is that 'the celebration of the Mystery of the Eucharist includes in a more perfect way that spiritual communion to which exposition should lead the faithful. Therefore there is no need for this further help'.[5] The prohibition applies only to Mass and exposition simultaneously taking place 'in the same area of the church or oratory'. Thus, e.g. Mass could be celebrated in the crypt while exposition took place in the main body of the church, or exposition could continue in a separate blessed Sacrament chapel while Mass was celebrated at the main altar of the church. However, where there is no such separate area and if exposition is prolonged over a day or several days, it should be interrupted during the celebration of Mass.[6] 1849

---

[1] Cf. GIRM 292: Fl I 196.

[2] Cf. DOL n.2203.

[3] EuM 60: Fl I 133.

[4] Cf. SCDW, *Holy Communion and Worship of the Eucharist outside Mass* 82–92: DOL nn.2208–2218.

[5] EuM 61: Fl I 134.

[6] Cf. ibid.

Can. 942 It is recommended that in these churches or oratories, there is to be each year a solemn exposition of the blessed Sacrament for an appropriate time, even if it be not continuous, so that the local community may more attentively meditate on and adore the eucharistic mystery. This exposition is to take place only if a fitting attendance of the faithful is foreseen, and the prescribed norms are observed.

1850 The practice of solemn exposition of the blessed Eucharist each year for 'an appropriate time' is recommended. No length of time is laid down and the period does not have to be continuous.[1] However, it should not be interrupted more than twice a day[2] and then only if sufficient numbers of the faithful cannot be present.

Can. 943 The minister of exposition of the blessed Sacrament and of the eucharistic blessing is a priest or deacon. In special circumstances the minister of exposition and deposition alone, but without the blessing, is an acolyte, an extraordinary minister of holy communion, or another person deputed by the local Ordinary, in accordance with the regulations of the diocesan Bishop.

1851 The ordinary minister of exposition of the blessed Sacrament is a priest or a deacon. *Only these* may give the eucharistic blessing. In special circumstances, e.g. in the absence of a priest or deacon or if they are impeded, an acolyte, an extraordinary minister of holy communion or another person specially deputed for this by the local Ordinary may expose the blessed Sacrament and replace it in the tabernacle: in houses of religious sisters it is not infrequent that the local Ordinary will depute the Superior or another of the sisters to fulfil this task.

Can. 944 §1 Wherever in the judgement of the diocesan Bishop it can be done, a procession through the streets is to be held, especially on the solemnity of Corpus Christi, as a public witness of veneration of the blessed Eucharist.

§2 It is for the diocesan Bishop to establish such regulations about processions as will provide for participation in them and for their being carried out in a dignified manner.

1852 The traditional practice of holding public eucharistic processions, especially on the solemnity of Corpus Christi, is encouraged 'as a public witness of veneration of the blessed Eucharist'. Since local conditions will vary considerably, even from one diocese to another, the judgement about whether to hold such processions, and the establishing of regulations concerning them, is left to the diocesan Bishop. The thrust of this canon is however to the positive effect that, unless it be considered impossible or seriously unwise, such processions are to be held.

---

[1] Although it is not required by the law, the devotion known as the 'Forty Hours Exposition', whereby in some countries solemn exposition of the blessed Sacrament was held annually in each parish for approximately that length of time over a two- to three-day period, should not be forgotten. Where it still exists, it should be actively encouraged; where it may have to some extent lapsed, serious thought should be given to its restoration.

[2] Cf. EuM 65: Fl I 135.

Part I The Sacraments

Chapter III
THE OFFERING MADE FOR THE CELEBRATION OF MASS

Can. 945 §1 In accordance with the approved custom of the Church, any priest who celebrates or concelebrates a Mass may accept an offering to apply the Mass for a specific intention.

When this part of the law was being revised the Commission referred to the historical background and noted how the practice of giving an offering derived from the custom of the faithful of bringing not only the bread and wine for the Mass but also other gifts for the support of the priests and to feed the poor. In this way the offering became associated with the celebration of the Eucharist.[1] The current Code uses the word *stips* (translated as 'offering') instead of the *stipendium* ('stipend') of the 1917 Code. The new word historically describes an offering for a public work, for the honour of God or for the poor, and so is a more fitting term for a Mass offering than was the previous one which could have connotations of payment in return for a service.[2] 1853

This canon recognises the right of a priest who celebrates or concelebrates Mass to accept an offering to apply the Mass for a specific intention. This is a strictly personal right – a point made clear in a private reply from the Congregation for the Clergy to an American Bishop who sought permission to assign Mass stipends and stole fees to a parish or institution rather than to the priest directly. The reply raised no objection as regards stole fees but stated that the Congregation could not grant the request for Mass stipends 'since it is part of the letter and the spirit of the law to give the Mass stipend directly to the celebrant'.[3] 1854

The application of a Mass for a specific intention must not be understood in any exclusive sense, as if this Mass were for that intention only. That intention must, as it were, be given priority and could be announced as such, but every Mass is offered for all mankind.[4] 1855

Can. 945 §2 It is earnestly recommended to priests that, even if they do not receive an offering, they celebrate Mass for the intentions of Christ's faithful, especially of those in need.

The Mass 'is the action of Christ and his Church in which the priest always acts for the salvation of the people'.[5] Hence it must never be seen as a private action of the priest. This paragraph emphasises this by recommending that, even if they do not receive an offering, priests should celebrate the Mass for the intentions of the faithful, especially those in need. 1856

Can. 946 Christ's faithful who make an offering so that Mass can be celebrated for their intention, contribute to the good of the Church, and by that offering they share in the Church's concern for the support of its ministers and its activities.

In making a Mass offering 'by which they contribute in a particular way to the needs of the Church and especially to the sustenance of its ministers ... the faithful unite themselves 1857

---

[1] Cf. Comm 4(1972) 57.
[2] Cf. ibid.
[3] RR 1984 1–2.
[4] Cf. GIRM 45: Fl I 173.
[5] Cf. GIRM 4: Fl I 162.

more closely with Christ offering himself as a victim, thus deriving more abundant fruit from the sacrifice'.[1] This canon, which is new, emphasises that the primary purpose of Mass offerings is to help provide support for the ministers and activities of the Church.

Can. 947 Even the semblance of trafficking or trading is to be entirely excluded from Mass offerings.

1858 The precept of Can. 898 that 'Christ's faithful are to hold the blessed Eucharist in the highest honour' has not always been obeyed and history shows that abuses can arise, particularly when money is involved. The Church is particularly sensitive to the abuse of simony. Much of the legislation on Mass offerings is concerned with avoiding 'even the semblance of trafficking or trading' in them, i.e. making any profit in relation to them. For this reason individual Bishops or Bishops' Conferences could well give serious thought to making particular regulations regarding practices in their respective territories which could be considered doubtful.

Can. 948 Separate Masses are to be applied for the intentions of those for each of whom an offering, even if small, has been made and accepted.

1859 The fundamental principle underlying this canon is that there must be as many Masses celebrated as there are offerings given and accepted. Essentially it repeats the norm of c.828 of the 1917 Code. Thus a celebrant may accept a single offering for a single Mass. Recently, however, this principle has been modified somewhat. The Congregation for the Clergy issued a decree in 1991 dealing with the so-called 'multi-intentional' or 'collective' Masses which were being celebrated in various parts of the world.[2]

1860 Briefly, this decree permits priests to celebrate one Mass for the intentions of several donors. However the Congregation places certain restrictions on such celebrations:

(a) the faithful must knowingly and voluntarily agree to have their intentions combined in a single celebration;

(b) the date, time and place of this celebration is to be publicly announced;

(c) such celebrations may occur, at most, only twice each week in any church;

(d) the celebrant may retain for himself only what amounts to the offering determined within the diocese; the remainder must be forwarded to the Ordinary as determined by Can. 951 §1.[3]

1861 Lest there be any doubt, this decree makes it clear that the principle of a single Mass for a single offering remains the fundamental norm: priests who accept an offering for Mass for a particular intention are obliged *in justice* to satisfy that obligation personally or to transfer it to another priest. The 'collective' Masses permitted by the decree ought not, however, to be confused with other legitimate practices such as the 'November Dead list', or membership of various Mass Associations and Missionary Unions which have, as one of the benefits of membership, the inclusion of one's intentions in a Mass celebrated every day, week or month for a specified period.[4]

---

[1] Pope Paul VI lit ap *Firma in Traditione* 15.VI.1974: Fl I 277.

[2] Cf. decr *Mos Iugiter* 22.II.1991: AAS 83(1991) 443–446; L'Osservatore Romano (English weekly ed) 25.III.1991; The Furrow (The Furrow Trust Ireland) 42(1991) 385–387. For a detailed account of the matter, cf. Manzanares *De stipendio pro missis ad intentionem 'collectivam' celebratis iuxta decretum 'Mos Iugiter'* Per 80 (1991) 579–608.

[3] Cf. *Mos Iugiter* 2 1; 2 2; 3 1–2.

[4] For a useful summary of the 1991 decree, cf. Dalton *Multi-intentional Mass Cards – the recent Decree* The Furrow 42(1991) 366–372. It is to be noted, however, that there is a substantial distinction between multi-intentional Mass cards and multi-intentional Mass *offerings*.

Part I The Sacraments

Can. 949 One who is obliged to celebrate and apply Mass for the intention of those who made an offering, is bound by this obligation even if through no fault of his own the offering received has been lost.

This canon repeats the norm of c.829 of the 1917 Code. An offering may be lost in many ways: through carelessness, theft or even devaluation of currency. It does not matter how the loss occurred: the obligation still remains.

Can. 950 If a sum of money is offered for the application of Masses, but with no indication of the number of Masses to be celebrated, their number is to be calculated on the basis of the offering prescribed in the place where the donor resides, unless the donor's intention must lawfully be presumed to have been otherwise.

Not infrequently it happens that a sum of money is given for Masses without any specification as to the number of Masses. This happens most commonly in wills. (Where the donor is still alive and available, the best course would be to approach him or her and have the number specified.) In the absence of any specification, the present canon provides a practical norm: the number of Masses is to be calculated by dividing the sum of money by the prescribed or customary offering of the place where the donor resides or resided at the time of e.g. the will. An exception to this rule arises when 'the donor's intention *must* (not *may*) lawfully be presumed to have been otherwise'. Thus, if during his or her lifetime the donor had habitually given an offering larger than the prescribed one, or if there was a special relationship between the donor and the priest, it should be presumed that the intention was to give an offering larger than the prescribed one. Such presumptions must obviously be properly based and not made lightly. The prescription of Can. 1300 about observing carefully the intentions of those who leave goods to pious causes must also be borne in mind.

Can. 951 §1 A priest who celebrates a number of Masses on the same day may apply each Mass for the intention for which an offering was made, subject however to the rule that, apart from Christmas Day, he may retain for himself the offering for only one Mass; the others he is to transmit to purposes prescribed by the Ordinary, while allowing for some compensation on the ground of an extrinsic title.

Can. 905 determines the number of times a priest may celebrate Mass on the same day. The present canon allows him to receive an offering for each Mass he celebrates on the same day but, except for Christmas Day when he may retain the offerings for all three Masses, he may not retain the offering for more than one Mass. Any others must be transferred to purposes prescribed by the Ordinary, 'while allowing for some compensation on the ground of an extrinsic title', e.g. expenses incurred in travelling to say the extra Mass. The Ordinary who determines how extra offerings are to be used is the Ordinary of the place where the Mass is celebrated.[1] A priest – and, it would seem, anyone else – who has the obligation of the *Missa pro populo* (see Cann. 388, 429, 534, 543 §2 2°) may retain a stipend for a second Mass celebrated on the same day.[2]

Can. 951 §2 A priest who on the same day concelebrates another Mass may not under any title accept an offering for that Mass.

This paragraph is specifically in the context of *concelebration* and, as such, is an exception to the norm of §1. The principle enunciated here was very clearly stated in the

---

[1] CCom reply 2.II.1987: AAS 79(1987) 1132.
[2] Cf. Comm 15(1983) 200–201 at Can. 896.

words of the declaration of the Congregation for Divine Worship in 1972: 'priests who celebrate Mass for the good of the faithful and who concelebrate at another Mass may on no account accept a stipend for the concelebrated Mass',[1] the manifest implication being that the two Masses are celebrated on the same day, whether or not the concelebrated Mass precedes the other. This therefore is a situation in which the transfer to the Ordinary of another stipend (see Can. 951 §1) simply does not arise.[2]

Can. 952 §1 The provincial council or the provincial Bishops' meeting is to determine by decree, for the whole of the province, what offering is to be made for the celebration and application of Mass, and it is unlawful for a priest to demand a larger sum. However, he may accept for the application of a Mass, an offering voluntarily made, which is greater, or even less, than that which has been determined.

1866 This paragraph represents a change from c.831 §1 of the 1917 Code which gave the local Ordinary the power to determine what offering was to be made for Masses. During the revision of the Code various options were considered before the present norm was determined.[3] Now the amount of the offering is to be determined either by the provincial council (see Can. 440) or by a meeting of the Bishops of the province. This puts the decision-making at a level intermediate between that of the individual Bishop and that of the Bishops' Conference. Presumably the reason is that, while it is desirable to have uniformity on this matter in a given area, conditions in the area covered by a Bishops' Conference might be too diverse to allow such uniformity in the whole region. Note that this canon does not require a uniform offering for all Masses: the Bishops could determine one amount for e.g. 'announced' or 'anniversary' Masses, and another for other Masses.

1867 A priest may certainly not demand more than the amount determined, but he may accept a greater or lesser offering which has been voluntarily made. Indeed in the case of the poor, charity will often demand – and is indeed frequently exercised – that he be prepared to take less than is the regular norm.

Can. 952 §2 Where there is no such decree, the custom existing in the diocese is to be observed.

1868 In default of a decree by the Bishops of the province, the custom existing in the diocese is to be followed. Indeed such custom could provide a valuable guide-line to the Bishops in determining the amount of the offering. It would be helpful, in practice, if from time to time diocesan Bishops were in some appropriate manner to make known what is the prescribed or the customary offering.

Can. 952 §3 Members of religious institutes of all kinds must abide by the decree or the local custom mentioned in §§ 1 and 2.

1869 All religious are subject to the Bishops' decree in this matter; they may not introduce their own amounts. This is principally to avoid the confusion and 'the semblance of trafficking and trading' that could result from not having uniformity of practice.

1870 The norms in this canon concern what were formerly called 'manual' Mass offerings, i.e. individual offerings for individual Masses. It does not deal with Mass offerings which derive from foundations, i.e. endowments to have Masses offered for a particu-

---

[1] SCDW decl *In Celebratione Missae* 7.VII.1972 3: Fl I 223.
[2] Cf. Pope Paul VI lit ap *Firma in Traditione* 3: Fl I 279.
[3] Cf. Comm 13(1981) 435 at Can. 117 §1; 15(1983) 201 at Can. 901.

Part I The Sacraments

lar intention either in perpetuity or for a length of years. The diocesan Bishop, in accordance with Can. 1304, is responsible for approving the acceptance of such a foundation and for determining the feasibility of carrying out its obligations and the sufficiency of the revenue.

Can. 953 No one may accept more offerings for Masses to be celebrated by himself than he can discharge within a year.

1871 This canon repeats the norm of c.835 of the 1917 Code and forbids a priest to accept more offerings for Masses to be celebrated by himself than he can discharge within a year. This does not, of course, forbid him to accept other offerings, on the understanding that they will be transferred in accordance with Can. 955.

Can. 954 If in certain churches or oratories more Masses are requested than can be celebrated there, these may be celebrated elsewhere, unless the donors have expressly stipulated otherwise.

1872 It may happen e.g. in a church at a place of pilgrimage, that more Masses will be requested than can be celebrated in that church. These Masses may be celebrated in any other church or oratory unless the donor has stipulated that they be said in this particular place. Before accepting such a stipulation, the person responsible should ensure that it can be fulfilled.

Can. 955 §1 One who intends to transfer to others the celebration of Masses to be applied, is to transfer them as soon as possible to priests of his own choice, provided he is certain that they are of proven integrity. He must transfer the entire offering received, unless it is quite certain that an amount in excess of the diocesan offering was given as a personal gift. Moreover, it is his obligation to see to the celebration of the Masses until such time as he has received evidence that the obligation has been undertaken and the offering received.

1873 A priest in a busy parish may well receive more requests to offer Mass than he can satisfy within a year. He will therefore see to the celebration of these by other priests. This canon lays down the rules about such transferral:

(a) he is to transfer the offerings 'as soon as possible';
(b) he is to transfer them to priests of his own choice whom he knows to be 'of proven integrity';
(c) he is to transfer the entire offering, unless it is quite certain that the amount in excess of the local offering was intended as a personal gift. This again is to prevent the 'trading or trafficking' mentioned in Can. 947. The phrase 'diocesan offering' means the offering determined for the particular diocese by the Bishops of the province or by diocesan custom;
(d) the responsibility of having the Masses celebrated remains that of the priest transferring the obligation until he is certain that the offerings have been received and that the obligations have been undertaken (see Can. 949). In practice, this simply imposes upon the priest receiving the transferred Masses the obligation to acknowledge his receipt and acceptance of them.

Can. 955 §2 Unless it is established otherwise, the time within which Masses are to be celebrated begins from the day the priest who is to celebrate them receives them.

1874 A priest is not to accept more offerings than he can celebrate in a year (see Can. 953), and this year begins to run when he accepts the obligation, unless there is clearly some other lawful stipulation. Accordingly, a priest to whom a number of Masses has been transferred, has a year to celebrate these, starting from the day on which he undertook to do so.

Can. 955 §3 Those who transfer to others Masses to be celebrated are without delay to record in a book both the Masses which they have accepted and those which they have passed on, noting also the offering for these Masses.

1875 Those who transfer Mass obligations are obliged to keep a record of the Masses received and transferred by themselves as well as of the offerings received, so that the full offering may be transferred in accordance with §1.

Can. 955 §4 Each priest must accurately record the Masses which he has accepted to celebrate and those which he has in fact celebrated.

1876 Although this obligation is distinct from that in §2, which is concerned with transferred Mass obligations, the same book could well be used for both purposes. Such a record is not just a necessary aid to the priest's memory; it also indicates any outstanding Mass obligations in the event of serious illness or death. The general thrust of the law, not only in this canon but throughout, is to insist that each individual priest keep an accurate record of the Mass obligations which he has undertaken and of the manner – whether by personal celebration or by transfer to other priests – in which he has fulfilled, or intends to fulfil, those obligations. A certain lack of attention to detail in this regard has been observed as a 'new phenomenon': it has to be recalled that, in accepting offerings for Mass, priests are undertaking an obligation binding in strict justice.

Can 956 Each and every administrator of pious causes or those in any way obliged to provide for the celebration of Mass, be they clerics or lay persons, are to hand over to their Ordinaries, in a manner to be determined by the latter, such Mass obligations as have not been discharged within a year.

1877 The predecessor of this canon, c.841 of the 1917 Code, made a distinction between 'manual' Masses and 'quasi-manual' Masses, specifying that the former had to be handed over to the Ordinary when a year after their acceptance had elapsed, while the year for the latter was reckoned as the calendar year. Both sorts of Masses are covered in the present canon, and it can be safely assumed that the two methods of reckoning the year, depending on the type of Mass obligation, still hold good. As well as individual priests, as regards their own personal Mass intentions, and administrators of pious causes, the canon obliges such people as parish priests whose parishes have accepted a gift with the condition that a certain number of Masses be offered, rectors of seminaries endowed with bursaries to which Mass obligations are attached, executors of wills to whom legacies for Masses have been committed, etc. If any of these have not discharged their obligations within the specified year, they are to hand them over to the Ordinary, who is to arrange to have the obligations fulfilled. In certain cases there may even be occasion for a reduction of Mass obligations in accordance with the rules of Can. 1308.

Can. 957 The duty and the right to see that Mass obligations are fulfilled belongs, in the case of the churches of the secular clergy, to the local Ordinary; in the case of churches of religious institutes or societies of apostolic life, to their Superiors.

1878 The duty and right of vigilance concerning the fulfilment of Mass obligations are assigned in this canon. For diocesan clergy these fall on the local Ordinary, for others on the appropriate Superior.

Part I The Sacraments

Can. 958 §1 The parish priest, as well as the rector of a church or other pious place in which Mass offerings are usually received, is to have a special book in which he is accurately to record the number, the intention and the offering of the Masses to be celebrated, and the fact of their celebration.

§2 The Ordinary is obliged to inspect these books each year, either personally or through others.

This canon is not directly concerned with what might be called the 'ordinary' parish, in which as a rule the individual priests keep each his own register or record of Mass-offerings received and their obligation discharged (see Can. 955 §4). What is in mind here are those churches, be they parochial or otherwise, and other such places 'in which Mass offerings are usually received', i.e. places in which the practice has developed of making Mass offerings almost as a matter of course. The obvious examples are places of special worship, such as pilgrimage centres, sanctuaries etc.; equally would be included certain houses of religious institutes where such a practice has become commonplace. It is for such 'churches or other pious places' that the law requires of those clerics in charge to keep 'a special book' or register in which are to be recorded the items detailed in §1. And the law imposes upon the relevant Ordinary (see Can. 134 §1) the obligation to inspect that register once every year, whether personally or through his delegate.   1879

Title IV
The Sacrament of Penance

INTRODUCTION

Vat. II called for the revision of the rite and formulae of the sacrament of penance 'so that they more clearly express both the nature and effect of the sacrament'.[1] The introduction to the *Order of Penance* situates the sacrament in the context of salvation history: '... not only did Jesus exhort men to do penance, to give up their sins and be converted to God with all their hearts. He also received sinners and reconciled them to the Father. He cured the sick as a sign of his power to forgive sins. He himself even died for our sins and rose from the dead for our justification. On the night he was betrayed, as he commenced his saving passion, he instituted the sacrifice of the new covenant in his blood for the remission of sins, and after his resurrection he sent his Spirit to the apostles that they might have the power to forgive sins or to retain them, and that they might accept the task of preaching penance and the remission of sins to all nations in his name'.[2] Although the Church is filled with Christ's divine gifts, its members are exposed to temptation and fall into sin and so even though it is holy, it is always in need of purification.[3]   1880

---

[1] SC 72: Fl I 22.

[2] MS 1: Fl I 33.

[3] Cf. MS 3: Fl I 34.

Can. 959 In the sacrament of penance the faithful who confess their sins to a lawful minister, are sorry for their sins and have a purpose of amendment, receive from God, through the absolution given by that minister, forgiveness of sins they have committed after baptism, and at the same time they are reconciled with the Church, which by sinning they wounded.

1879 This canon mentions a number of elements in the sacrament of penance, some to do with the penitent and one to do with the minister. The penitent must have contrition, which includes a purpose of amendment, and must confess his or her sins to a lawful minister. The minister gives absolution. Through this sacrament sins committed after baptism are forgiven by God and the sinner is simultaneously reconciled with the Church which has been wounded by the sin. The canon makes no mention of the element of satisfaction by which 'true conversion is completed';[1] this is dealt with by Can. 981. Neither does it describe absolution as 'judicial' as did the corresponding c.870 of the 1917 Code. This omission is not to deny the judicial aspect of this sacrament which indeed is referred to in Can. 978 §1, but serves to show that this aspect is not confined to absolution.[2] In any case the tribunal in question is one 'of mercy rather than one of strict and rigorous justice' and 'is comparable to human tribunals only by analogy'.[3]

Chapter I
THE CELEBRATION OF THE SACRAMENT

Can. 960 Individual and integral confession and absolution constitute the sole ordinary means by which a member of the faithful who is conscious of grave sin is reconciled with God and with the Church. Physical or moral impossibility alone excuses from such confession, in which case reconciliation may be attained by other means also.

1880 The *Order of Penance*, issued on 2 December 1973, contains three Rites of Penance: (1) the rite of reconciliation of individual penitents; (2) the rite of reconciliation of several penitents with individual confession and absolution; (3) the rite of reconciliation of several penitents with general confession and absolution. The first two are the only normal ways of celebrating the sacrament; the third is for use only in cases of grave necessity.[4] On this whole matter there has been some discussion among both priests and laity, and indeed in certain places a sometimes unfortunate variety in pastoral practice. It is to be noted that the terms under which each of the rites may be used are specifically and solely those which are determined in these Cann. 960–963, norms ultimately promulgated by the Legislator after a most extensive consultation throughout the Church. Even more importantly perhaps: the primary consideration is that penance is a sacrament and, as such, an act of worship which acknowledges not only the infinite mercy of God as witnessed by Christ's death on Calvary, but also the need for us sinners to avail ourselves of that mercy only by a true spirit of repentance and amendment. To use *any* of the rites of penance without this twofold essential acknowledgement would be an abuse of the sacrament.

---

[1] MS 6b: Fl I 38.

[2] Cf. Comm 10(1978) 50; 15(1983) 202 at Can. 913.

[3] Pope John Paul II ap exhort *Reconciliatio et Paenitentia* 2.XII.1984 (AAS 77(1985) 185–275) n.31 II: Origins 14(1984) 451.

[4] Cf. ibid. nn.32–33: Origins 14(1984) 453–454.

This canon repeats the rule of *Sacramentum Paenitentiae* about individual and complete confession being the only ordinary means of reconciliation for one in grave sin.[1] The question of completeness or integrity of confession is dealt with in Can. 988. Two exceptions to the 'ordinary means' prescribed by Can. 960 are the general absolution considered in Can. 961 and the possibility of an act of perfect contrition. Both of these are exceptional and are justified only in a case of 'physical or moral impossibility'. Physical impossibility would exist where there is imminent danger and no confessor is available, e.g. cases of serious illness where the patient is in a remote place, cases of major disaster where it is impossible for confessors to attend individually to all those in need. Moral impossibility would exist e.g. where the penitent fears with justification that complete confession could harm himself or some other person. 1881

Can. 961 §1 General absolution, without prior individual confession, cannot be given to a number of penitents together, unless

1° **danger of death threatens and there is not time for the priest or priests to hear the confessions of the individual penitents;**

2° **there exists a grave necessity, that is, given the number of penitents, there are not enough confessors available properly to hear the individual's confessions within an appropriate time, so that without fault of their own the penitents are deprived of the sacramental grace or of holy communion for a lengthy period of time. A sufficient necessity is not, however, considered to exist when confessors cannot be available merely because of a great gathering of penitents, such as can occur on some major feastday or pilgrimage.**

Although Can. 960 demands individual and integral confession of sins in the ordinary celebration of this sacrament, it is clear from the present canon that this requirement is not essential in the same way that contrition or absolution are. In certain circumstances general absolution without prior individual confession is permitted. However, the negative language of this canon makes it quite clear that these circumstances are to be regarded as quite exceptional. 1882

The first situation is when there is danger of death and there is not enough time for the priest or priests to hear the confessions of the individual penitents. In such a situation 'any and every priest has the faculty to give general absolution; if there is time, he should preface this with a very brief exhortation that each person be sure to make an act of contrition'.[2] The danger of death could arise from any cause such as sickness, accident, warfare, natural disaster etc. and the impossibility of attending to each penitent could come not only from the number of these but also from other factors causing inaccessibility. 1883

The second situation visualised is a more general one. There must be 'a grave necessity', and the canon explains this by saying that such a necessity exists when there is such a large number of penitents that they would be deprived of the sacramental grace of confession or of holy communion for a long time. It goes on to state that the unavailability of confessors due merely to a large gathering of people, such as on the occasion of a major feastday or pilgrimage, does not provide a sufficient necessity. Much less does the convoking of a large congregation for the express purpose of giving general absolution qualify.[3] The determining factor therefore, is not only the 1884

---

[1] SCDF Pastoral Norms *Sacramentum Paenitentiae* 16.VI.1972 I: DOL n.3039; CCC n.1484.
[2] Ibid. II: DOL n.3040.
[3] Cf. SCDF rep 20.I.1978: Fl II 62–63.

absolute number of penitents or even the proportion of penitents to priests available, but the length of time that the penitents would be deprived of the grace of this sacrament or of holy communion.

Can. 961 §2 It is for the diocesan Bishop to judge whether the conditions required in §1 n.2 are present; mindful of the criteria agreed with the other members of the Bishops' Conference, he can determine the cases of such necessity.

1885 The decision as to whether the conditions of §1 2° have been fulfilled in an individual case rests with the diocesan Bishop, who is to be guided also by the criteria agreed with the other members of the Bishops' Conference. These criteria will apply the conditions to the local situation. In particular, the latin word *diu* ('a lengthy period of time') must be interpreted.[1] Neither the individual Bishop nor the Bishops' Conference may change the required conditions or substitute other conditions or determine grave necessity according to their own criteria.[2] A priest has no power to decide in this matter except perhaps in a case when he is unable to contact the diocesan Bishop, in which situation he should be guided by the general principles of moral theology.[3] The language of this paragraph, speaking as it does of determining 'cases', strongly suggests that the Bishop should assess each situation individually, rather than lay down general rules.

Can. 962 §1 For a member of Christ's faithful to benefit validly from a sacramental absolution given to a number of people simultaneously, it is required not only that he or she be properly disposed, but also that he or she be at the same time personally resolved to confess in due time each of the grave sins which cannot for the moment be confessed.

1886 For the valid reception of general absolution this paragraph lays down two conditions. Firstly, as for any form of the rite of penance, the penitent must be properly disposed. The dispositions required are briefly described at Can. 987: '... they must be so disposed that, repudiating the sins they have committed and having the purpose of amending their lives, they turn back to God'. Secondly, the penitent must be personally resolved to confess in due time all the grave sins that he or she is unable to confess at present. Although during the drafting of the Code the Commission stated that the determination of what was 'due time' should be left to the commentators,[4] Can. 963 states that this confession is to be made 'as soon as possible', i.e. as soon as is possible for each individual penitent.

Can. 962 §2 Christ's faithful are to be instructed about the requirements set out in §1, as far as possible even on the occasion of general absolution being received. An exhortation that each person should make an act of contrition is to precede a general absolution, even in the case of danger of death if there is time.

---

[1] The directives issued by those Bishops' Conferences which have addressed this matter constitute a good example of the Code's wisdom in leaving the determination to the authority at local level: some determine *diu* to mean one or a number of months, others interpret it in terms rather of geographical or even climatic circumstances, others still state that (without prejudice to the right of the diocesan Bishop) the conditions for general absolution do not exist in their territories, and so on. The interested reader would profitably consult LCE Tavola per Paesi e Canoni at Can. 961; CN(USA) 12.

[2] Cf. Pope Paul VI Address to the Bishops of the USA 20.IV.1978: DOL n.3140.

[3] Cf. Comm 15(1983) 206 at Can. 915 §2.

[4] Cf. Comm 15(1983) 206 at Can. 916 §1.

Priests are obliged to instruct the faithful about the obligations contained in the first paragraph of this canon, as far as this is possible, and they should do this even on the occasion of general absolution. In addition, if time allows, even in danger of death, they are to exhort the penitents to make an act of contrition.

Can. 963 Without prejudice to the obligation mentioned in Can. 989, a person whose grave sins are forgiven by a general absolution, is as soon as possible, when the opportunity occurs, to make an individual confession before receiving another general absolution, unless a just reason intervenes.

Can. 989 prescribes that grave sins are to be confessed at least once a year. However, if someone has lawfully and validly received general absolution, he or she could be bound by this canon to confession even sooner if 'the opportunity occurs'. This should certainly be done before availing oneself of another general absolution, unless of course the same or similar conditions to those which justified the first general absolution again obtain. This would be most likely to occur in mission territories where one priest would have a vast area to cover. Those who have not committed grave sin are not obliged to confess their sins individually before receiving general absolution again.

Before passing from the foregoing explanation of the three Rites of Penance set out in the *Order of Penance* (2 December 1973), mention may be made of a practice which appears to be employed in some places. In general outline, it takes the following form: a liturgy of the Word, an examination of conscience, a recommendation that the faithful confess at least one sin, an individual confession to that effect, and the receipt of individual absolution. This form is sometimes used at penitential services, whether during Lent or on the occasion of a parish 'mission' or 'retreat'. Its justification is often on the ground that it does help to bring back to confession those who have ceased to frequent the sacrament. Having some of the elements of both rite 2 and rite 3, it has even been referred to as 'rite two-and-a-half'! Whatever about the alleged merits of such practice, it must be recalled that the Church expressly requires that 'the faithful are bound to confess, in kind and in number, all grave sins committed after baptism' (Can. 988 §1). There is moreover the fact of a real danger arising that a practice of this kind could lead to an erosion of the sense of personal responsibility for one's sins. The concepts of both sin and forgiveness can be trivialised. It may well be that it was just that which the Lutheran theologian Bonhoeffer had in mind when he referred to `cheap grace'. 'Cheap grace', he wrote, 'is the preaching of forgiveness without requiring repentance, baptism without Church discipline, communion without confession, absolution without personal confession.'[1] Pope John Paul II insists that 'it remains the obligation of pastors to facilitate for the faithful the practice of integral and individual confession of sins, which constitutes for them not only a duty but also an inviolable and inalienable right ...'[2]

Can. 964 §1 The proper place for hearing sacramental confessions is a church or oratory.

Since the sacrament of penance is not just a private affair between confessor and penitent, but has an important ecclesial dimension in that penitents 'are ... reconciled with the Church which they have wounded by their sins',[3] it is fitting that it be celebrated in a sacred place. This also emphasises its link with the Eucharist, the reception of which symbolises full communion with the Church.

---

[1] *The Cost of Discipleship* SCM London 1959 36.

[2] ap exhort *Reconciliatio et Paenitentia* n.33: Origins 14(1984) 454.

[3] LG 11: Fl I 362. Cf. also Comm 10(1978) 68 at Can. 157.

Can. 964 §2 As far as the confessional is concerned, norms are to be issued by the Bishops' Conference, with the proviso however that confessionals, fitted with a fixed grille between the penitent and the confessor, always be available in an open place, so that the faithful who so wish may freely use them.

1891 Bishops' Conferences are required to issue norms concerning confessionals. These norms will take into account local conditions and circumstances. They may, e.g. permit 'reconciliation rooms' or other suitable arrangements whereby confessor and penitent can more easily communicate. However they are required to have a 'traditional' confessional available and accessible to all who wish to use it. This will have a fixed grille so that penitents may confess anonymously. Note that unlike its predecessor, the present Code does not have particular rules for the hearing of women's confessions: it was decided to leave any norms in this regard to the discretion of the Bishops' Conference.[1]

Can. 964 §3 Except for a just reason, confessions are not to be heard elsewhere than in a confessional.

1892 The reason for hearing confessions elsewhere than in the designated place does not have to be a grave one but it must be *just*, i.e. not fictitious or trivial. Examples of just reasons would be: illness, deafness, claustrophobia, urgency, the desire to go to a particular confessor when a confessional is not available, etc. All of this Can. 964 reflects the practical wisdom of the Church, gathered over centuries, in this delicate area. It has a particular relevance in modern-day circumstances, when a sometimes hostile society would on occasion wish to assign to the administration of the sacrament of penance an occasion for abuse or enticement of the penitent. It goes without saying that every confessor will keep this insidious and perhaps even malicious danger in mind.

Chapter II
THE MINISTER OF THE SACRAMENT OF PENANCE

Can. 965 Only a priest is the minister of the sacrament of penance.

1893 This canon is almost identical with c.871 of the 1917 Code and affirms that only one who is in priestly orders can be minister of this sacrament. 'The Church exercises the ministry of the sacrament of penance through Bishops and priests, who call the faithful to conversion by preaching the word of God and who testify to the forgiveness of sins and impart it to them in the name of Christ and by the power of the Holy Spirit.'[2]

Can. 966 §1 For the valid absolution of sins, it is required that, in addition to the power of order, the minister has the faculty to exercise that power in respect of the faithful to whom he gives absolution.

1894 In addition to the power of order, a priest needs a specific authority to exercise that power in respect of those whom he absolves. The present Code no longer uses the term 'jurisdiction' to describe this specific authority. It prefers to use the word 'faculty' since what is involved is an exercise of sacramental power rather than of the

---

[1] Cf. Comm 10(1978) 69 at Can. 157 §2. For the manner in which Bishops' Conferences have hitherto dealt with this matter, cf. LCE Tavola per Paesi e Canoni at Can. 964.

[2] MS 9: Fl II 40.

Part I The Sacraments

power of governance.[1] The reason for retaining the traditional notion of faculties for hearing confession was, at least in part, in order to promote good order in the Church: if the need for them were suppressed, a Bishop could not remove them.[2] The requirement of faculties for valid absolution is a disciplinary provision which allows Church authorities to react to any such abuses as might arise.

Can. 966 §2 A priest can be given this faculty either by the law itself, or by a concession issued by the competent authority in accordance with Can. 969.

1895 The required faculty may come *either* from the law – as e.g. in the case of the Pope, Cardinals and Bishops (see Can. 967 §1) – *or* from a specific concession made by the competent authority as determined in Can. 969. Note also that Can. 144 (q.v.) is relevant in this context.

Can. 967 §1 Besides the Roman Pontiff, Cardinals by virtue of the law itself have the faculty to hear the confessions of Christ's faithful everywhere. Likewise, Bishops have this faculty, which they may lawfully use everywhere, unless in a particular case the diocesan Bishop has disapproved.

1896 The Pope and Cardinals have, by virtue of the law itself, the faculty to hear confessions without any restriction as to person or place. Bishops have the same faculty, with just one restriction: if, in a particular case, the local diocesan Bishop indicates his objection, they may not lawfully exercise this faculty; this restriction does not affect validity. The phrase 'in a particular case' means that a diocesan Bishop may not issue a general or 'blanket' disapproval.

Can. 967 §2 Those who have the faculty habitually to hear confessions, whether by virtue of their office or by virtue of a concession by the Ordinary of either the place of incardination or that in which they have a domicile, can exercise that faculty everywhere, unless in a particular case the local Ordinary has disapproved, without prejudice to the provisions of Can. 974 §§2-3.

1897 Traditionally the Church has required confessional faculties for reasons of discipline but, with the growth in travel between and within countries, there has been a desire to have this discipline relaxed in the interests of a more flexible and fruitful ministry. Accordingly, this canon provides that priests who have the faculty habitually to hear confessions whether by virtue of their office (see Can. 968 §1), or by virtue of concession by their own Ordinary or the Ordinary of the place where they have a domicile – can exercise that faculty *everywhere*. This is a very substantial change introduced by the current Code, with manifestly helpful pastoral implications. There is but one restriction, namely 'unless in a particular case the local Ordinary has refused' them permission to do so. From the reference to Can. 974 §2, it is clear that such a refusal would in effect be a revocation of faculties for that territory and accordingly that confessions heard in spite of such a refusal would be invalid. As in §1 such a refusal may be made *only* 'in a particular case', i.e. where a priest, or perhaps a group of priests, is deemed unfit to hear confessions.

Note that the general extension of faculties contained in this paragraph refers only to *habitual* faculties. A priest who has received faculties only for a particular occasion or for a particular group of people receives no more than that; his power is not

---

[1] Cf. Comm 9(1977) 235; 10(1978) 56.
[2] Ibid.

extended. Efforts during the drafting of this canon to restrict further the exercise of this faculty were resisted by the Commission.[1]

Can. 967 §3 In respect of the members and those others who live day and night in a house of an institute or society, this same faculty is by virtue of the law itself possessed everywhere by those who have the faculty to hear confessions, whether by virtue of their office or by virtue of a special concession of the competent Superior in accordance with Cann. 968 §2 and 969 §2. They may lawfully use this faculty, unless in a particular case some major Superior has, in respect of his own subjects, disapproved.

1899 This paragraph is concerned with priests who have the faculty to hear the confessions of members of religious institutes or clerical societies of apostolic life of pontifical right and of those who live night and day in a house of the institute or society. These may be priests of the institute or society, may belong to another institute or society or may be diocesan. The limited faculty that they have in respect of those mentioned, whether it comes by virtue of their office or by concession of the competent Superior, is extended to all houses of the institute or society. A major Superior may in a particular case deny a priest the right to exercise this faculty, but the wording of the canon indicates that such denial would affect only the lawfulness, not the validity, of such exercise.

Can. 968 §1 By virtue of his office, for each within the limits of his jurisdiction, the faculty to hear confessions belongs to the local Ordinary, to the canon penitentiary, to the parish priest and to those who are in the place of the parish priest.

1900 This canon lists those who have the faculty to hear confessions by virtue of the offices which they hold. In each case the faculty is limited by the extent of the office-holder's jurisdiction. Local Ordinaries, i.e. (in addition to Bishops who were considered at Can. 967 §1) Vicars general and episcopal Vicars, enjoy this faculty by law within the territory of their diocese. This applies also to their counterparts in those particular Churches which are equivalent to a diocese (see Can. 368). The jurisdiction of the canon penitentiary or of the priest appointed to fulfil this office (see Can. 508 §2) is described in Can. 508 §1. A parish priest and those who take his place (see Cann. 515–544) have faculties for the parish. Since all of the above have habitual faculties by virtue of their offices, they have the faculty to hear confessions everywhere in accordance with Can. 967 §2.

Can. 968 §2 By virtue of their office, the faculty to hear the confessions of their own subjects and of those others who live day and night in the house, belongs to the Superiors of religious institutes or of societies of apostolic life, if they are clerical and of pontifical right, who in accordance with the constitutions have executive power of governance, without prejudice however to the provision of Can. 630 §4.

1901 Superiors of religious institutes or of societies of apostolic life, if they are clerical and of pontifical right, who in accordance with the constitutions have executive power of governance (see Can. 596 §2), have the faculties to hear the confessions of their subjects and of those who live day and night in a house of the institute or society. The reference to Can. 630 §4 is a reminder that Superiors are not to hear the confessions of their subjects unless these spontaneously ask them to do so; this is in order to avoid conflict between the internal and external forums.

---

[1] Cf. Comm 15(1983) 208 at Can. 921 §2.

Can. 969 §1 Only the local Ordinary is competent to give to any priests whomsoever the faculty to hear the confessions of any whomsoever of the faithful. Priests who are member of religious institutes may not, however, use this faculty without the permission, at least presumed, of their Superior.

It is the local Ordinary who gives to any priest the faculty to hear the confessions of those in his territory. This grant of faculties, if given habitually to a priest of the diocese in question or to one who has a domicile there, can form the basis for the wider power given in Can. 967 §2. If the priest in question is a religious, he is not to exercise this faculty without the permission, at least presumed, of his Superior – normally this permission can be presumed; this stipulation is not for validity.

Can. 969 §2 The Superior of a religious institute or of a society of apostolic life, mentioned in Can. 968 §2, is competent to give to any priests whomsoever the faculty to hear the confessions of his own subjects and of those others who live day and night in the house.

A grant of a faculty more limited in its scope can be given by the Superiors of religious institutes or of societies of apostolic life of apostolic right, provided they have from their constitutions executive power of governance. It can be given to any priest and is limited to the subjects of the Superior in question and to those who live night and day in the house of the institute or society. Again, this faculty, if given habitually, can form the basis for the wider faculty granted by Can. 967 §2.

Can. 970 The faculty to hear confessions is not to be given except to priests whose suitability has been established, either by examination or by some other means.

Before a priest is given the faculty to hear confessions he must satisfy the competent authority that he is suitable to act as a confessor. Pope John Paul II sums up the qualities required in a confessor: '... the confessor must necessarily have the human qualities of prudence, discretion, discernment and a firmness tempered by gentleness and kindness. He must likewise have a serious and careful preparation ... in the different branches of theology, pedagogy and psychology, in the methodology of dialogue and above all in a living and communicable knowledge of the word of God. But it is even more necessary that he should live an intense and genuine spiritual life'.[1] Suitability can be established by an examination – e.g. just before ordination or just prior to taking up an appointment in a new diocese – or by some other method deemed appropriate by the competent Ordinary.

Can. 971 The local Ordinary is not to give the faculty habitually to hear confessions to a priest, even to one who has a domicile or quasi-domicile within his jurisdiction, without first, as far as possible, consulting that priest's own Ordinary.

This canon deals with the granting of the faculty to hear confessions to a priest who is not incardinated in the diocese or territory of the grantor. This could be a priest of another diocese or a priest member of a religious institute or society of apostolic life. In either case, even if the priest in question has a domicile or quasi-domicile within the territory, the local Ordinary is not to grant him *habitual* faculties without first having made every reasonable effort to consult the priest's own Ordinary. The reason for this is clearly to assist the grantor in satisfying himself as to the suitability of this priest to act as a confessor.

---

[1] ap exhort *Reconciliatio et Paenitentia* n.29: Origins 14(1984) 450.

Can. 972 The faculty to hear confessions may be given by the competent authority mentioned in Can. 969, for either an indeterminate or a determinate period of time.

1906   The faculty could be given indefinitely as e.g. in the case of a priest who is incardinated in the grantor's diocese and who intends to remain there. In the case of a religious priest who is ministering in a diocese, he might be given faculties for as long as he stays in the diocese. Both of these would be examples of indeterminate periods. On the other hand, a priest who is on probation might be given faculties for, say, a year, or a priest giving a retreat might be given them for the duration of the retreat. It will be for the competent authority to judge what is most appropriate in each case.

Can. 973 The faculty habitually to hear confessions is to be given in writing.

1907   The requirement that habitual faculties be given in writing allows for more supervision.[1] In many dioceses a printed *pagella* is issued, which grants not only the faculty to hear confessions but also such other faculties and permissions as may be relevant to the diocesan circumstances. The requirement of this canon is not for validity.

Can. 974 §1 Neither the local Ordinary nor the competent Superior may, except for a grave reason, revoke the grant of a faculty habitually to hear confessions.

1908   Since the revocation of habitual faculties is a serious matter, not only for the priest's ministry but also for his good name, it may not be done save for a serious and proven reason, such e.g. as serious misbehaviour by the priest while hearing confessions, the consistent giving by him of advice based on heterodox theology, a consistently scandalous lifestyle on his part, his withdrawal from the authority of his Bishop or Superior, etc.

Can. 974 §2 If the faculty to hear confessions granted by the local Ordinary mentioned in Can. 967 §2 is revoked by that Ordinary, the priest loses the faculty everywhere. If the faculty is revoked by another local Ordinary, the priest loses it only in the territory of the Ordinary who revokes it.

1909   A faculty granted by the local Ordinary of the place of incardination or domicile may, as Can. 967 §2 states, be exercised everywhere. If this local Ordinary revokes the faculty, the revocation is effective everywhere. If, on the other hand, another local Ordinary revokes the faculty in accordance with that same canon (q.v.) the priest loses the faculty only in the territory of the Ordinary who revoked it. The effect of either revocation, general or particular, is to render invalid an absolution given by such a priest in spite of the revocation.

Can. 974 §3 Any local Ordinary who has revoked a priest's faculty to hear confessions is to notify the Ordinary who is proper to that priest by reason of incardination or, if the priest is a member of a religious institute, his competent Superior.

1910   Precisely because revocation of confessional faculties is such a serious matter, the priest's proper Ordinary or his competent Superior must be informed. This is not simply a matter of courtesy; it also allows the Ordinary or Superior to try to remedy the situation which led to the revocation or, if this is not possible, it may even alert him to the need for a more general revocation of the confessional faculty.

---

[1] Cf. Comm 15(1983) 210 at Can. 927.

Can. 974 §4 If the faculty to hear confessions is revoked by his own major Superior, the priest loses everywhere the faculty to hear the confessions of the members of the institute. But if the faculty is revoked by another competent Superior, the priest loses it only in respect of those subjects who are in that Superior's jurisdiction.

This paragraph states, for a faculty granted by a religious Superior, a norm analogous to that of §2 for a faculty granted by a local Ordinary. If the revocation is made by the priest's own major Superior, the faculty cannot be used anywhere. But if it is made by another competent Superior, it takes effect only in respect of those who are in that Superior's jurisdiction.   1911

Can. 975 Apart from revocation, the faculty mentioned in Can. 976 §2 ceases by loss of office, by excardination, or by loss of domicile.

The faculty granted in Can. 967 §2 of hearing confessions anywhere depends on the fulfilment of one (or more) of three conditions: (a) the original faculty was based on the holding of an office; (b) it was granted by the Ordinary of incardination; or (c) it was granted by the Ordinary of the place of domicile. If the basis for these conditions ceases, so does the faculty. However, it is possible that a priest could have had the faculty on the basis of more than one condition, e.g. a parish priest would have the faculty by virtue of his office, but in many cases he would also have it by virtue of an earlier grant by the Ordinary of the diocese in which he was incardinated or had a domicile. Hence, if he were to resign his office, he would still retain his faculty, unless of course he was also excardinated or lost his domicile.   1912

Can. 976 Any priest, even though he lacks the faculty to hear confessions, can validly absolve any penitents who are in danger of death, from any censures and sins, even if an approved priest is present.

Just as in c.882 of the 1917 Code the law provides that when a penitent is in danger of death, any priest, even if he lacks the faculty to hear confessions, can validly and lawfully absolve him or her from any censures and sins, even if an otherwise approved priest is present. This reflects the Church's wish to provide the penitent in such circumstances with the fullest opportunity to receive the sacrament and with the widest choice in confessors. The phrase 'any priest' would include a priest under censure (see Can. 1335), a priest who has been laicised in accordance with Can. 290 3°, or one who is any way in an irregular situation in relation to the Church. The danger of death does not have to be imminent; it suffices e.g. that the penitent be suffering from a terminal illness.   1913

Can. 977 The absolution of a partner in a sin against the sixth commandment of the Decalogue is invalid, except in danger of death.

This norm takes its origin from the constitution of Pope Benedict XIV *Sacramentum Paenitentiae* of 1.VI.1741, and is substantially the same as that given in c.884 of the 1917 Code. Unless the penitent is in danger of death, absolution given by a priest to a partner in a sin against the sixth commandment is invalid. A decree of the Sacred Penitentiary issued on 22 January 1879 stated that this norm applies even if the sin was committed before the priest was ordained. Ignorance of the law on the part of the priest does not alter the invalidity of the absolution (see Can. 15 §1). The penalty for breaking this law is given in Can. 1378 §1: the priest incurs a *latae sententiae* excommunication reserved to the Apostolic See. A proposal to extend the norm of this canon to the absolution of partners in other grave sins was rejected by the Revision Commission.[1]   1914

---

[1] Cf. Comm 15(1983) 210 at Can. 931.

Can. 978 §1 In hearing confessions the priest is to remember that he is at once both judge and healer, and that he is constituted by God as a minister of both divine justice and divine mercy, so that he may contribute to the honour of God and the salvation of souls.

1915 This paragraph, which contains the only surviving reference to the tribunal aspect of the sacrament of penance (see Commentary on Can. 959), directs the confessor to remember his twofold function as judge and healer, minister of both divine justice and divine mercy. He must compromise neither function, and must not be over-strict in seeking justice or over-lax in being merciful. The two principles which should guide him are the honour of God and the salvation of souls.

Can. 978 §2 In administering the sacrament, the confessor, as a minister of the Church, is to adhere faithfully to the teaching of the magisterium and to the norms laid down by the competent authority.

1916 In administering the sacrament of penance the priest does not act in a personal capacity, but in the name of the Church to which he reconciles the sinner. Accordingly his manner of acting, his guidance of penitents and his discernment as a confessor must reflect the mind of the Church.[1] Serious and habitual deviation from the magisterium (see Can. 750) could constitute a grave reason which would justify the revocation of a priest's faculty to hear confessions in accordance with Can. 974 §1.

Can. 979 In asking questions the priest is to act with prudence and discretion, taking into account the condition and age of the penitent, and he is to refrain from enquiring the name of a partner in sin.

1917 Questioning during confession should be limited to what is necessary for the integrity of the confession and the need to provide guidance for the penitent. This will obviously call for prudence and discretion on the part of the confessor, who will *inter alia* have to take into consideration the age and condition of the penitent. This will be particularly true regarding sins against chastity. An instruction of the Holy Office in 1943 on this matter recommended that where there is danger to either priest or penitent in a particular line of questioning the requirement of integral confession should take second place to discretion.[2] The canon specifically forbids the priest to ask the name of a partner in sin.

Can. 980 If the confessor is in no doubt about the penitent's disposition and the penitent asks for absolution, it is not to be denied or deferred.

1918 Absolution is not a personal favour to be granted or withheld as the priest pleases. If he is in no doubt about the penitent's dispositions (see Can. 987) and is asked for absolution, he must give it and not deny or defer it. If he is in doubt or if he is certain that the person is not properly disposed, he should first of all try to bring about the proper frame of mind in the penitent. If he fails in this, he might be obliged to defer or even deny absolution in case otherwise absolution might be seen as something 'magical' and not dependent for fruitfulness on the penitent's dispositions.

Can. 981 The confessor is to impose salutary and appropriate penances, in proportion to the kind and number of sins confessed, taking into account, however, the condition of the penitent. The penitent is bound personally to fulfil these penances.

---

[1] Cf. MS 10: Fl II 40.
[2] SCHO instr *Ecclesia Numquam* 16.V.1943: CLD 3 381.

This canon essentially repeats c.887 of the 1917 Code. 'True conversion is completed by satisfaction for sin, by improvement of life and repair of the damage done. The work of satisfaction and its measure should be suited to the penitent, so that he should restore the order he had damaged and take suitable medicine for the malady which afflicted him.'[1] The two principles which should determine a suitable penance in an individual case are the gravity and number of the sins confessed and the condition of the penitent. The Introduction to the *Order of Penance* provides some guidelines: 'The penance imposed may fittingly take the form of prayer, or self-denial, but especially of service to the neighbour and works of mercy. By these latter the social aspect of sin and of its forgiveness are set in relief.'[2] The penitent has an obligation to carry out the penance personally.

Can. 982 A person who confesses to having falsely denounced to ecclesiastical authority a confessor innocent of the crime of solicitation to a sin against the sixth commandment of the Decalogue, is not to be absolved unless that person has first formally withdrawn the false denunciation and is prepared to make good whatever harm may have been done.

The offence of solicitation is described in Can. 1387. The Church regards a false accusation of such solicitation as a very serious matter since, due to the seal of confession, the priest has little if any opportunity to defend himself against it. Can. 1390 determines the penalties for false denunciation, and the present canon demands that absolution should not be given until the denunciation is formally withdrawn and the person making it is prepared to make good any harm that may have been done. These two requirements serve to ensure a real repentance and purpose of amendment.

Can. 983 §1 The sacramental seal is inviolable. Accordingly, it is absolutely wrong for a confessor in any way to betray the penitent, for any reason whatsoever, whether by word or in any other fashion.

Everything disclosed to the priest in the sacrament of penance, *whether absolution is given or not*, comes under the 'seal of confession'. The use of the latin word *nefas* ('absolutely wrong') shows how seriously the norm of this canon is regarded. Put simply, the priest is strictly forbidden to reveal by any means whatever anything the penitent may have disclosed to him. Even the penitent cannot release him from this obligation. 'The confessor, realising that, as God's minister, he knows the secret conscience of his brother, is under a most sacred obligation to maintain the sacramental seal.'[3] If a confessor needs in a particular case to consult an expert in moral theology or in canon law, he must in doing so be careful not in any way to connect the sin with the sinner. If there is a real danger of doing this, he must either forgo the consultation or receive the penitent's permission to disclose the matter in the limited fashion necessary. So serious has always been the Church's insistence on the absolute inviolability of this sacramental seal that in many civil jurisdictions it is recognised as being, technically, *privileged* information, not subject to scrutiny by the civil courts.

Violation of the seal may be direct or indirect. It is *direct* if the priest explicitly or equivalently reveals the sin and the sinner: thus e.g. he might name the person and tell what he or she had confessed, or he might mention the sin only but in such circumstances that his hearers can easily determine who the sinner is. It is *indirect* if

---

[1] MS 6c: Fl II 38.
[2] Ibid. 18: Fl II 43.
[3] Ibid. 10: Fl II 40.

there is a lesser danger of the sin and the sinner being identified. The distinction is of importance in relation to the penalties prescribed (see Can. 1388 §1).

Can. 983 §2 An interpreter, if there is one, is also obliged to observe this secret, as are others who in any way whatever come to a knowledge of sins from a confession.

1925 Can. 990 allows confession through an interpreter; this paragraph obliges him or her to the same secrecy as that of the priest. The very same obligation binds all others who have in any way got to know of sins from a confession. Although the obligation to secrecy is the same as that on the confessor and its violation is also subject to a penalty (see Can. 1388 §2), technically it is not referred to as the 'seal' but simply as a 'secret'.

1926 In 1988 the Congregation for the Doctrine of the Faith issued a decree which provided for the extreme excommunication *latae sententiae* on anyone who recorded on an instrument or otherwise published anything, whether true or false, said in sacramental confession.[1]

Can. 984 §1 The confessor is wholly forbidden to use knowledge acquired in confession to the detriment of the penitent, even when all danger of disclosure is excluded.

1927 Can. 983 forbids the disclosure of information gained during sacramental confession; the present paragraph forbids the confessor to use any information so gained to the penitent's detriment, even if there is no risk of disclosure. The basic principle is that it is never lawful to do what one would not have done but for the fact of having heard the confession. So a priest could not e.g. discriminate against employing someone on the sole basis of what that person had told him in confession; neither should he in preaching or lecturing use as a specific example that which he has heard in confession. Any such practice could give rise to the suspicion that he is careless about the seal – and even suspicion, however unfounded, is to be sedulously avoided in this area.[2]

Can. 984 §2 A person who is in authority may not in any way, for the purpose of external governance, use knowledge about sins which has at any time come to him from the hearing of confession.

1928 No one who exercises authority in the external forum, such as a Bishop, religious Superior, a member of staff in e.g. a seminary or a school etc., may use information which has come to him in the hearing of confessions. Thus, e.g. a Bishop who at some stage (even before he became a Bishop) heard a priest's confession, could not use any information, good or bad, gained from that confession in deciding to appoint or not to appoint that priest to a particular position. A suggestion that an exception be made when the use of such information would be to the penitent's advantage was rejected during the drafting of this canon, precisely because no one could judge in such a dangerous matter.[3]

1929 One certain principle which emerges from Cann. 983–984 is that information gained in the confessional should be regarded as not having been gained at all and, in so far as is humanly possible, should not *ever* be acted on or spoken of *in any way*.

---

[1] SCDF decr undated: AAS 80(1988) 1367.

[2] In this regard, cf. instr of the Holy Office 9.VI.1915 forbidding any use of confessional knowledge outside the confessional: CLD 1 413–414.

[3] Cf. Comm 10(1978) 67 at Can. 154 §2.

Can. 985 The director and assistant director of novices, and the rector of a seminary or of any other institute of education, are not to hear the sacramental confessions of their students resident in the same house, unless in individual instances the students of their own accord request it.

This canon is based on the same principles as Can. 984 §2 and is designed to avoid the danger of mixing the internal and external forums. Even though all the faithful are free to choose their own confessors (see Can. 991), there are obvious and common-sense reasons why those mentioned in this canon should not normally hear the confessions of the students under their direction. There will always be the danger of confusing confessional and extra-confessional knowledge, and there could be the suspicion that confessional knowledge was being used improperly, even if this were not in fact the case. Those mentioned may hear such confessions in an individual case if the students request this of their own accord. But even here they could, outside of a case of grave necessity, refuse to do so for fear of a conflict of roles in the external and internal forums. Can. 630 §4 has a similar rule regarding religious Superiors and their subjects.

1930

Can. 986 §1 All to whom by virtue of office the care of souls is committed, are bound to provide for the hearing of the confessions of the faithful entrusted to them, who reasonably request confession, and they are to provide these faithful with an opportunity to make individual confession on days and at times arranged to suit them.

The norm stated here is a specific example of the general principle stated in Can. 843 §1 that 'sacred ministers may not deny the sacraments to those who opportunely ask for them, are properly disposed and are not prohibited by law from receiving them'. The obligation falls on those who by office have the care of souls entrusted to them. These include parish priests (see Can. 528 §2), chaplains (see Can. 566 §1), religious Superiors (see Can. 630 §2) and those responsible for seminary formation (see Can. 240 §1). The obligation is not always to be fulfilled personally. Indeed in the case of religious Superiors and seminary rectors, this is normally forbidden (see Cann. 985, 630 §4). Those with the care of souls are to provide opportunity for confessions, both when reasonably asked for them and at times fixed to suit the convenience of the faithful. What is reasonable will depend very much on individual circumstances, but in this area above all a priest should presume that the request is reasonable unless the contrary is abundantly clear.

1931

Can. 986 §2 In an urgent necessity, every confessor is bound to hear the confessions of Christ's faithful, and in danger of death every priest is so obliged.

If there is an urgent necessity – e.g. if the penitent is conscious of being in mortal sin and wishes to repent without delay – every confessor is obliged to hear the confession. The urgency of the case automatically means that a request for confession is reasonable. In danger of death *any priest*, even e.g. one without the normal faculty to hear confessions, or a dispensed priest, not only can hear confession (in accordance with Can. 976) but is obliged to do so.

1932

Chapter III
THE PENITENT

Can. 987 In order that Christ's faithful may receive the saving remedy of the sacrament of penance, they must be so disposed that, repudiating the

sins they have committed and having the purpose of amending their lives, they turn back to God.

1933 Fruitful celebration of the liturgy requires 'that the faithful come to it with proper dispositions'.[1] This is especially true of the sacraments, and the present canon states in broad terms what is required in recipients of the sacrament of penance. Above all they must have a true sorrow for their sins. True sorrow necessarily involves 'repudiating the sins they have committed' and 'having the purpose of amending their lives', a desire for genuine conversion so that, having turned away from God in sin, they turn back to him in penance. The very fact of approaching this sacrament implies sorrow for sin and so a penitent should always be presumed to be in good faith. The sorrow may be far from perfect, and the confessor may have to help the penitent to come to a better understanding and acceptance of what he or she is doing.

Can. 988 §1 Each of Christ's faithful is bound to confess, in kind and number, all grave sins committed after baptism, of which after careful examination of conscience he or she is aware, which have not yet been directly pardoned by the keys of the Church, and which have not been confessed in an individual confession.

1934 This canon is concerned with what has been traditionally called the 'integrity' of confession. It determines what sins must be confessed. These are all grave[2] sins committed after baptism, of which the penitent is aware after a proper examination of conscience and which have not yet been directly pardoned by 'the keys of the Church'[3] and which have not been confessed in an individual confession. Sins committed before baptism are forgiven in that sacrament and need not be confessed. Sins not directly pardoned by the keys of the Church include those for which the penitent has made an act of perfect contrition or which have been inadvertently and inculpably omitted in a previous confession. In accordance with Can. 963 a person who has had grave sins forgiven by a general absolution is bound subsequently to confess these in an individual confession.

1935 All grave sins must be confessed 'in kind and in number' i.e. they must be identified, and the number of times each one was committed must be mentioned as far as this is reasonably possible; this is an area in which the prudent confessor must not be mathematical but rather exercise a particular sensitivity and understanding. Although the canon does not explicitly repeat the requirement of c.901 of the 1917 Code that the penitent also set out any circumstances which would change the nature of the sin, this is clearly still required by the general requirement to confess all grave sins fully and properly. The basic requirement is that the penitent approach the sacrament 'with a humble and contrite heart', genuinely seeking forgiveness for what he or she knows to

---

[1] SC 11: Fl I 6. Cf. CCC nn.1430–1433.

[2] The 1917 Code, following the usage of the Council of Trent, spoke of 'mortal' sins. The present canon follows the language of MS 7 (cf. Fl II 39) and speaks of 'grave' sins. There is no basis for thinking that there is any important change of doctrine here: cf. *Reconciliatio et Paenitentia* n.17: Origins 14(1984) 440.

[3] The phrase 'by the keys of the Church' is one established by a long tradition: in effect, it means 'through the power and ministry of the Church as committed to it by Jesus Christ its founder' (cf. John 20:22–23; Matt 18:15–18). Its use here (as indeed in c.902 of the 1917 Code) 'indicates the precise nature of the confessional obligation. By its very nature sin not only offends God but also wounds or diminishes the Church established by the Son of God as *inter alia* the visible sign of the redemptive work of His own death and resurrection': cf. Can. 959; ID n.2: Fl I 63; CCC nn.1455–1457.

have been wrongdoings, and truly pledging a resolve to do better in the future. The very antithesis of this approach would be any attitude which might even appear to consider the sacrament of penance as in any way, as it were, a mechanical instrument for the forgiveness of sins.

Can. 988 §2 It is recommended that Christ's faithful confess venial sins also.

Although the confession of venial sins is not obligatory it is recommended because 'those who fall into venial sin ... experiencing their weakness daily, receive through frequent confession the strength to arrive at the full freedom of the children of God'.[1]

1936

Can. 989 All the faithful who have reached the age of discretion are bound faithfully to confess their grave sins at least once a year.

On reaching the age of discretion, which is presumed to be at the age of seven (see Can. 97 §2), all the faithful are bound to confess their grave sins at least once a year. This is a minimal requirement rather than a desired norm; it had its origin at the Fourth Lateran Council. There is no obligation to confess even once a year if the person has committed only venial sins. Although in the past this obligation has been traditionally associated with the obligation to receive the Eucharist once a year at Paschal time (see Can. 920), there is in fact no necessary connection between the two, nor is there any specified or preferred time for fulfilling the obligation of annual confession.

1937

Can. 990 No one is forbidden to confess through an interpreter, provided however that abuse and scandal are avoided, and without prejudice to the provision of Can. 983 §2.

Confession through an interpreter is clearly an exceptional event. Apart from the difficulty of confessing sins clearly, the confessor will be seriously handicapped in discerning the state of soul of the penitent and in giving the necessary advice and counselling. However, such confession is allowed with due safeguards against abuse and scandal and, above all, with great care for the secrecy of what is confessed. Those chosen to act as interpreters in confession should be above reproach and should be made clearly aware of the serious obligation of secrecy laid upon them.

1938

Can. 991 All Christ's faithful are free to confess their sins to lawfully approved confessors of their own choice, even to one of another rite.

This canon reflects the Church's concern that the sacrament of penance be readily and easily available to all of Christ's faithful. It acknowledges the right of each of the faithful to the widest possible choice of confessor and allows them to approach even one of a different catholic rite. In certain circumstances the faithful could even approach a non-catholic minister whose Church is acknowledged to have a valid sacrament of penance (see Can. 844 §2). Cann. 240 §1 and 630 §1 acknowledge the specific rights of seminarians and religious in this matter.

1939

Chapter IV
INDULGENCES

Can. 992 An indulgence is the remission in the sight of God of the temporal punishment due for sins, the guilt of which has already been forgiven. A

---

[1] MS 7: Fl II 39.

member of Christ's faithful who is properly disposed and who fulfils certain conditions, may gain an indulgence by the help of the Church which, as the minister of redemption, authoritatively dispenses and applies the treasury of the merits of Christ and the Saints.

1940 This canon and those which follow are based principally upon the most recent formal papal pronouncement on the matter in 1967.[1] That document outlines the notion of the catholic doctrine on indulgences. 'Sins must be expiated. This may be done on this earth through the sorrows, miseries and trials of this life and, above all, through death. Otherwise the expiation must be made in the next life through fire and torments or purifying punishments.'[2] Just as the sin of one person harms others, so the holiness of one person helps others.[3] The doctrine of the Communion of Saints is shown in the way in which the faithful 'have always tried to help one another along the path which leads to the heavenly Father, through prayer, the exchange of spiritual goods and penitential expiation'.[4] 'The conviction was present in the Church that the pastors of the Lord's flock could set the individual free from the vestiges of sin by applying to him the merits of Christ and of the saints.'[5] It was from this conviction that grew the practice of indulgences. In a very real and significant sense the Church endorses the dictum that 'the good which people do lives after them'.

1941 The Church as minister of redemption applies to the faithful who are properly disposed and who fulfil certain conditions, such as saying certain prayers or performing certain works of charity or devotion, the 'treasury of the merits of Christ and the Saints'. This serves to expiate in whole or in part the temporal punishment due for sins which, note, have already been forgiven.

Can. 993 An indulgence is partial or plenary according as it partially or wholly frees a person from the temporal punishment due for sins.

1942 Indulgences are distinguished as being partial or plenary according as they remove part or all of the temporal punishment due for sins.[6] 'The faithful who at least with a contrite heart perform an action to which a partial indulgence is attached obtain, in addition to the remission of temporal punishment merited by the action itself, an equal remission of punishment through the Church's intervention.'[7] In order to gain a plenary indulgence – which can be done only once a day[8] – there are three requirements: sacramental confession, eucharistic communion and prayer for the Pope's intentions. Further, it is necessary to be free from all attachment to sin, even venial sin.[9]

---

[1] The doctrine on indulgences has had a long and, as is well known, a sometimes turbulent history in the Church. This commentary is not the place in which to rehearse or to study that history: in accordance with its practical and pastoral purpose, it limits itself to the current guidelines as given in those Cann. 992–997. For those wishing to pursue the matter, the starting–point now ought to be the ap con *Indulgentiarum Doctrina* of Pope Paul VI: cf. ID. Reference should also be made to the *Enchiridion indulgentiarum* issued by the Sacred Penitentiary 29.VI.1968 Vatican Press 1968: DOL nn.3193–3228. A particularly helpful statement may be found in CCC nn.1471–1479.

[2] ID 2: Fl I 63.
[3] Cf. ID 4: Fl I 65.
[4] ID 5: Fl I 65.
[5] ID 7: Fl I 69.
[6] Cf. ID Norm 2: Fl I 75.
[7] ID Norm 5: Fl I 75.
[8] Cf. ID Norm 6: Fl I 76.
[9] Cf. ID Norm 7: Fl I 76.

Can. 994 All members of the faithful can gain indulgences, partial or plenary, for themselves, or they can apply them by way of suffrage to the dead.

Just as the gaining of indulgences is based on the doctrine of the Communion of Saints, so their application is also part of the same teaching. They can be gained for oneself or applied for the dead who are still members of that Communion. 1943

Can. 995 §1 Apart from the supreme authority in the Church, only those can grant indulgences to whom this power is either acknowledged in the law, or given by the Roman Pontiff.

The power to grant indulgences is obtained in either of two ways: by law or by specific grant of the Roman Pontiff. The *Enchiridion Indulgentiarum* lists those who have the power by law and describes what indulgences they can grant. Bishops, Metropolitans, Patriarchs, Archbishops major and Cardinals all have various powers granted by law.[1] Requests for the power to grant other indulgences should be addressed to the Sacred Penitentiary.[2] 1944

Can. 995 §2 No authority below the Roman Pontiff can give to others the faculty of granting indulgences, unless the authority has been expressly given to the person by the Apostolic See.

This repeats the rule of norm 10 of the *Enchiridion Indulgentiarum*.[3] So e.g. a Bishop could not give a parish priest power to grant even such indulgences as are within the Bishop's power. 1945

Can. 996 §1 To be capable of gaining indulgences a person must be baptised, not excommunicated, and in the state of grace at least on the completion of the prescribed work.

§2 To gain them, however, the person who is capable must have at least the general intention of gaining them, and must fulfil the prescribed works at the time and in the manner determined by the terms of the grant.

This canon deals with the recipient of an indulgence. The person must first be capable of gaining an indulgence. He or she must be baptised, not excommunicated and in the state of grace, at least at the time of completing the prescribed work. The person must also have the intention of gaining the indulgence – thus avoiding any notion of automatic or 'magical' indulgences – and in addition must carry out the prescribed work as prescribed in the terms of the grant.[4] 1946

Can. 997 As far as the granting and the use of indulgences is concerned, the other provisions contained in the special laws of the Church must also be observed.

The Code does not go into any further detail with regard to indulgences, but leaves the more specific prescriptions to 'the special laws of the Church'. In this instance these will be found in the *Enchiridion Indulgentiarum*. 1947

---

[1] Cf. DOL nn.3204–3206.
[2] Ibid. n.3201.
[3] Ibid. n.3202.
[4] Ibid. n.3214.

Title V
The Sacrament of Anointing of the Sick

INTRODUCTION

1946 The Church teaches that the anointing of the sick is one of the seven New Testament sacraments instituted by Christ.[1] In the apostolic constitution *Sacram Unctionem* Pope Paul VI refers to Mark 6:13 and James 5:14–15 and to the liturgical tradition of anointing in both East and West. In referring e.g. to James 5:14 ('If one of you is ill ...'), there is an indication that this sacrament is primarily the sacrament of the sick, rather than the sacrament of the dying. The emphasis on this as a sacrament for the sick was retained in the Eastern liturgical tradition,[2] whereas in the West, as its former name indicates, the sacrament was seen more as for those on the point of death. The change in emphasis is reflected in the change of terminology introduced by Vat. II: '"Extreme Unction", which may also and more fittingly be called "Anointing of the Sick", is not a sacrament for those only who are at the point of death. Hence, as soon as any one of the faithful begins to be in danger of death from sickness or old age, the fitting time for him or her to receive this sacrament has already arrived'.[3]

1947 The special graces conferred by this sacrament are thus described in the introduction to the Rite of Anointing: 'The sacrament gives to the sick person the grace of the Holy Spirit by which the whole person is made healthy, is encouraged to trust in God and is given the strength to resist the temptations of the Evil One and avoid succumbing to anxiety about death. The sick are thus able not only to bear their affliction with courage but also to struggle to overcome it. Restoration to health may follow the reception of the sacrament if this will be in the interests of the sick person's salvation. If such be needed, the sacrament also offers the sick person the forgiveness of sin and the completion of Christian penance'.[4]

Can. 998 The anointing of the sick, by which the Church commends to the suffering and glorified Lord the faithful who are dangerously ill so that he may support and save them, is conferred by anointing them with oil and pronouncing the words prescribed in the liturgical books.

1948 The principal source for this introductory canon is Vat. II in its Constitution on the Church: 'By the sacred anointing of the sick and the prayer of the priests the whole Church commends those who are ill to the suffering and glorified Lord that he may raise them up and save them'.[5] In this sacrament our Lord continues, through the action of his Church, to show that concern for the bodily and spiritual welfare of the sick which he demonstrated during his earthly life and which he commended to his followers.[6] The essential elements of the sacrament are declared to be anointing with oil and pronouncing the prescribed words.

---

[1] Cf. Pope Paul VI ap con *Sacram Unctionem* 17.II.1966: Fl II 13.

[2] Cf. Ziegler *Let them Anoint the Sick* Liturgical Press Collegeville 1987 82. For details of Eastern sources, cf. op cit 169 note 41.

[3] SC 73: Fl I 22.

[4] OUI 6: Fl II 16.

[5] LG 11: Fl I 362. Cf. CCC n.1532.

[6] Cf. OUI 5: Fl II 16.

Part I The Sacraments

Chapter I
THE CELEBRATION OF THE SACRAMENT

Can. 999 The oil to be used in the anointing of the sick can be blessed not only by a Bishop but also by:

1° those who are in law equivalent to the diocesan Bishop;

2° in a case of necessity, any priest but only in the actual celebration of the sacrament.

Normally the oil used in this sacrament will be blessed by the diocesan Bishop during the Mass of the Chrism on Holy Thursday. The law also allows those who are equivalent in law to a diocesan Bishop, whether or not they are in episcopal orders, to do so: these are determined in Cann. 368 and 381 §2. To these may be added the diocesan Administrator whom Can. 427 §1 declares to enjoy the power of a diocesan Bishop, except in those matters 'which are excepted by the nature of things or by the law itself'. Since in certain circumstances a priest can now bless the oil for this sacrament, neither the nature of things nor the law seems to operate as an exception in this case. Finally, the law allows a priest to bless the oil, but with two restrictions: 1949

(a) there must exist 'a case of necessity': the degree of necessity is not determined but it would certainly exist e.g. if the oil blessed by the Bishop had run out or was not available in an emergency;

(b) he may bless it only during the actual celebration of the sacrament.

Can. 1000 §1 The anointings are to be carried out accurately, with the words and in the order and manner prescribed in the liturgical books. In a case of necessity, however, a single anointing on the forehead, or even on another part of the body, is sufficient while the full formula is recited.

The former extensive anointing of various parts of the body has now been reduced to two, on the forehead and on the hands. The sacramental form has been divided into two parts, one to be said while anointing the forehead, the other while anointing the hands. In a case of necessity, e.g. where time is short, a single anointing suffices while both parts of the form are said. This will normally and most suitably be on the forehead but another part of the body may be chosen.[1] In particular places the number of anointings may be increased and the places to be anointed may be changed in accordance with local tradition and culture. These changes will be found in the approved local adaptations of the rite of anointing.[2] 1950

Can. 1000 §2 The minister is to anoint with his own hand, unless a grave reason indicates the use of an instrument.

The anointing should be done by the minister with his own hand, unless a grave reason suggests otherwise, e.g. the danger of causing or receiving an infection: hence the permissibility of 'the use of an instrument'. 1951

Can. 1001 Pastors of souls and those who are close to the sick are to ensure that the sick are helped by this sacrament in good time.

---

[1] Cf. OUI 23: DOL n.3343.

[2] Cf. OUI 24: DOL n.3344.

1952 It is the desire of the Church that 'the faithful take part (in the sacraments) fully aware of what they are doing, actively engaged in the rite and enriched by it'.[1] This applies to the sacrament of anointing the sick as much as it does to the others. And in view of the teaching of Vat. II that this sacrament is not just for those at the point of death,[2] it is important that those responsible for conferring the sacrament and those who look after the sick whether at home or in hospital – should not unduly postpone the anointing. A reason formerly invoked for leaving it to the last minute, namely a desire not to frighten the sick person, is no longer valid. In practice there has been a real change of thinking about this sacrament; it is no longer inevitably associated with death, and sick people readily welcome its reception.

Can. 1002 The communal celebration of anointing of the sick, for a number of the sick together, who have been appropriately prepared and are rightly disposed, may be held in accordance with the regulations of the diocesan Bishop.

1953 The Rite of Anointing gives the local Ordinary the responsibility of supervising celebrations where a number of sick persons come together to be anointed.[3] This canon gives the responsibility to the diocesan Bishop as the moderator, promoter and guardian of the entire liturgical life of the diocese (see Can. 835 1). The principles which should guide him are given in the *Rite of Anointing*.[4] Some Conferences of Bishops have warned that 'the practice of indiscriminate anointing of numbers of people on these occasions simply because they are ill or have reached an advanced age is to be avoided'.[5]

Chapter II
THE MINISTER OF ANOINTING OF THE SICK

Can. 1003 §1 Every priest, but only a priest, can validly administer the anointing of the sick.

1954 This paragraph, which is in essentials identical with c.938 §1 of the 1917 Code, was the subject of much debate while the present Code was being drafted. The main point of difference was the inclusion or exclusion of the words 'only' and 'validly'. The resolution of this point obviously depends on the doctrinal principle involved, i.e. whether someone not ordained a priest could validly confer this sacrament. As an argument that such a person could do so, one consultor noted that the German Bishops had sought permission from the Holy See to allow deacons to anoint,[6] while another stated that the present view takes no account of the practice of the first eight centuries of the Church.[7] In the event it was decided not to resolve the theological debate and to retain the formula of the 1917 Code. Accordingly the position remains that *only* one who has been ordained a priest can *validly* confer this sacrament.

---

[1] SC 11: Fl I 7.
[2] Cf. SC 73: Fl I 22.
[3] Cf. OUI 17: DOL n.3337.
[4] Cf. OUI 83–95: LE 6342–6343.
[5] *Pastoral Care of the Sick* n.238.
[6] Cf. Comm 9(1977) 342 at Can. 186 §1.
[7] Cf. Comm 15(1983) 215 at Can. 956 §1.

Part I The Sacraments

Can. 1003 §2 All priests to whom has been entrusted the care of souls, have the obligation and the right to administer the anointing of the sick to those of the faithful entrusted to their pastoral care. For a reasonable cause, any other priest may administer this sacrament if he has the consent, at least presumed, of the aforementioned priest.

1955 The sacrament is normally to be conferred by the priest (usually, though not necessarily, of the parish) who has the pastoral care of the sick person. This will, among other things, allow him adequately to prepare the recipient and the family for the sacrament. However, a reasonable cause is sufficient to allow another priest to anoint, provided he has at least presumed the consent of the proper priest. Such consent could obviously be presumed in imminent danger of death and indeed readily in other less pressing circumstances.

Can. 1003 §3 Any priest may carry the holy oil with him, so that in a case of necessity he can administer the sacrament of anointing of the sick.

1956 The 1917 Code c.946 required the parish priest to keep the oil of the sick in a neat and properly ornamented place. He was forbidden to keep the oil in his house without the permission of the Ordinary. In 1965 local Ordinaries were empowered to allow priests carry the oil with them.[1] Now, although Can. 847 §2 rightly requires the parish priest to 'keep (the holy oils) carefully in fitting custody', each and every priest is allowed to carry the oil of the sick with him, without any specific permission of the Bishop, so that he may if needs be administer the sacrament in an emergency. A priest may therefore carry the holy oil on his person, in his car, etc. In doing so, however, he is obliged to ensure against even the appearance that the container of oil for use in conferring this sacrament is no more than merely 'another piece of baggage': he must acknowledge the long tradition of the Church which has seen the *olea sacra* as the object of a special veneration – precisely because this oil is the material of a sacrament.

Chapter III
THOSE TO BE ANOINTED

Can. 1004 §1 The anointing of the sick can be administered to any member of the faithful who, having reached the use of reason, begins to be in danger by reason of illness or old age.

1957 The 1917 Code in its c.940 §1 stated that this sacrament could not be given except to a member of the faithful, having the use of reason, who because of illness or old age was in danger of death. Despite the teaching of Pope Pius XI that it was not necessary to wait until a sick person was in imminent danger of dying before conferring the sacrament,[2] it was still in practice and in popular thinking considered as the sacrament of the dying. As has already been noted in the introduction to this sacrament, Vat. II has changed that popular perception. The present canon states the conditions for administering the sacrament:

(a) the person must be a baptised member of the faithful (in the case of members of other Churches or ecclesial communities, the rules of Can. 844 are to be followed);

---

[1] Cf. SCRit decr *Pientissima Mater Ecclesia*: DOL n.3314.
[2] Cf. Pope Pius XI lit ap *Explorata Res*: AAS 15(1923) 105.

(b) the person must have reached the use of reason (see also Can. 1005);

(c) he or she must be 'in danger by reason of illness or old age'. In danger of death from other reasons, e.g. before execution or battle, the sacrament is not to be administered. The change from 'danger of death' of the 1917 Code to 'danger' seems to have been intended to emphasise that this sacrament is not to be exclusively connected with the dying. The danger mentioned is still, however, understood to be danger of death.[1]

1958 Who then should be anointed? The *Rite of Anointing* lists a number of cases. In general, 'those who are dangerously ill through sickness or old age should receive this sacrament'.[2] More specifically, 'a sick person should be anointed before surgery whenever the surgery is necessitated by a dangerous illness'.[3] 'Elderly people may be anointed if they are weak, though not dangerously ill.'[4] 'Sick children may be anointed if they are sufficiently mature to be comforted by the sacrament.'[5] 'Sick people who have lost consciousness or have lost the use of reason may be anointed if, as befits Christians, they would have requested it if they had been in possession of their faculties.'[6]

1959 There are some cases where people should not be anointed. As mentioned under Can. 1002, there should not be indiscriminate anointing of large numbers of people at communal celebrations simply because they are ill or old. Likewise, those who are physically or mentally handicapped should not be anointed simply because they are handicapped and are not in any danger. Those who are already dead are not to be anointed. In such a case the priest 'should pray for the dead person... The priest must not in such circumstances administer the sacrament of anointing'.[7] If he is unsure whether the person is dead, the norm of Can. 1005 is to be followed.

Can. 1004 §2 This sacrament can be repeated if the sick person, having recovered, again becomes seriously ill or if, in the same illness, the danger becomes more serious.

1960 Since this sacrament does not imprint a character it can be repeated. This may be done in two situations:

(a) where the sick person recovers and later becomes ill again either from the same or from another illness;

(b) when within the same illness the danger becomes more acute. In the past this sacrament suffered from underuse; there is now some danger of overuse. Care must be taken lest such overuse should lead to lack of appreciation of the sacrament and cause it to be reduced in popular thinking to little more than a blessing.

Can. 1005 If there is any doubt as to whether the sick person has reached the use of reason, or is dangerously ill, or is dead, this sacrament is to be administered.

1961 Three doubtful situations are covered by this canon: doubts about whether the person has reached the use of reason, is dangerously ill or is dead. In c.941 of the 1917 Code

---

[1] Cf. Comm 15(1983) 215 at Can. 957 §1.
[2] OUI 8: Fl II 17.
[3] Ibid. 10.
[4] Ibid. 11.
[5] Ibid. 12.
[6] Ibid. 14.
[7] Ibid. 15.

the solution was to confer the sacrament conditionally. The present rule is that in such doubt the person is simply to be anointed without any condition.

During the drafting of the Code the question of anointing the mentally handicapped was discussed in considerable detail. The Commission did not provide specifically for them, stating that the Code legislates only for 'ordinary circumstances'. It went on to say that the question of the mentally handicapped is adequately covered by the commentaries of authors and by the *Rite of Anointing* itself. Finally it referred to the draft of the present canon dealing with doubtful cases.[1] From all of this it is certainly safe teaching that, in danger of death from illness or old age, the mentally handicapped may and should be anointed.

Can. 1006 This sacrament is to be administered to the sick who, when they were in possession of their faculties, at least implicitly asked for it.

Normally for the reception of any sacrament the recipient must ask for it; this sacrament is no exception. This canon deals specifically with the not uncommon case where the sick or elderly person has lost consciousness or is no longer lucid. In such circumstances, that person is to be anointed: 'if, as befits Christians, they would have asked for it if they had been in possession of their faculties'.[2] Unless in a particular case the contrary is clear, it should be presumed that a catholic would have so requested the sacrament.

Can. 1007 The anointing of the sick is not to be conferred upon those who obstinately persist in a manifestly grave sin.

Where a person is conscious, the ordinary means of reconciliation with the Church is the sacrament of penance. The conditions for this reconciliation are that the penitent repudiate his sins and, having the purpose of amending his life, turn back to God (see Can. 987). One who manifestly persists in grave sin obviously cannot receive absolution, nor can such a person be admitted to holy communion (see Can. 915). The present canon makes it explicit that such a person cannot receive anointing of the sick either, even though this sacrament does involve forgiveness of sin (see James 5:15). There is no 'magic' in such forgiveness; it depends upon the at least implicit repentance of the person.

If the person is unconscious and there is some basis for judging that he or she did desire reconciliation with the Church, then the person could be given the benefit of the doubt and anointed. In the absence of any basis for so judging, it would be at least imprudent to confer the sacrament, as doing so could cause scandal or could give the impression that the sacrament operated in some magical fashion and conferred grace regardless of the disposition of the recipient.

---

[1] Cf. Comm 15(1983) 215 at Can. 957 §1.
[2] OUI 14: Fl II 17.

Title VI
Orders

INTRODUCTION

1968 Although the layout of the material dealt with in this title is similar in both the previous and the current Codes, there are a number of important changes in the present law. These result from the teaching of Vat. II, which, while insisting on the essential difference between the two, puts the sacramental priesthood in the context of the common priesthood of all Christ's faithful.[1] They result also from the interim rules laid down by the Holy See between the Council and the promulgation of the Code. The most important of these latter were contained in the various mp documents of Pope Paul VI: *Sacrum Diaconatus Ordinem* (1967), restoring the permanent diaconate in the latin Church; *Ministeria Quaedam* (1972), abolishing the subdiaconate and the minor orders of porter and exorcist, and changing the two remaining minor orders, acolyte and lector, into ministries; *Ad Pascendum* (1972), introducing some norms for both diaconate and priesthood.[2] The term 'ordination' now refers only to the orders of episcopate, priesthood and diaconate, and the term 'cleric' applies only to members of these orders.

Can. 1008 By divine institution some among Christ's faithful are, through the sacrament of order, marked with an indelible character and are thus constituted sacred ministers; thereby they are consecrated and deputed so that, each according to his own grade, they fulfil, in the person of Christ the Head, the offices of teaching, sanctifying and ruling, and so they nourish the people of God.

1969 This canon summarises the theology of the sacrament of order and puts it into its proper context. It emphasises the position of those who are ordained, as members of Christ's faithful who are 'consecrated and deputed' to the service of the whole Body of Christ.

1970 The words 'by divine institution' replace 'by the institution of Christ' in the first draft of this canon because, as the Commission noted, Christ did not directly institute the priesthood and the diaconate.[3] Since the orders of episcopate, priesthood and diaconate are of divine institution, they cannot be abolished or substantially changed as the subdiaconate and the minor orders were.

1971 Although the Church's magisterium has never declared that ordination to the diaconate imprints a character, this is common doctrine and the present canon reflects it.[4] The imprinting of the character means that once ordination has been validly conferred, it cannot be repeated (see Can. 845 §1).

1972 Although there is but one sacrament of order, there are different grades in it. To emphasise the distinction between these grades, the words 'each according to his own grade' were added to the original draft of the canon.[5] Bishops, 'invested with the fulness of the sacrament of Orders',[6] and priests who are 'cooperators of the episcopal

---

[1] Cf. LG ch II: Fl I 359ff; CCC nn.1534–1535, 1554, 1592.
[2] SDO: DOL nn.2533–2546; MQ: Fl I 427ff; AP: Fl I 433ff.
[3] Comm 10(1978) 181 at Can. 190.
[4] Ibid.
[5] Ibid.
[6] LG 26: Fl I 381.

college ... under the authority of the Bishop',[1] exercise the threefold office of teaching, sanctifying and ruling in a fuller manner than deacons, 'who receive the imposition of hands "not unto the priesthood, but unto the ministry"',[2] and who do not participate directly in the power of ruling. The cleric is 'consecrated and deputed' to exercise this office 'in the person of Christ'. This recalls that he does not function by mandate of the community, but acts directly in the person of Christ himself.

Can. 1009 §1 The orders are the episcopate, the priesthood and the diaconate.

§2 They are conferred by the laying on of hands and the prayer of consecration which the liturgical books prescribe for each grade.

This canon lists the three grades of order and describes how the sacrament is to be conferred, i.e. 'by the laying on of hands and the prayer of consecration' proper to each grade. This follows the rules laid down by Pope Pius XII in 1947 in the ap con *Sacramentum Ordinis*, declaring what was required for validity.[3] It was that document which established *inter alia* that the *traditio instrumentorum* was not required for validity.

1973

Chapter 1
THE CELEBRATION OF ORDINATION AND THE MINISTER

Can. 1010 An ordination is to be celebrated during Mass, on a Sunday or holyday of obligation. For pastoral reasons, however, it may take place on other days also, even on ferial days.

The 1917 Code in c.1006 gave stricter and more detailed rules about the time for the conferring of orders. The present law allows a greater latitude: ordination is always to take place during Mass and, by preference, on a Sunday or holyday of obligation; for pastoral reasons it may take place on other days, e.g. to allow as many as possible to attend (see Can. 1011 §2).

1974

Can. 1011 §1 An ordination is normally to be celebrated in the cathedral church. For pastoral reasons, however, it may be celebrated in another church or oratory.

§2 Clerics and other members of Christ's faithful are to be invited to attend an ordination, so that the greatest possible number may be present at the celebration.

§1 represents a simplification of the rules of c.1009 of the 1917 Code. The normal place is the cathedral church, the mother church of the diocese, but for pastoral reasons another church or oratory may be used. Suitable reasons would be: the fostering of vocations in individual parishes, the convenience of parents, relatives and others attending, the size of the cathedral, etc.

1975

§2 enlarges on the prescription of the former Code (c.1009 §1) which called for invitation of the cathedral chapter or the local clergy. Now, not only clergy but also 'other members of Christ's faithful' are to be invited, so that the ceremony may truly

1976

---
[1] LG 28: Fl I 385.
[2] LG 29: Fl I 387.
[3] AAS 40(1947) 5ff: CLD 3 396ff. Cf. CCC n.1538.

reflect the fact that this is not just a private matter but a celebration of and for the Church community. Allowing for the presence of a suitable number will be an important factor in determining the time and place of an ordination. Both should be as convenient as possible for the largest possible number.

Can. 1012 The minister of sacred ordination is a consecrated Bishop.

1977 The use of the word 'consecrated' indicates that a Bishop-elect cannot ordain. The abolition of the subdiaconate, and the changing of the minor orders into ministries, has swept away past controversy about who could ordain to these. Now that orders comprise only episcopate, priesthood and diaconate, for the valid conferral of which a Bishop was always required, there is no longer room for dispute. A suggestion that the word 'only' (*unice*) be added to this canon was rejected by the Commission, presumably because the existing wording adequately reflected the tradition and practice in this matter.[1]

Can. 1013 No Bishop is permitted to consecrate anyone as Bishop, unless it is first established that a pontifical mandate has been issued.

1978 The original draft of this canon had an introductory section which put the reason for this prohibition in the context of the hierarchial communion between members of the College of Bishops and the head of the College. That section was suppressed because of disagreement on its exact force and because it might be taken as affecting not only lawfulness but also validity.[2] The law as it stands affects only the lawfulness of an episcopal consecration: the term 'is permitted' (*licet*) does not expressly prescribe nullity (see Can. 10). A violation of this law involves an automatic excommunication, reserved to the Holy See, for both the consecrating Bishop and the one consecrated (see Can. 1382).

Can. 1014 Unless a dispensation has been granted by the Apostolic See, the principal consecrating Bishop at an episcopal consecration is to have at least two other consecrating Bishops with him. It is, however, entirely appropriate that all the Bishops present should join with these in consecrating the Bishop-elect.

1979 The practice of having co-consecrators is a very ancient one and it expresses the collegiality and unity of the Bishops. The conciliar constitution on the Church says: 'Indeed, pointing to it (the collegiate character and structure of the episcopal order) also quite clearly is the custom, dating from very early times, of summoning a number of Bishops to take part in the elevation of one newly chosen to the highest sacerdotal office'.[3] The present canon repeats the substance of c.954 of the 1917 Code, with the addition of the strong recommendation that all the Bishops present should join in consecrating the Bishop-elect. Consecration by one Bishop only would be valid, but without a dispensation from the Holy See it would be unlawful. Reasons for seeking such a dispensation would e.g. be the long distances to be travelled, the fact that in a mission territory or where the Church is under persecution there may be so few Bishops available, etc.

Can. 1015 §1 Each candidate is to be ordained to the priesthood or to the diaconate by his proper Bishop, or with lawful dimissorial letters granted by that Bishop.

---

[1] Comm 10(1978) 182 at Can. 192.
[2] Ibid. at Can. 193.
[3] LG 22: Fl I 374ff.

§2 If not impeded from doing so by a just reason, a Bishop is himself to ordain his own subjects. He may not, however, without an apostolic indult lawfully ordain a subject of an oriental rite.

The general rule is that a candidate for the priesthood or the diaconate is to be ordained by his proper Bishop or else by another Bishop with lawful dimissorial letters granted by the proper Bishop (§1). The proper Bishop for secular clergy is determined by Can. 1016. Dimissorial letters are letters from the proper Ordinary authorising another Bishop to ordain one of his subjects and testifying to the candidate's fitness.

§2 obliges a Bishop to ordain his own subjects unless he is lawfully impeded. Reasons which could excuse from this obligation would e.g. be ill health, the long distance to be travelled and the expense involved in this, etc. There is one important exception to this rule. A Bishop may not, unless he has a special permission from the Holy See, ordain one who, although he is a subject, belongs to an oriental rite. This situation can arise where an oriental-rite hierarchy has not been established in the area in question. There, even though the candidate is certainly subject to the local latin-rite Bishop, he is normally to be ordained by a Bishop of his own rite. This exception is in keeping with the respect due to the Eastern Churches.[1] The rule affects only the lawfulness of the ordination, not its validity.

Can. 1015 §3 Anyone who is entitled to give dimissorial letters for the reception of orders may also himself confer these orders, if he is a Bishop.

This paragraph permits the person who can grant dimissorial letters for a candidate, to confer orders, provided however that he is himself a Bishop. This repeats the rule of c.959 of the 1917 Code. Can. 1018 determines who can grant dimissorial letters for the secular clergy, and Can. 1019 does the same for others. Examples of the application of this rule would be: a diocesan Administrator who is a Bishop and has the consent of the college of consultors, can ordain; a major Superior of a clerical religious institute of pontifical right who is a Bishop, can do the same.

Can. 1016 In what concerns the ordination to the diaconate of those who intend to enrol themselves in the secular clergy, the proper Bishop is the Bishop of the diocese in which the aspirant has a domicile, or the Bishop of the diocese to which he intends to devote himself. In what concerns the priestly ordination of the secular clergy, it is the Bishop of the diocese in which the aspirant was incardinated by the diaconate.

This canon, which determines who is the proper Bishop for ordination of the secular clergy, corresponds to c.956 of the 1917 Code, but it has removed the complication of considering the diocese of origin of the candidate. For a deacon the proper Bishop is *either* the Bishop of the diocese where the candidate has a domicile or the Bishop of the diocese where he intends to exercise his ministry. Reception of the diaconate incardinates the candidate into a diocese, and it is the Bishop of that diocese who is the proper Bishop for ordination to the priesthood.

Can. 1017 A Bishop may not confer orders outside his own jurisdiction except with the permission of the diocesan Bishop.

This canon simply reflects the general principle that a Bishop's authority can be exercised only within his own diocese. He may not confer orders, even on his own subjects, outside that territory unless he has the permission of the Bishop of the dio-

---

[1] Cf OE 1–6: Fl I 441ff.

cese in which the candidate is. This permission is quite distinct from the permission, given in dimissorial letters, to ordain another's subject. The prohibition does not affect the validity of orders conferred without such permission.[1]

Can. 1018 §1 The following can give dimissorial letters for the secular clergy:

   1° the proper Bishop mentioned in Can. 1016;

   2° the apostolic Administrator; with the consent of the college of consultors, the diocesan Administrator; with the consent of the council mentioned in Can. 495 §2, the Pro-vicar and Pro-prefect apostolic.

1985   The original draft of this paragraph was rather more complete in listing those who can give dimissorial letters for the secular clergy,[2] as indeed was c.958 §1 of the 1917 Code. The principle is that those who hold their offices permanently – the proper Bishop and the apostolic Administrator – can give the letters on their own authority, while those who hold temporary office must first receive the consent of another body: that of the college of consultors, in the case of the diocesan Administrator; that of the council mentioned in Can. 495 §2, in the case of a Pro-vicar or Pro-prefect apostolic. Others who are equivalent in law to a diocesan Bishop (see Can. 381 §2), such as Vicars and Prefects apostolic, Abbots and Prelates of territorial abbacies and prelatures, clearly have the same powers in this regard as the diocesan Bishop, while a Vicar general or other episcopal Vicar can give dimissorial letters only by special mandate of the Bishop (see Can. 134 §3).

Can. 1018 §2 The diocesan Administrator, the Pro-vicar and Pro-prefect apostolic are not to give dimissorial letters to those to whom admission to orders was refused by the diocesan Bishop or by the Vicar or Prefect apostolic.

1986   This prohibition is an extension of the traditional principle that what has been refused by a superior cannot be granted by an inferior. In the present canon it is applied to the case where a permanent holder of the office has done the refusal, and it forbids a temporary holder of the same office to grant the letters. The matter must be held over until the office is permanently filled.

Can. 1019 §1 It belongs to the major Superior of a clerical religious institute of pontifical right or of a clerical society of apostolic life of pontifical right to grant dimissorial letters for the diaconate and for the priesthood to his subjects who are, in accordance with the constitutions, perpetually or definitively enrolled in the institute or society.

1987   For a major Superior to grant dimissorial letters for a subject, both must belong either to a clerical religious institute or to a clerical society of apostolic life of pontifical right. This requirement rules out non-clerical institutes or societies and clerical institutes or societies which are not of pontifical right. Thus e.g. the major Superior of an institute of brothers cannot give dimissorial letters for a brother who is to be ordained for the service of the institute. In addition, the subject must be perpetually or definitively enrolled in the institute or society, by whatever means are prescribed in the constitutions, such as final profession of vows or other sacred bonds: e.g. if a religious in temporary vows is to be ordained, the major Superior cannot issue dimissorial letters for him; either he must wait until the candidate has

---

[1] Cf. Comm 15(1983) 217 at Can. 970.
[2] SS at Can. 199.

taken perpetual vows or he must receive permission from the Holy See to anticipate the final profession.

Can. 1019 §2 The ordination of all other candidates of whatever institute or society, is governed by the law applying to the secular clergy, any indult whatsoever granted to Superiors being revoked.

Where all the requirements of §1 have not been met, the ordination of all other candidates comes under the rules already given for the secular clergy. It is noteworthy that any indults given to the contrary in the past are revoked. Since the candidate is not destined for the service of a diocese, the dimissorial letters are to be granted by the Bishop of the place where the candidate has a domicile (see Can. 1016). In all such cases the Bishop must satisfy himself that the necessary formation for priesthood, and not just for consecrated life, has taken place.

Can. 1020 Dimissorial letters are not to be granted unless all the testimonials and documents required by the law in accordance with Cann. 1050 and 1051 have first been obtained.

The two canons to which reference is made here list the documents required (see Can. 1050) and the testimonials from those responsible for the candidate's formation (see Can. 1051). The obligation imposed by the present canon is a serious one, and the person issuing the dimissorial letters must satisfy himself of the authenticity and reliability of the testimonial and documents in question.

Can. 1021 Dimissorial letters may be sent to any Bishop in communion with the Apostolic See, but not to a Bishop of a rite other than that of the ordinand, unless there is an apostolic indult.

This canon repeats substantially c.961 of the 1917 Code and permits sending dimissorial letters to any Bishop in communion with the Holy See, except a Bishop of a rite different to that of the ordinand unless a special apostolic indult has been obtained to allow this. The restrictions which the former law imposed on religious Superiors regarding the Bishop to whom the letters were to be sent, have been abolished.[1] The law does not determine any particular Bishop to whom the letters are to be sent.[2]

Can. 1022 When the ordaining Bishop has received the prescribed dimissorial letters, he may proceed to the ordination only when the authenticity of these letters is established beyond any doubt whatever.

This canon also is substantially the same as its predecessor in the 1917 Code c.962. The only obligation that it places on the ordaining Bishop is to satisfy himself beyond any doubt that the dimissorial letters are genuine. In the drafting of this law there was some discussion about obliging that Bishop to enquire also about the personal qualities of the candidate, but this was not admitted into the text of the law.[3] However, the fact that the letters are authentic does not oblige the Bishop to ordain the candidate. Indeed if he has good reason to doubt that the candidate is suitable, then he should not ordain him (see Can. 1052 §3).

Can. 1023 Dimissorial letters can be limited or can be revoked by the person granting them or by his successor; once granted, they do not lapse on the expiry of the grantor's authority.

---

[1] Cf. 1917 Code cc.965–967.

[2] Cf. Bouscaren–Ellis 362.

[3] Cf. Comm 10(1978) 186 at Can. 204.

Book IV The Sanctifying Office of the Church

1992   There are two main points here. Firstly, the one who grants dimissorial letters can revoke them, or he can limit them e.g. by granting them only for a specified time or place, to a specific ordaining Bishop, or subject to a condition such as a further proof of fitness. Secondly, in accordance with the general principle expressed in Can. 46, the letters once granted, remain effective even though the grantor may have died or otherwise ceased from office.

Chapter II
THOSE TO BE ORDAINED

Can. 1024 Only a baptised man can validly receive sacred ordination.

1993   Two requirements for the valid *reception of orders* are given here: the candidate must have been baptised (see Can. 842 §1), and must be of the male sex. In recent times this second requirement has been widely discussed, and the question of the possible ordination of women has been repeatedly raised. A significant stage in this process was reached during the pontificate of Pope Paul VI in the latter half of the 1970s, specifically in the context of ecumenism.[1] The Pope's teaching was clear, namely that the Church did not consider itself as having the power to admit women to the priestly ministry. Despite that, the question continued to be raised. Accordingly, an even more definitive pronouncement (clearly endorsing that of his predecessor), addressed to the Bishops of the Church, was issued by Pope John Paul II in 1994,[2] the kernel of which is expressed in the following terms: '... in order that all doubt may be removed regarding a matter of great importance, a matter which *pertains to the Church's divine Constitution* itself, in virtue of *my ministry of confirming the brethren* (see Lk. 22:32) I declare that the Church has no authority whatsoever to confer priestly ordination on women and that this judgement is to be *definitively held by all the Church's faithful*' (n.4).

1994   The law therefore is clear: as stated in this canon, only a baptised man – not any woman – can validly receive sacred ordination. However, in interpreting this law it is important, especially in pastoral practice, to take clear account of the following points:

(a) The Pope's 1994 directive on this matter does not appear to be an infallible declaration (see Can. 749 §§1 and 3).

(b) It is nevertheless a clear exercise of the supreme teaching authority entrusted by Christ to the Apostle Peter and his lawful successors: it goes beyond any mere reaffirmation of the practice of the catholic Church in admitting only men to ordination to the priesthood. As such, it requires the 'religious submission of

---

[1] Cf. Pope Paul VI letters (30.XI.1975, 23.III.1976) to the then Anglican Archbishop of Canterbury: AAS 68(1976) 599–601: Origins 6(1976) 129–132; SCDF decl *Inter Insigniores* 15.X.1976: AAS 69(1977) 98–116: Fl II 331–345.

[2] Cf. lit ap *Ordinatio sacerdotalis* 22.V.1994: Origins 24(1994) 49–52: The Tablet London 248 (4.VI.1994) 720–721. That which motivated the Pope on this occasion was the fact that (in his own words) 'although the teaching that priestly ordination is to be reserved to men alone has been preserved by the constant and universal tradition of the Church and firmly taught by the magisterium in its more recent documents, at the present time in some places it is nonetheless still considered open to debate, or the Church's judgement that women are not to be admitted to ordination is considered to have a merely disciplinary force' (op cit n.4). Both of these assertions are firmly rejected in the papal document. Cf. also the official Presentation Note published in L'Osservatore Romano 23.V.94, reproduced in Origins 24(1994) 52–53; CCC n.1577.

Part I The Sacraments

intellect and will' of Can. 752. As of now, this is therefore the only norm which may lawfully be followed.[1]

(c) While insisting on this principle, the Pope's letter makes two further fundamentally relevant points:

  (i) there is no question whatever of reducing the place of women in the Church. On the contrary: 'the presence and the role of women in the life and mission of the Church, although not linked to the ministerial priesthood, *remain absolutely necessary and irreplaceable* ... the Church desires that christian women should become fully aware of *the greatness of their mission*. Today their role is of capital importance, both for the renewal and humanization of society and for the rediscovery by believers of the true face of the Church ... *They* (are the people) who passed on the Church's faith and *tradition by bringing up their children in the spirit of the Gospel*'.[2]

  (ii) the cause of ecumenism is in no way adversely affected by this decision. On the contrary: 'as regards ecumenical dialogue, which is a dialogue in the truth, the apostolic letter *Ordinatio sacerdotalis*, far from constituting an obstacle, can provide an opportunity for all Christians to deepen their understanding of the origin and theological nature of the episcopal and priestly ministry conferred by the Sacrament of orders'.[3]

A third requirement for the valid reception of orders, which this sacrament has in common with all sacraments received in adulthood, is the intention of the candidate to receive the order. The petition made in writing by him to be admitted as a candidate for orders in accordance with Can. 1034 §1, if sincerely and knowingly made and not revoked, is a sufficient expression of intention. **1995**

Can. 1025 §1 In order lawfully to confer the orders of priesthood or diaconate, it is required that, in the judgement of the proper Bishop or of the competent major Superior, the candidate, having completed the probation in accordance with the law, possesses the requisite qualities, that he is free of any irregularity or impediment, and that he has fulfilled the requirements set out in Cann. 1033-1039. Moreover, the documents mentioned in Can. 1050 must be to hand, and the investigation mentioned in Can. 1051 must have been carried out.

This paragraph summarises the basic requirements for lawful ordination. These are: **1996**

(a) the necessary programme of formation and probation must have been completed: Cann. 235–261, especially Cann. 235, 236 and 250;

(b) the candidate must have the qualities mentioned in Can. 1029;

(c) he must be free from all irregularities or impediments: Cann. 1040–1049;

(d) he must have completed the prerequisites of Cann. 1033–1039;

(e) the documents mentioned in Can. 1050 must be to hand;

(f) the investigation mentioned in Can. 1051 must have been made.

---

[1] Questions have been raised in various responsible quarters concerning the precise theological status of this papal teaching. This remains a matter of legitimate theological enquiry, to be pursued in accordance with SCDF instr *Donum Veritatis* (on the ecclesial vocation of the theologian) 24.V.1990: AAS 82(1990) 1550–1570: Origins 20(1990) 117–126. In this regard, cf. D. Connell (later Archbishop of Dublin) *Women Priests: Why Not* Apol 59(1986) 493–511. An illuminating ensuing correspondence may be consulted in CLSGBI Newsletter n.70(1987) 104–106 and n.73(1988) 117–119.

[2] *Ordinatio sacerdotalis* n.3, with its references to other papal teaching in this regard.

[3] Presentation Note: Origins 24(1994) 53.

Can. 1025 §2 It is further required that, in the judgement of the same lawful Superior, the candidate is considered beneficial to the ministry of the Church.

1997 Here is emphasised the fact that a man is ordained not for his own benefit but for that of the Church. Its requirement is in addition (*insuper*) to those enumerated in §1 and presupposes a satisfactory outcome thereof. In a situation where there is a shortage of priests, the ordination of any new member will clearly be 'beneficial to the ministry of the Church', but this in itself must never be so interpreted as to permit any lowering of the standards required of every candidate for the priesthood. There are two changes from the corresponding canon of the 1917 Code (c.969): that applied to the secular clergy only, and it required that the candidate be 'necessary or beneficial to the churches of the diocese'. The present law applies to all ordinands.

Can. 1025 §3 A Bishop ordaining his own subject who is destined for the service of another diocese, must be certain that the ordinand will in fact be attached to that other diocese.

1998 Even though the candidate is destined for the service of a diocese where he has not a domicile, the Bishop of that diocese is a proper Bishop for ordination (see Can. 1016). In order to be admitted as an aspirant for orders, the candidate must have submitted a written petition to this effect and the petition must have been accepted in writing by the Bishop in question (see Can. 1034 §1). In the case envisaged in this paragraph the Bishop who is in fact ordaining one of his own subjects must be certain that this acceptance has been given and not revoked; alternatively, and more simply, he could receive dimissorial letters from the Bishop of the diocese of service. This requirement is a safeguard of the general rule of Can. 265 that there should be no 'acephalous or "wandering" clergy'.

Article 1
The Requirements in those to be Ordained

Can. 1026 For a person to be ordained, he must enjoy the requisite freedom. It is absolutely wrong to compel anyone, in any way or for any reason whatsoever, to receive orders, or to turn away from orders anyone who is canonically suitable.

1999 This canon repeats c.971 of the 1917 Code, with the addition of the first sentence which states the basic principle of the necessity for freedom in the candidate. It contains two rules. Firstly, it is strictly forbidden to use compulsion of any kind or for any reason to induce a man to be ordained. This is a particular application of the rule of Can. 219 which states the right of all Christ's faithful to immunity from coercion in choosing a state in life. If a person is compelled to receive orders, the ordination could be invalid and could give rise to a process to have this declared (see Can. 290 1°). If the compulsion was not so severe as to render the ordination invalid, it could still be a sufficient reason for seeking a rescript of laicisation from the Holy See (see Cann. 290 3°, 1708–1712). Secondly, it also forbids the refusal of orders to one who is canonically suitable. 'Suitability' here includes all the requirements outlined in Can. 1025. Can. 1030 deals with the specific case of refusing to promote further a deacon who was destined for the priesthood.

Can. 1027 Aspirants to the diaconate and the priesthood are to be formed by careful preparation in accordance with the law.

Part I The Sacraments

The 'law' here refers to the Code (Cann. 232–264), to the Charter for Priestly Formation (see Can. 242), and to any local provisions made by the Bishops' Conference and the diocesan Bishop in accordance with the general law. 2000

Can. 1028 The diocesan Bishop or the competent Superior must ensure that before they are promoted to any order, candidates are properly instructed concerning the order itself and its obligations.

This canon is a specific application of the general rule on formation given in Can. 1027. It corresponds to c.996 §1 of the 1917 Code which specified an examination of the candidate. As well as a knowledge of the theology of the order, the candidate must receive proper instruction about its obligations (see Cann. 273–289). 2001

Can. 1029 Only those are to be promoted to orders who, in the prudent judgement of the proper Bishop or the competent major Superior, all things considered, have sound faith, are motivated by the right intention, are endowed with the requisite knowledge, enjoy a good reputation, and have moral probity, proven virtue and the other physical and psychological qualities appropriate to the order to be received.

The ultimate judgement about the fitness of a candidate rests with the proper Bishop or, in the case of religious, with the competent major Superior. However, before giving his decision, he must receive a report from the rector of the seminary or of the house of formation concerning the qualities listed in this canon (see Can. 1051). The qualities are clearly enumerated: sound faith, right intention, requisite knowledge, good reputation, moral uprightness, proven virtue, and 'the other physical and psychological qualities appropriate to the order to be received'. 2002

With regard to the last of these requirements, that of possessing the appropriate psychological qualities, many seminaries and religious institutes now have a system of psychological assessment of candidates for orders. Can. 642 does allow that the 'health, disposition and maturity' of candidates for a religious novitiate may, if necessary, be established by experts. It adds the precautionary words 'without prejudice to Can. 220', which refers to a person's right to a good reputation and to privacy. This is a caveat which must also be applied in the case of candidates for orders; the report of any psychological assessment should be treated with the utmost confidentiality and should not be used for any purpose other than that for which it was made. Not only that, but great care must be taken to ensure that no psychological assessment, from whatever school of psychological thought, should be allowed to become *the sole factor* in determining a candidate's fitness for ordination – and indeed, prior to that, much less in determining whether or not he be admitted to a seminary formation.[1] 2003

Can. 1030 Only for a canonical reason, even one which is occult, may the proper Bishop or the competent major Superior forbid admission to the priesthood to deacons subject to them who were destined for the priesthood, without prejudice to recourse in accordance with the law.

This canon follows logically from the preceding one and deals with the case of ordaining to the priesthood a deacon destined for that order. The obligation laid on the competent authority by Can. 1029 to ensure the fitness of the candidate does not cease when he is ordained deacon: it may happen e.g. that he was given the benefit of a doubt when admitted to the diaconate, or he may in the interval between the two 2004

---

[1] For a balanced assessment of this issue, cf. Costello *Psychology and the Discernment of a Vocation* (address to the Synod of Bishops 1990): Origins 20(1990) 346–348.

orders be first discovered to be lacking in one or more of the required canonical qualities. However, the fact of admission to the diaconate, while not conferring a right to the priesthood, does give the candidate at least a reasonable hope of becoming a priest. Hence the explicit mention of the candidate's legal right of recourse against a decision refusing him admission to the priesthood. This recourse could be to the Holy See or e.g. to the Superior General of a religious institute. In the comments on the first draft of this canon it was recommended that the appropriate superior should inform the candidate of the reasons for the refusal, so that he would have a realistic possibility of having recourse.[1] This suggestion did not find explicit expression in the law, but natural justice certainly demands that he be given at least the substance of such reasons.

2005 It is particularly to be noted that in this situation the proper Bishop or the competent major Superior may forbid admission to the priesthood 'only for a canonical reason', i.e. in consideration *only* of some canonical (as distinct from a merely personal) factor – an impediment, an irregularity or a censure: in effect, a failure to meet some or any of the requirements detailed in this Ch. II. This is so, however, even if the reason in question is 'occult', i.e. not capable of being proven in the external forum. The implied thrust of this canon is an admonition to the effect that the situation envisaged should be very much an exceptional one, that the norm rather should be the elimination of any such problem before admission to the diaconate.

Can. 1031 §1 The priesthood may be conferred only upon those who have completed their twenty-fifth year of age, and possess a sufficient maturity; moreover, an interval of at least six months between the diaconate and the priesthood must have been observed. Those who are destined for the priesthood are to be admitted to the order of diaconate only when they have completed their twenty-third year.

2006 For lawful reception of the priesthood, a man must have completed his twenty-fifth year of age; for the transitory diaconate he must have completed his twenty-third year: in effect, this means that the earliest day for ordination is the day after the man's twenty-fifth and twenty-third birthday respectively (see Can. 203 §2). In both cases, the age required is an increase of a year on that demanded in c.975 of the 1917 Code. In the case of the priesthood, the candidate must not only have attained the specified age but must also 'possess a sufficient maturity' (see Can. 1029).

2007 Between priesthood and diaconate a minimum interval of six months must have been observed – an increase of three months on the interval called for by c.978 §2 of the 1917 Code. The interval is to allow time for both the exercise of the order and for further formation (see Can. 1032 §2).

Can. 1031 §2 A candidate for the permanent diaconate who is not married may be admitted to the diaconate only when he has completed at least his twenty-fifth year; if he is married, not until he has completed at least his thirty-fifth year, and then with the consent of his wife.

2008 This paragraph distinguishes between those who are married and those who are single. In the case of the latter, the age is the same as for the priesthood, twenty-five. A married candidate must have completed his thirty-fifth year; in addition, the law also requires the consent of his wife, which must be attested in a document (see Can. 1050 3°). This is to ensure that the wife knows the nature and extent of the obligations to be undertaken by her husband. It is for the Bishop to draw up or approve an appropriate programme of instruction for this purpose.

---

[1] Cf. Comm 10(1978) 188 at Can. 209.

Part I The Sacraments

Can. 1031 §3 Bishops' Conferences may issue a regulation which requires a later age for the priesthood and for the permanent diaconate.

This rule allows for local circumstances which may urge a later age for ordination, and it allows the Bishops' Conference – not a diocesan Bishop – to make a regulation to this effect.[1]

Can. 1031 §4 A dispensation of more than a year from the age required by §§1 and 2 is reserved to the Apostolic See.

This is a limitation on the Bishop's general power of dispensing in accordance with Can. 87 §1. If the defect of age is less than a year, the Bishop can dispense; otherwise the Holy See must be approached. This paragraph repeats the regulation given in the mp *De Episcoporum Muneribus*.[2] A suggestion to the Revision Commission that Bishops be given the faculty to dispense from a defect of up to eighteen months was rejected, for the reason that the precise object of the law was to deter the ordination of very young men.[3] Although the law does not make specific provision for dispensation from the interval required in §1 of the present canon, the Bishop could grant such a dispensation for sufficient reason in accordance with Cann. 87 and 90.

Can. 1032 §1 Aspirants to the priesthood may be promoted to the diaconate only when they have completed the fifth year of the curriculum of philosophical and theological studies.

Can. 250 requires a minimum of six full years of philosophical and theological studies before ordination to the priesthood. The diaconate may not be conferred on aspirants to the priesthood before the completion of at least five of those years. *De Episcoporum Muneribus* expressly reserved to the Holy See the power of dispensing from the required length of time of study;[4] this reservation is not retained in the Code.

Can. 1032 §2 After completing the curriculum of studies and before being promoted to the priesthood, deacons are to spend an appropriate time, to be determined by the Bishop or by the competent major Superior, taking part in the pastoral ministry and exercising the diaconal order.

Even though the man in question is destined for the priesthood, the order of diaconate is seen as more than a merely initiatory stage. The order is exercised in its own right, and a suitable length of time for this is to be determined by the Bishop or major Superior – not simply arranged by the seminary or formation authorities. This period is to be spent 'in the pastoral ministry', in whatever appropriate form that may take, thereby giving the aspirant practical formation and experience. It may not be combined with any part of the minimum six-year curriculum of studies; whenever, and for whatever duration, it takes place, this period may not be other than an addition to the six years of study prescribed by Can. 250. It is particularly to be noted that this period of practical experience is still an integral part of the aspirant's *formation*, and must therefore remain subject to a continuing observation and evaluation. Merely e.g. to assign a deacon 'to work in a parish' for whatever length of time, be it continuous or intermittent, would not meet the demand of the law. The very least required

---

[1] As of 1990 only two Conferences – Nigeria and the Dominican Republic – had availed themselves of this authority: cf. LCE Tavola per Paesi e Canoni at Can. 1031.
[2] Cf. EM IX 6: AAS 58(1966) 470.
[3] Cf. Comm 15(1983) 218 at Can. 984.
[4] Cf. EM IX 7: AAS 58(1966) 470.

would be some form of structured liaison between the seminary or formation authorities and the parish priest in question. It would be for the respective Bishop or major Superior to determine the details.

Can. 1032 §3 An aspirant to the permanent diaconate is not to be promoted to this order until he has completed the period of formation.

2013 Can. 236 lays down a minimum period of three years for the training of those who aspire to the permanent diaconate, and it entrusts to local Bishops' Conferences the task of determining their instruction and formation.[1] They are not to be ordained until this period of formation has been completed.

Article 2
Prerequisites for Ordination

Can. 1033 Only one who has received the sacrament of sacred confirmation may lawfully be promoted to orders.

2014 It is obviously unfitting that one who has not completed christian initiation should be ordained. The canon makes it clear that confirmation is needed for the lawful reception of orders, not for validity.

Can. 1034 §1 An aspirant to the diaconate or to the priesthood is not to be ordained unless he has first, through the liturgical rite of admission, secured enrolment as a candidate from the authority mentioned in Cann. 1016 and 1019. He must previously have submitted a petition in his own hand and signed by him, which has been accepted in writing by the same authority.

§2 One who has by vows become a member of a clerical institute is not obliged to obtain this admission.

2015 With the abolition of first tonsure a new rite was introduced, the rite of admission as a candidate for orders. The present canon derives from the norms laid down for this rite in the mp *Ad Pascendum* of Pope Paul VI.[2] The aspirant must have been enrolled as a candidate by the appropriate authority unless he has become a member of a clerical institute by taking vows: in this latter case the profession of vows takes the place of the rite of admission. The proper authority for aspirants to the secular clergy is the proper Bishop for ordination as determined by Can. 1016. He is also the proper authority for members of non-clerical institutes and societies. Members of those clerical institutes or societies who are bound by promises, not vows, must be admitted to candidacy, and for these the proper authority is the major Superior. Before being admitted as a candidate, the aspirant must petition this in his own hand and must sign the petition. The competent authority must accept the petition, also in writing.

2016 The requirement in *Ad Pascendum* that '... those who aspire to the transitional diaconate will have completed their twentieth year and have begun their course of theological studies'[3] before being accepted as candidates, although not explicitly stated in the Code, still obtains.

---

[1] For the implementation of this faculty by the various Bishops' Conferences, cf. LCE Tavola per Paesi e Canoni at Can. 236.

[2] Cf. AP 1 a,b: Fl I 438.

[3] Ibid.

Part I The Sacraments

Can. 1035 §1 Before anyone may be promoted to the diaconate, whether permanent or transitory, he must have received the ministries of lector and acolyte, and have exercised them for an appropriate time.

§2 Between the conferring of the ministry of acolyte and the diaconate there is to be an interval of at least six months.

This canon reflects the older tradition of advancement through what were then the minor orders. More immediately, it is based on *Ministeria Quaedam*[1] and *Ad Pascendum*.[2] The purpose of receiving these ministries and of having a fitting time to exercise them is that the candidates may 'be better disposed for the future service of the word and the altar'.[3] The first draft of this canon repeated the rule of the two documents mentioned above, which reserved to the Holy See the power to dispense from receiving these ministries. This reservation has not been repeated in the Code, and it is clear from the deliberations of the Revision Commission that a diocesan Bishop can dispense from this law for a good and sufficient reason;[4] he can also dispense from the interval mentioned in §2. The faculty to dispense is not, however, an invitation to dispense, since a dispensation is of its nature designed for an exceptional situation (see Can. 85).

Can. 1036 For a candidate to be promoted to the order of diaconate or priesthood, he must submit to the proper Bishop or to the competent major Superior a declaration written in his own hand and signed by him, in which he attests that he is about to receive the sacred order freely and of his own accord and will devote himself permanently to the ecclesiastical ministry, asking at the same time that he be admitted to receive the order.

The 'proper Bishop' is determined by Cann. 1016 and 1019 §2, the 'competent major Superior' by Can. 1019 §1. A candidate for either the diaconate, whether permanent or transitory, or the priesthood must declare in a document written in his own hand and signed by him that he is receiving the order of his own accord and freely, and in the same document he is to ask to be admitted to the order. The declaration presupposes that the candidate knows the obligations he is undertaking (see Can. 1028). A candidate for the diaconate must also make the prescribed profession of faith (see Can. 833 6°).

Can. 1037 A candidate for the permanent diaconate who is not married, and likewise a candidate for the priesthood, is not to be admitted to the order of diaconate unless he has, in the prescribed rite, publicly before God and the Church undertaken the obligation of celibacy, or unless he has taken perpetual vows in a religious institute.

The obligation on clerics to observe celibacy is contained in Can. 277 §1. Can. 247 §1 decrees that clerical students are to be properly instructed in and prepared for this obligation. The present canon concerns a public undertaking of the obligation to be made by the candidate before receiving the order of diaconate. This rule was first introduced by *Ad Pascendum*.[5] It binds all candidates for the diaconate, except married men aspiring to the permanent diaconate and religious who have already taken perpetual vows. In the

---

[1] MQ 10–11: Fl I 431.
[2] AP 2,4: Fl I 438, 439.
[3] MQ loc cit.
[4] Cf. Comm 15(1983) 218 at Can. 988.
[5] Cf. AP 6: Fl I 439.

latter case the perpetual vow of chastity takes the place of this undertaking. The prescribed rite is contained in the rite of ordination to the diaconate.

Can. 1038 A deacon who refuses to be promoted to the priesthood may not be forbidden the exercise of the order he has received, unless he is constrained by a canonical impediment, or unless there is some other grave reason, to be estimated by the diocesan Bishop or the competent major Superior.

2020 This canon reflects the fact that, with the restoration of its permanent form, the diaconate is no longer seen as merely a step on the way to the priesthood but is given a positive recognition in its own right. If a deacon who was originally an aspirant to the priesthood, in due time finds that he cannot or should not proceed beyond the diaconate to which he is still committed, not only can he not be constrained to go on (see Can. 1026), but he may not be forbidden the exercise of the diaconate, *except in two cases*: (a) where he is prevented by an impediment from the exercise of his order (see Can. 1044), or (b) where, in the judgement of the Bishop or of the major Superior, there is some other grave reason against such exercise. In the latter case he has a right of recourse to the Holy See against a decision forbidding him to function as a deacon.

Can. 1039 All who are to be promoted to any order must make a retreat for at least five days, in a place and in the manner determined by the Ordinary. Before he proceeds to the ordination, the Bishop must have assured himself that the candidates have duly made the retreat.

2021 The ordination retreat is to be of a minimum of five consecutive days. The Ordinary is to decide the place and manner of the retreat. This retreat should never be regarded as the mere fulfilment of a legal requirement: rather must it always be seen in the context of an essential spiritual formation. The 1917 Code, at c.1011 §2, ordered the repetition of the retreat if for any reason the ordination had to be postponed for more than six months. The present Code does not repeat this rule, but the Ordinary could certainly impose a similar regulation. The ordaining Bishop, whoever he may be, is obliged to assure himself that this retreat has been duly made by the candidate.

Article 3
Irregularities and other Impediments

Can. 1040 Those bound by an impediment are to be barred from the reception of orders. An impediment may be simple; or it may be perpetual, in which case it is called an irregularity. No impediment is contracted which is not contained in the following canons.

2022 An impediment in the context of orders is a personal defect which by ecclesiastical law forbids the reception of an order or forbids the exercise of an order already received. Impediments may be either simple or perpetual; the latter, in accordance with canonical tradition, are called 'irregularities'. While retaining this distinction, the present law has abolished the former distinction between irregularities by offence and by defect. The lists of impediments given in the canons which follow (i.e. Cann. 1041, 1042 and 1044) are exhaustive. This is not to say that there are no other reasons for which a man may be barred from orders or forbidden their exercise. There are such, but a reliance on such reasons depends on the decision of the proper Bishop or competent major Superior, and the candidate may have recourse against this decision (see Can. 1030). The action of an impediment, on the other hand, is automatic. There is no recourse against it. It can cease to bind only in either of two situations:

(a) in the case of a simple impediment to the reception of orders, by the cessation of the defect causing it; (b) in the case both of a simple impediment and of an irregularity, by the grant of a dispensation by the competent authority.

Can. 1041 The following persons are irregular for the reception of orders:

> **1°** one who suffers from any form of insanity, or from any other psychological infirmity, because of which he is, after experts have been consulted, judged incapable of properly fulfilling the ministry;

2023 Two sources of irregularity are given here: insanity, and any other psychological infirmity. Insanity (*amentia*), which also gave rise to an irregularity in the 1917 Code, means an habitual lack of the use of reason.[1] The addition of other psychological infirmities considerably widens the scope of the irregularity. Under this head would be included a wide range of personality disorders. Whether an infirmity induces the irregularity in an individual case depends on whether or not it renders the person incapable of fulfilling the ministry. This calls for a judgement on the part of the proper Bishop or major Superior: in making this judgement he is obliged to consult competent experts. It should be noted, however, that the judgement is not left to the experts.[2] In declaring the existence of an irregularity on this head, as on others, he must have moral certainty about the candidate's habitual lack of the use of reason or his psychological unfitness for the ministry; this moral certainty must be based upon objective and, should the situation arise, provable evidence.

> **2°** one who has committed the offence of apostasy, heresy or schism;

2024 The terms 'apostasy', 'heresy' and 'schism' are defined in Can. 751. In order to incur the irregularity, the person must have committed a punishable offence; this means *inter alia* that his action must have been 'gravely imputable by reason of malice or culpability' (Can. 1321). Those born and baptised in other Churches or ecclesial communities can rarely be regarded as thus gravely culpable in this regard. However, under the 1917 Code, which the present law substantially repeats, the practice was to dispense such people *ad cautelam* because of a doubt concerning their good faith.[3] In view of the changed attitude in the Church in this regard, shown particularly in the Decree on Ecumenism of Vat. II, the general continuance of such a practice could not today be justified. In practice, this irregularity will normally arise in the case only of those who, having been baptised and probably, for some time at least, brought up as catholics, have then committed the offence of heresy, apostasy or schism, and later still returned to the Church.

> **3°** one who has attempted marriage, even a civil marriage, either while himself prevented from entering marriage whether by an existing marriage bond or by a sacred order or by a public and perpetual vow of chastity, or with a woman who is validly married or is obliged by the same vow;

2025 This irregularity arises from an attempted, and therefore invalid, marriage even if the ceremony was a civil one. It arises, not from all invalid marriages, but from five specified cases, namely where the man:

(a) was himself bound by an existing marriage;

(b) was bound by the impediment of orders;

---

[1] Cf. e.g. Wernz–Vidal I 321.
[2] Cf. e.g. Vermeersch–Creusen II 175.
[3] Cf. Comm 10(1978) 197 at Can. 224.

(c) was bound by the impediment of a public and perpetual vow of chastity;

(d) has attempted marriage with a woman who is validly married;

(e) has attempted marriage with a woman bound by a public and perpetual vow of chastity.

In cases (a) and (d), if the previous marriage was invalid and was subsequently so declared by an ecclesiastical decree of nullity, the irregularity does not arise.

4° one who has committed wilful homicide, or one who has actually procured an abortion, and all who have positively cooperated;

2026 Although this section does not use the word 'offence', it repeats almost verbatim the text of c.985 4° of the 1917 Code which put this irregularity under the heading of those incurred by offence. And both Can. 1044 §1 4° and Can. 1047 §2 1° refer to this irregularity as arising from an offence. One may therefore reasonably assume that, if the conditions necessary for the imputability of an offence are lacking, or if the mitigating circumstances mentioned in Cann. 1323 and 1324 §1 are operative, the irregularity is not incurred. This view is given added weight by the retention, after some debate, of the words *effectu secuto* (translated as 'actually') in the present text.[1] The irregularity is therefore incurred by those who commit the crime of homicide, those who actually procure an abortion, and those who directly cooperate in either offence. Accordingly, e.g. killing in lawful self-defence, or causing the expulsion of a foetus by means of a surgical procedure intended for another purpose, would not make a man irregular.

5° one who has gravely and maliciously mutilated himself or another, or who has attempted suicide.

2027 Establishing malicious intent in the case of one who has mutilated himself or attempted suicide presents obvious difficulties. In many such cases, the irregularity could well be that mentioned in 1° of the present canon, insanity or psychological disorder. The same may equally be true of one who has gravely mutilated another. The formation of a prudent judgement here clearly calls for very careful and sensitive adjudication.

6° one who has carried out an act of order which is reserved to those in the order of the episcopate or priesthood, while himself either not possessing that order or being barred from its exercise by some canonical penalty, declared or imposed.

2028 The 'act of order' mentioned here must be an act of ministry reserved to the priesthood or episcopate, e.g. celebrating Mass, hearing sacramental confession, ordaining. Merely posing as a priest or a Bishop would not suffice. Two cases are covered: (a) carrying out an act of order without having the order in question, e.g. a layman or a deacon pretending to celebrate Mass, a priest pretending to ordain; and (b) carrying out an act of order when, although the person possesses the order, he has been barred from its exercise by a canonical penalty which has been declared or imposed. Such a penalty would be excommunication, interdict or suspension. An automatic (*latae sententiae*) penalty which has not been declared, does not induce the irregularity. In danger of death, the prohibition arising from even a declared or imposed penalty is suspended (see Can. 1335), and so no irregularity arises.

Can. 1042 The following are simply impeded from receiving orders:

1° a man who has a wife, unless he is lawfully destined for the permanent diaconate;

---

[1] Cf. Comm 10(1978) 199 at Can. 225.

Part I The Sacraments

Whereas the irregularities in the previous canon arise from either a grave defect in the person or an offence committed by him, the simple impediments imply no such fault or defect. They are not perpetual and can cease with the cessation of the cause giving rise to them.

A married man may be admitted to the permanent diaconate; apart from that case, all men who have wives are simply impeded from the reception of orders. If the marriage bond ceases, either by the death of the wife or by an ecclesiastical dissolution, the impediment ceases also. Strictly speaking, if a marriage has been declared null the impediment does not exist and the man may be ordained. But other considerations may arise here. If the nullity of the marriage was due to a psychological defect in the man, he may be irregular by virtue of Can. 1041. Moreover, if he has young children, his obligations towards these might demand at least a postponement of ordination. This could arise also where the marriage bond has ceased. And whether or not the marriage was valid, the wife should be asked about her attitude to the ordination in case she has objections to raise that could later on jeopardize his ministry.

The Holy See sometimes dispenses from this impediment if the wife gives her consent and seeks admission to a religious institute or at least seriously undertakes not to interfere with her husband's ministry. In more recent times the Holy See has also in certain cases granted dispensations from this impediment to former ministers of other faiths, allowing them to be ordained and to continue to live with their wives.

2° one who exercises an office or administration forbidden to clerics, in accordance with Cann. 285 and 286, of which he must render an account; the impediment binds until such time as, having relinquished the office and administration and rendered the account, he has been freed;

In practice this is an impediment which will not often arise, if only because the aspirant's entry into the seminary will normally entail relinquishing all such offices and administration. If it does arise, the Ordinary can dispense if there be a good and sufficient reason. The impediment does not normally arise in the case of permanent deacons (see Can. 288).

3° a neophyte, unless, in the judgement of the Ordinary, he has been sufficiently tested.

A neophyte is one who has been recently baptised as an adult. In the present context the term also includes those who have been recently admitted to full communion with the Church. The reason for the impediment is to allow sufficient time to prove the person's stability in the faith. If the Ordinary judges that this has already been done, he may permit him to be ordained. Many seminaries have established a two- or three-year period before a convert may be admitted to begin his formation.

Can. 1043 Christ's faithful are bound to reveal, before ordination, to the Ordinary or to the parish priest, such impediments to sacred orders as they may know about.

This canon corresponds to Can. 1069 regarding marriage impediments. Since being married and being in orders are both matters of public status, the community is involved in ensuring that the candidates are fit. The obligation is a serious one; in some places, in order to bring it to the notice of the faithful, it is customary to call banns before ordination.

Can. 1044 §1 The following are irregular for the exercise of orders already received:

Book IV The Sanctifying Office of the Church

1° one who, while bound by an irregularity for the reception of orders, unlawfully received orders;

2° one who committed the offence mentioned in Can. 1041 n.2, if the offence is public;

3° one who committed any of the offences mentioned in Can. 1041 nn.3, 4, 5, 6.

2035 This paragraph indicates those who are irregular for the exercise of orders which they have already received. First come those who have unlawfully received an order while barred from doing so by an irregularity. Next are those who have committed the offence of apostasy, heresy or schism, but only if the offence is public. Lastly come those who have, even privately, committed any of the offences described in Can. 1041 3°, 4°, 5°, 6°. The last two groups of cases refer to offences committed after the reception of orders; offences committed beforehand are covered by 1° of this paragraph.

Can. 1044 §2 The following are impeded from the exercise of orders:

1° one who, while bound by an impediment to the reception of orders, unlawfully received orders;

2° one who suffers from insanity or from some other psychological infirmity mentioned in Can. 1041 n.1, until such time as the Ordinary, having consulted an expert, has allowed the exercise of the order in question.

2036 The first category consists of those who have received orders while bound by an impediment to such reception. Thus e.g. a man who, although married, unlawfully received the order of priesthood, is impeded from exercising his priesthood. The second category is comprised of those who suffer from insanity or some other psychological infirmity as mentioned in Can. 1041 1°. The existence of such an infirmity before ordination constitutes an irregularity; if the condition appears only after ordination, or at least if it only then becomes serious, it constitutes, not an irregularity for the exercise of orders, but a simple impediment. The reason is that there is always hope of a cure or of an improvement in the condition, and so it is seen as not necessarily being perpetual. However, even if the infirmity should cease or improve, the Ordinary's permission is needed before the cleric can exercise his order, and the Ordinary is to consult an appropriate expert before giving this permission. This permission, being provided for in the law, is not a dispensation.

2037 Since simple impediments are not of their nature perpetual, it would seem that an impediment to the exercise of orders contracted by unlawful reception of that order, would cease when the cause of the impediment has ceased. Thus e.g. a married man who has unlawfully received orders would cease to be bound by the impediment if his wife were to die.

Can. 1045 Ignorance of irregularities and impediments does not exempt from them.

2038 This canon repeats exactly c.988 of the 1917 Code, omitting the words 'whether by offence or by defect' since this distinction is no longer made. However, the common interpretation of the former law held that in the case of irregularities by offence, ignorance of the prohibition of the law exempted from these irregularities, by reason of lack of culpability.[1] This interpretation would seem still applicable – even though it is

---

[1] Cf. e.g. Vermeersch–Creusen II 171.

not easy to imagine a person not being aware that the offences mentioned in Can. 1041 are forbidden by law. Ignorance of the existence of the irregularity or impediment does not exempt.

Can. 1046 Irregularities and impediments are multiplied if they arise from different causes, not however from the repetition of the same cause, unless it is a question of the irregularity arising from the commission of wilful homicide or from having actually procured an abortion.

This is a substantial repetition of c.989 of the 1917 Code, with the addition of the final provision concerning abortion. Multiplication of irregularities or impediments is of importance only in seeking a dispensation from them. If they are multiplied, the number of offences must be mentioned in a petition for a dispensation; otherwise the dispensation could be invalid (see Can. 1049 §§1, 2). The clear rule now is that, with two exceptions, they are not multiplied by a repetition of the same cause, but only by the placing of different causes. Thus e.g. a man who several times attempted suicide, or pretended to celebrate Mass although not ordained a priest, would incur only one irregularity on each head. The exceptions are the offences of wilful homicide or actually procuring an abortion: in these cases there is a separate irregularity for each act of homicide or abortion.   2039

Can. 1047 §1 If the fact on which they are based has been brought to the judicial forum, dispensation from all irregularities is reserved to the Apostolic See alone.

§2 Dispensation from the following irregularities and impediments to the reception of orders is also reserved to the Apostolic See:

1° irregularities arising from the offences mentioned in Can. 1041 nn.2 and 3, if they are public;

2° an irregularity arising from the offence, whether public or occult, mentioned in Can. 1041 n.4;

3° the impediment mentioned in Can. 1042 n.1.

§3 To the Apostolic See is also reserved the dispensation from the irregularities for the exercise of an order received mentioned in Can. 1041 n.3 but only in public cases, and in n.4 of the same canon even in occult cases.

§4 The Ordinary can dispense from irregularities and impediments not reserved to the Holy See.

While the Code was being formulated there was some debate as to whether power to dispense from impediments to orders should be left to Bishops' Conferences, but the final decision was to reserve to the Holy See all cases except those of lesser importance.[1] §§1–3 of the present canon list the cases reserved to the Holy See; §4 leaves to the Ordinary the power to dispense from all others.   2040

In all cases, whether of irregularities or of impediments and whether these concern the reception or the exercise of an order, if the fact on which the irregularity or impediment is based has been brought to the judicial forum, i.e. before a court, dispensation is reserved to the Holy See (§1). The judicial forum here can be either ecclesiastical or civil.   2041

---

[1] Cf. Comm 10(1978) 195–196.

Book IV The Sanctifying Office of the Church

2042 §2 lists irregularities and one impediment to the *reception* of orders which are reserved to the Holy See:

(a) the irregularities arising from apostasy, heresy or schism (Can. 1041 2°) and from attempted marriage (Can. 1041 3°), but only if the offences in question are public, i.e. capable of being proven in the external forum;

(b) the irregularity arising from wilful homicide or abortion (Can. 1041 4°), even if the offence was occult;

(c) the impediment of marriage (Can. 1042 1°). This dispensation is sometimes granted in special cases.

2043 §3 concerns dispensations from irregularities to the *exercise* of an order already received, and it reserves two of these to the Holy See:

(a) the irregularity arising from an attempted marriage (Can. 1041 3°), but only in public cases;

(b) the irregularity arising from wilful homicide or abortion (Can. 1041 4°) even in occult cases.

Can. 1048 In the more urgent occult cases, if the Ordinary or, in the case of the irregularities mentioned in Can. 1041 nn.3 and 4, the Penitentiary cannot be approached, and if there is imminent danger of serious harm or loss of reputation, the person who is irregular for the exercise of an order may exercise it. There remains, however, the obligation of his having recourse as soon as possible to the Ordinary or the Penitentiary, without revealing his name, and through a confessor.

2044 This canon deals not with dispensation, but with a special case where a man, irregular for the exercise of an order already received, is nevertheless allowed to exercise it. There are three essential conditions: (a) the case must be an occult one; (b) it must be impossible for him to approach the appropriate dispensing authority; (c) there must be imminent danger of grave harm or loss of reputation in not exercising the order. The appropriate authority will be the Ordinary or, where dispensation is reserved to the Holy See, the Apostolic Penitentiary. The canon specifically refers to the two irregularities that are reserved to the Holy See, attempted marriage (Can. 1041 3°) and wilful homicide or abortion (Can. 1041 4°). In the case of the former, since the case being considered is an occult one, the Ordinary could dispense as the reservation applies only to public cases (see Can. 1047 §3), but the Penitentiary is also competent.

2045 Having exercised his order in accordance with this canon, the cleric is bound to have recourse as soon as possible to the Ordinary or to the Penitentiary. He may do this through a confessor and without revealing his identity. The confessor does not grant a dispensation; he merely assists in this,[1] and the powers of dispensation which he had under c.990 §2 of the 1917 Code have been abrogated.

Can. 1049 §1 In a petition to obtain a dispensation from irregularities or impediments, all irregularities and impediments are to be mentioned. However, a general dispensation is valid also for those omitted in good faith, with the exception of the irregularities mentioned in Can. 1041 n.4, or of others which have been brought to the judicial forum; it is not, however, valid for those concealed in bad faith.

2046 A petition for a dispensation must mention all the irregularities and impediments contracted. If some are omitted in good faith, i.e. through ignorance or inadvertence,

---

[1] Cf. Comm 10(1978) 202 at Can. 231.

Part I The Sacraments

a general dispensation still covers these, with the exceptions of the irregularity arising from wilful homicide or abortion (Can. 1041 4°) and of any other which has been brought before a court; these need specific dispensation. Irregularities or impediments knowingly concealed are not covered by a general dispensation.

Can. 1049 §2 If there is question of an irregularity arising from wilful homicide or from a procured abortion, for the validity of the dispensation even the number of offences must be stated.

The reason for this norm is twofold. Technically, the irregularity arising from this source is the only one which is multiplied by repetition of the same cause (see Can. 1046). In addition, the offences involved are so serious that dispensation from the irregularity will less easily be granted if the offences have been repeated. 2047

Can. 1049 §3 A general dispensation from irregularities and impediments to the reception of orders is valid for all orders.

This means that a general dispensation from irregularities and impediments given for the diaconate holds good for ordination to the priesthood and episcopate, unless of course a new irregularity is contracted in the meantime. 2048

Article 4
Documents required and the Investigation

Can. 1050 For a person to be promoted to sacred orders the following documents are required:

1° a certificate of studies duly completed in accordance with Can. 1032;

2° for those to be ordained to the priesthood, a certificate of the reception of the diaconate;

3° for those to be promoted to the diaconate, certificates of the reception of baptism, of confirmation and of the ministries mentioned in Can. 1035, and a certificate that the declaration mentioned in Can. 1036 has been made; if an ordinand to be promoted to the permanent diaconate is married, a certificate of his marriage and testimony of his wife's consent.

This canon simply provides a list of documents that are required before a man can be ordained. Other documents might be required in particular cases – such as any dispensations granted in the external forum from impediments or irregularities, dispensations from the age requirements of Can. 1031 or the interval required by Can. 1035 §2. 2049

Can. 1051 In the investigation of the requisite qualities of one who is to be ordained, the following provisions are to be observed:

1° there is to be a certificate from the rector of the seminary or of the house of formation, concerning the qualities required in the candidate for the reception of the order, namely sound doctrine, genuine piety, good moral behaviour, fitness for the exercise of the ministry; likewise, after proper investigation, a certificate of the candidate's state of physical and psychological health;

2° the diocesan Bishop or the major Superior may, in order properly to complete the investigation, use other means which, taking into account the circumstances of time and place, may seem useful, such as testimonial letters, public notices or other sources of information.

2050 The primary obligation to make the investigation called for in this canon falls on the proper Bishop or major Superior (see Can. 1025 §1). An obligatory part of this investigation is a certificate from the rector of the seminary or house of formation, concerning the qualities listed in this canon. The remarks made under Can. 1029 concerning the use of psychological assessments are relevant here. The same rector may be, and frequently is, charged with such additional optional enquiries as the Ordinary may consider necessary or useful to complete the investigation – such as publication of the banns (no longer obligatory), testimonial letters from the local clergy, private and confidential enquiries, references from former employers, etc.

Can. 1052 §1 For a Bishop to proceed to an ordination which he is to confer by his own right, he must be satisfied that the documents mentioned in Can. 1050 are at hand and that, as a result of the investigations prescribed by law, the suitability of the candidate has been positively established.

2051 In conferring orders a Bishop has a grave responsibility to be as certain as possible about the fitness of the candidate. Where he is the candidate's proper Bishop, he must ensure that the documents prescribed in Can. 1050 are at hand, that the investigations required by law have been carried out and that the candidate is positively established as suitable. The mere fact that nothing is known against him is not sufficient; his fitness must be positively shown to have been proven, in so far as is humanly possible.

Can. 1052 §2 For a Bishop to proceed to the ordination of someone not his own subject, it is sufficient that the dimissorial letters state that those documents are at hand, that the investigation has been conducted in accordance with the law, and that the candidate's suitability has been established. If the ordinand is a member of a religious institute or a society of apostolic life, these letters must also testify that he has been definitively enrolled in the institute or society and that he is a subject of the Superior who gives the letters.

2052 If the ordaining Bishop is not the candidate's proper Bishop he still has the same general obligations regarding the fitness of the candidate, but it suffices if the dimissorial letters state that the requirements of the law have been met. If the candidate is a member of a religious institute or society of apostolic life, the dimissorial letters must in addition testify that he has been definitively enrolled and that he is a subject of the Superior who grants the letters.

Can. 1052 §3 If, not withstanding all this, the Bishop has definite reasons for doubting that the candidate is suitable to receive orders, he is not to promote him.

2053 This paragraph emphasises the ordaining Bishop's responsibility, whether or not he is the ordinand's proper Bishop. Even if all the legal requirements have been carried out, if the Bishop has definite reasons for doubting the candidate's fitness, he may not ordain him. However, doubts which have no real basis, or which arise from scruples, are not sufficient (see Can. 1026); the Bishop must have good and definite reason for his doubts.

Part I The Sacraments

Chapter III
THE REGISTRATION AND EVIDENCE OF ORDINATION

Can. 1053 §1 After an ordination, the names of the individuals ordained, the name of the ordaining minister, and the place and date of ordination are to be entered in a special register which is to be carefully kept in the curia of the place of ordination. All the documents of each ordination are to be accurately preserved.

A proper record of each ordination, comprising the details listed in this canon, is to be made in a special register. This register is to be kept in the episcopal curia of the place of ordination, not in the place of the ordination itself – a point to be noted when e.g. the ordination is held in a parish church.   2054

Can. 1053 §2 The ordaining Bishop is to give to each person ordained an authentic certificate of the ordination received. Those who, with dimissorial letters, have been promoted by a Bishop other than their own, are to submit the certificate to their proper Ordinary for the registration of the ordination in a special register, to be kept in the archive.

One who is ordained by a Bishop other than his own is obliged to submit the certificate, which is to be given to all newly ordained, to his own Bishop for registration in a special register kept for this purpose. In practice, the curia of the place of ordination will usually notify the curia of the proper Bishop. But the primary obligation is laid on the newly ordained cleric, and he should be made aware of this.   2055

Can. 1054 The local Ordinary, if it concerns the secular clergy, or the competent Major Superior, if it concerns his subjects, is to send a notification of each ordination to the parish priest of the place of baptism. The parish priest is to record the ordination in the baptismal register in accordance with Can. 535 §2.

The law considers the baptismal register a vital source for the record of sacraments received and of information about a person's status (see Can. 535 §2). The obligation to see that notice of ordination is sent there is firmly placed on the local Ordinary for secular clergy, and on the competent major Superior for his subjects – not on the administrator of the cathedral, nor e.g. on the parish priest if the ordination has taken place in a parish church. Under the present law, notice of *each* order is to be sent; the 1917 Code in its c.1011 demanded this only for the subdiaconate.   2056

Title VII
Marriage

Can. 1055 §1 The marriage covenant, by which a man and a woman establish between themselves a partnership of their whole life, and which of its own very nature is ordered to the well-being of the spouses and to the procreation and upbringing of children, has, between the baptised, been raised by Christ the Lord to the dignity of a sacrament.

2057 The first canon on marriage reflects the development in thinking and teaching on this sacrament which has taken place since the promulgation of the 1917 Code. Firstly, it describes marriage at the outset as a 'covenant' rather than as a contract. This term, which is used to translate the Latin *foedus*, derives from Vat. II,[1] and it serves to broaden and enrich the concept of Christian marriage, by linking it (a) to the covenant between God and his chosen people and (b) to the Pauline model of the Church as the spouse of Christ. The term is not used to supplant the idea of marriage as a contract; indeed the Revision Commission makes it clear that the terms 'covenant' and 'contract' apply to the same reality.[2] The biblical and theological antecedents and associations of the first term are richer; they emphasise the personal nature of the commitment made in marriage.

2058 This emphasis on the personal is also reflected when the text speaks of the mutual consent of the parties as setting up a 'partnership of their whole life' whose essential purpose is 'the well-being of the spouses and the procreation and upbringing of children'. The phrase 'partnership of their whole life' has its origins in Roman law and has a long tradition in canonical usage. It implies not merely a physical sexual union, but a total union on all levels between equal partners. The 1917 Code did not explicitly give a description of marriage; rather, in its c.1081 §2 it defined the object of marital consent as a 'perpetual and exclusive right over the body, for acts which are of themselves suitable for the generation of children'. The present law has expanded the object of consent, and it clearly regards as essential certain elements which formerly might have been seen as pertaining to the perfection, rather than the essence, of marriage. The previous law distinguished between the primary (procreation and education of children) and secondary (mutual help and allaying of concupiscence) ends of marriage. The present law, following Vat. II, makes no such hierarchy of distinction.[3] Instead, both are seen as essential and related parts of the total self-giving which is marriage. This has important practical consequences, in that the capacity for this partnership of life and the willingness to commit oneself to it have a direct bearing on the validity of marriage.[4]

2059 When it takes place between baptised partners, the natural institution of marriage has been 'raised by Christ the Lord to the dignity of a sacrament'. This statement affirms the traditional belief of the Church that marriage is one of the seven sacraments. Even though this was not formally defined until the thirteenth century, marriage had from the earliest times been regarded as having a sacred dimension.

Can. 1055 §2 Consequently, a valid marriage contract cannot exist between baptised persons without its being by that very fact a sacrament.

2060 This paragraph, which repeats the wording of c.1012 §2 of the 1917 Code, states the principle that 'between baptised persons' there is no distinction between contract and sacrament. If two validly baptised persons marry, their marriage is necessarily a sacrament;

---

[1] GS 48: Fl I 950 (where the word *foedus* is translated 'contract'!).

[2] Cf. Comm 15(1983) 222 at Can. 1008 §2.

[3] GS 48: 'God ... has endowed (marriage) with various benefits and with various ends in view': Fl I 950. Cf. Comm 15(1983) 221 at Can. 1008 §1.

[4] This canon does not determine precisely what, in the context of a marriage's validity, constitutes the 'well-being of the spouses': this is a matter for the jurisprudence and practice of the Church's marriage tribunals. Nor does the canon spell out in detail what the 'upbringing of children' entails, involving generally (as it obviously must) their physical, moral, religious, intellectual and social education (cf. Can. 795): this too belongs partly to ecclesiastical jurisprudence, partly also to those other canons in the Code which deal with this same matter, e.g. Cann. 773–780, 793–794, 796–806 etc.

Part I The Sacraments

the sacrament is not something added to the contract: the contract itself constitutes the sacrament.[1] In the official discussions on the drafts of this paragraph there was extensive debate. The Revision Commission's position was that the law must reflect the teaching of the Church's magisterium as it stands, and that it is not its purpose to decide theological issues.[2] In particular, the law does not address the problem of marriages where the partners, although baptised, are to one degree or another lacking in faith. Can such people marry validly? In view of the inseparability of the sacrament and the contract, if they have sufficient faith to receive the sacrament validly, even if that faith is weak or careless and accordingly the fruits of the sacrament are far less than ideal, they can nevertheless marry validly.[3] To say this however is by no means to tell the whole story. From the pastoral point of view, it is essential that every effort be made, by all concerned – the parties themselves, their parents and families, their friends, the instructing priests etc. – to ensure as far as possible that the celebration of every marriage be made the occasion of expressing and, if needs be, of quickening the faith of the couple involved. It should never be forgotten that marriage, like all the sacraments, is a 'sign and a means by which faith is expressed and strengthened ...' (Can. 840), that it 'must proceed from and rest upon faith', and accordingly that 'sacred ministers are to strive to arouse and enlighten this faith ...' (Can. 836). This admonition of the Code is all the more pertinent today when marriage, subject as it is to so many economic, social and even family pressures, is under a distinct threat of being invited to overlook that which is its distinct and essential character in the Church, namely that it is a sacrament instituted by Christ.[4]

A different situation exists in respect of baptised people who explicitly reject the faith, who reject the sacramentality of marriage or who have never come to an act of faith. It is clear that they cannot receive the sacrament. It has been argued in some circles that since such people have a fundamental right to marry, they can marry validly and that in their case the sacrament and the contract are separated.[5] Whatever the merits of this argument in favour of changing the traditional teaching and changing the law, the law as it stands certainly regards the marriages of such people as invalid.[6]

2061

---

[1] The principle stated in this canon is a doctrinal or theological one, which has attracted varying opinions and about which a vast literature exists. For a comprehensive overview of the theological position after Vat. II, cf. Baudot *L'Inseparabilité entre le Contrat et le Sacrament de Mariage* Analecta Gregoriana Rome 1987. For some shorter studies, one may usefully consult e.g. Norris *Why the marriage of Christians is one of the seven Sacraments* Irish Theological Quarterly 51(1985) 37–51; Eid *Il matrimonio mistero della comunione: reflessioni teologico-canoniche* ME 109(1984) 437–446; Himes *The intrinsic sacramentality of marriage: the theological ground for the inseparability of validity and sacramentality in marriage* Jur 50(1990) 198–220; Beyer *Die christliche Ehe ist Sakrament* Iustus Iudex (Festgabe für Paul Wesemann) Ludgerus-Verlag 1990 185–198; Navarrete *Matrimonio, Contratto e Sacramento* ME 117(1993) 91–112.

[2] Cf. Comm 9(1977) 122 at Can. 242 §2; 15(1983) 222 at Can. 1008 §2.

[3] Cf. O'Callaghan *Faith and the Sacrament of Marriage* Irish Theological Quarterly 52(1986) 161–179; Finn *Faith and the Sacrament of Marriage: General conclusion from an historical study* Marriage Studies 3(1989) 95–111 CLSA Washington DC; Pompedda *Faith and the Sacrament of Marriage: lack of faith and matrimonial consent: juridical aspects* Marriage Studies 4(1990) 33–65, and Quaderni Studio Rotale 2(1987) 41–71 Libreria Leoniana Rome; Lane *Notes on the Sacramentality of Marriage*: Address to CLSGBI annual Conference 1990 6–10.

[4] Cf. de Lanversin *'Sécularisation' et sacrement de mariage* cit Iustus Iudex 215–234.

[5] Cf. e.g. Örsy in Theological Studies 43(1982) 390, and *Marriage in Canon Law* Wilmington Delaware 1986 57; O'Callaghan *Faith and the Sacrament of Marriage* Irish Theological Quarterly (1986) 178.

[6] Cf. Faltin *The exclusion of the sacramentality of marriage with particular reference to the marriage of baptized non-believers* cit Marriage Studies 4(1990) 66–104; Versaldi *Exclusio sacramentalitatis matrimonii ex parte baptizatorum non credentium: error vel potius simulatio* Per 79(1990) 421–440.

2062 For any marriage to be sacramental, both parties must have been validly and sacramentally baptised. If one party is not baptised, as e.g. in the case where a catholic marries an unbaptised person with a dispensation from the impediment of disparity of cult (see Can. 1086), there is no sacrament but the marriage is still a valid natural one. Such a marriage would become sacramental if the unbaptised party were later to receive baptism.

Can. 1056 The essential properties of marriage are unity and indissolubility; in christian marriage they acquire a distinctive firmness by reason of the sacrament.

2063 This canon is a repetition of c.1013 §2 of the 1917 Code, with a minor change in the order of the words. *Essential properties* are qualities that flow from the very nature of marriage in itself, so that without them there can never be a real marriage. There is question here then, not of an ideal to be aimed at, nor even of a moral imperative, but of ontological fact. The essential properties are unity and indissolubility.

2064 *Unity* involves the marriage of one man and one woman, and accordingly excludes all forms of polygamy, whether it be polygyny, where one man has several wives, polyandry where one woman has several husbands, or so-called 'group marriages' where several men 'marry' several women. It does not, of course, exclude successive marriages, where the former bond has been dissolved by death or other legitimate means. Without unity the total self-giving essential to marriage is impossible: a person with several spouses cannot give totally to any of them.

2065 *Indissolubility* is a property of all marriages, sacramental or natural. However, christian marriage, because it is a sacrament and because it therefore reflects the unbreakable union of Christ with his Church, is especially indissoluble. Nevertheless, in certain circumstances the Church does dissolve marriages where neither party, or even only one, is baptised. This is done 'in favour of the faith' of a catholic party (see Cann. 1142–1150). Even the valid marriage of two baptised people can in some situations be dissolved if the marriage was not consummated (see Cann. 1697–1706). The only marriages which are absolutely indissoluble are the consummated marriages of baptised parties (see Can. 1141).[1]

Can. 1057 §1 A marriage is brought into being by the lawfully manifested consent of persons who are legally capable. This consent cannot be supplied by any human power.

2066 The medieval debate about what precisely brought marriage into being – consent or consummation – was finally settled by Pope Alexander III who stated that consent alone made marriage, while affirming that consummation gave it absolute indissolubility. The present law repeats the wording of c.1081 §1 of the 1917 Code and it prescribes three general principles:

(a) There must be a real act of consent by both parties. This is absolutely necessary, and no human power, parents, family, state or church can supply this consent. Even when the requirement of renewal of consent is dispensed from in validating an invalid marriage, the true consent already given must still persist (see Cann. 1161ff). Where a marriage is arranged by parents or others, the parties must at least consent to the person chosen. The qualities required in the consent and the defects which render it inefficacious are discussed under the canons on matrimonial consent (see Cann. 1095ff).

---

[1] In granting the dissolutions mentioned above the Church acts in virtue of the divine authority given it by Christ. This authority is not granted to any civil power.

(b) The consent must be 'lawfully manifested'. Marriage is not merely a private matter between the spouses but has important implications for the whole of society. Accordingly, entrance into it is effected not by a purely private exchange of consent, but by a public ceremony involving certain legal or customary formalities. For a marriage where at least one party is a catholic, this means observing the canonical form of marriage (see Cann. 1108ff).

(c) The parties must be 'legally capable' of marriage, i.e. they must not be bound by any diriment impediment which renders them incapable of any marriage or of this particular marriage (see Cann. 1073–1094).

To these three requirements correspond, in general terms, the three ways in which a marriage may be invalid: defect of consent, defect of canonical form, and the existence of a diriment impediment.

Can. 1057 §2 Matrimonial consent is an act of will by which a man and a woman by an irrevocable covenant mutually give and accept one another for the purpose of establishing a marriage.

The ultimate object of the act of consent is the establishing of a marriage as described in Can. 1055 §1. The immediate object is the mutual giving and acceptance of the parties.[1] Because married life is of its essence a partnership, this mutuality must be present in the consent which sets it up. Consent given by one party only would be ineffective, at least until such time as the other also consented in accordance with the law. In the 1917 Code at c.1081 §2 the immediate object of the consent was the giving and accepting of 'a perpetual and exclusive right over the body for acts which are of themselves suitable for the generation of children'. The present law, in keeping with a more personalist approach, sees as the proper object of the consent not only the procreative dimension of marriage, but the whole of married life. 2067

Can. 1058 All can contract marriage who are not prohibited by law.

This canon repeats c.1035 of the 1917 Code where, however, it was located at the start of the canons on impediments. Its present position among the introductory canons to marriage serves to emphasise the fundamental nature of the right to marry. This is one of the most basic of human rights; it is not however absolute or unrestricted. For a greater good, some marriages may be prohibited by either natural or human law. The prohibition may be invalidating, as in the case of the impediments, or it may be simply prohibitory, as in the case of mixed marriages or where the local Ordinary acts in accordance with Can. 1077. Forbidding a marriage, whether by law or in an individual case, is done only for serious and well-founded reasons. 2068

Can. 1059 The marriage of catholics, even if only one party is a catholic, is governed not only by divine law but also by canon law, without prejudice to the competence of the civil authority in respect of the merely civil effects of the marriage.

Divine law binds everyone whether baptised or not, and so its prescriptions apply to all marriages. Can. 11 states the general principle that 'merely ecclesiastical laws bind those who were baptised in the catholic Church or received into it'. Hence in a marriage where both parties are non-catholic, they are not bound e.g. by the canonical form of marriage or by impediments which are of purely ecclesiastical law, such e.g. as those detailed in Cann. 1083, 1093. However, if one party is a catholic and the other is not, the marriage is subject to canon law, whether the non-catholic party is 2069

---

[1] Cf. GS 48: Fl I 950.

baptised or not. In framing this canon the Revision Commission made it quite clear that the wording was in no way to be taken as denying the competence of the Church with regard to the marriages of baptised non-catholics.[1] In fact, such competence is exercised by the Church's tribunals in regard to all the baptised in marriage nullity cases (see Can. 1671).

2070 This canon acknowledges, as did the corresponding c.1016 of the 1917 Code, the competence of the state regarding the 'merely civil effects' of a marriage. Such effects would concern e.g. registration, succession, inheritance, the name borne by a wife and by children, tax liability. In addition to the effects of a marriage, the civil authority frequently stipulates certain requirements concerning such things as the time and place of the ceremony, blood tests, prior notice and the like. As long as these do not conflict with the substance of marriage or its essential properties, they can and should be followed. The Church does not recognise civil legislation which is contrary to divine law or, in the case of catholics, which is contrary to canon law.

Can. 1060 Marriage enjoys the favour of law. Consequently, in doubt the validity of a marriage must be upheld until the contrary is proven.

2071 The presumption of law stated here simply means that if a couple have gone through a ceremony of marriage, they are presumed to be validly married. It also means that a valid marriage is presumed to exist *even where the fact of the ceremony has not been proved* but where marriage is 'in possession', i.e. where the parties and others genuinely believe they did in fact get married.[2] Moreover, this presumption is commonly held to apply both to the external and to the internal forum,[3] so that even a sincerely held belief that a particular marriage is not valid does not excuse from observing this law. On the other hand, this presumption is one – technically known as a 'simple presumption' – which can be displaced by contrary proof, i.e. by proof that, despite the fact that the couple have gone through a *marriage ceremony*, there existed at that time some substantial defect which prevented there coming into being the marriage envisaged by Can. 1055 §1, as regulated by Can. 1057.[4]

Can. 1061 §1 A valid marriage between baptised persons is said to be merely ratified, if it is not consummated; ratified and consummated, if the spouses have in a human manner engaged together in a conjugal act in itself apt for the generation of offspring: to this act marriage is by its nature ordered and by it the spouses become one flesh.

2072 The distinction made in this §1 is an important one, which can have very practical consequences. A valid marriage between two baptised people is:

– *merely ratified* if, albeit a valid one, it is not consummated by sexual intercourse;
– *ratified and consummated* if the spouses have had sexual intercourse together after their having exchanged matrimonial consent.

---

[1] Cf. Comm 15(1983) 223 at Can. 1012.

[2] Cf. Cappello V n.51.

[3] Cappello op cit n.53.

[4] This brings into clear focus the fundamental distinction – recognised not only by the canon law but so widely by the various civil laws – between the concepts of nullity and of divorce: the one being a proven recognition that no real marriage had ever existed, the other being a claim that, whether it did or not, it could and should be extinguished by the civil law. Note also that the presumption stated in this canon is without prejudice to the provision of Can. 1150 (see Can. 1608 §2): cf. Comm 15 (1983) 244 at Can. 1013.

While consummation is not a constitutive element of marriage, it does make a merely ratified marriage absolutely indissoluble (see commentary on Can. 1056). It is therefore essential to understand what in canon law constitutes the consummation of a marriage.[1]

Traditionally, consummation has been understood to occur when the following three elements take place: erection of the male penis, penetration by it of the female vagina, and ejaculation within the vagina. In accordance with the thinking of Vat. II,[2] a notable fourth element has been introduced in this canon, i.e. that this physical act of sexual intercourse be performed in a *human manner*: in other words, no longer is a marriage considered to be consummated by a mere physical act of sexual intercourse, independently of whether that was a human act or not: whether it was freely and willingly engaged in by both parties or was forced by one upon the other, whether it was just or unjust.[3] Thus e.g. sexual intercourse forced by a husband against his wife's expressed wish would certainly not constitute the consummation of their marriage.[4] What in this context is the position of contraceptive intercourse? The Revision Commission expressed the view that if the contraceptive means employed affect the act of intercourse itself, e.g. 'coitus interruptus', the marriage would not be consummated, whereas it would be if the means did not affect the act.[5] This leaves unresolved the question as to whether or not a marriage is consummated if e.g. a condom or a vaginal sheath is used: is this a 'human manner' of the exercise of the procreative act ordained by God in the context of marriage?: it is the view of this commentary that it is not. This and allied matters are ones which have yet to be more extensively explored and clarified by jurisprudence and practice.[6]

2073

Can. 1061 §2 If the spouses have lived together after the celebration of their marriage, consummation is presumed until the contrary is proven.

This is an eminently reasonable presumption of law and is of practical importance in cases where a marriage is alleged not to have been consummated. If the parties have lived together, even for a very brief period, the presumption can be displaced only by contrary proof.

2074

Can. 1061 §3 An invalid marriage is said to be putative if it has been celebrated in good faith by at least one party. It ceases to be such when both parties become certain of its nullity.

A *putative marriage* is one which is in fact invalid but which is believed to be valid by at least one of the parties. A reply of the Code Commission in 1949 regarding c.1015

2075

---

[1] The canonical definition does not necessarily coincide with that understood in some medical circles.

[2] Cf. GS 49: Fl I 952–953; Comm 6(1974) 191–192; Navarrete *De notione et effectibus consummationis matrimonii* Per 59(1970) 636–637.

[3] '... for a marriage to be consummated it is necessary that there be a human act on the part of both spouses; it is sufficient for it to be virtually voluntary, provided that it was not extorted through violence. No weight is given to other psychological elements which render the act easier or more loving': SCSac lit circ *De processu super matrimonio rato et non consummato* 20.XII.1986: ME 112 (1987) 423–428 (English trans in Woestman *Special Marriage Cases* St Paul Ottawa 1992 119–126). Cf. Commentary on this Circular Letter by Melli, under-secretary of SCSac: ME op cit 431; Woestman op cit 19–20.

[4] Cf. Comm 6(1974) 191–192.

[5] Cf. Comm 6(1974) 194–196.

[6] In the meantime, there is the clear practical directive of the Holy See that, should a Bishop be presented with a petition claiming that a marriage was not consummated by reason of the fact that the act of intercourse had not been carried out *in a human manner*, he is obliged, even before instituting a formal process in the case, to seek the guidance of the competent Congregation in Rome: cf. cit SCSac lit circ 20.XII.1986 n.2. See our commentary on Can. 1699 §2.

§4 of the 1917 Code, which this paragraph repeats, made it clear that 'celebrated' in this context means celebrated before the Church.[1] In order to qualify as a putative marriage, therefore, the marriage must be invalid by reason of an impediment, a defect of consent, or a defect of canonical form which was not total, e.g. where the person assisting at the marriage was not authorised to do so in accordance with Cann. 1108–1112, or where there were not two witnesses. A register office marriage of a catholic does not qualify as putative.

2076 In order to be putative, the marriage must have been celebrated in good faith by at least one party, and it remains so until both parties become certain of its invalidity, e.g. by a declaration by a competent tribunal. The principal effect of a putative marriage is to make legitimate such children as may be born of or conceived during it (see Can. 1137); even if at a later date a putative marriage is declared to have been in fact invalid, the children are and remain legitimate.

Can. 1062 §1 A promise of marriage, whether unilateral or bilateral, called an engagement, is governed by the particular law which the Bishops' Conference has enacted after consideration of such customs and civil laws as may exist.

2077 An engagement is a promise to marry, which may be made by one or both parties. This paragraph represents a simplification of the more detailed prescriptions of c.1017 §§1, 2 of the 1917 Code, and it leaves it to local Bishops' Conferences to make regulations concerning engagements: the guide-lines to be followed are local custom and civil law.[2]

Can. 1062 §2 No right of action to request the celebration of marriage arises from a promise of marriage, but there does arise an action for such reparation of harm as may be due.

2078 A promise to marry, whatever its moral force, does not give a right to bring an action before an ecclesiastical court to enforce fulfilment of the promise. Can. 1491 states that 'every right is reinforced ... by an action, unless otherwise expressly provided ...'. This is an example of such express provision; it is justified by the freedom required in consenting to marriage and by the practical impossibility of compelling such consent. However, the law does give a right of action where real damages have arisen, as a result of a reneguing on the promise, e.g. loss of good name, loss of property.

Chapter I
PASTORAL CARE AND THE PREREQUISITES FOR THE CELEBRATION OF MARRIAGE

Can. 1063 Pastors of souls are obliged to ensure that their own Church community provides for Christ's faithful the assistance by which the married state is preserved in its christian character and develops in perfection. This assistance is to be given principally:

---

[1] CCom rep 26.I.1949: cf. CLD 3 405.

[2] For the implementation of this faculty by Bishops' Conferences, cf. LCE Tavola per Paesi e Canoni at Can. 1062.

1° by preaching, by catechetical instruction adapted to children, young people and adults, indeed by the use of the means of social communication, so that Christ's faithful are instructed in the meaning of christian marriage and in the role of christian spouses and parents;

2° by personal preparation for entering marriage, so that the spouses are disposed to the holiness and the obligations of their new state;

3° by the fruitful celebration of the marriage liturgy, so that it clearly emerges that the spouses manifest, and participate in, the mystery of the unity and fruitful love between Christ and the Church;

4° by the help given to those who have entered marriage, so that by faithfully observing and protecting their conjugal covenant, they may day by day achieve a holier and a fuller family life.

The significance and pastoral importance of this canon – an entirely new formulation in the Code – can scarcely be overemphasised. The canon reflects the deep concern expressed by Vat. II about the pressures and dangers surrounding the institution of marriage in today's world, and it gives practical effect to the Council's intention 'to guide and encourage christians and all men who are trying to preserve and to foster the dignity and supremely sacred value of the married state'.[1] The canon is not just exhortatory; it places a serious obligation on pastors of souls, Bishops and parish priests in particular, to see that the local Church community gives proper and adequate support to preserving and developing the christian character of marriage. Although the immediate obligation is on the pastors, it falls ultimately on the whole Christian community. Hence it is not just opportune but necessary to involve the community in the different ways in which this support is to be given, whether as members of groups such as the Catholic Marriage Advisory Council, the Christian Family Movement and the like in various countries, or as individuals such as parents, teachers, catechists, married couples, etc. There is in this canon a clear call for the active participation of the laity, each in accordance with his or her own status, in the preparation of those, mainly the young, who wish to choose marriage as their vocation in life (see Cann. 225–229). The canon points to four principal ways in which all concerned, both clergy and laity, are obliged to cooperate in this supportive assistance. 2079

In the first place, there is the remote preparation for marriage, with a particular focus on 'the meaning of christian marriage and (on) the role of christian spouses and parents'. It is in the home that this process must begin, based upon the words and particularly the example of the originating parents. Thereafter, as the children pass through youth and into adulthood, it is to be consolidated and developed 'by preaching, by catechetical instruction[2] ... (and) indeed by the use of the means of social communication[3]...'. 2080

Next comes the particular preparation of those who are about to be married – a stage which is to focus on 'the holiness and the obligations of their new state'. This may 2081

---

[1] GS 47, 52: Fl I 949, 956–957.

[2] For a fuller understanding of this injunction, a careful study should be made of the many relevant canons concerning the Ministry of the Divine Word (Cann. 756–780) and Catholic Education (Cann. 793–821).

[3] It is noteworthy that, in this sensitive area of preparation for marriage, the Code should choose to refer specifically to the influence of the means of social communication – a reference which should activate a serious reconsideration in this context of Vat. II (IM: Fl I 283–292) and of the ensuing instr *Communio et Progressio* 29.I.1971: AAS 63(1971) 593–656: Fl I 293–349.

take various forms, each accommodated to local circumstances and cultures: formally organised pre-marriage courses; individual instruction by e.g. a priest, a catechist, a married couple or other appropriate person or agency; etc. The point to be stressed is that this is a specific and distinct obligation to be fulfilled, and that it is not to be confused with – even though it may occur at or about the same time as – the obligations prescribed by Cann. 1066–1067.

2082 The third level of preparation concentrates on the community aspect of marriage in ensuring a fruitful celebration of the marriage liturgy. In addition to its sanctifying role, the liturgy also has a valuable teaching function for the spouses and for the whole community. The couple to be married and those close to them should be actively involved in the preparation of the liturgy, not just in order to produce an impressive and smooth-running ceremony, but as a means of making them aware of, and helping them to participate in, the mystery of unity and fruitful love which is the special focus of this stage.

2083 Lastly, the canon speaks of the support to be given to those who have married – a support which must focus on the holiness of family life as a sign of God's grace, given to the couple by virtue of the sacrament which they have received, and as a witness to the whole community. The obligations of the community do not cease on the wedding day but extend to the whole married life. Such support will be of special importance in the early years of the marriage, particularly in the case of those whose faith is weak or who have difficulty in adjusting to their new state. It would be difficult to overemphasise the extent to which the support of the extended family and of the local community can assist in maintaining the level of commitment pledged by the couple on their wedding day. Equally, it will so often be the local community which can most effectively give public voice to those elements in society – hardship, inadequate housing, unemployment, crime, etc. – which frequently are critical factors in the erosion of marital and family life. While it is necessary to do so at times, it is not, however, enough to put the entire blame on social conditions alone. There is always required a clear appreciation, based on christian faith, of the inherent grace of the sacrament of marriage.[1]

Can. 1064 It is the responsibility of the local Ordinary to ensure that this assistance is duly organised. If it is considered opportune, he should consult with men and women of proven experience and expertise.

2084 In keeping with the real need for this assistance and with the clear obligation imposed by the previous canon, its organisation is not to be left to chance or opportunity. The local Ordinary is obliged to make the appropriate practical arrangements. In so doing, he may and, except in very unusual circumstances, should consult men and women who have expertise and experience in this area. Here again is a clear example of the Church's desire that the laity would actively participate in its mission of salvation (see Cann. 228 §2, 212 §3).

Can. 1065 §1 Catholics who have not yet received the sacrament of confirmation are to receive it before being admitted to marriage, if this can be done without grave inconvenience.

2085 The requirement of this paragraph, repeating the norm of c.1021 §2 of the 1917 Code, is not an absolute one.[2] However, since confirmation is one of the sacraments of full christian initiation (see Can. 842 §2), and since marriage is a sacrament of

---

[1] For a significant guide to the issues involved here, cf. FC nn.65–69: Fl II 868–874.
[2] Cf. Comm 15(1983) 225 at Can. 1018.

adulthood which carries with it grave obligations both in the living of a christian life and in the christian education of a family, it is obviously more than merely appropriate that those undertaking these responsibilities should be confirmed.

Can. 1065 §2 So that the sacrament of marriage may be fruitfully received, it is earnestly recommended that spouses approach the sacraments of penance and the blessed Eucharist.

While the reception of these two sacraments is 'earnestly recommended' in order to ensure the fruitful reception of marriage, by reason particularly of the intimate connection between the Eucharist and marriage,[1] there is nevertheless no absolute obligation to receive them. Those who are unwilling to receive them may not for that reason alone be refused the sacrament of marriage. However, such an unwillingness might well be indicative of a careless practice of the faith, perhaps even of a loss of faith – in which case the diligent priest will see the need for further sensitive pastoral care and evaluation. It is *only* in the situation where *both parties* 'show that they reject explicitly and formally what the Church intends to do when the marriage of baptised persons is celebrated'[2] that the sacrament has to be refused. If only one party makes such a rejection, it is left to the prudent judgement of the parish priest, taking all the circumstances into account, as to whether or not the marriage be permitted – save only for the situation in which the rejection of the Catholic faith is *notorious*, when the local Ordinary has then to be consulted and give permission (see Can. 1071 §1 4°).

Can. 1066 Before a marriage takes place, it must be established that nothing stands in the way of its valid and lawful celebration.

This canon, repeating c.1019 §1 of the 1917 Code, emphasises the fact that the right to marry stated in Can. 1058 is not an absolute one but is subject to limitations of both divine and ecclesiastical law. Before the marriage ceremony is allowed to take place, it must have been established that there is no legal obstacle to either its valid or lawful celebration. Establishing the legal freedom to marry is a matter of positive proof, not just a question of presumption or conjecture: in other words, positive steps must be taken to show that the parties are free to marry, and the person responsible for the preparation of the couple must be morally certain about their freedom. The manner of proof is covered generically in the two following canons.

Can. 1067 The Bishops' Conference is to lay down norms concerning the questions to be asked of the parties, and concerning the publication of marriage banns or other appropriate means of enquiry to be carried out as a pre-requisite for marriage. When he has carefully observed these norms the parish priest may proceed to assist at a marriage.

This canon replaces the detailed legislation of the 1917 Code and the Instruction of the Sacred Congregation of the Sacraments issued in 1941.[3] It leaves it to each Bishops' Conference to decide the precise manner of making the prenuptial enquiry in accordance with local conditions.[4] This does not in any way weaken the seriousness of the enquiry or the obligation of making it: apart from the cases covered in the next

---

[1] Cf. FC 57: Fl II 862–863.

[2] FC 68: Fl II 873; for a full understanding of the issues and sensitivities involved here, one should study carefully the entire text of FC 68: Fl II 872–874.

[3] Cf. AAS 33(1941) 297ff: CLD 2 253ff.

[4] For the manner in which many Bishops' Conferences have legislated in this regard, cf. LCE Tavola per Paesi e Canoni at Can. 1067; CN(USA) at Can. 1067 in Commentary (St Paul's) 1421.

canon, the parish priest may not proceed with the wedding until the enquiry has been properly carried out.

2089 The purpose of this enquiry is to establish: (a) that there are no impediments or prohibitions against the marriage; (b) that both parties are entering marriage freely; (c) that both parties understand the nature and obligations of the married state and are able, and actually intend, to accept these obligations.

2090 Frequently, as in the past, the details of the enquiry may be contained in a form which is to be completed before the wedding. In more recent times, some such forms have also indicated steps to be taken in the preparation of the engaged couple. It must always be remembered, however, that neither the preparation nor the enquiry is merely a matter of filling in a form. Indeed, any such impression would be an abuse of the Church's stance in this context: whatever the form or its structure, it can never be more than a record of a preparation and an enquiry already diligently carried out (see our commentary on Can. 1063).[1]

2091 The obligation of making the enquiry falls primarily on the parish priest whose special function it is to assist at the marriage (see Can. 530 4°). It may, however, be made by others, such as an assistant priest or a deacon in the parish, a qualified religious sister or other lay person who is 'entrusted with a share in the exercise of the pastoral care of (the) parish' (see Can. 517 §2); in the case where one or even both of the parties reside outside the parish or diocese in which the marriage is to take place, it may be made by one of the priests or other such person as mentioned above in the parish of residence.

Can. 1068 In danger of death, if other proofs are not available, it suffices, unless there are contrary indications, to have the assertion of the parties, sworn if need be, that they are baptised and free of any impediment.

2092 This canon governs the case where one or both of the parties is in danger of death, so that the normal pre-nuptial enquiry cannot be made. If there are no positive indications which would create a reasonable doubt about their baptism or their freedom to marry, then the assertion of the parties about these points is sufficient. The present law (unlike c.1019 §2 of the 1917 Code) requires that this assertion be made under oath *only* 'if need be', i.e. where there is a real doubt about the truthfulness of the parties.

2093 The motivation of those who marry in danger of death may be, at least in part, to secure some civil benefit, such as inheritance or a pension for the surviving spouse. In all such cases therefore the priest should be aware of the relevant civil requirements for the valid celebration of this marriage and, in so far as may be possible, ensure that they are complied with.

Can. 1069 Before the celebration of a marriage, all the faithful are bound to reveal to the parish priest or the local Ordinary such impediments as they may know about.

2094 In seeking to guard against the invalidity of a marriage, this rule (itself a repetition of c.1027 of the 1917 Code) acknowledges that marriage has not merely a personal dimension but also a serious social one. It obliges all the faithful – except obviously

---

[1] Two practical points may be noted: (i) the traditional reading of the banns of marriage (cf. 1917 Code cc. 1022–1026) is no longer of general obligation, but the local Bishops' Conference may decide to retain it; (ii) the former law required that the pre-nuptial enquiry include a baptismal certificate, of not more than six months old, of every catholic party to a marriage (cf. 1917 Code c.1021 §1; cit instr SCSac 1941 n.4c); while this injunction has not been explicitly stated in the current Code, it is certain that it still applies, not least by reason of the implications of Can. 535 §2.

those bound by the seal of confession or by the rules of professional confidence – to reveal, to the parish priest or another priest of the parish or to the local Ordinary, any impediment of which they have certain or very probable knowledge. In the course of pastoral instruction, whether from the pulpit or in the course of parish visitation or otherwise, this obligation should be clearly and unambiguously brought to the notice of the faithful, not least to parents. In this context it is of particular practical and pastoral importance to understand that the obligation is to make known to the appropriate minister not merely impediments in the strict sense of Can. 1083–1094, such e.g. as an existing marriage bond or a degree of consanguinity, but also other possibly invalidating factors, such e.g. as a serious psychiatric illness, an established history of gross personal immaturity, a manifestly serious problem with alcohol, indications that one or other party may be agreeing to marry only under duress (whether from the family or from any other source) or only on the condition that the couple will not have any children or that one or other would feel free to abandon the marriage 'if things don't work out well' between them, and so on. A particular caution should be exercised, especially in the 'Western world', in respect of those who would wish to marry at a very young age; this caution would be heightened if it should appear that the principal, if not the only, motivation for the marriage were the fact that the girl is already pregnant: experience bears heavily against the success of such a marriage. The faithful should be disabused of the notion – not uncommon today – that by expressing their reservations about a particular proposed marriage, they would in some way or other be considered as 'disloyal' or 'interfering': on the contrary, provided that they themselves are for good reasons conscientiously concerned about the sacrament of marriage and equally about the future happiness of the couple concerned, they could well be making a significant contribution to both, thereby helping to avoid what is often – for husband or wife or children – a devastating heartbreak in the future.[1]

2095 If, as a result of a communication, by whomsoever, an impediment or other invalidating factor were to be confirmed, two courses of action could be considered:

(a) the possibility of a dispensation from the impediment (see Cann. 1078–1080);

(b) the possibility that, in the case of an invalidating factor other than an impediment strictly so called, appropriate pastoral instruction and counselling could bring about a satisfactory resolution of the presenting problem.[2]

Should neither of these two options be available, the marriage may not be permitted (see also Can. 1077 §1).

Can. 1070 If someone other than the parish priest whose function it is to assist at the marriage has made the investigations, he is by an authentic document to inform that parish priest of the outcome of these enquiries as soon as possible.

2096 It is quite common for the parties to a marriage to live in different parishes. It is also common (though no longer prescribed) for a bride to be married in her native parish, even if she may have been living elsewhere for a considerable length of time. In such circumstances it is obviously more fitting that the preparation and investigation be made in the place of actual residence. When this happens, the results of the investigation are to be communicated in writing ('by an authentic document') to the parish priest or one of his assistant priests in the parish where the marriage is in fact to be

---

[1] It is understood that, in revealing their anxiety to the local priest or Ordinary, the faithful can be assured, in so far as may be necessary, of a total confidentiality.

[2] In most such situations it would be at least advisable to consult the local Ordinary.

celebrated.[1] Since it is *in that parish* – not in the parish of residence – that the ultimate responsibility rests to permit the marriage (see Can. 1067), it is clear that in practice the priest to whom the relevant documents are sent must be able to rely upon the care and judgement of the person who conducted the preparation and investigation and who transmits the documents, upon whom accordingly a considerable measure of responsibility rests. While in the majority of cases there are no problems to occasion serious anxiety, in some there certainly are. At least in these latter, the formal documents transmitted should be accompanied by a reasoned written assessment of the parties' freedom to marry and, particularly, of their aptitude for the reception of this sacrament.

Can. 1071 §1 Except in a case of necessity, no one is to assist without the permission of the local Ordinary at:

1° a marriage of *vagi*;

2° a marriage which cannot be recognised by the civil law or celebrated in accordance with it;

3° a marriage of a person bound by natural obligations towards another party or children, arising from a previous union;

4° a marriage of a person who has notoriously abandoned the catholic faith;

5° a marriage of a person who is under censure;

6° a marriage of a minor whose parents are either unaware of it or are reasonably opposed to it;

7° a marriage to be entered by proxy, as mentioned in Can. 1105.

§2 The local Ordinary is not to give permission to assist at the marriage of a person who has notoriously abandoned the catholic faith unless, with the appropriate adjustments, the norms of Can. 1125 have been observed.

2097 This canon details a number of situations in which the permission of the local Ordinary is required before any priest, deacon or other authorised person may assist at a marriage. The purpose clearly is to cater for abnormal situations in which, to ease the burden on the local parish priest, it is considered necessary to have the advice and sanction of the local Ordinary. The following preliminary points are to be noted in this regard:

(a) while not affecting the validity of the marriage, this permission is necessary for the lawfulness of its celebration, and the obligation to seek it is a serious one.

(b) this permission is not, however, required when there arises 'a case of necessity', i.e. not only a danger of death, but any situation in which an undue delay could involve a serious pastoral risk.[2] It will be for the person who is to assist at the marriage to make a prudent judgement in this regard, bearing in mind that the purpose of the rule is to protect both the sacrament and the ultimate well being of the partners. Accordingly a decision not to seek or not to await the required permission should not be taken lightly; it would obviously of course have to take account of local and cultural circumstances.

---

[1] The above–cited instr SCSac 1941 required that, whenever such investigations will have been conducted *in different dioceses*, the relevant documents be sent not directly to the parish of the marriage, but rather through the competent diocesan chancellery or curia. This rule no longer applies, unless an individual diocesan Bishop or Bishops' Conference should specifically determine otherwise.

[2] Cf. Comm 9(1977) 142 at Can. 257.

Part I The Sacraments

In the light of the foregoing, the following are the situations in which the prior permission of the local Ordinary is required.

2098 *A marriage of 'vagi'* (1°) i.e. of those who do not have a domicile or quasi-domicile anywhere (see our commentary on Can. 100, and Glossary at *vagus*). Various circumstances may determine that a person may be in that category, which often may e.g. pose a particular difficulty in establishing the person's freedom to marry. A special word may be said here in respect of *travelling people*, who are a feature of the culture in many countries. It is important to recognise that these people, however nomadic, have for the most part their own distinctive and clearly-formed code, often quite strict, in respect of marital relationships. This factor must be taken into account in any decision to accede or not to their request to be married in the Church.[1]

2099 *A marriage which cannot be recognised by the civil law or celebrated in accordance with it* (2°). The clear objective of this regulation is to obviate, in so far as may be possible, a clash between the canonical and the civil jurisdictions in the matter of the requirements for a valid marriage. The most frequent situation in this regard is when a person whose marriage is regarded by the civil law as valid but is canonically non-existent (whether by a declaration of nullity, a dispensation, or otherwise), wishes to enter 'another' marriage in accordance with the laws of the Church. It is manifest that in such a situation a clash of jurisdictions runs a serious risk of being to the detriment of one or other or both of the parties and of such children as they may have. Hence the wisdom of this canon in requiring that such situations be referred to the local Ordinary, who will best be able to evaluate the local relationship between Church and State in this regard and who will be able to direct accordingly. This will obviously be without prejudice to the Church's necessary freedom in the administration of the sacraments and of its stance vis-a-vis the civil authority in Can. 1059.[2]

2100 *A marriage of a person bound by natural obligations towards another party or children, arising from a previous union* (3°). This regulation, which had no explicit counterpart in the 1917 Code,[3] underlines a principle of natural law, which requires that if, for whatever reason, a person wishes to enter a marital union subsequent to an earlier one, steps must be taken to ensure that the proper provision which is due to the former partner or to children is not prejudiced by any subsequent marriage in the Church. It is the right and the obligation of the local Ordinary to insist on this before giving permission for the now-proposed marriage – so much so that if he is satisfied that the relevant party does not seriously intend to fulfil this duty, he is entitled to forbid the marriage, in accordance with the terms of Can. 1077 §1. For pastoral practice it is important to note that the authority entrusted to the local Ordinary here refers to *all* so-called second marriages: ranging from those of widowers and widows,

---

[1] In a number of dioceses it has been a commendable practice to nominate a priest as chaplain to the travelling people. There are significant possibilities in this initiative. Such an appointment could e.g. include a faculty to the appointed chaplain to exercise the authority assigned to the local Ordinary in this canon. It should also be noted that the prescription of this canon applies even to the case where only one of the parties is a *vagus*: cf. Chiappetta II n.3561.

[2] Cf. our commentary on Can. 1059. Two ancillary points may be made: (a) since there is in so many places today a considerable diversity between civil and canonical requirements concerning marriage, it is obviously appropriate that, for the good of society, serious consideration be given to the possibility of establishing in this regard appropriate 'agreements entered into by the Apostolic See with nations or other civil entities' (Can. 3); (b) in interpreting 'the civil law' of this canon, account would have to be taken also of cultural and even tribal traditions, which in some communities are, in effect, 'the civil law' within which the community has to operate.

[3] A formulation of it appeared in SCDF instr *Ut notum sit* 3.XII.1973 art 12: CLD 8 1183.

through those whose earlier marriage has been annulled or dispensed or merely civilly divorced, and even those which had been preceded by no more than a 'living together' situation with another person.[1]

2101 *A marriage of a person who has notoriously abandoned the catholic faith (4°).* This prescription repeats, with some modifications, the substance of c.1065 of the 1917 Code. It deals with the proposed marriages of those who – one or both – have by that time *abandoned* the catholic faith. This concept of 'abandonment of the catholic faith' is not to be confused with that of a 'defection from the catholic Church by a formal act' (see Cann. 1086 §1, 1117, 1124, and commentary thereon). Nor does it necessarily involve – though it would indeed be evidenced by – the deliberate joining of a non-catholic religion or sect. What this canon has principally in mind is the person who has, in effect, given up the practice of the faith in any real manner, thereby adopting a stance of practical agnosticism or even atheism. And the substantial requirement of the canon is that the local Ordinary's permission must be obtained – 'except in a case of necessity', as explained above – in every such case which is notorious i.e., in practice, where the abandonment is such that it is so publicly known that it can in no way be concealed or legally excused.[2]

2102 This prescription of law involves profound pastoral considerations, which were discussed in depth by the Revision Commission.[3] These are considerations which, in the context of those who wish to enter marriage, ever-increasingly in a current secularized society face every member of the Church, most particularly perhaps parents, priests and other pastors of souls. What is to be the policy and the pastoral approach in respect of those baptised catholics, requesting a Church marriage, whose faith is lukewarm or even very weak and whose practice is equally so or even almost non-existent? There are no clearer guidelines in this matter than the principles and considerations so clearly set out by Pope John Paul II in his apostolic exhortation in 1981 on 'The Christian Family in the Modern World'.[4] While this entire document will repay careful study by all who are concerned with the place and import of the family in today's society, the following extracts from its n.68 will form a valuable practical guide in the context of this canon:[5]

- '... in the celebration of this sacrament very special attention must be devoted to the moral and spiritual dispositions of those being married, in particular to their faith ...'

- 'in fact, the faith of the person asking the Church for marriage can exist in different degrees, and it is the primary duty of pastors to bring about a rediscovery of this faith and to nourish it and bring it to maturity'

- 'but pastors must also understand the reasons that lead the Church also to admit to the celebration of marriage those who are imperfectly disposed'

- '... it is true that in some places engaged couples ask to be married in Church for motives which are social rather than genuinely religious. This is not surprising (since) marriage ... by its very nature is also a social matter ... (and) it must not be forgotten that these engaged couples, by virtue of their baptism, are already really

---

[1] Cf. Comm 9(1977) 144–145 at c. As far as concerns a marriage declared null by an ecclesiastical court, cf. Can. 1689.

[2] Cf. 1917 Code c.2197 3°; Comm 9(1977) 144 at Can. 257 n.4 b.

[3] Cf. Comm 5(1973) 71 at 3° and 4°; 9(1977) 145 at f; Chiappetta II n.3565 note 5.

[4] Cf. FC: Fl II 815–898.

[5] Cf. Fl II 872–874.

Part I The Sacraments

sharers in Christ's marriage Covenant with the Church ... and therefore at least implicitly consent to what the Church intends to do when she celebrates marriage. Thus, the fact that motives of a social nature also enter into the request is not (of itself) enough to justify refusal on the part of pastors'.

At this point the papal message states that it would be unwise, and indeed quite possibly damaging, to lay down further criteria that would determine the precise level of faith to be required of those who wish to be married. The reason for this clearly is that so much depends upon the circumstances of each individual case. It goes on however to point out that:

– 'when, in spite of all efforts, engaged couples show that they reject explicitly and formally what the Church intends to do when the marriage of baptised persons is celebrated, the pastor of souls cannot admit them to the celebration of marriage. (In taking this decision) he has the duty ... to make it clear to those concerned that, in these circumstances, it is not the Church that is placing an obstacle in the way of the celebration that they are asking for, but themselves'.

2103 In summary, the position of a local Ordinary to whom a case of this kind is presented may be stated as follows:

(a) he simply may not give permission 'unless, with the appropriate adjustments, the norms of Can. 1125 have been observed' (Can. 1071 §2).[1]

(b) assuming that the observance of those norms will have been secured, he should be extremely reluctant to refuse his permission, lest 'the smoking flax be quenched'.

(c) a more critical situation arises when *both* parties have notoriously abandoned the catholic faith: should efforts to reawaken their faith (or even that of one of them) fail, he will – apart from the most exceptional circumstances – have no option but to refuse permission for the marriage.

The overall position is aptly stated by Pope John Paul II when he says that:

'Once more there appears *in all its urgency* the need for evangelization and catechesis before and after marriage, *effected by the whole Christian community*, so that every man and woman who gets married celebrates the sacrament of Matrimony not only validly but also fruitfully'.[2]

2104 *A marriage of a person who is under censure (5°).* One who is under the censure of either excommunication or interdict is 'forbidden to celebrate the sacraments ... and to receive the sacraments' (see Cann. 1331 §1 2°, 1332). On referral of the matter to the local Ordinary, his first step will be to see if the censure can in the circumstances be remitted; if so, the problem may disappear. If not, permission may be granted for the marriage only in the most exceptional circumstances, which will have taken into account not only the spiritual status of the censured party but also the danger to the faith of the other party.

2105 *A marriage of a minor whose parents are either unaware of it or are reasonably opposed to it (6°).* A minor is one who has not completed the eighteenth year of age (see Can. 97 §1). The marriages of the young have always had their special problems (see Can. 1072), because of the danger of their not having sufficient maturity of judgement to make a proper decision in getting married and the danger of their lacking the emotional stability to cope with the reality of married life. Hence the law has hedged such

---

[1] These are the norms governing permission for mixed marriages. The principal adjustment to be made will be a change of wording from 'the catholic party' to 'the practising catholic party'; other adjustments will take into account the knowledge the other party has of the faith and his or her goodwill.

[2] FC n.68: Fl II 873–874.

marriages with prudent precautions: the present rule repeats the substance of c.1034 of the 1917 Code. Parents are presumed to know their children well and to be able to judge their maturity for marriage, so their opposition to a marriage must be taken seriously and carefully investigated; the one who has the task of preparing the couple for marriage should not lightly conclude that their opposition is unreasonable. Only when, taking all the circumstances of the case into account, he is morally certain that it is unreasonable may he permit the marriage; otherwise the permission of the local Ordinary must first be sought. On the other hand, if the parents are unaware of the marriage, the obvious first step is to inform them; should the couple be unwilling to do this or to have it done, then the local Ordinary must be approached. In granting permission in any of the situations envisaged here, the Ordinary must ensure an appropriate and special preparation for that particular marriage.

2106 *A marriage to be entered by proxy, as mentioned in Can. 1105 (7°)*. A marriage by proxy means that one or both parties is not personally present at the ceremony but is represented by an agent or proxy in accordance with Can. 1105. In many countries, especially those following the Common Law tradition, the civil law does not allow such marriages – in which case the Ordinary's permission will be doubly needed (see this canon §1 2°). Proxy marriages, which are unusual, do raise special problems about the parties' knowledge of one another, the freedom and genuineness of their consent, and their preparation for marriage. Accordingly, permission for such a marriage will be granted only for very grave reasons. It is to be noted that certain local and particularly cultural factors may also well be relevant.

Can. 1072 Pastors of souls are to see to it that they dissuade young people from entering marriage before the age customarily accepted in the region.

2107 This canon, which repeats the provision of c.1067 §2 of the 1917 Code, especially when read in conjunction with Can. 1071 §1 2°, reflects a serious and well-justified concern for the marriages of the young. The experience of marriage tribunals e.g. shows that the immaturity of young people is responsible for the breakdown of many marriages (whether or not these marriages are later shown to be null and void). The customary age for marriage will vary from one culture to another, but it does represent a useful rule of thumb for gauging whether or not a young person has sufficient maturity for marriage. This canon lays a specific obligation on all pastors of souls positively to dissuade the young from entering marriage before this age. By a necessary implication, it strongly encourages all concerned – parents, family members, priests etc. – to advise such a deferral of the marriage as would allow for a more informed appraisal of the maturity of judgement and the emotional development required for marriage.[1]

Chapter II
DIRIMENT IMPEDIMENTS IN GENERAL

2108 The structure of the present Code in regard to matrimonial impediments is significantly different from that of its 1917 predecessor. Some of the earlier impediments have been simply suppressed; the requirements for others have been altered to a greater or lesser degree. Particularly to be noted is the abolition of the earlier distinction between impediments known as *diriment* i.e. which not only forbade a marriage but rendered it invalid, and those called *impedient* i.e. which simply forbade a marriage

---

[1] For a fuller understanding of the issues involved here, cf. Can. 1083 and the commentary thereon.

Part I The Sacraments

while allowing its validity; these latter have, as such, been abolished,[1] and the law now provides only for diriment impediments. As a result of this approach, the current Code (as compared with that of 1917) has, in fewer than half the number of canons, been able to deal with matrimonial impediments in two brief chapters: this Ch. II (Cann. 1073–1082), and the following Ch. III (Cann. 1083–1094).

This particular chapter, which is necessarily a technical one, may helpfully be considered under the following sub-headings:

- the concept of a diriment impediment (Can. 1073);
- the distinction between a public and an occult impediment (Can. 1074);
- the authority in the Church who is competent to declare or to establish a matrimonial impediment (Cann. 1075–1077);
- the situations in which an impediment may be dispensed by ecclesiastical authority (Cann. 1078–1082).

Can. 1073 A diriment impediment renders a person incapable of validly contracting a marriage.

The concept of a diriment impediment is provided by this canon. It is an objective circumstance attaching to a person which, in virtue of either divine or human law, makes that person *incapable* of validly contracting marriage – whether with anyone (as e.g. in the case of a person already married to another: see Can. 1085 §1), or with a certain person (as e.g. in the case of a person related by consanguinity in the direct line to that other person: see Can. 1091 §1). A diriment impediment is not to be interpreted as a restriction on the natural right to marry enjoyed by all: it is, rather, to be seen as a necessary regulation of the exercise of that right, in the specific interest of the spouses themselves, of the family and of the common good of society (see Can. 1058). Thus understood, this canon is a clear example of an *incapacitating law* (see Can. 10 and commentary thereon), which operates independently of the person's knowledge or will: in other words, it renders invalid even a marriage which is contracted in total good faith by one or both of the parties (see Can. 15 §1). This is so even if the impediment directly affects only one of the parties, as e.g. in the case of the impediment of age (see Can. 1083 §1): a marriage cannot be invalid for one partner and valid for the other.

Can. 1074 An impediment is said to be public, when it can be proved in the external forum; otherwise it is occult.

The distinction between a public and an occult impediment is singled out here (as it was in c.1037 of the 1917 Code) precisely because of the important implications which it has in various other parts of the law on marriage (see Cann. 1079 §3, 1080 §1, 1082, 1158). For an impediment to be public, the essential criterion is that it be *provable in the external forum*: it is not necessary that it be widely or publicly known. Its provability is determined by those criteria indicated in the relevant section of Book VII of the Code (see Cann. 1526ff) e.g. the testimony of two or more reliable witnesses or even of one so-called 'qualified' witness (see Can. 1573), authentic public records, the evidence of appropriate experts, etc. Thus an impediment might in fact be known only to very few and yet be public in the sense of this canon. Of course some impediments are

---

[1] Of the three impedient impediments in the 1917 Code, that based upon various vows (c.1058 §1) has been eliminated, that in respect of mixed marriages (c.1060) has been assigned a separate chapter with a new approach (cf. Cann. 1124–1129), and that based upon adoption (c.1059) has become a diriment impediment (cf. Can. 1094): cf. Comm 9(1977) 132–134 at Can. 260.

of their very nature public in that they are based on facts which are themselves public,[1] e.g. the impediments of consanguinity and affinity, sacred orders, public propriety, legal relationship: apart from being usually a matter of public knowledge, they are almost invariably susceptible to proof by authentic public records. In exceptional situations, however, even some of these might not in fact be provable and so would be technically occult, as e.g. in the case of consanguinity arising from an illicit union.

Can. 1075 §1 Only the supreme authority in the Church can authentically declare when the divine law prohibits or invalidates a marriage.

§2 Only the same supreme authority has the right to establish other impediments for those who are baptised.

Can. 1076 A custom which introduces a new impediment, or is contrary to existing impediments, is reprobated.

Can. 1077 §1 The local Ordinary can in a specific case forbid a marriage of his own subjects, wherever they are residing, or of any person actually present in his territory; he can do this only for a time, for a grave reason and while that reason persists.

§2 Only the supreme authority in the Church can attach an invalidating clause to a prohibition.

2112   *Who is the authority in the Church* competent either to declare or to establish a matrimonial impediment? Briefly, that power is vested exclusively in 'the supreme authority of the Church', i.e. the Pope alone, or the College of Bishops acting with the Pope as its head (see Cann. 331, 336). The purpose of these three Cann. 1075–1077 is first to establish that principle, and then to deal with some relevant considerations consequent upon it.

2113   The exclusive power vested in the supreme authority concerns two specific aspects:

(a) authentically to *declare* both the existence and the extent of impediments emanating from the divine law (see Can. 1075 §1) – and this in virtue of the prerogative of the Pope and the College of Bishops as the custodian of the deposit of faith.[2] In practice, it is not always easy to determine whether an impediment is of divine law or not. There is general consensus that certain impediments have a basis in divine law, such as an existing bond of marriage, impotence, consanguinity. It is equally certain that the precise legal formulation of these and, in some, the extent of the impediment is of ecclesiastical law, e.g. consanguinity in the direct line is generally accepted to be of divine law, whereas in the farther degrees of the collateral line it is certainly of merely ecclesiastical law.

b) 'to *establish* other impediments for those who are baptised' (see Can. 1075 §2): these are impediments of ecclesiastical law, which bind, in both the internal and the external forum, all the baptised[3] save only as provided for in Can. 11. This exclusive power extends not only to establishing impediments of merely ecclesiastical law, as e.g. the impediment of orders, but also to enlarging the extent of impediments of divine law as has been done e.g. in the case of the impediment of consanguinity.

---

[1] Cf. CCom rep 25.VI.1932: AAS 24(1932) 284: CLD 1 501 at c.1037.

[2] Authentic interpretations of these impediments issued by the PCI are made by virtue of authority delegated by the Pope.

[3] For the relationship between this Can. 1075 §2 and Can. 1059, cf. Chiappetta II n. 3579.

Part I The Sacraments

By reason of the principle stated in Can. 1075, it follows that no inferior authority in the Church – a particular Council (see Cann. 439ff), a Bishops' Conference (see Cann. 447ff) or a diocesan Bishop (see Cann. 381ff) – may establish a matrimonial impediment of any kind, diriment or impedient.[1] Relevant in this context is the authority granted by Can. 1077 §1 to local Ordinaries (see Can. 134 §2), not only to diocesan Bishops. While this might at first sight be seen as a power to establish an impedient impediment, it is in fact an essentially different disposition of law, surrounded as it is by the following conditions: 2114

(a) it may be imposed only 'in a specific case', not therefore by a law or a general decree, as e.g. by a prohibition of all marriages where the girl is pregnant and under eighteen years of age.[2]

(b) it may be imposed only as a temporary measure, not therefore for an indeterminate time, much less on a permanent basis. This is not to say that it could not be renewed at the end of the specified period if at that time the initial reason for imposing it were still to exist; equally, if that reason has certainly ceased, the prohibition itself expires.

(c) it may be imposed only for a grave reason. Such a reason would certainly be a serious likelihood that the marriage would be invalid; it must be noted, however, that invalidity is not always easily discernible beforehand, especially when its possible source is in the psychological condition of one or other of the parties or in their immaturity. Other grave reasons would be e.g. a well-grounded prospect of a turbulent and unhappy marriage, a real danger to the faith of the parties or their children, a serious physical or moral danger to the parties or to others, etc. A complete list is not possible: the local Ordinary must judge the gravity of each case, taking into account all the local and cultural circumstances, the natural right of the parties to marry, the dignity of the sacrament, and the dangers to be feared.

It is to be noted that the authority given to the local Ordinary by Can. 1077 §1 is exercisable in respect of: (a) his own subjects, i.e. those who have a domicile or quasi-domicile in the territory of his jurisdiction (see Can. 107 §1), whether or not they are at the time residing within that territory; (b) any other person, not his subject, who at the time is 'actually present in his territory', even if not a resident there. Moreover, since this law restricts the free exercise of the fundamental right to marry, its prescriptions are to be interpreted strictly (see Can. 18). Accordingly, it is clear *inter alia* that *only the local Ordinary* has this power of prohibition.[3] Parish priests and others with the task of preparing couples for marriage, no matter what their doubts or fears, may 2115

---

[1] In the course of the revision of the Code it was proposed, more than once, that Bishops' Conferences be empowered to establish for their respective territories both impedient and diriment impediments. This proposal was rejected, not least at the behest of so many individual Bishops and Bishops' Conferences who counselled that it would be pastorally unwise to abandon the principle of uniformity throughout the Church on this matter: cf. Comm 9(1977) 80 Q.III; 10(1978) 126 at c; 15(1983) 226 at Can. 1028.

[2] The diocesan Bishop could of course prescribe general regulations for the pastoral discipline of his diocese, to the effect that marriages may be celebrated *only* e.g. at certain times of the day, after a determined number of months of prior notice, in special circumstances (e.g. the young age of one or both of the parties) when the couple will have undertaken an appropriately special preparation or even undergone a specific examination regarding their fitness, etc.

[3] The prohibition referred to in this canon is quite distinct from that which may be imposed by a tribunal in a Judgement of nullity of marriage (cf. Can. 1685). The latter is not of its nature temporary, and the reason for which it was imposed, though not the prohibition itself, may well involve the invalidity of a subsequent marriage.

Book IV The Sanctifying Office of the Church

not themselves forbid a marriage. But they not only may but, particularly in cases which they judge to be seriously doubtful, certainly should approach the Ordinary. In circumstances of this latter kind, the Ordinary is obliged, before giving his decision, to weigh carefully the submission, and the opinion, of the priest who is in immediate touch with the actual situation. An obvious corollary is that the priest will have made his submission only after a most careful investigation. Finally, it is to be noted that any prohibition issued in virtue of this power can never of itself invalidate a marriage which might take place in defiance of such prohibition: 'only the supreme authority in the Church can attach an invalidating clause to a prohibition' (see Can. 1077 §2).

2116 Has *custom* (see Can. 23) any role in respect of matrimonial impediments? Can. 1076 prescribes in effect that no custom, of whatever antiquity or duration, may introduce an impediment which is either in addition to those already in the law itself or in any way contrary to any of them. This is the consequence of the express statement that any such custom 'is reprobated' (see Cann. 5 §1, 24 §2). Accordingly, the *only* role for custom in this context is as a guide to interpretation within the meaning of Can. 27.

2117 *The situations in which an impediment may be dispensed* by ecclesiastical authority are dealt with in the following canons:

- first, the general power in this regard enjoyed by the local Ordinary (see Can. 1078);
- then, the faculties enjoyed by various ecclesiastical authorities in the special circumstances of (a) danger of death (see Can. 1079) and (b) the emergency problem arising when an impediment is discovered only after everything has already been prepared for a wedding (see Can. 1080);
- finally, specific regulations concerning the recording of dispensations granted in virtue of the foregoing dispositions (see Cann. 1081–1082).

Can. 1078 §1 The local Ordinary can dispense his own subjects wherever they are residing, and all who are actually present in his territory, from all impediments of ecclesiastical law, except for those whose dispensation is reserved to the Apostolic See.

§2 The impediments whose dispensation is reserved to the Apostolic See are:

1° the impediment arising from sacred orders or from a public perpetual vow of chastity in a religious institute of pontifical right;

2° the impediment of crime mentioned in Can. 1090.

§3 A dispensation is never given from the impediment of consanguinity in the direct line or in the second degree of the collateral line.

2118 The general notion of dispensation from ecclesiastical laws is dealt with in Can. 85. This Can. 1078, dealing specifically with dispensation from matrimonial impediments, represents a substantial change from the previous law: under c.1040 of the 1917 Code dispensation from all diriment impediments was reserved to the Holy See, except in extraordinary circumstances or where the local Ordinary had special faculties. Such faculties were at that time usually granted for a five-year period and they varied in extent from place to place. In 1963 Pope Paul VI made an interim grant of faculties and privileges to Bishops, which included a rather wider general power of dispensing from matrimonial impediments.[1] In 1965 Vat. II allowed individual diocesan Bishops 'to dispense from the general law of the Church in particular cases those faithful over whom they normally exercise authority. It must, however, be to

---

[1] Cf. PM; CLD 6 370–378.

their spiritual benefit and may not cover a matter which has been specially reserved by the supreme authority of the Church'.[1] In 1966 Pope Paul VI issued a further document which *inter alia* specified the cases reserved to the Holy See.[2]

The power granted in this canon can be exercised by the local Ordinary (see Can. 134 §2); it is not confined to the diocesan Bishop. The dispensation can be given to his own subjects, irrespective of where they are residing, and to anybody actually present in his territory. The power, moreover, is *ordinary*, and so it can be delegated.[3] In ordinary circumstances the local Ordinary cannot dispense from impediments reserved to the Apostolic See. However, in danger of death and in the special circumstances of Can. 1080, the local Ordinary, and some others, have power to dispense from even some of these (see Cann. 1079, 1080).

Three impediments are declared reserved to the Apostolic See:

(a) the impediment arising from sacred orders, i.e. from the diaconate, priesthood or episcopate (see Can. 1087).

(b) the impediment arising from a public perpetual vow of chastity in a religious institute of *pontifical right* (see Can. 589). If the institute is of diocesan right, there is no reservation and the local Ordinary can dispense.[4] It is to be noted that the impediment affects only religious who have taken a *public* perpetual vow of chastity (see Cann. 654, 1192 §1). Those who have taken a *private* vow, even in a secular institute or in a society of apostolic life, are not bound by the impediment, much less by the reservation.[5]

(c) the impediment of crime (see Can. 1090).

Impediments of divine law cannot be dispensed, not even by the Apostolic See. In the case of the impediment of consanguinity (see Can. 1091), the Code does not decide the debated issue as to how far this is of divine or natural law. It simply states in Can. 1098 §3 that a dispensation is never given where one party is directly descended from the other in whatever degree, or where they are brother and sister, even of half-blood. This ruling clearly binds the local Ordinary.

Can. 1079 §1 When danger of death threatens, the local Ordinary can dispense his own subjects, wherever they are residing, and all who are actually present in his territory, both from the form to be observed in the celebration of marriage, and from each and every impediment of ecclesiastical law, whether public or occult, with the exception of the impediment arising from the sacred order of priesthood.

§2 In the same circumstances mentioned in §1, but only for cases in which not even the local Ordinary can be approached, the same faculty of dispensation is possessed by the parish priest, by a properly delegated sacred minister, and by the priest or deacon who assists at the marriage in accordance with Can. 1116 §2.

§3 In danger of death, the confessor has the power to dispense from occult impediments for the internal forum, whether within the act of sacramental confession or outside it.

---

[1] CD 8: Fl I 567. Cf. Can. 87 §1 and commentary thereon.
[2] Cf. EM; CLD 6 394–400.
[3] Cf. Can. 137; Comm 15(1983) 227 at Can. 1031 §1 n.1.
[4] Cf. Comm 9(1977) 346–347 at Can. 266 §2.
[5] Cf. Comm 15(1983) 227 at Can. 1031 §2 n.2.

§4 In the case mentioned in §2, the local Ordinary is considered unable to be approached if he can be reached only by telegram or by telephone.

2122 This canon, to which c.1043 of the 1917 Code partly corresponds, gives to the local Ordinary and, with some added restrictions, to others a power of dispensing from impediments of ecclesiastical law which is wider than that given in Can. 1078. The danger of death, which is needed for the valid use of this power, may come from such causes as serious illness, a dangerous surgical operation, a sentence of death, warfare, etc. The people concerned need not be at the point of death, but the danger must be proximate and real, not remote or fancied. The local Ordinary can dispense from all impediments of ecclesiastical law, except only that arising from the priesthood.[1] With this exception, he can dispense from all the reserved impediments of Can. 1078 §2, including that arising from the diaconate, but not from impediments which are certainly or probably of divine law: thus e.g. he cannot dispense from the impediment arising from the bond of a previous marriage, or from the impediment of consanguinity in the direct line or in the second degree of the collateral line.

2123 In danger of death the local Ordinary can also dispense from the canonical form of marriage, and his powers here are wider than those which he enjoys under Can. 1127 §2. In particular, he could grant a dispensation for the marriage of two catholics without insisting on the requirement that there be 'some public form of celebration'. He could even use this power in the unlikely event of there being no witnesses available or, more plausibly, to protect the good name of people believed to be validly married, by allowing the ceremony to take place in the presence of a priest alone without any other witness.[2]

2124 He can exercise these powers of dispensation both over his own subjects, wherever they are at the time, and over all those who happen to be present in his territory. The 1917 Code at c.1043 required that the dispensation could be given 'for peace of conscience or for the legitimation of children'. The present law lays down no specific reasons which would justify using this faculty: certainly the two mentioned above would do so, but any lesser just cause would also suffice.

2125 The same powers granted to the local Ordinary are also extended to others, but *only in cases where the local Ordinary cannot reasonably be reached*. It is not required that it be physically impossible to reach him; moral impossibility suffices, e.g. where the local Ordinary is gravely ill or absent from his territory or otherwise impeded; where approaching him would put the minister or the parties or a third party in serious danger of death, imprisonment or loss of good name; where there is danger of one of the parties dying if time is taken to ensure an approach to the Ordinary. In view of §4 of Can. 1079, which declares the local Ordinary unable to be approached if he can be reached only by telegram or telephone, the criteria for judging when he cannot be approached should be liberally interpreted. In practice, those to whom the faculty is

---

[1] Neither the 1975 draft of this canon (at Can. 286) nor its 1980 draft (at Can. 1032) contained the exception. It was introduced during the final plenary session of the Revision Commission in October 1981, and was incorporated into the 1982 draft submitted to the Pope.

[2] Apart from the danger of death, not even the diocesan Bishop can dispense from the canonical form of marriage: cf. CCom rep 14.V.1985: AAS 77(1985) 771: Comm 17(1985) 262 at III.

granted can use it whenever they conscientiously and reasonably judge that there is serious difficulty in approaching the local Ordinary either in person or by letter.[1]

Those who can dispense in such cases are: 2126

(a) the parish priest. By analogy with §1, this would be either the proper parish priest of one or both of the parties, or the parish priest of the place in which they actually are. He can dispense even if he does not assist at the wedding.

(b) a properly delegated sacred minister, i.e. a Bishop, a priest or a deacon who has been given general or particular delegation to assist at this marriage in accordance with Can. 1111. It is not necessary that the one who gives the dispensation actually assist at the marriage.

(c) the priest or deacon who assists at the marriage in accordance with Can. 1116 §2. This is a priest or deacon who, although not delegated to assist at the marriage, is to be called upon to be present where the so-called extraordinary form of marriage is used. This person's powers can be exercised *only* if he is in fact called upon to be present.

A lay person delegated to assist at marriages in accordance with Can. 1112, cannot dispense in these areas or in those envisaged in the following canon. Granting a dispensation is an exercise of the power of governance and, although Can. 129 §2 states that 'lay members of Christ's faithful can cooperate in the exercise of this same power', this must be done 'in accordance with the law'. The law has made no specific provision in this context, and so lay persons are excluded from dispensing, as indeed are clerics other than those specifically mentioned above. 2127

The dispensing powers of a confessor as such are rather different from those already outlined. The requirement that there be danger of death is the same. His powers are rather wider in that the local Ordinary does not have to be unavailable. They are more restricted in that they extend only to occult impediments,[2] and in that the dispensation holds good only for the internal forum. He may use his power either within the act of sacramental confession or outside it. If he uses it outside it, the granting of the dispensation is to be recorded in the special book kept in the secret archive of the Curia, and it could later hold good for the external forum if the impediment were to become public (see Can. 1082).[3] 2128

---

[1] Can. 1079 §4 derives from a reply of the then Code Commission in 1922: cf. CCom rep 12.XI.1922: AAS 14(1922) 662: CLD 1 502. In view of the technological advances over the intervening seventy years, it is certain that communication by radio, telex or fax may be added to the 'telegram or telephone' of §4. It is important, however, to recognise the point of this regulation. It is designed not only to assist in the emergency situation facing the parish priest and the others mentioned in §2, but principally to safeguard the necessary privacy and confidentiality of such a situation. It is not a declaration that these means of communication are to be regarded as extraordinary or unreliable in themselves: cf. Comm 9 (1977) 350 at Can. 269. The use of these means is not therefore forbidden by the law: rather is it a matter of a prudent judgement in each individual case, taking all the circumstances into account.

[2] In accordance with the traditional understanding of this faculty (cf. the approved commentaries on c.1044 of the 1917 Code), it is at least a probable, if not a certain, opinion that an *occult impediment* in this context is not only one which is defined as 'occult' in Can. 1074 but also one which, though possibly provable in the external forum, is in fact not publicly known at the time of the request for dispensation by the confessor. The salient factor here is that the situation envisaged involves for the penitent a real danger of death.

[3] There is a possibility – unlikely in ordinary circumstances, but in certain situations not to be excluded – that the confessor would qualify for the faculty granted by Can. 1079 §2, *not as confessor* but as 'the priest ... who assists at the marriage in accordance with Can. 1116 §2': cf. Comm 9(1977) 350 at Can. 269 b.

Can. 1080 §1 Whenever an impediment is discovered after everything has already been prepared for the wedding and the marriage cannot without probable danger of grave harm be postponed until a dispensation is obtained from the competent authority, the power to dispense from all impediments, except those mentioned in Can. 1078 §2 n.1, is possessed by the local Ordinary and, provided the case is occult, by all those mentioned in Can. 1079 §§2–3, the conditions prescribed therein having been observed.

§2 This power applies also to the validation of a marriage when there is the same danger in delay and there is no time to have recourse to the Apostolic See or, in the case of impediments from which he can dispense, to the local Ordinary.

2129   Passing to the *other type of urgent or emergency situation* this canon gives a power of dispensation which can be invoked when:

(a) 'everything has already been prepared for a wedding' before the impediment is discovered. This does not mean that absolutely every possible preparation has been completed. Some *substantial* preparations must have been made by the parties;[1] what is crucial is that the dispensation cannot be obtained in the normal way in time for the wedding to take place on the day planned.[2] The *discovery* of the impediment refers to its becoming known to the local Ordinary or parish priest:[3] thus, even if the parties were aware of the existence of the impediment and overlooked it or its relevance (not deliberately concealed it) until preparations were well advanced, this power could be used.

(b) 'the marriage cannot without probable danger of grave harm be postponed until a dispensation is obtained from the competent authority'. The *grave harm* in question could be either moral or material, and would include such as loss of good name, family dissensions, serious financial loss, etc. Nor does the harm have to be certain: sufficient is a prudent judgement by the one granting the dispensation that the harm is probable.[4]

2130   Subject to the conditions mentioned below in respect of those who are competent in this situation, the canon gives the power to dispense from all impediments except only those mentioned in Can. 1078 §2 1°, i.e. those arising from sacred orders or from a public perpetual vow of chastity in a religious institute of pontifical right. Some commentators on the corresponding c.1045 of the 1917 Code held that this power extended also to dispensing from the form of marriage. However, since Can. 1079 explicitly allows for dispensation from the form in danger of death, and the present canon does not mention it, that opinion is not now tenable.[5]

2131   Under this canon the following can dispense:

(a) *the local Ordinary*: since he can already dispense from all impediments, public or occult, except those reserved by Can. 1078 §2 to the Apostolic See, and since the impediments of Can. 1078 §2 1° are excluded by the present canon, *in practice* the only extra power he has in this situation is over the impediment of crime (see Can. 1090).

---

[1] Cf. SRRDec (Rota 14.III.1927) 19 70ff: CLD 2 278–280.
[2] Cf. SRRDec (Rota 25.V.1925) 17 195ff: CLD 2 277–278.
[3] Cf. CCom rep I.III.1921: AAS 13(1921) 178: CLD 1 502.
[4] CF. SRRDec (Rota 25.V.1925) 17 195ff: CLD 2 277–278.
[5] Cf. also in this regard CCom rep 14.V.1985: AAS 77(1985) 771: Comm 17(1985) 262 at III.

(b) *the parish priest; a sacred minister properly delegated to assist at the marriage; the priest or deacon who assists in accordance with Can. 1116 §2*: for each of these the power to dispense is subject to two conditions, namely that it be not possible to approach the local Ordinary (see Can. 1079 §2), and that the case be an occult one (see Can. 1090 §1) i.e. not that it concern an occult *impediment* in the case of Can. 1074, rather that the impediment (whether provable in the external forum or not) is in fact not publicly known.[1]

(c) *the confessor*: whose power is again subject to two conditions, namely that it is confined to dispensing only 'for the internal forum, whether within the act of sacramental confession or outside it' (see Can. 1079 §3), and that it is limited to occult impediments.

The same people mentioned above have the same powers, subject to the same conditions, when there is question of validating a marriage already contracted invalidly (§2). The validation of a marriage could be effected either by a simple validation (see Cann. 1156–1160) or by a retroactive validation (see Cann. 1161–1165): in some instances the granting of the latter is reserved to the Holy See. And even though a local Ordinary or other person may have the power to dispense in the circumstances envisaged in this canon, one is always free to have direct recourse to the Holy See to obtain the dispensation. 2132

Can. 1081 The parish priest or the priest or deacon mentioned in Can. 1079 §2, is to inform the local Ordinary immediately of a dispensation granted for the external forum, and this dispensation is to be recorded in the marriage register.

There are two distinct obligations here which arise when a dispensation is given for the *external forum* in the extraordinary circumstances of Cann. 1079 or 1080: 2133

(a) when it is given by one lower than the local Ordinary, he must inform the Ordinary that he has done so. This is a serious personal obligation, binding upon the parish priest (even if the dispensation was granted by another delegated for the marriage) and upon the priest or deacon of whom in Can. 1079 §2; and it is an obligation which must be fulfilled 'immediately' i.e. within a matter of a very few days.

(b) the dispensation must be recorded in the appropriate local marriage register. The dispensation is a matter of public law which concerns the very important matter of the validity of the marriage of two people. This rule is to ensure that in an urgent case, when it could so easily be overlooked, there is a proper record of the fact.

Can. 1082 Unless a rescript of the Penitentiary provides otherwise, a dispensation from an occult impediment granted in the internal non-sacramental forum, is to be recorded in the book to be kept in the secret archive of the curia. No other dispensation for the external forum is necessary if at a later stage the occult impediment becomes public.

This canon deals with the registration of dispensations granted by any competent authority *for the internal non-sacramental forum*. In some rare cases where there is special need for secrecy, the Apostolic Penitentiary will include in the rescript granting the dispensation a clause directing that it should not be registered locally and will itself keep a secret record of it. In all other cases, such dispensations are to be registered in a special book to be kept in the secret archive of the Curia; they are not to be noted in the ordinary local marriage register. If, later on, the impediment were to become public the dispensation would hold good for the external forum. 2134

---

[1] Cf. CCom rep 28.XII.1927: AAS 20(1928) 61: CLD 1 503.

2135 A dispensation granted by a confessor *for the internal sacramental forum*, i.e. within the act of sacramental confession, is not to be registered anywhere, nor reported to the local Ordinary: once granted, it immediately becomes subject to the inviolable sacramental seal (see Cann. 983–984). If the impediment were later to become public, a new dispensation for the external forum would be required (see 1917 Code c.1047).

Chapter III
INDIVIDUAL DIRIMENT IMPEDIMENTS

2136 In consequence of the suppression of those considered to be merely impedient impediments in the 1917 Code, those detailed in the following Cann. 1083–1094 are all diriment impediments (see Can. 1073 and Commentary thereon). Some are *of divine law* and accordingly bind everyone, even the non-baptised, nor has the Church any direct authority to dispense from them. Others are *of merely ecclesiastical law*: these bind only those who have been baptised in the catholic Church or received into it (see Cann. 11, 1059), not therefore the baptised who belong to a non-catholic church or ecclesial community; in appropriate circumstances they may be dispensed by the relevant canonical authority. Others still are of *mixed origin*: partly divine law and partly ecclesiastical law; the specific provisions in their regard are dealt with under the relevant canons which follow.

Can. 1083 §1 A man cannot validly enter marriage before the completion of his sixteenth year of age, nor a woman before the completion of her fourteenth year.

2137 The *impediment of non-age* is partly of natural law, partly of ecclesiastical law. Those who have not yet attained sufficient use of reason and discretion of judgement to give adequate matrimonial consent (whatever their age) are, by virtue of the natural law itself, incapable of contracting marriage. Ecclesiastical law here declares a minimum age below which people cannot marry validly, even if they have sufficient use of reason and discretion to meet the natural law requirements. This age is sixteen for a man and fourteen for a woman, the higher age for men reflecting the fact that adolescent boys usually mature later than girls; in effect, a man cannot marry validly until the day after his sixteenth birthday, nor a woman until the day after her fourteenth (see Cann. 202, 203).

2138 Given the high failure rate in marriages of the very young, and given the possibility that even at the ages of sixteen and fourteen the parties may not have sufficient discretion of judgement for valid consent, a dispensation from this impediment should be given only very rarely and then only for the most serious of reasons.[1]

2139 In the consultations during the revision of the Code there were calls for the minimum age to be raised. For a number of reasons these were rejected: because it was felt incorrect to restrict the natural right to marry, because of the difficulties that would arise in different cultures and local circumstances throughout the Church, because the present canon concerns only physical maturity whereas personal or psychological maturity is dealt with elsewhere in the law, most particularly in Can. 1095.[2] There was also a request to make the minimum age the same as that in the local civil law,

---

[1] This has long been the established interpretation in this matter: cf. e.g. Cappello V n.338, 2. Cf. also Chiappetta II n.3571.

[2] Cf. Comm 9(1977) 360 at Can. 282 §1; 15(1983) 228 at Can. 1036.

but the difficulties arising from the different requirements of the two laws were considered to be adequately covered by the new provision that marriages which cannot be recognised by the civil law or celebrated in accordance with it, need the permission of the local Ordinary (see Can. 1071 §1 2°). The appropriate ecclesiastical authority in each country will obviously be acquainted with the local civil requirements.

Can. 1083 §2 The Bishops' Conference may establish a higher age for the lawful celebration of marriage.

This is a new law and is in effect an optional impedient impediment which may be invoked by a Bishops' Conference (but not by an individual Bishop) in view of local circumstances.[1] It allows the raising of the age required for the *lawful* celebration of marriage, but it has no effect on the marriage's *validity*. It could be used e.g. to make the age the same as that required by local civil law. If the Bishops' Conference does so raise the age, dispensations from this law could be given, for sufficient reason, in the same ways and by the same people as detailed in Cann. 1078–1080.

2140

Can. 1084 §1 By reason of its very nature, marriage is invalidated by antecedent and perpetual impotence to have sexual intercourse, whether on the part of the man or on that of the woman, whether absolute or relative.

§2 If the impediment of impotence is doubtful, whether the doubt be one of law or one of fact, the marriage is not to be prevented nor, while the doubt persists, is it to be declared null.

The *impediment of impotence* has, over the centuries, been the subject of considerable debate and diverse opinions. The decisions even of the Holy See in individual cases in this regard have not always been consistent.[2] Accordingly, this particular area was subjected to a very incisive scrutiny and debate by the Revision Commission before its formulation of the present text.[3]

2141

In general terms, impotence means the inability to have sexual intercourse. In canonical terms, sexual intercourse involves three essential elements: (a) erection of the male member; (b) penetration, at least partial,[4] by it of the female vagina; (c) ejaculation within the vagina. If any of these three is impossible – for whatever reason, whether on the part of the male or on that of the female – there is impotence. This impotence will, however, invalidate a marriage only if it is antecedent, perpetual and certain:

2142

- impotence is *antecedent* if the condition was present at the time of marriage. If the condition were to arise only after this time, as a result of e.g. an accident or an illness or surgery, while the person would then be undoubtedly impotent, this would not in any way affect the validity of the marriage already contracted.

- impotence is *perpetual* if it cannot be cured by what are called 'ordinary means'. These are any lawful means which are available to the person concerned, and which do not involve a probable danger to life or a serious threat to the health of an otherwise healthy person. The actual availability of such means will depend upon circumstances, local, cultural, financial, etc. Thus, e.g. impotence caused by a defect which can be cured only by a dangerous surgical operation, or even by an ordinary operation which is not in fact available to the person in question, is regarded as perpetual.[1]

---

[1] For the manner in which this faculty has been used by the various Bishops' Conferences, cf. LCE Tavola per Paesi e Canoni at Can. 1083.
[2] Cf. Comm 6(1974) 179.
[3] Cf. Comm 6(1974) 177–198.
[4] Cf. SCHO decl I.III.1941: LE I 1599 2050.

– impotence is *certain* when it is not subject to any serious doubt, whether of law or of fact (see Can. 14). Since there is a fundamental human right to marry, the exercise of that right may not be impeded save only when there is established with *moral certainty* the existence of some condition, circumstance or situation which would render a particular person incapable of exercising it. In this context special attention must be paid to the prescription (which did not exist in the 1917 Code) of §2 of this canon. The text speaks for itself. What is important, however, is to realise that, by laying down this rule, the Code resolves a divergence of long standing between, on the one hand, an administrative practice based on c.1068 of the 1917 Code whereby those whose impotence was not certain were permitted to marry and, on the other, a judicial practice in a number of tribunals including the Roman Rota whereby their marriages were subsequently declared null on the ground of impotence.

2143 The impotence described above may be either organic or functional:

– it is *organic* if it is caused by the lack of, or a deformation in, the physical organs required for intercourse. Thus e.g. a man lacking a penis or a woman lacking a vagina would suffer from organic impotence.

– it is *functional* when the organs are physically intact but intercourse is impossible due to psychological or neurological problems, such e.g. as, in the male, inability to maintain an erection or, in the female, severe vaginismus: the Revision Commission laid particular stress on the necessity in this regard to secure the informed advice of competent medical and psychiatric experts.[2]

2144 Impotence may be either absolute or relative:

– it is *absolute* if a person is, for whatever proven reason, incapable of sexual intercourse with any partner, as would e.g. be the case of a man who lacks a penis or who could not ever sustain an erection, or of a woman who lacks a vagina[3] or who suffers from incurable vaginismus.

– it is *relative* if the person is incapable with a determined partner, though not perhaps with another, as would e.g. be the case if it were due to a gross disproportion in size between the organs of the people involved or, as may more commonly occur, if it were due to a woman's severe vaginismus with her partner, albeit perhaps not so with another. If the impotence is certain, it is invalidating whether it be absolute or relative.

2145 The majority opinion, both under the 1917 Code and now under its successor, maintains that the impediment of impotence as explained above is of the divine natural law[4] and, accordingly, that a dispensation from it may never be granted by any human authority, ecclesiastical or civil. That is the firm stance of this commentary.[5]

---

[1] There is therefore an element of relativity in the estimate of whether a particular instance of established impotence is or is not 'perpetual'. To illustrate the point, one may take a stark example by contrasting the position of an impotent person residing in a highly-developed 'Western' society, with wide availability of professional services and health-care, and another such a person in a seriously 'undeveloped' society, with little or no such resources. There will obviously be many situations intermediate between these two extremes, which will each have to be estimated on its own merits.

[2] Cf. Comm 6(1974) 197–198. For an informative guide on this matter of functional impotence, and indeed on the background to impotence in general, cf. Sheehy *Male Psychical Impotence in Judicial Proceedings* and the authorities cited therein: Jur 20(1960) 253–294.

[3] In this regard cf. in particular Comm 6(1974) 196.

[4] Cf. Comm 15(1983) 228–229 at Can. 1037.

[5] For academic purposes, it may be noted that this is not an unchallenged position, as is evidenced by the discussions in the Revision Commission: cf. Comm 7(1975) 54–56; 9(1977) 360–361. It would appear to have been in deference to this divergence of opinion that §1 of this canon substituted the phrase '*by its very nature*' for that of '*by the natural law itself*' of c.1086 §1 of the 1917 Code. Be that as it may, it is difficult, if not impossible, to see that there is any real difference in substance.

Can. 1084 §3 Without prejudice to the provisions of Can. 1098, sterility neither forbids nor invalidates a marriage.

Whereas impotence is the incapacity to have sexual intercourse as described above, sterility is a condition which, while not eliminating the possibility of intercourse, precludes the resultant conception of a child. Although 'marriage and married love are by nature ordered to the procreation ... of children',[1] the begetting of children is not totally within the control of the husband and wife. It is for this reason that their matrimonial consent is *not to the having of children, but to intercourse which is open to life*. Sterility may be caused by many factors, which themselves are for diagnosis and determination by the medical profession. Formerly it had been held by many, including some Judges of the Roman Rota, that impotence arose if there was an inability to ejaculate semen produced in the testicles. In 1977, however, in an epoch-making decision explicitly approved by Pope Paul VI, the Congregation for the Doctrine of the Faith declared against this opinion and made it clear that such inability amounted only to sterility[2]: in other words, the content of the ejaculate or its precise origin is irrelevant as far as impotence is concerned. From this it follows e.g. that, in the case of the man, neither vasectomy nor the atrophy or even the absence of the testicles would constitute impotence; in the case of the woman, impotence would not arise from the absence of or serious pathological damage to the post-vaginal organs, such as the uterus, the ovaries, the fallopian tubes.[3] It will therefore be appreciated that this particular decree has a profound effect upon the concept of impotence – a necessary corollary of which is its import for matrimonial jurisprudence in this context, not least as to whether or not the decree is retroactive in its effect.[4]

It is to be noted that in dealing with sterility in the context of a diriment impediment to marriage, this Can. 1084 §3 is 'without prejudice to the provisions of Can. 1098', dealing with deceit as a factor invalidating of marriage. There is here a clear and certain implication that deceit, in the terms of Can. 1098, concerning fertility would invalidate a marriage.[5] The same would be the case if one of the parties were to make the sexual fertility of the other a condition of his or her own consent (see Can. 1102).[6]

Can. 1085 §1 A person obliged by the bond of a previous marriage, even if not consummated, invalidly attempts marriage.

The impediment of the bond of a previous marriage is one both of natural law and of divine positive law, based upon the essential properties of marriage, namely unity and indissolubility (see Can. 1056). Accordingly a dispensation from it may not in any circumstance be granted, by either Church or State: this is so even in respect of two unbaptised people who were validly married to one another in accordance with the civil laws or customs of their own country or region.

---

[1] GS 50: Fl I 953.

[2] SCDF decr 13.V.1977: AAS 69(1977) 426. Cf. Comm 6(1974) 186–188 ad quartum.

[3] Cf. Chiappetta II n.3608.

[4] Cf. Chiappetta II note 11 at n.3608. For a thoroughly comprehensive up-to-date examination of all the implications of the Holy See's 1977 decree, cf. McGrath *A Controversy concerning Male Impotence* Analecta Gregoriana Rome 1988 (327 pp) – an authoritatively summary version of which is in: McGrath *De relatione iuridica Breve Sixti V 'Cum frequenter' diei 27 iunii 1587 inter et decretum Sacrae Congregationis pro Doctrina Fidei diei 13 maii 1977* Per 76(1987) 309–334.

[5] Cf. Comm 7(1975) 59 at Can. 1068 §3.

[6] Cf. Comm 9(1977) 361 at Can. 283 §3.

2149 The impediment exists if the following two conditions are verified:
- that the previous marriage was a valid one, religious or civil, sacramental or not, consummated or not;[1] it would not, however, be valid if contracted contrary to the law of the Church by a person bound by the canonical form of marriage as prescribed by Can. 1117.
- that the previous marriage still exists in law, i.e. that it has not been dissolved whether by the death of one of the partners,[2] or by an appropriate disposition of ecclesiastical authority, as in the case of a dispensation by the Pope in a non-consummated marriage (see Can. 1142), of the pauline privilege (see Can. 1143 §1), or where the Holy See grants a dissolution, 'in favour of the faith', of a natural bond between a baptised catholic and an unbaptised person (see Cann. 1148–1150). It is important to note that a civil divorce is of no canonical effect in this regard.

Can. 1085 §2 Even though the previous marriage is invalid or for any reason dissolved, it is not thereby lawful to contract another marriage before the nullity or the dissolution of the previous one has been established lawfully and with certainty.

2150 As a corollary to the statement of the impediment in §1, this paragraph lays down a practical ancillary rule. In effect, if it is proposed that 'the previous marriage is invalid or for any reason dissolved', a further marriage may not lawfully take place unless the appropriate authority – very often, the priest in the parish – will have possession of clear proof (not merely hearsay) that the earlier marriage was declared invalid or was lawfully dissolved. For pastoral practice, this means that the officiant at any subsequent marriage may proceed only on the basis of an authentic document or statement officially attesting to the invalidity or dissolution of the previous marriage. Should there be any doubt, the officiating priest or other authorised person must consult the diocesan Bishop or other competent local Ordinary.

Can. 1086 §1 A marriage is invalid when one of the two persons was baptised in the catholic Church or received into it and has not by a formal act defected from it, and the other was not baptised.

2151 *This impediment of disparity of cult* invalidates a marriage between a baptised catholic (subject to certain conditions) and an unbaptised person.[3] The reason for the impediment is twofold: the difficulty the catholic partner may encounter in practising his or her faith, and the danger that children of the marriage may not be brought up as catholics; at a deeper level, because such a marriage is not sacramental, it does not fully mirror either the covenant between God and his people or the relationship between Christ and the Church as christian marriage should.

2152 The impediment applies to an unbaptised person and 'one baptised in the catholic Church or received into it'. Who are to be regarded as having been baptised in the

---

[1] Should there be a positive and insoluble doubt about the validity of that previous marriage, any second marriage must be considered null and void: cf. CCom rep 26.VI.1947: AAS 39(1947) 374.

[2] In normal circumstances, the death of one of the parties will be easily verifiable and officially attested. In exceptional circumstances, there may be difficulties; in some such cases it may be necessary, or at least prudent, to apply to the diocesan Bishop for an official declaration of presumed death in accordance with Can. 1707.

[3] A catechumen (see Can. 206) is included here: a proposal to the Revision Commission that catechumens be excluded from the ambit of this impediment was not accepted, precisely by reason of the difficulty of determining when a person becomes a catechumen: cf. Comm 9(1977) 363 at Can. 285.

catholic Church? There is no difficulty where baptism has been received in adulthood: the intention of the recipient determines the matter. Neither is there a problem where the parents or guardians of an infant, be they catholic or not, consent to or ask for catholic baptism for the infant, nor where an infant is lawfully given catholic baptism in danger of death (see Cann. 867 §2, 868 §2). In all of these cases the person is regarded as baptised in the catholic Church. But what of a person unlawfully baptised in the catholic Church, where baptism has been given outside of danger of death without, or even contrary to, the consent of the parents, or without any hope that the child will be brought up a catholic? The common opinion of commentators on the 1917 Code was that such people are not regarded as having been 'baptised in the catholic Church' and so are not bound by this impediment.[1] This opinion would still hold good for the present law.

A new provision in the present Code exempts from the impediment those catholics who have by *a formal act defected from the Church* (the same phrase occurs in Cann. 1117, 1124). The law itself does not determine what constitutes such a formal act of defection, and in individual cases it may indeed be difficult to decide whether or not such an act has been placed.[2] Pending an official decision by the Pontifical Council for the Interpretation of Legislative Texts, this is clearly a matter in which guidance will mainly come from the jurisprudence of the ecclesiastical courts. In the meantime, the following may be stated as safe guidelines:

2153

(a) a formal act of defection from the catholic Church is a more restricted and limited concept than that of the notorious defection mentioned in Can. 171 §1 4°: accordingly, one who has *notoriously*, but *not formally*, abandoned or rejected the catholic faith would still be bound by the impediment of disparity of cult.[3]

(b) on the other hand, a formal defection would certainly be involved in the following situations:

– an open declaration of abandonment of the catholic faith, for whatever reason or motive: this, whether it be made in writing or orally, would have to be such that it is capable of unequivocal proof;

– an established heresy, apostasy or schism (see Can. 751);

– a formal enrolling, by whatever outward sign, in another religion, be it christian or not;

– a public affiliation to an atheistic ideology or movement which is manifestly opposed to the catholic faith;

(c) it is to be noted that in each of the foregoing instances a distinct act of *formality* is required, which itself is either unequivocably apparent or at least provable in the external forum; accordingly, a mere ceasing to practise one's catholic faith even over a considerable time, a regular attendance at the religious services of another religion or ecclesial communion, and the like, would not necessarily – and in the absence of contrary proof, certainly would not – establish the formal defection from the catholic church envisaged in this canon or in its analogous Cann. 1117, 1124.

---

[1] Cf. e.g. Bouscaren–Ellis 477; Cappello V n.412.

[2] For some preliminary studies on this matter, cf. Lenherr *Der Abfall von der Katholischen Kirche durch einen formalen Akt* AKK 152(1983) 107–125; Arya Arteaga *Bautizados en la Iglesia católica no obligados a la forma canónica del matrimonio: problemas que presenta* Proceedings of the 5th International Congress of Canon Law (Le Nouveau Code de Droit Canonique) Ottawa St Paul University 1984 897–930; Ludicke *Die Kirchengliedschaft und die plena communio* Festgabe Hugo Schwendenwein, Graz Verlag Styria 1986 377–391; Stenson *The concept and implications of the formal act of defection of Can. 1117* Stud Can 21(1987) 175–194; Doyle *The formal act of leaving the Catholic Church* CLSA Proceedings 1990 152–160.

[3] Cf. Chiappetta n.1017; Comm 10(1978) 96–97 at Can. 319 §1.

(d) if and when a formal act of defection has been properly established, to the satisfaction of the competent Bishop, parish priest or other appropriate ecclesiastical person, it should be notified for insertion in the register of baptisms and have effect in accordance with Can. 535 §2.[1]

Can. 1086 §2 This impediment is not to be dispensed unless the conditions mentioned in Cann. 1125 and 1126 have been fulfilled.

2154 The conditions mentioned here concern the promises to be made by the catholic party concerning his or her own faith and the catholic upbringing of children, and the instruction and information to be given to both parties which are required when permission is given for a mixed marriage (see Cann. 1125–1126). These conditions must be fulfilled before a dispensation is given from this impediment. While there are some of the view that a dispensation granted without the fulfilment of these conditions would be invalid – and, as a result, that the ensuing marriage would itself be invalid[2] – this opinion would not appear to be an acceptable guide in practice, taking account particularly of the text of the canon and of its antecedents. To say this does not, however, in any way take from the serious obligation to ensure the fulfilment of the prescribed conditions.

Can. 1086 §3 If at the time the marriage was contracted one party was commonly understood to be baptised, or if his or her baptism was doubtful, the validity of the marriage is to be presumed in accordance with Can. 1060, until it is established with certainty that one party was baptised and the other was not.

2155 The wording of this paragraph, almost identical with c.1070 §1 of the 1917 Code, is a particular application of Can. 1060. It states that in case of doubt about either the fact or the validity of a person's baptism, his or her marriage to a baptised person is presumed to be valid. This rule does not make such a marriage valid; the validity depends on the fact of baptism. It merely gives a presumption in law that the marriage is valid; this presumption can of course yield to contrary proof, but not to anything less. Its application will normally occur only when the doubt about baptism arises after marriage. If the doubt arises beforehand, it should be resolved either by establishing the fact of baptism by enquiry or even by conditional baptism, or else by a dispensation given as a precaution (*ad cautelam*).

Can. 1087 Those who are in sacred orders invalidly attempt marriage.

2156 *The impediment of sacred orders* is related to the obligation of clerical celibacy (see Can. 277 §1) and renders invalid a marriage attempted by a deacon, priest or Bishop. The tradition of clerical celibacy was well established in the latin Church long before – in fact since at least the early 4th century at the Council of Elvira – the first general invalidating law, which seems to have been in the Second Lateran Council in 1139. If the order was received invalidly there is, of course, no impediment. If it was received under the influence of grave fear or without knowledge of the obligation of celibacy,

---

[1] There are some countries in which a civil tax is imposed on the basis of one's allegiance to a given religious denomination or belief. There is evidence that, in order to avoid this tax, among others some catholics are prepared to, and in fact do, publicly declare that they have defected from their faith. Such a declaration, however made, is not *of itself* an adequate proof that it fulfils the *formal defection* in question here. Each case should be examined on its merits, in accordance with the principles outlined above. Only when such an examination will have yielded certainty that there has in fact been a formal defection should the appropriate insertion be made – or requested to be made – in the register of baptisms.

[2] Cf. e.g. Commentary (CLSA) 768–769.

Part 1 The Sacraments

the common teaching under the 1917 Code was that the obligation of celibacy did not bind and therefore neither did the impediment: that interpretation still holds good.

The impediment extends to married men who have been ordained deacons and are subsequently widowed. This is in accord with the mp *Ad Pascendum* of Pope Paul VI in 1972: 'In accordance with the traditional discipline of the Church, a married deacon who has lost his wife cannot enter a new marriage'.[1]

Dispensation from this impediment is reserved exclusively to the Apostolic See (see Cann. 1078 §2 1°, 291). It is not granted in the case of a Bishop and is not easily granted to priests. Even in danger of death the local Ordinary cannot dispense from the impediment in so far as it may concern a Bishop or a priest (see Can. 1079 §1).

Can. 1088 Those who are bound by a public perpetual vow of chastity in a religious institute invalidly attempt marriage.

The impediment of public perpetual vow of chastity has been substantially reformed in the current Code. In contrast with the 1917 Code which in its cc.1058 §1 and 1073 had a multiplicity of impediments in this context, this canon contains the one and only impediment now attached to a vow. In order to give rise to the impediment, the vow of chastity must fulfil three requirements:

(a) It must be *public*, i.e. 'accepted in the name of the Church by a lawful Superior' (Can. 1192 §1) and in accordance with the approved constitutions of an institute. It does not matter whether the vow is simple or solemn, or whether it is made in an institute of pontifical right or one of diocesan right.

(b) It must be *perpetual*, i.e. taken until death, as distinct from a temporary vow which is taken only for a determined period (see Can. 655).

(c) It must be *taken in a religious institute*. Thus, a commitment to chastity taken in a secular institute, even though it is perpetual and accepted by a lawful Superior and even though it may be made in the form of a vow, would not give rise to this impediment.[2]

If the institute in question is of pontifical right, dispensation from the impediment is reserved to the Apostolic See (see Can. 1078 §2 1°), but if it is of diocesan right, although the impediment is still a diriment one it can be dispensed from by the local Ordinary.[3]

Can. 1089 No marriage can exist between a man and a woman who has been abducted, or at least detained, with a view to contracting a marriage with her, unless the woman, after she has been separated from her abductor and established in a safe and free place, chooses marriage of her own accord.

Although this impediment has the same general purpose as Can. 1103 which deals with the effect of force and fear on the consent, namely to safeguard freedom of

---

[1] AP 6: Fl I 439. The first draft of this canon in 1975 carried an additional paragraph which explicitly included married-and-then-widowed deacons within the ambit of this impediment: cf. SS at Can. 287 §2. However, subsequent drafts, even including the final one of 1982, reversed that position: cf. Comm 9(1977) 365 at Can. 287 §2; 15(1983) 229–230 at Can. 1040 §2. In the event, when the Code was published and officially promulgated, the proposed second paragraph was simply omitted, thus restoring the discipline stated by Pope Paul VI.

[2] Cf. Comm 15(1983) 230 at Can. 1041.

[3] For competence to dispense in danger of death, cf. Can. 1079. It is to be noted that where the religious is also a cleric, a double impediment arises: cf. Can. 1087. Moreover, a dispensation from the impediment of this vow automatically involves the loss of the religious state: cf. Chiappetta n.3628 and note 15.

choice in getting married, its scope and effect are different from that canon. The impediment applies only to women, and its invalidating effect remains even if she freely consents to marriage, without all the conditions of the canon having been fulfilled: once the impediment arises, its effect becomes independent of the sole element of consent.

2162 There are two forms of the impediment: (a) abduction of the woman; (b) detention of her against her will. Both must be done with a view to contracting marriage with the woman in question, and both must involve some degree of violence, either physical or moral. The woman e.g. need not be physically tied up or locked in a room; she could be detained by blackmail or threats. The impediment ceases only when she has been established in a safe and free place, and there freely consents to marriage. This means that she must be physically and morally outside the abductor's power. A particular care should be exercised to ensure that a residual effect of the abductor's attraction has ceased to endure. Although the local Ordinary could dispense from this impediment, since it is not reserved, it is not easy to see what circumstances would justify him in doing so.

2163 During the consultations on the revision of this canon it was suggested that it be dropped entirely, on the ground that the situation envisaged in it was adequately covered by the canon on force and fear. However, the majority of the consultors decided to retain it because the abduction of a woman was not as infrequent as might at first be thought. Likewise, a proposal to extend the impediment to the abduction of a man by a woman was rejected.[1]

Can. 1090 §1 One who, with a view to entering marriage with a particular person, has killed that person's spouse, or his or her own spouse, invalidly attempts this marriage.

§2 They also invalidly attempt marriage with each other who, by mutual physical or moral action, brought about the death of either's spouse.

2164 *The impediment of 'crime'* as stated in this canon differs from that given in c.1075 of the 1917 Code. In the previous law the impediment had three degrees: the first involving adultery with a promise of, or attempt at, marriage; the second, adultery with coniugicide; the third, mutual cooperation in coniugicide. It now has only two degrees, in neither of which adultery plays any part. Both degrees involve coniugicide, which is the intentional and unlawful killing of the spouse of a valid marriage. The killing may be done physically by the person or persons in question, or it may be done morally, e.g. by hiring a killer, by persuading someone else to do it, or even by persuading the victim to commit suicide. Death caused by accident or by carelessness would not give rise to the impediment.

2165 In the first degree, the killing of the spouse is done by one party only. The other party may be ignorant of the deed or even opposed to it. The spouse killed may be the killer's own spouse or the spouse of his or her prospective partner. The killing must be done in order to enter a particular marriage: if e.g. a man were to kill his wife in order to marry another specific woman, the impediment would arise only between him and that other woman; it would not, as such, impede him from marrying someone else.

2166 In the second degree, the killing is done by the mutual physical or moral action of both parties to the prospective marriage. There must be in both parties an element of conspiracy and consent to the killing. Mere knowledge by one party of the other's intention to commit the crime, without consent, would not cause the impediment.

---

[1] Cf. Comm 9(1977) 366 at Can. 289.

Commentators on the previous law required that, in such a case, the killing be done with a view to marrying the accomplice.[1] The original draft of this canon had just one paragraph, which was identical with §1 of the present law. It was suggested that the words 'with a view to entering marriage' be deleted in order to give wider scope to the canon. However, the Revision Commission decided to distinguish between the case where a person committed coniugicide with a view to marriage and the case where there was mutual cooperation in the murder. Accordingly, even though the second paragraph of the canon is substantially the same as the 1917 law, the reason for its inclusion would seem to be to give wider scope to the impediment in the case of conspiracy to murder and to exempt this case from the qualification that the murder be done with a view to marriage.[2] If this were not so, there would be no need for a second paragraph to the canon; the case would be adequately covered by the first paragraph. So the mere fact of mutual cooperation by a man and a woman in the murder of the spouse of either, gives rise to the impediment. If, e.g. the wife of a sick man persuaded a doctor to end his suffering by taking his life, the impediment comes into being between them, even though at the time of the death neither had any intention of marrying the other.

Dispensation from this impediment is reserved to the Apostolic See in normal circumstances (see Can. 1078 §2 2°). Where the murder is publicly known the dispensation is not granted. A dispensation could be given in danger of death or where the impediment is discovered only when everything has been prepared for the wedding, by those mentioned in Cann. 1079 and 1080 and subject to the conditions mentioned in those canons. However, where the murder is known or at all likely to become known, prudence would dictate that, apart from danger of death, the dispensation should not be given.

Can. 1091 §1 Marriage is invalid between those related by consanguinity in all degrees of the direct line, whether ascending or descending, legitimate or natural.
§2 In the collateral line, it is invalid up to the fourth degree inclusive.

The impediment of consanguinity is based on blood relationship. Most, if not all, societies and legal systems have a prohibition on marriage between close blood relatives; the canon law is no exception. The reasons for the prohibition are the possible genetic consequences of such a union and a desire to protect the sanctity of the family. The extent of the impediment in canon law has not always been constant. Under the 1917 Code it extended as far as second cousins; the present law is more restricted.

The relationship on which the impediment is based is described in Can. 108. It is a blood relationship, i.e. the two people concerned are descended either one from the other, or from a common ancestor. In the first case, the relationship is in the direct line; in the second, it is in the collateral. Both lines are measured in degrees. 'In the direct line there are as many degrees as there are generations, that is, as there are persons, not counting the common ancestor' (Can. 108 §2). Thus, a father and daughter are related in the first degree of the direct line, a grandfather and granddaughter are related in the second degree of the direct line. 'In the collateral line there are as many degrees as there are persons in both lines together, not counting the common ancestor' (Can. 108 §3). This method of computation, based on Roman law, differs from that in the 1917 Code which followed a Germanic law system, and it allows more easily for a precise description of the relationship. The following diagram should be of help:

---
[1] Cf. e.g. Cappello V nn.496–497.
[2] Cf. Comm 9(1977) 366 at Can. 290.

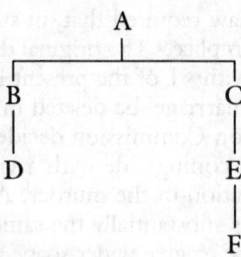

The degree is arrived at by counting from the first person involved back to the common ancestor and down to the second person and then subtracting one. So, to determine the degree in the case of B and C above, one starts with B, counts up to A and down to C, which gives three persons in all; subtract one, revealing that B and C (brother and sister) are related in the second degree. Similarly B and E (uncle and niece, or aunt and nephew) are related in the third degree, D and E (first cousins) in the fourth degree.

2170 The impediment extends to all degrees of the direct line and as far as the fourth degree in the collateral line. In the collateral line, therefore, for most practical purposes the impediment extends as far as first cousins. Reference to the diagram above will show that B and F (granduncle and grandniece, or grandaunt and grandnephew) are also related in the fourth degree and are therefore impeded from marrying; in most cases, however, the age difference involved would make such a marriage very unlikely.

2171 It should be noted that the relationship of consanguinity, and hence the impediment, does not depend on marriage, valid or otherwise. It depends solely on actual blood relationship, whether lawful or not. It should also be noted that the impediment makes no distinction between relationships of half blood and those of full blood. Thus e.g. the impediment between a full brother and sister is exactly the same as that between a half brother and sister; put another way, it makes no difference whether the 'common ancestor' was one person or two.

Can. 1091 §3 The impediment of consanguinity is not multiplied.

2172 If two people are descended from more than one common ancestor, the relationship between them is multiplied and can, in some cases, become quite complicated. Under the 1917 law (see c.1076 §2), if the relationship was multiplied in this way, so was the impediment. The present paragraph rules out any such multiplication. Thus e.g. if double first cousins (the children of two brothers and two sisters) wish to marry, the dispensation is simply from consanguinity in the fourth degree, as for simple first cousins. However, if a couple are multiply related, an application for a dispensation should be made for the closest degree of relationship: a dispensation given for the fourth degree would not be valid if the parties were also related in the third degree.

Can. 1091 §4 A marriage is never to be permitted if a doubt exists as to whether the parties are related by consanguinity in any degree of the direct line, or in the second degree of the collateral line.

2173 This paragraph, which repeats almost exactly c.1076 §3 of the 1917 Code, is in addition to the statement of Can. 1078 §3 that a dispensation is never given when such relationships *certainly* exist, and it precludes the seeking of a dispensation even when the relationship is *doubtful*.

2174 The question as to whether this impediment is of divine law and, if so, to what extent, is of practical importance principally in judging the validity or nullity of the marriages of non-catholics, and a detailed discussion of the question is beyond the scope of the present volume. Traditionally, it has been regarded as certainly of divine law in the first degree of the direct line and probably so in the other degrees as well. The status of the impediment in the second degree of the collateral line, i.e. between brother and sister, has been disputed.[1] Beyond this, the impediment is certainly of purely ecclesiastical law, as is demonstrated by the fact that dispensations have been given for all other degrees.

2175 Since the relationship on which it depends is a permanent one, this impediment does not cease. It can be dispensed from in the collateral line, up to and including the third degree, i.e. uncle and niece or aunt and nephew, and this dispensation can now be granted by the local Ordinary or, in the circumstances mentioned in Cann. 1079 and 1080, by those indicated there. Under the 1917 Code, dispensation from what is now the third degree of the collateral line was granted only by the Holy See and for such reasons as 'the prevention of notable scandal, the settlement of important questions affecting the succession of property, or the relief of involved or very distressing family conditions'.[2] The same criteria remain a good guideline today.

Can. 1092 Affinity in any degree of the direct line invalidates marriage.

2176 *The impediment of affinity* is based upon a relationship through a valid marriage. It exists between the man and the blood relations of the woman, and between the woman and the blood relations of the man. The blood relations of the man are related by affinity to the woman in the same line and degree, and vice versa. Thus e.g. the child of a man by a former union is related to his wife in the first degree of the direct line of affinity; the man's brothers are related to her in the second degree of the collateral line of affinity. Although the relationship takes account of the collateral line, the impediment is now confined to the direct line. So a man cannot marry his deceased wife's descendants or ancestors, nor can a woman marry those related in the same way to her deceased husband. This is a change from the 1917 Code, under which the impediment extended to what was then the second degree of the collateral line, i.e. as far as first cousins of the former spouse.

2177 This impediment is not reserved to the Holy See, and so the local Ordinary has the power to dispense from it. However, he should have a very serious reason for doing so; under the previous law a dispensation from affinity in the first degree of the direct line was granted only very rarely and in extraordinary circumstances.[3]

Can. 1093 The impediment of public propriety arises when a couple live together after an invalid marriage, or from a notorious or public concubinage. It invalidates marriage in the first degree of the direct line between the man and those related by consanguinity to the woman, and vice versa.

2178 *The impediment of public propriety* is similar to the impediment of affinity in that it affects a man and the blood relatives of his partner, and vice versa. It differs from it both in its basis and in its extent. The basis for affinity is a valid marriage; the basis for the impedi-

---

[1] Cf. e.g. Capello V n.519, who refers to replies of the SCHO given in 1916 which said that in specific cases couples in such unions 'were not to be disturbed' and that their 'separation was not to be insisted on'. Even more interestingly, LE V 7288 reports that in 1977 Pope Paul VI in a communication to the SCDF declared himself competent to grant a dispensation in such a case and in favour of granting it in a specific case, saying that the impediment in question could be considered of ecclesiastical, not divine, law.

[2] SCSac instr I.VIII.1931: AAS 23(1931) 413–415: CLD 1 514–516.

[3] Cf. e.g. Capello V n.539.

ment of public propriety is a stable union other than marriage. It may arise from living together after an invalid marriage, or from simple cohabitation without any ceremony; in the latter case the cohabitation must be notorious or public, i.e. it must be well known and not just a clandestine liaison. It differs in extent in that it extends only to the first degree of the direct line. So a man cannot marry his partner's daughter or mother; a woman cannot marry her partner's father or son. Under the 1917 Code in its c.1078 the impediment extended to the second degree of the direct line.

2179 The local Ordinary can dispense from this impediment for a grave reason, unless of course there is a positive doubt as to whether the couple to be married might be father and daughter or mother and son.

Can. 1094 Those who are legally related by reason of adoption cannot validly marry each other if their relationship is in the direct line or in the second degree of the collateral line.

2180 *The impediment of legal adoption* is now substantially different from that prescribed in c.1078 of the 1917 Code. There the fact and the extent of the impediment was made dependent on the relevant civil law: if the civil law had such an impediment, then the Church's law also had, and to the degree laid down in the civil law. Since the precise force of the local civil law was not always clear, there could be confusion as to the existence of an impediment in canon law. The present law has solved the problem by erecting legal relationship on the ground of adoption into an ecclesiastical impediment independent of any such provision in the civil law. The impediment comes into existence through (civil) legal adoption, but not through fostering or any extra-legal arrangement. It extends to all degrees of the direct line and to the second degree of the collateral line. Thus, a person cannot marry any of his or her adoptive descendants or ancestors, nor can an adopted brother and sister marry.

2181 This impediment would cease if the relationship on which it is based ceased, e.g. by order of a civil court. The local Ordinary can dispense from it, provided of course that there is no danger that the relationship in question may also be one of a prohibited degree of consanguinity.

2182 *The former impediment of spiritual relationship*, which existed between a person being baptised and the sponsor or the minister (see 1917 Code c.1079), has been abolished.

Chapter IV
MATRIMONIAL CONSENT

Can. 1095 The following are incapable of contracting marriage:

1° those who lack sufficient use of reason;

2183 Without the use of reason a person cannot know what marriage is or what he or she is purporting to undertake in getting married. The person is incapable of a responsible human act and so cannot consent validly. It is not the *content of the intellect* that is in question here – that is considered under Can. 1096 – but *the fundamental ability to know*. If this is lacking entirely or seriously inadequate, the person simply cannot consent. Such a lack may result from a more or less permanent condition such as severe mental handicap, a psychotic mental illness or brain damage, or it may be due to a temporary deprival of intellectual function caused e.g. by drunkenness or drug abuse.

§2° those who suffer from a grave lack of discretion of judgement concerning the essential matrimonial rights and obligations to be mutually given and accepted.

A full discussion of all the implications of this paragraph, including its historical development from the philosophy of St Thomas Aquinas and from the jurisprudence of the Roman Rota, is clearly outside the scope of the present work. It will suffice to identify and comment briefly on the principal issues involved. 2184

The concept of discretion of judgement is concerned, not so much with intellectual or cognitive ability, as with being able to use such intellectual ability in a practical way. Any valid human decision is based on the person's powers of judgement which in turn rest on his or her knowledge, experience and maturity. The more important the area in which the decision is to be made, the better the powers of judgement need to be. This is especially true where the area concerned has implications which go beyond oneself and involves long-term consequences. Obviously the powers of judgement needed e.g. to buy a house are greater than those needed to buy a pencil. Where the decision has life-long implications and intimately involves another person, as does the decision to marry, it is clear that reasonably mature adult powers of judgement are called for. A bright child could have an adequate intellectual grasp of what marriage is and even of the obligations it imposes, but the child could not judge in a practical way what the real personal implications of the married state are for him or her, and so could not validly consent to marry. 2185

Since marriage is made for mankind and must therefore be presumed to be within the compass of most people, minor defects of judgement will not suffice to invalidate matrimonial consent. The lack of discretion of judgement must be a *grave* one. It must remove the person's powers of judgement completely or at least so cloud them that he or she is incapable of consenting to marriage. The gravity of the defect will, in a concrete case, be measured by evaluating the person's personality and abilities, as derived from a range of evidence of behaviour and usually also from reports by psychological or psychiatric experts. 2186

The factors causing a lack of discretion of judgement may be more or less permanent, such e.g. as very low intelligence, brain damage, mental illness, personality disorder. Alternatively they may be of a more transitory nature, such e.g. as the influence of alcohol or other drugs, serious psychological pressure due e.g. to pregnancy. Whether lasting or transitory, the factors involved must be operative at the time of marriage; anything coming later can have no effect on the act of consent. The two sorts of factor are not mutually exclusive and it can indeed happen that e.g. a transitory psychological pressure will combine with a personality disorder to deprive a person of the needed discretion of judgement. 2187

The 'essential rights and obligations to be mutually given and accepted' are not defined in detail but may be found in broad terms in Can. 1055 §1. Husband and wife commit themselves in the covenant of marriage to 'a partnership of their whole life ... which of its very nature is ordered to the well-being of the spouses and to the procreation and upbringing of children'. So they must know of the nature of this partnership and its implications and be able to appreciate the practical demands that these will make on them. 2188

3° those who because of causes of a psychological nature, are unable to assume the essential obligations of marriage.

Whereas the first two sections of this canon are concerned with the *act of consent itself* – whether there was any real act at all (1°), or whether that act was made with sufficient powers of judgement (2°) – this third section deals with the *object of the act of* 2189 *consent*. If a person is incapable of fulfilling the essential obligations of marriage, he or she cannot validly consent to assume them and so the marriage will be invalid.[1] The canon covers inability which is due to 'causes of a psychological nature'; it does not, therefore touch on e.g. the inability to fulfil and hence to assume involved in the impediment of impotence which, although there may be a psychological element present, is seen as physical in nature.

2190 As remarked above, the law does not list the essential obligations of marriage in detail, but from Can. 1055 §1 it can be seen that they are wider than the object of consent as formulated in the 1917 Code in its c.1081 §2, where matrimonial consent was stated to be 'an act of the will by which both parties give and accept a right to the body, perpetual and exclusive, for the purpose of acts of themselves suitable for the begetting of children'. Now, consent is explicitly seen as covering the total relationship between the spouses and not just its physical aspects: 'Matrimonial consent is an act of the will by which a man and a woman by an irrevocable covenant mutually give and accept one another for the purpose of establishing a marriage' (Can. 1057 §2).

2191 It is not possible to identify all the possible ways in which a person might be unable to assume the essential obligations. Firstly, this is an area where jurisprudence is still developing and so there is no definitive list of what obligations are deemed to be essential; secondly, the psychological sciences themselves, on which depend the identification and evaluation of the 'causes of a psychological nature', are also an area of development. Apart from conditions such as nymphomania or satyriasis which are fairly clear-cut in the way in which they affect capacity for particular obligations in marriage, most examples of invalidity under this section will be concerned with the more general capacity for a true, conjugal relationship. This is a wide field indeed, and the ways in which a person can be incapable of the relationship are many and varied.

2192 The canon speaks of being 'unable' to assume the essential obligations of marriage. This implies a serious psychological defect in the person and not merely a diminished capacity. The person must be morally incapable of taking on the obligations inherent in marriage. This incapacity must have been present at the time of marriage, otherwise it could hardly affect the person's consent.[2] Proof of such an incapacity will usually involve – in addition to the testimony of appropriate witnesses – expert evidence about the nature and effects of the alleged psychological defect. Evidence of mere behaviour, no matter how depraved, is not *of itself* evidence of inability. It must be shown that the behaviour was the result of a serious psychological defect and was not caused by ill-will or moral weakness.[3]

Can. 1096 §1 For matrimonial consent to exist, it is necessary that the contracting parties be at least not ignorant of the fact that marriage is a permanent partnership between a man and a woman, ordered to the procreation of children through some form of sexual cooperation.

§2 This ignorance is not presumed after puberty.

---

[1] The canon uses the term 'assume' rather than 'fulfil' to emphasise that this is a *defect of consent*: the fulfilment of an obligation lies in the future and accordingly is not so directly connected with the act of consent as is the assumption of the obligation which is part of the act itself.

[2] It may on occasion occur that the disorder, while not yet florid in its symptoms, may be, as is said, 'latent', yet nevertheless of such nature that its destructive effects upon a marital life are inexorably inevitable: schizophrenia e.g. can in some cases be an instance. The determination of such a situation is obviously a matter for competent professional advice.

[3] Cf. Pope John Paul II Address to the Roman Rota 5.II.1987 n.7: AAS 79(1987) 1457.

This canon is concerned with ignorance i.e. with the lack of due knowledge. It lays down in a negative way the very minimum knowledge needed for valid matrimonial consent: the parties must know that marriage is (a) a permanent partnership which is (b) heterosexual i.e. between a man and a woman, and (c) ordered to the procreation of children through some form of sexual cooperation. The first two elements, generally speaking, do not cause any great difficulty. Most people who have reached the use of reason know that marriage is a permanent partnership between a man and a woman. The availability of easy divorce and the consequent growth of the so-called 'divorce mentality', however, could lead to ignorance about the permanence of the relationship.[1]

2193

The area where, more than in any other, due knowledge may be lacking is the third. In regard to this area, the 1917 Code in its c.1082 §1 simply required that the parties know that marriage was for the generation of children; it did not explicitly require any knowledge of sexual cooperation. However, the commentators were in general agreement that it was necessary that the parties realise that this came about through some form of bodily cooperation, and a Rotal judgement *coram* Mattioli,[2] generally recognised as a definitive statement on the point, makes it clear that this cooperation must be known to be a physically sexual one. It is not sufficient that the parties know that children result from some indeterminate bodily cooperation; they must know that this cooperation is sexual.[3] This does not mean that they must have a full knowledge of sexual techniques, but they must have some knowledge of the fact of sexual intercourse.

2194

After puberty the presumption is that people have the knowledge necessary for valid matrimonial consent. However, this presumption can yield to contrary proof.

2195

Can. 1097 §1 Error of person renders a marriage invalid.

Error is a false judgement, a defect in understanding. Can. 126 states that 'an act is invalid when performed as a result of ... error which concerns the substance of the act ...'. Error of person, i.e. error regarding the identity of the person, directly concerns the substance of the act of matrimonial consent. In consenting to marriage a person consents to marry *this* person, not any other. So if A consents to marry B and, by some means or other, C is substituted for B without A's knowledge, there is no marriage. Apart from marriages by proxy or where the parties do not personally know one another beforehand, it is not easy to imagine such error occurring in practice.

2196

Can. 1097 §2 Error about a quality of the person, even though it be the reason for the contract, does not render a marriage invalid unless this quality is directly and principally intended.

A 'quality' of a person – e.g. his or her health, financial, professional or social status etc. – is normally something extrinsic to the person and not part of his or her identity. Accordingly, error regarding such a quality has no real effect on the consent to marry, even if the error was the reason for marrying. So e.g. if a man consents to marry a woman in the mistaken belief that she is wealthy, and would not have married her if he had known that she was not, his error about the quality of her financial status does not, of itself at least, invalidate his consent.

2197

---

[1] It should perhaps be noted that the concept of a so-called 'marriage' between either homosexual or lesbian partners – promoted by a minority in some modern, particularly Western societies – is flagrantly contrary both to the law of nature and to Christian teaching.

[2] Cf. c. Mattioli 25.XI.1964: SRRDec 56(1964) 867ff: CLD 6 623–5.

[3] Cf. Comm 15(1983) 232 at Can. 1050 where the word 'sexual' is expressly substituted for 'bodily' (*corporali*).

2198 In its c.1083 the 1917 Code contained two exceptions to this rule. One of these, error concerning the servile status of the other party, has been suppressed. The other exception was where the error about a quality amounted in fact to an error about the identity of the person. Recent Rotal and local jurisprudence developed the idea of *error redundans*, not without some controversy as to when a quality ceased to be accidental and became intrinsic to the person's identity. Earlier drafts of the present canon continued with the older wording but, after some study of the matter, the Revision Commission decided on the present text as corresponding to the doctrine of St Alphonsus and to the present-day jurisprudence of the Roman Rota.[1] The law now formally recognises that a quality which is of itself accidental to a person's identity may become an essential part of that to which the other person consents, whether as identifying the person or simply as a *conditio sine qua non*: in either case, if the consent is to be invalid, it must be made under the influence of an error about a quality which was directly and principally intended; the quality, erroneously believed to be present, must be an intrinsic part of the object of consent. The determination of this is yet, as it were, in its jurisprudential infancy, and its development by the ecclesiastical courts, both pontifical and local, will be watched with interest over the coming years.[2]

Can. 1098 A person contracts invalidly who enters marriage inveigled by deceit, perpetrated in order to secure consent, concerning some quality of the other party, which of its very nature can seriously disrupt the partnership of conjugal life.

2199 Can. 125 §2 states the general principle that 'an act performed ... as a result of deceit, is valid, unless the law provides otherwise'. The present canon is an example of where the law does precisely that. This is a new law and reflects once more the personalist approach of post-Vat. II law on marriage. Since marriage is seen very much as a relationship of mutual self-giving and openness, obviously anything like deceit, which is of its nature inimical to and destructive of these qualities, should have no place in it. While considerations such as these provide good reason for the existence of this law, they do not determine the precise reason why and how deceit invalidates marriage. It may be that the person perpetrating the deceit thereby demonstrates a fundamental and even invalidating flaw in his or her own consent, but what invalidates under the present canon is the error produced by the deceit in the deceived party which renders his or her consent invalid.

2200 The canon identifies a number of conditions which must be met before this deceit is regarded as invalidating matrimonial consent:
(a) There must be real deceit. This implies that one person, usually but not always or necessarily one of the parties to the marriage, perpetrates real deceit on a contracting party. It is not sufficient merely to intend to deceive, without actually doing so. Nor would the consent be invalid if the person concerned was not in fact deceived. The deceit must have succeeded.

---

[1] Cf. Comm 15(1983) 232 at Can. 1051 §2.

[2] Meanwhile, cf. e.g. Di Felice *La recente giurisprudenza rotale circa 'l'error qualitatis redundans in errorem personae'* in Dilexit Iustitiam: Studia in honorem Aurelii Card. Sabattani Rome 1984 39–50; Di Felice *Error in personam – dolus* EIC 43/44 (1987–1988) 33–43; Hennessy *A Requiem for 'error redundans'* Jur 49 (1989) 146–181; Navarrete *Error circa personam et error circa qualitates communes seu non identificantes personam (Can. 1097)* Per 82(1993) 637–667. Relevant references to both Rotal and local jurisprudence may be found in the appropriate section of *Special Subject Index* compiled in the Dublin Regional Marriage Tribunal (ed. Aidan McGrath ofm) 22.VIII.1994, a copy of which may be sought from the Secretary of CLSGBI.

(b) The deceit must have been 'perpetrated in order to secure consent'. There must be a causal connection between the deceit and the consent, otherwise the consent would not be invalid. Deceit, therefore, perpetrated e.g. purely to preserve one's good name or to avoid embarrassment or the like, would not invalidate.

(c) The deceit must concern 'some quality of the other party, which of its very nature can seriously disrupt the partnership of conjugal life'. The object of the deceit must be a quality pertaining to the other party to the marriage. A quality pertaining to a third party would not qualify. This quality must of its nature be capable of gravely disrupting the married life. There is no list of such qualities. The Code itself identifies only one, sterility (see Can. 1084 §3), and those who framed the law decided to leave it to doctrine and jurisprudence to draw up such a list if necessary.[1] Such a list would include ongoing psychiatric illness or personality disturbance; serious medical conditions such as syphilis, AIDS; pregnancy by someone else; a criminal record or immoral lifestyle; a previous marriage whether canonically valid or not. It can be argued that the criteria for determining what qualities would qualify for inclusion here are not purely objective, even if the canon does use the phrase 'of its very nature'; in a concrete case a particular quality might not be seen by those involved as very serious, while another might. In other words, the importance of a quality and the disruptive effect it could have, will depend on subjective as well as on objective factors.

Since the promulgation of the Code in 1983 there has been some debate about whether this canon represents natural or purely ecclesiastical law. This is not just of academic importance. For if it is of Church law only, it would affect only marriages which have been contracted after this Code came into effect, i.e. 27 November 1983. If it reflects natural law, then it does not matter when the marriage was celebrated. Supporters of both points of view may be found even in the Roman Rota. Without entering into the debate, the fact that the view that it is of natural law finds support in the Rota means that this view can be safely followed in local tribunals. As time passes the debate will become more academic. 2201

Can. 1099 Provided it does not determine the will, error concerning the unity or the indissolubility or the sacramental dignity of marriage does not vitiate matrimonial consent.

This canon addresses the problem of the capacity for true matrimonial consent of those people who hold beliefs or opinions about marriage which are contrary to the teaching and law of the Church. Repeating the substance of c.1084 of the 1917 Code, the law makes clear that the simple fact of adherence to an erroneous concept of marriage does not, of itself, have any deleterious effect on the act of consent. On the other hand, if, in a particular case, the error in question has 'determined the will' of a person contracting marriage, then the act of consent will have been vitiated. Commentators on the 1917 Code had distinguished *simple error*, which remained in the intellect alone, from *error pervicax* which radically affected a person's will. Today, in the light of a better understanding of human psychology, such a neat distinction is no longer admissible: the cooperation between the intellect and will is much too complex and subtle. Contemporary authors stress the need to examine each case carefully on its merits to see whether or not a person's erroneous ideas affected his or her *intention* at the time of marriage.[2] It is quite possible for people to adhere to a set of beliefs about marriage 2202

---

[1] Cf. Comm 15(1983) 233 at Can. 1052.
[2] Cf. Stankiewicz *De errore voluntatem determinante (Can. 1099) iuxta rotalem iurisprudentiam* Per 79(1990) 469–481; una Montisvidei c. Stankiewicz 25.IV.1991: ME 118(1993) 377–380 nn.3–6.

in general, while intending something very different for their own marriage. Certainly, no simple presumption in favour of nullity can be drawn from the *mere fact* that a person has shown that he or she holds a belief or opinion at variance with the Church's teaching concerning the exclusivity or permanence or sacramental dignity of marriage. On the other hand, there is room for a possible proof that the erroneous belief or opinion did in fact 'determine the will' in the act of professing consent.

2203 Closely related to the question of those who hold erroneous beliefs about marriage is the problem of baptised non-believers, i.e. those people who, although baptised into the Church, do not in any way practise their faith. The principle of this canon may be applied to these persons: the mere fact that they do not practise their faith is no basis for concluding that their matrimonial consent is defective. Nevertheless, it has been noted that 'the personal faith of the contracting parties does not constitute the sacramentality of matrimony, but the absence of personal faith weakens the validity of the sacrament'.[1] There is need therefore to investigate each case carefully, in order to discover whether the party's failure to practise the faith is the result of negligence, indifference or conscious hostility, i.e. whether or not the lack of faith has 'determined the will'.

Can. 1100 Knowledge of or opinion about the nullity of a marriage does not necessarily exclude matrimonial consent.

2204 A marriage may be invalid due to the existence of a diriment impediment or due to a defect of canonical form or due to a defect of consent. The law accepts that a party's knowledge or opinion about the possible nullity of the marriage being contracted does not of itself exclude the consent of that party. In other words, the simple fact that a party knows or believes, rightly or wrongly, that his or her marriage is null due to an undispensed impediment or some defect in the canonical form does not *ipso facto* vitiate the consent expressed by that party. In these circumstances, the act of consent as such is regarded as naturally sufficient but, because of extraneous factors, it may be deprived of its juridical efficacy. If the party was correct in his or her belief about the nullity of the marriage, this may be validated later – even retroactively without any renewal of consent (see Can. 1163 §1) – provided the consent expressed originally persists.

Can. 1101 §1 The internal consent of the mind is presumed to conform to the words or the signs used in the celebration of a marriage.

2205 Marriage is brought into being by the consent of the parties (see Can. 1057 §1) which is essentially an internal act. In order to have consequences in the public domain, this internal act must be manifested in some external manner. Common sense and human reason expect that the external manifestation of consent is in full harmony with a person's real internal intention. The alternative would be chaos and anarchy, with no-one ever being sure of what another person really meant. The presumption stated in this canon is an obvious one: a person who goes through a form of marriage is understood to have intended what he or she said or did during the celebration.

Can. 1101 §2 If, however, either or both of the parties should by a positive act of will exclude marriage itself or any essential element of marriage or any essential property, such party contracts invalidly.

2206 The presumption contained in §1 may be overturned if it can be demonstrated that one or other of the parties did in fact exclude from their consent either marriage itself or

---

[1] International Theological Commission, Propositions on the Doctrine of Christian Marriage 2.3, in *Contemporary perspectives on Christian Marriage: Propositions and Papers from the International Theological Commission* ed. R. Malone and J.R. Connery Chicago 1984 15.

some essential property or element of marriage. This exclusion is known in ecclesiastical jurisprudence as *simulation*. Traditionally, a distinction has been drawn between total simulation and partial simulation. *Total simulation* occurs where a person goes through a form of marriage but, at the same time, intends to take on none of the obligations involved in marriage; such a person goes through the external form of marriage for some purpose extraneous to marriage e.g. a marriage of convenience for the sole purpose of obtaining citizenship in a country when there is no real intention of ever establishing a 'partnership of life'. *Partial simulation* occurs where a party excludes from the act of consent some essential element or essential property of marriage. In this case, there is consent to marriage but with one or more substantial reservations. According to Can. 1056, the essential properties of marriage are unity and indissolubility. The essential elements of marriage are not listed anywhere in the Code but may be deduced from the description of marriage contained in Can. 1055 §1 i.e. the ordering of marriage to the good of the couple and to the procreation and upbringing of children.

2207 Rotal jurisprudence has traditionally related cases of partial simulation to the three so-called 'goods of marriage' identified by St Augustine. Thus, a person who excludes the possibility in marriage of procreative intercourse is said, in technical terms, to have an intention *contra bonum prolis*; a party who while marrying reserves the right to have sexual relations with a third party is understood to have an intention *contra bonum fidei*; finally, a person who marries while reserving the right to dissolve the marriage should difficulties arise is said to have an intention *contra bonum sacramenti*.

2208 It must be noted that mere inadvertence or non-inclusion of the essential elements or properties of marriage does not constitute simulation. The canon speaks of an exclusion 'by a positive act of the will'. In many cases, this exclusion will be stated explicitly by the party concerned; in some instances, however, it might well be implicit in a general attitude to life which is hostile or contrary to the Church and its teaching. A person's behaviour in the marriage itself does not provide unequivocal proof of simulation. The intention to exclude marriage itself or one of its essential elements or properties must be concomitant with the act of consent in order to vitiate that consent. Experience shows that people do change their minds after marriage and behave in ways that are contrary to the obligations positively taken on in marriage.

2209 While it is not easy, proof in a case of alleged simulation is not impossible. Among the elements of proof required in any investigation are the following: an admission by the person who simulated consent; the testimony of witnesses who knew of that person's intentions and observed his or her behaviour at the time of the marriage; a clearly established motive for simulating consent despite proceeding with the marriage ceremony; a careful examination of all the circumstances surrounding the celebration of the marriage. Whether the case is one of total or of partial simulation, the presumption of law contained in §1 stands in the way of any facile conclusion in favour of nullity.

Can. 1102 §1 Marriage cannot be validly contracted subject to a condition concerning the future.

2210 A condition may be defined as a stipulation by which an agreement is made contingent upon the verification or fulfilment of some circumstance or event which is not yet certain. The practice of attaching such conditions to matrimonial consent has long posed a problem for the Church. During the process of revision, the complex provisions of c.1092 1°–3° of the 1917 Code were simplified.[1] No longer is there any need

---

[1] Cf. Comm 3(1971) 77–78; 7(1975) 39; 15(1983) 234 at Can. 1056 §1. A short history of the evolution of the text of Can. 1102 may be found in Robitaille *Conditioned consent: Natural Law and Human Positive Law* Stud Can 26(1992) 75–110.

to find out whether the condition concerning the future is licit or immoral, certain or impossible, against the substance of marriage or not: any condition concerning the future attached to matrimonial consent renders marriage invalid. Whether this norm is of the natural law or of positive ecclesiastical law is a matter of some debate. Insofar as there are divergences in this area between the Latin Code and the Code of Canons of the Eastern Churches, it can be argued that the invalidating force in marriages contracted subject to conditions is of positive law and that it applies only to marriages contracted after 27 November 1983; however, insofar as the contents of this paragraph are consistent with what has been the constant jurisprudence of the Roman Rota, it may be understood to be a norm of the natural law and thus affects marriages contracted before 27 November 1983.[1]

Can. 1102 §2 Marriage entered into subject to a condition concerning the past or the present is valid or not, according as whatever is the basis of the condition exists or not.

§3 However, a condition as mentioned in §2 may not lawfully be attached except with the written permission of the local Ordinary.

2211 A condition concerning the past makes the consent to marriage contingent upon verification of some historical fact about which the person is uncertain; a condition concerning the present makes consent contingent upon verification of some present circumstance or reality about which the person is uncertain. While the Code of Canons of the Eastern Churches, in its c.826, rules out the possibility of any licit or valid conditional marriages, the Latin Code retains these two possibilities. In cases of this nature, there is no question of 'suspended consent'; rather, at the time of marriage, the act of consent is understood to be effective if the condition has been verified or fulfilled, i.e. if the specific historical fact or the specific present reality has been verified.

2212 The canon also requires that any such condition concerning the past or the present may lawfully be attached only with the written permission of the local Ordinary. This provision is clearly an effort to make the attachment of such conditions to matrimonial consent much more difficult, since it provides the local Ordinary with an express opportunity to scrutinise the proposed condition and only then to decide whether or not it would be reasonable to permit its insertion.

Can. 1103 A marriage is invalid which was entered into by reason of force or of grave fear imposed from without, even if not purposely, from which the person has no escape other than by choosing marriage.

2213 Can. 125 establishes the general principles in respect of the validity of juridical acts placed under the influence of force and fear. The second paragraph of that canon speaks of the validity of acts performed as a result of fear 'unless the law provides otherwise'. This canon constitutes such an exception to the general norm. It is important to draw the distinction between *force and fear*: force refers to an external physical or moral impulse which cannot be resisted; fear refers to the trepidation of the mind which is the result of an impending danger or impending evil produced by physical or moral force. Consent extracted by physical force is always invalid since the individual concerned is deprived of any freedom to do otherwise. Consent given under the influence of fear may be invalid if the qualifications contained in the canon are verified in the particular circumstances.

---

[1] Cf. Notaro *Retroattività–irretroattività del Can. 1102 par. 1* Il consenso matrimoniale condizionato: Dottrina e giurisprudenza rotale recente Città del Vaticano 1993 61–71.

2214 In order to vitiate marital consent, the fear must be *grave*. This gravity may be objective in nature, i.e. the evil threatened or the danger perceived is such that it would intimidate a reasonable and resolute person, e.g. loss of life, physical injury, imprisonment, exile; or it may be subjective, i.e. when the evil threatened is not ordinarily viewed as grave but is understood to be such due to some special disposition of the person in question, or due to some particular circumstances e.g. extreme youth, gross immaturity, low intelligence, parental dependence. The fear must be *imposed from outside*. This excludes from the scope of this canon irrational fears which may arise from within a person's temperament or psyche. Of course, various psychological factors in the person's make-up may assist those who have to assess the gravity of the fear experienced in a given case. The canon points out that the fear may be imposed unintentionally, i.e. it is not necessary to establish that the one imposing the pressure intended to inspire fear in the other person; nor is it necessary to demonstrate that the person imposing pressure did so in order to obtain consent to marriage. It is sufficient that the party who experienced the fear understood that, in the circumstances, he or she had no option but to contract marriage in order to escape the impending evil or danger threatened.

2215 The grave fear experienced by the party must also be *the cause of the marriage*, i.e. consenting to marriage must be the only way perceived by the party of avoiding the danger or evil which is threatened; if the person was, in the circumstances, easily capable of doing something else to escape the pressure or eliminate the fear, this canon cannot be applied. A marriage is thus invalid only if it was contracted *because of fear*; it is regarded as valid if contracted *with fear*.

2216 Jurisprudence has distinguished two different types of fear: *common fear* which is inspired by threats made by a hostile or brutal person; *reverential fear* which is inspired by the expectation of harm arising out of the displeasure of someone to whom special reverence is owed, e.g. a parent, or superior; in reverential fear, there are often no threats: the gravity of the fear is related to the relationship of dependence upon the person respected and the expectation that this relationship will be undermined or destroyed unless consent is given to marriage.[1]

2217 In considering cases of alleged nullity on the ground of grave fear, an ecclesiastical court may reach moral certainty concerning nullity in two ways: a *direct* proof of nullity rests on the verification of the qualities of grave fear listed in the canon; an *indirect* proof rests on the demonstration of the party's aversion to marriage: this aversion refers strictly to a lack of desire to marry a particular partner; in order to have probative value, it must be shown to have existed at the time consent was expressed.

2218 Many canonists commenting on the 1917 Code held that this was a norm of purely ecclesiastical positive law, while a smaller number insisted that it was a norm of the natural law.[2] The Pontifical Commission for the Interpretation of the Code issued a response on 15.XI.1986 in which it indicated that this canon was to be applied to marriages of non-catholics as well as those of catholics.[3] This would seem to support the position that Can. 1103 is an expression of the natural law. However, there are some eminent canonists who believe that the issue has not been resolved and who contend that the Commission's response was over extensive rather than simply declarative.[4]

---

[1] In fact, in a survey of Rotal Judgments 1911–1942 it was discovered that the vast majority of cases of grave fear considered before the Rota involve the parents or grandparents of one of the parties: cf. Doheny *Canonical Procedures in Matrimonial Cases* I Milwaukee 1948 917–942.

[2] Gasparri e.g. favoured the view that the canon was of positive law (II nn.840–841), while Cappello considered that it was of natural law (V n.609).

[3] Cf. AAS 79(1987) 1132.

[4] Cf. Navarrete *Responsa Pontificiae Commissionis Codici Iuris Canonici authentice recognoscendo* Per 73(1988) 497–510. This has been translated into English, along with a contrary view, by Wrenn *Urban Navarrete S.J. and the response of the Code Commission on force* Jur 51(1991) 119–137.

Book IV *The Sanctifying Office of the Church*

Can. 1104 §1 To contract marriage validly it is necessary that the contracting parties be present together, either personally or by proxy.

2219 While Cann. 1095–1103 dealt with possible defects in the act of consent, Cann. 1104–1106 deal with specific matters relating to the manifestation of matrimonial consent. First and foremost, the law requires that the parties consenting to marriage must be present together in order to exchange consent validly; they may be present in person, i.e. be physically together in the one place at the same time, or they may be present by proxy, i.e. with someone there to represent the absent party. This requirement is a natural corollary of the canonical form of marriage (see Can. 1108). The present canon repeats almost verbatim c.1088 §1 of the 1917 Code, prior to which, it had been possible to contract marriage by letter.[1] The provisions of this canon are of positive ecclesiastical law. In 1949 the Holy Office stated that the necessity of personal presence or presence by proxy applied also to the marriages of baptised non-catholics.[2] However, in the light of Can. 11, it must be concluded that this norm applies only to those who were baptised or received into the catholic Church and have not defected from it by a formal act.

Can. 1104 §2 The spouses are to express their matrimonial consent in words; if, however, they cannot speak, then by equivalent signs.

2220 This paragraph enunciates an important principle concerning the manner of manifesting matrimonial consent. Ordinarily, this consent is to be expressed 'in words', i.e. some verbal formula must be used by both parties to indicate clearly and unequivocally their intention to contract marriage. While the Code does not require that a specific form of words be used, the civil law may demand a set formula. Provision is also made in the canon for parties who are unable to speak. In these circumstances, the verbal formula is to be replaced by 'equivalent signs'. Such signs must be unambiguous and clearly understood by the witnesses and by the one who asks for and receives the consent in the name of the Church.

Can. 1105 §1 For a marriage by proxy to be valid, it is required:

1° that there be a special mandate to contract with a specific person;

2° that the proxy be designated by the mandator and personally discharge this function.

2221 Specific matters concerning marriage by proxy are dealt with in this canon. In order for such a marriage to be valid, the law demands that the party who is unable to be present for the exchange of consent designate someone to represent him or her. This designation is to be done by means of a special document. The document must state clearly the purpose of the proxy, i.e. to express matrimonial consent on behalf of the mandator; the identity of the intended spouse is to be stated unambiguously in the mandate; so, too, must the identity of the person who has been designated by the mandator. The law makes it clear that this duty must be discharged personally by the proxy: it cannot be delegated to another, even with the consent of the mandator.

2222 The universal law gives no indication of any particular qualifications for a proxy. Thus, the proxy may be male or female, regardless of the gender of the absent spouse; there is no requirement that the proxy be a catholic, or even a christian; nor is there any specific indication about the age of a proxy. These are matters for which a local

---

[1] Cf. SRRDec una Ravennaten. 19.I.1910: AAS 2(1910) 297ff.
[2] Cf. CLD 3 446.

Ordinary may wish to legislate. Of course, he may also wish to add further specific requirements since all marriages to be entered by proxy are to be referred to the local Ordinary (see Can. 1071 §1 7°). It should be noted that marriages by proxy are not generally permitted in countries with a Common Law tradition; this is a further reason for referring such cases to the local Ordinary (see Can. 1071 §1 2°).

Can. 1105 §2 For the mandate to be valid, it is to be signed by the mandator, and also by the parish priest or local Ordinary of the place in which the mandate is given or by a priest delegated by either of them or by at least two witnesses, or it is to be drawn up in a document which is authentic according to the civil law.

Since the validity of a marriage by proxy depends upon the mandate appointing the proxy, it is essential that this document be valid. The canon foresees two ways in which this validity may be assured. Firstly, the mandate can be prepared as an ecclesiastical document which must be signed by the party appointing the proxy; this document must also be signed by the parish priest or local Ordinary of the place where the mandate is given or by a priest delegated by either of these or by at least two witnesses. Secondly, where such marriages are permitted by the law of the state, the mandate can be prepared as an authentic document according to civil law, with due observance of all the necessary formalities and requirements laid down by that civil law. 2223

Can. 1105 §3 If the mandator cannot write, this is to be recorded in the mandate and another witness added who is to sign the document; otherwise, the mandate is invalid.

The law makes special provision for a party who is unable to write and who wishes to appoint a proxy. In these circumstances, the validity of the mandate requires that the fact of the mandator's inability to write be recorded in the document itself which must then be signed by at least one further witness in addition to those mentioned in §2. 2224

Can. 1105 §4 If the mandator revokes the mandate, or becomes insane, before the proxy contracts in his or her name, the marriage is invalid, even though the proxy or the other contracting party is unaware of the fact.

While the proxy acts in the name of the one who appointed him or her, it is the mandator's consent which must be sufficient at the time of marriage. Hence if, before the proxy contracts the marriage on his or her behalf, the mandator revokes the mandate i.e. refuses to consent to marriage, or becomes insane i.e. is rendered incapable of consent, then the marriage will be invalid, even if the proxy or the other party knew nothing about it. However, this does not mean that, at the time of the marriage by proxy, the absent party must be fully aware and conscious of what is being done in his or her name; it is sufficient that he or she has not revoked the mandate or become incapable of consent. 2225

Can. 1106 Marriage can be contracted through an interpreter, but the parish priest may not assist at such a marriage unless he is certain of the trustworthiness of the interpreter.

The function of an interpreter is to translate what is being said in one language into another language which is intelligible to those who are concerned in what is happening. The one who is to receive the consent in the name of the Church or the witnesses may not be able to understand the language used by the parties. In these circumstances, the law sanctions the use of an interpreter. However, before permitting such 2226 a marriage to take place, the parish priest must be satisfied that the interpreter is worthy of trust, i.e. that he or she will translate faithfully and accurately what is being said from one language into the other; if after careful enquiry he is not thus satisfied, he may not assist at the marriage.

Can. 1107 Even if a marriage has been entered into invalidly by reason of an impediment or defect of form, the consent given is presumed to persist until its withdrawal has been established.

2227 The law draws a distinction between *natural consent* and *legal consent*. Cann. 1095–1103 explored the ways in which a marriage might be invalid due to a defect of consent. Those considerations apart, a marriage might be invalid due to an undispensed impediment or to a defect in canonical form. In these cases, the consent expressed by the parties may well be naturally sufficient but, because of the impediment or defect of form, it is deprived of its legal efficacy. The law here states an important presumption: the consent expressed in these circumstances is presumed to endure unless and until the contrary is established. This presumption is of immense significance in matters of simple and retroactive validation (see Cann. 1156–1165).

Chapter V
THE FORM OF THE CELEBRATION OF MARRIAGE

Can. 1108 §1 Only those marriages are valid which are contracted in the presence of the local Ordinary or parish priest or of the priest or deacon delegated by either of them, who, in the presence of two witnesses, assists, in accordance however with the rules set out in the following canons, and without prejudice to the exceptions mentioned in Cann. 144, 1112 §1, 1116 and 1127 §§2–3.

2228 While the consent of both parties is sufficient to establish a marriage according to the natural law, certain external solemnities are required for validity by positive ecclesiastical laws. These requirements are the result of the Church's struggle to eliminate the practice of clandestine marriages, i.e. marriages which took place without any external formalities and often without any proof of marriage in the external forum. The Fourth Lateran Council took action against these marriages by insisting that the banns be published on three successive days, by suspending any priest who blessed clandestine marriages and by imposing suitable penalties upon the parties concerned.[1] However, the Council did not declare these marriages invalid; indeed, the punitive action taken against all concerned would seem to imply a recognition that something valid but simply illicit had taken place.

2229 It was the Council of Trent, at its 24th session, which took decisive action against clandestine marriages. In the famous decree *Tametsi*, marriages were declared invalid unless they took place before the parish priest or another priest delegated by him and in the presence of two or three witnesses. As proof that a marriage had been celebrated according to law, each parish was required to have a book in which the names of the parties and the witnesses were to be inscribed, together with the date and time of the wedding.[2] This decree was to be promulgated in each parish and to come into

---

[1] Cf. Fourth Lateran Council con 51: *Conciliorum Oecumenicorum Decreta* Bologna 1991 258.

[2] Council of Trent Decree 'Tametsi': DS 1813–1816; full text in *Conciliorum Oecumenicorum Decreta* 755–757.

effect thirty days after its promulgation. Due to the upheaval in Europe caused by the Reformation, 'Tametsi' was not promulgated evenly throughout the world. So, for over three hundred years after the Council of Trent, in parts of the world clandestine marriages continued to take place; these were regarded as illicit but not invalid if 'Tametsi' had not been promulgated in the place where they took place. This situation was corrected by the Decree *Ne Temere* issued by the Sacred Congregation for the Council in 1907.[1] The provisions of 'Tametsi' were made universal law. Henceforth, any marriages celebrated by catholics without the assistance of the parish priest of the place of marriage or the local Ordinary or a priest delegated by either of them, or without the presence of two witnesses, were considered to be invalid. This legislation passed into cc.1094–1095 of the 1917 Code. Apart from a few minor alterations, it continues to form part of the current Code.

According to the present law, the canonical form of marriage consists in the declaration of consent by the parties, in the presence of two witnesses, before one of the following: 2230

(a) the local Ordinary (see Cann. 134 §§1–2, 368);

(b) the parish priest (see Cann. 519, 530 4°);

(c) a priest delegated by either of the above (see Can. 1111);

(d) a deacon delegated by the local Ordinary or the parish priest (see Can. 1111).

The proper delegation or appointment of the last two qualified witnesses is essential if the marriage is not to be null and void due to defect of form. The canon makes explicit reference to four canons which foresee possible exceptions to the universal demand for the canonical form of marriage: these include the case of common error or positive or probable doubt about the delegation of the one to receive the consent in the name of the Church (see Can. 144); the case of a lay person who is delegated in certain circumstances to act as the qualified witness (see Can. 1112 §1); the case of a marriage contracted before witnesses alone in certain foreseen circumstances (see Can. 1116); the case of a marriage where the appropriate ecclesiastical authority has granted a dispensation from canonical form (see Can. 1127 §§2–3). 2231

The participation of the deacon as a qualified witness is a post-Vat. II innovation. Originally, permanent deacons were permitted to assist at marriages only 'when no priest is present'.[2] In 1968, transient deacons were also permitted to assist.[3] By this time, the condition requiring the absence of a priest affected the licitness of the celebration, not its validity.[4] There are no guidelines or qualifications contained in the law concerning those who are to be witnesses at a marriage. Nevertheless, they should be of such an age and psychological condition that they are capable of understanding and fulfilling the role demanded of them. 2232

Can. 1108 §2 Only that person who, being present, asks the contracting parties to manifest their consent and in the name of the Church receives it, is understood to assist at a marriage.

The local Ordinary or parish priest or deacon or appointed lay person before whom the parties are to exchange their consent is said to 'assist' at a marriage. This paragraph 2233

---

[1] Cf. SCCo 'Ne Temere' 2.VIII.1907: ASS 40(1907) 527ff: DS 3468–3474.

[2] Cf. Pope Paul VI mp SDO 22 4: CLD 6 582.

[3] Cf. DVCom rep 26.III.1968: CLD 7, 133 – and this despite a private response given by SCDW on 30.VIII.1968 which denied that the norms of SDO could be applied to deacons preparing for priesthood: CLD 7 689.

[4] Cf. DVCom rep 4.IV.1969: CLD 7 134.

defines clearly what is understood by assistance in these circumstances. The qualified witness must first ask the parties to express their consent; this consent must then be received or accepted by the same qualified witness 'in the name of the Church'. The person who assists is not a passive listener or spectator. The Congregation for the Doctrine of the Faith has made it clear that the one who assists must have an 'active role' in the expression of consent;[1] this was also the understanding of the Commission which prepared the present text.[2]

Can. 1109 Within the limits of their territory, the local Ordinary and the parish priest by virtue of their office validly assist at the marriages not only of their subjects, but also of non-subjects, provided one or other of the parties is of the latin rite. They cannot assist if by sentence or decree they have been excommunicated, placed under interdict or suspended from office, or been declared to be such.

2234 By virtue of the law, the local Ordinary, within his diocese, can assist at the marriages of those who live in the diocese, or of those who are domiciled elsewhere but happen to be in his diocese. Similarly, by virtue of the law, the parish priest, within his parish, can assist at the marriages of his parishioners and of those who happen to be in his parish but who are domiciled elsewhere. The law adds an important limitation to this jurisdiction: at least one of the parties to the marriage must be of the latin rite. A local Ordinary or a parish priest of the latin rite may not assist validly at the marriage of two eastern-rite catholics. It is to be noted that the practice of receiving the sacraments in the latin rite, even over an extended period, does not entail a change of rite (see Can. 112 §2).

2235 The local Ordinary or parish priest cannot assist validly at a marriage if, by judicial sentence or decree, he himself has been excommunicated, or suspended, or placed under interdict, or if an automatic censure which he has incurred has been declared by the appropriate ecclesiastical authority. The loss of the power to assist at marriages is the natural consequence of these penalties (see Cann. 1331–1333).

Can. 1110 A personal Ordinary and a personal parish priest by virtue of their office validly assist, within the confines of their jurisdiction, at the marriages only of those of whom at least one party is their subject.

2236 This canon extends the principle of Can. 1109 to personal Ordinaries and personal parish priests, i.e. those who have jurisdiction over a specified group of persons e.g. military ordinaries, or parish priests of particular nationalities within a territory. Such Ordinaries and parish priests, by virtue of the law, can assist validly at marriages provided that one of the parties at least is their subject and provided the marriage takes place 'within the confines of their jurisdiction'. In order to assist validly at marriages outside of these circumstances, personal Ordinaries and parish priests require the proper delegation.

Can. 1111 §1 As long as they validly hold office, the local Ordinary and the parish priest can delegate to priests and deacons the faculty, even the general faculty, to assist at marriages within the confines of their territory.

2237 Priests and deacons may be delegated to assist at marriages by the local Ordinary or the parish priest. Two forms of delegation are envisaged in this canon: *general delega-*

---

[1] Cf. SCDF rep 28.XI.1975: CLD 8 820–821.

[2] Cf. Comm 8(1976) 36–37 at Can. 1094 §2; 10(1978) 86–87 at Can. 311.

tion given for all marriages, and *special delegation* given for one particular marriage. According to the canon, the local Ordinary can grant either kind of delegation for marriages to be celebrated within his diocese, while the parish priest can do so for marriages to be celebrated within his parish. The competence of the local Ordinary or parish priest to grant such delegation is dependent upon the office they hold. Should they retire or resign or otherwise lose their office, they also lose the power to delegate others to assist at marriages.

Can. 1111 §2 In order that the delegation of the faculty to assist at marriages be valid, it must be expressly given to specific persons; if there is question of a special delegation, it is to be given for a specific marriage; if however there is question of a general delegation, it is to be given in writing.

The conditions for a valid delegation to assist at marriages are set out clearly: 2238
(a) it must be given to determined persons; this determination may be by naming the individual or individuals concerned, or by specifying the office they hold;
(b) it must be given expressly: presumed or tacit delegation is not valid;
(c) if it is a special delegation, then it must somehow identify the specific marriage; this need not be done in writing – indeed, it can be given by word of mouth, but the fact of the delegation must be noted;
(d) if it is a general delegation, then it must be given in writing. The present text reflects a great deal of discussion on this point during the revision process.[1] A person with general delegation may sub-delegate it in individual cases (see Can. 137 §3).

Should there be any positive or probable doubt about the validity of the delegation or about the fact of its having been granted, or should there be common error about either of these matters, the Church supplies the necessary jurisdiction (see Can. 144). 2239

Can. 1112 §1 Where there are neither priests nor deacons, the diocesan Bishop can delegate lay persons to assist at marriages, if the Bishops' Conference has given its prior approval and the permission of the Holy See has been obtained.

Following Vat. II many Bishops petitioned the Holy See to ask if, in the absence of a priest or deacon, a lay person might be designated as the official witness at a marriage. After much study and reflection, the Congregation for the Sacraments issued a private instruction on the matter[2] containing norms by which, in exceptional circumstances, a lay person could be appointed to assist at marriages. These provisions have been incorporated into the current Code. A lay person may now be delegated to assist at a marriage, 'where there are neither priests nor deacons'. This phrase may be interpreted as meaning that the delegation may be given only where priests and deacons are not and will never be available, or as meaning that it may be given where priests and deacons are not available for some length of time. The latter interpretation is more in keeping with the practice of the Church prior to this Code.[3] By analogy with Can. 1116 §1 2°, the absence of a priest or deacon for more than a month is sufficient to warrant the delegation of a lay person. Moreover, it would appear that the absence of priests or deacons may also be interpreted as the absence of suitable or qualified priests or deacons, since permission has been given by the Holy See for lay persons to 2240

---

[1] Cf. Comm 3(1971) 78; 8(1976) 41 at Can. 1096 §2; 10(1978) 89 at Can. 313 §2. It is the view of this commentary that the requirement of a written delegation is for the validity of that delegation.
[2] Cf. instr *Sacramentalem indolem* 15.V.1974: CLD 8 815–818.
[3] Ibid.

assist at the marriages of emigrants and refugees who do not speak the language of the country.[1]

2241 The law lays down certain conditions which must be fulfilled before a Bishop can delegate a lay person to assist at a marriage. First and foremost, the Bishops' Conference must have given its approval of this course of action in the given circumstances. Then the permission of the Holy See must be obtained: this permission would obviously be included in the recognition given by the Holy See to the decisions of the Bishops' Conference (see Can. 455 §2). Indeed, the complementary legislation of some countries makes it clear that, having obtained the recognition of the Holy See for the Bishops' Conference decision, no further application to the Holy See by the diocesan Bishop is necessary.[2] Strangely, however, in some countries the Conference has approved the delegation of lay people in principle but in such terms that each Bishop must apply directly to the Holy See for permission before actually delegating anyone.[3]

2242 It must be noted that the faculty to delegate lay persons is given by law *only to the diocesan Bishop* and not to any other local Ordinary. Since the law has made no distinction, the lay person may be granted general delegation or special delegation, depending upon the precise circumstances.

Can. 1112 §2 A suitable lay person is to be selected, capable of giving instruction to those who are getting married, and fitted to conduct the marriage liturgy properly.

2243 The canon contains a brief description of the type of lay person considered suitable for the role of assisting at marriages. Should any of the qualities listed in this canon be missing in the delegated lay person, the validity of the marriage is not in any way affected. It must be remembered that the lay person is acting as a qualified witness and is in no way exercising the power of governance when he or she assists at a marriage.[4] Consequently, in conducting the liturgy of marriage, he or she may not do anything reserved to a priest or deacon.

Can. 1113 Before a special delegation is granted, provision is to be made for all those matters which the law prescribes to establish the freedom to marry.

2244 One of the fundamental purposes of a pre-nuptial investigation is to establish whether or not any impediment stands in the way of the parties' freedom to marry. The manner of this investigation is determined by the Bishops' Conference (see Can. 1067). According to the present canon, this inquiry is to be conducted before a special delegation is granted. While the law does not state it explicitly, there is no doubt that the responsibility for carrying out the investigation rests with the one who is to grant the delegation, i.e. the local Ordinary or the parish priest. He may carry it out himself or entrust it to someone else, but he must make sure that it is done. This norm of law applies to cases of special delegation only and not to those of general delegation. It is a provision which affects the lawfulness of marriage, not its validity.[5]

Can. 1114 One who assists at a marriage acts unlawfully unless he has satisfied himself of the parties' freedom to marry in accordance with the law and, whenever he assists by virtue of a general delegation, has satisfied himself of the parish priest's permission, if this is possible.

---

[1] Cf. SCSDW rep 20.I.1983: CLD 10 178–181.
[2] This is the case e.g. in Canada and Peru: cf. LCE 139, 558.
[3] Thus e.g. in Bolivia, Chile, India, Mexico, Venezuela: cf. LCE 105, 172, 345, 464, 727.
[4] Cf. Comm 15(1983) 236 at Can. 1066.
[5] Cf. Comm 10(1978) 89 at Can. 314.

In all cases involving a delegation to assist at a marriage, the priest or deacon or lay person must be convinced personally that the parties are in fact free to marry. The pre-nuptial investigation might well be carried out by someone else, but this does not absolve the one who is to assist from the responsibility of being sure that no impediment stands in the way of the valid celebration of the marriage. Moreover, if the priest or deacon assists by virtue of a general delegation, he is required to obtain the parish priest's permission. This is not delegation, nor does it pertain to the validity of the marriage. Rather it is an acknowledgement of the fact that the law entrusts the assistance at marriages in a special way to the parish priest (see Can. 530 4°). Such permission need not be explicit on every occasion; it may be tacit or presumed. 2245

Can. 1115 Marriages are to be celebrated in the parish in which either of the contracting parties has a domicile or a quasi-domicile or a month's residence or, if there is question of *vagi*, in the parish in which they are actually residing. With the permission of the proper Ordinary or the proper parish priest, marriages may be celebrated elsewhere.

This canon determines in principle the place, or better the territory, in which a particular marriage may be celebrated. According to c.1097 §2 of the 1917 Code, the proper place of marriage ordinarily was the parish of the bride. The present law is of much broader scope, giving the couple a wide choice. Thus the marriage may take place in any of the following places: the parish where either party has a domicile (see Can. 102 §1) or a quasi-domicile (see Can. 102 §2); the parish where either party has been resident for a month; some other place provided the permission of the proper Ordinary or parish priest has been obtained. Unlike the previous discipline (see c.1097 §1 3° of the 1917 Code), the marriage can take place in the parish of either spouse without any reference to the parish priest of the other partner. The sole exception to this concerns the marriage of *vagi* (see Can. 100): these are to be married in the parish where one or both of the parties is actually resident. Such marriages must be referred to the local Ordinary (see Can. 1071 §1°). 2246

Can. 1116 §1 If one who, in accordance with the law, is competent to assist, cannot be present or be approached without grave inconvenience, those who intend to enter a true marriage can validly and lawfully contract in the presence of witnesses only:

    1° in danger of death;

    2° apart from danger of death, provided it is prudently foreseen that this state of affairs will continue for a month.

Following on c.1098 of the 1917 Code, the law recognises the validity of marriages contracted before witnesses alone if a person competent by law to assist at marriages 'cannot be present or approached without grave inconvenience'. This is referred to as the extraordinary form of marriage. It is used validly and lawfully in two distinct sets of circumstances. Firstly, if one or both of the parties is in danger of death, i.e. if there is reason to believe that death may occur e.g. due to illness or injury or war. Secondly, outside the danger of death, if there is good reason to believe that no qualified witness will be available for a month. 2247

The law speaks about 'one who, in accordance with the law, is competent to assist' at marriages. This includes the local Ordinary, the parish priest, a priest or deacon delegated by either of them, and a lay person delegated in accordance with Can. 1112 §1. The fact that none of these people is actually present at a time when a marriage is to take place is not sufficient reason to use the extraordinary form of marriage; they 2248 must be physically absent from the place of marriage, understood in the sense that they are impeded from intervening for some considerable time, due to a grave inconvenience which may affect either the qualified witness or the parties themselves.[1]

2249 This extraordinary form may be used only by those parties 'who intend to enter a true marriage', i.e. who intend that the union which they enter in the presence of witnesses alone will have the full effects intended by the Church. Thus, if the circumstances foreseen by this canon are verified in either situation mentioned, a civil marriage between two catholics could have full canonical effects, provided that the couple intended to establish a true marriage. However, this canon does not cover the situation of two catholics who contract a merely civil marriage in either of the situations foreseen by the canon, but whose intention is later to enter marriage 'properly' before the Church whenever the opportunity arises: in that case, the parties do not intend there and then to enter a true marriage.

2250 Although the law permits consent to be exchanged without a qualified witness who asks for the consent and receives it in the name of the Church, it still requires that this consent be expressed in the presence of at least two witnesses. No qualifications are given for these witnesses but they must be capable of observing and understanding what takes place. These people have no role to play in asking for or receiving the consent of the parties. The Congregation for the Sacraments had indicated at one time that local Ordinaries should train lay people for the role of witnesses to marriage in the extraordinary form:[2] it was felt that these people could be of help to the parties wishing to enter marriage and could record the celebration of the marriage and make sure that it was properly registered. These instructions, however, have been rendered superfluous by the provisions of Can. 1112 §1.

Can. 1116 §2 In either case, if another priest or deacon is at hand who can be present, he must be called upon and, together with the witnesses, be present at the celebration of the marriage, without prejudice to the validity of the marriage in the presence of only the witnesses.

2251 It is possible that, although no priest or deacon competent to assist in accordance with the law is present, another priest or deacon may be at hand. The law makes it clear that such a cleric cannot assist at the marriage, since he is not duly delegated to do so. Nevertheless, such a person is to be invited to the celebration along with the witnesses. His presence at the celebration will enhance the liturgical and religious dimension of the marriage, but it has no effect whatever on the validity of the marriage before the witnesses. In these circumstances, the priest or deacon may not ask for or receive the consent of the parties.[3]

2252 No indication is given in the law concerning the rite for the celebration of marriage according to the extraordinary form. It is sufficient that the parties manifest clearly and unambiguously to the witnesses their intention to enter marriage as understood by the Church. This may be done within a liturgy of the Word. The witnesses are to

---

[1] Cf. CCom repp 10.XI.1925, 10.III.1928, 25.VII.1931, 3.V.1945: CLD 1 542, 3 454.

[2] Cf. SCS instr 7.XII.1971: CLD 7 755.

[3] During the preparation of this text, a proposal was submitted to the effect that, to the *priest or deacon* referred to in this §2, there be added a *lay person*, understood in the terms of Can. 1112. It was rightly pointed out by the Revision Commission that, if this were done, it would render nugatory the 'extraordinary form' of Can. 1116 – itself designed to meet a very real and practical pastoral situation – since the lay person envisaged in Can. 1112 would in fact be 'competent to assist' at the marriage in accordance with the law: cf. Comm 15(1983) 237 at Can. 1071 §2.

refrain from saying or doing anything during the celebration of marriage in this form which is reserved to a priest or deacon. After the marriage, the fact that it has taken place should be noted and the parish priest of the place of marriage should be informed as soon as possible. Responsibility for this rests with those enumerated in Can. 1121 §2.

Can. 1117 The form prescribed above is to be observed if at least one of the parties contracting marriage was baptised in the catholic Church or received into it and has not by a formal act defected from it, without prejudice to the provisions of Can. 1127 §2.

2253 This canon replaces the more complicated c.1099 of the 1917 Code. The canonical form of marriage prescribed in Can. 1108 is obligatory upon all those who have been baptised or received into the catholic Church, provided that they have not defected from it 'by a formal act'. Thus, if any member of the catholic Church should attempt to enter marriage without the participation of a competent priest or deacon and the presence of two witnesses in circumstances other than those foreseen in Cann. 1112 §1, 1116 §1 or 1127 §§1–2, that marriage will be regarded as invalid. On the other hand, a person who was baptised or received into the catholic Church and who subsequently defected from it by a formal act is not bound by the canonical form of marriage; if such a person contracts marriage without the presence of a competent priest or deacon and two witnesses, all else being equal, that marriage is regarded as valid.

2254 For an analysis of the concept and implications of *defection from the catholic Church by a formal act*, see our commentary on Can. 1086 §1.

Can. 1118 §1 A marriage between catholics, or between a catholic party and a baptised non-catholic, is to be celebrated in the parish church. By permission of the local Ordinary or of the parish priest, it may be celebrated in another church or oratory.

2255 While Can. 1115 determined the place of marriage in broad terms, this canon specifies the actual location of the celebration. Ordinarily, a marriage between two catholics or between a catholic and a baptised non-catholic is to take place in the parish church of either party, in accordance with Can. 1115. With the permission of the local Ordinary or the parish priest, the wedding may take place in another church or oratory.

Can. 1118 §2 The local Ordinary can allow a marriage to be celebrated in another suitable place.

2256 For a marriage to take place outside of that foreseen in §1, the permission of the local Ordinary is required. The 1917 Code, in its c.1109 §2, required that this permission could be given only in an extraordinary case and for a just and reasonable cause. During the preparation of this Code, it was felt that the Ordinary should be left free to consider each case on its own merits.[1] Nevertheless, the Commission made it clear that any such concession was indeed extraordinary.[2] 'Another suitable place' could include a hall, a private house, a church belonging to another denomination etc.

Can. 1118 §3 A marriage between a catholic party and an unbaptised party may be celebrated in a church or in another suitable place.

2257 In the case of a non-sacramental marriage, the law permits the celebration to take place in a church or another appropriate place. No special permission is required from

---

[1] Cf. Comm 10(1978) 104 at Can. 329 §2.
[2] Cf. Comm 15(1983) 237 at Can. 1073 §2.

the local Ordinary for these marriages. However, the parish priest should be careful to follow any diocesan regulations on the matter. Care should be taken by the parish priest – and by the local Ordinary in the cases foreseen in §2 – when giving permission to celebrate marriages outside a church, since in some countries the marriage can have civil effects only when celebrated in a specially licensed building.

Can. 1119 Apart from a case of necessity, in the celebration of marriage those rites are to be observed which are prescribed in the liturgical books approved by the Church, or which are acknowledged by lawful custom.

2258 As a sacrament, marriage is to be celebrated with 'great reverence and due care' (Can. 840). However, in conformity with the general principle of Can. 2, the Code does not determine the liturgical rites to be followed in the celebration of marriage. These are to be found in the liturgical books approved by the competent ecclesiastical authority (see Can. 1120); they may be found also in legitimate local customs which have been received by the appropriate authority (see Can. 23). The *Rite of Marriage* issued in 1969 foresaw different forms of the liturgical celebration of marriage, some within the Mass, others within a liturgy of the Word.[1] Whatever the precise details of any rite used, the law recognises that the liturgical requirements may have to be set aside in 'a case of necessity', e.g. a marriage celebrated in danger of death, or according to the extraordinary form (see Can. 1116), or with a dispensation from canonical form (see Can. 1127 §§2–3).

Can. 1120 The Bishops' Conference can draw up its own rite of marriage, to be reviewed by the Holy See, in keeping with the usages of the place and people, adapting these to the christian spirit; however the law must be observed which requires that the person assisting at the marriage, being present, is to ask for and receive the expression of the contracting parties' consent.

2259 Each Bishops' Conference is given the faculty to draw up a rite of marriage for its own territory. This ritual is to take account of local customs and traditions, making sure that these are in harmony with christianity. The *Rite of Marriage* provides general guidelines for the preparation of these local rituals, which are then to be submitted to the Holy See for approval.[2] Whatever form the local rite of marriage takes, one element which cannot be omitted or substantially altered is the role of the one who assists: the qualified witness must ask for and receive the consent of the parties in the name of the Church (see Can. 1108 §2).

Can. 1121 §1 As soon as possible after the celebration of marriage, the parish priest of the place of celebration or whoever takes his place, even if neither has assisted at the marriage, is to record in the marriage register the names of the spouses, of the person who assisted and of the witnesses, and the place and date of the celebration of the marriage; this is to be done in the manner prescribed by the Bishops' Conference or by the diocesan Bishop.

2260 A natural corollary of the requirement of canonical form is the need to register the celebration of marriage. The Council of Trent insisted that each parish priest should have a register in which marriages were to be recorded.[3] According to the present law, the responsibility for the registration of marriages rests with the parish priest or whoever is

---

[1] *Rite of Marriage* 19.III.1969 nn. 6, 8: DOL nn. 2974, 2976.

[2] *Rite of Marriage* nn.12–16: DOL nn. 2980–2984.

[3] Decree 'Tametsi': *Conciliorum Oecumenicorum Decreta* 757.

acting in his place e.g. a parochial administrator (see Cann. 539–540). He must record the fact of the marriage along with all the relevant details, even if someone else actually assisted at the marriage. Thus, a duly delegated priest or deacon or lay person who assists at a wedding has no obligation in law to register the marriage. Of course, it is not necessary that the parish priest carry out the registration himself; he may entrust all such work to one of his assistant priests or to a secretary; it remains however his responsibility to make sure that this is done as soon as possible after the wedding.

The canon indicates the minimum details that should be noted in the register: the names of the spouses, the name of the person who assisted, the names of the witnesses, and the date and place of the marriage. The Bishops' Conference may establish a standard procedure for the registration of marriages within its territory; the Conference may even demand that further information be recorded, e.g. the address of the parties at the time of the marriage. If such a standard procedure has been established, the parish priest should observe it carefully in registering marriages; if a standard national procedure has not been established, he is to follow the regulations of his own diocese.   **2261**

Can. 1121 §2 Whenever a marriage is contracted in accordance with Can. 1116, the priest or deacon, if he was present at the celebration, is bound as soon as possible to inform the parish priest or the local Ordinary about the marriage entered into; otherwise the witnesses, jointly with the contracting parties, are so bound.

Should a marriage be celebrated according to the extraordinary form (see Can. 1116), the local Ordinary or the parish priest must be informed about its celebration and given all the relevant details. The responsibility for doing this rests with a priest or deacon who was present at the marriage, although not competent to assist canonically (see Can. 1116 §2); if no cleric was present, then the responsibility falls on the witnesses conjointly with the parties. It is to be noted that the obligation in this case rests equally upon all concerned; however, if one carries out what the law requires, all the others are absolved from the obligation (see Can. 140 §1). The necessary information must be communicated to the proper authority as soon as possible after the celebration of the marriage.   **2262**

Can. 1121 §3 In regard to a marriage contracted with a dispensation from the canonical form, the local Ordinary who granted the dispensation is to see to it that the dispensation and the celebration are recorded in the marriage register both of the curia, and of the proper parish of the catholic party whose parish priest carried out the inquiries concerning the freedom to marry. The catholic spouse is obliged as soon as possible to notify that same Ordinary and parish priest of the fact that the marriage was celebrated, indicating also the place of celebration and the public form which was observed.

When a marriage is contracted in accordance with Can. 1127 §2, the responsibility for registering the marriage lies with the local Ordinary who granted the dispensation from form. He is to make sure that the fact of the dispensation and the celebration of the marriage are recorded in the diocesan curia as well as in the proper parish of the catholic party: this is understood to be the parish where the parish priest (or his representative) carried out the pre-nuptial investigation. However, in order that these facts may be registered, the law obliges the catholic party to give the necessary information to the Ordinary and to the parish priest.   **2263**

2264 Initially, it had been proposed that each Bishops' Conference should be left to prepare its own norms for the registration of these marriages. However, it was decided that it was better to determine in the Code what was to be done since this would ensure uniformity of practice throughout the Church.[1]

Can. 1122 §1 A marriage which has been contracted is to be recorded also in the baptismal registers in which the baptism of the spouses was entered.

§2 If a spouse contracted marriage elsewhere than in the parish of baptism, the parish priest of the place of celebration is to send a notification of the marriage as soon as possible to the parish priest of the place of baptism.

2265 The parish priest of the place where the marriage has been celebrated has the responsibility, not only of registering the fact of the marriage, but also of making sure that the marriage is recorded in the baptismal registers of both parties in accordance with Can. 535 §2. If both parties are catholics and were baptised in his parish, then he can make the necessary registration himself. However, if the marriage takes place outside the parish of baptism of either party (which, given the current mobility of population, is by no means a rare occurrence), the parish priest of the place of celebration must notify the parish priest of the place or places of baptism, who in turn is obliged to acknowledge to the sender the receipt of the notification and the fact of its implementation. If one of the parties was a baptised non-catholic, there is no obligation for the parish priest to inform the relevant authority. As with the registration of the marriage itself, the entry of the marriage in the baptismal register is to be done as a matter of urgency.

Can. 1123 Whenever a marriage is validated for the external forum, or declared invalid, or lawfully dissolved other than by death, the parish priest of the place of the celebration of the marriage must be informed, so that an entry may be duly made in the registers of marriage and of baptism.

2266 It is important that any change in a person's canonical status is carefully recorded, particularly when the alteration is related to marriage. The parish priest of the place of marriage is to be informed of the following alterations:

(a) if a marriage has been validated for the external forum, whether this is done by a renewal of consent (Cann. 1156–1160) or retroactively (Cann. 1161–1165);

(b) if a marriage celebrated in his parish has been declared invalid by an ecclesiastical tribunal;

(c) if a marriage has been dissolved because of non-consummation (Can. 1142) or in favour of the faith.

In the cases mentioned under (b) and (c) above it is clear that the obligation to inform the parish priest of the place of marriage rests upon the competent ecclesiastical tribunal or, depending upon local practice, the diocesan curia. As for the cases mentioned under (a) above, the obligation would sometimes rest upon the parish priest or assistant priest involved, as in cases of simple validation; sometimes upon the diocesan curia, as in cases of retroactive validation. To ensure that the important rule of this canon be not neglected, a good case can be made for a specific regulation in each diocese, determining a uniform practice, especially in respect of the cases mentioned at (a) above.

2267 The law requires that the parish priest who has been informed of these events should record them in the register of marriages and also in the register of baptism in accordance with Can. 535 §2.

---

[1] Cf. Comm 10(1978) 99–100 at Can. 321 §3.

Part I The Sacraments

Chapter VI
MIXED MARRIAGES

Can. 1124 Without the express permission of the competent authority, marriage is prohibited between two baptised persons, one of whom was baptised in the catholic Church or received into it after baptism and has not defected from it by a formal act, the other of whom belongs to a Church or ecclesial community not in full communion with the catholic Church.

A mixed marriage refers to a marriage between a catholic party (i.e. one who was baptised or received into the catholic Church and has not defected from it by a formal act) and a person who belongs to a Church or ecclesial community not in full communion with the catholic Church. This latter phrase includes christians from the Orthodox Eastern Churches and from the Churches of the Reformation.   2268

The Church has always been conscious of problems which may arise when catholics marry outside the Church. Such marriages were understood to be a threat to the faith of the catholic party. Consequently, the Church has striven to protect its members by making laws against these marriages. The strict discipline against mixed marriages made its way into c.1060 of the 1917 Code; this considered them to be 'most severely forbidden', and dispensations from the impediment were regarded as wholly exceptional. Moreover, the practice of the Church in many places implied more than a little disapproval of such marriages, decreeing that they should take place not in a church but in its sacristy, without any element of celebration, much less of pomp.   2269

As the number of mixed marriages grew in the twentieth century, the application of this strict discipline became more relaxed. A major watershed in the development of the present legislation was Vat. II with its decree on ecumenism and its declaration on religious freedom. In fact, Pope Paul VI anticipated the results of the Council by extending to local Ordinaries the faculty of dispensing from the impediments of mixed religion and disparity of cult.[1] On 18 March 1966 the Sacred Congregation for the Doctrine of the Faith issued the Instruction *Matrimonii Sacramentum*, which contained a procedure for the preparation of mixed marriages. The catholic party was to promise to make sure that the children would be baptised as catholics; the non-catholic party was to be informed of this promise and of the obligation of the catholic party to preserve his or her own faith; the non-catholic party was to be invited to make a promise that he or she would not impede the fulfilment of this obligation.[2] Four years later, following an evaluation of this procedure, Pope Paul VI addressed the matter in the apostolic letter *Matrimonia mixta*. The same promises were to be given by the catholic party and communicated to the non-catholic party, but the universal law no longer required that the non-catholic be invited to make any promise, although the Bishops' Conference could add other prescriptions.[3] Perhaps the major innovation of *Matrimonia mixta* was that it made clear that any mixed marriage entered without a dispensation was illicit rather than invalid;[4] furthermore, the local Ordinary was given the faculty to dispense from canonical form if there were serious difficulties concerning its observance.[5]   2270

---

[1] Cf. Pope Paul VI mp *Pastorale Munus* 30.XI.1963 nn.19–20: AAS 56(1964) 8.
[2] SCDF instr *Matrimonii Sacramentum* 18.III.1966 n.I: Fl I 476–477.
[3] Pope Paul VI mp *Matrimonia Mixta* 7.I.1970 nn.4–7: Fl I 512.
[4] Ibid. n.1: Fl I 511.
[5] Ibid. n.9: Fl I 512.

2271 These post-conciliar changes in the discipline have been incorporated into the Code. Mixed marriages are still viewed as something exceptional: they are still prohibited 'without the express permission' of the competent ecclesiastical authority (see Can. 1125), although failure to obtain this permission does not affect the validity of the marriage. The Church continues to perceive these marriages as being potentially dangerous to the faith of the catholic party and the children. Moreover, differences between the spouses in the matter of faith and religious practice are not conducive to the realisation of marriage as a partnership of the whole life.

Can. 1125 The local Ordinary can grant this permission if there is a just and reasonable cause. He is not to grant it unless the following conditions are fulfilled:

> 1° the catholic party is to declare that he or she is prepared to remove dangers of defecting from the faith, and is to make a sincere promise to do all in his or her power in order that all the children be baptised and brought up in the catholic Church;
>
> 2° the other party is to be informed in good time of these promises to be made by the catholic party, so that it is certain that he or she is truly aware of the promise and of the obligation of the catholic party;
>
> 3° both parties are to be instructed about the purposes and essential properties of marriage, which are not to be excluded by either contractant.

2272 Although they have become more common, mixed marriages remain an exception in the eyes of the law. The local Ordinary *can* grant the necessary permission for such a marriage, but he is not bound to do so. Indeed, he may give the permission only if there is 'a just and reasonable cause'. The canon does not contain any indication of what constitutes such a cause; the judgement concerning the sufficiency of a cause in any particular case is left to the local Ordinary. Even if a sufficient cause is found to exist, the Ordinary is not to grant the required permission unless the conditions listed in the canon are fulfilled:

> 1° The catholic party must acknowledge the potential danger to his or her faith and must declare his or her readiness to remove that danger. The same party must promise to do 'all in his or her power' to ensure the baptism and education of the children as catholics. This phrase must be interpreted carefully in the light of the Council's teaching on ecumenism and religious freedom: it is not to be understood in an absolute sense as if the non-catholic party had no rights in the matter. Any decision on the religious upbringing of the children must take account of the potential effects on the marriage relationship itself as well as on the faith commitment and rights of the non-catholic party. Clearly these are matters which ought to be discussed fully with both parties before marriage, so that misunderstanding may be avoided and possible conflict prevented.
>
> 2° In keeping with the conciliar teaching and the evolution of legislation after the Council, no promises or undertakings are required of the non-catholic party. The law demands that this person 'be informed in good time' of the promises made by the catholic party. This is a further acknowledgement of the non-catholic party's equal rights within the marriage. Before a mixed marriage takes place, the non-catholic party must be in no doubt concerning the undertakings given by the catholic party and the obligations entailed.
>
> 3° Finally, both parties are to receive special instruction on the nature of marriage. Ordinarily, this is done by the parish priest in the course of preparing a couple for

marriage (see Can. 1063). Yet, since members of other christian Churches sometimes have views on marriage different from catholic teaching, the law requires that both parties be fully informed of the purposes (see Can. 1055 §1) and essential properties (see Can. 1056) of marriage. The aim of this teaching is to ensure that both parties consent to marriage as understood and taught by the Church.

Can. 1126 It is for the Bishops' Conference to prescribe the manner in which these declarations and promises, which are always required, are to be made, and to determine how they are to be established in the external forum, and how the non-catholic party is to be informed of them.

Since different circumstances obtain in various parts of the world, the Code leaves it to the Bishops' Conference to make specific determination of the matters dealt with in Can. 1125. In particular, they are to decide the manner in which the Catholic party makes the declarations and promises required by Can. 1125 1°. These may be given in written form, or orally before a witness who will testify to what has taken place: it is necessary that some proper record be made so that there may be objective proof of the promises and declarations in the external forum. Sensitive to local circumstances, the Bishops' Conference is also to determine the manner in which the promises and declarations of the catholic party are to be communicated to the other party 'in good time'.[1]

Can. 1127 §1 The provisions of Can. 1108 are to be observed in regard to the form to be used in a mixed marriage. If, however, the catholic party contracts marriage with a non-catholic of Oriental rite, the canonical form of marriage is to be observed for lawfulness only; for validity, however, the intervention of a sacred minister is required, while observing the other requirements of law.

For validity, a mixed marriage must be celebrated according to the canonical form mentioned in Can. 1108. However, the law makes an exception to this norm for marriages which are celebrated between a catholic and a non-catholic of Oriental rite: in these cases, the requirement of the canonical form pertains only to the lawfulness of the celebration, not to its validity. All that is necessary for validity in such a marriage is the 'intervention of a sacred minister'. According to the constant jurisprudence of the Apostolic Signatura on this point, a sacred minister is a validly ordained cleric, i.e. a Bishop, priest or deacon.[2] The special provisions for these marriages is rooted in the Council's decree on Eastern Churches[3] and the decree of the Congregation for Oriental Churches *Crescens Matrimoniorum*.[4] Since their purpose is to foster better relations with the Eastern Churches and pay respect to their practice and tradition, it is fair to conclude that the 'intervention of a sacred minister' should be understood in their terms. It should be noted that the Code of Canons of the Eastern Churches does not permit marriages to be blessed by deacons; among the non-catholic Churches of the East, only the Coptic Church permits this.[5]

The constant practice of the Eastern Churches shows that the 'intervention' by a sacred minister has to do with his blessing of a marriage; indeed, without this bless-

---

[1] For the manner in which Bishops' Conferences have dealt with this matter, cf. LCE Tavola per Paesi e Canoni at Can. 1126; CN(USA) pp. 16, 35–45.
[2] The following decisions of the Apostolic Signatura have dealt with this question: 28.XI.1970: Apol 44(1971) 24–25; 7.VII.1971: Apol 44(1971) 578–580; 18.IV.1972: Apol 45(1972) 383–385.
[3] OE 18: Fl I 447–448.
[4] SCOC *Crescens Matrimoniorum* 22.II.1967: Fl I 481–482.
[5] Cf. Pospishil *Eastern Catholic Marriage Law* Brooklyn 1991 391.

ing a marriage is understood to be invalid in Eastern christian eyes. Hence, the simple physical presence of a sacred minister is not sufficient: he must intervene actively in some way and bless the marriage; no particular liturgical rite is necessary, however.[1] Since no mention is made of them in the canon, it would appear that the presence of witnesses at these marriages pertains only to lawfulness rather than to validity.

Can. 1127 §2 If there are grave difficulties in the way of observing the canonical form, the local Ordinary of the catholic party has the right to dispense from it in individual cases, having however consulted the Ordinary of the place of the celebration of the marriage; for validity, however, some public form of celebration is required. It is for the Bishops' Conference to establish norms whereby this dispensation may be granted in a uniform manner.

2276 *Matrimonia mixta* gave local Ordinaries the power to dispense from the canonical form in mixed marriages, if there was some serious difficulty concerning the observance of that form. This post-conciliar legislation now forms part of the Code. The competent authority to grant this dispensation is the local Ordinary of the catholic party, i.e. the Ordinary of the place where the catholic party has a domicile or quasi-domicile or is actually resident. The power to dispense is granted to the Ordinary 'for individual cases', so he cannot issue a general dispensation for all mixed marriages. However, since the power to grant this dispensation is ordinary, it may be delegated to others; this will be of benefit in those regions where mixed marriages are very common.[2] In the preparation of the text of the present canon, the Commission rejected the idea that permission be also required from the local Ordinary of the place of marriage.[3] According to the canon, that Ordinary must simply be consulted.

2277 Of course, the dispensation is to be given only 'if there are grave difficulties in the way of observing the canonical form'. Such difficulties include the total opposition of the non-catholic party to the canonical form, the rejection of the canonical form by a large number of friends or family members of one or other of the parties, the close relationship or friendship between one of the parties and the non-catholic minister, etc. It is for the local Ordinary to weigh up the circumstances and decide if the reason given warrants the granting of the dispensation. Whatever the reason, the parties are obliged, under pain of invalidity, to manifest their consent in some public form, religious or civil. Moreover, they are bound to communicate to the local Ordinary and the parish priest the relevant details of their marriage (see Can. 1121 §3) so that it might be registered.

2278 In order to avoid an uneven practice within a given territory in the matter of granting dispensations from the canonical form, the law leaves it to the respective Bishops' Conference to draw up suitable norms to regulate the granting of this dispensation.[4]

2279 Lest there be any confusion, it must be stressed that the faculty of granting a dispensation from the canonical form is given to the local Ordinary for mixed marriages only. As the Commission for Interpretation made clear, outside the case of urgent danger of death, the diocesan Bishop cannot dispense from the canonical form in accordance with Can. 87 §1.[5]

---

[1] Cf. Pont Comm Int Cod Orient. rep 3.V.1953: CLD 4 16.

[2] Cf. Comm 15(1983) 239 at Can. 1081 §3 2°.

[3] Cf. Comm 15(1983) 239 at Can. 1081 §3 1°.

[4] For the manner in which Bishops' Conferences have dealt with this matter, cf. LCE Tavola per Paesi e Canoni at Can. 1127; CN(USA) p.17.

[5] Cf. CCom rep 14.V.1985: AAS 77(1985) 771.

Can. 1127 §3 It is forbidden to have, either before or after the canonical celebration in accordance with §1, another religious celebration of the same marriage for the purpose of giving or renewing matrimonial consent. Likewise, there is not to be a religious celebration in which the catholic assistant and non-catholic minister, each performing his own rite, together ask for the consent of the parties.

In order to avoid any misunderstanding and confusion, the law does not permit the double celebration of a mixed marriage, whether another celebration precedes or follows the canonical form or whether the priest and a non-catholic minister officiate jointly at the marriage together. It is essential to understand what precisely is prohibited:

(a) the canonical form of marriage may not be preceded or followed by another ceremony in which matrimonial consent is given and received. Consent to marriage is given once, and cannot be revoked in order to be given again. A second ceremony for the exchange of consent is superfluous and could of course result in widespread and dangerous confusion. That is not to say that a couple may not seek to have the minister of the non-catholic party pray with them and bless their union, but any semblance of an exchange of consent during such a rite is to be excluded.

(b) a joint ceremony conducted by the catholic minister and the non-catholic minister in which each asks for the consent of the parties is also forbidden. If the canonical form is observed, there is nothing to prevent the non-catholic minister from carrying out some function during the ceremony, e.g. reading a lesson, pronouncing a blessing etc. Similarly, if the canonical form has been dispensed, the catholic minister may take part in the celebration by reading from Scripture, saying some prayers etc.

This provision of law does not prohibit the practice in some countries – and in individual cases in others – of having a purely civil ceremony before the canonical form of marriage, on the understanding that such a ceremony, while rightly fulfilling the civil law, does not in any way establish the couple as married in the eyes of the catholic Church.

Can. 1128 Local Ordinaries and other pastors of souls are to see to it that the catholic spouse and the children born of a mixed marriage are not without the spiritual help needed to fulfil their obligations; they are also to assist the spouses to foster the unity of conjugal and family life.

Pope John Paul II has stated: 'Couples living in a mixed marriage have special needs, ... In the first place, attention must be paid to the obligations that faith imposes on the catholic party with regard to the free exercise of the faith and the consequent obligation to ensure, as far as is possible, the baptism and upbringing of the children in the catholic faith. There must be borne in mind the particular difficulties inherent in the relationships between husband and wife with regard to religious freedom ...'.[1] The pastoral care of these couples with special needs is entrusted to the local Ordinary and the parish priest. They must be solicitous for the welfare and harmony of such families and must provide whatever support is needed by the catholic party and the children in the living of their faith. This may e.g. be done through parish-based or diocesan programmes for inter-Church families.

Can. 1129 The provisions of Cann. 1127 and 1128 are to be applied also to marriages which are impeded by the impediment of disparity of worship mentioned in Can. 1086 §1.

---

[1] FC 78: Fl II 883.

2283 This canon, concerning marriages celebrated with a dispensation from the impediment of disparity of cult speaks for itself. What has been said above concerning the dispensation from canonical form (Can. 1127 §2), double celebrations of marriage (Can. 1127 §3), and the pastoral care of the families of mixed marriages (Can. 1128) is all equally applicable to these marriages.

Chapter VII
THE SECRET CELEBRATION OF MARRIAGE

Can. 1130 For a grave and urgent reason, the local Ordinary may permit that a marriage be celebrated in secret.

2284 The Church established the canonical form of marriage in order to eliminate the abuses associated with clandestine marriages, i.e. marriages of which no proof exists in the external forum. A very different phenomenon is a marriage celebrated in secret, what was known in the 1917 Code as a 'marriage of conscience'. Unlike the clandestine marriage, this marriage is celebrated according to the canonical form, but in secret, i.e. without the usual publicity. The law gives the power to *the local Ordinary* to permit such marriages: this term includes the Vicar general, something which c.1104 of the 1917 Code expressly excluded. Since the law does not specify, the one competent to give permission may be the local Ordinary of the domicile or quasi-domicile or residence of either party, or that of the place of marriage.

2285 Marriages celebrated in secret must always be understood to be very exceptional. Therefore, the law requires a grave and urgent reason, e.g. the marriage of a couple already living together and publicly accepted as husband and wife; the loss of pension benefits for a widow or widower should the marriage become known publicly; a civil law prohibiting the celebration of marriage between different categories of people; a civil law prohibiting the religious celebration of marriage. It is for the local Ordinary to determine whether or not a reason is grave and urgent enough to warrant such an exceptional celebration.

Can. 1131 Permission to celebrate a marriage in secret involves:

1° that the investigations to be made before the marriage are carried out in secret;

2° that the secret in regard to the marriage which has been celebrated is observed by the local Ordinary, by whoever assists, by the witnesses and by the spouses.

2286 The fact that permission has been given for a marriage to be celebrated in secret in no way absolves the priest or deacon involved from making the required investigations into the freedom of the parties to marry or from preparing them for the celebration of the sacrament. In the circumstances, however, great care is to be taken in order to preserve the secret. This secret binds the following persons: the local Ordinary, the person who assists at the marriage, the witnesses and the parties themselves. It is clear from the law that the obligation of secrecy is, for the local Ordinary, a *relative* one (see Can. 1132); the obligation on the others is *absolute*. If however the parties should freely decide together to make known the fact of their marriage, all the others are released from the obligation.

Part I The Sacraments

Can. 1132 The obligation of observing the secret mentioned in Can. 1131 n.2 ceases for the local Ordinary if from its observance a threat arises of grave scandal or of grave harm to the sanctity of marriage. This fact is to be made known to the parties before the celebration of the marriage.

Before a marriage is celebrated in secret, the local Ordinary must inform the couple of the limits of his obligation to maintain the secret. He is no longer bound by the secret if its observance leads either to a threat of grave scandal (e.g. if the couple, having been married in secret, pretended publicly to live in open concubinage), or to a threat of grave harm to the sanctity of marriage (e.g. if one or both parties, although married in secret, attempted publicly to contract marriage with someone else). In these circumstances, the Ordinary is bound to make known the fact of the marriage celebrated in secret. During the drafting of this canon, it was decided that it was no longer opportune to retain mention of the specific problems listed in c.1106 of the 1917 Code, i.e. failure to baptise the children of such a marriage or neglect of their christian education.[1] In fact, warning a couple beforehand of the limits placed by the law upon the local Ordinary's observance of the secret should go a long way to preventing any grave scandal or grave harm.

2287

Can. 1133 A marriage celebrated in secret is to be recorded only in a special register which is to be kept in the secret archive of the curia.

Marriages celebrated in secret are not to be entered in the ordinary parish register of marriages, but in a special register for such marriages. This is to be kept in the secret archive of the diocesan curia (see Cann. 489–490). Since the canon does not make any mention of it, no record of these marriages is to be made in the register of baptism of the parties. Of course, should the secret cease, the appropriate registrations are to be made.

2288

Chapter VIII
THE EFFECTS OF MARRIAGE

Can. 1134 From a valid marriage there arises between the spouses a bond which of its own nature is permanent and exclusive. Moreover, in christian marriage the spouses are by a special sacrament strengthened and, as it were, consecrated for the duties and the dignity of their state.

During the revision of the Code, it was proposed that this canon should be omitted completely because its content was entirely doctrinal. However, it was agreed that its omission would seriously weaken this whole chapter on the effects of marriage.[2] The canon sets forth clearly the principal effect of the valid exchange of matrimonial consent, i.e. a permanent and exclusive bond between the spouses. The properties of permanence and exclusivity belong to all valid marriages whether natural i.e. where one or both parties is not baptised, or sacramental i.e. where both parties are baptised. All valid marriages are thus held to be intrinsically indissoluble, i.e. they cannot be dissolved by the will of the parties or by any civil authority. However, in certain circumstances, some marriages may be dissolved by the vicarious power of Christ

2289

---

[1] Cf. Comm 10(1978) 102–103 at Can. 326.
[2] Cf. Comm 10(1978) 104 at Can. 330.

entrusted to the Pope as in cases of non-consumption (Can. 1142), of the pauline privilege (Can. 1143), and of the privilege of the faith.

2290 The second half of the canon recalls the Church's teaching on the sacramentality of marriage. In this special sacrament 'Christ abides with the couple who in his name have become an indissoluble unity. The purpose of his abiding presence ... is to make their love increasingly resemble his own love for the Church, so that it will truly become mutual dedication in absolutely faithful love'.[1] Vat. II itself is explicit in stating that, 'fulfilling their conjugal and family role by virtue of this sacrament, spouses are penetrated with the spirit of Christ and their whole life is suffused by faith, hope and charity; thus they increasingly further their own perfection and their mutual sanctification, and together they render glory to God'.[2] Although the sacrament of marriage does not confer a character, its efficacy remains permanently.[3]

Can. 1135 Each spouse has an equal obligation and right to whatever pertains to the partnership of conjugal life.

2291 Following the general principle of the equality of all the faithful (see Can. 208), this canon establishes the more specific principle of the equality of the spouses in what pertains to the rights and obligations of marriage.[4] Indeed, at an early stage in its labours, the Revision Commission decided that, given the situation of women in some parts of the world, it seemed opportune to affirm in the new Code the equality of husband and wife.[5] Unlike c.1111 of the 1917 Code, the equality of which this canon speaks refers to the partnership of conjugal life in all its aspects and not simply to 'acts proper to conjugal life'. It is of the utmost importance to distinguish the basic equality in principle from the various ways in which this equality is lived and expressed in different cultures.

Can. 1136 Parents have the most serious obligation and the primary right to do all in their power to ensure their children's physical, social, cultural, moral and religious upbringing.

2292 According to Can. 1055 §1, marriage of its very nature is ordered to the procreation and upbringing of children. Those spouses whose marriage has been blessed with the gift of children have, according to the present canon, 'the most grave obligation' to do all they can for the proper education of their children. This upbringing has many dimensions, none of which ought to be neglected: physical, social, cultural, moral and religious. This is a serious obligation which is incumbent upon both parents equally. The canon also speaks of the parents having the 'primary right' to bring up their children. This expression echoes other canons dealing with the responsibility for educating children (see Cann. 774 §2, 793). Consequently, only in very exceptional circumstances, e.g. the manifest incapacity of both parents, may another agency such as the Church or the State intervene and take over the role of rearing the children. When parents exercise this right and fulfil this obligation, they share actively in the sanctifying mission of the Church (see Can. 835 §4).

Can. 1137 Children who are conceived or born of a valid or of a putative marriage are legitimate.

---

[1] Häring in Vorgrimler V 235.
[2] GS 48: Fl I 951.
[3] Cf. Pope Pius XI encl *Casti Connubii* 31.XII.1930: AAS 22(1930) 555, 583: ND 1833.
[4] Cf. Comm 10(1978) 105 at Can. 331.
[5] Comm 5(1973) 75–76 at Can. 1111.

Part I The Sacraments

A marriage is said to be *valid* if consent has been expressed lawfully by two legally capable parties (see Can. 1057 §1); it is said to be *putative* if it was celebrated in good faith by at least one party although in fact it was invalid (see Can. 1061 §3). The juridical effects of both types of marriage are identical insofar as they refer to the children born of them: such children are always regarded as legitimate. This is a matter which causes some concern to parties seeking a declaration of the nullity of their marriage; they must be assured that, should their marriage be declared invalid, the status of the children born of that marriage is in no way affected. 2293

During the revision process, objections were raised about the appropriateness of retaining the concept of illegitimacy within the Code. The provisions of the 1917 Code concerning illegitimates[1] were not incorporated into the new Code, so why retain the concept? However, the Commission decided to include the notion in the Code, since it might have consequences in particular law and in order to highlight the sanctity of marriage.[2] 2294

Can. 1138 §1 The father is he who is identified by a lawful marriage, unless by clear arguments the contrary is proven.

§2 Children are presumed legitimate who are born at least 180 days after the date the marriage was celebrated, or within 300 days from the date of the dissolution of conjugal life.

Two closely related presumptions of law are contained in this canon. These are to be used in cases where the legitimacy of a child is doubtful or in question. Firstly, the law presumes that the husband of a woman who has a child is in fact the father of that child. Of course, this presumption may be overturned by evidence to the contrary, e.g. if the couple never had sexual intercourse, or if the husband was sterile or had been away at the material time, etc. This presumption does not apply if the couple had not been lawfully married, even though they may have cohabited. The second presumption provides a means of deciding whether or not a child, in a particular case, may be accepted as the legitimate child of a married couple. Thus, if the child was born within 180 days of the celebration of the marriage, it is presumed to be legitimate; similarly, if the child was born within 300 days of the termination of conjugal life, it is also presumed legitimate. The times mentioned in the canon are identical to those of c.1115 §2 of the 1917 Code, although that referred to months rather than days. Commentators on that Code made it clear that these terms are not so absolute that the legitimacy of a child born within them cannot be impugned.[3] If the first presumption should fall due to contrary evidence, the second presumption cannot be invoked. 2295

Can. 1139 Illegitimate children are legitimated by the subsequent marriage of their parents, whether valid or putative, or by a rescript of the Holy See.

Children born of a couple who are not married can be made legitimate or become *legitimated* in two ways: 2296
(a) if their parents contract a marriage (even if afterwards it is declared invalid), or if their existing union is validated;

---

[1] Under the 1917 Code, illegitimate children were precluded from becoming Cardinals (c.232 §2 1°), Bishops (c.331 §1 1°), abbots and prelates *nullius* (c.320 §2), major Superiors (c.504); they were also prohibited from admission to seminaries (c.1363 §1), and the reception of orders (cc.984 1°, 991 §3).
[2] Cf. Comm 10(1978) 106 at Can. 333; 15(1983) 240 at Cann. 1091–1094.
[3] Cf. e.g. Cappello V n.749.

(b) if the Holy See grants a rescript.[1] Such a provision is sometimes included in a dispensation from priestly obligations in cases where the priest has entered a civil marriage and has children.

Can. 1140 As far as canonical effects are concerned, legitimated children are equivalent to legitimate children in all respects, unless it is otherwise expressly provided by the law.

2297 The contents of this canon might appear to be somewhat superfluous since the present Code makes no distinction between children who are legitimate and those who are legitimated. According to some canons of the 1917 Code, subsequent legitimation did not remove the bar to certain offices.[2] As has been noted already, none of these provisions has been included in this Code. However, the canon does appear to permit particular law to make such a distinction in cultural or other such circumstances as might make it appropriate.

Chapter IX
THE SEPARATION OF THE SPOUSES

Article 1
The Dissolution of the Bond

Can. 1141 A marriage which is ratified and consummated cannot be dissolved by any human power or by any cause other than death.

2298 In a clear and unambiguous manner, this canon states the Church's teaching on the indissolubility of marriage, which is firmly rooted in the teaching of Christ himself (see Matt 19:6; Mark 10:9). This doctrine was clarified in the 12th-century dispute between the schools of Paris and Bologna concerning the efficient cause of marriage (see our commentary on Can. 1061 §1). The outcome of that debate forms the basis for the present canon: consent makes marriage, consummation by sexual intercourse makes marriage indissoluble. Thus a valid marriage between two baptised christians and consummated by an act of sexual intercourse performed 'in a human manner' (Can. 1061 §1) is absolutely indissoluble, i.e. it cannot be dissolved intrinsically by the will of the couple, nor can it be dissolved extrinsically by any human agency, civil or ecclesiastical. Only death can dissolve such a union. It is to be noted that 'a marriage which is ratified' includes all valid marriages between baptised christians, not just those celebrated according to the canonical form.

Can. 1142 A non-consummated marriage between baptised persons or between a baptised party and an unbaptised party can be dissolved by the Roman Pontiff for a just reason, at the request of both parties or of either party, even if the other is unwilling.

2299 Implicit in the teaching of Can. 1141 is that certain marriages may be dissolved by causes other than death. The Code addresses one such case, that of the ratified mar-

---

[1] Such a rescript was granted in recent times in the case of the children of Princess Caroline of Monaco whose second husband was accidentally killed before their marriage could be validated.

[2] E.g. c.232 §2 1° prohibited illegitimates from becoming Cardinals, even if subsequently legitimated.

Part I The Sacraments

riage which has not been consummated by sexual intercourse. As a valid marriage, it is *intrinsically indissoluble*, i.e. it cannot be dissolved by the couple. However, according to law, such a marriage may be dissolved by the Pope. This has been part of the practice of the Church since at least the 12th century. Pope Pius XII explained that the Pope can dissolve non-consummated marriages by virtue of his 'ministerial' or 'vicarious' power; the use of this power is indeed extraordinary; its use is designed exclusively for the salvation of souls.[1]

Either party may freely petition the Holy See for such a dissolution, even if the other party is unwilling. The process is administrative in nature. It is set forth in Cann. 1697–1706. The principal purpose of the procedure is to establish with moral certainty that the marriage in question has not been consummated by sexual intercourse. This may be demonstrated in one or more of three ways: 2300

(a) by the physical argument, i.e. by showing with the assistance of medical experts that the woman is still a virgin or that, given the state of the sexual organs of either party or both, sexual intercourse could not have taken place;

(b) by the moral argument, i.e. using the sworn testimony of the parties and of witnesses who knew of the fact of non-consummation at a non-suspect time, as well as witnesses to the credibility of the parties, documents and other indications to arrive at moral certainty concerning the non-consummation;

(c) by demonstrating from evidence beyond dispute that the parties did not spend sufficient time together to engage in sexual intercourse, e.g. showing that they separated immediately after the celebration of the marriage.

Of course, the simple fact of non-consummation is not a sufficient reason for dissolving the bond of marriage: the law requires also a just cause, a reason for doing something as extraordinary as dissolving a valid marriage. The most common of these causes include the collapse of the marital relationship between the spouses without any remaining hope of reconciliation (a possibility which must always be carefully investigated before any process is commenced), or the fact that one of the spouses has obtained a civil divorce and contracted a subsequent civil marriage. 2301

Can. 1143 §1 In virtue of the pauline privilege, a marriage entered into by two unbaptised persons is dissolved in favour of the faith of the party who received baptism, by the very fact that a new marriage is contracted by that same party, provided the unbaptised party departs.

This canon deals with yet another category of marriages which may be dissolved by causes other than death. The so-called *Pauline Privilege* derives its name from a response given by the apostle Paul to specific questions concerning the marriage of Christians with pagans in Corinth. The apostle states: 'If a brother has a wife who is an unbeliever, and she is content to live with him, he must not send her away; and if a woman has an unbeliever for her husband, and he is content to live with her, she must not leave him ... However, if the unbelieving partner does not consent, they may separate; in these circumstances, the brother or sister is not tied ...' (1 Cor 7:12–13, 15). 2302

By virtue of this 'privilege', the law permits the dissolution of a marriage celebrated between two non-baptised parties if, after one has received baptism, the other 'departs' or leaves the marriage (see §2). This practice had entered the Church's legislation on marriage by the late middle ages. Repeating c.1126 of the 1917 Code, this 2303

---

[1] Pope Pius XII Address to Roman Rota 3.X.1941: AAS 33(1941) 424–426.

paragraph makes it clear that the marriage is dissolved by the fact that a new marriage has been contracted by the baptised party; the first marriage is dissolved in favour of the faith of that party. The validity of the subsequent marriage, however, is made dependent upon the fulfilment of the requirements of Cann. 1144–1147. The pauline privilege may be used only in cases where, at the time of the marriage, both parties were not baptised and where one party subsequently has been baptised validly.[1]

Can. 1143 §2 The unbaptised party is considered to depart if he or she is unwilling to live with the baptised party, or to live peacefully without offence to the Creator, unless the baptised party has, after the reception of baptism, given the other just cause to depart.

2304 The simple fact of the baptism of one party cannot be used as a reason for dissolving the marriage. The law requires that the unbaptised party must 'depart'. In this paragraph, the precise canonical meaning of that term is given: if, as a consequence of his or her partner's baptism, the unbaptised party finds that he or she can no longer live with the Christian party, he or she is considered to have departed from the marriage; this is also the case if, as a result of the baptism of his or her partner, the unbaptised party is unwilling 'to live peacefully without offence to the Creator', i.e. that his or her demands or behaviour make it impossible for the Christian party to carry out the obligations or responsibilities of the faith. In the latter case, although it might be the Christian party who actually leaves as a consequence of his or her partner's behaviour, the law understands that the unbaptised party has departed. Nevertheless, the law stresses that the baptised party must not have given the unbaptised party 'just cause' to depart. So, if the baptised party were to commit adultery, causing the unbaptised party to leave, the pauline privilege cannot be invoked.

Can. 1144 §1 For the unbaptised person validly to contract a new marriage, the unbaptised party must always be interpellated whether:

1° he or she also wishes to receive baptism;

2° he or she at least is willing to live peacefully with the baptised party without offence to the Creator.

2305 Cann. 1144–1147 refer to the procedure to be followed in cases of dissolution of marriage by virtue of the pauline privilege.

2306 The first of these canons sets out what is required by law for the valid celebration of a new marriage by the party who has been baptised, namely the so-called 'interpellations' or questions to be asked of the unbaptised party. Prior to any interpellation, it must be established beyond doubt that, at the time of the first marriage, both parties were indeed unbaptised and that one of them subsequently has been baptised or at least has the immediate intention of being baptised. The contents of the interpellations are given:

(a) the unbaptised must be asked if he or she also desires to be baptised;

(b) if the response to the first question is in the negative, the unbaptised must be asked if he or she is willing to live in peace with the baptised party 'without offence to the Creator', as explained above.

---

[1] The Church does not require that the converted party be baptised a catholic (cf. SCDF rep 30.VIII.1976: CLD 8 837–840). However, it does require that the baptism received is valid. Further information concerning the Churches whose baptism is presumed valid and those whose baptism is not accepted as valid may be found in Woestmann *Special Marriage Cases* Ottawa 1992 39–40, note 12.

Should the response to both questions be negative, the law considers the unbaptised party to have 'departed' from the marriage in the sense of Can. 1143. In such a situation, the baptised party is free to contract a new marriage. Great care must be taken when considering the responses given by the unbaptised party, particularly when evaluating his or her sincerity.

Can. 1144 §2 This interpellation is to be done after baptism. However, the local Ordinary can for a grave reason permit that the interpellation be done before baptism; indeed he can dispense from it, either before or after baptism, provided it is established, by at least a summary and extra-judicial procedure, that it cannot be made or that it would be useless.

Ordinarily these interpellations are to take place after one of the parties has received baptism. Yet, if there is a serious reason, the local Ordinary may permit them to take place before baptism, e.g. if there is a reason to believe that the other party will also desire to be baptised. The law makes the validity of any new marriage depend on these interpellations, since they are the means by which the departure of the unbaptised party is verified. Of course, the law recognises that it might not be always possible to carry out such an investigation, especially if the couple have already separated and the unbaptised party is hostile to the Church or is living at an unknown address. In such a situation, the local Ordinary may dispense from the interpellations after baptism has been received or, if the circumstances so warrant, even before baptism. This dispensation can be granted only if it can be shown 'by a summary and extra-judicial' form of investigation that the interpellations cannot be carried out or that no good purpose would be served by them. Dispensing from the interpellation does not absolve the local Ordinary from acquiring all the other necessary information, e.g. that both parties were not baptised at the time of the first marriage; that the unbaptised party has not received baptism in the meantime; that the unbaptised is not willing to live peacefully with the other party. Such information may be obtained from the testimony of relatives and friends, or it may be deduced from documents, e.g. the certificate of a subsequent civil marriage contracted by the unbaptised party. 2307

Can. 1145 §1 As a rule, the interpellation is to be done on the authority of the local Ordinary of the converted party. A period of time for reply is to be allowed by this Ordinary to the other spouse, if indeed he or she asks for it, warning the person however that if the period passes without any reply, silence will be taken as a negative response.

§2 Even an interpellation made privately by the converted party is valid, and indeed it is lawful if the form prescribed above cannot be observed.

§3 In both cases there must be lawful proof in the external forum of the interpellation having been done and of its outcome.

The law recognises that the interpellations can be conducted in two ways. The first is the formal investigation undertaken by the local Ordinary of the baptised party. He is to question the unbaptised party, either personally or, as is more common, through a delegate, in accordance with Can. 1141 §1. If need be, he may allow the party some time to consider before making a formal response. If a response is given, it must be noted. Should the unbaptised party respond affirmatively to the interpellation, the Ordinary must do what he can to ascertain the sincerity of the person concerned before declaring that the baptised party may not contract a new marriage. Should the unbaptised party fail to give a response within the allotted time, the Ordinary is to interpret this silence as a negative answer; however, he must have warned the unbaptised party of this in advance. The second manner of conducting the interpellations 2308 takes the form of a private interrogation of the unbaptised party concerning his or her intentions carried out by the converted party. In order to rule out any semblance of collusion, this ought to be done in writing or in the presence of witnesses. It would appear from the canon that such an alternative approach is always valid but lawful only if the formal investigation by the local Ordinary cannot be carried out.

2309 Whichever form of the interpellations is used in a given case, the law requires that the fact of the interpellation and its outcome must admit of proof in the external forum. Consequently, there should be a written record of the questions asked and the responses received, e.g. in a letter to the unbaptised person, in a formal declaration by the local Ordinary, or in a sworn deposition by the baptised party who carried out a private interpellation.

Can. 1146 The baptised party has the right to contract a new marriage with a catholic:

1° if the other party has replied in the negative to the interpellation, or if the interpellation has been lawfully omitted;

2° if the unbaptised person, whether already interpellated or not, who at first persevered in peaceful cohabitation without offence to the Creator, has subsequently departed without just cause, without prejudice to the provisions of Cann. 1144 and 1145.

2310 If the unbaptised party responds negatively to the interpellations, or fails to respond within the designated time (see Can. 1145 §1), or if the interpellations have been lawfully dispensed and the fact of departure has been clearly demonstrated, the law gives to the baptised party the right to enter a new marriage with a catholic. The same right is given even if, after baptism, the unbaptised party did live peacefully with the converted party but subsequently departed. In accordance with provisions of Cann. 1144–1145, the fact of this later departure must be established and there must be proof that the baptised party did not provide the unbaptised party with a 'just cause' for departure (see Can. 1143 §2).

Can. 1147 However, the local Ordinary can for a grave reason allow the baptised party, using the pauline privilege, to contract marriage with a non-catholic party, whether baptised or non-baptised; in this case, the provisions of the canons on mixed marriages must also be observed.

2311 By virtue of the pauline privilege, according to the previous canon, the baptised party has the right to enter a new marriage with a catholic partner. The present canon gives to the local Ordinary the faculty to permit such a person to enter a new marriage with a baptised non-catholic or even with an unbaptised person. This derogation from the norm of law requires a grave reason, e.g. the regularisation of an already existing civil marriage. In all such cases, the local Ordinary is to see to it that the norms concerning mixed marriages (Cann. 1124–1129) are observed. Great care must be exercised in these cases to remove or minimise any risk or threat or danger to the faith of the newly baptised party.

Can. 1148 §1 When an unbaptised man who simultaneously has a number of unbaptised wives, has received baptism in the catholic Church, if it would be a hardship for him to remain with the first of the wives, he may retain one of them, having dismissed the others. The same applies to an unbaptised woman who simultaneously has a number of unbaptised husbands.

By virtue of c.1125 of the 1917 Code the provisions of three apostolic constitutions promulgated in the 16th century were made universal law. These documents were contained in an appendix to that Code.[1] They had been issued to resolve specific questions concerning the marriages of non-Christian peoples whom the missionaries were encountering in Africa, Asia and the Americas. The present Code makes no reference to these constitutions. However, in this and the following canon, their provisions are repeated with some modifications.

The first situation addressed in the present Code is that of polygamy and polyandry, i.e. an unbaptised person seeking baptism who is simultaneously married to several spouses. According to the canon, a man who has a number of unbaptised wives is to choose one of them when he is baptised into the catholic Church. Ordinarily, he is to choose the first wife. This was the requirement of the 1917 Code; only if he could not remember which was the first could a man in this position choose another of his wives. However, the current law permits him to select one of the others if it would be a hardship for him to remain with the first. Should he select someone other than his first wife, his subsequent marriage in accordance with this canon dissolves his prior natural bond of marriage. This norm applies equally to polyandrous women.

In all cases, the other spouses who are not chosen are 'dismissed'. This question was debated fully by the Revision Commission in 1978. It was argued that the concept of sending wives away could have serious detrimental effects upon a tribe and a family. Indeed, the view was expressed that the dismissal of a wife appeared to be contrary to natural justice. At the time, it was felt that this was a matter for the Congregation for the Doctrine of the Faith. A proposal to omit any reference to the dismissal of the spouses was defeated at the meeting.[2] The notion of dismissal must be understood in the light of the provisions of §3.

Can. 1148 §2 In the cases mentioned in §1, when baptism has been received, the marriage is to be contracted in the legal form, with due observance, if need be, of the provisions concerning mixed marriages and of other provisions of law.

The law requires that a newly baptised person who has chosen one of his or her several spouses must enter marriage with the chosen spouse in a legitimate form, i.e. observing the canonical form or some other public form if a dispensation from canonical form has been granted. There is no requirement that the other party is to be baptised. The provisions of the law concerning mixed marriages and disparity of cult are, in so far as they are relevant, to be observed (see Cann. 1086, 1124–1129).

Can. 1148 §3 In the light of the moral, social and economic circumstances of place and person, the local Ordinary is to ensure that adequate provision is made, in accordance with the norms of justice, christian charity and natural equity, for the needs of the first wife and of the others who have been dismissed.

While it does not recognise the validity of polygamous unions, the Church is aware that from such marriages arise serious obligations of natural justice. The law entrusts the local Ordinary with the responsibility of making sure that adequate provision is

---

[1] The apostolic constitutions were: *Altitudo* promulgated by Pope Paul III on 1.VI.1537; *Romani Pontificis* promulgated by Pope Pius V on 2.VIII.1571; *Populis* promulgated by Pope Gregory XIII on 25.I.1585.
[2] Cf. Comm 10(1978) 114 at Can. 344 §1.

made for the needs of the first wife and the others who have been dismissed. This provision clearly includes the welfare of the children involved. Whereas in §1 there was an explicit reference to the case of polyandrous women, no such reference is made here to the dismissed husbands of these women. During the preparation of the Code, some of the consultors observed that this canon placed an intolerable burden upon the local Ordinary. It was pointed out that this would be indeed a heavy burden if it were stated that the Ordinary himself had to make provision for the dismissed wives; however, the law simply requires him to ensure that provision is made for these people.[1]

Can. 1149 An unbaptised person who, having received baptism in the catholic Church, cannot re-establish cohabitation with his or her unbaptised spouse by reason of captivity or persecution, can contract another marriage, even if the other party has in the meantime received baptism, without prejudice to the provisions of Can. 1141.

2317 The apostolic constitution of Gregory XIII *Populis* provided for a different situation. During the 16th century, it became clear that the deportation of slaves from Africa to America meant that married couples were often separated with little or no chance of them ever restoring their married life. By virtue of this constitution, the Pope granted to local Ordinaries, parish priests and Jesuit confessors the faculty to dispense from their earlier marriages such people who, after baptism, sought to marry catholics. With this constitution as its foundation, the canon permits the remarriage of those who had been married before their baptism as catholics and whose conjugal life was disrupted with little hope of restoration by captivity or persecution. The new marriage dissolves the prior bond. This is also the case even if the other party has in the meantime also received baptism – provided that the couple have not managed to re-establish even temporarily their marital life and engaged in sexual intercourse. This provision of law was omitted from the earlier drafts of the current Code[2] but was restored at the meeting of the consultors in 1978.[3] It is possible to envisage the application of this norm among the many people displaced in today's world as a result of warfare and internal political strife.

Can. 1150 In a doubtful matter the privilege of the faith enjoys the favour of the law.

2318 According to Can. 1060, marriage enjoys the favour of law and, in doubt, the validity of the marriage is to be upheld. The provision of this canon would appear to qualify that principle somewhat. However, it must be understood that this canon refers only to those non-sacramental marriages in which a dissolution is being sought in accordance with Cann. 1143–1149. There is no presumption in favour of the invalidity of these marriages; rather, the canon establishes a practical principle: if, during the process for the dissolution of a marriage in accordance with the pauline privilege or according to the provisions of Cann. 1148–1149, a doubt arises concerning certain facts, the law gives the benefit of the doubt to the faith of the baptised party. Such doubtful matters would include a lack of clarity as to the cause of the departure of the unbaptised party, an uncertainty as to the sufficiency of the cause for dispensing from the interpellations, uncertainty concerning the sincerity of the responses of the unbaptised party, etc. In these situations, the law permits the celebration of the new

---

[1] Cf. Comm 10(1978) 115 at Can. 344 §2.
[2] Cf. Comm 5(1973) 85.
[3] Cf. Comm 10(1978) 112, 115–116.

marriage and the dissolution of the prior natural bond to proceed. However, should the doubtful matter concern the validity of the baptism of one or other of the parties, the principle of this canon may not be invoked since the norms of Cann. 1143–1149 cannot be applied in such a case.[1]

Other Privilege of the Faith cases

The dissolution of natural-bond marriages which take place in accordance with the provisions of Cann. 1143–1149 do not require the intervention of the Pope. Cases concerning the pauline privilege do involve the local Ordinary; cases concerning the situations envisaged by Cann. 1148–1149 involve only the general invigilatory attention of the local Ordinary. In Church law and practice, however, another form of dissolution of natural-bond marriages exists: this concerns marriages where one of the parties was baptised at the time of the celebration of the marriage. Like the other cases dealt with in Cann. 1143–1149, this procedure was drawn up in answer to specific situations, i.e. what to do when a catholic seeks to marry a person who was married before, but whose previous marriage was non-sacramental since only one party was baptised. This is not regulated by any norm within the Code, although varying provisions had been made for it in earlier drafts.[2] 2319

Before the 1917 Code, no specific provision was necessary in this matter since the impediment of disparity of cult applied to the marriages of all the baptised, whether catholic or not. This meant that, unless a dispensation had been granted, all such marriages were regarded as invalid. In the 1917 Code c.1070 §1, the invalidating force of this impediment was restricted to marriages involving one party baptised into the catholic Church. So, when presented with a situation involving a catholic seeking to marry someone bound by a natural-bond marriage, Ordinaries could no longer resort to a declaration of the nullity of the former union. Instead, they sought the assistance of the Holy See. In 1924 Pope Pius XI responded affirmatively to three such requests: they concerned marriages which had been celebrated between a baptised non-catholic and an unbaptised party; in each case, one of the parties to that marriage now sought to become a catholic and marry a catholic.[3] In the years following the Second World War, Pope Pius XII responded affirmatively to many other requests, even involving marriages celebrated with a dispensation from the impediment of disparity of cult between a catholic and an unbaptised person.[4] 2320

In order to regulate the procedure followed in these applications, the Holy Office issued a series of Norms in 1934.[5] These remained in force until 1973 when the 2321

---

[1] Cf. SCSO rep 10.VI.1937: CLD 2 343.

[2] Cf. Comm 5(1973) 86; 9(1977) 117; 15(1983) 240–241 at Can. 1104. Even though the final draft approved by the Revision Commission in 1982 (at c.1150) had certain provisions in this regard, the matter was simply omitted in the promulgated text of 1983 – most likely, it would appear, because the issues inolved were seen to be doctrinal rather than juridical. In consequence of that omission, omitted also in the promulgated text were the corresponding canons in Book VII of the 1982 draft (at cc.1707–1710) which had proposed certain procedural norms in the handling of such cases.

[3] Cf. SCSO repp 2.IV.1924: LE I 679–681; 10.VII.1924: CLD 1 552–553; 5.XI.1924: CLD 1 553–554.

[4] Cf. SCSO repp 18.VII.1947: LE II 2428: CLD 3 485; 10.VIII.1947: LE II 2432; 30.I.1950: LE II 2730–2731: CLD 3 486–488; 2.II.1955: LE II 3353–3354: CLD 4 347–350; 9.VII.1955: LE II 3397–3398; 8.VIII.1955: LE II 3400–3401: CLD 4 350–352; 12.III.1957: LE II 3591–3592.

[5] These norms were never promulgated in AAS. Even at the time of the publication of LE I in 1966 the text could not be made public. However, the norms were contained in LE II 3354–3355.

Congregation for the Doctrine of the Faith issued a new instruction on the whole subject, together with procedural norms for preparing such cases.[1] Since the promulgation of the Code of Canon Law in 1983, although no reference to these cases is to be found in the Code, these norms are still in force and to be followed.

Article 2
Separation while the Bond remains

Can. 1151 Spouses have the obligation and the right to maintain their common conjugal life, unless a lawful reason excuses them.

2322 A common conjugal life lies at the very heart of marriage. By this means a couple are able to establish a partnership of their whole lives and fulfil the obligations they have assumed, e.g. their mutual welfare and the procreation and upbringing of children. Consequently, the canon speaks of spouses having the *duty* as well as the right to preserve this life in common. However, marital disharmony is a fact of life, and the law must make some provision for those unfortunate situations where this common life cannot be maintained. In broad terms, the canon recognises that a couple may end their life together 'for a lawful reason' (see Cann. 1152 §1, 1153 §1). Such a separation, however, does not affect the indissolubility of the bond of marriage. Although they may live apart, temporarily or permanently, neither party is free to enter a new marriage. During the process of revision, it was suggested that all references to this type of separation should be omitted from the Code and the matter be left to local Bishops' Conferences. Eventually, it was decided to retain these broad principles within the Code; it was felt that they should remain since the major reason which justified the separation of spouses, namely adultery (see Can. 1152 §1), was rooted in sacred Scripture.[2]

Can. 1152 §1 It is earnestly recommended that a spouse, motivated by christian charity and solicitous for the good of the family, should not refuse to pardon an adulterous partner and should not sunder the conjugal life. Nevertheless, if that spouse has not either expressly or tacitly condoned the other's fault, he or she has the right to sever the common conjugal life, provided he or she has not consented to the adultery, nor been the cause of it, nor also committed adultery.

2323 Adultery is committed when a married person engages in an act of sexual intercourse with someone other than his or her spouse. Like c.1129 §1 of the 1917 Code, this canon recognises that, in a case of adultery, the innocent party has the right to put an end to the common conjugal life. However, the present legislation prefaces this acknowledgement with an appeal for forgiveness, calling on the party who has been offended to exercise christian charity, consider the good of the family, and not sunder the conjugal life. The right of the innocent spouse to separate is carefully qualified by the law: he or she must not have condoned the adultery, either expressly or tacitly (see §2); he or she must not have consented to the adultery, i.e. must not have failed to do what was possible to prevent it; he or she must not have given the other party cause for committing adultery, e.g. by unreasonably and unjustly refusing sexual intercourse with the other party; he or she also must not have committed adultery.

---

[1] Cf. SCDF instr *Ut notum est* 6.XII.1973. This was not promulgated in AAS but an English translation is to be found in CLD 8 1177–1184.

[2] Cf. Comm 10(1978) 118 at Can. 347.

Can. 1152 §2 Tacit condonation occurs if the innocent spouse, after becoming aware of the adultery, has willingly engaged in a marital relationship with the other spouse; it is presumed, however, if the innocent spouse has maintained the common conjugal life for six months, and has not had recourse to ecclesiastical or to civil authority.

A party is understood to have condoned the adultery of his or her spouse *expressly* if he or she has openly and explicitly pardoned that spouse. A party is understood to have condoned that adultery *tacitly* if he or she has engaged willingly in a marital relationship, i.e. in sexual intercourse, with the adulterous spouse after the adultery has been discovered. This tacit condonation is presumed by the law if the innocent spouse has preserved the common conjugal life for six months after learning of the adultery and has not approached the competent ecclesiastical or civil authority to request a separation or divorce. The presumption of law, however, may be overturned by contrary evidence, e.g. if the adulterous spouse prevented the other party from leaving or from approaching the appropriate authority. 2324

Can. 1152 §3 Within six months of having spontaneously terminated the common conjugal life, the innocent spouse is to bring a case for separation to the competent ecclesiastical authority. Having examined all the circumstances, this authority is to consider whether the innocent spouse can be brought to condone the fault and not prolong the separation permanently.

The law requires that the innocent spouse who has separated because of the other party's adultery should, within six months of the actual separation, present a case for formal separation before the competent ecclesiastical authority. In accordance with Can. 1692 §1, this authority is the diocesan Bishop or the local tribunal. The principal duty enjoined upon this authority is to make yet another effort to effect a reconciliation between the parties and bring the separation to an end, an injunction that is repeated in Can. 1695. Should the Bishop or tribunal fail in this attempt, the procedures laid down in Cann. 1692–1696 are to be followed. 2325

Can. 1153 §1 A spouse who occasions grave danger of soul or body to the other or to the children, or otherwise makes the common life unduly difficult, provides the other spouse with a lawful reason to leave, either by a decree of the local Ordinary or, if there is danger in delay, even on his or her own authority.

As well as adultery, the law acknowledges that there are other reasons why one spouse might end the common conjugal life. In c.1131 §1 of the 1917 Code these were specified in some detail. Now, however, the Code speaks in general terms: a spouse has just cause to put an end to the common life if the other party constitutes a danger to him or her or to the children, or behaves in such a way that the common life is rendered exceptionally difficult. In such a situation, the person has the right to seek a decree of separation from the local Ordinary. The law also gives the spouse the authority to act on his or her own initiative and end the common life at once if there is any danger in delay. While no details are provided in the canon, it must be emphasised that the law is referring to serious problems which may result in serious harm to the party or to the children; the terms of the canon do not include the tensions, misunderstandings, and arguments between the spouses which can be overcome by the spouses themselves alone or with the intervention of a counsellor. 2326

Can. 1153 §2 In all cases, when the reason for separation ceases, the common conjugal life is to be restored, unless otherwise provided by ecclesiastical authority.

2327 In the light of the general principle of Can. 1151, as soon as the cause for separation ceases, the couple should restore their common conjugal life. This may not be possible immediately, given the pain and suffering which may have accompanied the separation. However, the intervention of an outside agent, e.g. a counsellor, a priest, etc. may be of assistance. In a particular case, given the gravity of the situation which led to the separation, the ecclesiastical authority may determine that a couple should not resume life together, i.e. the Bishop or tribunal may decree a permanent separation if there is no hope of a remedy. Clearly, the law does not intend couples to institute permanent separation on their own authority.

Can. 1154 When a separation of spouses has taken place, appropriate provision is always to be made for the due maintenance and upbringing of the children.

2328 It is important to remember that separation does not dissolve the bond of marriage. Therefore, the obligations essential to marriage are still incumbent on the spouses, even if they live apart. This is especially true of the obligations of the spouses towards their children. Without entering into any specifics, the law lays down a general principle concerning the welfare of children in cases where their parents have separated: provision for their support and upbringing must always form a part of any settlement after a separation. The stance of the Church in this regard is that, while itself assisting by its authority in making clear the moral principles and obligations involved, the *enforcement* of a settlement such as is envisaged here is probably in most cases more effectively entrusted to the civil authority.[1]

2329 As every priest experienced in pastoral practice will realise, the various provisions required in respect of the children are most often the most delicate to be resolved in a separation agreement, and thereafter to be implemented. Circumstances obviously vary from one case to another and, in some, the resolution of difficulties can be quite amicable and just. By way of general observation, however, two established facts should be borne in mind. In the first place, there is the clear *right* of each of the parents to make the best possible provision for their children in what is, unfortunately, a second-best situation; there is an equal *obligation* on the two parents to attain that end. Secondly, experience has established that, given the searing emotional circumstances of many marital separations, there is a real and often frightening danger that one or other parent will, in self-interest, attempt to use a child or children as a bargaining factor against the other partner. Whatever the civil courts may perforce have to determine in these circumstances, any such approach by a parent would be a betrayal of both the right and the obligation stated in this canon.

Can. 1155 The innocent spouse may laudably readmit the other spouse to the conjugal life, in which case he or she renounces the right to separation.

2330 Even though he or she may have justly instituted a separation from the other spouse in accordance with the law, the innocent party may re-establish common conjugal life at any time on his or her own initiative, whether or not the reason for the separation has ceased, whether or not the ecclesiastical authority has decreed otherwise. This willing readmission to the conjugal life of the other party means that the innocent party gives up the right to separation acknowledged in Cann. 1152 §1 and 1153 §1. Any further separation must take place in accordance with the law, i.e. it must have a new cause.

---

[1] Cf. Comm 15(1983) 241 at Can. 1108.

Formal separation cases of the kind provided for in Cann. 1152–1155 are far from common. Most couples whose marriages break down institute definitive separations on their own initiative, without any reference to ecclesiastical authority or the provisions of the Code of Canon Law. Yet such behaviour on their part does not, of itself, affect the juridical status of these persons within the Church, unless they have entered a subsequent civil marriage or established a quasi-conjugal relationship with another party.

Chapter X
THE VALIDATION OF MARRIAGE

Article 1
Simple Validation

Can. 1156 §1 To validate a marriage which is invalid because of a diriment impediment, it is required that the impediment cease or be dispensed, and that at least the party aware of the impediment renews consent.

While consent alone makes marriage, according to the canon law marriage may be invalid in three distinct ways:

- through the existence at the time of marriage of a diriment impediment which has not been dispensed;
- through a grave defect in the consent of one or both of the parties;
- through a defect in the form in which the consent was manifested.

It happens sometimes that parties who are aware that their marriage is invalid for one of the above reasons seek to have their situation rectified by the Church. This process is known as *validation*. The canons of this article make specific provisions for the three types of nullity just indicated.

Should a marriage be invalid due to the existence of an undispensed diriment impediment, the law requires two conditions to be fulfilled before such a marriage is validated. *Firstly*, the impediment in question should have ceased or should have been dispensed, e.g. in a case where no dispensation from the impediment of cult was granted at the time of the marriage, the impediment ceases if the unbaptised party receives baptism; if the competent authority intervenes at a later stage the impediment is dispensed. The *second* condition to be fulfilled is that the party or parties who knew of the existence of the impediment must renew their consent to marriage. The manner and form of this renewal is dealt with in the following canons.

Can. 1156 §2 This renewal is required by ecclesiastical law for the validity of the validation, even if at the beginning both parties had given consent and had not afterwards withdrawn it.

The law presumes that matrimonial consent once given perseveres until its withdrawal has been established (see Can. 1107). Nevertheless, this canon makes it clear that ecclesiastical law requires a new act of consent if an invalid marriage is to be truly validated. That this obligation is binding on all catholics is clear from Can. 11; however, the situation concerning non-catholics is not quite so clear. Commenting on the 1917 Code, some experts took the view that neither the unbaptised nor baptised non-catholics were bound to observe this requirement.[1] Others, however, basing their argument on c.12 of the 1917 Code, asserted that all the baptised were bound to renew consent in a case of validation.[2] The provisions of Can. 11 of the present Code would appear to support the former of those two interpretations. In the case of the validation of a mixed marriage, should the non-catholic party have difficulty with the idea of renewing consent, perhaps the best solution to the situation, provided there is reason to believe that the consent of the other party perseveres, is a retroactive validation without any renewal of consent (see Cann. 1161–1165). Of course, if a non-catholic party is willing in the circumstances to renew consent, there is no problem, provided that the nature of the invalidity has been properly explained as well as the nature of the renewal of consent (see Can. 1157).

Can. 1157 The renewal of consent must be a new act of will consenting to a marriage which the renewing party knows or thinks was invalid from the beginning.

2335 Before dealing with the manner in which the renewal of consent is to be carried out, the law addresses the question of the nature of this renewal. According to this canon, it is understood to be a 'new act of will consenting to a marriage', i.e. it is an act distinct from the consent expressed at the time of the original celebration of the marriage. Thus a reaffirmation that the original consent continues or perseveres is not regarded as sufficient. This act is required of the party or parties who know or think that their marriage was invalid from the beginning. In other words, there must be a genuine acceptance by each renewing party that, whatever his or her personal opinion or conviction, the marriage was in the eyes of the Church's law null and void from the start, and that he or she is in the circumstances willing to abide by that law. This canon must be read and understood in the light of the comments made on Can. 1156 §2. Clearly, great care and sensitivity must be exercised by the pastoral ministers involved with such couples: they must explain carefully the concepts of nullity and validation; they must ensure that there is no ambiguity about what is happening in the mind of the one renewing consent.

2336 Excluded from the possibility of fulfilling the requirement of this canon would be a person whose fixed frame of mind would be, e.g. 'No matter what anyone – even the catholic Church – says, I am married to X and have been for ... years, but if you want me to go through this ritual of renewing my marriage vows, I'm prepared to do so'. Such a person would be incapable of 'a new act of will consenting to a marriage' which he or she 'knows or thinks was invalid from the beginning'. The only solution in such a situation would be a retroactive validation, as suggested in our commentary on Can. 1156 §2 – provided, having carefully considered all the circumstances of the particular case, even this could be considered advisable. Hence, again, an injunction for great care and sensitivity on the part of the pastoral ministers directly involved.

Can. 1158 §1 If the impediment is public, consent is to be renewed by both parties in the canonical form, without prejudice to the provision of Can. 1127 §2.

2337 The renewal of consent takes different forms depending on the nature of the diriment impediment which rendered the marriage invalid in the first place. Thus, if the impediment is public, i.e. if it can be proved in the external forum (see Can. 1074), both parties are required to renew consent in accordance with Can. 1108, i.e. a duly

---

[1] Cf. e.g. Cappello V n.845.

[2] Cf. e.g. Navarrete *De convalidatione matrimonii (Cann. 1133–1141)* Romae 1964–1965 n.82.

authorised minister is to ask for and receive in the name of the Church the matrimonial consent of both parties in the presence of two witnesses. The law envisages the possibility that, if there are difficulties concerning the observation of the canonical form, a dispensation might be granted provided that some form of public exchange of consent would take place (see Can. 1127 §2). In a mixed marriage, if the non-catholic party is unable or unwilling to renew consent in this way, even with a dispensation from canonical form, and if the perseverance of both parties' consent is probable (see Can. 1161 §3), the provisions of Cann. 1161–1165 should be applied.

Can. 1158 §2 If the impediment cannot be proved, it is sufficient that consent be renewed privately and in secret, specifically by the party who is aware of the impediment provided the other party persists in the consent given, or by both parties if the impediment is known to both.

If the impediment which rendered the marriage invalid is occult, i.e. if it cannot be proved in the external forum (see Can. 1074), then the law does not demand the renewal of consent according to the canonical form. Instead, once the impediment in question has ceased or has been dispensed in the internal forum, it is sufficient that the party who is aware of the impediment renews his or her consent to marriage privately and in secret. This may be done in a simple form of words, indicating love and commitment to the other party who remains unaware of the existence of the impediment; however, it must be clear that the other party actually perseveres in his or her consent to marriage. If both parties happen to know of the existence of such an occult impediment, once it has ceased or been dispensed, the law asks that both renew their consent, again privately and in secret, demonstrating either verbally or in some other way the endurance of their love and commitment to each other. There is no necessity for the presence of a sacred minister or any witnesses, nor should any record be made of such a renewal. Whoever has been consulted by the party or parties about this matter in the internal forum (e.g. their parish priest or confessor) ought to explain these matters carefully. 2338

Can. 1159 §1 A marriage invalid because of a defect of consent is validated if the party who did not consent, now does consent, provided the consent given by the other party persists.

Marriage may be invalid due to a defect of consent in either or both parties, e.g. due to simulation (Can. 1101 §2), grave fear (Can. 1103), condition (Can. 1102). In such instances, the marriage is validated when the party whose consent was defective actually expresses an integral act of matrimonial consent. Again, the law adds the proviso concerning the perseverance of the consent given by the other party. Should this have been withdrawn in the meantime, the validation of the marriage cannot take place. The manner of renewing consent in cases of defect of consent is specified in the following paragraphs. 2339

Can. 1159 §2 If the defect of the consent cannot be proven, it is sufficient that the party who did not consent, gives consent privately and in secret.

This provision finds a parallel in Can. 1158 §2. If the defect of consent was purely internal, i.e. if it cannot be proved in the external forum and if it was not known to the other party, then the law regards it as sufficient for that party to renew his or her consent privately and in secret. He or she may do so verbally or in some other way so that love and commitment to the other party is expressed. In the light of the provisions of §1 of this canon, such a private and secret renewal can be done only if the consent of the other party persists. Whoever is consulted in the internal forum about the whole matter will obviously exert every effort in assisting the party in determining this. 2340

Can. 1159 §3 If the defect of consent can be proven, it is necessary that consent be given in the canonical form.

2341 Should the defect of consent admit of proof in the external forum, then the law requires that consent be renewed according to the canonical form (see Can. 1108). Since this norm is obviously a parallel to Can. 1158 §1, the comments on that canon are pertinent here also. No mention is made in this canon of a possible dispensation from form; yet given the similarities between this canon and Cann. 1158 §1 and 1160, it seems logical to conclude that, in the appropriate circumstances, such a dispensation could be given in accordance with Can. 1127 §2.

Can. 1160 For a marriage which is invalid because of defect of form to become valid, it must be contracted anew in the canonical form, without prejudice to the provisions of Can. 1127 §2.

2342 A marriage may also be invalid due to a defect of form. This canon concerns those marriages in which the canonical form is required for validity, i.e. it does not include marriages between two non-catholics whether baptised or not (see Can. 1117), nor marriages between a catholic and a non-catholic of Oriental rite (see Can. 1127 §1), nor those where a dispensation has been granted in accordance with Can. 1127 §2. The form of marriage may be defective in several ways, i.e. if the marriage involving at least one catholic party was celebrated (without a dispensation) in a register office or before a non-catholic minister, or if it was celebrated without at least two witnesses, or if the priest or deacon or lay person who asked for and received the consent of the parties was not duly delegated.

2343 Whatever the precise cause in any particular case, the law prescribes that the marriage must be *contracted anew* according to the canonical form. If a dispensation is given in such a case, the couple must exchange their consent afresh in some public form, in conformity with Can. 1127 §2. The problem of mixed marriages highlighted in connection with Can. 1156 §2 affects the application of this norm as well: is this prescription obligatory on non-catholic parties? i.e. must they also contract their marriage anew? Since this is a norm of ecclesiastical law, it would appear from Can. 11 that they are not so obliged; however, the canonical form cannot be observed unless the duly delegated minister assists, i.e. asks for and receives the consent of the parties, not simply an affirmation of the perseverance of the consent of the non-catholic party.[1] In order to avoid any ambiguity and the risk of an invalid validation, should the non-catholic party manifest an inability or unwillingness to make a new act of matrimonial consent, a retroactive validation should be considered.

Article 2
Retroactive Validation

Can. 1161 §1 The retroactive validation of an invalid marriage is its validation without the renewal of consent, granted by the competent authority. It involves a dispensation from an impediment if there is one, and from the canonical form if it had not been observed, as well as a referral back to the past of the canonical effects.

---

[1] An affirmation of the perseverance of consent by the non-catholic party is said to be sufficient in these circumstances by Doyle, Commentary (CLSA) 826, and by Wrenn (Annul) 118.

An invalid marriage may also be validated by the competent ecclesiastical authority without any renewal of consent by the parties. This form of validation, known as *sanatio in radice* (literally 'healing in the root'), is in fact a retroactive validation. This juridical institution appeared first at the beginning of the 14th century.[1] It is based on the fact that, at the time of marriage, both parties expressed consent which was 'naturally sufficient' but which, due to the presence of a diriment impediment or to the non-observance of the canonical form, was juridically ineffective. According to the canon, this *sanatio* has a threefold effect: it validates the consent to marriage originally expressed by the parties; it brings with it a dispensation from the diriment impediment which rendered the marriage invalid or a dispensation from canonical form if this had not been observed; it makes the canonical effects of the validation retroactive, i.e. it refers them back to the time of the marriage itself.

Can. 1161 §2 The validation takes place from the moment the favour is granted; the referral back, however, is understood to have been made to the moment the marriage was celebrated, unless it is otherwise expressly provided.

It is important to note that the rectification of the original union dates from the moment the favour was granted by the competent authority; it does not date from the time the parties learned of the favour or from the time of their acceptance; indeed, such a validation may take place without either party knowing of it (see Can. 1164). The canonical effects of this type of validation, however, are understood to pertain to this validated union from the date of the original exchange of consent. Although it is no longer mentioned explicitly, as it was in c.1138 §1 of the 1917 Code, this retroactivity is effected by a 'legal fiction'.

Can. 1161 §3 A retroactive validation is not to be granted unless it is probable that the parties intend to persevere in conjugal life.

The institution of retroactive validation is clearly very useful for resolving difficult situations. However, the law adds a timely warning: before granting any retroactive validation, the competent authority is to ascertain the probability that the parties intend to persevere in their original matrimonial consent. The law does not require certainty; however, the probability must have a foundation in objective reality. An already difficult situation may be rendered even more fraught by an over-zealous use of retroactive validation.

Can. 1162 §1 If consent is lacking in either or both of the parties, a marriage cannot be rectified by a retroactive validation, whether consent was absent from the beginning or, though given at the beginning, was subsequently revoked.

According to Can. 1057 §1, consent is the sole efficient cause of marriage and cannot be supplied by any human power. The use of the institution of retroactive validation presupposes the existence at the time of the original marriage of a naturally sufficient act of consent given by both parties and the perseverance of both parties in that same consent. So, if at the time of marriage the consent of one or both of the parties was defective, e.g. due to grave fear, or simulation, or condition, such a marriage cannot be validated in this way. Furthermore, even though a naturally sufficient consent was given at the time of marriage, if one of the parties subsequently alters his or intentions concerning marriage, e.g. by an intention against fidelity or against the possibility of children, the marriage cannot be validated retroactively since the original consent does not persist.

---

[1] Cf. Cappello V n.858.

Can. 1162 §2 If the consent was indeed absent from the beginning but was subsequently given, a retroactive validation can be granted from the moment the consent was given.

2348 In the case of a marriage which was invalid due to a defect in the consent expressed by either or both of the parties, a retroactive validation in the sense of Can. 1161 §2 cannot be granted. Nevertheless, the law permits the validation of such a union if naturally sufficient consent was given subsequently by the party or parties concerned. In this case, the canonical effects are not referred back to the time of the marriage; instead, they are understood as dating from the time when an integral act of matrimonial consent was made by the party or parties whose consent was defective in the first place.

Can. 1163 §1 A marriage which is invalid because of an impediment or because of defect of the legal form, can be validated retroactively, provided the consent of both parties persists.

2349 This canon states explicitly what is implied in the text of Can. 1161 §1, namely that a retroactive validation may be given in marriages which are invalid because of a diriment impediment or a defect of canonical form. Such a validation brings with it a dispensation from the impediment; therefore, the impediment in question must admit of dispensation, i.e. it must be an impediment of positive ecclesiastical law, e.g. consanguinity of the fourth degree in the collateral line (see Can. 1091 §2); moreover, care must be taken since the dispensation from some impediments is reserved to the Holy See (see Can. 1078 §2). Should the cause of the invalidity have been a defect in the canonical form, the retroactive validation carries with it a dispensation from that form, so that the canonical effects may be referred back to the time of the marriage. Whether an impediment or a defect of form was involved, the law requires as an absolute prerequisite the perseverance of the original consent given by both parties.

Can. 1163 §2 A marriage which is invalid because of an impediment of the natural law or of the divine positive law, can be validated retroactively only after the impediment has ceased.

2350 An impediment of the natural law or of divine positive law cannot be dispensed. Consequently, a marriage which is invalid due to such an impediment cannot be validated retroactively unless this impediment has ceased to exist. Effectively, this canon is referring to the impediments of prior bond of marriage and impotence: if the previous spouse of one of the parties dies, the impediment will have ceased; similarly, if a person who suffered from antecedent and perpetual impotence at the time of marriage should have the condition remedied by extraordinary means, the impediment is understood to have ceased (e.g. in the case of a woman who, at the time of the marriage, lacked a vagina, but afterwards underwent surgery for the construction of an artificial vagina). In such situations, the marriage may be validated retroactively, but the canonical effects can only date from the time the impediment ceased.

Can. 1164 A retroactive validation may validly be granted even if one or both of the parties is unaware of it; it is not, however, to be granted except for a grave reason.

2351 It is possible that a retroactive validation may be granted in a marriage where one or even both of the parties is not aware of it. This may arise where one party, knowing that the marriage is null, seeks to have it regularised without causing any upset to the other party; it may also arise where the cause of the invalidity is the negligence of the parish priest or local Ordinary, e.g. where the assisting minister lacked the proper delegation, or where a dispensation asked for was not actually granted due to inadvertence; in the latter case, the marriage may be validated retroactively without either party ever knowing that their union was in fact invalid. However, to do this in such cases requires a 'grave reason' e.g. the calming of the conscience of the party who knew of the invalidity, or the avoidance of scandal. Of course, as with all cases of retroactive validation, an absolute requirement is the perseverance of the consent of both parties. Should any doubt arise concerning the sufficiency of the reason in a particular case where one or both of the parties did not know of the invalidity, the retroactive validation is valid in conformity with the principle enunciated in Can. 90 §2.

Can. 1165 §1 Retroactive validation can be granted by the Apostolic See.

2352 The instrument of retroactive validation was reserved solely to the Holy See by c.1141 of the 1917 Code. According to the current legislation, the Holy See remains competent to consider any request for such a validation. Indeed, the Holy See remains the only competent authority to deal with certain categories of retroactive validation, e.g. the validation of a large number of marriages invalid for the same reason,[1] the validation of a marriage invalid because of an impediment whose dispensation is reserved to the Holy See, the validation of a marriage where an impediment of natural law or divine positive law has ceased.

Can. 1165 §2 It can be granted by the diocesan Bishop in individual cases, even if a number of reasons for nullity occur together in the same marriage, assuming that for a retroactive validation of a mixed marriage the conditions of Can. 1125 will have been fulfilled. It cannot, however, be granted by him if there is an impediment whose dispensation is reserved to the Apostolic See in accordance with Can. 1078 §2 or if there is question of an impediment of the natural law or of the divine positive law which has now ceased.

2353 Although the 1917 Code reserved retroactive validations to the Holy See alone, in practice this faculty was granted to local Ordinaries by the Sacred Congregation for the Propagation of the Faith.[2] This was extended to all local Ordinaries by Pope Paul VI.[3] The present canon sets forth the limitations of the Bishop's authority in this matter: he may grant a retroactive validation in individual cases only; he may do so even though the marriage may have been invalid on a number of headings; he must make sure that the provisions of law concerning mixed marriages are observed in the retroactive validation of such a marriage. The law makes it abundantly clear that the diocesan Bishop can not grant a retroactive validation if the impediment in question is one that is reserved to the Holy See; nor can he do so if there was an impediment of natural law or divine positive law which has now ceased. The canon speaks of the 'diocesan Bishop', not of the 'local Ordinary'. Accordingly, this faculty is given by law solely to those who are diocesan Bishops and to those who are equivalent in law to a diocesan Bishop (see Cann. 381 §2, 368). This does not include the Vicar general or Vicar episcopal, although the Bishop may give these the faculty to grant retroactive validations by special mandate (see Can. 134 §3).

---

[1] A general retroactive validation was granted for England by Pope Julius III in 1554, for France by Pope Pius VII in 1801 and 1809, and for the whole Church by Pope Pius X in 1912: cf. Cappello V n.858.

[2] SCPF Decennial Faculties 1.1.1920, Formula Prima n.9: LE I 251; Formula Secunda nn.16–17: ibid 253; Formula Tertia nn.22–23: ibid 256.

[3] Pope Paul VI mp EM 15.VI.1966 18: CLD 6 399.

PART II

THE OTHER ACTS OF DIVINE WORSHIP

Title I
Sacramentals

Can. 1166 Sacramentals are sacred signs by which, somewhat after the fashion of the sacraments, effects, especially spiritual ones, are signified and are obtained through the intercession of the Church.

2354 This definition of sacramentals is different to that given in c.1144 of the 1917 Code, which referred to them as 'things or actions'. Now, following Vat. II they are described as 'sacred signs which bear a resemblance to the sacraments'.[1] This is not to say that sacramentals are somehow the same as the sacraments; it is rather to make the point that they are 'somewhat like the sacraments' precisely in that they too *signify* the spiritual effects to which they are directed. The difference of course is that they bring about their effects 'through the intercession of the Church', not – as in the case of the sacraments – by their own inherent action arising from their institution by Christ *(ex opere operato)*.[2] In this general context Vat. II has an illuminating comment when it observes that the liturgy of the sacraments and sacramentals sanctifies almost every event of the lives of the faithful: 'there is scarcely any proper use of material things which cannot thus be directed toward the sanctification of people and the praise of God'.[3]

Can. 1167 §1 Only the Apostolic See can establish new sacramentals, or authentically interpret, suppress or change existing ones.

2355 In the course of the revision process it was submitted that this paragraph could be considered too exacting, for the reason that the Apostolic See would not be able to have sufficient knowledge and experience of all the socio-cultural circumstances and needs throughout the world to allow it adequately to interpret, suppress or change existing sacramentals or introduce new ones. However, the Revision Commission rejected this on the ground that the very importance of the matter i.e. a public act of

---

[1] SC 60: Fl I 20.

[2] The particular terminology of this canon arose as a result, during the revision process, of a consultation with the SCSDW which underlined the link in sacramental theology between the twin concepts of *sign* and *sacredness*: cf. Comm 13(1981) 442 at Can. 362. Cf. also Can. 834 §1, and Can. 840 where the sacraments are described as not only 'signs' but in themselves 'means' by which *inter alia* 'our sanctification is brought about'.

[3] SC 61: Fl I 20.

the Church, required that it be reserved to the Apostolic See.[1] On the other hand, it is certainly open to Bishops' Conferences to make submissions to the Apostolic See concerning sacramentals which would have a specific reference to local conditions or circumstances.[2]

Can. 1167 §2 The rites and the formulae approved by ecclesiastical authority are to be accurately observed when celebrating or administering sacramentals.

This substantially repeats c.1148 §1 of the 1917 Code, though the words 'and the formulae' have been added. The prescription of this paragraph clearly involves an obligation to do precisely what it says; its non-observance would therefore obviously be unlawful. But the text itself does not – as c.1148 §2 of the 1917 Code did – raise any question as to whether or not the non-observance would render *invalid* the sacramental in question. Some commentators have expressed the view that, while the *rites* are required for lawfulness only, the non-observance of the *formulae* would render the sacramental invalid and consequently of no effect whatever.[3] On the other hand, there is the fact that the Revision Commission deliberately, it would seem, omitted any reference to validity, even though it had been positively invited to do so by the Congregation for the Sacraments and Divine Worship.[4]

2356

Can. 1168 The minister of the sacramentals is a cleric who has the requisite power. In accordance with the liturgical books and subject to the judgement of the local Ordinary, certain sacramentals can also be administered by lay people who possess the appropriate qualities.

Going beyond c.1146 of the 1917 Code, and conforming to Vat. II,[5] this canon establishes the twofold general principle:

2357

(a) that the ordinary minister of the sacramentals is a cleric i.e. a Bishop, a priest or a deacon – each in accordance with his appropriate competence as established by law (see Can. 1169);

(b) that in certain circumstances some sacramentals may be administered by qualified lay people – in accordance with liturgical law (including local liturgical law) and subject to the judgement of the local Ordinary: one could think of examples such as parents blessing their children, a eucharistic minister blessing a communicant, any lay person conducting a burial service, etc. It is clear that this matter will be governed by local circumstances and conditions and that, while allowing a due discretion to those 'working on the ground', the judgement of the local Ordinary will in the last analysis be the determining factor.

Can. 1169 §1 Consecrations and dedications can be validly carried out by those who are invested with the episcopal character, and by priests who are permitted to do so by law or by legitimate grant.

---

[1] Cf. Comm 15(1983) 243 at Can. 1121 §1.

[2] Cf. ibid.

[3] Cf. Chiappetta II n. 3892; Commentary (St Paul's) 733 at Can. 1167.

[4] Cf. Comm 13(1981) 442 at Can. 364 (rectius 363). In practice, the point is perhaps more theoretical than real – the more so since the efficacy of the sacramentals depends so fundamentally on the intercession of the whole Church. The clear obligation of Can. 1167 §2 remains.

[5] Cf. SC 79: Fl I 23.

§2 Any priest can impart blessings, except for those reserved to the Roman Pontiff or to Bishops.

§3 A deacon can impart only those blessings which are expressly permitted to him by law.

2358 While c.1147 §1 of the 1917 Code spoke only of 'consecration', and some intervening liturgical books substituted for it the term 'dedication',[1] §1 of this canon uses both terms in the same context. In this terminology a *consecration* is a solemn rite in which either a person[2] or a thing[3] becomes permanently destined to worship and the service of God. Normally the rite involves the use of sacred oils. A *dedication*, which is not substantially distinct from a consecration, is the term properly applied to the rite involving sacred places, in particular churches and altars for which a special rite is included in the *Roman Pontifical*.[4] The persons and the things thus set aside thereby become, both juridically and liturgically, 'sacred persons' and 'sacred things'.[5]

2359 For validity, the *minister of consecrations and dedications* is:

(a) a Bishop – though it must be noted that 'the dedication of a place belongs to the diocesan Bishop and those equiparated to him in law' (Can. 1206; see Cann. 368, 381 §2);

(b) a priest 'permitted to do so by law or by legitimate grant' (see e.g. Can. 1206).

2360 A *blessing* is a less solemn rite, generally involving the recital of certain prayers followed by a sprinkling with holy water, but without the use of sacred oils. Blessings fall into two traditionally-accepted categories; they are:

(a) *constitutive* when, along the same lines as consecrations, they render 'sacred' some place or thing, e.g. a church (see Can. 1217 §1), an oratory or a private chapel (see Can. 1229), an altar (see Can. 1237 §1), a cemetery (see Can. 1240 §1), etc.

(b) *invocative* when, without in any way altering the nature of their object, they invoke the favour and protection of God upon certain persons (e.g. the sick, the attendant worshippers at the end of Mass), upon certain places (e.g. a newly acquired family home, a factory, a school), upon certain things (e.g. a motorcar/automobile, a fishing fleet, etc.)

The current regulations and rites of blessings which may be imparted are contained in the *Roman Ritual*[6] and in its approved local vernacular translations.

2361 The *minister of a blessing* is 'any priest' (*a fortiori*, any Bishop) 'except for those blessings reserved to the Roman Pontiff or to Bishops' (§2). Vat. II prescribed that 'reserved blessings shall be very few ... (and) shall be in favour only of Bishops or Ordinaries'.[7] This prescription is reflected in the list of reserved blessings to be found in the Ceremonial of Bishops.[8] Two practical points may be noted: (i) any reservation affects

---

[1] E.g. RDCA.

[2] E.g. the consecration of a virgin (cf. Can. 604): cf. *The Rite of Consecration to a Life of Virginity* SCDW 31.V.1970 Vatican Press 1970: DOL nn.3253–3262.

[3] E.g. the consecration of oils (cf. Can. 847 §1), of chrism (cf. Can. 880 §2): cf. *The Rite of the Blessing of Oils and Rite of Consecrating the Chrism* SCDW 3.XII.1970 Vatican Press 1971: DOL nn.3861–3872.

[4] Cf. RDCA nn.4361–4445.

[5] Cf. Chiappetta II n.3894.

[6] *Rituale Romanum: De Benedictionibus, editio typica 1984* Vatican Press.

[7] SC 79: Fl I 23.

[8] *Caeremoniale Episcoporum, editio typica 1984* Vatican Press; *Ceremonial of Bishops* ICEL The Liturgical Press Collegeville Minnesota 1989.

only the lawfulness of the blessing – not its validity unless this is expressly stated;[1] (ii) in respect of the blessing of *places*, the prescription of Can. 1207 is to be observed.

A *deacon* may also be a *minister of a blessing* but, in accordance with §3 of this canon, only of 'those blessings which are expressly permitted to him by law'.[2] A deacon is empowered to give the blessing after exposition of the Blessed Sacrament,[3] after giving holy communion to the sick,[4] and on the occasions of baptism and marriage.[5]

Can. 1170 While blessings are to be imparted primarily to catholics, they may be given also to catechumens and, unless there is a prohibition by the Church, even to non-catholics.

This canon considers those to whom blessings may be given. Its attitude is significantly positive, to the effect namely that, in the absence of any specific prohibition by the Church, an appropriate blessing may be given to any and every person:

(a) primarily to *catholics*, who 'have the *right* to be assisted by their Pastors from the spiritual riches of the Church ...' (Can. 213).

(b) to *catechumens*, who, though not yet baptised, 'are linked with the Church in a special way ...' (Can. 206 §1): a particular point in this regard was made in the course of the revision process.[6]

(c) to *non-catholics*, whether baptised or not, believers or not, all of whom are children of God whom the Saviour came to redeem.[7] At the practical level, pastoral prudence must obviously be exercised in this regard and any real danger of scandal avoided.

(d) even to *excommunicated persons* who, though forbidden to receive the sacraments (see Can. 1331 §1 2°), are not prohibited from receiving the sacramentals. The same would apply to those who, for other reasons based upon the sacramental theology of the Church, are excluded from the reception of the Blessed Eucharist (such e.g. as their involvement in irregular marital unions, in persistently grave violations of justice whether public or private, in manifest violations of the Fifth Commandment, etc.) Once again here, pastoral prudence and understanding will ensure that scandal be avoided.

---

[1] Cf. 1917 Code c.1147 §3; Chiappetta II n.3896.

[2] For the background to this regulation, cf. Comm 12(1980) 387 at Can. 4; DVCom rep 13.XI.1974: AAS 66(1974) 667: LE V 4330 6878–6879.

[3] Cf. *Holy Communion and Worship of the Eucharist outside Mass* SCDW 21.VI.1973 Vatican Press 1973: DOL n.2217; cf. Can. 943.

[4] Cf. *Pastoral Care of the Sick: Rites of Anointing and Viaticum* SCDW 7.XII.1972 Vatican Press 1972: DOL n.3349.

[5] Cf. *Rite of Baptism for Children* SCDW Vatican Press 1973: DOL nn.2299–2306; *Rite of Marriage* SCRit 19.III.1969 Vatican Press 1969: Not 5(1969) 216–220: DOL nn.2969–2984.

[6] Cf. Comm 12(1980) 387 at Can. 5; *Rite of Christian Initiation of Adults* SCDW 6.I.1972 Vatican Press 1972: DOL n.2345.

[7] Cf. Comm 15(1983) 244 at Can. 1124. For further background material in this regard, cf. Comm 12(1980) 387 at Can. 5; 13(1981) 443 at Can. 366. Noteworthy is the *omission* from the promulgated text of a phrase, inherited from c.1149 of the 1917 Code, which indicated the purpose for which blessings might be given to non–catholics, i.e. 'so that they might receive the light of faith or, with that, bodily health' – a phrase which, despite considerable debate in the Revision Commission, survived into the 1982 Draft which was submitted to the Holy Father; its obviously deliberate omission by the Legislator is clearly a reflection of the thrust of Vat. II.

Can. 1171 Sacred objects, set aside for divine worship by dedication or blessing, are to be treated with reverence. They are not to be made over to secular or inappropriate use, even though they may belong to private persons.

2364 Since, by dedication and by some blessings, certain objects become *sacred objects* (see Can. 1169 §§1 and 2), 'set aside for divine worship', this canon insists that, 'even though they may belong to private persons', they 'are to be treated with reverence'. This has implications even beyond the religious one of a necessary reverence. Their sacred character imposes a certain limitation on the proprietary rights of those who possess them: thus 'they are not to be made over to secular or inappropriate use': a typical example would be that of an oratory or private chapel which, in the words of Can. 1229, must 'be freed from all domestic use'.[1]

Can. 1172 §1 No one may lawfully exorcise the possessed without the special and express permission of the local Ordinary.

§2 This permission is to be granted by the local Ordinary only to a priest who is endowed with piety, knowledge, prudence and integrity of life.

2365 The exorcism 'of the possessed', with its long history in the Church, going back to the time of Christ,[2] remains one of the sacramentals. As its predecessor c.1151 of the 1917 Code, and indeed the centuries-old tradition of canon law, this canon treats this delicate matter with great care and caution. It makes two specific points:

(a) no such exorcism may be carried out without 'the special and express permission of the *local Ordinary*': no such permission may ever be presumed, nor may it be granted by any other Ordinary such as that of a religious institute or of a society of apostolic life (see Can. 134 §2);

(b) this permission may be granted by the local Ordinary 'only to a priest who is endowed with piety, knowledge, prudence and integrity of life'.[3]

Title II
The Liturgy of the Hours

2366 This brief three-canon Title draws significant attention to a vital element in the life of the Church, i.e. the need for prayer. *The Liturgy of the Hours* – commonly known as 'the Divine Office' or 'the Breviary' – has had a long and important history, stemming from the admonition of Christ on the necessity of praying always and not losing heart (see Luke 18:1). The stress here is on the need for communal or public prayer, in addition to that private or personal prayer which is incumbent upon every individual. In effect, *The Liturgy of the Hours* is the Church itself at prayer.

---

[1] For further relevant implications in this regard, cf. Cann. 397 §1, 1269, 1376.

[2] Cf. the substantial document *Christian Faith and Demonology* issued by SCDW 26.VI.1975: Fl II 456–485. It is to be noted that the exorcism referred to in this canon is other than that involved in the administration of the sacrament of Baptism, for which the appropriate minister of that sacrament is competent.

[3] In this regard cf. the strict admonition of SCDF lit circ 29.IX.1985: AAS 77(1985) 1169–1170: Comm 18(1986) 46–47: CLD 11 276–277.

Can. 1173 In fulfilment of the priestly office of Christ, the Church celebrates the liturgy of the hours, wherein it listens to God speaking to his people and recalls the mystery of salvation. In this way, the Church praises God without ceasing, in song and prayer, and it intercedes with him for the salvation of the whole world.

This canon highlights the theological thinking which lies behind the canonical norms in respect of the Liturgy of the Hours, itself the public and official prayer of the Church. In particular, in the Divine Office the Church: 2367

- listens to God speaking to his people;
- recalls the mystery of salvation;
- praises God without ceasing;
- intercedes with God for the salvation of the whole world.[1]

Can. 1174 §1 Clerics are obliged to recite the liturgy of the hours, in accordance with Can. 276 §2 n.3; members of institutes of consecrated life and of societies of apostolic life are obliged in accordance with their constitutions.

§2 Others also of Christ's faithful are earnestly invited, according to circumstances, to take part in the liturgy of the hours as an action of the Church.

It is in the light of the foregoing comments on Can. 1173 that the prescriptions of this canon are to be interpreted. The obligation to which it refers (§1) and the invitation which it extends (§2) can be properly understood solely in the light of a clear understanding not only of the place but also of the vital importance of this official prayer in the name of the whole Church. 2368

The obligation is therefore placed upon those who, by their calling and status, are already committed officially to pray in the name of the Church. This obligation is incumbent upon: 2369

(a) *Clerics* i.e. Bishops, priests, deacons aspiring to the priesthood, whether belonging to the diocesan or the non-diocesan ('religious') clergy (see Can. 276 §2 3°). This is an absolute obligation.

(b) *Non-clerical members* of institutes of consecrated life and of societies of apostolic life. The extent of this obligation is that determined by the specific constitutions of the respective institutes or societies (see Can. 663 §3).

(c) *Permanent deacons*, to the extent determined by the appropriate Bishops' Conference.[2]

The extent to which this obligation is, or is not, a grave one, i.e. obliging under pain of serious sin, is discussed by commentators. A not uncommon opinion is that the recitation of Lauds and Vespers (Morning Prayer and Evening Prayer) fulfils the sub- 2370

---

[1] After Vat. II the Divine Office was revised and reordered along the lines prescribed by SC 83–101: Fl I 24–28. For the principal documents implementing this revision, cf. Pope Paul VI ap con *Laudis Canticum* I.XI.1970: AAS 63(1971) 527–535: DOL nn.3415–3429; SCDW *General Instruction on the Liturgy of the Hours* 2.II.1971 (now to be found in Vol I of the Breviary): DOL nn.3431–3714. Both of these documents will repay careful study. Cf. also Comm 15(1983) 242 at Can. 1120.

[2] For the manner in which Bishops' Conferences have hitherto determined this matter, cf. LCE Tavola per Paesi e Canoni at Can. 276: the majority have prescribed Lauds and Vespers (Morning Prayer and Evening Prayer).

stantial obligation.[1] Be that as it may, the view of this commentary is that any such minimalist approach fails to capture the spirit of the law, namely that 'in fulfilment of the priestly office of Christ, the Church celebrates the liturgy of the hours ... ' (Can. 1173). In effect, the Church prays, and wants to pray. To those who, by their very vocation, are committed to praying for and on behalf of the Church, the obligation of reciting the Divine Office integrally every day should be seen as a precious privilege – one of which they should generously avail themselves in all but the most exceptional circumstances.

2371 Since the Church is not merely clerics and religious but *all of Christ's faithful* (see Cann. 204 §1, 207), an earnest invitation is extended (§2) to everyone, according to their individual circumstances and possibilities, to participate in one way or another in the official prayer of the Church: 'if the prayer of the Divine Office becomes genuine personal prayer, the relation between the liturgy and the whole christian life becomes clearer'.[2] What is clearly in mind here are principally those occasions when the faithful come together to reflect, to meditate and to pray, such as retreats, missions, special group Masses, and the like. Even one 'Hour' of the Divine Office could well be used; obviously a fruitful participation would require an appropriate preparation and catechesis.[3]

Can. 1175 In carrying out the liturgy of the hours, each particular hour is, as far as possible, to be recited at the time assigned to it.

2372 This canon gives very practical effect to the injunction of Vat. II which, while requiring that 'the traditional sequence of the hours ... be restored so that, as far as possible, they may again become also in fact what they have been in name', at the same time recognised that 'account must be taken of the conditions of modern life in which those who are engaged in apostolic work must live'.[4] That the individual hours of the Divine Office be, 'as far as possible, recited at the time assigned to it' is obvious to those who are aware of its history in the life of the Church. The most obvious example is today, as it has always been, the practice of monks, nuns and others whose very vocation and life-style involve choral recitation of the Office. At the other end of the clerical spectrum are those whose whole-time commitment is to the active ministry of the apostolate, particularly in parishes and in certain allied missionary endeavours. It is recognised that their work-schedule is often such as to make the ideal in this regard impossible in practice. The thrust of this canon is to require of them that they would do the best possible, within that milieu, to spread their recitation of the Divine Office through the day, 'since the purpose of the office is to sanctify the day'.[5]

---

[1] Cf. e.g. Chiappetta II n.3912, who not unreasonably bases his position on SCDW *General Instruction on the Liturgy of the Hours* n.29, 2. But cf. also SC 89 (a) and 96: Fl I 25 and 29.

[2] Pope Paul VI ap con *Laudis Canticum* n.8: DOL n.3427.

[3] It is even envisaged that, in certain circumstances, the Code's invitation could profitably be taken up in the environment of the family, 'this domestic sanctuary': SCDW op cit n.27, 2.

[4] SC 88: Fl I 25. Cf. also SC 89–99: Fl I 25–28; Comm 15(1983) 243 at Can. 1120 b.

[5] SC 88: Fl I 25. A perceptive footnote (j) to Fl I 25 points to a practice which both Vat. II and this canon aim to reform and, so far as possible, to reverse.

Part II The Other Acts of Divine Worship

Title III
Church Funerals

When compared with its counterpart in cc.1203–1242 of the 1917 Code, this Title is considerably shortened and simplified. Taking as its starting point the injunction of Vat. II that 'funeral rites should express more clearly the paschal character of Christian death',[1] its general thrust is aptly expressed in the revised *Rite of Funerals*: 2373

> 'At the funerals of its children the Church confidently celebrates Christ's paschal mystery. Its intention is that those who by baptism were made one body with the dead and risen Christ may with him pass from death to life. In soul they are to be cleansed and taken up into heaven with the saints and elect; in body they await the blessed hope of Christ's coming and the resurrection of the dead... Because of the communion of all Christ's members with each other, all of this brings spiritual aid to the dead and the consolation of hope to the living. As they celebrate the funerals of their brothers and sisters, Christians should be intent on affirming with certainty their hope for eternal life.'[2]

Can. 1176 §1 Christ's faithful who have died are to be given a Church funeral according to the norms of law.

The law states clearly a *right* of Christ's faithful (see Cann. 204 §1, 1183 §1): they 'are to be given a Church funeral'. This is a public right, which cannot therefore be arbitrarily renounced – at least as to its substance, whatever about minor details of the ceremonial itself. It is moreover a right which carries with it a corresponding *obligation* both on the family or other representatives of the deceased to see to the funeral arrangements, and on the parish priest (or one of his assistant priests) to conduct the Church funeral (see Can. 530 5°). The only restriction which 'the norms of law' place upon this right is that prescribed by Can. 1184. 2374

Can. 1176 §2 Church funerals are to be celebrated according to the norms of the liturgical books. In these funeral rites the Church prays for the spiritual support of the dead, it honours their bodies, and at the same time it brings to the living the comfort of hope.

This paragraph makes a vital practical point in highlighting the threefold specific purpose of a Church funeral. Every such funeral is designed: 2375

(a) primarily, to pray 'for the spiritual support' of the person who has died, i.e. earnestly to ask that God's infinite mercy would admit this person to the eternal life merited by the death and resurrection of Christ. 'It is therefore a holy and wholesome thought to pray for the dead, that they may be loosed from sins';[3]

---

[1] SC 81: Fl I 24.

[2] SCDW 15.VIII.1969 nn.1–2: DOL nn.3373–3374.

[3] 2 Maccabees 12:46 (Douay), testifying to even the Old Testament's significant insistence on prayers for the dead so that, precisely in view of a resurrection, they might be forgiven their sins: at that time the fullness of the revelation in Christ had yet to come. For a perhaps fuller flavour of the text, cf. the RSV and the Jerusalem Bible renderings of 2 Maccabees 12:43–45.

(b) to honour this dead body which in life, by reason of baptism, had been a temple of the Holy Spirit – a salutary reminder;

(c) to bring 'to the living' – obviously, in the first place, to the family, friends and other close associates of the person who has died – 'the comfort of hope', that Christian hope which carries the certainty of reunion in eternal life.

The whole tenor of this paragraph makes clear what a fundamental misrepresentation and pastoral error it would be to consider any Church funeral as little more than an occasion for a eulogy, however merited, of the person who had died.[1]

Can. 1176 §3 The Church earnestly recommends that the pious custom of burial be retained; it does not however forbid cremation, unless this is chosen for reasons which are contrary to christian teaching.

2376 Reflecting the constant tradition of the Church, even back to apostolic times, this paragraph clearly indicates that 'the pious custom of burial' should, in so far as possible, be the norm.

> 'All necessary measures must be taken to preserve the practice of reverently burying the faithful departed. Accordingly, through proper instruction and persuasion Ordinaries are to ensure that the faithful refrain from cremation and not discontinue the practice of burial except when forced to do so by necessity.'[2]

2377 It is well known that under the legislation of the 1917 Code (see cc.1203, 1240 §1 5°) the cremation of the faithful was strictly forbidden and visited by penal measures. The reason for this was never that cremation was wrong in itself; it was, rather, that principally from the time of the French Revolution cremation had been positively advocated by liberal and atheistic movements as a sectarian instrument to promote anticlericalism and, in effect, to deny the resurrection of the body, merited by Christ's own death and resurrection. In the changed circumstances of the middle of this century Pope Paul VI reviewed the matter and, in the light of prevailing social, economic and environmental conditions, decided to lift the automatic ban on cremation, and to prohibit it solely when, in the words of this canon, it 'is chosen for reasons which are contrary to christian teaching'.[3] The current evidence would appear to suggest that choice is nowadays rare.

2378 'Funeral rites are to be granted to those who have chosen cremation, unless there is evidence that their choice was dictated by anti-Christian motives ...'[4] The precise determination of those rites is a matter for the appropriate Bishops' Conference, issuing its own *Rite of Funerals*.[5]

---

[1] The 'norms of the liturgical books' referred to may be found, and profitably studied, in SCDW 15.VIII.1969: *Rite of Funerals* DOL nn.3373-3397, and in the appropriate local adaptations.

[2] SCHO instr *Piam et constantem* of 8.V.1963, approved by Pope Paul VI 5.VII.1963: AAS 56(1964) 822-823: DOL nn.3366-3370, at n.3367.

[3] The reasoning behind this norm is clearly set out in *Piam et constantem* loc cit, which would merit careful study.

[4] *Piam et constantem* loc cit: DOL n.3387.

[5] A problem arises in the not infrequent situation in which the cremated ashes of a deceased are returned for burial in the country of his or her origin, specifically in the parish of origin. Should there be a formal funeral service? The liturgy does not provide for this. A practical solution would appear to be a Requiem Mass for the deceased in the chosen church, in association with a burial of the ashes in the grave of the family's choice.

Part II The Other Acts of Divine Worship

Chapter I
THE CELEBRATION OF FUNERALS

Unlike the more restrictive regulations of the 1917 Code, a feature of this Chapter is the element of a considerably simplified choice which it offers in respect both of the church in which one's funeral may be celebrated, and of the place of one's burial.

Can. 1177 §1 The funeral of any deceased member of the faithful should normally be celebrated in the church of that person's proper parish.

§2 However, any member of the faithful, or those in charge of the deceased person's funeral, may choose another church; this requires the consent of whoever is in charge of that church and a notification to the proper parish priest of the deceased.

§3 When death has occurred outside the person's proper parish, and the body is not returned there, and another church has not been chosen, the funeral is to be celebrated in the church of the parish where the death occurred, unless another church is determined by particular law.

In normal circumstances, the church is to be the one 'of that person's proper parish' (§1), i.e. the parish in which he or she has had a domicile or quasi-domicile (see Can. 107 §1) – in effect, what is usually called the person's *own* parish; this will clearly have to be adjusted in respect of the travelling people (see Can. 107 §2). However, that rule must now be read in the light of the wide choice offered by §2, whereby 'another church' – *any other church*[1] – may be chosen either by the person in question (e.g. in a will or otherwise expressed before death), or by the family of the deceased or those in charge of the funeral arrangements (e.g. the executors of the will). There are just two simple requirements: (a) that 'whoever is in charge' of the chosen church (be that a parish priest, a religious Superior, a seminary rector, etc.) would agree: it is envisaged that that consent would be readily forthcoming in all but the most exceptional circumstances; (b) that the parish priest of the deceased person's own parish would be simply informed.

When death occurs outside the person's own parish – as will in modern times not infrequently happen (e.g. in hospital, while travelling abroad, as a result of an accident away from home, etc.) – it is envisaged that, whenever possible and practicable, the body will be returned for the funeral either to the home parish or to the other church chosen in accordance with §2. The rule of §3 provides *solely* for the situation in which, for whatever reason, that normal procedure turns out to be impossible. In such a situation, the funeral is to be celebrated 'in the church of the parish where the death occurred', provided only that the local ecclesiastical law of that place has not determined otherwise.[2]

Can. 1178 The funeral of a diocesan Bishop is to be celebrated in his own cathedral church, unless he himself has chosen another church.

This canon speaks for itself. In the light of Can. 1242, the same rule applies to a *retired* diocesan Bishop.

Can. 1179 Normally, the funerals of religious or of members of a society of apostolic life are to be celebrated in their proper church or oratory: by the Superior, if the institute or society is a clerical one; otherwise, by the chaplain.

---
[1] The restrictions imposed by c.1225 of the 1917 Code have been removed.
[2] Cf. Comm 15(1983) 244–245 at Can. 1128 n.2.

2383   This canon concerns the funerals of those who are members either of an institute of consecrated life (see Can. 573ff) or of a society of apostolic life (see Can. 731ff). The norm is that their funerals be celebrated in their own church or oratory: 'by the Superior, if the institute or society is a clerical one; otherwise, by the chaplain'. But this rule is not a hard and fast one: the word 'normally' clearly allows that for special reasons other appropriate arrangements could be made. It is to be noted that members of secular institutes (see Cann. 710–730) must follow not this regulation but rather that of the other faithful as prescribed in the foregoing Can. 1177.[1]

Can. 1180 §1 If a parish has its own cemetery, the deceased faithful are to be buried there, unless another cemetery has lawfully been chosen by the deceased person, or by those in charge of that person's burial.

§2 All may, however, choose their cemetery of burial unless prohibited by law from doing so.

2384   Turning to the place of burial, this canon follows the pattern of those preceding it. In the absence of any other disposition, the norm is that 'if a parish has its own cemetery, the deceased faithful are to be buried there' (§1). However, as in the matter of the church of the funeral, the law allows that another cemetery may have been chosen, as in the terms of Can. 1177 §2. Moreover, it states that 'all may ... choose their cemetery of burial, unless prohibited by law from doing so' (§2): this choice would appear to be open also to religious.[2]

Can. 1181 The provisions of Can. 1264 are to be observed in whatever concerns the offerings made on the occasion of funerals. Moreover, care is to be taken that at funerals there is to be no preference of persons, and that the poor are not deprived of a proper funeral.

2385   Besides making explicit reference to the directive of Can. 1264 2°, this canon underlines once again the Church's care for the poor – a point significantly made in Can. 848.

Can. 1182 After the burial an entry is to be made in the register of the dead, in accordance with particular law.

2386   Can. 535 §1 prescribes that there be in every parish *inter alia* a register of deaths. Precisely what that should record is a matter for 'particular law', in effect the regulation either of the Bishops' Conference or of the diocesan Bishop.

Chapter II
THOSE TO WHOM CHURCH FUNERALS ARE TO BE ALLOWED OR DENIED

Can. 1183 §1 As far as funerals are concerned, catechumens are to be reckoned among Christ's faithful.

2387   This simple regulation is in keeping with the special status of catechumens as established by Vat. II[3] and as defined in Can. 206 (see also Can. 788). They have therefore the right to a church funeral, as the parish priest has the corresponding obligation to provide it; the permission of the local Ordinary is not required.

---

[1] Cf. Comm 15(1983) 245 at Can. 1130.
[2] Cf. Comm 12(1980) 353.
[3] Cf. AGD 14: Fl I 828–829.

Can. 1183 §2 Children whose parents had intended to have them baptised but who died before baptism, may be allowed Church funerals by the local Ordinary.

This rule modifies the more rigid stance of c.1239 §1 of the 1917 Code. Two important conditions are however required:

(a) it applies only to 'children whose parents had intended to have them baptised': the *real* intention of the parents is a crucial factor; in normal circumstances (though there could indeed be intervening exceptional situations) it should conform to the obligation placed upon them by Can. 867; a vague undetermined intention to have the child baptised 'at some time in the future' would certainly not fulfil this condition.

(b) it requires the express permission of the local Ordinary, whose obligation it is to be assured that the first condition above has indeed been fulfilled. The *Rite of Funerals*, while providing for the appropriate liturgical celebration in these circumstances, carries an injunction to the effect that the permission may be granted only if the local Ordinary is satisfied that it will not either tend to undermine the Church's teaching on the necessity of baptism or lead to a practice of delaying baptism. In certain situations this matter will clearly call for a sensitive and understanding dialogue with the parents.

Can. 1183 §3 Provided their own minister is not available, baptised persons belonging to a non-catholic Church or ecclesial community may, in accordance with the prudent judgement of the local Ordinary, be allowed church funerals unless it is established that they did not wish this.

The ecumenism fostered by Vat. II is responsible for this further development in the law, whereby a Church funeral may be granted to '*baptised* persons belonging to a non-catholic Church or ecclesial community'. The conditions are simple and readily understandable, namely:

(a) that 'their own minister is not available';[1]

(b) that, whether or not such minister be available at the time, they themselves had not already made it clear that they did not wish this particular funeral rite.

It is entrusted to the prudent judgement of the competent local Ordinary, whose permission is required, to determine whether these conditions have been fulfilled.[2]

Can. 1184 §1 Church funerals are to be denied to the following, unless they gave some signs of repentance before death:

1° notorious apostates, heretics and schismatics;

2° those who for anti-christian motives chose that their bodies be cremated;

---

[1] The unavailability of 'their own minister' can clearly occur in many and differing circumstances. It is perhaps worth noting that in some – by no means all – mixed marriages, the non-catholic partner would have had the practice over the years of accompanying his or her spouse to the family Sunday Mass etc. In the absence of positive evidence to the contrary, it would be reasonable in such a situation to presume that the non-catholic minister was, in the sense of this canon, 'not available'.

[2] The granting of permission for a Church funeral implies the celebration of a funeral or exsequial Mass, itself a public function. In this regard consideration should be given to SCDF decr *Accidit in diversis* 11.VI.1976: AAS 68(1976) 621–622: Fl II 59–61: DOL nn.1074–1077. The opinion of some commentators, e.g. Chiappetta II n.3939, that some of the restrictive clauses of that decree have been superseded by this canon is certainly a tenable one.

3° other manifest sinners to whom a Church funeral could not be granted without public scandal to the faithful.

§2 If any doubt occurs, the local Ordinary is to be consulted and his judgement followed.

2390 The denial of a Church funeral to one of its members has always been an extremely sensitive issue in the Church's law. Even in the 1917 Code (cc.1239–1242) a considerable care was exercised to seek a balance between, on the one hand, a necessary discipline and, on the other, a true understanding of the mercy of God, revealed principally in the death and resurrection of Christ. In seeking to strike that same balance, the present Code takes account of two very relevant factors, namely that:

(a) the *primary* purpose of a Church funeral is to pray 'for the spiritual support of the dead' (see our commentary on Can. 1176 §2): this consideration alone induces a strong reluctance to deny such a funeral to any of its members;

(b) all *'liturgical actions* (of which funerals are certainly one) are not private but are celebrations of the Church itself as the "sacrament of unity" ... (which) concern the whole body of the Church, making it known and influencing it' (Can. 837 §1). When therefore the law decrees that certain persons are to be denied a Church funeral, its reluctant decision is directed solely at those who, by their conduct in life, have deliberately and irrevocably chosen to secede from the unity and community of the Church.

It is in the light of these considerations that this Can. 1184 has to be understood and applied.[1] This explains also why – as in c.1240 §1 of the 1917 Code – the denial of a Church funeral to those named in §1, does not apply if 'they gave *some signs* of repentance before death'. This is a phrase which has long been interpreted by canonists in the most charitable and generous sense. Almost any positive sign which would indicate the person's continued belief in God's mercy, however apparently flawed by previous personal conduct, would suffice – even e.g. by his or her making the sign of the cross, by responding to an invocation of God's mercy, or the like.

2391 Taking the foregoing considerations into account, only the following are to be denied a Church funeral:

(a) *apostates, heretics and schismatics* (see Cann. 751, 1364), but *only* if their offences will have been *notorious* i.e. either in some way publicly declared by ecclesiastical authority, or in fact so well known that it would be impossible to deny or doubt them:[2] anything less would not justify the denial of a funeral;

(b) those who have chosen that their bodies be *cremated*, but *only* if they will have made the decision 'for anti-christian motives' (see our commentary on Can. 1176 §3);

(c) *other manifest sinners*, but *only* if the granting of a Church funeral to them would cause 'public scandal to the faithful'. Among such 'manifest sinners' would be included e.g. those who had publicly espoused atheistic ideologies, those who were publicly known to have been members of a group or society whose purpose was to inveigh against the Church, etc. Under the 1917 Code (c.1240 §1 6°) some would have included in this category those who had been living in an invalid or otherwise irregular marital union. Before making a judgement on that situation, or others of its like, one must take account of the Letter from the Sacred Congregation for the Doctrine of the Faith issued on 29.V.1973 which *inter alia* reads as follows:

---

[1] It must therefore be clearly understood that the denial of a Church funeral is *never* a penal measure in respect of a person's conduct during life.

[2] For the conditions under which a person is liable to penal sanctions, cf. Cann. 1321–1330.

'the celebration of ecclesiastical burial should be made easier for those catholics to whom it had been denied by the provisions of c.1240 (of the 1917 Code). As an amendment to this canon to the extent required, a new set of regulations will be promulgated as soon as possible. On the basis of the new arrangement the celebration of liturgical funeral rites will no longer be forbidden in the case of the faithful who, even though involved in a clearly sinful situation before their death, have maintained allegiance to the Church and have given some evidence of repentance. A necessary condition is that there be no public scandal for the rest of the faithful. It will be possible to lessen or forestall such scandal ... to the extent that pastors explain in an effective way the meaning of a Christian funeral. Then the majority will see the funeral as an appeal to God's mercy and as the Christian community's witness to faith in the resurrection of the dead and life eternal.'[1]

From all of this clearly emerges the law's reluctance to deny a Church funeral except in the most publicly scandalous of situations – with the clear obligation on priests, in perhaps sometimes difficult situations, to explain to their people 'the meaning of a Christian funeral'.

It will be easily appreciated that in this area there may well arise a doubt as to how best to act in a given situation. In §2 of this canon a clear directive is provided: 'the local Ordinary is to be consulted and his judgement followed'. In making his decision the relevant Ordinary will obviously be guided by the foregoing considerations.

Can. 1185 Any form of funeral Mass is also to be denied to a person who has been excluded from a Church funeral.

If in virtue of Can. 1184 a person has been denied a Church funeral, it follows that 'any form of funeral Mass is also to be denied', i.e. a Mass celebrated *publicly in association with the funeral*. There is however no prohibition on the celebration of a private Mass for the repose of the person's soul, that to him or her also God's mercy may be extended. Nor, it would appear, is there a prohibition (as there was in c.1241 of the 1917 Code) on the celebration of even a public Mass on the occasion of the anniversary of the death, provided always that this would not cause scandal to the faithful.[2]

Title IV
The Cult of the Saints, of Sacred Images and of Relics

Can. 1186 To foster the sanctification of the people of God, the Church commends to the special and filial veneration of Christ's faithful the Blessed

---

[1] DOL n.3398, reported also in CLD 8 862–863. By way of follow-up to that Letter, cf. SCDF decr 20.IX.1973 which declared that 'a funeral is not to be forbidden for public sinners if before death they have given some evidence of repentance and there is no danger of scandal to others of the faithful': DOL n.3399: CLD 8 864. Cf. also Comm 12(1980) 356.

[2] Cf. Chiappetta II n.3944.

Mary ever-Virgin, the Mother of God, whom Christ constituted the Mother of all. The Church also promotes the true and authentic cult of the other Saints, by whose example Christ's faithful are edified and by whose intercession they are supported.

2394 Once again Vat. II has provided the inspiration of this canon, in which the veneration of the Blessed Virgin Mary and of the Saints is earnestly encouraged, precisely 'to foster the sanctification of the people of God'.[1] Highlighted is 'the special and filial veneration ... (of) the Blessed Mary ever-Virgin, the Mother of God, whom Christ constituted the Mother of all', she 'who occupies a place in the Church which is the highest after Christ and also closest to us'.[2] Fostered also is 'the true and authentic cult of other Saints by whose example Christ's faithful are edified and by whose intercession they are supported': in effect, that the faithful should pray to the Saints and ask their help on their own pilgrimage to eternal life.

Can. 1187 Only those servants of God may be venerated by public cult who have been numbered by ecclesiastical authority among the Saints or the Blessed.

2395 This canon speaks for itself: the 'public cult' to which it refers is defined in Can. 834 §2. Despite considerable and protracted discussion in the Revision Commission, the Code does not determine the distinction – if there be any of substance – between the cult of the Saints and that of the Blessed.[3] The veneration by public cult is permitted only of those 'who have been numbered by ecclesiastical authority among the Saints or the Blessed' – whether this *numbering* has been done either by the recognition of an immemorial cult (as in the case of many through earlier ages), or by the formal process of canonisation or beatification.[4] On the other hand, however, there is no reason – in fact, quite the contrary – why the faithful might not pray, but *privately*, not only *for* but also *to* those who by widespread popular consent have led lives of singular service to God and to the Church: they are surely to be included among those 'by whose example Christ's faithful are edified ...' (Can. 1186).

---

[1] Cf. SC 103–104: Fl I 29; LG 52–69: Fl I 413–423. For the development of this text through the Revision Commission, cf. Comm 12(1980) 372 at Can. 54; 15(1983) 246 at Cann. 1137ff; 16(1984) 99 at Can. 70

[2] LG 54: Fl I 414. It is important to recognise – as Vat. II has stressed more than once (cf. SC 103: Fl I 29; LG 66–67: Fl I 421–422) – that devotion to the Blessed Virgin is not, as it were, independent of and a kind of adjunct to the mystery of salvation but is, rather, essentially linked with the redemptive work of Christ: 'She is inseparably linked with her Son's saving work' (SC 103: Fl I 29). This is not the only reference in the Code to the pre-eminence of devotion to the Blessed Virgin: cf. Cann. 246 §3, 276 §2 5°, 663 §4. For recent papal statements in this regard, cf. Pope Paul VI ap exhort *Signum Magnum* 13.V.1967: AAS 59(1967) 465–475; ap exhort *Marialis cultus* 2.II.1974: AAS 66(1974) 113–168; Pope John Paul II encl *Redemptoris Mater* 25.III.1987: AAS 79(1987) 361–433: Origins 16(1987) 745–766.

[3] Cf. Comm 12(1980) 372–373 at Can. 55 §2; 15(1983) 247 at Can. 1138 §2; even though the final draft, submitted to the Pope in 1982 (at Can. 1187 §2), did carry a specific reference to this matter, it does not appear in the promulgated text – from which it would be reasonable to conclude that the Legislator did not wish to resolve in a code of law that which was manifestly a matter of divergent views among liturgical scholars.

[4] For the most recent regulations for the processing of causes for beatification and canonisation, cf. Pope John Paul II ap con *Divinus perfectionis Magister* 25.I.1983: AAS 75(1983) 349–355: CLD 10 266–273; SCCS Norms etc. 7.II.1983: AAS 75(1983) 396–404: CLD 10 273–282.

Can. 1188 The practice of exposing sacred images in churches for the veneration of the faithful is to be retained. However, these images are to be displayed in moderate numbers and in suitable fashion, so that the christian people are not disturbed, nor is occasion given for less than appropriate devotion.

It has for centuries been the tradition of the Church to acknowledge and to promote the practice of the veneration of so-called 'sacred images' i.e. statues, sculptures, paintings and the like, which depict in artistic form either the overall history of salvation or the contribution thereto from this or that organisation or person. Equally, it has been the Church's tradition firmly to warn against trivial or popularist aberrations in this regard.[1] This is precisely the point made in this balanced canon, clearly reflecting Vat. II.[2]

Can. 1189 The written permission of the Ordinary is required to restore precious images needing repair: that is, those distinguished by reason of age, art or cult, which are exposed in churches and oratories to the veneration of the faithful. Before giving such permission, the Ordinary is to seek the advice of experts.

Subject to this regulation are those sacred images (see Can. 1188) which are:

– *precious* in the sense defined in the canon;

– *exposed* in churches and oratories.

When any of these is in need of repair or restoration, written permission to carry it out must first be sought from the competent Ordinary i.e. the local Ordinary, in respect of churches and oratories belonging to a diocese or its equivalent; the appropriate major Superior, in respect of those which are the property of the institutes or societies determined in Can. 134 §1. In other situations, it would appear to be a matter also for the local Ordinary. But even the competent Ordinary may not give the requested permission without having himself had 'the advice of experts' (not just any *one*) in the sphere involved.[3]

Can. 1190 §1 It is absolutely wrong to sell sacred relics.

§2 Distinguished relics, and others which are held in great veneration by the people, may not validly be in any way alienated nor transferred on a permanent basis, without the permission of the Apostolic See.

Sacred *relics* are in a different category to sacred images, since the former, if properly authenticated, are part (however minute) of the mortal remains of those martyrs and saints who have been formally acknowledged by the Church as having lived lives of heroic virtue and accordingly are proposed as an example and a support for all of Christ's faithful. It is for this reason that §1 – using a terminology employed on only

---

[1] Cf. Chiappetta II n.3950 and the sources cited therein.

[2] Cf. SC 125: Fl I 35.

[3] In a diocesan situation the local Ordinary will obviously think, at least initially, of the Commission on Sacred Art as recommended by Vat. II: SC 126: Fl I 35. Attention should moreover be given to the lit circ *Opera artis* issued to the Presidents of Bishops' Conferences by SCC 11.IV.1971: AAS 63(1971) 315-317: DOL nn.4327-4334. It is also to be noted that the 'precious images' involved here are subject to the regulations of Cann. 1220 §2, 1283 2°-3°, 1292 §2 and, in the context of prescription, 1270.

three other occasions in the Code[1] – declares the sale of sacred relics to be 'absolutely wrong' and in no way to be countenanced or tolerated. The rule of §2 applies only to sacred relics which are *distinguished*[2] or are the object of especial *public veneration* and, apart from their alienation (see Cann. 1291–1294), it concerns only their *permanent* transfer to another, not any merely temporary one.

Can. 1190 §3 The provision of §2 applies to images which are greatly venerated in any church by the people.

2399 The 'images' referred to here are those described above at Can. 1188 – but not all such: only those which in a given church are and, for the most part, long have been the object of a deep-rooted and widespread popular veneration. Some of these may well be in themselves of considerable artistic, historical or other such value. But the issue here is not merely one of monetary value: the images in question are considered to be an integral part of the general patrimony of that church. Hence the application of the same requirement as in §2 of this canon concerning alienation and permanent transfer, a violation of which could involve the penal sanction of Can. 1377.

Title V
Vows and Oaths

Chapter I
VOWS

Can. 1191 §1 A vow is a deliberate and free promise made to God, concerning some good which is possible and better. The virtue of religion requires that it be fulfilled.

§2 Unless they are prohibited by law, all who have an appropriate use of reason are capable of making a vow.

§3 A vow made as a result of grave and unjust fear or of deceit is by virtue of the law itself invalid.

2400 The definition of a vow in §1 is the traditional one, itself already enshrined in c.1307 §1 of the 1917 Code.[3] The essential elements of a vow are clear. A vow is:

– a promise, not any mere wish or desire;

– deliberately and freely made;

---

[1] Significantly, in respect of the blessed Eucharist (Can. 927), of the seal of sacramental confession (983 §1), and either of forcing a person to receive ordination or of repelling a suitable candidate from doing so (Can. 1026). A violation of this regulation could well involve the penal sanction of Can. 1376.

[2] Cf. 1917 Code c.1281 §2. This rule does not therefore apply to the minute and enclosed relics which are often in the possession of private persons, though of course these also would come under the prohibition of §1 of the present canon.

[3] The recognised commentators on the 1917 Code in this regard remain therefore a secure guide. Cf. also Chiappetta II n.3959; Commentary (St Paul's) 744 at Can. 1191. For the progress of this and its following canons on vows through the Revision Commission, cf. Comm 12(1980) 374–376.

- to God, and to Him alone;
- accordingly to be fulfilled by reason of the virtue of religion;
- in respect of something which is in itself positively good, not merely indifferent, and which is both possible of attainment and, in all the circumstances, the 'better option' for the person in question.

From this it is quite clear that no vow – whether in religious life or otherwise – should ever be either taken or admitted without the most serious prior consideration on the part of all concerned. This is all the more manifest when one considers the import of §2, which rightly permits the making of a vow to 'all who have an appropriate use of reason': the use of reason as required by Can. 97 §2, obviously; but much more: that use of reason which is *appropriate to*, in the sense of adequately understanding and appreciating, the meaning and implications of the vow in question.

A vow is, in the terms of the law, a 'juridical act' (see Cann. 124–128). It is accordingly subject to the rules governing such acts. In accordance with those rules, §3 of this canon declares invalid, and therefore of no effect, a vow which may have been made under the influence of:

- grave and unjust fear, from whatever source;
- deceit, of whatever kind.

Though not specifically mentioned in this canon, it would appear that a substantial ignorance or error would, in virtue of Can. 126, also invalidate a vow.[1]

Can. 1192 §1 A vow is public if it is received in the name of the Church by a lawful Superior; otherwise, it is private.

§2 It is solemn if it is recognised by the Church as such; otherwise, it is simple.

§3 It is personal if it promises an action by the person making the vow; real, if it promises some thing; mixed, if it has both a personal and a real aspect.

Vows may be of various kinds, as stated in this canon, itself for the most part reflecting c.1308 of the 1917 Code but with significant differences as to their implications.

(a) *A vow may be public or private (§1)*
- it is **public** if it is received 'in the name of the Church' and specifically by a Superior determined for this purpose by the law.
- it is **private** if it is made otherwise than in those circumstances.[2]

The publicity or otherwise attaching to the occasion of making the vow is not the criterion of this distinction. Thus e.g. a vow made in accordance with the approved constitutions of a religious institute, but without any publicity, would be a public vow, whereas e.g. a vow of chastity made by an individual at his or her own choice would remain a private one no matter what publicity surrounded the occasion.

(b) *A vow may be solemn or simple (§2)*
- it is **solemn** if it is 'recognised by the Church as such';
- it is **simple** if it is not thus recognised.

Under the 1917 Code this distinction had a significant importance which in itself it no longer has: e.g. in the previous legislation a solemn vow was a diriment impediment invalidating marriage, whereas a simple vow while impeding marriage did not,

---

[1] Cf. Chiappetta II n.3960.

[2] For an instructive discussion on this distinction, cf. Comm 12(1980) 375–376.

apart from very exceptional circumstances, invalidate it (see 1917 Code cc.1073, 1058); in this same context of marriage, the current Code makes no reference to the distinction but substitutes the straightforward norm of Can. 1088. In fact, this distinction has no longer any juridical relevance in the general law of the Church. However, after considerable discussion in the Review Commission it was decided to retain it in view of the possibility that some religious Institutes might wish to incorporate it into their own particular constitutions.[1]

(c) *A vow may be personal, real or mixed* (§3)

- it is **personal** if it 'promises an action by the person making it', e.g. to assist at daily Mass, to recite certain prayers, to abstain from this or that, etc.
- it is **real** if it 'promises some thing', e.g. to make a certain donation to the poor, to give the gift of a precious personal possession to a church or to a charitable organisation, etc.
- it is **mixed** if it 'has both a personal and a real aspect', e.g. personally to bring a precious personal possession as an offering to a charitable organisation or cause, etc.

In so far as they arise nowadays, most vows are personal. The others considered here should not, however, be forgotten.

Can. 1193 Of its nature a vow obliges only the person who makes it.

2403 This canon states a clear and obvious principle: if a person makes a vow, that vow *as such* binds only that person. Under c.1310 §2 of the 1917 Code, however, that obligation had been, as far as a *real* vow was concerned (see Can. 1192 §3), extended to include the heirs of the person who had made the vow. For very good reasons the Revision Commission rejected that position, thus in effect abolishing that part of the previous legislation.[2]

Can. 1194 A vow ceases by lapse of the time specified for the fulfilment of the obligation, or by a substantial change in the matter promised, or by cessation of a condition upon which the vow depended or of the purpose of the vow, or by dispensation, or by commutation.

2404 This canon lists six circumstances in which the obligation undertaken by a vow ceases to bind. The first four are intrinsic to the vow itself, e.g. the lapse of time specified for its fulfilment, the cessation of a condition upon which the vow depended, etc.[3] The last two are extrinsic causes: dispensation (see Can. 1196) and commutation (see Can. 1197).

Can. 1195 A person who has power over the matter of a vow can suspend the obligation of the vow for such time as the fulfilment of the vow would affect that person adversely.

2405 Unlike c.1312 of the 1917 Code, this canon deals only with the *temporary suspension* of a vow's obligation, specifically by the person who has power over *the matter of the vow*, not necessarily over the person making the vow.[4] The very good reason behind

---

[1] For a fuller understanding of this matter, cf. Comm 12(1980) 376 at Can. 60; 15(1983) 73 at Can. 580; 16(1984) 120–132. Cf. also Chiappetta I nn.2523–2524.

[2] Cf. Comm 5(1973) 45; 12(1980) 376.

[3] For further elaboration, cf. the approved commentators on the 1917 Code at c.1311; Chiappetta II n.3967; Commentary (Urbanianum) 691.

[4] The 1917 Code in its c.1312 §1 did e.g. allow any religious Superior in certain circumstances simply to cancel the obligation of a vow made by one of that Superior's subjects – and this in virtue of the then-named 'dominative power' (*protestas dominativa*), a term which finds no place in the current Code. For the explanation of this change, cf. Comm 5(1973) 45; 12(1980) 377 at Can. 63.

this regulation is that no one may promise to God something which is prejudicial to the rights of others. Thus e.g. a religious Superior could suspend the vow of a novice, or indeed of even an outsider, if the fulfilment of that vow were to be harmful to or disruptive of the good order of the religious house – precisely because the Superior has the obligation and the right (the 'power over') to promote and protect that good order. This power of suspension is temporary, in the sense that it can be exercised only for as long as the fulfilment of the vow remains prejudicial to the person with power over the matter of the vow; should that situation change – a possibly unlikely scenario – the obligation of the vow would revive in the person who had made it.

Can. 1196 Besides the Roman Pontiff, the following can for a just reason dispense from private vows, provided the dispensation does not injure the acquired rights of others;

1° **the local Ordinary and the parish priest, in respect of all their own subjects and also of** *peregrini*;

2° **the Superior of a religious institute or of a society of apostolic life, if these are clerical and of pontifical right, in respect of members, novices and those who reside day and night in a house of the institute or society;**

3° **those to whom the faculty of dispensing has been delegated by the Apostolic See or by the local Ordinary.**

This canon concerns *only* dispensations from *private vows* (see Can. 1192 §1). Dispensations in the matter of public vows are dealt with in Cann. 688 §2, 691–692, 701, 728, 743 etc. Besides the Roman Pontiff, whose competence extends to the universal Church (see Can. 331), the following can dispense from private vows:

2406

- **the local Ordinary and the parish priest:**[1] in respect not only of their own subjects, be they within their territory or not, but also of passers-by (*peregrini*: see Can. 100 and Glossary) who happen to be within their territory.[2]

- **the Superior** of a religious institute or of a society of apostolic life provided it be **clerical**[3] **and of pontifical right**: in respect not only of their members and their novices, but also of 'those who reside day and night in a house of the institute or society', such e.g. as housekeepers and other such lay persons of the staff resident in the house.[4]

- those to whom **the faculty of dispensing** has been **delegated** either by the Apostolic See or by the local Ordinary;[5] it may not be delegated by the parish priest.

As in the case of all dispensations, those considered here may be granted only for a just reason and provided the acquired rights of others (see Can. 4) are respected.

---

[1] The granting of this authority to the parish priest (not to assistant priests in a parish) is an example of the provision catered for in Can. 89.

[2] The proposal that this same authority be given to confessors was rejected by the Revision Commission: cf. Comm 12(1980) 377 at Can. 64.

[3] Cf. Can. 129 §1.

[4] It would appear that this faculty of dispensation would extend also even to other clerics resident in the house, say e.g. for the purpose of convalescence after illness, further studies in the locality, etc.

[5] The 1917 Code c.1313 3° had limited this power of delegation to the Apostolic See.

Can. 1197 What has been promised by private vow can be commuted into something better or equally good by the person who made the vow. It can be commuted into something less good by one who has authority to dispense in accordance with Can. 1196.

2407 This canon speaks for itself in regard to the very exceptional situation which it considers. No one should change the object of a private vow 'into something better or equally good' without the serious advice of a competent spiritual director.

Can. 1198 Vows taken before religious profession are suspended as long as the person who made the vow remains in the religious institute.

2408 Once a person makes a formal profession, even temporary, in a religious institute or society of apostolic life, *any vow* made before that is automatically thereby suspended. It will remain suspended for as long as the person remains a professed member of that institute or society. It is only if the person subsequently leaves the institute or society that the obligation of the earlier vow would once again become operative, subject of course to the provisions of Can. 1196.

Chapter II
OATHS

Can. 1199 §1 An oath is the invocation of the divine Name as witness to the truth. It cannot be taken except in truth, judgement and justice.

2409 This canon deals with what is technically known as an *assertory* oath. An oath, as evidenced by its definition here, is a very serious matter. It is the invocation of 'the divine Name as witness to the truth'. This means that the person making an oath is in effect saying to God, the creator of the universe: 'You may disown me if what I now say is not the truth as I know it' – a frightening prospect for anyone who believes in God. The taking of an oath is a common feature in both ecclesiastical and civil courts. In both cases it is, and can only be, an act of religion: otherwise it would make no sense whatever. There is evidence that in recent years it has in some quarters become trivialised, and often reduced to a mere formality. Anyone who professes to take an oath otherwise than 'in truth, judgement and justice' is simply not taking an oath, and must be adjudged as such by any court, whether ecclesiastical or civil.

Can. 1199 §2 An oath which is required or accepted by the canons cannot validly be taken by proxy.

2410 This paragraph speaks for itself. A person who commits perjury is subject to a penal sanction (see Can. 1368).

Can. 1200 §1 A person who freely swears on oath to do something is specially obliged by the virtue of religion to fulfil that which he or she asserted by the oath.

§2 An oath extorted by deceit, force or grave fear is by virtue of the law itself invalid.

2411 This and the succeeding canons deal with a *promissory* oath i.e. one whereby the person solemnly undertakes to do something or to provide some service. The obligation to fulfil such a promise derives not merely from the acceptance of ordinary human decency and trust, but specifically from the virtue of religion (§1). This assumes *inter alia* that the oath be made in total freedom – so much so that if were to be *extorted* by deceit, force or grave fear (§2) it would be of no binding effect whatever.[1] As in the case of a vow (see Can. 1191 §3), an oath made under the influence of substantial ignorance or error would also be invalid.

Can. 1201 §1 A promissory oath is determined by the nature and condition of the act to which it is attached.

§2 An act which directly threatens harm to others or is prejudicial to the public good or to eternal salvation, is in no way reinforced by an oath sworn to do that act.

The principle enunciated in §1 of this canon is a simple but fundamental one. Even though a promise made under oath endows it with the additional demand of the virtue of religion, it does not thereby in any way *alter the substance* of that which was promised. Thus e.g. an oath-bound promise to do something within a specified time-limit does not make that promise obligatory after that limit has passed, no more than a promise dependant upon the fulfilment of a certain condition obliges if that condition is not in fact fulfilled, etc. An application of the same principle operates in the prescription of §2: a solemn promise 'which directly threatens harm to others, or is prejudicial to the public good or to eternal salvation' is the very antithesis of an act of religion, and accordingly 'is in no way reinforced by an oath sworn to do that act' – indeed, on the contrary. 2412

Can. 1202 The obligation of a promissory oath ceases:

1° **if it is remitted by the person in whose favour the oath was sworn;**

2° **if what was sworn is substantially changed or, because of altered circumstances, becomes evil or completely irrelevant, or hinders a greater good;**

3° **by the cessation of the purpose or the condition under which the oath may have been made;**

4° **by dispensation or commutation in accordance with Can. 1203.**

The obligation of a promissory oath ceases in substantially the same circumstances as in those applicable to a vow (see Cann. 1194, 1196 and relevant footnotes). 2413

Can. 1203 Those who can suspend, dispense or commute a vow have, in the same measure, the same power over a promissory oath. But if dispensation from an oath would tend to harm others and they refuse to remit the obligation, only the Apostolic See can dispense the oath.

The first sentence of this canon is a simple referral in the context of an oath to those canons which authorise, '**in the same measure**', the suspension, dispensation or commutation of a vow (see Cann. 1195–1197). In the second sentence, however, one exception is made, in respect namely of 'a *dispensation* from an oath (which) would tend to harm others and they refuse to remit the obligation' (see Can. 1202 §1 1°). In such a situation 'only the Apostolic See can dispense the oath' – a rare situation perhaps but one which, if it were to arise, should not be disregarded.[2] 2414

---

[1] For the relationship between the terminology employed here and that in Can. 1191 §3 concerning a vow, cf. Comm 12(1980) 378 at Can. 68 §2. Note also that the prescription of §2 of this canon applies equally to an assertory oath.

[2] Cf. Comm 12(1980) 380 at Can. 71.

Can. 1204 An oath is subject to strict interpretation, in accordance with the law and with the intention of the person taking the oath or, if that person acts deceitfully, in accordance with the intention of the person to whom the oath is made.

2415 For the concept of *strict interpretation* see Can. 18. An oath is subject to such interpretation, and particularly 'in accordance ... with the intention of the person taking the oath': the obligation of an oath depends essentially on what precisely that person intended. The only exception would be 'if that person acts deceitfully' i.e. swore an oath to do something which he or she had no real intention of carrying out. In such a situation – and this rule stresses again the seriousness of any oath, since it invokes the name of God – the oath must be interpreted in accordance with the intention and understanding of the beneficiary.

PART III

SACRED PLACES AND TIMES

Title I
Sacred Places

Can. 1205 Sacred places are those which are assigned to divine worship or to the burial of the faithful by the dedication or blessing which the liturgical books prescribe for this purpose.

This is the first of nine canons which introduce the five brief chapters in this title, and give the general norms concerning their subject matter. The definition of sacred places is the same as that in c.1154 of the 1917 Code, other than that the term 'dedication' is used here in place of 'consecration', on the ground that dedication is theologically the more accurate term.[1] The use of the two forms, dedication and blessing, is consistent with usage in the liturgical books, particularly the *Rite of Dedication of a Church and an Altar*.[2] This Rite, particularly in its introductory paragraphs, gives an overview of the theological background to this title of the Code. The revised *Roman Ritual* 31.V.1984 provides norms regarding blessings; the revised *Caeremoniale Episcoporum* 14.IX.1984 lists the blessings which are reserved to the Roman Pontiff or to Bishops.

2416

Can. 1206 The dedication of a place belongs to the diocesan Bishop and to those equivalent to him in law. For a dedication in their own territory they can depute any Bishop or, in exceptional cases, a priest.

Can. 1169 §1 states the general law on those who can validly carry out a dedication: this canon is an application of the principle. Those 'equivalent in law' to a diocesan Bishop are indicated in Can. 381 §2. In 'exceptional cases', when it is impossible or difficult for the Bishop or his equivalent to perform the ceremony, he may depute a priest of his choice to carry out the dedication: this is a change from c.1155 of the 1917 Code, which reserved this function to a Bishop.

2417

Can. 1207 Sacred places are blessed by the Ordinary, but the blessing of churches is reserved to the diocesan Bishop. Both may, however, delegate another priest for the purpose.

The blessing of a church (see Can. 1214) is reserved to the diocesan Bishop: an example of the reservation of a blessing as provided for in Can. 1169 §2. Other sacred places, such as oratories, private chapels, shrines and cemeteries may be blessed by the Ordinary. However, for all blessings of sacred places, including churches, a priest may also be delegated. This is a less restrictive norm than that of the preceding canon where, in the case of a dedication, a priest could be deputed only in exceptional cases.

2418

---

[1] Comm 12(1980) 325 at Can. 1.

[2] DOL nn.4361–4445.

Can. 1208 A document is to be drawn up to record the dedication or blessing of a church, or the blessing of a cemetery. One copy is to be kept in the diocesan curia, the other in the archive of the church.

2419 The prescription of this canon – which concerns only churches and cemeteries – conforms to other norms of the Code which require that acts, particularly those which of their nature are designed to have a juridical effect, must be in writing (see Can. 474, etc.). The regulation is an important one, and its implementation is subject to visitation by the Ordinary: apart from their obvious historical value, these records could well be crucial in certain legal situations (see e.g. Cann. 1222, 1376). For the diocesan archive, see Cann. 486–488; for that of a church, not merely a parish church, see Can. 491 §1; Can. 535 §4 deals specifically with the parish archives.

Can. 1209 The dedication or the blessing of a place is sufficiently established even by a single unexceptionable witness, provided no one is harmed thereby.

2420 In the absence of a written document, the testimony of a witness may suffice to establish the dedication or blessing; a 'single unexceptionable witness' is the same term as that used in Cann. 876 and 894 in regard to proving the conferral of baptism and of confirmation – though the practical application of this measure will obviously be far less likely than in the case of those two sacraments.

Can. 1210 In a sacred place only those things are to be permitted which serve to exercise or promote worship, piety and religion. Anything which is discordant with the holiness of the place is forbidden. The Ordinary may however, for individual cases, permit other uses, provided they are not contrary to the sacred character of the place.

2421 The canon draws much of its thinking from Vat. II[1] and from the 1970 *General Instruction on the Roman Missal*.[2] A strong thrust of these sources is that sacred places, their furnishings and their works of art, should be liturgically and artistically of a high quality, and yet adapted to present-day needs. All 'should worthily and beautifully serve the dignity of worship'.[3] *Anything* out of harmony with the holiness of a sacred place is forbidden.

2422 Uses other than the direct exercise or promotion of worship, piety and religion are permitted, but for individual cases, and then only with the permission of the Ordinary. Such individual cases might e.g. involve events such as a musical concert[4] or a flower festival: in proper circumstances, there is in fact a real sense in which such events do exercise and promote worship, piety and religion. At times, it might be appropriate to allow other religious groups to hold services in a church or other sacred place. However, the use of churches for political rallies is firmly excluded.

Can. 1211 Sacred places are violated by acts done in them which are gravely injurious and give scandal to the faithful when, in the judgement of the local Ordinary, these acts are so serious and so contrary to the holiness of the place that worship may not be held there until the harm is repaired by means of the penitential rite which is prescribed in the liturgical books.

---

[1] SC 124–128: Fl I 35–36
[2] GIRM 254: Fl I 189.
[3] SC 122: Fl I 34.
[4] Cf. SCDW letter on concerts in churches 5.XI.1987: Origins 17(1988) 468–470.

Part III Sacred Places and Times

The 1917 Code in cc.1172 and 1207 concerned itself only with the violation of a church and a cemetery, and it enumerated four specific acts by which violation could occur. This canon concerns *all* the sacred places defined in Can. 1205, and it does not mention any specific acts. Rather, it leaves it to the local Ordinary to determine when such a violation has occurred. In effect, a sacred place is violated – though it does not thereby lose its dedication or blessing – when the local Ordinary declares that an act has occurred *within it* which is gravely offensive and has caused real scandal to the faithful, to the extent that it would be contrary to the sacred character of the place to hold any further form of worship there until the harm, not least to the feelings and consciences of the people, would have been repaired by a liturgical ceremony of repentance. The profanation of the blessed Eucharist is an obvious example, as would be the malicious desecration of graves in a cemetery. Anyone responsible for such a violation is subject to a 'just penalty' (Can. 1376; see also Can. 1367). The faithful are to be invited to participate in the appropriate penitential rite, thus to have the opportunity to express their abhorrence of the violation of what is *their* sacred place.[1]

2423

Can. 1212 Sacred places lose their dedication or blessing if they have been in great measure destroyed, or if they have been permanently made over to secular usage, whether by decree of the competent Ordinary or simply in fact.

The loss of dedication or of blessing is more radical than the violation dealt with in Can. 1211. It occurs in two situations:

2424

(a) if the sacred place has been 'in great measure' destroyed, as e.g. by an act of war or by fire; on occasion, the major reconstruction of, say, a church may raise the question as to whether the building is merely a restored one or is in effect a new one: the decision on this matter would be for the Ordinary;

(b) if the sacred place has been 'permanently made over to secular usage': at times, particularly in respect of ancient buildings, this will have occurred as a matter of established fact; alternatively, the place may be so made over by a decision of the appropriate Ordinary, whose decree to this effect itself brings about the loss of dedication or of blessing. For the application of this principle to churches in particular, see Can. 1222.

Can. 1213 Ecclesiastical authority freely exercises its power and functions in sacred places.

This statement of ecclesiastical authority in respect of its sacred places is distinctly different in tone from that of the corresponding canon in the 1917 Code,[2] thereby reflecting a more realistic attitude to contemporary society. It is an unequivocal statement of the Church's right *freely*, i.e. without interference by the civil authority, to exercise its own 'powers and functions', particularly in the fulfilment of its threefold mission of governing, of teaching and of sanctifying. To that extent, the canon firmly rejects the conduct of those governments – of which there are even current lamentable instances – whereby e.g. a Bishop's pastoral letter to his flock is required to be subject to prior civil approval, even worse where a church is simply confiscated and converted to a quite other use.

2425

At the same time, the canon implicitly recognises that these sacred places cannot properly function without reference to the appropriate civil and administrative regula-

2426

---

[1] Cf. Comm 12(1980) 329–331.

[2] Cf. 1917 Code c.1160, which opens with a claim of the exemption of all sacred places from the civil authority.

tions governing public order of the country or society in which they exist.[1] Thus e.g. those in charge of sacred places such as churches and cemeteries must take care to observe the relevant civil legislation in respect of planning, public safety, public health and the like – and indeed where necessary to have an adequate insurance against the civil risks involved.[2]

Chapter I
CHURCHES

Can. 1214 The term church means a sacred building intended for divine worship, to which the faithful have right of access for the exercise, especially the public exercise, of divine worship.

2427 The term 'church' is best understood in conjunction with the terms 'oratory' and 'private chapel' as defined in the next chapter; the term 'public oratory' is no longer used. Central to this canon is the definition of a church as a sacred place to which the faithful have 'right of access', as distinct from the 'use by all the faithful as its principal purpose' of which c.1161 of the 1917 Code spoke. Although the canon speaks of access by 'the faithful', it can happen that a church will be *primarily* at the service of the faithful of a certain rite, or language, or culture: such churches are sometimes known as 'national' churches. This does not, however, alter the basic right of access by whomsoever of the faithful, inherent in the very definition of any church (see also Can. 1221).

Can. 1215 §1 No church is to be built without the express and written consent of the diocesan Bishop.

§2 The diocesan Bishop is not to give his consent until he has consulted the council of priests and the rectors of neighbouring churches, and then decides that the new church can serve the good of souls and that the necessary means will be available to build the church and to provide for divine worship.

§3 Even though they have received the diocesan Bishop's consent to establish a new house in a diocese or city, religious institutes must obtain the same Bishop's permission before they may build a church in a specific and determined place.

2428 This canon is not substantially different from c.1162 of the 1917 Code, save only that the consent now required is that of the diocesan Bishop (§1), not of any other local Ordinary (see Can. 134 §2). It is again stressed that this consent must be express and in writing. The purpose of requiring this consent is to ensure not merely the authority of the Bishop, but also the benefit of his prudent judgement in respect of the appropriate distribution of places of worship in each diocese.[3] This required consent is not to be given save under the conditions laid down in §2, namely that the Bishop:

---

[1] In this regard, cf. the principle running through the Code in e.g. Cann. 22, 1286, 1290.

[2] The 1917 Code in c.1179 claimed the right to asylum in a church: no such claim is made in the current law.

[3] The canon applies not only to the building of a new church, but also to the designation of an existing building as, from that time, a church.

- must first consult (see Can. 127) the council of priests (see Can. 495) and (a point sometimes overlooked) 'the rectors of neighbouring churches', who will for the most part comprise the neighbouring parish priests;
- must be satisfied that 'the new church can serve the good of souls' i.e. that the purpose in building it is a pastoral one, not any other;
- must equally be satisfied that the necessary financial means are available, including obviously the continuing means to service the debt arising (as so often is the case) from a loan taken out to fund the construction etc. of the church in question (see Can. 1284 §2 5°).

The establishment of a house of *any* religious institute requires 'the prior written consent of the diocesan Bishop' (Can. 609 §1). In the case of a *clerical* religious institute, that permission carries with it 'the right to have a church', but *only* 'subject to the provisions of (this) Can. 1215 §3' (Can. 611 3°), which itself requires an *additional* permission of the Bishop which would authorise that institute to 'build a church *in a specific and determined place*' (§3). Before granting such permission, the diocesan Bishop would be required to fulfil the conditions, as explained above, in §2 of this canon. 2429

Can. 1216 In the building and restoration of churches the advice of experts is to be used, and the principles and norms of liturgy and of sacred art are to be observed.

Can. 1210 has already treated this general area in the context of all sacred places. Here the focus is specifically on churches. Vat. II introduced the regulation that there be diocesan commissions for sacred liturgy and, as far as possible, for sacred art.[1] Many of the experts this canon has in mind would already be members of such commissions. The same Constitution on the Liturgy carries an illuminating chapter on *Sacred Art and Sacred Furnishings*, while the *General Instruction on the Roman Missal* has a chapter dealing with the arrangement and decoration of churches for the celebration of the blessed Eucharist.[2] These texts contain a valuable overview of 'the principles and norms of liturgy and of sacred art' to which this canon refers. 2430

Can. 1217 As soon as possible after completion of the building the new church is to be dedicated or at least blessed, following the laws of the sacred liturgy.
§2 Churches, especially cathedrals and parish churches, are to be dedicated by a solemn rite.

Once the building of a new church has been completed, the ideal is that, before the Mass or other sacred functions are celebrated there, it 'be dedicated or at least blessed' (§1). This indeed is the normal procedure, but it can happen in some circumstances that for pastoral reasons the liturgy may have to be celebrated in a new church before even its blessing can be conveniently arranged.[3] In any event, the blessing or dedication must be done 'as soon as possible' and, specifically, in accordance with 'the laws of the sacred liturgy'.[4] The ideal is that *all churches* should be solemnly dedicated, not simply blessed (§2) – an ideal to be particularly striven for in respect of *cathedral and parish churches*, precisely by reason of their especially significant place in the life of every diocese. This ideal may not always, however, be possible to achieve in practice, 2431

---

[1] Cf. SC 45–46: Fl I 16.
[2] Cf. SC 122–130: Fl I 34–36; GIRM 253–280: Fl I 189–194.
[3] For the minister of the appropriate dedication or blessing, cf. Cann. 1206–1207.
[4] Cf. RDCA: DOL nn.4369–4434.

depending upon a variety of customary, cultural, social, economic etc. circumstances. The final decision must rest with the diocesan Bishop.

Can. 1218 Each church is to have its own title. Once the church has been dedicated this title cannot be changed.

2432 The concept here is well understood among the faithful: theirs (particularly their parish church) is e.g. the Church of the Blessed Trinity, of the Incarnation or the Resurrection, of Our Blessed Lady (under any recognised one of her titles), of St Peter or St John, of the Guardian Angels, of any one of the Saints etc. This is the *title* given to the church on the occasion of its dedication or blessing when, to the glory of God, it is placed under the special protection of its own titular.[1] It is only when a church has been dedicated, not just blessed, that this title 'cannot be changed', though recourse to the Holy See in the matter is obviously always open.

Can. 1219 All acts of divine worship may be carried out in a church which has been lawfully dedicated or blessed, without prejudice to parochial rights.

2433 Once a church has been lawfully dedicated or blessed all acts of divine worship – the celebration of Mass, the conferring of sacraments and sacramentals etc. – may be carried out in it, obviously under the guidance and directives of the diocesan Bishop (see Cann. 835 §1, 838 §§1 and 4). This norm is, however, subject to 'parochial rights', which themselves are enumerated in Can. 530 (see also Cann. 558–560, 858 §2). It is also in fact subject to what may be determined by lawful privileges or approved customs.[2]

Can. 1220 §1 Those responsible are to ensure that there is in churches such cleanliness and ornamentation as befits the house of God, and that anything which is discordant with the holiness of the place is excluded.

§2 Ordinary concern for preservation and appropriate means of security are to be employed to safeguard sacred and precious goods.

2434 The regulation of §1 substantially repeats c.1178 of the 1917 Code. The church is, literally, 'the house of God': accordingly, not only is anything discordant with its sacred character to be excluded (see also Can. 1210), but it is positively to be characterised by a befitting cleanliness and a becoming ornamentation. The obligation to ensure this rests primarily on the parish priest or rector (see Can. 562), but it is one to be actively shared by all 'those responsible' i.e. the faithful, such as parishioners etc., who frequent the church.[3] In §2 stress is laid upon the need for the careful maintenance of the church structure, in all its components – a factor which in modern times is often a serious financial concern, especially in parishes. Moreover, in view of the current vulnerability of churches to acts of wanton destruction and of theft, particularly in regard to 'sacred and precious goods', the law makes a particular point of insisting that 'appropriate means of security', including modern technological means, be employed to combat these dangers insofar as possible.[4] Detailed regulations regarding the security of the tabernacle and of the blessed Sacrament are given in Can. 938.

---

[1] RDCA: DOL n.4372; SCDW Norms 19.III.1973: AAS 65(1973) 276–279: Not 9(1973) 263–266: DOL nn.3971–3985.

[2] Cf. Comm 12(1980) 336 at Can. 12.

[3] Cf. ibid. 337 at Can. 13.

[4] Cf. Pontifical Commission for Sacred Art lit circ 6.VI.1961: LE III 2989 4216–4217; SCC lit circ *Opera artis* 11.IV.1971: DOL nn.4327–4334.

Can. 1221 Entry to a church at the hours of sacred functions is to be open and free of charge.

This canon absolutely prohibits the imposition of any financial charge – even one which, though not strictly imposed, might be strongly canvassed – as a condition of:

– *entry to a church*

– *at the hours of sacred functions.*

The canon is therefore a corollary to the right of the faithful stated in Can. 1214. It is *not* concerned with those voluntary offerings which may be sought from the faithful in the course of a Mass or other such sacred function: that is a matter for regulation by the parish priest or rector, in accordance with the directives of the diocesan Bishop.[1] It is accepted that when a church is used not specifically for worship, but rather as an appropriate building for other permissible purposes, it would not be unreasonable to require an admission charge.[2]

Can. 1222 §1 If a church cannot in any way be used for divine worship and there is no possibility of its being restored, the diocesan Bishop may allow it to be used for some secular but not unbecoming purpose.

§2 Where other grave reasons suggest that a particular church should no longer be used for divine worship, the diocesan Bishop may allow it to be used for a secular but not unbecoming purpose. Before doing so, he must consult the council of priests; he must also have the consent of those who could lawfully claim rights over that church, and be sure that the good of souls would not be harmed by the transfer.

This canon, which should be read in conjunction with Can. 1212, envisages two situations:

(a) the first is when a church has, for whatever reason, come to such a state of deterioration, disrepair or even ruin that it may in no way be used for divine worship, nor are there means available to have it repaired or restored, the diocesan Bishop may by an appropriate decree convert it to some secular use, provided this latter be not altogether unbecoming to that which had once been the house of God;[3]

(b) the second situation is when the concern is not with the structural condition of the church itself, but rather that other circumstances have so altered as strongly to suggest 'that a particular church should no longer be used for divine worship'. A typical instance in modern Western conditions can arise when e.g. there occurs a substantial movement of population from inner cities. Here again the diocesan Bishop may decree the conversion of a particular church to a secular use as above, subject however to the following conditions:

– that he first *consults* the council of priests;

– that he secures the prior consent of 'those who could lawfully claim rights over that church';

– that he be assured that no harm to the good of souls would thereby occur.

---

[1] In interpreting this canon, one must also take account of Can. 560 and, more particularly, of Can. 937 in regard to the prescribed daily accessibility of churches for prayer before the blessed Sacrament.

[2] Cf. Can. 1210 and commentary thereon; Comm 12(1980) 338 at Can. 15.

[3] Some secular uses will always of their very nature be unbecoming e.g. those which are immoral, nefarious, disruptive of the social order, etc.; in other situations, the criterion of what is 'unbecoming' may well be determined by local social and cultural circumstances.

In both of the foregoing situations the building and/or its site could then be sold or otherwise disposed of from ecclesiastical ownership.[1]

Chapter II
ORATORIES AND PRIVATE CHAPELS

Can. 1223 An oratory means a place which, by permission of the Ordinary, is set aside for divine worship, for the convenience of some community or group of the faithful who assemble there, to which however other members of the faithful may, with the consent of the competent Superior, have access.

Can. 1224 §1 The Ordinary is not to give the permission required for setting up an oratory unless he has first, personally or through another, visited the place destined for the oratory and found it to be becomingly arranged.

§2 Once this permission has been given, the oratory cannot be converted to a secular usage without the authority of the same Ordinary.

2437 Can. 1223 provides a change in the definition of an oratory from that given in c.1188 of the 1917 Code.[2] An oratory now is distinguished from a church in two fundamental respects:

(a) whereas a church is 'a sacred building ... to which (all) the faithful have right of access' (see Can. 1214), an oratory is 'a place which, by permission of the Ordinary, is set aside (as of right) *for the convenience of some community or group of the faithful* ...': this is its specific and distinctive purpose – even though other members of the faithful may also be granted access to it by the competent Superior, who could therefore attach conditions of access, e.g. as to times, numbers, etc.

(b) whereas a church is essentially a sacred place, and in fact becomes such by a strictly required dedication or blessing (see Can. 1217), an oratory becomes a sacred place *only if* it is blessed (see Can. 1205), and the law goes no farther (see Can. 1229) than to state that it is *appropriate* that an oratory be blessed.[3]

2438 The 'community or group of the faithful' for whom an oratory may be established admits of a wide variety of possibilities: seminaries, religious communities, schools, hospitals, ships, military camps, recreational centres, shopping centres, even locations 'along highways and at train and bus stations and airports'.[4] For all this extensive variety of possibilities, it must be clearly understood that no oratory, in whatever location and whether it be blessed or not, may be established *without the prior permission of the*

---

[1] The concern expressed in Can. 1220 §2 for the care and preservation of precious goods and of works of art would clearly be a relevant consideration when the question of the change of use of a church arises. For a more detailed commentary on this Can. 1222, cf. Liturgy 8(1990) 71–76 (reprinted in Newsletter of CLSGBI 83 Sept 1990 28–36).

[2] The previous division of oratories into *public, semi-public and private or domestic* has been abolished.

[3] Cf. Comm 12(1980) 339 at Can. 18.

[4] Cf. SCB Directory on the Pastoral Ministry of Bishops *Ecclesiae imago* 22.II.1973 Vatican Press 1973: DOL n.2666.

Part III Sacred Places and Times

Ordinary as defined in Can. 134 §1 and including a military Ordinary, each in accordance with his own sphere of competence.[1]

Can. 1224 prescribes the conditions according to which the appropriate Ordinary may give permission for the establishment of any oratory: note that a positive prior inspection, 'personally or through another' selected by him, is an absolute requirement (§1). Should circumstances subsequently so change as to suggest or require that the oratory 'be converted to a secular usage', the permission of the same Ordinary is required before this may be given effect (§2).

Can. 1225 All sacred celebrations may take place in a lawfully constituted oratory, apart from those which are excluded by the law, by a provision of the local Ordinary, or by liturgical norms.

Once an oratory has been established by the permission of the competent Ordinary *all sacred services* may be celebrated in it *except only* those which are specifically excluded

– by the law;
– by a particular provision of the local Ordinary (see Can. 134 §2) in virtue of his overall responsibility for the liturgy within his jurisdiction (see Cann. 835 §1, 838 §4);
– by liturgical norms e.g. those concerning the celebration of the Mass of the Lord's Supper on Holy Thursday.[2]

Can. 1226 The term private chapel means a place which, by permission of the local Ordinary, is set aside for divine worship, for the convenience of one or more individuals.

Can. 1227 Bishops can set up for their own use a private chapel which enjoys the same rights as an oratory.

Can. 1228 Without prejudice to the provision of Can. 1227, the permission of the local Ordinary is required for Mass and other sacred celebrations to take place in any private chapel.

The term *private chapel*[3] is a new one, introduced by the present Code. Although its concept corresponds to that of the 'private or domestic oratory' of the 1917 Code c.1188 §2 3°, the conditions under which it may be established and used are less restrictive. The following are the salient points to be noted in its regard:

(a) the distinctive element of a private chapel – and this particularly distinguishes it from an oratory (see Can. 1223) – is that it is for the convenience of one or more individuals (Can. 1226), more often than not, of a family; it is a feature more common in some countries than in others.

(b) its establishment necessarily requires the permission of the local Ordinary (Can. 1226); the other 'religious' Ordinaries of Can. 134 §1, while they may establish

2439

2440

2441

---

[1] The question of permission to reserve the blessed Sacrament *in any oratory* is a separate and additional issue, governed by Can. 934 §1 2°, which requires the permission of the *local Ordinary* (Can. 134 §2). In regard to the so-called 'Prayer Rooms' which have become a recent feature of some places such as seminaries, religious houses, hospitals etc., the blessed Sacrament may be reserved in them only if permission for this will have been granted at least by the Ordinary referred to in Can. 936.

[2] Cf. The Roman Missal 1975 n.243.

[3] Cf. Comm 12(1980) 339–340 at Can. 18.

an oratory in any house under their jurisdiction (see Can. 1223), may not establish a private chapel in the sense defined here.

(c) it must be set aside or reserved for divine worship only (Cann. 1226, 1229) and accordingly not available for any domestic use (Can. 1229); divine worship would include e.g. private or family prayer, recitation of the Divine Office, reading of and meditation on the Scriptures, etc.

(d) for the celebration of Mass and of other sacred functions – e.g. a baptism, a marriage, a funeral – in a private chapel, a special permission of the local Ordinary, over and above that given for the chapel's establishment, is required (Can. 1228); in granting such permission, the local Ordinary could obviously lay down appropriate conditions, e.g. as to the frequency or the days on which Mass might be celebrated, as to the circumstances which might surround a funeral, etc.; if this permission is to be granted for the habitual or frequent (as distinct from an occasional) celebration, it is required that the chapel be blessed (see Can. 932 §1; 1917 Code c.1194). Equally, the reservation of the blessed Sacrament in a private chapel would also require a special permission of the local Ordinary (see Can. 934 §1 2°), which would not of itself be in any way implied in a permission to celebrate Mass there.[1]

2442 The law accords to a Bishop a special standing in this regard (Can. 1227), be he diocesan, auxiliary or retired. He may have a private chapel for his own use, as of right, without therefore the need to have the permission of any local Ordinary.[2] Even more: such a chapel is, in effect, an oratory, since it 'enjoys the same rights as an oratory', and may accordingly be used by the Bishop for any purpose permitted by the law in an oratory, e.g. the celebration of a marriage. Moreover, it enjoys by law the right to have the blessed Sacrament reserved in it (see Can. 934 §1 2°).

Can. 1229 It is appropriate that oratories and private chapels be blessed according to the rite prescribed in the liturgical books. They must, however, be reserved for divine worship only and be freed from all domestic use.

2443 Neither an oratory nor a private chapel may be dedicated; while it is not even required that they be blessed, it is certainly, in the words of this canon, 'appropriate' that they be, 'according to the rite prescribed in the liturgical books'.[3] The minister of the blessing of an oratory is the Ordinary, of the blessing of a private chapel the local Ordinary (see Can. 134 §§1, 2): either may delegate another priest to do so (see Can. 1207). Whether blessed or not, an oratory or a private chapel, once lawfully established and thus 'reserved for divine worship only', may not be put to any domestic use.

Chapter III
SHRINES

Can. 1230 The term shrine means a church or other sacred place which, with the approval of the local Ordinary, is by reason of special devotion frequented by the faithful as pilgrims.

---

[1] A practical recommendation would strongly advise that any permission by the local Ordinary in respect of these canons should be specific and in writing.

[2] Cf. Comm 12(1980) 340 at Can. 21.

[3] Cf. RDCA ch V: DOL nn.4428–4432.

The regulation of shrines is a new element, not found in the 1917 Code. The canonical concept of a shrine had been most recently defined by Pope Pius XII in 1956.[1] This canon provides its definitive definition: it is

- a church or other sacred place;
- by reason of special devotion frequented by the faithful *as pilgrims*: it is this element which specifically characterises a shrine;
- approved as such by the local Ordinary.

All through the history of the Church shrines have come into being, as it were, precisely by reason of popular devotion. It is only later, after a careful and often prolonged investigation, that they receive, or do not receive as the case may be, the official approval of the Church – normally, at least in the first place, that of the diocesan Bishop.[2]

Can. 1231 For a shrine to be described as national, the approval of the Bishops' Conference is necessary. For it to be described as international, the approval of the Holy See is required.

Can. 1232 §1 The local Ordinary is competent to approve the statutes of a diocesan shrine; the Bishops' Conference, those of a national shrine; the Holy See alone, those of an international shrine.

§2 The statutes of a shrine are to determine principally its purpose, the authority of the rector, and the ownership and administration of its property.

Can. 1233 Certain privileges may be granted to shrines when the local circumstances, the number of pilgrims and especially the good of the faithful would seem to make this advisable.

Categories. Shrines may be diocesan, national or international, requiring the approval respectively of the local Ordinary, of the Bishops' Conference and of the Holy See (Can. 1231): the criterion obviously will be the origin of the majority of the pilgrims: thus e.g. Lourdes, with its influx of pilgrims from all parts of the world, is clearly an international shrine.

Statutes. It is appropriate, though not strictly required, that each shrine would have its own statutes (see Can. 94), which would determine the purpose of the shrine, the authority of whoever is in charge, and the ownership or administration of its property (Can. 1232 §2). Such statutes would usually be accredited to the group or, frequently, the religious community who have the custody and care of the shrine, and again they require the approval respectively of the authorities listed in Can. 1332 §1.[3]

Privileges. It is not unusual that, particularly in the spiritual interests of the faithful and for the good of souls, special privileges are granted to certain shrines (Can. 1233), in respect e.g. of liturgical functions, faculties in the hearing of confessions, indulgences, etc.[4]

---

[1] Cf. rep S. Congregation for Studies 8.II.1956: LE II 2558 3455.

[2] The shrine of Our Lady at Lourdes is a typical example of this process. Others, such e.g. as Medjugorje, clearly now a place of devout pilgrimage, are still at the stage of investigation by the Church. For the general background of this matter as discussed by the Revision Commission, cf. Comm 12(1980) 341ff.

[3] The bodies to which these statutes are accredited *may* become *juridical persons* in the Church (cf. Can. 113 §2) only if the statutes are approved by the competent authority (cf. Can. 117). Cf. also Comm 12(1980) 343–344 at Can. 26.

[4] For the law on privileges, cf. Cann. 76–84.

Can. 1234 §1 At shrines the means of salvation are to be more abundantly made available to the faithful: by sedulous proclamation of the word of God, by suitable encouragement of liturgical life, especially by the celebration of the Eucharist and penance, and by the fostering of approved forms of popular devotion.

§2 In shrines or in places adjacent to them, votive offerings of popular art and devotion are to be displayed and carefully safeguarded.

2446 *The essential significance and pastoral role* of shrines in the life of the Church is aptly summed up in §1 of this canon: their purpose is, and is only, that 'the means of salvation ... be more abundantly made available to the faithful',[1] principally by:
- the preaching of the word of God;
- the celebration of the Eucharist;
- the hearing of confessions;[2]
- the fostering of approved forms of popular devotion.[3]

2447 At many shrines it is customary for pilgrims, whether individually or in groups, to donate gifts – known as *votive offerings* – in thanksgiving for blessings or favours received. These may at times be of little or no monetary or artistic value; equally however it can and does happen that they are of significant merit, not necessarily of very great monetary value but frequently of considerable personal value e.g. expensive watches, jewellery, paintings, sculptures etc. It is to these that §2 refers, prescribing that, either at the shrines themselves or in places adjacent to them, they be put on public display and in such manner that their security is assured.[4]

Chapter IV
ALTARS

2448 The following five brief canons – considerably simplified by comparison with their predecessors in the 1917 Code cc.1197–1202 – deal with only the basic canonical legislation concerning altars. The more detailed norms are left to liturgical law, principally to the *General Instruction on the Roman Missal*[5] and to the *Rite of Dedication of a Church or an Altar*,[6] to which the reader's attention is directed, both in view of the

---

[1] It is regrettable that pilgrimages to shrines, particularly national and international ones, are sometimes portrayed as little more than tourist attractions. Those responsible should always be reminded that such pilgrimages are essentially and necessarily occasions of a religious and spiritual nature, designed solely to help people in their striving for God.

[2] In his address at the Marian Shrine of Zapopan in Mexico 30.I.1979 Pope John Paul II described such shrines as 'places of conversion, of penance and of reconciliation with God': AAS 71(1979) 230 at n.3.

[3] For an instructive and illuminating treatment of 'popular devotion', cf. Pope Paul VI ap exhort *Evangelii nuntiandi* 8.XII.1975 n.48: AAS 68(1976) 37–38: Fl II 731–732, where the Pope concludes that 'when it is wisely directed, popular piety ... can make a constantly increasing contribution towards bringing the masses of our people into contact with God in Jesus Christ'. Cf. also Can. 839 §2.

[4] It is to be noted that, in virtue of Can. 1292 §2, some at least of these votive offerings may require the permission of the Holy See for their valid alienation.

[5] Cf. GIRM nn.259–270: Fl I 191–192.

[6] Cf. RDCA ch IV nn.1–30: DOL nn.4398–4427.

latter document's illuminating exposition of the theological understanding of an altar (nn.1–4) and in respect of the specific practical directives. Central in both documents is the idea that the altar is 'the centre of the thanksgiving that the Eucharist accomplishes'. 'The (main) altar should be so placed and constructed that it is always seen to be *the sign of Christ himself*, the place at which the saving mysteries are carried out, and the centre of the assembly, to which the greatest reverence is due.'[1]

Can. 1235 §1 The altar or table on which the eucharistic Sacrifice is celebrated is termed fixed if it is so constructed that it is attached to the floor and therefore cannot be moved; it is termed movable, if it can be removed.

§2 It is proper that in every church there should be a fixed altar. In other places which are intended for sacred celebrations, the altar may be either fixed or movable.

Can. 1236 §1 In accordance with the traditional practice of the Church, the table of a fixed altar is to be of stone, indeed of a single natural stone. However, even some other worthy and solid material may be used, if the Bishops' Conference so judges. The support or the base can be made from any material.

§2 A movable altar can be made of any solid material which is suitable for liturgical use.

An altar may be either *fixed or movable*, as clearly defined in Can. 1235 §1. It is to be noted that these definitions are both different from those in c.1197 §1 1° of the 1917 Code: gone e.g. is the concept of a movable altar as an 'altar stone'.[2] In a church, it is proper – not therefore absolutely required – that the altar be a fixed one; in an oratory or a private chapel, it may be either fixed or movable (Can. 1235 §2). 2449

'In new churches it is better to erect only one altar ... (which) signifies the one Saviour Jesus Christ and the one Eucharist of the Church. But an altar may also be erected in a chapel (somewhat separated, if possible, from the body of the church) where the tabernacle for the reservation of the blessed Sacrament is situated. On weekdays, when there is a small gathering of people, Mass may be celebrated at this altar. The merely decorative erection of several altars in a church must be entirely avoided.'[3] 2450

In regard to *the materials to be used in the construction of an altar*, the detailed instructions are left to the liturgical law as cited in the introduction to this Chapter. Can. 1236 specifies three general guidelines: 2451

– the table of a fixed altar is, by preference, to be not only of stone but of one natural stone, in accordance with the traditional practice of the Church;

– however, if the appropriate Bishops' Conference should decide otherwise, it may be of any other worthy and solid material;[4]

---

[1] EuM n.24: Fl I 116–117.

[2] A movable altar is not to be confused with the table which, in accordance with Can. 932 §2, may on occasion be used for the celebration of Mass.

[3] RDCA ch IV n.7: DOL n.4404.

[4] For the manner in which Bishops' Conferences have interpreted this faculty, cf. LCE Tavola per Paesi e Canoni at Can. 1236: many have simply remitted to the diocesan Bishop the judgement as to what is another 'worthy and solid material'; some have suggested alternatives; there is no doubt that e.g. a durable wood, an appropriate metal, a modern synthetic concrete amalgam would be permissible.

– a movable altar may be of any solid material which is suitable for liturgical use: a criterion in this regard is that such material be 'acceptable to local traditions and culture'.[1]

Can. 1237 §1 Fixed altars are to be dedicated, movable ones either dedicated or blessed, according to the rites prescribed in the liturgical books.

§2 The ancient tradition of placing relics of Martyrs or of other Saints beneath a fixed altar is to be retained, in accordance with the norms prescribed in the liturgical books.

Can. 1238 §1 An altar loses its dedication or blessing in accordance with Can. 1212.

§2 Altars, whether fixed or movable, do not lose their dedication or blessing as a result of a church or other sacred place being made over to secular usage.

2452 The following are the principal points to be noted about these two canons concerning the dedication and blessing of altars:
– only fixed altars are required to be dedicated: in fact the dedication of the altar is the principal part of the whole rite of dedication of a church; movable altars may be either dedicated or blessed (Can. 1237 §1);
– the relics referred to in Can. 1237 §2 – of martyrs (preferably) or of other saints – are permitted only in the case of fixed altars: they are to be securely placed beneath the altar, not on it or inserted into its table;
– any altar, fixed or movable, loses its dedication or blessing in the same manner as does any sacred place (Cann. 1238 §1, 1212), but no altar loses either by reason only of the fact that the church, oratory or private chapel in which it stands is made over to secular usage (Can. 1238 §2): thus e.g. if a church were to be closed down and sold, in accordance with Can. 1212, its altar could be transferred to another church etc. without any need to have it dedicated or blessed again;
– the rites for the dedication or the blessing of an altar are to be found in the prescribed liturgical books already cited above.

Can. 1239 §1 An altar, whether fixed or movable, is to be reserved for divine worship alone, to the exclusion of any secular usage.

§2 No corpse is to be buried beneath an altar; otherwise, it is not lawful to celebrate Mass at that altar.

2453 'The altar, on which the sacrifice of the Cross is made present under sacramental signs, is also the Lord's table which the people are invited to share when they come to Mass. It is also the centre from which thanksgiving is offered to God through the celebration of the Eucharist.'[2] It is for these reasons that every altar, whether fixed or movable, 'is to be reserved for divine worship alone, to the exclusion of any secular usage' (§1), i.e. any use, however lawful or worthy in itself, other than that of worship.

2454 The prohibition on the burial of a corpse 'beneath an altar', with the consequent exclusion of the celebration of Mass at such an altar (§2), applies only to a burial directly beneath and, as it were, in association with the altar. It does not exclude a burial somewhere nearby, much less a burial in the crypt of a church even if this be, as it often is, beneath an altar.[3]

---

[1] GIRM n.264: Fl I 191.
[2] GIRM n.259: Fl I 191. Cf. EuM n.24: Fl I 116–117.
[3] Cf. Chiappetta II n.4060. Cf. also Can. 1242.

Part III Sacred Places and Times

Chapter V
CEMETERIES

Can. 1240 §1 Where possible, the Church is to have its own cemeteries, or at least an area in public cemeteries which is duly blessed and reserved for the deceased faithful.

§2 If, however, this is not possible, then individual graves are to be blessed in due form on each occasion.

The 1917 Code c.1206 expressed a direct and uncompromising claim to the Church's right to own its own cemeteries. Recognising the change over the intervening years in social circumstances and in particular the clearly justifiable interest of the civil law in this regard, the current Code deals with the matter rather differently. It is satisfied to allow its rightful claim to that ownership to be encompassed within the general terms of Can. 1254 §1 and, in respect of cemeteries, to lay down the following practical directives:[1]

(a) where possible – and this would include where permitted by the civil law – the Church is 'to have its own cemeteries' (§1);

(b) if this is not possible, the Church is to have 'at least an area in public cemeteries'. Both this area and the Church's own cemeteries are to be 'duly blessed and reserved for the deceased faithful' (§1);

(c) if even that is not possible, then 'individual graves are to be blessed in due form on each occasion' (§2), in accordance with the appropriate funeral rite (see Can. 1176 §§1–2).

Can. 1241 §1 Parishes and religious institutes may each have their own cemetery.

§2 Other juridical persons or families may each have their own special cemetery or burial place which, if the local Ordinary judges accordingly, is to be blessed.

The following are entitled, but not obliged, to have each a cemetery of its own (§1):

– parishes: this is common practice particularly in rural parishes (see also Can. 1180 §1);

– religious institutes, not only those strictly so called but also secular institutes and societies of apostolic life: in fact many such institutes, both of men and of women, do have their own privately-owned cemeteries, located within the grounds of one or a number of their houses.[2]

In both situations the cemetery must be blessed. In all cases care must be taken to ensure compliance with the relevant civil regulations, concerning e.g. public health etc.

The following are also entitled, but not obliged, to have each a cemetery or burial place (i.e. a so-called tomb or vault) of its own (§2):

– other ecclesiastical juridical persons, both public and private (see Cann. 113 §2 – 116);

---

[1] Cf. Comm 12(1980) 348–349 at Can. 31.

[2] Instead of having their own cemetery on their own property, many religious institutes have their own reserved plot within larger and even publicly-owned cemeteries; the same is true of some dioceses, in respect of some or all of their priests.

– private families: a practice common in some countries and cultures, rare or almost unknown in others.

Whether or not these may be blessed will depend upon the judgement of the local Ordinary, who will take all the local circumstances into account. Should the local Ordinary consider it not appropriate that such cemeteries be blessed, then the individual graves 'are to be blessed in due form on each occasion' (Can. 1240 §2). Once again compliance with the civil law should be ensured.

Can. 1242 Bodies are not to be buried in churches, unless it is a question of the Roman Pontiff or of Cardinals or, in their proper churches, of diocesan Bishops even retired.

2458 The burial of bodies in churches – and also in oratories[1] – is prohibited save *only* in the case of the Pope, of Cardinals and, in their own churches, of diocesan Bishops[2] even if retired. Coadjutor and Auxiliary Bishops are excluded, unless in a particular case there be a special reason to seek a specific authorisation from the Holy See;[3] excluded also are those others mentioned in c.1205 §2 of the 1917 Code.

Can. 1243 Appropriate norms are to be enacted by particular law for the management of cemeteries, especially in what concerns the protection and the fostering of their sacred character.

2459 As will have been clear both in the immediately preceding canons and in those concerning funerals (Cann. 1176–1185), the Church's primary concern in respect of cemeteries is that they be *sacred places* in which the bodies of the dead would be *respected and honoured*. Recognising that the conditions in which this objective can best be achieved may well vary from country to country, perhaps even from diocese to diocese, the Code wisely assigns to 'particular law' – be it national, provincial or diocesan – to determine the specific local arrangements of the management of cemeteries.[4]

Title II
Sacred Times

2460 The concept of certain special *Sacred Times* has been in the tradition and devotion of the Church from its very early days. It has always carried the implication that some particular days throughout the year are to be set aside as 'feast days' or 'holy days', and that others are equally to be set aside as 'days of penance' – both in recognition of the dependence of God's people upon their Saviour Jesus Christ. This was clearly reflected in the 1917 Code in its cc.1243–1254. It is even more significantly illuminated by Vat. II in its Constitution on the Sacred Liturgy,[5] which should be carefully

---

[1] Cf. SCCo 10.XII.1927: LE I 796 917.

[2] Included here also are those equivalent in law to diocesan Bishops: cf. Cann. 368, 381 §2.

[3] Cf. Comm 12(1980) 349 at Can. 31.

[4] Local legislation may find some relevant pointers in some of cc.1209–1214 of the 1917 Code.

[5] Cf. SC 102–111: Fl I 28–31.

studied in order the better to understand the following canons of this title. Cann. 1244–1245 deal in the essential logistical details, Cann. 1246–1253 with the substance and practice.

Can. 1244 §1 Only the supreme ecclesiastical authority can establish, transfer or suppress holydays or days of penance which are applicable to the universal Church, without prejudice to the provisions of Can. 1246 §2.

§2 Diocesan Bishops can proclaim special holydays or days of penance for their own dioceses or territories, but only for individual occasions.

The *exclusive* authority of the Holy See is clearly stated in §1: even the authority granted to Bishops' Conferences in Can. 1246 §2 may be exercised only if it has the approval of the Holy See. The authority of diocesan Bishops 'to proclaim special holydays or days of penance' (§2) extends also to those equivalent to them in law (see Cann. 368, 381 §2) and to a diocesan Administrator (see Can. 427 §1). It is subject to two limitations:

- it is strictly territorial, i.e. it binds only those belonging to the diocese or other such territory while they are in it, and *vagi*; it does not bind *peregrini* (see Can. 13 §§2 and 3, and Glossary);
- it may be exercised only 'for individual occasions', e.g. at a time of war, of famine, of seriously threatening weather conditions etc. or indeed in thanksgiving for deliverance from any such; this authority may not be so exercised as to establish an additional permanent holyday or day of penance.

Can. 1245 Without prejudice to the right of diocesan Bishops as in Can. 87, a parish priest, in individual cases, for a just reason and in accordance with the prescriptions of the diocesan Bishop, can give a dispensation from the obligation of observing a holy-day or day of penance, or commute the obligation into some other pious works. The Superior of a pontifical clerical religious institute or society of apostolic life has the same power in respect of his own subjects and of those who reside day and night in the house.

The authority to dispense from, or to commute, the obligation of observing a holy-day or day of penance can have significant practical and pastoral consequences. This authority is, in virtue of Can. 87, enjoyed as of right by every *diocesan Bishop* and by those equivalent to him in law (see Cann. 368, 381 §2). Perhaps more relevant from the point of view of day-to-day pastoral practice is the fact that, in virtue of this canon, it is enjoyed also by every *parish priest* and by those equivalent to him in law, e.g. the administrator of a mensal parish, those referred to in Cann. 516 §1, 517–520 and, in this respect, the rector of a seminary (see Can. 262). This parochial authority is governed by the following conditions:

- that there be a justifiable reason, not a merely trivial one, for the granting of the dispensation or the commutation (see Can. 90): in most normal circumstances this will exist;
- that the parish priest use this authority 'in accordance with the prescriptions of the diocesan Bishop', which in normal practice will mean that it be in tune with the known general policy of the Bishop;
- that the dispensation or the commutation be granted 'in individual cases' which, in this situation, means not merely to individual persons but also e.g. to families and even, if the circumstances would seem to call for it, to the entire parish.[1]

---

[1] Cf. Comm 12(1980) 358 at Can. 43.

It is to be noted, moreover, that the parish priest may use this faculty in respect both of his own parishioners, be they in the parish or away from it, and of *peregrini* and *vagi* (see Can. 91, and Glossary).[1]

2463 This same authority to dispense or commute is entrusted also to every *Superior*, whether major or local, of a religious institute or a society of apostolic life which is *clerical and of pontifical right*. The exercise of the faculty by such a Superior is, however, limited to those who are his own subjects and to those who habitually reside in the house to which the Superior is assigned.

Chapter I
HOLYDAYS

Can. 1246 §1 Sunday, on which by apostolic tradition the paschal mystery is celebrated, is to be observed in the universal Church as the primary holyday of obligation. The following feast days are also to be observed as holydays of obligation: the Nativity of Our Lord Jesus Christ, the Epiphany, the Ascension, Corpus Christi, Mary the Mother of God, her Immaculate Conception, her Assumption, St Joseph, the Apostles SS Peter and Paul and All Saints.

§2 However, the Bishops' Conference may, with the prior approval of the Apostolic See, suppress certain holydays of obligation or transfer them to a Sunday.

2464 Worship is an integral and essential part of christian living. In its §1 this canon prescribes for the universal Church those specific days through the year which the faithful are obliged to devote in a special manner to the honour and worship of God, thereby acknowledging both the dependence of every creature upon its Creator and the grateful praise which is due for the gift of salvation, earned by the passion, death and resurrection of Jesus Christ. Primary among those days is every Sunday: 'by a tradition handed down from the apostles, which took its origin from the very day of Christ's resurrection, the Church celebrates the paschal mystery every seventh day, which day is appropriately called the Lord's Day or Sunday ... the original feast day ... (and itself) the foundation and kernel of the whole liturgical year'.[2] To the Sundays as holydays of obligation are added the ten other feast days enumerated in this canon.[3] The obligation itself is detailed in Cann. 1247–1248.

2465 In accordance with the tenor of Vat. II, the Code recognises that the prescribing of holydays of obligation for the universal Church may, by reason of local circumstances or cultures, require prudent adjustment in this territory or that. Accordingly §2 of this canon entitles the appropriate Bishops' Conferences to 'suppress certain holydays of obligation or transfer them to a Sunday', provided they each have 'the prior approval of the Apostolic See'.[4]

---

[1] The exercise of this faculty is one which can be communicated in any practical manner e.g. face to face, by telephone, by letter, through a third person etc.: cf. Chiappetta II n.4079. The parish priest can exercise it, for a just cause, even in respect of himself (see Can. 91).

[2] SC 106: Fl I 29–30.

[3] In using the term 'feast days' (translated here as 'holydays') the Code is considering only the juridical obligation attaching to those days, not the liturgical division of such days into 'solemnities' and 'feasts'. Cf. also Comm 12(1980) 359–360 at Can. 45.

[4] For the manner in which Bishops' Conferences have availed themselves of this faculty, cf. LCE Tavola per Paesi e Canoni at Can. 1246; CN(USA) 18.

Can. 1247 On Sundays and other holydays of obligation, the faithful are obliged to participate in the Mass. They are also to abstain from such work or business that would inhibit the worship to be given to God, the joy proper to the Lord's Day, or the due relaxation of mind and body.

In this context of 'holydays', the obligation to observe Sundays and the other days specified in Can. 1246 is a twofold one. The faithful are obliged:

(a) *to assist at Mass*, i.e. to be present and, in so far as may be appropriate or possible, to participate in the celebration of the sacrifice which sacramentally represents the institution of the Eucharist, with all its implications of Christ's death and resurrection;[1]

(b) *to abstain from* 'such work or business that would inhibit the worship to be given to God, the joy proper to the Lord's Day, or the due relaxation of mind and body'. Modern commercial and economic pressures may not lie easily with this directive, but this canon is a clear call to Christ's faithful to assert their fundamental belief in the spiritual values of the Gospel of Christ – values which may well be out of accord with the current trend towards material possessions as some kind of ultimate value, a value which nonetheless can so easily turn out to be nugatory.

Can. 1248 §1 The obligation of participating in the Mass is satisfied by one who assists at Mass wherever it is celebrated in a catholic rite, either on the holyday itself or on the evening of the previous day.

§2 If it is impossible to participate in a eucharistic celebration, either because no sacred minister is available or for some other grave reason, the faithful are strongly recommended to take part in a liturgy of the Word, if there be such in the parish church or some other sacred place, which is celebrated in accordance with the provisions laid down by the diocesan Bishop; or to spend an appropriate time in prayer, whether personally or as a family or, as occasion presents, in a group of families.

'The obligation of participating in the Mass is satisfied' (§1):

(a) *wherever Mass is celebrated in a catholic rite*

– there is no restriction whatever in respect of the place in which the Mass may be celebrated;[2]

– what of a catholic who, on a Sunday or holyday of obligation, may for a good reason – e.g. because of a public office, of a family relationship, of friendship, even of a wish to be better informed – attends Mass in an Orthodox Church on a Sunday or holyday of obligation? It is certainly a tenable view that, in accordance with the *Directory concerning Ecumenical Matters* of 1967, such a catholic will thereby have satisfied the obligation of assisting at Mass as determined by this canon.[3]

---

[1] Reflecting the eucharistic theology of Vat. II, the Code normally speaks of 'participating' in, rather than 'assisting' at, the Mass, e.g. Cann. 663 §2, 866, 917, 923; cf. SC 14: Fl I 7–8. Here however it deliberately uses the phrase 'to assist at Mass', thereby indicating that the canonical obligation is fulfilled if one is simply present at Mass; in doing so, it in no way diminishes the objective that those present should participate in the celebration in as full a measure as possible. Cf. Comm 12(1980) 362 at Can. 47.

[2] The 1917 Code c.1249 excluded most 'private oratories' – the equivalent of the 'private chapels' of the current Code (see Cann. 1226, 1228): that restriction is no longer operative.

[3] Cf. SPUC *Ad totam Ecclesiam* 14.V.1967: AAS 59(1967) 574ff nn.47, 50: Fl I 497, 498.

(b) *either on the holyday itself or on the evening of the previous day*
- the 'holyday itself' clearly means from the midnight which begins the day to the midnight which closes it;
- what is 'the evening of the previous day'? Despite the view of some commentators that this should be interpreted as beginning only at 1400 hours (2 pm) on that day,[1] it is the firm view of this commentary that the evening of the previous day begins at midday (12 noon) on that day itself. In some dioceses there is a local regulation to the effect that the so-called vigil or anticipated Mass may not be celebrated before, say, 5 pm or 6 pm: this is normally for pastoral reasons, e.g. to facilitate weddings or funerals in parish or other churches. Those regulations do not in any way concern the time prescribed for fulfilling the obligation to assist at Mass: thus e.g. if in such a diocese a person were to attend a nuptial Mass in the early afternoon on a Saturday, that person would thereby have fulfilled the obligation of §1 of this canon.[2] When a vigil Mass properly so called is in fact celebrated 'on the evening of the previous day', it is to be the Mass liturgically proper to the following day, implying a homily, prayers of the faithful, etc.[3] It is to be noted, however, that when a Sunday and another holyday of obligation occur on two successive days, the assistance at no more than an evening Mass on the first of two such days does not fulfil the dual obligation.[4]

2468 The content of §2 of this canon is entirely new: it did not form part even of the final draft of the 1982 Code which was submitted to the Pope. It takes account of a situation which already exists in some regions of the Church and which could well become more widespread in the years to come. What the paragraph states is not a canonical obligation, but rather a *strong recommendation* that, if by reason of the circumstances described it is *impossible* to assist at Mass, the faithful would:
- either take part in a liturgy of the Word, to be held in accordance with the directives of the diocesan Bishop;
- or spend some time in prayer, personal, family or interfamily.[5]

The current practical guide in this regard is the 1988 *Directory for Sunday celebrations in the absence of a priest*,[6] which prescribes that it is for the diocesan Bishop, acting in accordance with the norms and tenor of this Directory, and having consulted the Council of Priests (see Can. 495), to determine if and under what conditions appropriate to the diocese a Sunday assembly without Mass is to be held on a regular basis. This Directory will repay careful study.[7]

---

[1] Cf. e.g. Chiappetta II n.4087.

[2] Note that the obligation to abstain from the 'work or business' referred to in Can. 1247 pertains only to the holy day itself, not to the previous evening.

[3] Cf. EuM 28: Fl I 119. Cf. also SCDW rep May 1974: LE V 4296 6814–6815.

[4] Cf. Comm 12(1980) 359 at Can. 44.

[5] Noteworthy throughout the Code is an emphasis on the significance and importance of family prayer, e.g. Cann. 226, 528 §2, 851 2°.

[6] Cf. SCDW 2.VI.1988: Origins 18(1988) 302–307. Cf. also Comm 22(1990) 324–326; CLA 64(1990) 77.

[7] It would appear that, in appropriate circumstances, the distribution of Holy Communion could be permitted in association with the Sunday assembly envisaged in this canon and in the Directory: cf. Cann. 230 §3, 910 §2, 918.

Part III Sacred Places and Times

Chapter II
DAYS OF PENANCE

Adequately to understand this brief Chapter one must begin by a careful study of the *Apostolic Constitution on Penance* issued by Pope Paul VI in 1966[1] – one of the most significant, if not always the most attended to, pastoral documents of our time. The 1917 Code concerned itself simply with fast and abstinence: what are they? – when are they to be observed? – who are bound by them? This current Code, embodying the spirit and vision of Vat. II as perceived by Pope Paul VI, widens the horizon: it sees fast and abstinence to be but part, though still an enduring important part, of the larger concept of penance. In effect, it stresses the fundamental fact that penance is an integral, albeit not the only, component of christian life, precisely by reason of the fact that the followers of Christ have been redeemed by His passion, death and resurrection. It is for this reason that Can. 1249 begins with the statement that *'all Christ's faithful are obliged by divine law ... to do penance'*. For the christian, penance is not the kind of 'optional extra' which might perhaps indicate a particularly laudable commitment by this person or that: it is an essential ingredient required of all by the law of God. It is this understanding which is the key to the interpretation of the following canons. **2469**

Can. 1249 All Christ's faithful are obliged by divine law, each in his or her own way, to do penance. However, so that all may be joined together in a certain common practice of penance, days of penance are prescribed. On these days Christ's faithful are in a special manner to devote themselves to prayer, to engage in works of piety and charity, and to deny themselves, by fulfilling their obligations more faithfully and especially by observing the fast and abstinence which the following canons prescribe.

While the divine law obligation to do penance rests upon each individual member of Christ's faithful, this canon points to the desirability – and the help to each which would ensue as a consequence – that 'all ... be joined together in a certain common practice of penance'. In saying this, the canon reflects the teaching of Vat. II that the Church is not just a conglomerate of individuals but is rather a *unified body*, in Christ.[2] The obligation to do penance is not therefore a merely individualistic one: in the Church it implies a communitarian or social requirement which itself expresses the unity and the community of Christ's Church. Hence the reason why specific 'days of penance are prescribed' for all. **2470**

The change of emphasis in the concept of penance is reflected in the manner prescribed in this canon for the observance of the official days of penance. On those days the faithful are called upon to devote them in a special manner: **2471**

– to prayer;
– to engage in works of piety and charity;
– to deny themselves, in a twofold way:
(a) by fulfilling the obligations of their state in life more faithfully, accepting in a true spirit of christian self-denial the inconveniences, the trials, the uncertainties, often the very real sufferings of life;

---

[1] Cf. ap con *Paenitemini* 17.II.1966: AAS 58(1966) 177–198; Fl II 1–12. For those in the pastoral ministry, the importance of reading and absorbing this document cannot be overemphasised.
[2] Cf. LG 1–17 passim: Fl I 350–369.

(b) especially by observing the prescribed fast and abstinence.[1]

Can. 1250 The days and times of penance for the universal Church are each Friday of the whole year and the season of Lent.

2472 This canon states the simple directive that 'the days and times of penance for the universal Church are':
- *each Friday* of the whole year, commemorating the crucifixion and death of Christ on the first Good Friday;
- *the season of Lent* – from Ash Wednesday to midday on Holy Saturday – itself the immediate preparation for the celebration of the Resurrection on Easter Sunday.

To all and each of these days is to be applied the directive 'to do penance', as explained above at Can. 1249. As a matter of pastoral practice, both the clergy and the laity could well from time to time be reminded that, even apart from Lent, every Friday of the year calls for some expression of the penance to which we are all, by divine law, obliged.

Can. 1251 Abstinence from meat, or from some other food as determined by the Bishops' Conference, is to be observed on all Fridays, unless a solemnity should fall on a Friday. Abstinence and fasting are to be observed on Ash Wednesday and Good Friday.

Can. 1252 The law of abstinence binds those who have completed their fourteenth year. The law of fasting binds those who have attained their majority, until the beginning of their sixtieth year. Pastors of souls and parents are to ensure that even those who by reason of their age are not bound by the law of fasting and abstinence, are taught the true meaning of penance.

2473 These two canons concentrate on the two forms of penance – fasting and abstinence – which are specifically a matter of legal obligation in the Church. While in no way taking from the overall moral obligation 'to do penance', they lay down the following regulations in respect of fasting and abstinence:
(a) *abstinence from meat* – or from some other food as determined by the local Bishops' Conference (see Can. 1253 below) – is to be observed on all Fridays, unless a 'solemnity', as determined by Can. 1246,[2] should fall on a Friday;
(b) *abstinence*, as defined above, *and fasting*[3] are to be observed on Ash Wednesday, initiating the penitential season of Lent, and on Good Friday, commemorating the passion and death of our Lord Jesus Christ;

---

[1] In using here the word 'especially' the Code does not intend to give to fast and abstinence as such a greater value than the other forms of penance indicated: it intends rather to point out the specifically legal obligation of this particular form of community penance, while the other forms mentioned, no less an exigency of christian penance, are entrusted to the personal choice of the individual: cf. Comm 12(1980) 364, 366 at Can. 48; for the background to the thinking behind this canon, cf. especially ap con *Paenitemini* ch II §§1–3: Fl II 5.

[2] Cf. Chiappetta II n.4103.

[3] For detailed regulations concerning both abstinence and fasting, cf. ap con *Paenitemini* ch III nn.1–2: Fl II 8. It is also to be noted that 'nothing is changed either regarding the vow of any physical or moral person or regarding the constitutions and rules of any approved religious congregation or institute': ibid. V: loc cit.

Part III Sacred Places and Times

(c) *the law of abstinence binds* those who have a sufficient use of reason (see Can. 11) and who have completed their fourteenth year,[1] i.e. from midnight on their fourteenth birthday (see Can. 203 §2), and it endures throughout their lives;

(d) *the law of fasting binds* those who have attained their majority, i.e. from midnight on their eighteenth birthday (see Cann. 97 §1, 203 §2) and it endures until the beginning of their sixtieth year, i.e. until midnight on their fifty-ninth birthday (see Can. 203 §2).

Can. 1252 concludes with a pastoral directive, itself borrowed from Pope Paul VI in his already-cited apostolic constitution (ch III, IV). *Pastors of souls*, principally Bishops and priests, and, very significantly, parents 'are to ensure that even those who by reason of their age are not bound by the law of fasting and abstinence, are taught the true meaning of penance' as an integral part of christian living. The true contemporary spirit of this injunction is aptly expressed in the words of Pope Paul VI: 2474

'.... in our time there are special reasons whereby, according to the demands of various localities, it is necessary to inculcate some special form of penitence in preference to others. Therefore, where economic well-being is greater, so much more will the witness of asceticism have to be given in order that the sons of the Church may not be involved in the spirit of the "world", and at the same time the witness of charity will have to be given to the brethren who suffer poverty and hunger beyond any barrier of nation or continent. On the other hand, in countries where the standard of living is lower, it will be more pleasing to God the Father and more useful to the members of the Body of Christ if Christians – while they seek in every way to promote better social justice – offer their suffering in prayer to the Lord in close union with the Cross of Christ.

'Therefore, the Church, while preserving – where it can be more readily observed – the custom (observed for many centuries with canonical norms) of practising penitence also through abstinence from meat and fasting, intends to ratify with its prescriptions other forms of penitence as well, provided that it seems opportune to Bishops' Conferences to replace the observance of fast and abstinence with exercises of prayer and works of charity.'[2]

Can. 1253 The Bishops' Conference can determine more particular ways in which fasting and abstinence are to be observed. In place of abstinence or fasting it can substitute, in whole or in part, other forms of penance, especially works of charity and exercises of piety.

In the course of the revision of the Code the question of fast and abstinence was considered at some length; in particular, it was asked whether abstinence should be confined to abstaining only from meat, as had been the traditional practice in the Church. It was decided that, since abstinence from meat was significant in the cultures and traditions of only certain peoples, it would not be appropriate to require it of others for whom abstinence from some other form of food would be a more meaningful penance.[3] Arising from that discussion came the proposal, now adopted in this 2475

---

[1] Not, as in c.1254 §1 of the 1917 Code, from the completion of their seventh year.
[2] op cit ch III: Fl II 7.
[3] Cf. Comm 12(1980) 364 at Can. 48.

Book IV The Sanctifying Office of the Church

canon, that while stating a general law for the universal Church, provision should be made for the adjustment of both abstinence and fast in order the more profitably to accord with local conditions and circumstances. Hence the prescription of this canon, the terms of which permit Bishops' Conferences:

(a) *to determine more particular ways* in which fast and abstinence are to be observed;

(b) *to substitute*, in whole or in part, other forms of penance, especially works of charity and exercises of piety.[1]

---

[1] For the manner in which a great number of Bishops' Conferences have availed themselves of this faculty, itself requiring the prior review of the Holy See (cf. Can. 455 §2), cf. LCE Tavola per Paesi e Canoni at Cann. 1251, 1253; CN(USA) 19, 29–34.

BOOK V

THE TEMPORAL GOODS OF THE CHURCH

Can. 1254 §1 The catholic Church has the inherent right, independently of any secular power, to acquire, retain, administer and alienate temporal goods, in pursuit of its proper objectives.

In the matter of property, the catholic Church claims an innate right to engage in four specific activities, each and all four for the purpose of carrying out and advancing the 'proper objectives' of the Church (see Can. 1254 §2), and all 'independently of any secular power'.[1] These are to *acquire*, to *retain or possess* (see Can. 634 §1), to *administer*, and to *alienate* temporal goods: 2476

(a) the right to acquire temporal goods, which is specified in Can. 1259.

(b) the right to retain or possess temporal goods: the concept of ownership (*dominium*) is somewhat different in canon law from that which is found in a number of civil jurisdictions. A test of complete ownership would be to examine whether the four acts listed in this canon can be carried out in respect of a particular fund or piece of property: e.g. it can and does happen that such goods are simply entrusted to the Church, without full ownership being transferred; in such instances, while the Church (through one of its juridical persons) may acquire, possess and administer such goods, it does not have an unfettered right to alienate them.[2]

(c) the right to administer temporal goods applies primarily to the discharging of the duties of an administrator, whoever he or she might be. The purpose of administration in this context is to see to the protection of the goods and to their production of appropriate revenues.

(d) the right to alienate temporal goods includes the right to convey them or to transfer their title to another person, whether physical or juridical.

That these rights may be exercised independently of the civil authority is the assertion of an inviolable canonical principle, one which can e.g. find practical expression in concordats entered into 'by the Apostolic See with nations or other civil entities' (Can. 3). There is at the same time a recognition that the civil authority has itself not only the right but the obligation to prescribe norms for the ordered administration and protection of property – a recognition found e.g. in Cann. 1284 §2 2°–3°, 1290, where, to ensure a desirable harmony, the canon law itself directs that the appropriate civil law be observed. 2477

Equally, however, it is well known that certain civil jurisdictions do not acknowledge this independent right of *the Church as such* to acquire, retain, administer and alienate its own property. To cater for such situations, it is accepted practice – and this is particularly true in countries of the Common Law tradition – that the various 2478

---

[1] This initial canon may usefully be compared with Cann. 747, 1311 and 1401, each of which asserts the fundamental rights of the Church in the area under consideration.

[2] A parallel is to be found in the Common Law tradition, itself in this regard inherited from the Canon Law.

ecclesiastical entities (be they dioceses, religious institutes, parishes, etc.) vest their property in corporations, trustees, companies or the like, all of which are recognised by the appropriate civil law. In this way it is possible, without any Church–State controversy, to conduct the normal measure of property transactions. It is important however to recognise that such practical arrangements do not in themselves affect the fundamental principle of this canon; nor do they, within the Church, in any way alter the regulations imposed by canon law.

Can. 1254 §2 These proper objectives are principally the regulation of divine worship, the provision of fitting support for the clergy and other ministers, and the carrying out of works of the sacred apostolate and of charity, especially for the needy.

2479 Here is stated what are the 'proper objectives' for the attainment of which the Church claims the right to own and administer property.[1] They must be emphasised:
- the regulation of divine worship, a primary objective;
- the support of those engaged in divine worship, a clear corollary;
- the carrying out of apostolic works, a necessary consequence: education, care of the sick, missionary endeavours, family programmes etc.;
- the charitable care of the needy: the poor, the dispossessed, those who have lost hope, those who feel abandoned by what they see to be an affluent world, and so on.

The list is not exhaustive: 'principally', the canon says. Can. 298 addresses the same question: it adds 'works of the apostolate ... which animate the temporal order with the christian spirit' – a special need of today, not least in the area of social and political endeavour.[2] Accordingly, ecclesiastical property which is not in fact devoted to one or other of these purposes is not rightly held, and should therefore be reassigned. The Church is opposed to the accumulation of property, of whatever kind, which serves no purpose other than to provide unnecessary security.

Can. 1255 The universal Church, as well as the Apostolic See, particular Churches, and all other public and private juridical persons are capable of acquiring, retaining, administering and alienating temporal goods, in accordance with the law.

2480 The canon lists five categories of 'persons' who may carry out the four fundamental activities in respect of temporal goods: all are 'moral' or 'juridical' persons. The five categories are:

(a) 'the universal Church': see Can. 113 §1

(b) 'the Apostolic See': see Cann. 113 §1, 361[3]

(c) 'particular Churches': see Can. 368

(d) 'other public juridical persons': see Can. 116

(e) 'private juridical persons': see Can. 116

The canon stipulates that, in carrying out their respective activity in regard to property, each is to act 'in accordance with the law', i.e. either the Code itself and, according to the circumstances, the relevant particular or proper law. It is understood that in an appropriate situation the relevant civil law should if possible also be observed.

---

[1] The text is taken from PO 17: Fl I 895. Cf. also AA 8, GS 42: Fl I 775–776, 942–943.

[2] Cf. also Cann. 114 §2, 222 §1, 394.

[3] The various institutes of the Roman Curia are currently governed by PB: AAS 80(1988) 841–934.

Individuals, or associations which do not have juridical status, may of course own and administer property. They do not, however, come within the ambit of this Book V of the Code. They are governed, rather, by the norms relating to private individuals, be they clerics or lay people (see Can. 207). 2481

Can. 1256 Under the supreme authority of the Roman Pontiff, ownership of goods belongs to that juridical person which has lawfully acquired them.

This canon establishes the fundamental principle that the 'ownership of goods belongs to that juridical person which has lawfully acquired them'. No one, in whatever position of authority, is entitled to contravene this principle. Its application is indeed 'under the supreme authority of the Roman Pontiff', but this in no way implies that the Pope is the owner of all the temporal goods of the Church.[1] 2482

Not only is the principle of this canon a fundamental one; it has major practical applications. Thus e.g. property acquired by a parish – say, a parochial house – belongs exclusively to that parish, not to the diocese, even where, for purposes of the civil law, all parochial property is vested in e.g. a corporation or a diocesan trust; should it occur that it be appropriate to convert it to a diocesan, as distinct from a parochial use, it must be purchased or leased or in some other lawful manner conveyed. The same would be true of property, of whatever kind, acquired e.g. by a religious house, vis-a-vis the province or the institute concerned, unless the constitutions provide otherwise (see Can. 634 §1). The canon refers to goods 'lawfully acquired' by the juridical person in question. The illegitimate acquisition of property does not give a right to ownership (saving the norm of Can. 1268 on prescription, if the act took place in good faith). Thus e.g. if a parish were *forced* to surrender any of its property to the diocese, such property would not 'lawfully' belong to the diocese, and an action could be instituted for its return (see Can. 1491). It is clearly desirable that any such situation be avoided. 2483

Can. 1257 §1 All temporal goods belonging to the universal Church, to the Apostolic See or to other public juridical persons in the Church, are ecclesiastical goods and are regulated by the canons which follow, as well as by their own statutes.

Here is enunciated the principle that all temporal goods belonging not only to the universal Church or to the Apostolic See but to all *public* juridical persons are, technically, 'ecclesiastical goods'.[2] It is essential that all administrators of ecclesiastical goods be aware of this canonical principle. In the perspective of canon law, the various forms of civil recognition have as their primary purpose the protection of the canonical ownership (see Cann. 1274 §5, 1284 §2 2°). 2484

As a consequence of this principle of ownership, all ecclesiastical goods must be 'regulated', i.e. governed and administered, by a twofold source of law, namely (a) the 'canons' of this Book V, and (b) the respective applicable 'statutes' (see Can. 94). Thus e.g. in the constitutions of each religious institute there should be a chapter on the administration of temporal goods, outlining the right of ownership, the norms for administration, and so on; equally, each diocese should have a policy regarding the administration of goods belonging to parishes, e.g. the amount of money a parish priest may spend without recourse to higher authority, etc. 2485

---

[1] Cf. Can. 1273.
[2] SCRIS 7.X.1974: CLD 9 370; cf. SCCE 2.I.1974: CLD 9 369. Cf. also Maida *Ownership, Sponsorship and Control of Catholic Institutions* Harrisburg, Pennsylvania Catholic Conference 1975 21–22.

Can. 1257 §2 Unless it is otherwise expressly provided, temporal goods belonging to a private juridical person are regulated by its own statutes, not by these canons.

2486 The temporal goods belonging to *private* juridical persons are not considered to be 'ecclesiastical goods' and thus are not, as such, subject to the canons of Book V and similar norms. However, it could reasonably be assumed that if the statutes of a private juridical person did not provide for such matters, the general principles of law would apply.[1]

2487 The goods of private juridical persons, then, are not regulated by the canons of Book V unless otherwise expressly stated.[2] Nevertheless, because the right to property is acknowledged to private juridical persons, this right can be vindicated through the ecclesiastical courts. There are some exceptional situations, among which may be mentioned: Can. 1263: taxing private juridical persons in cases of grave necessity; Can. 1265 §1: the prohibition against taking up collections without the permission of the Ordinary; Can. 1266: private oratories could be subject to mandatory collections; Can. 1267: it is presumed that gifts are intended for the juridical person; Can. 1269: prescription is foreseen for sacred objects; Can. 1280: the requirement of having a finance committee.

Can. 1258 In the canons which follow, the term Church signifies not only the universal Church or the Apostolic See, but also any public juridical person in the Church, unless the contrary is clear from the context or from the nature of the matter.

2488 The term 'Church' (*Ecclesia*) is used in different senses throughout the Code, depending on the context: thus e.g. in Book II, on the People of God, it has a very specific meaning; in Book IV, on the Sanctifying Office of the Church, it can have varying meanings, again according to varying contexts – compare Can. 834 §2 with Can. 838 §1. The precise point of this canon is to determine the specific meaning which the term is to bear in the current Book V.[3]

Title I
The Acquisition of Goods

Can. 1259 The Church may acquire temporal goods in any way in which, by either natural or positive law, it is lawful for others to do this.

---

[1] This matter was discussed at length by the Commission during the process of revising the Code, with particular reference to associations of the laity, such as the St Vincent de Paul Society, the Knights of Columbus, etc. For an instructive summary, cf. Comm 12(1980) 391–392, 398–399. Cf. also ibid. 124–125.

[2] In the USA and in Canada, and in the context particularly of catholic hospitals and other such health-care institutions, questions have been raised concerning the practical advisability of having these bodies regarded as private rather than as public juridical persons. On this issue cf. Morrisey *Juridic Status: Canonical Provisions, Possible Applications* Health Progress 67(1986) 41–45; Modde *Private Association: Opportunity for Laity* ibid. 46–50; Howarth *Juridic Person or Private Association: Choosing a Canonical Structure* ibid. 51. This is a matter for determination by the competent local authority, within the general lines enacted in the Code.

[3] For a relevant discussion on this matter, cf. Comm 12(1980) 399 at Can. 2.

This canon, itself adopted unchanged from the 1917 Code (c. 1499 §1), speaks of 'any way' in which it is lawful to acquire property not only by natural law, but also by positive law i.e. either by canon law or by civil law. A number of ways are recognized in canon law: free-will donations (Can. 1261); taxation (Can. 1263); fund raising (Can. 1265); prescription (Can. 1268); deriving income from existing goods (Cann. 1271, 1274); contracts to purchase (Can. 1290). Other means, recognised by civil law, might on occasion give right to the acquisition of goods, e.g. occupancy, the results of intellectual labour (patent rights, copyrights), acts of forfeiture, succession, marriage, insolvency, intestacy, gift or sale, court order, accession (increase, augmentation, addition) whether natural or artificial, improvements to existing property, results of artistic work.

In speaking of ways in which it is 'lawful' to acquire goods, the canon presupposes that the acquisition is also valid. Thus, an act of possession which is not valid would not generally constitute a licit means of acquiring goods, e.g. forcible retention, robbery, blackmail, and similar procedures.

Can. 1260 The Church has the inherent right to require from Christ's faithful whatever is necessary for its proper objectives.

Can. 222 is the counterpart of the present canon and has traditionally been recognised as among the precepts of the Church.

In referring to the 'inherent right' – the same word that is used in Can. 1254 – the canon underlines that this right does not depend on the good will of others. Of course, the *use* of the right might be restricted in some fashion by civil legislation or, in some countries, it might even be enhanced by public taxation laws (the well-known *Kirchensteuer* is an example). As regards the limitation of the use of the right, in some areas there are mortmain laws which have for their object the control of possessions of religious corporations or trusts: no lands are to be given to charities unless certain requisites are observed. Other places have restrictions concerning donations which are to be given to recognised charitable organizations if they are to qualify for taxation exemptions.

Can. 1261 §1 Christ's faithful have the right to donate temporal goods for the benefit of the Church.

Here the law recognises the *right* (as distinct from the obligation, already dealt with in Cann. 222 and 1260) of the faithful to donate temporal goods to the Church. A donation is a voluntary transfer of property: it may be *inter vivos*, or *mortis causa*, or *propter nuptias* (a dowry). Usually such a donation is irrevocable; in certain circumstances, however, it can take the form of a donative trust, to the effect namely that unless the donation is used for the purpose specified, it must be returned to the donor. In this context also it is important to ensure that any such gift has a 'clean title', i.e. that the donor is free to make it without any legal incumbrances.

Can. 1261 §2 The diocesan Bishop is bound to remind Christ's faithful of the obligation mentioned in Can. 222 §1, and in an appropriate manner to urge it.

Taking Can. 222 into account, the correlative obligation of the diocesan Bishop is obvious. The 'appropriate manner' in which he will fulfil this obligation will clearly be dependent upon the local circumstances, of which he in association with his priests is the appointed arbiter.

Can. 1262 The faithful are to give their support to the Church in response to appeals and in accordance with the norms laid down by the Bishops' Conference.

2495 In so far as possible to achieve a measure of uniformity in each region, appeals are to be carried out in accordance with the norms established by the respective Bishops' Conferences.[1] In practice, the Conference will often remit the specific details to the diocesan Bishop, while confining itself to such general directives as would deal e.g. with a schedule of national appeals, with matters which ought not to be the object of collections in churches, with rendering a subsequent account to the faithful, etc.

Can. 1263 The diocesan Bishop, after consulting the finance committee and the council of priests, has the right to levy on public juridical persons subject to his authority a tax for the needs of the diocese. This tax must be moderate and proportionate to their income. He may impose an extraordinary and moderate tax on other physical and juridical persons only in a grave necessity and under the same conditions, but without prejudice to particular laws and customs which may give him greater rights.

2496 This canon is a substantial innovation in the Church's law; there was no real equivalent in the previous Code.[2] It became necessary by reason of various stipulations in Vat. II which clearly demanded a new approach to the funding of undertakings entrusted to the diocese itself.[3] The thrust of the Council was that these must be shared diocesan activities, no longer the confine of e.g. individual parishes. While preserving the principle enunciated in Can. 1256, the Code here reminds especially public juridical persons that their right to ownership involves also an obligation to the wider ecclesial community. It does this by specifying the rights of a diocesan Bishop to impose taxes for diocesan purposes. Two types of taxes are dealt with: one ordinary, the other extraordinary.[4]

2497 The *ordinary tax* may be imposed only by the diocesan Bishop, or by one who is equivalent to him in law (see Can. 381 §2): not therefore by any other local Ordinary.[5] Before imposing the tax he must consult with both his finance committee and his council of priests. The consent of these bodies is not required, only their advice (see Can. 127).

2498 This tax may be levied only on 'public juridical persons' (parishes are the obvious, though not the only, example), not on individuals. Moreover these juridical persons are those only which are 'subject to (the diocesan Bishop's) authority'. External schools of pontifical religious institutes are not so subject.[6] Neither are religious institutes, whether pontifical or diocesan, because of their autonomy of governance (see Can. 586),[7] nor private associations of the faithful, nor supra-diocesan institutes such as the Bishops' Conference, the Conference of major Superiors, and the like.

---

[1] Cf. LCE Tavola per Paesi e Canoni at Can. 1262: the great and interesting variety of practice in the various regions of the Church comes through clearly.

[2] Cf. 1917 Code cc.1502, 1504–1506.

[3] One thinks e.g. of the funds required to provide, where necessary: for the support of the clergy serving the diocese; for their social security; for retired priests; for the assistance of poorer dioceses; for a diocesan office or organ to deal with such as education, catechetics, communication; for matrimonial tribunals, and so on.

[4] For the background to this canon and its evolution, cf. Comm 12(1980) 401–403; 16(1984) 28–30.

[5] Apart from quite extraordinary circumstances, the diocesan Administrator, elected in accordance with Can. 421 §1, would not be empowered to impose this tax: cf. Cann. 427 §1, 428.

[6] Cf. Reply of PCI 24.I.1989: AAS 81(1989) 991 ad II.

[7] Cf. Kealey *Diocesan Financial Support: its history and canonical status* Rome (Pont. Gregorian University) 1986 333.

Title I The Acquisition of Goods

The tax is to be 'moderate and proportionate to the income' of the respective juridical persons. It is for the Bishop to determine whether the tax is based on gross or on net income. Sometimes a combination of procedures is adopted: parishes that do not have a debt could have their tax rated on gross revenue; parishes with a debt might have their tax rated on gross revenue less any capital paid back on the debt. The Bishop could also determine a sliding scale in proportion to the revenue. **2499**

The *extraordinary tax* can be applied for special needs, e.g. to cover the expenses of a papal visit, to build or substantially to repair the cathedral, to build a new seminary. The Code speaks of a 'grave necessity': not therefore of any need that might arise; on the other hand, it does not have to be one of an exceptionally serious nature. This tax may be levied not only on the public juridical persons who are subject to the ordinary tax, but also on private juridical persons (see Can. 116) and even on individuals. The 'same conditions' apply as those required to levy the ordinary tax, in particular that the Bishop would first consult his finance committee and his council of priests. In view of its extraordinary nature, this tax may not be permanent.[1] The canon provides also for particular and exceptional circumstances: 'without prejudice to particular laws and customs ...'. In view here are certain situations, of historical origin, whereby in some places, whether by lawful custom or e.g. by a document of foundation, a public juridical person would have contracted to pay a regular sum for the needs of the diocesan Bishop, should this sum be greater than that required by this extraordinary tax, the law here requires that it would still, by reason of the Bishop's acquired right, have to be paid. **2500**

The 1917 Code in c.1506, had stipulated that no tax could be levied on Mass stipends. It was certainly the opinion of the Revision Commission that this rule should be maintained.[2] In fact, it was not included in the promulgated text and, subject to any future determination by the Pontifical Council for the Interpretation of Legislative Texts, the earlier rule still obtains. It would certainly be an abuse if a Bishop were arbitrarily to designate to another, however worthy, purpose the entire amount of a stipend which is understood by the donor to be given for the support of the celebrant. **2501**

Can. 1264 Unless the law prescribes otherwise, it is for the provincial Bishops' meeting to:

1° determine the taxes, to be approved by the Apostolic See, for acts of executive authority which grant a favour, or for the execution of rescripts from the Apostolic See;

2° determine the offerings on the occasion of the administration of the sacraments and sacramentals.

The Code assumes that the Bishops of each ecclesiastical province meet on a regular basis, to carry out the overall purpose entrusted to them by Can. 431. In this canon two specifications of that purpose are dealt with: to determine certain 'taxes' and to determine certain 'offerings'.[3] **2502**

The *taxes* are those to be required on the occasion of 'acts of executive authority' (see Cann. 135 §4 – 138), namely (a) those 'which grant a favour' e.g. a dispensation: it is **2503**

---

[1] Cf. Comm 16(1984) 28 at Can. 1213.
[2] Cf. Comm 5(1973) 95 n.5; 12(1980) 402; Sch 1982 at Can. 1263.
[3] To complete the picture cf. Cann. 952, 1181, 1221 – a corollary is to be found in Can. 848; cf. also Can. 264 §2.

standard practice today in the majority of dioceses either to make no charge or to make only a nominal charge for such favours; (b) those 'for the execution of rescripts from the Apostolic See', which itself normally charges a tax for the issue of its rescripts: again, it would seem to be unusual for a diocese to impose a further tax for the mere execution of such a rescript. It is to be noted that should a provincial Bishops' meeting determine either of these taxes, the positive 'approval' of the Holy See would be required before they would be legally binding. Finally, these taxes are quite different from those established to cover the expenses in judicial proceedings (see Can. 1649).

2504 The *offerings*, which are clearly to be distinguished from taxes, are those which may be requested 'on the occasion of the administration of the sacraments and sacramentals', e.g. baptism, marriage, funerals – a source which in certain regions provides a substantial part of the support of the clergy.[1] If the respective Bishops have not in provincial assembly determined the amounts to be requested, then, by analogy with Can. 952 §2, the custom of the diocese is to be followed.

Can. 1265 §1 Without prejudice to the right of mendicant religious, all private juridical or physical persons are forbidden to quest for any pious or ecclesiastical institute or purpose without the written permission of their proper Ordinary and of the local Ordinary.

2505 It is to be noted that, apart from 'the right of mendicant religious' (see §2), the conditions prescribed here apply only to 'private juridical or physical persons'. They do not therefore apply to public juridical persons as such, but they would apply to their individual members, e.g. the members of a parish or of a non-mendicant religious institute. The clear purpose of this ruling is to control indiscriminate, and even bogus, appeals to the faithful.[2] Those who are asked to contribute to so-called charitable campaigns are entitled – an entitlement which they should exercise – to make certain that the written authorisation prescribed here has been given. It is important that the authorising authority should, in giving the requisite permission, specify how and by whom the funds collected are to be administered.

Can. 1265 §2 The Bishops' Conference can draw up rules regarding questing, which must be observed by all, including those who from their foundation are called and are 'mendicants'.

2506 While the Conference is not obliged to draw up such rules, many have in fact already done so.[3] Should a particular Conference choose not to act in this regard, then clearly the matter would be regulated by the norms applicable in each diocese.

Can. 1266 In all churches and oratories regularly open to Christ's faithful, including those belonging to religious institutes, the local Ordinary may order that a special collection be taken up for specified parochial, diocesan, national or universal initiatives. The collection must afterwards be carefully forwarded to the diocesan curia.

2507 The reference here is to a *special* collection – as distinct from regular collections, from various types of appeals and from the diocesan tax – which may be for a specified parochial, diocesan, national or universal initiative. The special nature of this collec-

---

[1] Cf. the important considerations in this regard outlined in Comm 12(1980) 403 at Can. 6.
[2] Cf. Comm 12(1980) 404 at Can.7.
[3] Cf. LCE Tavola per Paesi e Canoni at Can. 1265.

tion implies that the local Ordinary would use it only with moderation.[1] The initiative in question need not be exclusively for religious ends, but could also be for humanitarian purposes e.g. to alleviate famine, to cater for the homeless or other such social need, etc. The collection may be prescribed in any and every church or oratory (see Cann. 1214, 1223) which is regularly and officially open to the faithful for worship.[2] The prior consultation referred to in Can. 1263 is not required in respect of such a collection.

Can. 1267 §1 Unless the contrary is clear, offerings made to Superiors or administrators of any ecclesiastical juridical person, even a private one, are presumed to have been made to the juridical person itself.

This paragraph sets out an important principle, expressed in the form of a presumption (see Can. 1584). Every presumption does of course yield to proof of the contrary: hence the phrase 'unless the contrary is clear'; this would cater for the received policy in many dioceses in respect e.g. of stole fees, clergy dues, Christmas and Easter offerings, etc. But apart from such accepted customary practices, the practical principle is clear: unless the offering made is clearly designated to be exclusively for the personal use of the recipient, it must be handed over to the juridical person in question, e.g. the parish, the religious house or institute, the approved charity, etc.[3] The word 'Superior' is used not only in the sense of Can. 617 but also in the sense of Can. 118. — 2508

Should the recipient simultaneously represent two juridical persons, e.g. a parish priest who is also the superior of a religious house, it is essential that it be clearly understood whether the offering is made to the one or to the other: to the parish or to the institute. Equitable and practical commonsense must be the guide here. — 2509

Can. 1267 §2 If there is question of a public juridical person, the offerings mentioned in §1 cannot be refused except for a just reason and, in matters of greater importance, with the permission of the Ordinary. Without prejudice to the provisions of Can. 1295, the permission of the Ordinary is also required for the acceptance of offerings to which are attached some qualifying obligation or condition.

Offerings made to a public juridical person cannot be refused except for a just (not necessarily a grave or very grave) reason and, in matters of greater importance, with the permission of the Ordinary (not necessarily the local Ordinary); accordingly in the case of a clerical institute of pontifical right, the major Superior's permission would suffice (see Can. 134 §1). — 2510

The canon does not state what are such 'matters of greater importance'. Certainly, any sums which go beyond the minimum amount determined by the Bishops' Conference for purposes of alienation (see Can. 1292 §1) would be subject to this provision. The publicity, or the general circumstances, attached to a gift could also make it a matter of such greater importance, even though the sum involved might be relatively small. — 2511

It must be noted that an Ordinary – or any person for that matter – is *never* obliged to accept a gift, of whatever nature or provenance. There can well be a 'just cause' which would justify the refusal of a gift, e.g. its origin, the reputation of the donor, the nature of the gift as e.g. if it were to be from a place of ill repute, the circum- — 2512

---

[1] Cf. Comm 12(1980) 405 at Can. 8.

[2] Complementary to this canon is Can. 791 4° which is often implemented by way of a special collection.

[3] For another application of this same principle cf. Can. 531.

stances surrounding it as a gift from someone whose parents or children were in dire need, etc.

2513 The last clause of §2 means that the norms regarding the alienation of temporal goods must be observed (e.g., prior consent of certain bodies, etc.) when a *condition* is attached that would make the patrimonial state of the juridical person less secure (see Can. 1295). The prudent practice today is to refuse gifts with *perpetual* conditions attached, no matter how enticing the gift. Even conditions with a duration of, say, about twenty years may rightly be considered excessively onerous, precisely because – unlike in times past – financial values can now so very rapidly undergo substantial change. In general, when there is question of the acceptance of a gift with a condition of substantial duration, the gift should be accepted only if it incorporates a reasonable provision that, if needs be, the purpose of the gift may be adjusted, e.g. at the discretion of the diocesan Bishop or other such appropriate authority.

2514 The law here applies only to public juridical persons, not to individuals. However, a religious institute could well establish a policy to the effect that *individual* members do not accept legacies which entail obligations or conditions that could be contrary to the vow or to the spirit of poverty e.g. a gift given on condition that the member may, each year, take an extended vacation.

Can. 1267 §3 Offerings given by the faithful for a specified purpose may be used only for that purpose.

2515 Here again is enuntiated a fundamental principle: that which is given, and accepted, for a specific purpose may be devoted to that purpose – and to no other, however worthy or deserving that other might be. This same principle of absolute respect for the intention and wishes of the donor is a significant feature of the Church's law.[1] It is only where the purpose of the offering is stated in general, rather than specific, terms – e.g. 'for the diocese', 'for the charitable works of the institute' – that the recipient would have a discretionary power to apply the proceeds as would be considered appropriate within the terms of the gift or offering made.

2516 As a practical norm, the recipients of any such offerings, great or small, should try in so far as possible to ensure that they be consulted in advance about the precise wishes of the donor, and where appropriate to suggest a possible adjustment should circumstances change substantially in the future. The majority of donors, and their advisors, would not only understand but would welcome such guidance.

Can. 1268 The Church recognises prescription, in accordance with Cann. 197-199, as a means both of acquiring temporal goods and of being freed from their obligations.

2517 In the context of temporal goods, prescription is generally defined as a manner of acquiring the ownership of property, or of discharging debts, by the passage of time and under the conditions regulated by law. The matter is dealt with in detail by Cann. 197-199 (q.v.). The present canon specifically extends to the area of temporal goods the principles and norms enunciated there, and it is to be read in conjunction with the following two canons, 1269-1270.

Can. 1269 Sacred objects in private ownership may be acquired by private persons by prescription, but they may not be used for secular purposes unless they have lost their dedication or blessing. If, however, they belong to a public ecclesiastical juridical person, they may be acquired only by another public ecclesiastical person.

---

[1] By way of example, in diverse situations cf. Cann. 122, 123, 616 §1, 1284 §2 3°, 1299 §2.

Title I The Acquisition of Goods

Sacred objects are those set aside for divine worship by dedication or blessing (see Can. 1171) and even if, being in 'private ownership' i.e. in that of an individual or of a private juridical person (see Can. 116), they are not 'ecclesiastical goods' (see Can. 1257 §1), they must be treated with reverence and accordingly not put to any improper use. The purpose of this canon is to protect that position. 2518

The canon prescribes that: (a) those sacred objects which are in private ownership *may* by prescription be acquired by private individuals; although the matter is not formally addressed in the canon, it is evident that such objects may also be acquired prescriptively by juridical persons; (b) those in the ownership of a public juridical person (see Can. 116) may thus be acquired *only* by another public juridical person: thus e.g. a chalice owned by a parish, even if used exclusively by the parish priest, may not by prescription be acquired after his death by his relatives; (c) in either event, the sacred object, whatever its nature, may not be devoted to any 'secular', or non-religious, purpose unless it itself will 'have lost (its) dedication or blessing'. 2519

Can. 1270 Immovable goods, precious movable goods, rights and legal claims, whether personal or real, which belong to the Apostolic See, are prescribed after a period of one hundred years; for those which belong to another public ecclesiastical juridical person, the period for prescription is thirty years.

Here are determined certain so-called 'privileged' prescription-times in respect of (a) specified properties and rights, and (b) specified ecclesiastical owners. In regard to the *former*, the canon mentions three categories: immovable goods, such as land or buildings; precious movable goods i.e. 'precious by reason of their artistic or historical significance' (Can. 1292 §2);[1] rights and legal claims whether personal i.e. concerning one's relationship to another person physical or juridical, or real, i.e. concerning real property. In regard to the *latter*, the canon determines that if any of the specified properties and rights belong to the Apostolic See, a period of one hundred years is required before they may be acquired by prescription; if to any other public juridical person (see Can. 116), a period of thirty years.[2] In all situations other than those prescribed in this canon, the time-span for prescription is to be that determined by the relevant civil law.[3] 2520

Can. 1271 By reason of their bond of unity and charity, and according to the resources of their dioceses, Bishops are to contribute to the provision of those means which the Apostolic See may from time to time need to exercise properly its service to the universal Church.

This is a clear reflection of the teaching of Vat. II.[4] The general manner of fulfilling this prescription is to have an annual diocesan collection for 'Peter's Pence' or its equivalent, the proceeds of which are to be forwarded to Rome. However, in special 2521

---

[1] Apart from the fact that it itself can so much vary from time to time and from place to place, monetary value is clearly not a sole determinant here; thus e.g. the personal possession of a founder or foundress of a religious institute, such as a prayer-book, a diary, a rosary etc. would indeed be 'precious' in this context even though in itself of no particular artistic merit or monetary value.

[2] For an instructive insight into the discussions at the Revision Commission cf. Comm 12(1980) 407 at Can. 12.

[3] This is without prejudice to the special privilege enjoyed by some religious institutes even before the 1917 Code and protected by c.4 of that Code e.g. the property of the Benedictines required a 60-year term for prescription, that of the Mendicant Orders and of the Cistercians a 100-year term: cf. Wernz–Vidal IV *De Rebus* II n.825; Vermeersch–Creusen II n.831; Regatillo II n.295; Vromant n.141 ad 4. In virtue of Can. 4 of the current Code, each such privilege remains in effect.

[4] LG 23: Fl I 376–378.

circumstances, the Apostolic See could call upon diocesan Bishops and even upon religious institutes to assist it.[1]

Can. 1272 In those regions where benefices properly so called still exist, it is for the Bishops' Conference to regulate such benefices by appropriate norms, agreed with and approved by the Apostolic See. The purpose of these norms is that the income and as far as possible the capital itself of the benefice should by degrees be transferred to the fund mentioned in Can. 1274 §1.

2522 It was the wish of Vat. II to abolish the system of 'benefices' in the Church, or at very least so to reform it that the right to an income attached to a particular office should be regarded as secondary, and that the principal emphasis in law be given to the ecclesiastical office itself.[2] The text speaks of 'benefices properly so called' (see 1917 Code c.1409). In fact, these are not a particularly significant feature of the English-speaking world, for which therefore this canon has not a major relevance.[3] On the other hand, such benefices still have a distinct significance – on historical, technical and even political grounds – in a number especially of European countries.[4] Hence the decision by the Legislator to prescribe this transitional norm, whereby the appropriate Bishops' Conferences are required to determine, 'by degrees' (*paulatim*), that 'the income and, *as far as possible*, the capital itself of the benefice' – a more substantial step – be assigned to the special fund prescribed in Can. 1274 §1 'for the support of the clergy who serve the diocese'.[5] It is to be noted that these decisions of the relevant Bishops' Conferences are to be 'agreed with' (i.e. there is room for discussion) 'and approved by the Apostolic See'. It is equally to be noted that Bishops' Conferences are *obliged* to bring about this reform intended by Vat. II. It is clear, finally, that no new benefices may be established.

Title II
The Administration of Goods

Can. 1273 The Roman Pontiff, by virtue of his primacy of governance, is the supreme administrator and steward of all ecclesiastical goods.

---

[1] This canon was invoked by the Secretariat of State in a letter of 25.III.1987 which appealed to diocesan Bishops to come to the aid of the Holy See in the matter of a budget deficit; in like manner Can. 640 was invoked in a similar letter to religious Institutes on 29.VI.1987. In this context cf. also Can. 529 §2 concerning the obligation of every parish priest to ensure that his parishioners 'feel themselves to be members (not only of the diocese but also) of the universal Church' and accordingly, to the extent that they can afford it, willing to support the apostolic mission of the See of Peter.

[2] Cf. PO 20: Fl I 899; ES I 8: Fl I 596; AAS 63(1971) 921.

[3] Under the 1917 Code there were two views as to whether or not parishes in many English-speaking countries were 'benefices properly so called', the majority view being that they were not. It is certain that the current Code does not regard any parish as a benefice: contrast 1917 Code c.451 §1 with Cann. 515 §1 and 519.

[4] For the background here cf. Comm 5(1973) 96 n.10; 9(1977) 269; 12(1980) 412 at Can. 17; 16(1984) 31 at Can. 1223.

[5] For the response of Bishops' Conferences to this requirement cf. LCE Tavola per Paesi e Canoni at Can. 1272.

Title II The Administration of Goods

2523 Administration of property may well be compared to the general notion of governance of persons. Just as the proper function of government is to strive for the well-being of persons and thus to help them achieve their proper purpose in life and in society, so too the administration of property consists in taking care that property which has lawfully been acquired is preserved and is used for the purpose for which it was assigned. This canon sees the Roman Pontiff precisely in this context: his role here is specifically 'by virtue of his primacy of governance',[1] thus underlining the unity of the Church which must itself be manifest in the manner in which all ecclesiastical property is administered 'in pursuit of (the Church's) proper objectives' (Can. 1254 §1).

2524 It is not however a question of the Pope being the owner of all ecclesiastical goods,[2] not even as it were the concurrent owner with those juridical persons to whom the property belongs (see Can. 1256). It is rather that, in virtue of his overall authority of governance, he enjoys the power to invigilate and to steward all other administrators of property in the Church. In the ordinary course, the Roman Pontiff exercises this power:

- through the relevant general laws of the Church, principally in the Code;
- by reserving to himself either the more serious acts of administration or the administration of particular ecclesiastical goods[3] e.g. Cann. 1292 §2, 638 §3.

In addition, it is not infrequent in practice for the Holy See to be called upon either to oversee or to determine difficult or controversial individual acts of administration in various places throughout the Church.

2525 Whenever a particular act of administration is specifically reserved to the Holy See, the authority of all other relevant administrators – be they Bishops, religious Superiors, parish priests, or whomsoever – is superseded, and accordingly the permission of the Holy See is required for the valid canonical transaction of the matter. As far as property belonging to the universal Church or to the Apostolic See itself is concerned, the Roman Pontiff exercises his role as supreme administrator and steward through the relevant organs of the Roman Curia.[4]

2526 The word 'steward' (*dispensator*) used in this canon very aptly describes the role not only of the Roman Pontiff but of every administrator of ecclesiastical property. In the Church the concept of ownership, of which administration is a corollary, carries with it the notion of responsible stewardship, precisely because the right of the Church to own and otherwise to deal with temporal goods is solely with a view to the pursuit of its proper objectives as outlined in Can. 1254 §2.

Can. 1274 §1 In every diocese there is to be a special fund which collects offerings and temporal goods for the purpose of providing, in accordance with Can. 281, for the support of the clergy who serve the diocese, unless they are otherwise catered for.

2527 This canon must be read in conjunction with Can. 1272 which, itself reflecting Vat. II, prescribes the abolition of benefices. Recognising the need for alternative means to support those in the Church's ministry and in a practical way to meet current financial

---

[1] Cf. Can. 331. To make the point, this phrase was added to the text of what had been c.1518 of the 1917 Code.
[2] Cf. Comm 12(1980) 412–413 at Can. 18.
[3] Cf. Comm 5(1973) 97 n.15.
[4] Cf. PB Artt 171–179.

circumstances, Vat. II undertook an overall review,[1] to which legislative effect is finally given in the five paragraphs of this canon, dealing respectively with: the support of the clergy; their social security; the remuneration of those employed by the Church and the provision for various diocesan needs; the possibility of financial cooperation among dioceses; the advisability of ensuring that funds set up for these various purposes would have appropriate standing in civil law.

2528 The fund prescribed in §1 is destined specifically for the support of the clergy 'who serve the diocese' i.e. obviously secular priests and permanent deacons, but also religious priests who serve the diocese[2] e.g. by being entrusted with a parish.[3] It is obligatory to establish this fund, unless the support of the clergy is 'otherwise catered for', as would be the case if e.g. the civil government were to pay a salary to priests (as does occur in a number especially of European countries); even in this latter situation, however, it may be necessary to establish a fund of this kind to supplement the support of the clergy, in accordance with terms of Can. 281 §1. The principal source of this fund will of course be the voluntary offerings of the faithful, to which however may in the relevant circumstances be added the proceeds referred to in Can. 1272 (see also Can. 1303 §2). All of this is a matter for the diocesan Bishop to determine, bearing in mind the specific circumstances of his own diocese. In any event, the fund itself, howsoever formed, should be given juridical personality in accordance with Cann. 114–116.

Can. 1274 §2 Where there is as yet no properly organised system of social provision for the clergy, the Bishops' Conference is to see that a fund is established which will furnish adequate social security for them.

2529 The prescription of §2 applies *only* 'where there is as yet no properly organised system of social provision for the clergy', such as health-care, arrangements for retirement, and the like. There are countries or regions in which such provision is already made, even by the relevant ecclesiastical authorities. More significantly perhaps, there are many countries in which the State or a State-agency offers such a service: in that situation, it would meet this regulation if the Bishops' Conference were by general decree (Can. 455) to 'see to it' that the clergy would join the appropriate scheme, prescribing the financial arrangements necessary to accord with the regulations, or even perhaps leaving it to each individual diocesan Bishop so to arrange.

2530 It is only in the absence of any such provision that the alternative prescribed by §2 would arise, namely that the Bishops' Conference itself establish a special fund, to be financed proportionally by the constitutive dioceses. In this case, the fund should be governed by appropriate statutes, which would *inter alia* set out the method whereby the fund would be operated and the role of each of the Bishops involved, as e.g. in the case of interdiocesan seminaries (Can. 237) or of interdiocesan tribunals (Can. 1423).[4]

Can. 1274 §3 To the extent that it is required, a common reserve is to be established in every diocese by which the Bishop is enabled to fulfil his obligations towards other persons who serve the Church and to meet various needs of the diocese; this can also be the means by which wealthier dioceses may help poorer ones.

---

[1] PO 21: Fl I 889–900, which had been given interim effect in ES I 8: Fl I 596–597.

[2] Cf. Comm 12(1980) 408–410; 16(1984) 31–32 at Can. 1225 §1.

[3] When a parish is entrusted to a religious institute, account would also have to be taken of the terms of the contract agreed between the diocesan Bishop and the competent religious Superior.

[4] For the response of Bishops' Conferences to this requirement, cf. LCE Tavola per Paesi e Canoni at Can. 1274.

In every diocese, in addition to the clergy who directly serve the Church's ministry, there are at least two other groups or agencies for whom financial provision must be made. The first – 'other persons who serve the Church' – are principally those lay people who are in fact *employed* to assist the pastoral ministry of the clergy (as distinct from those many others who voluntarily put their generous services, mostly on a part-time basis, at the disposal of the Church's concerns and activities). These people 'have the *right* to a worthy remuneration', in accordance with the terms of Can. 231 §2 (q.v.). The second concern of this §3 is the 'various needs of the diocese' itself (as distinct in the main from the specific needs of individual parishes), e.g. education, formation of the clergy, social services, youth, marriage, liturgy, etc. 2531

It is to fund these two purposes that §3 prescribes the establishment of a common reserve, but only 'to the extent that it is required'. Provided the objective of this law is achieved, the Bishop has therefore a choice between such a common fund and some other appropriate measure of funding according to the circumstances of the diocese. He might indeed have the choice of a mixture of both: it is conceivable e.g. that a common reserve (or reserves) would be established to cater for the various needs of the diocese and for the remuneration of those laity who are employed by the central diocesan administration, while at the same time prescribing rules to ensure that the laity employed in individual parishes be remunerated from parish funds in a manner which would meet their right as determined by Can. 231 §2. So much may depend on local circumstances, but the essential point is that the Bishop ensures that, whatever method is adopted, the clear objective of this law be integrally achieved. Should any form of common fund be decided upon, it too should be given formal juridical personality, or at least its own set of rules and of procedures. 2532

Finally, should a form of common reserve be determined, consideration must also be given to deciding whether this be the appropriate fund from which 'wealthier dioceses may help poorer ones', thus reflecting the teaching of St Paul (2 Cor 8:14) and the call of Vat. II. But if not from such a fund, it clearly remains incumbent upon the more financially secure dioceses to devise other means of fulfilling their manifest obligation in this regard. 2533

Can. 1274 §4 Depending on differing local circumstances, the purposes described in §§2 and 3 might better be achieved by amalgamating various diocesan funds, or by cooperation between various dioceses, or even by setting up a suitable association for them, or indeed for the whole territory of the Bishops' Conference itself.

This §4 is at best exhortatory, reflecting the similar approach of Vat. II.[1] It proposes various possible means whereby the important purposes dealt with in §§2 and 3 might perhaps, depending on local circumstances, better be achieved. This is clearly a technical matter, calling for the assistance of persons competent to judge not only financial affairs but also the relevant ecclesiastical circumstances.[2] 2534

Can. 1274 §5 If possible, these funds are to be established in such a manner that they will have standing also in the civil law.

---

[1] Cf. PO 21: Fl I 900.

[2] By analogy with Can. 1274 §4 a number of dioceses have made a move to consolidate the funds belonging to parishes in one central fund, to enable the diocese to have added funds with which to operate and thereby e.g. to secure a higher rate of investment interest. Such practice is canonically allowable, provided however – and this is very important – that the parochial ownership of the respective funds is integrally understood and preserved, and that each parish gets its strictly proportionate share of the interest accruing: cf. Can. 1256.

2535 It is an obviously sensible procedure that, if at all possible, the funds referred to in the previous paragraphs of this canon be given 'standing also in the civil law'; just how this is to be done – whether by incorporation, by trust, by the device of 'reserved powers', or by whatever – will clearly depend upon the structures available in the relevant civil law. The point to be stressed is that whatever civil means is employed does not in any way alter the canonical or ecclesiastical ownership as determined by Can. 1256.[1]

Can. 1275 A reserve set up by a number of different dioceses is to be administered according to norms opportunely agreed upon by the Bishops concerned.

2536 This refers particularly to the possibilities envisaged in Can. 1274 §4. The norms to be 'opportunely agreed upon by the Bishops concerned' could determine such as the composition of the board of directors, provision for the distribution of assets, a system of reporting (budgets, audited accounts, etc.), appropriate reserve clauses, provision for the dissolution of the fund if necessary, and the like. The Bishops' Conference as such does not have competence in this regard.[2]

Can. 1276 §1 Ordinaries must carefully supervise the administration of all the goods which belong to public juridical persons subject to them, without prejudice to lawful titles which may give the Ordinary greater rights.

2537 The canon applies to all Ordinaries, both local and personal (see Can. 134 §1). Their role is a supervisory one: it does not as such entail intervention in the actual administration itself. It is applicable 'to public juridical persons subject to them'.[3] It is therefore an act of the power of governance or jurisdiction (see Can. 129 §1), enabling them to inspect the administration and, if needs be, to introduce corrective measures (see Can. 1279 §1). This is however 'subject to lawful titles which may give the Ordinary *greater* rights', e.g. by delegation of the Holy See or by the statutes.

Can. 1276 §2 Taking into account rights, lawful customs and the circumstances, Ordinaries are to regulate the whole matter of the administration of ecclesiastical goods by issuing special instructions, within the limits of universal and particular law.

2538 The manner by which Ordinaries are obliged 'to regulate the whole matter of the administration of ecclesiastical goods' is to issue 'special instructions'. These, obviously to be 'within the limits of universal and particular law', will depend upon the local circumstances, be these diocesan or religious. Particular points of reference may be found in Cann. 537 and 635 §2. In issuing such instructions, the Ordinary must also have an eye to the relevant civil legislation, endeavouring as far as possible or desirable to accord with it. He must also take into account 'rights' which may have been lawfully established, perhaps for many years, and 'lawful customs'.[4]

---

[1] A significant feature of all the elements of Can. 1274 is its stress upon the need to adjust its prescriptions to the circumstances and needs of the local Church. For a valuable insight into the evolution of the canon, cf. Comm 5(1973) 96 n.14; 9(1977) 271; 12(1980) 407–411 at Can. 16; 15(1984) 31–32 at Can. 1225.

[2] Cf. Comm 15(1984) 32 at Cann. 1226, 1225 §1 n.2.

[3] The same authority is enjoyed in respect of associations of the faithful (cf. Can. 305 §2), autonomous monasteries and religious houses of diocesan right (cf. Can. 637).

[4] Bearing in mind that 'custom is the best interpreter of laws' (Can. 27), Ordinaries would be well advised in this regard to take accurate account of Cann. 23–28.

Title II The Administration of Goods

Can. 1277 In carrying out acts of administration which, in the light of the financial situation of the diocese, are of major importance, the diocesan Bishop must consult the finance committee and the college of consultors. However, in addition to the cases specifically expressed in the universal law or in the documents of foundation, for acts of extraordinary administration he needs the consent of the committee and of the college of consultors. It is for the Bishops' Conference to determine what are to be regarded as acts of extraordinary administration.

The administration of money and of other property is a normal and ordinary part of the regime of every diocese. The Code assumes this, recognising it to be governed by the general norms of this Book V. This canon, however, singles out two forms of administration which call for specific attention. It distinguishes and regulates: 2539

(a) 'acts of administration ... of major importance';

(b) 'acts of extraordinary administration'.

The criterion of an act of administration of *major importance* is simply 'the financial situation of the diocese', which will obviously vary from one diocese to another, and certainly from one country to another: that which e.g. might well be considered 'ordinary' in a diocese of two million Catholics could well be of 'major importance' in a very much smaller diocese. It will be for the diocesan Bishop himself, aided by advisors who will be aware that administrators are essentially 'stewards' (see Can. 1273), to determine what is, in all the circumstances, such an act of major importance. Having made a conscientious decision in that regard, the Bishop is then obliged to 'consult the finance committee and the college of consultors' (see Cann. 492 §1, 502 §1). While he is not obliged to accept the advice given, he would act invalidly if he did not seek it and, in the absence of an overriding reason, illegally and imprudently if he simply rejected it (see Can. 127 §2 2°). 2540

The criterion of an act of *extraordinary administration* is quite different: here it is simply that which has been determined as such by an approved decree of the relevant Bishops' Conference.[1] There is a long tradition in this regard, as evidenced particularly by the decision of the Sacred Congregation for the Propagation of the Faith 21.VII.1856,[2] the norms of which have in large measure been followed ever since. The current Code has changed that situation. While of course allowing that the earlier guidelines from the Holy See would be taken into account, it has firmly placed upon the relevant Bishops' Conferences the obligation to determine, in view of its own current circumstances, those acts of administration which are to be regarded as *extraordinary*. An examination of the various confirmed decrees issued by Conferences to date shows that a variety of approaches has been taken: some use a listing of categories of acts, others use a basic sum of money or value as indicative of extraordinary administration, while still others use a mixed approach.[3] 2541

The diocesan Bishop cannot validly carry out any act which has been determined as one of 'extraordinary administration', unless he will first have had the consent (by at 2542

---

[1] As far as religious institutes are concerned, cf. Can. 638 §1. A further factor to be borne in mind, in all cases, is 'the documents of foundation', namely the specific conditions under which a particular fund may have been established, which itself may have determined other conditions for acts of extraordinary administration.

[2] CIC (1917) Fontes 7 n.4841. Cf. SCCon 13.VII.1963: CLD 6 822–832.

[3] Cf. LCE Tavola per Paesi e Canoni at Can. 1277. As of 1990 all but 7 (4 of them English-speaking!) of the 46 Conferences listed had fulfilled their obligation in this regard.

least an absolute majority) both of the diocesan finance committee and of the college of consultors (see Can. 127 §§1 and 2 1°). The only exceptions are those 'expressly provided for in the universal law' e.g. Can. 1292, or 'stated in the documents of foundation' i.e. the statutes or rules under which a particular fund or endowment was established.[1]

Can. 1278 Besides the duties mentioned in Can. 494 §§3 and 4, the diocesan Bishop may also entrust to the financial administrator the duties mentioned in Cann. 1276 §1 and 1279 §2.

2543 The duties inherent in the office of the diocesan financial administrator are detailed in Can. 494 §§3 and 4. The point of this canon is to permit the diocesan Bishop, if he so wishes, to extend those duties to two further areas, namely: the supervision of the administration of monies and all other property belonging to public juridical persons subject to himself, e.g. parishes (Can. 1276 §1); the actual administration itself of the goods belonging to those public juridical persons for which no administrator has been lawfully provided (Can. 1279 §2), this latter being a renewable three-year appointment. These two further duties are to be carried out subject to the direct responsibility of the Bishop himself.[2]

Can. 1279 §1 The administration of ecclesiastical goods pertains to the one with direct power of governance over the person to whom the goods belong, unless particular law or statutes or legitimate custom state otherwise, and without prejudice to the right of the Ordinary to intervene where there is negligence on the part of the administrator.

2544 This paragraph establishes an important principle, itself simple and clear, namely that the responsibility for the administration of all ecclesiastical goods (see Can. 1257 §1) rests firmly upon the individual who immediately governs the juridical person to whom the goods belong.[3] Thus e.g. it is the parish priest who carries the ultimate responsibility for the administration of all parochial property (see Can. 532); equally, the local Superior of an individual religious house. The issue here is the simple one of ultimate responsibility. This is in no way altered by the fact that various ancillary or supportive means may be either prescribed or devised to assist in the fulfilment of this obligation – such e.g. as a parish finance committee (see Can. 537), or a financial administrator (or bursar) in a religious institute or province or local community (see Can. 636).[4]

2545 The law does envisage the possibility of exceptions to this principle, each based upon local conditions and circumstances: it mentions 'particular law or statutes or legitimate custom'. The exception would be valid only if any of these were to make it clear that the ultimate administrative responsibility had been transferred to someone other than 'the one with direct power of governance over the (juridical) person to whom the goods belong': Can. 636 §1 e.g. is not such an exception.

---

[1] For an insight into the evolution of Can. 1277, cf. Comm 12(1980) 414 at Can. 21; 15(1984) 33 at Can. 1228.

[2] Cf. Comm 5(1973) 97 n.19; 12(1980) 414–415 at Can. 22.

[3] Cf. Can. 118. This simple principle supersedes the more complex arrangements of the 1917 Code in cc.1521, 1182–1184: cf. Comm 5(1973) 97 nn.20–21.

[4] In some religious institutes a recent practice has been to centralise all administration in the office of the provincial or the general financial administrator. While such practice may indeed have practical advantages in current circumstances, it does not relieve the appropriate superior of the responsibility for the administration of the goods of the juridical person under his or her control – nor in consequence in any way remove his or her authority to enquire into and scrutinise the details of the administration.

Finally, this §1 allows (along the lines indicated in Can. 1276) for the intervention of the respective Ordinary, be he local or personal, 'where there is negligence on the part of the administrator'. In such a situation it would be within the Ordinary's competence to correct errors, to insist upon a different method of administration and, if needs be, even to apply punitive measures.

Can. 1279 §2 Where no administrators are appointed for a public juridical person by law or by the documents of foundation or by its own statutes, the Ordinary to which it is subject is to appoint suitable persons as administrators for a three-year term. The same persons can be reappointed by the Ordinary.

This is designed to cater for the exceptional situation in which from no recognised source is any administrator appointed for a public juridical person. In that situation, the competent Ordinary, local or personal, 'is to appoint suitable persons as administrators': it could be one person; in the case of a public juridical person subject to the diocesan Bishop, it could be the diocesan financial administrator (see Can. 1278). The appointment is for a term of three years, which however is renewable for such subsequent terms as the Ordinary may wish.[1]

Can. 1280 Every juridical person is to have its own finance committee, or at least two counsellors, who are to assist in the performance of the administrator's duties, in accordance with the statutes.

Every juridical person, public and private, is subject to the norm that its statutes provide for a sharing of responsibility in its financial affairs; hence this canon, prescribing 'its own finance committee or at least two counsellors', whose function would be 'to assist in the performance of the administrator's duties'. It would appear that the role of the committee or of the counsellors is advisory only, not definitive – with the very strong implication that the administrator would be at least imprudent to act against the advice given, especially if it were unanimous.

Can. 1281 §1 Without prejudice to the provisions of the statutes, administrators act invalidly when they go beyond the limits and manner of ordinary administration, unless they have first received in writing from the Ordinary the faculty to do so.

This canon, in its three paragraphs, determines the competence of administrators in respect of acts of extraordinary administration (§1), the criterion for the determination of such acts being laid down in §2, while §3 rules on the responsibility in canon law which juridical persons may or may not have in respect of the fiscal conduct of their administrators.[2]

This §1 establishes the fundamental principle that any administrator who for whatever reason wishes to 'go beyond the limits and manner of ordinary administration' must have the prior written permission to do so from the competent Ordinary; otherwise,

---

[1] Although the decision of the Code Commission that the term *iterum* in Can. 917 (the same term used in this paragraph) means 'only once again' (cf. CCom 26.VI.1984: AAS 76(1984) 746) there is no reason to believe that the same interpretation applies here.

[2] The canon treats of the same problem as that dealt with in c.1527 of the 1917 Code, and in its §2 clarifies one particularly delicate and potentially contentious aspect, namely what precisely are those 'acts (which) go beyond the limits and manner of ordinary administration' – a matter not faced as such by the 1917 Code. The academic reader could profitably study this canon's evolution – not unlike that of Can. 1277 – in Comm 5(1973) 98 n.22; 12(1980) 416–418 at Can. 25.

the administrative act will be canonically null and void.[1] There is no suggestion here that prudent administrators may not at times quite sensibly propose an act of extraordinary administration, e.g. a major repair or reconstruction project. The simple point of the law is that this requires something more than the authority vested in every administrator to deal with the day-to-day affairs under his or her control; it is a matter of the prudent and controlled administration characteristic of every reasonable society.

Can. 1281 §2 The statutes are to determine what acts go beyond the limits and manner of ordinary administration. If the statutes are silent on this point, it is for the diocesan Bishop, after consulting the finance committee, to determine these acts for the persons subject to him.

2551 It is the statutes which are to determine those acts which are to be considered as of 'extraordinary administration'. There is therefore a clear responsibility on whatever ecclesiastical authority establishes a juridical person and approves its statutes (see Cann. 113–118) to ensure that such a stipulation is clearly contained within the statutes. This is very much the same kind of obligation as that imposed on Bishops' Conferences by Can. 1277 (q.v.).

2552 It is only when 'the statutes are silent on this point' – whether by reason of an original neglect or, as more often is the case, when a juridical person is simply established by the law itself – that it becomes a matter 'for the diocesan Bishop, after consulting the (diocesan) finance committee, to determine these acts for the persons subject to him'. A parish is a typical example: in many dioceses, a scale of authorised expenditure for parishes, without the need to refer to the Bishop, has been established. The point of this §2 is that there is an obligation on the Bishop that this or its equivalent be done.

Can. 1281 §3 Except and insofar as it is to its benefit, a juridical person is not held responsible for the invalid actions of its administrators. The juridical person is, however, responsible when such actions are valid but unlawful, without prejudice to its right to bring an action or to have recourse against the administrators who have caused it damage.

2553 The responsibility of a juridical person for the acts of its administrator may be summarised as follows:

(a) if the act is both valid and lawful, the juridical person itself is exclusively responsible;

(b) if the act is invalid (see §1), the juridical person is not responsible (the administrator is, and may be legally pursued accordingly), save only to the extent that the juridical person may have profited by that invalid act;

(c) if the act is valid in itself, but unlawful e.g. because the administrator neglected to fulfil a prescribed procedure or condition which was not however required for validity, the juridical person is responsible – but it has the right either to bring an action for damages against the administrator in the ecclesiastical courts (see Cann. 128, 1389 §2), or to have recourse to the appropriate ecclesiastical superior.

2554 This picture again highlights the need for a clear determination of what is an act which goes beyond the limits of ordinary administration (see §2). It also highlights the need for attention to the civil law consequences in matters of this kind: it raises e.g. the advisability of taking out liability insurance, to protect both the juridical person (e.g. a parish, a religious house) and its administrators.[2]

---

[1] In its own turn, this could have far-reaching effects for the Church in civil law also: on this important aspect, cf. Commentary (CLSA) 875 col.1.

[2] Cf. Comm 12(1980) 417 at Can. 25.

Title II The Administration of Goods

Can. 1282 All persons, whether clerics or laity, who lawfully take part in the administration of ecclesiastical goods, are bound to fulfil their duties in the name of the Church, in accordance with the law.

Here the reference is to the goods of public juridical persons. The duties of their administrators, be they clerical or lay, are to be carried out 'in the name of the Church'. Although they may not be acting precisely 'by virtue of an ecclesiastical office' (Can. 1289), these administrators are in a very real sense participating in the Church's apostolate.[1] As such, they differ from the role of persons entrusted with the administration of secular goods. Their purpose is not one of profit; rather it is to protect and to provide resources for the pursuit of the Church's proper objectives (see Can. 1254 §2).

2555

Can. 1283 Before administrators undertake their duties:

1° they must take an oath, in the presence of the Ordinary or his delegate, that they will well and truly perform their office;

2° they are to draw up a clear and accurate inventory, to be signed by themselves, of any immovable goods, of those movable goods which are precious or in any way of cultural value, and of any other goods, with a description and an estimate of their value; and they are to review any inventory already drawn up;

3° one copy of this inventory is to be kept in the administration office and another in the curial archive; any change which takes place in the property is to be noted on both copies.

This canon, which requires little elucidation, prescribes the practical steps to be taken before any administrator takes up his or her office. The taking of an oath (1°) – in a simple formula to be determined by the Ordinary – underlines the importance which the law attaches to ensuring in so far as possible the attainment of the objectives of the Church's temporal goods (see Can. 1254). As for the term 'precious' (2°), see Cann. 638 §3, 1189, 1292 §2.

2556

At the practical level, this canon has a special relevance when there is a change of administrator, e.g. the appointment of a new parish priest, or the election of a new local or provincial (or even general) religious superior. There would appear to be evidence that this has not always been done. It is the clear obligation of the competent Ordinary to ensure that it be done.

2557

Can. 1284 §1 All administrators are to perform their duties with the diligence of a good householder.

§2 Therefore they must:

1° be vigilant that no goods placed in their care in any way perish or suffer damage; to this end they are, to the extent necessary, to arrange insurance contracts;

2° ensure that the ownership of ecclesiastical goods is safeguarded in ways which are valid in civil law;

3° observe the provisions of canon and civil law, and the stipulations of the founder or donor or lawful authority; they are to take special care

---

[1] Cf. PO 17: Fl I 894–896; AA 10: Fl I 777–778; AGD 41: Fl I 854–855.

that damage will not be suffered by the Church through the non-observance of the civil law;

4° seek accurately and at the proper time the income and produce of the goods, guard them securely and expend them in accordance with the wishes of the founder or lawful norms;

5° at the proper time pay the interest which is due by reason of a loan or mortgage, and take care that in due time the capital is repaid;

6° with the consent of the Ordinary, make use, for the purposes of the juridical person, of money which is surplus after payment of expenses and which can be profitably invested;

7° keep accurate records of income and expenditure;

8° draw up an account of their administration at the end of each year;

9° keep in order and preserve in a fitting and secure archive the documents and records establishing the rights of the Church or institute to its goods; where conveniently possible, place authentic copies in the archive of the curia.

2558 The governing principle is stated succinctly in §1, reflecting Vat. II;[1] the reference to the 'good householder' parallels that to the 'steward' in Can. 1273. In effect, the canon reproduces c.1523 of the 1917 Code; such changes as it makes concern mainly details or methods of administration, introduced solely by way of example.[2] The detailed prescriptions of §2 represent sensible and practical applications of the governing principle, and for the most part they call rather for attention than for explanation. The following specific points may be mentioned briefly.

2559 The question of adequate insurance, on all forms of ecclesiastical property (1°), is vital: a parish priest e.g. would be held to be seriously negligent in his administration if the parish church or a parochial house, destroyed by fire, were found to have been quite inadequately insured. There is a stress on the need to comply with the relevant civil law as a means to protect Church property (2°–3°): hence the obvious need that every ecclesiastical administrator use the service of a competent legal advisor – solicitor, attorney or howsoever entitled. There is an equal stress on the need to attend carefully to 'the wishes of the founder' or donor (3°–4°): goods, whether by way of property or of money, given to and accepted by an ecclesiastical administrator for a specific purpose, may be used for that purpose only; this prescription should alert the administrator to the need for prudence and careful consideration before accepting such gifts. The question of the investment of so-called 'surplus money' is addressed (6°): this requires 'the consent of the (respective) Ordinary', which however is needed only if there is question of converting such money into *stable capital*, not for the ordinary deposit of money into a bank account from which interest would accrue. The need to 'keep accurate records' and securely to preserve 'the documents and records' is underlined (7°–9°): it is the strict duty of every administrator – parish priest, religious superior or whomsoever – to ensure both accurate records and their secure protection in an adequate filing-cabinet or other archive. An annual account by the administrator is prescribed (8°): this is probably best regulated by particular or proper law or directive.

---

[1] Cf. PO 17: Fl I 894–896.

[2] Cf. Comm 5(1973) 98 n.25; 12(1980) 419 at Can. 28. Accordingly, the recognised commentators on the 1917 Code at c.1523 remain relevant here.

Title II The Administration of Goods

Can. 1284 §3 It is earnestly recommended that administrators draw up each year a budget of income and expenditure. However, it is left to particular law to make this an obligation and to determine more precisely how it is to be presented.

While the general law, in this new prescription exemplifying the Vat. II principle of accountability, 'earnestly recommends' that an annual budget be drawn up, it wisely leaves to particular law to determine whether or not this be made an obligation and, if so, the precise form it should take. If it be made an obligation, the particular law should also determine the manner in which the budget is to be prepared for approval. By analogy with the prescription of Can. 493, the appropriate finance committee (see Can. 1280) ought to be involved in the preparation and the monitoring of this budget. The law refers specifically to income and expenditure; it does not expressly apply to investments, although these could be integrated in consolidated balance sheets which may in due time be made public (see Can. 1287 §2). 2560

Can. 1285 Solely within the limits of ordinary administration, administrators are allowed to make gifts for pious purposes or christian charity out of the movable goods which do not form part of the stable patrimony.

The canon acknowledges what clearly ought to be a feature of those who administer Church property, namely a readiness within reasonable limits to make donations to pious or charitable purposes – 'pious' to include the traditional 'corporal and spiritual works of mercy' and of course divine worship. The 'reasonable limits' are laid down: (a) that the donations be 'within the limits of ordinary administration' (see Can. 1277); (b) that they be made only from 'the movable goods which do not form part of the stable patrimony': this clearly excludes e.g. a gift of land, or of an investment which would be part of the fixed assets of, say, a parish or a religious house. To make a donation outside these limits without observing the prescribed formalities, would be not only illicit but invalid (see Can. 1281 §3). But within these limits the law positively permits that e.g. a parish priest might sanction the moderate use of ordinary parochial funds to make donations to charity, whether by himself personally or through one of his assistant priests.[1] It should also be recognised that there is a long and laudable tradition whereby, quite apart from such public funds as are envisaged here, priests do so much from their personal and often meagre resources to help the poor, the needy and the underprivileged in our society. 2561

Can. 1286 Administrators of temporal goods:

1° in making contracts of employment, are accurately to observe also, according to the principles taught by the Church, the civil laws relating to labour and social life;

2° are to pay to those who work for them under contract a just and honest wage which would fittingly provide for their needs and those of their dependents.

The prescription of this canon is a corollary of the right enshrined in Can. 231 §2.[2] It places upon all administrators a clear obligation to ensure that, in respect of those whom the Church employs, at whatever level – diocesan, parochial, religious etc.– 2562

---

[1] There is a marked and obviously significant contrast between the tone of this canon and the somewhat negative tone of its counterpart in the 1917 Code c.1535 (cf. Comm 5(1973) 98–99 n.26).
[2] Cf. Comm 5(1973) 99 n.27; 12(1980) 420 at Can. 30; 15(1984) at Can. 1237.

they observe integrally the relevant civil law, particularly in the matter of contracts of work. In some countries, where the problem is widespread, this could have a particular relevance in respect of those would-be employees who, by reason of their immigration status, do not have the right to employment. This obligation is however to be fulfilled 'according to the principles taught by the Church'.[1] As such, it would not therefore bind if the civil law in question were to be manifestly immoral or unjust (see Can. 22); in this regard, the matter of unlawful discrimination – say, on the ground of creed, sex, colour and the like – could be a very relevant consideration.

Can. 1287 §1 Where ecclesiastical goods of any kind are not lawfully withdrawn from the power of governance of the diocesan Bishop, their administrators, both clerical and laity, are bound to submit each year to the local Ordinary an account of their administration, which he is to pass on to his finance committee for examination. Any contrary custom is reprobated.

2563 This is an implementation of Can. 1284 §2 8° save where specifically excepted e.g. Can. 637, the administrators of all public juridical persons – not only parishes – are to render an annual written account of their administration to the local Ordinary. The purpose is that he would thereby be enabled to fulfil the obligation placed upon him by Can. 1276 – and in this connection it is to be noted that 'any contrary custom is reprobated' (see Can. 24 §2). On receipt of such account, the local Ordinary is obliged to submit it to the diocesan finance committee (see Cann. 492–493), for examination and report. Should any irregularities emerge from this examination, it would be the right and the obligation of the diocesan Bishop to take appropriate remedial measures.

2564 Specifically excepted from this particular obligation are those administrators who are not subject to the direct vigilance of the diocesan Bishop (see Can. 1276). These however must render account to their own appropriate authorities (see Cann. 319, 636) and abide by whatever directives might in consequence be given.

Can. 1287 §2 Administrators are to render accounts to the faithful concerning the goods which the faithful have given to the Church, in accordance with the norms to be laid down by particular law.

2565 The appropriate particular law is obliged to determine the manner in which financial statements are to be made public, e.g. by the Bishops' Conference (if it were authorised to do so: see Can. 455 §1), the diocesan Bishop, the constitution or statutes of the juridical person. The rule concerns only those goods donated by the faithful (see Can. 1267 §3), not of income arising from other sources, such as investment income and the like. If public accounts are to be issued, it would be appropriate (and in some cases necessary) that the particular law specify that they be audited accounts.

Can. 1288 Administrators may not, in the name of a public juridical person, either institute or contest legal proceedings in a civil court without first having obtained the written permission of their proper Ordinary.

2566 Without the prior written permission of the *proper* Ordinary (see Can. 107 §1), no administrator may as such become either the plaintiff or the defendant in civil legal proceedings. The purpose of the canon is to enable the Ordinary to decide whether or

---

[1] The Church's social teaching on labour matters is most recently set out by Pope John Paul II in encl *Centesimus Annus* I.V.1991: AAS (83)1991 793–867: Origins 21(1991–1992) 1, 3–24. Cf. also SCCE lit circ *Guidelines for the Study and Teaching of the Church's Social Doctrine in the Formation of Priests* Origins 19(1989–1990) 169, 171–192.

not it would be possible or preferable to resolve the matter otherwise than by a court action, thus avoiding a dangerous precedent or misleading publicity or the like. The rule applies only in cases where the juridical person – and not e.g. an insurance company – is a *direct* party to the action. It is generally accepted that actions before 'small claims courts' and various types of similar procedures do not come within this prescription. If an administrator were to act in disregard of the rule, it could be asked if the act is not only unlawful but invalid: see Cann. 1277, 1281; in any event, the norm of Can. 128 would apply.

Can. 1289 Although they may not be bound to the work of administration by virtue of an ecclesiastical office, administrators may not arbitrarily relinquish the work they have undertaken. If they do so, and this occasions damage to the Church, they are bound to restitution.

A number of administrators of church property become such precisely by reason of the ecclesiastical office which they hold, e.g. parish priests. Some however assume the task by another route e.g. designated by the Ordinary in the circumstances of Can. 1279 §2, or in virtue of the relevant statutes or of some other appropriate norm. The point of this canon is to insist that, whether they come by the one route or the other, no administrator may 'arbitrarily' i.e. capriciously, simply relinquish or walk away from 'the work (they) have undertaken'. In simple terms, a person who accepts the office of administrator is thereby understood automatically to accept the obligations inherent in the task (see Can. 1283 §1). Accordingly, if precisely by a capricious relinquishing of that task, damage is occasioned 'to the Church', and specifically to the administration in question, that person would be 'bound to restitution' – an obligation which might well on occasion be pursued through the civil courts, particularly if an appropriate insurance against such an eventuality had been set in place. 2567

Title III
Contracts and Especially Alienation

Can. 1290 Without prejudice to Can. 1547, whatever the local civil law decrees about contracts, both generally and specifically, and about the voiding of contracts, is to be observed regarding matters which are subject to the power of governance of the Church, and with the same effect, provided that the civil law is not contrary to divine law, and that canon law does not provide otherwise.

This is an application of the general principle enuntiated in Can. 22, which in the matter of the law of contract has had a long-established place in canonical jurisprudence.[1] In effect, this regulation 'canonises' and makes its own, 'with the same effect', whatever the local civil law requires concerning contracts. There is a twofold proviso: (a) that the civil law in question 'is not contrary to divine law'; (b) that the canon law 2568

---

[1] Cf. 1917 Code c.1529, and its sources. The opinions of the recognised commentators on that canon have therefore an abiding value.

itself, even by way of particular law, 'does not provide otherwise' for specific aspects or transactions.[1]

2569 In practice, the rule is to the effect that whenever the question arises either of entering or of voiding a contract in respect of property in the control of the Church, the appropriate administrator should seek the advice of a civil lawyer competent in this field and be guided by the advice given. Hence, obviously, the need for care and prudence in selecting the lawyer in question.

2570 The reference to Can. 1547 concerns proof by witnesses, so that it would be clearly seen that such proof remains canonically admissible, even though it might not, in face of e.g. an apparently contrary document, be recognised by the civil law: the situation envisaged by Can. 1299 §2 is a case in point.

Can. 1291 The permission of the authority competent by law is required for the valid alienation of goods which, by lawful assignment, constitute the stable patrimony of a public juridical person, whenever their value exceeds the sum determined by law.

2571 Cann. 1291–1296 deal with the alienation of ecclesiastical property. In terms of their practical application, they do present a much more workable criterion than that prescribed by the corresponding canons of the 1917 Code.[2] However, the principle, enunciated in this canon, remains the same: namely, that the permission of the competent superior is an essential prerequisite if property, of whatever kind, constituting the fixed capital of a public juridical person (see Can. 116), the value of which is greater than that which the canon law determines for this purpose, is to be validly alienated. The elements of this principle may be briefly explained as follows.

2572 In itself, the term *alienation* simply means the transfer of the ownership of property from one person to another, e.g. by sale or by gift. In this context, however, it has long had an acknowledgedly wider meaning. It includes not only the direct transfer of ownership, but 'any transaction whereby the patrimonial condition of the juridical person may be jeopardised' (Can. 1295). Such a transaction would include the obvious examples such as mortgage, lien, option, lease etc., and of course any act whereby Church property would be subjected to either a permanent or a long-term burden as e.g. in the case of borrowing money. Manifestly included also would be the dissipation of so-called immovable goods, e.g. a fund, for a purpose other than that for which it was donated or designed. Equally would be included the disposal of objects of a worth which is special by reason of their market value or their artistic, historical, consecrated or votive nature.[3]

2573 The alienation involved here is that only which concerns the *fixed capital* ('the stable patrimony') of the juridical person in question. Buildings and land are the most frequent and obvious examples. They are not however the only examples. It should be noted that money in itself is a medium of exchange and as such is considered perishable; even if temporarily invested, it remains free capital – in effect, cash on hand for day-to-day or ordinary running expenses. On the other hand, money can, and in today's world often does, become part of the fixed capital, principally by being invested in property or in secure holdings such as stocks, bonds, deposits and the like. In the context of alienation, this transfer of money from free to fixed capital may occur only in one or the other of the following two ways:

---

[1] Cf. Vermeersch–Creusen II n.850.

[2] Cf. 1917 Code cc.1530–1543; Comm 5(1973) 100–101 nn.33–40.

[3] On this concept of alienation there is unanimity among the recognised commentators on both the current Code and its 1917 predecessor at c.1533. For a more detailed treatment, these should be consulted.

Title III Contracts and especially Alienation

(a) by the wish or directive of the donor: if a person gives money to be devoted to a specified purpose, it must be used for that purpose only. More often than not, it will be invested in a security which will allow for the fulfilment of the purpose in question e.g. the charitable needs of a diocese or of a parish, the building of a church in a parish or in a mission, the formation of diocesan seminarians or of novices in a religious institute, etc.[1]

(b) by the formal designation of it *as such* by the competent ecclesiastical or religious authority. Thus e.g. 'if the annual surplus of a parish has been profitably invested in readily negotiable securities, deposited, or set aside for future needs by a Bishop or Pastor, such surplus does not *necessarily and automatically* become stable, invested or fixed capital subject to the restrictions of alienation. In cases of doubt, the presumption would seem to be that the money would not be considered invested or fixed capital'.[2]

2574 Both the *competent Superior* and the *value* in question are determined by Cann. 1292 §1 and, for religious institutes, 638 §3 (q.v.).

Can. 1292 §1 Without prejudice to the provisions of Can. 638 §3, when the amount of the goods to be alienated is between the minimum and maximum sums to be established by the Bishops' Conference for its region, the competent authority in the case of juridical persons not subject to the diocesan Bishop is determined by the juridical person's own statutes. In other cases, the competent authority is the diocesan Bishop acting with the consent of the finance committee, of the college of consultors, and of any interested parties. The diocesan Bishop needs the consent of these same persons to alienate goods which belong to the diocese itself.

2575 This paragraph does two things: (a) it prescribes that it is for the Bishops' Conference to determine what, in the matter of alienation, the Code calls 'the minimum and maximum sum to be established for its region';[3] (b) it prescribes who, within those limits, is the authority whose consent is so required that without it an alienation would be invalid.[4] These represent a significant change from the norm of the 1917 Code (see cc.1530 §1 3°, 1532 §§1–3) and do introduce a more practical regulation in terms of current financial conditions.

2576 As for the authority whose consent is required, the matter may be summarised as follows:

(a) For juridical persons not subject to the diocesan Bishop, their own statutes are to be the determining factor. What are envisaged here, besides religious institutes, are juridical persons of a supra-diocesan nature e.g. a national or a regional seminary, a national university, and the like.

---

[1] The same would be the case if land or a building were donated on the condition that it be sold and the proceeds devoted to a specified purpose: while this sale itself would not constitute alienation, the money accruing would be presumed to become part of the fixed capital and thus subject to the conditions governing alienation.

[2] Doheny *Practical Problems in Church Finance* Milwaukee 1941 43. When appropriately adjusted to the prescriptions of the current Code, Doheny's work remains a valuable guide.

[3] On the response of Bishops' Conferences to this requirement, cf. LCE Tavola per Paesi e Canoni at Can. 1292. Many of the Conferences have expressly ruled that the sums determined are to be index-linked, thus imposing on the Conference itself an obligation to review the matter at regular, if not prescribed, intervals and formally to promulgate the revised sums.

[4] It follows of course that if the amount is below the minimum limit, then it is for the local administrator (as in Can. 1279 §1) to decide what best to do, subject to his or her general obligation to render account of the stewardship.

(b) For juridical persons subject to the diocesan Bishop – the typical, but not only, example is a parish – the consent of the Bishop himself is required. However, before he may give his consent, he in turn is required to have the consent of: (i) the diocesan finance committee (see Can. 492); (ii) the college of consultors (see Can. 502 §1); (iii) any 'interested parties' – a group sometimes forgotten: e.g. in the case of parochial property, the parish priest would certainly be one such (see Can. 532); in other cases, each to be examined in its own circumstances, it might well be the original donor or the lawful representative thereof, or anyone who might retain an acknowledged legal interest in the property in question. The point to be observed is that, unless he will have had the consent of all three of the groups mentioned, the Bishop's own consent would be invalid.

(c) The consent of the three groups mentioned in (b) above is equally required if there is question of alienating 'goods which belong to the diocese itself' i.e. as distinct from goods belonging to other juridical persons subject to the diocesan Bishop.[1]

2577 All the prescriptions of this paragraph are 'without prejudice to the provisions of Can. 638 §3' (q.v.) which, in the context of alienation, has its own special regulations in respect of religious institutes (see also Cann. 718, 741).

Can. 1292 §2 The additional permission of the Holy See is required for the valid alienation of goods whose value exceeds the maximum sum, or if it is a question of alienation of something given to the Church by reason of a vow, or of objects which are precious by reason of their artistic or historical significance.

2578 This paragraph deals with the alienation of two further kinds of goods, i.e. (a) those whose value is in excess of the maximum determined by the Bishops' Conference of the region in question, and (b) those which are in themselves of a special significance in the Church. It determines that in each case the permission of the Holy See is required *in addition to that prescribed by §1*.

2579 As far as the goods mentioned in (a) are concerned, application for permission must be made to the relevant organ of the Holy See. In so far as the application concerns a proposed alienation of property subject to the diocesan Bishop, the Congregation for the Clergy is the appropriate organ; in so far as it concerns a religious institute, the application must be submitted to the Congregation for Institutes of Consecrated Life and Societies of Apostolic Life. It is to be noted that, in this latter case, the practice of the Holy See has been to require at least a 'nihil obstat' from the diocesan Bishop of the place where the property is located.

2580 Those goods mentioned in (b) are in a special category: they are those 'given to the Church by reason of a vow' (see Can. 1191), or 'objects which are precious by reason of their artistic or historical significance' (see Can. 1189).

Can. 1292 §3 When a request is made to alienate goods which are divisible, the request must state what parts have already been alienated; otherwise, the permission is invalid.

2581 The point of this paragraph is that when permission is sought for a particular alienation (a transaction which of its nature jeopardises the patrimonial condition of the juridical person in question: see Can. 1295), the permitting authority must, on pain

---

[1] For the illuminating background to this matter, cf. Comm 12(1980) 423–424 at Can. 37 §1; 15(1984) 35–36 at Can. 1243 §1.

of invalidity, be informed of the extent to which the property in question is already encumbered. The reference is to 'goods which are divisible'. The obvious example is money which in fact forms part of the fixed capital, e.g. if a parish seeks permission to ask a bank for a substantial loan, say to build a new church, it is clearly relevant that the permitting authority would know the extent to which that parish is already indebted to the bank, say by reason of an earlier loan for some other purpose. Money is not, however, the only example. The same principle would apply if it were a question of encumbering land or buildings with an *additional* mortgage, lien, lease or the like. The principle would also apply if goods had previously been alienated on a piecemeal basis in order to avoid on any occasion exceeding the maximum sum.

Can. 1292 §4 Those who must give advice about or consent to the alienation of goods are not to give this advice or consent until they have first been informed precisely both about the economic situation of the juridical person whose goods it is proposed to alienate and about alienations which have already taken place.

Those whose advice or consent is to be sought in the matter of alienation (see Can. 1292 §1) must clearly be informed in advance of the overall indebtedness of the juridical person involved. This paragraph imposes on them the obligation to insist on being given that information, as a condition to their giving the advice or consent.

Can. 1293 §1 To alienate goods whose value exceeds the determined minimum sum, it is also required that there be:

1° a just reason, such as urgent necessity, evident advantage, or a religious, charitable or other grave pastoral reason;

2° an evaluation in writing by experts of the goods to be alienated.

The principle has already been established (see Can. 1292 §1) that 'to alienate goods whose value exceeds the determined minimum sum', the permission of the competent authority is required, and for validity. This paragraph points to the considerations which must be taken into account in determining whether or not that permission be given.

There must, in the first place, be 'a just reason'. Five examples are given, obviously not exhaustive: (a) an urgent necessity, e.g. a tax burden, another debt to be paid; (b) an evident advantage, e.g. a good price offered for buildings and lands that are not absolutely necessary; (c) a religious reason, e.g. to put the property to use as a retreat centre or the like; (d) a charitable reason, e.g., to assist a group working in the justice or similar apostolate which needs a place to serve as its headquarters; (e) another grave pastoral reason, e.g. to borrow money to build a diocesan pastoral centre, to set up a home for the elderly or disadvantaged, or the like.

Secondly, there must be 'an evaluation in writing by experts' on the goods in question. It is generally accepted, both under the 1917 Code (c.1530 §1 1°) and under the current law, that at least two such evaluations must be presented to the authority who is to make the decision as to whether or not to grant the required permission.

Can. 1293 §2 To avoid loss to the Church, any other precautions drawn up by lawful authority are also to be followed.

This caters for the fact that, since the universal law cannot be expected to foresee all particular circumstances, it may well happen that local regulations exist concerning alienation e.g. a diocesan, provincial or national law, the constitution or the statutes of the particular juridical person. Relevant also are the prescriptions of the civil law, e.g. feasibility studies, zoning regulations, public interest laws, environmental protection norms, etc. All such directives must be taken into account.

Can. 1294 §1 Normally goods must not be alienated for a price lower than that given in the valuation.

2587 The term 'normally' indicates that there may be exceptions to this rule. At times, notwithstanding the market price, there may be question of determining what reasonable offer is in fact available and which circumstances indicate acceptance or not. Thus, e.g. in the case of a building or land which has become an expensive liability, it might be prudent to dispose of it at a price somewhat under its market value in order to avoid greater expenses at a later date. It could also happen that a juridical person might be willing to alienate goods for less than their full worth in order to offer them at a lower price to another charitable or apostolic purpose. The decision on these matters is for the authority whose permission is required for alienation.

Can. 1294 §2 The money obtained from alienation must be carefully invested for the benefit of the Church, or prudently expended according to the purposes of the alienation.

2588 Since alienation of its nature involves the disposal of part of fixed capital (see Can. 1291), it is important that, when it takes place, the diminution of the fixed capital be limited to the minimum possible: hence the rule of this paragraph, which prescribes that the money accruing must be *either*:

(a) 'carefully invested for the benefit of the Church': the most obvious way would be to reconvert it by investment into fixed capital; this however is not absolutely required – it may be invested as working capital; *or*

(b) 'prudently expended according to the purposes of the alienation': envisaged here is the situation in which the alienation would have been done with a view to funding a serious pastoral endeavour or objective (see Can. 1293 §1 1°); the point is that the money may not under any circumstances be devoted to any other purpose, however laudable in itself – unless of course there be a surplus, in which case it too must be invested in accordance with (a) above.

Can. 1295 The provisions of Cann. 1291–1994, to which the statutes of juridical persons are to conform, must be observed not only in alienation, but also in any transaction whereby the patrimonial condition of the juridical person could be adversely affected.

2589 The implications of this canon are dealt with under Can. 1291 above (q.v.). In general, it may be noted that, in determining whether or not jeopardy is involved, three elements concerning the Church's interest should be considered: ownership, control, patronage or sponsorship. In order to protect whichever of these elements is involved – particularly if it be control – consideration will have to be given to the relevant prescriptions of the civil law. In this connection, it is often necessary to ensure that certain 'reserved powers', effectively protecting the Church's interests, are incorporated into the appropriate legal documents, such as contracts, indentures, leases etc. This canon can be of particular relevance when certain joint ventures or collaborative endeavours take place and when the goods belonging to various juridical persons are commingled, e.g. when two or more parishes jointly operate an educational, charitable or social undertaking, or when two or more religious institutes operate a hospital or other health-care institution.[1]

---

[1] Cf. Catholic Health Association of the USA *The Search for Identity: Canonical Sponsorship of Catholic Healthcare* St Louis 1993 esp. 38–48, 56–58.

Title III Contracts and especially Alienation

Can. 1296 When alienation has taken place without the prescribed canonical formalities, but is valid in civil law, the competent authority must carefully weigh all the circumstances and decide whether, and if so what, action is to be taken, namely personal or real, by whom and against whom, to vindicate the rights of the Church.

The canon recognises the fact that a transaction could be recognised in civil law, without the prescribed canonical formalities having been observed. If indeed the contract is valid civilly, then it is a matter for the competent authority, e.g. the diocesan Bishop, the religious superior, to decide in what best manner possible the rights of the juridical person in question may be vindicated. The canon speaks of the 'action', if any, to be taken: the reference here is to a formal court procedure, but this does not preclude the authority from deciding, in view of 'all the circumstances', to deal with the matter administratively rather than judicially. However, should the latter be chosen, it then becomes a matter of deciding whether to proceed through the civil or through the canonical forum, the latter being possibly the more appropriate if the case simply concerns two ecclesiastical juridical persons; whether the action be for damages against the responsible party ('personal') or for repossession of that which was invalidly alienated ('real'); who precisely should take the action, and against whom. All of this is a matter for the prudent judgement of the competent authority, and the canon does not exclude the possibility that in a given situation the prudent course might be to take no action of any kind, other perhaps than that prescribed by Can. 1377 (q.v.). 2590

Precisely because of the principal issue raised by this canon, namely the divergence which may, and in current circumstances not infrequently does, exist between the formalities required on the one hand by the canon law and on the other by the relevant civil law, especially in regard to the validity of transactions such as alienation, it is imperative that the competent ecclesiastical authorities explore and adopt such measures as may be available in order to exclude or at least to minimise the risk of a clash between the two jurisdictions. A practical means of ensuring this can often be the insertion into the statutes or constitution of the juridical person, or perhaps into the very contract itself of the alienation, a clause to the effect that the transaction would be null, even in the civil law, if the conditions for validity at canon law had not been integrally observed.[1] 2591

Can. 1297 It is the duty of the Bishops' Conference, taking into account the local circumstances, to determine norms about the leasing of ecclesiastical goods, especially about permission to be obtained from the competent ecclesiastical authority.

A lease is a contract by which property, whether movable or immovable, is let to another for use for a determined time at a specified price or rent. Unlike the 1917 Code which carried very detailed prescriptions (c.1541), the current law simply obliges Bishops' Conferences to regulate the matter in view of local circumstances; they are to pay particular attention to determining the authority who is competent to give permission for leasing transactions – a permission which is required for validity.[2] 2592

---

[1] In some, but relatively few, countries an agreement on such matters may have come about by way of concordat with the Holy See (see Can. 3).

[2] On the response of Bishops' Conferences to this requirement, cf. LCE Tavola per Paesi e Canoni at Can. 1297.

Can. 1298 Unless they are of little value, ecclesiastical goods are not to be sold or leased to the administrators themselves or to their relatives up to the fourth degree of consanguinity or affinity, without the special written permission of the competent authority.

2593 This norm of prudence, required obviously for liceity only, is in keeping with the general policy of the Code (e.g. Cann. 478 §2, 492 §3, 1448) which seeks to eliminate potential conflicts of interest.

Title IV
Pious Dispositions in General and Pious Foundations

Can. 1299 §1 Those who by natural law and by canon law can freely dispose of their goods may leave them to pious causes either by an act *inter vivos* or by an act *mortis causa*.

2594 This paragraph states a basic principle of the Church's position in respect of donations which people may wish to make to what are here called 'pious causes' – in effect, those causes which constitute any part of the Church's 'proper objectives' as exemplified in Can. 1254 §2. Behind this principle is the doctrine that, where such pious causes are concerned, that which is primarily to be protected is the wish or intent of the donor – a doctrine which permeates the succeeding canons in this Title IV. Accordingly, all those who are entitled either by natural law or by canon law freely to dispose of their own property, may give that property, of whatever kind, to the pious cause of their choice. Prohibited by natural law would be e.g. those who lack the use of reason, who are coerced, who are subject to serious error or fraud; by canon law, those who e.g. are subject to the special regulations governing religious (see Can. 668). This principle applies, in the words of Can. 1254 §1, 'independently of any secular power' i.e. of the relevant civil law. Thus e.g. if a person were too young to make a will according to the civil law but was canonically of age, the canon law would still recognise, and in so far as possible seek to implement, the wish contained in such a will to donate property to a pious cause.

2595 This capacity or entitlement to dispose of property may be exercised in the following ways:

(a) by an act *inter vivos* i.e. a transaction which takes place between one person and another, either a physical or a juridical person: the most frequent, though not the only, example is a gift;

(b) by an act *mortis causa* i.e. either by a will (or last testament),[1] or by a so-called *donatio mortis causa* which is a gift given during life but specifically in anticipation

---

[1] Some commentators have held that the *per actum mortis causa* (precisely the same phrase was used in the 1917 Code c.1513 §1) did not include a will in the context of this canon. That view would not however appear to have gained general acceptance: cf. Hannan *The Canon Law of Wills* Catholic University of America 1934 nn.58–60; Vermeersch–Creusen II n.835; Vromant nn.160–162.

of the donor's death e.g. during a serious illness on the part of the donor: it is therefore conditional and revocable, and it becomes the full property of the recipient only on the donor's death.[1]

Can. 1299 §2 In dispositions *mortis causa* in favour of the Church, the formalities of the civil law are as far as possible to be observed. If these formalities have been omitted, the heirs must be advised of their obligation to fulfil the intention of the testator.

The paragraph applies both to a will and to a *donatio mortis causa*. Precisely in order to avoid controversy after the donor's death, it prescribes that, where possible, the formalities required by the relevant civil law are to be observed. It recognises however that circumstances can at times be such as to make it impossible or extremely difficult to fulfil the civil requirements – in which case it will usually be impossible to enforce the donor's wish in the civil forum. There remains nonetheless an obligation in conscience upon the heirs to carry out the donor's intention,[2] assuming of course that this is known for certain. Not only that, but anyone who is in a position to do so, cleric or lay person, is obliged by this canon to bring that obligation to the notice of the heirs.

Can. 1300 The intentions of the faithful who give or leave goods to pious causes, whether by an act *inter vivos* or by an act *mortis causa*, once lawfully accepted, are to be most carefully observed, even in the manner of the administration and the expending of the goods, without prejudice to the provisions of Can. 1301 §3.

Here once more is the law's insistence on the primacy of the donor's wishes in the matter of property or money given or left to pious causes (see Can. 1299 §1). The conditions which may be laid down in the gift or legacy are to be 'most carefully observed' by whomsoever is concerned; if details such as the manner of administration or how the money is to be expended are prescribed, these too must, in so far as possible, be followed to the letter. This rule presupposes that the gift or legacy will have been 'lawfully accepted'.[3] This highlights the obligation upon all recipients of such gifts, particularly upon the administrators of public juridical persons, to ensure that the conditions attaching to the gift are reasonably capable of fulfilment – an admonition which applies particularly to gifts which may carry a long-term condition.[4] The only restriction on the rule is that it is 'without prejudice to the provisions of Can. 1301 §3' which establish the position of the Ordinary in this regard (q.v.).[5]

Can. 1301 §1 The Ordinary is the executor of all pious dispositions whether made *mortis causa* or *inter vivos*.

§2 By this right the Ordinary can and must ensure, even by making a visitation, that pious dispositions are fulfilled. Other executors are to render him an account when they have finished their task.

---

[1] The concept of a *donatio mortis causa* is not recognised in all civil jurisdictions.
[2] Cf. CComm 17.II.1930: AAS 22(1930) 196.
[3] This condition did not appear in the 1917 Code c.1514: for the reason for its insertion here cf. Comm 5(1973) 102 n.44.
[4] In this regard the prescription of Can. 1267 §2 is instructive and important.
[5] Cf. also Can. 325 §2.

§3 Any clause contrary to this right of the Ordinary which is added to a last will, is to be regarded as non-existent.

2598 A feature of the process whereby gifts are given, particularly if they are made by will, is that an executor is nominated, whose function it is to ensure that the wish of the donor is integrally implemented. In stating in §1 that 'the Ordinary (see Can. 134 §1) is *the* executor of all pious dispositions...', the Code re-states a long-standing tradition in canon law.[1] In a sense, it uses the word 'executor' in a manner not normally understood in transactions of this kind. It recognises that executors in the ordinary sense will often, if not always, be nominated. But it makes the point that as far as 'all pious dispositions' are concerned, the Ordinary has an overriding authority to ensure that even nominated executors do fulfil the task entrusted to them.

2599 It is for this reason that §2 insists that 'the Ordinary can and must ensure ... that pious dispositions are fulfilled', and that 'other executors are to render him an account when they have finished their task'. He can fulfil this task 'even by making a visitation', which in effect often means asking for the relevant documents and having them carefully examined. It is up to the Ordinary himself to issue, if necessary, specific directives in this regard.

2600 Should it occur that anyone would, in a will, add a clause specifically rejecting this right of the Ordinary, such a clause 'is to be regarded as non-existent' (§3). While the likelihood of such an occurrence is probably remote, the point of this canon is to state clearly the canon law – whatever might, on occasion, be the reaction at the bar of the civil forum.

Can. 1302 §1 Anyone who receives goods in trust for pious causes, whether by an act *inter vivos* or by last will, must inform the Ordinary about the trust, as well as about the goods in question, both movable and immovable, and about any obligations attached to them. If the donor has expressly and totally forbidden this, the trust is not to be accepted.

2601 This prescription – which must surely apply also to gifts received *mortis causa* (see Can. 1299 §1) – concerns only *trustees* of goods, of whatever kind, given in whatever way to a pious cause. If such a trust is accepted e.g. by a parish priest, by a religious Superior, by a law firm, even by a bank, there arises an obligation upon the trustee to inform the Ordinary (see §3 below), not only of the trust but of its details as specified in this paragraph. Should it happen that the donor would not make the gift except upon a condition which would 'expressly and totally' forbid the fulfilment of this obligation, then the trust may simply not be accepted.

Can. 1302 §2 The Ordinary must demand that goods left in trust be safely preserved and, in accordance with Can. 1301, he must ensure that the pious
2602 **disposition is executed.**

Upon being informed in accordance with §1, there arises for the Ordinary the correlative obligation determined in this paragraph.[2]

Can. 1302 §3 When goods given in trust to a member of a religious institute or society of apostolic life, are destined for a particular place or diocese

---

[1] Cf. e.g. Vromant n.164.

[2] A similar provision is found in a number of civil jurisdictions: in some e.g. a statutory 'Commissioner(s) of Charities' is established, with the right and obligation to supervise the execution of all charitable trusts and to require regular reports.

Title IV Pious Dispositions in General and Pious Foundations

or their inhabitants, or for pious causes, the Ordinary mentioned in §§1 and 2 is the local Ordinary. Otherwise, when the person is a member of a pontifical clerical institute or of a pontifical clerical society of apostolic life, it is the major Superior; when of other religious institutes, it is the member's proper Ordinary.

Who is 'the Ordinary mentioned in §§1–2'? 2603

(a) In most cases it is the local Ordinary (see Can. 134 §2) even when the goods are given in trust to a member of a religious institute or society of apostolic life but are destined for a particular place or diocese or are for pious causes generally.

(b) It is the major Superior (see Can. 134 §1) for cases other than those detailed in (a) above, when the goods are given in trust to a member of a *pontifical clerical institute* or of a *pontifical clerical society* of apostolic life.

(c) It is the member's proper Ordinary (see Cann. 103, 107 §1) when the goods are given in trust to a member of any other religious institute or society of apostolic life – assuming of course that the goods have not any of the destinations mentioned in (a) above; should they have, the local Ordinary is the competent authority.[1]

(d) Since this paragraph makes no reference to a secular institute, it would appear that the general prescription of Can. 1302 §1 would apply in that case.

Can. 1303 §1 In law the term pious foundation comprises:

1° autonomous pious foundations, that is, aggregates of things destined for the purposes described in Can. 114 §2, and established as juridical persons by the competent ecclesiastical authority.

2° non-autonomous pious foundations, that is, temporal goods given in any way to a public juridical person and carrying with them a long-term obligation, such period to be determined by particular law. The obligation is for the juridical person, from the annual income, to celebrate Masses, or to perform other determined ecclesiastical functions, or in some other way to fulfil the purposes mentioned in Can. 114 §2.

The concept of a 'pious foundation' has long been a feature of canonical legislation. 2604 Traditionally, it is understood to be an arrangement whereby property, of whatever kind, is donated or willed to a juridical person for some religious or charitable purpose, on the understanding that the capital thus transferred be invested on a long-term basis and that the annual income accruing from that investment be devoted to the fulfilment of the precise purpose intended by the donor. Such a concept clearly requires regulation by the law. The 1917 Code did this in its own way, attuned to the circumstances of the time.[2] The current Code, while integrally maintaining the same basic concept, puts the matter in the context of today and prescribes regulations which are considered to be more accommodated to current economic conditions.[3]

Abandoning the distinction in the 1917 Code between 'foundations' (cc.1544ff) and 2605 'institutes' (cc.1489ff), this paragraph distinguishes two kinds of pious foundations:

---

[1] Cf. Comm 12(1980) 430 at Can. 48.
[2] Cf. 1917 Code cc.1544ff, 1489ff; Hannan op cit nn.750–760; Vermeersch–Creusen II n.865; Vromant nn.360–362.
[3] For an instructive background cf. Comm 5(1973) 102; 12(1980) 423–424, 431–432; 15(1984) 35–36 at Can. 1243 §1.

autonomous (1°) and non-autonomous (2°). To appreciate this distinction clearly it is necessary to understand the concept dealt with in Can. 114 (q.v.). An *autonomous* foundation is that which arises when a new juridical person is set up as a trust for the specific purpose of accepting and administering a donation or bequest in favour of some work 'of piety, of the apostolate or of charity whether spiritual or temporal' (Can. 114 §2). Of its nature such a foundation is 'perpetual', in the sense that it is not subject to any given time-span. A *non-autonomous* foundation, on the other hand, is that which arises when a donation or bequest is made to an existing juridical person e.g. a parish, a religious house, in trust and on condition that the annual income accruing would, on a long-term basis, be devoted to the specified purpose determined by the donor: 'to celebrate Masses, or to perform other determined ecclesiastical functions, or in some other way to fulfil the purposes' of piety, of the apostolate or of charity already mentioned (see Can. 114 §2) e.g. to help fund an aspirant to the priesthood, to support the local branch of the St Vincent de Paul Society, to promote a missionary endeavour, etc.

2606 What is meant by a 'long-term obligation'? The 1917 Code (c.1544 §1) had spoken of 'a perpetual or a long-term' obligation, but the Revision Commission deliberately decided that a perpetual obligation was no longer appropriate to modern economic circumstances.[1] It would appear certain, therefore, that it is no longer permissible to accept a perpetual foundation, and that the Ordinary may not give permission (see §2 below) for such a foundation. This is particularly relevant in respect of the so-called 'foundation Masses'. The only possible exception might be a case in which the donor or testator would expressly insert a clause allowing the competent Ordinary a discretion in certain circumstances to alter either the purpose of the foundation or the assignment of its revenue.

2607 Under the 1917 Code, 'long-term' was variously interpreted by the commentators, ranging up to fifty years, with forty being perhaps the most agreed figure. Now, it is to be specifically 'determined by particular law', diocesan, provincial or national: hence an obligation arising from this canon upon the appropriate particular legislator, who will take account both of the previous practice and of the existing local economic conditions. In the light of current circumstances, it would seem that a period in excess of about twenty–twenty-five years would reasonably qualify as 'long-term'. A very practical consequence is that such local legislation be so promulgated that it be effectively made known not only to would-be donors or testators, but also and perhaps particularly to their legal advisors – solicitors, law firms and the like – thus hopefully avoiding conflicts with the civil law in the future.

Can. 1303 §2 If the goods of a non-autonomous pious foundation are entrusted to a juridical person subject to the diocesan Bishop, they are, on the expiry of the time, to be sent to the fund mentioned in Can. 1274 §1, unless some other intention was expressly manifested by the donor. Otherwise, the goods fall to the juridical person itself.

2608 In the case of non-autonomous foundations, what is to happen to the capital when the time (as determined in accordance with §1 2° above) expires? The rule is clear:

(a) if the capital had been assigned either to a diocese itself or to a juridical person subject to the diocesan Bishop e.g. a parish, then it is simply to be transferred to the special fund for the support of the clergy prescribed by Can. 1274 §1 (q.v.); the only exception would be – and it would have to be respected – if the donor

---

[1] Cf. Comm 5(1973) 102; 12(1980) 432.

had expressly directed that the capital be at that stage devoted to some other purpose, even perhaps to remain for the benefit of the juridical person in question. Donors should be made clearly aware of their entitlement in this regard.

(b) if the capital had been assigned to a juridical person not subject to the diocesan Bishop e.g. a religious house or institute, it would automatically become the property of that juridical person, to be used as it might, within the canon law, think fit.[1]

Can. 1304 §1 For the valid acceptance of a pious foundation by a juridical person, the written permission of the Ordinary is required. He is not to give this permission until he has lawfully established that the juridical person can satisfy not only the new obligations to be undertaken, but also any already undertaken. The Ordinary is to take special care that the revenue fully corresponds to the obligations laid down, taking into account the customs of the region or place.

No juridical person may validly accept any pious foundation without first having sought and obtained the permission, which must be in writing, of the appropriate Ordinary (as defined in Can. 134 §1). Before giving such permission, the Ordinary is obliged:

(a) so to investigate the situation that he becomes satisfied that the juridical person can in fact fulfil the obligations attaching to the foundation; an essential part of his investigation will be to take account of already-existing obligations, to ensure that those proposed will neither overstretch the resources nor be incompatible with existing ones: a Mass foundation is a particular case in point.

(b) to take 'special care that the revenue fully corresponds to the obligations laid down': for this he must take into account 'the customs of the region or place', a point which again could have a special relevance to a Mass foundation; most of all, this requirement imposes on the Ordinary the obligation to make the best possible assessment – with the help of appropriate experts, if necessary – of the real value which the capital will have over the length of time the foundation will endure.

The practical application of this regulation could well ensure the avoidance of so many problems in this area which have occurred in the past – not least in those situations where it has been discovered, many years later, that the capital revenue is quite inadequate to meet the obligations of the foundation.[2]

Can. 1304 §2 Other conditions for the establishment or acceptance of a pious foundation are to be determined by particular law.

This is not merely an option for particular legislators, particularly Bishops, but an obligation. Taking account of 'the customs of the region or place' (§1 above), they are empowered and obliged to prescribe such 'other conditions for the establishment or acceptance of a pious foundation' as may in their judgement, in the light of local circumstances, be needed properly to regulate this matter. They would certainly be entitled, if they thought it appropriate or necessary, to prescribe conditions necessary for validity.

---

[1] This commentary would take the view that, if in this situation the donor had expressly directed otherwise, his or her directive should prevail: attention to the donor's wishes is the thrust of the current law.
[2] Cf. Comm 5(1973) 102 nn.48–49; 9(1977) 273; 12(1980) 432 at Cann. 50–51; 15(1984) 37 at Can. 1255.

Can. 1305 Money and movable goods which are assigned as an endowment are immediately to be put in a safe place approved by the Ordinary, so that the money or the value of the movable goods is safeguarded; as soon as possible, they are to be carefully and profitably invested for the good of the foundation, with an express and individual mention of the obligation undertaken, in accordance with the prudent judgement of the Ordinary when he has consulted those concerned and his own finance committee.

2611 This, a practical rule of prudence, speaks for itself: it reflects the thinking behind Cann. 1284 and 1294 §2. It is to be noted that it concerns not only the manner of safeguarding and investing the endowment, but also the manner in which its fruits are to be assigned to the purpose of the endowment: this latter calls for a 'prudent judgement of the Ordinary', who is required first to seek the opinion both of 'those concerned' – manifestly in the first place those who have established the endowment – and of his own finance committee.

Can. 1306 §1 All foundations, even if made orally, are to be recorded in writing.

§2 One copy of the document is to be carefully preserved in the curial archive and another copy in the archive of the juridical person to which the foundation pertains.

2612 This is an important practical regulation. When one is dealing with a pious foundation, whether it be autonomous or non-autonomous, one is obviously dealing with a matter of a long term of years. With the passage of years, oral arrangements tend to be forgotten or variously understood. It is essential therefore that they be committed to writing from the very beginning (§1): such a document should carry not only the basic assignment, but also such conditions as the donor might wish to have incorporated for the future, e.g. a change of purpose, a discretion to the Ordinary, etc. Equally important is that authentic copies of this original document be carefully preserved (§2).

Can. 1307 §1 When the provisions of Cann. 1300–1302 and 1287 have been observed, a document showing the obligations arising from the pious foundations is to be drawn up. This is to be displayed in a conspicuous place, so that the obligations to be fulfilled are not forgotten.

§2 Apart from the book mentioned in Can. 958 §1, another book is to be kept by the parish priest or rector, in which each of the obligations, their fulfilment and the offering given, is to be recorded.

2613 Since pious foundations are of their nature long-term, stretching in many cases over a long number of years, it is important that a document be drawn up detailing precisely what obligations they imply. It is equally important that such a document – which clearly may have to be up-dated from time to time – should be readily accessible to all concerned (hence 'displayed in a conspicuous place' – often, in the case of foundation Masses, in the sacristy), precisely 'so that the obligations to be fulfilled are not forgotten' (§1). The 'book mentioned in Can. 958 §1' refers to manual Masses; the 'other book' mentioned in §2 of this canon refers to foundation Masses. The purpose of these rather detailed norms is to bring discipline at a practical level into a matter which has occasioned many problems in the past. The key to the success of that purpose is the extent to which, in particular, local Ordinaries will take such measures as are designed to ensure that the requirements of the universal law are fulfilled.

Title IV Pious Dispositions in General and Pious Foundations

Can. 1308 §1 The reduction of Mass obligations, to be made only for a just and necessary reason, is reserved to the Apostolic See, without prejudice to the provisions which follow.

The fundamental principle is clearly stated: 'the reduction of Mass obligations ... is reserved to the Apostolic See', save only as otherwise provided in the subsequent paragraphs of this canon and in Can. 1309.[1] 'Reduction' means a diminution in the number of Masses which are required to be celebrated for a given intention. No such reduction, by whomsoever, may be permitted save *'for a just and necessary reason'*, the merits of which would be determined by the permitting authority. The principle itself applies to all Mass obligations, whether they be 'manual' or 'foundation', though the question would obviously in the main arise in respect of the latter. 2614

Can. 1308 §2 If this is expressly provided for in the document of foundation, the Ordinary may reduce Mass obligations on the ground of reduced income.

§3 In the case of foundation Masses, whether in legacies or howsoever founded, which are separately endowed, the diocesan Bishop has the power, because of the diminution of income and for as long as this persists, to reduce the obligations to the level of the offering lawfully current in the diocese. He may do this, however, only if there is no one who has an obligation to increase the offering and can actually be made to do so.

§4 The diocesan Bishop has the power to reduce the obligations or legacies of Masses which bind an ecclesiastical institute, if the revenue has become insufficient to achieve in a fitting manner the proper purpose of the institute.

§5 The supreme Moderator of a clerical religious institute of pontifical right has the powers given in §§3 and 4.

These paragraphs provide for the *only* exceptions to the rule that the Holy See alone may reduce Mass obligations. They concern foundation, not manual, Masses. 2615

In virtue of §2, the appropriate Ordinary may reduce the Mass obligations 'on the ground of reduced income', but *only* 'if this is expressly provided for in the document of foundation'. In practice, it is highly desirable that donors be advised and encouraged to insert a clause to this effect into the document of foundation, be this a will, a formal agreement, a letter or whatever other appropriate means may be used in making the donation. In the past, the absence of such a very reasonable stipulation has occasioned disproportionately unreasonable difficulty and, at times, conflict. 2616

§3 deals with foundations which were given *solely* for the purpose of having Masses celebrated, whether they were established as autonomous foundations in the strict sense of Can. 1303 §1 1°, or as part of a non-autonomous foundation (Can. 1303 §1 2°) with however the specific stipulation that a determined part of the funding money be devoted exclusively to the celebration of Masses.[2] In this situation only the dioce- 2617

---

[1] The absolute reservation to the Apostolic See was a feature of the 1917 Code, cc.1551, 1517 §2. The exceptions to this rule were first introduced in 1963 by Pope Paul VI (PM I 11-12: AAS 56(1964) 5-12: CLD 6 372ff) and subsequently confirmed in substance by the same Pope in 1974 (mp *Firma in traditione*: AAS 66(1974) 308-311: CLD 8 530-533). These two papal documents are the principal sources of Cann. 1308 §§2-5 and 1309.

[2] The phrase 'quae sint per se stantia' (which had its origin in PM n.11) has posed problems both of interpretation and of translation. Few commentators have faced the issue. Chiappetta II n.4257 (a) has an illuminating comment. Salvo meliore iudicio the explanation given in the text is the stance of this commentary. Hence also the rendering – 'which are separately endowed' – in the translation of §3.

san Bishop (and the supreme Moderator of a clerical religious institute of pontifical right: see §5) is authorised to reduce the Mass obligations, subject to the following conditions:

(a) that it be on the sole basis of 'the diminution of income';

(b) that the criterion of the reduction be 'the level of the offering lawfully current in the diocese' (see Cann. 950, 952): the Bishop may not reduce the number of Masses below the number calculated by that standard;

(c) that the reduction be operative only 'for as long as (the diminution of income) persists': it could happen e.g. that the value of the shares in which the money was invested would rise later, to the extent that the original obligation could be reassumed – in which case the earlier reduction would cease to have effect;

(d) that there be 'no one who has an obligation to increase the offering and can actually be made to do so': this envisages a situation in which the document of foundation would have charged someone with the obligation to ensure, should the income be diminished in the future, that the foundation be itself supplemented to offset the diminution; in practice, the situation is an unlikely, though not an impossible, one: to attempt to enforce this condition would always call for a very sensitive judgement, and perhaps indeed for the intervention of the civil law – an action not to be encouraged save in the most grave of situations.

2618 §4 envisages yet another situation, namely where a foundation is established for a multiple purpose: primarily for the support of some 'ecclesiastical institute', with however a supplementary obligation attached for the celebration of Masses for the donor's specified intentions. For long this has been and continues to be a regular occurrence, e.g. a foundation to support the formation of a student or students in a seminary or in a religious institute, a foundation to support a chaplain to an ecclesiastical university, and many other such. Under the legislation of the 1917 Code it had caused serious practical problems, particularly in the recent past in view of rapidly changing economic conditions. This paragraph, reflecting PM n.12, authorises the diocesan Bishop (and, again, the supreme Moderator of a clerical religious institute of pontifical right: see §5) to reduce the number of Masses prescribed by the donor. In these circumstances, the criterion of the reduction is more extensive than that in §3 i.e. 'because of diminution of income'. For the cases considered under §4, the criterion is: 'if the revenue has become insufficient to achieve *in a fitting manner* the proper purpose of the institute'. The case of a foundation to support the formation of a student in a seminary or in a religious institute would be a typical example if the financial burden of having to celebrate the number of Masses prescribed are such as to make it impossible to support the formation of a seminarian (the primary object of the foundation) 'in a fitting manner' (clearly a matter for the authority to decide), then the number of Masses could be reduced, even if needs be to one per year. What the Bishop or Moderator could not do would be abolish the Mass obligation altogether.

Can. 1309 Where a fitting reason exists, the authorities mentioned in Can. 1308 have the power to transfer Mass obligations to days, churches or altars other than those determined in the foundation.

2619 A feature of Mass foundations often is that not only a certain number of Masses be celebrated, but that they be celebrated on prescribed days e.g. the first Friday of every month, or in a prescribed church e.g. the local parish or religious church, or even at a prescribed altar in a particular church e.g. the altar of our Blessed Lady. The point of this canon is to give to 'the authorities mentioned in Can. 1308' a reasonable discre-

Title IV Pious Dispositions in General and Pious Foundations

tion – 'where a fitting reason exists' – to adjust not only those explicitly mentioned, but any such ancillary conditions, to the practical circumstances of a given time or place.[1] The authorities in question are, in the appropriate circumstances, all of those mentioned in Can. 1308. There is no question here of reducing the Mass obligations.

Can. 1310 §1 The intentions of the faithful for pious causes may be reduced, moderated or commuted by the Ordinary, if the founder has expressly conceded this power to him, but only for a just and necessary reason.

§2 If it has become impossible to carry out the obligations because of reduced income, or for any other reason arising without fault on the part of the administrators, the Ordinary can diminish these obligations in an equitable manner, with the exception of the reduction of Masses, which is governed by the provisions of Can. 1308. He may do so only after consulting those concerned and his own finance committee, keeping in the best way possible to the intention of the founder.

§3 In all other cases, the Apostolic See is to be approached.

In effect, this canon deals with possible alterations in the terms of pious foundations *other than those which imply the celebration of Masses*, e.g. for the formation of a seminarian, for the maintenance of a number of beds in a hospital, for the assistance of the poor in a given institution, etc. For such a situation it gives certain powers, subject to specified conditions, to the Ordinary (§§1–2), and it determines that all other cases, which do not meet these conditions, must be referred to the Holy See (§3). 2620

The authority given to the appropriate Ordinary in §1 is to *reduce* whatever obligation may have been placed by the donor, to *moderate* i.e. adjust it, or to *commute* it i.e. to substitute for it another cognate one. He may exercise this authority only 'if the founder has expressly conceded this power to him', and even then 'only for a just and necessary reason' (see Can. 1308 §§1–2), which in current economic conditions may well arise, with diminution of income, rising costs and other such substantial changes. Here again is a pointer to the wisdom of advising would-be donors to make express provision in the original document (whatever form it may take) for a situation such as is envisaged. 2621

§2 envisages a situation in which 'because of reduced income, or *for any other reason* arising without fault on the part of the administrators' 'it has become *impossible* (not merely difficult) to carry out the obligations' of the foundation. In such a situation the appropriate Ordinary is empowered to 'diminish (not to eliminate) these obligations'. Before doing so, however, he must consult: (a) 'those concerned' – in effect, officials of the institution in question and, if possible, such members of the family or heirs of the donor as may be available; (b) 'his own finance committee'. The Ordinary is not obliged to follow the advice given by any or all of these persons, but his action in diminishing the obligations would be invalid if he did not at least consult them (see Can. 127 §2 2°). It is to be noted, once again, that the stress of the law is that, in so far as possible, 'the intention of the founder' be kept paramount. 2622

In all of this matter, it is important also that an eye be kept on the requirements of the relevant civil law, so that, in so far as possible, any conflict may be avoided. It is equally important to recognise that the canon law stands on its own principles and prescriptions – a point which has been recognised as valid and effective in many civil jurisdictions. 2623

---

[1] Cf. mp *Firma in traditione* locc citt; Comm 12(1980) 434 at Can. 56.

BOOK VI

SANCTIONS IN THE CHURCH

PART I

OFFENCES AND PUNISHMENTS IN GENERAL

Title I
The Punishment of Offences in General

Can. 1311 The Church has its own inherent right to constrain with penal sanctions Christ's faithful who commit offences.

This inherent right is derived from the nature of the Church 'as a visible organisation'.[1] The principle limits this right to the spiritual realm, in accordance with the teaching of Vat. II that the 'political community and the Church are autonomous and independent of each other in their own fields'.[2] 2624

Christ's faithful are defined in Can. 204 §1, understood in the light of Cann. 11 and 205. Thus only those baptised who are in full communion with the catholic Church and who have a sufficient use of reason are subject to penal sanctions. This provision is further specified by Can. 1323 1°, which states that no one is liable to a penalty who has not completed the sixteenth year of age. 2625

The right to impose punishments in respect of offences committed is to be exercised in accordance with Cann. 1317 and 1341, i.e. to the extent that pastoral considerations require them. 2626

Can. 1312 §1 The penal sanctions in the Church are:

1° medicinal penalties or censures, which are listed in Cann. 1331–1333;

2° expiatory penalties, mentioned in Can. 1336.

The law does not here attempt to define these two types of penal sanctions. It alludes to them by descriptive title; they are specified in detail in the canons mentioned. 2627

---

[1] LG 8: Fl I 357.
[2] GS 76: Fl I 984.

Medicinal penalties (censures, i.e. excommunication, interdict, and suspension) are designed to bring about the correction of an offender's behaviour and his or her reintegration into the full life of the Church community. *Expiatory* penalties seek to compensate for harm done to the life of the Church;[1] their remission does not depend on repentance or amendment of life by the offender.

Can. 1312 §2 The law may determine other expiatory penalties which deprive a member of Christ's faithful of some spiritual or temporal good, and are consistent with the Church's supernatural purpose.

2628 The list of expiatory penalties given in Can. 1336 is not exhaustive. This paragraph indicates that there are others which may be determined by Church authority, as e.g. by a particular council or by a diocesan Bishop. In so doing, the paragraph also states the nature of all ecclesiastical penal sanctions, not just expiatory penalties. The reference to the supernatural purpose of the Church indicates that penal law and its application within the Church should always be understood in the light of the pastoral purpose of all ecclesiastical law, rather than in terms of secular models of criminal law.

Can. 1312 §3 Use is also made of penal remedies and penances: the former primarily to prevent offences, the latter rather to substitute for or to augment a penalty.

2629 These matters are summarily described in Cann. 1339–1340. Their provision indicates the flexibility of ecclesiastical penal law. Prevention is to be preferred to punishment. There is a considerable measure of discretion allowed, to forgo or to reduce or increase punishment of the offender as the circumstances of the offence may suggest.

Title II
Penal Law and Penal Precept

Can. 1313 §1 If a law is changed after an offence has been committed, the law more favourable to the offender is to be applied.

§2 If a later law removes a law, or at least a penalty, the penalty immediately lapses.

2630 Two basic principles of ecclesiastical penal law are given here. The first, in §1, deals with the situation when 'a law is changed after an offence has been committed'. This may be understood as an extension of Can. 18, which states that penal law is to be interpreted strictly, i.e. in such a way as not to enlarge the scope of its application. The second principle, in §2, provides that in all cases where a later law abrogates a former one or at least the penalty attached to it, the penalty ceases to exist, even though the offence may have been committed while the earlier law was in force. In respect of censures, this is a distinct mitigation of the severity of c.2226 §3 of the 1917 Code.

---

[1] In the 1917 Code these were termed vindictive penalties (c.2216 2°): the deliberate change of terminology underlines the less harsh, and indeed more accurate, approach of the current law.

Can. 1314 A penalty is for the most part *ferendae sententiae*, that is, not binding upon the offender until it has been imposed. It is, however, *latae sententiae*, so that it is incurred automatically upon the commission of an offence, if the law or precept expressly lays this down.

Ecclesiastical penalties may be incurred in two ways: (a) those, called *ferendae sententiae*, which are imposed by the competent ecclesiastical authority; (b) those, called *latae sententiae* or 'automatic', which are incurred by the very commission of the offence in question: they can arise only 'if the law or precept expressly lays this down'. The formulation of this canon reflects n.9 of the principles proposed by the 1967 Synod of Bishops concerning the revision of the Code of Canon Law: this was to the general effect that the number of penal laws be reduced and, in particular, that the number of automatic penalties be kept as few as possible, limited to the most grievous of offences:[1] in fact they have been very considerably reduced. 2631

Can. 1315 §1 Whoever has legislative power can also make penal laws. A legislator can, however, by laws of his own, reinforce with a fitting penalty a divine law or an ecclesiastical law of a higher authority, observing the limits of his competence in respect of territory or persons.

Penal laws can be laid down only by those who have legislative power of governance in the Church, and only for their own territory or subjects. Vicars general and judicial Vicars do not have such authority: they may only impose penalties which are already provided for in a law, after an appropriate administrative or judicial process. Legislators have, in addition, a discretionary power to enforce by way of fitting penalty a divine law or any law of a higher ecclesiastical authority: thus e.g. a diocesan Bishop could, if it were necessary, attach a penalty to the violation of an approved general decree of the Bishops' Conference which did not itself prescribe any penalty. In view however of the general thrust of the Code in the matter of penal law, this power should be exercised only with great caution and if no other effective means are available (see Cann. 1317–1318). 2632

Can. 1315 §2 A law can either itself determine the penalty or leave its determination to the prudent decision of a judge.

A penal law may either specify a particular penalty for a given offence, or require that a penalty be imposed e.g. a 'just penalty', while leaving the determination of the specific penalty to the discretion of the judge in the case. In either situation, a penalty is obligatory, subject however to the norm of Can. 1344. On occasion, the law may leave it to the discretion of the judge dealing with a particular offence to decide whether a penalty is to be imposed at all (see Can. 1343). 2633

Can. 1315 §3 A particular law can also add other penalties to those laid down for a certain offence in a universal law; this is not to be done, however, except for the gravest necessity. If a universal law threatens an undetermined penalty or a discretionary penalty, a particular law can establish in its place a determined or an obligatory penalty.

Those enjoying legislative power may legislate penalties *in addition* to those set down in the universal law for a stated offence. They are, however, strongly admonished to use such power with extreme discretion, only 'for the gravest necessity'. But they may, to meet a particular local need, determine penalties which the universal law has left indeterminate, or make obligatory those which would otherwise be discretionary. 2634

---

[1] Cf. Comm 2(1969) 84–85; cf. also Can. 1318.

Can. 1316 Diocesan Bishops are to take care that as far as possible any penalties which are to be imposed by law are uniform within the same city or region.

2635 Because Vat. II emphasises the diocesan Bishop's governing power within his own diocese, there is the possibility that in the formulation and application of penal law there could be a notable discrepancy between the laws of neighbouring dioceses. This was a matter of some detailed discussion at the Revision Commission,[1] where the prevailing view was that while it was essential to maintain the legislative autonomy of the diocesan Bishop, based as it is on divine law, it was necessary also as far as possible to safeguard against the harm to the faithful which could result from a diversity of penal laws in contiguous districts or regions. Hence this canon, urging diocesan Bishops to act in concert with their neighbours in this regard. It is noteworthy that not only the same region but even 'the same city' is mentioned: not a few large modern cities encompass a number of dioceses.

Can. 1317 Penalties are to be established only in so far as they are really necessary for the better maintenance of ecclesiastical discipline. Dismissal from the clerical state, however, cannot be laid down by particular law.

2636 Like the preceding canons, this law urges restraint in the discretionary use of local penal legislation. Matters of ecclesiastical discipline should, whenever possible, be dealt with by other pastoral means. Only when the maintenance of ecclesiastical order absolutely demands it should there be a last resort to penal sanctions. There is, however, one case which may never, no matter what the circumstances, be dealt with by particular law, i.e. dismissal from the clerical state. Because of the distinct status of clerics in the Church, and since this penalty is the most severe that can be inflicted on a cleric, the grounds for such dismissal are restricted exclusively to those determined by the universal law.[2]

Can. 1318 A legislator is not to threaten *latae sententiae* penalties, except perhaps for some outstanding and malicious offences which may be either more grave by reason of scandal or such that they cannot be effectively punished by *ferendae sententiae* penalties. He is not, however, to constitute censures, especially excommunication, except with the greatest moderation, and only for the more grave offences.

2637 The reduction in the universal law of the number of *latae sententiae* penalties (to seventeen), and especially of excommunications (to seven), should serve as a model for particular legislators. Again the emphasis is on strict moderation in the exercise of discretionary penal power. Even when they are necessary, penalties should normally be *ferendae sententiae* (see Can. 1314). An automatic penalty may be established by a local legislator only if three conditions are fulfilled, namely that there be question: (a) not only of an 'outstanding' offence but of one which is 'malicious', i.e. gravely imputable by reason of *malice*: excluded therefore are offences imputable by reason only of *culpability* (see Can. 1321 §1); (b) of an offence which is particularly serious precisely by reason of the scandal which it causes among the faithful; (c) of an offence for which only an automatic penalty could be effective. In effect, therefore, a local legislator is

---

[1] Cf Comm 8(1976) 171–172 at Can. 6.

[2] In the current Code, there are only the following: Cann. 1364 §2, 1367, 1370 §1, 1387, 1394 §1, 1395 §1, 1395 §2, 1397. No other may be added, not even in a situation where there may be an accumulation of other penalties.

severely restricted in his use of any automatic penalty.[1] He is even more restricted in his use of censures, particularly excommunication, which simply may not be established save 'with the greatest moderation and only for the more grave offences'.

Can. 1319 §1 To the extent to which one can impose precepts by virtue of the power of governance in the external forum, to that extent can one also by precept threaten determined penalties, with the exception of perpetual expiatory penalties.

§2 A precept to which a penalty is attached is not to be issued unless the matter has been very carefully considered, and unless the provisions of Cann. 1317 and 1318 concerning particular laws have been observed.

A precept differs from a law in that it is concerned with the welfare of a specific person or persons, as opposed to the common good of the whole community (see Can. 49). In so far as someone in authority[2] has the power to issue such precepts in the external forum, thus far can he attach a penalty to a precept. The penalty may not, however, be a *perpetual* expiatory penalty (see Can. 1336 §1). As in the case of penalties attached to laws, moderation in the threat and imposition of penalties by precept is strongly urged, and the provisions of Cann. 1317 and 1318 apply.

Can. 1320 In all matters in which they come under the authority of the local Ordinary, religious can be constrained by him with penalties.

Matters in which religious come under the authority of the local Ordinary concern 'the care of souls, the public exercise of divine worship and other works of the apostolate' (Can. 678). The application of the principle of this canon, which appeared only in the later drafts,[3] will obviously have to take account also of Cann. 678 §3, 679–681.

Title III
Those who are Liable to Penal Sanctions

Can. 1321 §1 No one can be punished for the commission of an external violation of a law or precept unless it is gravely imputable by reason of malice or of culpability.

§2 A person who deliberately violated a law or precept is bound by the penalty prescribed in the law or precept. If, however, the violation was due to the omission of due diligence, the person is not punished unless the law or precept provides otherwise.

§3 When there has been an external violation, imputability is presumed, unless it appears otherwise.

---

[1] Cf. Comm 8(1976) 173 at Can. 8.

[2] Governing authorities within the Church include those mentioned in Cann. 134 and 620.

[3] This canon was not part of the 1973 draft discussed at Comm 8(1976) 174; it first appeared in the 1980 draft. It has been suggested that it was the retention of the institution of exemption in Can. 591, which led to the explicit enunciation of the principle of the local Ordinary's power over religious in the matter of penalties: cf. Commentary (Urbanianum) 757.

2640 Even though the approach of this Code in the domain of penal law is somewhat different to that of its predecessor, many of the fundamental concepts and the practical consequences remain substantially unchanged.[1] An accurate appreciation of this canon is crucial to the understanding of a *punishable* offence. For such an offence to be verified, it is necessary that the threefold constitutive elements identified in the 1917 Code be present, namely the objective, the subjective and the legal components.[2]

2641 The *objective* element is the 'external violation of a law or precept' (§1). The violation must be external in the sense that, *if* someone were present, it would be perceived; it must admit of proof in the external forum. Accordingly, no merely internal act of mind or will, e.g. of heresy, would be subject to penalty.

2642 The *subjective* element requires that the violation in question be 'gravely imputable by reason of malice or of culpability'. The act by which a law or precept was violated must, in the first place, be attributable to a particular person. Great care is needed if one is properly to understand the concept of imputability in this context. It is *juridical*, not simply moral, imputability: that which is damaged by the violation of the law or precept is not specifically the moral order, the order of sin, but rather the public or social order: hence the imposition of a penalty which renders the offender accountable to the public authority of the Church in the external forum. This juridical imputability must be rooted in either *malice* or *culpability*. Malice may be understood as the deliberate intention of violating a law or precept; culpability, on the other hand, involves the 'omission of due diligence', i.e. the law or precept was violated through culpable ignorance of the law or neglect of one's legal responsibilities.

2643 The *legal* component of an offence means that not every external violation of a law or precept is punishable, even if gravely imputable by reason of malice or culpability. Only the violation of a law which expressly provides for a penal sanction may be punished; thus, e.g. clerics 'are obliged to observe perfect and perpetual continence ... and are therefore bound to celibacy' (Can. 277 §1), but not every external violation of this law is subject to a penalty: only those for which the law so provides, as e.g. in Cann. 1394–1395. Hence the long-established maxim: 'nullum crimen, nulla poena sine lege'.[3]

2644 By contrast with the 1917 Code (see cc.2199, 2203 §1, 2229 §3 2°), the present Code establishes a very important principle: that, ordinarily, only those violations of a law or a precept which arise out of *malice* are to be punished.[4] Thus, if it is proved that someone violated a law or precept *deliberately*, i.e. with malice, then that person is subject to whatever penalty is prescribed in the law or precept. On the other hand, if it is proved that the violation was not deliberate but rather the consequence of culpable ignorance or negligence, then the person does not incur a penalty so-called – unless the law or precept provides otherwise, as it does, e.g. in Cann. 1326 §1 3°, 1389 §2. In saying this, the law is in no way implying that a recalcitrant person is freed from the discipline which any society, including the Church, must require. It is, rather, making the point – essential to a proper understanding of this Book VI on penal sanctions – that, in the matter of maintaining the requisite discipline, the imposition of penalties has indeed its place, but that it is not to be regarded as a substitute for the ordinary administrative regulation of discipline in the Church.

---

[1] Accordingly, the approved commentators on the 1917 Code in this regard remain a distinctly relevant guide.

[2] The three were contained by way of practical definition in c.2195 in the 1917 Code.

[3] In this context cf. also Can. 1399.

[4] Cf. Comm 2(1970) 103.

Once the objective element of an offence has been established, i.e. the external violation of a law or precept to which a penalty has been attached, the law presumes the subjective element. In other words, as soon as an act or omission which violates a law or precept has been established as a fact, the law presumes that the person in question was juridically responsible; in effect, the presumption of innocence ceases. This provision of law constitutes a major shift from the position adopted in c.2200 §2 of the 1917 Code whereby malice was presumed once the fact of an external violation of the law had been established. Under the current law, only imputability is presumed; if the cause of the imputability should turn out to be culpability, not malice, then no penalty may be inflicted (§2). However, this presumption gives way to appearances to the contrary, i.e. if, given the fact of an external violation of a law or precept, some explanation other than malice or culpability *appears* probable from the facts, then the onus of establishing and proving imputability remains on the appropriate ecclesiastical authority.[1]

Can. 1322 Those who habitually lack the use of reason, even though they appeared sane when they violated a law or precept, are deemed incapable of committing an offence.

Those who habitually lack the use of reason are considered to be juridically incapable of personal responsibility (see Can. 99). The present canon is a necessary corollary of this principle. The current law stands in a distinct contrast with c.2201 §§1-2 of the 1917 Code: there, a distinction had been drawn between those who 'actually' lacked the use of the reason and those who were 'habitually insane': the former were considered by the then law as being incapable of crime, while the latter were simply *presumed* to be incapable because they sometimes had 'lucid intervals' or seemed to be sane in their reasoning. However, the Revision Commission, eschewing the distinction of the earlier Code, wished to make clear that neither category of person can be considered to be juridically capable of crime.[2] Thus, if it is certain that someone habitually lacks the use of reason, that person cannot be punished for any act or omission which would usually carry a penalty with it, even if at the time he or she appeared to be sane: such persons are quite simply excluded from the provisions of the Church's penal law.

Can. 1323 No one is liable to a penalty who, when violating a law or precept:

1° **has not completed the sixteenth year of age;**

2° **was, without fault, ignorant of violating the law or precept; inadvertence and error are equivalent to ignorance;**

3° **acted under physical force, or under the impetus of a chance occurrence which the person could not foresee or if foreseen could not avoid;**

4° **acted under the compulsion of grave fear, even if only relative, or by reason of necessity or grave inconvenience, unless, however, the act is intrinsically evil or tends to be harmful to souls;**

---

[1] Cf. Comm 2(1970) 103; cf. also de Paolis *Quaestiones miscellaneae II: nonnullae quaestiones circa librum VI CIC* Per 73(1984) 485; Hughes *The presumption of imputability in Canon 1321 §3* Stud Can 21(1987) 33-35; McDonough *A gloss on Canon 1321* Stud Can 21 (1987) 383-384; Beal *To be or not to be: that is the question; the rights of the accused in the canonical penal process* CLSA Proceedings 1991 82.
[2] Cf. Comm 8(1976) 177 at Can. 11.

5° acted, within the limits of due moderation, in lawful self-defence or defence of another against an unjust aggressor;

6° lacked the use of reason, without prejudice to the provisions of Cann. 1324 §1 n.2 and 1325.

7° thought, through no personal fault, that some one of the circumstances existed which are mentioned in nn.4 or 5.

2647 The pre-eminently pastoral purpose of the Church's penal law is seen in the many people whom the law exempts or excuses from penalties. In addition to those who habitually lack the use of reason, this canon identifies seven other categories of people who are not liable to a penalty even if they violate a law or precept.

1° Lack of sufficient age is an obvious reason to exempt someone from a penalty. The law fixes the minimum age for incurring ecclesiastical penalties at sixteen: anyone below that age, even if the author of an act which violates a law or precept, cannot incur a penalty as such.

2° If someone is ignorant of a law or precept, or is unaware of it, or in error about it, through no fault of his or her own, then that person is exempt from an ecclesiastical penalty. In accordance with Can. 15, however, ignorance or error concerning a law is not to be presumed. It must therefore be established that this particular person did act in ignorance, inadvertence or error about the law or precept and must show that this was genuinely inculpable, i.e. that he or she could not in the circumstances have done anything about it.

3° Those who act as a result of physical force, or as a consequence of a chance occurrence, are not subject to punishment. This provision of law must be seen as a corollary to the principle of Can. 125 §1 whereby an act performed as the result of outside force is considered not to have taken place. In order to be juridically imputable, an act must have been performed freely and without the constraint of some external force. A 'chance occurrence' also restricts the freedom of an act: a set of fortuitous circumstances which were unforeseen or, at least, unavoidable, may constrain a person to act in such a way as to be in violation of a law or precept. Such a person is not liable to a penalty.

4° A person's real freedom to act may also be limited by grave fear or by necessity or by grave inconvenience. Grave fear, resulting from a threat of present or future evil, does not render the person incapable of an act of free will[1] but it does diminish that person's responsibility. Circumstances may require that someone violate a law or precept in order to prevent personal harm or damage or harm or damage to others. In such a case, the person is constrained by necessity to act against the law. Similarly, if the observation of a law or precept would lead to serious trouble for the offender or for others, the violation is caused by grave inconvenience and the person is exempt from penalty. It is for the appropriate ecclesiastical authority to decide whether or not the fear, necessity or inconvenience involved was in fact grave. The canon adds that none of these three exempting causes is sufficient to exclude the possibility of a penalty if the act in question is intrinsically evil or if is harmful to souls.

5° In the face of unjust aggression one has the right to defend oneself and others. If such defence results in a violation of a law or precept, provided that the defence in question did not exceed the limits of due moderation, the person concerned is not liable to any penalty.

---

[1] Cf. Comm 16(1984) 40 at Can. 1274.

Part I Offences and Punishments in General

6° Since those who are habitually lacking in the use of reason (see Can. 1322) are juridically incapable of committing an offence, it is not surprising to find that the law exempts from penalties those who actually lack the use of reason. However, the law qualifies this exemption: if the *actual* lack of the use of reason was the result of culpable drunkenness or some other similar mental disturbance (e.g. drug or solvent abuse), the person is indeed liable to punishment for the offence committed (see Cann. 1324 §1 2°, 1325).

7° If someone genuinely and without any personal fault believed that the circumstances described in 4° and 5° obtained at the time of a violation of a law or precept, then that person is also exempted from ecclesiastical penalties, provided always of course that the act in question was not intrinsically evil or harmful to souls.

Can. 1324 §1 The perpetrator of a violation is not exempted from penalty, but the penalty described in the law or precept must be diminished, or a penance substituted in its place, if the offence was committed by:

1° one who had only an imperfect use of reason;

2° one who was lacking the use of reason because of culpable drunkenness or other mental disturbance of a similar kind;

3° one who acted in the heat of passion which, while serious, nevertheless did not precede or hinder all mental deliberation and consent of the will, provided that the passion itself had not been deliberately stimulated or nourished;

4° a minor who has completed the sixteenth year of age;

5° one who was compelled by grave fear, even if only relative, or by reason of necessity or grave inconvenience, if the act is intrinsically evil or tends to be harmful to souls;

6° one who acted in lawful self-defence or defence of another against an unjust aggressor, but did not observe due moderation;

7° one who acted against another person who was gravely and unjustly provocative;

8° one who erroneously, but culpably, thought that some one of the circumstances existed which are mentioned in Can. 1323 nn.4 or 5;

9° one who through no personal fault was unaware that a penalty was attached to the law or precept;

10° one who acted without full imputability, provided it remained grave.

Another clear indication that the welfare of the individual lies at the heart of the Church's penal law comes from the categories of person listed in this canon. These are people who are not exempted from ecclesiastical penalties but who find themselves affected by a wide variety of extenuating circumstances. Many of these circumstances are closely related to those contained in Can. 1323. Thus the following are to be punished, but with a lesser penalty than that contained in the law or precept which was violated:

2648

1° those whose use of reason is impaired but not habitually defective;

2° those whose use of reason is actually defective as a result of some culpable behaviour such as drunkenness or other substance abuse;

3° those who acted under the impulse of passion (e.g. anger, hatred, jealousy, sexual desire) – provided that this passion had not been deliberately excited;

4° those who are aged between sixteen and eighteen;

5° those who did something intrinsically evil or harmful to souls but as a result of grave fear, necessity or grave inconvenience;

6° those who failed to observe due moderation in their self-defence or in defence of others against unjust aggression;

7° those who violated a law or precept while reacting to grave and unjust provocation, i.e. those who acted against another person under the influence of anger or resentment provoked by that person;

8° those who believed that the circumstances mentioned in Can. 1323 4° or 5° obtained at the time but who ought to have known that they did not in fact obtain;

9° those who, through no fault of their own, did not know that a penalty was attached to a particular law or precept which they had violated;

10° those whose personal responsibility for their actions has been diminished by some other demonstrable factor, provided that this still amounted to grave imputability.

Can. 1324 §2 A judge can do the same if there is any other circumstance present which would reduce the gravity of the offence.

2649 Faced with offenders who find themselves affected by any of the extenuating circumstances listed in §1, the ecclesiastical authority is required to reduce the penalty to be imposed. The law gives a similar faculty to a judge in a penal process; he may impose a lesser penalty if any of the circumstances mentioned in §1 are verified or if he is satisfied that some other circumstance is present which would render the offence less serious.

Can. 1324 §3 In the circumstances mentioned in §1, the offender is not bound by a *latae sententiae* penalty.

2650 In order to incur a *latae sententiae* penalty, the law demands full imputability on the part of the offender. Consequently, if any of the circumstances listed in Can. 1323 §1 is verified, no automatic penalty is incurred: thus, e.g. if a woman had an abortion as a result of grave fear, she does not incur the penalty prescribed in Can. 1398. However, the competent authority may always impose some suitable lesser penalty or a penance.

Can. 1325 Ignorance which is crass or supine or affected can never be taken into account when applying the provisions of Cann. 1323 and 1324. Likewise, drunkenness or other mental disturbances cannot be taken into account if these have been deliberately sought so as to commit the offence or to excuse it; nor can passion which has been deliberately stimulated or nourished.

2651 The factors mentioned in this canon do not constitute a basis for exempting from penalties or imposing a lesser penalty. Indeed, what is described here is culpable behaviour: the person could have acted otherwise but, through deliberate action or wilful omission or neglect, chose to behave in such a way that resulted in the violation of a law or precept. Thus, ignorance of a law or precept or of a penalty attached thereto cannot result in an exemption from a penalty or be considered as an extenuating circumstance if it is crass or supine, i.e. due to laziness, negligence or complete lack of interest, or if it is affected, i.e. if it was cultivated with the purpose of violating the law or precept. Drunkenness or some other similar disturbance of the mind cannot be used as an excuse if induced by someone either with the express intention of committing an offence or in the clear knowledge that it would be very likely to lead to the commission of an offence. Likewise, a passion which has been deliberately excited cannot be used to seek exemption from or diminution of an ecclesiastical penalty.

Can. 1326 §1 A judge may inflict a more serious punishment than that prescribed in the law or precept when:

1° a person, after being condemned, or after the penalty has been declared, continues so to offend that obstinate ill-will may prudently be concluded from the circumstances;

2° a person who is established in some position of dignity, or who, in order to commit an offence, has abused a position of authority or an office;

3° an offender who, after a penalty for a culpable offence was constituted, foresaw the event but nevertheless omitted to take precautions to avoid it which any careful person would have taken.

In addition to circumstances which reduce imputability, the law also recognises some circumstances which would make an offence even more serious and worthy of a penalty more serious than that prescribed in the law or precept. The law gives the power to a judge in a penal process to inflict a more serious penalty if one or other of the following aggravating circumstances is verified: 2652

1° *obstinate ill-will*: this is to be deduced from the behaviour of someone who has continued to commit the same offence even though a penalty has already been imposed or declared; this is similar but quite distinct from the multiplication of offences mentioned in Can. 1346;

2° *abuse of power*: an offence is reckoned to be much more serious when it is committed by someone to whom a position of authority or influence has been entrusted and who has taken advantage of that position precisely to commit the offence;

3° *lack of due diligence*: a culpable offence is understood to have been more serious if the offender, through his or her own carelessness, failed to take the precautions to avoid it that any prudent person would take; this is an incisive example of a modification of the general principle of law, stated in Can. 1321 §2, which exempts from punishment those who offend due to the omission of due diligence.

Can. 1326 §2 In the cases mentioned in §1, if the penalty constituted is *latae sententiae*, another penalty or a penance may be added.

While §1 authorises the judge in a penal case to impose a more serious penalty, this paragraph deals with what is to be done when aggravating circumstances are verified in connection with a *latae sententiae* penalty. The law provides that the judge or the appropriate ecclesiastical authority has the discretion to add a further penalty or a suitable penance to what has already been incurred automatically. 2653

Book VI Sanctions in the Church

Can. 1327 A particular law may, either as a general rule or for particular offences, determine excusing, attenuating or aggravating circumstances, over and above the cases mentioned in Cann. 1323-1326. Likewise, circumstances may be determined in a precept which excuse from, attenuate or aggravate the penalty constituted in the precept.

2654 Whoever has legislative power or the power of governance in the Church, in conformity with Cann. 1315 and 1319, has the authority not only to issue penal laws and penal precepts but also to establish within such laws and precepts excusing, extenuating or aggravating circumstances in addition to those contained in universal law (Cann. 1323-1326).

Can. 1328 §1 One who in furtherance of an offence did something or failed to do something but then, involuntarily, did not complete the offence, is not bound by the penalty prescribed for the completed offence, unless the law or a precept provides otherwise.

§2 If the acts or their omissions of their nature lead to the carrying out of the offence, the persons responsible may be subjected to a penance or to a penal remedy, unless he or she had spontaneously desisted from the offence which had been initiated. However, if scandal or other serious harm or danger has resulted, the perpetrator, even though spontaneously desisting, may be punished by a just penalty, but of a lesser kind than that determined for the completed crime.

2655 The 1917 Code in its cc.2212-2313 and 2235 contained some rather complicated regulations concerning 'attempted' and 'frustrated' offences. Early in the process of revision, however, the Commission established the principle that in the new Code attempted or frustrated offences were not to be punished by penalty but only by penances or penal remedies.[1] Thus, only an act which has been completed, which has attained its desired or intended aim, may be punished by the imposition or the incurring of a penalty. Consequently, if someone, for whatever reason, did not actually complete the offence, even if this was interrupted against the perpetrator's will, that person is not bound by the penalty prescribed in the law or precept, unless it is expressly provided otherwise (§1). Furthermore, if someone spontaneously desists from an offence which has been begun, that person is to be given a suitable penance or penal remedy, unless the acts or omissions concerned will have led to scandal or other serious harm or damage – in which case the offender may be punished with a penalty, but one less serious than that established in the law or precept for the completed offence (§2).

Can. 1329 §1 Where a number of persons conspire together to commit an offence, and accomplices are not expressly mentioned in the law or precept, if *ferendae sententiae* penalties were constituted for the principal offender, then the others are subject to the same penalties or to other penalties of the same or lesser gravity.

§2 In the case of a *latae sententiae* penalty attached to an offence, accomplices, even though not mentioned in the law or precept, incur the same penalty if, without their assistance, the crime would not have been committed, and if the penalty is of such a nature as to be able to affect them; otherwise, they can be punished with *ferendae sententiae* penalties.

---

[1] Cf. Comm 2(1970) 103-104.

Not all violations of ecclesiastical laws or precepts are the work of individuals: sometimes a number of people cooperate in the offence. This canon addresses the issue of the punishment of these collaborators or accomplices.[1] The general principle of law is that all who did in fact formally cooperate in an offence are to be punished. Their punishment, however, depends upon a number of distinctions made within the canon:

(a) *ferendae sententiae* penalties (§1): when the penalties mentioned in the law must be imposed upon the principal offender by the competent ecclesiastical authority and where the law makes no specific provision for cooperators or accomplices, this canon determines either that all involved are subject to the same penalties or, if the situation merits it, to penalties of the same or of a lesser gravity. In making a decision about the punishment of such accomplices, the relevant authority will obviously keep in mind the provisions of Cann. 1322–1326;

(b) *latae sententiae* penalties (§2): when the penalty for the offence is incurred automatically by virtue of the law, all accomplices incur the same penalty as the principal offender, even if the law or precept does not make any express provision for accomplices. However, one must be clear about what is meant here by 'accomplice': it is someone without whose assistance an offence would not have been committed.[2] If the persons concerned were not accomplices in this strict sense, or if the penalty imposed by the law could not affect them (e.g. if the penalty incurred by the principal offender was suspension and the accomplices were not clerics), the canon declares that they are to be punished with *ferendae sententiae* penalties. Again, when imposing these, the appropriate authority will have to take cognisance of Cann. 1322–1326.

Can. 1330 An offence which consists in a declaration or in some other manifestation of will or of doctrine or of knowledge, is not to be regarded as effected if no one actually perceives the declaration or manifestation.

A person can be punished only for an external violation of a law or precept. This canon focuses on the meaning of the qualification 'external'. A declaration or other kind of manifestation which is clearly contrary to a law or precept is not considered to be an offence unless it was *actually perceived* by someone. Thus, e.g., a person cannot be punished for heresy (see Can. 1364 §1), perjury (see Can. 1368), blasphemy (see Can. 1369), or teaching condemned doctrine (see Can. 1371 1°) unless someone else will have actually perceived it. The formulation of this canon was the subject of considerable debate during the revision process.[3] In the light of Can. 17 it is clear that an offence such as is contemplated here is 'perceived' when, rather than kept in the mind of the alleged perpetrator, it is expressed in such a way – whether orally, in writing or otherwise – that any normal observer would be able to testify to its declaration.

---

[1] The current canon reduces and simplifies the complicated norms of its predecessor: cf. cc.2209 §§1–7, 2231 of the 1917 Code.

[2] Thus, e.g. included in the penalty prescribed by Can. 1398 for abortion are those without whose help the abortion could not have taken place, such as those who persuaded the woman to have the abortion, those who paid for it, those who actually performed the operation, etc.

[3] Cf. Comm 8(1976) 168–169 at Can. 2.

Book VI Sanctions in the Church

Title IV
Penalties and Other Punishments

Chapter I
CENSURES

Can. 1331 §1 An excommunicated person is forbidden:

1° to have any ministerial part in the celebration of the Sacrifice of the Eucharist or in any other ceremonies of public worship;

2° to celebrate the sacraments or sacramentals and to receive the sacraments;

3° to exercise any ecclesiastical offices, ministries, functions or acts of governance.

2658 This Chapter, dealing with censures, hearkens back to Can. 1312 §1 1° and, in particular, to the concept that censures are of their very nature *medicinal* penalties, designed to bring about the correction of an offender's behaviour and that person's reintegration into the full life of the Church's community. It is essential to keep this concept in mind when dealing, as this canon does, with excommunication, itself the most serious penalty in the Church, involving as it does the exclusion of a person from communion with the rest of the Church. This exclusion obviously, and necessarily, reflects the seriousness of the offence. Yet it must never be forgotten that its purpose is not of its nature punitive: rather is it designed, precisely by highlighting the gravity of the damage, to induce the offender to reconsider his or her actions and to return to full communion with the Church. This canon spells out in some detail the consequences of excommunication for the person concerned, distinguishing what is common to all forms of excommunication (§1) and what is particular to those excommunications which have been imposed or declared (§2).

2659 Those who incur excommunication become the subject of a threefold prohibition:

1° they may not have any *ministerial* participation in the Mass or in any other liturgical celebrations; this prohibition affects Bishops, priests and deacons as well as lay ministers (see Can. 230); it prevents them from exercising their ministry in any act of worship 'offered in the name of the Church' (Can. 834 §2). The penalty does not forbid them to attend Mass or other public acts of worship, or to take part in private acts of prayer and devotion;

2° they are also forbidden to celebrate the sacraments or sacramentals and, significantly, they are forbidden to receive the sacraments. This latter prohibition was a subject of considerable debate within the Revision Commission; eventually there was a firm decision to retain this overall prohibition.[1]

3° they are prevented from exercising any offices, ministries[2] or other functions they may have within the Church; they are also prohibited from carrying out any acts of

---

[1] Cf. Comm 9(1977) 147 at Can. 16 §1 b, 149 note 1, 213 at II, 321–322; 16(1984) at Can. 1282 §2.
[2] This includes the lay ministries introduced by Pope Paul VI in 1972: cf. Comm 9(1977)149–150 at Can. 16 §1 c.

jurisdiction or governance: this includes all acts of the internal and external forum, ordinary and delegated power, legislative, administrative and judicial power.

The prohibitions contained in §1 of this canon affect the legality of the actions concerned, not their validity. Moreover, in interpreting them, account must always be taken of the rule of Can. 1335.

Can. 1331 §2 If the excommunication has been imposed or declared, the offender:

1° **proposing to act in defiance of the provisions of §1 n.1 is to be removed, or else the liturgical action is to be suspended, unless there is a grave reason to the contrary;**

2° **invalidly exercises any acts of governance which, in accordance with §1 n.3, are unlawful;**

3° **is forbidden to benefit from privileges already granted;**

4° **cannot validly assume any dignity, office or other function in the Church;**

5° **does not enjoy the benefits of any dignity, office, function or pension held in the Church.**

The *imposition* by an ecclesiastical authority of an excommunication *ferendae sententiae*, or the *declaration* of an excommunication incurred *latae sententiae*, reinforces the consequences outlined in §1 and highlights the extent of an excommunicated person's exclusion from the community of the faithful:

1° those who, in defiance of an excommunication, attempt to exercise their liturgical ministry in celebrating Mass or leading some other act of public worship, are 'to be removed': in practical effect, this means that the relevant authority is formally to insist, under obedience, that they desist from any such conduct. The canon goes further in prescribing that, as an alternative, 'the liturgical action is to be suspended' – presumably in the very course of its happening – wisely however adding: 'unless there is a grave reason to the contrary', which in most current circumstances there almost certainly would be, not least because of the danger thereby to cause even greater scandal among the faithful.

2° those who attempt to exercise acts of *jurisdiction* would do so not merely illegally but invalidly – whether these be acts of the internal or external forum, ordinary or delegated power, legislative, administrative or judicial power. In accordance with Can. 976, however, this does not prevent an excommunicated priest from validly and lawfully absolving penitents who are in danger of death. On the other hand, by virtue of Can. 1109, such a priest cannot validly assist at a marriage. In cases of common error, of course, the Church supplies the necessary jurisdiction (see Can. 144).

3° they are prohibited from using ecclesiastical privileges for their benefit, even though they retain a privilege which is understood to be perpetual (see Can. 78 §1).

4° by reason of the prohibition contained in §1 3°, they cannot legally exercise any office or function which they already hold; by virtue of this paragraph, they are prevented from validly assuming any new dignity or office or function within the Church.

Book VI Sanctions in the Church

5° even though they are in possession of some ecclesiastical dignity, office, function or pension, they cannot enjoy the benefits of the same; the application of this penalty must, however, carefully bear in mind the provisions of Can. 1350.

2662 Besides the effects enumerated in this canon, excommunication may also affect a person's legal capacity to vote (see Can. 171 §1 3°), membership of public associations of the faithful (see Can. 316), and capacity to gain indulgences (see Can. 996 §1). Moreover, the special permission of the local Ordinary is required before such a person can contract marriage within the Church (see Can. 1071 §1 5°).

Can. 1332 One who is under interdict is obliged by the prohibition of Can. 1331 §1 nn.1 and 2; if the interdict was imposed or declared, the provision of Can. 1331 §2 n.1 is to be observed.

2663 A lesser form of censure is an interdict.[1] This is a penalty whereby offenders are excluded from certain sacred actions, while remaining in communion with the Church. The canon draws a distinction between the common effects of interdict and the effects of an interdict which has been imposed or declared by the competent ecclesiastical authority. All those persons under interdict are forbidden to participate as ministers in the celebration of the Mass or other acts of public worship, and they are prohibited from celebrating the sacraments and sacramentals and from receiving the sacraments; if the interdict has been imposed or declared, then those attempting to celebrate Mass or other acts of worship as ministers are to be prevented from doing so, if possible, in the same way as excommunicates (see Can. 1331 §2 1°). What has been said above concerning excommunicated persons applies also to those under interdict; unlike excommunication, however, an interdict has no effect on the exercise of ecclesiastical offices or functions or the enjoyment of privileges, pensions etc.

2664 Other consequences of an interdict are to be found elsewhere in the Code: thus, e.g. a person under interdict requires the special permission of the local Ordinary in order to contract marriage (see Can. 1071 §1 5°); moreover, if they are under an interdict which has been imposed or declared (see Can. 1109), then – without prejudice to the principle of Can. 144 concerning common error etc. – the local Ordinary or the parish priest cannot validly assist at their marriage or delegate other priests or deacons to do so.[2]

Can. 1333 §1 Suspension, which can affect only clerics, prohibits:

1° all or some of the acts of the power of order;

2° all or some of the acts of the power of governance;

3° the exercise of all or some of the rights or functions attaching to an office.

§2 In a law or a precept it may be prescribed that, after a judgement which imposes or declares the penalty, a suspended person cannot validly perform acts of the power of governance.

---

[1] In the past a distinction was drawn between a local interdict and a personal interdict (see c.2268–2277 of the 1917 Code). The local interdict was rejected by the Revision Commission and only the personal interdict was retained: cf. Comm 16(1984) 42 at Can. 1283.

[2] *Latae sententiae* interdicts are incurred by those who commit the offences mentioned in Cann. 1370 §2, 1397, 1378 2§, 1390 §1, 1394 §2. *Ferendae sententiae* interdicts may be imposed on those who commit the offences mentioned in Cann. 1373, 1374, 1380.

§3 The prohibition never affects:

1° any offices or power of governance which are not within the control of the Superior who establishes the penalty;

2° a right of residence which the offender may have by virtue of office;

3° the right to administer goods which may belong to an office held by a person suspended, if the penalty is *latae sententiae*.

§4 A suspension prohibiting the receipt of benefits, stipends, pensions or other such things, carries with it the obligation of restitution of whatever has been unlawfully received, even though this was in good faith.

While excommunication and interdict can affect all members of Christ's faithful who commit certain offences, the third type of censure, suspension, affects only clerics, i.e. Bishops, priests and deacons. The effects of suspension vary considerably depending upon how the censure was incurred.[1] Thus a cleric who is suspended may find that he is forbidden either completely or partially to exercise his power of order, his power of jurisdiction, or the rights and duties attached to his office. In each case, the extent of the suspension must be specified by law or by the competent ecclesiastical authority (see Can. 1334).

In general, a suspended cleric who acts in defiance of the suspension acts *illicitly*. Nevertheless, if the penal norm so prescribes, any acts of governance performed after a suspension has been imposed or declared are regarded as invalid (§2). The imposition or declaration of a suspension has no effect on the validity of acts of the power of order.[2]

The effects of a suspension are not without limits, however (§3). Thus, the suspension of a cleric has no effect on any offices or power of governance which are not subject to the authority of the Superior who established the penalty, e.g. the suspension of a religious cleric by a diocesan Bishop does not affect any office the religious may hold within his institute. Nor does suspension affect a cleric's right of residence in a certain place by reason of his office, e.g. a parish priest who is suspended cannot be required to leave the parochial house. In a similar way, if the suspension was incurred *latae sententiae*, a cleric who is suspended does not lose the right to administer temporal goods which pertain to the office he holds, e.g. a parish priest in this position can continue to administer the affairs of the parish. However, if the penalty is *ferendae sententiae*, the appropriate ecclesiastical authority may well determine otherwise.

Of course, if the suspension expressly prohibits the cleric from receiving income associated with his office, the law obliges the cleric to make restitution of all that which he unlawfully received, even if it was obtained in good faith (§4). This provision of law must be applied in such a way that a cleric is not deprived of what is required for the necessities of life (see Cann. 281 §1, 1350 §1).

Can. 1334 §1 The extent of a suspension, within the limits laid down in the preceding canon, is defined either by the law or precept, or by the judgement or decree whereby the penalty is imposed.

---

[1] It is to be noted that suspension can only be incurred as a censure. The former procedure whereby an Ordinary could suspend a cleric *ex informata conscientia* (cc.2186–2194 of the 1917 Code) has been abrogated.

[2] By virtue of Can. 1109, of course, a suspended cleric cannot validly assist at marriages, nor can he delegate others to do so.

Book VI Sanctions in the Church

§2 A law, but not a precept, can establish a *latae sententiae* suspension without an added determination or limitation; such a penalty has all the effects enumerated in Can. 1333 §1.

2669 While the effects of excommunication and interdict are specified in the law (see Cann. 1331, 1332), the precise effects of suspension in each case are not. This canon requires that the extent of a *ferendae sententiae* suspension is to be determined by the law or penal precept by which the penalty is established in the first place, or in the judgement or decree whereby the penalty is actually imposed.[1] On the other hand, if the law does not specify or determine the effects of a *latae sententiae* suspension, then it is understood to include all the effects listed in Can. 1333 §1, i.e. the cleric is prohibited from all the acts of the power of order, from all the acts of the power of governance, and from all the rights or functions pertaining to his office.[2] Such an indeterminate suspension can be established only by a law, never by a precept. Whether the effects of a suspension are specified or not, however, they can never exceed the limits contained in Can. 1333 §3.

Can. 1335 If a censure prohibits the celebration of the sacraments or sacramentals or the performance of an act of governance, the prohibition is suspended whenever this is necessary to provide for the faithful who are in danger of death. If a *latae sententiae* censure has not been declared, the prohibition is also suspended whenever one of the faithful requests a sacrament or sacramental or an act of the power of governance; for any just reason it is lawful to make such a request.

2670 In order not to deprive the faithful of what they need or desire for their own spiritual welfare, the law provides for the suspension of the effects of some censures in certain situations. The censures involved all contain a prohibition of the celebration of the sacraments or sacramentals or of the performance of an act of governance. Such a prohibition is suspended if the person affected by the censure is required to attend to the needs of the faithful in danger of death, e.g. a priest who is excommunicated or under interdict or under a general suspension may celebrate the sacraments for such people. If the censure affecting the person is *latae sententiae* and has not been declared, then the prohibition is suspended on any occasion when one of the faithful makes a request to receive a sacrament or a sacramental or an act of the power of governance. There is no similar suspension of the effects of a censure which has been incurred *ferendae sententiae* or which has been declared. This canon is a practical illustration of the principle *suprema lex, salus animarum* (Can. 1752) and must always be read in conjunction with Cann. 1352 and 1357.

---

[1] *Ferendae sententiae* suspension is to be imposed on those who commit the offences mentioned in Cann. 1380, 1387, 1395 §1; other *ferendae sententiae* censures including suspension are to be imposed on those who committed the offences mentioned in Cann. 1372, 1385, 1390 §2. In each of these cases, the effects of the suspension must be determined in the judgement or decree. The Code contains one example of a determinate *latae sententiae* suspension in Can. 1383 whereby a cleric who was ordained without lawful dimissorial letters is suspended from the order received, but he may exercise other orders received legitimately.

[2] Indeterminate *latae sententiae* suspensions are incurred by those who commit the offences mentioned in Cann. 1370 §2, 1378 §2, 1390 §1, 1394 §1.

Part I Offences and Punishments in General

Chapter II
EXPIATORY PENALTIES

Can. 1336 §1 Expiatory penalties can affect the offender either forever or for a determined or an indeterminate period. Apart from others which the law may perhaps establish, these penalties are as follows:

1° **a prohibition against residence, or an order to reside, in a certain place or territory;**

2° **deprivation of power, office, function, right, privilege, faculty, favour, title or insignia, even of a merely honorary nature;**

3° **a prohibition on the exercise of those things enumerated in n.2, or a prohibition on their exercise inside or outside a certain place; such a prohibition is never under a pain of nullity;**

4° **a penal transfer to another office;**

5° **dismissal from the clerical state.**

Whereas censures are aimed at the correction of offenders and their reconciliation or rehabilitation, expiatory penalties are aimed at the reparation of the harm done to the body of the faithful and a deterrence of further offences. Consequently, depending upon the nature and circumstances of the offence, an expiatory penalty may affect the offender in perpetuity, or for a specified period of time, or even for an indeterminate period.

The temporal scope of such a penalty must be established clearly in the decree or judgement by which such a penalty is imposed. Five examples of this type of penalty are listed in the canon. This list is not exhaustive. The universal or particular legislator may decide to add other expiatory penalties, e.g. dismissal from a religious institute.

At an initial glance, the list of penalties given in this canon might seem to affect only clerics. However, since lay people may now hold certain ecclesiastical offices, they may be affected by some of these penalties. Cann. 1337–1338 provide further details concerning the penalties mentioned in 1°–3°. It must be noted that not every transfer of office (4°) is the result of an offence (see Cann. 190–191). To be considered an expiatory penalty, the transfer must have been imposed after the appropriate procedures. Dismissal from the clerical state (5°) is a most serious punishment; its effects are set out in Cann. 290–293. It is regarded as so serious that it cannot be established as a penalty by particular law (see Can. 1317).

Can. 1336 §2 Only those expiatory penalties may be *latae sententiae* which are enumerated in §1 n.3.

One of the guiding principles of the revision of the Code was the reduction of *latae sententiae* penalties. In this paragraph, the law restricts automatic expiatory penalties to those enumerated in §1 3°, i.e. the prohibition of the exercise of a power, office, function etc. Thus, a person may be prohibited from the exercise of an ecclesiastical office by means of an automatic penalty; such a person may not, however, be deprived of the office itself by means of such a penalty.

Can. 1337 §1 A prohibition against residing in a certain place or territory can affect both clerics and religious. An order to reside in a certain place can affect secular clerics and, within the limits of their constitutions, religious.

§2 An order imposing residence in a certain place or territory must have the consent of the Ordinary of that place, unless there is question of a house set up for penance or rehabilitation of clerics, including extra-diocesans.

2675   This canon makes more specific the scope of the penalty mentioned in Can. 1336 §1 1°. As a result of such a penalty, a cleric or a religious may be forbidden to reside in a particular place. This prescription affects secular clerics without distinction or qualification; however, in the case of religious, the decree or judgement imposing such a penalty must take account of the constitutions of the particular institute. From the wording of this canon, it is clear that such a penalty cannot be applied to lay people but only to deacons, priests, Bishops and religious. It would appear that, given the principle of Can. 18, this penalty cannot be applied to members of secular institutes or societies of apostolic life, although it has been argued by some that it may, by analogy, be applied to these also.[1]

2676   If the penalty prescribes residence in a particular place or territory, the law requires that the Ordinary of that place must give his prior consent. The only exception foreseen by the canon is where the cleric or religious is ordered to take up residence in an institution already established for the rehabilitation of clerics.

Can. 1338 §1 The deprivations and prohibitions enumerated in Can. 1336 §1 nn.2 and 3 never affect powers, offices, functions, rights, privileges, faculties, favours, titles or insignia, which are not within the control of the Superior who establishes the penalty.

§2 There can be no deprivation of the power of order, but only a prohibition against the exercise of it or of some of its acts; neither can there be a deprivation of academic degrees.

§3 The norm laid down for censures in Can. 1335 is to be observed in regard to the prohibitions mentioned in Can. 1336 §1 n.3.

2677   This canon establishes the parameters for those penalties mentioned in Can. 1336 §1 2°–3°, i.e. those which involve a deprivation of some power, office or function, etc., or a prohibition of the exercise of the same. Firstly, as is the case in Can. 1333 §3 1°, a Superior cannot impose a penalty which deprives someone of office, etc., or prohibits the exercise of an office, etc., which does not come under the jurisdiction of the same Superior, e.g. a Bishop cannot deprive a priest of privileges granted by the Holy See or forbid him to exercise those privileges. Secondly, these expiatory penalties mentioned in Can. 1336 §1 2°–3° can never involve the deprivation of the power of order: once this has been validly received, it cannot be taken away or repeated (see Can. 845 §1). However, the penalty may restrict the exercise of this power of order, wholly or in part, e.g. a prohibition on hearing confessions or preaching in public. Thirdly, such penalties cannot deprive a person of an academic degree which has been awarded. This does not mean, of course, that the penalty cannot restrict the exercise of any power, office, function etc., obtained by reason of such a degree. Finally, so that the people of God may not be deprived of what is necessary for their welfare, the law provides for the suspension of the effects of those expiatory penalties listed in Can. 1336 §1 3° in certain circumstances. Thus, if the penalty prohibited the exercise of the power of order or the power of governance, that prohibition is suspended in order to provide for those members of the faithful who are in danger of death. Moreover, if the penalty incurred was *latae sententiae* and has not been declared, the prohibition, whatever it is, is suspended whenever any member of the faithful, for any just reason, requests a sacrament or sacramental or an act of governance.

---

[1] Cf. Chiappetta I n.4408 note 8.

Chapter III
PENAL REMEDIES AND PENANCES

Can. 1339 §1 When someone is in a proximate occasion of committing an offence or when, after an investigation, there is a serious suspicion that an offence has been committed, the Ordinary either personally or through another can give that person a warning.

§2 In the case of behaviour which gives rise to scandal or serious disturbance of public order, the Ordinary can also reprove the person, in a way appropriate to the particular conditions of the person and of what has been done.

§3 The fact that there has been a warning or a correction must always be proven, at least from some document to be kept in the secret archive of the curia.

2678 Whereas c.2306 of the 1917 Code indicated four kinds of penal remedy (i.e. warning, correction, precept and vigilance), the present canon mentions only two, warning and correction (or reproof). Penal remedies are not penalties in the strict sense: rather, they are preventive interventions by the concerned authority (see Can. 1312 §3). The Ordinary can issue a warning (§1) in order to prevent someone subject to his authority from committing an offence or, if there is an objective reason to believe that an offence has already been committed, to ensure against its recurrence. Such a warning may be given by the Ordinary personally or through a delegate.

2679 In addition to the warning, the Ordinary can also reprove or correct someone (§2) if that person's behaviour is such that it gives rise to scandal or a serious disturbance of the public order. Such correction is to be proportionate, i.e. it must always take account of the specific circumstances of the individual concerned and the type of behaviour involved.

2680 Whether the penal remedy taken is a warning or a correction, the law requires that some written proof be kept of the action taken – whether in a letter or in a written record of what was done orally: in either form, a brief indication of the motives for the penal remedy should be given.[1] Such documents are to be carefully lodged in the secret archive of the curia (see Can. 486 §2).

Can. 1340 §1 A penance, which can be imposed in the external forum, is the performance of some work of religion or piety or charity.

2681 A penance is the performance of a work of religion, piety or charity which has been *imposed* on someone. As such it has a distinctly penal flavour, but it is of a much less serious nature than a censure or an expiatory penalty. Such a penance is to be imposed in the external forum; it must not be confused with the penances imposed in the internal sacramental forum (see Can. 981). In accordance with Can. 1312 §3, a penance may be imposed on a person in place of a penalty (see Cann. 1324 §1, 1343), or in conjunction with a penalty (see Can. 1326 §2), or as part of the process of remission of a penalty (see Can. 1358 §2).

Can. 1340 §2 A public penance is never to be imposed for an occult transgression.

---

[1] Cf. Comm 16(1984) 44 at Can. 1291 §1.

2682 In keeping with the ancient practice of the Church, public penances may be imposed only for public offences. If a person has committed an offence which is occult, i.e. not known or not widely known, the penance imposed by the appropriate authority cannot be such that it would be, or would be likely to become, known in the external forum. Indeed, even in the case of some public offences, the correction of the individual is best served by the imposition of a private penance. This is a matter in which great prudence and discretion is called for on the part of the authority in question.

Can. 1340 §3 According to his prudent judgement, the Ordinary may add penances to the penal remedy of warning or correction.

2683 While penances are understood to be a much milder form of punishment, they can add a certain extra force to the warning or reproof issued by the Ordinary in accordance with Can. 1339 §§1–2. It is for the Ordinary to decide in each individual case whether or not to add such penances.

Title V
The Application of Penalties

Can. 1341 The Ordinary is to start a judicial or an administrative procedure for the imposition or the declaration of penalties only when he perceives that neither by fraternal correction nor reproof, nor by any method of pastoral care, can the scandal be sufficiently repaired, justice restored and the offender reformed.

2684 This opening canon voices an essential element in the philosophy of the Church concerning the application of penalties – a philosophy given its initial thrust by Pope Pius XII,[1] and subsequently endorsed by Vat. II which itself introduced a new outlook and a new spirit into the penal law of the Church. This canon stresses two major principles of the revised penal law: restraint in the use of penalties, and discretion in their application. In a situation where a person has behaved in a reprehensible fashion, the law urges caution: penalties are to be imposed *only as a last resort*. When the Ordinary is made aware of such behaviour, he is to seek to redress the situation by fraternal correction or by a more formal reproof, or by some other means of pastoral care. He is obliged to explore every reasonable measure whereby, without having recourse to penal action, a satisfactory pastoral resolution may be found. To ignore this obligation would in many cases be to run the risk of achieving none of the three objectives listed in the closing words of this canon.

2685 Should all other efforts to repair scandal, restore justice and reform the offender fail to produce the desired effect, then and only then may the Ordinary institute a formal procedure (judicial or administrative) for the imposition or declaration of the appropriate penalty. It is also to be noted that, should a formal judicial penal procedure be selected – as indeed, on occasion, it may have to be – the outcome will no longer be

---

[1] Cf. Pope Pius XII allocutions 5.XII.1954 and 5.II.1955: AAS 47(1955) 60–71, 72–85: *The Pope Speaks* II 1955 17ff.

Part I Offences and Punishments in General

within the control of the Ordinary: it automatically transfers to the (normally) collegiate tribunal entrusted with the case (see Can. 1425 §1 2°, §2).

Can. 1342 §1 Whenever there are just reasons against the use of a judicial procedure, a penalty can be imposed or declared by means of an extra-judicial decree; penal remedies and penances however may in any case whatever be applied by a decree.

At the Revision Commission it was first felt that, if a penalty had to be imposed or declared, the only manner of doing so should be by way of a formal judicial procedure, i.e. by the setting up of a tribunal which would (in accordance with the current Cann. 1721–1728) adjudicate on the matter. This original proposal would have excluded the imposition of a penalty in an administrative manner – in effect i.e. by an extra-judicial or administrative decree by the diocesan Bishop.[1] In the event, it was decided that room should be found for both possibilities: hence this Can. 1342 §1. While very rightly expressing a preference for a judicial procedure in the matter of imposing penalties, it does recognise that if – *but only if* – there is a good reason, based on objective reality, for acting administratively e.g. the need to act quickly in a particular situation, the possibility is open of imposing or declaring a penalty 'by means of an extra-judicial decree'. In so far as this extra-judicial procedure may be adopted, particular care must be taken to ensure that the right of defence of the accused person, consonant with his or her position in the Church, be integrally protected. 2686

There are no restrictions on the application of penal remedies or penances: they may always be applied administratively by decree of the Ordinary. If a penance is to be applied in place of a penalty or in conjunction with a penalty, it would obviously be preferable that this be done as part of the judicial process. 2687

Can. 1342 §2 Perpetual penalties cannot be imposed or declared by means of a decree; nor can penalties which the law or precept establishing them forbids to be applied by decree.

Certain penalties may never be imposed or declared by administrative decree, even if 'just reasons' exist against the use of the judicial process. The first of such is the perpetual penalty, i.e. a penalty whose effect is perpetual, e.g. dismissal from the clerical state (Can. 1336 §1 5°), deprivation of office in some circumstances (Can. 1336 §1 2°), prohibition of the exercise of power in some circumstances (Can. 1336 §1 3°), etc.; in fact, dismissal from the clerical state requires a collegiate tribunal of at least three judges (Can. 1425 §1 2°). Since the consequences of such a penalty are so serious, it is only right that, by requiring a formal judicial process, the law should afford full protection to the rights of the accused. Secondly, the law forbids the use of the administrative procedure in the case of penalties where the law or precept by which they are established explicitly prohibits their application by extra-judicial decree. 2688

Can. 1342 §3 What the law or decree says of a judge in regard to the imposition or declaration of a penalty in a trial, is to be applied also to a Superior who imposes or declares a penalty by an extra-judicial decree, unless it is otherwise clear, or unless there is question of provisions which concern only procedural matters.

In the judicial process, the important central figure is that of the judge; in the administrative procedure, it is the relevant Superior, i.e. the local Ordinary, or the major Superior in the case of members of institutes of consecrated life and societies of 2689

---

[1] Cf. Comm 9(1977) 161 at Can. 28 §1.

apostolic life.[1] In order to avoid any confusion and to promote justice and equity in the matter of the application of penalties, the law provides the principle of equivalence between the judge in the judicial process and the Superior in the administrative procedure. Consequently, what is said of the judge is to be understood as applying also to the Superior in the canons which follow and in other penal laws or precepts, except where it is clear that such an application would have no meaning, or where the law or decree treats of matters of a procedural nature only.

Can. 1343 If a law or precept gives the judge the power to apply or not to apply a penalty, the judge may also, according to his own conscience and prudence, modify the penalty or in its place impose a penance.

2690 The Code contains several canons where the punishment of an offence is facultative rather than obligatory (see e.g. Cann. 1364 §1, 1375, 1384, 1390 §2, 1391, 1393). According to this canon, in these cases, the judge (or Superior – see Can. 1342 §3) is given full discretion to apply a penalty or not. Moreover, even in the application of the penalty, he has the discretion of modifying the penalty suggested by the law; he may even substitute a penance in place of the penalty if the circumstances warrant it. The granting of this discretion was challenged during the work of revision: it was said that it was excessive. However, the Commission made it clear that this canon does not in any way permit arbitrary behaviour on the part of the judge in the application of penalties; rather, the law gives a faculty to the judge to decide what is best and equitable in the circumstances of a given case[2] – a principle which clearly illustrates an accurate appreciation of the role of a judge.

Can. 1344 Even though the law may use obligatory words, the judge may, according to his own conscience and prudence:

1° defer the imposition of the penalty to a more opportune time, if it is foreseen that greater evils may arise from a too hasty punishment of the offender;

2° abstain from imposing the penalty or substitute a milder penalty or a penance, if the offender has repented and repaired the scandal, or if the offender has been or foreseeably will be sufficiently punished by the civil authority;

3° may suspend the obligation of observing an expiatory penalty, if the person is a first-offender after a hitherto blameless life, and there is no urgent need to repair scandal; this is, however, to be done in such a way that if the person again commits an offence within a time laid down by the judge, then that person must pay the penalty for both offences, unless in the meanwhile the time for prescription of penal action in respect of the former offence has expired.

2691 Further illustrating the Code's appreciation of the role of an ecclesiastical judge (as mentioned in our commentary on the preceding canon), this canon extends a degree of discretion to the judge even in cases where 'the law may use obligatory words' in respect of the application of a penalty – in some civil law jurisdictions referred to as a 'mandatory sentence', where in fact no discretion is permitted to the judge. The canon

---

[1] The Revision Commission described these Superiors as 'omnes qui potestatem habent ferendi decreta poenalia': Comm 9(1977) 162 at Can. 28 §3.
[2] Cf. Comm 9(1977) 162 at Can. 29.

insists that this discretion be exercised 'according to (the judge's) own conscience and prudence', not impulsively or on the basis of any whim. Moreover, the situations in which it may be exercised are clearly determined, as follows:

1° The imposition of a penalty may be postponed if its application too soon would create an even worse situation, e.g. if it would lead to widespread scandal. In such a case, the penalty is not suspended, but only delayed: when the threat of 'greater evils' has passed, the penalty is to be imposed upon the offender.

2° Since the fundamental aim of penalties is the reform of the offender or the repair of damage or scandal, if both these ends have been achieved prior to the application of a penalty, the judge is given discretion either to abstain from imposing a penalty altogether or to substitute a less serious penalty or even a penance – another good example of the essentially pastoral nature of the Church's penal law. Moreover, the same discretion is given to the judge in cases where the offender has already been punished sufficiently by the civil authority or where such punishment is justifiably foreseen. In this case, too, the purpose of the penal law has been achieved and there is no need to add to the affliction of the one being punished.[1]

3° If the offender has a clean record prior to the offence, and if there is no urgent need to repair scandal, the judge has the faculty of suspending *expiatory* penalties. This is a situation in which the penalty is indeed incurred but where its observance by the offender is deferred, *pending the verification of certain conditions*: thus, if the offender commits the offence again within a period of time established by the judge, then he or she incurs a double penalty, i.e. one for each offence. The only exception to this is where prescription has extinguished any penal action in respect of the first offence (see Can. 1363).

Can. 1345 Whenever the offender had only an imperfect use of reason or committed the offence out of fear or necessity or in the heat of passion or with a mind disturbed by drunkenness or a similar cause, the judge can refrain from inflicting any punishment if he considers that the person's reform may be better accomplished in some other way.

In Can. 1324, the Code establishes the principle that those who act with diminished imputability are not exempted from penalties but are to be punished in a less severe manner, depending upon the nature of the offence. The present canon is closely related to this principle: it gives the judge the faculty to refrain from imposing a penalty in particular circumstances provided there is reason to believe that the reform of the offender can be achieved better by means other than punishment. The circumstances referred to in the canon are those contained in Can. 1324 §1 1°–3° and 5°. This is a clear application of the fundamental principle underlying the whole Code, namely that the supreme law is the salvation of souls (see Can. 1752): if the desired effect can be attained by other means, the judge has the discretion under the law to set aside punitive action. 2692

Can. 1346 Whenever the offender has committed a number of offences and the sum of penalties which should be imposed seems excessive, it is left to the prudent decision of the judge to moderate the penalties in an equitable fashion.

A further discretion is given to the judge in the case of someone who has committed a number of offences. If the judge considers that the accumulation of penalties in a 2693

---

[1] Cf. Comm 9(1977) 163 at Can. 30a.

particular case is too much for the offender, he has the faculty to adjust the penalties to a more equitable situation. This discretion refers only to the imposition of *ferendae sententiae* penalties. A person who offends several times against laws containing *latae sententiae* penalties incurs a penalty for each new offence, whether or not the penalties are declared.

Can. 1347 §1 A censure cannot validly be imposed unless the offender has beforehand received at least one warning to purge the contempt, and has been allowed suitable time to do so.

§2 The offender is said to have purged the contempt if he or she has truly repented of the offence and has made, or at least seriously promised to make, appropriate reparation for the damage and scandal.

2694 Since the purpose of medicinal penalties is the reform of the offender, the law requires that every effort be made to attain this end before the imposition of penalties. Thus the validity of a censure (see Cann. 1331–1335) is made contingent upon the issuing of a warning to the offender by the appropriate ecclesiastical authority. The law requires that at least one warning be given, urging the offender to 'purge the contempt' and providing a suitable time in which to repent. The meaning of the technical term *purging contempt* is given in §2: it consists of two elements:

(a) the repentance of the offender, i.e. an expression of genuine regret and sorrow concerning the offence committed;

(b) the making of appropriate restitution for any damage done or scandal caused, or at least the making of a serious promise to do this.

If someone has purged contempt in this way, the judge may abstain from inflicting a penalty altogether or may substitute a less onerous penalty (see Can. 1344 2°). The provisions of this canon refer only to *ferendae sententiae* censures; they cannot be extended to expiatory penalties or to *latae sententiae* censures.

Can. 1348 When the person has been found not guilty of an accusation, or where no penalty has been imposed, the Ordinary may provide for the person's welfare or for the public good by opportune warnings or other means of pastoral care, and even, if the case calls for it, by the use of penal remedies.

2695 A penal process may end in different ways, e.g.

(a) there is proof of an offence having been committed and of imputability, and a penalty is imposed;

(b) there is no proof of an offence having been committed and the accused is acquitted, therefore there is no penalty;

(c) there is proof of an offence having been committed but not proof of imputability, so no penalty is imposed.

2696 This canon highlights the fact that sometimes, even if the person was acquitted or if no penalty can be imposed in accordance with Cann. 1322–1323, the ecclesiastical authority may need to take some disciplinary action. By virtue of this canon, the Ordinary[1] is given the faculty in such cases to issue warnings about the behaviour of a person or to make use of other means of pastoral care in order to provide for the individual and common good, e.g. by insisting on appropriate counselling and care in a

---

[1] An earlier draft had spoken of the judge as having this faculty, but it was eventually decided that this action is best taken by the Ordinary: cf. Comm 9(1977) 165 at Can. 32.

Part I Offences and Punishments in General

situation where alcoholism or other such was involved.[1] If the matter was particularly serious, even where no offence has been proved, the Ordinary may issue a formal warning or even a reproof in accordance with Can. 1339 §§1–2.

Can. 1349 If a penalty is indeterminate, and if the law does not provide otherwise, the judge is not to impose graver penalties, especially censures, unless the seriousness of the case really demands it. He may not impose penalties which are perpetual.

Throughout Part II of this Book VI are many canons where a penalty, although prescribed, is not determined: the offender is to be punished 'with a just penalty' (see Cann. 1365, 1368, 1369, 1371, etc.). While the law gives the judge a wide degree of discretion in the matter of reducing penalties, this canon places limits on his discretion in the matter of imposing penalties where a particular one is not determined. Thus, he is not to inflict a more serious penalty unless the particular circumstances of the case warrant it; thus e.g. censures are not to be imposed except in the most serious situations, or unless the law provides for such a possibility (see Cann. 1366, 1373, 1385, 1388 §2). In these situations, the judge is strictly forbidden to impose a perpetual penalty, no matter how serious the offence. 2697

Can. 1350 §1 In imposing penalties on a cleric, except in the case of dismissal from the clerical state, care must always be taken that he does not lack what is necessary for his worthy support.

§2 If a person is truly in need because he has been dismissed from the clerical state, the Ordinary is to provide in the best way possible.

According to Can. 281 §1, clerics have the right to receive sufficient remuneration in order to provide for their necessities, taking due account of the nature of their office and the conditions prevalent in society. The fact that a cleric incurs a penalty, whether automatically or otherwise, does not affect that right, provided that the penalty involved is not dismissal from the clerical state. Whatever other punishment is inflicted upon a cleric, it may never be to the detriment of 'his worthy support'. 2698

Dismissal from the clerical state, however, involves the extinction of the cleric's strict right to support. Yet it does not remove all the obligations of the Ordinary towards the cleric concerned. The Code reminds the Ordinary of his duty to make sure that the dismissed cleric is provided for 'in the best way possible'. In actual practice, this provision of law is to be interpreted as generously as the circumstances of all concerned will permit, bearing in mind that 'equity and evangelical charity' (Can. 702 §2) may never be overlooked. 2699

Can. 1351 A penalty binds an offender everywhere, even when the one who established or imposed it has ceased from office, unless it is otherwise expressly provided.

As a general norm, ecclesiastical penalties are universally binding on those who have incurred them: they affect these persons everywhere, not merely within the territory of the person who imposed the penalty. Moreover, they do not lose their force whenever the authority which established or imposed them has ceased: thus e.g. a penalty does not cease simply because the Bishop who imposed it resigns or otherwise ceases from office. However, as the canon itself indicates, the law or precept establishing the penalty or the decree of judgement imposing it may provide otherwise, e.g. a person 2700

---

[1] It is relevant in this context to mention the offence of paedophilia by a cleric: in this matter, cf. our commentary on Can. 1395 §2.

may be punished by being forbidden to exercise a particular function within a certain diocese, or a penalty may have been imposed by the Bishop or Superior with the clause 'at our pleasure' (*ad beneplacitum nostrum*) or the like attached, in which case it ceases to oblige if the one who imposed it ceases from that office.

Can. 1352 §1 If a penalty prohibits the reception of the sacraments or sacramentals, the prohibition is suspended for as long as the offender is in danger of death.

2701 Since the supreme law in the Church is the salvation of souls (see Can. 1752) and the purpose of penalties is to reform the offender and make good the damage done by the offence or the scandal caused, the law wisely foresees some circumstances in which some penalties may be suspended: they are, after all, only a means to an end. Thus, if a person under excommunication or interdict is in danger of death, he or she may have access to the sacraments or sacramentals according to his or her necessity, and may receive the sacraments of penance, Eucharist, anointing and confirmation. However, should the danger of death truly pass, the obliging force of the penalty returns, unless in the meantime the person in question will have received remission of the penalty in accordance with the relevant terms of Cann. 1355–1361. This norm is closely related to the principles of Cann. 1335 and 1338 §3.

Can. 1352 §2 The obligation of observing a *latae sententiae* penalty which has not been declared, and is not notorious in the place where the offender actually is, is suspended either in whole or in part to the extent that the offender cannot observe it without the danger of grave scandal or loss of good name.

2702 Outside the danger of death, the Code foresees another situation in which a penalty is to be suspended, i.e. where a person has incurred a *latae sententiae* penalty which has not been declared and which is not known to anyone, and where the observance of the penalty would result in serious scandal or the loss of the person's good name. In such circumstances, the penalty is not remitted, rather it is simply suspended, and this suspension lasts as long as the situation persists. In the meantime, there is nothing to hinder the person from seeking the full remission of the penalty in the normal way. Should the penalty become notorious, or should the risk of scandal or infamy cease, then the obligation of observing the penalty is restored.

Can. 1353 An appeal or a recourse against judgements of a court or against decrees which impose or declare any penalty, has a suspensive effect.

2703 When a penalty has been imposed or declared by a tribunal, the person affected by it has the right of appeal to a tribunal of higher instance (see Can. 1628). This tribunal may be the ordinary tribunal of second instance (see Cann. 1438–1439) or the Apostolic Tribunal of the Roman Rota (see Cann. 1443–1444). Similarly, if the penalty has been imposed or declared by an extra-judicial decree, the person affected has the right to have recourse to a higher authority (see Can. 1737), i.e. against a decree of the Bishop, a priest has the right of recourse to the Congregation for the Clergy and, if needs be, from there to the Apostolic Signatura; against a decree of the major Superior, a religious can have recourse to the Congregation for Institutes of Consecrated Life and Societies of Apostolic Life and, again if needs be, to the Apostolic Signatura.

2704 The current law has considerably simplified the rather complex norms in this regard of the 1917 Code. It is important that the principle of this canon be clearly understood: it establishes that *no matter what penalty may be either imposed or declared*, the very fact of an appeal or (as the case may be) a recourse against it automatically suspends its effect and, pending the outcome of the appeal or recourse, eliminates any obligation to observe it: in a word, the status quo, before the penalty, is maintained in its entirety. This is an illuminating insight into the Church's current attitude to penal law and into the concern for the rights of the individual, cleric or lay person (see Cann. 220–221). It is also important that those who feel themselves genuinely aggrieved by being subjected to a penalty should be made aware of this right to appeal or recourse. Experience has taught that a very serious consideration is given to these matters, particularly by the competent organs of the Holy See.

Finally in this regard, it must be noted that the fact that a penalty is suspended in accordance with the foregoing does not prevent the competent local authority (Bishop or major Superior) from taking non-penal steps which in his judgement, knowing the local situation (better perhaps than any law might be able to do) are necessary either for the welfare of the individual or, more particularly perhaps, for the welfare of the faithful in his care: thus e.g. he might judge it necessary or prudent to withdraw from a particular priest the faculty to hear confessions or to preach the word of God. 2705

Title VI
The Cessation of Penalties

Can. 1354 §1 Besides those who are enumerated in Cann. 1355–1356, all who can dispense from a law which is supported by a penalty, can also remit the penalty itself.

§2 Moreover, a law or precept which establishes a penalty can also grant to others the power of remitting the penalty.

Penalties can cease in a variety of ways: 2706

(a) through the death of the person affected;

(b) through completion of the terms of the penalty;

(c) through prescription;

(d) through remission, which is the most common form of cessation.

Whereas the 1917 Code in c.2236 §1 distinguished between the 'dispensation' of expiatory penalties and the 'absolution' of censures, the present Code refers simply to the remission of penalties, whatever the type. The opening canon of this Title establishes the broad principles concerning those who may grant this remission. It contains a reference to Cann. 1355–1356, which establish the limits of the authority of the Ordinary concerning penalties. In addition to these, the law gives the power to remit penalties to 'all those who can dispense from a law which is supported by a penalty'. This includes the one who made the law or precept establishing the penalty, his successor in office and hierarchical superior. Moreover, the law or precept establishing the penalty may identify others to whom it gives the power to remit the penalty, e.g. the Vicar forane for his own territory. Insofar as this power to remit penalties belongs to the external forum, it can be delegated to others by the authorities concerned.

Can. 1354 §3 If the Apostolic See has reserved the remission of a penalty to itself or to others, the reservation is to be strictly interpreted.

2707 While the 1917 Code had many more, in the present Code only five penalties are reserved to the Apostolic See; they are all *latae sententiae* excommunications (see Cann. 1367, 1370 §1, 1378 §1, 1382, 1388 §1). The present canon makes it clear that, wherever the law reserves the remission of the penalty to the Apostolic See or to another authority (e.g. the local Ordinary, the legislator, etc.), the reservation must be interpreted strictly (see Can. 18): by virtue of the law, no one else is capable of remitting such a penalty validly in the external forum. When dealing with a penalty reserved to the Apostolic See, remission in the external forum is to be sought from the appropriate Congregation in Rome. When circumstances call for it, remission in the internal forum from such a penalty may always be sought from the Apostolic Penitentiary.[1]

Can. 1355 §1 Provided it is not reserved to the Apostolic See, a penalty which is established by law and has been imposed or declared, can be remitted by the following:

1° **the Ordinary who initiated the judicial proceedings to impose or declare the penalty, or who by decree, either personally or through another, imposed or declared it;**

2° **the Ordinary of the place where the offender actually is, after consulting the Ordinary mentioned in n.1, unless because of extraordinary circumstances this is impossible.**

2708 This and the following canon establish the scope of the power of the Ordinary in the matter of remitting penalties. Always provided that the penalty is not reserved to the Holy See, the following have the power to remit penalties established by law (whether universal or particular) and which have been imposed or declared:

(a) the Ordinary (see Can. 134 §1) who initiated the judicial penal process according to Can. 1721 §1;

(b) the Ordinary who imposed or declared the penalty by administrative process in accordance with Can. 1720;

(c) the Ordinary of the place where the person affected by the penalty *actually is*; in this case, that local Ordinary must first consult the Ordinary who began the judicial process or imposed or declared the penalty by extra-judicial decree. While in normal circumstances this prior consultation is required for the validity of the remission (see Can. 127 §2 2°), it may be omitted if 'because of extraordinary circumstances (it) is impossible': the judgement in this regard is left to the local Ordinary in question. Moreover, even when the requisite consultation does take place, no more is required for validity (whatever else may be required by prudence and wisdom – a not unimportant consideration); it is not required that the Ordinary consulted give his consent to the proposed remission.[2] Since this power to remit penalties belongs to ordinary executive power, each of the Ordinaries mentioned in this canon can delegate it to another, in accordance with Can. 137 §1.

---

[1] From time to time the Apostolic Penitentiary issues letters to Bishops and major Religious Superiors informing them of the procedures to follow when seeking remission of penalties procedures to be communicated to their priests in a discreet fashion: for examples of such a letter cf. CLD 11 49–52, 52–57.

[2] Cf. Comm 16(1984) 45 at Can. 1307.

Can. 1355 §2 Provided it is not reserved to the Apostolic See, a *latae sententiae* penalty established by law but not yet declared, can be remitted by the Ordinary in respect of his subjects and of those actually in his territory or of those who committed the offence in his territory. Moreover, any Bishop can do this, but only in the course of sacramental confession.

The remission of *latae sententiae* penalties which are established by law, whether universal or particular, are not reserved to the Holy See, and are not officially declared, may be granted by the Ordinary (see Can. 134 §1) in respect of three categories of people: 2709

(a) the subjects of the Ordinary, i.e. all those who are under his jurisdiction, whether he be the local Ordinary or a personal Ordinary in the case of members of clerical religious institutes of pontifical right and their equivalent (see Can. 134 §1);
(b) those living within the territory of the local Ordinary (see Can. 134 §2), even if they are not his subjects;
(c) those who committed the offence within the territory of the local Ordinary, even if they are not his subjects or are not actually living within his territory.

While the above authority of Ordinaries clearly pertains to the external forum – and, as such, may of course be delegated (see Can. 137 §1) – this canon goes on to add a new pastoral element, not found in the 1917 Code. *Any Bishop* (residential, auxiliary, titular, retired) may remit any of the penalties detailed in this canon 'in the course of sacramental confession'. In practice, this opens to the faithful, cleric or layperson, the possibility of going to confession, for this purpose, to any Bishop whom he or she may happen to be able to approach. It is understood of course that the remission of a penalty granted in these circumstances applies only to the internal, and indeed sacramental, forum. 2710

Can. 1356 §1 A *ferendae* or a *latae sententiae* penalty established in a precept not issued by the Apostolic See, can be remitted by the following:

1° **the Ordinary of the place where the offender actually is;**

2° **if the penalty has been imposed or declared, the Ordinary who initiated the judicial proceedings to impose or declare the penalty, or who by a decree, either personally or through another, imposed or declared it.**

§2 Before the remission is granted, the author of the precept is to be consulted, unless because of extraordinary circumstances this is impossible.

Since a penal *precept* is established for an individual or a number of individuals (as distinct from the general application of a penal *law*), the power to remit a penalty attached to such a precept is manifestly more restricted. This canon provides for two possibilities for their remission – on the understanding that the precepts in question have not been 'issued by the Apostolic See': 2711

(a) the local Ordinary of the place where the person affected by the penalty *actually* is can remit all such penalties, howsoever incurred, whether declared or not;
(b) in addition to the local Ordinary, but only if the penalty has been imposed or declared by a judicial or administrative process, the same power to remit is granted to the Ordinary who initiated the judicial or administrative process for the imposition or declaration of the penalty contained in the precept. The Ordinary in this case may be any of those mentioned in Can. 134 §1. Moreover, the faculty of remission is granted to him whether he initiated the judicial or administrative penal process either personally or through another.

2712 The canon (§2) requires that, before remission, the Ordinary in question must consult the author of the penal precept – as in the case mentioned at Can. 1355 §1 2°; and subject to the same conditions as explained above in our commentary on that canon.

Can. 1357 §1 Without prejudice to the provisions of Cann. 508 and 976, a confessor can in the internal sacramental forum remit a *latae sententiae* censure of excommunication or interdict which has not been declared, if it is difficult for the penitent to remain in a state of grave sin for the time necessary for the competent Superior to provide.

2713 Whereas the previous canons of this Title dealt in the main with the competent authority to remit penalties in the external forum, this canon deals with those who have the power to remit them in the internal sacramental forum, and it sets out clearly the terms of that faculty:

(a) The one who remits penalties in this way must be a 'confessor'; therefore the remission can take place only during the celebration of the sacrament of penance. Can. 508 already deals with the faculties of the canon penitentiary of a diocese; Can. 566 §2 grants similar faculties to various chaplains; Can. 976 grants this faculty to any priest when the person seeking remission is in danger of death. This present canon grants the faculty to any ordained priest with the requisite faculty to hear confessions (see Can. 966).

(b) In these circumstances, the priest may remit only *latae sententiae* excommunications or interdicts, provided they have not been declared. Thus, excluded from the faculty given here are all *ferendae sententiae* penalties whether imposed by judicial process or extra-judicially, and all *latae sententiae* penalties which have been declared either judicially or extra-judicially. It is to be noted that even reserved censures may be remitted in this way, provided that the prescriptions of §2 are observed.

(c) This faculty is granted to the confessor subject to the condition that he may remit the censure if the penitent would find it difficult 'to remain in a state of grave sin' while awaiting the decision of the competent authority. Commentators on the 1917 Code, referring to a parallel c.2254 §1, stated that one day's delay was enough to constitute this hardship or even, in the case of clerics or religious, a few hours.[1] In pastoral practice, it should normally be possible for an understanding and competent confessor so to advise and encourage the penitent that he or she would wish to have immediate absolution from sin and remission of penalty. It has long been the tradition of the Church to regard those who come to the sacrament of penance – personally difficult as it may be for some – to be inspired, under God's grace, by none other than a sincere wish to be reconciled with God and with the Church.

Can. 1357 §2 In granting the remission, the confessor is to impose upon the penitent, under pain of again incurring the censure, the obligation to have recourse within one month to the competent Superior or to a priest having the requisite faculty, and to abide by his instructions. In the meantime, the confessor is to impose an appropriate penance and, to the extent demanded, to require reparation of scandal and damage. The recourse, however, may be made even through the confessor, without mention of a name.

---

[1] Cf. Cappello *De censuris* n.124 4°; Vermeersch–Creusen III 454 1 2°.

2714 It will be appreciated that the special faculty given to the confessor in §1 of this canon is specifically designed to provide an immediate peace of mind and of conscience to a repentant person. While thus achieving that pastoral aim, the law wishes also to stress the public gravity of the offences which gave rise to the automatic excommunication or interdict involved here: the excommunication incurred for the offence of abortion (see Can. 1398) would be a not untypical example. Hence this §2 which prescribes the necessary steps consequent upon the remission granted in the internal sacramental forum, the confessor is obliged as follows:

(a) to inform the penitent that he or she must have recourse, within one month, to the appropriate ecclesiastical authority who has power to remit the penalty in the external forum, i.e. as the case may be, a priest with the requisite faculty, the Ordinary mentioned in Cann. 1355–1356, or the appropriate Congregation etc. of the Holy See. The canon does state that this recourse 'may be made through the confessor, without mention of a name': in fact, this is by far the more usual practice, not least because the ordinary penitent would have no idea as to how to go about this procedure. The confessor would get in touch with the appropriate authority, normally in writing, not in any way revealing the identity of the penitent but rather by the use of a fictitious first name (it is understood that *Titius and Bertha* are still in good standing, though in these non-classical days *John and Mary* would do equally well!); the confessor would then obviously arrange for the penitent to return to him, in order to pass on whatever instructions would have been received from the authority in question – instructions which the penitent would be obliged to observe.

(b) to inform the penitent that failure to make this recourse (the obligation of which, as indicated above, will normally be assumed by the confessor) would mean that the penalty would be renewed.

(c) to impose on the penitent a penance appropriate to the gravity of the offence committed: this would normally be a substantial penance (no mere recitation of a few conventional prayers), yet not one which would in any way expose the penitent to any public notice. Moreover, in so far as the situation may require it, he must ask the penitent to do what is reasonably possible, in all the circumstances, to repair the scandal and the spiritual harm to others which may have been caused by the offence (see Can. 1347 §2).

The implementation of these conditions will clearly call for a firm but understanding and sympathetic approach on the part of the confessor.

Can. 1357 §3 The same duty of recourse, when they have recovered, binds those who in accordance with Can. 976 have had remitted an imposed or declared censure or one reserved to the Apostolic See.

2715 In accordance with Can. 976, a penitent who is in danger of death can receive from any priest a remission from 'any censures'; obviously this remission pertains only to the internal forum. Should the penitent recover later, he or she is bound by virtue of this §3 to have recourse to the competent authority in the manner described in §2, *but only if* the internal forum remission received was from a censure that was imposed or declared, or reserved to the Holy See.

Can. 1358 §1 The remission of a censure cannot be granted except to an offender whose contempt has been purged in accordance with Can. 1347 §2. However, once the contempt has been purged, the remission cannot be refused.

2716 Since censures are medicinal penalties whose purpose is to bring about the reform of the offender, they can be remitted only if in fact the person in question has been reformed, i.e. 'if he or she has truly repented of the offence and has made, or at least seriously promised to make, reparation for the damage and scandal' (Can. 1347 §2). If the competent authority is not satisfied that this is the case, the requested remission of a censure is to be refused. On the other hand, if that authority is indeed satisfied that the offender's contempt has been thus purged, remission of the censure cannot be denied. Indeed, where a remission is denied, the individual concerned has the right of recourse (see Cann. 1732ff).

Can. 1358 §2 The one who remits a censure can make provision in accordance with Can. 1348, and can also impose a penance.

2717 If the circumstances so warrant it, the one who remits a censure is granted the faculty of taking further disciplinary steps to care for the good of the individual concerned and for the common good, i.e. he may issue a warning or reproof in accordance with Can. 1339 or even impose a penance in accordance with Can. 1340. It must be stressed that this particular canon refers only to censures, and not to the remission of expiatory penalties which must not only take account of the reform of the offender but also consider any injustice caused by the offence and the damage or scandal caused to others.

Can. 1359 If one is bound by a number of penalties, a remission is valid only for those penalties expressed in it. A general remission, however, removes all penalties except those which in the petition have been concealed in bad faith.

2718 This canon speaks for itself and requires no detailed explanation – save perhaps to remark that the principle governing it accords with that which, dealing with rescripts, is enunciated in Can. 63 §1.

Can. 1360 The remission of a penalty extorted by grave fear is invalid.

2719 Although the general norm stated in Can. 125 §2 is in favour of the validity of a juridical act which has been performed out of grave fear, the law 'may provide otherwise'. The remission of penalties is one such exceptional provision: if 'extorted by grave fear' any remission granted is invalid and the penalty or penalties remain in force.

Can. 1361 §1 A remission can be granted even to a person who is not present, or conditionally.

2720 While the physical presence of a person is required for the reception of sacramental absolution and thus for the remission of censures in the internal sacramental forum (see Can. 1357), this is not required for the remission of penalties in the external forum. A penalty may be remitted by the competent authority even in the case of someone who is absent: a typical, but by no means only, such a situation is that of a penalty reserved to the Holy See. Moreover, a remission may be granted subject to a condition, upon the fulfilment of which, whenever required, will depend the efficacy of the remission.

Can. 1361 §2 A remission in the external forum is to be granted in writing, unless a grave reason suggests otherwise.

2721 In keeping with the general norms of Cann. 37 and 51, the remission of penalties in the external forum is normally to be given in writing, so that if needs be it can be proven. There may, however, in a particular case be 'a grave reason' which would suggest otherwise, e.g. the risk of pernicious or damaging publicity, the danger of a lawsuit in a civil court, etc.

Can. 1361 §3 Care is to be taken that the petition for remission or the remission itself is not made public, except in so far as this would either be useful for the protection of the good name of the offender, or be necessary to repair scandal.

Even if affected by a penalty, a person remains entitled to the preservation of his or her good reputation (see Can. 220). Hence great care should be taken that both the request for remission of a penalty and the remission itself remain strictly confidential communications between the individual and the proper authority. Where recourse is made by a confessor on behalf of a penitent, this confidentiality is assured by the use of conventional pseudonyms and the general anonymity of the petition and the response (see Can. 1357 §2). If the penitent insists on having recourse personally, he or she must be informed of the need to proceed very carefully. The canon does foresee that communications in this regard might be published if this were necessary to protect the good name of an offender who has purged his or her contempt, or to repair the scandal caused. It is considered, however, that any such situation should be highly exceptional and contemplated only with the greatest reserve and care.

Can. 1362 §1 A criminal action is extinguished by prescription after three years, except for:

1° offences reserved to the Congregation for the Doctrine of the Faith;

2° an action arising from any of the offences mentioned in Cann. 1394, 1395, 1397, 1398, which is extinguished after five years;

3° offences not punished by the universal law, where a particular law has prescribed a particular period of prescription.

§2 Prescription runs from the day the offence was committed or, if the offence was enduring or habitual, from the day it ceased.

Prescription (see Can. 197) can affect either the 'criminal action', i.e. the action to establish guilt and inflict a penalty, or the 'penal action', i.e. the action to execute the penalty which has been imposed or declared.[1] As a rule, the Ordinary loses the right to institute a criminal action concerning an offence three years after that offence has been committed. After that time, he cannot initiate a judicial penal process (see Cann. 1717–1728) or proceed extra-judicially to impose or declare a penalty (see Cann. 1342, 1720) in respect of that offence. As is made clear by Can. 198, the offender's good faith is not required during that period.

However, the canon foresees three exceptions to this general rule:

(a) any offence reserved to the Congregation for the Doctrine of the Faith is not affected by prescription. Thus a criminal action in respect of such an offence may be initiated at any time after the offence was committed. There is, regrettably, no official list of the offences thus reserved. Pending the repair of this lacuna, it is widely considered that they include those enumerated in Cann. 1364, 1371 1°, 1378 §1.

(b) a criminal action is extinguished only after five years for the following offences:
 – attempted marriage by a cleric or a religious in perpetual vows (Can. 1394);
 – serious sexual offences committed by a cleric (Can. 1395);

---

[1] Cf. Comm 9(1977) 173–174 at Can. 47.

- murder, abduction, imprisonment, mutilation, etc. (Can. 1397);
- the actual procurement of an abortion (Can. 1398).

(c) in the case of an offence punished by particular law but not by universal law, the criminal action is extinguished after three years unless the relevant particular law has established a different norm.

2725 Prescription in these cases is to be carefully calculated. If it is a matter of a single offence, the period of prescription begins on the day after the offence was committed (see Can. 203 §1); on the other hand, if the offence is ongoing, e.g. the education of children in a non-catholic religion, or if it is part of a series of offences, e.g. continued sexual offences by a cleric, prescription begins on the day after the offence ceased or the day after the last offence took place.

Can. 1363 §1 An action to execute a penalty is extinguished by prescription if the judge's decree of execution mentioned in Can. 1651 was not notified to the offender within the periods mentioned in Can. 1362; these periods are to be reckoned from the day the condemnatory judgement became an adjudged matter.

§2 The same applies, with the necessary adjustments, if the penalty was imposed by an extra-judicial decree.

2726 Whereas the preceding canon dealt with prescription concerning the criminal action, this canon focuses on its effects on the penal action, i.e. the action to impose or execute a penalty. At the end of the judicial penal process, the judge's decree for the execution of the condemnatory sentence (see Can. 1651) must be communicated to the offender within the time limits specified in Can. 1362 §1. Failure to do so results in the extinction of the penal action, i.e. the competent authority will no longer be able to impose a penalty in respect of the offence committed. According to this canon, the periods for prescription are calculated as beginning on the day after the condemnatory sentence became an adjudged matter (see Cann. 203 §1, 1641). Can. 1344 1° and 3° provide for circumstances in which the imposition of a penalty may be deferred or suspended for particular reasons. Should that deferral or suspension exceed the time periods set in Can. 1362 §1, no penalty may be imposed for that offence. In its §2 this canon makes it clear that the norm of §1 applies also to penalties imposed by the administrative process.

PART II

PENALTIES FOR PARTICULAR OFFENCES

Title I
Offences against Religion and the Unity of the Church

Having in Part I of this Book VI outlined the principles governing the various aspects and implications of penal law in the Church, the Code turns here to an enumeration and an explanation of the particular offences which come within the general law. It is recognised, of course, that there may be other offences specified in particular law – diocesan, Bishops' Conference, religious constitutions, etc.: these too are governed by the principles of Part I, except only in so far as an *approved* alternative prescription may be incorporated into the particular law itself. Throughout must be borne in mind the twofold purpose which lies at the heart of our penal law, namely the salvation of souls, and the reparation in so far as possible of the harm which criminal action inflicts upon the People of God. 2727

Can. 1364 §1 An apostate from the faith, a heretic or a schismatic incurs a *latae sententiae* excommunication, without prejudice to the provision of Can. 194 §1 n.2; a cleric, moreover, may be punished with the penalties mentioned in Can. 1336 §1 nn.1, 2 and 3.

According to Can. 751, 'heresy is the obstinate denial or doubt, after baptism, of a truth which must be believed by divine and catholic faith'; apostasy is described as 'the total repudiation of the christian faith'; schism is defined as 'the withdrawal of submission to the Supreme Pontiff or from communion with the members of the Church subject to him'. Before a penalty can be incurred for any of these offences, the act must be gravely imputable and externally manifested (see Cann. 1321 §1, 1330 and our commentary thereon). 2728

One who is guilty of any of these offences incurs a *latae sententiae* excommunication. This was a matter of very considerable debate during the revision of the Code. In its final draft of 1982 the Commission proposed (in its then c.1364 §1) that the penalty should indeed be excommunication but that it be *ferendae sententiae*. In the event, the promulgated text opted to retain the stance of c.2314 of the 1917 Code, retaining the automatic penalty but eliminating the previous reservation to the Holy See.[1] 2729

If the offender is a cleric, the law gives the competent authority the faculty to add further penalties, namely the expiatory penalties listed in Can. 1336 §1 1°–3°. Such 2730

---

[1] For an instructive background to this matter, cf. Comm 9(1977) 305 at Can. 48 §1; 16(1984) 46–47 at Can. 1316.

additional penalties must be imposed by using either the judicial penal process or the administrative process.

2731 The canon contains an explicit reference to Can. 194 §1 2° which deals with the automatic removal from ecclesiastical office of someone who has publicly defected from the catholic faith or from communion with the catholic Church. It is to be noted that this is not an effect of the excommunication incurred for heresy, apostasy or schism; rather is it a provision of the law itself.[1]

Can. 1364 §2 If a long-standing contempt or the gravity of scandal calls for it, other penalties may be added, not excluding dismissal from the clerical state.

2732 In addition to the penalties prescribed in §1, one guilty of apostasy, heresy or schism may be punished further if the case is one of long-standing contempt or a cause of grave scandal to the faithful. The competent authority may impose 'other penalties' upon such persons, whether they are lay or cleric. In the case of a lay person, these are not specified. In the case of a cleric, however, such obstinate behaviour may result in the imposition of dismissal from the clerical state. Whatever the details of an individual case, these extra penalties may be imposed following either a judicial or an extra-judicial process, never arbitrarily. They cannot be established as *latae sententiae* penalties by particular law.

Can. 1365 One who is guilty of prohibited participation in religious rites is to be punished with a just penalty.

2733 This canon raises the question of what, under the 1917 Code, was known as a prohibited *communicatio in sacris*, the most notable example of which was that Code's c.1258 (see also its c.731 §2). Vat. II changed that perspective, as is illustrated e.g. in Cann. 844, 933, 1124–1129. Yet, the problem remains: there is still a 'prohibited participation in religious rites', illustrating the Church's obligatory opposition to practices who go contrary to its very nature as the Church of Christ, such e.g. as would be matters referred to in Cann. 844, 908. It is to such as these that the present canon refers, and it is the transgression of such which, if proven and are juridically imputable, would be subject to the penalty mentioned.

2734 While the penalty itself is obligatory, its nature is not determined in the canon. In determining which penalty ought to be imposed, the authority must take account of several factors, e.g. the gravity of the offence, its frequency, scandal caused; in addition, the impact of any penalty on the ecumenical dialogue in the area and the relevant norms of the Bishops' Conference will have to be weighed carefully. Finally, the authority will bear in mind the discretion accorded by Can. 1344.

2735 This is one of the canons of the Code which highlights the importance, and at the same time the delicacy, of the Church's apostolate towards ecumenism – an essential movement but one which, if the Church is to remain true to itself and to the ultimate success of the ecumenical movement, leaves it with no option but to maintain its fundamental dogmas.

Can. 1366 Parents, and those taking the place of parents, who hand over their children to be baptised or brought up in a non-catholic religion, are to be punished with a censure or other just penalty.

---

[1] Cf. Comm 16(1984) 48 at Can. 1316.

In accordance with Cann. 774 §2, 867 and 868, catholic parents are obliged to have 2736
their children baptised as catholics and educated in the catholic faith. Under c.2319 of
the 1917 Code, parents who gave their children for baptism or education in another
faith were punished by *latae sententiae* excommunication reserved to the Ordinary.
These penalties were abolished by Pope Paul VI.[1] The present discipline leaves it to
the competent authority to impose 'a censure or other just penalty'.

Three offences are mentioned in this canon: 2737

- baptism of children in another faith or denomination;
- education of children in another faith or denomination;
- baptism and education of children in another faith or denomination.

The offence must be committed by parents, whether natural or adoptive, or by those
who take the place of parents e.g. foster parents, guardians etc., in respect of the children who are actually in their care, whether these children are legitimate or
illegitimate, adopted or fostered.

The penalty is to be imposed on those who have deliberately violated this law. 2738
However, great care must be taken in assessing such a situation, especially if it involves
a mixed marriage. The competent authority must be satisfied that there has been a
deliberate violation of the law which is juridically imputable. In the ordinary course
this would not include the decision of parents, taken for a variety of reasons, to send
their children to non-catholic schools for their education. If an appropriate penalty is
to be imposed, the authority must bear in mind the options presented by Can. 1344.

**Can. 1367 One who throws away the consecrated species or, for a sacrilegious
purpose, takes them away or keeps them, incurs a *latae sententiae* excommunication reserved to the Apostolic See; a cleric, moreover, may be punished with
some other penalty, not excluding dismissal from the clerical state.**

As 'the summit and source of all worship and christian life' (Can. 897), the blessed 2739
Eucharist is to be held 'in the highest honour' (Can. 898). Desecration of the
Eucharist is a most heinous offence. This canon indicates what precisely constitutes
the offence: it may be committed in one of three ways:

(a) throwing away the consecrated species: this entails throwing or scattering the
consecrated Hosts or the Precious Blood into an inappropriate place, e.g. on to
the floor of the Church, into a bin, on to the ground. No offence is committed
by one who, through inadvertence, allows a Host, for example, to fall to the
ground while distributing Holy Communion. The offence necessarily involves an
action motivated by disrespect for the sacrament or hatred for the Church.

(b) taking the consecrated species out of its proper place for sacrilegious purposes:
this entails removing the Eucharistic species (usually consecrated Hosts) from the
tabernacle or from the Church for obscene or superstitious reasons, e.g. for use in
satanic, magical or disrespectful rites. The offence is not committed by someone
who, without due authorisation, removes the blessed Sacrament from the tabernacle for devotional purposes or distribution among the faithful.

(c) keeping the consecrated species for sacrilegious reasons: this entails someone
retaining the blessed Sacrament for nefarious purposes such as those mentioned
in (b) above. The offence is not committed by someone who, out of misguided
devotion, retains the blessed Sacrament in his or her personal keeping in contravention of the rule of Can. 935.

---
[1] Cf. Pope Paul VI mp *Matrimonia mixta* 7.I.1970 n.15: Fl I 514.

2740 The penalty incurred for this offence, no matter how it was committed, is very severe: *latae sententiae* excommunication reserved to the Apostolic See. Moreover, if the offender was a cleric, other penalties may be added by the competent authority, including dismissal from the clerical state. In the external forum, the remission of such a penalty may be granted only by the Congregation for the Doctrine of the Faith;[1] in the internal forum, remission may be sought from the Apostolic Penitentiary. According to an instruction from the Congregation of the Sacraments in 1938, in cases where the blessed Sacrament had been desecrated during a sacrilegious theft, an administrative process was to be instituted against the parish priest or rector of the church.[2] This is not mentioned in the Code, but the instruction is cited as one of the sources for Can. 938 §3 concerning the security of the tabernacle. Where it might be thought necessary, such a process could still be instituted.

Can. 1368 A person who, in asserting or promising something before an ecclesiastical authority, commits perjury, is to be punished with a just penalty.

2741 According to Can. 1199 §1, 'an oath is the invocation of the divine Name as witness to the truth'. Anyone taking an oath takes upon themselves a serious obligation before God to tell the truth. Deliberate violation of this obligation is known as perjury. It may be committed in one of two ways: firstly, by knowingly telling lies having taken an oath to tell the truth; secondly, by promising under oath to do something which one has no intention of actually doing. While perjury is always a most serious sin, it is an offence only when it is committed 'before an ecclesiastical authority' – not therefore when committed before a civil court. The taking of an oath is required by the Code on certain occasions, e.g. on assuming certain offices (see Cann. 380, 1454), during the ordinary contentious process (see Cann. 1532, 1562 §2, etc.). If perjury is committed on such an occasion, the canonical offence may arise: the competent authority must establish that there was indeed an external violation of the law which was gravely imputable. When so satisfied, he is to impose a 'just penalty', bearing in mind the discretion given by Can. 1344.

Can. 1369 A person is to be punished with a just penalty, who, at a public event or assembly, or in a published writing, or by otherwise using the means of social communication, utters blasphemy, or gravely harms public morals, or rails at or excites hatred of or contempt for religion or the Church.

2742 The offence mentioned in this canon is rather complex insofar as it may be committed in a number of ways. It must consist of one of the following actions:

- uttering blasphemy in the strict sense, i.e. speaking impiously or contemptuously of God; some commentators consider blasphemy to include speaking in this fashion against the blessed Virgin Mary or the Saints.[3]
- doing something which is gravely harmful or offensive to public morals, e.g. committing an act of obscenity, promoting pornography, etc.
- making direct attacks on the faith and on the Church.
- inciting others to have a hatred or contempt for the faith or the Church.

---

[1] Cf. PB n.52: CCLA 1216–1217.

[2] Cf. SCS instr 26.V.1938 (AAS 30(1938) 198–207) n.10 b: CLD 2 386.

[3] Cf. Chiappetta II n.4481.

For the offence to be committed, this behaviour must take place:

(a) at a public event or meeting, or
(b) in a piece of writing that has been published, or
(c) in some other use of the means of social communication, such as television, radio, cinema.

Once the competent authority has been satisfied that the offence as contained in the canon has been committed and is gravely imputable, he is required by law to impose a 'just penalty'. In doing so, he is to bear in mind the discretion granted in Can. 1344. 2743

Title II
Offences against Church Authorities and the Freedom of the Church

Can. 1370 §1 A person who uses physical force against the Roman Pontiff incurs a *latae sententiae* excommunication reserved to the Apostolic See; if the offender is a cleric, another penalty, not excluding dismissal from the clerical state, may be added according to the gravity of the crime.

§2 One who does this against a Bishop incurs a *latae sententiae* interdict and, if a cleric, he incurs also a *latae sententiae* suspension.

§3 A person who uses physical force against a cleric or religious out of contempt for the faith, or the Church, or ecclesiastical authority or the ministry, is to be punished with a just penalty.

Physical force may result in injury or damage to the person of the Pope (e.g. the result of a gunshot, or a blow), or to his liberty (e.g. if he was kidnapped or imprisoned against his will), or to his dignity (e.g. if someone spat at him, or tore his clothes). Anyone guilty of such physical force against his person – for whatever reason – incurs a *latae sententiae* excommunication reserved to the Holy See. Such an offence is a serious assault on the supreme authority within the Church; the gravity of the offence is matched by the severity of the penalty. Moreover, if the offender was a cleric, the Apostolic See can add a further penalty, including dismissal from the clerical state. 2744

A similar act against the person of a Bishop results in a *latae sententiae* interdict if committed by a lay person, and in a *latae sententiae* suspension if committed by a cleric. In the light of the principle enunciated in Can. 18, the offence can be committed only against the person of a Bishop (residential, auxiliary, titular, retired) who has actually received episcopal ordination. 2745

The canon is completed by provisions for those who use physical force against a priest or deacon or religious. In these cases, the offence must be committed 'out of contempt for the faith, or the Church, or ecclesiastical authority or the ministry'. Consequently, such an action perpetrated out of personal hatred or revenge or self-defence does not fall under the scope of this canon. If the competent authority is 2746 satisfied that the offence has been committed and is gravely imputable, the offender is to be punished with a just penalty (see Can. 1344). Since this canon must be interpreted strictly in accordance with Can. 18, the offence concerns all members of religious institutes (see Can. 607) but only the clerical members of secular institutes or societies of apostolic life.

Can. 1371 The following are to be punished with a just penalty:

1° **a person who, apart from the case mentioned in Can. 1364 §1, teaches a doctrine condemned by the Roman Pontiff, or by an Ecumenical Council, or obstinately rejects the teaching mentioned in Can. 752 and, when warned by the Apostolic See or by the Ordinary, does not retract;**

2° **a person who in any other way does not obey the lawful command or prohibition of the Apostolic See or the Ordinary or Superior and, after being warned, persists in disobedience.**

2747 Three separate offences are dealt with in this canon:

(a) teaching a doctrine which has been condemned by the Pope or by an Ecumenical Council and refusing to desist or retract when warned to do so by the Apostolic See or the Ordinary; this offence is quite distinct from that of heresy (see Can. 1364);

(b) obstinately rejecting a doctrine which the Pope or the College of Bishops declare on a matter of faith or morals when they exercise their authentic magisterium, even though they do not intend to proclaim that doctrine by definitive action (see Can. 752), and refusing to retract this rejection when so warned by the Apostolic See or the Ordinary;

(c) persistently failing to obey the lawful commands or prohibitions of the Pope, the Ordinary or one's legitimate Superior.

2748 Common to all three offences is obstinacy, i.e. persistence in the offensive behaviour after a warning has been given and failure to make the necessary retraction or obey the injunctions of the competent authority. In all cases, provided the required warnings have been issued and provided all that pertains to proof and imputability have been carried out, the offender is to be punished by a just penalty. This is to be imposed either by the Apostolic See (i.e. the Congregation for the Doctrine of the Faith)[1] or, as the case may demand, by the Ordinary (i.e. the offender's local or proper Ordinary).

Can. 1372 A person who appeals from an act of the Roman Pontiff to an Ecumenical Council or to the College of Bishops, is to be punished with a censure.

2749 According to Can. 331, the Pope 'by virtue of his office, ... has supreme, full, immediate and universal ordinary power in the Church'. Consequently, 'there is neither appeal nor recourse against a judgement or decree of the Roman Pontiff' (Can. 333 §3) and 'the First See is judged by no one' (Can. 1404). During the fourteenth and fifteenth centuries efforts had been made to establish the principle of the supremacy of the Ecumenical Council in the authority of the Church,[2] but these efforts did not

---

[1] Cf. PB n.51.
[2] Council of Constance sess IV–V 30 March and 6 April 1415: *Conciliorum Oecumenicorum Decreta* 408–409.

succeed.[1] Any appeal against an act of the Pope would suggest the existence in the Church's structure of a higher authority, a clear contradiction of the principle of Can. 331 and an assault on the position and authority of the Roman Pontiff. It is important to note that the offence concerns an effort to seek redress against an act of the Roman Pontiff, not an act of the Roman Curia unless of course that act has received a *specific confirmation* by the Pope (see Can. 1405 §2). Moreover, the appeal or recourse must be made to the Ecumenical Council if it is in session or, in some other way, to the College of Bishops. One who has offended in this way is to be punished by the imposition of an excommunication or an interdict or a suspension, as considered appropriate in the circumstances.

Can. 1373 A person who publicly incites his or her subjects to hatred or animosity against the Apostolic See or the Ordinary because of some act of ecclesiastical authority or ministry, or who provokes the subjects to disobedience against them, is to be punished by interdict or other just penalties.

This canon is concerned solely with offences which may be committed by those who are *in a position of authority*: this would clearly include Bishops, Bishops' Conferences, local ecclesiastical Councils, religious Superiors and religious Chapters, etc.; it is at least probable that it would also include catholic civil political leaders. The thrust of the canon concerns those who, in one way or another, would attempt to influence 'his or her subjects' to oppose the authority of the Church. 2750

The canon deals with two specific offences. The first has to do with the *public* incitement of one's subjects to hatred or animosity towards the Apostolic See or the Ordinary, as the result of some act of ecclesiastical government or ministry performed by either, e.g. a statement by the Pope or the Ordinary concerning a major social issue. The incitement may take the form of published writings, public speeches, radio or television interventions, and the like. The second offence has to do with the provocation of one's subjects to actual disobedience of the directives of the Apostolic See or the Ordinary on a particular issue – more than simple protest at a particular policy of the ecclesiastical authority concerned. 2751

In both offences, it must be clear that the intention of the person in authority was to incite opposition or provoke disobedience, i.e. there must be some form of deliberate aim to oppose the legitimate authority of the Church: the mere fact that a person's subjects reacted in a certain way following a statement of their superior would not alone constitute unequivocal proof of this offence. The punishment foreseen by the Code for such offences is serious: the canon obliges the competent ecclesiastical authority to inflict an 'interdict or other just penalties'. The severity of the actual penalty will depend on the extent of the harm done to the good of the faithful by the offence. 2752

Can. 1374 A person who joins an association which plots against the Church is to be punished with a just penalty; one who promotes or takes office in such an association is to be punished with an interdict.

According to c.2335 of the 1917 Code, anyone who enrolled in the freemasons or similar societies incurred a *latae sententiae* excommunication. The present canon is much broader than its predecessor in the terminology it uses: there is no specific mention of freemasonry; rather the canon speaks of 'an association which plots against the Church'. During the revision process, there was a strong movement for the retention of explicit mention of freemasonry in this canon. The German Bishops, 2753

---

[1] Cf. Pope Pius II Bull *Exsecrabilis* 18.I.1460: DS 1375.

in particular, wanted this because of the incompatibility between freemasonry and the christian faith. In the event, it was decided to adopt the present wording: this was more in keeping with the principle of reducing automatic penalties; it included adherence to atheistic communism which was often much more damaging to the Church than freemasonry; and it took account of the fact that freemasonry was not felt to be the same all over the world, so that particular law could deal more accurately with this matter.[1]

2754 In the meantime, the Congregation for the Doctrine of the Faith had reiterated the effects of c.2335 of the 1917 Code for those who joined masonic groups.[2] On the day before the present Code came into effect, the same Congregation repeated the Church's negative decision concerning freemasonry, pointing out that those who enrol in such movements are in serious sin and prohibited from receiving Communion. Moreover, it reminded local ecclesiastical authorities that they could not make any judgement concerning masonic societies which derogated from the Church's negative decision.[3] This is still a matter of some difference of opinion among canonists, and it would appear that it is one which will have to be resolved at a local level, depending in great measure on the precise status and impetus of the freemason institution in the area.

2755 The canon details two offences related to membership of such organisations, for each of which a different penalty is to be imposed:

(a) in the case of someone who enrols in such an association, a just penalty is to be imposed;

(b) in the case of someone who promotes membership of such an association or accepts office within it, the penalty to be imposed is an interdict, since this activity is more directly involved and accordingly more harmful to the authority of the Church.

Can. 1375 Those who hinder the freedom of the ministry or of an election or of the exercise of ecclesiastical power, or the lawful use of sacred or other ecclesiastical goods, or who intimidate either an elector or one who is elected or one who exercises ecclesiastical power or ministry, may be punished with a just penalty.

2756 This canon contains a brief catalogue of various offences against freedom within the Church. The competent ecclesiastical authority is to impose a just penalty on the following:

– anyone who deliberately and successfully prevents the free exercise of an ecclesiastical ministry;

– anyone who deliberately and successfully prevents the free exercise of ecclesiastical authority or the discharge of an ecclesiastical office;

– anyone who deliberately and successfully prevents the free conduct of an ecclesiastical election;

– anyone who deliberately and successfully obstructs the free and lawful use of sacred goods (see Can. 1171) or ecclesiastical goods (see Can. 1257 §1);

---

[1] Cf. Comm 16(1984) 49 at Can. 1326; Congregatio Plenaria 1981 150–168 (this includes the full text of the German Bishops' submission dated May 1980), 308–333 (this includes the full discussion of the matter at the final Plenary Session of the Commission).
[2] Cf. SCDF instr 17.II.1981: CLD 9 1003–1004.
[3] Cf. SCDF instr 26.XI.1983: CLD 10 285.

- anyone who deliberately intimidates another who is participating in an ecclesiastical election, whether actively or passively, whether or not the intimidation succeeds;
- anyone who deliberately intimidates another who exercises or discharges some ecclesiastical office or power, whether or not the intimidation succeeds;
- anyone who deliberately intimidates another who is engaged in an ecclesiastical ministry, whether or not the intimidation succeeds.

Can. 1376 A person who profanes a sacred object, movable or immovable, is to be punished with a just penalty.

Anything which has been set aside for divine worship through dedication or blessing is regarded by law as a sacred object (see Can. 1171). These are to be treated at all times with reverence and may never be made over to secular or inappropriate uses. Sacred objects may be movable (e.g. sacred vessels, vestments, statues, holy oils, etc.) or immovable (e.g. an altar, a church, a cemetery). This canon complements Can. 1171's exhortation to treat these objects with the greatest respect by making it clear that it is an offence to use any such object for profane purposes, i.e. for any purpose other than those liturgical and devotional uses for which they were dedicated or blessed. Depending on the nature and gravity of the profanation, the sacredness of the object involved, and the amount of harm and scandal caused, the competent authority is to punish the offender with a just penalty, bearing in mind the discretion granted by Can. 1344. The consequences of the profanation of a sacred place are especially serious (see Can. 1211).

Can. 1377 A person who without the prescribed permission alienates ecclesiastical goods, is to be punished with a just penalty.

Ecclesiastical goods are understood to be all those temporal goods 'belonging to the universal Church, to the Apostolic See or to other public juridical persons in the Church' (Can. 1257 §1). These are to be administered in accordance with the law of the Church. Alienation refers to the transfer of ownership of these goods to another, as well as to 'any dealings by which the patrimonial condition of the juridical person may be jeopardised' (Can. 1295). For the validity of such transactions, the law lays down that the permission of the competent ecclesiastical authorities, at the appropriate level, must be obtained beforehand (see Cann. 638 §3, 1291–1292).

Moreover, by virtue of this canon the person who maliciously or culpably fails to obtain the required permission is understood to have committed a canonical offence. In such a situation, the competent ecclesiastical authority must impose a penalty, taking into account the gravity of the situation resulting from the alienation and any scandal caused. Although it is invalid in canon law, the transaction may be valid according to the local civil law; in this case, the ecclesiastical authority will decide to take whatever action is appropriate in the circumstances to vindicate the rights of the Church (see Can. 1296).

Title III
Usurpation of Ecclesiastical Offices and Offences committed in their Exercise

Can. 1378 §1 A priest who acts against the prescription of Can. 977 incurs a *latae sententiae* excommunication reserved to the Apostolic See.

2760 According to Can. 977, 'the absolution of a partner in a sin against the sixth commandment of the Decalogue is invalid, except in danger of death': apart from that danger, any priest who knowingly attempts to absolve an accomplice in such a sin commits a very serious offence. The essential elements of this offence are:
- an external sin against the sixth commandment which takes place between the priest and another person, i.e. it must be much more than a purely internal sin;
- knowingly hearing the sacramental confession of this accomplice and attempting to give absolution.

2761 This canon must be interpreted strictly: accordingly, no offence is committed in the following circumstances:
- if the priest listens to the confession but does not give absolution;
- if the priest absolves the accomplice without in any way realising that he or she was in fact his accomplice;
- if the priest does not specifically recognise the accomplice or has doubts concerning his or her identity.

2762 In keeping with Can. 1321 §§1–2, there must be malice or culpability on the part of the priest before any penalty can be incurred. The canon lays down a *latae sententiae* excommunication reserved to the Apostolic See for this offence, a clear indication of the gravity with which the Church views such an offence.

Can. 1378 §2 The following incur a *latae sententiae* interdict or, if a cleric, a *latae sententiae* suspension:

1° a person who, not being an ordained priest, attempts to celebrate Mass;

2° a person who, apart from the case mentioned in §1, though unable to give valid sacramental absolution, attempts to do so, or hears a sacramental confession.

§3 In the cases mentioned in §2, other penalties, not excluding excommunication, can be added according to the gravity of the offence.

2763 Two separate offences related to the priestly ministry are covered by §2 of this canon. The first has to do with the celebration of Mass. Since only a validly ordained priest[1] can celebrate Mass (see Can. 900 §1), anyone else attempting to do so commits a very serious offence. This offence is not committed by a priest who celebrates Mass even though excommunicated, suspended, dispensed or dismissed from the clerical state: a celebration of this kind would be valid, though unlawful. The offence involved here is that of a lay man or woman, or even a deacon, who goes through the rites prescribed for the Mass in an attempt to celebrate the Eucharist, whether publicly or in private.

---

[1] The term used is *sacerdos*, which includes priests and Bishops.

The second offence dealt with in this paragraph concerns the celebration of the sacrament of penance. Only a priest is the minister of this sacrament (see Can. 965); in addition to the power of orders, the law requires that the priest also have the faculty to absolve sins (Can. 966 §1). Consequently, any lay person, or deacon, or priest who has not the faculty to absolve, who purports to hear a sacramental confession and give sacramental absolution commits a serious offence. The fact that, in the case of a priest, the law itself may in certain circumstances supply the necessary jurisdiction (see Can. 144) would not seem to alter the position of a priest who, knowing that he has not the faculty to absolve, would deliberately set out to hear a sacramental confession and to give absolution. The position could be different if, given the circumstances of a particular case, the priest, knowing his law, were deliberately to decide to rely upon the faculty provided by Can. 144.

The law prescribes an automatic punishment for both these offences: lay people who commit such offences incur a *latae sententiae* interdict; a deacon or a priest incurs a *latae sententiae* suspension. Furthermore, a deacon who has committed either of these offences is irregular for the reception and exercise of orders (see Cann. 1041 6°, 1044 §1 3°).

In accordance with §3 of this canon, should the competent authority consider it necessary, further penalties may be imposed on such offenders, taking account of the gravity of what was done. Because of the intrinsic seriousness of any offence involving the celebration of the sacraments, the law foresees the possibility that the competent authority may decide to impose excommunication on an offender in a particular case.

Can. 1379 A person who, apart from the cases mentioned in Can. 1378, pretends to administer a sacrament, is to be punished with a just penalty.

A person can pretend to administer a sacrament in various ways:

(a) if he does not have the required order or faculty, e.g. the cases described in Can. 1378 §§1–2, someone not a priest who attempts to anoint the sick or administer confirmation in danger of death, someone not a Bishop who attempts to ordain another, etc.;

(b) if materials are used other than those required, e.g. baptising in milk, or anointing with water; a somewhat similar situation arises if a person distributes unconsecrated hosts at Holy Communion;

(c) if the person does not have the proper intention when administering the sacrament, e.g. if he or she deliberately intends not to do 'what the Church intends' in baptising an infant.

In all of these cases, the sacrament will have been invalid, and the minister concerned will have committed an offence.[1] The law prescribes that such persons should be punished with a just penalty, leaving the determination of the penalty to the competent authority.

Can. 1380 A person who through simony celebrates or receives a sacrament, is to be punished with an interdict or suspension.

According to c.727 §1 of the 1917 Code, simony may be defined as the deliberate intention to buy or sell for a temporal price something which is intrinsically sacred such as the sacraments, ecclesiastical jurisdiction, consecration, blessing, indulgences, etc. While the present Code does not explicitly incorporate these canons on

---

[1] In the case of a minister who withheld the proper intention, it will not be possible to prove an external violation of this law unless the minister openly admits the offence. Not included in this canon are those spouses of whom at least one has simulated consent, or a minister who has assisted at a wedding knowing that he did not have due delegation: cf. Chiappetta II n.4499.

Book VI Sanctions in the Church

simony, it does include the negative consequences of this offence, e.g. according to Can. 149 §3, the provision of an office by simony is invalid. Anyone who deliberately sets out to celebrate a sacrament in return for material gain, e.g. money or other goods, and anyone who deliberately receives the sacrament having expended temporal goods for that purpose is said to have committed the canonical offence of simony.

2770 This offence is not to be confused with the legitimate practice of making and receiving offerings on the occasion of sacramental celebrations. In order to prevent abuses and misunderstanding, the law regulates this practice (see Cann. 531, 848, 945 §2, 952, 1181), particularly to ensure that the poor are not deprived of the services of the clergy for reasons of penury.

2771 For the offence of simony, the law prescribes a *ferendae sententiae* penalty: the competent authority, satisfied that there has been an external violation of the law which is gravely imputable, must impose an interdict; if the offender is a cleric, the authority has the further faculty of imposing a suspension: since the law makes no qualification of this, the suspension is understood to be general (see Can. 1333 §1).

Can. 1381 §1 Anyone who usurps an ecclesiastical office is to be punished with a just penalty.

§2 The unlawful retention of an ecclesiastical office after being deprived of it, or ceasing from it, is equivalent to usurpation.

2772 'An ecclesiastical office is any post which by divine or ecclesiastical disposition is established in a stable manner to further a spiritual purpose' (Can. 145 §1). The requirements for the provision of an ecclesiastical office are contained in Cann. 146–183. If these norms are not followed, the office is to be regarded as vacant. Usurpation of an ecclesiastical office is said to take place when someone attempts to occupy an office for which provision has not been made in accordance with the relevant law (§1).

2773 Equivalent to usurpation (§2) is the unlawful retention of an office after the person concerned has been deprived of it (see Can. 196) or after the office has ceased in accordance with the law, i.e. upon expiry of the predetermined term of office, or resignation, or transfer or removal (see Cann. 184–195).

2774 The law requires that such offenders be punished. It leaves the determination of the actual penalty to the competent authority. This must be decided according to the particular circumstances of each case. In doing so, the authority will also be mindful of the discretion granted by Can. 1344.

Can. 1382 Both the Bishop who, without a pontifical mandate, consecrates a person a Bishop, and the one who receives the consecration from him, incur a *latae sententiae* excommunication reserved to the Apostolic See.

2775 One of the prerequisites for a lawful episcopal ordination is the issuing of an apostolic mandate (see Can. 1013) since, according to Can. 377 §1, the Supreme Pontiff freely appoints Bishops or confirms those lawfully elected. An episcopal ordination without such a mandate would normally be valid, but it constitutes a grave breach of the law and is a very serious offence. Both the Bishop who ordains and those who are ordained incur a *latae sententiae* excommunication reserved to the Apostolic See. The 1917 Code in its c.2370 had prescribed automatic suspension as the penalty; however, Pope Pius XII decided that the penalty ought to be a *latae sententiae* excommunication reserved in a very special way to the Apostolic See.[1]

Can. 1383 A Bishop who, contrary to the provision of Can. 1015, ordained someone else's subject without the lawful dimissorial letters, is prohibited from conferring orders for one year. The person who received the order is *ipso facto* suspended from the order received.

Prior to ordaining to the diaconate or to the priesthood those who are not his subjects, a Bishop must receive dimissorial letters (see Cann. 1015 §1, 1019 §1) from the proper Ordinary of the ordinands. These are issued after all has been done to ascertain the suitability of these candidates for ordination (see Cann. 1020, 1050–1051). If a Bishop proceeds to ordain someone without these letters, he will have committed an offence. In the matter of the penalty, the law makes a distinction between the Bishop who ordains and those who are ordained:

(a) the ordaining prelate incurs an automatic prohibition from conferring orders[2] for one year;

(b) those ordained in this way are automatically suspended from the exercise of the order received on that occasion.

Can. 1384 A person who, apart from the cases mentioned in Cann. 1378–1383, unlawfully exercises the office of a priest or another sacred ministry, may be punished with a just penalty.

Cann. 1378–1383 deal with particularly serious offences related to the exercise of sacred ministry and ecclesiastical office. This canon establishes as an offence any other unlawful exercise of priestly office or sacred ministry. The law leaves it to the competent authority to determine whether or not a 'just penalty' is to be imposed. There was no corresponding canon in the 1917 Code. It is clear that, depending upon the local pastoral situation, a distinct sensitivity must be employed in deciding that a penalty is called for, bearing in mind particularly the discretion granted by Can. 1343.

Can. 1385 A person who traffics for profit in Mass offerings is to be punished with a censure or other just penalty.

The offering made for the celebration of the Mass is very carefully regulated by Cann. 945–958. According to Can. 947, even the appearance of trafficking or trading in these offerings must be excluded. This canon reinforces such an exclusion by prescribing a punishment for those who offend in this way. The offence is committed when someone benefits unlawfully from the money or goods received for the celebration of the Mass, e.g.:

2776

2777

2778

---

[1] Cf. SCSO decr 9.IV.1951: CLD 3 649. This penalty was declared in the case of Archbishop Pierre Martin Ngô-dinh-Thuc who ordained priests and Bishops in 1976 and again in 1983: cf. SCDF decr 17.IX.1976: CLD 8 1216–1217; decr 12.III.1983: CLD 10 285–287. In 1988, Archbishop Marcel Lefebvre and those ordained by him incurred this same penalty of automatic excommunication reserved to the Holy See and this penalty was formally declared by the Congregation for Bishops: cf. SCB decr I.VII.1988: Origins 18(1988) 151; Pope John Paul II lit ap *Ecclesia Dei adflicta* 2.VII.1988: AAS 80(1988) 1495–1498: Origins 18(1988) 149–152. In that declaration, however, it is stated that the co-consecrating Bishop incurred a *latae sententiae* excommunication for schism (see Can. 1364). Consequently, it would appear that the penalty prescribed in this canon affects only the principal consecrating Bishop and those who receive consecration from him.

[2] Although the latin text uses the singular (*ordinem conferre*), the clear sense would appear to involve a prohibition from the conferring of *any order*: hence the translation 'conferring orders'.

- a priest who accumulates offerings against the prescriptions of Can. 948 and the decree *Mos iugiter*[1];
- a priest who takes more than one offering each day against the prescription of Can. 951;
- a priest who requires an offering higher than that established in accordance with Can. 952;
- a priest who retains part or all of the offering when transferring the obligation of celebrating Mass in accordance with Cann. 955 §1, 956.

The offence may also be committed by those who have the responsibility of receiving offerings for Mass at churches, shrines and places of pilgrimage.

2779 When satisfied that there has been an external violation of the law which is gravely imputable, the competent authority is obliged to impose on the offender a censure or some other just penalty, to be determined by the gravity and frequency of the offence and the harm or scandal caused.

Can. 1386 A person who gives or promises something so that some one who exercises an office in the Church would unlawfully act or fail to act, is to be punished with a just penalty; likewise, the person who accepts such gifts or promises.

2780 Bribery is a deliberate attempt to persuade someone to do or to omit something in return for money or some other recompense; what is to be done or omitted must be in favour of the one offering the bribe. Anyone who attempts to bribe a person exercising ecclesiastical office commits the offence mentioned in this canon; so, too, does the person who accepts the bribe. The competent authority is obliged to punish both parties with a just penalty, bearing in mind the discretion permitted by Can. 1344.

2781 Subornation of this kind must not be confused with the acceptable practice of giving something as an expression of gratitude after some favour has been received. It is to be noted, however – as Can. 1456 makes clear – that judges and all who work in ecclesiastical tribunals are forbidden to accept any gifts on the occasion of a trial; indeed, special penal provisions are made for advocates and procurators who offend in this way (see Cann. 1488–1489).

Can. 1387 A priest who in confession, or on the occasion or under the pretext of confession, solicits a penitent to commit a sin against the sixth commandment of the Decalogue, is to be punished, according to the gravity of the offence, with suspension, prohibitions and deprivations; in the more serious cases he is to be dismissed from the clerical state.

2782 The offence of solicitation is committed by a priest who seeks to persuade a penitent to commit a sin against the sixth commandment. Liability for the penalty involved requires that the solicitation take place in any one of the following situations:

(a) 'in confession', i.e. during the actual celebration of the sacrament of penance;

(b) 'on the occasion of confession', i.e. immediately before or after the celebration of the sacrament of penance;

(c) 'under the pretext of confession', i.e. in a place designated for the celebration of the sacrament of penance or a place used by the priest on the understanding that he is going to celebrate the sacrament of penance.

---

[1] SCC decr *Mos iugiter* 22.II.1991: AAS 83(1991) 443–446; Origins 20 705–706.

The offence is committed whether the priest encourages the penitent to sin either with 2783
the priest himself or with any third party; he may commit the offence by words, signs,
gestures or writing.[1] The offence consists of the action of the priest: it is not necessary
that the penitent accede to the suggestions made; consequently, even if nothing further occurs, the offence has been committed and the priest is liable to the penalty.

As soon as the competent authority has been informed, action must be taken. 2784
According to c.904 of the 1917 Code, the penitent was obliged to denounce the confessor to the local Ordinary or the Holy Office within one month; failure to do meant that the penitent incurred a *latae sententiae* excommunication (see c. 2368 §2 of the 1917 Code); this obligation no longer exists. While the Congregation for the Doctrine of the Faith is competent to deal with these cases in so far as they may be reported to it,[2] the matter may normally be dealt with at local level, once the local Ordinary has been made aware of the offence. The penalty for the offence is severe: the priest is to be suspended, involving the general suspension envisaged by Can. 1333 §1; in addition, the competent authority must also prescribe appropriate prohibitions and deprivations (see Can. 1336 §1 1°–3°) – and 'in the more serious cases (the priest) is to be dismissed from the clerical state'. In all of this matter, however and before any affective action is taken, the local Ordinary must exercise the greatest care and specific investigation to ensure that the allegations made to him are well-founded and true; in this context, he will obviously bear in mind the risks envisaged by Cann. 1390 §1, 982.

Can. 1388 §1 A confessor who directly violates the sacramental seal incurs a *latae sententiae* excommunication reserved to the Apostolic See; he who does so only indirectly is to be punished according to the gravity of the offence.

According to Can. 983 §1, the seal of sacramental confession 'is inviolable': the con- 2785
fessor may never, for any reason, divulge what he has learned in the course of celebrating the sacrament. Should he do so, he commits a most serious offence. The canon distinguishes between direct and indirect violation of the seal:

– direct violation occurs when a confessor deliberately[3] discloses the identity of the penitent and the contents of a confession, either explicitly or implicitly;
– indirect violation occurs when the confessor negligently says or does or fails to do something which leads others to conclude or suspect the identity of the penitent and the content of the confession.

In the case of direct violation, the law imposes a *latae sententiae* excommunication 2786
reserved to the Holy See – in effect, to the Congregation for the Doctrine of the Faith.[4] In the case of indirect violation, the competent authority is required by law to impose a penalty 'according to the gravity of the offence': in doing so, that authority will bear in mind the provisions of Can. 1349.

Can. 1388 §2 Interpreters and the others mentioned in Can. 983 §2, who violate the secret, are to be punished with a just penalty, not excluding excommunication.

---

[1] Cf. Pope Benedict XIV ap con *Sacramentum Poenitentiae* 1.VI.1741 n.1: Document V attached to the 1917 Code (Document III in editions after 8.XII.1945).
[2] Cf. PB n.52.
[3] Cf. Comm 16(1984) 50 at Can. 1340.
[4] Cf. PB n.52.

2787 While the sacramental seal primarily binds the confessor, all others, including interpreters, who in any way, lawfully or unlawfully, come to know the contents of a confession are also bound (see Can. 983 §2). Should they violate this obligation, the law requires that the competent authority punish them with a just penalty; since anything pertaining to the sacrament of penance is a very grave matter, the penalty imposed, according to the circumstances of the case, may be excommunication.

2788 In 1973, the Sacred Congregation for the Doctrine of the Faith, by virtue of special authority granted by the Pope, decreed that anyone who obtained the contents of confessions and sought to publish or divulge them was excommunicated automatically.[1] In the context of a widely publicised case, this sanction was repeated by the same Congregation in 1988: 'whoever by any technical instrument records or publishes in the mass media what was said in sacramental confession by the confessor or the penitent, real or feigned, by himself or herself or another, incurs *latae sententiae* excommunication'.[2]

Can. 1389 §1 A person who abuses ecclesiastical power or an office, is to be punished according to the gravity of the act or the omission, not excluding by deprivation of the office, unless a penalty for that abuse is already established by law or precept.

§2 A person who, through culpable negligence, unlawfully and with harm to another, performs or omits an act of ecclesiastical power or ministry or office, is to be punished with a just penalty.

2789 All power in the Church, whether of order or of jurisdiction, and every role or office, is to be exercised for the good of the faithful. The Code contains several penalties for specific abuses of ecclesiastical power and office (see e.g. Cann. 1378 §1, 1382, 1383, 1387, etc.). This canon establishes a general principle in respect of any abuse of such power or office (§1). The text must be interpreted strictly in accordance with Can. 18, i.e. there must be a deliberate misuse of one's authority or position which results in injustice or injury to others. In these cases, the law obliges the competent authority to punish the offender with a penalty proportionate to the gravity of the offence. Because of the nature of the offence, the law foresees the possibility that the offender might be deprived of his or her office or power.

2790 Harm or injury may also be caused to the faithful by the culpable negligence of those who exercise power or ministry or any function within the Church (§2). This offence occurs when someone, without due diligence, illicitly does or omits something in the exercise of his or her authority or ministry which results in harm to another. Such an offence must be punished with a just penalty. Moreover, in accordance with Can. 128 the person responsible is obliged to make reparation for whatever harm or damage has resulted from his or her abuse or negligence, and anyone who has suffered as a consequence of one of the offences described in this canon can institute an action for compensation in accordance with Can. 1729 §1.

---

[1] Cf. SCDF decr 23.II.1973: CLD 8 1214–1215.

[2] Cf. SCDF decr: AAS 80(1988) 1367. The decree does not carry a date but it states that it is effective from the date of promulgation, i.e. 23.IX.1988.

Title IV
The False Accusation

Can. 1390 §1 A person who falsely denounces a confessor of the offence mentioned in Can. 1387 to an ecclesiastical Superior, incurs a *latae sententiae* interdict and, if a cleric, he also incurs a suspension.

Since the offence mentioned in Can. 1387 is a particularly serious one, any priest guilty of that offence must certainly be reported to the competent authority. On the other hand, it must be noted that, in this situation as in many others, a confessor is in a very delicate and vulnerable position, being clearly open to the risk of a false accusation against which he may, precisely because he is a confessor, be unable to defend himself. The law, accordingly, recognises the need to protect against this danger: hence the serious offence detailed in this canon, which itself endorses a long-standing canonical tradition.[1]

The offence consists of the following elements:

- an accusation that a particular priest has committed the offence described in Can. 1387;
- there is no basis in truth for this allegation, i.e. it is a false accusation;
- the accusation is made deliberately by someone who knows that it is false;
- the accusation is made formally to an ecclesiastical Superior of the priest, e.g. his own Ordinary, local or personal, the Ordinary of the place where the offence is alleged to have occurred, the Holy See.

The accusation need not be made by the person who was allegedly solicited; it may be made by another who claims to know what happened.

The penalty established for this offence is grave: a *latae sententiae* interdict and, if the accuser is a cleric, a *latae sententiae* suspension (see Can. 1333 §1). Moreover, in accordance with Can. 982, a person guilty of this offence cannot be absolved sacramentally until the false denunciation is withdrawn and a promise given to repair the harm caused.

Can. 1390 §2 A person who calumniously denounces an offence to an ecclesiastical Superior, or otherwise injures the good name of another, can be punished with a just penalty, not excluding a censure.

§3 The calumniator can also be compelled to make appropriate amends.

Two quite distinct, though related, offences are mentioned here:

(a) the calumnious denunciation of a person to an ecclesiastical Superior for something of which that person is actually innocent; this offence covers the false denunciation of any offence except that of Can. 1387 (dealt with in §1 of this canon);

(b) unjustifiably injuring the good name of another person, whether by the spoken or written word or even by gesture.

Since the right to one's good name is a basic right acknowledged in Can. 220, it is appropriate that those who deliberately undermine it should be punished. The canon requires the competent authority to impose a just penalty on offenders; depending upon the circumstances of the case, this may include a censure.

---

[1] Cf. Pope Benedict XIV cit ap con *Sacramentum Poentitentiae* 1.VI.1741 n.3; 1917 Code c.2363.

2796 If the damage or harm caused by the false denunciation or the injury to the person's good name is serious, the competent authority can oblige the offender to make an adequate satisfaction.

Can. 1391 The following can be punished with a just penalty, according to the gravity of the offence:

    1° a person who composes a false public ecclesiastical document, or who changes or conceals a genuine one, or who uses a false or altered one;

    2° a person who in an ecclesiastical matter uses some other false or altered document;

    3° a person who, in a public ecclesiastical document, asserts something false.

2797 Public ecclesiastical documents are understood by Can. 1540 §1 as 'those which an official person draws up in the exercise of his or her function in the Church and in which the formalities required by law have been observed'. Since such documents normally 'constitute acceptable evidence of those matters which are directly and principally affirmed in them' (Can. 1541), it is of great importance that they be accurate and authentic.

2798 This canon speaks of a number of possible offences related to these documents:

    (a) the composition of a document which is totally false, i.e. the forgery of a public ecclesiastical document;

    (b) the deliberate and malicious alteration of such a document;

    (c) the deliberate and malicious concealment of such a document;

    (d) the deliberate use of such a document knowing that it has been forged or altered;

    (e) the deliberate use in an ecclesiastical matter of any other document which has been so forged or altered;

    (f) the deliberate assertion in a public ecclesiastical document of something which is not true.

2799 In all of these possible offences, the composition, alteration or concealment of a document must be done with a view to creating falsehood, from whatever motive. Once an external violation of the law and grave imputability have been established, the competent authority must punish the offender with a penalty which is proportionate to the offence, i.e. related to the amount of harm or damage or scandal caused.

Title V
Offences against Special Obligations

Can. 1392 Clerics or religious who practise commerce or trade contrary to the provisions of the canons, are to be punished according to the gravity of the offence.

Part II Penalties for Particular Offences

By virtue of Cann. 286 and 672 all clerics and members of religious institutes are forbidden to engage in commerce or trade, '*except* with the permission of the lawful ecclesiastical authority'. In general, this activity is rightly considered to be incompatible with the vocation of a cleric or religious, although it is recognised that, for purposes of necessary administration, it may on occasion be required that some clerics or religious engage to some extent in such activity: hence the requirement of a special permission – an element not recognised in the otherwise parallel c.142 of the 1917 Code. 2800

Those who violate this regulation 'are to be punished according to the gravity of the offence'.[1] This offence can be committed only by a Bishop, priest or deacon or by a professed member of a religious institute. Exempt from such an offence are the non-clerical members of secular institutes and societies of apostolic life; in virtue of Can. 288, permanent deacons are also exempt. 2801

Can. 1393 A person who violates obligations imposed by a penalty, can be punished with a just penalty.

Anyone who incurs a penalty is obliged to abide by the requirements of that penalty, e.g. to desist from the reception of the sacraments (Can. 1331 §1), to reside in a certain place (Can. 1336 §1 1°), to relinquish the exercise of an office (Can. 1336 §1 3°), etc. If such a person violates these obligations, the competent authority has the faculty to punish him or her with a just penalty, this being a new offence. However, a penalty is not mandatory in this case; it is sufficient – and certainly pastorally advisable – if the competent authority could succeed in having the offender resume the observation of the previous penalty. 2802

Can. 1394 §1 Without prejudice to the provisions of Can. 194 §1 n.3, a cleric who attempts marriage, even if only civilly, incurs a *latae sententiae* suspension. If, after warning, he has not reformed and continues to give scandal, he can be progressively punished by deprivations, or even by dismissal from the clerical state.

According to Can. 277 §1 'clerics are obliged to observe perfect and continual continence for the sake of the Kingdom of heaven, and are therefore bound to celibacy'. This requirement of law is reinforced by the undertaking of the obligation of celibacy at ordination to the diaconate (see Can. 1037), and of course sacred orders constitute a diriment impediment to marriage (see Can. 1087). Should a cleric attempt to marry, either civilly or canonically, he is guilty of an offence, known as *attempted marriage*: a civil marriage would be invalid due to lack of form, a canonical marriage due to the diriment impediment of orders. 2803

A cleric who is guilty of this offence incurs a *latae sententiae* suspension. The law makes further provision: if, after warning, the cleric persists in his conduct and gives scandal, the competent authority may add further penalties, *including that of dismissal from the clerical state*. Reference is also made to Can. 194 §1 3°, which provides for the automatic removal from ecclesiastical office of a cleric who attempts marriage, provided only that the reason for the removal be supported by a declaration of the competent ecclesiastical authority (see Can. 194 §2). 2804

No mention is made in this canon of the partner to such an attempted marriage. However, in virtue of Can. 1329 §2 the competent authority could impose a penalty on her since, without her cooperation and the expression of her consent, the offence 2805

---

[1] For the circumstances in which in 1950 the then Sacred Congregation for the Council found it necessary to deal much more severely with this matter, cf. that Congregation's decr 22.III.1950: CLD 3 68–69.

could not have taken place. Such a penalty is of course facultative, not mandatory, and indeed should be imposed, if at all, only with the greatest discretion and sensitivity – in fact, only if there is no other way in which justice can be done.

Can. 1394 §2 Without prejudice to the provisions of Can. 694, a religious in perpetual vows who is not a cleric but who attempts marriage, even if only civilly, incurs a *latae sententiae* interdict.

2806 The offence described in this paragraph is the same as that mentioned in §1. The offender is a religious in perpetual vows who is not a cleric, i.e. only those men and women who have made perpetual vows in a religious institute; therefore the canon does not apply to those who are temporarily professed, or those who are perpetually professed or incorporated in secular institutes and societies of apostolic life.

2807 A religious who is guilty of such an offence incurs a *latae sententiae* interdict. In this case, in virtue of Can. 1329 §2 this automatic penalty also affects the partner, unlike the suspension mentioned in §1.

2808 Can. 694 provides for the automatic dismissal of religious from their institute if they contract marriage or attempt to do so: this includes those in temporary profession, as well as members of secular institutes (see Can. 729) and of societies of apostolic life (see Can. 746). As this §2 has explicitly stated, the penalty involved here is 'without prejudice to the provisions of Can. 694', i.e. this penalty still applies, in addition to the ruling of Can. 694.

Can. 1395 §1 A cleric living in concubinage, other than in the case mentioned in Can. 1394, and a cleric who continues in some other external sin against the sixth commandment of the Decalogue which causes scandal, is to be punished with suspension. To this, other penalties can be progressively added if after a warning he persists in the offence, until eventually he can be dismissed from the clerical state.

2809 Two separate offences are set out in this paragraph:

(a) *a cleric living in concubinage*: this involves a permanent or quasi-permanent and continuing relationship between the cleric and a woman, whether married or single, which involves the component of their having sexual intercourse together[1] – irrespective of where this relationship is conducted, in the residence of the cleric or in any other place or places.

(b) *a cleric who, continuing in some other external sin against the sixth commandment, causes scandal*: the 1917 Code in its c.2359 §2 listed a number of such sins; they are obviously included here, as are any of such ilk – adultery, sodomy, incest, etc. While all of these are manifestly sinful, the component element of the punishable *offence* detailed in this paragraph is the continuing commission of such a sin *which causes scandal* – a matter to be determined by the local Ordinary

2810 A cleric guilty of either of these offences is to be punished by suspension, in the sense of Can. 1333 §1. Moreover, if the cleric concerned has been warned about his situation and has failed to reform his behaviour, the competent authority can add further penalties; in fact, if the circumstances so warrant it, such a cleric may be dismissed from the clerical state, but only if the requirements of law in this regard will have been observed (see Cann. 1342 §2, 1425 §1 2°a).

---

[1] Cf. Wernz–Vidal VII n.495d; Vermeersch–Creusen nn.367, 560(2); Coronata II n.2054; Regatillo II n.1015.

Part II Penalties for Particular Offences

Members of religious institutes, secular institutes and societies of apostolic life are to be dismissed from their institutes if they are guilty of an offence of this kind (see Cann. 695 §1, 729, 746). In these cases, the procedure outlined in Can. 695 §2 is to be followed; when the members involved are clerics, Can. 1395 must also be observed.

Can. 1395 §2 A cleric who has offended in other ways against the sixth commandment of the Decalogue, if the offence was committed by force, or by threats, or in public, or with a minor under the age of sixteen years, is to be punished with just penalties, not excluding dismissal from the clerical state if the case so warrants.

This §2 deals with other kinds of offence against the obligation of clerical celibacy:

(a) if the cleric offends against the sixth commandment with another person by using force or threats, e.g. by committing rape or some other form of sexual assault;

(b) if the cleric offends against the sixth commandment in a public place or in a place to which the public has access; in this case, if the other party was willingly involved, he or she may be punished in accordance with Can. 1329;

(c) if the cleric offends against the sixth commandment with a minor under the age of sixteen years.

The matter of imputability is of fundamental importance in considering each of these offences, and not least the third mentioned above. Before imposing any penalty for such an offence, the ecclesiastical authority must be morally certain that there has been an external violation of the law which is gravely imputable in the sense explained above at Can. 1321 §1. Among the factors which may seriously diminish imputability in such cases is *paedophilia*. This is described as 'the act or fantasy of engaging in sexual activity with pre-pubertal children as a repeatedly preferred or exclusive method of achieving sexual excitement'.[1] Those who have studied this matter in detail have concluded that proven paedophiles are often subject to urges and impulses which are in effect beyond their control.[2]

When the facts of a particular case are examined carefully, it may well emerge that the cleric did indeed commit a sexual offence, or a number of them, with a minor; as such, he may be liable to punishment by the criminal law of the State; nevertheless, because of the influence of paedophilia, he may not be liable, by reason of at least diminished imputability, to any canonical penalty, or perhaps to only a mild penalty, to a formal warning or reproof, or to a penal remedy.[3] In dealing with such cases, the ecclesiastical authority must tread very carefully, balancing the harm done to the victims, the rights of the cleric in canon law, and the overall good of the Church in its striving for justice for all.

---

[1] American Psychiatric Association *Diagnostic and Statistical Manual of Mental Disorders* (ed 3) Washington DC 1987 266.

[2] Cf. Doyle *The canonical rights of priests accused of sexual abuse* Stud Can 24(1990) 353–354; Berlin and Krout *Paedophilia: diagnostic concepts, treatment and ethical considerations* American Journal of Forensic Psychiatry 7(1986) 20; Paulson *The clinical and canonical considerations in cases of paedophilia: the Bishop's role* Stud Can 22(1988) 88.

[3] Cf. Cann. 1339 §2, 1348. Can. 1348 mentions, in particular, 'other solicitous means', which would obviously include the intervention by the diocesan Bishop who would personally, and alone, talk to the cleric and strongly advise him concerning the steps to be taken to deal with the problem, giving an assurance of his willingness to provide any reasonable help in what may be necessary by way of treatment, counselling, etc. Apart from quite exceptional cases, any form of threat – which would almost certainly be counter-productive – should have no place in such an interview.

2815 In the first place, a clear distinction must be drawn between two not untypical situations, namely: (a) that of a cleric of such paedophile orientation that he stands accused of having, over a number of years and even up to the present time, sexually abused a minor or minors under sixteen years of age; and (b) that of a cleric who stands accused of having, a number of years previously – perhaps, ten, fifteen, twenty – sexually abused such a minor, on one or a number of occasions, but who since the alleged offence has led a blameless clerical life. No real system of justice – least of all that of the canon law – can equate these two situations, particularly in the manner in which it deals with them. Nor should this juridical and pastoral view be adversely influenced by the sometimes excessive statements of some psychologists and psychiatrists, to the effect that once such an offence, of however long ago, has been established, the ecclesiastical authority has on its hands an incurable paedophile. Experience has proven that the disregard of this interpretation of the law has itself led to yet further injustice. In particular, it would appear to be imprudent of any episcopal authority to be dependent upon the advice of any one psychiatric expert. It should be noted that in fact, whatever else, the advice of a *psychological* expert should always be sought. It will then be for the Bishop to balance the advice he is thus given and, in his own prudent judgement, to act accordingly.

2816 Secondly, serious consideration should always be given by the diocesan Bishop before the use of the penal process (see Cann. 1717ff) is involved in these cases. It should be used as a first response only in exceptional circumstances. It should never be used by way of threat of dismissal from the clerical state – not least because, in normal circumstances, the outcome of the penal process would not be in the Bishop's personal control. There is the further consideration – relevant perhaps in some countries more than others – that the premature use of the penal process could lead to a requirement by the civil authorities of 'discovery' of the documents used in the canonical process. In accordance with Can. 1344 2°, the competent ecclesiastical authority may refrain from seeking to punish an offending cleric in such a case 'if the offender has been or foreseeably will be sufficiently punished by the civil authority'.[1]

2817 Religious who offend against Can. 1395 §2 must be dismissed from their institute in accordance with Can. 695 §1, unless the relevant Superior judges that it is not absolutely necessary. In such a case, the Superior must ascertain that sufficient provision can be made otherwise for the amendment of the offender and the reparation of the harm and scandal caused.

2818 Those clerics who are found guilty of any of the offences listed in this paragraph are to be punished with a just penalty, i.e. the offender must be punished, but the determination of the penalty is left to the competent authority who will be more familiar with the precise details and circumstances of the offence. Because of the intrinsic gravity of these offences, the authority may even proceed towards dismissal from the clerical state, provided always that all the requirements of law in this regard are carefully observed (see Cann. 1342 §2, 1425 §1 2°a).

Can. 1396 A person who gravely violates the obligations of residence to which he is bound by reason of an ecclesiastical office, is to be punished with a just penalty, not excluding, after a warning, deprivation of the office.

---

[1] To protect the essential rights of the victims, the ecclesiastical authority should always consider acting in some way other than the formal penal process. In this context, cf. Morrisey *Procedures to be applied in cases of alleged sexual misconduct by a priest* Stud Can 26(1992) 39–73; Beal *Administrative leave: Canon 1722 revisited* Stud Can 27(1993) 293–320; Cafardi *Stones instead of bread: sexually abusive priests in ministry* Stud Can 27(1993) 145–172. Some dioceses have already published a policy to be followed in these matters: in the formulation of such policies, it is important that the principles outlined here be carefully borne in mind.

The obligation of residence is incumbent on many who hold office in the Church, e.g. diocesan Bishops (Can. 395), their equivalents in law (Can. 381 §2), their coadjutors and auxiliaries (Can. 410); the diocesan Administrator (Can. 429), parish priests (Can. 533 §1), members of a group of priests to whom a parish has been entrusted (Can. 543 §2 1°), assistant priests in a parish (Can. 550 §1), religious Superiors (Can. 629). Any such person who repeatedly, habitually or notoriously is absent from the place of residence is guilty of this offence, assuming it is shown to be gravely imputable. 2819

The principle of the obligation of residence is none other than to assist these office-holders in the discharge of their office for the good of those in their care; accordingly, the violation of this obligation is a serious matter. The competent authority – be that the Holy See or the Ordinary – is required to punish such offenders with a just penalty; if the circumstances so warrant it, this may include deprivation of the office – in which case the judicial penal process must be used (see Can. 1342 §2). 2820

Title VI
Offences against Human Life and Liberty

Can. 1397 One who commits homicide, or who by force or by fraud abducts, imprisons, mutilates or gravely wounds a person, is to be punished, according to the gravity of the offence, with the deprivations and prohibitions mentioned in Can. 1336. In the case of the homicide of one of those persons mentioned in Can. 1370, the offender is punished with the penalties there prescribed.

This canon speaks of a number of offences against human life and liberty: 2821

(a) to kill another human being. The canon speaks of 'homicide' without any qualification,[1] i.e. the offence consists of any act or omission by which another person dies, provided of course it is imputable by reason of malice or culpability (Can. 1321 §1), e.g. murder (wilful homicide where there is malice aforethought), some cases of reckless driving, placing bombs, misuse of firearms, etc. This offence also includes euthanasia, i.e. 'an action or omission which of itself or by intention causes death, in order that suffering may in this way be eliminated. Euthanasia's terms of reference, therefore, are to be found in the intention of the will and in the methods used'.[2] This is to be clearly distinguished from the legitimate practice of alleviating pain, even though the treatment administered may reduce the person's life expectancy.

(b) by force or fraud to abduct and detain another person, i.e. to take someone and hold him or her against their will, either by physical force or by duping that person into going somewhere and not permitting him or her to return. This is a direct assault on human liberty and manifestly a very serious matter.

(c) by force or fraud to mutilate another person, i.e. to wound a person to such an extent that a part or parts of the body is severed. This offence includes both delib-

---
[1] Unlike Can. 1041 4° which speaks of 'wilful homicide' or murder.
[2] SCDF decl *Iura et bona* 5.V.1980: Fl II 512.

erate violence against the other person and a surgical intervention for which the person (or the parent or lawful guardian) has not given consent.

(d) by force or fraud to wound another person seriously. No injury is specified in the canon. The competent authority must decide whether or not the injury is serious in the circumstances; anything which compromises life or bodily integrity would certainly be understood as serious. Obviously excluded from this offence would be injuries caused in the course of legitimate self-defence.

2822 Anyone guilty of one of these offences is to be punished by the competent ecclesiastical authority. The penalties mentioned are the expiatory penalties of Can. 1336; these are to be applied 'according to the gravity of the offence'. Moreover, since the criminal law of the State may also be involved, the ecclesiastical authority may decide not to impose any penalty or to impose a less severe one, in accordance with Can. 1344 2°.

2823 Should the particular offence involve the killing of the Pope or of a Bishop, a cleric or a religious, the offender is to be punished in accordance with the penalties set out in Can. 1370, i.e. *latae sententiae* excommunication if the victim is the Pope, *latae sententiae* interdict if the victim is a Bishop, just penalties imposed by the competent authority if the victim is a cleric or a religious.

2824 In accordance with Cann. 695, 729, 746, members of religious and secular institutes and of societies of apostolic life are to be dismissed if they are guilty of any of the offences listed in this canon.

Can. 1398 A person who actually procures an abortion incurs a *latae sententiae* excommunication.

2825 Traditionally abortion has been defined as the deliberate premature ejection of a living non-viable foetus from the womb of the mother. This practice has been forbidden to Christians from the earliest days of the Church.[1] Over the intervening centuries, the question of abortion has been the subject of many interventions by the teaching authority of the Church.[2] An ecclesiastical penalty has been attached to this offence for many centuries. A further relevant consideration in this regard is the authentic interpretation of this canon issued in 1988, whereby it was decided that 'abortion, mentioned in Can. 1398, is to be understood ... also of the killing of the ... foetus, in whatever way or at whatever time from the moment of conception it may be procured'.[3]

2826 In the light of the foregoing, the canonical offence is constituted by any action resulting directly in the ejection of an immature foetus from the womb or the death of the foetus in the womb. It is not constituted by surgical interventions in which the death of the foetus is a foreseen side-effect, e.g. the necessary removal of a cancerous uterus. Neither, obviously, does the offence arise in the case of a spontaneous abortion or miscarriage. Finally, this canon determines that the offence arises only if the action in question will have actually achieved its objective. An unsuccessful attempt to expel the foetus from the womb or to kill the foetus in the womb, although gravely sinful, does not amount to this canonical offence.

---

[1] A valuable summary of the Church's teaching against abortion in the early Church is to be found in the SCDF decl *Quaestio de abortu* 18.XI.1974 n.6: Fl II 443.

[2] The most recent has been that of Pope John Paul II in his encyclical *Evangelium Vitae* 25.III.1995: Origins 24(1995) 689–727, particularly (but by no means exclusively) in nn.58–62. In this document the Pope is at pains to point out, *inter alia*, precisely how much his teaching is in total harmony both with that of his predecessors (cf. n.62) and with Vat. II (cf. GS 51: Fl I 955). No reputable canonist can purport to interpret this Can. 1398 without having first carefully studied this most recent teaching of the magisterium, and not least its specific references to the consistent tradition in this matter. Released with this encyclical was a brief official *Summary*, which is a valuable point of reference: cf. Origins loc cit 728–730.

[3] PCI rep 23.V.1988: AAS 80(1988) 1818.

Who are subject to the penalty prescribed in this canon? A number of people are always involved in the carrying out of an abortion: the pregnant mother, sometimes the father of her child, her family, friends and advisors, those who in one way or another make possible access to the abortive service, the surgeon who performs the operation, the attendant nurses and other such supportive staff, politicians and legislators who promote this service, etc. A clear distinction must always be drawn between, on the one hand, those who thereby act sinfully and, on the other, those who incur the canonical penalty. An instructive guide in this matter may be found in the encyclical *Evangelium Vitae* when it states:

> 'sometimes it is precisely the mother herself who makes the decision and asks for the child to be eliminated, and who then goes about having it done.
>
> 'It is true that the decision to have an abortion is often tragic and painful for the mother insofar as the decision to rid herself of the fruit of conception is not made for purely selfish reasons or out of convenience, but out of a desire to protect certain important values such as her own health or a decent standard of living for the other members of the family. Sometimes it is feared that the child to be born would live in such conditions that it would be better if the birth did not take place. Nevertheless, these reasons and others like them, however serious and tragic, can never justify the deliberate killing of an innocent human being.
>
> 'As well as the mother, there are often other people too who decide upon the death of the child in the womb. In the first place, the father of the child may be to blame, not only when he directly pressures the woman to have an abortion, but also when he indirectly encourages such a decision on her part by leaving her alone to face the problems of pregnancy. In this way the family is thus mortally wounded and profaned in its nature as a community of love and in its vocation to be the "sanctuary of life". Nor can one overlook the pressures which sometimes come from the wider family circle and from friends. Sometimes the woman is subjected to such strong pressure that she feels psychologically forced to have an abortion. Certainly in this case moral responsibility lies particularly with those who have directly or indirectly obliged her to have an abortion. Doctors and nurses are also responsible when they place at the service of death skills which were acquired for promoting life.
>
> 'But responsibility likewise falls on the legislators who have promoted and approved abortion laws and, to the extent that they have a say in the matter, on the administrators of the health care centres where abortions are performed. A general and no less serious responsibility lies with those who have encouraged the spread of an attitude of sexual permissiveness and a lack of esteem for motherhood, and with those who should have ensured – but did not – effective family and social policies in support of families, especially larger families and those with particular financial and educational needs. Finally, one cannot overlook the network of complicity which reaches out to include international institutions, foundations and associations which systematically campaign for the legalisation and spread of abortion in the world. In this sense abortion goes beyond the responsibility of individuals and beyond the harm done to them, and takes on a distinctly social dimension. It is a most serious wound inflicted on society and its culture by the very people who ought to be society's promoters and defenders.'

2828 The penalty incurred by those who are guilty of this offence is a *latae sententiae* excommunication. This penalty may be remitted by the Ordinary (see Can. 1355 §2). In some dioceses, the diocesan Bishop grants the faculty to absolve from it to all priests to whom he has accredited the faculty to hear confessions in accordance with Can. 969 §1. The decision to make such a grant will obviously have been made by the Bishop in the light of the actual circumstances existing in his own diocese – not necessarily applicable to any other particular diocese.[1]

Title VII
General Norm

Can. 1399 Besides the cases prescribed in this or in other laws, the external violation of divine or canon law can be punished, and with a just penalty, only when the special gravity of the violation requires it and necessity demands that scandals be prevented or repaired.

2829 This Book VI of the Code closes with a final canon by way of a general norm. While the Code does include many specific penalties for specific offences, it recognises that it is not possible to anticipate every possibility. For this reason, it establishes that a penalty can be inflicted for an external violation of divine or canon law, even though this is not prescribed in universal or particular law. Some might see this as a dangerous principle, inviting arbitrary action on the part of ecclesiastical authorities which would offend against the right of the faithful enunciated in Can. 221 §3. This is not so: the canon strictly qualifies this faculty, requiring that two specific conditions must be fulfilled before any such action can be taken:

(a) the violation involved must be of a special gravity, i.e. it must be objectively very serious, not just to the dislike of the authority concerned;

(b) there must be a genuine need to prevent or to repair scandal as a result of the offence. If either of these conditions is not verified in a particular case, the Superior cannot impose a canonical penalty (see Can. 18). Moreover, although the penalty is not determined by the canon, there are clear guidelines elsewhere in Book VI which every authority must use in deciding which, if any, penalty is appropriate in the circumstances (see Cann. 1342 §2, 1347 §1, 1349 etc.). These provisions are specifically designed to protect the faithful against any arbitrary or unjust use of the principle contained in the canon.

---

[1] For some further consequences of the offence of abortion, cf. Cann. 695 §1, 729, 1041 4°, 1044 §1 3°.

BOOK VII

JUDICIAL PROCEDURES

PART I

TRIALS IN GENERAL

Can. 1400 §1 The objects of a trial are:

1° to pursue or vindicate the rights of physical or juridical persons, or to declare juridical facts;

2° to impose or to declare penalties in regard to offences.

Unlike the 1917 legislation in its c.1552 §1, the current Code presupposes rather than expressly defines the term 'trial'.[1] Derived from the latin *iudicare* or *ius dicere*, it signifies the legal discussion and settlement by an ecclesiastical tribunal of a controversy in a matter in which the Church has the right to judge.

The object of trials is here divided into two categories: the pursuit or the vindication of rights or the declaration of juridical facts, and the examination of offences with a view to deciding whether or not to impose or to declare a specific penalty. In the 1917 Code, the former were referred to as 'contentious' trials; the latter, 'penal' ones.[2] Rights of *physical* persons to be pursued or vindicated would include such as the recognition of a state of life (e.g. the validity of orders or of marriage or of religious profession), in fact the recognition of any other right acknowledged by ecclesiastical law. In practice, the rights of *juridical* persons would more often than not concern matters relating to the ownership or administration of temporal goods. The declaration of *juridical facts* might e.g. refer to a decision that an alleged contract had or had not been entered into, that a purportedly official certificate is or is not authentic, and so on. There are special norms in the Code regarding the processing of penal trials (see Cann. 1717–1731). Moreover there are special rules to be observed in the processing of trials concerning the public good (see e.g. Cann. 1430, 1536, 1691, 1696, 1728).

Can. 1400 §2 Disputes arising from an act of administrative power, however, can be referred only to the Superior or to an administrative tribunal.

Disputes arising out of an act of administrative power are not to be brought before the ordinary ecclesiastical courts, but are rather to be treated in accordance with the special procedure outlined in Cann. 1732–1739. Administrative procedure for recourse is new in the current Code, although a precedent can be found in the ap con *Regimini Ecclesiae universae*.[3] This exclusion of the courts as a first step in seeking

2830

2831

2832

---

[1] Cf. Comm 10(1978) 127 at Can. 1.

[2] Cf. 1917 Code c.1552 §2, the substance of which is in fact repeated in the current text. The recognised commentators on the 1917 Code in this regard remain therefore a secure guide to the interpretation of this paragraph.

[3] Cf. REU art 106.

redress against an administrative decree does not, however, preclude the ultimate recourse to the Supreme Tribunal of the Apostolic Signatura (see Can. 1445 §2).[1]

Can. 1401 The Church has its own and exclusive right to judge:

1° cases which refer to matters which are spiritual or linked with the spiritual;

2° the violation of ecclesiastical laws and whatever contains an element of sin, to determine guilt and impose ecclesiastical penalties.

2833 The Church spells out in this canon *its own* and *exclusive* judicial domain. It reserves to itself judicial competence

- in spiritual matters, e.g. the validity of a baptism or of an ordination or of a marriage, the effects of a vow, etc.

- in temporal matters which are essentially linked with spiritual matters, e.g. the right of presentation or of election to an ecclesiastical office, matters concerning ecclesiastical property or pious dispositions and foundations, etc.

- in matters concerning the violation of ecclesiastical laws (see Cann. 7–22).

- in matters containing 'an element of sin', where this is relevant to the determination of imputability in the context of imposing an ecclesiastical penalty.[2]

2834 This declaration of the rights of the Church, which are independent of any other authority, finds a parallel in corresponding statements at the beginning of other books of the Code (see Cann. 747, 1254, 1311). The fact that such rights are not always recognised or respected by the civil authorities is another matter, which has to be dealt with in the best way possible in accordance with the legal and cultural circumstances of each situation.

Can. 1402 All tribunals of the Church are governed by the canons which follow, without prejudice to the norms of the tribunals of the Apostolic See.

2835 This canon is self-explanatory. There are three tribunals of the Apostolic See, to the functioning of which, in addition to the rules outlined in Cann. 1442–1445, special norms (not contained in the Code) apply: the Apostolic Penitentiary (which deals exclusively with the internal forum), the Supreme Tribunal of the Apostolic Signatura, the Tribunal of the Roman Rota.[3] All other tribunals are obliged by the succeeding norms of this Book VII.

Can. 1403 §1 Cases for the canonisation of the Servants of God are governed by special pontifical law.

---

[1] The reference in this §2 to an *administrative tribunal*, together with that in Can. 149 §2, are the sole remnants of the proposal – which played a significant part in the process of revising this part of the Code – which sought to establish a system of local administrative tribunals in the Church. The draft canons designed to give effect to that proposal were abandoned almost on the eve of the Code's promulgation. For an instructive summary of the background and the implications, cf. Chiappetta II nn. 4571–4574, 5312–5314.

[2] This same phrase 'contains an element of sin' (*inest ratio peccati*) was used in the 1917 Code at c.1553 §1 2°, the recognised commentators on which remain a valued guide. 'Sin' is used not in the strictly theological sense and thus confined to the internal forum, but rather in the broader sense of that which offends or disturbs the good of religion, the mission and purpose of the Church: cf. Chiappetta II n.4576. Cf. also Can. 1321 and our commentary thereon: this is a particularly difficult and sensitive area of interpretation.

[3] Cf. PB 117–130.

§2 The provisions of this Code are also applied to these cases whenever the special pontifical law remits an issue to the universal law, or whenever norms are involved which of their very nature apply also to these cases.

These cases constitute a category of their own, outside the norm of the ordinary judicial process in the Church. They are regulated by a 'special pontifical law', which is indeed very detailed and exacting – not least by reason of the fact that one of the major elements is the determination of divine intervention through miracles.[1] For all that such cases are governed by the special procedure laid down in the pontifical law (§1), that law may on occasion expressly remit a particular item of the process to the general procedural norms of the Code, in which case these latter obviously apply; the same would be true where the special norms themselves 'of their very nature' require the application of the general procedural rules (§2), e.g. proof from witnesses or from experts (see Cann. 1547–1581). 2836

Title I
The Competent Forum

Can. 1404 The First See is judged by no one.

It is a fundamental principle, based upon divine law, that the First See – the Roman Pontiff (see Cann. 331–333 §2) – cannot be judged by any human power, ecclesiastical or civil. This is a prerogative which, being the supreme judge in the Church, even the Pope himself cannot renounce. 2837

A consequence is that 'there is neither appeal nor recourse against a judgement or a decree of the Roman Pontiff' (Can. 333 §3). In a particularly difficult or sensitive situation, there is however always the possibility of requesting the Pope that he might reconsider the matter – subject of course to his own ultimate decision. 2838

This immunity of the Roman Pontiff applies not only to those acts and documents emanating from the Pope personally and in his own name, but also to those issued 'by other persons or institutions whose acts he makes his own by express approbation or acceptance':[2] this is the case when e.g. certain documents of the Roman Curia are approved by the Pope, as the technical phrase has it, 'in specific form' (*in forma specifica*), thereby making such documents formal papal acts (see Can. 1405 §2). 2839

Can. 1405 §1 In the cases mentioned in Can. 1401, the Roman Pontiff alone has the right to judge:

    1° Heads of State;

    2° Cardinals;

---

[1] Cf. Pope John Paul II ap con *Divinus perfectionis Magister* 25.I.1983: AAS 75(1983) 349–355: CLD 10 267–273; SCCS *Normae* 7.II.1983: AAS loc cit 396–404: CLD loc cit 273–281.
[2] Comm 10(1978) 219 at Can. 4.

Book VII Judicial Procedures

3° Legates of the Apostolic See and, in penal cases, Bishops;

4° other cases which he has reserved to himself.

2840 The law here reserves to the Roman Pontiff the exclusive right to judge the cases of:

– *Heads of State*, and their spouses – not, as was the situation under the 1917 Code (c.1557 §1 1°), their children or those with the right of immediate succession.[1]

– *Cardinals*, by reason of their status, from the moment of their proclamation in Consistory (see Can. 351 §2).

– *Legates of the Apostolic See* (see Can. 362).

– *Bishops* but only in respect of offences (as in Book VI of the Code) allegedly committed by them: this comprises all Bishops, whether diocesan, titular or retired, and those Prelates equivalent in law to diocesan Bishops (see Cann. 368, 381 §2).

To this list is added (4°) such other cases as the Pope may from time to time decide to reserve to himself, whether on his own initiative or at the request of an interested party.

2841 In practice, the Pope does not normally judge these cases personally; they are, rather, delegated by him to other judges e.g. of the Apostolic Signatura or of the Roman Rota, who then act in the Pope's name and by his direct authority.

Can. 1405 §2 A judge cannot review an act or instrument which the Roman Pontiff has specifically confirmed, except by his prior mandate.

2842 This rule is a direct consequence of Can. 1404. It relates also to Can. 333 §3, in specifying that the only judge (or any other body) who can review a papal decision is one who has received the 'prior mandate' of the Pope himself. This provides for the situation in which – e.g. on the advent of new evidence or some such circumstance – the Pope could authorise the reopening of a case already decided by an organ of the Roman Curia and at the time approved *in forma specifica*.[2]

Can. 1405 §3 It is reserved to the Roman Rota to judge:

1° Bishops in contentious cases, without prejudice to Can. 1419 §2;

2° the Abbot primate or the Abbot superior of a monastic congregation, and the supreme Moderator of a religious institute of pontifical right;

3° dioceses and other ecclesiastical persons, physical or juridical, which have no Superior other than the Roman Pontiff.

2843 This extends somewhat the competence of the Roman Rota (see 1917 Code c.1557 §2). No other tribunal may judge, at least in first instance, those enumerated here:

– *Bishops*, but only 'in contentious cases' i.e. those referred to in Can. 1400 §1 1° above.[3] The sole exception is, that referred to in Can. 1419 §2 (q.v.).

---

[1] In the course of the revision of the Code it was suggested that this particular reservation was little more than a medieval vestige which could profitably be omitted. It was decided however that such cases, though very rare, do still occur even today, and that the reservation be maintained, not in any sense to confer a special privilege but rather to ensure that these cases be given the wholly independent and objective judgement which the Pope can ensure – a judgement which might, understandably, have to face the hazard of unwarranted or undue pressure at a local level; cf. Comm 10(1978) 220 at Can. 5 §1.

[2] An interesting recent example of the principle involved here is the famous Galileo case: cf. Card. Paul Poupard *Galileo: Report on Papal Commission's Findings*: Origins 22(1992–1993) 374–376. Cf. also Pope John Paul II allocution 31.X.1992 *Lessons of the Galileo Case*: Origins 22(1992–1993) 369, 371–373.

[3] For penal cases, cf. Can. 1405 §1 3° : the term 'Bishops' is to be understood here as in that previous reference.

Part I Trials in General

- *Abbot primate or Abbot superior of a monastic congregation* (see Can. 620): in all cases, contentious or penal.
- *Supreme Moderator of a religious institute of pontifical right*, be it clerical or lay, male or female: again in all cases. Excluded from this reservation is the supreme Moderator of a secular institute or of a society of apostolic life.
- *Dioceses directly subject to the Roman Pontiff*, including those other such entities equivalent to dioceses (see Can. 368).
- *Other ecclesiastical persons, whether physical or juridical*, in like manner directly subject.[1]

2844 It is important to note that the prescription of this paragraph applies only to those cases in which the persons enumerated are cited as respondents, not when they themselves are plaintiffs.[2]

2845 Before proceeding to a commentary on the remaining canons of this Title, it is necessary to outline the concept of judicial competence in canon law. Briefly, the position is that no one may be summoned before an ecclesiastical tribunal unless the judge of that tribunal is determined by the Code to be competent to deal with the case in question (see Can. 1407 §1). The normal bases of that competence are determined by Cann. 1408–1414. There are special norms governing cases of marriage nullity (see Can. 1673).

2846 All other judges are, canonically speaking, *non-competent*, a concept which may technically be either absolute or relative. *Absolute* non-competence, which is concerned principally with the public good, affects substantially the validity of the judgement, which is accordingly 'null with a nullity which cannot be remedied' (Can. 1620 1°; see also 1621). *Relative* non-competence, on the other hand, is concerned rather with matters of procedural detail and, while it does involve the validity of the judgement, the nullity is such that it can be remedied, often with little difficulty (see Cann. 1407 §2, 1460, 1619, 1623, 1626).

Can. 1406 §1 If the provision of Can. 1404 is violated, the acts and decisions are considered not to have taken place.

§2 In the cases mentioned in Can. 1405, the non-competence of other judges is absolute.

2847 Acts and decisions taken in attempting to judge the Roman Pontiff (§1) are not only null but are considered non-existent (*pro infectis*): they are utterly devoid of any legal consequence and may not be pursued in any court. The circumstances referred to in §2 – namely the cases reserved by Can. 1405 – are such that any other judge attempting to deal with those cases would be absolutely non-competent, in the sense explained above.

Can. 1407 §1 No one can be brought to trial in first instance except before a judge who is competent on the basis of one of the titles determined in Cann. 1408–1414.

§2 The non-competence of a judge who has none of these titles is described as relative.

2848 Since not every tribunal is competent to accept any and every case presented to it, this paragraph prescribes the norm which ensures the proper and ordered administration of justice. This it does by determining certain 'titles of competence', each of which is assigned to a particular territory, depending on the nature or subject-matter of the

---

[1] The substance of Can. 1405 §3 appears in PB 129.
[2] Cf. Chiappetta II n.4597.

case. It is only a judge who possesses one of these titles who is canonically competent to hear and decide a given case. The titles themselves are determined, in an exclusive enumeration, in Cann. 1408–1414. It is to be noted that the prescription of this paragraph applies only to a tribunal of first instance, which will normally be a diocesan (see Can. 1419) or an interdiocesan (see Can. 1423) one.[1]

Can. 1407 §3 The plaintiff follows the forum of the respondent. If the respondent has more than one forum, the plaintiff may opt for any one of them.

2849 The person who introduces a case is generally known as the plaintiff; the other party is then known as the respondent. As has already been indicated and as is illustrated in the succeeding Cann. 1408–1414, there may in any given case be a number of competent tribunals ('forums'): in this connection, see Can. 1415. On the other hand, there may on occasion be only one title of competence. In keeping with a long-established canonical principle, itself designed to ensure the greatest possible degree of equity and fairness, the forum in the latter situation must be that of the respondent, not of the plaintiff. Hence the law here that 'the plaintiff follows the forum of the respondent': perhaps the clearest, though not the only, example is where the plaintiff has a domicile in one place and the respondent in another. It is only in the situation where 'the respondent has more than one forum', each equally competent, that 'the plaintiff may opt for any one of them', according to his or her choice.

Can. 1408 Anyone can be brought to trial before the tribunal of domicile or quasi-domicile.

2850 This is one of the most frequently relevant titles of competence.[2] A plaintiff may submit a plea 'before the tribunal of domicile or quasi-domicile' which, in virtue of Can. 1407 §3, must be that of the respondent, unless the law determines otherwise (in this regard see Can. 1673 3°). For the relevant law on domicile and quasi-domicile, see Cann. 102–106. It is to be noted that, unlike the situation under the 1917 Code (c.93 §1), a wife does not now necessarily have the domicile of her husband (see Can. 104).

Can. 1409 §1 A person who has not even a quasi-domicile has a forum in the place of actual residence.

2851 This refers to the *vagus* of Can. 100. The tribunal before which such a person may be summoned is the place where he or she actually resides at any given time.

Can. 1409 §2 A person whose domicile, quasi-domicile or place of actual residence is unknown, can be brought to trial in the forum of the plaintiff, provided no other lawful forum is available.

2852 This is a new prescription, not found in the 1917 Code – introduced, it may be thought, by reason of the new frequency with which the situation it confronts is found in cases of nullity of marriage.[3] In the circumstance it envisages, 'the forum of the plaintiff' is the competent one, i.e. that in which the plaintiff has a domicile or quasi-domicile or, if he or she be a *vagus*, that in which the plaintiff actually resides at the moment. However, this rule – which is an exception to the general principle

---

[1] At second and at third instance there is no question of choice on the basis of the nature or subject-matter of a particular case; the tribunals themselves are specifically determined by law: cf. Cann. 1438–1439, 1444.

[2] The singular domiciliary forum of competence provided for in the 1917 Code c.1562 has been suppressed: cf. Comm 10(1978) 223 at Can. 8.

[3] In this regard, cf. Can. 1673, not only in 3° but also in 4°.

stated in Can. 1407 §3 – is subject, for validity, to the condition that no other competent forum is open to the respondent on the basis of any of the other titles as set out in the following canons.[1]

Can. 1410 Competence by reason of subject matter means that a party can be brought to trial before the tribunal of the place where the subject matter of the litigation is located, whenever the action concerns that subject matter directly, or when it is an action for the recovery of possession.

This title of competence applies only to real, as distinct from personal, actions. A *real* action concerns the vindication of a particular 'thing' (*res*), e.g. land, buildings, other forms of property even mobile, an ecclesiastical office or privilege, etc.; into this category falls also an action for 'the recovery of possession' of some such 'thing' of which one may have unlawfully been deprived (see Cann. 1496 §1, 1500). A *personal* action, on the other hand, concerns the vindication of some act which one has a right to receive from another person, e.g. payment of a debt, compensation for damages, fulfilment of any other particular personal obligation. The point of this canon is to determine that when there is question of a real action, the competent tribunal *may* be that of the place in which the 'thing' ('the subject matter of the litigation') is located. It need not, however, necessarily be so: the plaintiff remains free to choose another competent forum, such e.g. as that of the respondent's domicile or quasi-domicile (Can. 1408).[2]   2853

Can. 1411 §1 Competence by reason of contract means that a party can be brought to trial before the tribunal of the place in which the contract was made or must be fulfilled, unless the parties mutually agree to choose another tribunal.

In the case of contract, the plaintiff has a choice among the following three competent tribunals: 2854

- that of the place where the contract was made;
- that of the place in which the contract is to be carried out;
- such other tribunal as the parties may mutually agree to select, e.g. that of the respondent's domicile.[3]

Can. 1411 §2 If the case concerns obligations which arise from some other title, the party can be brought to trial before the tribunal of the place in which the obligation arose or in which it is to be fulfilled.

Should the action concern an obligation other than a contractual one, e.g. from a will, from a court judgement, either of the first two tribunals mentioned in §1 above is competent, i.e. where the obligation arose or where it is to be fulfilled – but not any other tribunal, even if agreed upon by the parties. The situation envisaged here could exist e.g. when an endowment fund is based in one diocese and its revenues are to be partly disbursed in a new diocese which itself has in the meantime been created by division from the first.   2855

---

[1] When the forum of the plaintiff is selected in virtue of this canon, it might be considered advisable – though it is not always necessary – for the tribunal to appoint a procurator to represent the interests of the respondent: cf. Can. 1481 §§1 and 3. In this same context cf. also Ap Sig rep 6.IV.1973: RR 1984 61–63.

[2] Under the 1917 Code c.1560 1°, the option given here did not apply to an action for the recovery of possession.

[3] Contrary to the rule of the 1917 Code c.1565 §2, the agreement of the parties need not be made at the time of the contract but may be made at any time before the action: cf. Comm 10(1978) 225 at Can. 11.

Can. 1412 A person accused in a penal case can, even though absent, be brought to trial before the tribunal of the place in which the offence was committed.

2856 This canon refers only to cases in which an offence has allegedly been committed i.e. cases in which a penalty may be involved. The reason for the possibility of holding the trial before the tribunal of the 'place in which the offence was committed' is that it is there the facts of the alleged offence might more readily be ascertained and any associated scandal repaired. However, the place of the respondent's domicile or quasi-domicile would also be a basis of competence.[1]

Can. 1413 A party can be brought to trial:

1° in cases concerning administration, before the tribunal of the place in which the administration was exercised;

2° in cases concerning inheritances or pious legacies, before the tribunal of the last domicile or quasi-domicile or residence of the person whose inheritance or pious legacy is at issue, in accordance with the norms of Cann. 1408–1409. If, however, only the execution of the legacy is involved, the ordinary norms of competence are to be followed.

2857 Unlike the 1917 Code c.1560 3°– 4°, which prescribed a necessary forum for actions concerning both the administration of ecclesiastical property and those matters involving inheritances and pious legacies, this canon *offers* in each situation an optional forum, i.e. one which may be chosen by the plaintiff unless he or she finds another competent forum, e.g. that of the respondent's domicile, more convenient or appropriate.[2] Accordingly it allows:

– in matters of *administration*, 'the tribunal of the place in which the administration was exercised' or carried out; if it were carried out in a number of places, that in which its substantial part was conducted and, if there were none such, that among them to be chosen by the plaintiff.

– in matters of *inheritances or pious legacies*, 'the tribunal of the last domicile or quasi-domicile or residence' of the deceased person (see Cann. 1408–1409), i.e. of the place which immediately preceded the testator's death, irrespective of wherever the last will was made.[3] If however the only question to be resolved is 'the execution of the legacy', e.g. to ensure that its clear terms are complied with, then the case is to be dealt with in accordance with 'the ordinary norms of competence'.

Can. 1414 By reason of connection, cases which are inter-connected are to be heard by one and the same tribunal and in the same process, unless this is prohibited by a provision of the law.

2858 Any number of cases are said to be 'inter-connected' not on the merely subjective basis that the parties are the same in each, but rather on the objective ground that the matter to be dealt with in each is the same, e.g. the annulment of a marriage and the education of the children, the case of a person involved in multiple marriages, an action against two debtors each individually and collectively liable, a penal action against a number of accomplices in the same offence. The point of this canon is that

---

[1] Cf. Comm 10(1978) 225 at Can. 1.
[2] Cf. Comm 10(1978) 226 at Can. 13.
[3] Cf. Chiappetta II n.4611; CCLA 876 at Can. 1413.

such cases are to be heard not only 'by one and the same tribunal' but also 'in the same process'[1] – the only restriction being 'unless this is prohibited by a provision of the law', e.g. if the situation were such that the non-competence of the judge in one of the inter-connected cases was absolute (see Cann. 1405–1406). In prescribing this ground of competence for the kind of situation which it envisages, the Code is ensuring against possibly divergent decisions in one and the same matter, not to mention the practical considerations in the saving of time and expense. In effect, this prescription could, in an appropriate case, give to a judge a competence which he would not have on any other title.

Can. 1415 By reason of prevention, if two or more tribunals are equally competent, the tribunal which has first lawfully summoned the respondent has the right to hear the case.

This canon does not in any real sense prescribe a title of judicial competence. Rather, it looks at the situation which may arise when the same case is submitted at more or less the same time before two or even more tribunals which, in accordance with Can. 1407 §1, are equally competent to hear the case. What the canon does is simply to provide a practical rule in such a situation, namely that 'the tribunal which has first lawfully summoned the respondent has the right to hear the case', to the exclusion thereby of any other tribunal which might otherwise be competent (see Can. 1512). 2859

Can. 1416 A conflict of competence between tribunals subject to the same appeal tribunal is to be resolved by the latter tribunal. If they are not subject to the same appeal tribunal, the conflict is to be settled by the Apostolic Signatura.

This again is a canon of practical decision, in a situation which could arise if there were between two or more tribunals a conflict as to which was competent to hear and adjudicate upon a particular case; it could also arise if two or more tribunals were to declare themselves non-competent. The rule itself is simple: 2860

– if the tribunals in dispute are 'subject to the same appeal tribunal' – which, more often than not, they will be – the matter in dispute 'is to be resolved' by that appeal tribunal, the decision of which will then be definitive;

– if the situation is otherwise, 'the conflict is to be settled by the Apostolic Signatura' (see Can. 1445 §1 4°), to which therefore the case must clearly be referred by the competent local authority.[2]

---

[1] This is a clarification, if not an extension, of the prescription of the 1917 Code c.1567: for background material on this matter cf. the useful summary in CCLA 877 at Can. 1414.

[2] In the course of the revision of the Code it was observed that the rule requiring the submission of such conflicts to the Apostolic Signatura does not in any way eliminate the possibility that the judges in conflict concerning competence would among themselves resolve that conflict 'by a more profound (thorough, insightful) juridical investigation': Comm 16(1984) 54 at Can. 1368 §1 – a very practical observation which ought to be given the most serious consideration.

Title II
Different Grades and Kinds of Tribunals[1]

Can. 1417 §1 Because of the primacy of the Roman Pontiff, any of the faithful may either refer their case to, or introduce it before, the Holy See, whether the case be contentious or penal. They may do so at any grade of trial or at any stage of the suit.

§2 Apart from the case of an appeal, a referral to the Apostolic See does not suspend the exercise of jurisdiction of a judge who has already begun to hear a case. The judge can, therefore, continue with the trial up to the definitive judgement, unless the Apostolic See has indicated to him that it has reserved the case to itself.

2861 In providing that any of the faithful, i.e. those validly baptised even if not catholic, may call upon the Holy See to adjudicate upon his or her case, whatever, or at whichever stage, it may be, the Code makes a statement which is not only juridical but profoundly theological, with centuries of tradition behind it: 'because of the primacy of the Roman Pontiff'. Apart from the situation of a case already decided at a lower level and of a consequent formal appeal by the plaintiff to a tribunal of the Holy See (§2), this principle is not designed to interfere with the operation of lower tribunals; it is rather simply to state the right of every one of the faithful to seek the help of the Pope in matters involving a judicial investigation, and it implies an acceptance of the decision of the Holy See in regard to the submission made to it. The only situation in which such a submission would suspend the competence of a local tribunal would be if and when the Holy See has formally notified such a local tribunal that 'it has reserved the case to itself'. In the absence of such a notification, the local tribunal may, and should, 'continue with the trial up to (and including) the definitive judgement'.[2]

Can. 1418 Every tribunal has the right to call on other tribunals for assistance in instructing a case or in communicating acts.

2862 This canon establishes a clear *right* of 'every tribunal', even in respect of a tribunal of higher grade, 'to call on other tribunals for assistance' in the various matters which may arise in the instruction of a case, whether these be in respect of so-called 'rogatory commissions' or of any other reasonable request for cooperation or exchange of information. For the tribunal requested, this is not merely a matter of supplying a courtesy; it is, rather, a matter of fulfilling a legal obligation. Among those who have had experience of the operation of ecclesiastical tribunals, the almost universal verdict is one of deep appreciation of the cooperation of their colleagues. It would not be unreasonable if the tribunal which is requested to help were to charge a modest fee for its service.

---

[1] For an informative summary of the different grades and kinds of tribunals, cf. CCLA 878–879 at Title II; Chiappetta II n.4617.

[2] For a technicality to be observed in this regard, cf. Comm 10(1978) 190, and 228 at Can. 16 §2. For the theological background to this canon, cf. especially the dogmatic constitution of the First Vatican Council *Pastor Aeternus* 18.VII.1870 Session IV: DS n.3063.

Part I Trials in General

Chapter I
THE TRIBUNAL OF FIRST INSTANCE

Article 1
The Judge

Can. 1419 §1 In each diocese and for all cases which are not expressly excepted in law, the judge of first instance is the diocesan Bishop. He can exercise his judicial power either personally or through others, in accordance with the following canons.

§2 If the case concerns the rights or temporal goods of a juridical person represented by the Bishop, the appeal tribunal is to judge in first instance.

This canon enunciates a basic principle: the diocesan Bishop, in virtue of his power of governance (see Cann. 375, 381 §1), is the judge in first instance of every case arising in his diocese, apart from those cases which are 'expressly excepted in law' (see e.g. Cann. 1404–1405). The same is true of those prelates who are equivalent to diocesan Bishops (see Cann. 368, 381 §2). The canon goes on, however, to state that this judicial power may be exercised 'either personally or through others, in accordance with the following canons'. In fact and in normal practice, the diocesan Bishop exercises his judicial function through the judicial Vicar or 'Officialis' whom he is obliged to appoint in virtue of Can. 1420. **2863**

The only exception to the rule that the Bishop be the adjudicator of a case arising within his diocese is that dealt with in §2, i.e. 'if the rights or temporal goods of a juridical person represented by the Bishop', e.g. the diocesan Curia, a diocesan trust, were in question: in such a situation, 'the appeal tribunal', which will normally be that of the Metropolitan, is to determine the issue; should the situation concern a metropolitan see itself, the determining tribunal will be that which, with the approval of the Apostolic See, the Metropolitan has designated 'in a stable fashion' (Can. 1438 2°). **2864**

Can. 1420 §1 Each diocesan Bishop is obliged to appoint a judicial Vicar, or 'Officialis', with ordinary power to judge. The judicial Vicar is to be a person distinct from the Vicar general, unless the smallness of the diocese or the limited number of cases suggests otherwise.

§2 The judicial Vicar constitutes one tribunal with the Bishop, but cannot judge cases which the Bishop reserves to himself.

The appointment of a judicial Vicar or 'Officialis' is a matter not of choice but of obligation for every diocesan Bishop, as for every prelate equivalent in law to him. Once appointed, the judicial Vicar has ordinary, not just delegated, power: his office is equivalent, in effect, to that of a Vicar general, though in a different field (see Cann. 131 §1, 135 §3). He is therefore 'to be a person distinct from the Vicar general', save only where 'the smallness of the diocese or the limited number of cases' in effect dictates otherwise. **2865**

Since the judicial Vicar 'constitutes one tribunal with the Bishop', it is not possible to enter an appeal to the Bishop against a decision of the diocesan tribunal, nor may the Bishop alter in any way a decision or judgement given by the judicial Vicar or his collegiate tribunal. The Bishop may, however, *reserve* certain cases – and, it would appear, certain types or categories of cases – to *himself*, i.e. to be judged by himself personally either as a sole judge or as the presiding judge of a collegiate tribunal. Any **2866** such reservation should be expressly stated and may not be presumed. The effect of this reservation is to remove from the judicial Vicar the authority to judge the case or cases in question.[1]

Can. 1420 §3 The judicial Vicar can be given assistants, who are called associate judicial Vicars or 'Vice-officiales'.

§4 The judicial Vicar and the associate judicial Vicars must be priests of good repute, with a doctorate or at least a licentiate in canon law, and not less than thirty years of age.

§5 When the see is vacant, they do not cease from office, nor can they be removed by the diocesan Administrator. On the coming of the new Bishop, however, they need to be confirmed in office.

2867 According to the needs of the diocese the Bishop may appoint one or a number of associate judicial Vicars, who equally enjoy ordinary power, in the exercise of which their specific task is to assist the judicial Vicar. Both the judicial Vicar and his associate(s) are required to have the qualities detailed in §4. The requisite academic qualifications are more exigent than in the 1917 Code.[2]

2868 It is appropriate, in view of their offices, that the judicial Vicar and his associate judicial Vicar(s) should have an effective stability of tenure. Accordingly:

– they may be removed from office only 'for a lawful and grave reason' (Can. 1422) no longer, as under the 1917 Code c.1573 §5, at the mere will or pleasure of the Bishop (*ad nutum Episcopi*).

– even when the See is vacant, 'they do not cease from office' (§5), unlike the case of a Vicar general (see Can. 481 §1); should the same person hold both the office of judicial Vicar and that of Vicar general (see Can. 1420 §1), then he ceases from the latter office but retains the former, even if he himself were to be elected the

---

[1] Apart from the 'personal reservation' authorised by Can. 1420 §2, may the Bishop delegate the hearing of a particular case to a judge or judges not possessing ordinary power? There are two views on this question, some commentators maintaining that he may, others that he may not. The former view is at least tenable, if not the more probable: cf. Chiappetta I-II nn.862, 4631; CCLA 881 at Can. 1419. In practice, the proper ordering of the judicial function in a diocese would require, as a minimum, that in advance of any such delegation the Bishop would consult with his diocesan judicial Vicar; any executive arrangement which would in effect exclude such a consultation would be, to say the least, administratively unwise.

[2] The former Code c.1573 §4 required that these office-holders possess a doctorate in canon law 'or be otherwise expert'; the current law demands that they have 'at least a licentiate in canon law', whether or not they have any other theological qualification or practical judicial expertise arising from experience: cf. Comm 10(1978) 230 at Can. 19 §4. The same requirement holds for other judges to be appointed by the Bishop in accordance with Can. 1421. All of this reflects an obviously laudable attempt by the legislator – in face particularly of the recent practice in some tribunals, especially in matrimonial cases – to maintain a high level of canonical expertise among those who administer justice in the Church. It must, however, be recognised that in current circumstances, in some parts of the Church particularly, it is not always possible to achieve the ideal of merely academic qualification: there is still a case to be made for those who, in the terms of the 1917 Code, are 'otherwise expert'. Such situations do require the authorisation of the Apostolic Signatura (Can. 87 §1; cf. Comm 16 (1984) 55 at Can. 1373 §3) which, it has to be said, has shown itself to be understanding of and sympathetic to submissions in this regard. In this difficult jurisprudential situation, the best way forward would appear to be by way of a mutually trusting cooperation between local tribunals and the Apostolic Signatura.

interim diocesan Administrator (see Can. 421 §1) – unless of course he himself were then to choose to appoint a new judicial Vicar.[1]

– they cannot be removed from office by the interim diocesan Administrator, not even, it would appear, for the 'lawful and grave reason' of Can. 1422; on the accession of the next Bishop however, 'they need to be confirmed in office' (§5): while this confirmation may be implicit or tacit,[2] it is preferable that it would be in writing and would specify the duration of the appointment.

Can. 1421 §1 In each diocese the Bishop is to appoint diocesan judges, who are to be clerics.

§2 The Bishops' Conference can permit that lay persons also be appointed judges. Where necessity suggests, one of these can be chosen in forming a college of judges.

§3 Judges are to be of good repute, and possess a doctorate, or at least a licentiate, in canon law.

To carry out the functions assigned to him in the law, the judicial Vicar requires the active assistance of other judges: hence the obligation on each diocesan Bishop 'to appoint diocesan judges' (§1). The norm is that they 'be clerics', i.e. Bishops, priests or deacons, to be freely chosen by the Bishop from either the diocesan or the religious clergy, or even from clergy outside the diocese.[3] Subject however to the authorisation of the competent Bishops' Conference, they may also be lay persons (§2), men or women.[4] Lay persons thus appointed may form one, but only one, member of a collegiate tribunal, whether of three or of five, not however a sole judge in any case.[5] 2869

Can. 1422 The judicial Vicar, the associate judicial Vicars and the other judges are appointed for a specified period of time, without prejudice to the provision of Can. 1420 §5. They cannot be removed from office except for a lawful and grave reason.

In accordance with the requirement of stability, to which reference was made above at Can. 1420, the judicial Vicar, his associates and all other judges, clerical and lay, must be appointed for a specific term – a minimum, one would think, of three years, preferably perhaps of five (which would seem to be the current practice of the Holy See); the term is always renewable. In the course of that term they may be removed from office only 'for a lawful and grave reason', which clearly would have to be identified and established: some such reasons are indicated in Can. 1457 §1; others, even in relation to personal conduct, could arise. 2870

---

[1] The contrary prescription of the 1917 Code c.1573 §7 has been dropped. Cf. also Comm 10 (1978) 230 at Can. 19 §6.

[2] Cf. Chiappetta II n.4634.

[3] Unlike under the 1917 Code (c.1574 §1), there is no upper limit to the number of judges who may be appointed – this will simply be determined by the needs of the diocese – but in view of Can. 1425 §2 they may not be fewer than four.

[4] The possibility of having the laity as judges in an ecclesiastical tribunal is a major change from the legislation of the 1917 Code; in the sense of Can. 207 §1, 'lay persons' includes non-clerical male religious and all religious Sisters. This change was first introduced by Pope Paul VI in CM n.V §1. Cf. Comm 10(1978) 231 at Can. 20 §1; 16(1984) 54–55 at Can. 1373 §2. The fundamental background is dealt with in our commentary on Can. 129 §2. For the manner in which Bishops' Conferences have availed themselves of this faculty, cf. LCE Tavola per Paesi e Canoni at Can. 1421.

[5] Cf. Comm 10(1978) 231 at Can. 20 §1. As for the qualities required in these diocesan judges (§3), cf. n.2867 above note 2.

Book VII Judicial Procedures

Can. 1423 §1 With the approval of the Apostolic See, several diocesan Bishops can agree to establish one tribunal of first instance in their dioceses, in place of the diocesan tribunals mentioned in Cann. 1419-1421. In this case the group of Bishops, or a Bishop designated by them, has all the powers which the diocesan Bishop has for his tribunal.

§2 The tribunals mentioned in §1 can be established for all cases, or for some types of cases only.

2871 This canon provides for the establishment of interdiocesan or regional tribunals. The provision is intended to cater for the situation which can arise when in any number of contiguous dioceses, be they of the same province or not, the Bishops concerned consider it advisable to pool their resources in the matter of discharging their judicial obligations, i.e. through their tribunals. Such a situation can arise by reason e.g. of the scarcity of qualified tribunal personnel, the need to introduce a greater efficiency and expedition especially when a large number of cases are calling for attention, etc. For such circumstances the canon provides an option; it does not impose an obligation.

2872 Should the Bishops concerned agree to avail themselves of this option, the first step is to seek 'the approval of the Apostolic See'. In practice, this means the submission of a request, detailing the problem and the proposed solution, to the Supreme Tribunal of the Apostolic Signatura, which has shown itself to be understanding of these matters and willing to accommodate the diocesan Bishops involved.[1] On receipt of the requisite approval, the new regional tribunal is to be erected by decree of the Bishops themselves. The details of its structure and operation will obviously depend in great measure upon the prevailing local circumstances. The following points of law are to be noted:

(a) the new tribunal is one of first instance and as such takes the 'place of the pre-existing diocesan tribunals mentioned in Cann. 1419-1421' (§1); the question of its tribunal of appeal will obviously have had to be settled in the prior negotiations with the Holy See: it could be e.g. a local metropolitan tribunal or a tribunal specifically set up for this purpose, whether on a regional or even a national basis.

(b) the administration of the new tribunal is entrusted either to 'the group of Bishops' involved, or to 'a Bishop (presumably one of themselves) designated by them', normally designated the 'Moderator'; practice has shown the latter to be the more efficient and better option but, whichever option is chosen, the group or the individual Bishop has all the powers which the diocesan Bishop has for his tribunal' (§1), to the exclusion therefore of all others.[2]

(c) the new tribunal 'can be established for all cases, or for some types of cases only' (§2); this would have to be specified in the statutes approved by the Holy See and incorporated into the decree of erection. If it be for all cases, the judicial Vicar of the new tribunal becomes, in effect, the judicial Vicar of each of the constituent dioceses. If, on the other hand, it be for some types of cases only – cases of marriage nullity being in current circumstances the most likely possibility – the judicial Vicar of each of the constituent dioceses retains his authority and sole competence in respect of all other judicial cases in his diocese; this is so even in respect of the judicial Vicar of one of the constituent dioceses who may be nominated judicial Vicar of the new regional tribunal.

---

[1] Cf. PB art 124 4°; Ap Sig norms *Ut causarum iudicialium* 28.XII.1970: AAS 63(1971) 486-492: CLD 7(1968-1972) 920-926, which norms have now been modified in this canon.

[2] In this regard cf. CCom rep 28.II.1986, cited at Can. 1673 3°: AAS 78(1986) 1323.

Part I Trials in General

Can. 1424 In any trial a sole judge can associate with himself two assessors as advisers; they may be clerics or lay persons of good repute.

In any trial which may be heard by a sole judge (for the contrary situation, see Can. 1425 §§1 and 2), that sole judge may, at his own discretion, 'associate with himself (a maximum of) two assessors as advisers'. If the judge decides to avail himself of such assistance, the only function of the assessors is advisory, particularly e.g. on a matter calling for a special expertise: they have no judicial function and accordingly have no vote in the decision of the court. Provided they be 'of good repute' and – as the matter clearly demands – of appropriate expertise, they may be 'clerics or lay persons' men or women.[1] In their regard, appropriate account would have to be taken of the prescriptions of Cann. 1448–1449, 1454–1455.

Can. 1425 §1 The following matters are reserved to a collegiate tribunal of three judges, any contrary custom being reprobated:

1° contentious cases: a) concerning the bond of sacred ordination; b) concerning the bond of marriage, without prejudice to the provisions of Cann. 1686 and 1688;

2° penal cases: a) concerning offences which can carry the penalty of dismissal from the clerical state; b) concerning the imposition or declaration of an excommunication.

In many forms of judicial trial in the Church, the case may be heard by a sole judge. This paragraph, however, prescribes that in certain cases there must be a collegiate tribunal of, at minimum, three judges, namely:

(a) *in contentious cases concerning*

- 'the bond of sacred orders', i.e. cases where the claim is that a particular ordination was null and void.
- 'the bond of marriage', i.e. cases where the claim is that a particular marriage was null and void; in this regard, however, account must also be taken of the documentary process of Cann. 1686, 1688.

(b) *in penal cases concerning*

- 'offences which can carry the penalty of dismissal from the clerical state': these are *only* those dealt with in Cann. 1364 §2, 1367, 1370 §1, 1387, 1394 §1, 1395, 1397.
- 'the imposition or declaration of an excommunication': imposition refers to *ferendae sententiae* excommunication, declaration to that which is *latae sententiae* (see Can. 1314).

Note that any existing custom which may be contrary to this regulation is hereby reprobated, with the consequences detailed in Cann. 5 §1 and 28. This however must now be read in the light of the prescription of §4 below of this same canon.[2]

Can. 1425 §2 The Bishop can entrust the more difficult cases or those of greater importance to the judgement of three or of five judges.

---

[1] Cf. Comm 10(1978) 223 at Can. 23.
[2] Under the 1917 Code c.1892 1°, the use of a fewer number of judges than that prescribed would have resulted in an irremediable nullity of the court's judgement; in the current law the resulting nullity is 'simply remediable' (Can. 1622 1°).

2875 In respect of the cases dealt with in §1, the assignment of a minimum of three judges is mandatory. There can also, however, be other cases in which it would appear advisable or helpful to have more than a sole judge: for such cases those namely which are 'more difficult' or 'of greater importance' – this paragraph gives the competent Bishop (not the judicial Vicar, unless he has from the Bishop a general mandate in this regard) the option of assigning either three or even five judges. This could well be an advisable, even an impelling, option in e.g. a particularly complex or sensitive case, whether contentious or penal.[1]

Can. 1425 §3 The judicial Vicar is to assign judges in order by rotation to hear the individual cases, unless in particular cases the Bishop has decided otherwise.

2876 The general principle enacted in this paragraph is quite clear. Within the limits of that principle, each local tribunal is entitled to work out and to adapt its own practice.

Can. 1425 §4 In a trial at first instance, if it should happen that it is impossible to constitute a college of judges, the Bishops' Conference can for as long as the impossibility persists, permit the Bishop to entrust cases to a sole clerical judge. Where possible, the sole judge is to associate with himself an assessor and an auditor.

2877 This paragraph introduces a major change in the law on judicial procedure. It reflects a recognition of the fact that in the current circumstances of some first instance tribunals – principally, it would appear, by reason of the substantial increase in the number of marriage-nullity cases, partly also by reason of the decrease in the number of available competent judicial personnel – it may be necessary to permit to a sole judge the determination of a case which otherwise, ideally, would be heard by a collegiate court. The law now permits the assignment by the competent Bishop[2] of any case, including any of those enumerated in §1 of this canon, to a sole judge, subject however to the following conditions:

(a) that the competent Bishops' Conference, by decree in accordance with Can. 455, permits this arrangement, but only 'for as long as the impossibility persists'.[3]

(b) that the sole judge be a cleric.

2878 It is recommended, not required, that 'the sole judge is to associate with himself an assessor and an auditor'. What this means, in effect, is that the judge would be well advised, depending on the circumstances, to enlist the help of one ('an assessor') more experienced than himself in whatever technical matters might be involved, and of one ('an auditor') who would carry out the task of taking the evidence of the various persons concerned (see also Can. 1424).

Can. 1425 §5 Once judges have been designated, the judicial Vicar is not to replace them, except for the gravest of reasons, which must be expressed in a decree.

---

[1] Some commentators have proposed that if a collegiate tribunal of five judges has, in accordance with this canon, determined a case at first instance, then a five-judge court must also be assigned at second instance (cf. Can. 1441). Pending any authentic interpretation, such a view cannot be regarded as obligatory.

[2] The Bishop could obviously delegate this authority to the relevant judicial Vicar.

[3] For the varying extent to which Bishops' Conferences have availed themselves of this faculty, cf. LCE Tavola per Paesi e Canoni at Can. 1425. In view of the time-restriction imposed by the canon, it is clear that the relevant decree should include a clause for its obligatory review within a specified time.

Once a judge or judges have been assigned to a particular case, the judicial Vicar may not replace either or any of them 'except for the gravest of reasons', e.g. serious illness, the encroachment of other demanding duties, an unexpected conflict of interest, or the like. Should such a situation arise, the judicial Vicar is obliged to issue a formal decree to this effect, giving the precise reason for the substitution and nominating the substitute judge.[1]

2879

Can. 1426 §1 A collegiate tribunal must proceed in a collegiate fashion and give its judgement by majority vote.

When a case is heard by a collegiate tribunal, the effective decision is that of the majority of the judges, but all are obliged to sign it. Unlike the 1917 Code, however, the current law provides for the possibility of a written dissenting judgement which, if there be an appeal, must be forwarded to the appeal tribunal (see Can. 1609 §4).

2880

Can. 1426 §2 As far as possible, the judicial Vicar or an associate judicial Vicar must preside over the collegiate tribunal.

This paragraph expresses an ideal, which in fact is often possible of achievement. Equally, however, it acknowledges the possibility that, principally because of the number of cases before a tribunal – more often than not, marriage-nullity cases – this ideal cannot be achieved. If possible, the judicial Vicar or one of the associate judicial Vicars is to be the 'presiding judge' in a collegiate tribunal; if this be not possible, one of the judges appointed to form the college is to be nominated to preside over and to order the conduct of the trial.

2881

Can. 1427 §1 If there is a controversy between religious or houses of the same clerical religious institute of pontifical right, the judge at first instance, unless the constitutions provide otherwise, is the provincial Superior or, if an autonomous monastery is concerned, the local Abbot.

§2 Without prejudice to a different provision in the constitutions, when a contentious matter arises between two provinces, the supreme Moderator, either personally or through a delegate, will be the judge at first instance. If the controversy is between two monasteries, the Abbot superior of the monastic congregation will be the judge.

§3 Finally, if a controversy arises between physical or juridical persons of different religious institutes or even of the same clerical institute of diocesan right or of the same lay institute, or between a religious person and a secular cleric or a lay person or a non-religious juridical person, it is the diocesan tribunal which judges at first instance.

This canon, specifically inserted despite some proposals to the contrary,[2] regulates the procedure to be adopted when a controversy in the context of religious life calls for judicial determination. It is based on three principles:

2882

– it determines only the judge of first instance;
– it grants judicial power only to clerical religious institutes of pontifical right (see Cann. 588 §2, 589);[3]

---

[1] It would appear that the giving of the reason(s) is not required for the validity of this decree: cf. Comm 10(1978) 234 at Can. 24 §5.

[2] Cf. Comm 10(1978) 235 at Can. 26.

[3] Excluded as such from the exercise of judicial power are therefore lay institutes (Can. 588 §3), clerical religious institutes of diocesan right (Can. 589), secular institutes (Can. 710), and societies of apostolic life (Can. 731) even those which are clerical and of pontifical right. Some commentators have questioned the exclusion of the last-mentioned and even suggested that this is a *lacuna iuris* to be supplied on the basis of analogy with Can. 1427 §1: cf. e.g. Chiappetta II n.4653 note 8.

– for the situations dealt with in §§1 and 2, it allows that other arrangements may be sanctioned by the constitutions of the institute in question.

2883 In the light of those principles, the canon determines who is to be the judge in the following situations:

(a) if the controversy is between either religious or houses of the same institute, it is the provincial Superior (§1);

(b) if the controversy is between members of an autonomous monastery (see Can. 613), it is the local Abbot (§1);

(c) if the controversy is between two provinces of the same institute, it is the supreme Moderator, who may judge either personally or through his delegate (§2);

(d) if the controversy is between two autonomous monasteries, it is the Abbot superior of the monastic congregation (§2);

(e) if the controversy is between any of the following, the diocesan tribunal, whose competence will be determined in accordance with Cann. 1407–1415, is to judge (§3), viz

  (i) physical or juridical persons of different religious institutes;

  (ii) physical or juridical persons of the same clerical institute of diocesan right or of the same lay institute;

  (iii) a religious person, of whatever kind, and a secular cleric;

  (iv) a religious person and a lay person;

  (v) a religious person and a non-religious juridical person.

Article 2
Auditors and Relators

Can. 1428 §1 The judge or, in the case of a collegiate tribunal, the presiding judge, can designate an auditor to instruct the case. The auditor may be chosen from the tribunal judges, or from persons approved by the Bishop for this office.

§2 The Bishop can approve clerics or lay persons for the role of auditor. They are to be persons conspicuous for their good conduct, prudence and learning.

§3 The task of the auditor is solely to gather the proofs in accordance with the judge's commission and, when gathered, to submit them to the judge. Unless the judge determines otherwise, however, an auditor can in the meantime decide what proofs are to be collected and the manner of their collection, should any question arise about these matters while the auditor is carrying out his or her role.

2884 In every trial it is necessary that a certain volume of evidence be gathered, for the consideration and ultimate determination of the court. This task can be undertaken by the judge himself or, in the case of a collegiate tribunal, by the presiding judge. In many situations however, especially in busy matrimonial tribunals, it is customary and helpful for the court to avail itself of the facility afforded by this canon whereby an *Auditor* is designated by the (presiding) judge. The specific task of the auditor is 'to instruct the case' (§1), i.e. 'to gather the proofs in accordance with the judge's commission and, when gathered, to submit them to the judge' (§3). The auditor as such does not have any power of decision over the matter at issue before the court, but – in the absence of any contrary instruction from the judge (which would be very unusual) – does have a distinct and valuable discretionary power in determining what evidence or proof is to be collected and how precisely this is to be sought in the circumstances (§3). Although the judge would normally provide the auditor with a list of those persons whose testimony is to be sought, those documents which are required, etc. and with appropriate questionnaires drawn up by the defender of the bond, the auditor must be aware of the possibility of other elements of proof, even e.g. of a new ground of nullity, which might come to light during the instruction of the case: a characteristic of an effective auditor is the capacity to discern at once and to evaluate accurately such new elements of proof as might arise in the course of the trial, and to act accordingly without the need to refer back to the judge.[1]

2885 The auditor may be chosen either 'from the tribunal judges' (see Can. 1421) – even from among the judges of the collegiate tribunal assigned to the case in question – or 'from persons approved by the Bishops for this office' (§1). Those to be approved may be either clerics or lay persons (§2) whether men or women.[2] Though they are not required to have a specific academic qualification, they must be persons 'conspicuous for their good conduct, prudence and learning': the *learning* in question would certainly have to comprise a basic knowledge of the subject under investigation e.g. Christian marriage, its nature and properties etc. and of the procedural rules involved in the trial.[3] The Bishop's approval is required for the validity of the procedural acts to be carried out by the auditor, though he could of course – and in practice often does – delegate this power of approval to the judicial Vicar.

2886 At first sight, this Can. 1428 might appear to suggest that in any particular case there may be only one auditor. This is true only to the extent that, in accordance with §1, only one person may be designated by the (presiding) judge 'to instruct the (entire) case' on behalf of the court. But there are many situations in which someone other than that person will in fact take the evidence required by way of proof and, to that extent, fulfil the task of 'auditor' as determined in §3. This will always occur e.g. when it is necessary for the instructing auditor to seek evidence by way of rogatorial commission from persons residing in another jurisdiction (see Can. 1418). Equally, however, there is no reason why the judge should not designate other auditors within his own jurisdiction to assist the instructing auditor in the actual taking of evidence. This has in fact become a feature in many contemporary tribunals and has greatly benefited the efficiency and expedition of tribunal work; it is a sphere in which the laity in particular can play a valuable role.

Can. 1429 The presiding judge of a collegiate tribunal is to designate one of the judges of the college as *ponens* or *relator*. This person is to present the case at the meeting of the judges and set out the judgement in writing. For a just reason the presiding judge can substitute another in the place of the *ponens*.

---

[1] In view of the nature of the auditor's office, it would clearly never be lawful to nominate to that task one who is already the defender of the bond (or in an appropriate situation the promotor of justice) or the advocate in the same case.

[2] Cf. Comm 10(1978) 236 at Can. 27. A significant and particularly helpful development in recent tribunal practice has been the nomination of lay persons as auditors, who not only can supply a need where there is a shortage of clergy, but also can fruitfully – for themselves and for others – exercise the apostolate which is their prerogative as lay members of Christ's faithful: cf. Cann. 225, 228, 231 §1.

[3] Especially to be commended is the initiative launched in recent years, with episcopal approval, by a number of both regional and diocesan tribunals whereby there is provided a structured but simple programme of appropriate training for those, clerics and laity, who are willing to offer their services, on a part-time unpaid basis, to the apostolate of service to the Church specifically through its matrimonial tribunals.

2887 When a case is being heard by a collegiate tribunal, the presiding judge is obliged to designate one of their number (not excluding a lay judge appointed in accordance with Can. 1421 §2) as the so-called *ponens* or *relator*. He may designate himself; he may, and often profitably does, designate the judge whom he has designated as the auditor in accordance with Can. 1428 §1; he may not validly designate any judge who does not form part of the college in question. The function of the *ponens* is twofold:[1] having studied every aspect of the case, to present it and express his own opinion on it at the meeting of the judges at which the collegiate decision is pronounced (see Can. 1609); and then subsequently to draw up the written judgement of the court in accordance with the terms of Can. 1610 §§2–3. For any good reason, the presiding judge may substitute one of the other judges, including himself, for the *ponens* originally chosen: it is customary e.g. at least to offer this when the *ponens* finds himself in a minority position in respect of the court's decision (see Can. 1426 §1).

Article 3
The Promotor of Justice, the Defender of the Bond and the Notary

2888 Pivotal to the judicial system of the Church are the offices of the *promotor of justice* and of the *defender of the bond*. Subsequent canons spell out the details of their respective functions, obligations, interventions and so on; the present canons (1430–1436) establish the general principles and fundamental norms governing these offices.

Can. 1430 A promotor of justice is to be appointed in the diocese for penal cases, and for contentious cases in which the public good may be at stake. The promotor is bound by office to safeguard the public good.

Can. 1431 §1 In contentious cases it is for the diocesan Bishop to decide whether the public good is at stake or not, unless the law prescribes the intervention of the promotor of justice, or this is clearly necessary from the nature of things.

§2 If the promotor of justice has intervened at an earlier instance of a trial, this intervention is presumed to be necessary at a subsequent instance.

2889 The specific function of the promotor of justice is to be the official guardian and custodian of the public good (Can. 1430), i.e. the good of the Church, of its rights and laws, and the general good of the community. Can. 1430 makes it obligatory that such an officer be appointed in each diocese (see also Can. 1435). The intervention of the promotor is required:

(a) *in all penal cases*, since the offences under investigation are of their nature a disruption of due order and discipline in the community; in these cases, the promotor acts as plaintiff (see Can. 1721 §1).

(b) *in those contentious cases in which the public good may be at stake*: while contentious cases are in themselves private, a number of them can be such as to affect also the public good, e.g. cases concerning juridical persons, those concerning persons under age or of reduced mental capacity, etc.[2] In fact, the intervention of the promotor is determined in one or another of the following situations (Can. 1431 §1):

---

[1] For a special competence exercisable by the *ponens* in a marriage-nullity case, cf. Can. 1677.

[2] The public good is also at stake in every marriage-nullity case (cf. Can. 1691), but its protection is considered to be adequately guaranteed by the necessary presence of the defender of the bond.

- when the law itself prescribes it, e.g. Cann. 1431 §2, 1674 2°, 1696.
- when it 'is clearly necessary from the nature of things': it would appear that it is for the judge in the case to decide whether or not this clear necessity is verified.
- in the absence of either of the above situations, when the diocesan Bishop himself decides, in view of the actual circumstances within his jurisdiction, that the case in question is such as to put the public good at stake: in this context the question of public scandal could well be a determining factor.

2890 When the promotor of justice has been involved 'at an earlier instance of a trial', then it is *presumed* – not obligatory if this presumption is, in the unlikely event, overturned by contrary proof – that the promotor's intervention will be 'necessary at a subsequent instance', in which case it will be the promotor of justice of that latter instance tribunal.

Can. 1432 A defender of the bond is to be appointed in the diocese for cases which deal with the nullity of sacred ordination or the nullity or dissolution of marriage. The defender of the bond is bound by office to present and expound all that can reasonably be argued against the nullity or dissolution.

2891 Like the promotor of justice, the defender of the bond is also an official guardian of the public good, this time specifically in protecting the special bond which arises both from sacred ordination (diaconate, priesthood, Episcopate) and from marriage. Accordingly, this canon makes it equally obligatory that such an officer be appointed in each diocese (see also Can. 1435), with the specific task of intervening in any case concerning the nullity of ordination (see Cann. 1708–1712), or either the nullity (see Cann. 1671–1691) or the dissolution of marriage e.g. on the ground of non-consummation (see Cann. 1697–1706) or in favour of the faith.[1] In any such case, it is the defender's obligation 'to seek out, expose and clarify everything which can weigh in favour of the bond'. While strictly bound so to do, the defender may not on the other hand 'elaborate and make up at all cost an artificial defence ... He has the right to declare that, after a careful, thorough and conscientious examination of the record, he has found no reasonable objection to propose against the plea of the plaintiff or petitioner'.[2] But he should not ever go further than that, much less express any view in favour of either the nullity or the dissolution.

Can. 1433 In cases in which the presence of the promotor of justice or of the defender of the bond is required, the acts are invalid if they were not summoned. This does not apply if, although not summoned, they were in fact present or, having studied the acts, were able, at least before the judgement, to fulfil their role.

2892 In any case in which is required the intervention of the promotor of justice or of the defender of the bond, it is essential that these officers be officially summoned to attend every formal act of the court at which their presence is required by law – so much so that if they are not summoned, the acts in question, e.g. the examination of the parties or of the witnesses, are invalid and may not therefore be in any way taken into account by the court in coming to its decision. Note that what is prescribed is that the officer be *summoned*, not that he or she be present: thus e.g. if the defender of the bond had been summoned but for some good reason could not or chose not to be present on

---

[1] Cf. SCDF Normae 6.XII.1973 artt 4 §1, 7 §1: LE V 4244.
[2] Pope Pius XII address to Roman Rota 2.X.1944: AAS 36(1944) 281ff: CLD 3 612–622 at 615. Cf. also Pope John Paul II address to Roman Rota 26.I.1988: AAS 80(1988) 1178–1185 at 1183–1185: CLSN 74 (June 1988) 15–22; Grocholewski *Duty of the Defender of the Bond* RR 1992 125–127.

the occasion in question, the act would be perfectly valid and effective. The purpose of the rule clearly is to ensure that no formal act of the court take place without official advance notice thereof being given to the promotor and/or the defender.

2893 The rule does not, however, apply in either of the following two situations:
- if, though not summoned, they were in fact present, on their own initiative;
- if, though not summoned nor in fact present, they were given – *at least* before the court makes its decision, preferably much earlier – an appropriate opportunity so to inspect and study all the relevant acts of the case that they could make what they would regard as submissions to the court consonant with their role and their obligation under the law.[1]

Can. 1434 Unless otherwise expressly provided:

1° whenever the law directs that the judge is to hear the parties or either of them, the promotor of justice and the defender of the bond, if they are engaged in the trial, are also to be heard;

2° whenever, at the submission of a party, the judge is required to decide some matter, the submission of the promotor of justice or of the defender of the bond engaged in the trial has equal weight.

2894 On the assumption that they are engaged in the trial, this canon gives to both the promotor of justice and the defender of the bond the same rights as those enjoyed by the parties
– 'unless otherwise expressly provided' – in respect of the following two situations:
- 'whenever the law directs that the judge is to hear the parties or either of them', the promotor and/or the defender must also be given the opportunity to make such submissions as they may consider appropriate;
- whenever in the course of the trial the judge is requested by one of the parties to determine a particular issue, e.g. an incidental matter (see Cann. 1587–1591), the promotor and/or the defender must be invited to comment, and their observations are to be given 'equal weight' to that of the party's request.[2]

Can. 1435 It is the Bishop's responsibility to appoint the promotor of justice and defender of the bond. They are to be clerics or lay persons of good repute, with a doctorate or a licentiate in canon law, and of proven prudence and zeal for justice.

2895 The promotor and the defender are to be appointed:
- in the case of a diocesan tribunal, by the diocesan Bishop or by the prelate who in law is equiparated to him (see Cann. 368, 381 §2);
- in the case of a regional or interdiocesan tribunal, by the Bishop assigned as its Moderator.

They may be either clerics, or lay persons men or women,[3] provided however that they be of good repute, of established prudence, and hold either a doctorate or a licentiate in canon law: should a person with this academic qualification not be available, one who is truly versed in these matters and who has already had experience could well be

---

[1] This latter exception to the rule of Can. 1433 – which was not available under the 1917 Code c.1587 – is a welcome acknowledgement of the practicalities which exist in many contemporary and especially matrimonial tribunals.

[2] For a relevant comment in this regard, cf. Comm 10(1978) 239 at Can. 33 §2.

[3] Cf. Comm 10(1978) 239 at Can. 35 §1; 16(1984) 57 at Can. 1389.

considered – with, if needs be, the appropriate dispensation from the Apostolic Signatura. It is no longer necessary that, as in the 1917 Code c.1589 §2, the promotor of justice in a tribunal of a religious institute be a member of that institute.[1]

Can. 1436 §1 The same person can hold the office of promotor of justice and defender of the bond, although not in the same case.

§2 The promotor of justice and the defender of the bond can be appointed for all cases, or for individual cases. They can be removed by the Bishop for a just reason.

This canon speaks for itself and requires little elucidation. The offices of promotor and defender, both being guardians of the public good, are clearly not incompatible one to the other – save only where they might both be involved in the same case (§1): the typical example would be in a marriage-nullity case in which the promotor of justice would be the plaintiff in accordance with Can. 1674 2°. Each of these officers may be appointed either 'for all cases or for individual cases' (§2): the norm is that they be appointed for all cases. Their removal from office is a matter for the appropriate Bishop (§2), provided he has a 'just cause' for doing so (which need not imply any reflection whatever upon their competence: they could simply be required for another function e.g. a parish, a teaching post, in the diocese or region). It would appear, however, that they may not be removed, *sede vacante*, by the diocesan Administrator, but that they would obviously require the confirmation of the incoming Bishop, for the same reason as that prescribed for the judicial Vicar and his associate judicial Vicars (see Can. 1420 §5, and 1917 Code c.1590 §1). 2896

Can. 1437 §1 A notary is to be present at every hearing, so much so that the acts are null unless signed by the notary.

§2 Acts drawn up by notaries constitute public proof.

The presence of a notary[2] at every judicial hearing is so essential that 'the acts are null unless signed by the notary' (§1). There is, however, nothing in the law which would prevent the office of notary being assigned to another officer, e.g. an auditor, in a particular judicial proceeding; in fact, this is not infrequently a practical necessity, especially in marriage-nullity proceedings. Records drawn up and attested by an approved notary constitute public ecclesiastical documents (§2: see Can. 1540 §1). 2897

Chapter II
THE TRIBUNAL OF SECOND INSTANCE

Can. 1438 Without prejudice to the provision of Can. 1444 §1 n.1:

1° an appeal from the tribunal of a suffragan Bishop is to the tribunal of the Metropolitan, without prejudice to the provisions of Can. 1439;

2° in cases heard at first instance in the tribunal of the Metropolitan, the appeal is to a tribunal which the Metropolitan, with the approval of the Apostolic See, has designated in a stable fashion;

---

[1] Cf. Comm 10(1978) 239 at Can. 35 §2.

[2] The office and function of notaries – primary among whom is the diocesan Chancellor – are set out in Cann. 482–485.

3° **for cases dealt with before a provincial Superior, the tribunal of second instance is that of the supreme Moderator; for cases heard before the local Abbot, the second instance court is that of the Abbot superior of the monastic congregation.**

2898 A tribunal of second instance is that which is established for the purpose of receiving and determining appeals lodged against decisions made 'at first instance' by a so-called lower court. In determining such appeals the second-instance tribunal is entitled either to confirm the first decision, or to reverse it in whole or in part. Not every tribunal can be one of second instance; clearly there must be a certain order observed in this regard: it is this order which this canon determines. Subject only to one overriding principle, namely that it is always open to a litigant to bring an appeal even in second instance before the Roman Rota (see Can. 1444 §1 1°), the order is as follows:[1]

(a) from a decision of a suffragan Bishop's diocesan tribunal, the appeal is to be to the diocesan tribunal of the metropolitan Bishop of the province.[2]

(b) from a decision of a metropolitan Bishop's diocesan tribunal, the appeal is to be to that tribunal (often, though not necessarily, among the suffragan dioceses) selected on a permanent basis by the Metropolitan and approved as such by the Holy See.

(c) from a decision of a religious tribunal in the terms of Can. 1427 §1, the appeal is to be:

  (i) to the tribunal of the supreme Moderator of the institute, in those cases decided by a provincial Superior;

  (ii) to the tribunal of the Abbot superior of the monastic congregation, in those cases decided by a local Abbot.[3]

Can. 1439 §1 If a single tribunal of first instance has been constituted for several dioceses, in accordance with the norm of Can. 1423, the Bishops' Conference must, with the approval of the Apostolic See, constitute a tribunal of second instance, unless the dioceses are all suffragans of the same archdiocese.

§2 Even apart from the cases mentioned in §1, the Bishops' Conference can, with the approval of the Apostolic See, constitute one or more tribunals of second instance.

§3 In respect of the second instance tribunals mentioned in §§1-2, the Bishops' Conference, or the Bishop designated by it, has all the powers that belong to a diocesan Bishop in respect of his own tribunal.

2899 While Can. 1423 (q.v.) provides for the establishment, if needs be, of first-instance interdiocesan or regional tribunals, §1 of this canon makes the requisite corresponding provisions for the respective tribunals of appeal:

(a) if the interdiocesan tribunal encompasses *solely* a number of dioceses all of which are suffragans of the same archdiocese, the appeal tribunal is to be that of the metropolitan archdiocese; this would obviously not be the case if the archdiocese were itself a part of the interdiocesan tribunal, in which situation the provision of (b) below would apply.

---

[1] Principally by reason of the prescription of Can. 431 §2, the order specified here has modified that of the 1917 Code c. 1594 §3.

[2] A special arrangement exists where there is a regional or interdiocesan tribunal at first instance: cf. Can. 1439.

[3] The canon does not determine the tribunal of second instance in respect of the situations envisaged in Can. 1427 §2, but this obviously cannot be other than the Roman Rota or some other higher tribunal determined, with the approval of the Holy See, in the respective constitutions.

(b) if the interdiocesan tribunal encompasses a number of dioceses belonging to different ecclesiastical provinces, the Bishops' Conference is obliged to establish, with the approval of the Apostolic Signatura, another tribunal which would hear appeals from the regional tribunal.[1]

A different but analogous situation is considered in §2 which, without imposing an obligation to do so, entitles Bishops' Conferences to establish 'one or more tribunals of second instance', having first secured the approval of the Apostolic Signatura. The situation envisaged is where interdiocesan tribunals do not exist – rather, a number of individual diocesan tribunals – and where one appeal tribunal, or even a small number, would facilitate the efficiency and the uniformity of the appeal procedure.[2]

It should be noted in this general context that the Holy See is open to proposals which, while not strictly within the ambit of §1 or §2 of this canon, would appear more effectively to meet the local requirements of this or that country or region. Thus e.g. in Southern Africa, where there are four regional tribunals, there is an approved arrangement of appeal from one to another; in the USA, some appeal tribunals are that of the Metropolitan, some otherwise at a provincial level, others still by way of special arrangement to meet special needs.[3]

In so far as any of the second-instance tribunals referred to in §§1 and 2 may be set up, it then becomes a matter either for the appropriate Bishops' Conference or, as would seem considerably preferable, a Bishop designated by the Conference to act in effect as moderator of such tribunal, with 'all the powers that belong to a diocesan Bishop in respect of his own tribunal' (§3). Other arrangements approved by the Holy See would have to be accommodated accordingly.

Can. 1440 If competence by reason of the grade of trial, in accordance with the provisions of Cann. 1438 and 1439, is not observed, then the non-competence of the judge is absolute.

This canon states, in effect, that in an appeal from a tribunal of first instance to an appeal tribunal other than one of those determined by Cann. 1438–1439, the non-competence of the appeal judge is absolute, with the accompanying irremediable nullity determined by Can. 1620 1°. In an appropriate situation, however, one should consult Cann. 1419 §2 and 1683.

Can. 1441 The tribunal of second instance is to be constituted in the same way as the tribunal of first instance. However, if a sole judge has given a judgement in first instance in accordance with Can. 1425 §4, the second instance tribunal is to act collegially.

In stating that the tribunal of second instance must be constituted 'in the same way' as the first-instance tribunal, the canon is referring to the number of judges, whether one or a collegiate number (three or five), and to the presence or absence of either the

---

[1] Often, and especially where there are a number of regional tribunals in a country, the second-instance tribunal takes the form of a national appeal tribunal, as e.g. in Australia, Canada, Ireland.

[2] Cf. Comm 10(1978) 243 at Can. 40 §2. This situation exists in a number of countries, such e.g. as in England and Wales and in some parts of the USA.

[3] In the course of the revision of the Code, many even serious attempts were made to admit a general permission for tribunals of third, and therefore for the most part of final, instance at local level. None of these was accepted, principally on the ground that such an arrangement would, in effect, eliminate the Apostolic tribunal of the Roman Rota which has *inter alia* the important function of ensuring as far as possible a uniformity of jurisprudence throughout the Church: cf. Comm 10(1978) 243 at Can. 40; 16(1984) 59 at Can. 1397 §3.

defender of the bond or the promotor of justice or of both. Thus e.g. if a sole judge had determined the case at first instance, a sole judge would suffice on appeal, save only in respect of cases in which the sole first-instance judge had been assigned in virtue of Can. 1425 §4;[1] equally, if for whatever reason a collegiate tribunal had been employed at first instance, a collegiate tribunal must also be employed at second. This canon does not apply to the tribunals of the Apostolic See (see Can. 1402) which are governed by their own specific norms.

Chapter III
THE TRIBUNALS OF THE APOSTOLIC SEE

Can. 1442 The Roman Pontiff is the supreme judge for the whole catholic world. He gives judgement either personally, or through the ordinary tribunals of the Apostolic See, or through judges whom he delegates.

2905 By virtue of his office, the Pope has 'supreme, full, immediate and universal ordinary power in the Church' (Can. 331). This power may be distinguished as legislative, executive and judicial. There is no human authority higher within the Church. He can rightly be described as the 'supreme judge for the whole catholic world'. According to the canon, the Pope may exercise his supreme judicial power in three ways:

(a) he may do so personally, reserving a particular case for his own attention; this is in fact extremely rare;

(b) he may do so by entrusting a case to the ordinary tribunals of the Holy See; this refers to the Supreme Tribunal of the Apostolic Signatura and the Tribunal of the Roman Rota; it does not include the Apostolic Penitentiary which deals with cases of the internal forum only; nor does it include the tribunal of the Vicariate of Rome which is a tribunal of the diocese of Rome rather than of the Holy See;

(c) he may delegate other judges, depending upon the nature of the case to be dealt with and other circumstances.

Can. 1443 The ordinary tribunal constituted by the Roman Pontiff to receive appeals is the Roman Rota.

2906 The historical origins of the Roman Rota lie in the Apostolic Chancellery of the 12th century where individual cases were prepared and discussed by curial officials, often in the presence of the Pope. Gradually, he permitted some of these officials to decide the issue in some cases. Over the centuries, the Rota took on the structure of a tribunal, consisting of a college of judges (Auditors) appointed by the Pope, although often nominated by the governments of certain countries. The reorganisation and development of the Roman Curia in the 16th century resulted in an eclipse of the power of the Rota; many issues previously decided by its judges were entrusted to the various Congregations. With the fall of Rome in 1870, the judicial activity of the Rota practi-

---

[1] Can. 1425 in its §1 reserves certain first-instance cases, including those concerning the bond of marriage, to a collegiate tribunal of three judges. In its §4 however it takes account of the exceptional local situation where 'it is impossible to constitute a college of judges', and for such it empowers the appropriate Bishops' Conference to 'permit the (individual) Bishop to entrust cases to a sole clerical judge'. It is in respect of precisely that situation that the present canon insists that there must be a collegiate court (of at least three judges) at the second-instance appeal. As far as concerns marriage-nullity cases in this regard, cf. Comm 16(1984) 58 at Can. 1393.

Part I Trials in General

cally came to an end.[1] Pope Pius X restored the Rota in 1908, as a tribunal to consider judicial recourses made to the Holy See, providing it with its own special law.[2] Further norms were issued in 1934;[3] these were updated in 1969[4] in the light of *Regimini Ecclesiae Universae* and again in 1982.[5]

The Rota is composed of a number of judges (Auditors) appointed by the Pope and drawn from various parts of the world. The tribunal is presided over by a dean who is appointed by the Pope from among the Auditors for a specific period of time.[6] Ordinarily the judges sit in rotation; the dean constitutes a *turnus* of three Auditors to deal with each case.[7] Sometimes, however, a greater number of judges is assigned to a particular case[8] and, occasionally, a case is considered by all the Auditors.[9] The function of the Rota, as specified in the following canon, is to hear appeals made to the Holy See in judicial processes. 2907

Can. 1444 §1 The Roman Rota judges:

1° in second instance, cases which have been judged by ordinary tribunals of first instance and have been referred to the Holy See by a lawful appeal;

2° in third or further instance, cases which have been processed by the Roman Rota itself or by any other tribunal, unless there is a question of an adjudged matter.

This canon specifies which cases the Roman Rota is to hear insofar as it is the ordinary tribunal of the Holy See constituted to hear appeals. In second instance, the Rota hears those cases judged at first instance by ordinary tribunals and referred to the Holy See by a legitimate appeal (see Cann. 1628–1640). The Rota also judges cases in third or further instance if they have already been judged by the Rota itself or by any other tribunal, except where those cases have become adjudged matter (see Can. 1641). The faculty to consider cases at third instance is also given to other tribunals. Some of these have it habitually, e.g. the Rota of the Nunciature of Spain, the Tribunal of the Primate of Hungary, etc.; other tribunals have this faculty given to them occasionally, but only for each specific case, by the Apostolic Signatura in virtue of a special concession. 2908

Can. 1444 §2 This tribunal also judges in first instance the cases mentioned in Can. 1405 §3, and any others which the Roman Pontiff, either on his

---

[1] Various theories have been advanced concerning the name 'Rota' (Latin for 'wheel'); these include the trolley that was used to bring the cases around to the judges, and the fact that the judges sat around a table when in session. For further information concerning the origins and history of the Roman Rota, cf. *New Catholic Encyclopedia* XII 683–685; Roberti (Proc) I 346–354; Wernz-Vidal VI 113–114.

[2] Cf. ap con *Sapienti consilio* 29.VI.1908: AAS 1(1909) 7–19; *Regulae servandae in iudiciis apud S. Romanae Rotae Tribunal* 2.VIII.1910: AAS 2(1910) 783–850.

[3] *Normae S. Romanae Rotae Tribunalis* 29.VI.1934: AAS 26(1934) 449–491: LE I 1547–1567.

[4] *Nuove norme del Tribunale della Sacra Romana Rota* 25.V.1969: LE V 5550–5558: CLD 8 1055–1078.

[5] *Normae Sacrae Romanae Rotae*: 16.I.1982: AAS 74(1982) 490–517: LE VI 8356–8370: CLD 10 219–248. New norms for the Roman Rota were promulgated on 18 April 1994: AAS 86(1994) 508–540. These came into force on 1 October 1994 and replace completely the earlier norms. In an audience of 23 February 1995, Pope John Paul II approved these norms *in forma specifica*: AAS 87(1995) 366.

[6] PB 127.

[7] *Normae SRR* 1982 18.

[8] E.g. a case of nullity of marriage was heard by nine Auditors in 1986 because the matter was complicated and of great importance: cf. una Romana coram Serrano 27.I.1986: SRR Dec 78 49–75.

[9] *Normae SRRT* 1934 141.

own initiative or at the request of the parties, has reserved to his tribunal and has entrusted to the Roman Rota. These cases are judged by the Rota also in second or further instances, unless the rescript entrusting the task provides otherwise.

2909 Although, of its nature, the Roman Rota is an appeal tribunal, this canon points out that certain cases are reserved for judgement at the Rota in first instance. Some are reserved by law i.e. those cases listed in Can. 1405 §3; others may be reserved from time to time by the Pope, acting either on his own initiative or at the request of the parties. Appeals from such first instance judgements are to be dealt with by the Rota unless something else was stated expressly in the rescript reserving first instance judgement to the Rota.

Can. 1445 §1 The Supreme Tribunal of the Apostolic Signatura hears:

1° plaints of nullity, petitions for total reinstatement and other recourses against rotal judgements;

2° recourses in cases affecting the status of persons, which the Roman Rota has refused to admit to a new examination;

3° exceptions of suspicion and other cases against Auditors of the Roman Rota by reason of things done in the exercise of their office;

4° the conflicts of competence mentioned in Can. 1416.

§2 This same tribunal deals with controversies which arise from an act of ecclesiastical administrative power, and which are lawfully referred to it. It also deals with other administrative controversies referred to it by the Roman Pontiff or by departments of the Roman Curia, and with conflicts of competence among these departments.

§3 This Supreme Tribunal is also competent:

1° to oversee the proper administration of justice and, should the need arise, measures against advocates and procurators;

2° to extend the competence of tribunals;

3° to promote and approve the establishment of the tribunals mentioned in Cann. 1423 and 1439.

2910 Like the Roman Rota, the origins of the Apostolic Signatura lie in the practice of the Apostolic Chancellery of the 12th century, whereby some officials were entrusted with the task of preparing requests for favours to be presented to the Pope. These officials (*referendarii*) had the task of deciding which cases were a matter of a simple concession and which required prior full judicial investigation. When they were ready, these documents were submitted to the Pope for his signature. In the 15th century, the faculty of signing some of these decisions was entrusted by Pope Eugene IV to these same *referendarii*, who were then set up as a stable group. Pope Sixtus IV divided the office into the *Signatura iustitiae* and the *Signatura gratiae*; to the former were reserved judicial matters, to the latter, administrative matters.

2911 With the organisation of the Roman Curia of the 16th century, the functions of the *Signatura gratiae* were taken over, by and large, by the Congregations. This office eventually disappeared early in the 19th century. On the other hand, the *Signatura iustitiae* assumed more and more the role of a supreme court for the papal states.

With the fall of Rome in 1870, the *Signatura* lost almost all its remaining functions.[1] In 1908, Pope Pius X restored both sections of the former Signatura as the Supreme Tribunal of the Apostolic Signatura, giving it special norms.[2] These were updated in 1968 in the light of *Regimini Ecclesiae Universae*.[3]

According to the current norms, the tribunal of the Signatura is composed of twelve cardinals nominated by the Pope, one of whom is designated by him as Prefect.[4] The Prefect is assisted in his task by the Secretary, the Promotor of Justice, the Defender of the Bond. The Tribunal is divided into two sections: the First Section deals with judicial matters, the Second Section handles all administrative matters. The supreme tribunal has a threefold competence which is set forth in this canon.

(a) *Judicial competence*: The Apostolic Signatura is not an appeal tribunal: it judges challenges of various kinds (other than ordinary appeals) against decisions of the Rota (§1 1°–2°), challenges made against Auditors of the Rota in the performance of their duties (§1 3°), and conflicts of competence between first instance tribunals which are not subject to the same appeal tribunal (§1 4°). These cases are dealt with by the First Section.

(b) *Contentious administrative competence*: the Signatura handles all controversies arising from administrative acts; thus it is the place of final recourse against an administrative decree (see Cann. 1732–1739); it adjudicates in any administrative conflicts which are referred to it by the Pope or by one of the departments of the Curia; it is also the competent forum should any disputes of competence arise between various departments of the Curia.[5] These matters are handled by the Second Section of the Signatura.

(c) *Administrative competence*: it is here that the Signatura exercises its widest influence. In fulfilling its task of overseeing the proper administration of justice, the Signatura has regular contact with all the tribunals of the Church, receiving from them an annual report of the tribunal's activity as well as petitions for various matters. The law entrusts to the Signatura the duty of disciplining advocates and procurators if this is necessary. It is the Signatura which must be approached if, for particular reasons, a tribunal is to deal with a case for which it is not competent by law. The Signatura is also given the responsibility to promote and establish interdiocesan tribunals of first and second instance. Other responsibilities, not specified in the Code, include dealing with petitions to the Holy See requesting the commission of a case to the Rota or some other favour related to the administration of justice, and the granting of the faculty to lower tribunals to judge appeals ordinarily reserved to the Holy See.[6] These duties, while administrative in nature, are closely related to the judicial activity of the Church; they are discharged by the First Section of the Signatura.

2912

---

[1] For further information on the origins and history of the Apostolic Signatura, cf. *New Catholic Encyclopedia* XIII 209–210; Roberti (Proc) I 378–382; Wernz–Vidal VI 116–118.

[2] ap con *Sapienti consilio* 29.VI.1908: AAS 1(1909) 7–19; *Regulae servandae in iudiciis apud Supremum Signaturae Apostolicae Tribunal* 6.III.1912: AAS 4(1912) 187–206.

[3] *Normae speciales in Supremo Tribunali Signaturae Apostolicae ad experimentum servandae* 23.III.1968: LE III 5321–5332: CLD 7 246–272.

[4] In more recent times, the Pope has nominated several Bishops as members of the Signatura.

[5] PB 123.

[6] PB 124 2°, 4°.

Book VII Judicial Procedures

Title III
The Discipline to be Observed in Tribunals

Chapter I
THE DUTIES OF THE JUDGES AND OF THE OFFICERS OF THE TRIBUNAL

Can. 1446 §1 All Christ's faithful, and especially Bishops, are to strive earnestly, with due regard for justice, to ensure that lawsuits among the people of God are as far as possible avoided, and are settled promptly and without rancour.

2913 The avoidance of contention and litigation is a fundamental Christian principle.[1] Stated clearly and broadly here, it finds echoes throughout the rest of Book VII.[2] The canon makes it clear that the duty to avoid litigation rests on all the baptised, but above all it rests on the Bishops. There is to be no sweeping of matters under the carpet. Rather, a judicial process is to be avoided but 'with due regard to justice'. In other words, the rights of the parties involved must be respected fully. All disputes between Christians are to be resolved in a spirit of generosity and forgiveness.

Can. 1446 §2 In the early stages of litigation, and indeed at any other time as often as he discerns any hope of a successful outcome, the judge is not to fail to exhort and assist the parties to seek an equitable solution to their controversy in discussions with one another. He is to indicate to them suitable means to this end and avail himself of serious-minded persons to mediate.

2914 Once a judicial process has commenced, the judge has a special responsibility to seek ways of resolving the issue before a judgement is given. If he discerns any real hope of success, he is urged to encourage mediation between the disputing parties, using the assistance of other responsible persons if necessary.

Can. 1446 §3 If the issue is about the private good of the parties, the judge is to discern whether an agreement or a judgement by an arbitrator, in accordance with the norms of Cann. 1713–1716, might usefully serve to resolve the controversy.

2915 As one method of avoiding unnecessary trials, the Code suggests referring a matter to an independent arbiter. However, this may be done only in cases where the private good of the parties is in question (see Can. 1715 §1). In accordance with Can. 1691, this means that this procedure may not be invoked in marriage cases, although the law requires the judge in those cases to do his utmost to reconcile the parties and restore conjugal life (see Cann. 1676, 1695).

Can. 1447 Any person involved in a case as judge, promotor of justice, defender of the bond, procurator, advocate, witness or expert cannot subsequently, in another instance, validly determine the same case as a judge or exercise the role of assessor in it.

---

[1] Cf. Matt 5:25, 39–41.
[2] Cf. Cann. 1659 §1, 1676, 1695, 1713, 1718 §1 3°, 1718 §4, 1720, 1733, 1742 §1, 1748.

The law must ensure that anyone acting as a judge is above reproach. Therefore, someone who has taken part in a case at one instance in any of the capacities enumerated in the canon cannot, in another instance, serve as judge or act as an assessor. A breach of this norm will render the judgement irremediably null (see Can. 1620 1°). This prohibition is an added guarantee of the objectivity of the judicial procedures of the Church.

Can. 1448 §1 The judge is not to undertake the hearing of a case in which any personal interest may be involved by reason of consanguinity or affinity in any degree of the direct line and up to the fourth degree of the collateral line, or by reason of guardianship or tutelage, or of close acquaintanceship or marked hostility or possible financial profit or loss.

§2 The promotor of justice, the defender of the bond, the assessor and the auditor must likewise refrain from exercising their offices in these circumstances.

In order to guarantee the impartiality and integrity of the tribunal's operations, the law obliges the major officials of the tribunal (i.e. judges, promotor of justice, defender of the bond, assessor and auditor) to abstain from dealing with cases in which they may have any personal interest. The list of reasons contained in the canon is not exhaustive. Once the official in question becomes aware of the personal interest, he is to disqualify himself from further involvement in the case. Failure to do so may lead to an objection from the parties (see Can. 1449).

Can. 1449 §1 In the cases mentioned in Can. 1448, if the judge himself does not refrain from exercising his office, a party may object to him.

§2 The judicial Vicar is to deal with this objection. If the objection is directed against the judicial Vicar himself, the Bishop in charge of the tribunal is to deal with the matter.

§3 If the Bishop is the judge and the objection is directed against him, he is to refrain from judging.

§4 If the objection is directed against the promotor of justice, the defender of the bond or any other officer of the tribunal, it is to be dealt with by the presiding judge of a collegial tribunal, or by the sole judge if there is only one.

If a judge has become aware of some personal interest in a case in accordance with Can. 1448 and has not refrained from carrying out his duties, a party has the right to lodge an objection to him. This is to be done before the joinder of the issue unless the information emerges only afterwards (see Can. 1459 §2). Similar objections may be raised by the parties against the promotor of justice, the defender of the bond and any other tribunal official. This canon identifies the competent authority to deal with such objections:

(a) if the exception is made against one of the tribunal judges, it is the judicial Vicar who must decide the matter (§2);

(b) if the objection is raised about the judicial Vicar, then the Bishop who is responsible for the tribunal must deal with it (§2);

(c) if the exception is made against the promotor of justice, the defender of the bond, or any other of the tribunal officials, the presiding judge of a collegiate tribunal or a sole judge is to determine the issue;

(d) if the Bishop has reserved a case to himself (see Cann. 1419 §1, 1420 §2) and an objection is lodged against him, the law itself solves the problem: he is to abstain from judging the case.[1]

---

[1] Other authorities are competent to deal with exceptions in particular cases, e.g. exceptions against Rotal Auditors are heard by the Apostolic Signatura (see Can. 1445 §1 3°).

Can. 1450 If the objection is upheld, the persons in question are to be changed, but not the grade of trial.

2919 Once the objection has been received by the competent authority, the process is suspended until the incidental question has been resolved. If the exception is not accepted, the matter is closed (see Can. 1629 4°–5°) and the process will resume. On the other hand, should the competent authority accept the objection lodged, then the person against whom it was raised is to be replaced. The process will then continue at the original instance.

Can. 1451 §1 The objection is to be decided with maximum expedition, after hearing the parties, the promotor of justice or the defender of the bond, if they are engaged in the trial and the objection is not directed against them.

2920 In order to prevent undue delay and avoid possible injustice, the law requires that the incidental question of an exception against tribunal personnel be determined 'with maximum expedition' (see Can. 1629 5°). The parties are to be consulted as are the promotor of justice and the defender of the bond, if they are involved, unless, of course, the objection was lodged against them. Such matters can be dealt with efficiently by the oral contentious process (see Cann. 1656–1670).

Can. 1451 §2 Acts performed by a judge before being objected to are valid. Acts performed after the objection has been lodged must be rescinded if a party requests this within ten days of the admission of the objection.

2921 This canon establishes the principle that acts performed by a judge against whom an objection has been directed are valid. However, the law makes a distinction: any acts posited before the objection was lodged are valid and remain so; any acts performed after the objection was lodged may be rescinded at the request of a party, provided that this request is made within ten days of a decision accepting the objection.

Can. 1452 §1 In a matter which concerns private persons exclusively, a judge can proceed only at the request of a party. In penal cases, however, and in other cases which affect the public good of the Church or the salvation of souls, once the case has been lawfully introduced, the judge can and must proceed *ex officio*.

2922 In any judicial process, the role of the judge is fundamental. The law makes clear the limits of the judge's activity within the process: he may not do anything in a case concerning private persons except at the request of one of the parties; on the other hand, in penal cases and in other cases concerning the public good of the Church,[1] he may and, in some cases, he must act on his own initiative. In these latter cases, even if both parties lose interest, the judge may proceed with the investigation and the trial in order to safeguard the public good of the Church.

Can. 1452 §2 The judge can also supply for the negligence of the parties in bringing forward proofs or in opposing exceptions, whenever this is considered necessary in order to avoid a gravely unjust judgement, without prejudice to the provisions of Can. 1600.

2923 Since the primary concern of the judge is the pursuit of truth and the administration of justice, he may on occasion find himself in the position of introducing proofs or lodg-

---

[1] These include cases of nullity of marriage and nullity of sacred orders.

ing objections. While such activity belongs properly to the parties, the judge *may* intervene if he foresees that, without it, an unjust judgement might ensue. While it does not impose an obligation on the judge,[1] this faculty itself highlighting a contrast with those systems of civil law which are confined to an adversarial procedure – is a valuable option which, particularly in marriage-nullity cases, can greatly advance the search for objective truth. Normally, this supplementary activity should take place before the conclusion of the case (see Can. 1599). However, in certain circumstances, the law permits the presentation of further proofs even after the conclusion (see Can. 1600).

Can. 1453 Judges and tribunals are to ensure that, within the bounds of justice, all cases are brought to a conclusion as quickly as possible. They are to see to it that in the tribunal of first instance cases are not protracted beyond a year, and in the tribunal of second instance not beyond six months.

Cases pending before a tribunal ought to be processed as quickly as possible in accordance with the old adage, *justice delayed is justice denied*. This canon reduces the time-scale of a judicial process, over two instances, to one and a half years.[2] However, this does not affect the validity of a process which lasts longer. While delays in a particular case are often caused by the parties themselves, the law exhorts judges and tribunals to do all they can within the limits of justice to keep the length of processes to a minimum.[3]

Can. 1454 All who constitute a tribunal or assist in it must take an oath to exercise their office properly and faithfully.

The serious nature of the work of a tribunal is underlined by the requirement of an oath. This is demanded of all those who constitute a tribunal (i.e. judges, assessors, auditors, promotor of justice, defender of the bond, notaries) as well as those who assist in any way in the work of the tribunal, e.g. experts, interpreters, secretaries. No formula is provided but the oath should mention the obligation to fulfil faithfully whatever task is given them within the tribunal, in addition to the obligation to maintain secrecy (see Can. 1455).

Can. 1455 §1 In a penal trial, the judges and tribunal assistants are bound to observe always the secret of the office; in a contentious trial, they are bound to observe it if the revelation of any part of the acts of the process could be prejudicial to the parties.

Concerning the obligation to maintain secrecy, the Code makes a clear distinction between penal cases and contentious cases. Because of the delicate nature of what is involved in a penal case and the risk of harming a person's reputation, the obligation to observe secrecy is always binding. In contentious cases, on the other hand, secrecy is to be observed only if it is clear that harm or damage to the parties would follow the disclosure of some procedural act. No explicit mention is made of marriage-nullity cases in

---

[1] During the revision of the Code, it was suggested that the judge be obliged to act in order to supply for the negligence of parties. However, this was rejected by the Commission since it would place too great a burden on the judge: cf. Comm 10(1978) 253 at Can. 53 §2.

[2] In the 1917 Code c.1620 set the limits at two years in first instance and one year in second instance.

[3] The Pope recalled the duty of the tribunals to do what they could to overcome delays in processes: 'I know very well that the duration of the process does not depend only on the judges who must decide; there are many other factors which can cause delays. But you, to whom the task of administering justice has been entrusted ... must do your best to ensure that the process be carried out with the promptness which the good of souls demands and which the new Code of Canon Law prescribes ...' (Pope John Paul II address to Roman Rota 30.I.1986 n.6: CLSGBI Newsletter 69(March 1987) 6).

this canon. Inasmuch as they are cases concerning the public good, the outcome of such processes cannot be regarded as secret. However, all information obtained by tribunal personnel in the course of the investigation must remain strictly confidential.

Can. 1455 §2 They are also obliged to maintain permanent secrecy concerning the discussion held by the judges before giving their judgement, and concerning the various votes and opinions expressed there, without prejudice to the provisions of Can. 1609 §4.

2927　The judges of the tribunal are obliged particularly to observe permanent secrecy concerning what happens at their deliberative session. Since the tribunal 'must proceed in a collegiate fashion and give its judgement by majority vote' (Can. 1426 §1), it is in the best interests of justice that the discussion between the judges and the opinions expressed during the session remain secret. The only exception foreseen by the law is that of 'a judge who does not wish to accede to the decision of the others'; in conformity with Can. 1609 §4 (q.v.), he can require that his dissenting opinion be forwarded to the higher tribunal, if there is an appeal.

Can. 1455 §3 Indeed, the judge can oblige witnesses, experts, and the parties and their advocates or procurators, to swear an oath to observe secrecy. This may be done if the nature of the case or of the proofs are such that revelation of the acts or proofs would put at risk the reputation of others, or give rise to quarrels, or cause scandal or have any similar untoward consequence.

2928　The obligation to observe secrecy may be extended to cover persons who are not formally part of the tribunal. This is to be done when, in the view of the judge, the disclosure of information concerning the events under investigation or the process itself would have gravely negative consequences such as damage to a person's reputation, quarrels and disagreements between the parties or the witnesses or their families and friends, or grave scandal to the faithful. If he foresees such a danger, the judge has the authority to impose an oath of secrecy on witnesses, experts, the parties and their procurators or advocates.[1] This provision of law is of particular importance in marriage nullity cases, given the delicate and often confidential nature of the proofs presented.

Can. 1456 The judge and all who work in the tribunal are forbidden to accept any gifts on the occasion of a trial.

2929　The impartiality and objectivity of the tribunal and the judicial process must remain at all times above suspicion. For this reason, the law prohibits judges and all tribunal officials from accepting any gifts on the occasion of a trial. Anyone who breaches this norm is liable to a just penalty (see Can. 1386).

Can. 1457 §1 Judges can be punished by the competent authority with appropriate penalties, not excluding the loss of office, if, though certainly and manifestly competent, they refuse to give judgement; if, with no legal support, they declare themselves competent and hear and determine cases; if they breach the law of secrecy; or if, through deceit or serious negligence, they cause harm to the litigants.

2930　Because of their central role in settling disputes and controversies for the good of souls, the Church requires the highest possible standards of professional behaviour

---

[1] This obligation to observe secrecy is without prejudice to the provisions of Can. 1598 §1 concerning the publication of the acts. Of course, in order to avoid any of the serious dangers mentioned in Can. 1455 §3, the judge may decide that some act or acts may not to be made available to the parties.

from its judges. Hence, neglect or abuse of office constitutes a most serious offence for which the offender can be punished. The canon identifies four principal offences:

(a) if judges refuse to give judgement when they are certainly and manifestly competent to do so; this is a fundamental denial of justice;

(b) if judges hear and determine cases after declaring themselves competent although they have no legal basis for doing so; such an offence undermines the impartiality and objectivity of the Church's judicial activity;

(c) if the judges violate the law of secrecy (see Can. 1455); this may lead to the most serious negative consequences for the parties and for the Church;

(d) if, through deliberate deceit or neglect of their responsibilities within the process, the judges cause harm to the parties in a case.

Appropriate penalties are to be imposed upon any judge found guilty of such an offence. In some cases, this will entail his removal from office. Whatever the penalty, it is to be imposed by the competent authority; thus, in the case of first instance judges, this means the diocesan Bishop or the Bishop or group of Bishops responsible for an interdiocesan tribunal (see Can. 1423); in the case of appeal tribunal judges, this means the Metropolitan or the Bishops' Conference or the Bishop designated by the Conference if it is a national or interdiocesan appeal tribunal (see Can. 1439); if the Bishop himself is the judge who has offended, the matter should be referred to the Pope (see Can. 1405 §1 3°). The circumstances of each case will determine whether the penalties are to be imposed administratively or judicially. 2931

Can. 1457 §2 Tribunal officers and assistants are subject to the same penalties if they fail in their duty as above. The judge also has the power to punish them.

The high standard of behaviour required of judges is also expected of all tribunal officials and assistants. The same penalties are to be applied if they are guilty of neglect of duty or abuse of office. In their case, the offences will have to do with the violation of secrecy and harm to the parties caused by deceit or negligence in the discharge of their duties. Tribunal officials (i.e. auditors, assessors, promotor of justice, defender of the bond, notaries) and assistants (e.g. interpreters, secretaries, etc.) are to be appropriately punished by the judge of their own tribunal. 2932

Chapter II
THE ORDERING OF THE HEARING

Can. 1458 Cases are to be heard in the order in which they were received and entered in the register, unless some case from among them needs to be dealt with more quickly than others. This is to be stated in a special decree which gives supporting reasons.

The hearing of a case consists in the acceptance of a petition, the gathering of relevant evidence, discussion and decision by the judges. Justice is served best if cases are dealt with according to an objectively identifiable order. The law prescribes that the order of hearing is to be based on when the case was received by the tribunal. This preserves the tribunal from allegations of favouritism or bias. However, there are exceptions to this norm: some cases, e.g. those concerning the public good and penal cases, of their nature ought to be dealt with more quickly than others; sometimes 2933 urgent circumstances will require a speedy resolution of the case, e.g. danger of death or other emergency. In such cases, the judge is to issue a decree exempting the case from the usual order of hearing and giving the reasons in support of the decision.

Can. 1459 §1 Defects which can render the judgement invalid can be proposed as exceptions at any stage or grade of trial; likewise, the judge can declare such exceptions *ex officio***.**

2934 An exception may be defined as a positive opposition lodged against the persons involved in a judicial process or against the manner in which the case is being dealt with. These exceptions are described as *dilatory* if their effect is to delay the action, or *peremptory* if their effect is to extinguish the action altogether. This canon provides that exceptions concerning acts which may render the judgement invalid (see Cann. 1620, 1622) can be proposed at any time during the process and at any instance. Such exceptions may be lodged by either of the parties, by the promotor of justice or the defender of the bond, if they are involved in the case, and *ex officio* by the judge himself.

Can. 1459 §2 Apart from the cases mentioned in §1, exceptions seeking a delay, especially those which concern persons and the manner of trial, are to be proposed before the joinder of the issue, unless they emerge only after it. They are to be decided as soon as possible.

2935 All dilatory exceptions, apart from those concerned with the possible nullity of the sentence, are to be proposed early in the process, i.e. prior to the joinder of the issue. A dilatory exception may be lodged at a later stage only if the reason for the exception emerged after the joinder of the issue had taken place. In order to avoid undue delays in the overall process, exceptions are to be dealt with as quickly as possible.

Can. 1460 §1 If an exception is proposed against the competence of the judge, the judge himself must deal with the matter.

§2 Where the exception concerns relative non-competence and the judge pronounces himself competent, his decision does not admit of appeal. However, a plaint of nullity and a total reinstatement are not prohibited.

§3 If the judge declares himself non-competent, a party who complains of being adversely affected can refer the matter within fifteen canonical days to the appeal tribunal.

2936 A particular category of dilatory exceptions concerns the competence of the judge. These may be proposed by either of the parties, by the promotor of justice or the defender of the bond, if they are involved. The canon requires that any exceptions concerning competence are to be dealt with by the judge himself, not by another judge at the same instance nor by a judge of a higher instance (§1). If the exception concerns relative non-competence (see Can. 1407 §2) and the judge declares himself to be competent to hear the case, no appeal is possible against his decision. However, an aggrieved party may seek to lodge a plaint of nullity against that decision or seek total reinstatement (§2). By contrast, if the judge declares that he is in fact not competent, an aggrieved party has the right of recourse to the appeal tribunal within fifteen canonical days (§3).

Can. 1461 A judge who becomes aware at any stage of the case that he is absolutely non-competent, is bound to declare his non-competence.

2937 A judge is said to be absolutely non-competent if he attempts to judge a case which has been reserved to a higher authority because of the nature of the case itself or by reason of the persons involved (see Can. 1405), or if he attempts to deal with a case which has passed legitimately to a higher instance by means of an appeal or some other recourse (see Can. 1440). When a judge becomes aware of his absolute non-competence, no matter at what point of the trial, he is obliged by law to declare that lack of competence and cease all involvement in the process. Failure to do so will result in an irremediably null judgement (see Can. 1620 1°).

Can. 1462 §1 Exceptions to the effect that an issue has become an adjudged matter or has been agreed between the parties, and those other peremptory exceptions which are said to put an end to the suit, are to be proposed and examined before the joinder of the issue. Whoever raises them subsequently is not to be rejected, but will be ordered to pay the costs unless it can be shown that the objection was not maliciously delayed.

The effect of a *peremptory* exception is to extinguish an action pending before the tribunal or to prevent that action being instituted in the future. Some peremptory exceptions are said 'to put an end to the suit'; these arise e.g. if an issue has already become an adjudged matter (see Can. 1641) or if an agreement or reconciliation has been effected with the assistance of an arbiter (see Cann. 1713–1716). According to the canon, these exceptions must be lodged and examined before the joinder of the issue. However, the law permits them to be raised subsequently. In that event, the party proposing the exception will be ordered to pay the judicial expenses unless he or she can demonstrate that the delay in raising the objection was not malicious. 2938

Can. 1462 §2 Other peremptory exceptions are to be proposed in the joinder of the issue and treated at the appropriate time under the rules governing incidental questions.

Other peremptory exceptions prevent the prosecution of the action for the moment by seeking to declare invalid some essential element of the action. These exceptions are to be raised at the joinder of the issue. They are to be dealt with not immediately but are to be considered as incidental questions (see Cann. 1587–1591) at the proper time. 2939

Can. 1463 §1 Counter actions can validly be proposed only within thirty days of the joinder of the issue.

§2 Such counter actions are to be dealt with at the same grade of trial and simultaneously with the principal action, unless it is necessary to deal with them separately or the judge considers this procedure more opportune.

A counter action which has the purpose of 'removing or mitigating the plaintiff's plea' (Can. 1494), in order to be valid, must be instituted before the judge within thirty days of the joinder of the issue. Since this provision of law offers an opportunity to the respondent to bring his own action against the plaintiff, it is only reasonable that the law places strict time limits. Counter actions are to be handled by the same judge and in the same trial as the original or principal action, unless it is evident that they ought to be considered separately or the judge decides that it would be more appropriate to do so in the circumstances. 2940

Can. 1464 Questions concerning the guarantee of judicial expenses or the grant of free legal aid which has been requested from the very beginning of the process, and other similar matters, are normally to be settled before the joinder of the issue.

All other subordinate matters in a case are to be decided before the joinder of the issue. These would include the question of a deposit for judicial expenses and the granting of free legal aid. Such issues are to be determined in accordance with particular legislation (see Can. 1649 §1). 2941

Chapter III
TIME LIMITS AND POSTPONEMENTS

Can. 1465 §1 The so-called *fatalia legis*, that is time-limits set by law for the extinguishing of rights, cannot be extended, nor can they validly be shortened except at the request of the parties.

2942 Three kinds of time-limit may be distinguished. These are:
- *legal* if they are established by the law itself;
- *judicial*, if they are determined by the judge;
- *conventional*, if they are agreed by the parties.

Legal deadlines, known traditionally as the *fatalia legis*, are peremptory. In other words, when the time limit set by law has expired, the right may no longer be vindicated before the tribunal. Thus e.g. if an appeal is not lodged with the judge within fifteen days, it cannot be admitted (see Can. 1630 §1). Some legal deadlines, however, are not peremptory. In other words, when the time specified by law has elapsed, the right is not extinguished, e.g. if the judges defer a decision for more than the week permitted by Can. 1609 §5 the case itself does not come to an end on that account. Peremptory legal deadlines can never be extended for any reason. However, the law permits them to be shortened on occasion, but only at the request of the parties.

Can. 1465 §2 After hearing the parties, or at their request, the judge can, for a just reason, extend before they expire times fixed by himself or agreed by the parties. These times can never validly be shortened without the consent of the parties.

2943 Unlike time-limits established by law, judicial and conventional deadlines may be extended before they expire. Such an extension may only be granted by the judge for a just reason, either at the request of the parties, or *ex officio* if the parties have been consulted beforehand. These time limits cannot validly be shortened for any reason unless both parties in the case give their positive consent.

Can. 1465 §3 The judge is to ensure that litigation is not unduly prolonged by reason of postponement.

2944 While the law permits the judge in some cases to extend certain time limits, he must make sure that this causes no unnecessary delay in the process so that the case is concluded within the time foreseen by the law (see Can. 1453).

Can. 1466 Where the law does not establish fixed times for concluding procedural actions, the judge is to define them, taking into consideration the nature of each act.

2945 The law itself establishes time-limits concerning the most important procedural acts, e.g. Cann. 1505 §4, 1506, 1630 §1, 1633, 1734 §2, 1737 §2. However, in the course of a case, if a judge should discover that no time-limit has been set for a particular procedural act, he may set a deadline himself. In doing so, he is to keep in mind the nature of the act and the particular circumstances of the case.

Can. 1467 If the day appointed for a judicial action is a holiday, the fixed term is considered to be postponed to the first subsequent day which is not a holiday.

2946 In canon law, time is to be calculated according to the provisions of Cann. 201–203. When reckoning procedural time-limits, especially if they are peremptory, holidays (civil and religious) are an important factor to be kept in mind. In order to safeguard the rights of parties, if a day assigned as the canonical deadline coincides with a holiday in the tribunal, then the expiry of the time-limit is understood to be postponed until the first subsequent day on which the tribunal is working.

Chapter IV
THE PLACE OF TRIAL

Can. 1468 As far as possible, the place where each tribunal sits is to be an established office which is open at stated times.

When the tribunal is located at a fixed location which is open at specified times, the faithful can have easy access to the judicial activity of the Church, either personally or by means of the postal system. Wherever they are established, the tribunal offices should be large enough to accommodate all the essentials of judicial procedure securely and in reasonable comfort, e.g. interviews, typing of documents, filing of cases, meetings of judges.

Can. 1469 §1 A judge who is forcibly expelled from his territory or prevented from exercising jurisdiction there, can exercise his jurisdiction and deliver judgement outside the territory. The diocesan Bishop is, however, to be informed of the matter.

§2 Apart from the circumstances mentioned in §1, the judge, for a just reason and after hearing the parties, can go outside his own territory to gather proofs. This is to be done with the permission of, and in a place designated by, the diocesan Bishop of the place to which he goes.

Ordinarily, a judge may exercise his judicial power only within the territory of his jurisdiction.[1] However, the Code provides for two situations in which a judge may, in fact, exercise his authority in another territory:

(a) the first situation (§1) is that of a judge who has been expelled from his territory by force or who has been prevented from exercising his jurisdiction there by force: according to this canon, he may continue to act as judge and issue a judgement outside his own territory. The law requires that such a judge inform the diocesan Bishop of the place in which he is functioning; there is no requirement that this Bishop's consent or permission be sought or obtained;

(b) the second situation (§2) is that of a judge who may, for a just reason and after consulting the parties, find it necessary or useful to go outside his own jurisdiction in order to collect proofs. In this case, the permission of the diocesan Bishop of the other place is required and, in addition, the proofs are to be gathered in a place designated by that same Bishop. Normally, however, the judge should seek the assistance of the local tribunal in collecting proofs outside his own jurisdiction, in accordance with Can. 1418.

---

[1] 'Extra territorium ius dicenti impune non paretur' (l.20 D.2,1); 'Iudex extra territorium est privatus' (*Regula iuris communis*).

Book VII Judicial Procedures

Chapter V
THOSE WHO MAY BE ADMITTED TO THE COURT AND THE MANNER OF COMPILING AND PRESERVING THE ACTS

Can. 1470 §1 Unless particular law prescribes otherwise, when cases are being heard before the tribunal, only those persons are to be present whom the law or the judge decides are necessary for the hearing of the case.

2949 A judicial process is a *public* act of the Church. This does not mean that each and every person has open access to the tribunal when it is in session. It means rather that access is given to those who are necessary to the process, those whom the law or, in an individual case, the judge considers essential to the process. At different stages of the process, depending on the nature of the case and upon any relevant provision of particular law, this means the presence before the tribunal of the following: the parties, their parents, guardians or curators, witnesses, experts, advocates, procurators, defender of the bond, promotor of justice, notaries (see Cann. 1478 §1, 1559, 1560 §1, 1561, 1578 §3, 1663 §2, 1678). The presence of these individuals during proceedings belongs to the phases of the process prior to the discussion and decision. In accordance with Cann. 1455 §2 and 1609, that stage of the process concerns the judges alone and must always remain secret.

Can. 1470 §2 The judge can with appropriate penalties take to task all who, while present at a trial, are gravely lacking in the reverence and obedience due to the tribunal. He can, moreover, suspend advocates and procurators from exercising their office in ecclesiastical tribunals.

2950 The law entrusts the judge with the responsibility of ensuring that those admitted to the tribunal during judicial proceedings behave themselves in a correct and fitting manner. He has the authority and power to punish anyone who is guilty of serious misconduct before the tribunal. This includes, if necessary, the power to suspend from office advocates and procurators.

Can. 1471 If a person to be interrogated uses a language unknown to the judge or the parties, an interpreter, appointed by the judge and duly sworn, can be employed in the case. Declarations are to be committed to writing in the original language, and a translation is to be added. An interpreter is also to be used if a deaf and dumb person must be interrogated, unless the judge prefers that replies to the questions he has asked be given in writing.

2951 The judge may engage the services of an interpreter if necessary in two situations:
   (a) when the person to be questioned speaks only a language which is not understood by the judge or the parties;
   (b) when the person to be questioned is deaf or dumb and the judge prefers not to have the person submit written answers to his questions.

In these situations, the interpreter must be appointed to the task formally by the judge and must take the oath to 'exercise their office properly and faithfully' (see Can. 1454). The responses of the person questioned are always to be written down. In the case of someone speaking another language, the written record of the interview must be in the original language with a translation attached. This provides an added guarantee of the accuracy of the interrogation.

Part I Trials in General

Can. 1472 §1 Judicial acts must be in writing, both those which refer to the merits of the case, that is, the acts of the case, and those which refer to the procedure, that is, the procedural acts.

In order to publish the acts to the parties (see Can. 1598 §1) and to provide the judges with all that they need to make a just decision (see Can. 1608), the law requires that all judicial acts are to be committed to writing. This canon introduces the distinction between those acts pertaining to the merits of the investigation itself – the 'acts of the case' – and those acts which pertain to the various steps or stages of the process – the 'procedural acts'. This distinction is important when considering the effects of abatement or peremption (see Can. 1522) and renunciation (see Can. 1525): in both instances, the procedural acts are extinguished, but the acts of the case itself are not affected. 2952

Can. 1472 §2 Each page of the acts is to be numbered and authenticated.

All those who have access to judicial acts in the course of a process must be confident that they have a complete and accurate record of all that took place. For this reason, each page of the acts – the acts of the case and the procedural acts – is to be numbered and authenticated. 2953

Can. 1473 Whenever the signature of parties or witnesses is required in judicial acts, and the party or witness is unable or unwilling to sign, this is to be noted in the acts. At the same time the judge and the notary are to certify that the act was read verbatim to the party or witness, and that the party or witness was either unable or unwilling to sign.

The signature of the parties or their procurators is required e.g. if either wishes to renounce a trial at any stage (see Can. 1524 §3); the signature of witnesses is required on the written record of their testimony (see Can. 1569 §2). In any situation where the party or the witness refuses to sign the relevant document or is unable to do, this must be noted in the acts. Moreover, the law obliges the judge and the notary to certify that the document in question was read word for word to the party or witness and that the said person was not able or was unwilling to sign it. 2954

Can. 1474 §1 In the case of an appeal, a copy of the acts is to be sent to the higher tribunal, with a certification by the notary of its authenticity.

When a judgement is appealed, a copy of the acts – the acts of the case and the procedural acts – are to be transmitted to the appeal tribunal. This copy must be properly certified as authentic by the notary. 2955

Can. 1474 §2 If the acts are in a language unknown to the higher tribunal, they are to be translated into another language known to it. Suitable precautions are to be taken to ensure that the translation is accurate.

Should it happen that the original acts are written in a language which the appeal tribunal does not understand, the lower court has the duty to ensure that all the acts are translated into a language known to the appeal judges. Every effort must be made to ensure that the translation is faithful and accurate, leaving no room for ambiguity and doubt. By analogy with Can. 1471, the translator should be appointed formally and required to take the oath of office in the same way as an interpreter; by further analogy with the same canon, an authentic copy of the acts in the original language should accompany the translation which is forwarded to the appeal tribunal. 2956

Can. 1475 §1 When the trial has been completed, documents which belong to private individuals must be returned to them, though a copy of them is to be retained.

§2 Without an order from the judge, notaries and the chancellor are forbidden to hand over to anyone a copy of the judicial acts and documents obtained in the process.

2957   Confidentiality demands that everything pertaining to a judicial process must be preserved carefully within the tribunal.[1] As soon as a case has been completed,[2] any documents which private individuals may have presented to the tribunal in the course of its proceedings are to be returned to them. However, the law requires that a copy of these documents, duly authenticated, must be retained in the archives. The law forbids notaries and the chancellor from giving to the parties or other interested persons a copy of any juridical acts or documents acquired for the purpose of the court, unless they are ordered to do so by the judge.

Title IV
The Parties in the Case

Chapter I
THE PLAINTIFF AND THE RESPONDENT

INTRODUCTION

2958   The plaintiff in a case is the one who initiates the action. This does not have to be the person whose right is to be asserted or whose juridical status is to be declared. In criminal cases the plaintiff will be the promotor of justice (see Can. 1721); in cases of nullity of ordination it could be the Ordinary (see Can. 1708). The respondent is the one who is called on to respond either to a particular charge or at least to the summons of the court. In marriage-nullity cases, although these are technically classed as contentious cases, in fact it is the validity of the marriage which is being directly challenged and not the person of the respondent. Hence the use of the term 'respondent' in these cases, although correct, must always be understood in an analogous sense. Strictly speaking, the term 'plaintiff' is used of a person seeking something as of

---

[1] The Code does not prescribe any time-limit for the retention of judicial acts. However, the Apostolic Signatura did permit a particular tribunal to destroy the original acts of matrimonial cases after ten years from the conclusion of the process, provided that original sentences and decrees were preserved and the other judicial acts were stored on microfilm so that they could be reproduced if necessary (cf. RR 1990 22). This is a matter for a common-sense decision, consonant with the facilities available to each tribunal.

[2] A case may be considered as completed in a variety of ways: when the issue becomes adjudged matter (Can. 1641), when two conforming sentences have been issued in a case involving status of persons (Can. 1644 §1), when there is renunciation of the action, or an agreement between the parties resolving the matter at issue.

Part I Trials in General

right, while the term 'petitioner' is reserved for one asking for the grant of a favour. Hence, in a marriage-nullity case it is correct to speak of the 'plaintiff', because the person is seeking as of right to have his or her juridical status judicially declared, while in a case of non-consummation of marriage it is more correct to speak of a 'petitioner' because here the person is seeking the grant, not of a right, but of a favour, i.e. dispensation from the bond of marriage.

Any trial, whether civil or canonical, involves, together with the judge, at least two parties. If there is no plaintiff or no respondent, then the trial is irremediably null (see Can. 1620 4°)   2959

Can. 1476 Any person, baptised or unbaptised, can plead before a court. A person who is lawfully summoned must respond.

In the older law there were certain restrictions on who could introduce a suit, but some relaxations on these had been introduced even before the present Code.[1] Now, in keeping with the doctrine of Vatican II about the essential equality of all human beings,[2] any person, baptised or not, can plead before an ecclesiastical court in any type of case. This does not, of course, give everybody the right to be the plaintiff in any and every particular case; thus e.g. in a marriage-nullity case this matter is determined by Cann. 1674–1675.   2960

A person who has the right to bring a particular action – the so-called 'processual capacity' – is not obliged to exercise that right. But a respondent who has been lawfully summoned to appear in court has no option: he or she is bound to respond.   2961

Can. 1477 Even though the plaintiff or the respondent has appointed a procurator or advocate, each is always bound to be present in person at the trial when the law or the judge so prescribes.

The law relating to procurators and advocates is to be found in Cann. 1481–1489. Even if such people have been appointed, the law or the judge may require the personal presence of either party at the trial, e.g. a party might have to attend personally to take an oath (see Can. 1199 §2) or to answer further questioning required by the judge (see Cann. 1530–1531).   2962

Can. 1478 §1 Minors and those who lack the use of reason can stand before the court only through their parents, guardians or curators, subject to the provisions of §3.

§2 If the judge considers that the rights of minors are in conflict with the rights of the parents, guardians or curators, or that these cannot sufficiently protect the rights of the minors, the minors are to stand before the court through a guardian or curator assigned by the judge.

Because minors, i.e. those under 18 years of age, even though they have the use of reason, are considered not to be mature enough fully to handle their affairs in the exercise of their rights, they are subject in this regard to their parents, guardians or curators (see Can. 98 §2). The present canon represents a specific instance of this, in allowing them to stand before a court only through those charged with upholding   2963

---

[1] These concerned particularly the capacity to accuse a marriage of nullity. Non-catholics, whether baptised or not, and apostates, were barred from this, and there were severe restrictions on excommunicated people and on those who were the culpable cause of nullity. A reply of DVCom issued on 8.I.1973 (AAS 65(1973) 59: CLD 8 1092–1093) made it clear that non-catholics could now act as plaintiffs in marriage cases without special permission. The present Code has lifted the restrictions on all cases.

[2] Cf. LG 29: Fl I 929–930.

their interests. However, if a judge considers that the rights of a minor are in jeopardy, either because of a conflict of interests between the rights of the minor and those of the parents, guardians or curators, or because these people are unable properly to protect them, then he himself is to assign a guardian or curator who will represent the minor in court.[1]

Can. 1478 §3 However, in cases concerning spiritual matters and matters linked with the spiritual, if the minors have the use of reason, they can plead and respond without the consent of parents or guardians; indeed, if they have completed their fourteenth year, they can stand before the court on their own behalf; otherwise, they do so through a curator appointed by the judge.

2964 This paragraph contains an important exception to the norm of §1. In order to allow them complete freedom in such cases, minors can act as plaintiffs or respondents in 'cases concerning spiritual matters and matters linked with the spiritual' (see Can. 1401 1°) without the consent of their parents or guardians and, if they are over 14 years old, they do not need a curator to stand before the court. If they are under this age or have not the use of reason, the judge is to appoint a curator. One practical example of this exception in operation would be the right of a minor to stand before the court in a marriage-nullity case either as plaintiff or respondent.

Can. 1478 §4 Those barred from the administration of their goods and those of infirm mind can themselves stand before the court only to respond concerning their own offences, or by order of the judge. In other matters they must plead and respond through their curators.

2965 In normal circumstances those who are barred from the administration of their own goods and those of infirm mind can be plaintiffs or respondents only through their curators. However, in two instances they may personally be respondents: in penal cases concerning their own offences, or in any case when the judge orders it. The judge is here given discretion to decide on the capability of the person so to act and on the opportuneness of his or her so doing.

Can. 1479 A guardian or curator appointed by a civil authority can be admitted by an ecclesiastical judge, after he has consulted, if possible, the diocesan Bishop of the person to whom the guardian or curator has been given. If there is no such guardian or curator, or it is not seen fit to admit the one appointed, the judge is to appoint a guardian or curator for the case.

2966 It can happen that a minor or a person of diminished capacity will have a civilly appointed guardian or curator. This person may be admitted by an ecclesiastical judge also. Before doing so the judge is, if possible, to consult the diocesan Bishop of the person so represented, but the consent of the Ordinary is no longer needed as it was in the 1917 Code (c.1651 §1). In the absence of a civilly appointed guardian or curator, or if it is not judged appropriate to admit the person who has been appointed, the judge himself is to appoint a guardian or curator for the case.

Can. 1480 §1 Juridical persons stand before the court through their lawful representative.

---

[1] The law does not make a rigid distinction between guardians and curators and often the terms are used interchangeably. Where there is a distinction, the term 'guardian' is used generally for one who looks after the interests of those who are under age, while a 'curator' does the same for those of diminished mental capacity.

A juridical person (see Cann. 113–123) of its nature cannot act for itself in court and so must do so through its lawful representative. Who this is will be determined by universal or particular law or by the statutes of the juridical person (see Can. 118): thus e.g. the diocesan Bishop acts for the juridical person which is the diocese (Can. 393), a parish priest for a parish (Can. 532).

Can. 1480 §2 In the case where there is no representative or the representative is negligent, the Ordinary himself, either personally or through another, can stand before the court in the name of juridical persons subject to his authority.

If the interests of a juridical person are in danger due to the lack of a legal representative or because of negligence on his or her part, the Ordinary to whose authority the juridical person is subject, can represent the juridical person before the court either personally or through a delegate.

Chapter II
PROCURATORS AND ADVOCATES

Can. 1481 §1 A party can freely appoint an advocate and procurator for him or herself. Apart from the cases stated in §§2 and 3, however, a party can plead and respond personally, unless the judge considers the services of a procurator or advocate to be necessary.

§2 In a penal trial the accused must always have an advocate, either appointed personally or allocated by the judge.

§3 In a contentious trial which concerns minors or the public good, the judge is *ex officio* to appoint a legal representative for a party who lacks one; matrimonial cases are excepted.

'An advocate is a person approved by the diocesan Bishop and appointed by a party to safeguard the rights of that party by arguments regarding the law and the facts.'[1] 'A procurator or proxy is one who, by legitimate mandate, performs judicial business in the name of someone else.'[2] There is no conflict between the two functions and so they can be, and often are, exercised by one and the same person.[3] In his allocution to the Roman Rota in 1944 Pope Pius XII spoke of the function of the advocate and described his ultimate duty as 'the discovery, ascertainment, and legal assertion of the truth, the objective fact'.[4]

The general principle of the canon is that advocates and procurators are a matter of option to the parties, unless the judge or the law demands otherwise. The judge may do so in order to protect the rights of a person whom he foresees may otherwise not be sufficiently safeguarded (§1). In penal trials the law demands that the accused person must have an advocate, either chosen personally or appointed by the judge (§2). In contentious trials which concern minors or the public good (§3), the law

---

[1] Wrenn *Procedures* CLSA Washington DC 1987 24.
[2] op cit 26.
[3] A proposed paragraph explicitly allowing this was dropped as 'superfluous': cf. Comm 10(1978) 269 at Can. 88 §4.
[4] Pope Pius XII allocution to Rota 2.X.1944: AAS 36(1944) 286: CLD 3 617.

again demands a 'legal representative' (*defensor*) and if there is none such, the judge is to appoint one. Matrimonial cases are a notable exception to this rule: even though such cases do concern the public good, the parties retain the option of appointing an advocate or not.[1] This does not, however, preclude the judge, in his discretion, from appointing an advocate or a procurator in a particular marriage case: one could think e.g. of his deciding to do so in the case of a non-cooperative respondent, thus to ensure the latter's right of defence.

Can. 1482 §1 A person can appoint only one procurator; the latter cannot appoint a substitute, unless this faculty has been expressly conceded.

§2 If, however, several procurators have for a just reason been appointed by the same person, these are to be so designated that the first to act excludes the others.

2971 Since a procurator is a person's personal representative, the *alter ego* acting in his or her name, the general rule is that there should be not more than one. He or she may not appoint a substitute unless this has been expressly provided for in the original appointment (§1). It may, however, occur that in certain circumstances it might be advisable so to provide from the beginning – for 'a just reason', e.g. in case one should not be available when needed. It is this situation which is catered for in §2, which prescribes that in such a situation the original document of appointment must expressly state that the procurator who first acts thereby excludes the others from doing so.

Can. 1482 §3 Several advocates can, however, be appointed together.

2972 Because of the nature of the advocate's function there is no conflict or confusion caused by having more than one. Indeed, in a case with a number of complex issues involved, it could be desirable to have several advocates, each expert in a particular area.

Can. 1483 The procurator and advocate must have attained their majority and be of good repute. The advocate is also to be a catholic unless the diocesan Bishop permits otherwise, a doctor in canon law or otherwise truly skilled, and approved by the same Bishop.

2973 This canon lays out the qualities needed in a procurator and an advocate. For both functions, the person must be at least 18 years of age and must be of good repute. No further qualities are needed in a procurator. An advocate, in addition, should normally be a catholic, although the diocesan Bishop may allow otherwise. He or she must also either have a doctorate in canon law or be otherwise well versed in it, and must be approved by the diocesan Bishop.[2] This approval allows that person to function at the diocesan level only; in order to plead a case before the appropriate

---

[1] This principle was determined only after considerable discussion in the course of the revision of the Code: cf. Comm 10(1978) 268 at Can. 87 §2; 16(1984) 61 at Can. 1433 §3. It was ultimately agreed that both the public good and the genuine interests of the parties were adequately protected by the fact that the defender of the bond is a necessary participant and that a minimum number of three judges is required.

[2] On 12.VII.1993 the Apostolic Signatura, in its administrative capacity as supervisor of tribunal practice, issued a declaration which, though of its nature private, clearly has implications of more general application. In respect of the particular situation presented, it declared that a person who is living in an irregular marital union may not be admitted as an advocate in a marriage-nullity case before a diocesan tribunal, and indeed that that irregular status would itself justify the Bishop-Moderator in removing the person in question from the list of advocates approved for his tribunal. For the text of this Declaration and an instructive Commentary, cf. Burke *Commentarium de responsione in casu particulari de idoneitate advocatorum qui in unione irregulari vivunt ad patrocinium in causis nullitatis matrimonii exercendum* Per 82(1993) 699–708.

appeal court, the advocate needs the approval of the Bishop who is head of that tribunal.

Can. 1484 §1 Prior to undertaking their office, the procurator and the advocate must deposit an authentic mandate with the tribunal.

§2 To prevent the extinction of a right, however, the judge can admit a procurator even though a mandate has not been presented; in an appropriate case, a suitable guarantee is to be given. However, the act lacks all force if the procurator does not present a mandate within the peremptory time-limit to be prescribed by the judge.

In normal circumstances both the procurator and the advocate must deposit a 'mandate', i.e. a formal document of appointment, with the tribunal before beginning to exercise their functions. This mandate must be authentic, i.e. signed by the mandator, and dated and witnessed by an independent person. The mandate of a procurator must be specifically for judicial purposes: a general mandate to carry out business for the mandator would not suffice. The lack of a lawful mandate causes irremediable nullity of the judgement (see Can. 1620 6°). In one particular case, namely where a delay might occasion the extinction of a right, whether of the plaintiff or of the respondent, the judge may admit a procurator even though a mandate has not been duly presented; if necessary in such a case, a suitable guarantee is to be given. If a procurator is admitted to act in these circumstances, he or she must present a proper mandate within the time-limit set by the judge; otherwise any act performed by such a would-be procurator is invalid. 2974

Can. 1485 Without a special mandate, a procurator cannot validly renounce an action, an instance or judicial acts, nor can a procurator settle an action, bargain, submit to arbitration, or in general do anything for which the law requires a special mandate.

Even though a procurator has a valid mandate for judicial purposes, there is need of a special mandate to perform certain acts, notably acts which could seriously affect the mandator's rights. If he or she acts in the cases listed or outlined in this canon without such a special mandate, the action is invalid. 2975

Can. 1486 §1 For the dismissal of a procurator or advocate to have effect, it must be notified to them and, if the joinder of the issue has taken place, the judge and the other party must be notified of the dismissal.

Although a party may have withdrawn the mandate of his or her procurator or advocate, this has no effect until the dismissal has been made known to the persons concerned and so any acts done by them prior to this notification are valid. If the trial has already reached the stage of the joinder of the issue, the judge and the other party must also be informed of the dismissal. 2976

Can. 1486 §2 When a definitive judgement has been given, the right and duty to appeal lie with the procurator, unless the mandating party refuses.

The advocate's function ceases with the giving of the definitive judgement in a case and so requires a new mandate to proceed any further, unless this was already specifically given in the original mandate. The procurator, on the other hand, by virtue of the original mandate, has the right and, where the mandator's interests demand this, the duty to appeal unless the mandator positively does not wish to do so.[1] 2977

---

[1] As already noted at Can. 1481 §1, it is frequent practice, especially in marriage-nullity cases, that the one person be appointed both advocate and procurator – in which case the possible conflict adverted to in respect of this paragraph simply does not arise.

Can. 1487 For a grave reason, the procurator and the advocate can be removed by a decree of the judge given either *ex officio* or at the request of the party.

2978 The reason for the judicial dismissal of a procurator or an advocate must be not only just but grave.[1] This is because of the implications such dismissal has for the person's professional competence and integrity. Examples of a grave reason would be serious dishonesty, neglect of duty, gross incompetence. The judge's decree may be given *ex officio*, if e.g. he himself becomes aware of dishonesty, or at the request of the party in question.

Can. 1488 §1 Both the procurator and the advocate are forbidden to influence a suit by bribery, seek immoderate payment, or bargain with the successful party for a share of the matter in dispute. If they do so, any such agreement is invalid and they can be fined by the judge. Moreover, the advocate can be suspended from office and, if this is not a first offence, can be removed from the register of advocates by the Bishop in charge of the tribunal.

2979 Three types of financial dishonesty by the procurator or advocate are mentioned here: bribery to win a case, seeking unduly large fees, bargaining for a share in the matter in dispute. Any such agreement is invalid in law, and the perpetrator can be fined by the judge. An advocate who is guilty of any of these offences may be suspended from office and, unless it be only a first offence, the Bishop who has charge of the tribunal may remove him or her from the panel of advocates.

Can. 1488 §2 The same sanctions can be imposed on advocates and procurators who fraudulently exploit the law by withdrawing cases from tribunals which are competent, so that they may be judged more favourably by other tribunals.

2980 This is a new disposition of law, designed to combat a certain type of unlawful 'forum shopping', where the procurator or advocate withdraws a case from a competent forum so as to introduce it to another where it is hoped more easily to gain a favourable outcome. Pope Paul VI referred to abuses in this area in connection with marriage cases, where the second tribunal was approached on the basis of 'artificially created domiciles or fictitious permanent residences'.[2] Those advocates and procurators guilty of such practices can be punished with the sanctions mentioned in §1.

Can. 1489 Advocates and procurators who betray their office because of gifts or promises, or any other consideration, are to be suspended from the exercise of their profession, and are to be fined or punished with other suitable penalties.

2981 This canon prescribes the penalties – suspension from office, fines or other suitable penalties – for advocates and procurators who for any reason whatever 'betray their office'. Since the principal part of their office is to represent and safeguard the rights of their mandator, the principal way in which they would betray this office would be in acting against the mandator's interests.

Can. 1490 In each tribunal, as far as possible, permanent legal representatives are to be appointed, who receive a salary from the tribunal and who are to exercise the office of advocate and procurator, especially in matrimonial cases, for parties who may wish to choose them.

---

[1] Cf. Comm 10(1978) 271 at Can. 97.
[2] Pope Paul VI allocution to the Rota 28.I.1978: AAS 70(1978) 183: CLD 9 922.

Part I Trials in General

This canon is new and calls for the establishing in every tribunal of a panel of legal representatives, paid by the tribunal and available to act as procurators and advocates, especially in marriage cases. While the advantages of such a system are obvious, the words 'as far as possible' recognise that such a panel of permanent paid officials may not be within the compass of many local tribunals, either because of a lack of trained personnel or for financial reasons. Nevertheless, in the interests of justice and equity, even if the exact letter of the canon cannot be observed, each tribunal is obliged to make what efforts it can to make available trained and independent legal representatives.

Title V
Actions and Exceptions

Chapter I
ACTIONS AND EXCEPTIONS IN GENERAL

Can. 1491 Every right is reinforced not only by an action, unless otherwise expressly provided, but also by an exception.

An action is the power acknowledged by the law whereby a person can seek the judicial protection of his or her rights. An exception is related to an action: it permits the respondent in a case to adduce rights or circumstances designed to counter the claims of the plaintiff in whole or in part; it is in effect a counter-claim by the respondent to the claim of the plaintiff. The norm of the present canon is that where there is a right, there is a corresponding action to defend it 'unless otherwise expressly provided', and that the right may also be defended by an exception. An example of where the law expressly provides otherwise can be found in Can. 1062 §2 which disallows an action to require the celebration of marriage arising from a promise of marriage.

Can. 1492 §1 Every action is extinguished by prescription in accordance with the law, or in any other lawful way, with the exception of actions bearing on personal status, which are never extinguished.

With the exception of actions which have to do with personal status,[1] all actions are subject to extinction, that is the cessation of the right to bring the action. They may be extinguished by legal prescription (see Cann. 197–199, 1270), by any other lawful way, such as renunciation, or by the loss or cessation of the substantive right on which the action was based. The basic reason behind this rule is to prevent the insecurity and uncertainty which could arise from the possibility of bringing an action in perpetuity. The exception in favour of actions which bear on personal status is to provide an adequate safeguard for the important rights on which these are based.

Can. 1492 §2 Without prejudice to the provision of Can. 1462, an exception is always possible, and is of its nature perpetual.

---

[1] These include cases about sacred ordination and religious status and marriage cases.

2985 Unlike an action, an exception 'is of its nature perpetual' and can always be introduced. An exception is a defensive measure and can be introduced only after an action has been already brought. It is important that the respondent always have a right of defence. Can. 1462, to which the present canon refers, gives the rules for bringing peremptory exceptions.

Can. 1493 A plaintiff can bring several actions simultaneously against another person, concerning either the same matter or different matters, provided they are not in conflict with one another, and do not go beyond the competence of the tribunal that has been approached.

2986 A plaintiff is not limited to one action at a time. He or she can bring several against the same person simultaneously, either concerning the same matter or even concerning different matters. An example of more than one action concerning the same matter would be where a declaration of nullity of marriage is sought on several grounds. There are two conditions before actions can be cumulated in this fashion: (a) there must be no conflict between the different actions, as there would be e.g. in challenging the validity of a marriage on the grounds of force and fear and also simulation of consent; (b) all the actions must be within the competence of the tribunal that has been approached.

Can. 1494 §1 A respondent can institute a counter action against a plaintiff before the same judge and in the same trial, either by reason of the case's connection with the principal action, or with a view to removing or mitigating the plaintiff's plea.

§2 A counter action to a counter action is not admitted.

2987 A counter action is a method of defence whereby a respondent, in answer to the plaintiff's petition, brings an action of his or her own against the plaintiff. The original action and the counter action are heard in the same trial, thus allowing for a more expeditious way of settling the dispute. Two types of counter action are contemplated here: those connected with the principal action, the plaintiff's petition, and those aimed at removing or mitigating the plea. However, the two types are related in that both are connected to the plaintiff's plea and both have as their ultimate purpose the removal or mitigation of the petition. The law forbids (§2) a counter action to a counter action, in order to avoid a potentially endless case.

Can. 1495 The counter action is to be proposed to the judge before whom the original action was initiated, even though he has been delegated for one case only, or is otherwise relatively non-competent.

2988 Because of the connection between a counter action and the original petition, the two are to be heard by the same judge. Where he is not competent to hear the counter action, either because he was delegated for one case only or because he is otherwise relatively non-competent, the law extends his competence to cover the counter action. In cases of absolute non-competence (see Cann. 1406 §2, 1440) there is no such extension of competence.

Chapter II
ACTIONS AND EXCEPTIONS IN PARTICULAR

Can. 1496 §1 A person who advances arguments, which are at least probable, to support a right to something held by another, and to indicate an

imminent danger of loss unless the object itself is handed over for safekeeping, has a right to obtain from the judge the sequestration of the object in question.

§2 In similar circumstances, a person can obtain a restraint on another person's exercise of a right.

Sequestration of an object means the handing of the object to a third party for safekeeping. It can be used to prevent loss in the case of an object whose ownership is in dispute until the dispute is resolved. If a person advances at least probable arguments which indicate (a) his or her right to the object in question and (b) an imminent danger of loss of the object unless it is put in safekeeping, the judge is obliged to issue a decree of sequestration (§1). If *mutatis mutandis*, these same conditions are fulfilled, a person may be forbidden by the judge to exercise a right or to exercise it in full, until the main controversy is settled (§2).

Can. 1497 §1 The sequestration of an object is also allowed for the security of a debt, provided there is sufficient evidence of the creditor's right.

§2 Sequestration can also extend to the assets of a debtor which, on whatever title, are in the keeping of others, as well as to the loans of the debtor.

This canon allows for sequestration as security for a debt, provided that there is sufficient evidence of the creditor's right. The sequestration can be of some object in the debtor's possession, or of personal assets which are in the keeping of others, or even of loans that he or she has made.

Can. 1498 The sequestration of an object, and restraint on the exercise of a right, can in no way be decreed if the loss which is feared can be otherwise repaired, and a suitable guarantee is given that it will be repaired.

Sequestration and restraint on the exercise of a right are to be regarded as extraordinary procedures and cannot be decreed if the loss which is feared can be made good in some other way and a suitable guarantee is given that this will in fact be done.

Can. 1499 The judge who grants the sequestration of an object, or the restraint on the exercise of a right, can first impose on the person to whom the grant is made an undertaking to repay any loss if the right is not proven.

It is not only the person who seeks sequestration or restraint who has to fear a loss; the other party may also justifiably have the same fear. Hence this law allows the judge to protect him or her by making the original party undertake to repay any loss if the claimed right is not in due course proven in court.

Can. 1500 In matters concerning the nature and effect of an action for possession, the provisions of the civil law of the place where the thing to be possessed is situated, are to be observed.

An action for possession is one which seeks either the restitution of something which has been lost or the peaceful possession of an object. In this area, as in a number of others, the law 'canonises' the civil law of the place where the object in dispute is located: it is to *that* law alone that recourse is to be had in actions of this kind, not only as to the effect of such an action but also as to its very nature.[1]

---

[1] This is a substantial change from the 1917 Code which not only defined the nature of this action (c. 1688 §2) but retained it within the canonical ambit, in a series of detailed norms (cc. 1693–1700). Cf. Comm 11(1979) 78–80.

PART II

THE CONTENTIOUS TRIAL

Section I
THE ORDINARY CONTENTIOUS TRIAL

Title I
The Introduction of the Case

Chapter I
THE PETITION INTRODUCING THE SUIT

INTRODUCTION

2994 This second part of Book VII deals with contentious cases. Although in origin, and also often enough in fact, the term 'contentious' implies a dispute between persons, this is not always the case. Indeed, in the most common type of case before the Church's tribunals today, the marriage case, it often happens that both parties are in agreement, not only about wanting the nullity of the marriage declared, but even on the exact grounds on which the plea is based, so that there is in fact no legal dispute between them. Even so, these cases are still called contentious and, apart from special rules in some areas, they come under the regulations laid down here.

Can. 1501 A judge cannot investigate any case unless a plea, drawn up in accordance with canon law, is submitted either by a person whose interest is involved, or by the promotor of justice.

2995 A judge may never introduce a case on his own initiative. He must await a plea from either a person whose interest is involved in the matter in dispute or, in cases involving the public good, from the promotor of justice. This plea is to be drawn up in accordance with the canons which follow. If there is no such plea, any judgement given is irremediably null (see Can. 1620 4°). The principle underlying this canon persists throughout the case: the judge may not go beyond the request made in the petition, nor may he decide on matters not contained in it or not determined at the joinder of the issue.

Can. 1502 A person who wishes to sue another must present a petition to a judge who is lawfully competent. In this petition the matter in dispute is to be set out and the intervention of the judge requested.

2996 The plea already referred to is to be made in the form of a petition (*libellus*). The form and content of this document are prescribed in Can. 1504. It is to be presented to a competent judge. The general rules of competence are regulated by Cann. 1404–1416. Competence for marriage cases is determined by Can. 1673 and for ordination cases by Can. 1709 §1. The two essential elements of the petition are the setting out of the matter in dispute, e.g. the nullity of a marriage, and the request for the intervention of the judge.

Can. 1503 §1 A judge can admit an oral plea whenever the plaintiff is impeded from presenting a petition or when the case can be easily investigated and is of minor significance.

§2 In both cases, however, the judge is to direct a notary to record the matter in writing. This written record is to be read to, and approved by, the plaintiff, and it takes the place of a petition written by the plaintiff as far as all effects of law are concerned.

Normally a plea to a tribunal is to be in writing, but in two cases a judge can admit an oral plea: (a) where the plaintiff is impeded from presenting a written petition, e.g. by illness or illiteracy, (b) where the case is a simple one of minor significance. Whenever the judge admits an oral plea in accordance with §1, he is to have a notary record it in writing. The written record is then to be read to and approved by the plaintiff and thereafter this document becomes, for all legal purposes, the petition (§2). 2997

Can. 1504 The petition by which a suit is introduced must:

1° state the judge before whom the case is being introduced, what is being sought and from whom it is being sought;

The judge, or at least the tribunal, should be named. This allows determination of competence. Next to be expressed is the thing being sought, e.g. payment for work done. The person from whom the thing is sought, the respondent, must also be designated. 2998

2° indicate on what right the plaintiff bases the case and, at least in general terms, the facts and proofs to be evinced in support of the allegations made;

The right on which the plaintiff bases the case could be e.g. a contract or, in a marriage case, a ground of nullity such as force and fear. The petition must also indicate the facts and proofs which will be brought to support the plea: these need not be set out in detail; the 'in general terms' of the canon means that there be sufficient to satisfy the judge that this is not a frivolous application, that there is a substance behind it – the details of which have of course yet to be proven during the hearing. 2999

3° be signed by the plaintiff or the plaintiff's procurator, and bear the day, the month and the year, as well as the address at which the plaintiff or the procurator resides, or at which they say they reside for the purpose of receiving the acts;

The petition must be signed either by the plaintiff in person or by his or her procurator. It must also be dated, giving the day, month and year on which it was signed. The plaintiff's address or that of the procurator, or at least a mailing address for either, must be given so that the acts of the case can be communicated.[1] 3000

4° indicate the domicile or quasi-domicile of the respondent.

This is required for the purpose both of communication and of establishing competence (see Cann. 1407 §3, 1408, 1673 2°). 3001

---

[1] In some cases the plaintiff's domicile or quasi-domicile may be needed in order to establish competence (cf. Cann. 1409 §2, 1673 3°) but, strictly speaking, this need not be included in the petition.

Can. 1505 §1 Once he has satisfied himself that the matter is within his competence and the plaintiff has the right to stand before the court, the sole judge, or the presiding judge of a collegiate tribunal, must as soon as possible by his decree either admit or reject the petition.

3002 Acceptance or rejection of a petition is made either by the sole judge or, if the case is heard by a collegiate tribunal, by the presiding judge of that tribunal. Before deciding on acceptance or rejection, in accordance with the terms of §2 below, the judge must satisfy himself: (a) of his own legal competence to hear the case (see Cann. 1404–1415, 1673); (b) of the plaintiff's right to stand before the court (see Cann. 1476–1480).[1]

Can. 1505 §2 A petition can be rejected only if:

1° the judge or the tribunal is not legally competent;

2° it is established beyond doubt that the plaintiff lacks the right to stand before the court;

3° the provisions of Can. 1504 nn.1-3 have not been observed;

4° it is certainly clear from the petition that the plea lacks any foundation, and that there is no possibility that a foundation will emerge from a process.

3003 From the language of this paragraph it is clear that the rejection of a petition should be the exception rather than the rule.[2] The reasons for such rejection are given here; none other is admissible. The first two, lack of legal competence on the part of the judge or of the tribunal, and lack of the right to stand before the court on the part of the plaintiff, have already been mentioned in §1. The next reason for the rejection of the petition is the lack of certain requirements of form and content, as demanded by Can. 1504 1°–3° e.g. neglecting to name the judge or tribunal before whom the case is to be heard, lack of signature, and the like. A petition may also, however, be rejected if from the petition it is certain that the plea lacks any foundation in law or in fact and that there is no possibility that such a foundation will emerge later in the process (4°). From the nature of the case it will be obvious that such certainty will not be easily reached at this stage of a case. The precise difficulty facing a tribunal at this point is to determine the extent to which the current law permits a measure of investigation which goes beyond the mere examination of a written document entitled a 'petition'. There is a strong case to be made in favour of something more substantial than any such examination.[3]

---

[1] In the course of the revision of the Code, a proposal to have the judge decide also on the respondent's right to stand before the court was rejected as irrelevant to accepting or rejecting the petition: cf. Comm 11(1979) 84 at Can. 141 §1.

[2] ' ... generatim reiectio libelli rarissime fit ...' (... in general the rejection of a petition happens very rarely ...): Comm 11 (1979) 88 at Can. 142 §1. Cf. Churchill *The Admission and Rejection of the Libellus in the Canonical Tradition and Especially According to the 1983 Code of Canon Law* Rome PUG 1993.

[3] In marriage cases in particular, many, if not most, first-instance tribunals have established the practice of a preliminary informal investigation before accepting or rejecting a petition. This is not to prejudge in any way the merits of the case itself, but simply to establish whether the plaintiff's plea has a genuinely substantial *fumus boni iuris*. For a significant discussion of the merits and legitimacy of such a practice – both of which seem beyond question – cf. Sheehy *Introducing a Case of Nullity of Marriage: The New Code and the Practice of Local Tribunals* in *Dilexit Iustitiam: Scripta in honorem Aurelii Card. Sabattani* ed. Grocholewski–Carcel Orti Vatican City 1984 339–347. The author states that 'every Tribunal is obliged, before it makes a judgement on the acceptability or otherwise of a request for a decree of nullity, not only to enquire if the fact or facts alleged would or would not, if proven, amount to nullity, but also to estimate prudently if in the circumstances of the case there is, or is not, a real possibility that the fact or facts alleged can be proven', and he concludes that a brief investigation will be 'almost invariably conducted as a preliminary to a decision about accepting or rejecting a plea, bearing in mind that the sole purpose of such investigation is to determine not the merits of the plea, but only whether or not it establishes a prima facie case for nullity': op cit 345.

Can. 1505 §3 If a petition has been rejected by reason of defects which can be corrected, the plaintiff can draw up a new petition correctly and present it again to the same judge.

Where the rejection is due to formal rather than substantial defects, e.g. omitting the date or the signature, these can be corrected and the petition may again be presented to the same judge, without any need for recourse against the rejection.

Can. 1505 §4 A party is always entitled, within ten canonical days, to have recourse, based upon stated reasons, against the rejection of a petition. This recourse is to be made either to the tribunal of appeal or, if the petition was rejected by the presiding judge, to the collegiate tribunal. A question of rejection is to be determined with maximum expedition.

Either party to a case has the right, within ten canonical days (see Can. 201 §2), to have recourse against the rejection of a petition. If the petition was rejected by the presiding judge of a collegiate tribunal, the recourse is to be made to the full collegiate tribunal. If the rejection was made by a sole judge, the recourse is to the appeal tribunal.[1] Wherever the recourse is made, it is to be heard with the least possible delay ('with maximum expedition'): as such its outcome is not susceptible of any further recourse or appeal (see Can. 1629 5°). If the recourse overturns the rejection of the petition, the case is to be returned for hearing to the original tribunal.[2]

Can. 1506 If within one month of the presentation of a petition, the judge has not issued a decree admitting or rejecting it in accordance with Can. 1505, the interested party can insist that the judge perform his duty. If, notwithstanding this, the judge does not respond, then after ten days from the party's request the petition is to be taken as having been admitted.

This canon is designed to protect the rights of the parties in the event of negligence on the part of the judge. If a month has elapsed from the presentation of the petition and the judge has not issued a decree either accepting or rejecting it, the interested party can insist that he do so. If he or she takes this course and the judge does not answer within ten more days, then the petition is regarded as having been accepted. This is in effect automatic acceptance by the law itself.

Chapter II
THE SUMMONS AND THE INTIMATION OF JUDICIAL ACTS

Can. 1507 §1 In the decree by which a plaintiff's petition is admitted, the judge or the presiding judge must call or summon the other parties to court to effect the joinder of the issue; he must prescribe whether, in order to agree the point at issue, they are to reply in writing or to appear before him.

---

[1] Although the law makes no explicit provision for the acceptance or rejection of a petition by the whole collegiate tribunal, it certainly does not forbid it; such a procedure is therefore not only permissible but may well be advisable, particularly in a difficult or complicated case, not least in the sphere of marriage nullity – the more so because of the reason given by the Revision Commission in rejecting a proposal that in all cases involving a collegiate tribunal the rejection should be done collegially: cf. Comm 11 (1979) 84 at Can. 141 §1. In such a situation the recourse can only be to the appeal tribunal.

[2] Cf. Comm 11(1979) 85 at Can. 141 §4.

Book VII Judicial Procedures

If, from their written replies, he perceives the need to convene the parties, he can determine this by a new decree.

3007 Having by decree admitted the plaintiff's petition, the judge is obliged *in the same decree* to summon the other party or parties in order to effect the joinder of the issue, i.e. the determination of the precise point or points at issue. This summons is of crucial importance, in that it informs the respondent of the plaintiff's plea and allows him or her the opportunity of defence. If the summons is not lawfully communicated (but see Can. 1510), the acts of the case are null, and the denial of the right of defence to either party results in irremediable nullity of the judgement (see Can. 1620 7°). The judge is to determine whether the parties are to reply in writing or to appear before him, in order to determine the point at issue. If he allows written replies, he may however by a later decree call the parties to appear before him, if at that stage he considers this to be necessary.[1]

Can. 1507 §2 If a petition is deemed admitted in accordance with the provisions of Can. 1506, the decree of summons to the trial must be issued within twenty days of the request of which that canon speaks.

3008 When, in the exceptional situation catered for in Can. 1506, the admission of the petition is made automatically by the law, the decree summoning the other party or parties to the trial must be made within twenty days of the plaintiff's request 'that the judge perform his duty', which in effect means within ten days of the date of automatic admission.

Can. 1507 §3 If the litigants in fact present themselves before the judge to pursue the case, there is no need for a summons; the notary, however, is to record in the acts that the parties were present in court.

3009 If all the parties to a case appear without being summoned, there is no need for a summons since the purpose for which it exists will already have been fulfilled. However the notary is to record in writing that the parties were present, so that there can in future be no doubt of this fact. It will be appreciated that this situation is not of frequent occurrence.

Can. 1508 §1 The decree of summons to the trial must be notified at once to the respondent, and at the same time to any others who are obliged to appear.

3010 The decree of summons is to be notified immediately to the respondent or respondents, to the plaintiff and, if their presence is demanded by the law, to the promotor of justice and to the defender of the bond. For the manner of notification, see Cann. 1509–1510.

Can. 1508 §2 The petition introducing the suit is to be attached to the summons, unless for grave reasons the judge considers that the petition is not to be communicated to the other party before he or she gives evidence.

3011 Normally the petition is to be attached to the summons, so that the respondent may have an opportunity to prepare a defence. The right of the respondent to see a copy of the petition at this stage is not, however, an absolute one: for 'grave reasons' the judge may direct that the petition not be communicated to the respondent until after he or she has given evidence; the judge has an absolute discretion in this regard. Such a grave reason would comprise e.g. the risk of a civil action especially in the context

---

[1] This paragraph embodies a number of significant practical changes from the 1917 Code: in this regard, cf. Sheehy op cit **346 c**).

of defamation, the danger that the respondent would attempt to interfere with the proposed proofs or witnesses, and the like. This is a delicate area, particularly in respect of marriage-nullity cases, in which the judge must exercise a special sensitivity and prudence. However, even if the actual petition is not communicated to the respondent, the plaintiff's plea and the title on which he or she makes it must always be communicated. It is only the proofs on which the plaintiff relies which may at this stage be withheld from the respondent.[1] The matter of full disclosure properly arises only on the occasion of the publication of the acts, as determined by Can. 1598 §1.

Can. 1508 §3 If a suit is brought against a person who does not have the free exercise of his or her rights, or the free administration of the matters in dispute, the summons is to be notified to, as the case may be, the guardian, the curator, the special procurator, or the one who according to law is obliged to undertake legal proceedings in the name of such a person.

In the case of a suit against those who lack the capacity to stand before the court in their own right (see Cann. 1478–1480), the summons is to be notified to the appropriate legal representative as determined by law or by the court.

Can. 1509 §1 With due regard to the norms laid down by particular law, the notification of summonses, decrees, judgements and other judicial acts is to be done by means of the public postal service, or by some other particularly secure means.

§2 The fact and the manner of notification must be shown in the acts.

The summons and other judicial acts are to be communicated in a secure fashion. This is primarily to ensure that they are received by those to whom they are sent, and also to prevent what might be sensitive personal information falling into wrong hands. The law does not absolutely determine what means are to be used. If there is particular law it is to be followed, otherwise the judge is to determine the method to be used. He is recommended to use the public postal service, and since §2 demands that a record be kept of the fact and the manner of delivery, the local registration service with proof of delivery should be used. Where a particular tribunal still has its own messengers, these could be used to make local deliveries.

The law no longer makes an explicit provision for cases where the respondent's address is unknown: the 1917 Code allowed for summons by edict in such a case (c.1720); this is not excluded by the present Code, but in practice this method is very rarely a fruitful one. The judge could instruct that other steps be taken: to urge the plaintiff to make more diligent enquiries – through family sources, through the relevant parochial clergy, through public records of various kinds, and the like – can often prove fruitful.

Can. 1510 A respondent who refuses to accept a document of summons, or who circumvents the delivery of a summons, is to be regarded as lawfully summoned.

The purpose of this norm is to prevent a respondent from delaying the trial or putting it off indefinitely. If he or she either refuses to accept the summons or takes

---

[1] A decision of the Apostolic Signatura of 6.IV.1971 held that a respondent does not have the right to see the plaintiff's petition either when he or she receives the summons or at the time of the joinder of the issue: cf. LE IV 5987–5989. It is significant to note also that among the considerations which led to giving the judge his present discretion in this matter, was the danger in Common Law countries of a civil suit which might have serious consequences for the administration of justice in the Church: cf. Comm 16(1984) 62 at Can. 1460 §1; Sheehy op cit 347.

steps to avoid receiving it, then the respondent is for all legal purposes to be regarded as having been summoned. Note that it must be certain that the respondent knew of the summons and refused to receive it: thus e.g. if someone else at the same address refused to accept a registered letter, so that the respondent never in fact got to know of it, the norm of this canon would not operate.

Can. 1511 Without prejudice to the provision of Can. 1507 §3, if a summons has not been lawfully communicated, the procedural acts are null.

3016 If the respondent has not been lawfully summoned, or has not voluntarily appeared without a summons, the procedural acts in the case, though not the acts concerning the merits of the case (for this distinction see Can. 1472 §1), are null. In addition, the judgement would be irremediably null by virtue of Can. 1620 4° and 7°.

Can. 1512 Once a summons has been lawfully communicated, or the parties have presented themselves before a judge to pursue the case:
  1° the matter ceases to be a *res integra*;

3017 When the summons has been lawfully communicated, in fact or equivalently, the trial begins and a number of important consequences results. The first of these is that the matter in question, whether it be a thing or a right, ceases to be in a situation of peaceful possession and formally becomes the object of litigation.

  2° the case becomes that of the judge or of the tribunal, in other respects lawfully competent, before whom the action was brought;

3018 This canon does not supply legal competence – that has to come from elsewhere (see Cann. 1404–1414, 1673) – but it does apply the principle of prevention and makes the judge or tribunal before whom the action has been brought, solely competent, to the exclusion of all others who up to that point may have been competent.

  3° the jurisdiction of a delegated judge is confirmed so that it does not lapse on the expiry of the authority of the person who delegated;

3019 The jurisdiction over the case held by a delegated judge is confirmed in such a way that it continues even if the person who delegated him, e.g. the judicial Vicar, loses his authority, e.g. by expiry of his term of office, by death or resignation.

  4° prescription is interrupted, unless otherwise provided;

3020 Prescription (see Cann. 197–199), whether as a means of extinguishing a right or of acquiring one, is interrupted, unless the law determines otherwise.

  5° the suit begins to be a pending one, and therefore the principle immediately applies 'while a suit is pending, no new element is to be introduced'.

3021 While the suit is pending no changes may be made regarding the object of the dispute which could damage the interests of the parties: thus e.g., if the ownership of a piece of property is in dispute, once the suit is pending this property may not be sold or leased nor may its value be in any way reduced.

Title II
The Joinder of the Issue

Can. 1513 §1 The joinder of the issue occurs when the terms of the controversy, as derived from the pleas and the replies of the parties, are determined by a decree of the judge.

§2 The pleas and the replies of the parties may be expressed not only in the petition introducing the suit, but also either in the response to the summons, or in statements made orally before the judge. In more difficult cases, however, the parties are to be convened by the judge, so as to agree the question or questions to which the judgement must respond.

3022 The joinder of the issue is the determination by the judge's decree of the terms of the controversy, i.e. the points at issue in the case. These must be determined in any trial, contentious or penal, and even in incidental cases if these are to be decided by a judgement (see Can. 1590 §1). The judgement in the case must address itself to all the points decided on in the joinder of the issue. The terms of the controversy are to be determined by the judge from the plaintiff's plea and from the replies, written or oral, of the parties made in response to the summons (see Can. 1507 §1). In many cases, therefore, the parties do not have to appear either personally or through a procurator, but in more difficult cases the parties are to be convened by the judge in order to agree the precise points at issue.

Can. 1513 §3 The decree of the judge is to be notified to the parties. Unless they have already agreed on the terms, they may within ten days have recourse to the same judge to request that the decree be altered. This question, however, is to be decided with maximum expedition by a decree of the judge.

3023 This notification is necessary in order that the parties may learn legally of the object of the trial, something not always expressed clearly and in precise legal terms in the petition.[1] Unless the parties have already agreed on the points at issue, they have ten days within which they may have recourse to the same judge to have them altered if they disagree with them. The judge is to decide this recourse 'with maximum expedition', which means that there is no further recourse from this decision (see Can. 1629 5°).

Can. 1514 Once determined, the terms of the controversy cannot validly be altered except by a new decree, issued for a grave reason, at the request of the party, and after the other parties have been consulted and their reasons considered.

3024 When the terms of the controversy have been determined by the judge's decree, they cannot validly be changed unless the following conditions have been met:
(a) There must be a grave reason. This could be e.g. the coming to light of new facts which substantially alter the nature of the case.
(b) The change must be made at the request of one of the parties. This would include a request made by the promotor of justice or by the defender of the bond if these are involved in the case (see Can. 1434 2°). The judge cannot make such a change *ex officio*.

---

[1] Cf. Comm 16(1984) 64 at Can. 1465 §3.

(c) Any other interested parties, including the promotor of justice and the defender of the bond, if these are involved (see Can. 1434 1°), are to be consulted. The judge is not bound by what these have to say nor does he need their consent.[1]

(d) The judge is to weigh up the gravity of the reasons adduced by the party requesting the change and the arguments advanced by the other interested parties; he is then to decide the matter by a decree, either rejecting the request or redefining the matter at issue.

Can. 1515 Once the joinder of the issue has occurred, the possessor of another's property ceases to be in good faith. If, therefore, the judgement is that he or she return the property, the possessor must return also any profits accruing from the date of the joinder, and must compensate for damage.

3025 After the joinder of the issue has taken place, the possessor of another's property is no longer in peaceful possession; he or she is now legally aware that the property is the object of a judicial dispute and so good faith, necessary for acquiring title to the object by prescription, ceases. If the judgement is that the property be returned, any profits accruing from the date of the joinder must also be returned and any damage must be compensated for.

Can. 1516 Once the joinder of the issue has occurred, the judge is to prescribe an appropriate time within which the parties are to present and complete the proofs.

3026 Can. 1453 demands that all cases by brought to a conclusion as quickly as possible. However, no two cases will be exactly alike in the length of time needed, and so the present canon gives the judge discretion in determining the time within which the parties are to present and complete the proofs. At the request of the parties, the judge could extend the time available, always ensuring that there is no undue delay (see Can. 1465).

Title III
The Trial of the Issue

Can. 1517 The trial of the issue is initiated by the summons. It is concluded not only by the pronouncement of the definitive judgement, but also by other means determined by law.

3027 The trial of the issue, the judicial process itself by which rights are protected, begins with the summons. The normal way in which it is concluded is the definitive judgement on the matter in dispute, but there are other ways in which it can be concluded according to law. These include abatement (Cann. 1520–1523), renunciation (Cann. 1523–1524) and the non-judicial procedures of agreement, reconciliation and arbitration (Cann. 1713–1716). A trial can also be suspended without being concluded (Cann. 1518–1519).

---

[1] The 1917 Code (c. 1731 1°) demanded the consent of the respondent before a judge could agree to changing the petition once the joinder of the issue had taken place.

Can. 1518 If a litigant dies, or undergoes a change in status, or ceases from the office in virtue of which he or she was acting:

> 1° if the case has not yet been concluded, the trial is suspended until the heir of the deceased, or the successor, or a person whose interest is involved, resumes the suit;
>
> 2° if the case has been concluded, the judge must proceed to the remaining steps of the case, having first summoned the procurator, if there is one, or else the heir of the deceased or the successor.

During a trial a party may die, undergo a change in status which changes his or her capacity to stand before the court (e.g. a person may lose the use of reason), or may cease from the office in virtue of which he or she was acting (e.g. a priest might cease to be parish priest of the parish whose rights he was defending). If any of these changes takes place, the consequences depend on whether the case has been concluded in accordance with Can. 1599. If the case has not been concluded, the trial is suspended until the dead person's heir, the successor in office or a person who has an interest in the case resumes the suit. If the case has been concluded, the judge is to proceed to the remaining steps of the case but must first summon the procurator of the deceased person or of one who has changed status, if there is one, or the heir of the deceased person or the successor to the one who has ceased from office as appropriate. This canon is also to be observed when a spouse dies during a marriage-nullity case (see Can. 1675 §2).

Can. 1519 §1 If the guardian or the curator or the procurator required in accordance with Can. 1481 §§1 and 3, ceases from office, the trial is suspended for the time being.

§2 However, the judge is to appoint another guardian or curator as soon as possible. He can appoint a procurator ad litem if the party has neglected to do so within the brief time prescribed by the judge himself.

This canon deals with the suspension of a trial because of the cessation from office of a guardian, curator or procurator required by law. Such a suspension is to be a brief one and in order to effect this, the judge is to appoint another guardian or curator as soon as possible. In the case of a required procurator (see Can. 1481 §§1 and 3), if the party concerned does not appoint one in the time allotted, the judge may appoint one for the purposes of this trial.

Can. 1520 If over a period of six months, no procedural act is performed by the parties, and they have not been impeded from doing so, the trial is abated. Particular law may prescribe other time limits for abatement.

Abatement means the extinction of a particular trial, but not the loss of the right to bring the action again.[1] If within the time limits established by the law – six months in the present canon, but particular law may specify a longer or shorter period – the parties, while not impeded from doing so, have placed no judicial act, the trial is abated. The neglect must be by the parties; neglect by the judge has no such effect. One purpose of this norm is to prevent undue delay in trials because of neglect or malice.

---

[1] Not only may the action be brought again but when it is reintroduced, this does not have to be before the original tribunal. It may be brought before any tribunal competent at the time of resumption: cf. CCom rep 29.IV.1986: AAS 78(1986) 1324.

Can. 1521 Abatement takes effect by virtue of the law itself, and it is effective against everyone, even minors and those equivalent to minors; moreover, it must be declared even *ex officio*. This, however, is without prejudice to the right to claim compensation against those guardians, curators, administrators and procurators who have not proved that they were without fault.

3031   Abatement is automatic in operation. The judge is bound to declare it without waiting to be petitioned to do so, but his declaration is just that – a declaration; it does not, as it were, impose abatement as a sort of penalty. Abatement is effective against everyone, even minors and those equivalent to minors in law. However these have a right to bring an action for damages against their negligent legal representatives. Note that in this case the law presumes that the legal representatives were negligent and so it is for these to prove that they were without fault.

Can. 1522 Abatement extinguishes the procedural acts, but not the acts of the case. The acts of the case may indeed be employed in another trial, provided the case is between the same persons and about the same matter. As far as those outside the case are concerned, however, these acts have no standing other than as documents.

3032   The procedural acts in a case, such as decrees, the summons, the joinder of the issue etc., are extinguished, but not the acts of the case. If precisely the same case – i.e. between the same persons and about the same matter – is later reintroduced, the acts of the case (i.e. those concerning the merits of the case, such as proofs etc.) may be used. For those not concerned in the original case, however, these acts have documentary value only.

Can. 1523 When a trial has been abated, the litigants are to bear the expenses which each has incurred.

3033   Since the abatement is due to the inactivity of the parties, they have to bear the expenses that they have incurred.

Can. 1524 §1 The plaintiff may renounce a trial at any stage or at any grade. Likewise, both the plaintiff and the respondent may renounce the procedural acts either in whole or only in part.

3034   A trial can be concluded by renunciation of the trial. The plaintiff may renounce the trial at any stage or grade. The respondent, if he or she has appealed the definitive judgement, can renounce the appeal (see Can. 1636 §1). Both parties may renounce the procedural acts in whole or in part. Renunciation of all the procedural acts would be tantamount to renunciation of the trial.

Can. 1524 §2 To renounce the trial of an issue, guardians and administrators of juridical persons must have the advice or the consent of those whose agreement is required to conduct business which exceed the limits of ordinary administration.

3035   This norm, which is designed to protect juridical persons from possible serious loss, requires the guardians or administrators to have either the advice or consent (whichever is appropriate) of those whose agreement is needed for acts exceeding the limits of ordinary administration (see Cann. 1276–1277, 638).

Can. 1524 §3 To be valid, a renunciation must be in writing, and must be signed either by the party, or by a procurator who has been given a special mandate for this purpose; it must be communicated to the other party, who must accept or at least not oppose it; and it must be admitted by the judge.

For the validity of renunciation a number of conditions must be met: 3036

(a) It must be done in writing and signed either by the party, or by a procurator who must have a special mandate for this purpose.
(b) It must be communicated to the other party, who must either agree to it or at least not oppose it; thus e.g. if a respondent objects to the plaintiff's renunciation of the trial and wishes the trial to continue, the renunciation would have no effect. However, if in such a case the respondent feared that the plaintiff would be less than energetic in prosecuting the case, it would always remain open for the respondent to become the plaintiff in a new case.
(c) The judge must admit the renunciation by a decree. If he saw that serious injustice could result from the renunciation, the judge could refuse to admit it.

Can. 1525 Once a renunciation has been admitted by the judge, it has the same effects for the acts which have been renounced as has an abatement of the trial. Likewise, it obliges the person renouncing to pay the expenses of those acts which have been renounced.

The effects on the acts which have been validly renounced is the same as in the case of abatement (see Can. 1522): procedural acts are extinguished either in whole, if the trial or all the procedural acts are renounced, or in part, if only some of the acts are renounced; the acts of the case remain and can be used if the same case is later reintroduced. The party who makes the renunciation is liable for the expenses incurred in the acts renounced. 3037

Title IV
Proofs

INTRODUCTION

This title deals with the instruction of the case, the central part of the process in which the proofs which support the claims of the parties are gathered. From these proofs the judge is to reach the degree of certainty which will enable him to pronounce authoritatively on the case in his definitive judgement. 3038

After four introductory canons, the Code treats of six different types of proof: (1) The declarations of the parties; (2) Documentary proof; (3) Witnesses and testimony; (4) Experts; (5) Judicial access and inspection; (6) Presumptions. 3039

Can. 1526 §1 The onus of proof rests upon the person who makes an allegation.

This paragraph follows the maxim of Roman law *affirmanti incumbit probatio* ('the burden of proof falls on him who makes an allegation'). If the plaintiff, or anyone else in a trial who alleges something, e.g. the respondent in making an exception, does not provide adequate proof, the judge will have no option but to declare the allegation not proven. 3040

Can. 1526 §2 The following matters do not require proof:

1° **matters which are presumed by the law itself;**

2° **facts alleged by one of the litigants and admitted by the other, unless their proof is nevertheless required either by law or by the judge.**

3041 Two types of matter do not require proof:

(a) Matters presumed by the law itself, e.g. the validity of a marriage (see Can. 1060), perduration of matrimonial consent (see Can. 1107). These presumptions are not absolute and can be overthrown by contrary proof.

(b) Facts alleged by one party and admitted by the other, unless either the law or the judge requires proof. The law requires such additional proof in cases concerning the public good (see Can. 1536 §2) and especially in marriage-nullity cases (see Can. 1679). In these cases the declarations and confessions of the parties, even when they are in agreement, provide only partial proof and need further 'indications and supportive elements' (see Can. 1679).[1]

Can. 1527 §1 Any type of proof which seems useful for the investigation of the case and is lawful, may be submitted.

3042 The law does not determine in detail what proofs are admissible and what are not. It simply states in general terms that any type of proof may be submitted provided it seems useful for the investigation of the case and is lawful. It is for the judge to decide whether a particular proof is to be admitted or not. He should keep in mind not only the requirements of this paragraph, but also such considerations as the delays that may be occasioned by certain methods of proofs.[2]

Can. 1527 §2 If a party submits that a proof, which has been rejected by the judge, should be admitted, the judge is to determine the matter with maximum expedition.

3043 If the judge rejects a particular proof, the party who has submitted it may request that it be admitted. The judge is then to determine, 'with maximum expedition', whether or not to admit it. Against his decision in this regard there can be no recourse (see Can. 1629 5°).

Can. 1528 If a party or a witness refuses to testify before the judge, that person may lawfully be heard by another, even a lay person, appointed by the judge, or asked to make a declaration either before a public notary or in any other lawful manner.

3044 This canon is new and is based on Art. 5 of an instruction of the Congregation for the Doctrine of the Faith concerning dissolution of marriages in favour of the faith and of non-consummated marriages.[3] The judge should weigh up the reasons for the refusal to testify before the judge. It might be because of personal acquaintance, or because a non-catholic has some scruples in coming before a catholic ecclesiastical judge, or it might be that the person is totally refusing to cooperate in the case. In

---

[1] The 1917 code c.1747 enumerated a third category of matters which did not need proof, 'notorious facts'. This category was dropped because not all facts which are considered notorious are true and because if the facts are truly notorious, proof of them will be rather easy: cf. Comm 11(1979) 98 at Can. 167.

[2] The 1917 Code c.1749 forbade the admission of proofs which could cause delay, unless no other sufficient proofs were available.

[3] SCDF instr *Ut Notum Sit* Art. 5: LE V 6704.

Can. 1540 §2 Public civil documents are those which are legally regarded as such in accordance with the laws of each place.

Public civil documents are those that qualify as such under the local civil law. They would include such documents as birth certificates, civil marriage or divorce certificates, etc. 3060

Can. 1540 §3 All other documents are private.

Any documents which do not qualify as public are private. This is a vast and varied category of documents and includes practically any written or recorded material which can be of help in deciding the point at issue. 3061

Can. 1541 Unless it is otherwise established by contrary and clear arguments, public documents constitute proof of those matters which are directly and principally affirmed in them.

Public documents, whether ecclesiastical or civil, are proof of those matters directly and principally contained in them. A document can state some things directly and principally, as e.g. a baptismal certificate states that baptism was conferred on a particular person in a particular place on a particular day; the same document can state other things in an indirect way, e.g. the same certificate might give the date of birth and the fact of subsequent confirmation. The certificate would give full proof of the first facts, partial proof of the second. 3062

The presumption of law stated in this canon stands unless there are clear contrary arguments to overthrow it. Such arguments could prove e.g. that the document was not authentic, that its contents were in fact false, that it was incomplete, that it was not in proper legal form. 3063

Can. 1542 A private document, whether acknowledged by a party or admitted by a judge, has the same probative force as an extrajudicial confession, against its author or the person who has signed it and against persons whose case rests on that of the author or signatory. Against others it has the same force as have declarations by the parties which are not confessions, in accordance with Can. 1536 §2.

In order to have any probative force, a private document must either be acknowledged by the party against whom it is brought forward or be admitted by the judge. Against the author or the signatory, or against those whose case rests on that of the author or signatory, such a private document has the probative force of an extrajudicial confession i.e. 'the judge, having considered all the circumstances, (is) to evaluate the weight to be given to' it (see Can. 1537). Against other persons, it has the same weight as declarations of the parties which are not confessions in accordance with Can. 1536 §2 (q.v.). 3064

Can. 1543 If documents are shown to have been erased, amended, falsified or otherwise tampered with, it is for the judge to evaluate to what extent, if any, they are to be given credence.

Documents can be altered in many ways – malicious, innocent, accidental, due to natural causes. Instead of giving detailed prescriptions of what to do in each case the law leaves it to the judge's conscience to decide what value to attribute to an altered document, public or private. Some alterations will be obviously harmless, such as the accidental misspelling of the name of a person or a place, and the judge could ignore these. Others may be less innocent and could render the document totally void of probative value. The judge could invoke the services of an expert, as e.g. in the case of a doubt regarding the authenticity of a signature or in deciphering an old and faded document. 3065

Article 2
The Production of Documents

Can. 1544 Documents do not have probative force at a trial unless they are submitted in original form or in authentic copy and are lodged in the office of the tribunal, so that they may be inspected by the judge and the opposing party.

3066 Two conditions must be fulfilled before any document can have probative force:

(a) It must be submitted in original form or in authentic copy so that there is no doubt about its authenticity. Today photocopies and even faxcopies are generally accepted as authentic, but the judge would be entitled to demand that even these be compared with the originals and individually authenticated by a notary.

(b) It must be lodged in the tribunal office so that the judge and the opposing party can inspect it and, in the case of the latter, possibly enter an exception.

Can. 1545 The judge can direct that a document common to each of the parties is to be submitted in the process.

3067 Documents can be common to both parties, e.g. wills, contracts between them, prenuptial agreements. The judge, with due regard to the following canon, can decree that such a document be produced in a trial.

Can. 1546 §1 No one is obliged to exhibit documents, even if they are common, which cannot be communicated without danger of the harm mentioned in Can. 1548 §2 n.2, or without the danger of violating a secret which is to be observed.

§2 If, however, at least an extract from a document can be transcribed and submitted in copy without the disadvantages mentioned, the judge can direct that it be produced in that form.

3068 In two cases there is no obligation to produce documents, even those which are common: (a) where there is reason to fear 'loss of reputation, dangerous harassment or some other grave evil' for the person concerned, his or her spouse or blood or marriage relations (see Can. 1548 §2); (b) where there is danger of violating a secret which should be observed. However, even in these cases, if part of the document can be produced without these dangers, the judge may decree that this be done, thus serving the cause of justice while avoiding the dangers mentioned.

Chapter III
WITNESSES AND TESTIMONY

Can. 1547 Proof by means of witnesses is admitted in all cases, under the direction of the judge.

3069 This canon establishes the general principle that proof by means of witnesses is allowed in all cases.[1] In view of the statement of Can. 1527 §1, which allows any type of proof which seems useful, the present canon might seem superfluous. It was retained however because of the 'canonisation' of the local civil law of contracts (see Can. 1290) lest some civil systems might not allow proof by witnesses in all such cases.[2]

---

[1] The one exception, from the very nature of the case, is the documentary process in marriage-nullity cases dealt with in Cann. 1686–1688.

[2] Cf. Comm 11(1979) at Can. 189.

Proof by witnesses is always subject to the direction of the judge. Given the numerous ways in which the testimony of witnesses can be inaccurate, such as malice, bias, error, forgetfulness, poor observation etc., the judge is always called on to make a prudent assessment of the sincerity and the objectivity of this evidence.

Can. 1548 §1 Witnesses must tell the truth to a judge who lawfully questions them.

For this obligation to bind, leaving aside the exceptions mentioned in §2 of the present canon, the judge must lawfully question the witness. This means that the questioning must be done by a legally competent judge, his delegate, an auditor or by a person whom the law allows to do this (see Cann. 1528 and 1661). In addition, the questions must be lawful and must fulfil the requirements of Can. 1564.

Can. 1548 §2 Without prejudice to the provisions of Can. 1550 §2 n.2 the following are exempted from the obligation of replying to questions:

   1° clerics, in those matters revealed to them by reason of their sacred ministry; civil officials, doctors, midwives, advocates, notaries and others who are bound by the secret of their office, even on the ground of having offered advice, in respect of matters subject to this secret;

   2° those who fear that, as a result of giving evidence, a loss of reputation, dangerous harassment or some other grave evil will arise for themselves, their spouses, or those closely related to them by consanguinity or affinity.

Two classes of people are exempted from answering the judge's questions: (1) those bound by the secret of their office; (2) those who fear some grave evil to themselves or those close to them, if they give evidence. The first class includes clerics and the reference to Can. 1550 §2 1° is a reminder that a priest can never give evidence about what he has heard in sacramental confession. In addition, it includes civil officials, members of the medical and legal professions and anyone who is bound by the secret of his or her office. The exemption applies only to those matters subject to the secret of their office and could cease if and when the obligation of secrecy ceases. The second class are those who fear a loss of reputation, dangerous (not just any) harassment or any other grave evil, of whatever nature, not only to themselves but also to their spouses and even to those otherwise closely related to them.[1] In neither class, however, is a mere assertion of exemption sufficient: the judge must be satisfied that the claim is well-founded in the terms of this canon.

Article 1
Those who can be Witnesses

Can. 1549 Everyone can be a witness, unless expressly excluded, whether wholly or in part, by the law.

The general principal is that anyone can be a witness unless the law excludes him or her, in whole or in part. The following canon lists those excluded by the Church's law.

---

[1] A proposal that the law determine the degree of consanguinity which would give rise to this exemption was not admitted and instead the matter was left to the judge's discretion: cf. Comm 11(1979) 109 at Can. 190 §2.

Others, e.g. the insane, would be excluded by natural law. The exclusion can be total, as e.g. in the case of the judge in the case, or partial as e.g. in the case of a priest who could testify to some matters but not to what he had heard in sacramental confession.

Can. 1550 §1 Minors under the age of fourteen years and those who are of feeble mind are not admitted to give evidence. They can, however, be heard if the judge declares by decree that it would be appropriate to do so.

3074 Those under 14 and those of feeble mind are deemed not to have sufficient discretion to be of value as witnesses and so the general rule is that they are to be excluded. However the final decision is left to the judge: he may decree that such people be admitted if he deems this 'appropriate'. He might do so e.g. where no other evidence is available, where they could testify to simple but important facts, etc.

Can. 1550 §2 The following are deemed incapable of being witnesses:

> **1° the parties in the case or those who appear at the trial in the name of the parties; the judge and his assistant; the advocate and those others who in the same case assist or have assisted the parties;**

3075 Neither the parties, those who appear for them (procurators, guardians, curators or other legal representatives) or the advocates who are assisting them or have assisted them in this particular case, can be admitted as witnesses. The principal reason seems to be the difficulty which these people might have in being fully objective in the matter. Likewise the judge and his assistant – an assessor, instructor or auditor – is excluded so as to safeguard his or her independence.

> **2° priests, in respect of everything which has become known to them in sacramental confession, even if the penitent has asked that these things be made known. Moreover, anything that may in any way have been heard by anyone on the occasion of confession, cannot be accepted even as an indication of the truth.**

3076 Priests are absolutely forbidden to testify to matters which have become known to them during sacramental confession, even if the penitent has given permission or even asked that the priest testify to them. This rule is intended as a defence of the sacramental seal and as a safeguard against even the suspicion of the betrayal of the secret of confession. In addition, no knowledge gained by anyone, including the penitent, on the occasion of sacramental confession can be admitted as evidence; it may not in any way whatever be taken into account by the judge, 'even as an indication of the truth'.

Article 2
The Introduction and the Exclusion of Witnesses

Can. 1551 A party who has introduced a witness may forgo the examination of that witness, but the opposing party may ask that the witness nevertheless be examined.

3077 Witnesses may be proposed by the parties, the promotor of justice, the defender of the bond[1] and, in accordance with the terms of Can. 1452, by the judge himself. Where a party has proposed a witness and later forgoes the examination of this witness, the opposing party has nevertheless the right to request that this witness be

---
[1] Cf. Can. 1434 and Comm 11(1979) 111 at Can. 194.

examined. Indeed the judge himself, if e.g. he suspects that the motives for forgoing the examination are not worthy ones, could and, generally speaking, should proceed to examine the witness.

Can. 1552 §1 When proof by means of witnesses is sought, the names and domicile of the witnesses are to be communicated to the tribunal.

The reason for this norm is primarily so that the witnesses can be identified and properly cited. It can also serve the secondary function of helping to establish competence in marriage nullity cases (see Can. 1673 4°). 3078

Can. 1552 §2 The propositions on which the interrogation of the witnesses is requested, are to be submitted within the time-limit determined by the judge; otherwise, the request is to be deemed abandoned.

The propositions or points on which the witnesses are to be questioned (see Can. 1533) are to be submitted (by the parties, the promotor of justice or the defender of the bond) within the time-limit laid down by the judge. Failure to do this is equivalent to forgoing the examination of the witnesses concerned. 3079

Can. 1553 It is for the judge to curb an excessive number of witnesses.

Although the parties are free to nominate witnesses, it can happen that the point at issue can be satisfactorily decided without hearing all of them. In such a case, or indeed whenever he deems that further evidence of witnesses would be unnecessary or useless, the judge can decree that no more witnesses be heard, thus *inter alia* avoiding excessive expense and an unduly long trial. The party has the right to have recourse against this decision and, if he or she does so, the judge is to decide the matter 'with maximum expedition' (see Can. 1527 §2), which means that there is no further recourse against that decision (see Can. 1629 5°). 3080

Can. 1554 Before witnesses are examined, their names are to be communicated to the parties. If, in the prudent opinion of the judge, this cannot be done without great difficulty, it is to be done at least before the publication of the proofs.

All the parties to a case have the right to know the names of the witnesses, no matter by whom proposed, so that they can, if necessary, raise objections to them or ask to have them excluded (see Can. 1555). In the 1917 Code c.1763 the obligation of communicating the names rested with the parties themselves. The present law does not specify who is to do this,[1] and so it could be done either by the judge or by the parties. This does not imply any right of the parties to know the current address(es) of the witnesses; there are situations in which such disclosure would be at least inadvisable and possibly even perilous. It is to be noted that the names are to be communicated 'before witnesses are examined' – unless the judge in his prudence considers that this cannot be done 'without great difficulty', of whatever kind, e.g. if a particular witness would refuse, or be disinclined, to give evidence if his or her name were to be made known in advance. Should a judge take this course of action – which is clearly the exception rather than the rule – there would still remain the requirement that the parties be informed of the names of the witnesses 'at least before the publication of the proofs'.[2] 3081

---

[1] Cf. Comm 11(1979) 112 at Can. 197.

[2] In the normal practice in marriage-nullity cases, the prescription of this canon does not cause a problem; more often than not the spouses are much more concerned about the outcome of the case than about the procedures adopted in arriving at the ultimate decision: in effect, many of them implicitly waive their right to know the names of the witnesses. The particular point of the canon is to insist that in every trial the right be made known to all the interested parties, including the spouses in a marriage-nullity case, and that, if they wish to exercise it, it is to be protected in accordance with the terms of the canon.

Can. 1555 Without prejudice to the provisions of Can. 1550, a party may request that a witness be excluded, provided a just reason for exclusion is established before the witness is examined.

3082 Can. 1550 provides for the exclusion of certain witnesses by the law itself; the present canon allows a party to request the judge to exclude a witness. In order that a witness be excluded, there must be a just reason and the request must be made before the witness has in fact been examined. The mere fact that a party does not want a witness examined or personally dislikes or mistrusts the witness, or any such, is not a sufficient reason. The party must advance a good and well-founded reason for such a serious step, e.g. evidence of the witness's established or well known untruthfulness, unreliability, bias, etc. The decision to exclude any witness remains that of the judge.

Can. 1556 The summons of a witness is effected by a decree of the judge lawfully notified to the witness.

3083 The judge's decree summoning a witness should name the place, date and time of the examination. It is to be communicated to the witness in accordance with Can. 1509. In the practice of most local tribunals this is done by way of an official letter from the tribunal.

Can. 1557 A properly summoned witness is to appear, or to make known to the judge the reason for being absent.

3084 Once lawfully summoned, the witness is obliged either to appear or to inform the judge of any lawful reason for not doing so. Such a reason could be any of the exempting factors of Can. 1548 §2; it could also include such as grave personal inconvenience, illness, infirmity, etc. It is common and sensible practice in many tribunals to have the parties approach beforehand the witnesses proposed by them, in order to secure their cooperation. In a situation where a witness, on receipt of an official written summons to appear, may be overawed or frightened or hesitant or even directly unwilling to cooperate, it can often be helpful if the tribunal would ask an understanding and sympathetic priest of the parish to call on the person at home, to allay what more often than not is an unnecessary or exaggerated anxiety; in this same context, the experienced tribunal will recognise that many ordinary folk tend not to reply to official letters, especially those which at first sight appear to be in one way or another menacing!

Article 3
The Examination of Witnesses

Can. 1558 §1 Witnesses are to be examined at the office of the tribunal unless the judge deems otherwise.

§2 Cardinals, Patriarchs, Bishops, and those who in their own civil law enjoy a similar favour, are to be heard at the place selected by themselves.

§3 Without prejudice to the provisions of Cann. 1418 and 1469 §2, the judge is to decide where witnesses are to be heard for whom, by reason of distance, illness or other impediment, it is impossible or difficult to come to the office of the tribunal.

3085 The normal place for the examination of witnesses is the tribunal office (§1). This is not merely more convenient for the tribunal staff; it ensures a certain valuable solemnity in the proceeding. The judge, however, is allowed a wide discretion in choosing another place when this is necessary or more convenient.[1] This is particularly evidenced in the norms of §3. Where a witness lives outside the judge's territory there are two options regarding his or her testimony. The more usual one is for the judge to request the tribunal of the place to undertake the task (see Can. 1418). Alternatively, with the permission of the diocesan Bishop of the place to which he goes, he could leave his territory in order to gather the evidence personally (see Can. 1496 §2). Where the witness lives in the judge's territory but there are reasons such as distance or illness or other impediment, which make it impossible or difficult for the witness to come to the tribunal office, the judge is to decide where he or she is to be heard: in practice, this is usually done by arrangement with the Auditor concerned.

Repeating the substance of c.1770 §2 1° of the 1917 Code, §2 lists those who, because of the dignity of their office, have the right to select the place in which to give their evidence. These are Cardinals, Patriarchs, Bishops and those who enjoy a similar privilege in civil law. **3086**

Can. 1559 The parties cannot be present at the examination of the witnesses unless, especially when there is question of a private interest, the judge has determined that they are to be admitted. Their advocates or procurators, however, may attend, unless by reason of the circumstances of matter and persons, the judge has determined that the proceedings are to be in secret.

In general the parties, but not the promotor of justice or the defender of the bond, are forbidden to be present at the examination of the witnesses, unless the judge permits otherwise. He may do so especially, but not only, in cases concerning a private interest. He may not do so in marriage-nullity cases (see Can. 1678 §2).[2] The reason for the prohibition is to avoid disputes and to safeguard the witnesses from possible intimidation. The parties' advocates or procurators may attend, unless the judge has forbidden this. **3087**

Can. 1560 §1 The witnesses are to be examined individually and separately.

§2 If in a grave matter the witnesses disagree either among themselves or with one of the parties, the judge may arrange for those who differ to meet or to confront one another, but must, in so far as possible, eliminate discord and scandal.

The general rule is that witnesses are to be examined one at a time and separately. The reason is so that the testimony of one will not influence that of others.[3] However, exceptionally, in an important matter, if the witnesses differ from one another or from one of the parties, the judge may allow a confrontation between those who differ in order to arrive at the truth. If he does take this step the judge is to ensure as far as possible that there be no discord or scandal. Note that such a confrontation is not a right of the parties but remains completely at the judge's discretion. **3088**

---

[1] A proposal that this canon explicitly allow examination of a witness by telephone was not admitted because of the danger of abuse and the possibility of doubts about the identity and freedom of the witness. However the consultors did add that the practice of taking a deposition by telephone was not reprobated by the canon. From this it would seem that in a case of necessity this means could be used. Cf. Comm 11(1979) 114 at Can. 202.

[2] Cf. also Comm 11(1979) 114 at Can. 203.

[3] Cf. Comm 11(1979) 114-115 at Can. 204. Occasionally it happens that elderly and often timid parents, particularly of one of the parties in a marriage-nullity case, will request that they be allowed to give their evidence together, rather than separately. If he is satisfied that their motive is solely one of mutual support on what can be for them a distinctly traumatic occasion, the experienced judge must consider such a request with a sympathetic understanding and exercise his discretion accordingly.

Can. 1561 **The examination of a witness is conducted by the judge, or by his delegate or an auditor, who is to be attended by a notary. Accordingly, unless particular law provides otherwise, if the parties or the promotor of justice or the defender of the bond or the advocates who are present at the hearing have additional questions to put to the witness, they are to propose these not to the witness, but to the judge, or to the one who is taking the judge's place, so that he or she may put them.**

3089 The rule of general law is that the examination of a witness is done only by the judge or by one who takes his place in this function in accordance with the law, i.e. his delegate or an auditor, attended by a notary. Just as Can. 1533 allows the parties, the promotor of justice, the defender of the bond and the parties' advocates to propose initial propositions upon which the parties are to be questioned, the present canon allows these same people, if they are present at the examination in accordance with Can. 1559, to propose supplementary questions to be put to the witnesses, but only by the judge or the one who takes his place. The canon, however, allows for particular law which may permit that the questions be put directly rather than through the judge. There is in fact a strong case to be made for the enactment of such legislation, particularly at a national or at least a provincial level, thus to avoid a potentially harmful divergence of practice between one local tribunal and another.

Can. 1562 §1 **The judge is to remind the witness of the grave obligation to tell the truth and nothing but the truth.**

3090 Can. 1548 §1 obliges witnesses to 'tell the truth to a judge who lawfully questions them'. The present canon directs the judge to remind them in specific form about this obligation: they are 'to tell the whole truth and nothing but the truth' and this obliges whether or not they take an oath to this effect.

Can. 1562 §2 **The judge is to administer an oath to the witness in accordance with Can. 1532. If, however, a witness refuses to take an oath, he or she is to be heard unsworn.**

3091 For the value of an oath in evidence, see the comments made at Can. 1532. The judge is to administer an oath to a witness in the same circumstances as he would to a party in accordance with Can. 1532, i.e. in cases where the public good is involved, the oath is to be administered unless a grave reason suggests otherwise; in cases concerning private matters, it is for the judge to decide whether or not to administer it. The oath can be either one to tell the truth or one confirming the truthfulness of what has been said. The canon allows for the taking of an unsworn deposition from someone who refuses to take an oath, e.g. for reasons of conscience or even of a divergent religious belief.

Can. 1563 **The judge is first of all to establish the identity of the witness. The relationship which the witness has with the parties is to be probed, and when specific questions concerning the case are asked of the witness, enquiry is to be made into the sources of his or her knowledge and the precise time the witness came to know the matters which are asserted.**

3092 The judge has firstly to establish the identity of the witness. This he will do through asking his or her name, address, date of birth, occupation, etc. In a case of doubt, he could seek additional proof of identity, such as a passport or other document with a photograph, or he could have the person formally identified by someone he knows to be beyond suspicion. Next he is to establish the relationship between the witness and the parties. This will be useful not only in showing possible bias, but also in showing how well the witness is versed in the facts of the case. Obviously a close relative or associate of a party would probably know more about the party than a comparative stranger.

The canon goes on to give important rules about establishing the sources of the witness's knowledge and the exact time that he or she acquired this knowledge. Thus e.g. in a case where a marriage is alleged to be null because of an exclusion of the *bonum prolis*, it will be very important, evidentially, to discover from whom the witness heard of the alleged exclusion, whether it was from the alleged excluder or from someone else, and perhaps even more important to discover when he or she heard of it; obviously if the witness heard of it before the marriage, or at least before there was any question of a nullity case, the evidence will be more telling than if the knowledge was acquired just before the witness was summoned to appear at the tribunal.

3093

Can. 1564 The questions are to be brief, and appropriate to the understanding of the person being examined. They are not to encompass a number of matters at the same time, nor be captious or deceptive. They are not to be leading questions, nor give any form of offence. They are to be relevant to the case in question.

This canon describes in both positive and negative terms the questions that are to be put to witnesses. They are to be *brief*: by the end of a question that is too long the witness may well have forgotten the precise point he or she is being asked about and may even be too polite to say so! They are to be *appropriate* to the understanding of the person being examined: so e.g. highly literary or abstract language should be avoided in questioning someone who is illiterate or not very intelligent. They should be *simple*, in the sense that each question should deal with one point and not with many simultaneously. They should *not be captious or deceptive*, i.e. designed to trick the witness. *Leading questions*, i.e. questions which suggest an answer, must be avoided. Questions should *never be in any way offensive* to the parties or others, including the witness, who take part in the case. Above all, the questions should be relevant to the case in question: it is quite possible to ask interesting questions and to get interesting information that has little or nothing to do with the case! The whole area of questioning is one where the judge must exercise the greatest care, skill and prudence. Too often inept questioning can result in depositions which are almost useless, even though the witness has information that is relevant to the case and is willing to communicate it.

3094

Can. 1565 §1 The questions are not to be made known in advance to the witnesses.

§2 If, however, the matters about which evidence is to be given are so remote in memory that they cannot be affirmed with certainty unless they are recalled beforehand, the judge may, if he thinks this can safely be done, advise the witness in advance about certain aspects of the matter.

Normally a witness is not to be told in advance what questions he or she will be asked. This is a safeguard against collusion and a means of ensuring replies that are spontaneous rather than studied. In order to ensure that the witnesses do not gain advance knowledge of the questions, the judge could impose an oath of secrecy in accordance with Can. 1455 §3. The second paragraph of the canon allows for an exception with regard to matters that are from so long ago that it would be unreasonable to expect a witness to recall them accurately without an opportunity to refresh his or her memory. In such a case, if he deems that it can be safely done, the judge may give the witness advance notice of some aspects of the matters about which he or she will be questioned.

3095

Book VII Judicial Procedures

Can. 1566 The witnesses are to give evidence orally. They are not to read from a script, except where there is a question of calculations or accounts. In this case, they may consult notes which they have brought with them.

3096 Prepared written answers are forbidden not only by this canon but also by Can. 1565 §1, because they require prior notice of the questions to be asked. Particularly prohibited is the known practice of some local tribunals whereby a written questionnaire is sent by post to a witness who is asked simply to write his or her replies and then to return the document. However, when the witnesses are being questioned on matters of calculations or accounts, they may consult notes because it is difficult to rely on memory alone for accuracy in such matters; obviously they may also consult notes, diaries etc. to refresh their memory.

Can. 1567 §1 The replies are to be written down at once by the notary. The record must show the very words of the evidence given, at least in what concerns those things which bear directly on the matter of the trial.

3097 The witness's answers are to be written down immediately by the notary. A delay in doing so could cause inaccuracy or even outright error. Where the answers concern those things which bear directly on the matters of the trial, the exact words used by the witness must be recorded; for less important matters an accurate precis of his or her statements will suffice. This is an area where the skill and experience of the judge or auditor is such a practical factor.

Can. 1567 §2 The use of a tape-recorder is allowed, provided the replies are subsequently committed to writing and, if possible, signed by the deponents.

3098 This paragraph explicitly allows the use of a tape-recorder in taking evidence, subject to the condition that the replies are subsequently committed to writing and, insofar as possible, signed by the witness. The requirement that the recording be written out is not just one of convenience – although it is quicker and easier to read a written deposition than to listen to a recorded one – but, more importantly, in order to guarantee accuracy. There is a danger that tape-recordings could be tampered with.[1]

Can. 1568 The notary is to mention in the acts whether the oath was taken or excused or refused; who were present, parties and others; the questions added *ex officio*; and in general, everything worthy of record which may have occurred while the witnesses were being examined.

3099 This canon lists specifically and generically what the notary is to record in the acts in addition to the answers to the questions. Specifically, he or she is to mention whether the oath was taken, excused or refused (see Can. 1562 §2): this may have importance in helping decide the value of the witness's evidence. The notary is also to record who was present at the session, the parties, the promotor of justice, the defender of the bond, procurators, advocates etc. (see Can. 1559). Questions asked *ex officio,* i.e. additional questions either proposed by the judge or put by him at the request of others in accordance with Can. 1561, are also to be recorded in full. In general, the notary is to mention anything worthy of record which may have happened during the examination of the witnesses, e.g. that a witness refused to answer a particular question, that an interpreter was used in accordance with Can. 1471, etc.

Can. 1569 §1 At the conclusion of the examination, the record of the evidence, either as written down by the notary or as played back from the

---

[1] Cf. Comm 16(1984) 66 at Can. 1519 §2.

tape-recording, must be communicated to the witness, who is to be given the opportunity of adding to, omitting from, correcting or varying it.

§2 Finally, the witness, the judge and the notary must sign the record.

When the evidence of a witness has been taken, he or she is to be allowed either to read or have read the written record of the evidence or to hear the play-back of the tape-recording. The witness is then to be given the opportunity to add to, omit from, correct or vary the record so that it most faithfully represents what he or she intended to say. Finally, the record is to be signed by the witness, the judge and the notary.[1]

Can. 1570 Before the acts or the testimony are published, witnesses, even though already examined, may be called for re-examination, either at the request of a party or *ex officio*. This may be done if the judge considers it either necessary or useful, provided there is no danger whatever of collusion or of inducement.

While this is not of frequent occurrence, witnesses who have already been examined may be recalled for further questioning either at the judge's own initiative or at the request of a party, subject to certain conditions: (a) The re-examination must be done before the publication of the acts or of the testimony; after this the more stringent rules of Can. 1600 apply. (b) The judge must consider this step either necessary or useful, e.g. he might do it in cases of contradictory evidence or where he believes that a witness was not fully examined and has further evidence of value to give. (c) There must be no danger either of collusion, i.e. an unlawful agreement between a witness and an opposing party, or of inducement i.e. an offer of money or the like to the witness to get him or her to give favourable or more favourable evidence.

Can. 1571 Witnesses must be refunded both the expenses they may have incurred and the losses they may have sustained by the reason of their giving evidence, in accordance with the equitable assessment of the judge.

Witnesses are to be compensated both for expenses incurred, e.g. by travel, accommodation, and for any losses sustained, e.g. loss of earnings, in connection with giving evidence. It is for the judge to assess the amount to be paid, in accordance with the norms established by the Bishop who is moderator of the tribunal (see Can. 1649 §1 2°). Not infrequently in practice witnesses do in effect waive their right in this regard, but the experienced judge will remain alert to the tribunal's obligation in the matter, especially in respect of witnesses who, by reason of the financial loss envisaged in this canon, might reasonably be reluctant to give evidence.

Article 4
The Credibility of Evidence

Can. 1572 In weighing evidence the judge may, if it is necessary, seek testimonial letters, and is to take into account:

1° the condition and uprightness of the witness;

This canon, after providing in a case of necessity for testimonial letters, i.e. a written statement by someone of undoubted integrity and knowledge about the witness's credibility, offers to the judge a number of common-sense helps in weighing up the

---

[1] If the witness cannot or will not sign, the prescriptions of Can. 1473 are to be followed.

value of evidence. The first of these is the condition and uprightness of the witness, taking into consideration such factors as his or her age, cultural background, education, mental ability and, above all, his or her honesty.

2° whether the knowledge was acquired at first hand, particularly if it was something seen or heard personally, or whether it was opinion, rumour or hearsay;

3104 The source of the witness's knowledge is very important. Obviously whatever the witness has learned at first hand, being less likely to distortion in transmission, is more valuable than what he or she has heard or believes.

3° whether the witness is constant and consistent, or varies, is uncertain or vacillating;

3105 The manner in which evidence is given can also be a guide to its value. If the witness is constant and consistent, the evidence is more likely to be accurate than if he or she varies the statements which are inconsistent with one another or with other evidence and proofs. Likewise if the witness is uncertain, it is hard to accept the evidence as objectively reliable.

4° whether there is corroboration of the testimony, and whether it is confirmed or not by other items of proof.

3106 It is clear that evidence which is corroborated by other independent testimony or confirmed by other items of proof, is more valuable than that which is singular and stands quite alone.

Can. 1573 The deposition of one witness cannot amount to full proof, unless the witness is a qualified one who gives evidence on matters carried out in an official capacity, or unless the circumstances of persons and things persuade otherwise.

3107 This canon follows the old legal maxim *testis unus, testis nullus*, 'a single witness is no witness'. However, it does admit two exceptions, one of them rather broad. The first is the case of a 'qualified witness', e.g. a priest testifying to something done in the exercise of his office, such as officiating at a marriage. The second and broader exception is where 'the circumstances of persons and things persuade otherwise': so e.g. the evidence of an individual of particular and proven uprightness and honesty, even if it is uncorroborated, could be allowed by the judge to give full proof; equally if there are indications or circumstantial factors other than corroborative evidence to support the testimony of a single witness, and there is no proof of the contrary, the judge could reach the required moral certainty.

Chapter IV
EXPERTS

Can. 1574 The services of experts are to be used whenever, by a provision of the law or of the judge, their study and opinion, based upon their art or science, are required to establish some fact or to ascertain the true nature of some matter.

3108 An expert is one with special technical knowledge or skills which he or she places at the services of the judge in order to establish a fact or to ascertain the true nature of some matter. In today's tribunals the most common expert is the psychological or psychiatric expert frequently employed in marriage-nullity cases,[1] but there can be many other kinds in all sorts of cases, e.g. theological, medical, legal, artistic, financial experts. Their services are to be used whenever the law calls for them or the judge deems it opportune. There may be one expert, or, especially in more complex or difficult cases, there may be several. An example of where the law itself calls for the services of experts is in marriage-nullity cases concerning impotence or defect of consent by reason of mental illness (see Can. 1680).

The function of experts is not to decide the point at issue – that belongs solely to the judge – nor is it merely to testify to what they have seen and heard, as with an ordinary witness. Rather it is to provide the court with the benefit of their professional expertise in a particular area and so aid the judge in coming to a conclusion. Thus, e.g. a psychiatric expert would not decide on the nullity of a marriage but would give his considered opinion about the mental state of one or both parties and about how that state could affect their powers of knowledge and consent; or an art expert could be called to decide whether a painting in dispute was an original or a copy, but it would not be for him or her to decide the question of ownership. 3109

Can. 1575 It is for the judge, having consulted the parties or at their request, to appoint the experts or, if such is the case, to accept reports already made by other experts.

It is solely the judge's function to appoint experts or to acknowledge reports already made by other experts. He may do this *ex officio*, in which case he is to consult the parties (and also the promotor of justice and the defender of the bond, if these are involved in the case), or he may do so at the request of the parties.[2] 3110

Can. 1576 Experts can be excluded or objected to for the same reasons as a witness.

Although an expert is appointed by the judge, he or she remains in essence a witness and so is subject to the same rules about exclusion and objection as any other witness (see Cann. 1550 and 1555). The present canon makes certain and explicit what would otherwise have been a reasonable assumption. 3111

Can. 1577 §1 The judge in his decree must define the specific points to be considered in the expert's task, taking into account whatever may have been suggested by the litigants.

The judge is to indicate as precisely as possible the points to be covered by the expert. In some cases, e.g. in the psychological or psychiatric area, it will not always be possible in advance to be completely precise, but even here the expert is not mandated to range over every possibility, however interesting, but must confine himself to the points at issue. In defining the scope of the expert's task the judge is to take into consideration whatever suggestions are made by the parties and by the promotor of justice and the defender of the bond. 3112

---

[1] For a valuable comprehensive and up-to-date study on this matter, cf. McGrath *At the Service of the Truth: Psychological Sciences and their relation to the Canon Law of Nullity of Marriage* Stud Can 27(1993) 379–400.

[2] The present Code does not explicitly repeat the provision of c.1797 §1 of the 1917 Code which obliged experts to take an oath faithfully to fulfil their office. However, they would certainly come within the ambit of Can. 1454 which demands such an oath from all who assist in a tribunal.

Can. 1577 §2 The expert is to be given the acts of the case, and any documents and other material needed for the proper and faithful discharge of his or her duty.

3113 In order to carry out his or her duty properly, the expert may need access to the acts of the case and to other documents and material; if this is the case, the judge is to allow such access. Note however that this rule is confined to those acts and documents which are *needed* for the discharge of the expert's task. Indeed it can and does happen, especially in the psychiatric and psychological domains, that the expert would prefer to be unencumbered beforehand by whatever information may already be in the hands of the tribunal.

Can. 1577 §3 The judge, having consulted the expert, is to determine a time for the completion of the examination and the submission of the report.

3114 In order to avoid undue delay, the judge is to fix a time-limit for the completion of the expert's task. However, he is first to consult the expert, as he or she will be the one who knows best how long the task is likely to take.[1]

Can. 1578 §1 Each expert is to complete a report distinct from that of the others, unless the judge orders that one report be drawn up and signed by all of them. In this case, differences of opinion, if there are such, are to be carefully noted.

3115 Where there is more than one expert in a case, they are to produce separate reports, unless the judge orders a common report signed by all of them. In such a case any differences of opinion between the experts are to be carefully noted.[2]

Can. 1578 §2 Experts must clearly indicate the documents or other appropriate means by which they have verified the identity of persons, places or things. They are also to state the manner and method followed in fulfilling the task assigned to them, and the principal arguments upon which their conclusions are based.

3116 The expert is to indicate the documents or other means used to identify persons, places or things, the manner and method used and the principal arguments on which the conclusions are based. This information will aid the judge in estimating how pertinent and reliable the conclusions are.

Can. 1578 §3 The expert may be summoned by the judge to supply any further explanations which seem necessary.

3117 It may be that there is some conflict between the reports of two or more experts, or between an expert and other proofs; or it can happen that the report is not clear or is couched in very technical language. For these or other similar reasons, the judge can always call upon the expert to appear before him for the purpose of clarification; if this be not possible, e.g. by reason of distance or such impediment, a written clarification may be sought.

---

[1] The time-limit can, if necessary, be extended, but only after hearing from the parties (cf. Can. 1465 §2).

[2] The use of the word 'signed' implies that the reports of experts are written, even though the Code nowhere explicitly makes this obligatory. The 1917 Code at c.1801 §1 allowed the report to be written or made orally before the judge, in which latter case it was to be written down and duly signed. A proposal that the reports be made in writing was not admitted by the Revision Commission (cf. Comm 11(1979) 122 at Can. 227 §3). An oral report is certainly still permissible.

Can. 1579 §1 The judge is to weigh carefully not only the experts' conclusions, even when they agree, but also all the other circumstances of the case.

§2 When he is giving the reasons for his decision, the judge must state on what grounds he accepts or rejects the conclusions of the experts.

The judge is in no way bound by the conclusions of experts in a case, but he is obliged to consider these carefully as a valuable form of proof. Obviously, the conclusions of experts are the more telling if they are independent and agree with one another, or if they are supported by other elements of proof. In his judgement the judge must state why he accepts or rejects these conclusions. Where experts disagree, the judge is free to seek further reports from them, or to appoint a further expert in order to elucidate the matter.[1]

Can. 1580 Experts are to be paid their expenses and honorariums. These are to be determined by the judge in a proper and equitable manner, with due observance of particular law.

This canon corresponds to Can. 1571, which has regard to ordinary witnesses, and has a necessary addition concerning professional fees. These are to be determined in accordance with Can. 1649 §1 1°.

Can. 1581 §1 The parties may designate their experts, to be approved by the judge.

The possible designation of private experts by the parties in a case is new in the present Code. Such experts have to be approved by the judge, which does give them a certain 'official' quality, but would not put them on the same level as experts appointed by the judge. Their function resembles that of advocates in that it is to further and protect the interests of the party who designates them. For this reason they cannot be regarded as wholly independent and their conclusions should be weighed up in the same way as the evidence of witnesses nominated by the parties.

Can. 1581 §2 If the judge admits them, these experts can inspect the acts of the case, in so far as required for the discharge of their duty, and can be present when the appointed experts fulfil their role. They can always submit their reports.

If admitted by the judge, these private experts can, but only 'in so far as their task demands it', examine the acts of the case and they can be present while the experts appointed by the judge fulfil their role. They are not allowed to inspect the reports of the appointed experts or to be present when these are questioned about their reports.[2] They are always allowed to submit their own reports.

Chapter V
JUDICIAL ACCESS AND INSPECTION

Can. 1582 If, in order to decide the case, the judge considers it opportune to visit some place, or inspect some thing, he is to set this out in a decree.

---

[1] This was explicitly allowed by c.1803 §1 of the 1917 Code. The fact that this paragraph was not repeated in the present Code in no way limits the judge's powers in this regard: cf. Comm 11(1979) 124 at Can. 231.

[2] Cf. Comm 11(1979) 124 at Can. 233 bis.

> After he has heard the parties, the decree is to give a brief description of what is to be made available for this access.

3122 This fifth form of proof is of rare application. If in a particular case the judge considers it useful to visit a place or inspect some object which has to do with the case, he is to issue a decree stating this and specifying the time and date for the access. He is to consult the parties and to lay down what is to be made available for this access and to decide who is to be present. If what is to be inspected is a place, e.g. a church, a shrine, a cemetery etc., the judge will go there; if it is an object this can, if feasible, be brought to the tribunal.

> **Can. 1583** After the inspection has been carried out, a document to this effect is to be drawn up.

3123 This document will record the fact of the inspection, how, when and where it took place and who was present, and it should be properly dated and signed.

Chapter VI
PRESUMPTIONS

> **Can. 1584** A presumption is a probable conjecture about something which is uncertain. Presumptions of law are those stated in the law; human presumptions are those made by a judge.

3124 This canon gives a succinct definition of a presumption: 'a probable conjecture about something which is uncertain'. Based on experience or on probability, a presumption makes deductions from certain facts and circumstances about other facts which are doubtful. Presumptions can be stated in the law, in which case they are called presumptions of law, e.g. Can. 1060 which presumes the validity of a marriage until the contrary is proven; or they may be human presumptions, made by the judge from his experience and from probability: thus, e.g. a judge might presume from the fact of possession of an object that the possessor is the owner.

3125 A presumption, whether of law or human, can be overthrown either directly or indirectly. It is overthrown directly by showing that the fact which is presumed is false: e.g. if the possessor of an object is presumed to be its owner, this presumption would be overthrown directly by showing that someone else had in fact valid title to the object. A presumption is overthrown indirectly by showing that the facts on which the presumption is based are false: thus in the example just given, the presumption of ownership would be overthrown indirectly if it were shown that the person alleged to be in possession of the object was not in fact the possessor.[1]

> **Can. 1585** A person with a presumption of law in his or her favour is freed from the onus of proof, which then falls on the other party.

3126 A presumption of law is not strictly speaking a form of proof, but if a person has a presumption of law in his or her favour, he or she is relieved of the burden of proof once the facts on which the presumption is based have been established: thus e.g. given the fact of the celebration of a marriage ceremony, a party seeking a declaration of its nullity must overthrow the presumption of the validity of that marriage, while a

---

[1] The former distinction in presumptions of law between presumptions *iuris et de iure* (which could be overthrown only indirectly) and presumptions *iuris simpliciter* (which could be overthrown by either method) has now been abolished: cf. Comm 11(1979) 127 at Can. 240.

party who wishes to maintain its validity need prove nothing. Note that the presumption of law in favour of validity in this case may indeed be contrary to the fact, but if it is, this must be proven.

Can. 1586 The judge is not to make presumptions which are not established by the law, other than on the basis of a certain and determined fact directly connected with the matter in dispute.

The judge may always use relevant presumptions of law. In forming his own, human presumptions he must be guided by prudence and experience and not act in an arbitrary manner. In particular, he must base his presumptions on a certain and determined fact, and this fact (or facts) must be directly connected with the matter in dispute. 3127

Title V
Incidental Matters

Can. 1587 An incidental matter arises when, after the case has begun by the summons, a question is proposed which, even though not expressly raised in the petition which introduced the case, yet so affects the case that it needs to be settled before the principal question.

As considered in this title, an incidental matter is a question which arises after the summoning of the parties and before the issuing of the judgement, and which, although not explicitly included in the petition, so affects the case that it needs to be settled before the principal question. Other incidental questions are possible, e.g. before the summons there could be questions regarding the legal competence of the tribunal, the processual capacity of the plaintiff, etc.; after the judgement there could be questions regarding judicial expenses.[1] 3128

Can. 1588 An incidental matter is proposed before the judge who is competent to decide the principal case. It is raised in writing or orally, indicating the connection between it and the principal case.

An incidental matter can be raised, either orally or in writing, before the judge who is competent to decide the principal case. The person proposing it must indicate the connection between it and the principal case. It can be proposed by the parties, the promotor of justice or the defender of the bond, if these intervene in the case,[2] by a third party intervening in accordance with Cann. 1596–1597 or by the judge himself.[3] 3129

Can. 1589 §1 When the judge has received the petition and heard the parties, he is to decide with maximum expedition whether the proposed incidental matter has a foundation and a connection with the principal matter, or whether it is to be rejected from the outset. If he admits it, he must decide whether it is of such gravity that it needs to be determined by an interlocutory judgement or by a decree.

---
[1] Cf. Comm 11(1979) 128 at Can. 243.
[2] Ibid.
[3] Ibid.

3130 On receiving the petition proposing the incidental matter, the judge is to hear the parties (and the promotor of justice and the defender of the bond if they are intervening in the case) with a view to deciding whether the proposed incidental matter (a) has any real foundation and (b) is connected to the principal matter. If his decision on either of these points is in the negative, he is to reject the petition forthwith. Since he is to decide this matter 'with maximum expedition', no appeal is possible against his decision (see Can. 1629 5°). If the judge admits the incidental matter, he is to decide whether it is to be determined by an interlocutory judgement (in more serious matters) or simply by a decree (in matters of less importance).

Can. 1589 §2 If, however, he concludes that the incidental matter is not to be decided before the definitive judgement, he is to determine that account be taken of it when the principal matter is decided.

3131 It may well happen that it is quite clear that the outcome of the incidental matter will have no effect on the main question. In such a case, in order to avoid undue delay, the judge may decide to postpone determining the incidental matter until the definitive decision of the main question.

Can. 1590 §1 If the incidental matter is to be decided by judgement, the norms for an oral contentious process are to be observed unless, because of the gravity of the issue, the judge deems otherwise.

§2 If it is to be decided by decree, the tribunal can entrust the matter to an auditor or to the presiding judge.

3132 If the incidental matter is to be determined by a judgement, normally the rules for the oral contentious process (see Cann. 1656–1670) are to be followed. However, the judge may decide, because of the seriousness of the point at issue – e.g. a point which could be decisive of the main question – to determine it according to the norms of the ordinary contentious process. If the case is to be decided by decree, the whole tribunal, if the case is being heard by a collegiate tribunal, need not be involved. The tribunal can entrust the matter to the auditor or to the presiding judge, who should in his decree give, at least in summary form, the reasons motivating his decision (see Cann. 51, 1617).

Can. 1591 Before the principal matter is concluded, the judge or the tribunal may for a just reason revoke or alter an interlocutory judgement or decree. This can be done either at the request of a party or *ex officio* by the judge after he has heard the parties.

3133 Interlocutory judgements or decrees on incidental matters given before the end of the principal case have a provisional character and are open to revocation or alteration. This can be done for a just reason either at the request of a party, or by the judge himself after hearing the parties (and the promotor of justice and the defender of the bond, if these are involved in the case).

Chapter I
THE NON-APPEARANCE OF PARTIES

Can. 1592 §1 If a respondent is summoned but does not appear, and either does not offer an adequate excuse for absence or has not replied in accordance with Can. 1507 §1, the judge is to declare the person absent from the

process, and decree that the case is to proceed to the definitive judgement and to its execution, with due observance of the proper norms.

If a respondent has been duly summoned but does not answer to the summons, or does not at least offer a sufficient excuse for his or her absence, the judge has no option but to issue a decree declaring him or her absent from the process and stating that the case is to proceed to the definitive judgement and its execution in accordance with the normal rules. This provision is in some contrast to the more severe rule of the 1917 Code (cc.1842–1851) where the respondent in such circumstances was to be declared to be in contempt and, unless he or she purged that contempt, lost all right to intervene in the case. Yet it is to be noted that, on the issue of the decree envisaged here, 'the case is to proceed to the definitive judgement and to its execution', thus effectively eliminating the respondent unless in the meantime he or she would make effective amends. This is therefore an important norm of law in the context of the right of defence – especially, because of their preponderance, in marriage-nullity cases.

Can. 1592 §2 Before issuing the decree mentioned in §1, the judge must make sure, if necessary by means of another summons, that a lawful summons did reach the respondent within the canonical time.

It can happen that the summons did not in fact reach the respondent and so the judge, before issuing the decree mentioned above, must make sure that the respondent was duly summoned. He may take whatever steps he deems necessary or useful for this purpose – registered post, evidence of delivery, personal contact; if necessary, he may even issue another summons. It is important to note that one of the most effective methods of intervention in this regard is to enlist the active assistance of the local parochial clergy.

Can. 1593 §1 If the respondent thereafter appears before the judge, or replies before the trial is concluded, he or she can bring forward conclusions and proofs, without prejudice to the provisions of Can. 1600; the judge is to take care, however, that the process is not deliberately prolonged by lengthy and unnecessary delays.

Even after being declared absent the respondent may appear. If he or she does so before the conclusion of the case, since the instruction stage of the process is still in progress, he or she is quite free to advance proofs and conclusions. If the process has reached the conclusion of the case, then the new conclusions and proofs may be admitted only in accordance with Can. 1600. In all cases the judge is to take care that the process is not deliberately prolonged by a late-appearing respondent. He must carefully balance the respondent's right of defence against the plaintiff's right to a reasonably expeditious trial.

Can. 1593 §2 Even if the respondent has neither appeared nor given a reply before the case is decided, he or she can challenge the judgement; if the person can show that he or she was impeded by a legitimate cause and was without fault in not being able to prove this hitherto, a plaint of nullity can be lodged.

The respondent's right of defence is protected here, even if he or she has not appeared before the case is decided. The sentence is to be communicated to the respondent and he or she retains the right of appeal. If (but only if) the respondent can show that there was good reason for not appearing before this, and that he or she was without fault in not indicating this earlier, then he or she can lodge a plaint of nullity against the sentence.

Can. 1594 If the plaintiff does not appear on the day and at the hour arranged for the joinder of the issue, and does not offer a suitable excuse:

1° the judge is to summon the plaintiff again;

2° if the plaintiff does not obey the new summons, he or she is presumed to have renounced the trial in accordance with Cann. 1524–1525;

3° if the plaintiff should want to intervene at a subsequent stage in the process, the provisions of Can. 1593 are to be observed.

3138 This canon deals with the situation where the plaintiff does not answer to the summons. The judge is firstly to summon him or her again. If there is still no reply the plaintiff is presumed to have renounced the trial in accordance with Can. 1524 and with the effects mentioned in Can. 1525. If the case still goes ahead, because the respondent does not accept the renunciation (see Can. 1524 §3), the rules of Can. 1593 are applied to the plaintiff if he or she later wishes to intervene in the case. Once again, however, it must be stated that, in practice, common sense should rule, and that a personal contact by whatever appropriate means e.g. through the parochial clergy, can often be much more effective than any number of written communications – by whatever official title they may be called.

Can. 1595 §1 A party, whether plaintiff or respondent, who is absent from the trial, and who does not establish the existence of a just impediment, is bound to pay the expenses which have been incurred in the case because of this absence, and also, if need be, to indemnify the other party.

§2 If both the plaintiff and the respondent were absent from the trial, they are jointly bound to pay the expenses of the case.

3139 If a party who is absent from a case does not show that his or her absence was legitimate, then he or she is bound to pay any expenses incurred in the case due to the absence and also, if this arises, to make good any losses incurred by the other party. If both parties are absent, both are jointly bound to pay the expenses of the case. The implementation of this manifestly equitable rule will be a matter for the experience and ingenuity of each local tribunal.

Chapter II
THE INTERVENTION OF A THIRD PARTY IN A CASE

Can. 1596 §1 Any person with a legitimate interest can be allowed to intervene in a case in any instance of the suit, either as a party defending his or her own right or, in an accessory role, to help one of the litigants.

3140 A third party in a case is one who is not, or at least was not originally, involved in the case. He or she may be involved in order to protect personal rights: (a) as a party, when he or she will act as co-plaintiff or co-respondent; (b) independently of, or even in opposition to, both parties. Moreover, a third party may be involved in an accessory manner, purely in order to help one of the parties. If the person's interest in the case is legitimate, he or she can be allowed to intervene in the case. This is allowed at any instance of the case, although in a penal trial a harmed party can intervene only at first instance (see Can. 1729 §2).

Can. 1596 §2 To be admitted, however, the person must, before the conclusion of the case, produce to the judge a petition which briefly establishes the right to intervene.

In order to be lawfully admitted to intervene, the person must submit to the judge a petition, briefly showing his or her right to do so. This must be done before the conclusion of the case. It is then for the judge to decide whether or not the intervention be permitted.

Can. 1596 §3 A person who intervenes in a case is to be admitted at that stage which the case has reached. If the case has reached the proof stage, a brief and peremptory time-limit is to be assigned within which to bring forward proofs.

A third party intervenes at the stage at which he or she finds the case. However, if the proof stage has already been reached, the judge is to assign a brief and peremptory time-limit within which he or she is to produce any proofs that are requested.

Can. 1597 A third party whose intervention is seen to be necessary must be called into the case by the judge, after he has consulted the parties.

Can. 1596 deals with the intervention of a third party on his or her own initiative. The present canon envisages the case where such intervention is perceived as necessary, either in order to protect the person's rights or as providing needed clarification of the point at issue. If this is the case, it is the judge who, having first consulted the parties, is to call the person into the case. Since the person is thus called by the judge and does not therefore come on his or her own initiative, he or she cannot be regarded as a party to the case.

Title VI
The Publication of the Acts, the Conclusion of the Case and the Pleadings

Can. 1598 §1 When the evidence has been assembled, the judge must, under pain of nullity, by a decree permit the parties and their advocates to inspect at the tribunal office those acts which are not yet known to them. Indeed if the advocates so request, a copy of the acts can be given to them. In cases which concern the public good, however, the judge can decide that, in order to avoid very serious dangers, a given act is not to be shown to anyone. He must take care, however, that the right of defence always remains intact.

This paragraph raises one of the most delicate issues in the procedural law of the Church, particularly in the context of marriage-nullity cases. It will be noted that the paragraph is in two parts, first a general rule, and then a permitted exception in certain circumstances:

- *the general rule* is that when proofs in a case have been assembled, the judge is obliged to issue a decree (known as the 'Decree of Publication') which permits the parties and their advocates 'to inspect', i.e. to read through, 'those acts which are not yet known to them'. This inspection to be done only 'at the tribunal office'; moreover, 'if the advocates so request, a copy of the acts can be given to them'.
- *the exception* to that rule arises when, 'in cases which concern the public good' and 'in order to avoid very serious dangers', the judge decides that 'a given act' is to remain secret and not be shown to anyone; in coming to any such decision, the judge must however ensure 'that the right of defence always remains intact'.

3145 To understand this twofold regulation, account must be taken of its history through the revision process which preceded the promulgation of the current Code. Many submissions were made, from various parts of the Church, which pointed out the dangers inherent in allowing full and open access to all the acts, particularly in marriage-nullity cases (constituting as they do the great majority of the cases before the Church's tribunals): dangers said to arise, e.g., when in certain countries either the parties or the witnesses could be open to a civil action for defamation and accordingly, in the absence of a guarantee of confidentiality, might withhold evidence which could well be distinctly relevant;[1] or when the acts of an ecclesiastical trial might be demanded *sub poena* by the civil authorities; etc.[2]

3146 In the light of this background, the following points may be made:

(a) *In regard to the general rule*:

(i) this rule is rightly designed to protect the right of defence which belongs to every person (not merely the respondent but also the plaintiff) who appears before an ecclesiastical tribunal: that right must be acknowledged and protected in regard to every such person who wishes to invoke it. The rule does not however impose upon any person an obligation to invoke that right: it is important in this regard that any merely doctrinaire position should not be allowed to obscure the practical realities.[3]

(ii) insofar as anyone may wish to invoke the right, he or she and the appropriate advocate, is entitled, but only at the tribunal office – obviously therefore under a certain supervision – to read through 'those acts which are not yet known to them', which in practice will normally be the major portion of the evidence before the court.

(iii) if he or she requests it, the respective advocate may be given a copy of the acts. There is a manifest implication in the law that, in such a situation, the advocate is strictly forbidden to give that or any copy to his or her client: the clear purpose of the regulation is to permit the advocate – the professional

---

[1] It is a proven fact that the understanding of confidentiality before the ecclesiastical marriage-nullity courts is a significant factor in enabling those courts to secure a more accurate picture of the truth than is the case before many corresponding civil courts, especially among those in which the so-called 'adversarial procedure' is the norm.

[2] Cf. Comm 11(1979) 134 at Can. 257. A particularly instructive account of the dangers envisaged may be found in the proceedings of the final plenary session of the Pontifical Commission for the Revision of the Code in October 1981: cf. *Acta et Documenta Pontificiae Commissionis Codici Iuris Canonici Recognoscendo: Congregatio Plenaria 20-29 Oct. 1981* Vatican Press 1991 469–479.

[3] In the practice of first-instance matrimonial courts it is a rare occurrence for either of the parties to seek to see the evidence – not because they are not aware of their right to do so, but much more because in the vast majority of cases their concern at that stage is focused almost exclusively upon the forthcoming decision of the court. This practical situation should not of course in an appropriate situation deflect the sensitive judge from reminding the relevant party of his or her right.

representative committed not only to the interests of the client but also to the search for truth which is the objective of the court's endeavour – the maximum possibility of submitting to the court whatever reasonable defence he or she may wish to present.

(b) *In regard to the exception*:

(i) this is admissable only 'in cases which concern the public good' – as distinct from cases which concern *only* the personal good or interest of two individual litigants (see Cann. 1452 §1, 1536 §1): marriage-nullity cases do concern the public good;

(ii) equally, it is admissable only 'to avoid very serious dangers', such e.g. as those indicated above, especially but not only in respect of the civil law;

(iii) assuming the foregoing twofold condition, the admissability of this exception depends upon the specific decision of the judge, to whom in this respect the law gives an unfettered discretion, subject only to 'the right of defence';

(iv) it permits the judge to exclude from even a party's inspection 'a given act' (*aliquod actum*): in practical terms, it would seem that this must be understood to mean not merely the evidence (or part of it) of a particular witness or expert, but such part or parts of the total evidence as the judge, taking account of the overall situation, may decide to be withheld, in order 'to avoid very serious dangers';

(v) as far as 'the right of defence' is concerned, this must obviously be rigorously maintained. It has to be understood, however, that this is not an absolute and unrestricted right, and that in some situations it may have to give way to the public interest of the Church and the good of souls: *(salus) animarum ... in Ecclesia suprema semper lex esse debet* (Can. 1752);

(vi) the canon permits the judge to require that a certain part or parts of the evidence 'are not to be shown to anyone' (*nemini manifestandum*); this would not however preclude the judge from prescribing that the evidence in question be made available to a party's advocate, on condition that it be not shown to the party: a procedure of this kind would in an appropriate case clearly allow the judge to fulfil his obligation to ensure 'that the right of defence always remains intact'.[1]

Can. 1598 §2 To complete the proofs, the parties can propose others to the judge. When these have been assembled, the occasion arises anew for the decree mentioned in §1, if the judge considers it necessary.

When the acts have been inspected, it may become clear that further proofs are needed. The parties can request from the judge that these be acquired. When this has been done, there may be need for a repetition of the decree mentioned in §1, so that both parties are aware of the content of the new proofs: this is a matter for the judge to decide.

Can. 1599 §1 When everything concerned with the production of proofs has been completed, the conclusion of the case is reached.

---

[1] For an instructive summary of the background to Can. 1598 §1, cf. Commentary (CLSA) 991–992. Other relevant studies could profitably include: Grocholewski *Alcune questioni attuali concernenti lo stato e l'attività dei tribunali, con particolare riguardo alla situazione negli USA* ME 114(1989) 347–371; Johnson *Publish and be damned – the dilemma of implementing the canons on publishing the acts and the sentence* Jur 49(1989) 210–240; Nau *Publish and be damned – one practitioner's experience* Jur 51 (1991) 442–450; Farret *Publication des actes et publication de la sentence dans les causes de nullité de mariage* Stud Can 25(1991) 115–138; Bernhard *A propos de la publication de la sentence dans les procédures en déclaration de nullité de mariage* in Iustus Iudex Ludgerus-Verlag 1990 387–399; Hilbert *De publicatione actorum* Per 81(1992) 521–533.

§2 This conclusion occurs when the parties declare that they have nothing further to add, or when the canonical time allotted by the judge for the production of proofs has elapsed, or when the judge declares that he considers the case to be sufficiently instructed.

§3 By whichever way the case has come to its conclusion, the judge is to issue a decree declaring that it is concluded.

3148 The conclusion of the case is the formal ending of the instruction phase of the case. It is marked by a decree of the judge and can be brought about in any one of three ways: (a) by a declaration of the parties that they have nothing more to add to the proofs; (b) by the elapse of the time allowed by the judge for the production of proofs; (c) by a declaration of the judge that the case is sufficiently instructed. In normal practice, this comes about by a combination of (a) and (c) above.

Can. 1600 §1 Only in the following situations can the judge, after the conclusion of the case, still recall earlier witnesses or call new ones, or make provision for other proofs not previously requested:

1° in cases in which only the private good of the parties is involved, if all the parties agree;

2° in other cases, provided that the parties have been consulted, that a grave reason exists, and that all danger of fraud or subornation is removed;

3° in all cases, whenever it is probable that, unless new proof is admitted, the judgement will be unjust for any of the reasons mentioned in Can. 1645 §2 nn. 1-3.

3149 Once the conclusion of the case has been reached and decreed, further proofs or re-examination of earlier ones are admitted only in accordance with the rules given here. In cases involving only the private good of the parties, the consent of all the parties is a prerequisite (1°). In other cases, the parties must be consulted, there must be a grave reason and there must be no danger of fraud or subornation (2°). In all cases, however, such further proofs may be admitted if otherwise the judgement will probably be unjust for any of the causes mentioned in Can. 1645 §2 1°-3°, i.e. where the judgement is based on false evidence, where documents subsequently discovered demand a contrary decision, where the judgement was given through the deceit of one party (3°).

Can. 1600 §2 The judge can, however, order or admit the presentation of a document which, without fault of the interested party, could not perhaps be presented earlier.

3150 A document which perhaps could not have been presented earlier, may be admitted by the judge either at the request of a party or on the judge's own initiative.

Can. 1600 §3 New proofs are to be published according to Can. 1598 §1.

3151 The rules of Can. 1598 §1 (q.v.) are to be observed in regard to evidence admitted after the original conclusion of the case.

Can. 1601 When the case has been concluded, the judge is to determine a suitable period of time for the presentation of pleadings and observations.

3152 After the definitive conclusion of the case the judge is to assign a suitable period of time for the presentation of pleadings by the parties and their advocates and for observations by the defender of the bond and the promotor of justice. One month for each would normally be regarded as reasonable. For the rules governing the extension or the shortening of this time-limit, see Can. 1465.

Can. 1602 §1 Pleadings and observations are to be in writing unless the judge, with the consent of the parties, considers it sufficient to have a discussion before the tribunal in session.

Normally pleadings and observations are to be in writing,[1] but with the consent of the parties, the judge can allow an oral discussion before the tribunal.

Can. 1602 §2 If the pleadings and the principal documents are to be printed, the prior permission of the judge is required, and the obligation of secrecy, where it exists, is still to be observed.

For the printing – not just the customary typing – of the pleadings and the principal documents of the case, the judge must give permission beforehand. This could arise e.g. if it were proposed to insert this material into a canonical or other journal, or to use it in a thesis for an academic degree. In any event, if the permission is granted, it must be such as will ensure the observance of any particular obligation of secrecy as may exist, as e.g. from Can. 1598 §1.

Can. 1602 §3 The directions of the tribunal are to be observed in questions concerning the length of the pleadings, the number of copies and other similar matters.

Relatively minor matters such as those mentioned here are left to the approved norms of the individual tribunal.

Can. 1603 §1 When the pleadings and observations have been exchanged, each party can make reply within a brief period of time determined by the judge.

When the pleadings and observations have been submitted and communicated to all concerned, the parties are to be assigned a brief period of time – say, about ten days – to make any replies they may wish; they may well, as they not infrequently do, declare that they have nothing to add.

Can. 1603 §2 This right is given to the parties once only, unless for a grave reason the judge considers that the right to a second reply is to be given; if this right is given to one party, it is to be considered as given to the other as well.

The right of reply is normally given once only, in order to prevent endless and useless delays. However, if there is a grave reason, e.g. in a very complex case, the judge may allow a second reply. If this is granted to one party, it is automatically granted to the other as well. No reply beyond a second is permitted.

Can. 1603 §3 The promotor of justice and the defender of the bond have the right to respond to every reply of the parties.

Except in penal trials where the accused person has the right to the final reply (see Can. 1725), the promotor of justice and the defender of the bond have the right to respond to every submission and reply of the parties.

Can. 1604 §1 It is absolutely forbidden that any information given to the judge by the parties or the advocates, or by any other persons, be excluded from the acts of the case.

Any decision reached by the judge must be on the exclusive basis of the acts of the case: *Quod non est in actis non est in mundo* ('What is not found in the acts has no real

---

[1] This facilitates the judge in weighing them up fully before coming to a decision: cf. Comm 11 (1979) 137 at Can. 261 §1.

existence'). While the judge may not always be able to avoid being given private information, from whatever source, this canon gives clear notice that no such information may be in any way taken into account in deciding the case, unless the judge decides to incorporate it formally into the official record of the case.

Can. 1604 §2 If the pleadings in the case are made in writing, the judge may, in order to clarify any outstanding issues, order that a moderate oral discussion be held before the tribunal in session.

3160 When the pleadings are in writing, as they usually will be in accordance with Can. 1602 §1, the judge may allow a short oral supplementary discussion in order to clarify any points that still need this.

Can. 1605 The notary is to be present at the oral discussion mentioned in Cann. 1602 §1 and 1604 §2, so that, if the judge so orders, or the parties so request and the judge consents, the notary can immediately make a written report of what has been discussed and concluded.

3161 The notary must be present at the discussions mentioned in Can. 1602 §1, which takes the place of written pleadings, and in Can. 1604 §2, the supplementary discussion. It is for the judge to decide, either on his own initiative or at the request of the parties, whether the notary is to make a written report of the discussion. If the issues are complex or the discussion is in any way lengthy, the fact of having a written report would at least be helpful in coming to a final decision and in writing the judgement.

Can. 1606 If the parties neglect to prepare their pleadings within the time allotted to them, or if they entrust themselves to the knowledge and conscience of the judge, and if at the same time the judge perceives the matter quite clearly from the acts and the proofs, he can pronounce judgement at once. He must, however, seek the observations of the promotor of justice and the defender of the bond if they were engaged in the trial.

3162 The parties may neglect to draw up or submit any pleadings or they may entrust themselves to the learning and conscience of the judge. If the judge has a clear view and understanding of the case from the acts and the proofs, he may immediately proceed to pronounce his judgement. However, if the promotor of justice or the defender of the bond are involved in the case, he must ask for their observations.

Title VII
The Pronouncements of the Judge

Can. 1607 A principal case which has been dealt with in judicial fashion is decided by the judge by a definitive judgement. An incidental matter is decided by an interlocutory judgement, without prejudice to Can. 1589 §1.

3163 A judgement or sentence is 'a legal pronouncement by which the judge decides a case proposed by the parties and processed judicially'.[1] If the matter decided is the princi-

---
[1] 1917 Code c.1868 §1.

pal case, the sentence is definitive; if it is an incidental matter, it is interlocutory. In accordance with Can. 1589 §1, an incidental matter may also be decided by a decree of the judge. After the definitive judgement the process is complete, and the case passes from the competence of the judge who gave the judgement – if appropriate, to the appeal tribunal.

Can. 1608 §1 To give any judgement, the judge must have in his mind moral certainty about the matter to be decided in the judgement.

In order to arrive at a just decision the judge must have what is called 'moral certainty' about the matter to be decided. Moral certainty, which is a specifically canonical term, was well described by Pope Pius XII in an allocution to the Rota in 1942. He places moral certainty between the two extremes of absolute certainty and quasi-certainty or probability. Moral certainty 'is characterised *on the positive side* by the exclusion of well-founded or reasonable doubt, and in this respect it is essentially distinguished from the quasi-certainty which has been mentioned; *on the negative side,* it does admit the absolute possibility of the contrary, and in this it differs from absolute certainty. The certainty of which we are now speaking is necessary and sufficient for the rendering of a judgement ... Only thus is it possible to have a regular and orderly administration of justice, going forward without useless delays and without laying of excessive burdens on the tribunal as well as on the parties'.[1] Moral certainty 'is understood to be objective, that is, based on objective motives; it is not a purely subjective certitude, founded on sentiment or on this or that merely subjective opinion ...'.[2]

3164

Can. 1608 §2 The judge must derive this certainty from the acts and from the proofs.

The judge's certainty, and hence his judgement, must be based on the acts of the case and the proofs: *Quod non est in actis non est in mundo*. He cannot base it just on opinion or purely private knowledge. Any information given to the judge must be included in the acts of the case (see Can. 1604 §1).

3165

Can. 1608 §3 The judge must weigh the proofs in accordance with his conscience, with due regard for the provisions of law about the efficacy of certain proofs.

In arriving at the necessary certainty the judge is to weigh up the proofs in accordance with his conscience. In doing this he is to be guided *inter alia* by statements of the law concerning the weight to be attributed to the various kinds of proof, e.g. Cann. 1526 §2, 1541.

3166

Can. 1608 §4 A judge who cannot arrive at such certainty is to pronounce that the right of the plaintiff is not established and is to find for the respondent, except in a case which enjoys the favour of law, when he is to pronounce in its favour.

If the judge cannot arrive at moral certainty about the plaintiff's plea, i.e. if he finds himself in a state of uncertainty as to whether the plea is proven or not, he is positively obliged to pronounce that the plaintiff's claim is not established and is accordingly to find in favour of the respondent. There is one *important exception* to this rule, i.e. where the case in question 'enjoys the favour of law'. Significantly for practical pur-

3167

---

[1] CLD 3 607–608.
[2] Ibid. 608.

poses, this includes all marriage cases (see Can. 1060): if therefore the judge cannot reach certainty about a plaintiff's allegation of nullity, he must find against that allegation and accordingly, in effect, in favour of the validity of the marriage; this is so even if the respondent also is in favour of nullity, as not infrequently occurs.

Can. 1609 §1 The presiding judge of a collegiate tribunal decides the day and time when it is to meet for discussion. Unless a special reason requires otherwise, the meeting is to be at the tribunal office.

§2 On the day appointed for the meeting, the individual judges are to bring their written conclusions on the merits of the case, with the reasons in law and in fact for reaching their conclusions. These conclusions are to be added to the acts of the case and to be kept in secrecy.

§3 Having invoked the divine Name, they are to offer their conclusions in order, beginning always with the *ponens* or *relator* in the case, and then in order of precedence. Under the chairmanship of the presiding judge, they are to hold their discussion principally with a view to establishing what is to be stated in the dispositive part of the judgement.

3168 This canon deals with the way in which collegiate tribunals are to discuss the case and arrive at a decision. The presiding judge is to determine the day and time of the meeting. The place is normally to be the tribunal office, 'unless a special reason requires otherwise' (§1). Each judge is to bring to the meeting his or her written conclusions on the case and the reasons in law and in fact for the conclusions drawn (§2). These conclusions become part of the acts of the case but are to be kept secret in the archives of the tribunal. The procedure at the meeting is described in §3. It opens with a prayer for God's guidance. Then, beginning with the *ponens*, the judges in order of precedence state their conclusions. There follows a discussion, the outcome of which is to determine what is to be said in the dispositive part of the judgement, i.e. the part which states the decision of the court. The presiding judge is to direct this discussion.

3169 All of the foregoing regulations assume that in every tribunal the judges can with reasonable convenience meet together as prescribed: where this is in fact the case, it must be done. There are however situations – especially in respect of some interdiocesan or regional tribunals – where that kind of meeting, at the central tribunal office, is either simply not possible, or possible only at great inconvenience and expense; this can occur e.g. in regional areas which cover a vast extent of territory and accordingly involve substantial distances of travel. In such situations it would not be unreasonable, or against the purpose of the law, that an appropriate alternative arrangement be made, e.g. that, under the guidance of the presiding judge, all the judges would first exchange among themselves their written conclusions and then, if needs be, arrange for a subsequent exchange of views e.g. by telephone or fax. Modern conditions do, in certain circumstances, call for some such alternative arrangement. In so far as it may be thought necessary, it must however ensure that the basic intent of the law, and particularly the integrity and confidentiality of the prescribed procedure, be kept integrally intact. Short-cuts, in the sole interest of local convenience, are not permissible.

Can. 1609 §4 In the discussion, each one is permitted to depart from an original conclusion. A judge who does not wish to accede to the decision of the others can demand that, if there is an appeal, his or her conclusions be forwarded to the higher tribunal.

3170 A judge is not bound by the written conclusion that he or she brought to the meeting. If as a result of the discussion, he or she gains a different insight into the point at issue and achieves moral certainty about a different conclusion, he or she is quite free to depart from the original conclusion. The decision of the court is always that of the majority of its members.

This §4 does, however, introduce a new element which did not exist under the 1917 Code. A judge who has come to a decision which dissents from the majority is now permitted, if he or she so chooses, to require that, in the event of an appeal, this dissenting opinion be made available to the appeal tribunal. The superior court would obviously have to take serious account of any such dissent.

Can. 1609 §5 If the judges do not wish, or are unable, to reach a decision in the first discussion, they can defer their decision to another meeting, but not beyond one week, unless the instruction of the case has to be completed in accordance with Can. 1600.

Two possibilities are envisaged when the judges are unwilling or unable to reach a decision at the first meeting: (a) there is no more instruction to be done in the case, but simply a need for more time to study the case; (b) further supplementary proofs are needed in order to reach a decision. In the first case, the decision may be deferred to a second meeting, which is to take place not more than a week after the first. In the second, the rules of Can. 1600 about new evidence after the conclusion of the case are to be followed, and the new meeting is to be set at a suitable date.

Can. 1610 §1 If there is a sole judge, he will draw up the judgement.

§2 In a collegiate tribunal, the *ponens* or *relator* is to draw up the judgement, using as reasons those tendered by the individual judges in their discussion, unless the reasons to be preferred have been defined by a majority of the judges. The judgement must then be submitted to the individual judges for their approval.

§3 The judgement is to be issued not later than one month from the day on which the case was decided, unless in a collegiate tribunal the judges have for grave reasons stipulated a longer time.

This canon determines who writes the judgement, how it is to be done and when. If there is a sole judge, obviously it is he who writes the judgement (§1). In a collegiate tribunal (§2), the drawing up of the judgement is one of the two main functions of the *ponens* (see Can. 1429). In doing so he is to state the reasons determined by the judges during their discussion; if the decision is not a unanimous but a majority one, the reasons are to be those agreed by the majority. In all cases the written judgement is to 'be submitted to the individual judges (even those dissenting) for their approval' – unless, as not infrequently occurs in practice, all the judges agree in advance to leave the matter to the *ponens*.

Normally, a judgement is to be issued no longer than one month from the date of decision (§3). In the case of a sole judge, this rule should if at all possible be observed. In a collegiate tribunal, however, the judges may 'for grave reasons' stipulate a longer time. Such reasons could e.g. be the unusual sensitivity or complexity of the case concerned; they could also have regard to the pressures upon judges in, say, a busy marriage tribunal.

Can. 1611 The judgement must:

1° **define the controversy raised before the tribunal, giving appropriate answers to the individual questions;**

2° **determine the obligations of the parties arising from the trial and the manner in which these are to be fulfilled;**

3° set out the reasons or motives, both in law and in fact, upon which the dispositive part of the judgement is based;

4° apportion the expenses of the suit.

3175 This canon is concerned with the contents of the sentence. First and foremost, it must decide the issue before the tribunal, answering all the individual questions (if there be more than one) admitted at the joinder of the issue: a total failure to do this would result in the incurable nullity of the judgement (see Can. 1620 8°). Next, it is to determine any obligations falling on the parties as a result of the trial and is to specify how these are to be carried out, e.g. determining the handing over of property from one person to another, determining the duties of the spouses toward their children in a marriage which has been declared invalid, etc. This requirement is closely related to the first one and will depend upon it. Thirdly, the judgement must be motivated, i.e. it must set forth, if only in a summary form, the reasons in law and in fact for the decision; failure to comply with this norm would result in the remediable nullity of the judgement (see Can. 1622 2°). Finally, the judgement should apportion the expenses involved in the trial; in many local tribunals this matter will already have been dealt with by the established and approved practice of the tribunal itself.

Can. 1612 §1 The judgement, after the invocation of the divine Name, must state in order the judge or tribunal, and the plaintiff, respondent and procurator, with names and domiciles duly indicated. It is also to name the promotor of justice and the defender of the bond if they were engaged in the trial.

§2 It must then briefly set out an outline of the facts, with the conclusions of the parties and the formulation of the doubt.

§3 Then follows the dispositive part of the judgement, prefaced by the reasons which support it.

§4 It ends with the date and the place in which it was given, and with the signature of the judge or, in the case of a collegiate tribunal, of all the judges, and of the notary.

3176 This canon deals with the formal layout of the judgement. Firstly (§1), it should invoke the divine Name, using a formula such as 'In the Name of God. Amen.' Next, it is to list the judge or the tribunal, the plaintiff, the respondent and the procurator(s), with appropriate identifications. If the promotor of justice and the defender of the bond are engaged in the trial, they too are to be named.[1] The next part of the judgement (§2) is a brief recital of the facts of the case, to which are added the conclusions or claims made by the parties and the formulation of the doubt. The dispositive part of the judgement is the statement of the actual decision (§3). This statement must be accompanied with the reasons in law and in fact which gave rise to it. The judge will normally state the relevant law and will often tease out its implications for this particular sort of case. Then he applies these principles of law to the actual facts of the case, showing precisely on what grounds the decision is based. Rulings regarding expenses would also be made here and, in marriage cases, any prohibition against a further marriage (see Can. 1685). The final formalities of the judgement are described in §4. Note that the omission of the required signatures, or of the year, month and day and the place where the judgement was given, would cause remediable nullity of the judgement (see Can. 1622 3° and 4°).

---

[1] A proposal to omit many of the elements required here, on the ground that they are already contained in the acts, was rejected, since 'it is the judgement, not the acts, which is given to the parties' Comm 11(1979) 141 at Can. 270 §1 – a position theoretically defensible, if not always demanded by the situation at the practical level.

Can. 1613 The rules set out above for a definitive judgement are to be adapted also to interlocutory judgements.

Although interlocutory judgements are more limited in scope than definitive judgements, they are still judgements. They will not be as elaborate as the definitive judgement, but they should in general follow, with any necessary adaptations, the rules laid down above. In particular, they should always state the reasons for the decision reached.

Can. 1614 A judgement is to be published as soon as possible, with an indication of the ways in which it can be challenged. Before publication it has no effect, even if the dispositive part may, with the permission of the judge, have been notified to the parties.

It is only after it has been published that a judgement has any juridical effect. Therefore, to avoid undue delays, the law requires that the judgement be published 'as soon as possible'. The law does not stipulate any actual time limit since special circumstances in a given case may demand an interval between the issuing of the judgement (see Can. 1610 §1) and its publication. The decree of publication must inform the parties that the decision of the court may be challenged by means of a plaint of nullity (see Cann. 1621, 1623) or by an appeal (see Can. 1628).[1] Even if the outcome of the case has been communicated to the parties beforehand, the judgement can have no juridical effect until it is published in accordance with the law.

Can. 1615 The publication or notification of the judgement can be effected by giving a copy of the judgement to the parties or to their procurators, or by sending them a copy of it in accordance with Can. 1509.

The 1917 Code in c. 1877, permitted three methods of publication of the judgement to the parties:

(a) they could read the text of the judgement in the tribunal office;

(b) they could have the text read to them in the tribunal office;

(c) they could receive a copy of the decision.

According to the present canon, publication takes place when the parties or their procurators are handed a copy of the judgement or receive a copy through the mail or by some other secure means (see Can. 1509 §1). During the process of revision, the Commission rejected suggestions that publication of the judgement might be effected by reading the text to the parties[2] or by issuing the judgement to the advocate alone.[3] Pope John Paul II has noted that the right of both parties to be informed of the judgement is an integral part of the right of defence.[4]

Given the requirements of law, it is clear that great care must be exercised by judges when writing their judgements. The difficulties encountered when considering the question of the publication of the acts are just as relevant in the matter of the publica-

---

[1] 'To guarantee still more the right of defence the tribunal is bound to indicate to the parties the ways in which the judgement can be challenged (cf. Can. 1614). It seems opportune to recall that the court of first instance, in fulfilling this duty, must also indicate the possibility of approaching the Roman Rota as the court of second instance': Pope John Paul II address to R. Rota 26.I.1989: AAS 81 (1989) 922–927 n.7; CLSGBI Newsletter 77 (March 1989) 11.

[2] Comm 11(1979) 142–143 at Can. 273.

[3] Comm 16(1984) 68–69 at Can. 1567.

[4] Pope John Paul II address to R. Rota 26.I.1989: op et locc cit.

tion of the judgement. Although the law makes no explicit mention of an exception to its norm, it would seem at least probable, by analogy with Can. 1598 §1 (q.v.), that 'a given part' of the judgement might in exceptional cases be restricted by the judge and not communicated to the parties.[1]

Can. 1616 §1 A judgement must be corrected or completed by the tribunal which gave it if, in the text of a judgement, there is an error in calculations, or a material error in the transcription of either the dispositive part or the presentation of the facts or the pleadings of the parties, or if any of the items required by Can. 1612 §4 are omitted. This is to be done either at the request of the parties or *ex officio*, but always after having consulted the parties and by a decree appended to the foot of the judgement.

§2 If one party is opposed, an incidental question is to be decided by a decree.

3181 Any minor errors or omissions in a judgement that has already been drawn up are to be corrected in a decree appended to the original judgement, after the parties and the defender of the bond or promotor of justice (see Can. 1434 1°) have been consulted. The correction of such errors and omissions may be requested by the parties or demanded *ex officio* by the tribunal which made the judgement. Errors which affect the substance of the judgement itself do not lie within the competence of the tribunal once the judgement has been given.

3182 If one of the parties objects to the proposed corrections, then the matter is to be dealt with as an incidental question, and determined by a decree which must accord with Can. 1617.

Can. 1617 Other pronouncements of a judge apart from the judgement, are decrees. If they are more than mere directions about procedure, they have no effect unless they give at least a summary of their reasons or refer to motives expressed in another act.

3183 Apart from the judgement, the judge may make a formal pronouncement by means of a decree. This decree may be simply procedural, directing that a case move forward to the next stage of the process, e.g. the decree of publication of the acts (see Can. 1598 §1). Or, it may determine a particular question, in which case, in order to be effective juridically, the decree must contain a brief expression or reference to the motives for the decision, e.g. the decree by which a petition is rejected (see Can. 1505 §1).

Can. 1618 An interlocutory judgement or a decree has the force of a definitive judgement if, in respect of at least one of the parties, it prevents the trial, or brings to an end the trial itself or any instance of it.

3184 Although quite distinct from definitive judgements, interlocutory judgements and decrees of the judge may, on occasion, have the force of a definitive judgement. This occurs when the judge's pronouncement effectively prevents a trial taking place or resolves a question which puts an end to the trial itself or any instance of it. Since, for all practical purposes, such interlocutory judgements or decrees decide the case, they are subject to appeal (see Can. 1629 4°).

---

[1] Cf. Daneels *The Right of Defence* Stud Can 27(1993) 90.

Part II The Contentious Trial

Title VIII
Challenging the Judgement

Chapter I
THE PLAINT OF NULLITY OF THE JUDGEMENT

Can. 1619 Without prejudice to Cann. 1622 and 1623, whenever a case concerns the good of private individuals, acts which are null with a nullity established by positive law are validated by the judgement itself, if the nullity was known to the party making the plaint and was not raised with the judge before the judgement.

By way of introduction to this chapter the Code establishes a new and an important general principle, namely that the nullity of procedural acts is validated by the judgement itself, provided however that three conditions are verified:

(a) the causes of the nullity must be one of positive ecclesiastical law, e.g. the failure to notarise the acts (see Can. 1437 §1);[1]

(b) the nullity must have been known to the party making the plaint of nullity and not raised with the judge before the judgement was given;

(c) the matter must concern the good of private individuals.[2]

This principle does not affect the types of nullity listed in Can. 1622 which are considered 'remedied' if a plaint of nullity has not been lodged within the required time (see Can. 1623) or if the judge has dealt with the matter himself (see Can. 1626 §2).

Can. 1620 A judgement is null with an irremediable nullity, if:

1° it was given by a judge who was absolutely non-competent;

2° it was given by a person who has no power to judge in the tribunal in which the case was decided;

3° the judge was compelled by force or grave fear to deliver judgement;

4° the trial took place without the judicial plea mentioned in Can. 1501, or was not brought against some party as respondent;

5° it was given between parties of whom at least one has no right to stand before the court;

6° someone acted in another's name without a lawful mandate;

7° the right of defence was denied to one or other party;

8° the controversy has not been even partially decided.

---

[1] Accordingly a nullity arising from the natural law is not included, e.g. where the right of defence has been denied.

[2] It has been proposed that the 'good of private individuals' is to be distinguished from the 'private good': cf. CCLA 1002. This opinion would not however appear tenable in view of the clear statement ('de bono privato') of the Revision Commission: cf. Comm 16(1984) 60 at Can. 1571.

3186 This canon indicates eight cases where a judgement is null and cannot be validated. The defects which are listed affect the very nature of the process.

1° Not every ecclesiastical judge may decide a given case. The Code contains general rules on the competent forum (see Cann. 1404–1416) and more specific rules concerning cases of nullity of marriage (see Cann. 1671–1673).

2° To be a judge, a person must be appointed to that office in a tribunal in accordance with Can. 1421. No one can claim that office for himself or herself, no matter how qualified.

3° In accordance with Can. 125 §1, any act performed as a result of force is invalid. On the other hand, in accordance with Can. 125 §2, an act performed as a result of grave fear is accepted as valid *unless the law provides otherwise*: this is an excellent example of the law making such provision.

4° A petition (see Can. 1501) and a respondent (see Cann. 1502, 1504 2° and 4°, 1507–1512, etc.) are essential to any process. The absence of either deprives the process and subsequent judgement of any possible validity.

5° In accordance with Can. 1478 §1, those who do not have the right to stand before the court are minors and those who lack the use of reason. Such persons must be represented by their parents or guardians, curators or procurators.

6° Anyone representing another must be appointed validly by that party or *ex officio* by the judge in accordance with the law (see Cann. 1481–1485, 1723). Any defect in this regard may undermine the right of defence.

7° According to the jurisprudence of the Supreme Tribunal of the Apostolic Signatura, the right of defence consists of the following elements:

  (a) the faculty of bringing forward proofs in a trial;

  (b) the faculty of knowing what proofs the other party has brought forward;

  (c) the faculty of producing his or her own deductions, allegations and defences;

  (d) the faculty of responding, at least once, to the deductions, allegations and defences advanced by the other party.[1]

This right of defence is understood to be required by the very nature of the process. Therefore, if any of these elements is denied to any party to the controversy,[2] then the judgement will be irremediably invalid.

8° In accordance with Can. 1611 1°, a judgement must define the controversy; if it does not respond to the terms of the controversy as determined at the Joinder of the Issue (see Can. 1513 §1), at least in part, the judgement can have no force.

3187 When any of the defects listed in this canon is discovered, the whole process must begin again at the point where the invalidity occurred. Such action is also to be taken in the case envisaged by Can. 1669 which might be added to the list of causes of irremediable nullity.

Can. 1621 In respect of the nullity mentioned in Can. 1620, a plaint of nullity can be made in perpetuity by means of an exception, or within ten years

---

[1] Ap Sig Nullitatis matrimonii: incidentalis, coram Sabattani 17.I.1987 n.14: ME 113(1988) 273–274; Per 77(1988) 341. Further insights into the right of defence in the jurisprudence of the Apostolic tribunals may be found in Daneels *The Right of Defence* Stud Can 27(1993) 77–95; Erlebach *La nullità della sentenza giudiziale 'ob ius defensionis denegatum' nella giurisprudenza rotale* Roma 1991 265ff.

[2] This is understood as including not only the plaintiff and the respondent, but also the defender of the bond and the promotor of justice if they intervene in a particular case: cf. Comm 11(1979) 128 at Can. 243.

of the date of publication of the judgement by means of an action before the judge who delivered the judgement.

A plaint of nullity against a judgement on the basis of any of the reasons listed in Can. 1620 may be proposed in two ways: **3188**

(a) by means of an exception: in accordance with Can. 1492 §2, such a plaint can always be made;

(b) by means of an action, i.e. by presenting a petition seeking the declaration of the nullity of the judgement before the judge who delivered it; this must be done within ten years of the publication of that judgement.

Can. 1622 A judgement is null with a nullity which is simply remediable if:

1° contrary to the requirements of Can. 1425 §1, it was not given by the lawful number of judges;

2° it does not contain the motives or reasons for the decision;

3° it lacks the signatures prescribed by the law;

4° it does not contain an indication of the year, month, day and place it was given;

5° it is founded on a judicial act which is null and whose nullity has not been remedied in accordance with Can. 1619;

6° it was given against a party who, in accordance with Can. 1593 §2, was lawfully absent.

Apart from the more serious situations where the nullity of a sentence is judged to be irremediable, the Code foresees other less serious situations where the sentence may be null, but with a nullity which may be remedied by the law itself: **3189**

1° if, in a contentious or penal case, the judgement was given by fewer than three judges (see Can. 1425 §1);

2° if, contrary to Can. 1611 3° and 1612 §3, the judgement does not contain the reasons in law and in fact upon which the decision is based;

3° if the signatures required by Can. 1612 §4 are omitted and the judgement has not been corrected in accordance with Can. 1616 §1;

4° if the date and place of decision required by Can. 1612 §4 are omitted and have not been corrected in accordance with Can. 1616 §1;

5° if the judgement is based on an invalid procedural act of positive law which has not been remedied in accordance with Can. 1619;

6° if the judgement was given against a respondent who was lawfully absent in accordance with Can. 1593 §2; in this case, the sentence may be challenged only after the respondent has established the legitimacy of his or her absence from the process.

Can. 1623 In the cases mentioned in Can. 1622, a plaint of nullity can be proposed within three months of notification of the publication of the judgement.

A sentence invalid according to Can. 1622 is remedied by the law itself unless a plaint of nullity has been proposed to the judge who handed down the decision within three months of the notification of the publication of the same sentence. **3190**

Can. 1624 The judge who gave the judgement is to consider the plaint of its nullity. If the party fears that the judge who gave the judgement is

biased, and consequently considers him suspect, he or she can demand that another judge take his place in accordance with Can. 1450.

3191 Since a plaint of nullity as such is not an appeal against the substance of a judgement, it must be heard by the judge who gave the original decision. A different judge at the same level will hear the plaint of nullity in a situation where the party proposing the plaint fears that the original judge is or may be biased.

Can. 1625 Within the time-limit established for appeal, a plaint of nullity can be proposed together with the appeal.

3192 A plaint of nullity may be entered not merely on its own but also combined with an appeal against the substance of a judgement. This must be done within fifteen canonical days from the time of the notification of the publication of the judgement (see Can. 1630 §1). In this case, the plaint of nullity will not be heard by the original judge or by another at the same instance, but by the appropriate appeal tribunal (see Cann. 1438–1439, 1444–1445).

Can. 1626 §1 A plaint of nullity can be made not only by parties who regard themselves as injured, but also by the promotor of justice and the defender of the bond, whenever they have a right to intervene.

3193 If either or both of the parties feel aggrieved by the judgement, they are free to lodge a plaint of nullity. So, too, may the promotor of justice and the defender of the bond if they have been involved in the case.

Can. 1626 §2 Within the time-limit established in Can. 1623, the judge himself can retract or correct an invalid judgement he has given, unless in the meantime an appeal joined to a plaint of nullity has been lodged, or the nullity has been remedied by the expiry of the time-limit mentioned in Can. 1623.

3194 The judge may not propose a plaint of nullity against his own judgement. However, when he discovers that the judgement is invalid, the law permits him to retract or correct it, subject to two conditions:

(a) that the retraction or correction take place before the three month time-limit set by Can. 1623; after that date, the sentence is automatically remedied by the law and cannot be retracted or corrected;

(b) that an appeal combined with a plaint of nullity has not been lodged; in this case, the judgement must be forwarded to the appeal tribunal as it was originally published.

Can. 1627 Cases concerning a plaint of nullity can be dealt with in accordance with the norms for an oral contentious process.

3195 When a plaint of nullity alone has been lodged against a judgement, the oral contentious process (see Cann. 1656–1670) may be used – a point particularly to be noted for the practical convenience of many tribunals. Of course, in accordance with Can. 1656 §1, the ordinary contentious process must be used if one of the parties should request it.

Chapter II
THE APPEAL

Can. 1628 Without prejudice to the provisions of Can. 1629, a party who considers himself or herself to be injured by a judgement has a right to

appeal from the judgement to a higher judge; in cases in which their presence is required, the promotor of justice and the defender of the bond have likewise the right to appeal.

An appeal may be defined as the referral of a judgement given by a lower tribunal to a higher tribunal (see Cann. 1438–1439, 1444), so that it may be overturned or modified. It differs radically from the plaint of nullity since it challenges not the validity of the original sentence but its substance. This canon specifies who has the right to make an appeal: either of the parties, or the defender of the bond or the promotor of justice may do so, if they believe their interests have been harmed, i.e. if they think that the decision has not given them the justice they feel to be their due. The canon adds the reminder that this right of appeal is limited by what is prescribed in the following Can. 1629. 3196

Can. 1629 No appeal is possible against:

1° a judgement of the Supreme Pontiff himself, or a judgement of the Apostolic Signatura;

2° a judgement which is null, unless the appeal is lodged together with a plaint of nullity, in accordance with Can. 1625;

3° a judgement which has become an adjudged matter;

4° a decree of the judge or an interlocutory judgement, which does not have the force of a definitive judgement, unless the appeal is lodged together with an appeal against the definitive judgement;

5° a judgement or a decree in a case in which the law requires that the matter be settled with maximum expedition.

Notwithstanding the fundamental right of appeal, there are some situations in which an appeal is not permitted. This canon mentions five types of decisions from which there is no appeal. 3197

1° Since 'the First See is judged by no one' (Can. 1404), 'there is neither appeal nor recourse against a judgement or a decree of the Roman Pontiff' (Can. 333 §3). Likewise, since the Apostolic Signatura is designated as the *supreme* tribunal of the Church (see Can. 1445), there can be no appeal to 'a higher judge'.

2° If a judgement is null, it has no juridical force. For this reason, an appeal is not possible. However, the law does permit an appeal to be lodged if it is combined with a plaint of nullity (see Can. 1625).

3° When a judgement has become 'an adjudged matter', the case is effectively closed and the matter resolved (see Cann. 1641–1644). Nevertheless, within certain limits the law permits an aggrieved party to seek a total reinstatement (Cann. 1645–1648) or a new presentation of the case if it concerns the status of persons (Can. 1644). The principle here is stated in Can. 1643, in virtue of which no case concerning the status of persons ever becomes an adjudged matter: the particular practical relevance here is of course marriage-nullity cases.

4° If a decree of the judge or an interlocutory judgement has not prevented the trial or brought it to an end (see Can. 1618), no appeal is possible against such decisions unless it is combined with an appeal against the definitive judgement.

5° When the law requires that an issue be resolved 'with maximum expedition' (see Cann. 1451 §1, 1505 §4, 1513 §3, 1527 §2, 1589 §1, 1631); the purpose of the law in respect of these practical situations is precisely to ensure against any frivolous, capricious or unnecessary delay in the proceedings; hence the exclusion of an appeal. This is a point particularly to be noted in the practice of matrimonial proceedings.

Can. 1630 §1 The appeal must be lodged with the judge who delivered the judgement, within a peremptory time-limit of fifteen canonical days from notification of the publication of the judgement.

§2 If it is made orally, the notary is to draw up the appeal in writing in the presence of the appellant.

3198 An appeal is to be made by the aggrieved party to the judge who issued the judgement within fifteen canonical days of the notification of the publication of the judgement. This peremptory time-limit is to be calculated according to Cann. 203 §1, 1465 §1, 1467. Generally an appeal is first made in writing but if it is made orally, then it must be consigned to writing by the notary in the presence of the party making the appeal.

Can. 1631 If a question arises about the right of appeal, the appeal tribunal is to determine it with maximum expedition, in accordance with the norms for an oral contentious process.

3199 Any question concerning the right of a party to make an appeal is to be settled 'with maximum expedition'. The issue is to be determined by the tribunal of appeal. Since it is a serious matter (Can. 1589 §1), the oral contentious process is to be used in accordance with the terms of Can. 1590.

Can. 1632 §1 If there is no indication of the tribunal to which the appeal is directed, it is presumed to be made to the tribunal mentioned in Cann. 1438 and 1439.

§2 If the other party has resorted to some other appeal tribunal, the tribunal which is of the higher grade is to determine the case, without prejudice to Can. 1415.

3200 In order to resolve any eventual conflict of competence in the matter of appeals, the canon offers two guiding principles:

(a) if the appeal does not contain any explicit indication of the tribunal to which it is directed, the law presumes it to be directed to the ordinary tribunal of second instance (see Cann. 1438–1439);

(b) in the event of the parties appealing the case to different and equally competent tribunals, the case is to be determined by the higher of the two. Such a solution does not in any way undermine the principle of prior summons established in Can. 1415.

Can. 1633 The appeal is to be pursued before the appeal judge within one month of its being forwarded, unless the originating judge allows the party a longer time to pursue it.

3201 Not alone must the appellant give notice of appeal to the tribunal from which the original judgement was given (see Can. 1630 §1), he or she must also prosecute that appeal before the tribunal to which the appeal has been directed. This prosecution of the appeal must take place within thirty days (see Can. 202 §1) from the date of the notice of appeal, unless the judge who issued the original judgement has granted an extension to the appellant. In cases of nullity of marriage, the process and time-limits are rather different (see Can. 1682 §1).

Can. 1634 §1 To pursue the appeal, it is required and is sufficient that the party request the assistance of the higher judge to amend the judgement

which is challenged, enclosing a copy of the judgement and indicating the reasons for the appeal.

In order to prosecute the appeal, a party must send the following to the appeal tribunal: 3202
- a request that the tribunal come to the aid of the party in his or her effort to reform the original judgement;
- a copy of the original judgement;
- an indication, at least in summary form, of the reasons for the appeal.

Can. 1634 §2 If the party is unable to obtain a copy of the appealed judgement from the originating tribunal within the canonical time-limit, this time-limit is in the meantime suspended. The problem is to be made known to the appeal judge, who is to oblige the originating judge by precept to fulfil his duty as soon as possible.

If for any reason the party wishing to make an appeal cannot obtain a copy of the judgement within the prescribed time-limits (see Cann. 1630 §1, 1633),[1] these time-limits are temporarily suspended. The appellant must inform the appeal judge of the problem; he is then to issue a precept obliging the original judge to carry out his responsibility. 3203

Can. 1634 §3 In the meantime, the originating judge must forward the acts to the appeal court in accordance with Can. 1474.

The judge who issued the original judgement has the obligation to send a notarised copy of the acts to the appeal court, together with a statement of authenticity (Can. 1474 §1). If necessary, the acts are to be translated into a language known by the higher tribunal (Can. 1474 §2). 3204

Can. 1635 The appeal is considered to be abandoned if the time-limits for an appeal before either the originating judge or the appeal judge have expired without action being taken.

If an appeal has not been lodged at the original tribunal within fifteen days of the publication of the judgement (Can. 1630) or if the appeal has not been pursued before the appeal tribunal within one month or the longer period established by the original judge (Can. 1633), the law considers that appeal to have been abandoned. Consequently, the case becomes an adjudged matter (see Can. 1641 2°) and a decree of execution of the original judgement is to be issued, except in cases of nullity of marriage (see Can. 1682 §2). 3205

Can. 1636 §1 The appellant can renounce the appeal, with the effects mentioned in Can. 1525.

An appeal can be withdrawn by the appellant. To be valid, this renunciation must be in writing, signed by the appellant or his or her procurator, accepted or at least not opposed by the other party and admitted by the judge (see Can. 1524 §3). The one renouncing the appeal assumes the obligation of paying the expenses (Can. 1525). If the appeal is renounced, the sentence may be executed, again except in cases of nullity of marriage (see Can. 1682 §2). 3206

---

[1] It is difficult to understand what the reason might be for the appellant or the appropriate procurator not having a copy of the judgement, in the light of the prescription of Can. 1615. It is possible that this paragraph, taken verbatim from c.1884 §2 of the 1917 Code, is a relic of publication by solemn reading of the judgement (c.1877). Chiappetta suggests that this situation might arise if the party lost or mislaid the copy provided at the publication: op cit n.5083.

Can. 1636 §2 Unless the law provides otherwise, an appeal made by the defender of the bond or the promotor of justice, can be renounced by the defender of the bond or the promotor of justice of the appeal tribunal.

3207 In the appeal court, both the defender of the bond and the promotor of justice may renounce an appeal which was proposed by their respective counterparts in the original tribunal. To be valid, such a renunciation must be in writing and must be accepted by the judge (see Can. 1524 §3).

Can. 1637 §1 An appeal made by the plaintiff benefits also the respondent, and vice versa.

3208 When an appeal is lodged by one of the parties, the law recognises that both enjoy the same equal rights in the process, and *both* are equally affected by the outcome of the appeal.

Can. 1637 §2 If there are several respondents or plaintiffs, and the judgement is challenged by or against only one of them, the challenge is considered to be made by all and against all whenever the thing requested is indivisible or the obligation is a joint one.

3209 This paragraph establishes an important principle in those cases where the object of the litigation is something indivisible such e.g. as ownership or inheritance, or is a joint obligation: if a case involved several plaintiffs or several respondents, they do not all have to lodge individual appeals against a judgement; if an appeal is lodged by one of the parties or against one of the parties, the law considers that the appeal has been made 'by all and against all'.

Can. 1637 §3 If one party challenges a judgement in regard to one ground, the other party can appeal incidentally on the other grounds, even if the canonical time-limit for the appeal has expired. This incidental case is to be appealed within a peremptory time-limit of fifteen days from the day of notification of the principal appeal.

3210 In cases where one of the parties has challenged one ground of the judgement, in keeping with the principle enunciated in §1, the other party may lodge an appeal against other grounds in the original judgement – but only as an incidental question. Such an incidental appeal may be lodged after the time-limit for appeal has elapsed (Can. 1630 §1), provided that it is lodged within a further time-limit of fifteen days from the date of notification of the principal appeal. If the principal appeal is not admitted by the appeal tribunal, any incidental appeals submitted by the other party cannot be considered.

Can. 1637 §4 Unless it is established otherwise, an appeal is presumed to be against all the grounds of the judgement.

3211 The law requires the appellant to indicate at least briefly the reasons for an appeal (see Can. 1634 §1). However, if he or she does not specify precisely on which ground the judgement is being challenged, the law presumes that all grounds are being appealed and the appeal court must examine the entire judgement.

Can. 1638 An appeal suspends the execution of the judgement.

3212 When an appeal is made, a twofold effect ensues:
(a) the judgement must be referred to 'a higher judge' (see Can. 1628);
(b) the judgement cannot be executed until the matter is resolved by the appeal tribunal.

Although the principle is stated more clearly and simply than in the 1917 Code (c.1889), the law does foresee some situations where the principle does not apply fully. Thus, for example, a recourse to a higher tribunal for a new presentation of a case after two conforming sentences does not *ipso iure* suspend the execution of the judgement (Can. 1644 §2); moreover, in certain circumstances, the original judge or the appeal judge may order the provisional execution of a judgement or subject its execution to a guarantee (see Can. 1650 §§2–3).

Can. 1639 §1 Without prejudice to the provision of Can. 1683, a new ground cannot be introduced at the appeal grade, not even by way of the useful accumulation of grounds. So the joinder of the issue can concern itself only with the confirmation or the reform of the first judgement, either in part or in whole.

§2 New proofs are admitted only in accordance with Can. 1600.

The task of the appeal court is straightforward: it must either confirm or reform wholly or partially the decision of the original court. Consequently, a new basis for petitioning cannot be added at the appeal level since this would substantially alter the object of the process. The only exception to this principle provided for by the law concerns the introduction of a new ground of nullity of marriage at the appeal grade (see Can. 1683). New evidence may be presented during the appeal, however; this may be admitted by the judge but only in accordance with the provisions of Can. 1600.

Can. 1640 With the appropriate adjustments, the procedure at the appeal grade is to be the same as in first instance. Unless the proofs are to be supplemented, however, once the issue has been joined in accordance with Cann. 1513 §1 and 1639 §1, the judges are to proceed immediately to the discussion of the case and the judgement.

The procedure to be followed in considering a case at appeal is to be identical to that of first instance, insofar as that is possible or necessary. Since appeals are to be dealt with without undue delay (see Can. 1453), unless new proofs are to be admitted (see Can. 1639 §2), once the joinder of issue has taken place at appeal (see Cann. 1513 §1, 1639 §1), the judges are to proceed at once to discuss the case and reach a decision (see Cann. 1601–1606).

Title IX
Adjudged Matter and Total Reinstatement

Chapter I
ADJUDGED MATTER

Can. 1641 Without prejudice to Can. 1643, an adjudged matter occurs when:

1° there are two conforming judgements between the same parties about the same matter and on the same grounds;

2° no appeal was made against the judgement within the canonical time-limit;

3° the trial has been abated or renounced in the appeal grade;

4° a definitive judgement has been given from which, in accordance with Can. 1629, there is no appeal.

3215 The purpose of a judicial process is to resolve a problem. This resolution comes when an issue becomes what is known as an 'adjudged matter'. This means that the question proposed in the trial has been answered and the case is now closed. According to the Code, this can happen in any one of four ways:

1° when two tribunals have given conforming sentences in the same case, i.e. when a case involving the *same* parties about the *same* object on the *same* ground has been resolved in the *same* way by two tribunals at different instances. It is important to note that the jurisprudence of the Rota has interpreted this principle to include 'equivalent conformity' of sentence in marriage-nullity cases.[1]

2° when the parties have failed to lodge an appeal within fifteen canonical days from the notification of the publication of the judgement (see Can. 1630 §1) or when the appeal was not prosecuted within one month of its being lodged (see Can. 1633).

3° when the appellant has failed to perform a required procedural act over a period of six months (see Can. 1520) or when he or she has renounced the trial at the appeal level (see Cann. 1524–1525).

4° when the definitive judgement is one of those mentioned in Can. 1629 which do not admit of appeal.

Can. 1642 §1 An adjudged matter has the force of law and cannot be challenged directly, except in accordance with Can. 1645 §1.

3216 This canon establishes the principle that a matter resolved in conformity with any of the four situations foreseen in Can. 1641 has the firmness or the stability of law. Such a decision may not be challenged directly by plaint of nullity or appeal. Instead, only the extraordinary challenge of total reinstatement is permitted (see Can. 1645 §1).

Can. 1642 §2 It has the effect of law between the parties; it gives the right to an action arising from the judgement and to an exception of an adjudged matter; to prevent a new introduction of the same case, the judge can even declare such an exception *ex officio*.

3217 Such is the force of the adjudged matter that it is considered to 'have made law' between the parties to the controversy. This means that they have a right to the execution of the judgement and, if necessary, to introduce an exception 'to the effect that an issue has become an adjudged matter' in accordance with Can. 1462 §1. Should it be necessary to prevent the case being introduced a second time, the law gives the judge also the right to declare such an exception.

Can. 1643 Cases concerning the status of persons never become an adjudged matter, not excepting cases which concern the separation of spouses.

3218 The canon proposes an important exception to the principle just enunciated: the norms governing adjudged matter do not apply to cases which concern the status of persons. These include cases of nullity of marriage (Cann. 1671–1691), nullity of

---

[1] Cf. McGrath *Conformity of sentence in marriage nullity cases* Stud Can 27(1993) 5–22.

ordination (Cann. 1708–1712), separation of spouses (Cann. 1692–1696), etc. This canon ought not, however, be read in isolation from what follows.

Can. 1644 §1 If two conforming judgements have been given in cases concerning the status of persons, recourse to a tribunal of appeal can be made at any time, to be supported by new and serious proofs or arguments which are to be submitted within a peremptory time-limit of thirty days from the time the challenge was made. Within one month of receiving the new proofs and arguments, the appeal tribunal must declare by a decree whether or not a new presentation of the case is to be admitted.

In the light of Can. 1643, cases of the status of persons are always open to challenge. However, they do not admit of the ordinary challenges of plaint of nullity or appeal. Instead, an application may be made requesting a new presentation of the case – but only on the basis of the submission of 'new and serious proofs or arguments'. These are to be proposed to the appeal tribunal within a peremptory time-limit thirty days from the lodging of this extraordinary challenge. The question must be dealt with by the judges as a matter of urgency: the law gives them only one month in which to decide whether or not to grant, on the basis of these same 'new and serious proofs or arguments', a new presentation of the case.

Can. 1644 §2 Recourse to a higher tribunal to obtain a new presentation of the case does not suspend the execution of the judgement, unless the law provides otherwise or the appeal tribunal orders a suspension in accordance with Can. 1650 §3.

Even though the double conforming judgement in a case of status of persons does not become adjudged matter in the strict sense, the decision does have a certain stability. Consequently, a recourse to obtain a new presentation of the case does not have suspensive effect; the judgement may be executed unless the law prescribes a suspension (which this Code itself does not) or unless the appeal tribunal decrees a suspension in conformity with Can. 1650 §3. Interestingly, a new presentation of the case may be granted even if a further marriage had taken place as a consequence of a double conforming judgement in favour of the nullity of a previous bond. The Revision Commission felt that to exclude the possibility of such a challenge would be contrary to natural law and the provisions of Can. 1643.[1]

Chapter II
TOTAL REINSTATEMENT

Can. 1645 §1 Against a judgement which has become an adjudged matter there can be a total reinstatement, provided it is clearly established that the judgement was unjust.

Since adjudged matter has the strength or the firmness of law, it cannot be challenged directly by a plaint of nullity or by an ordinary appeal. However, the law permits that

---

[1] Cf. Comm 16(1984) 76 at Can. 1636 §1. If, as a result of the new presentation, the original decision in favour of nullity were in due time reversed, what of an intervening marriage which, on the basis of the earlier conforming judgements, had in fact taken place? For all that such a marriage had been both permitted and entered into in all good faith, it would nevertheless be invalid, in accordance with Can. 1085. The ensuing pastoral problem is certainly one which should be referred to the diocesan Bishop.

adjudged matter may still be challenged if the injustice of the judgement can be clearly established. This remedy is known as total reinstatement; it amounts to restoring a situation juridically to the way it had been prior to the judgement. The challenge is directed not so much against the substance of the judgement as against the injustice it has caused.[1]

Can. 1645 §2 Injustice is not, however, considered clearly established unless:

1° the judgement is so based on proofs which are subsequently shown to be false, that without those proofs the dispositive part of the judgement could not be sustained;

2° documents are subsequently discovered by which new facts demanding a contrary decision are undoubtedly proven;

3° the judgement was given through the deceit of one party to the harm of the other;

4° a provision of a law which was not merely procedural was evidently neglected;

5° the judgement runs counter to a preceding decision which has become an adjudged matter.

3222 A vague allegation of injustice is not sufficient reason for seeking a total reinstatement. The law requires that the injustice be 'clearly established'. In this paragraph, the demonstration of such injustice is limited to five possible situations:

1° if the dispositive part of the judgement was based on proofs which have subsequently been shown to be false;

2° if documents hitherto unknown are discovered which shed light on facts in such a way that a contrary decision is required;

3° if the substance of the decision was based on deceit perpetrated by one party in the case against the other party;

4° if there was evident neglect of some provision of a law which was not merely procedural;[2]

5° if the decision contradicts a previous judgement which has become an adjudged matter.

Can. 1646 §1 Total reinstatement based on the reasons mentioned in Can. 1645 §2 nn.1-3, is to be requested from the judge who delivered the judgement, within three months from the day on which these reasons became known.

---

[1] It has been suggested by some authors that total reinstatement may be used in cases of marriage-nullity: cf. Wrenn *Procedures* Washington 1987 79; Commentary (CLSA) 1004. This is not a view shared by the majority of authors: cf. Schwendenwein *Das Neue Kirchenrecht Gesamtdarstellung* Graz 1983 502; Garcia Failde *Nuevo Derecho Procesal* Salamanca 1984 248; Chiappetta n.5100. These base their position on the fact that total reinstatement is possible only where there is an adjudged matter: this necessarily excludes all cases referred to in Can. 1643. This whole issue is discussed thoroughly in Johnson *Making restitution in marriage cases: can it be done?* Jur 51(1991) 155–182.

[2] Cf. una Opolien., praeiudicialis: restitutionis in integrum adversus reiectionem libelli et avocationis causae ad R. Rotam, decretum coram Stankiewicz 10.X.1985: *Quaderni Studio Rotale* II 91–97, in which total reinstatement was refused. This was overturned in a decree coram Bruno, 23.V.1986 op cit 99–105, on the basis that the judges at first instance had clearly neglected the prescriptions of Can. 1505 §2 4°.

§2 Total reinstatement based on the reasons mentioned in Can. 1645 §2 nn.4 and 5, is to be requested from the appeal tribunal within three months of notification of the publication of the judgement. In the case mentioned in Can. 1645 §2 n. 5, if the preceding decision is not known until later, the time-limit begins at the time the knowledge was obtained.

This canon specifies the judge who is competent to consider a request for total reinstatement and sets out the time-limits within which such a request may be made. Thus, if the manifest injustice is based on false evidence, or newly discovered documents, or deceit by one party against the other, the request must be made to the judge who delivered the sentence being challenged. This must be presented to the judge within three months from the date of the discovery of the relevant facts. 3223

If the manifest injustice is based on a neglect of the law or a contradiction with a previous judgement which has become an adjudged matter, then the request for total reinstatement must be made to the appropriate appeal tribunal. In these cases, the request must be submitted within three months from the notification of the publication of the judgement, except where the earlier decision was not known until later: in this case, the time-limit runs from the date of that judgement's discovery. 3224

Can. 1646 §3 The time-limits mentioned above do not apply for as long as the aggrieved party is a minor.

Whatever the reason for requesting a total reinstatement, if the injured party is a minor, the time-limits specified in this canon do not apply until he or she has completed his or her eighteenth year of age (see Can. 97 §1). 3225

Can. 1647 §1 A plea for total reinstatement suspends the execution of a judgement which has not yet begun.

§2 If there are probable indications leading the judge to suspect that the plea was made to cause delays in execution, he may decide that the judgement be executed. The person seeking total reinstatement is, however, to be given suitable guarantees that, if it is granted, he or she will be indemnified.

If a judgement has not yet been executed, a petition seeking a total reinstatement suspends the execution. However, the law enables the judge to act at once and decree the execution of the judgement if he has good reason to suspect that the petition for total reinstatement is only a delaying tactic. In such a situation, the judge is to take precautionary measures in order to prevent harm or damage to the petitioning party should the total reinstatement be granted. 3226

Can. 1648 Where total reinstatement is granted, the judge must pronounce on the merits of the case.

If the total reinstatement is not granted, then the original judgement retains its force and effects. However, if the total reinstatement is granted, the matter is returned to the situation obtaining prior to that judgement: the controversy remains to be resolved. This canon prescribes that the same judge who grants total reinstatement must then proceed to give judgement on the merits of the original case. 3227

Title X
Judicial Expenses and Free Legal Aid

Can. 1649 §1 The Bishop who is responsible for governing the tribunal is to establish norms concerning:

1° declarations that parties are liable for the payment or reimbursement of judicial expenses;

2° the honorariums for advocates, experts and interpreters, and the expenses of witnesses;

3° the granting of free legal aid and the reduction of expenses;

4° the payment of damages owed by a person who not merely lost the case, but was rash in having recourse to litigation;

5° the money to be deposited, or the guarantee to be given, for the discharging of expenses and payment of damages.

3228 Whereas the 1917 Code (see cc.1908–1916) devoted nine canons to the matter of judicial expenses and free legal aid, the present Code has only this one canon, leaving detailed provisions to particular law. It is for the moderator of each tribunal, taking into account local circumstances, to establish the appropriate norms governing the matters listed in 1°–5° of this canon. Although not required by law, it might well be appropriate if the Bishops of the same Bishops' Conference were to issue similar norms in these matters.

Can. 1649 §2 No distinct appeal exists from a pronouncement concerning expenses, honorariums and damages. The parties can, however, have recourse within ten days to the same judge, who can change the sum involved.

3229 When the expenses of a case are determined within the judgement (see Can. 1611 4°), no distinct appeal against the judge's pronouncement is possible. The judge's decision can always be challenged along with an appeal against the substance of the judgement. However, in a case where there is no appeal, the law permits the parties to have recourse to the judge within fifteen days of the notification of the judge's decision. Similar action may be taken by the parties when the judge has determined this issue in accordance with Can. 1464. Having received and considered such a recourse, the judge may adjust the sum of money involved.

Title XI
The Execution of the Judgement

Can. 1650 §1 A judgement which becomes an adjudged matter can be executed, without prejudice to the provision of Can. 1647.

The execution of a judgement is a judicial act whereby the legal consequences of a decision are put into effect. The law establishes the norm that only a judgement which has become an adjudged matter may be executed, foreseeing an exception in the case where a total reinstatement is sought prior to the execution (see Can. 1647 §1).

Can. 1650 §2 The judge who delivered the judgement and, if there has been an appeal, the appeal judge, can either *ex officio* or at the request of a party order the provisional execution of a judgement which has not yet become an adjudged matter, adding if need be appropriate guarantees when it is a matter of provisions or payments concerning necessary support. They can also do so for some other just and urgent reason.

Even if there is not yet an adjudged matter, the judge can order the provisional execution of the judgement. This may be done by the judge who delivered the original sentence, or by the appeal judge if there has been an appeal. Provisional execution may be decreed on the judge's own initiative or at the request of one of the parties. In doing so, the judge may add appropriate guarantees where a person's basic support is concerned or where some other just cause demands it.

Can. 1650 §3 If the judgement mentioned in §2 is challenged, the judge who must deal with the challenge can suspend the execution or subject it to a guarantee, if he sees that the challenge is probably well founded and that irreparable harm could result from execution.

The provisional execution of a sentence may be challenged. In such an event, the judge may suspend the execution or make it subject to certain guarantees if he believes that the challenge is justified and in order to prevent serious damage that cannot otherwise be repaired.

Can. 1651 Execution cannot take place before there is issued the judge's executing decree directing that the judgement be executed. Depending on the nature of the case, this decree is to be either included in the judgement itself or issued separately.

The execution of a judgement requires not only an adjudged matter but also a decree of the judge ordering its execution. This decree may form an integral but distinct part of the judgement itself,[1] or it may be issued by the judge separately.

Can. 1652 If the execution of the judgement requires a prior statement of accounts, this is to be treated as an incidental question, to be decided by the judge who gave the judgement which is to be executed.

When, in a given case, financial accounts must be rendered if a judgement is to be properly executed, the matter is to be dealt with as an incidental question (see Cann. 1587–1591) by the judge who issued the sentence which is to be executed.

Can. 1653 §1 Unless particular law provides otherwise, the Bishop of the diocese in which the first instance judgement was given must, either personally or through another, execute the judgement.

§2 If he refuses or neglects to do so, the execution of the judgement, at the request of an interested party or *ex officio*, belongs to the authority to which the appeal tribunal is subject in accordance with Can. 1439 §3.

---

[1] This would appear to be the case in sentences or decrees declaring the nullity of a marriage. The wording of Can. 1684 §1 seems to render unnecessary any separate executory decree such as that required formerly by PME 202 §6.

3235 The actual execution of a judgement is entrusted to the competent ecclesiastical authority. First and foremost, the responsibility belongs to the diocesan Bishop of the place of the first instance decision; he must execute the sentence personally or through a delegate.

3236 Should the diocesan Bishop fail to carry out his responsibility, the law entrusts the execution of the judgement to the authority to which the appeal tribunal is subject; this may be the Metropolitan (see Can. 1438 1°) or the one designated to hear appeals from the tribunal of the Metropolitan (see Can. 1438 2°) or the Bishops' Conference or the Bishop designated by the Conference (see Can. 1439 §3). In this case, the relevant authority may act to execute the sentence *ex officio* or at the request of an interested party.

Can. 1653 §3 Between religious, the execution of the judgement is the responsibility of the Superior who gave the judgement which is to be executed, or who delegated the judge.

3237 In the case of a judgement concerning religious, the responsibility for the execution of the judgement lies with the appropriate major Superior (see Can. 1427 §§1–2) or his or her delegate.

Can. 1654 §1 The executor must execute the judgement according to the obvious sense of the words, unless in the judgement itself something is left to his discretion.

3238 Unless the judgement itself has granted the executor some latitude in the matter, the judgement is to be executed 'according to the obvious sense of the words', a clear reference to the general principle of Can. 17. This prevents an executor from distorting or undermining in any way the decision made by the judge.

Can. 1654 §2 He can deal with exceptions concerning the manner and the force of the execution, but not with the merits of the case. If he has ascertained from some other source that the judgement is null or manifestly unjust according to Cann. 1620, 1622 and 1645, he is to refrain from executing the judgement, and is instead to refer the matter to the tribunal which delivered the judgement and to notify the parties.

3239 The authority mentioned in Can. 1653 is prohibited from dealing with the merits of the case. However, he or she can consider any exceptions raised concerning the manner and force of the judgement's execution. The executor is obliged by the law to abstain from executing the judgement if convinced that the judgement itself is invalid (see Cann. 1620, 1622) or manifestly unjust (see Can. 1645). In this case, the matter must be brought to the attention of the tribunal which issued the sentence and the parties must be informed.

Can. 1655 §1 In real actions, whenever it is decided that a thing belongs to the plaintiff, it is to be handed over to the plaintiff as soon as the matter has become an adjudged matter.

§2 In personal actions, when the respondent is condemned to hand over a movable possession or to pay money, or to give or do something, the judge in the judgement itself, or the executor according to his discretion and prudence, is to assign a time-limit for the fulfilment of the obligation. This time-limit is to be not less than fifteen days nor more than six months.

3240 This canon regulates the time-limits for the fulfilment of obligations imposed in the judgement:

(a) in a real action (i.e. one which concerns property, movable or immovable), the law requires that the object of the dispute is to be handed over to the plaintiff immediately the judgement becomes adjudged matter;

(b) in a personal action (i.e. one which concerns the rights or obligations of a person), the judge or, at his discretion, the executor is to fix a time-limit for the fulfilment of the obligation in question – a period of not less than fifteen days and not more than six months.

Section II
THE ORAL CONTENTIOUS PROCESS

INTRODUCTION

There is nothing corresponding to this section in the 1917 Code. Its remote roots are to be found in the con *Saepe* of Pope Clement V 13.XII.1306, and its more proximate source is Pope Pius XII's mp *Sollicitudinem Nostram* 6.I.1950 which revised procedural law for the Eastern Churches.[1] The oral contentious process is different, not because of the material treated but because of its structure. It reduces or eliminates those elements in a trial not strictly needed for justice, in order to expedite the whole procedure; in essence it is, as its name suggests, an oral rather than a written process. The heart of the procedure is the oral trial or hearing, in which witnesses are heard, documents produced, evidence examined, arguments presented and the decision given. It contrasts with the ordinary contentious process where everything must be written down, with consequent delays. 3241

This section is not intended to be complete in itself. It presupposes the norms for trials in general (Cann. 1400–1500) and many of those contained in the section on the ordinary contentious process (Cann. 1501–1655) where special provisions have not been made for the oral process.[2] 3242

Can. 1656 §1 The oral contentious process dealt with in this section can be used in all cases which are not excluded by law, unless a party requests the ordinary contentious process.

The general principle is that the oral contentious process can be used unless the law excludes it or one of the parties requests the ordinary contentious process. The law expressly forbids its use in marriage-nullity cases (Can. 1690) and does so equivalently, by requiring the ordinary contentious process, in the process for the dispensation from a ratified and non-consummated marriage (Can. 1702), in cases for the declaration of the nullity of sacred ordination (Can. 1710), in penal trials (Can. 1728 §1). Cases reserved by law (Can. 1425 §1) or by the Bishop (Can. 1425 §2) to a collegiate tribunal cannot be heard using the oral process, since this presupposes that there is just one judge (Can. 1657). 3243

---

[1] Cf. Comm 4(1972) 60–61; 8(1976) 192.
[2] Cf. Can. 1670.

3244 This process is not just permitted but is normally to be used in cases of incidental matters which are to be decided by judgement (Can. 1590) and in cases concerning the separation of spouses (Can. 1693 §1). Its use is obligatory in deciding questions about the right to appeal (Can. 1631). A plaint of nullity of judgement may be dealt with by this process (Can. 1627).

Can. 1656 §2 If the oral process is used in cases other than those permitted by the law, the judicial acts are null.

3245 If the oral process is used when this is forbidden by law, then not only the judgement but all the judicial acts are null.[1]

Can. 1657 The oral contentious process takes place in the first instance before a sole judge, in accordance with Can. 1424.

3246 The oral process is heard by a sole judge at first instance. This is in keeping with the purpose of this type of process which is to simplify and so speed up the process. In accordance with Can. 1424 the judge may utilize the services of two assessors. At second instance the case would also be heard by a sole judge in accordance with the norm of Can. 1441 which prescribes that the second instance tribunal is to be constituted in the same way as the tribunal of first instance.

Can. 1658 §1 In addition to the matters enumerated in Can. 1504, the petition which introduces the suit must:

1° set forth briefly, fully and clearly the facts on which the plaintiff's pleas are based;

2° indicate the proofs by which the plaintiff intends to demonstrate the facts and which cannot be brought forward with the petition; this is to be done in such a way that the proofs can immediately be gathered by the judge.

§2 Documents on which a plea is based must be attached to the petition, at least in authentic copy.

3247 The petition in the oral process must be rather more complete than that in the ordinary process. The reason is that since the oral process involves one hearing only, the judge will have to gather the proofs beforehand and so will need detailed indications of what these are. Accordingly the canon prescribes that the facts on which the pleas are based be set forth, not just in general terms, but 'briefly, fully and clearly'. The proofs themselves are to be indicated and any documents supporting the plea are to be attached to the petition, at least in authentic copy.

3248 The oral petition of Can. 1503 is not ruled out, but it should be sufficiently complete to allow the judge to carry out the necessary pre-trial investigations.

Can. 1659 §1 If an attempt at mediation in accordance with Can. 1446 §2 has proven fruitless, the judge, if he deems that the petition has some foundation, is within three days to add a decree at the foot of the petition. In this decree he is to order that a copy of the plea be notified to the respondent, with the right to send a written reply to the tribunal office within fifteen days.

§2 This notification has the effects of a judicial summons that are as mentioned in Can. 1512.

---

[1] The nullity of judgement here is more probably irremediable: see footnote to Can. 1669.

For as long as there is any hope of success, the judge is always to attempt a peaceful solution (Can. 1446 §2). If this fails and if he decides that there is a basis for the petition, he is within three days to add a decree at the foot of the petition, ordering that it be communicated to the respondent, who has the right to reply within fifteen days. In this reply the respondent can present contrary proofs and counter arguments, as well as exceptions or even a counter action. The notification of the petition with its attached decree to the respondent has all the five effects of a judicial summons mentioned in Can. 1512. 3249

Can. 1660 If the exceptions raised by the respondent so require, the judge is to assign the plaintiff a time-limit for a reply, so that from the material advanced by each he can clearly discern the object of the controversy.

If the respondent's reply contains exceptions or even a counter action, and if this leaves the object of the controversy less than clear, the judge is to give the plaintiff the opportunity to reply within a specified time. 3250

Can. 1661 §1 When the time-limits mentioned in Cann. 1659 and 1660 have expired, the judge, after examining the acts, is to determine the point at issue. He is then to summon all who must be present to a hearing, which is to be held within thirty days; for the parties, he is to add the formulation of the point at issue.

After the time-limits mentioned in Can. 1659 (fifteen days for the respondent to reply) and Can. 1660 (whatever fitting time may have been given to the plaintiff) have expired, the judge is to determine the point at issue and to formulate it accordingly. He is then to summon all those who must be present to a hearing which is to be held within thirty days. Those to be summoned include the parties, witnesses, experts and, if the case calls for them, the promotor of justice and the defender of the bond.[1] In addition to the summons the parties are to receive a copy of the formulation of the point at issue. 3251

Can. 1661 §2 In the summons the parties are to be informed that, to support their assertions, they can submit a short written statement to the tribunal at least three days before the hearing.

When they are summoned, the parties are also to be notified that they may submit a brief written statement in support of their assertions. This – yet another way of promoting a more expeditious trial – must be submitted at least three days before the hearing. 3252

Can. 1662 In the hearing, the questions mentioned in Cann. 1459–1464 are considered first.

Before proceeding to the main point at issue, a number of preliminary matters may first have to be considered and decided. These are given in Cann. 1459–1464 and include such questions as exceptions which would render the judgement invalid, exceptions seeking a delay, exceptions concerning legal competence, exceptions that the issue has become an adjudged matter and other such peremptory exceptions. Further questions could include counter actions, judicial expenses and free legal aid. 3253

Can. 1663 §1 The proofs are assembled during the hearing, without prejudice to the provision of Can. 1418.

---

[1] Although marriage and ordination nullity cases cannot be tried by the oral process, the process may be used to decide incidental matters arising during such cases. In this eventuality the defender of the bond and, perhaps, the promotor of justice would take part.

3254 Normally all the proofs are to be presented during the hearing. If it is impossible for witnesses to be present, the judge could take their depositions beforehand or, if they are outside the jurisdiction of the tribunal, he could request that their testimony be taken by a rogatory commission in accordance with Can. 1418.

Can. 1663 §2 A party and his or her advocate can assist at the examination of the other parties, of the witnesses and of the experts.

3255 In the ordinary contentious process the parties are not normally allowed to be present at the questioning of witnesses (Can. 1559) or of other parties (Cann. 1534 and 1559). The judge can also determine that their advocates may not be present either (Can. 1559). However, in the oral process both the parties and their advocates are allowed to be present at the examination of parties, witnesses and experts.[1]

Can. 1664 The replies of the parties, witnesses and experts, and the pleas and exceptions of the advocates, are to be written down by the notary in summary fashion, restricting the record to those things which bear on the substance of the controversy. This record is to be signed by the persons testifying.

3256 Although the process is an oral one, the notary is to put in writing the substance of the depositions of the parties, witnesses and experts, as well as the pleas and exceptions made by the advocates. Each person who testifies is to sign the record of his or her testimony as a guarantee of its accuracy. The written record serves to aid the judge in writing the judgement and will provide material which will be indispensable for the appeal tribunal.

Can. 1665 Proofs which were not submitted or requested in the plea or reply can be admitted by the judge only in accordance with Can. 1452. After the hearing of even one witness, however, the judge can decide upon new proofs only in accordance with Can. 1600.

3257 The parties should present or request their proofs with the petition or with the replies mentioned in Cann. 1659 §1 and 1660 or even, perhaps, with the short written statement allowed by Can. 1661 §2. After this, proofs can be admitted by the judge only in accordance with Can. 1452, i.e. in order to supply for the negligence of the parties should this be necessary to avoid a gravely unjust judgement. After even one witness has been examined, the judge can allow new proofs only in accordance with Can. 1600 which details the requirements for new proofs after the conclusion of the case in the ordinary contentious process.

Can. 1666 If all the proofs cannot be collected during the hearing, a further hearing is to be set.

3258 Normally the oral process takes place with one hearing only. However, if this is not sufficient to allow for the collection of all the proofs, the judge is to appoint another day for a further hearing.

Can. 1667 When the proofs have been collected, an oral discussion is to take place at the same hearing.

3259 When all the proofs have been collected the parties' advocates are to present their arguments orally. The parties themselves can intervene in this discussion, as can the promotor of justice and the defender of the bond if these latter are present. The judge will preside over the discussion and keep it within proper limits.

---

[1] Even in the oral process the judge could, in a particular case and for sufficient reason, exclude the parties and their advocates: cf. Comm 4(1972) 63 8 g.

Can. 1668 §1 Unless it emerges from the discussion that something needs to be added to the instruction of the case, or that there is something which prevents the judgement from being correctly delivered, the judge is forthwith, on completion of the hearing, to decide the case privately. The dispositive part of the judgement is to be read immediately in the presence of the parties.

§2 Because of the difficulty of the matter, or for some other just reason, the decision of the tribunal can be deferred for up to five canonical days.

§3 The full text of the judgement, including the reasons for it, is to be notified to the parties as soon as possible, normally within fifteen days.

At the end of the discussion, unless further instruction of the case is needed or there is some other obstacle to giving the judgement immediately, the judge retires to reach his decision privately, with the assistance of the assessors who may have taken part with him. He will then write down the dispositive part of the judgement – i.e. his decision on the matter at issue – and return and read this in the presence of the parties (§1). 3260

It may happen that the judge needs more time to arrive at and announce his decision, either because of the complexity of the case or for some other just reason: in such a situation he may defer giving his decision for up to five canonical days (see Can. 201 §2). 3261

The judge is then to draw up a full written judgement (in accordance with the norms of Can. 1612) in which the reasons for his decision are to be set out. This judgement is to be communicated to the parties 'as soon as possible, normally within fifteen days'; this time-limit may for a good reason be extended, but only for a matter of days. Only when this has been done has the judgement any juridical effect (see Can. 1614). 3262

Can. 1669 If the appeal tribunal discerns that a lower tribunal has used the oral contentious process in cases which are excluded by law, it is to declare the judgement invalid and refer the case back to the tribunal which delivered the judgement.

Can. 1656 §2 declares invalid all the judicial acts in a case where the oral process was used unlawfully. This necessarily means that the judgement itself is invalid and so, if the appeal court discovers this, it is to send the case back to the first instance tribunal. The nullity of sentence here is generally held to be irremediable, even though this case is not specifically mentioned in Can. 1620.[1] 3263

Can. 1670 In all other matters concerning procedure, the provisions of the canons on ordinary contentious trials are to be followed. In order to expedite matters, however, while safeguarding justice, the tribunal can, by a decree and for stated reasons, derogate from procedural norms which are not prescribed for validity.

Obviously this brief section does not contain all the norms governing procedure in the oral contentious process. Where there are no special provisions, the norms for ordinary contentious trials are to be followed. However, since the principal aim of the oral process is to expedite trials, the judge is allowed considerable discretion in derogating from these procedural norms. He may do so provided that he safeguards justice, acts by decree which gives his reasons, and provided also that the norms in question are not prescribed for validity. 3264

---

[1] Cf. Grocholewski in Commentary (Urbanianum) 951; Madero CCLA 1029; Chiappetta II n.5148. All of these would hold that the nullity is irremediable. Wrenn, on the other hand, states that it is remediable on the basis of Can. 1622 n.5: cf. Commentary (CLSA) 1007.

PART III

CERTAIN SPECIAL PROCESSES

Title I
Matrimonial Processes

Chapter I
CASES CONCERNING THE DECLARATION OF NULLITY OF MARRIAGE

Article 1
The Competent Forum

Can. 1671 Matrimonial cases of the baptised belong by their own right to the ecclesiastical judge.

Can. 1401 1° declares that the 'Church has its own and exclusive right to judge cases which refer to matters which are spiritual or linked with the spiritual'. The marriage of the baptised is a sacrament (Can. 1055 §1) and so is clearly a spiritual matter. A marriage where only one party is baptised is not a sacrament, but is still a spiritual matter and so the Church also claims competence over cases concerning such marriages. The present canon no longer explicitly states the exclusivity of the Church's competence over marriage cases involving the baptised as did c.1960 of the 1917 Code, since such terminology 'smacks of disputes and dissensions and is of little service to ecumenism',[1] but Can. 1401 1° makes it clear that the Church does still claim exclusive competence over these cases.

Can. 1672 Cases concerning the merely civil effects of marriage pertain to the civil authority, unless particular law lays down that, if such cases are raised as incidental and accessory matters, they may be heard and decided by an ecclesiastical judge.

This canon acknowledges the competence of the civil authority in cases concerning the purely civil effects of marriage, such as inheritance rights, property settlements, custody of children, etc. It does provide for such matters to be settled by an ecclesiastical court, but only if they are raised as incidental to a marriage-nullity case and if particular law so provides. Such a provision of particular law could result from a concordat between the Holy See and the civil authority in question.

Can. 1673 The following tribunals are competent in cases concerning the nullity of marriage which are not reserved to the Apostolic See:

1° the tribunal of the place where the marriage was celebrated;

---

[1] Comm 11(1979) 256 at Can. 335.

The Holy See reserves to itself all cases involving heads of State (Can. 1405 §1 1°) and may reserve others (Can. 1405 §1 4°). Apart from these, the present canon gives four grounds of competence for marriage-nullity cases. These are by no means mutually exclusive, and accordingly the plaintiff may have a choice of tribunal. 3267

The first tribunal which is declared competent is the tribunal of the place where the marriage took place. The place of marriage has traditionally been competent; this is a specific example of the competence by reason of contract mentioned in Can. 1411 §1. The tribunal in question will be the diocesan (or equivalent) tribunal or else an inter-diocesan or regional tribunal. 3268

2° the tribunal of the place where the respondent has a domicile or quasi-domicile;

This ground of competence is in accordance with the traditional legal maxim *actor sequitur forum rei*: 'the plaintiff follows the tribunal of the respondent'. Whatever advantage is to be gained from having the tribunal local – ease of access, possible language advantages, etc. – accrue to the respondent. 3269

3° the tribunal of the place where the plaintiff has a domicile, provided that both parties live within the territory of the same Bishops' Conference, and that the judicial Vicar of the domicile of the respondent, after consultation with the respondent, gives consent;

In this case the tribunal of the plaintiff's domicile is competent, subject however to two essential conditions: (a) both parties must live within the territory of the same Bishops' Conference – if they do not, this ground of competence simply does not arise; (b) the judicial Vicar of the respondent's domicile must consult with the respondent, and only then give his consent. This consent must be explicit, and it cannot be presumed.[1] The judicial Vicar in question is the judicial Vicar of the diocese in which the respondent has a domicile, not therefore necessarily the judicial Vicar of an inter-diocesan tribunal; if there is no diocesan judicial Vicar, the consent of the Bishop is required.[2] 3270

4° the tribunal of the place in which in fact most of the proofs are to be collected, provided that consent is given by the judicial Vicar of the domicile of the respondent, who must first ask the respondent whether he or she has any objection to raise.

This ground of competence can be a convenient one, allowing the tribunal of the place where most of the proofs are to be collected, and hence where most of the work must be done, to hear the case. Its terms must, however, be accurately understood. The judicial Vicar of the respondent (as in 3° above) must give his consent, but prior to doing so he is obliged, *per se vel per alium*, to ask the respondent whether he or she has any objection to having the case heard in that tribunal. If the respondent has no objection, the judicial Vicar may freely give his consent, provided that he himself considers it reasonable and prudent to do so in the circumstances. If, on the other hand, the respondent does object, the Vicar ought to withhold his consent, unless he judges the respondent's objection to be wholly unreasonable. It is clear therefore that this consent may never be presumed. 3271

In estimating what is the place where most of the proofs are to be collected, account must be taken, not only of the witnesses and other proofs nominated by the plaintiff, 3272

---

[1] Cf. Ap Sig rep 27.IV.1989 in RR 1989 45–48.
[2] CCom rep 28.II.1986: AAS 78(1986) 1323.

but also of other proofs, such as those nominated by the respondent or sought *ex officio* by the judge. It should be particularly borne in mind that it is not the number of proofs which is important in arriving at the decision, but rather the weight to be attributed to each of them.[1]

3273 What is to be done when it is clearly desirable that a case be heard by the tribunal of the place where most of the proofs are to be collected, but the respondent's place of residence is unknown and so it is impossible to ask him or her if there are any objections to be raised? This question was raised with the Apostolic Signatura in 1973 under the corresponding norm of *Causas Matrimoniales* and the reply was that the tribunal of the place of most of the proofs could hear the case without any special permission. The reasons given were that the basic purpose of the norm was to allow cases to be processed more easily and more quickly and that the consent of the Ordinary was required to safeguard the rights of the respondent and the public good. The public good was not in danger in the sort of case envisaged.[2] That reasoning applies equally to the present law, and so in such a case the tribunal of most of the proofs could proceed validly and lawfully to hear the case.[3] This would seem to apply also not only when the respondent's place of residence is unknown (as in the case stated), but also when the respondent obdurately refuses to cooperate in any way.

Article 2
The Right to Challenge the Validity of Marriage

Can. 1674 The following are capable of impugning the validity of a marriage:

1° the spouses themselves;

2° the promotor of justice, when the nullity of the marriage has already been made public, and the marriage cannot be validated or it is not expedient to do so.

3274 Before a judge can investigate any case, a plea must be presented 'by a person whose interest is involved, or by the promotor of justice' (Can. 1501). The present canon determines who can present such a plea in marriage-nullity cases, and it represents a considerable simplification of the law of the 1917 Code, omitting some disqualifications given there. First and foremost the validity of a marriage can always be impugned by the spouses themselves (1°). This holds good whether they are baptised or not, whether they were the cause of the invalidity or not, and whether or not they are excommunicated.[4] The promotor of justice can also impugn the validity of a marriage (2°), but only in the exceptional circumstances where the following two situations coalesce: (a) the fact of nullity must already have become so publicly known that the public good may, in the promotor's judgement, be involved; (b) it must be impossible, or at least not expedient, to validate the marriage.

---

[1] Cf. Ap Sig decl 30.XII.1988: AAS 81(1989) 892–894; Jur 50(1990) 307–309.

[2] Ap Sig decr 6.IV.1973: Per 62(1973) 590–591; Apol 46(1973) 301–302.

[3] In a footnote to his article *The 'Forum of Most of the Proofs'* Jur 50 (1990) 305, Daneels, the Promotor of Justice at the Apostolic Signatura, states that the declaration of the Ap Sig of 6.IV.1973 'by its nature can be applied to the current canon 1673 4°'.

[4] Cf. Daneels *Il Diritto di Impugnare il Matrimonio (Cann. 1674–1675)* in *Il Processo Matrimoniale: Canonico* Libreria Editrice Vaticana 1988 144–146.

Can. 1675 §1 A marriage which was not challenged while both spouses were alive, cannot be challenged after the death of either or both of the spouses, unless the question of validity is prejudicial to the resolution of another controversy in either the canonical or the civil forum.

A marriage is dissolved by the death of one or both of the spouses; hence the general rule is that the validity of such a marriage should not be open to challenge. However, the law recognises that there can be cases where important consequences depend on the validity or invalidity of these marriages and so it allows them to be challenged in certain circumstances. If a decision on the question of validity is necessary to decide another controversy, in either the canonical or civil forum, then the marriage may be challenged even after the death of one or both spouses. An example would be where a question of inheritance depends on the legitimacy of an heir which in turn depends on the validity of the parents' marriage. The canon does not explicitly determine who can challenge the validity of the marriage in these cases, but it seems clear that the challenge could be made by the children of the marriage, heirs and others with a legitimate interest in the case.[1]

Can. 1675 §2 If a spouse should die during the course of a case, Can. 1518 is to be observed.

If a spouse dies during a case, Can. 1518 considers two possibilities: (a) if the case has not yet been concluded, the trial is to be suspended until 'a person whose interest is involved' resumes the suit. This could be the other spouse or an heir; (b) if the case has been concluded, the judge should proceed to the remaining steps of the trial, having first summoned the procurator, if there is one, or a representative of the deceased person.[2]

Article 3
The Office of Judges

Can. 1676 Before he accepts a case and whenever there appears to be hope of success, the judge is to use pastoral means to persuade the spouses that, if it is possible, they should perhaps validate their marriage and resume their conjugal life.

This canon is in keeping with the general principle of Can. 1446 about avoiding disputes and seeking solutions other than trials. In the context of marriage-nullity cases, the specific application of that principle, enshrined in this canon, is aptly expounded by a recent commentator in the following terms:

> 'An interesting instance of the pastoral influence of Vat. II on the new Code of Canon Law appears in the very approach of the Code to any plea for a declaration of nullity of marriage. A new canon, Can. 1676, puts ecclesiastical Judges on notice that, before accepting a case, they should always have an eye to the possibility of reconciliation between the couple whose differences have led one of them to approach the Marriage Tribunal.

> 'Those with experience in this matter will of course know that by the time a Tribunal is approached, it is often too late to consider reconciliation as a prac-

---
[1] Cf. Daneels art cit 150.
[2] Cf. Daneels art cit 151.

tical possibility, and the Code wisely obliges the Judge to attempt it only "whenever there appears to be hope of success". Nevertheless, the law remains as a salutary reminder that no Tribunal, certainly none of first instance, should ever take on a case without first at least considering whether there is room for pastoral measures aimed at restoring the conjugal life of the couple.

'This raises yet another point. In those instances where there is indeed a well-founded hope of a successful pastoral intervention, who should make that intervention? The Code says that "the Judge is to use pastoral means". In practice, the "Judge" will normally mean the Officialis. It can hardly be, however, that he should do this personally.

'Experience has taught that ecclesiastical Judges, especially if they be priests, are wise not to confuse – and particularly not to have others confuse – on the one hand, their judicial role and, on the other, their pastoral concern in other spheres. It would seem therefore that, in an appropriate case, the judge would prudently fulfil the obligation placed upon him by the law if he assigned the conduct of the pastoral intervention to some person or group other than himself, with a request that he be given a report in due course.'[1]

Can. 1677 §1 When the petition has been accepted, the presiding judge or the *ponens* is to proceed to the notification of the decree of summons, in accordance with Can. 1508.

3278 Once the petition has been accepted, either the presiding judge or the *ponens* is to notify the respondent and others who are obliged to appear, of the decree of summons to the trial 'in accordance with Can. 1508', i.e. he is to do so 'at once' (Can. 1508 §1), and a copy of the petition is to be attached to the summons 'unless for grave reasons the judge considers that the petition is not to be communicated to the other party before he or she gives evidence' (Can. 1508 §2). In this general context, see especially our commentary on Cann. 1507–1508.

Can. 1677 §2 On the expiry of fifteen days from the notification, the presiding judge or the *ponens* shall, unless one or other party requests a session for the joinder of the issue, within ten days by his decree determine *ex officio* the formulation of the doubt or doubts and notify the parties.

3279 When the parties have received notification of the summons they have fifteen days in which to request that the joinder of the issue take place at a formal session of the court, at which the parties can be at least represented. Either party can make such a request which, if made, should normally be granted. In fact, it is unusual in practice, especially in marriage-nullity cases, for either party to make this request. If none such is made within the prescribed time-limit, then the judge is himself, within a further ten days, i.e. within twenty-five days from the receipt by the parties of the notification of summons, to determine the terms of the precise issue to be decided by the court and to communicate these terms to the parties.

Can. 1677 §3 The formulation of the doubt is not only to ask whether the nullity of the particular marriage is proven, but also to determine the ground or grounds upon which the validity of the marriage is being challenged.

---

[1] Sheehy *Introducing a case of nullity of marriage: the new Code and the practice of local tribunals*: *Dilexit Iustitiam* ed. Grocholewski–Cartel Orti Vatican City 1984 339–340.

The formulation of the doubt must be specified i.e. it must determine the ground or grounds on which it is alleged this particular marriage is invalid; it is not sufficient that it ask generically whether the marriage is invalid. This does not mean that a ground originally alleged may not subsequently, in the course of the trial, be modified, dropped or substituted by another. What it does imply, however, is that if any such later alteration be considered necessary or advisable, it would then be required, for validity, that the prescribed procedure for the joinder of the issue be repeated, so that both parties and the defender of the bond be made clearly aware of the new situation (see Cann. 1513–1514).

Can. 1677 §4 After ten days from the notification of the decree, if the parties have not lodged any objection, the presiding judge or the *ponens* is by a new decree to arrange for the instruction of the case.

Within this period of ten days the parties are free to raise any objections they may have to the formulation of the doubt and can request that it be altered (see Can. 1513 §3). After this it can be changed only in accordance with Can. 1514. If there are no objections, the instruction of the case i.e. the formal enquiry into it, follows.

Article 4
Proofs

Can. 1678 §1 The defender of the bond, the legal respresentatives of the parties and, if involved in the trial, the promotor of justice also, have the right:

1° to be present at the examination of the parties, the witnesses and the experts, without prejudice to Can. 1559;

2° to inspect the judicial acts, even if they are not yet published, and to examine documents produced by the parties.

Those mentioned here have the right to be present at the examination of the parties, the witnesses and the experts. However the judge may, in accordance with Can. 1559 'determine that the proceedings are to be in secret' and disallow the presence even of the defender of the bond and the promotor of justice.[1] These same persons have also the right to inspect the judicial acts even before publication and to examine documents produced by the parties, i.e. they must on reasonable request be permitted fully to acquaint themselves of the state of the case as it proceeds.[2]

Can. 1678 §2 The parties cannot assist at the examination mentioned in §1 n.1.

The parties are not permitted to be present at the examination mentioned in §1 1°. This is to ensure the complete freedom of the other party, the witnesses and the experts during their examination. The parties' rights are protected by their legal representatives who can be present and can also inspect the acts.

---

[1] Cf. Comm 11(1979) 262–263 at Can. 342.
[2] The canon speaks of 'documents produced by the parties': what of documents secured *ex officio* by the court itself, e.g. written reports received from psychiatric, psychological or other medical experts? It would seem that such documents are equally open to the access referred to here, not least because their submission to the court will have required the consent of the party in question.

Can. 1679 Unless there are full proofs from other sources, then in addition to other indications and supportive elements, in order to weigh the depositions of the parties in accordance with Can. 1536 the judge is, if possible, to hear witnesses to the credibility of the parties themselves.

3284 Although the confessions and declarations of the parties do not of themselves have the force of full proof (see Can. 1536), in a marriage-nullity case they will often be of particular importance since, of the nature of the case, they will have knowledge hidden from anyone else. This will be particularly true in cases of simulation and deceit. Their testimony will however need corroboration, and one important source of this will be the evidence of character witnesses. The judge is instructed to seek such testimony if this can be done.

Can. 1680 In cases concerning impotence or defect of consent by reason of mental illness, the judge is to use the services of one or more experts, unless from the circumstances this would obviously serve no purpose. In other cases, the provision of Can. 1574 is to be observed.

3285 Can. 1574 calls for the use of experts 'whenever, by a provision of the law or of the judge, their study and opinion, based upon their art or science, are required to establish some fact or to ascertain the true nature of some matter'. The present canon is an example of where their use is called for by the law. In two cases this is mandatory: cases of impotence (where expert medical testimony is needed) and cases of defect of consent by reason of mental illness, unless, in both cases, the use of an expert would serve no purpose, i.e. either because there is manifestly nothing for the expert to investigate, or because the matter is already fully proven.

3286 There has been some controversy as to whether expert testimony is required by the law in the case of the defects of consent mentioned in Can. 1095 2° and 3°. This hinges on what is meant by the term 'mental illness', and many have argued that because more or less transitory personality disorders can cause nullity and because these are not 'mental illnesses' in the strict sense, there is no established need for experts in these cases. The view of this commentary is that it would be at least rash for a judge to decide in advance that in a particular case he is not faced with a mental illness, however that is to be defined. Moreover, he needs the services of the expert to decide what effect the person's condition, however it may be termed, has had on his or her consent. To prejudge either of these issues is to trespass on the expert's field and to risk making inadequately based decisions. This is not to say that expert evidence is always needed in these cases; it may well happen that the case is adequately proven without the expert evidence, especially where the disorder in question is florid and obviously manifest.[1]

3287 Whether or not the law requires the use of experts, the judge can always decide, in accordance with Can. 1574, that this is necessary in any marriage-nullity case.

Article 5
The Judgement and the Appeal

Can. 1681 Whenever in the course of the instruction of a case a very probable doubt arises that the marriage has not been consummated, the tribunal

---

[1] For a detailed commentary on this point, cf. McGrath *At the service of the truth: psychological sciences and their relation to the Canon Law of nullity of marriage* Stud Can 27(1993) 379–400, and the many authors cited therein.

can, having with the consent of the parties suspended the nullity case, complete the instruction for a dispensation from a non-consummated marriage, and in due course forward the acts to the Apostolic See, together with a petition for a dispensation from either or both of the spouses, and with the opinions of the tribunal and of the Bishop.

This canon permits the transition from the judicial process of nullity to the administrative investigation of a possibly non-consummated marriage. The grounds of nullity are not strictly relevant but the possibility would arise most readily in cases of impotence, defect of consent, or force and fear. There must be a 'very probable doubt' that the marriage was not consummated and both parties must consent to the suspension of the nullity case, even though only one of them need petition for a dispensation from the non-consummated marriage. Once the nullity issue has been suspended the case is completed in accordance with Cann. 1697–1706. 3288

Can. 1682 §1 The judgement which has first declared the nullity of a marriage, together with the appeals, if there are any, and the other judicial acts, are to be sent *ex officio* to the appeal tribunal within twenty days of the publication of the judgement.

The 1917 Code at c.1986 obliged the defender of the bond to appeal the first judgement which declared the nullity of a marriage. In the present Code this has been replaced by an automatic recourse whereby the tribunal which gave the judgement, *whether at first or second instance*, is itself obliged to send the judgement, the judicial acts and any appeals there may be, to the appropriate appeal tribunal within twenty days of the publication of the judgement. From this it can be seen that, even though there is this automatic recourse, the parties and the defender of the bond still retain their right of appeal in accordance with Cann. 1628–1640. 3289

Can. 1682 §2 If the judgement in favour of the nullity of the marriage was given in first instance, the appeal tribunal, after weighing the observations of the defender of the bond and, if there are any, of the parties, is by its decree either to ratify the decision without delay, or to admit the case to ordinary examination in the new instance.

If the judgement in favour of nullity was given in first instance, the appeal tribunal has two options. After weighing the observations of its own defender of the bond and, if there are such, of the parties, either it may by decree confirm the decision of the first instance tribunal immediately,[1] or it may admit the case to the full normal hearing at second instance. Obviously where the first option can be used – when the case is quite clear – there is a great saving of time and work. It is to be noted that this option of ratifying by decree is available only when the judgement in favour of nullity was given *at first instance*. If it was given at second instance, the third instance court must admit the case to ordinary examination. 3290

Can. 1683 If a new ground of nullity of marriage is advanced in the appeal grade, the tribunal can admit it and give judgement on it as at first instance.

A ground of nullity not hitherto advanced may be proposed at an appeal court and, if the tribunal admits it, this ground is then decided as at first instance. This could allow a ratification by decree by the third instance court, which would be hearing this ground as at second instance. 3291

---

[1] The decree must express, at least in summary form, the reasons in law and in fact on which the decision is based – cf. DVCom rep 14.II.1974: AAS 66(1974) 463; CLD 8 109.

Can. 1684 §1 After the judgement which first declared the nullity of the marriage has been confirmed on appeal, either by decree or by another judgement, those whose marriage has been declared invalid may contract a new marriage as soon as the decree or the second judgement has been notified to them, unless there is a prohibition of this appended to the judgement or decree itself, or imposed by the local Ordinary.

3292 When the first sentence declaring nullity has been confirmed, whether by decree or by another judgement, as soon as the parties have had the decree of judgement notified to them (but not before), they are free to contract a new marriage,[1] unless this has been expressly prohibited. This prohibition, or *vetitum* as it is called, may be attached to the judgement or decree or it may be imposed by the local Ordinary in virtue of Can. 1077 §1. A prohibition may be imposed by the tribunal e.g. in cases of absolute impotence, cases involving mental illness or serious personality disorder, cases of simulation. Some prohibitions, e.g. in the case of absolute impotence, or serious mental illness, will of their nature be well-nigh irremovable since the condition which gave rise to them is a permanent one. Others may be lifted in the course of time, e.g. with growing maturity or after appropriate therapy. Strictly speaking, if a prohibition has been imposed by a tribunal, its removal should also be judicial, but in practice most tribunals remit the task of removal to the local Ordinary. A prohibition does not of itself affect the validity of a subsequent marriage, but the condition which gave rise to it may well render a second marriage invalid just as it did the first one.

3293 There is some evidence of a tendency to disregard, or at least to regard as of little importance, the implications of a *vetitum*, often on the simplistic ground that it does not affect the validity of a subsequent marriage. From a pastoral point of view, any such tendency is dangerously imprudent and unhelpful. The purpose of a *vetitum* is twofold: (a) to protect the sacrament of marriage, and (b) to alert a future possibly unsuspecting or perhaps even deceived spouse to the problems which occasioned the breakdown of the previous union. The removal of a *vetitum* by the competent local Ordinary or his delegate should never therefore be simply a matter of course – it should always involve a serious investigation, normally demanding expert advice; moreover, even apart from the obvious cases of irremediable defect, there will certainly be cases in which the prudent judgement of the Ordinary will dictate a refusal to remove the prohibition and consequently a decision not to permit the then-proposed marriage.[2]

Can. 1684 §2 The provisions of Can. 1644 are to be observed even if the judgement which declared the nullity of the marriage is confirmed not by a second judgement, but by a decree.

3294 Cases concerning the status of persons – and these include marriage cases – never become an adjudged matter (see Can. 1643). Accordingly, the rules of Can. 1644 concerning the reopening of such cases and the suspension of the execution of the judgement are to be observed even when the first judgement was confirmed not by another judgement but by a decree.

---

[1] This is a modification of the rule of c.1987 of the 1917 Code which prescribed that, subject to a decision by the defender of the bond not to appeal further, the parties might enter a new marriage only 'when a period of ten days had elapsed' from their being informed of the decision. The reason for the removal of this apparently prudent limitation is not clear.

[2] Any such decision by one local Ordinary must be respected by any other local Ordinary whom the parties might subsequently approach in this regard; it ought not to be reversed except for a very grave reason: in this regard cf. in particular Can. 65.

Can. 1685 As soon as the judgement is executed, the judicial Vicar must notify it to the Ordinary of the place where the marriage was celebrated. This Ordinary must ensure that a record of the decree of nullity of the marriage, and of any prohibition imposed, is as soon as possible entered in the registers of marriage and baptism.

Can. 535 §2 lays down that the baptismal register is to contain a note concerning the canonical status of the person, and in particular concerning his or her marriage. The present canon directs the judicial Vicar of the tribunal which gave the second judgement or decree in favour of nullity[1] to notify the Ordinary of the place where the marriage was celebrated that a decree of nullity has been issued. In turn, that Ordinary is to ensure that the decree of nullity, together with any prohibition imposed, is recorded as soon as possible in the relevant marriage and baptismal registers, whether or not these be within his jurisidiction.[2]

Article 6
The Documentary Process

Can. 1686 On receiving a petition in accordance with Can. 1677, the judicial Vicar or a judge designated by him, can omit the formalities of the ordinary process and, having summoned the parties, and with the intervention of the defender of the bond, declare the nullity of the marriage by a judgement, if from a document which is not open to any contradiction or exception there is certain proof of the existence of a diriment impediment or a defect of form, which it is equally certain has not been dispensed from, or of the lack of a valid proxy mandate.

The process referred to here is a simplified and shortened procedure which can be used only in certain well-defined circumstances:

(a) it can be used only in certain types of cases, i.e. where the marriage is alleged to be invalid by reason of a diriment impediment, a defect of form or the lack of a valid proxy mandate. Marriages which may be invalid due to a defect of consent are excluded.[3] In the first two cases mentioned, the investigation must assure itself that no dispensation was given, e.g. in consanguinity, or in form (see Can. 1127 §§1–2).

(b) The invalidity of the marriage must be proved with certainty by a document which is beyond exception or objection. In cases of defect of form, if the parties who were bound by the form attempted marriage before a non-catholic minister or civil official, even this process is not necessary, and the matter can be dealt with in the course of the normal premarriage investigation.[4]

The judge is to summon the parties (normally a written intimation will be sufficient); the defender of the bond is to be involved and make appropriate observations; finally, the judge is to issue a judgement, stating the reasons in law and in fact for his decision.

---

[1] In practice as between first and second instance tribunals, this obligation is often as a matter of efficient convenience fulfilled in collaboration with the judicial Vicar at first instance.

[2] Experience has taught that the importance of this cross-registration cannot be overstressed. In terms of the pastoral implications involved, its implementation should therefore be a particular concern of every local Ordinary.

[3] Cf. Comm 11(1979) 269 at Can. 351.

[4] Cf. CCom rep 20.VI.1984: AAS 76(1984) 747.

Book VII Judicial Procedures

If he finds himself unable to issue an affirmative decision using the documentary process, he does not issue a negative decision but should rather remit the case to the ordinary process.

Can. 1687 §1 If the defender of the bond prudently judges that the defects mentioned in Can. 1686, or the lack of dispensation, are not certain, he must appeal to the judge of second instance. The acts must be sent to the appeal judge and he is to be informed in writing that it is a documentary process.

§2 A party who considers himself or herself injured retains the right of appeal.

3298 In contrast to the automatic recourse required by Can. 1682 in ordinary cases, there is no such requirement in the documentary process. However, the defender can appeal against the sentence if he prudently considers that the defects mentioned in Can. 1686 are not established or that there is some doubt about the lack of a dispensation (§1). The parties, if they consider themselves injured, also retain their right of appeal (§2). If there is an appeal, the acts of the case are to be sent to the appeal tribunal with a formal written notification that the case is a documentary one (§1).

Can. 1688 The judge of second instance, with the intervention of the defender of the bond and after consulting the parties, is to decide in the same way as in Can. 1686 whether the judgement is to be ratified, or whether the case should rather proceed according to the ordinary course of law, in which event he is to send the case back to the tribunal of first instance.

3299 In the event of an appeal the sole judge at second instance is to decide the case, with the intervention of the defender of the bond, in accordance with the procedure of Can. 1686. He may decide to ratify the decision of first instance, or he may decide that the case should be heard according to the ordinary full process, in which event he is to send it back to the tribunal of first instance for hearing there. As with the judge of first instance, he does not issue a negative decision.

Article 7
General Norms

Can. 1689 In the judgement the parties are to be reminded of the moral and also the civil obligations by which they may be bound, both towards one another and in regard to the support and upbringing of their children.

3300 The granting of a decree of nullity in no way removes the natural or civil obligations between the parties (e.g. the duty to provide support) or towards their children. Accordingly, in the judgement the parties are to be formally and specifically reminded of these obligations. This is true whether the judgement comes from the full ordinary process or from the documentary process. It is a feature of the new Code to which adequate attention should be directed.

Can. 1690 Cases for the declaration of nullity of marriage cannot be dealt with by the oral contentious process.

3301 Can. 1425 §1 1° reserves the hearing of marriage-nullity cases (apart from those dealt with in Cann. 1686 and 1688), to a collegiate tribunal, thereby implicitly ruling out

Part III Certain Special Processes

the use of the oral contentious process in such cases. This canon makes that prohibition explicit.[1] The oral process referred to is that dealt with in Cann. 1656–1670.

Can. 1691 In other matters concerning the conduct of the process, the canons concerning processes in general and concerning the ordinary contentious process are to be applied, unless the nature of the case demands otherwise; the special norms concerning cases dealing with the status of persons and cases pertaining to the public good are also to be observed.

Marriage-nullity cases are ordinary contentious processes for which special norms have been laid down. Accordingly the rules for trials in general (Cann. 1400–1500) and those for the ordinary contentious process (Cann. 1501–1655) are to be applied to them, 'unless the nature of the case demands otherwise'. The canon also calls attention to the need to observe the special norms for cases concerning the status of persons (e.g. Can. 1492 §1) and cases concerning the public good (e.g. Can. 1598 §1), since marriage-nullity cases come under both these headings.   3302

Chapter II
CASES CONCERNING THE SEPARATION OF SPOUSES

Can. 1692 §1 Unless lawfully provided otherwise in particular places, the personal separation of baptised spouses can be decided by a decree of the diocesan Bishop or by the judgement of a judge in accordance with the following canons.

The duty of married couples to live a conjugal life and the reasons for separation, permanent or temporary, are dealt with in Cann. 1151–1155. Leaving aside any provisions of particular law, there are two methods of legal separation: administrative, by a decree of the diocesan Bishop and judicial, by the judgement of a judge in accordance with the canons which follow.   3303

Can. 1692 §2 Where the ecclesiastical decision does not produce civil effects, or if it is foreseen that there will be a civil judgement not contrary to the divine law, the Bishop of the diocese in which the spouses are living can, in the light of their particular circumstances, give them permission to approach the civil courts.

§3 If the case is also concerned with the merely civil effects of marriage, the judge is to endeavour, having observed the provision of §2, to have the case brought before the civil court from the very beginning.

In a separation of a married couple there will always be important considerations of division of property, maintenance, custody and maintenance of children etc. Since canon law, for the most part, has no civil effects and is in any event without the means of enforcing any provisions a judge may make on these matters, the law allows the Bishop to give permission for the couple to approach the civil courts in order to secure their rights in these matters. Indeed, where the main area of concern is the merely civil   3304

---

[1] The reasons given for this prohibition were that since the oral contentious process is altogether new, it would be dangerous to have a sudden change of such gravity in so serious matter, and that with the simplifications introduced in the ordinary process the argument that this process is needed to speed up cases loses much of its cogency: Comm 11(1979) 271 at Can. 354.

effects of marriage, the judge is to try to have the case brought before the civil court from the start. In practice (except perhaps in countries operating under a concordat with the Holy See), requests to have the matter dealt with by the civil courts are about as rare as canonical judicial separation cases, in effect almost non-existent.

Can. 1693 §1 The oral contentious process is to be used, unless either party or the promotor of justice requests the ordinary contentious process.

§2 If the ordinary contentious process is used and there is an appeal, the tribunal of second instance is to proceed in accordance with Can. 1682 §2, observing what has to be observed.

3305 The choice of whether to proceed administratively or judicially is for the Ordinary to decide, either *ex officio* or at the request of the parties.[1] The process of choice in judicial separation cases is the oral contentious process of Cann. 1656–1670. The ordinary contentious process may be used if either party or the promotor of justice requests this. In the event of an appeal, if the oral process was used at first instance, it will also be used at second; if the ordinary contentious process was used, the appeal is to proceed in accordance with Can. 1682 §2 i.e. the first instance decision may be confirmed by decree or, if this is deemed necessary, the case is admitted to ordinary examination at the second instance.

Can. 1694 In matters concerning the competence of the tribunal, the provisions of Can. 1673 are to be observed.

3306 The rules for legal competence in judicial separation cases are the same as those for marriage-nullity cases as stated in Can. 1673.

Can. 1695 Before he accepts the case, and whenever there appears to be hope of success, the judge is to use pastoral means to induce the spouses to be reconciled and to resume their conjugal life.

3307 This canon corresponds to Can. 1676 concerning marriage-nullity cases and obliges the judge, whenever there appears to be a hope of success, to avail of pastoral means to effect a reconciliation and a resumption of common life.

Can. 1696 Cases of separation of spouses also concern the public good; the promotor of justice must, therefore, always intervene, in accordance with Can. 1433.

3308 Since separation cases concern the public good, the promotor of justice is to be summoned. If he is not summoned or did not in fact fulfil his role, the acts of the case are null (see Can. 1433).

Chapter III
THE PROCESS FOR THE DISPENSATION FROM A RATIFIED AND NON-CONSUMMATED MARRIAGE

Can. 1697 The spouses alone, or indeed one of them even if the other is unwilling, have the right to seek the favour of a dispensation from a ratified and non-consummated marriage.

---

[1] CCom rep 25.VI.1932: AAS 24(1932) 284; CLD I 554.

Part III Certain Special Processes

A marriage which is 'merely ratified' in the sense of Can. 1061 §1 can be dissolved, or, to use the technical term, dispensed from. Only the parties have the right to seek this dispensation, either both together, or just one of them even if the other objects. Only in the case where one party opposes the petition is there a respondent in the case. The procedure is administrative, not judicial, and it is controlled by an instructor, not a judge, usually at diocesan level. When the case has been properly instructed at local level, the petition and the acts are sent to the Congregation for Divine Worship and the Discipline of the Sacraments, which may or may not recommend to the Pope the granting of the dispensation.[1]

3309

Can. 1698 §1 Only the Apostolic See gives judgement on the fact of the non-consummation of a marriage and on the existence of a just reason for granting the dispensation.

The local process is confined to instructing the case in accordance with the regulations. Only the Apostolic See – through the Congregation for Divine Worship and the Discipline of the Sacraments – is legally competent to judge whether in fact a particular marriage was not consummated and whether there is a sufficient reason for granting the dispensation.

3310

Can. 1698 §2 The dispensation, however, is granted by the Roman Pontiff alone.

The vicarious power by which the Roman Pontiff can grant this dispensation is stated in Can. 1142. A suggestion that this power be extended to Bishops was not admitted, as it was judged 'opportune that the Roman Pontiff should grant such a dispensation personally'.[2]

3311

Can. 1699 §1 The diocesan Bishop of the place of domicile or quasi-domicile of the petitioner is competent to accept the petition seeking the dispensation. If the request is well founded, he must arrange for the instruction of the process.

Although the petition is addressed to the Holy Father, the diocesan Bishop of the domicile or quasi-domicile of the petitioner (or petitioners) is legally competent to accept it and to arrange for the instruction of the case. He does not need prior authorisation from the Apostolic See to do either. In the case where the question of non-consummation arises during a marriage-nullity case, the tribunal which was hearing the marriage case is to proceed with the instruction of the non-consummation case (see Can. 1681).

3312

Can. 1699 §2 If, however, the proposed case has special difficulties of a juridical or moral order, the diocesan Bishop is to consult the Apostolic See.

The purpose of this norm is not to limit the Bishop's authority but rather to provide assistance in cases of special difficulty of either a juridical or a moral order. A circular letter issued by the Congregation of Sacraments in 1986 gave examples of cases with such special difficulties. They included cases where intercourse was performed only with contraceptives, where there was penetration without ejaculation, where a child

3313

---

[1] A lit circ from SCSac of 20.XII.1986 *De Processu Super Matrimonio Rato et non Consummato*: ME 112 (1987) 423–429, explains succinctly the process of preparing the case according to the Code. For an English translation, cf. Woestman *Special Marriage Cases* Ottawa St Paul University 1990 119–126.

[2] Comm 11(1979) 275 at Can. 363.

was conceived by absorption without penetration, where there was artificial insemination, where there was danger of scandal or financial harm attaching to the grant of the dispensation.[1]

Can. 1699 §3 Recourse to the Apostolic See is available against the decree of a Bishop who rejects the petition.

3314 If the diocesan Bishop refuses to entertain the petition, recourse may freely be had to the Congregation, setting out the reasons for the complaint.

Can. 1700 §1 Without prejudice to the provisions of Can. 1681, the Bishop is to assign the instruction of these processes, in a stable manner or case by case, to his own tribunal or to that of another diocese, or to a suitable priest.

3315 The Bishop is given wide powers of choice in the instruction of non-consummation cases. He can assign these cases, either in a stable manner or case by case, to his own tribunal, to the tribunal of another diocese (or to an interdiocesan or regional tribunal) or to a suitable priest. The options given here can be useful in allowing different cases to be assigned to different instructors for reasons of prudence or for pastoral considerations. However, when the possibility of a non-consummation case arises during a nullity case, it must be instructed by the tribunal which was hearing the nullity case (see Can. 1681).

Can. 1700 §2 If, however, a judicial plea has been introduced to declare the nullity of the same marriage, the instruction of the process is to be assigned to the same tribunal.

3316 The canon envisages the case where nullity and non-consummation of the same marriage are alleged simultaneously. In such a situation, both cases are to be instructed by the one tribunal.

Can. 1701 §1 In these processes the defender of the bond must always intervene.

3317 The defender of the bond must intervene in these cases in accordance with Can. 1433. His function is to raise any objections, about substantial issues or about procedural matters, that can reasonably be made to the dissolution of the marriage.

Can. 1701 §2 An advocate is not admitted, but the Bishop can, because of the difficulty of a case, allow the petitioner or respondent to have the assistance of an expert in the law.

3318 Since the procedure involved here is an administrative one seeking a favour, not a judicial one to obtain a right, there is no place in it for an advocate. However, the Bishop can allow either party to have the services of a legal expert if the case is a difficult one. This expert does not present pleadings as an advocate would in a nullity case; he simply advises the party or parties.

Can. 1702 In the instruction of the process both spouses are to be heard. As far as possible, and provided they can be reconciled with the nature of these processes, the canons concerning the collection of proofs in the ordinary contentious process and in cases of nullity of marriage are to be followed.

3319 Since the parties are often the only people who know all the facts, it is obviously important that both of them be heard. Two essential facts have to be proved: the fact

---

[1] Cf. Woestman op cit 121.

Part III Certain Special Processes

of non-consummation, and the existence of a sufficient reason for the granting of a dispensation. Where there is no physical evidence of non-consummation and the basis for proving it is what is called the 'moral argument', it will be important to have witnesses as to the moral character and credibility of the parties (see Can. 1679). If the principal evidence of non-consummation is physical, medical experts will obviously have to be called to attest to this fact. Although the process is not a judicial one, the present canon states that, as far as possible and insofar as they can be reconciled with the non-consummation process, the canons on the collection of proof in the ordinary process (Cann. 1526–1583) and in the marriage nullity process (Cann. 1678–1680) are to be followed.

Can. 1703 §1 There is no publication of the acts, but if the judge sees that, because of the proofs tendered, a serious obstacle stands in the way of the plea of the petitioner or the exception of the respondent, he is prudently to make it known to the party concerned.

§2 To the party requesting it the judge can show a document which has been presented or evidence which has been received, and he can set a time for the production of arguments.

Since this is not a judicial procedure, there is no publication of the acts.[1] However, the instructor – in this canon referred to as the judge – may inform the party concerned of any serious obstacle in the way of the petitioner's plea or the respondent's exception. Likewise, he can show the party who requests it a document presented or evidence received, and can set a time for the matter to be discussed.[2]

Can. 1704 §1 When the instruction is completed, the instructor is to give all the acts, together with a suitable report, to the Bishop. The Bishop is to express his opinion on the merits of the case in relation to the alleged fact of non-consummation, the adequacy of the reason for dispensation, and the opportuneness of the favour.

§2 If the instruction of the process has been entrusted to another tribunal in accordance with Can. 1700, the observations in favour of the bond of marriage are to be prepared in that same tribunal. The opinion spoken of in §1 is, however, the province of the Bishop who gave the commission and the instructor is to give him, together with the acts, a suitable report on the case.

On the completion of the instruction, the defender of the bond is 'to put forward and explain everything that can be reasonably proposed against the granting of the dispensation'.[3] Where another tribunal has been given the task of the instruction, it is the defender of the bond of this tribunal who should intervene and make his observations. The instructor sends all the acts, together with a suitable report, to the Bishop who is to give his opinion on the case under three headings: the alleged fact of non-consummation, the adequacy of the reason for the dispensation and the opportuneness of the favour. In all cases, this is the Bishop who gave the original commission. However, when the case resulted from a transfer from the judicial to the administrative procedure, the opinion is to be drawn up by the Bishop of the relevant

---

[1] Cf. Comm 11(1979) 277–278 at Can. 368.
[2] There is some dispute as to whether the legal expert mentioned in Can. 1701 §2 can examine the acts of the case. In view of Can. 1705 §3 which allows him to do so in the specific case mentioned there, there seems to be no good reason why he should not do so: cf. Chiappetta II n.5235.
[3] Cf. Woestman op cit 124.

tribunal, having where appropriate sought the advice of the petitioner's Bishop, at least in regard to the opportuneness of granting the dispensation.[1]

Can. 1705 §1 The Bishop is to transmit all the acts to the Apostolic See, together with his opinion and the observations of the defender of the Bond.

3322 The Bishop is to send all the acts, together with his own opinion and the observations of the defender of the bond to the Apostolic See, specifically to the Congregation for Divine Worship and the Discipline of the Sacraments.[2]

Can. 1705 §2 If, in the judgement of the Apostolic See, a supplementary instruction is required, this will be notified to the Bishop, with a statement of the items on which the acts are to be supplemented.

3323 The Congregation may decide that the instruction of the case is incomplete and in this case it will notify the Bishop, stating the points on which supplementary instruction is needed. Such supplementary material should be returned to the Holy See with a minimum of delay.

Can. 1705 §3 If, however, the answer of the Apostolic See is that the non-consummation is not proven from the proofs submitted, then the expert in law mentioned in Can. 1701 §2 can inspect the acts of the case, though not the opinion of the Bishop, in the tribunal office, in order to decide whether anything further of importance can be adduced to justify another submission of the petition.

3324 If the decision of the Apostolic See is negative, the expert in law mentioned in Can. 1701 §2 may inspect the acts of the case – not however the Bishop's opinion. He or she may then, if it is considered fit, propose anything of importance which might justify another submission of the petition, such as further evidence, the re-examination of this person or that, etc. It is to be noted that the legal expert mentioned is not the only person who may conduct such a review: obviously it may be done by the Bishop himself, and of course at his request by any of his advisers, not least by his judicial Vicar.

Can. 1706 The rescript of dispensation is sent by the Apostolic See to the Bishop. He is to notify the parties of the rescript, and also as soon as possible direct the parish priests of the place where the marriage was contracted and of the place where baptism was received, to make a note of the granting of the dispensation in the registers of marriage and baptism.

3325 If the Congregation judges the non-consummation of the marriage proved and the reason for the dispensation adequate, it will present the case to the Pope, who, if he judges it opportune, will grant the dispensation. This is notified to the Bishop by rescript. In the grant of the dispensation, there may be a clause forbidding one or other party to contract another marriage. Removal of this prohibition may be reserved to the Congregation, or it may be remitted to the Bishop subject to the conditions laid down in the rescript. The Bishop is required to notify the parties of the rescript and of its terms. He is furthermore to see to it as soon as possible that the fact of the dispensation is duly noted in the marriage and baptismal registers.[3]

---

[1] op cit 125.

[2] The acts should be typed, the pages numbered, bound and indexed, and there should be three copies authenticated by a notary.

[3] In this regard cf. commentary on Can. 1684 §1 and footnote thereto.

Chapter IV
THE PROCESS IN THE CASE OF THE PRESUMED DEATH OF A SPOUSE

Can. 1707 §1 Whenever the death of a spouse cannot be proven by an authentic ecclesiastical or civil document, the other spouse is not regarded as free from the bond of marriage until the diocesan Bishop has issued a declaration that death is presumed.

This canon has no precedent in the 1917 Code, but is based on and summarises the procedure which was then in force.[1] When a spouse is believed or alleged to be dead, before the surviving spouse is regarded as free from the bond of marriage – and therefore free to marry again – the death must be proved by an authentic death certificate, ecclesiastical or civil, or the diocesan Bishop of the surviving spouse must issue a declaration presuming that death has taken place. One possible exception to this rule would be the special provision of Can. 1068 allowing the parties in danger of death to declare their freedom to marry, under oath if necessary. However, in this case one party or the other would have to know, and not just believe, that the former spouse was dead before being able to make the necessary declaration.

Can. 1707 §2 The diocesan Bishop can give the declaration mentioned in §1 only if, after making suitable investigations, he has reached moral certainty concerning the death of the spouse from the depositions of witnesses, from hearsay and from other indications. The mere absence of the spouse, no matter for how long a period, is not sufficient.

Before issuing the declaration mentioned in §1 the Bishop must reach moral certainty (i.e. a degree of certainty which though perhaps short of absolute certainty, excludes all reasonable doubt) about the fact of death. He does this by an appropriate investigation which will involve hearing from witnesses, weighing up rumour and hearsay which is based on facts, forming presumptions from such circumstances as the person's relationship with his or her family, his or her normal mode of behaviour, his or her possible involvement in natural or other disasters, etc. On its own, the absence of the spouse for however long a time is not a canonical proof or even presumption, but if e.g. the absence is shown to have begun at the time of some disaster, or if such an absence is altogether out of keeping with what is known of the person's character and behaviour, then weight can certainly be attributed to it. The intervention of the defender of the bond is not mandatory in these cases,[2] but it is not excluded and in certain situations the Bishop may well consider it helpful.

Can. 1707 §3 In uncertain and involved cases, the Bishop is to consult the Apostolic See.

If after the appropriate investigation the Bishop is still uncertain, or if the case is a particularly involved one, he is to consult the Apostolic See, specifically the Congregation for Divine Worship and the Discipline of the Sacraments, whose worldwide experience can provide a sure guide.

---

[1] This is to be found in the SCHO instr *Matrimonii Vinculo* of 1868: cf. Gasparri *Codicis Iuris Canonici Fontes* Rome 1926 4 306–309; Woestman op cit 139–142. For a discussion on the relationship between this document and the present Code, and for an overview of the present law, cf. Said *De Processu Praesumptae Mortis Coniugis* in *Dilexit Iustitiam* ed. Grocholewski–Cartel Orti Rome 1984 433–455.

[2] Cf. Comm 11(1979) 282 at §4.

Title II
Cases for the Declaration of Nullity of Sacred Ordination

Can. 1708 The right to impugn the validity of sacred ordination is held by the cleric himself, or by the Ordinary to whom the cleric is subject, or by the Ordinary in whose diocese he was ordained.

3329 The corresponding title in the 1917 Code dealt not only with nullity of sacred ordination, but also with cases concerning the obligations arising from ordination. These latter are now dealt with administratively in accordance with Cann. 290–293. The right to challenge the validity of an individual's ordination is acknowledged only to three persons: the man himself, the Ordinary, diocesan or religious, to whom he is subject, and the Ordinary *in whose territory he was ordained*. Others who believe a particular ordination to be invalid cannot challenge it themselves but could, and indeed should, bring the matter to the attention of the appropriate Ordinary.[1]

Can. 1709 §1 The petition must be sent to the competent Congregation, which will decide whether the case is to be determined by that Congregation of the Roman Curia, or by a tribunal designated by it.

3330 The petition impugning the validity of an ordination must be sent to the Congregation for Divine Worship and the Discipline of the Sacraments, the dicastery competent to judge such cases.[2] The Congregation may decide to settle the case administratively, or may decide on doing so judicially, when it will designate a tribunal to adjudicate the case.

Can. 1709 §2 Once the petition has been sent, the cleric is by the law itself forbidden to exercise orders.

3331 If a cleric has serious doubts about the validity of his ordination, he himself should avoid exercising his orders because of the probable invalidity of his acts. Once he becomes aware that a petition in this regard has been sent to the Holy See, the law itself forbids him any further exercise of his orders.

Can. 1710 If the Congregation remits the case to a tribunal, the canons concerning trials in general and the ordinary contentious trial are to be observed, unless the nature of the matter requires otherwise and without prejudice to the provisions of this title.

3332 The judicial process which examines the validity of ordination is a particular form of contentious trial and so follows the rules for all contentious trials, in so far as these are applicable to the case and are in keeping with the canons of the present title. In particular it should be noted that, as prescribed by Can. 1425 §1 1°, this process calls for a collegiate tribunal of three judges.[3]

---

[1] There is some dispute about the right of the promotor of justice to impugn the validity of ordination: cf. Chiappetta II n.5256. He could certainly bring the matter to the Ordinary's attention.

[2] Cf. PB art 68.

[3] It seems fitting that all three judges should be priests, although this is not explicitly laid down in the Code. Cf. Can. 483 §2 where in a case in which the reputation of a priest could be involved, even the notary must be a priest.

Can. 1711 In these cases the defender of the bond has the same rights and is bound by the same duties as the defender of the bond of marriage.

The function of the defender of the bond in ordination cases is the same as that in marriage cases. He is to raise any objections, whether about substantial issues or about procedural matters, which can reasonably be made to the declaration of nullity of ordination. No explicit mention is made here of the promotor of justice. This does not mean that he is excluded; rather it is for the Ordinary to decide whether his intervention is required (see Can. 1431 §1).

Can. 1712 After a second judgement confirming the nullity of the sacred ordination, the cleric loses all rights proper to the clerical state and is freed from all its obligations.

When a second judgement confirming the nullity of ordination has been issued, the effects noted here take place: the cleric loses all rights proper to the clerical state and also ceases to be bound by all its obligations, including the obligation of celibacy. Strictly speaking, since the ordination in question was declared null, the individual in question never had the rights nor was bound by the obligations.

Since cases of this kind concern the status of persons, they never become an adjudged matter (see Can. 1643) and so even after two conforming sentences, if there is new and serious evidence, there may be recourse to an appeal tribunal (see Can. 1644 §1).

Title III
Ways of Avoiding Trials

Can. 1713 In order to avoid judicial disputes, settlement or reconciliation can profitably be adopted, or the controversy can be submitted to the judgement of one or more arbiters.

Can. 1446 speaks of the duty of all of Christ's faithful, but especially of Bishops and judges, to see to the settling of disputes among the people of God promptly and without rancour. This general principle is reiterated in Can. 1676 with specific regard to marriage-nullity cases and in Can. 1695 regarding separation cases. Two methods of avoiding trials are proposed in the present canon:

(a) Reconciliation or settlement. Settlement has been defined as 'An agreement or compromise between litigants to settle the matters in dispute between them and conclude their litigation. The terms of the settlement may be incorporated in a consent to judgement to which the court grants authority, or in a contract between the parties'.[1]

(b) Arbitration: 'submission of a dispute to the decision of a person, other than a court of competent jurisdiction'.[2]

---

[1] Walker *The Oxford Companion to Law* Oxford 1980 s.v. *settlement*.
[2] Ibid. s.v. *arbitration*.

In a settlement the parties agree between themselves on the terms resolving their disagreement, with or without the help of one or more mediators. In binding arbitration the parties agree beforehand to accept the decision of the arbiter or arbiters.

Can. 1714 The norms for settlements, for mutual promises to abide by an arbiter's award, and for arbitral judgements are to be selected by the parties. If the parties have not chosen any, they are to use the law established by the Bishops' Conference, if such exists, or the civil law in force in the place where the pact is made.

3337 The norms for settlements and arbitration can be: (a) those agreed and chosen by the parties themselves; (b) those determined by the local Bishops' Conference, if there are such;[1] (c) those of the local civil law.

Can. 1715 §1 Settlements and mutual promises to abide by an arbiter's award cannot validly be employed in matters which pertain to the public good, and in other matters in which the parties are not free to make such arrangements.

3338 Certain matters are excluded from the solutions being considered here. Matters pertaining to the public good cannot be the subject of settlement or arbitration: thus e.g. they cannot be used in marriage-nullity cases. Neither can they be used in private cases where the parties are not free to make such arrangements, e.g. where a person has not the use of reason and so cannot manage his or her own affairs.

Can. 1715 §2 Whenever the matter concerned demands it, in questions concerning temporal ecclesiastical goods the formalities established by the law for the alienation of ecclesiastical goods are to be observed.

3339 Although in cases concerning temporal ecclesiastical goods (see Can. 1257 §1) settlement and arbitration may be used, the formalities required by the law for their alienation must be observed (see Cann. 1291–1298, 638, 741, 1190).

Can. 1716 §1 If the civil law does not recognise the force of an arbitral judgement unless it is confirmed by a judge, an arbitral judgement in an ecclesiastical controversy has no force in the canonical forum unless it is confirmed by an ecclesiastical judge of the place in which it was given.

§2 If, however, the civil law admits of a challenge to an arbitral judgement before a civil judge, the same challenge may be brought in the canonical forum before an ecclesiastical judge who is competent to judge the controversy at first instance.

3340 This canon enacts canonical legislation parallel to the local civil legislation in two instances. Where an arbitral judgement needs judicial confirmation in civil law, the same is true in ecclesiastical law. And where the civil law admits of a challenge to an arbitral judgement, canon law allows the same before an ecclesiastical judge. The rules of this canon bind whether the norms being used are chosen by the parties themselves, are those of the local Bishops' Conference or are those of the local civil law.

---

[1] As an example of legislation by a Bishops' Conference, the Bishops' Conference of the USA approved a document 'On due Process' on conciliation and arbitration in 1969. After some changes introduced by the Secretariat of State in 1971 (cf. CLD 7 899–900), the document was published by USCC Publications, Washington DC. It has to be said, however, that the overall legislation by Bishops' Conferences in this regard has been meagre.

PART IV

THE PENAL PROCESS

INTRODUCTION

A penal process is a judicial process to investigate the allegation of an offence and to determine whether or not to impose or declare a penalty for that offence.[1] The present law on penal processes represents a substantial simplification and shortening of the previous law in this regard. Most significantly, it is marked by a concern not only for justice and order in the Church – an essential ingredient – but also for the rights and good name of the individual accused and particularly for his or her right of defence. There is in the new Code a distinct tone, reflecting the thinking of Vat. II, that a penal process should be very much a last resort – a tone which finds explicit expression in Cann. 1341 and 1342 §1. Experience would seem to bear out the wisdom of this injunction.

3341

Chapter I
THE PRELIMINARY INVESTIGATION

Can. 1717 §1 Whenever the Ordinary receives information, which has at least the semblance of truth, about an offence, he is to enquire carefully, either personally or through some suitable person, about the facts and circumstances, and about the imputability of the offence, unless this enquiry would appear to be entirely superfluous.

Before starting a penal process, the Ordinary[2] must first have received information, which has at least the semblance of truth, that an offence has been committed; he may not act arbitrarily or on the basis of vague rumour. Having received such information, he is to set up a preliminary and purely administrative investigation about the facts and circumstances of the case, and about the imputability of the offence.[3] This enquiry may be carried out by the Ordinary in person or, more usually, by some other suitable person, man or woman.[4] If the enquiry reveals no offence or only a very doubtful one, or if it shows clearly that the offence was not imputable, the process will go no further. On the other hand, if the preliminary investigation appears to be totally superfluous, because of the already existing notoriety of the facts, it may be omitted. The intervention of the promotor of justice is not required at this stage,[5] although the Ordinary could presumably allow him to be present if he judges it useful.

3342

---

[1] For the elements constitutive of a canonical offence, cf. Can. 1321 and 1917 Code c.2195; for the distinction between *imposing* and *declaring* a penalty, cf. Can. 1314.

[2] The term 'Ordinary' includes all of those enumerated in Can. 134 §1: cf. Comm 12(1980) 189 at Can. 380 §1.

[3] For the law on imputability of offences, cf. Cann. 1321–1330.

[4] Cf. Comm 12(1980) 189–190 at Can. 380 §1.

[5] Cf. Comm 12(1980) 190 at Can. 381.

Can. 1717 §2 Care is to be taken that this investigation does not call into question anyone's good name.

3343 This rule, repeating the substance of c.1943 of the 1917 Code, is of fundamental and vital importance. It enjoins that the preliminary investigation be carried out with such care, discretion and even secrecy as not even to 'call into question', much less to damage *anyone's* good name. Since penal processes are a comparitively rare event in the Church's life, even the rumour that such might be brought against a particular person could be very damaging indeed, and contrary to the prescription of this paragraph.

Can. 1717 §3 The one who performs this investigation has the same powers and obligations as an auditor in a process. If, later, a judicial process is initiated, this person cannot take part in it as a judge.

3344 The investigator has the same powers and obligations as an auditor in a process, i.e. he or she is to gather the evidence (or more correctly in this case, the indications that a process should or should not be initiated) in accordance with the instructions given, and then to present them to the Ordinary (see Can. 1428 §3). In the 1917 Code at c.1946 §1 the investigator was also required to give an opinion about the case. This is not explicitly required in the present law; neither however is it excluded. What is clear is that the ultimate decision (see Can. 1718) rests with the Ordinary personally. Should he in fact decide upon a penal process, then to ensure as great a degree of judicial impartiality as possible, the investigator cannot validly act as a judge in that process.

Can. 1718 §1 When the facts have been assembled, the Ordinary is to decree:

1° **whether a process to impose or declare a penalty can be initiated;**

2° **whether this would be expedient, bearing in mind Can. 1341;**

3° **whether a judicial process is to be used or, unless the law forbids it, whether the matter is to proceed by means of an extra-judicial decree.**

3345 After the preliminary investigation the first decision the Ordinary has to make is whether the facts collected warrant a penal process. They may show the innocence of the accused person, or at least insufficient reason to proceed to a penal process, or they may show a lack of imputability: in any of these cases there will be no penal process, although other measures such as pastoral help, vigilance and warnings may be used. If there is sufficient reason to initiate a penal process, the Ordinary must then decide whether this would be expedient, having due regard to Can. 1341 which calls for the administrative or judicial imposition of penalties *only* when it is established that other specified methods of repairing scandal, restoring justice and reforming an offender would be unavailing. If he deems that such other methods might serve, these must be tried first. Should even those fail, he has finally to determine whether a judicial process or an extra-judicial decree is to be used. He must bear in mind here that the law forbids certain penalties to be imposed extra-judicially (see Can. 1342 §2) and, if these are to be invoked, there must be a formal penal process. A suggestion that the accused be allowed to demand a formal process was not admitted by the Revision Commission.[1]

Can. 1718 §2 The Ordinary is to revoke or change the decree mentioned in §1 whenever new facts indicate to him that a different decision should be made.

---

[1] Cf. Comm 12(1980) 191 at Can. 381 §1 1°.

There is nothing immutable about the decree (which indeed should be a formal written decree) issued by the Ordinary after the preliminary investigation; there is no question of a *res judicata*. Consequently, if further facts should later come to light, whether in favour of or against holding a penal procedure, the Ordinary is obliged to revoke or change that decree.

Can. 1718 §3 In making the decrees referred to in §§1 and 2, the Ordinary, if he considers it prudent, is to consult two judges or other legal experts.

In making, changing or revoking any of the decrees mentioned in §§1 and 2, the Ordinary should (unless he considers it imprudent to do so) consult two judges or other legal experts: there is here a clear insistence on canonical expertise and experience. In such a delicate and difficult area, prudence would normally urge that he does so consult, particularly if he is not himself skilled in this part of the law.

Can. 1718 §4 Before making a decree in accordance with §1, the Ordinary is to consider whether, to avoid useless trials, it would be expedient, with the parties' consent, for himself or the investigator to make a decision, according to what is good and equitable, about the question of damages.

Where there may be question of harm arising from an alleged offence and consequent damages, the Ordinary, before making the decree called for by §1, may explore the option of an informal, equitable solution on the question of these damages. The motive for doing so will be to avoid unnecessary trials, but the consent of all those involved, the accused person or persons and those harmed by the alleged offence, is needed. The Ordinary himself, or the investigator delegated by him, may in such a case give a just and equitable decision about damages.

Can. 1719 The acts of the investigation, the decrees of the Ordinary by which the investigation was opened and closed, and all those matters which preceded the investigation, are to be kept in the secret curial archives, if they are not necessary for the penal process.

Since the material under consideration here is of a very sensitive nature and could, even if not substantiated, be damaging to a person's reputation, it must be kept in the secret archive mentioned in Can. 489 – 'if they are not necessary for the penal process': in practice, the acts of the preliminary investigation will more often than not, if integral justice is to be done, have to be taken into account in an ensuing penal trial.

Chapter II
THE COURSE OF THE PROCESS

Can. 1720 If the Ordinary believes that the matter should proceed by way of an extra-judicial decree:

1° he is to notify the accused of the allegation and the proofs, and give an opportunity for defence, unless the accused, having been lawfully summoned, has failed to appear;

The law seems to favour a penal process over an administrative decree as a means of imposing or declaring a penalty, since it requires that there be just reasons against using the judicial procedure before an extra-judicial decree may be used (see Can. 1342 §1). Note again that certain penalties cannot be imposed by an extra-judicial process (see Can. 1342 §2). If the Ordinary chooses the latter option, he must notify the accused person of the allegation and the proofs. He must also allow the accused an opportunity for defence, unless he or she, having been lawfully summoned, fails to appear. The right of defence afforded here must be real, with sufficient time and access to legal help being allowed, and it serves to prevent extra-judicial penalties being imposed or declared in any sort of arbitrary manner.

    2° together with two assessors, he is accurately to weigh all the proofs and arguments;

3351 The Ordinary must avail himself of the services of two assessors in weighing up carefully all the proofs and arguments in the case, including any defence submitted by the accused. He is not bound to follow their advice – this is not a collegiate tribunal.

    3° if the offence is certainly proven and the time for criminal proceedings has not elapsed, he is to issue a decree in accordance with Cann. 1342–1350, stating at least in summary form the reasons in law and in fact.

3352 Can. 1362 determines the time-limits for the extinction of criminal actions. When the time-limit for the particular offence has elapsed, the Ordinary cannot use either a penal judicial process or an extra-judicial decree to impose or declare a penalty. If the offence is certainly proven, the Ordinary is to issue a decree, imposing or declaring the penalty, in accordance with the rules laid down in Cann. 1342–1350 and he is to give at least a summary of the reasons in law and in fact for the decree.

Can. 1721 §1 If the Ordinary decrees that a penal judicial process is to be initiated, he is to pass the acts of the investigation to the promotor of justice, who is to present to the judge a petition of accusation in accordance with Cann. 1502 and 1504.

3353 In a penal judicial process the part of the plaintiff, without whom there can be no trial, is taken by the promotor of justice (see Can. 1501). The Ordinary is to give him the acts of the preliminary investigation, and he is to present to the judge a formal petition drawn up in accordance with the general rules on petitions (see Cann. 1502 and 1504).[1]

Can. 1721 §2 Before a higher tribunal, the promotor of justice constituted for that tribunal adopts the role of plaintiff.

3354 If the case is appealed to a higher tribunal, the plaintiff is the promotor of justice appointed for that higher tribunal, and so the function in the case of the first promotor ceases.

Can. 1722 At any stage of the process, in order to prevent scandal, protect the freedom of the witnesses and safeguard the course of justice, the Ordinary can, after consulting the promotor of justice and summoning the accused person to appear, prohibit the accused from the exercise of the sacred ministry or of some ecclesiastical office and position, or impose or forbid residence in a certain place or territory, or even prohibit public par-

---

[1] Since the preliminary investigation will have already established a prima facie case against the accused, it follows that the judge cannot reject the petition on the ground that the plea lacks any foundation (Can. 1505 §2 4°). The only reasons for which he might reject it would be the absence of the formalities required in Can. 1504 1°–4°, or, which would be rather unlikely in this case, the lack of legal competence (Can. 1505 §2 3° and 1°).

ticipation in the blessed Eucharist. If, however, the reason ceases, all these restrictions are to be revoked; they cease by virtue of the law itself as soon as the penal process ceases.

The restrictions envisaged here are precautionary, not penal. They may be invoked *only* for the reasons stated: to avoid scandal, protect the freedom of witnesses and safeguard the course of justice. It is not the judge who invokes them, but the Ordinary and he may do so at any stage of the trial, having first consulted the promotor of justice and having summoned the accused to appear. Presumably the latter proviso is to allow the accused to request mitigation or to give suitable guarantees about his or her conduct which might obviate the need for the restrictions. Even though the restrictions are purely precautionary, they could have serious effects on the person's reputation; accordingly they should be applied only when necessary and, in any event, they are to be lifted as soon as the reason for them ceases. They cease automatically when the penal process is finished.[1]   3355

Can. 1723 §1 When the judge summons the accused, he must invite the latter to engage an advocate, in accordance with Can. 1481 §1, but within the time laid down by the judge.

Can. 1481 §1 allows a party in a case free choice of advocate, and the present canon directs the judge to invite the accused to do this within a time-limit to be determined by the judge.   3356

Can. 1723 §2 If the accused does not do this, the judge himself is to appoint an advocate before the joinder of issue, and this advocate will remain in office for as long as the accused has not engaged an advocate.

Can. 1482 §2 makes it mandatory for the accused in a penal trial to have an advocate, 'either appointed personally or allocated by the judge'. This is to ensure that his or her rights of defence are properly safeguarded. If the accused refuses to appoint an advocate or simply neglects to do so, the judge is to appoint one before the joinder of the issue, and this advocate remains in office until such time as the accused may appoint one personally.   3357

Can. 1724 §1 At the direction or with the consent of the Ordinary who decided that the process should be initiated, the promotor of justice in any grade of the trial can renounce the instance.

§2 For validity, the renunciation must be accepted by the accused person, unless he or she has been declared absent from the trial.

Since the promotor takes the part of plaintiff in a penal process any renunciation of the instance must formally be done by him. However, he may renounce it only at the direction of the Ordinary who decided that the case be initiated or, at least, with his consent. The renunciation is not valid unless it is accepted by the accused, except where the latter has been declared absent from the trial in accordane with Can. 1592. The right of the accused not to accept the renunciation of the instance by the promotor of justice is in contrast to the absence of any right on his or her part to demand a penal process (see the remarks under Can. 1718 §1). The reason is, presumably, that the actuality of a penal process is more damaging to a person's good name than the mere possibility of such a step, and so the accused has the right to seek a judicial acquittal by insisting that the case be finished by a definitive judgement.   3358

---

[1] The present Code makes no disposition about recourse against these restrictions but, using c. 1958 of the 1917 Code, which covered the same area, to supply for the *lacuna legis*, it would seem that no recourse is possible: 'contra eadem non datur iuris remedium', except perhaps recourse to the Holy See.

Book VII Judicial Procedures

Can. 1725 In the argumentation of the case, whether done in writing or orally, the accused person or the advocate or procurator of the accused, always has the right to speak last.

3359 Whatever advantage results from having the last word in the argumentation of the case is given to the accused, either personally or through his or her legal representatives. This is in contrast to the general right accorded to the promotor of justice in contentious cases of replying to every reply of the parties (see Can. 1603 §3).

Can. 1726 If in any grade or at any stage of a penal trial, it becomes quite evident that the offence has not been committed by the accused, the judge must declare this in a judgement and acquit the accused, even if it is at the same time clear that the period for criminal proceedings has elapsed.

3360 If it becomes quite clear at any grade or stage of the trial that the accused did not commit the offence alleged, the judge must formally declare this in a judgement and acquit the person. The very fact of having been brought to trial in a criminal case is damaging to a person's good name, and so he or she has a right to whatever the law can do to restore it. It is not sufficient to stop the process; there must be a formal declaration of innocence by the judge, and this must be done even if the time-limit for bringing a criminal action has elapsed.

Can. 1727 §1 The offender can appeal, even if discharged in the judgement only because the penalty was facultative, or because the judge used the power mentioned in Cann. 1344 and 1345.

3361 The offender, i.e. an accused person who has been found guilty in a penal process, can appeal in three cases: (a) when a penalty is imposed or declared; (b) when no penalty was imposed because the law or precept gave the judge power to apply it or not (see Can. 1343); (c) where the judge has applied the powers given him in Cann. 1344–1345. Can. 1344 gives the judge wide powers in certain circumstances to postpone a penalty, to abstain from imposing it, to substitute a milder penalty or penance, to suspend the obligation of observing an expiatory penance. Can. 1345 allows him to refrain from imposing a penalty when there was diminished imputability.

Can. 1727 §2 The promotor of justice can appeal whenever he considers that the reparation of scandal or the restitution of justice has not been sufficiently provided for.

3362 As plaintiff in the case and as the one specially charged with safeguarding the public good (see Can. 1430), the promotor of justice can also appeal if he considers that either the scandal caused by the offence or the restitution of justice has not been adequately provided for.[1]

Can. 1728 §1 Without prejudice to the canons of this title, and unless the nature of the case requires otherwise, in a penal trial the judge is to observe the canons concerning judicial procedures in general, those concerning the ordinary contentious process, and the special norms about cases which concern the public good.

3363 The special norms for penal trials do not exhaust the procedures to be followed in them; the norms for contentious judicial procedures in general are also to be applied,

---

[1] Both the offender and the promotor of justice can also bring a plaint of nullity of judgement or can apply for a total reinstatement (*restitutio in integrum*), in accordance with the general norms about trials: cf. Comm 12(1980) 198 at Cann. 394 and 345.

unless the nature of the case requires otherwise. The judge is also to observe the special norms about cases involving the public good, e.g. Cann. 1562 §2, 1598 §1.

Can. 1728 §2 The accused person is not bound to admit to an offence, nor may the oath be demanded of the accused.

The accused has the right to remain silent when questioned about the alleged offence; this is an exception to the general rule of Can. 1531 §1 which obliges a party who is lawfully questioned 'to respond and to tell the whole truth'. Nobody is bound to incriminate himself or herself. This does not, of course, prevent the accused from voluntarily confessing to the alleged crime. The oath, either to tell the truth, or confirming the truth of what has been said, cannot be demanded of the accused.[1]

3364

Chapter III
THE ACTION FOR DAMAGES

Can. 1729 §1 In accordance with Can. 1596, a party who has suffered harm from an offence can bring a contentious action for damages in the actual penal case itself.

Can. 128 directs that anyone who unlawfully causes harm to another by an act which is deceitful or culpable, is obliged to repair the damage done. Although an action to have this done could be initiated separately from the penal process, the present canon provides for the contentious case for damages to be heard together with the penal case about the crime from which the harm arose. The reference to Can. 1596 is to the general norm governing the intervention of a third interested party in a case.

3365

Can. 1729 §2 The intervention of the harmed party mentioned in §1 is no longer admitted if the intervention was not made in the first instance of the penal trial.

If the injured party decides to combine the action for damages with the criminal trial, this must be done at first instance; it may not be done at a later stage. This, of course, in no way impedes the bringing of a separate action even after the penal proces has been completed.

3366

Can. 1729 §3 An appeal in a case concerning damages is made in accordance with Cann. 1628-1640, even if an appeal cannot be made in the penal case itself. If, however, there is a double appeal, there is to be only one trial, even though the appeals are made by different persons, without prejudice to the provision of Can. 1730.

A case for damages is subject to the normal rules of appeal, even when it has been combined with a penal process. There can be an appeal even if the judgement of the penal process is not appealed. If both cases are appealed, even though the appeals are made by different persons, e.g. the offender in the penal process and the injured party in the case for damages, both appeals are to be heard in the same trial. The reference to Can. 1730 covers the case where the judge decides the penal case first in order to avoid undue delay.

3367

---

[1] While it is certain that the oath cannot be demanded of the accused, it is not stated whether he or she could voluntarily ask to make a sworn statement; assuming that no coercion of any kind is involved, it is difficult to see how such a request could lawfully be refused.

Book VII Judicial Procedures

Can. 1730 §1 To avoid excessive delay in a penal trial, the judge can postpone the trial concerning damages until he has given a definitive judgement in the penal trial.

3368 If when an action for damages has been combined with a penal trial, the judge foresees that excessive delays may result to the penal trial by hearing both cases together, he is allowed to postpone the trial for damages until after the definitive judgement in the other trial.

Can. 1730 §2 When the judge does this he must, after giving judgement in the penal trial, hear the case concerning damages, even though the penal trial is still pending because of a proposed challenge to it, or even though the accused has been acquitted, when the reason for the acquittal does not take away the obligation to make good the damages.

3369 If the judge takes the option given him in §1 of postponing the case for damages, he is to hear this case as soon as he has given judgement in the penal trial. He is to do this even though the penal trial is still pending, e.g. because of an appeal or a complaint of nullity of judgement by the offender. He is to do it even if the accused has been acquitted, so long as the reason for the acquittal does not remove the basis for the action for damages, as would be the case e.g. if the accused was acquitted because it was shown that he or she did not commit the offence alleged.

Can. 1731 A judgement given in a penal trial, even though it has become an adjudged matter, in no way creates a right for a party who has suffered harm, unless this party has intervened in accordance with Can. 1729.

3370 This canon is an application of the general principle stated in Can. 16 §3 that a court judgement 'binds only those persons and affects only those matters for which it was given'. Even if a person is found guilty of an offence by which another person was injured, this creates no right for the injured person unless he or she has combined the action for damages with the criminal trial in accordance with Can. 1729. The reason for the exception is the combination of cases which, as it were, brings the intervening party within the scope of the criminal trial.

PART V

THE MANNER OF PROCEDURE IN ADMINISTRATIVE RECOURSE AND IN THE REMOVAL OR TRANSFER OF PARISH PRIESTS

Section I
RECOURSE AGAINST ADMINISTRATIVE DECREES

Can. 1732 Whatever is laid down in the canons of this section concerning decrees, is also to be applied to all singular administrative acts given in the external forum outside a judicial trial, except for those given by the Roman Pontiff himself or by an Ecumenical Council.

This canon introduces the general question of recourse against administrative acts. It establishes the principle that the subsequent norms concerning recourse against 'decrees' are to be understood as applicable to all forms of singular administrative acts, i.e. decrees, precepts, rescripts, privileges and dispensations (see Cann. 48–93). In practice, it is important to note that it is the content of a document or communication – whether or not it is given a title such as decree, precept, rescript etc. – which constitutes it a singular administrative act in the sense of Cann. 35–93 and therefore of this canon. Thus e.g. a Bishop's letter appointing a parish priest, or imposing a suspension upon a priest, would be a singular administrative act and accordingly subject in appropriate circumstances to challenge through administrative recourse. Certain singular administrative acts are not covered by the provisions of these canons, however. By implication, all such acts in the internal forum, whether sacramental or non-sacramental, are not included. Explicitly excluded are singular administrative acts issued by the Pope[1] or by an Ecumenical Council.[2]

Can. 1733 §1 When a person believes that he or she has been injured by a decree, it is greatly to be desired that contention between that person and the author of the decree be avoided, and that care be taken to reach an equitable solution by mutual consultation, possibly using the assistance of serious-minded persons to mediate and study the matter. In this way, the controversy may by some suitable method be avoided or brought to an end.

§2 The Bishops' Conference can prescribe that in each diocese there be established a permanent office or council which would have the duty, in

---

[1] These include singular administrative acts issued originally by a dicastery of the Roman Curia (not however the Secretariat of State) and confirmed later by the Pope *in forma specifica*.

[2] The Apostolic Signatura, which in its *sectio altera* also deals with recourse against administrative acts (cf. Can. 1445 §2), has a more extensive competence than envisaged in this section of the Code: cf. Ap Sig decision I.XII.1970: Apol 44(1971) 610–622: Per 61(1972) 169–183; Grocholewski *Atti e ricorsi amministrativi* Apol 57(1984) 259–279.

accordance with the norms laid down by the Conference, of seeking and suggesting equitable solutions. Even if the Conference has not demanded this, the Bishop may establish such an office or council.

§3 The office or council mentioned in §2 is to be diligent in its work principally when the revocation of a decree is sought in accordance with Can. 1734 and the time-limit for recourse has not elapsed. If recourse is proposed against a decree, the Superior who would have to decide the recourse is to encourage both the person having the recourse and the author of the decree to seek this type of solution, whenever the prospect of a satisfactory outcome is discerned.

3372 It is a fundamental principle of Christian life that litigation be avoided if at all possible (see Matt 18:15–17). This principle finds expression in Can. 1446 and in the present canon. When someone feels aggrieved by an administrative act, in order to avoid conflict the law urges the parties involved to find an equitable solution by means of mutual consultation, using the good offices of third parties as mediators if necessary (§1). To assist in this task, the law proposes the possibility of the establishment in each diocese of an office or council for the resolution of such disputes. The primary responsibility for the establishment of these offices or councils rests with the Bishops' Conference.[1] In the absence of any decision by the Conference, the local Bishop may decide to set up such a body in his own diocese; the principles to govern its activity are set out in §3.

Can. 1734 §1 Before having recourse, the person must seek in writing from its author the revocation or amendment of the decree. Once this petition has been lodged, it is by that very fact understood that the suspension of the execution of the decree is also being sought.

3373 This is a preliminary step before the hierarchical recourse against an administrative act. The canon calls it a 'petition'; some authors, however, refer to it as a 'preliminary recourse'. The party challenging the decision seeks a change of mind on the part of the authority, asking that the decree be revoked or amended. Such a petition may also include a specific request that the execution of the decree be suspended. However, even if this suspension is not thus explicitly sought, the canon points out that the petition itself is to be understood as containing such a request, and on receipt of the petition the author of the decree must address the question.

Can. 1734 §2 The petition must be made within the peremptory time-limit of ten canonical days from the time the decree was lawfully notified.

3374 A *peremptory* time-limit, also called *fatalia legis* (see Can. 1465 §1), means that if the procedure is not used within the time-limit set, the person in question forfeits the opportunity to use it, in which case the person has no choice but to try for an out-of-court settlement (see Cann. 1713–1716, 1733) or to resort directly to hierarchical recourse (see Can. 1737). *Canonical* days are interpreted in accordance with Can. 201 §2.

Can. 1734 §3 The norms in §§1 and 2 do not apply:

1° in having a recourse to the Bishop against decrees given by authorities who are subject to him;

---

[1] For the manner in which some Bishops' Conferences have dealt with this matter, cf. LCE Tavola per Paesi e Canoni at Can. 1733: the majority, apparently, would prefer that the matter be remitted to the local Bishop.

2° in having recourse against the decree by which a hierarchical recourse is decided, unless the decision was given by the Bishop himself;

3° in having recourse in accordance with Cann. 57 and 1735.

However, the formalities prescribed in §§1 and 2 of this canon, those namely concerning the petition and the peremptory time-limit, are considered unnecessary and do not therefore apply in the following situations: 3375

(a) whenever recourse is made to the Bishop against a decision or directive issued by an authority who is administratively subject to him, e.g. a parish priest, a Vicar general, an episcopal Vicar, a Vicar forane, an officer of the curia etc.; in such a situation the Bishop may be approached immediately and directly, without further reference to the authority who issued the decision – though it would obviously be at least courteous, perhaps even helpful, first to discuss the matter with the authority in question;

(b) whenever a prior recourse in the same case has already been determined by an authority superior to the one who issued the decree or decision in the first place; a typical example would be where the Congregation for the Clergy had upheld a Bishop's administrative penalty of suspension on one of his priests: should the priest still consider himself aggrieved, he could at once have recourse to the Apostolic Signatura without making any request to the Congregation; the principle here does not however apply when the decision in the prior recourse had been that of 'the Bishop himself' (as e.g. in the situation envisaged in 1° of this paragraph);

(c) whenever recourse is made in accordance with either Can. 57 (referring to a Superior's failure to respond, itself to be interpreted as a negative answer) or Can. 1735 (referring to a Superior's refusal to withdraw the original decision or to modify it in an acceptable manner).

Can. 1735 If, within thirty days from the time the petition mentioned in Can. 1734 reaches the author of the decree, the latter communicates a new decree by which either the earlier decree is amended or it is determined that the petition is to be rejected, the period within which to have recourse begins from the notification of the new decree. If, however, the author of the decree makes no decision within thirty days, the time-limit begins to run from the thirtieth day.

When a petition or preliminary recourse has been received, the authority has thirty days within which to respond. This time is to be understood as *continuous*, not *canonical* (see Can. 201). The time to have recourse begins from the official notification of the authority's reply or, in the absence of a reply, from the thirtieth day after the petition was received by the authority. 3376

Can. 1736 §1 In those matters in which hierarchical recourse suspends the execution of a decree, the petition mentioned in Can. 1734 also has the same effect.

There are six instances in the Code whereby recourse against a decision does, by the mere fact of its being made, suspend the execution of a decree: 3377

(a) the dismissal of a member of a religious institute (Can. 700);
(b) the dismissal of a member of a secular institute (Can. 729);
(c) the dismissal of a member of a society of apostolic life (Can. 746);
(d) the imposition or declaration of a penalty (Can. 1353);

Book VII Judicial Procedures

(e) the removal of a parish priest (Can. 1747 §3);

(f) the transfer of a parish priest (Can. 1752).

The present canon points out that, in these cases, the petition or preliminary recourse of Can. 1734 has precisely the same suspensive effect.

Can. 1736 §2 In other cases, unless within ten days of receiving the petition mentioned in Can. 1734 the author of the decree has decreed its suspension, an interim suspension can be sought from the author's hierarchical Superior. This Superior can decree the suspension only for serious reasons and must always take care that the salvation of souls suffers no harm.

3378 Apart from the above six cases mentioned expressly in the law, the general principle is that the execution of a decree is not automatically suspended by a petition for its revocation or amendment. The author of the decree *may* decide to suspend the execution. If this has not been done within the time-limit of ten days, the Superior to whom recourse will be made may so suspend the decree's execution, but only if the one making the recourse asks for it and if the same Superior is satisfied that there are grave reasons to do so and no risk of harm to the good of souls. This suspension is temporary only, until such time as the hierarchical recourse itself is dealt with.

Can. 1736 §3 If the execution of the decree is suspended in accordance with §2 and recourse is subsequently proposed, the person who must decide the recourse is to determine, in accordance with Can. 1737 §3, whether the suspension is to be confirmed or revoked.

3379 Since the suspension mentioned in Can. 1736 §2 is temporary, it must be confirmed or revoked when the recourse itself is studied.

Can. 1736 §4 If no recourse is proposed against the decree within the time-limit established, an interim suspension of execution in accordance with §§1 and 2 automatically lapses.

3380 The suspension lapses at the end of the time-limit for the recourse (fifteen canonical days: see Can. 1737 §2) or when the plaintiff officially notifies the authority that he or she is abandoning the recourse.

Can 1737 §1 A person who contends that he or she has been injured by a decree, can for any just motive have recourse to the hierarchical Superior of the one who issued the decree. The recourse can be proposed before the author of the decree, who must immediately forward it to the competent hierarchical Superior.

3381 Recourse against an administrative act can be made by *anyone*, of whatever status, religious or civil, who believes that he or she has been injured by that act. The law states this principle in the broadest of terms, permitting recourse 'for any just motive' and without specifying what is meant by 'injured'. It will be for the hierarchical authority involved to determine the sufficiency of the motive and whether or not such a claim has any basis in objective reality. Recourse is made to the hierarchical Superior of the author of the decree (e.g. from a Bishop to the appropriate Roman Congregation), either directly, or through the author of the decree who is strictly obliged to transmit the recourse immediately to the superior: should this not happen, the direct approach remains intact.

Can. 1737 §2 The recourse is to be proposed within the peremptory time-limit of fifteen canonical days. In the cases mentioned in Can. 1734 §3, the

Part V Procedure for Administrative Recourse

time-limit begins to run from the day the decree was notified; in other cases, it runs in accordance with Can. 1735.

A person who does not act during that period of time specified by law, loses the right to lodge a hierarchical as well as a contentious-administrative recourse; whatever administrative decision was in the process of being challenged could then stand and remain operative. **3382**

Can. 1737 §3 Even in those cases in which recourse does not by law suspend the execution of the decree, or in which the suspension is decreed in accordance with Can. 1736 §2, the Superior can for a serious reason order that the execution be suspended, but is to take care that the salvation of souls suffers no harm.

Even if the execution of the decree has not been suspended, either by the law itself or by its author or by the Superior at the request of the one presenting the recourse (see Can. 1736), the hierarchical Superior can still decree its suspension, provided that there is a serious reason and no risk of harm to the good of souls: this will obviously be a matter for the superior to determine in the light of the circumstances of each individual case. **3383**

Can. 1738 The person having recourse always has the right to the services of an advocate or procurator, but is to avoid futile delays. Indeed, an advocate is to be appointed *ex officio* if the person does not have one and the Superior considers it necessary. The Superior, however, can always order that the one having recourse appear in person to answer questions.

The choice or appointment of an advocate or procurator (see Cann. 1481–1490) is an important means of caring for the rights and legitimate interests of the person making the recourse; indeed the Superior is obliged to see to this 'if considered necessary'. Having an advocate or procurator does not, however, exempt a plaintiff from appearing in person before the Superior if that be required. Furthermore, using an advocate or procurator must not be to the detriment of justice, such as e.g. would occur if it occasioned frivolous or 'futile delays'. **3384**

Can. 1739 In so far as the case demands, it is lawful for the Superior who must decide the recourse, not only to confirm the decree or declare that it is invalid, but also to rescind or revoke it or, if it seems to the Superior to be more expedient, to amend it, to substitute for it, or to obrogate it.

The superior authority to which the recourse has been made and which is competent to decide the issue has very wide powers to resolve the matter: it may *confirm* the original decision; it may declare that decision *null and void*; it may *quash* the original decision by rescinding it or revoking it; it may *amend* the decision, revoking or partially altering its contents; it may *replace* the original with a decree of its own. **3385**

Two special points should be noted in respect of those administrative recourses which are made to the Holy See: **3386**

(a) When the appropriate Roman Congregation declares that a particular decree of e.g. a Bishop is to be revoked, it does not thereby necessarily mean that the matter ends there. Rather, recognising that the Congregation may not be fully aware of all the local circumstances, it still leaves it to the Bishop to deal with the matter, but in some way other than that which has been found unjust or inappropriate.

(b) In a situation where the appropriate Roman Congregation upholds an episcopal or other such decree, there still remains open to the plaintiff to have further recourse to the *sectio altera* of the Apostolic Signatura, whose decision will be final.[1]

Section II
THE PROCEDURE FOR THE REMOVAL OR TRANSFER OF PARISH PRIESTS

Chapter I
THE PROCEDURE FOR THE REMOVAL OF PARISH PRIESTS

Can. 1740 When the ministry of any parish priest has for some reason become harmful or at least ineffective, even though this occurs without any serious fault on his part, he can be removed from the parish by the diocesan Bishop.

3387 This final section of the Code is devoted to the administrative procedures for the removal and transfer of parish priests. While the concept of such procedures might appear initially to be negative, the underlying principle in both cases is positive, namely the pastoral welfare of the faithful. This basic point is made clearly in this canon which deals with the matter of removal: a parish priest may be removed only if his ministry has become harmful or at least ineffective. It is for the diocesan Bishop to determine whether or not this is the case in a given situation. Since this is an administrative procedure, not a penal process, the personal responsibility of the parish priest is not relevant. In accordance with the law, only the diocesan Bishop or his equivalent (see Can. 381 §2) may remove a parish priest. A Vicar general or an episcopal Vicar would require a special mandate to do so (see Can. 134 §3). Moreover, the provisions of this canon refer only to those holding the office of parish priest as such (see Can. 515 §1), not to others such as rectors of churches (see Can. 563), chaplains (see Can. 572) including military ones.[2] They apply only to those parish priests who belong to the diocesan clergy or to a secular institute whose priests are incardinated in a diocese (see Can. 715 §1).

Can. 1741 The reasons for which a parish priest can lawfully be removed from his parish are principally:

1° a manner of acting which causes grave harm or disturbance to ecclesiastical communion;

2° ineptitude or permanent illness of mind or body, which makes the parish priest unequal to the task of fulfilling his duties satisfactorily;

3° the loss of the parish priest's good name among upright and serious-minded parishioners, or aversion to him, when it can be foreseen that these factors will not quickly come to an end;

---

[1] Cf. PB 123 §1. Cf. also LE III 5321–5332; CLD 7 246–272.
[2] Cf. Comm 15(1984) 90.

Part V Procedure for Removal or Transfer of Parish Priests

4° grave neglect or violation of parochial duties, which persists after a warning;

5° bad administration of temporal goods with grave harm to the Church, when no other remedy can be found to eliminate this harm.

3388 This canon presents five of the more common reasons (not necessarily all the reasons) why a parish priest may be removed as follows:

(a) behaviour by the parish priest which is harmful to 'ecclesiastical communion' (1°), in effect to the good of the Church, such e.g. as public participation in partisan politics, a continued manifest opposition to the decisions of ecclesiastical authority, lack of leadership whereby dissension is left to grow in the parish, etc.

(b) inability to fulfil 'his duties satisfactorily' (2°), whether arising from ignorance or lack of experience or from an 'illness of mind or body' which is judged to be of such permanence as to make him 'unequal to the task'.

(c) 'the loss of the parish priest's good name' (3°) by reason of his conduct, whether at a personal level (e.g. a persistent abuse of alcohol) or in his undue association with others (e.g. a subversive organisation, another individual). In this regard a judgement may be made, not on the basis of complaints made by a small even if vociferous minority in the parish, rather on that of opinions expressed generally by parishioners known to be sincere catholics committed to the Church; moreover, a removal on this ground would be justified only when it is clear that the situation in question 'will not quickly come to an end'.

(d) a serious and persistent 'neglect or violation of parochial duties' (4°) such as those enumerated in Cann. 528–535; in such a situation, however, a removal would be justified only if the Bishop had first given a formal warning which in the event was either disregarded or rejected.

(e) such 'bad administration of temporal goods' (i.e. financial and property administration) that 'grave harm to the Church' results (5°); a removal on this ground would, however, be justified only 'when no other remedy can be found to eliminate this harm': on occasion e.g. it might well be possible charitably to induce an otherwise exemplary parish priest, not blessed with administrative ability at a financial level, to transfer this aspect of his parochial obligations to one of his capable assistant priests.

3389 Since it is the diocesan Bishop who must decide that a given reason is sufficient in order to proceed, he must be careful to interpret the reasons listed here strictly, not extensively: the whole tenor of the canon has this thrust. He must ensure that, in a particular situation, the reason has a solid basis in objective reality and will admit of proof in the external forum. While this list is not exhaustive, the same principle of interpretation would govern the application of other cognate reasons.

Can. 1742 §1 If an investigation shows that there exists a reason mentioned in Can. 1740, the Bishop is to discuss the matter with two parish priests chosen from a group stably established for this purpose by the council of priests at the proposal of the Bishop. If he then believes that he should proceed with the removal, the Bishop must, for validity, indicate to the parish priest the reason and the arguments, and persuade him in a fatherly manner to resign his parish within fifteen days.

3390 The procedure for the removal of a parish priest as outlined in this canon contains four fundamental steps:

(a) there must be a preliminary investigation by the Bishop to establish the existence of a 'reason' for removal consistent with the contents of Cann. 1740–1741;

(b) the Bishop must, for the validity of the procedure, then discuss the matter with two parish priests; these are chosen from a group established in a stable form within the diocese for this purpose;[1] the group is set up 'by the council of priests at the proposal of the Bishop';[2]

(c) if the Bishop then believes that removal is the only appropriate action, he is obliged to indicate to the parish priest the reason and the arguments for his removal;

(d) the Bishop must then seek to persuade the parish priest to resign from his office within fifteen (presumably canonical) days.

After this request by the diocesan Bishop, the parish priest has three options: (i) accept the offer and submit his resignation (see Can. 1743); (ii) not answer or reject the offer without giving reasons (see Can. 1744); or (iii) reject the offer giving reasons (see Can. 1745).

Can. 1742 §2: For parish priests who are members of a religious institute or a society of apostolic life, the provision of Can. 682 §2 is to be observed.

3391 This paragraph makes the point that the removal of a parish priest who belongs to a religious institute or to a society of apostolic life, is governed not by these present canons but rather by Can. 682 §2, which gives a simple discretionary authority both to the diocesan Bishop and to the competent religious Superior.

Can. 1743 The resignation of the parish priest can be given not only purely and simply, but even upon a condition, provided the condition is one which the Bishop can lawfully accept and does in fact accept.

3392 Faced with the request of the Bishop at the end of the preliminary process, the parish priest may resign *purely and simply*, notifying his decision to the Bishop either in writing or orally before two witnesses (see Can. 189 §1). The parish priest may, however, resign *conditionally*. A conditional resignation cannot be effective without its formal acceptance by the Bishop. The fulfilment of any condition attached to such a resignation must lie within the competence of the Bishop (e.g. 'that I be allowed to remain in the parochial house'), and if it is to be effective, the Bishop must, within three months (see Can. 189 §3) in fact accept the resignation and the condition attached. Non-fulfilment of the condition would render the resignation invalid. Moreover, until it takes effect, the parish priest can revoke the resignation (see Can. 189 §4).

Can. 1744 §1 If the parish priest has not replied within the days prescribed, the Bishop is to renew his invitation and extend the canonical time within which a reply is to be made.

---

[1] The requirement that the group be 'stably established' excludes a situation whereby such a group might simply be set up *ad hoc* for individual cases. It is to be a permanent body and obviously should be known as such even if, hopefully, its services will not frequently be required. Its membership, not determined by the Code, should clearly be more than two.

[2] In this particular regard the Bishop must not merely consult but in fact receive the *consent* of the council of priests – itself primarily a consultative body (cf. Can. 500 §2) – to the nomination of those priests whom he proposes for appointment to the "group stably established for this purpose" in the diocese. The priests proposed must themselves be parish priests (Can. 515 §1), though not necessarily members of the council. Should the Vicar general or an episcopal Vicar be also a parish priest, it would be against the spirit of the law that either be appointed to this group, since they are by their very office committed to be of one mind with the Bishop (cf. Can. 480): the thrust of this canon is that in this particularly sensitive situation the Bishop be given sound but independent advice. The Bishop is not of course obliged to follow the advice given but he would clearly have an obligation to take it seriously into account.

§2 If it is clear to the Bishop that the parish priest has received this second invitation but has not replied, even though not prevented from doing so by any impediment, or if the parish priest refuses to resign and gives no reasons for this, the Bishop is to issue a decree of removal.

Having invited the parish priest to resign in accordance with Can. 1742 §1, if the Bishop has received no reply from the parish priest within fifteen days, he is obliged to make a further attempt, extending the time-limit for a response. However, if after this has elapsed, there is still no answer, or if the parish priest has replied by refusing to resign and gives no reasons for his decision, then the Bishop must proceed to issue the decree of removal in accordance with the relevant prescriptions of Cann. 35–58.

3393

Can. 1745 If, however, the parish priest opposes the case put forward and the reasons given in it, but advances arguments which seem to the Bishop to be insufficient, to act validly the Bishop must:

1° invite him to inspect the acts of the case and put together the objections in a written answer, indeed to produce contrary proofs if he has any;

2° after this, complete the instruction of the case, if this is necessary, and weigh the matter with the same parish priests mentioned in Can. 1742 §1, unless, because of some impossibility on their part, others are to be designated;

3° finally, decide whether or not the parish priest is to be removed, and without delay issue the appropriate decree.

If, after the Bishop has invited him to resign in accordance with Can. 1742 §1, the parish priest responds with arguments against his removal, the Bishop must proceed in accordance with this canon. Clearly, if he admits the reasoning of the parish priest in his reply, then there is no need to proceed further and the parish priest will be left in his place. However, if the Bishop is not satisfied concerning the sufficiency of the arguments advanced by the parish priest, he must then act carefully in conformity with the provisions of the canon. This requires that the parish priest be invited to examine the acts of the case and submit in writing objections and contrary proofs. Although the parish priest may choose not to avail himself of this invitation, it may never be omitted since it belongs to his right of defence. The Bishop must complete the instruction of the case, if it is necessary; this will entail a further inspection of the documentation by the parish priest and of additional submissions by him if he so wishes. A new discussion of the whole case must now take place between the Bishop and the two parish priests mentioned in Can. 1742 §1 or their substitutes. Finally, the Bishop must make a decision and issue the relevant decree, either confirming the parish priest in office or removing him. If the decision is in favour of removal, the parish priest may lodge a hierarchical recourse in accordance with Cann. 1734–1739, the effect of which is to suspend the decision pending the outcome of the recourse.[1]

3394

Can. 1746 When the parish priest has been removed, the Bishop is to ensure that he is either assigned to another office, if he is suitable for one, or is given a pension in so far as the case requires this and the circumstances permit.

Removal from office does not substantially alter the Bishop's obligation to provide for the parish priest's welfare. This he must fulfil either by assigning him to a new office

3395

---

[1] Cf. CCom rep I.VII.1971: AAS 63(1971) 860 at nn.14–15.

or by making appropriate arrangements concerning his income. In fact, it should be borne in mind that, when embarking on a process of removal, the Bishop should from the beginning seriously consider and, if possible, even at that early stage offer an alternative whereby the parish priest would be supported with his dignity intact.

Can. 1747 §1 A parish priest who has been removed must abstain from exercising the function of a parish priest, leave the parochial house free as soon as possible, and hand over everything pertaining to the parish to the person to whom the Bishop has entrusted it.

§2 If, however, it is a question of a sick man who cannot be transferred elsewhere from the parochial house without inconvenience, the Bishop is to leave him the use, even the exclusive use, of the parochial house for as long as this necessity lasts.

§3 While recourse against a decree of removal is pending, the Bishop cannot appoint a new parish priest, but is to make provision in the meantime by way of a parochial administrator.

3396   The practical consequences of a decree of removal for the parish priest are clear: he must relinquish all exercise of the office; he must vacate the parochial house as soon as possible; he must hand over to his replacement everything pertinent to the running of the parish. However, the law foresees two situations where some or all of these consequences do not follow immediately. In the first place, it acknowledges that a parish priest who is ill, although removed from office, may well have to retain the use of the parochial house – in which situation the Bishop is obliged to allow him to do so. Secondly, a recourse lodged against the decree of removal, in accordance with Cann. 1734–1739, suspends the removal pending the outcome of the recourse. In the interval, no new parish priest may be appointed. The Bishop may, however, consider it appropriate to appoint a parochial administrator in the interim.

Chapter II
THE PROCEDURE FOR THE TRANSFER OF PARISH PRIESTS

Can. 1748 The good of souls or the necessity or advantage of the Church may demand that a parish priest be transferred from his own parish, which he governs satisfactorily, to another parish or another office. In these circumstances, the Bishop is to propose the transfer to him in writing and persuade him to consent, for the love of God and of souls.

3397   The procedure for the transfer of a parish priest is an application of the general principles found in Cann. 190–191. The tone of this procedure is overwhelmingly positive. First of all, the canon makes clear that transfer is not to be viewed as a criticism of the ministry of a parish priest: the one to be transferred is a parish priest who has already exercised his ministry in a satisfactory manner. The purpose of the transfer is to deploy his talents elsewhere for the good of souls and to the benefit of the Church. According to this canon, the Bishop is to propose such a transfer in writing. In fact and in normal practice, this can and where possible ought to be done by way of a preliminary personal interview between the Bishop and the parish priest in question, before the matter is formally committed to writing.

Can. 1749 If the parish priest proposes not to acquiesce in the Bishop's advice and persuasion, he is to give his reasons in writing.

Faced with a proposed transfer, the parish priest may well choose to accept it 'for the love of God and of souls'. However, should he propose not to accept the request, then the procedure outlined in these canons is to be used. Can. 190 §2 recognises the right of a person 'to present reasons against the transfer' of an office. However, in the case of a parish priest, the law *requires* that he put his reasons against the proposed transfer in *writing*.

3398

Can. 1750 Despite the reasons put forward, the Bishop may judge that he should not withdraw from his proposal. In this case, together with two parish priests chosen in accordance with Can. 1742 §1, he is to weigh the reasons which favour and those which oppose the transfer. If the Bishop still considers that the transfer should proceed, he is again to renew his fatherly exhortation to the parish priest.

The Bishop is to consider the reasons put forward by the parish priest against the proposed transfer. If he accepts the priest's reasons, he should inform the priest to that effect. On the other hand, if the Bishop does not accept the reasons presented by the parish priest, he is to consult the two parish priests mentioned in Can. 1742 §1, and seek their advice. If, after this consultation, the Bishop decides to go ahead with the transfer, he is to renew his efforts to persuade the parish priest to accept the proposed transfer.

3399

Can. 1751 §1 If, when these things have been done, the parish priest still refuses and the Bishop still believes that a transfer ought to take place, the Bishop is to issue a decree of transfer stating that, when a prescribed time has elapsed, the parish shall be vacant.

§2 When this time has elapsed without result, he is to declare the parish vacant.

Should the parish priest refuse this renewed exhortation, then the Bishop, if he believes that he should continue with the procedure, is to issue a decree of transfer stating that, at the end of a specified period of time, the parish will be vacant. In accordance with Can. 191 §1, the office of parish priest will become vacant automatically when the priest concerned obtains canonical possession of his new office. However, if the parish priest does not leave his parish in order to take possession of his new ecclesiastical office during the time period stated in the Bishop's letter, the Bishop is required by law to issue a *further* decree at the end of that period declaring the parish vacant.

3400

Can. 1752 In cases of transfer, the provisions of Can. 1747 are to be applied, always observing canonical equity and keeping in mind the salvation of souls, which in the Church must always be the supreme law.

The effects of a decree of transfer are identical to those of a decree of removal: the priest who has been transferred is required to abstain from exercising the function of a parish priest, leave the parochial house, and hand over everything pertaining to the office to his successor. As in the case of removal, a decree of transfer may not be immediately effective: the Bishop may decide to permit a priest who is ill to remain in the parochial house for as long as is necessary; or the priest may institute recourse against the decree which will suspend its execution. The predominantly positive tone of the whole process is affirmed with the call to the observance of canonical equity and the reminder that the fundamental law of the Church must always be the salvation of souls. Pointing in the direction of that law will always be the application of commonsense, of patient forbearance and of christian charity.

3401

TABLE OF CANONS

		Canon nos
BOOK I: GENERAL NORMS		1–203
Title I	Ecclesiastical Laws	7–22
Title II	Custom	23–28
Title III	General Decrees and Instructions	29–34
Title IV	Singular Administrative Acts	35–93
Chapter I	Common Norms	35–47
Chapter II	Singular Decrees and Precepts	48–58
Chapter III	Rescripts	59–75
Chapter IV	Privileges	76–84
Chapter V	Dispensations	85–93
Title V	Statutes and Ordinances	94–95
Title VI	Physical and Juridical Persons	96–123
Chapter I	The Canonical Status of Physical Persons	96–112
Chapter II	Juridical Persons	113–123
Title VII	Juridical Acts	124–128
Title VIII	Power of Governance	129–144
Title IX	Ecclesiastical Offices	145–196
Chapter I	The Provision of Ecclesiastical Office	146–183
Article 1	Free Conferral	157
Article 2	Presentation	158–163
Article 3	Election	164–179
Article 4	Postulation	180–183
Chapter II	Loss of Ecclesiastical Office	184–196
Article 1	Resignation	187–189
Article 2	Transfer	190–191
Article 3	Removal	192–195
Article 4	Deprivation	196
Title X	Prescription	197–199
Title XI	The Reckoning of Time	200–203
BOOK II: THE PEOPLE OF GOD		204–746
Part I: Christ's Faithful		204–329
Title I	The Obligations and Rights of all Christ's Faithful	208–223
Title II	The Obligations and Rights of the Lay Members of Christ's Faithful	224–231

Table of Canons

Title III	Sacred Ministers or Clerics	232–293
Chapter I	The Formation of Clerics	232–264
Chapter II	The Enrolment or Incardination of Clerics	265–272
Chapter III	The Obligations and Rights of Clerics	273–289
Chapter IV	Loss of the Clerical State	290–293
Title IV	Personal Prelatures	294–297
Title V	Associations of Christ's Faithful	298–329
Chapter I	Common Norms	298–311
Chapter II	Public Associations of Christ's Faithful	312–320
Chapter III	Private Associations of Christ's Faithful	321–326
Chapter IV	Special Norms for Lay Associations	327–329

Part II: The Hierarchical Constitution of the Church — 330–572

Section I: The Supreme Authority of the Church — 330–367

Chapter I	The Roman Pontiff and the College of Bishops	330–341
Article 1	The Roman Pontiff	331–335
Article 2	The College of Bishops	336–341
Chapter II	The Synod of Bishops	342–348
Chapter III	The Cardinals of the Holy Roman Church	349–359
Chapter IV	The Roman Curia	360–361
Chapter V	Papal Legates	362–367

Section II: Particular Churches and their Groupings — 368–572

Title I	Particular Churches and the Authority Constituted within them	368–430
Chapter I	Particular Churches	368–374
Chapter II	Bishops	375–411
Article 1	Bishops in General	375–380
Article 2	Diocesan Bishops	381–402
Article 3	Coadjutor and Auxiliary Bishops	403–411
Chapter III	The Impeded or Vacant See	412–430
Article 1	The Impeded See	412–415
Article 2	The Vacant See	416–430
Title II	Groupings of Particular Churches	431–459
Chapter I	Ecclesiastical Provinces and Ecclesiastical Regions	431–434
Chapter II	Metropolitans	435–438
Chapter III	Particular Councils	439–446
Chapter IV	Bishops' Conferences	447–459
Title III	The Internal Ordering of Particular Churches	460–572
Chapter I	The Diocesan Synod	460–468
Chapter II	The Diocesan Curia	469–494
Article 1	Vicars General and Episcopal Vicars	475–481
Article 2	The Chancellor, other Notaries and the Archives	482–491
Article 3	The Finance Committee and the Financial Administrator	492–494

Chapter III	The Council of Priests and the College of Consultors	495–502
Chapter IV	The Chapter of Canons	503–510
Chapter V	The Pastoral Council	511–514
Chapter VI	Parishes, Parish Priests and Assistant Priests	515–552
Chapter VII	Vicars Forane	553–555
Chapter VIII	Rectors of Churches and Chaplains	556–572
Article 1	Rectors of Churches	556–563
Article 2	Chaplains	564–572

Part III: Institutes of Consecrated Life and Societies of Apostolic Life 573–746

Section I: Institutes of Consecrated Life 573–730

Title I	Norms Common to All Institutes of Consecrated Life	573–606
Title II	Religious Institutes	607–709
Chapter I	Religious Houses and their Establishment and Suppression	608–616
Chapter II	The Governance of Institutes	617–640
Article 1	Superiors and Councils	617–630
Article 2	Chapters	631–633
Article 3	Temporal Goods and their Administration	634–640
Chapter III	The Admission of Candidates and the Formation of Members	641–661
Article 1	Admission to the Novitiate	641–645
Article 2	The Novitiate and the Formation of Novices	646–653
Article 3	Religious Profession	654–658
Article 4	The Formation of Religious	659–661
Chapter IV	The Obligations and Rights of Institutes and of their Members	662–672
Chapter V	The Apostolate of Institutes	673–683
Chapter VI	The Separation of Members from the Institute	684–704
Article 1	Transfer to another Institute	684–685
Article 2	Departure from the Institute	686–693
Article 3	The Dismissal of Members	694–704
Chapter VII	Religious raised to the Episcopate	705–707
Chapter VIII	Conferences of Major Superiors	708–709
Title III	Secular Institutes	710–730

Section II: Societies of Apostolic Life 731–746

BOOK III: THE TEACHING OFFICE OF THE CHURCH 747–833

Title I	The Ministry of the Divine Word	756–780
Chapter I	Preaching the Word of God	762–772
Chapter II	Catechetical Formation	773–780
Title II	The Missionary Activity of the Church	781–792

Table of Canons

Title III	Catholic Education	793–821
Chapter I	Schools	796–806
Chapter II	Catholic Universities and other Institutes of Higher Studies	807–814
Chapter III	Ecclesiastical Universities and Faculties	815–821

| Title IV | The Means of Social Communication and Books in Particular | 822–832 |

| Title V | The Profession of Faith | 833 |

BOOK IV: THE SANCTIFYING OFFICE OF THE CHURCH — 834–1253

Part I: The Sacraments — 840–1165

Title I	Baptism	849–878
Chapter I	The Celebration of Baptism	850–860
Chapter II	The Minister of Baptism	861–863
Chapter III	The Persons to be Baptised	864–871
Chapter IV	Sponsors	872–874
Chapter V	Proof and Registration of Baptism	875–878

Title II	The Sacrament of Confirmation	879–896
Chapter I	The Celebration of Confirmation	880–881
Chapter II	The Minister of Confirmation	882–888
Chapter III	The Persons to be Confirmed	889–891
Chapter IV	Sponsors	892–893
Chapter V	Proof and Registration of Confirmation	894–896

Title III	The Blessed Eucharist	897–958
Chapter I	The Celebration of the Eucharist	899–933
Article 1	The Minister of the Blessed Eucharist	900–911
Article 2	Participation in the Blessed Eucharist	912–923
Article 3	The Rites and Ceremonies of the Eucharistic Celebration	924–930
Article 4	The Time and Place of the Eucharistic Celebration	931–933
Chapter II	The Reservation and Veneration of the Blessed Eucharist	934–944
Chapter III	The Offering made for the Celebration of Mass	945–948

Title IV	The Sacrament of Penance	959–997
Chapter I	The Celebration of the Sacrament	960–964
Chapter II	The Minister of the Sacrament of Penance	965–986
Chapter III	The Penitent	987–991
Chapter IV	Indulgences	992–997

Title V	The Sacrament of Anointing of the Sick	998–1007
Chapter I	The Celebration of the Sacrament	999–1002
Chapter II	The Minister of Anointing of the Sick	1003
Chapter III	Those to be Anointed	1004–1007

Table of Canons

Title VI	Orders	1008–1054
Chapter I	The Celebration of Ordination and the Minister	1010–1023
Chapter II	Those to be Ordained	1024–1052
Article 1	The Requirements in those to be Ordained	1026–1032
Article 2	Prerequisites for Ordination	1033–1039
Article 3	Irregularities and other Impediments	1040–1049
Article 4	Documents required and the Investigation	1050–1052
Chapter III	The Registration and Evidence of Ordination	1053–1054
Title VII	Marriage	1055–1165
Chapter I	Pastoral Care and the Prerequisites for the Celebration of Marriage	1063–1072
Chapter II	Diriment Impediments in General	1073–1082
Chapter III	Individual Diriment Impediments	1083–1094
Chapter IV	Matrimonial Consent	1095–1107
Chapter V	The Form of the Celebration of Marriage	1108–1123
Chapter VI	Mixed Marriages	1124–1129
Chapter VII	The Secret Celebration of Marriage	1130–1133
Chapter VIII	The Effects of Marriage	1134–1140
Chapter IX	The Separation of the Spouses	1141–1155
Article 1	The Dissolution of the Bond	1141–1150
Article 2	Separation while the Bond remains	1151–1155
Chapter X	The Validation of Marriage	1156–1165
Article 1	Simple Validation	1156–1160
Article 2	Retroactive Validation	1161–1165

Part II: The Other Acts of Divine Worship — 1166–1204

Title I	Sacramentals	1166–1172
Title II	The Liturgy of the Hours	1173–1175
Title III	Church Funerals	1176–1185
Chapter I	The Celebration of Funerals	1177–1182
Chapter II	Those to whom Church Funerals are to be allowed or denied	1183–1185
Title IV	The Cult of the Saints, of Sacred Images and of Relics	1186–1190
Title V	Vows and Oaths	1191–1204
Chapter I	Vows	1191–1198
Chapter II	Oaths	1199–1204

Part III: Sacred Places and Times — 1205–1253

Title I	Sacred Places	1205–1243
Chapter I	Churches	1214–1222
Chapter II	Oratories and Private Chapels	1223–1229
Chapter III	Shrines	1230–1234
Chapter IV	Altars	1235–1239
Chapter V	Cemeteries	1240–1243

Title II	Sacred Times	1244–1253
Chapter I	Holydays	1246–1248
Chapter II	Days of Penance	1249–1253

BOOK V: THE TEMPORAL GOODS OF THE CHURCH 1254–1310

Title I	The Acquisition of Goods	1259–1272
Title II	The Administration of Goods	1273–1289
Title III	Contracts and especially Alienation	1290–1298
Title IV	Pious Dispositions in General and Pious Foundations	1299–1310

BOOK VI: SANCTIONS IN THE CHURCH 1311–1399

Part I: Offences and Punishments in General 1311–1363

Title I	The Punishment of Offences in General	1311–1312
Title II	Penal Law and Penal Precept	1313–1320
Title III	Those who are liable to Penal Sanctions	1321–1330
Title IV	Penalties and other Punishments	1331–1340
Chapter I	Censures	1331–1335
Chapter II	Expiatory Penalties	1336–1338
Chapter III	Penal Remedies and Penances	1339–1340
Title V	The Application of Penalties	1341–1353
Title VI	The Cessation of Penalties	1354–1363

Part II: Penalties for Particular Offences 1364–1399

Title I	Offences against Religion and the Unity of the Church	1364–1369
Title II	Offences against Church Authorities and the Freedom of the Church	1370–1377
Title III	Usurpation of Ecclesiastical Offices and Offences committed in their Exercise	1378–1389
Title IV	The False Accusation	1390–1391
Title V	Offences against Special Obligations	1392–1396
Title VI	Offences against Human Life and Liberty	1397–1398
Title VII	General Norm	1399

BOOK VII: JUDICIAL PROCEDURES 1400–1752

Part I: Trials in General 1400–1500

Title I	The Competent Forum	1404–1416

Title II	Different Grades and Kinds of Tribunals	1417–1445
Chapter I	The Tribunal of First Instance	1419–1437
Article 1	The Judge	1419–1427
Article 2	Auditors and Relators	1428–1429
Article 3	The Promotor of Justice, the Defender of the Bond and the Notary	1430–1437
Chapter II	The Tribunal of Second Instance	1438–1441
Chapter III	The Tribunals of the Apostolic See	1442–1445
Title III	The Discipline to be Observed in Tribunals	1446–1475
Chapter I	The Duties of the Judges and of the Officers of the Tribunal	1446–1457
Chapter II	The Ordering of the Hearing	1458–1464
Chapter III	Time-Limits and Postponements	1465–1467
Chapter IV	The Place of Trial	1468–1469
Chapter V	Those who may be admitted to the Court and the Manner of Compiling and Preserving the Acts	1470–1475
Title IV	The Parties in the Case	1476–1490
Chapter I	The Plaintiff and the Respondent	1476–1480
Chapter II	Procurators and Advocates	1481–1490
Title V	Actions and Exceptions	1491–1500
Chapter I	Actions and Exceptions in General	1491–1495
Chapter II	Actions and Exceptions in Particular	1496–1500

Part II: The Contentious Trial   1501–1670

Section I: The Ordinary Contentious Trial   1501–1655

Title I	The Introduction of the Case	1501–1512
Chapter I	The Petition introducing the Suit	1501–1506
Chapter II	The Summons and the Intimation of Judicial Acts	1507–1512
Title II	The Joinder of the Issue	1513–1516
Title III	The Trial of the Issue	1517–1525
Title IV	Proofs	1526–1586
Chapter I	The Declarations of the Parties	1530–1538
Chapter II	Documentary Proof	1539–1546
Article 1	The Nature and Reliability of Documents	1540–1543
Article 2	The Production of Documents	1544–1546
Chapter III	Witnesses and Testimony	1547–1573
Article 1	Those who can be Witnesses	1549–1550
Article 2	The Introduction and the Exclusion of Witnesses	1551–1557
Article 3	The Examination of Witnesses	1558–1571
Article 4	The Credibility of Evidence	1572–1573
Chapter IV	Experts	1574–1581

Table of Canons

Chapter V	Judicial Access and Inspection	1582–1583
Chapter VI	Presumptions	1584–1586

Title V	Incidental Matters	1587–1597
Chapter I	The Non-Appearance of Parties	1592–1595
Chapter II	The Intervention of a Third Party in a Case	1596–1597

Title VI	The Publication of the Acts, the Conclusion of the Case and the Pleadings	1598–1606

Title VII	The Pronouncements of the Judge	1607–1618

Title VIII	Challenging the Judgement	1619–1640
Chapter I	The Plaint of Nullity of the Judgement	1619–1627
Chapter II	The Appeal	1628–1640

Title IX	Adjudged Matter and Total Reinstatement	1641–1648
Chapter I	Adjudged Matter	1641–1644
Chapter II	Total Reinstatement	1645–1648

Title X	Judicial Expenses and Free Legal Aid	1649

Title XI	The Execution of the Judgement	1650–1655

Section II: The Oral Contentious Process — 1656–1670

Part III: Certain Special Processes — 1671–1707

Title I	Matrimonial Processes	1671–1716
Chapter I	Cases concerning the Declaration of Nullity of Marriage	1671–1691
Article 1	The Competent Forum	1671–1673
Article 2	The Right to Challenge the Validity of Marriage	1674–1675
Article 3	The Office of Judges	1676–1677
Article 4	Proofs	1678–1680
Article 5	The Judgement and the Appeal	1681–1685
Article 6	The Documentary Process	1686–1688
Article 7	General Norms	1689–1691
Chapter II	Cases Concerning the Separation of Spouses	1692–1696
Chapter III	The Process for the Dispensation from a Ratified and Non-Consummated Marriage	1697–1706
Chapter IV	The Process in the Case of the Presumed Death of a Spouse	1707

Title II	Cases for the Declaration of Nullity of Sacred Ordination	1708–1712
Title III	Ways of Avoiding Trials	1713–1716

Part IV: The Penal Process — 1717–1731

Chapter I	The Preliminary Investigation	1717–1719
Chapter II	The Course of the Process	1720–1728
Chapter III	The Action for Damages	1729–1731

Table of Canons

**Part V: The Manner of Procedure in Administrative
Recourse and in the Removal or Transfer of Parish Priests 1732–1752**

Section I: Recourse Against Administrative Decrees   1732–1739

**Section II: *The Procedure for the Removal or Transfer
of Parish Priests***   1740–1752

  Chapter I   The Procedure for the Removal of Parish Priests 1740–1747
  Chapter II   The Procedure for the Transfer of Parish Priests   1748–1752

Concordance of Canons
1983 Code – 1917 Code

BOOK I

1983	1917
1	1
2	2
3	3
4	4
5	5
6	6
7	8 §1
8 §1	9
9	10
10	11
11	12
12	13
13	8 §2; 14
14	15
15	16
16	17
17	18
18	19
19	20
20	22
21	23
22	1529
23	25–26
24	27
25	28
26	5; 28; 30
27	29
28	30; 5
29–39	–
40–47	54–59
48	–
49	24
50–59	–
60	36 §1
61	37
62	38
63 §§1–2	42 §§1–2
63 §3	41; 48
64	43
65	44

BOOK I

1983	1917
66	47
67	48
68	51
69	52
70	54 §2
71–72	–
73	60 §2
74	–
75	62
76	63
77	67–68
78	70; 74; 75
79	71
80	72
81	73
82	76
83	77
84	78
85	80
86	–
87	81
88	82
89	83
90	84
91	–
92	85
93	86
94–95	–
96	87
97	88
98	89
99	88 §3
100	91
101	90
102	92
103	–
104	93 §1
105	93
106	95
107	94

Concordance 1983 Code – 1917 Code

BOOK I

1983	1917
108	96
109	97
110	–
111	101
112	98
113	99–100
114	100 §1
115	100 §2
116–118	–
119	101
120	102
121	–
122	1500
123	1501
124	1680
125	103
126	104
127	105
128	–
129	196
130	196
131	197; 200 §2
132	–
133	203
134	198
135	201 §2; 205 §1
136	201
137	–
138	201 §1
139	204
140	205
141	206
142	207
143	208
144	209
145	145
146	147 §1
147	148
148	–
149	153; 729
150	154
151	155
152	156
153	150
154	151
155	158
156	159
157	152

BOOK I

1983	1917
158–163	1455–1466
164	160
165	161
166	162
167	163; 168
168	164
169	165
170	166
171	167
172	169
173	171
174	172
175	173
176	174
177	175; 176 §1
178	176 §2
179	177
180	179
181	180
182	181
183	182
184	183
185–186	–
187	184
188	185
189	186; 187 §1; 189 §1; 190 §2; 191 §1
190	193
191	194
192–195	2147–2161
196	192
197	1508
198	1512
199	1509
1200	31
201	35
202	32
203	34

BOOK II

1983	1917
204–206	–
207	107
208–212	–
213	682
214–231	–
232	1352

982

Concordance 1983 Code – 1917 Code

BOOK II		**BOOK II**	
1983	**1917**	**1983**	**1917**
233	1353	288	–
234	1353–1354	289	141
235	972	290–293	211–214
236	–	294–297	–
237	1354; 1357	298	684–685
238	–	299–302	–
239	1358–1359	303	702–703
240	1361	304	688–689
241	1363	305	690
242	–	306	692
243	1357	307	693–694
244–245	–	308	696 §1
246	1367	309	697 §1
247	–	310–311	–
248	1364 §§1 and 3	312	686
249	1364 §2	313	–
250	1365	314	689
251–252	–	315	–
253	1366	316	693; 696
254–258	–	317	698 §1 and 4
259	1357	318	698 §3
260	1360 §2	319	691
261	1369	320	696
262	1368	321–330	–
263	–	331	218 §1
264	1355–1356	332	219–221
265	111 §1	333	228 §2
266	111 §2	334–337	–
267	112	338	222; 226
268	–	339	223
269	117; 115	340	229
270	116	341	227
271	–	342–347	–
272	113	348	–
273	127	349	230
274	118; 128	350	231 §1
275	–	351	232 §1; 235
276	124–126	352	237
277	132–133	353	233
278	–	354	–
279	129–131	355	239 §§2–3
280	134	356	238
281–282	–	357	240 §1; 239
283	143; 418; 465	358	266
284	136 §1	359	241
285	137–140	360	242–264
286	142	361	7
287	139 §4	362	265

Concordance 1983 Code – 1917 Code

BOOK II 1983	1917	BOOK II 1983	1917
363–364	–	421	432 §§1–3
365	267 §1 1°	422	432 §4
366	269 §3	423	443
367	268	424	133 §2
368	215	425	434
369	–	426	435 §2
370	319–327	427	435 §1; 438
371	293–318	428	436; 435 §3
372–376	–	429	440
377	329 §2	430	443
378	331	431–434	–
379	333	435	272
380	332 §2	436	274
381	334 §1	437	275; 277–278
382	333; 334 §§2–3	438	271
383–387	–	439	281
388	339	440	283
389	–	441	–
390	357	442	284
391	335 §1	443	286
392	336 §§1–2	444	287
393	1653 §1	445	290
394	–	446	291
395	338	447–459	–
396	343 §§1–2	460	356–362
397	344 §§1–2	461	356
398	346	462	357
399	340 §§1 and 3	463	358
400	341 §1; 342; 299	464	359
401–402	–	465	361
403	350; 352	466	362
404	353	467–468	–
405	351 §§1–2	469	363
406–407	–	470	366 §2; 372 §1
408	351 §§3–4	471	364
409	355 §§1–2	472	365
410	354	473–474	–
411	–	475	366
412	429 §1	476	–
413–414	429	477	366 §§2–3
415	429 §5	478	367
416	430 §1	479	368
417	430 §2	480	369
418	430 §3	481	371
419	431	482	372
420	309 §2; 317	483	373
		484	374
		485	373 §5

Concordance 1983 Code – 1917 Code

BOOK II		BOOK II	
1983	**1917**	**1983**	**1917**
486	375	555	447–449
487	377	556	479
488	378	557	480
489	379	558	481
490	379 §3; 382	559	482
491	383	560	483
492	1520	561	484 §1
493–502	–	562	485
503	391 §1	563	486
504	392	564–572	518–530
505	410	573–576	–
506	393; 394 §1	577	488 2°
507	393 §2; 394	578	–
508	401	579–580	492
509	404	581	–
510	402	582	494
511–514	–	583	–
515	215–216	584	493
516	216 §3	585–586	–
517–518	–	587	489
519	451	588	488 4°
520	452; 471	589–590	–
521	453	591	615–616
522	454	592–595	–
523	455	596	501
524	458–459	597	538
525	–	598–608	–
526	460	609–616	492–498
527	461	617–620	–
528	–	621	488 6°
529	467–468	622	502
530	462	623	504
531	463 §3	624	505
532	–	625	507
533	465	626	507
534	466	627	516 §1
535	470	628	511; 512
536–539	–	629	508
540	473	630	518–530; 876
541	475; 458; 472; 1923 §2	631–633	501; 507
		634–640	531–537
542	453; 454; 458; 459	641	543
543–544	–	642	538
545	476 §§1–2	643	542 §1
546–552	471–478	644	542 §2
553	445	645	544
554	446	646–649	553–558
		650–652	559–570

Concordance 1983 Code – 1917 Code

BOOK II	
1983	**1917**
653	571
654–658	572–586
659–661	587–591
662	593
663	595
664	–
665	606 §2
666	–
667	597–607
668	580–683; 569; 594 §2
669	596
670	–
671	592
672–683	–
684	632–634
685	635
686–693	637–645
694	646
695–704	647–672
705	627
706	628
707	629
708–730	–
731–746	673–681

BOOK III	
747	1322
748	1322 §2; 1351
749	1323
750	1323 §1
751	1325
752	1324
753	1326
754	1324
755	–
756	1327
757	1329
758	1334
759	1333
760	1347
761	–
762–772	1337–1348
773–780	1329–1336
781–792	1349–1351
793	1113; 1372 §2; 1335
794–795	–

BOOK III	
1983	**1917**
796–806	1372; 1375; 1379; 1381–1383
807–821	1376–1380
822	–
823	1385; 1384
824	1384 §2; 1385
825	1385; 1391
826	1390
827	–
828	1389
829	1392
830	1393
831	1386
832	1386
833	1406

BOOK IV	
834–839	–
840	731 §1
841	733
842	737 §1
843–844	–
845	732
846	733
847	734
848	736
849	737 §1
850	737 §2; 755; 759
851	752
852	–
853	757
854	758
855	761
856	–
857	771; 773
858	774
859	775
860	776
861	738; 743
862	739
863	744
864	745
865	745 §2 2°; 752
866	753 §2
867	770; 771
868	750
869	732 §2

986

Concordance 1983 Code – 1917 Code

BOOK IV		BOOK IV	
1983	**1917**	**1983**	**1917**
870	749	918	863
871	747	919	808; 858
872	762; 769	920	859–860
873	764	921	864
874	765–766	922	865
875	–	923	866
876	779	924	814–815
877	777	925	852
878	778	926	816
879	–	927	817
880	780–781	928	819
881	791	929	811
882	782 §§1–2	930	–
883	782–784	931	820–821
884	785	932	822
885	785 §§1–2	933	823
886	783	934	1265
887	784	935	1265 §3
888	792	936	1267
889	786	937	1266
890	787	938	1268–1269
891	788	939	1270; 1272
892	793–794	940	1271
893	795–796	941	1274
894	798	942	1274–1275
895	798	943	1274
896	799	944	1274
897	801	945	824
898	1273	946	–
899	–	947	827
900	802	948	828
901	809	949	829
902	803	950	830
903	804	951	824
904	805	952	831–832
905	806	953	835
906	813	954	836–833
907–908	–	955	837–840
909	810	956	841
910	845	957	842
911	850; 397 §3; 514 §1; 847–849	958	843
		959	870
912	853	960–963	–
913	854	964	908–910
914	854 §§4–5	965	871
915	855	966	872
916	807; 856	967	873
917	857	968	873 §§1–2

Concordance 1983 Code – 1917 Code

BOOK IV		BOOK IV	
1983	**1917**	**1983**	**1917**
969	874	1016	956
970	877	1017	–
971	–	1018	958
972	878 §1	1019	964
973	879 §1	1020	960
974	880 §1	1021	961
975	–	1022	962
976	882	1023	963
977	884	1024	968 §1
978	888 §1	1025	968 §1
979	888 §2	1026	971
980	886	1027	972 §1
981	887	1028–1029	–
982	894; 904	1030	970
983	889	1031	975
984	890	1032	976
985	891	1033	974 §1 1°
986	892	1034	–
987	–	1035	974 §1 5°–6°; 978 §2
988	901–902		
989	906	1036	992
990	903	1037	–
991	905	1038	973 §2
992	911	1039	1001
993	–	1040	973 §3; 983
994	930	1041	984–985
995	913–914	1042	987
996	925	1043	999
997	–	1044	968 §2
998	937	1045	988
999	945	1046	989
1000	947	1047	990 §1
1001	944	1048	990
1002	–	1049	991
1003	935; 938–939; 946	1050	993
		1051	995–996
1004	940	1052	997
1005	941	1053	1010
1006	943	1054	1011
1007	942	1055	1012
1008	948	1056	1013 §2
1009	949	1057	1081
1010	1006	1058	1035
1011	1009	1059	1016
1012	951	1060	1014
1013	953	1061	1015
1014	954	1062	1017
1015	955; 958–959	1063–1064	–

Concordance 1983 Code – 1917 Code

BOOK IV		BOOK IV	
1983	**1917**	**1983**	**1917**
1065	1033	1111	1095 §2; 1096 §1
1066	1019 §1	1112	–
1067	1022	1113	1096 §2
1068	1019 §2	1114	1097 §1 1°–2°
1069	1027	1115	1097 §1 3°
1070	1029	1116	1098
1071	1032; 1034	1117	1099
1072	1067 §2	1118	1009
1073	1036 §2	1119	1100
1074	1037	1120	–
1075	1038	1121	1103 §§1 and 3
1076	1041	1122	1103 §2
1077	1039	1123	–
1078	–	1124–1129	1060–1064
1079	1043–1044	1130	1104
1080	1045	1131	1105
1081	1046	1132	1106
1082	1047	1133	1107
1083	1067 §1	1134	1110
1084	1068	1135	1111
1085	1069	1136	1113
1086	1070	1137	1114
1087	1072	1138	1115
1088	1073	1139	1116
1089	1074 §§1–2	1140	1117
1090	1075 §§2–3	1141	1118
1091	1076	1142	1119
1092	1077 §1	1143	1120; 1123; 1126
1093	1078	1144	1121
1094	1080	1145	1122
1095	88 §3; 1081–1082; 1089 §3; 1982; 2201	1146	1123–1124
		1147–1149	1125
		1150	1127
1096	1082	1151	1128
1097	1083	1152	1129–1130
1098	–	1153	1131
1099	1084	1154	1132
1100	1085	1155	1130
1101	1086	1156	1133
1102	1092	1157	1134
1103	1087 §1	1158	1135
1104	1088	1159	1136
1105	1089; 1091	1160	1137
1106	1090–1091	1161	1138
1107	1093	1162	1140
1108	1094	1163	1139
1109	1095 §1 1°	1164	–
1110	1095 §1 2°	1165	1141

Concordance 1983 Code – 1917 Code

BOOK IV

1983	1917
1166	1144
1167	1145; 1148 §2
1168	1146
1169	1147
1170	1149
1171	1150
1172	1151
1173	135; 610
1174	135; 610 §1; 1475
1175	33 §1
1176	1215; 1203; 1240 §1
1177	1216–1218
1178	1219 §2
1179	1221
1180	1205; 1208; 1223
1181	1234–1235
1182	1238
1183	1239
1184	1240
1185	1241
1186	1255 §1
1187	1277
1188	1279
1189	1280
1190	1281
1191	1307
1192	1308 §§1–2 and 4
1193	1310
1194	1311
1195	1312 §2
1196	1313
1197	1313–1314
1198	1315
1199	1316
1200	1317 §§1–2
1201	1318
1202	1319
1203	1320
1204	1321
1205	1154
1206	1155–1157
1207	1156–1157; 1163
1208	1158
1209	1159 §1

BOOK IV

1983	1917
1210	–
1211	1172
1212	1170; 1187
1213	1160
1214	1161
1215	1162
1216	1164 §1
1217	1165 §§1 and 3
1218	1168 §1
1219	1171
1220	1178
1221	1180
1222	1187
1223	1188
1224	1192 §§1–3
1225	1191; 1193
1226	1190
1227	1189
1228	1194–1195
1229	1196
1230–1234	–
1235	1197
1236	1198 §§1–3
1237	1198 §4; 1199 §1
1238	1170; 1187; 1200
1239	1202
1240	1206
1241	1208
1242	1205 §2
1243	–
1244	1244
1245	1245
1246	1247
1247	1248
1248	1249
1249	–
1250	1252
1251	1250–1252
1252	1254
1253	–
1254	1495 §1
1255	1495 §2
1256	1499 §2
1257	1497 §1
1258	1498
1259	1499 §1
1260	1496
1261–1262	–

990

Concordance 1983 Code – 1917 Code

BOOK V		BOOK VI	
1983	**1917**	**1983**	**1917**
1263	1502; 1504–1506	1315	2220–2221; 2223; 2226 §§2–3
1264	1507	1316	–
1265	1503	1317	2214 §2
1266–1267	–	1318	2241 §2
1268	1508	1319	2220
1269	1510	1320	–
1270	1511	1321	2195; 2200 §§1–2
1271–1272	–		
1273	1518	1322	2201 §§1–2
1274–1275	–	1323	2202–2205; 2230
1276	1519	1324	2206; 2229 §§2 and 3 2°–3°; 2204; 2230; 2205 §§2 and 4; 2202 §2; 2199; 2223
1277–1281	–		
1282	1521 §2		
1283	1522		
1284	1523		
1285	1527	1325	2229 §§1 and 3 1°; 2201 §3; 2206
1286	1524		
1287	1525	1326	2223
1288	1526	1327	–
1289	1528	1328	2212; 2235
1290	1529	1329	2209; 2231
1291	1530 §1 3°	1330	–
1292	1532	1331	2257–2267
1293	1530 §1 1°–2°	1332	2268
1294	1531	1333	2278–2285
1295	1533	1334	2278 §2
1296	1534	1335	2284
1297	1541	1336	2291
1298	1540	1337	2301; 2302
1299	1513	1338	2306–2310
1300	1514	1339	2307–2309
1301	1515	1340	2312–2313
1302	–	1341	2214 §2
1303	1544	1342	1933 §4
1304	1546	1343	2223 §2
1305	1547	1344	2223 §3
1306	1548	1345	2223 §3 3°
1307	1549	1346	2224 §2
1308–1310	1551	1347	2242
		1348	2223 §3 3°
BOOK VI		1349	2223 §1
1311	2214 §1	1350	2229 §3; 2303 §2
1312	2215–2216; 2241; 2286	1351	2226 §4
		1352	2232 §1; 2252
1313	19; 22; 23; 2219 §1; 2226 §2	1353	2243 §2; 2287
		1354	2236–2237
1314	2217 §2	1355	2237; 2253; 2245; 2236

Concordance 1983 Code – 1917 Code

BOOK VI		BOOK VII	
1983	**1917**	**1983**	**1917**
1356	2236	1400	1552 §2; 1601
1357	2254	1401	1553
1358	2242 §3	1402	1555
1359	–	1403	1991; 2141
1360	2238	1404	1556
1361	2239 §§1–2	1405	1557
1362	1703; 2240	1406	1558
1363	1703; 2240	1407	1559
1364	2314	1408	1561
1365	2316	1409	1563
1366	2319 §1 3°–4° §2	1410	1564
		1411	1565
1367	2320	1412	1566
1368	2323	1413	1560
1369	2323; 2331 §2	1414	1567
1370	2343	1415	1568
1371	2317; 2331 §1	1416	1612
1372	2332	1417	1569
1373	2344	1418	1570 §2
1374	2335	1419	1572
1375	2237; 2334; 2345; 2390	1420	1573
		1421	1574
1376	2346	1422	1574 §2
1377	2347	1423	–
1378	1267; 2366	1424	1575
1379	–	1425	1576
1380	2371	1426	1577
1381	2394; 2401	1427	1579
1382	2370	1428	1580–1582
1383	2373 §1	1429	1584
1384	–	1430	1586
1385	2324	1431	–
1386	2407	1432	1586
1387	2368	1433	1587
1388	2369	1434	–
1389	2404–2414	1435	1589
1390	2363 §1	1436	1588; 1590
1391	2360; 2362	1437	1585 §1
1392	2380	1438	1594
1393	–	1439–1440	–
1394	2388	1441	1595–1596
1395	2359	1442	1597
1396	2381	1443	1598 §1
1397	2354	1444	1599
1398	2350 §1	1445	1603
1399	2222 §2	1446	–
		1447	1571
		1448	1613
		1449	1614
		1450	1614–1615

Concordance 1983 Code – 1917 Code

BOOK VII

1983	1917
1451	1616
1452	1618; 1619 §1
1453	1620
1454	1621
1455	1623
1456	1624
1457	1625
1458	1627
1459	1628
1460	1610
1461	1611
1462	1629
1463	1630
1464	1631
1465	1634
1466	–
1467	1635
1468	1636; 1638
1469	1637
1470	1640
1471	1641; 1642 §2
1472	1642 §1; 1643 §1
1473	1643 §§2–3
1474	1644
1475	1645
1476	1646
1477	1647
1478	1648; 1650
1479	1651
1480	1649; 1653
1481	1655
1482	1656
1483	1657; 1658
1484	1659 §1; 1660–1661
1485	1662
1486	1664
1487	1663
1488	1665
1489	1666
1490	–
1491	1667
1492	1701; 1705 §1
1493	1669–1671
1494	1690
1495	1692
1496	1672

BOOK VII

1983	1917
1497	1673
1498	1674
1499	–
1500	1693–1700
1501	–
1502	1706
1503	1707
1504	1708
1505	1709
1506	1710
1507	1711
1508	1713; 1715
1509	1720; 1877
1510	1718
1511	1894 §1
1512	1725; 1854
1513	1729 §1; 1850 §3
1514	1731
1515	1731 3°
1516	1731 2°
1517	1732
1518	1733; 1972
1519	1735
1520	1736
1521	1737
1522	1738
1523	1739
1524	1740
1525	1741
1526	1747–1748
1527–1529	–
1530	1742
1531	1743
1532	1744
1533	1745
1534	–
1535	1750
1536	1751
1537	1753
1538	1752
1539	1812
1540	1813
1541	1816
1542	1817
1543	1818
1544	1819
1545	1822
1546	1823

Concordance 1983 Code – 1917 Code

BOOK VII		BOOK VII	
1983	**1917**	**1983**	**1917**
1547	1754	1595	1851
1548	1755	1596	1852; 1898–1901
1549	1756	1597	1853
1550	1757	1598	1858–1859
1551	1759	1599	1860
1552	1761	1600	1861
1553	1762	1601	1862
1554	1763	1602	1863–1864
1555	1764	1603	1865
1556	1765	1604	1866
1557	1766	1605	1866
1558	1770	1606	1867
1559	1771	1607	1868
1560	1772	1608	1869
1561	1773	1609	1871
1562	1767	1610	1872
1563	1774	1611	1873
1564	1775	1612	1874
1565	1776	1613	1875
1566	1777	1614	1876
1567	1778	1615	1877
1568	1779	1616	1821
1569	1780	1617–1619	–
1570	1781	1620	1892
1571	1787	1621	1893
1572	1789	1622	1894
1573	1791	1623	1895
1574	1792	1624	1893; 1895–1896
1575	1793	1625	1895
1576	1796	1626	1897
1577	1799	1627	–
1578	1801–1802	1628	1879
1579	1804	1629	1880
1580	1805	1630	1881–1882
1581	–	1631–1632	–
1582	1806–1810	1633	1883
1583	1811	1634	1884
1584	1825	1635	1886; 1890
1585	1827	1636	–
1586	1828	1637	1887–1888
1587	1837	1638	1889
1588	1838	1639	1891
1589	1839	1640	–
1590	1840	1641	1902
1591	1841	1642	1904
1592	1942; 1843–1845	1643	1903
1593	1846–1848	1644	1903
1594	1849	1645	1905

Concordance 1983 Code – 1917 Code

BOOK VII		BOOK VII	
1983	**1917**	**1983**	**1917**
1646	1906	1709	1993; 1997
1647	1907	1710	1993
1648	–	1711	1996
1649	1908–1916	1712	1998 §1
1650	1917	1713	1925 §1; 1929
1651	1918	1714	1926; 1930
1652	1919	1715	1927
1653	1920	1716	–
1654	1921	1717	1935–1946
1655	1922	1718	1942; 1940
1656–1670	–	1719	1946 §2 1°–2°
1671	1960	1720	1933 §4
1672	1961	1721	1934; 1937
1673	1557 §1 1°	1722	1956; 1957
1674	1971 §1 1°–2°	1723–1739	–
1675	1972	1740	2147 §1
1676	1965	1741	2147; 2157
1677–1680	–	1742	2148; 2158
1681	1963 §2	1743	2150
1682	1986	1744	2149; 2161
1683	–	1745	2151–2153; 2159
1684	1987		
1685	1988	1746	2161 §2; 2154
1686	1990	1747	2156; 2161
1687	1991	1748	2162
1688	1992	1749	2164
1689–1696	–	1750	2165
1697	1973	1751	2167
1698–1707	–	1752	–
1708	1994 §1		

CONTRIBUTORS

Barry,	Rev. John A., PhD, JCD *Associate Judicial Vicar* Halifax Regional Tribunal	(Cann. 1400–1475)
Bourgon,	Rev. Robert, JCL *Associate Judicial Vicar* Toronto Regional Tribunal	(Cann. 1526–1586)
Browne,	Rev. Raymond, JCL *Associate Judicial Vicar* Galway Regional Marriage Tribunal	(Cann. 1205–1253)
Coyle,	Sr Margaret SCIC, JCL *Chancery Official* Whitehorse Yukon	(Cann. 1476–1525)
Kelly,	Rev. Donal, JCL *Judge* Dublin Regional Marriage Tribunal *olim Professor of Canon Law* St Patrick's College Carlow	(Cann. 834–878 1008–1165 1656–1716)
McAreavey,	Rev. John, JCD *Professor of Canon Law* St Patrick's College Maynooth	(Cann. 879–1007)
McGrath,	Rev. Aidan OFM, JCD *Judge* Dublin Regional Marriage Tribunal *President of the Canon Law Society GBI*	(Cann. 96–196 204–367)
McLean,	Rev. Brian, PLB, STB, JCL *Judge* Scottish National Tribunal	(Cann. 1166–1204)
Martin,	Rev. John SJ, PhD, JCD *Professor of Canon Law* Regis College Toronto	(Cann. 1311–1399 1717–1731)
Mendonça,	Rev. Augustine, MA, MPs, PhD, JCD *Titular Professor of Canon Law* Saint Paul University Ottawa	(Cann. 1–95 197–203)

Contributors

Morrisey,	Rev. Francis G. OMI, PhD, JCD *Titular Professor of Canon Law* (*olim Dean*) Saint Paul University Ottawa *Consultor to Pontifical Council* for the Interpretation of Legislative Texts	(Cann. 747–833 1254–1310)
Read,	V. Rev. Gordon, MA, BD, JCL *Chancellor and Judicial Vicar* Diocese of Brentwood	(Cann. 368–572)
Ryan,	Sr Marcella SC, JCL *Judge* Halifax Regional Tribunal *Director of Formation* Sisters of Charity Halifax	(Cann. 1587–1655)
Thériault,	Michel, MLS, JCD *Associate Professor of Canon Law* Saint Paul University Ottawa	(Cann. 1732–1752)
Williamson,	Sr Enid OSM, MA, JCD *Judge* Westminster Metropolitan Tribunal	(Cann. 573–746)

Glossary

advena	the term to describe a person when he or she is actually present in the place where he or she has a quasi-domicile.
ferendae sententiae	the term to describe one of the two forms of penalty, namely, that which is imposed by the judgement of a court or by the decree of a Superior, when a person has been found guilty of an offence (cf. *latae sententiae* below).
incola	the term to describe a person when he or she is actually present in the place where he or she has a domicile.
inter vivos	the term to describe a legal arrangement whereby, during lifetime, a person at once transfers property to another person or corporate body (cf. *mortis causa* below).
latae sententiae	the term to describe one of the two forms of penalty, namely, that which is automatically incurred on committing an offence, without the intervention of a judge or Superior (cf. *ferendae sententiae* above).
mortis causa	the term to describe a legal arrangement made by a person during lifetime, whereby only after his or her death property is transferred to another person or corporate body (cf. *inter vivos* above).
motu proprio	the term to describe a rescript (cf. Can. 59 §1) which grants a favour not on the request of a petitioner, but on the sole initiative of the granting authority.
peregrinus	the term to describe a person when he or she is outside the place where he or she has a domicile or quasi-domicile, while still retaining that domicile or quasi-domicile. The plural is *peregrini*.
presbyterium	the term to describe the body of priests who are dedicated to the service of a particular Church, under the authority of the Bishop or other Superior equivalent to a Bishop.
vagus	the term to describe a person who has neither a domicile nor a quasi-domicile anywhere. The plural is *vagi*.

INDEX

All references are to paragraph numbers.

A

Abatement:
expenses of case following, 3033
manner and effect of, 3031–3032
no procedural act for six months, 3030

Abbacy, territorial:
definition of, 763

Abbot:
as judge in religious cases, 2882–2883
in charge of territorial abbacy, 764
right of Rota to judge, 2843
tribunal cases before, 2898

Abbot Primate:
right of Rota to judge, 2843
role and authority of, 1224

Abduction:
description, 2161–2162
penalty for crime of, 2819

Abortion:
dispensation from irregularity: formalities, 2046–2048
irregularity for orders, 2026
multiplication of irregularities arising from, 2039
penalty for, 2825–2828

Abrogation:
by later law, 64–66
by new Code, 17–19
non-abrogation of agreements, 7–8

Absolution:
bogus, 2762
doubt about penitent's disposition, 1920
false denunciation of confessor, 1922
in danger of death, 1915
individual, as ordinary means of reconciliation, 1882–1883
minister's requirements for valid, 1896
of accomplice, 1916

Absolution, general:
judgement of conditions by Bishop, 1887
requirements for giving, 1884–1886
requirements for receiving, 1888–1891

Abstinence:
from meat on Fridays, 2473
nature of law, 2474

Abuse:
of ecclesiastical power, penalty for, 2789

of position or office, 2652

Acceptance:
of simple election, 321

Access, judicial:
norms for, 3122–3123

Accomplice:
absolution of, 1916
nature of punishment of, 2656
penalty for absolution of, 2760–2762
punishment of, 2656

Accounts, annual:
of administration, 2559

Accused:
acquittal of, 3360
always to have advocate in trial, 2970
right to appeal, 3361
right to silence, 3364
right to speak or write last, 3359

Acephalous clergy: cf. **Clergy**

Acolyte:
as minister of exposition, 1851
capacity of laity to supply certain functions of, 488
capacity of lay men to be given ministry of, 486
extraordinary minister of Holy Communion, 1789–1790
ministry to be received and exercised before diaconate, 2017

Acta Apostolicae Sedis:
promulgation in, 23–24

Act, administrative:
conditions attached to, 98
effects of, 97
equivalent to decree, 3371
error in execution, 106
executed in writing, 96
executor of, 101–102, 105
expiry of, 107
extension of, 95
interpretation of, 94
revocation of, 108

Act *inter vivos*:
disposal of goods by, 2595
Ordinary as executor of pious dispositions by, 2598–2600

Act *mortis causa*:
disposal of goods by, 2594–2596
legal formalities of, 2596
Ordinary as executor of pious dispositions by, 2598–2600

Action:
extinguished by prescription, 2984
reinforces a right, 2983

Actions, counter:
brought by respondent against plaintiff, 2987
opposing counter action not admitted, 2987
proposed before judge of original action, 2988
timing of, 2940
treatment of, 2940

Actions, criminal:
extinction of, 2723–2724

Actions, for damages:
procedure, 3365–3370

Actions, for possession:
civil law provisions to be followed, 2993

Actions, liturgical:
not private, 1641
rites to be observed, 4–6

Actions, personal:
execution of judgement, 3240

Actions, real:
execution of judgement, 3240

Actions, rescinding:
possible due to ignorance or error, 262

Acts:
judicial, to be signed by notary, 2897
publication or re-publication of, 1622

Acts of case:
all information supplied to judge to be included in, 3159
inspection of, 3144–3146
in writing, sealed, pages numbered, 2953
judges' conclusions preserved in, 3168–3169
null, validated by judgement, 3185

Acts, curial:
drawn up by Chancellor, 958–959
to have juridical effect, to be signed by Ordinary, 942

Acts, harmful:
diminution of penalties, 2648
liability to penalties, 2647

Acts, juridical:
harm caused by malice, 270
invalidity of, 2847
in writing, 2952

999

Index

Acts, juridical: *(contd)*
  not to be handed to anyone, 2957
  null if no lawful summons, 3016
  null, validated by judgement, 3185
  performed through fear or deceit, 259–260
  performed through ignorance or error, 261–262
  presumption of validity of, 258
  signature of parties or witnesses, 2954
  to record fact and manner of summons, 3013
  validity of, 255–257
  when not subject to dispensation, 173

Acts, procedural:
  in writing, sealed, pages numbered, 2952–2953
  null if no lawful summons, 3016
  null, validated by judgement, 3185

Acts, publication of:
  decree of, 3144–3146
  none in non-consummation cases, 3320

Adjudged matter: cf. **Matter: adjudged**

Ad mentem clause: cf. **Prohibiting clause**

Administration, acts of extraordinary:
  consent of Finance Committee and College of Consultors for, 2540–2542
  definition of, for Religious Institutes, 1265

Administration, acts of major importance:
  consultation with Finance Committee and College of Consultors about, 2540–2542

Administration, acts of ordinary:
  of Religious Institutes to determine same, 1265
  those who may perform, 1266

Administration, Apostolic:
  definition of, 766

Administration, diocesan:
  co-ordination of, 940–941

Administration, parish:
  cann. 1281–1288 to be observed, 1055
  harmful, 3388

Administration of temporal goods:
  see also **Temporal Goods**
  controlled by one with power of governance, 2544–2546
  done in name of Church, 2555

duties of Administrator, 2558–2559
invalid acts of, 2549–2550
level of acts beyond ordinary, 2551–2552
making gifts for pious purposes, 2561
manner of, 2558–2559
supervision by Ordinary of, 2537–2538

Administrative Act: cf. **Act**

Administrator, Apostolic:
  dimissorial letters, 1985

Administrator, Diocesan:
  appointment of parish priests *sede vacante*, 1039
  cessation from office, 864
  dimissorial letters, 1986
  elected within eight days of vacancy, 851
  excardination and incardination by, 563
  may not appoint canons, 1011
  missa pro populo, 863
  norms of 165–178 for election of, 856
  not financial administrator, 855
  notification to Apostolic See of election, 853
  obligations and powers of, 861
  officials not removed by, 2868
  only one elected, 854
  profession of faith, 1630
  qualities of, 857–858
  removal, resignation, death, 864
  residence, 863
  when appointed by Metropolitan, 851–852, 859

Administrator, Financial:
  appointment and duties of, 986–987
  duties specially entrusted to, 2543
  need in seminary of, 504–505
  not diocesan Administrator, 855

Administrator, Financial (Religious):
  necessity of and role in each Institute, Province and local Community, 1262
  to render account of administration, 1263

Administrator of Juridical Person:
  offerings belong to juridical person, 2508–2509

Administrator, Parochial:
  appointment of, 1074
  appointment pending recourse in parish priest removal case, 3396
  obligations of, 1075

Administrator of Pious Causes:
  obligations for Mass offerings, 1877

Administrator of Temporal Goods:
  see also **Temporal Goods**
  accounts to faithful, 2565
  annual accounts to Ordinary, 2563–2564
  appointment of, 2547
  assisted by Finance Committee, 2548
  duties of, 2558–2559, 2662
  duties performed in the name of the Church, 2555
  gifts by, 2561
  invalid acts of, 2549–2550
  lease or sale of ecclesiastical goods to self or relatives, 2593
  legal proceedings, 2566
  negligence, 2546
  no arbitrary resignation of, 2567
  requirements in, 2556
  responsibilities for invalid acts of, 2553

Admission:
  invalid, to novitiate, 1278
  of candidate to novitiate, 1276
  of petitions and summons, 3007
  of postulation, 321

Adopting parents: cf. **Parents**

Adoption:
  impediment of legal relationship, 2180
  status of adopted children, 223

Adult:
  admission to baptism, 1695
  baptised in non-Catholic ecclesial community, 1707–1709
  baptism in danger of death, 1698
  baptism to be referred to Ordinary, 1694
  conditional baptism, 1710
  confirmation of, 1735–1738
  confirmed after baptism, 1699
  place for baptism of, 1683
  proof of the baptism of, 1722
  role of sponsor in baptism of, 1714

Adultery:
  by guilty spouse, 2323
  condonation of, 2324

Advena:
  description, 202

Advice:
  collegial, required by Superior, 263–266
  individual, required, 267
  required by Superiors according to Constitutions, 1240
  sincerely given, 268

Index

Advocate:
appointment by plaintiff and respondent, 2962
appointment of several, 2972
can be suspended by judge, 2950
cannot be judge in same case in another instance, 2916
dismissal of, 2976
exemption from testifying, 3072
forbidden to accept bribes, seek immoderate payment, 2979
honorarium for, 3228
incapable of being witness in trial, 3075
information supplied to judge to be included in acts, 3159
mandate for taking office, 2974
misbehaviour of, 2979
oath to exercise office properly and faithfully, 2925
obligation to secrecy, 2928
presence at hearing of oral contentious process, 3255
presence at interrogations, 3087
proposal of questions by, 3089
qualities of, 2973
removal by judge, 2978
removal of cases to more favourable Tribunals, 2980
right to inspect acts, 3144–3146
to be salaried by Tribunals, 2982
used in penal process, 3356–3357
Marriage Processes:
none in non-consummation cases, 3318
right to be present at evidence sessions and inspect all acts, 3282

Affinity:
bar for judge, 2917
bar for promotor, defender, assessor, auditor, 2917
description and calculation of, 220–222
impediment of, 2176–2177

Age:
for confirmation, 1754–1755
for Holy Communion, 1794–1795
for liability to penalty, 2647
for marriage, 2137–2139
higher age for marriage decreed by Bishops' Conference, 2140
infant, 196
majority and minority, 196

Age, old:
anointing of sick, 1959–1961

Aggravating circumstances: cf. *Circumstances*

Aggregates of Persons: cf. **Persons**
Aggregates of Things: cf. **Foundation**

Aggregation:
of one Institute of Consecrated Life to another, 1138–1140

Aggressor, unjust:
defence against, and penalty, 2647
diminution of penalty, 2648

Agreements:
between Bishop and Religious Superior, 1367–1368
norms drawn from ecclesiastical and civil law, 3337
use of to avoid judicial disputes, 3336

Alienation: See also *Temporal Goods, alienation of*
by Religious, 1267
penalty for wrongful, 2759

Altar:
blessing or dedication of, 2452
construction of, 2451
description of, 2450
fixed, in every church, 2449
for celebration of Mass, 1832
loss of dedication, 2452
no burials under, 2454
relics in fixed, 2452
reserved for divine worship, 2453

Anchorites:
existence and description, 1186

Animadversions: cf. **Observations**

Animosity:
penalty for incitement against Apostolic See or Ordinary, 2750–2752

Anointing:
in confirmation, 1729–1730

Anointing of the Sick:
communal form of, 1955
description of, 1950
doubt about age of reason, state of health, 1963–1964
for those in danger, 1959–1961
in good time, 1954
manner of administration of, 1952–1953
obligations of chaplain, 1108
only by priest, 1956
repetition, 1962
those who ask (implicitly), 1965
when not to anoint, 1966–1967

Apostasy:
definition, 1508
irregularity, 2024
penalty for, 2728–2731

Apostate:
penalty upon, 2728–2731
refused Church funeral, 2390–2392

Apostolate:
Bishop to foster and co-ordinate, 812

proper object of Church, 2479
training in exercise of, 539

Apostolic Letters:
auxiliary Bishop, 826
coadjutor Bishop, 826
required for canonical possession, 792–794

Apostolic Life, Societies of:
admission, probation, incorporation into and formation in, 1477
assistance in local catechesis, 1544
catechetical formation in the schools of, 1550
description of, 1470–1471
departure and dismissal of temporary members, 1486
dimissorial letters for subjects of, 1987
dismissal of definitively incorporated member, 1491
divine office within, 2369–2370
effects of incorporation into, 1479
establishment of house and community, 1474
evangelical counsels, 1472
funerals of members of, 2383
governance of, 1476
granting faculties to hear confessions, 1901, 1903, 1905
incardination into, 1478
indult for departure of members, 1487
juridical personality, 1484
members' ability to acquire, possess, administer and dispose of goods, 1485
obligations of members, 1482
oversight of Mass obligations by Superior, 1878
permission to live outside the Society, 1490
residence in common life, 1483
right to oratory and reservation of Blessed Sacrament, 1475
subject to Moderator and Diocesan Bishop, 1480
Superiors and dispensation from holydays and days of penance, 2462–2463
Superiors and dispensation of oaths, 2414
Superiors and dispensation of vows, 2406
Superior's right to bring Viaticum, 1791
studies and ordination, 1478
transfer of members, 1488–1489

Apostolic See:
agreements made by, 7–8

1001

Apostolic See: (contd)
  as author of rescript, 146
  definition of, 750
  expired rescripts of, 150–151
  penal laws enacted by, 17–18
  permission to enter an autonomous Ritual Church, 226
  privilege granted by, 171
  Ecclesiastical Processes:
    approval of appeal courts, 2898
    approval of regional tribunals, 2871–2872
    approval of several courts of appeal, 2900
    consulted by Diocesan Bishop on complicated non-consummation cases, 3313
    consulted in presumption of death cases, 3328
    only Apostolic See decides on fact of non-consummation, 3310
    recourse to, against Bishop's rejection of hearing for non-consummation petition, 3314
    reference of tribunal cases to, 2861
    special norms for tribunals of, 2835
    suspension of jurisdiction of judge, 2861
    tribunals of, 2905–2912
  Judgement:
    judgement on faith in non-Catholic Churches, 1659
    ordering of public worship by, 1642
    permission for alienation or transfer of relics, 2398
    publication of liturgical texts and review of translations, 1643
  Marriage:
    approval of delegation of laity for marriage, 2240–2242
    impediments reserved to, 2120
    retroactive validation, 2352
  Orders:
    dispensation of irregularities and impediments to order, 2040–2043
    dispensation of lack of age for ordination, 2010
    dispensation of rule for co-consecrators given by, 1979
  Penalties:
    for disobedience to lawful command or prohibition of, 2747–2748
    for incitement to disobedience to, 2751–2752
    reservations of penalties to, 2739–2740, 2744, 2760–2762, 2775, 2785–2786
  Religious Life:
    approval of Institutes of Pontifical Right, fusion, union and confederation, 1160
    gives permission for establishment of Institutes of Consecrated Life, 1143–1145, 1137
    permission for changes in Institutes, 1146
    suppression of Institutes and disposal of goods, 1147
  Teaching Role of the Church:
    academic degrees in universities and faculties, 1603
    approval of books on scriptures and translations, 1614
    constitution, approval, direction of ecclesiastical universities and faculties, 1602
    profession of faith, 1630
    to foster and direct ecumenism, 1514–1515
  Temporal Goods:
    capable of acquiring, retaining, administering, alienating, 2780
    monitoring taxes on acts of administrative authority or execution of rescripts, 2503
    permission for certain acts of alienation, 2578–2580
    reduction of Mass obligations, 2614
    reduction of other obligations, 2620
    regulation of remaining benefices, 2522
    to be supported by dioceses, 2521
    transfer of Mass obligations, 2619
  Worship:
    approval etc. of shrines, 2445
    changes of holydays, 2465
    dispensation of oaths, 2414
    dispensation of vows, 2406
    establishes, interprets, suppresses and changes sacramentals, 2355
    establishment, transfer, suppression of holydays and days of penance, 2461
Appeal:
  abandonment of, 3205
  against judgement or penalty with suspensive effects, 2703–2705
  against negative decision on competence, 2936
  against rejection of petition, 3005
  against two conforming sentences, 3219
  basis for, 2898
  by several parties, 3209
  certified copy of acts sent on, 2955
  from judgement to higher court, 3196
  grounds of, 3210–3211
  in penal process, 3361–3362
  judgement not remedied after appeal lodged, 3194
  lodged with judge who gave judgement, 3198
  made by plaintiff benefits respondent and vice versa, 3208
  new evidence at appeal stage, 3213
  new ground at appeal stage, 3213
  no appeal against award of honoraria, expenses, damages, 3229
  no appeal possible against affirmative decision on competence, 2936
  no appeal possible in certain cases, 3197
  oral appeal recorded in writing by notary, 3198
  penalty for appeal from Roman Pontiff to Ecumenical Council or College of Bishops, 3749
  plaint of nullity made with, 3192
  procedure for, 3214
  questions on right of, 3199
  requirements to pursue, 3202
  renunciation of, 3206–3207
  right of, lies with procurator, 2977
  suspends execution of judgement, 3212
  to be pursued within one month, 3201
  translation of acts, 2956
  Marriage Processes:
    against two conforming sentences, 3294
    judgement, acts and appeal to next tribunal, 3289
    to second instance tribunal in documentary process, 3298
Appellant:
  all appeals drawn up in writing by notary in presence of, 3198
  renunciation of appeal by, 3206

Index

Appointment:
  to ecclesiastical office, 321
Arbitration:
  adoption of civil and ecclesiastical law to pursue, 3340
  use of to avoid disputes, 3336
  used in matters of public good, 3338
  norms established by Bishops' Conference, 3337
Arbitrator:
  settlement of litigation by, 2915
Archive, Curial:
  description and security of, 970
  historical, 980–981
  preservation of Cathedral and Church documents in, 980
  preservation of curial acts in, 958–959
  record of blessing or dedication of church kept in, 2419
  record of foundation preserved in, 2612
  records of Church or Institute's rights preserved in, 2559
  register of ordination preserved in, 2055
Archive, parish:
  confirmation register kept in, 1761
  nature and care of, 1061–1064
  record of dedication or blessing of church kept in, 2419
Archive, secret Curial:
  accessibility of, 977–979
  acts of preliminary penal investigation preserved in, 3349
  description of, 975
  key of, 977
  record of penal remedy kept in, 2680
  removal of document from, 979
Archpriest: cf. **Vicar Forane**
Art, Sacred:
  observations of principles of in Church building, 2430
Ash Wednesday:
  abstinence and fasting, 2473
Assessor:
  cannot act in another instance in same case, 2916
  cases which cannot be dealt with by, 2917
  forbidden to accept gifts, 2929
  incapable of being witness in trial, 3075
  obligation to secrecy, 2926–2928
  to take oath to exercise office faithfully, 2925
  use of as advisers to sole judge, 2873

Assets:
  of debtor can be secured by sequestration, 2990
Assistant Priest: cf. **Priest, Assistant**
Associate Judicial Vicar: cf. **Vice-Officialis**
Association:
  of monasteries of cloistered nuns with Institutes of men, 1211
  which plots against the Church, penalty for joining etc, 2753–2755
Associations:
  admission to, 644–647
  clerical, 633–634
  concept and purpose of, 622–624
  concept of private, 625–628
  concept of public, 630–632
  dismissal from, 648
  joined to Institutes of Consecrated Life, 652
  of clergy, 576–579
  right of association for Christ's faithful, 453
  rights and privileges of membership, 643
  right to make rules and appointments, 649
  statutes and title, 637–639
  supervision by Ordinary and Apostolic See, 640–641
  third order, 635–636
  use of description 'Catholic', 629
Associations, Lay:
  cooperation between, 690
  esteem for, 689
  formation of members, 691
Associations of Parents:
  to help in Catholic education, 1573
Associations, private:
  administration of goods of, 684
  autonomy of, 679
  direction of by Christ's faithful, 676
  ecclesiastical approval of, 678
  extinction and suppression of, 686–688
  juridical personality of, 677
  legacies to, 685
  moderators and officers of, 681
  overseeing of, 680
  spiritual counsellor to, 682–683
Associations, Public
  accountability of, 671
  administration of goods of, 671
  appointment of commissioner of, 668
  appointment of moderator, chaplain, ecclesiastical assistant, 663–664

  approval of statutes by competent authority, 658
  authority competent to establish, 653–654
  dismissal from, 662
  juridical person, 657
  members holding office in political parties, 667
  moderators of, 666
  removal of moderator of, 669
  requirements for establishment of, 655–656
  suppression of, 672–675
  those inadmissible to join, 660–661
Attenuating Circumstances: cf. **Circumstances**
Auditor:
  appointment of in collegiate tribunal, 2884–2886
  cases which cannot be dealt with by, 2917
  conduct of examination of witness, 3089
  forbidden to accept gifts, 2929
  incapable of being witness in trial, 3075
  obligations of secrecy, 2926–2927
  qualities of, 2885
  role of, 2884, 2886
  sole judge cases, 2878
  to take oath to exercise office properly and faithfully, 2925
Author:
  appropriate authority for censorship of, 1611–1612
Authorities, Civil: cf. **Civil**
Authorities, State: cf. **State**
Authority, Supreme: cf. **Supreme**
Autonomy:
  scientific, of universities, 1594
Autonomy, canonical:
  recognised in Institutes of Consecrated Life, 1150
  to be preserved in aggregation of Institutes, 1139–1140
Avoidance of judicial disputes:
  for temporal goods, norms for alienation used, 3339
  norms for use, 3337
  use of agreements, reconciliation, arbitration in, 3336
  when arbitration cannot be used, 3338

B

Banns:
  of marriage, 2090 note

Index

Baptism:
  as function of parish priest, 1052
  capacity of laity to confer, 488
  description and necessity of, 1670
  ecclesiastical law binds those baptised Catholics, 30–31
  entry into latin Church by, 224–225
  incorporation into Church by, 193
  no repetition of, 1662
  required to receive other sacraments, 1651
  with confirmation and eucharist as sacraments of initiation, 1652
  Celebration:
    church or oratory, 1682
    immersion or pouring, 1679
    norms for adults apply to all non-infants, 1677
    not in hospital, 1688
    not in private houses, 1687
    place for adult and infant, 1683
    place in difficult circumstances, 1686
    proper preparation for, 1675–1676
    recommended celebration on Sunday or Easter Vigil, 1681
    rite of, 1674
  Minister:
    of adult, 1694
    ordinary minister of, 1690
    other ministers, 1691–1692
    within territory of minister, 1693
  Proof:
    notification to proper parish priest, 1726
    proof of, 1722
    recording of, 1723–1725
  Sponsor:
    requirements in sponsor, 1717–1720
    role of sponsor, 1714–1715
  Subject:
    abandoned infant, 1711
    aborted foetuses, 1712
    admission of adult to, 1696–1697
    adult in danger of death, 1698
    after baptism adult to be confirmed, 1699
    deferment of, 1702–1703
    foundling, 1711
    in doubt of, 1705–1706
    infant in danger of death, 1700
    lawful, of infant, 1701
    proper subject of, 1695
    time of for infant, 1700
  Various:
    doubt and disparity of cult, 2155
    renewal of baptismal promises at confirmation, 1750
    same sponsor at confirmation as at, 1759

Baptism, Conditional:
  grounds for real doubt of original, 1707–1708
  in case of real doubt of original, 1705–1706

Bargaining:
  by advocate and procurators for share of award prohibited, 2979

Benefactors:
  safeguarding wishes of in amalgamation, 247
  safeguarding wishes of in division, 250

Benefice:
  to be regulated by Conference of Bishops, 2522

Benefits, medical:
  rights of laity employed by Church to, 490

Bishop:
  appointment by Roman Pontiff, 777
  consecration of holy oils, 1666
  definition of, 773–774
  episcopal consecration, 785
  norms for one previously a religious, 1428–1431
  principally exercises sanctifying office in the Church, 1636
  profession of faith, 786–787
  qualities of, 782–784
  right to be present at Ecumenical Council, 713
  selection of, 778–779
  Baptism:
    ordinary minister of baptism, 1690
    to decide whether to baptise an adult, 1694
  Confirmation:
    chrism consecrated by, 1730
    giving faculty to confirm to other priests, 1741–1742
    ordinary minister of confirmation, 1733
  Eucharist, Penance, Anointing:
    blessing oil of the sick, 1951
    faculty to hear confessions everywhere, 1898
    ordinary minister of holy communion, 1788
  Orders:
    may not ordain in doubt of candidate's suitability, 2053
    may not ordain outside jurisdiction, 1984
    may rely on dimissorial letters for suitability of ordinand, 2052
    minister of sacred ordination, 1977
    no consecration without pontifical mandate, 1978
    ordaining Bishop to authenticate dimissorial letters, 1991
    ordaining Bishop to ensure ordinand will be attached to appropriate diocese, 1998
    ordaining Bishop to provide certificate of ordination, 2055
    regulation of deacons' pastoral year, 2012
    requirements at episcopal consecration, 1979
    to be satisfied of ordinand's suitability, 2051
    to ensure ordinand has made a retreat, 2021
    to ordain own subjects, 1981
  Other Acts of Divine Worship:
    blessings, 2361
    burial of retired diocesan Bishops in churches, 2458
    dedication of places, 2417
    place of funeral, 2382
  Penalties:
    disobedience of lawful command or prohibition of, 2747–2748
    penalty for consecrating without pontifical mandate, 2775
    penalty for ordaining without dimissorial letters, 2776
    penalty for striking, 2745
    remitting penalty in sacramental confession, 2710
  Procedural Law:
    can establish conciliation office, 3372
    determining place of evidence, 3086
    duty to avoid disputes, 2913
    in case of exception of suspicion, 2918
    powers of in charge of regional and other tribunals, 2899
    Roman Pontiff has right to judge in penal cases, 2840
    Rota has right to judge in contentious cases, 2843
    who represents juridical person has tribunal case dealt with by appeal court, 2864
  Teaching Role:
    infallibility and teaching

Index

role, 1500–1501
moderators of ministry of the word in their churches, 1518
part of authentic magisterium, 1512
preaching to reach non-believers, 1536
promotion of ecumenism, 1516
right to judge writings on faith and morals, 1609
right to preach everywhere, 1525
solicitude in teaching those outside their ordinary pastoral care, 1536
special solicitude for missionary activity, 1554
see also **Moderator of Tribunal**

Bishop, Auxiliary:
ad limina visit for Diocesan Bishop, 819–820
and impeded See, 843
appointment of, 780
assists Diocesan Bishop, 830
assumes power before appointment of Diocesan Administrator, 849
deliberative vote at particular councils, 888–889
made episcopal Vicar, 832
made Vicar general, 831
nature of vote at Bishops' Conference determined by statutes, 908
notification to Apostolic See of death of Diocesan Bishop, 853
residence, 840
resignation of, 841
rights and obligations of, 829
role *sede vacante*, 838–839
special faculties, 824
summoned to diocesan synod, 925
taking possession, 826–828
to consult with Diocesan Bishop, 833–834
to perform pontifical and other functions of Diocesan Bishop, 835

Bishop, Coadjutor:
ad limina for Diocesan Bishop, 819–820
appointment of, 779
assists Diocesan Bishop, 830
deliberative vote at particular council, 888–890
deliberative vote at Bishops' Conference, 908
episcopal rights and functions of, not to be given habitually to others, 836
impeded, 843
made Vicar general, 831
residence of, 840
resignation of, 841
right of succession and special faculties, 824
succeeds Diocesan Bishop, 837
summoned to diocesan synod, 925
taking possession, 826–828
to consult with Diocesan Bishop, 833–834
to perform pontifical and other functions for Diocesan Bishop, 835

Bishop, Diocesan:
canonical possession, 791–792
definition of, 775
duty to foster and promote vocations, 492
those equivalent to, 790
and Religious:
authority to deal with abuses in Religious Institutes, 1373
barring a Religious from the diocese, 1364
confirmation of decree of dismissal for Religious, 1420
consultation with Religious Superior on religious apostolic work, 1363
dismissal from an autonomous monastery, 1419
entry into religious enclosure, 1336
extension of indult of exclaustration, 1385
necessity of contracts with Religious Superiors, 1367–1368
permission to leave during temporary profession, 1395
requests of perpetually professed to depart from Institute, 1404
right of visitation to churches or oratories of Religious and their schools, 1371–1372
right to visit certain religious houses, 1242
vigilance over an autonomous monastery, 1212
works entrusted to Religious Institutes under his authority, 1366
and establishment and Suppression of Religious Houses:
consent for establishment of Religious houses, 1203
implications of consent to Religious house, 1207
permission for change in apostolic works of Religious house, 1208
suppression of Religious house, 1214
and Institutes of Consecrated Life:
approval of constitutions of diocesan right, 1170–1171
dispensation from constitution of Institutes (diocesan right), 1172
duty to discern and promote new gifts of Consecrated Life, 1193
establishment of Institutes of Consecrated Life, 1136–1137
establishment of Institutes of diocesan right, 1160
special care of Institutes of diocesan right, 1169
and societies of Apostolic Life:
consent to establishment of house of, 1474
consent to schools conducted by Religious, 1579
relationship with members of, 1480–1481
special obligations in missionary territories, 1566
Councils and Synods:
communicates decrees of diocesan synod to Metropolitan and Bishops' Conference, 932
deliberative vote at Bishops' Conference, 908
deliberative vote at particular council, 888
dissolves council of priests, 998
establishes parish councils, 1065–1066
presides over diocesan synod, 923–924
sole legislator at diocesan synod, 931
suspends or dissolves diocesan synod, 933
Penalties:
to ensure uniformity of penalties within the same cities, 2635
Procedural Law:
approval of advocate by, 2973
approval of panels of judges, 2885
consulted about curator or guardian appointed by civil authority, 2966
entrusts difficult tribunal cases to collegiate tribunal, 2875
establishes regional tribunals, 2871–2872
execution of a judgement, 3235–3236

1005

Bishop, Diocesan: *(contd)*
  first instance judge in each case, 2863
  sole judge cases, 2877
  to appoint defender and promoter, 2895
  to appoint diocesan judges, 2869
  to appoint Officialis, 2865
  to be informed when non-diocesan judge exercises jurisdiction in his territory, 2948
  to confirm appointment of Officialis, 2868
Procedures, Marriage:
  civil separation, 3304
  difficult non-consummation cases, 3313
  dispensation from unconsummated union, 3312
  legal separation, 3303
  notification of non-consummation rescript, 3325
Relationship with Auxiliaries:
  assisted by coadjutor and auxiliary, 835–836
  to consult with coadjutor and auxiliary, 833–834
  to receive apostolic letters of auxiliary Bishop, 826–828
Sacraments:
  lays down liturgical regulations, 1645
  norms for administration of sacraments to non-catholics, 1661
  public worship, ordering of, 1642
(Anointing):
  blessing oil of sick, 1951
  communal, 1955
(Baptism):
  permission for baptism outside church or in hospital, 1688
  regulation of age of baptismal sponsors, 1718
(Confirmation):
  conferral of on subjects, 1744
  himself to confirm, 1741
  location of register, 1761
  mandate to confirm, 1736
  permission to confirm, 1746
  prohibition on confirmation by, 1746
(Eucharist):
  minister of exposition, 1851
  outdoor processions, 1852
(Marriage):
  delegation of lay persons to assist at marriage, 2240–2242
  norms concerning registration of marriage, 2260–2261
  retroactive validation granted by and conditions, 2353
(Orders):
  permission required for another Bishop to ordain in diocese, 1984
  proper Bishop for candidate to orders, 1983
  refusal of dimissorial letters, 1986
  to ensure ordinands are properly instructed in the order and its obligations, 2001
(Other Acts of Divine Worship):
  blessing of churches, 2418
  burial of in churches, 2458
  consultation required to give building permission, 2428
  dedication of sacred place, 2417
  dispensation from and obligations of, holydays or days of penance, 2462
  holydays and days of penance, 2461
  liturgy of the word where no Mass, 2468
  permission for religious church, 2429
  permission for secular use of a church, 2436
(Penance):
  conditions for general absolution, 1887
  refusal to allow other Bishops to hear confessions in diocese, 1898
Special Role in particular Church:
  acts in the name of the diocese, 809–811
  ad limina visit, 819–820
  care for the unbaptised, 798
  concern for priests, 799
  ecumenism, 798
  emeritus, 823
  pontificalia, 806
  power, legislative, executive, judicial, 807
  presides over the Eucharist in Cathedral, 805
  provision for other rites, 797
  provision for retirement, 823
  quinquennial report, 818
  residence of, 813
  resignation of, 821–822
  solicitous for all the faithful, 796
  to celebrate the *missa pro populo*, 804
  to foster ecclesiastical discipline, 808
  to foster the apostolate, 812
  to foster vocations, 800
  to promote holiness, 803
  to teach and defend the faith, 801–802
  visitation not to be burdensome, 817
  visitation of diocese 814–815
  visitation of persons and institutions, 816
Teaching Role:
  establishment of schools by, 1580–1581
  overseeing and regulation of religious formation and education, 1585
  overseeing of Catholic doctrine in universities and faculties, 1596
  profession of faith, 1630
  provision of institutes of higher studies, 1607
  right to overseeing of Catholic schools, 1588
  selection of candidates for university and faculties, 1605
  spiritual and pastoral provision for university students, 1599
Temporal Goods:
  alienation, permission for, 2575–2577
  annual accounts of juridical persons, 2563–2564
  consent and consultation required for acts of extraordinary administration and acts of major importance, 2539–2542
  reduction of Mass obligations, 2615–2618
  reserve fund to pay for laity and other purposes, 2531–2533
  right to levy taxes, 2496–2501
  special duties committed to Financial Administrator, 2543
  to remind faithful of duty to support the Church, 2494
  transfer of Mass obligations, 2619

Bishop, Proper:
  dimissorial letters, 1985
  judgement of qualities of candidate for ordination, 1996
  judgement that candidate is beneficial to ministry of Church, 1997
  of candidate for diaconate and priesthood defined, 1983
  refusal of admission to orders by, 2004–2005

Index

required qualities for the ordinand, 2002–2003
to ordain his candidate to the priesthood or diaconate, 1980
to receive handwritten petition for orders from ordinand, 2018

Bishop, Suffragan:
appeal from court of, 2898

Bishop, Titular:
definition of, 776
deliberative vote at particular councils, 888–890
nature of vote at Bishops' Conference determined by statutes, 908

Bishops' Provincial Meetings: cf. **Meeting**

Bishops, Synod of: cf. **Synod**

Blasphemy:
penalty for, 2742

Blessed Virgin Mary:
veneration of, 2394

Blessing:
loss of, 2424
priest as minister of, 2361
of churches as soon as possible, 2431
of church or cemetery, record of, 2419
of individual graves, 2455
of oratories and private chapels, 2443
of sacred places and churches, 2418
of special cemeteries, 2456
proof of, 2420
recipients of, 2363

Blessing, Nuptial: cf. **Nuptial**

Bodies: cf. **Corpses**
cf. **Participatory Bodies**
cf. **Consultative Bodies**

Body and Blood of Christ:
holyday of obligation, 2464–2465
procession on feast of, 1852

Bond of previous marriage:
impediment, 2148–2150

Bonds, Sacred:
for incorporation into secular Institutes, 1457–1461
means of professing evangelical councils, 1125–1126
temporary, 1457–1461

Books:
censors appointed to make judgement on, 1624–1626
for recording Mass intentions, 1879
proper authority for permission or approval of, 1611–1612

publication of religious textbooks, 1619
record of foundation Masses, 2613
re-publication of, 1622
submission of books to local Ordinary, 1620

Books, Liturgical:
prerogative of Apostolic See to publish, 1616, 1643
re-publication of, 1617
to be followed in the celebration of sacraments, 1664
translation of and Bishops' Conferences, 1644

Bread:
holy communion under species of, 1821
unleavened, 1822
used in Mass, 1816–1818

Brethren, Separated: cf. **Separated Brethren**

Bribery:
penalty for, 2780
special penalties for advocate and procurator, 2979

Budget:
to be drawn up annually by Administrator of temporal goods, 2560

Burial:
not in churches, 2458
to be retained, though cremation permitted, 2376

Business:
penalty for clerics or religious engaging in, 2800–2801

C

Calumniator:
to make amends, 2796

Candidate for Orders: cf. **Ordinand**

Candidate to Novitiate: cf. **Novitiate**

Canon Penitentiary:
confessional faculties from the law, 1902
faculties of, 1010
not certain persons, 952

Canonical Possession: cf. **Possession**

Canonisation:
special norms for, 2836

Canons:
appointment of by Bishop, 1011–1012
salary, dress of, 1008

Canons, Cathedral:
norms concerning, 1005–1013
summoned to diocesan synod, 925

Canons Regular:
religious house of with own

moderator is autonomous, 1209

Cantor:
capacity of laity to exercise role of, 487

Cardinal:
as legate *a latere*, 746
assisting Roman Pontiff, 703
cooperation with Roman Pontiff, 744
evidence by, place of giving, 3086
faculty to hear confessions everywhere, 1898
freedom from control of the local Bishop, 745
in petto, 739
offices held by, 733
profession of faith, 1630
publication of names of new, 738
residence in Rome, 744
residence outside Rome, 745
resignation of, 742
Roman Pontiff has right to judge, 2840
selection of, 737
suburbicarian or titular Churches, 745

Care, pastoral:
to be exercised on taking possession of parish, 1042

Case:
order of hearing, 2933
those allowed to be present during hearing of, 2949

Case, contentious: see also **Actions**
all can be referred to Apostolic See, 2861
appointment of representative in, 2970
certain cases reserved to collegiate tribunal, 2874
use of promotor of justice, 2889

Case, Penal:
accused always to have advocate, 2970
certain cases reserved to collegiate tribunal, 2874
judge proceeds *ex-officio* after introduction of, 2922
place of trial in, 2856
promotor of justice, use of, 2889

Case, Principal:
decided by definitive judgement, 3163

Cases, Matrimonial:
death of spouse during trial, 3276
for civil effects civil law applies, 3266
marriage cannot be challenged after death of spouse, 3275

Index

Cases, Matrimonial: *(contd)*
  of baptised heard by ecclesiastical judge, 3265
  who may challenge validity of marriage, 3274
Cases, Spiritual:
  Church's right to judge, 2833
Catechesis:
  care for, 1540
  formation to be given by all available means, 1551
  pastors have duty to attend to, 1539
  responsibility of parents for their children, 1540
  those who are to assist in, 1544
Catechetics:
  in and out of schools, 1575
  obligation of Bishop to establish norms concerning, 1541
  role of Bishop in, 801
Catechisms:
  preparation of to assist in teaching the faith, 1541
  publication of, 1619
Catechists:
  conferring baptism, 1691
  description, 1557
  formation of, 1558
  local Ordinary to ensure training of, 1552
  to assist in local catechesis, 1544
Catechumenate:
  admission to, 1562, 1676
  Bishops' Conference to establish norms for, 1563
  for an adult in preparation for baptism, 1697
Catechumens:
  and blessings, 2363
  description of, 431
  formation of, 1563–1564
  treated as faithful for funeral purposes, 2387
Cathedral:
  Bishop's funeral in, 2382
  reservation of Blessed Sacrament in, 1835–1836
Catholic (Title):
  use of adjective for description of schools, 1584
  use of adjective to describe universities, 1593
Cause, excusing:
  physical and moral impossibility for individual confession, 1883
Cause, pious:
  disposal of goods to, 2594–2595
  goods in trust for to be notified

to Ordinary, 2601
  regulations for administrators for Mass offerings, 1877
Celibacy, obligation of:
  dispensation from, 604–606
  preparation of seminarians for, 523
  remains on loss of clerical state, 604–606
  special regulations about, 575
Cemetery:
  belonging to juridical person, 2457
  blessing of (record), 2419
  burials in parish, 2384
  choice of, 2384
  Church cemeteries, 2455
  management of, 2459
Censors: 1624–1626
Censorship:
  right of pastors of Church to judge writings on faith and morals, 1609–1610
Censure:
  absolved in danger of death by any priest, 1915
  medicinal penalty, 2627
  moderation in establishing, 2637
  moderation in imposing, 2697
  reference of person under censure to local Ordinary for marriage, 2104
  remission of by confessor, 2713
  remission of following purged contempt, 2716
Certainty, Moral:
  derived from acts of case and proofs, 3165
  required for judge to reach conclusion, 3164
  without, decision against plaintiff, 3167
Certificate:
  concerning canonical status, 1062
Chancellor: see also **Notaries**
  and Bishop taking possession, 793
  appointment of, 958
  assistant to Chancellor, 958
  lists of those to head diocese when Bishop is impeded, 843
  not to hand over juridical acts, 2957
  profession of faith, 1630
  qualities of, 961
  removal of, 964–965
  signature on juridical acts, 942–943
  witnesses presentation of apostolic letters of auxiliary Bishop, 826
  witnesses presentation of apostolic letters of coadjutor Bishop, 826

witnesses presentation of apostolic letters when Bishop is impeded, 828
Chance occurrence: cf. **Occurrence**
Chapel, Bishops':
  reservation of Blessed Eucharist in, 1836
  same rights as for an oratory, 2442
Chapel, Private:
  blessing of, 2443
  description of, 2441
Chaplaincies: cf. *University Centres*
Chaplains:
  appointment of, 1107
  appointment to lay Religious Institutes, 1110
  celebrates liturgical functions in lay Religious Institute, 1110
  description of, 1106
  faculties and powers given to, 1108–1109
  removal of, 1116
  relations with parish priest, 1115
  right and duty to take Viaticum to the sick, 1791
  special purpose of, 1111
  to non-parochial church attached to community or group, 1114
Chapter, Cathedral:
  can be given functions of College of Consultors, 1003
  establishment and suppression of, 1006
  harmony between parish priests and chapter of capitular church, 1013
  members have consultative vote at particular council, 888–890
  parishes not to be united with, 1013
  parish priests of a capitular church, 1013
  presidency of, 1009
  role of, 1005
  statutes, 1007–1008
Chapter, Collegiate:
  harmony between parish priest and, 1013
  parishes not to be united with, 1013
  parish priest of collegiate church, 1013
  presidency of, 1009
  role of, 1005
  statutes of, 1007–1009
Chapter, General:
  composition, role, function of, 1251–1255
Chapter, Religious:
  own law determines detail, 1256

Index

Character:
  imprinted by baptism, confirmation and order, 1662, 1671, 1728, 1971
Charity, works of:
  part of sanctifying office of the Church, 1646
  proper object of the Church, 2479
Chastity: see also **Counsels, Evangelical**
  description, 1181
  perpetual vow of as marriage impediment, 2159–2160
Children:
  funerals for unbaptised, 2388
  legitimated, equivalent to legitimate, 2297
  natural obligations to, 2100
  obligations to children of previous marriage, 3300
  preparation for First Holy Communion, 1797–1800
  presumed legitimate, 2295
  requirements to receive Holy Communion, 1794–1795
  special norms for receiving Holy Communion in danger of death, 1796
  upbringing of as an end of marriage, 2058
Children, adopted:
  registration of baptism of, 1725
Children, illegitimate:
  legitimation of, 2296
Children, legitimate:
  born of putative marriages, 2293
Chrism: 1729–1730
Christians:
  duties and rights of, 192
Christmas Day:
  acceptance of Mass offerings on, 1864
Christ's faithful: cf. **Faithful**
Church (building):
  altar fixed in every, 2449
  blessing of, 2417–2418
  building of requires Diocesan Bishop's permission, 2428
  burial of Roman Pontiff, Cardinals, Bishops in, 2458
  celebration of baptism in, 1682
  celebration of confirmation in, 1731
  celebration of sacred ordinations in, 1975
  cleanliness and ornamentation of, 2434
  consultation by Bishop about building of church, 2428
  definition of, 2427
  document recording blessing or dedication of, 2419
  expert advice required for building, 2430
  reservation of Blessed Sacrament in, 1835–1836
  reservation of Blessed Sacrament in church of religious house, 1839
  secularisation of, 2436
  security of and contents, 2434
  to be open and free to the faithful, 1840, 2435
  to have own title, 2432
  use of for divine worship, 2433
Church, autonomous ritual:
  entry into, 224–225
  reception of sacraments in, 227
  those deemed to be members of, 226
Church, Capitular:
  alms given to, 1013
  harmony between parish priest of and chapter, 1013
  parish priest of, 1013
Church, Cathedral:
  celebration of sacred orders in, 1975
  solemn rite of dedication, 2431
Church, Eastern Orthodox:
  members of receiving sacraments from Catholic ministers, 1658–1659
Church, Latin:
  entry into by baptism, 224
  return to, 226
Church, non-catholic:
  and papal legates, 754
  consultation about members receiving sacraments from Catholic ministers, 1661
Church, Parish:
  liturgy of word in lieu of Mass, 2468
  place of baptism of adult and infant, 1683
  reservation of Blessed Eucharist in, 1835–1836
  solemn rite of dedication, 2431
  to have baptismal font, 1684
Church, Particular:
  acquiring, retaining, administering, alienating temporal goods, 2480
  and celebration of plenary council, 881
  and papal legates, 754
  definition of, 758
  differentiated by rite, 768
  government of by Bishop, 807
  grouped together in ecclesiastical provinces, 866
  juridical personality of, 769–770
  power of Roman Pontiff over, 700
Church, The:
  Sacraments:
  incorporation by baptism into, 1670–1671
  regulation of sacraments by, 1650
  sacraments entrusted to, 1648
  sanctifying office exercised through liturgy, 1633
  Teaching role:
  authority of in religious education, 1585
  exercise of its office through social communications, 1608
  missionary nature of, 1553
  right and obligation to preach gospel to all peoples, 1494
  rights and duties in education, 1571
  right to establish and direct schools, 1577
  right to establish and govern universities, 1590
  right to establish ecclesiastical universities and faculties, 1601
  right to proclaim moral principles, 1495
  Temporal Goods:
  capable of acquiring, retaining, administering, alienating, 2480
  manner of acquisition of goods, 2489–2490
  right to acquire, retain, administer, alienate, 2476
  right to require from faithful what is necessary for its proper objectives, 2491–2492
  Various:
  penalty for fomenting hatred against, 2742
  right and duty to train candidates for sacred ministries, 491
  right to judge, 2833
Church, Universal:
  instruction of seminarians in the needs of, 536
  Roman Pontiff's power over, 695–696
Churches, Titular:
  of Cardinals, 745
Circumstances:
  aggravating, for penalty, 2652
  attenuating, for penalty, 2648
  excusing, for penalty, 2647

Civil Authorities:
competence over civil effects of marriage, 2070
no rights to appoint Bishops, 781
punishments by taken into account, 2691

Civil Society: cf. **Society, Civil**

Clause:
invalidating: attached by Supreme Authority of the Church, 2115

Clergy:
acephalous or 'wandering clergy' not permitted, 547–548
support of, derived from special fund, 2527–2528
support of, is proper objective of Church, 2476

Cleric:
enrolment again after loss of clerical state, 612
exemption from testifying in court, 3072
invitation to ordinations of, 1976
only clerics affected by suspension, 2665
part of Christ's faithful, 433
penalty for attempting marriage, 2803–2804
penalty for living in concubinage etc., 2809–2810
penalty for physical force against, 2746
penalty for sexual crimes by, 2812–2818
requirements for their participation in media programmes, 1628
support of punished clerics, 2698–2699
suspended *a divinis* when invalidity of orders is sought, 3331
those attached to parishes to assist in catechesis, 1544
unity, 568
writing in certain periodicals requires permission, 1627
Clerical State: dismissal from:
as penalty for apostasy, heresy, schism, 2730
for attempted marriage, 2803–2804
for living in concubinage etc., 2809–2810
for scattering sacred species, 2740
for sexual crimes against minors, 2812–2818
for solicitation, 2782–2784
for striking Roman Pontiff, 2744
loss of, 603

Clerical Society of Apostolic Life:
excardination from, 555
incardination by diaconate into, see also **Apostolic Life, Societies of**

Clerics:
Capacities of:
to obtain offices, 566
Movement of:
incardination follows five years residence, 553–554
permission for, 559
recall to diocese, 562
rights in connection with, 561
suitable preparation of, 538
Obligations of:
avoidance of scandal, 574
celibacy and continence, 572
fraternal union and cooperation between clergy, 568
instruction of seminarians about, 524
special reverence and obedience to Pope and Bishop, 565
not to assume public office, 593
not to be involved in commerce or trade, 596–597
not to take an active role in political parties or in running trade unions, 599
not to undertake lay administration, 594
not to volunteer for military service, 601
to accept and fulfil office given, 567
to acknowledge and promote mission of laity, 569
to avoid the unbecoming, 591
to avoid what is alien to their state, 592
to continue studies after ordination, attend pastoral courses and study other allied sciences, 580–581
to esteem special associations of the clergy, 578
to follow a simple way of life, 586
to foster peace and harmony, 598
to refrain from associations irreconcilable with the clerical state, 579
to reside in the diocese, 588
to seek holiness, through daily Mass, divine office, retreats, devotion to BVM, 570–571, 2369
to take advantage of all exemptions afforded by the state from public civil offices, 602
to wear appropriate ecclesiastical dress, 590
Recommendations for:
annual holidays, 589
distribution of surplus goods and money, 587
some form of common life commended, 582
Remuneration for:
appropriate to conditions of, 583–584
Rights:
of association, 576
to remuneration, special welfare, care in old age and in sickness, 583–584

Codes:
of Institutes of Consecrated Life, 1151

Collections (documents):
publication or re-publication of, 1622

Collections (financial):
local Ordinary may order special, 2507
permission required for, 2505
rules made by Bishops' Conference, 2506

College:
of Bishops:
binding force of decrees of, 717
ecumenical councils, 713
infallibility of, 1498–1502
membership and description of, 705–707
missionary activity, direction of, 1554
penalty for appeal from Roman Pontiff to, 2749
power of, 708–709
Roman Pontiff, 695–696, 705
to foster and direct ecumenism, 1514–1515
ways of exercising its office, 710
of Cardinals:
announcement of new Pontiff by senior Cardinal deacon, 743
eastern patriarchs, 735
election-of new dean, 740
orders within, 734–736
ordination of Roman Pontiff by dean or sub-dean, 743
power *sede vacante*, 747
presided over by dean or sub-dean, 740
priests and deacons, 734–736

profession of faith, 1630
publication of names of new
  Cardinals in presence of, 738
role and competence of, 732-733
Of Consultors:
consent for alienation,
  2575-2577
consent of required for
  extraordinary acts of
  administration, 2541-2542
consent of required by diocesan
  administrator for excardination,
  incardination, 563
consent to diocesan administrator
  giving dimissorial letters, 1985
consultation of on appointment/
  removal of Financial
  Administrator, 986
consultation on acts of
  administration of major
  importance, 2540
elects Diocesan Administrator
  within eight days of vacancy of
  See, 851
elects priest to administer diocese
  when See is impeded, 843
establishment of, 999
functions of can be given to
  Chapter, 1003
functions of Council of Priests
  sede vacante fulfilled by, 1001
governance of diocese before
  appointment of Diocesan
  Administrator, 849
presidency of, 1001
profession of faith, 1630
receives apostolic letters of
  coadjutor Bishop, 826
receives apostolic letters when
  Diocesan Bishop is impeded,
  828
of Judges:
impossibility of forming, 2877
with one lay judge, 2869
see also **Collegiate Tribunal**
Command:
disobedience to lawful command of
  Apostolic See or Superior,
  2747-2748
Commandment, Sixth:
absolution of accomplice, 1916
false denunciation of confessor,
  1922
Commendatory Letters: cf. **Letters**
Commentator:
capacity for laity to exercise role of,
  487
Committee:
Diocesan Finance:

consent required for alienation,
  2576
consent required for extraordinary
  administrative acts, 2542
consulted on administrative acts
  of major importance, 2540
consulted on appointment and
  removal of Financial
  Administrator, 986
financial plan of, 987
responsibilities of, 984-985
term of office of members, 982
those excluded, 982
to appoint new Financial
  Administrator if elected as
  Diocesan Administrator, 855
Financial (of Juridical Person):
at least two counsellors to assist in
  administration of goods, 2548
consent required for alienation,
  2575-2577
consulted by Diocesan Bishop on
  setting levels of administration,
  2551-2552
examination of annual accounts,
  2563-2565
Parish Finance:
nature, ownership and
  establishment of, 1067-1068
Permanent (Bishops' Conference):
prepares and executes business
  of Bishops' Conference, 914
Common life:
commended for clerics, 582
Communal:
anointing of the sick, 1955
Communicatio in Sacris: cf.
  Participation, prohibited
Communication of acts:
right of tribunal to call for
  assistance of another tribunal to,
  2862
Communications, Social: cf. **Social
  Communications**
Communion, ecclesiastical:
disturbance of, 3388
established, strengthened,
  manifested by sacraments,
  1648-1649
Communion, Holy:
adequate preparation for first,
  1546
admission to, 1793
Bishop, priest, deacon, ordinary
  ministers of, 1788
capacity of laity to distribute, 488
confession before if in grave sin,
  1803
deprivation of for lengthy period,
  1887

distribution, time of, 1828
extraordinary ministers of,
  1789-1790
first reception of by convert, 1699
frequency of reception (precept),
  1809
number of times received on the
  same day, 1804
parish priest to judge about
  disposition and age for children
  to receive first, 1800
received under species of bread or
  wine or both, 1821
reception of during Mass or outside
  it, 1805
reception of in any Catholic rite,
  1815
requirements for children to
  receive, 1795
those not admitted to, 1801-1802
Community:
General:
assistance to be given to those in
  preparation for and within
  marriage, 2079-2083
capable of receiving law, 74
general decrees, 81-82
introducing a custom, 69
pastoral care when not yet a
  parish, 1023-1024
non-catholic ecclesial:
baptised member as witness
  at baptism, 1721
celebration of Mass in church of,
  1833-1834
concelebration of Mass forbidden
  with ministers of, 1786
doubt of valid baptism in,
  1707-1709
funeral of members of, 2389
Religious:
desirability and role of Financial
  Administrator in, 1262
to live in a lawfully constituted
  religious house, 1200-1201
Competence:
by reason of connection, 2858
by reason of contract, 2854
by reason of prevention, 2859
by reason of subject matter, 2853
conflicts of, 2860
exception against heard by judge,
  2936
extension of given by *Signatura*,
  2912
for plaintiff and respondent, 2849
in matrimonial cases, 3267-3273
in non-consummation cases,
  3312-3314

Index

Competence: *(contd)*
in separation cases, 3306
non-competence of tribunals, 2847
of judge, 2848
relative non-competence, 2848

Compromise:
in elections, 363–366

Concelebration:
acceptance of offering for, 1854
by priests, 1772–1774
non acceptance of offering for second Mass (concelebrated), 1865
with non-catholic ministers not permitted, 1786

Conciliation between Parties:
attempt at before administrative recourse procedure, 3372
judge to attempt before matrimonial procedure commences, 3277
to be attempted before separation of spouses decreed, 3307

Conclusion of Case:
decreed when all evidence produced, 3148
defined, 3148
further proofs after, 3149–3151
further stages, 3152
in oral contentious case, 3260

Concordat:
and papal legates, 755

Concordat cum originali:
given by Ordinary of place of publication, 1617

Concubinage:
notorious public, 2178–2179
penalty for cleric living in, 2809–2810

Condition:
determination of validity of marriage with past or present, 2211–2212
invalid marriage with future, 2210
to marriage, local Ordinary's permission required for, 2212

Confederation:
of Institutes of Consecrated Life, 1143–1145

Conference, Bishops':
and establishment of ritual particular Church, 768
and papal legates, 754
provisions for retired Bishop, 823

Church Structures:
conference of Major Religious Superiors, cooperation with, 1432–1433
establishment of norms for councils of priests, 990
functions of College of Consultors can be passed to Chapter, 1003
limited term for parish priest, 1034–1035
retirement or maintenance of priests, norms for, 1072–1073

Council:
convenes plenary council, fixes place, elects president, determines business, 883
decides celebration of plenary council, 881

Laity and Clergy:
approval of for inter-diocesan seminary, 502
dispensation from laws made by, 179–180
ecclesiastical dress, 590
establishment of national associations, 653–654
provisions of for training candidates for permanent diaconate, 500
rules for divine office for permanent deacons, 571
to draw up Programme of Priestly Formation, 516

Nature:
approval of the Apostolic See for variations, 897
constituted by, 897
consultation with Apostolic See, 917
decrees, power to make, 910
description of, 896
election of president and vice-president, 904
establishment, suppression, alteration of by Apostolic See, 898
frequency of meetings, 907
general secretary, duties of, 915–916
juridical personality of, 899
membership of, 900
minutes sent to the Apostolic See, 913
promulgation of decrees, 911
relationship with Diocesan Bishops, 912
relations with other, 917
required votes, 911
shown decrees of diocesan synods, 932
statutes of, 902–903
those with deliberative or consultative vote, 908

Procedural law:
appeal arrangements for regional and other tribunals, 2899–2902
conciliation office, 3372
lay judges, 2867
sole judge cases, 2877–2878

Sacraments:
administration of baptism, norms for, 1679
administration of sacraments to non-catholics, norms for, 1661
age for confirmation, 1754–1755
confessionals, 1893
confirmation register, 1761
conditions for general absolution, 1885–1887
delegation of lay persons for witnessing marriage, approval of, 2240–2242
engagement to marry, 2077
form of marriage, dispensation of, 2276–2279
ordination, age of, 2009
power to alter age for marriage, 2140
pre-nuptial enquiries and banns of marriage, 2088–2091
promises and declarations in, mixed marriage, 2273
registration of baptism of adopted children, 1725
registration of marriage, 2260–2261
rite of initiation, adaptation, 1676
rite of marriage, 2259

Teaching Role of Church:
authentic magisterium, part of, 1512
catechetical office, 1543
catechisms, publication of, 1542
catechumenate, norms for, 1562–1563
censors, lists of, 1624
clerics and religious involved in media programmes, 1628
ecumenism, promotion of, 1516
examination of books and sacred scriptures, 1614
gospel message on radio and TV, norms for, 1537
institutes of higher studies, provisions for, 1607
laity, provision of norms for preaching by, 1528
location of universities on territory of, 1594

overseeing of doctrine in Catholic universities, 1596
publication of versions of sacred scriptures by, 1614–1615
religious formation and education, norms about, 1585
right to judge writings on faith and morals, 1609
translation of liturgical books, 1644

Temporal Goods:
acts of extraordinary administration, 2539–2542
amalgamation of funds, 2534
collections, rules for, 2506
leasing ecclesiastical goods, 2592
levels for alienation, 2575–2577
remaining benefices, 2522
social security fund, 2529–2530
support of the Church, norms for, 2495

Worship, other acts of:
changes in holydays of obligation, 2465
fixed altars, 2449
national shrines, approval of, 2445
nature of Friday penance, 2473–2475
statues of national shrines, 2445

Conference of Major Religious Superiors:
to have own statutes, 1434
usefulness and purpose of, 1432–1433

Conferral:
free, 335
of ecclesiastical office, 321

Confession:
Extra-judicial:
evaluated by judge, 3056
no value if based on error of fact or force or grave fear, 3057

Judicial:
description of, 3053
legal effect of in cases of public good, 3055
legal effects of in private matters, 3054

Sacramental:
and seal, 1923–1924
and use of interpreter, 1925–1926
elsewhere than in a confessional, 1894
faculties only to suitable priests, 1906
general absolution without prior individual, 1884–1886

habitual faculties for, 1910
individual before a second general absolution, 1890
individual, integral, 1882–1883
obligation to hear confessions of faithful, 1931
place of, 1892
preceding first Holy Communion, 1799
preparation for first, 1546
prior to Mass or Holy Communion, 1803
role of confessor, 1917
use of knowledge acquired through, 1927–1929

Confessional:
description and place of, 1893

Confessional Seal: cf. *Seal*

Confessor:
choice of confessional by penitent, 1893
dispensing power in danger of death, 2128
doubt about penitent's disposition, 1920
false denunciation of, 1922
free choice by faithful, 1939
imposition of penances, 1921
in seminary, 508
number of, and general absolution, 1886
no vote in admission of students to orders, 509
obligation to hear confessions of faithful, 1932
penalty for false denunciation of, 2791–2793
power to remit penalties, 2713–1714
questions in confessional, 1919
recourse in case of irregularity or impediment, 2044–2045
sacramental seal, 1923–1924
role of, in confessional, 1917–1918

Confirmation:
function of parish priest in regard to, 1052
non-repetition because of character, 1662
obligations of chaplain, 1108–1109
of adults after baptism, 1699
preparation for, 1546
sacrament of, described, 1728
with baptism and eucharist, sacraments of initiation, 1652

Celebration:
celebrated in church during Mass, 1731–1732

chrism to be used in, 1729–1730
manner of administering, 1729

Minister:
any priest, in danger of death, 1739
Bishop as ordinary minister, 1733
equivalent to Diocesan Bishop, 1734
grant of special power to priest by Bishop, 1741–1743
in exempt places, 1748
place of by priests with special faculties, 1747
priest who baptises adult, 1736
priest with special faculty, 1733
territory in which confirmation may be administered, 1746–1747

Subject:
age of candidate, 1754–1755
candidate for, 1749
requirements in candidate, 1750–1751
time of and instruction for, 1752–1753

Various:
proof of, 1760
registration of, 1761
required for marriage, ordination, 2085, 2014
role of sponsor, 1756
same sponsor as at baptism, 1759

Conflict of competence:
how resolved, 2860

Coniugicide: cf. **Crime: impediment of**

Conjugal:
act, definition of, 2073
life, judge to attempt reconciliation of spouses for, 3277

Connection:
judicial competence by reason of, 2858

Consanguinity:
description of impediment, 2168–2171
prevents judge from hearing case, 2917
prevents promotor, defender, assessor, auditor dealing with a case, 2917
reckoning of, 216–219
when dispensation from impediment not given, 2121

Consecrated Life: cf. **Life, Consecrated**

Index

Consecrated Species: cf. Species, Consecrated
Consecration:
Episcopal:
newly appointed Bishop, 785, 792
not without pontifical mandate, 1978
penalty if without pontifical mandate, 2775
requirements for co-consecrators, 1979
Eucharistic:
wrong to consecrate one element alone; or outside Mass, 1823
Consecrations: (Sacramentals) minister of, 2359
Consent:
of group or college, 263–265
of individuals, 267
of the will and diminution of penalty, 2648
Defective:
in case of mental illness: need for services of expert, 3285–3287
Matrimonial:
deceit used to obtain, 2199–2201
description of, 2066–2067
description of renewal of, 2335
knowledge or opinion about nullity, 2204
makes marriage, 2066
manifestation of to minister who seeks it, 2233
not vitiated by error about unity etc. of marriage, 2202–2203
presumption of, 2205, 2227
renewal of required for validation, 2332–2334, 2339
Required:
for Bishop for acts of extraordinary administration, 2539–2542
for Bishop, for alienation of diocesan goods, 2575–2576
by Diocesan Administrator, of College of Consultors for excardination/incardination, 563
by Superior of Council, 1240
of Bishop to build church, 2428–2429
of parents for baptism of children, 1701
Consistory: 741
Conspiracy to commit crime:
punishment for, 2656
Constitutions:

dispensation from Institutes of Consecrated Life, 1172
manner of observance of evangelical counsels, 1179–1180
of Institutes of Consecrated Life, 1151–1155
Consultation:
advice sincerely given, 268
manner of acting upon, 267
with College or groups of persons, 267
Cases of Consultation:
acts of administration of major importance, 2539–2542
alienation, 2575–2582
by Bishop and Conference of Priests about Pastoral Council, 1065–1066
by Bishops' Conference about sacraments to non-catholics, 1660–1661
by Bishop with College or Consultors and Financial Council on: appointment and removal of Financial Administrator, 986–987
by Bishop with Council of Priests and Rectors on building a church, 2428–2429
by Bishop with Finance Council on limits of ordinary administration, 2551–2552
by local Ordinary with priest's own Ordinary about faculties, 1907
tax on diocese, 2496–2501
Consultative Bodies or Groups:
Bishops' Conference, 895–896,
College of Consultors, 999–1002
Conciliation Council, 3372
Council of Priests, 988–998
Diocesan Finance Committee, 982–987
Episcopal Council of Bishops, Vicars general and Vicars episcopal, 941
Finance Committee of juridical person, 2548
Missionary council, 987
Parish Finance Committee, 1067–1068
Pastoral council, 1014–1018
Permanent committee of Bishops' Conference, 914
Roman Curia, 748–749
Superiors' Council, 1238–1239
Consultative Bodies (Religious):
manner of working, 1257
Consultors, College of: cf. College
Consummated Marriage: cf.

Marriage
Consummation:
description of, 2072–2073
presumption of, 2074
Contempt:
increasing penalty, 2732
manner of purging, 2694
of religion, penalty for, 2742
penalty for striking cleric out of, 2746
to be purged before remission of penalty, 2716
warning to offender to purge, 2694
Contentious Case: cf. Case
Contract:
competence for judicial trial by reason of, 2854
observance of civil law in regard to, 2568–2570
of employment, 2562
payment of those under, 2562
valid contract of marriage is a sacrament, 2060–2062
Contrition, act of:
to precede reception of general absolution, 1889
Controversy:
appropriate tribunal for religious, 2882–2883
once agreed, terms not to be altered, 3024
Contumacy: cf. Contempt
Convalidation: cf. Validation
Corpses:
no burial beneath altars, 2454
no burial in churches, 2458
Correction, Fraternal:
consequences of failure of to have effect, 2684–2685
Council:
and infallibility, 1500
and profession of faith, 1630
and Roman Pontiff, 711
business dealt with by, 712
force of decrees of, 716
formed by College of Bishops, 708
penalty for appeal from Roman Pontiff to, 2749
presence of Bishops at and their vote, 713
presence of non-Bishops at, 714
suspension and dissolution of, 715
Episcopal:
establishment and work of, 941
Missionary:
establishment of in vicariate and prefecture apostolic, 989
Parish:
nature of vote, 1066

1014

Index

nature, purpose and establishment of, 1065
Particular:
all summoned must attend, 891
Bishops with deliberative vote, 888–890
decrees of, 894
invited guests at, 890
others with consultative vote, 888–890
part of the authentic magisterium, 1512
profession of faith, 1630
proxy possible at, 892
purpose of, 893
right to judge writings, 1609
Pastoral:
elects laity for pastoral synod, 925
establishment and functions of, 1014
frequency of meetings, 1018
lapse of, 1016
membership of, 1015
qualities of members, 1015
selection of members, 1015
term of, 1016
vote of and presidency over, 1018
Plenary:
celebrated on decision of Bishops' Conference, 881, 883
dispensation from laws made by, 179
place, president, business determined by Bishops' Conference, 883–884
Priests':
consulted by Bishop, 921, 1021, 1054, 1065, 2428, 2436, 2497
dissolution of, 998
election to, 992, 993
establishment, description, role, 988
lapses *sede vacante*, 997
membership of, 991
members to be summoned to Diocesan Synod, 925
role of Diocesan Bishop and, 994–995
statutes of, 990
vote of, 995
Provincial:
authority over ecclesiastical province, 869
decree about Mass offerings, 1866
dispensation from laws made by, 179

not held during vacancy of Metropolitan See, 882
role of Metropolitan in, 885–886
vote of members at, 880–890
when decided upon by Bishops of Province, 882
when decided upon by Bishops' Conference, 881
Counsels, Evangelical:
divine gift to the Church, 1129
interpretation of and legislation about, 1130–1131
professed in Institutes of Consecrated Life, 1125
profession of for Consecrated Life, 1124
taken by some members of Societies of Apostolic Life, 1472
Counteractions: cf. *Actions*
Court, Civil:
permission to approach for civil separation, 3304
Covenant, Marriage:
description of, 2057
made by giving consent, 2066–2067
Cremation:
choice of for anti-christian motives, 2391
permitted, 2376–2378
Crime, Impediment of:
description of, 2164–2166
dispensation reserved to Apostolic See, 2118
Criminal Actions: cf. Actions
Culpability:
required for imputability, 2642–2644
Cult, Disparity of:
description of impediment of, 2151–2153
dispensation of impediment of, 2154
doubt as to baptism, 2155
observance of special norms, 2274–2283
Curator:
and domicile or quasi-domicile, 212
appointed by civil authority, 2966
effect of cessation from office, 3029
replacement of, 3029
represents minors in court actions, 2963
Curia:
Diocesan:
appointment to, 937
Chancellor and Vice-Chancellor as Secretaries of, 958

composition of, 935–936
requirements of office-holders, 938
Roman:
composition and role of, 748–749
conflicts of competence dealt with by *Signatura*, 2912
practice of, 58–63
refusal of rescript by, 136–137
resignation of Cardinals of, 742
Custom:
and engagement to marry, 2077
and introduction of new impediment to marriage, 2116
and Mass offerings, 1853
approved, 97
as interpreter of law, 78
contrary to divine law, 71
introduced by community, 69–70
observance of law, in marriage celebration, 2258
Customs:
Centennial:
not suppressed, 14–15
prevailing over canonical law, 75–77
revocation of, 79–80
Contrary:
and force of law, 75–77
not suppressed by Code, 14–15
revocation of, 79–80
Immemorial:
not suppressed by Code, 14–15
prevailing over canonical law, 75–77
revocation of, 79–80
Particular:
reprobation of, 14–15, 72–73
revocation of, 79–80
suppression of, 14–15
Suppression of:
contrary customs, 14–15
if not reasonable, 72–73
Universal:
which suppressed, 14–15

D

Damage:
caused by crime, repair of, 2694
contentious action to make good, 3365
Damages:
arising from promise of marriage, 2078
no appeal against award of, 3229
norms for compensation for, 3228
norms on payment of, 3228

Index

Danger:
  anointing of those in, 1959–1960
Day:
  definition of, 417
  see also **Ferial Day**
Deacon:
  assistant at marriage (Can.1116), duty to notify, 2262
  daily Mass, 570
  delegation of, for marriage, 2237
  dispensing power in danger of death, 2126
  dispensing power when all ready for marriage, 2129–2132
  exercising diaconal order for priesthood, 2012
  homily reserved to priests and deacons, 1529
  in charge of parish, 1026
  minister of exposition of Blessed Sacrament, 1851
  not to say eucharistic prayer at Mass, 1785
  ordinary minister of baptism, 1690
  ordinary minister of holy communion, 1788
  presence of delegated deacon at marriage, 2230–2232
  profession of faith, 1630
  share in sanctifying office of the Church, 1638
  to notify local Ordinary of dispensations given, 2133
  to serve the faithful in the ministry of the word, 1519
  to use proper vestments in the celebration of Mass, 1825
  who refuses to be promoted to priesthood, 2020
  Married:
    age and requirement for ordination, 2008
    appropriate remuneration for, 585
  Permanent:
    age and requirement for ordination as, 2008
    obligations of, 600
    period of formation before ordination, 2013
    profession of faith, 1630
    recitation of divine office, 570
Dean: cf. **Vicar Forane**
Deanery: cf. **Vicariate Forane**
Death:
  Danger of:
    absolution by any priest in, 1915
    absolution of accomplice in, 1916
    act of contrition before general absolution in, 1889
    baptism of adult in, 1698
    baptism of infant in, 1700
    baptism of infant in when parents opposed, 1704
    confirmation in, 1735–1739, 1755
    dispensation of marriage impediment by local Ordinary in, 2122–2124
    dispensing power of parish priests and others in, 2125–2126
    general absolution in, 1884–1885
    holy communion to children in, 1796
    marriage before two witnesses only in, 2247–2250
    obligation to hear confessions in, 1932
    requirements for marriage in, 2092–2093
    requirement to confirm in, 1750–1751
    suspension of effects of penalty in, 2701
    Viaticum for those in, 1811–1813
  Of Spouse Presumed:
    consultation with Apostolic See, 3328
    procedure and requirements, 3326–3327
Deceit:
  as ground for nullity, 2199–2201
  influencing juridical acts, 259–260
  invalidates an oath, 2411
  invalidates a vow, 2401
  obligation to repair harm in case of, 269–271
Decisions, judicial:
  invalidity of, 2847
Declaration:
  by Catholic party in mixed marriage, 2272
Decree:
  application of penalty by extra-judicial, 2686–2687
  force of decree of judge, 3183, 3184
  issuing an administrative act, 93
  perpetual penalties cannot be applied by, 2688
  petitioner commences recourse procedure, 3373–3374
  suspension of pending recourse, 3377–3378
  Cessation of:
    by revocation, 90
  General:
    author of, 83–85
    definition of, 82
  General Executory:
    binding force of, 88
    cessation of, 90
    description of, 86–87
    promulgation of, 87
  Singular:
    cessation of, 123
    contrary, 114
    deemed to be known, 119
    description of, 109
    effect of, 113
    effects of presumed negative answer, 122
    execution of, 116
    force of, 117
    manner of issue of, 112
    oral or written, 118
    presumption of a negative answer, 121
    requirements before issuing, 111
    time-limits, 120
Dedication: see also **Sacramentals**
  loss of, 2424
  minister of, 2358–2359
  of church as soon as possible, 2431
  of sacred places, 2417
  proof of, 2420
  record of dedication of church, 2419
  solemn rite, for church, 2431
Defect of Form:
  special documentary process to establish, 3296–3299
Defection:
  Formal Act of:
    and impediment of disparity of cult, 2153
    mixed marriage permission in case of, 2268
    removes need for form of marriage, 2253–2254
  From Ecclesiastical Communion:
    bar to admission to public associations, 660–661
  Notorious:
    prevents voting, 358
Defence:
  of self or another and diminution of penalty, 2648
  of self or another and liability to penalty, 2647
  Right to:
    of religious accused of offences in can.696, 1415–1416
    of religious accused of specific

crimes, 1412
to be ensured for parties in case, 3144–3146

Defender of the Bond:
appointment and role of, 2891, 2896
can appeal from judgement to higher court, 3196
can be promoter in a different case, 2896
cannot be judge in same case in further instance, 2916
can propose questions to be put to parties, 3051
cases with which defender cannot deal, 2917
consulted before judgement, 3162
examination of witness, 3098
forbidden to accept gifts, 2929
intervention of, in hearing of legal objection, 2920
invalidity of acts if not cited, 2892–2893
objection to, 2918
obligation of secrecy, 2926
of appeal court can renounce appeal, 3207
qualities of, 2895
raising plaint of nullity, 3193
removal of, 2896
right of response to advocate/parties, 3158
submissions of, 2894
to be heard, 2894
to take oath to exercise office faithfully and properly, 2925
Marriage Procedure:
inspection of acts, 3282
observations of in non-consummation cases, 3322
presence at evidence sessions, 3282
role of in special documentary process, 3296–3299

Deferment:
of baptism, 1702–1703

Definition of Doctrine: cf. **Doctrine**

Delegation:
by local Ordinary of parish priest for marriage, 2237–2238
interpretation of, 303
lapse of, 308–309
of executive power, 302
of several persons acting individually, 306
of several persons collegially, 306
requirements for special delegation for marriage, 2244
successive, 307
to dispense, 172
General:
description of, for marriage, 2238
permission of parish priest for lawful assistance at marriage, 2245

Deliberation, mental:
and diminution of penalty, 2648

Deprivation:
constitution of expiatory penalties, 2671–2673
extent of effect of, 3677
for abduction, imprisonment, mutilation, wounding, 2821
for abuse of ecclesiastical office, 2789
for cleric or religious attempting marriage, 2803–2804
for solicitation, 2782–2784
for violation of law of residence, 2819–2820
of office, 406

Derogation:
by a later law, 7–8, 64–66

Desecration:
description of, 2423

Devotion:
fostering at shrines, 2446

Diaconate:
age and maturity required for, 2006
candidate publicly undertakes obligation of celibacy, 2019
candidate to be ordained by proper Bishop, 1980
dimissorial letters for religious, 1987
effects incardination, 549–550
judgement of proper Bishop or Major Superior of qualities of candidates, 1996
judgement that candidate is beneficial to the Ministry of the Church, 1997
only for baptised man, 1993–1994
proper Bishop of secular candidates, 1983
refusal of admission to priesthood, 2004–2005
retreat to be made before ordination, 2021
studies required for promotion to, 2011
Permanent:
age and requirements for admission to, 2008
candidates require period of formation, 2012–2013
formation of and regulations for those preparing for, 499–500
unmarried candidate publicly undertakes obligation, 2019

Dignity of Marriage, Sacramental:
error concerning, 2202–2203

Diligence, due:
omission of and imposition of penalty, 2642

Diminution of Penalty:
circumstances for, 2648

Diocesan Bishop: cf. **Bishop**

Diocesan Right:
house to inform local Ordinary of financial affairs, 1264
Institute of Consecrated Life, description of, 1160–1161
Institute of Consecrated Life of in special care of Diocesan Bishop, 1169
Institute of requires consent of Diocesan Bishop for alienation, 1268

Diocese:
annual celebration of day for missions, 1567
annual contribution to missions, 1567
as domicile or quasi-domicile, 208
defined territory, 762
definition of, 760–761
diocesan Bishop, judge in first instance, 2863–2864
establishment of special fund for support of clergy, 2527–2528
levy of tax for support of, 2496–2501
no exemption, 867
priest as promoter of missionary activities in, 1567
richer to assist poorer ones, 2531–2533
Rota's right to judge, 2843–2844
selection of candidates for universities and ecclesiastical faculties, 1605
to supply Apostolic See with necessary support, 2521
vocations to missions to be promoted, 1567

Director, Spiritual:
for seminarians, 522
need for in seminary, 506
no vote on admission to orders of seminary students, 509

Diriment Impediment: cf. **Impediment to Marriage**

Index

Discipline:
- Bishop to foster, 808
- maintenance of, in seminary, 507
- training for priesthood outside seminaries, 497

Discretion:
- annual confession from age of, 1937
- confirmation administered at age of, 1754–1755
- lack of due: invalidates marriage, 2184–2188
- use of by judge in penal cases, 2690–2691

Discussion, oral:
- norms for, 3161
- of pleadings can be allowed by judge, 3160
- oral contentious process, 3259

Dismissal: Religious, dismissal of

Dismissal from Clerical State:
- as an increased penalty for apostasy, heresy, schism, 2732
- as expiatory penalty, 2673
- cases concerning, reserved to Collegiate Tribunal, 2874
- effects of decree of, for Religious, 1421
- for attempted marriage, 2803–2804
- for living in concubinage etc., 2809–2811
- for scattering sacred species, 2740
- for sexual crimes against minors, 2812–2818
- for solicitation, 2782–2784
- for striking Roman Pontiff, 2744
- manner of, 603
- not in particular law, 2636
- support of one dismissed from clerical state, 2698–2699

Disobedience:
- penalty for incitement to, against Apostolic See or Ordinary, 2750–2752
- to lawful command of Apostolic See or Superior, penalty for, 2747–2748

Dispensation:
- and juridical acts, 173
- by Ordinary in doubt of fact, 41
- by priests or deacons, 181
- cessation of, 187
- description of, 172
- from disparity of cult, requirements, 2154
- from ecclesiastical laws, 182–183
- from form of marriage, 2276–2281
- from marriage impediments reserved to Apostolic See, 2120
- from obligation of holydays and days of penance, 2462–2463
- from universal and particular law, 174–176
- given in situations of doubt, 184
- granted by priest or deacon to be granted by rescript, 125
- in danger of death, 2122–2128
- interpretation of, 186
- notified to local Ordinary, 2133
- of impediment of consanguinity, 2121, 2173–2175
- of irregularities and impediments to order, 2040–2048
- of marriage impediments by local Ordinary, 2118–2120
- Ordinary's power to grant, 175, 170–180
- those who can be dispensed, 185
- when all is ready for marriage, 2129–2132

From non-consummation:
- change from nullity to, 3288
- only Roman Pontiff grants, 3311
- parties alone have right to seek, 3309

Disposed, properly:
- no doubt about disposition, and absolution, 1920
- to receive absolution, 1933
- to receive general absolution, 1888

Disposition, pious:
- fulfilment of overseen by Ordinary, 2598–2600, 2602
- Ordinary is executor of, 2598

Dissolution of Marriage:
- by reason of non-consummation, 2299–2301
- by reason of Pauline Privilege, 2302–2318
- must be lawfully established, 2150
- other privilege of the faith cases, 2319–2321
- to be notified to parish priest for registration in baptismal register, 2266–2267
- use of defender in cases of, 2891

Disturbance, mental:
- and diminution of penalty, 2648
- and judge's discretion, 2692
- deliberately sought, 2651
- expert(s) to be used in case of 3285–3287

Division:
- of Institute of Consecrated Life, 1141–1142

Doctorate:
- required for advocate, 2973
- required for defender and promoter, 2895
- required for judges, 2869
- required for Officialis and vice-Officialis, 2867

Doctors:
- exemption from testifying in court, 3072

Doctrine:
- penalty for teaching condemned, 2747–2748

Catholic:
- basis for formation and education in Catholic schools, 1583
- overseeing of in Catholic universities and faculties, 1596

Defined:
- requirements for, 1502
- to be believed by divine and Catholic faith, 1503–1505

Documents:

General:
- acceptability of public, 3062–3063
- altered or falsified, 3065
- judge directs submission of, 3067
- manner of production of, 3066
- obligations of pious foundations, 2613
- penalty for falsification, 2797–2799
- private, 3061
- probative force of private, 3064
- production of and secrecy, 3068
- proof by means of, 3058
- public civil, 3060
- public ecclesiastical, 3059
- record of foundation, 2612
- return of personal and private documents to owners, 2957
- supporting petition in oral contentious process, 3247

Curial:
- accessibility of, 972–973
- destruction of, 976
- historical, 980
- relating to Cathedral and churches, 980
- removal of, 974
- removal of from secret archives, 979

Domicile:
- acquisition of, 205–206
- forum for one without, 2851
- forum for one without known, 2852
- forum of trial in case of inheritance or legacy, 2857

Index

incola, peregrinus, vagus, 202
laws binding those with, 34
loss of, 213–214
loss of and cessation of habitual
    confessional faculties, 1914
of members of Religious Institutes,
    210
of minors, 212
of spouses, 211
parish of domicile for marriage,
    2246
parish priest and Ordinary of, 215
parochial or diocesan, 208
place of and faculties to hear
    confessions, 1899–1900
trial before tribunal of, 2850
Donors: cf. *Intentions*
Doubt:
General:
about meaning of administrative
    act, 94
about meaning of law, 55
in case of dispensation, 184
of validity or fact of baptism,
    1705–1710
revocation not presumed, 67
Of Fact:
as to impotence, 2142
Church supplies in, 313–314
Ordinary's ability to dispense in,
    41
Of Law:
as to impotence, 2142
Church supplies in case of,
    313–314
laws do not oblige when there is,
    39–40
Doubt, formulation of: cf.
Formulation
Drunkenness:
culpable, and diminution of
    penalty, 2648
effects of deliberate, on
    responsibility of a crime, 2651
offence committed because of, and
    judge's discretion, 2692
Due Diligence: cf. *Diligence*
Duty: cf. *Obligation*

E

Eastern Patriarchs: cf. *Patriarchs*
Easter Vigil:
celebration of baptism on, 1681
Ecclesiastical Goods: see also
Temporal Goods
penalty for hindering lawful use of,
    2756
penalty for wrongful alienation of,
    2758–2759

Ecumenism:
fostering of by diocesan Bishop,
    798
promotion of by College of
    Bishops, 1514
training of seminarians in, 536
Editions:
first and subsequent, approval by
    authority, 1623
Education:
Catholic:
by Religious Institute, 1579
Church's right in, 1571
duties of pastors and
    arrangements for, 1571
ensuring Catholic education in or
    out of schools, 1575
in Catholic schools, 1583
in schools (general), 1573
nature and manner of, 1572
promotion of, 1569
provision of, 1570
subject to Church authority,
    1585
Moral:
provision of in schools, 1576
Religious:
provision of in schools, 1576
subject to Church authority,
    1585
Effects, Civil:
of marriage, governed by civil law,
    2069–2071
Elderly, the:
no eucharistic fast for, 1808
Election:
by compromise, 363–365
cessation of compromise, 366
collegial acts, rules for, 239–242
conduct of, 362
confirmation of, 321, 372–375
immediate acquisition of rights to
    office, 371
invalid by reason of lack of freedom
    at, 357
no lobbying at, 1237
notification and acceptance of,
    368–370
of Superior of autonomous
    monastery 1235
one vote each at, 355
penalty for hindrance of freedom
    of election, 2756
result of, 367
right of in case of parish priest,
    1036
summoning of voters, 350–352
those incapable of voting at, 358
timing of, 248

valid vote, 360
who may vote, 353–356
Emeritus:
as a title, 389
Endowment:
to be safeguarded and invested,
    2611
Engagement (to marry):
governed by particular law, 2077
Episcopal Conference: cf. *Bishops'*
Conference
Episcopal Vicar: cf. *Vicar*
Equity, canonical:
observance of in removal of or
    transfer of parish priests, 3401
observance of laws with, 60
Error:
General:
about a person as ground for
    nullity, 2196–2198
about diminishing circumstances
    for penalty, 2648
about law, 42
about unity or indissolubility or
    sacramental dignity of
    marriage, 2202–2203
equivalent to ignorance for
    violation of law, 2647
influence on juridical act,
    261–262
not presumed, 43
Common:
the Church supplies in situations
    of, 313–314
Eucharist, Blessed: see also **Mass**
active role of faithful, 1765
and marriage, 2086
carrying of, 1838
celebration and concelebration of,
    1772–1775
celebration and reservation of in
    oratory of Society of Apostolic
    Life, 1475
celebration at shrines, 2446
celebration in seminary as centre of
    life, 522
description of, 1764, 1766
exposition of Blessed Sacrament,
    1848
manner of celebration of, 1768
obligation of diocesan Bishop to
    preside over, 805
penalty for scattering, 2739–2740
place of reservation, 1835–1837
prayer before, 1840
procession of Blessed Sacrament,
    1852
reservation marked by lamp, 1847
tabernacle, 1841–1845

Index

Eucharist, Blessed: *(contd)*
  with baptism, confirmation sacraments of initiation, 1652

Evangelisation:
  to be used to prepare for the sacraments, 1654

Evidence:
  collected by auditor, 2884–2886
  collection of, in oral contentious process, 3254
  completion of, 3147
  credibility witnesses, 3284
  discussion of evidence in oral contentious process, 3259
  minors and the feeble minded not admitted to give, 3074
  recorded by notary in oral contentious process, 3256
  weighing by judge, norms for, 3103–3107, 3166
  witnesses unable to sign, 2954

Examination:
  prior to the grant of confessional faculties, 1906
  Judicial:
    manner of examination of witnesses, 3089
    manner of questioning and giving evidence, 3094–3096

Excardination:
  and cessation of habitual confessional faculties, 1914
  rules for, 551–556, 558–563

Exception: see also *Objection*
  allegation of adjudged matter, 2938
  always possible and perpetual, 2985
  dealing with other peremptory, 2939
  of an adjudged matter, 3216
  plaintiff can bring several simultaneously, 2986
  raised by respondent in oral contentious process, 3250
  reinforces a right, 2983
  timing of submission of, 2934–2935

Exclaustration, indult of:
  effects of, 1391–1393
  for cloistered nuns, 1387
  for perpetually professed, 1385–1386
  imposition of, 1388–1390

Exclusion:
  of marriage or essential properties of marriage, 2206–2209

Excommunication:
  Bishop or priest under cannot assist at marriage, 2235
  constituting the penalty of, 2635
  declared or imposed, 2661–2662
  effects of, 2658–2660
  for abortion, 2825–2828
  for absolution of accomplice, 2760–2763
  for apostasy, heresy, schism, 2728–2731
  for attempting to say Mass or to absolve, 2763–2766
  for consecration of Bishop without pontifical mandate, 2775
  for (direct) violation of sacred seal, 2785–2786
  for scattering sacred species, 2739–2740
  for striking Roman Pontiff, 2744
  imposition or declaration of, reserved to Collegiate Tribunal, 2874
  prevents voting, 358
  remission of, by confessor, 2713
  those under, not admitted to Holy Communion, 1801
  when imposed or declared, is bar to admission to public association, 660–661

Excusing Cause: cf. *Cause*

Excusing Circumstances: cf. *Circumstances*

Execution:
  by executor's successor, 105
  error in, 106
  of administrative acts, 96
  of judgement, 3230–3240
  valid, 99–100

Executor:
  manner of execution of administrative act, 99–100
  must proceed according to mandate, 103
  obligation to act, 101–102
  of administrative acts, 96
  of all pious dispositions, the Ordinary, 2598–2600
  substitution of executor, 104
  to account for administration, 2599

Exempt Places: cf. *Places*

Exemption:
  of seminary from parish governance, 543

Exhortation, fatherly:
  in removal of parish priest cases, 3390
  in transfer of parish priest cases, 3399

Exorcism:
  Permission required for, 2365

Exorcist:
  qualities required in, 2365

Expenditure:
  annual budget of, to be drawn up by administrator, 2560
  record of, 2559

Expenses:
  judgement apportions, 3175
  judicial, borne by litigants for abated trial, 3033
  judicial, following renunciation of trial, 3037
  no appeal against award of, 3229
  norms for payment of judicial, 3228
  obligation to pay if no appearance, 3139
  of experts to be paid, 3119
  of witnesses to be paid, 3102
  questions concerning judicial, settled before joinder of issue, 2941
  reduction of, 3228

Expert:
  cannot be judge in same case in further instance, 2916
  defender, advocate, promoter, present at evidence session of, 3282
  evidence of, 3108–3121
  honorarium for, 3228
  in assistance and support for marriage, 2084
  in case of impotence or lack of consent because of mental illness, 3285–3287
  in case of insanity or psychological infirmity after ordination, 2036
  in case of insanity or psychological infirmity for ordination, 2023
  obligation to secrecy, 2928
  presence of parties and advocate at examination of, in oral contentious process, 3255
  to take oath to exercise office properly and faithfully, 2925
  In Law:
    allowed in non-consummation cases in place of advocate, 3318, 3324

Exposition of Blessed Sacrament: cf. *Blessed Sacrament*

Expulsion of Religious, instant:
  special urgent reasons required for, 1424–1425

Extension of Law:
  not retroactive, 50–51

Index

External Forum: cf. Forum
Extinction of actions:
  by means of prescription, 2984

F

Fact:
  declaration of juridical, by a trial, 2831
  ignorance or error about notorious, not presumed, 43
Faculties:
  Confessional:
    cessation of, 1914
    consultation by local Ordinary prior to granting, 1907
    effects of revocation by local Ordinary, 1911
    given by law or competent authority, 1897
    given for determinate or given in writing, 1909
    indeterminate time, 1908
    given only to suitable priests, 1906
    granted by Religious Superiors, 1901, 1905
    habitual, to hear confessions everywhere, 1899–1900
    necessary to hear confessions, 1896
    revocation of, 1913
    those who have them from law, 1902–1903
  Ecclesiastical (Universities):
    canonical effects of degrees in, 1603
    Church's right to have, 1601
    constitution and direction belongs to Apostolic See, 1602
    cooperation between faculties and universities, 1606
    deans of theology and canon law to have consultative vote at particular councils, 888–890
    location of, within territory of Bishops' Conference, 1594
    mandate for teachers of theology, 1598
    observance of principles of Catholic doctrine in, 1596
    of theology in Catholic universities, 1597
    rectors of, to have consultative vote at particular councils, 888–890
    right of laity to acquire further knowledge of sacred sciences, 483
    spiritual and pastoral care of students, 1599
    statutes approved by Apostolic See, 1602
    teachers, appointment and removal, 1595
  Habitual:
    governed by rules for delegation, 284
    lapse of, 285
    possessed by Vicar general and episcopal Vicar, 955
Faith:
  never lawful to force others to embrace, 1497
  profession of, 1630
  And Morals:
    books on, displayed for sale, 1621
    declarations upon, 1511
    judgement on matters of, by censor, 1624–1626
    norms for taking part in media programmes on, 1628
    protection of, by pastors of Church, 1609
    submission of books on, for censorship, 1620
    use of textbooks on, 1620
    writings by Religious on, 1629
  Bad:
    concealment of penalties, 2718
Faithful:
  General:
    accounts to be rendered to, 2565
    and publication of versions of sacred scriptures, 1615
    and the use of means of social communication, 1608
    at particular councils have consultative vote, 888–890
    community introducing custom, 69
    definition of, 424–430
    division into clerics and laity, 433
    equality of dignity and action, 437
    exercise of rights regulated by ecclesiastical authority, 471
    harm from use of social communication, 1609
    lay members to be summoned to diocesan synod, 925–926
    need to avoid disputes, 2913
    obligation to observe ecclesiastical decrees, 1513
    permission to publish prayer books for use of, 1618
    responsibility in missionary activity, 1553
    role of in the apostolate, 812
  Sacraments, the:
    part of the faithful in the sanctifying office of the Church, 1639
    present corporately at liturgy, 1641
    reception by, from non-catholic ministers, 1657
    reception of, from Catholic ministers, 1655–1656
    reverence of, for the sacraments, 1649
  (Anointing and Sacred Order):
    bound to reveal known impediments to orders, 2034
    invitation, to sacred ordinations, 1976
    pastor's obligation to anoint the sick, 1957
    some receive the sacrament of order, 1969–1972
  (Baptism, Confirmation, Eucharist)
    as extraordinary ministers of Holy Communion, 1789–1790
    bound to receive confirmation, 1752–1753
    participation in Mass and reception of Holy Communion in any Catholic rite, 1815
    paschal precept, 1810
    praying before Blessed Sacrament, 1840
    presence of, at exposition, 1850
    presence of at least one member of, at Mass, 1782–1784
    role of, in the celebration of the Eucharist, 1767
    spiritual nourishment in Eucharist, 1766
    to be taught how to baptise, 1692
    to receive Holy Communion at least once a year, 1809
    Viaticum, in danger of death, 1811
  (Marriage):
    community assistance to marriage state, 2079–2083
    obligation to reveal marriage impediments, 2094
  (Penance):
    choice of confessional, 1893
    disposition for confession, 1933
    free choice of confessor, 1939
    gaining indulgences, 1940–1941
    indulgences for self or another, 1943

Faithful: *(contd)*
  instruction about general absolution, 1889
  obligation of priest to hear confessions of, 1932
  obligations to confess grave sin, 1934–1935
  obligation to confess grave sins annually, 1937
  recommended to confess venial sins, 1936
  valid reception of general absolution, 1888
  Obligations of:
    a holy life and promotion of Church's growth, 441
    consent of authority to use of term 'Catholic', 455
    obedience to teaching of the sacred pastors, 443
    proper preparation for the sacraments, 1654
    reminder of by Diocesan Bishop, 2494
    the common good and the exercise of faithful's rights, 470–471
    to make their views known to their pastors, 445–447
    to preserve communion within the Church, 438–440
    to promote social justice, 469
    to provide for the needs of the Church, 467–468, 2494
    to support the Church, 2495
  Rights of:
    to be judged and punished according to law, 465–466
    to christian education, 456
    to collaborate in spreading the gospel, 442
    to donate goods for the benefit of the Church, 2493
    to establish pious or charitable associations, 453
    to follow own form of spirituality, 450–452
    to freedom in choosing a state of life, 459–461
    to good reputation and privacy, 462–463
    to make known their needs to their pastors, 444
    to make their views known to their pastors, 445–447
    to obtain spiritual assistance from their pastors, 448–449
    to promote and support apostolic action, 454
    to research in the sacred sciences, 457–458
    to vindicate and defend their rights, 464–466
    to worship God, 450–451
  Worship, other acts of:
    funerals of catechumens, 2387
    obligation to do penance, 2470–2471
    oratories open to access of faithful, with consent, 2437
    place of funeral, 2380–2381
    to be given Church funeral, 2374
    urged to venerate BVM, 2394
    veneration of sacred images, 2396
False denunciation:
  of confessor, penalty for, 2791–2793
Falsification:
  of ecclesiastical documents, penalty for, 2797–2799
Families:
  duty to foster vocations, 492
  joint preparation of, for baptism, 1675–1676
Fast, Eucharistic:
  for one hour, 1806
  for sick and elderly and those nursing them, 1808
  provisions for priests saying two or more Masses, 1807
Fasting:
  nature of law, 2473
  observance of Ash Wednesday and Good Friday, 2473
Favour of Law: cf. **Law, Favour of**
Fear:
  influencing juridical act, 259–260
  offence committed by reason of, 2692
  unjust, invalidates oath, 2411
  unjust, invalidates vow, 2401
  Grave:
    diminution of penalty, 2648
    invalidates marriage, 2213–2218
    liability to penalty, 2647
    remission of penalty extorted by, is invalid, 2719
Feastday:
  and general absolution, 1886
  list of holydays of obligation, 2464
Federation:
  of Institutes of Consecrated Life, 1145
***Ferendae Sententiae* Penalty:**
  and conspiracy, 2656
  description of, 2631
  for accomplices, 2656
  remission of by Ordinary, 2711–2712
Ferial Day:
  celebration of sacrament of Order on, 1974
Financial Administrator: cf. **Administrator**
Financial Committee (Diocesan): cf. **Committee**
Financial Support: cf. **Support**
Font, Baptismal:
  in another church or oratory, 1685
  in parish church, 1684
Foetus:
  baptism of aborted, 1712–1713
Force:
  and liability to penalty, 2647
  in abduction, imprisonment, mutilation, wounding, 2821
  invalidates marriage, 2213
  invalidates oath, 2411
  invalidates vow, 2401
  involved in sexual crime by cleric, 2812
  Of Law:
    and custom, 71–73
    authentic interpretation with the same, 48–51
    interpretation by court judgement lacks, 52
    of contrary custom, 75–77
    of custom, 74
    retroactive declaration of, 51
Form of Marriage: cf. **Marriage**
Formation:
  doctrinal, for seminarians, 525
  duty of laity to acquire, 489
  for candidates to permanent diaconate, 2013
  in Catholic religion subject to Church authority, 1585–1586
  in Catholic school, 1582–1584
  of students in the concern for universal Church, 538
  of the young, 1576
  pastoral, for seminarians, 526, 535
  provided in minor seminaries, 494
  spiritual, in seminary, 519
  spiritual, to equip candidate for pastoral ministry, 520
  writings on catechetical, 1619
  Houses of:
    provision of confessors in, 1248
  Religious:
    completion of, after first profession, 1315–1316
    elements of, 1318
    nature and duration of,

Index

defined in constitutions, 1316
special, for those going on to orders, 1317
to continue throughout religious life, 1320

Formulation of Doubt:
in marriage cases, 3279–3280

Forum:
External:
dispensation in, when occult impediment becomes public, 2135
Internal:
dispensation from occult impediment in internal non-sacramental, 2134
remission of penalties, in internal sacramental, 2713–1714
remission of penalty by Bishop, 2709–2710
Judicial:
for one without domicile or quasi-domicile, 2851
for plaintiff, 2849
use of judicial, of plaintiff, 2852

Foundation:
Autonomous:
description of, 232
description of pious, 2604–2605
Non-autonomous:
description of pious, 2605
Pious:
conditions for valid acceptance of, 2609
document showing obligations of, 2613
record of, kept in archives, 2612
to be recorded in writing, 2612

Founders:
observance of the mind of, 2559
safeguarding wishes of, in amalgamation, 246–248
safeguarding wishes of, in division, 249–252

Foundling:
baptism of, 1711
place of origin of, 203

Fraternal Correction: cf. Correction, Fraternal

Fraud:
involved in commission of crime, 2821–2824

Free Legal Aid: cf. Legal Aid

Freedom:
establishment of, for lawful assistance at marriage, 2245
establishment of, to marry in danger of death, 2092–2093
establishment of, to marry before special delegation is given, 2244
of investigation of truths, 802
of seminary students to approach any confessor, 508

Friday:
day of penance, 2472

Fund:
Reserve:
amalgamation of, on interdiocesan basis, 2534, 2536
establishment and purpose of, 2531, 2533
to have civil law standing, 2535
Social Security:
establishment of, to aid clergy, 2529–2530
to have civil law standing, 2535
Special:
establishment, purposes and use of, 2527–2528
to receive capital from non-autonomous pious foundations, 2608
transfer of benefice's income to, 2522

Funerals:
for Christ's faithful, 2374
function of parish priest at, 1052
manner of celebration, 2375
of catechumens, 2387
offerings made on the occasion of, 2385
of non-catholics, 2389
of unbaptised children, 2388
place of, 2380–2384
refusal of Church funeral, 2390–2392
refusal of *requiem* Mass, 2393

Fusion:
of Institutes of Consecrated Life, 1143–1144

G

General Absolution: cf. Absolution, General

General Secretary: cf. Conference, Bishops'

Godparents:
obligations of, 1540

Good Friday:
abstinence and fasting, 2473

Goods, Patrimonial:
distribution of on extinction of juridical person, 253
division of, 249–252

Good, Public:
safeguarded by promotor of justice, 2889
use of promoter decided by Bishop, 2889

Gospel, Proclamation of:
preparation of seminarians for, 525

Governance:
Acts of:
and excommunication, 2659–2661
validity of those done under censure, 2670
Delegated Power of:
directly granted, 281
exceeding limits of mandate, 286
proof of delegation, 283
Ordinary power of:
attached to office, 280
legislative, executive and judicial, 294
proper or vicarious, 282
Power of:
cooperation in by laity, 275–276
enjoyed by Superior of clerical Religious Institute of Pontifical Right, 1174
exercised by clerics, 272–274
exercised in external or internal forum, 277–278
exercise invalid by reason of suspension, 2666
exercise prohibited by suspension, 2665
ordinary and delegated, 280
proper or vicarious, 282
required for exercise of some offices, 566

Grave necessity: cf. Necessity

Graves:
in public cemeteries, to be blessed, 2455

Grille:
confessional 1893

Guardian:
and domicile or quasi-domicile, 212
appointed by civil authority, 2966
appointment of, 199–200
assigned by judge, 2963
effect of cessation of, from office, 3029
replacement of, 3029
represents minors in court action, 2963

Guardianship:
prevents promotor, defender, auditor, assessor, dealing with case, 2917
relationship of, prevents judge from hearing case, 2917

1023

Index

Guilt:
Church's right to judge, 2833–2834

H

Handicapped:
catechetical formation for mentally and physically, 1548

Hands, imposition of: cf. **Imposition**

Harassment:
danger of, arising from testifying in court, 3072

Hatred:
penalty for incitement to, against Apostolic See or Ordinary, 2750–2752
penalty for stirring up, against religion, 2742

Heads of State:
judged only by Roman Pontiff, 2840–2841

Hearing, the:
order of cases, 2933
those allowed to be present at, 2949
use of interpreter in judicial, 2951

Heirs:
obligation of, 2596

Heresy:
definition of, 1507
irregularity for orders, 2024
penalty for, 2729–2731

Heretic:
penalty for, 2729–2731
refused Church funeral, 2391

Hermits:
existence and description of, 1186–1188

Hierarchical Recourse: cf. **Recourse**

Hindrance:
penalty for, to the freedom of exercising the ministry or election, 2756

Holy Communion: cf. **Communion**

Holy See: see also **Apostolic See**
definition of, 750
difficulty in recourse to, 177–178
national rites of marriage to be reviewed by, 2259
permission of, required for acts of alienation by Religious, 1267
representation by papal legate, 754
to approve Programme of Priestly Formation, 516

Holy Spirit:
gift of conferred in confirmation, 1728

Holydays:

for assistant priests, 1088
for coadjutor and auxiliary Bishops, 840
for Diocesan Bishops, 813
for parish priests, 1058
postponement of judicial action by reason of, 2946

Homicide, wilful:
dispensation from irregularity: formalities, 2047
irregularity for orders, 2026
multiplication of irregularity, 2039

Homiletics:
training in, for seminarians, 1536

Homily:
at all Masses on Sundays and holydays, 1530
most important form of preaching, 1529
role of Bishop, 801–802
strongly recommended at daily Mass, 1531

Honorarium:
for advocate, experts, interpreters, 3228
no appeal against award of, 3229

Hospital:
no baptism in, 1688–1689

Hospital Chaplains: cf. **Chaplains**

Hosts, consecrated:
in pyx or ciborium, frequent renewal of, 1846

Hours: cf. **Office, Divine**

House:
Parochial:
continued use of, by sick but removed parish priest, 3396
Religious:
capacity to acquire, possess, administer, alienate temporal goods, 1258
description of a lawfully constituted, 1200–1201
establishment of, 1203
implication of diocesan Bishop's approval of, 1207
of canons regular or monks sometimes autonomous, 1209
requirements for the establishment of, 1204–1206
suppression of, 1213–1218
use of, and consent of diocesan Bishop, 1208

Human Rights: cf. **Rights**

I

Ignorance:
and violation of law, 2647
effect of crass, supine, affected, 2651
influence on juridical act, 261–262
not presumed, 43
of law, 42
of nature of marriage as grounds for nullity, 2193–2194
of penalty and its diminution, 2648

Illness:
anointing to be performed during, 1959–1962
of parish priests, 3388

Images, Sacred:
restoration of precious, 2397
veneration by faithful and manner of display, 2396

Immersion:
baptism by, 1679

Impeded:
From exercise of Orders:
one bound by impediment to orders already unlawfully received, 2036
one suffering from insanity or psychological infirmity 2036
From receiving Orders:
man with a wife living, 2029–2031
neophytes, 2033
one who exercises an office or administration forbidden to clerics, 2032
See:
definition of, 842
government of diocese during period of, 843

Impediment:
To Marriage:
custom and introduction of new, 2116
description of, 2110
dispensation in danger of death, 2122–2128
dispensation of ecclesiastical, by local Ordinary, 2118–2119
dispensation of occult, 2134–2135
established by Church, 2113
freedom from, to marry in danger of death, 2092–2093
obligation of faithful to reveal, 2094
of consanguinity when not dispensed, 2121
presumed consent in spite of, 2227
public, occult, 2111
reserved to Apostolic See, 2120
special documentary process to

Index

establish undispensed
3296–3297
validation of marriage invalid by
reason of diriment,
2332–2333
(In Detail):
abduction, 2161–2163
affinity, 2176–2177
age, 2137–2139
bond of previous marriage,
2148–2150
consanguinity, 2168–2175
crime, 2164–2167
disparity of cult, 2151–2155
impotence, 2141–2147
legal relationship, 2180–2182
public propriety, 2178–2179
sacred orders, 2156–2158
vow of chastity, 2159–2160
To Orders:
candidates for ordination to be
free of, 1996
dispensation of, 2040–2043
exercise of orders in case of,
2044–2045
formalities for dispensation of,
2046–2048
ignorance of, does not exempt,
2038
in deacon who refuses ordination
to priesthood, 2020
multiplication of, 2039
simple or perpetual, 2022
the faithful bound to reveal,
2034
those bound by, barred from
reception of orders, 2022
see also **Impeded**: *from exercise
of Orders*:
see also **Impeded**: *from
receiving Orders*:
Imposition of Hands:
manner of conferring Sacred
Orders, 1973
Impotence:
impediment of, 2141–2147
use of services of experts in case
of, 3285–3287
Imprimatur:
granting/not granting by local
Ordinary, 1624–1626
Imputability:
actions without full, and
diminution of penalty, 2648
enquiry by Ordinary, in penal
process, 3342
presumption of, 2644–2645
required for crime to be punished,
2642

Inability to Assume:
obligations of marriage,
2189–2192
Inadvertence:
equivalent to ignorance for
violation of law, 2647
Incardination:
description of and norms for,
547–563
determines proper Bishop for
ordination, 1983
following transfer from Religious
Institute, 1406
following transfer from Secular
Institute, 1443
following transfer from Society of
Apostolic Life, 1478
place of, in connection with confessional faculties, 1899–1900
Incidental Matters: cf. *Matter*
Incitement:
to hatred of Apostolic See or
Ordinary, penalty for, 2750–2752
Incola:
description of, 202
Income:
budget of to be drawn up annually
by administrator, 2560
celebration of Mass from income of
pious foundation 2604
seeking payment of, by
administrator, 2559
records of, kept by administrator,
2559
Inconvenience, grave:
and diminution of penalty, 2648
and liability to penalty, 2647
Incorporation:
into Secular Institute, 1457–1461
into Society of Apostolic Life, 1479
Indissolubility:
error about indissolubility of
marriage, 2202–2203
essential property of marriage,
2065
Individual Confession: cf.
Confession: *Sacramental*
Indulgence:
description and nature of,
1940–1941
gained by faithful, 1943
granted by the law or Roman
Pontiff, 1944–1945
partial or plenary, 1942
requirements to gain and use,
1946–1947
Infallibility:
no doctrine defined unless
manifestly demonstrated, 1502

of College of Bishops, 1498, 1500
of Supreme Pontiff, 1498–1499
Infant:
baptism of abandoned or foundling,
1711
baptism of, in danger of death,
1700
description of, 196
incapable of responsibility, 196,
1677
lawful baptism of, 1701–1703
place of baptism of, 1682
role of sponsor for baptism,
1714–1715
time of baptism, 1700
Infirmity:
physical or psychological, of
Religious, 1397
those with infirmity of mind in
court, 2965
Psychological:
as irregularity for Orders, 2023
impedes exercise of Orders, 2036
Inheritance:
place of action in case of, 2857
Initiation:
continued, in confirmation, 1728
role of sponsor in assisting in
christian, 1714–1715
stages of sacramental, 1675–1676
Sacraments of:
baptism, eucharist and confirmation,
1652
Insanity:
impedes exercise of orders, 2036
irregularity for reception of orders,
2023
of Religious, 1398
Inspection:
of acts by parties and advocates,
3144–3146
Institute:
Clerical Religious:
ability to have a church, 1207
and confessional faculties from
the law, 1903
description of, 1157–1158
governance of Superiors of
pontifical right, 1174
Major Superior granting dimissorials,
1987
Superior of – right to take
Viaticum to the sick, 1791
Superiors of, granting
confessional faculties, 1905
of Consecrated Life:
aggregation of, 1138–1140
authority of Superiors and
Chapters 1173

Index

Institute: *(contd)*
- autonomy of, 1150
- call to this state of life, 1127–1128
- changes in, 1146
- Church has responsibility to make to flourish, 1130
- constitutions of, 1151–1154
- diocesan Bishop approves constitutions of those of diocesan right, 1170
- division of etc, 1141–1142
- established by diocesan Bishop, 1136–1137
- fraternal life of each, 1185
- fusion and union, confederation and federation, 1143–1145
- incardination into, 548, 555–556
- manner of observance of evangelical counsels, 1179
- membership of, through profesion of evangelical counsels, 1125–1126
- members of, to bear witness to the gospel, 1520
- members to assist in local catechesis, 1544
- members to be summoned to diocesan synod, 925
- members to observe evangelical counsels, 1180
- members to play special part in missionary activity, 1555
- nature and preservation of patrimony of, 1133–1135
- of diocesan right in care of Bishop, 1160, 1169
- of pontifical right subject to Apostolic See, 1168
- pontifical right or diocesan right, 1160–1161
- provisions concerning apply equally to both sexes, 1194
- requirements for admission to, 1176–1178
- special obedience to Supreme Authority of the Church, 1163
- special responsibilities of Supreme Moderators, 1166–1167
- status of members of, 1127
- suppression and disposal of goods, 1147–1149
- varieties of, in the Church, 1132
- withdrawal from governance of local Ordinary, 1164–1165

Lay: description of, 1159
- participates in pastoral mission of Church, 1357

Religious, Apostolate of:
- activity to be animated by religious spirit, 1356
- activity to be performed in communion with the Church, 1356
- activity to proceed from intimate union with God, 1356
- consists in witness of Consecrated Life, 1354
- contemplative institutes not to be involved in active apostolate, 1355
- cooperation between different institutes in connection with the apostolate, 1365
- for public divine worship and care of souls subject to Bishop, 1360
- in exercise of apostolate religious is subject to Superior, 1361–1362
- works entrusted by Diocesan Bishop subject to contract with Superior, 1367–1368
- works entrusted to Religious under his authority by Diocesan Bishop, 1366

Religious – General:
- capacity to acquire, possess, administer, alienate temporal goods, 1258
- description of, 1196–1198
- domicile or quasi-domicile of members, 210
- incardination into, by diaconate, 550
- necessity for and role of financial administrator in, 1262
- obligation of equity and charity in dismissal of Religious, 1423
- obligation to give collective witness to charity and poverty, 1275
- own law to determine valid act of extraordinary administration, 1265
- requires special norms and constitutions for administration of goods, 1261
- Superiors to be summoned to diocesan synod, 925

Religious – Teaching Role in the Church:
- members of in connection with media programmes, 1627–1628
- right of diocesan Bishop to oversee and inspect schools, 1588
- selection of suitable candidates for university and ecclesiastical faculties, 1605
- Superiors to ensure catechetical formation in their schools, 1550
- with education as purpose, 1579
- writings by members of, on doctrine and morals, 1629

Religious – The Sacraments:
- and faculties to hear confessions, 1901
- and Mass offerings, 1869–1870
- funerals of members of, 2383
- members of, and revocation of habitual confessional faculties, 1910–1913
- obligation to divine office by members of, 2369
- overseeing of Mass obligations by Superior, 1878
- permission from diocesan Bishop to build Church, 2429
- Superior dispensing holydays and days of penance, 2463
- Superiors and dispensation of oaths, 2414
- Superiors and dispensation of vows, 2406
- Superiors giving confessional faculties, 1903
- to have own cemeteries, 2456
- use of confessional faculties by members of, 1904

Secular:
- administration of goods of, 1447
- clerics incardinated into diocese, 550, 1443
- clerics incardinated into Institute, 1444
- constitutions of, 1438
- description of, 1435–1436
- designation of Supreme Moderator, 1446
- effect of consecration as member of, 1437
- governance of, 1446
- life of members within Institute, 1445
- manner of living of members, 1442
- obligations of members, 1448–1449
- overall purpose of members, 1439
- purpose of clerical members, 1441
- purpose of lay members, 1440
- role of Moderators, 1446

1026

Secular – Admission and manner of living:
- association of with other members of the faithful, 1463
- continued formation after incorporation, 1462
- definitive and permanent incorporation, 1460–1461
- degree of maturity required for admission, 1453
- departure from, during or after temporary incorporation, 1464
- dismissal from, 1467
- effect of indult to depart, 1466
- first incorporation into Institute, 1457–1459
- impediments to admission, 1452
- invalid admission, 1451
- probation for candidates, 1454–1456
- right and manner of admission of members, 1450
- transfer from, 1468–1469

Institutes of Higher Studies:
- establishment by Bishops' Conferences and Diocesan Bishops of, 1607
- provisions for, 1590–1600

Institutes of Religious Sciences:
- Church's right to have, 1601
- provision of, by Bishops' Conferences and Diocesan Bishops, 1607
- right of laity to acquire fuller knowledge of the sacred sciences, 483

Instruction:
- *Catechetical*:
  - on the meaning of christian marriage and role of spouses and parents, 2080
  - to prepare for the sacraments, 1654
- *Of Case*:
  - auditor appointed for, 2884
  - right of tribunal to call for assistance of another tribunal in, 2862

Instructions:
- cessation of, 92
- description of, 92
- force of, 92

Insurance:
- arrangement of insurance contracts for ecclesiastical goods, 2559
- right of laity employed by Church to, 490

Integral Confession: cf. **Confession:** *Sacramental*

Intention, donor's:
- alteration of, 2620–2623
- in establishing the number of Masses to be said for an offering, 1863
- observance of, 2559, 2597
- recording of, in Mass book in parish, 1879
- stipulation of place of celebration of Mass, 1872

Intercourse, sexual:
- inability to have, 2141–2147

Interdict:
- Bishop or priest under, cannot assist at marriage, 2235
- effects of, 2663–2664
- for false denunciation of confessor, 2793
- for incitement to hatred or disobedience to Apostolic See or Ordinary, 2752
- for joining, promoting, taking office in associations which plot against the Church, 2755
- for non-priest attempting to absolve, 2765
- for non-priest attempting to celebrate Mass, 2765
- for religious attempting marriage, 2807
- for simony, 2771
- for striking a Bishop, 2745
- remission of, by confessor, 2713–2715
- those under, not admitted to holy communion, 1801

Internal Forum: cf. *Forum*

Interpellations:
- to be made in the case of the Pauline Privilege, 2305–2310

Interpretation:
- *of Administrative Acts*:
  - wide, 94
- *of Laws*:
  - authentic, 45–51
  - by court judgement for administrative act, 52
  - and custom, 78
  - strict, 56–57

Interpreter:
- and sacramental seal, 1925–1926
- penalty for, for violation of sacramental seal, 2787–2788
- sins may be confessed through, 1938
- use of, to contract marriage, 2226
- use of, in judicial hearings, 2951

Interrogation: see **Examination:** *Judicial*

Intervention:
- of third party in case, 3140–3143

Inter vivos: cf. **Act,** *inter vivos*

Intimidation:
- penalty for, of an elector or in one's exercise of ecclesiastical power, 2756

Invalidity of judgement:
- norms for treatment of, 3185–3195
- proposed by means of exceptions, 2934–2935

Investment:
- of endowment capital, 2611
- of funds derived from alienation, 2588
- of surplus money, 2559

Irregular:
- for exercise of orders received, 2035
- for reception of orders, 2023–2028

Irregularity:
- candidate for orders to be free of, 1996
- description of, 2022
- dispensation of, 2040–2043
- enumeration of, 2023–2028
- exercise of orders in case of, 2044–2045
- formalities for dispensation of, 2046–2048
- ignorance of, does not exempt, 2038
- multiplication of, 2039

J

Joinder of Issue:
- agreement of question(s) to be determined by trial, 3022
- counter actions to be proposed within 30 days, 2940
- description of, 3022
- determination of point at issue in oral contentious process, 3251
- exceptions proposed before, 2935
- for appeal cases, 3213
- has effect on possession of property, 3025
- intimated to parties by a decree, 3023
- judge prescribes time limits for instruction, 3026
- judicial expenses, free legal aid settled before, 2941
- once agreed, terms of controversy not changed, 3024
- proofs not collected before, 3045
- summons of other parties to effect, 3007

Index

Judge:
  and Penalties:
    determination of penalty by, 2633
    diminishing the penalty, 2649
    exercise of discretion in infliction of penalties, 2690–2691
    inflicting heavier penalties than in the law, 2652–2653
  and Tribunals:
    appointed by diocesan Bishop, 2869
    appoints an auditor, 2884–2886
    period of office and removal of, 2870
    possibility of lay, 2869
    prohibition of use of sole, 2904
    replacement of, 2879
    requirements for, 2869
    use of assessor and auditor, 2873, 2877–2878,
  Competence:
    embargo on powers of, 2842
    jurisdiction not suspended, 2861
    relative non-competence of, 2848
  Duties of:
    cannot act in another instance of the same case, 2916
    cases judge may not act in, 2917
    forbidden to accept gifts, 2929
    obligation of secrecy, 2928
    proceeds at request of private party or *ex officio*, 2922
    objection against, 2918
    punishment for not observing trial norms, 2930–2931
    to ensure prompt conclusion of cases, 2924
    to persuade litigants to settle their cases, 2914
    to take oath to exercise office properly and faithfully, 2925
    validity of acts of, in case of legal objection, 2921
    who deals with exceptions of suspicion against, 2918
  Evidence of Parties and Documents:
    direct production of transcribed documents, 3068
    direct submission of documents, 3067
    evaluation of changed or falsified documents by, 3065
    evaluation of extra-judicial confession, 3056
    inspection of documents by, 3066
    one other than judge taking evidence, 3044
    proofs not collected before joinder of issue, 3045
    rejection of proof by, 3043
    submission of private document by, 3064
    to administer oath of truthfulness, 3049–3050
    to evaluate refusal to answer questions, 3048
    to question parties, 3046
  Experts:
    accepts or not, experts appointed by parties, 3120
    appoints experts, 3110
    can summon expert for further explanations, 3117
    defines terms of reference for work of experts, 3112
    determines time for work of experts, 3114
    establishes experts' expenses, 3119
    exclusion of experts by, 3111
    reasons to be given for evaluation of expert evidence, 3118
    weighs experts' opinion, 3118
  General Procedural Matters:
    admission and hearing of exceptions by, 2935
    allows person to be present at hearing, 2949
    can take evidence outside own diocese, 2948
    extension or shortening of canonical time limits, 2943
    function of, when expelled from jurisdiction, 2948
    hears exceptions against his own competence, 2936
    to certify acts have been read to party or witness, 2954
    to declare absolute non-competence, 2937
    to determine undefined time limits, 2945
  Incidental matters:
    decision of incidental matters by, 3130–3131
    declaration of respondent's absence, 3134
    description of, 3128
    obligations if plaintiff does not appear, 3138
    to determine intervention of third party in case, 3142
    to ensure summons of respondent within canonical time limits, 3135
  Inspection and Presumptions:
    local inspection by, 3122–3123
    not to make presumptions not in law, 3127
  Introduction of case and first stages:
    accepts or rejects petition as soon as possible, 3002
    can only investigate a case when there is a formal plea, 2995
    determination of time limits for instruction, 3026
    direct oral plea to be recorded in writing, 2997
    discretion as to petition accompanying summons, 3011
    duty to summon other parties on acceptance of petition, 3007–3009
    obligation to accept/reject petition within a month, 3006
    replacement of guardian, for curator or procurator, 3029
  Marriage Procedures:
    judgement to permit legal separation, 3303
    role in documentary process, 3296–3297
    to attempt conciliation between parties before matrimonial proceedings, 3277
    to decide on need for credibility witnesses, 3284
  of Appeal:
    appeal to proceed within one month, 3201
    can order provisional execution of judgement, 3231
    role of appeal in documentary process, 3299
    to deal with cases where appellant has difficulty in obtaining judgement, 3203
  Oral Contentious Process:
    before sole, 3246
  Parties:
    admitting guardian or curator appointed by civil authority, 2966
    appoints advocate for accused, 2970
    appoints curator or guardian, 2963–2964
    can oblige parties to attend court, 2962
    discretion as to special mandate of procurator, 2974
    removal of procurator and advocate by, 2978
    sanctions and fines advocate and

Index

procurators, 2979–2980
Plaints of Nullity:
  can order provisional execution of judgement, 3231
  deals with challenges against decree of provisional execution, 3232
  remedies an invalid judgement, 3194
  to forward acts of case to appeal court, 2955–2956, 3204
  total reinstatement to be sought from appeal court, 3223–3224
  total reinstatement to be sought from one who gave unjust judgement, 3223
Presiding:
  and collegiate tribunal, 2881
  appoints *ponens* or *relator*, 2887
  chairs discussion of case by judges, 3168–3169
  decrees commencement of case, 3281
  determines time and place of meeting for decision, 3168–3169
  duty to summon other parties on acceptance of petition, 3007
  formulation of doubt, 3279
  hearing of objection of suspicion, 2918
  nature of formulation of doubt, 3280
  notification of summons to parties in matrimonial process, 3278
  obligation of secrecy, 2926–2928
  to accept or reject petition as soon as possible, 3002
  to take oath to exercise office properly and faithfully, 2925
Pronouncement of Judgement:
  individual to produce own reasons for decision, 3168
  preparation and signature of judgement, 3173, 3176
  requires moral certainty to give judgement, 3164
  substantive decrees require summary of reasons, 3183
  to decide against plaintiff if no moral certainty, 3167
  to derive certainty from acts and proofs of case, 3165
  to find for respondent if no moral certainty, 3167
  to weigh evidence to reach a decision, 3166
Publication and Conclusion:
  can decree or allow further evidence after conclusion, 3149–3151
  decrees conclusion of case, 3148
  decrees discussion of pleadings, 3160
  decrees time allowed for pleadings and observations, 3152
  norms for observations and pleadings, 3156–3158
  permits parties and advocates to inspect acts of case, 3144–3146
  proceeds to judgement, 3162
Witnesses:
  determines time for submission of questions, 3079
  notification of witnesses' names to parties, 3081
  summons witnesses by decree of judge, 3083
  those incapable of giving witness in trial, 3075
  to moderate numbers of witnesses, 3080
Witnesses, examination of:
  conduct of examination of witnesses, 3094–3095
  determines confrontation of witnesses, 3088
  determines place of interrogation of witnesses, 3085–3086
  determines who is at present at, 3087
  manner of, 3089
  norms for weighing evidence, 3103–3107
  oath of truthfulness for, 3091
  to determine expenses for witnesses, 3102
  to establish identity of witnesses and source of information, 3092–3093
  to recall witness for further examination, 3101
  to remind witness of obligation of truthfulness, 3090
  to sign record of evidence, 3100
  witnesses questioned by, manner of, 3089

Judgement:
  Discretion of:
    lack of concerning rights and duties of marriage, 2184–2188
  Interlocutory:
    decides incidental matter, 3131, 3163
    force of, 3184
    revocation of, 3133
    rules for, 3177
  Production of:
    based on reasoning of judges, 3173
    contents of, 3176
    deferment, 3172
    exceptions against, 2934
    judge proceeds to, 3162
    manner of, 3168–3172
    manner of publication and notification of, 3179–3180
    moral certainty required for, 3164
    prepared in writing by *ponens* or *relator*, 2887, 3173, 3176
    principal case decided by definitive, 3163
    punishment for refusal to give, 2930–2931
    requirements in, 3175
    time limit for issue of, 3174
    to be published as soon as possible, 3178
  Steps against:
    adjudged matter can be executed, 3230
    appeal suspends execution, 3212
    can be appealed against to higher court, 3196
    correction of, 3181
    full, in oral contentious process, to be notified within fifteen days, 3262
    invalid, in oral contentious process, 3263
    irremedial nullity, 3186–3187
    null acts validated by, 3185
    plaint of nullity, 3190
    plea for total reinstatement, 3226
    recourse against two conforming sentences, 3220
    remediable nullity, 3189
    remedied by judge, 3194
    requirements for injustice of, 3222
    sent to appeal tribunal, 3289–3290
    total reinstatement against unjust, 3221

Judicial Expenses: cf. **Expenses,** *judicial*
Judicial Vicar: cf. **Officialis**
Juridical Acts: cf. **Acts,** *juridical*
Jurisdiction, power of: see also *Governance, Power of*
  exercised by clerics, 272–274
Jurisprudence:
  and interpretation of the law, 61

Index

Justice:
overseeing of administration of by *Signatura*, 2912
restoration of, is part object of penal procedure, 2684–2685

K

Key:
to archive of diocese, 970–971
to secret archive, 977
to tabernacle, safekeeping of, 1845

Keys:
pardoned by the keys of the Church, 1934

Knowledge:
manifestation of for an offence, 2657
non-use of, from confessional, 1927–1929
of christian teaching etc., laity to acquire, 481–484
of judge, 3162
of languages for clerical students, 526
of marriage nullity, does not necessarily exclude consent, 2204
of nature of marriage, 2193–2195
required in candidates for ordination, 2002–2003
source of, in witnesses, 3093, 3104

L

Laicisation:
by rescript of Apostolic See, 603

Laity:
General:
and the administration of sacramentals, 2357
as missionary catechists, 1557–1558
assistance to parish priests given by, 1028–1029
cooperation with pastors in ministry of the word, 1521
consultation with, about appointment of parish priests, 1038
delegation of to assist at marriage, 2240–2243
not to say eucharistic prayer at Mass, 1785
part of Christ's faithful, 433–434
to assist in local catechesis and to preach, 1544
use of as judge assessors, 2873

Capacities of:
for experts to act as advisers to sacred pastors, 479–480
temporary assigned role of lector, commentator, cantor, 486–488
to be judges, defenders or promoters, 2869
to fulfil certain ecclesiastical functions, 478
to preach, 1528
to receive ecclesiastical mandate to teach, 484

Obligations of:
of all Christ's faithful, 472–473
of the married to build up the People of God, 475
to acquire formation appropriate to their role, 489
to educate their children, 476
to permeate and perfect temporal order, 474
to spread the message of salvation, 473

Rights of:
of parents to the education of their children, 476
overall rights of Christ's faithful, 472
to acquire knowledge of christian teaching, 481–482
to acquire fuller knowledge of Sacred Sciences, 483
to freedom in secular affairs, 477
to proper remuneration for Church work, 490
to spread message of salvation, 473

Language:
used in eucharistic celebration, 1824

Latae Sententiae **Penalty:**
addition of other penalties to, 2653
description of, 2631
can be established by law without determination or limitation, 2669
excommunication for abortion, 2828
excommunication for absolution of accomplice, 2762
excommunication for apostasy, heresy, schism, 2729–2731
excommunication for scattering sacred species, 2740
excommunication for striking Roman Pontiff, 2744
excommunication for violation of

confessional seal, 2786
for abortion, 2828
for accomplices, 2656
interdict for religious in perpetual vows attempting marriage, 2807–2808
interdict/suspension for false denunciation of confessor, 2793
interdict/suspension for striking Bishop, 2745
remission by confessor, 2713–2715
remission by Ordinary, 2708–2712
suspension for clerics attempting marriage, 2804
suspension of effect of, 2702
temporary cessation of, 2670
threatened by legislator, 2637
where penalty diminished, not incurred, 2650

Latin:
Church: Code concerns only, 1–3
member through baptism, 224–225
member may return to, 226

Language:
knowledge of by Church students, 526
used in eucharistic celebration, 1824

Law:
Canon:
abrogation of, 17–20
custom, contrary to, 75–77
dispensation from, 174–178
governs marriage of Catholics, 2069–2070
promulgation of, 23–25
relation between civil law and, 2568–2570
use of textbooks on, 1620

Cessation of:
effect upon Instructions, 91–92

Civil:
adoption, 223
and prescription, 407–409
appointment of guardians, 199–200
competence over civil effects of marriage, 2069–2070
contracts and observance of, 2568–2570
contracts of employment under, 2662
effects of, 68
formalities of for acts *mortis causa*, 2596
marriages referred to local Ordinary, 2099

1030

minors, 212
norms for actions for possession, 2993
safeguarding ecclesiastical goods in, 2559

Divine:
and civil law, 68
and contrary custom, 71
governs marriages of Catholics, 2069–2070
on marriage, declared by Church, 2112–2113
penalties attached to, 2632
relation between civil law and, 2568–2570

Ecclesiastical:
Church's right to judge violation of, 2833–2834
dispensation from, 182–184
dispensation of impediments of by local Ordinary, 2118–2119
penalty attached to, 2632
understanding of, 53–55
who are bound by, 30–31

Exception to:
interpreted strictly, 56–57

Favour of:
enjoyed by marriage, 2071
in case of doubt of baptism, 2155
privilege that the faith enjoys, 2318

Liturgical, 4–6

Natural:
disposal of goods according to, 2594–2595

Observance of:
and general executory decrees, 86

Penal:
deliberate violation of involves penalty, 2640–2645
determinate and indeterminate, 2633
granting powers to remit penalties, 2706
legislator's power to make, 2632
violation of, but no liability to penalty, 2647

Supreme:
salvation of souls as Church's goal, 3401

Universal disciplinary:
binding force of, 32–34
derogation of, 64–66
dispensation by Ordinary, 174–178
interpretation of, 58–63
no dispensation by a priest or deacon, 181

penalties laid down by, 2634
promulgation of, 23–24

Violation of:
Church's right to judge, 2833–2834
deliberate violation of, involves penalty, 2642
imputability presumed, 2644
requirement for punishment of external violation of, 2641
requirement of use of reason for violation of, 2646

Laws:
enacted in similar matters, 58–63

Disciplinary:
abrogation of, 17–20

Exemption from:
for those in territory where law not in force, 33

Incapacitating and invalidating:
description of, 28–29
obligation of, 39–41

Particular:
abrogated, 18
and interpretation, 58–63
and *Peregrini*, 37
can add penalties to the law, 2634
dispensation from by Diocesan Bishop, 175
excusing, extenuating or aggravating circumstances for crimes, 2654
manner of promulgation of, 25
presumed to be territorial, 35–36

Personal:
Peregrini bound by, 37

Procedural:
no dispensation from, 175

Laws, Interpretation of: cf. Interpretation of Laws

Laymen:
capacity to receive ministries of acolyte and lector, 486

Lector:
capacity for laity to exercise temporary role as, 487
capacity of laymen to be given ministry of, 486
certain functions of, 486
ministry to be received and exercised before diaconate, 2017

Legacy:
place of trial in case of, 2857

Legal Aid, Free:
norm for granting, 3228
time for dealing with questions concerning, 2941

Legate, Papal:
appointment, transfer, recall of, 751
cessation of role of, 757
exemption from local Ordinary's power, 756
legatus a latere, 746
not member of local Bishops' Conference, 900
rights of, 756
role of, 752–753
Roman Pontiff has right to judge, 2840–2841
tasks of, 754–755

Legislation:
and prescription, 407–409

Legislator:
and general decrees, 81–82
approval by, for a custom, 69–70, 75–77
as interpreter of law, 45–47
authorisation to make general decrees, 83–85
can threaten penalty by a precept, 2638
has power to make penal law, 2632
mind of, 55
restrictions on, in threatening penalties, 2637

Legitimacy:
arises from putative or valid marriage, 2293–2294
presumed, 2295

Lent:
season of penance, 2472

Letters, Commendatory:
produced by visiting priest, 1776

Letters, Dimissorial:
any Bishop who can issue can also ordain, 1982
limitation or revocation or lapsation of, 1992
Major Superiors granting, 1987
only granted when all the necessary documents obtained, 1989
penalty for ordaining without, 2776
sent to any Bishop in communion with Rome, 1990
to be authenticated before ordination, 1991
those who can grant, 1985–1988
to be issued by candidate's proper Bishop, 1980

Letters, Testimonial:
about witnesses, 3103

Levy, Diocesan:
for diocesan upkeep, 2496–2501
for seminary upkeep, 545–546

Index

Licentiate:
- required for defender and promotor, 2895
- required for judges, 2869
- required for Officialis and Vice-Officialis, 2867

Ligamen, Impediment of: cf. **Marriage,** *Bond of*

Life: see also **Apostolic Life, Societies of**
see also **Institute** *of Consecrated Life*
Consecrated:
- approval of new forms, 1193
- definition and description of, 1121–1124
- laity or clerics, 434
- the state neither clerical nor lay, 1156

Fraternal:
- lived by members of Religious Institutes, 1196–1198
- within its Institute of Consecrated Life, 1185

Religious:
- description of, 1195

Litigants: see also **Parties in trials**
- consequences of harm caused to, by court personnel, 2930–2931
- legal consequences of parties dying, changing status or office during trial, 3028
- to bear costs of abated trial, 3033

Litigation:
- not to be unduly prolonged, 2944

Liturgy:
- community celebration of, 1641
- marriage, fruitful celebration of, 2082
- means of exercise of Church's sanctifying office, 1633
- observance of principles in Church building, 2430
- ordering and guidance of by Apostolic See, 1642–1645
- parish priest must direct, 1048–1049
- Superiors to lead, 1223
- training in, 530

Liturgy of the Hours:
- description, 2367
- manner of celebration, 2372
- obligation of, 2368–2370

Loan:
- security of, secured by sequestration, 2990

M

Magisterium:
- adherence to teaching of by confessor, 1918
- judgement of books according to teaching of, 1624–1626
- solemn or ordinary and universal teaching, 1503–1505

Majority, Age of:
- definition, 196
- full exercise of rights, 198

Malice:
- required for imputability, 2642, 2644–2645

Mandate:
- capacity of laity to receive, 484
- of advocate and procurator, 2974
- required by teachers of theology in universities and Catholic faculties, 1598
- required for valid proxy, 2221–2225
- special documentary process to establish lack of valid proxy, 3296–3297
- special, required for certain acts by a procurator, 2975

Pontifical:
- no consecration of Bishop without, 1978
- penalty for consecration of Bishop without, 2775

Special:
- when required by Episcopal Vicar, 954
- when required by Vicar General, 954

Marriage:
General:
- Catholics – governed by divine and canon law, 2069–2070
- covenant of man and woman to establish, 2067
- definition of putative, 2075
- definition of ratified, 2072
- description of consummated and ratified, 2072–2073, 2298
- effects of, 2289–2297
- fruitful reception of, 2086
- made by consent, 2066
- no right of action from promise of marriage, 2078
- presumption of consummation, 2074
- presumption of validity of marriage, 2071
- promise of, governed by particular law, 2077
- registration, 2260–2264
- support for those in, 2083
- through interpreter, 2226
- unity and indissolubility, essential properties of, 2063–2065
- valid, as sacrament, 2060–2062
- who can contract, 2068

Assistance at:
- function of parish priest, 1052
- requirements for lawful, 2245

Attempted:
- irregularity for order, 2025
- penalty for cleric attempting, 2803–2805

Bond of:
- case reserved to collegiate tribunal, 2874
- previous, impediment of, 2148–2150
- use of defender, 2891

Consent:
- by proxy, 2221–2225
- conditions, 2211–2212
- exclusion of marriage itself or essential properties, 2206–2209
- force or grave fear, 2213–2218
- presence of parties for proxy, 2219
- presumed to conform to words or signs, 2205
- those incapable of contracting, 2183–2192

Consummated:
- and ratified marriage is indissoluble, 2298

Form of:
- assistance at, by delegated lay persons, 2240–2243
- description and requirements for valid celebration of, 2228–2233
- dispensation of, 2276–2279
- dispensation of in danger of death, 2122–2123
- for subjects of personal Ordinary or parish priest, 2236
- freedom of parties to be established before special delegation, 2244
- in parish Church, Church or Oratory, 2255
- in presence of two witnesses only, 2247–2252
- lawful assistance at, 2245
- marriage elsewhere than in Parish Church, Church or Oratory, 2256–2257
- observation of when one party catholic, 2253
- place of celebration of, 2246
- presumed consent in spite of

Index

defect of, 2227
registration after dispensation, 2263–2264
to be observed in mixed marriage, 2274–2275
validation of union defective by lack of, 2342–2343
Impediment:
diriment, defined, 2110
list of, 2180–2181
prohibition of marriage by local Ordinary, 2114–2115, 2140
Mixed:
dispensation of form for, 2274, 2281
pastoral care of, 2282
permission from local Ordinary for, 2271
permission granted for just and reasonable cause, 2272
non-consummated:
dispensation of, 2299–2301
Pastoral Care of:
assistance by pastors, 2079–2083
cases to be referred to local Ordinary, 2097–2106
dissuasion of young from marrying, 2107
nothing to stand in way of lawful celebration of, 2087
proxy, permission of local Ordinary for, 2106
proxy, requirements, 2219–2225
Ratified:
and consummated marriage is indissoluble, 2298
Secret:
description and requirements for, 2284–2288
Mass:
General:
active role of faithful at, 1765
confirmation during celebration of, 1731
daily celebration of by priests, 571
description of, 1764, 1766
for the people (*Missa pro populo*), 804, 1060, 1078, 1087
Minister:
celebration and concelebration, 1772–1775
daily celebration of by priests, 1777
deacons and laity not to say eucharistic prayer, 1785
number of celebrations permitted for priests, 1778–1781
preparation before, 1787
presence of faithful at celebration of, 1782–1784
priest may celebrate for anyone, 1771
priests not to concelebrate with non-catholic ministers, 1786
visiting priest, 1776
Offerings (Stipends):
avoidance of trafficking in, 1858
calculation of number of to be said for offering, 1863
celebration and concelebration of and acceptance of, 1853
celebration elsewhere than requested, 1872
custom to be observed, 1868
determination of amount of, 1866
intention for Christ's faithful, 1856
not affected by prescription, 413
number which may be accepted, 1871
obligations of administrator of pious causes, 1877
only one offering to be retained daily, 1864
penalty for unlawful trafficking in, 2778–2779
purpose of, 1857
recording of those accepted, 1876
Religious Institutes also bound by local decree or custom, 1869–1870
rules for transmission of and obligations of priest, 1873
separate intention for each offering made, 1859–1861
special book for recording, 1879
time within which Mass to be celebrated, 1874
vigilance by Ordinary or Superior, 1878
Participation:
confession prior to, if in grave sin, 1803
participation in celebration of any Catholic rite, 1815
reception of Holy Communion at, 1804–1805
Rites and Ceremonies:
celebrated in bread and wine, 1816
celebration by sick or elderly priests, 1826
language of, 1824
proper vestments to be used, 1825
wrong to consecrate one species alone or outside, 1823
Time and Place of celebration:
altar for celebration of, 1832
celebration of, time of, 1828
place of celebration, 1829–1834
Various Provisions:
celebration of and excommunication, 2659
celebration of and interdict, 2663
celebration of sacrament of orders during, 1974
obligation to celebrate arising from pious foundation, 2605
obligation to participate in, 2466
permission for celebration in private chapel, 2441–2442
place for fulfilment of obligation, 2467
reduction of Mass obligations, 2614–2618
transfer of Mass obligations, 2619
Matter:
Adjudged:
cases of, 3215
exceptions concerning, 2938
has force of law, 3216
in relation to penal sanctions, 2726
judgement which has become adjudged can be executed, 3230
legal effects of, 3217
status cases never become, 3218
total reinstatement against judgement which has become, 3221
Incidental:
decided by interlocutory judgement, 3163
decision of by judge, 3130–3131
description of, 3128
concerning execution of judgement, 3234
manner of raising, 3129
norms for decision of, 3132
raised concerning correction of judgement, 3182
raised in connection with appeal, 3210
Maturity:
development of in seminary, 519
in ordination candidates, 2006
Means of Social Communication: cf. **Social Communications, means of**

1033

Index

Mediation:
  attempt at prior to judicial action, 3249

Meeting, Provincial Bishops':
  decree on Mass offerings, 1866
  list of candidates for episcopate, 778
  taxes for offerings for administration of sacramentals, 2502–2504

Metropolitan:
  authority over ecclesiastical province, 869
  bound to request pallium within three months, 879
  competent to oversee faith and ecclesiastical discipline, 875
  convenes and arranges provincial council, 885–887
  new pallium on transfer, 878
  occasions when he appoints Diocesan Administrator, 852, 859
  powers of, 877
  presides over ecclesiastical province, 874
  reference of impeded See to Apostolic See, 845
  rules for wearing pallium, 878
  shown diocesan synod decrees, 932
  special functions of, 876
  those to govern diocese when See is impeded, 843
  visitations, 875

Midwives:
  exemption from testifying in court, 3072

Military Service:
  clerics not to volunteer for, 601

Mind:
  internal consent of presumed in marriage, 2205
  those of feeble, exempted from testifying, 3074
  those with infirmity of, in court, 2965

Minister:
  of anointing of sick, 1957
  of penance, requirements for, 1896
  of sacrament of penance is a priest, 1915
  of sacred orders is Bishop, 1977
  Catholic:
    administering sacraments to Catholics, 1655–1656
    administering sacraments to non-catholics, 1660
    administering sacraments to Orthodox Church members and others similar, 1658–1659
  Extraordinary:
    minister of exposition, 1851
    of Holy Communion, acolyte or other lay person, 1789–1790
    taking viaticum to the sick, 1792
  Non-catholic Minister:
    administering sacraments to Catholics, 1657
  Ordinary:
    Bishop, priest, deacon, for baptism, 1690
    of confirmation, Bishop, priest, deacon, 1788
    when ordinary minister for baptism is impeded, 1691–1692
  Sacred:
    constitution of by sacrament of order, 1969–1972
    dispensing power in danger of death, 2126
    dispensing when all is ready for marriage, 2131
    duty to arouse and enlighten the faith, 1640
    fostering of vocations to, 492
    not to refuse the sacraments to those properly disposed, 1653
    participation of for validity in mixed marriages with oriental rite party, 2274–2275
    reverence for sacraments, 1649
    right and duty of Church to train candidates as, 491
    to notify local Ordinary of dispensation given, 2133

Ministry:
  General:
    Bishop to foster vocations to, 800
    diversity of, represented in council of priests, 993
    eucharist and ministry of priest, 1766
    fitness for exercise of, 2050
    of acolyte and lector, 485–487
    of acolyte and lector before diaconate, 2017
    penalty for hindering free exercise of, 2756
  Ecclesiastical:
    excommunication and exercise of, 2659
    penalties for force against hindering, 2746, 2756,
    remuneration of clergy in, 583–584
    remuneration of married deacons 585
  Of the word:
    Bishop and, 801, 808
    Bishops are Moderators of, 1518
    christian worship and, 1640
    deacons and, 1519
    founded on scripture etc., 1522
    lay people can exercise, 486–487, 1521
    priests and, 1519
  Pastoral:
    assistant priests with parish priest in, 1080–1081, 1084–1086
    clergy to seek knowledge for, 581
    contemplative Institutes and, 1355
    knowledge of languages in preparation for, 526
    offering to assistant priests in, 1089
    parish priest and, 1029
    rectors of Churches and, 1100
    seminarians to be prepared for, 520
  Sacred:
    Bishop's permission to establish Religious House rights, 1207
    christian community to foster vocations to, 492
    clerical members of Secular Institutes and, 1440
    duty and right of Church to train candidates for, 491
    exemption from testifying in regard to, 3072
    men of mature years called to, 493
    penalty for unlawful exercise of, 2777
    prohibition from exercise of, penal process, 3355
    requirements in aspirants to, 511–512
    seminaries for students to, 501
  Students for:
    must be judged beneficial to, 1997
    pastoral formation of, 535
    spiritual formation of, 520
    theological formation of, 530
    unable to fulfil ministry, 2023

Minor:
  appointment of advocate for, 2970
  canonical time limits for total reinstatement for minor do not apply, 3225

conflict between rights of and
   those representing them, 2963
description of, 196
domicile or quasi-domicile of,
   212
exemption from testifying in
   court, 3074
norms affecting exercise of rights,
   2964–2965
over sixteen and diminution of
   penalty, 2648
reference of minor to local
   Ordinary for marriage, 2105
represented by parents,
   guardians, curators, 2963
sexual crimes against, 2812–2818
Missa pro populo:
   and team ministry, 1078
   assistant priests and, 1085
   Diocesan Administrator to say,
   863
   Diocesan Bishop to say, 804
   parish priest to say, 1060
Missionaries:
   description of, 1556
   manner of working, 1560
   object of work, 1561
   provisions made by Diocesan
   Bishop binding all, 1566
Missionary Activity:
   description of, 1559
Missionary Work:
   training seminarians in, 536
Missions, Parish:
   parish priests to arrange, 1535
Moderation, due:
   in lawful self-defence and liability to
   penalties, 2647
   in lawful self-defence (lack of) and
   diminution of penalty, 2648
Moderator:
   Curial:
      appointment and work of, 941
      to be notified of juridical acts,
      943
      usually the Vicar General, 941
   Supreme:
      and departure from secular
         institutes of permanently
         incorporated members, 1465
      and reduction of Mass
         obligations, 2618
      and right of admission of
         members to secular institutes,
         1450
      authority of, 1229
      cases before, 2898
      consent to members to reside
         outside society, 1490

designated by election, 1234
elected by general chapter, 1253
election of, 1234–1235
granting indult of exclaustration,
   1385–1386
indult for departure of members
   of Society of Apostolic Life,
   1487
of secular institute, 1446
period of office, 1231
permission to leave during
   temporary profession, granted
   by, 1395
procedure to be observed in trial
   of religious, 1418
re-entry of religious after lawful
   departure, 1399
request to depart by perpetually
   professed, 1402–1403
right of accused religious to
   communicate directly with,
   1417
Rota's right to judge, 2843
special responsibilities of,
   1166–1167
suppression of religious house,
   1213–1215
transfer of Mass obligations,
   2619
transfer of member of Society of
   Apostolic Life, 1488
Team Ministry:
   acts in the name of the parish,
   1078
   has faculties for marriage and
   powers to dispense of a parish
   priest, 1078
   of religious, 1030
   of seculars, 1025
   only one, 1041
   replacement of, 1079
Monastery:
   enclosure or cloister, 1333
   establishment of, for cloistered
   nuns, 1203
   of cloistered nuns, own confessors,
   1248
   of cloistered nuns, own rule of
   life, 1211
   Autonomous:
      alienation – consent of local
         Ordinary required, 1268
      entrusted to special care of
         diocesan Bishop, 1212
      involved in controversy, 2883
      procedure for dismissal from,
         1419
      required to render accounts
         annually to local Ordinary,
         1264

right of diocesan Bishop to visit,
   1242
suppression of, 1218
Monks:
   autonomy of religious house
   with own Moderator, 1209
Monstrance:
   use of for exposition, 1848
Month:
   definition of, 417
Moral Certainty: cf. **Certainty,
Moral**
Morals: see also **Faith** *and* **Morals**
   penalty for harm to public,
   2742–2743
Mother, unmarried:
   registration baptism of child of,
   1724
Motu Proprio:
   administrative act, 97
   rescript, 131
Murder:
   matrimonial impediment,
   2164–2167
   penalty for, 2821–2824
Mutilation:
   grave, malicious, irregularity for
   orders, 2027
   penalty for, 2821–2822

N

Name:
   Baptismal:
      not alien to christian sentiment,
      1680
   Good:
      loss of by parish priest, 3388
      protection of, 2722
      right to, 462
      safeguarding in penal process,
      3343
      suspension of effect of penalty if
      danger of harm, 2702
Necessity:
   baptism in case of, 1674, 1678
   determination of and general
   absolution, by Diocesan Bishop,
   1887
   grave, and general absolution,
   1886
   grave, and liability to penalty,
   2647
   offence committed out of, and
   judge's discretion, 2692
   urgent and obligation to hear
   confession, 1932
Needy, support of:
   proper object of the Church,
   2479

Index

Negligence:
  in conduct of trial, judge can supply, 2923

Neophytes:
  continued formation of, 1565
  when impeded from reception of orders, 2033

Newspapers:
  faithful not to write in certain, 1627

Non-catholics: see also **Separated Brethren**
  as recipients of blessings, 2363
  as parents opposed to infant baptism, 1704
  funerals of, 2389
  may be invited as observers to diocesan synod, 926

Non-christian:
  part of the Bishop's flock, 798

Non-competence:
  appeal against decision of, 2936
  by reason of wrong grade of trial, 2903
  exception of relative, 2936
  judge's obligation in case of absolute, 2937
  of tribunals, 2847
  relative non-competence of judge, 2848

Non-consummation Process:
  acceptance by Bishop, 3312
  action on refusal by Apostolic See, 3324
  change of nullity case into, 3288
  difficult cases referred to Holy See, 3313
  further instruction requested by Apostolic See, 3323
  instruction of case, 3315–3321
  obligation of Bishop if Apostolic See grants dispensation, 3325
  recourse to Apostolic See against rejection, 3314
  rights of parties to seek dispensation, 3309
  transmission of acts to Apostolic See, 3322

Notary:
  Chancellor and Vice-Chancellor, 958–959
  evidence recorded in oral contentious process, 3256
  exemption from testifying in court, 3072
  not to pass on judicial acts, 2957
  public proof of signed acts, 2897
  records oral plea in writing, 2997
  removal of, 964–965
  role of, 960–961
  role of in evidence session, 3097–3100
  specific task of, 963
  to be present at discussion of pleadings, 3161
  to be present at every judicial hearing and sign acts, 2897
  to certify acts read over to party or witnesses, 2954
  to draw up appeal in writing, 3198
  to record attendance of parties at trial, 3009
  to sign juridical acts, 942
  when notary must be a priest, 961

Notorious Rejection of Catholic Faith:
  penalty for, 2747–2748
  reference of marriage case to local Ordinary, 2101–2103
  when public, bar to admission to public associations, 660–661

Novice:
  completion of novitiate, 1305–1306
  confession to a director or assistant director of novices, 1930
  cooperation with director, 1299
  dispensation of vows, 2406
  dispensations of oaths, 2414
  effects of absence of, 1290
  example of community in formation of, 1300
  freedom to depart, dismissal of, 1302–1304
  manner of formation, 1298
  occupation of, 1301
  role of in novitiate, 1282
  ruled by a director, 1293

Novices:
  Director of:
    assistants to, 1295
    not to hear confessions of, 1930
    requirements in and role of, 1294, 1296
    responsibilities of, 1297
  Assistant Director of:
    not to hear confessions of, 1930

Novitiate:
  additional period(s) of apostolic activity during, 1287–1288
  completion of, 1305–1306
  description and purpose of, 1282
  establishment, transfer, suppression of, 1283
  formation of novices according to law of Institute, 1292
  invalidation of, 1290
  location of valid, 1284–1285
  novices ruled by director, 1293
  occupation of novices during, 1301
  required duration of, 1286, 1289
  Candidate to:
    proofs required – baptism, confirmation, freedom, 1281
    requirements in, 1277
    right to admit belongs to Major Superior, 1276
    secular cleric as, after consultation with proper Ordinary, 1280
    special requirements for clerics and others, 1281
    when eligible, 1278

Nullity of Marriage:
  must be lawfully established, 2150
  recorded in baptismal register, 2265
  removal of possibility of putative marriage, 2075–2076
  use of defender in cases of, 2891
  Grounds of:
    deceit, 2199–2201
    error about quality of person, 2197–2198
    error of person, 2196
    exclusion of marriage or essential elements or property of, 2206–2209
    force or grave fear, 2213–2218
    ignorance, 2193–2195
    inability to assume the obligations of marriage, 2189–2192
    invalid proxy mandate, 2223
    marriage with condition, 2210–2212
    those lacking grave discretionary judgement, 2184–2188
    those lacking use of sufficient reason, 2183

Nullity, Plaint of: cf. **Plaint of Nullity**

Nuns:
  establishment of monastery of, 1203
  exclaustration of, 1387
  monasteries of – own rule of life, 1211
  provision of ordinary confessors for, 1248
  suppression of autonomous monastery, 1218

O

Oath:
  cessation of promissory, 2413
  definition of, 2409

Index

description of promissory oath, 2412
inefficacy of, 2412
interpretation of, 2415
invalidated by deceit, force, grave fear, 2411
not taken by proxy, 2410
obligation of, 2411
of truthfulness by parties in judicial process, 3049–3050
suspension, dispensation, commutation of, 2414

Obedience: see also **Counsels, Evangelical**:
description of, 1183–1184
duty of, not lost by prescription, 413
of clergy to Roman Pontiff and Ordinary, 565
of faithful to pastors, 443
of religious raised to episcopate, 1429
promotion of voluntary, by Superior, 1220–1222

Objection, Legal:
consequence if upheld, 2919
manner of hearing against members of court, 2918
procedure against judgement when plaint of nullity raised, 3191
to be expeditiously decided, 2920

Objectives, proper:
of the Church, 2479
the Church's right to what is necessary for its, 2492

Objects, Precious:
alienation of, 2578–2580

Objects, Sacred:
acquisition of, 2518–2519
penalty for profanation of, 2757
use of, 2364

Obligation, Holydays of:
Bishop to preside at Eucharist on, 805
changes in, 2465
dispensation of, 2462–2463
establishment of by Diocesan Bishop, 2461
nature of the obligation, 2466
number of Masses that may be celebrated on, 1781
ordination on, 1974
place for fulfilment of, 2467
transfer, suppression, establishment of by Apostolic See, 2461

Obligations:
Attaching to temporal goods:
prescription as a means of being freed from, 2517
Matrimonial:
inability to assume, 2189–2192
lack of discretion of judgement concerning, 2184–2188
Natural:
children of former unions, 2100

Obreption:
definition of, 132

Obscurity:
of meaning of law, 55

Observations of Defender or Promotor:
exchange of reply to pleadings, 3156–3158
in writing, 3153
length of, 3155
printed, 3154
time allowed for presentation of, 3152

Obstinacy:
obstinate ill-will, 2652

Occurrence, chance:
and liability to penalty, 2647

Offence:
change of law after commission of, 2630
enquiry by Ordinary into alleged offence, 3342
giving rise to scandal, 2655
incapability of commission of, 2646
incomplete, 2654
multiplication of, 2693
publicity of, 2657
punishment of by trial, 2831
reduction of gravity of, 2649

Offender:
warned to purge contempt, 2694

Offerings of faithful: see also *Mass Offerings*
funerals, 2385
made to juridical persons, 2508–2514
observance of specific purpose, 2515–2516
on the administration of the sacraments, 1668

Office:
Ecclesiastical:
description of, 316–318
excommunication, 2659–2660
incompatible offices, 328
loss, cessation of habitual confessional faculties, 1914
loss of, 386–388, 390
obtained by canonical provision, 320
penalty for unlawful retention of, 2772–2774
penalty for usurpation of, 2772–2774
requirements for, 323–324
rights and duties of, 319
suspension of, 2665–2668
with care of souls, 326–327
Sanctifying:
carried out by means other than the liturgy, 1646
carried out specially in the liturgy, 1633
exercised principally by Bishops, 1635–1636

Officialis:
assigns judges by rotation, 2876
cessation from office, 2868
exercises judicial power, 807
forbidden to accept gifts, 2929
for each diocese, distinct from Vicar general, 2865
given assistance as necessary, 2867
in case of exception of suspicion, 2918
notifies nullity to Ordinary of place of celebration, 3295
obligation of secrecy, 2926–2928
one tribunal with a Bishop, 2866
period of office and removal, 2870
presides over collegiate tribunal, 2881
profession of faith, 1630
qualities of, 2867
replacement of judges, 2879
responsibility in documentary process, 3296–3297
takes oath to exercise office properly and faithfully, 2925
to be summoned to diocesan synod, 925–926

Officials, Civil:
exemption from testifying in court, 3072

Oils, Holy:
blessing of the oil of the sick, 1951
carrying oil of the sick, 1958
custody of, 1667
made from olives or other plants, 1666

Omission:
of due and reasonable precautions, 2652

Onus of Proof:
removed from one with presumption of law in his/her favour, 3126

Opinion:
about nullity of marriage does not

Index

Opinion: *(contd)*
  necessarily exclude consent, 2204
  of learned authors, 62
Oral Contentious Process: cf.
  Process: *Oral Contentious*
Oratory:
  all sacred services therein, 2440
  blessing of, 2443
  celebration of baptism in, 1682
  celebration of sacred ordination in, 1975
  conversion to secular use, 2439
  description of, 2437
  display of books for sale in, 1621
  reservation of Blessed Sacrament in, 1835–1836
  reservation of Blessed Sacrament in Religious, 1839
  right to, in House of Society of Apostolic Life, 1475
Order:
  Power of:
    and suspension, 2665–2668
    required for exercise of some offices, 566
    required for valid absolution, 1896
  Sacrament of:
    constituted by episcopate, priesthood and diaconate, 1973
    description of, 1969–1972
    manner in which conferred, 1973
    non-repetition of because of character, 1662
Order, Public:
  peregrini bound by laws concerning, 37
Orders:
  admission to: who votes on, 509
  exercise of in case of irregularity or impediment, 2044–2045
  impediment of, not dispensed, 2122
  impediment of to marriage, 2156–2158
  marriage impediment arising from, 2120
  notification to be made following reception of, 2056
  one forbidden to exercise, 2020
  received, evidence of, 2055
  registration after reception of, 2054
  required documentation before reception of, 2049
  required investigation before reception of, 2050
  those with impediment barred from reception of, 2022

Ordinances:
  description of, 191
  those bound by, 191
Ordinand: requirements for:
  confirmed, 2014
  content of petition, 2018
  documentation to be assembled, 2049
  formation prescribed by law, 2000
  has publicly undertaken obligation of chastity, 2019
  investigation to be satisfactorily carried out, 2050
  makes retreat before ordination, 2021
  properly instructed in the order and obligations thereof, 2001
  received ministries of acolyte and lector, 2017
  requirements in, 2002–2003
  requisite freedom, 1999
  rite of enrolment, petition, submitted, and accepted, 2015
Ordinary:
  concordat cum originali by Ordinary place of publication, 1617
  description of, 289–293
  issue of commendatory letters by, 1776
  of place of publication to judge writings, 1612
  permission of for Reservation in Religious House, 1839
  to sign juridical curial acts, 942–943
Penalties:
  application of penance as sanction, 2683
  obligation to apply penal remedies, 2678–2680
  obligation to commence procedures for, 2684–2685
  penalty for incitement to disobedience to, 2750–2752
  provision for punished or dismissed clerics, 2699
  warning by Ordinary even when no strict crime, 2695–2696
  who can remit penalties, 2708–2710
Procedures:
  can represent juridical persons, 2986
  decisions over penal process, 3345–3348
  enquiry by into alleged offences, 3342
  nullity entered into registers, 3295

Sacraments:
  dispensed irregularities and impediments to orders, 2040–2043
  exercise of orders with irregularity or impediment, 2044–2045
  regulations for preordination retreat, 2021
  revelation of impediment to orders, 2034
  ruling about transmission of Mass offerings, 1864
  submission of certificate of ordination to, 2055
  to inspect parish Mass offering book annually, 1879
Temporal Goods:
  appointment of administrator of goods, 2547
  correct ordinary in pious causes, 2603
  executor of all pious dispositions, 2598
  goods left in trust for pious causes, 2601
  may change intention of donors of pious causes, 2620–2621
  more than ordinary acts of administration, 2549–2550
  obligations for goods in trust for pious causes, 2602
  permission of, to accept pious foundation, 2609
  permission required to refuse offerings, 2510–2514
  reduction of Mass obligations, 2615–2618
  reduction of other obligations, 2622
  right to intervene in administration of goods, 2544–2546
  safeguarding of endowment goods, 2611
  supervision of temporal goods, 2537–2538
  to ensure pious dispositions are fulfilled, 2599
  transfer of Mass obligations, 2619
Worship, other acts of:
  blessing of sacred places, 2418
  determination of loss of dedication or blessing, 2424
  requirements for permission for oratory, 2437–2438
  uses of sacred places, 2421–2422
Ordinary, Local:
  autonomy of Institutes of Consecrated Life, 1150

Index

description of, 290–292
Penalties:
  can constrain Religious by means of, 2639
  consent required for penalty of residence, 2675–2676
  who can remit penalties, 2708
Sacraments: Baptism and Eucharist:
  appointing ministers of exposition, 1851
  appointing persons to baptise, 1691–1692
  permission for reservation, 1835–1836
  permission to establish baptismal font, 1685
  priest unable to stand at public celebration of Mass, 1826
  regulation of prayers, pious and other sacred practices, 1647
Sacraments: Celebration of Marriage:
  assists at marriage by virtue of office, 2234–2235
  condition attached to marriage consent, 2212
  delegation of priests or deacons by, 2237–2238
  dispenses from form of marriage, 2276–2279
  permission for mixed marriages, 2268–2272
  permission to celebrate marriage outside Church, 2256
  registration norms for dispensation from form of marriage, 2263–2264
  requirements for secret marriage, 2286–2288
  secret, 2284–2285
  to be informed of marriage under can. 1116, 2247–2250, 2262
Sacraments: Marriage Impediments:
  dispensing power in marriage cases of, 2118–2121
  dispensing power of for marriage impediments in danger of death, 2122–2124
  dispensing when he cannot be reached, 2125–2126
  forbidding marriage, 2114–2116
  omnia parata, 2129–2132
  to be notified of dispensation given by priest or deacon, 2133
Sacraments: Marriage Procedures:
  decree of separation by, 2326
  power to dispense interpellations, 2307
  to ensure provision for former spouse(s), 2316

Sacraments: Pastoral Care of Marriage:
  cases to be referred to for permission, 2097–2106
  responsibility to support marriage, 2084
  revelation to of impediments to marriage, 2094
Sacraments: Penance and Orders:
  competent to grant confessional faculties, 1904
  consultation before granting habitual confessional faculties, 1907
  has confessional faculties from the law, 1902
  refusal to allow priests to hear confessions, 1899
  required notification following ordination, 2056
  revocation of habitual confessional faculties, 1910–1913
Teaching Office:
  appointment of censors, 1624
  author's local Ordinary to judge writings, 1612
  care in appointment of teachers of religion, 1586
  granting *imprimatur*, 1624–1626
  permission to clerics for certain writings, 1627
  profession of faith, 1630
  publication of prayer books, 1618
  publication of works on catechetical formation, 1619
  removal and appointment of religious teachers, 1587
  re-publication of liturgical books or translations, 1617
  submission of books to for censorship, 1620
  supervision of academic standards, 1589
  to ensure training of catechists, 1552
Temporal Goods:
  annual accounts of juridical persons to be inspected, 2563–2564
  ordering special collections, 2507
  permission for making collections, 2505
Worship, other acts of:
  approval of diocesan shrine, 2445
  delegation to dispense vows, 2406

desecration of sacred place, 2423
dispensation of oaths, 2414
dispensation of vows, 2406
judgement of blessing of special cemeteries, 2423
judgement on granting Church funerals to manifest sinners, 2389
laity administering sacramentals, 2357
permission for exorcism, 2365
permission for funerals for non-catholics, 2389
permission for funerals for unbaptised children, 2388
permission for Mass in private chapel, 2441
permission for private chapel, 2441
permission for restoration of precious images, 2397
qualities of exorcist, 2365
regulates services in oratory, 2440
Ordinary, personal:
  validly assists at marriage of subject, 2236
Ordinary, proper:
  permission for legal proceedings to be taken in administration of goods, 2566
  permission of for marriage outside parish, 2246
  permission to make collections, 2505
Ordination, Sacred: see also **Ordinand**
  candidate for must be confirmed, 2014
  evidence of, 2055
  make known impediments to Ordinary before, 2034
  minister is Bishop, 1977
  notification to be made following, 2056
  once valid, never becomes invalid, 603
  only for a baptised man, 1993–1994
  oriental rite subject, 1981
  place to be celebrated, 1975
  registration or reception of, 2054
  required documents to be assembled before, 2049
  required investigation to be carried out before, 2050
  retreat to be made before, 2021
  those to be invited to, 1976
  when to be celebrated, 1974

1039

Index

Ordination, Sacred: *(contd)*
  Examination of bond of sacred:
    case referred to collegiate tribunal, 2874
    clerics suspended a *divinis* after petition, 3331
    petition sent to Apostolic See, 3330
    right to impugn validity of, 3329
    use of defender of the bond, 2891

Origin, Place of:
  of child and neophyte, 203–204
  of *vagus*, 203–204

P

Pallium:
  conferred by senior Cardinal Deacon, 743
  new pallium required on transfer of Metropolitan, 878
  requested by Metropolitan, 878
  rules for wearing, 878

Pamphlets:
  faithful not to write in certain, 1627

Parents:
  Catechesis and Education:
    choice of Catholic schools by, 1575
    cooperation between teachers and, 1573
    freedom of choice of school, 1574
    obligation for catechesis of children, 1540
    right and obligation to educate children, 476, 1569
    right to assistance of civil society, 1570
    schools to help in Catholic education, 1573
  Penalties:
    for baptism or upbringing of children in non-catholic religion, 2738
  Procedures:
    parents can represent minors, 2963
  Sacraments:
    adoptive, and baptism of child, 1725
    baptism of infants without permission of, 1704
    consent of, for baptism of an infant, 1701
    conscience of, 1576
    duty of, in preparation of children for first Holy Communion, 1798–1800
    instruction of, prior to child's baptism, 1676
    not to be sponsors at baptism, 1720
    obligation for baptism of infants, 1700
    obligation to ensure instruction for confirmation, 1752–1753
    reasons for deferment of baptism, 1702–1703
    responsibility in choosing a name, 1680
    role of sponsor with parents in baptism of infants, 1714–1715
    share in sanctifying office of Church, 1639

Parish:
  as domicile or quasi-domicile, 208
  boundaries: establishment, suppression, alteration of, 1021
  care of, by non-priest, 1026
  conducted as team ministry, 1025
  description of, 1019–1020
  enjoys juridical personality, 1022
  entrusted to Religious, 1030
  establishment of parish council in, 1065–1066
  establishment of parish finance committee in, 1067–1068
  may have own cemetery, 2456–2457
  only one parish priest in, 1041
  place for marriage, 2246
  part of a particular church, 771
  registers of, 1061–1064
  religious agreement between Bishop and Superior, 1031
  seal of, 1063
  territorial and personal, 1027
  to be conferred when vacant, 1037–1038
  vacancy of, 1074

Parish Priest:
General Functions:
  appointed to parish, 1020
  appointment by Diocesan Bishop, 1036
  appointment to capitular/parish church, 1013
  consultation about suitability of, 1037–1038
  description and authority of, 1028–1029
  duty to foster vocations, 492
  juridical person is not parish priest, 1030
  one parish priest in a parish, 1040–1041
  ordained a priest, 1032
  parochial care of one parish, 1040
  qualities of, 1033
  role of parish priest for capitular church, 1013
  seminary rector equivalent to, 543
  suitability to be assessed, 1033
  term of office, 1034–1035
Other functions:
  acts in person of the parish, 1055
  assisted by Finance Committee, 1067–1068
  assisted by Parish Council, 1065–1066
  cessation from office, 1069–1071
  consulted over appointment of assistant priest, 1083
  obligations, general, 1045–1051
  obligations, specific, 1052–1060, 1545–1549
  relations with chaplain, 1115
  resignation of, 1072–1073
  specific functions, 1052
Personal:
  when personal parish priest validly assists at marriage, 2236
Process, Removal:
  alternative office or pension for removed, 3395
  argumentation of case, 3394
  conditional or absolute resignation of, 3392
  decree of removal, 3393–3394
  discussion of case with two consultors, 3390
  legal effects of removal, 3396
  reasons to general for removal, 3387
  renewed invitation to resign, 3393
  specific reason for removal, 3388–3389
Process, Transfer:
  decree of transfer, 3400
  discussion of case with two consultors, 3399
  observance of equity in, 3401
  parish becomes vacant, 3400
  reasons for transfer, 3397
  written reasons of parish priest against transfer, 3398
Proper:
  and diocesan domicile or quasi-domiciles, 215
  permission of, for marriage outside parish, 2247
  proper parish priest and funerals, 2380–2381

Index

Sacraments: Baptism and Confirmation:
appointing sponsors for baptism, 1717
arrangement for baptism, 1700
consulted for establishment of baptismal font, 1685
obligation of parish priest in regard to baptism, 1676
power to confirm in danger of death, 1739
recording baptism, 1723
recording baptisms of illegitimate children, 1724
registration of confirmation, 1761
responsibility in the choice of name, 1680
to be notified of confirmation, 1762
to teach the faithful how to baptise, 1692

Sacraments: Eucharist, Penance, Orders:
confessional faculties from the law, 1902
disclosure of impediments to orders, 2034
preparation, examination of children for Communion, 1800
registration of ordination in baptismal register, 2056
right and duty to take Viaticum to the sick, 1791
to keep special parish Mass Offering book, 1879

Sacraments: Marriage:
advised of preparation for marriage by another priest, 2096
assists at marriage by virtue of office, 2234–2235
disclosure of impediment for marriage, 2094–2095
dispensing power of parish priest in danger of death, 2125–2126
notification of, 2265
obligation of registration rests on, 2260–2261
permission to celebrate marriage outside the Parish church, 2255
power to dispense impediments *omnia parata*, 2131
preliminaries to assistance at marriage, 2088–2091
presence of for valid celebration of marriage, 2228–2233
registration of marriage when form dispensed, 2263
to be informed of marriage under can. 1116, 2262
to notify local Ordinary of marriage dispensations, 2133
trustworthiness of interpreter in the celebration of marriage, 2226

Other Provisions:
consultor for Bishop in removal cases, 3390, 3394
consultor for Bishop in transfer cases, 3399
dispensation from holydays of obligation and days of penance, 2462
dispensation of oaths, 2414
dispensation of vows, 2406

Teaching Role:
cooperation in proclaiming Gospel, 1519
obligation to ensure catechetical formation of adults, young persons and children, 1544
preaching to reach nonbelievers, 1536
profession of faith, 1630
solicitude in teaching those outside ordinary pastoral care, 1536
to arrange retreats and missions, 1535

Participation, prohibited:
penalty for in religious rites, 2733–2735

Participatory Bodies (Religious)
manner of working, 1527

Parties in trials:
Commencing Stages:
appoint advocate, procurator, or plead personally, 2971
can request removal of advocate or procurator, 2978
refusal of to sign acts, to be noted, 2954
requests judge to proceed, 2922
right to raise objections against court personnel, 2918

Early Stages:
pleas, 3022
renunciation of trial by, 3034
the presence of parties dispenses needs for summons, 3009

Evidence Stage:
bound to answer, tell truth, 3047
can designate own experts, 3120–3121
can propose additional questions for witnesses, 3089
can propose questions to be asked, 3051
confrontation of parties with witnesses, 3088
oath of truthfulness administered to, 3049–3050
incapable of being witness, 3075
may request exclusion of witness, 3082
not to be present at the interrogation of witnesses, 3087
to be given in advance the names of the witnesses, 3081
to be questioned by judge, 3046
when party refuses to answer and testify, 3044, 3048

Later Stages:
appeal against judgement to higher court, 3196
evidence in oral contentious process, 3255
can request correction of a judgement, 3182
can seek change of judge to consider plaint of nullity, 3191
information supplied to be included in the acts, 3159
liability for judicial expenses, 3228
recourse against award of expenses and damages, 3229
right to inspect acts of case, 3144–3146
to receive copy of judgement, 3179–3180

Marriage Procedures:
cannot be present at evidence sessions, 3283
credibility of parties, 3284
obligation of party towards children of previous union, 3300
right of appeal in documentary process, 3298

Partnership:
of man and woman in marriage covenant, 2057–2059
permanent, in marriage, 2193

Passion:
effects of deliberately stimulated or nourished, 2651
heat of passion and diminution of penalty, 2648
offence committed in heat of, and judge's discretion, 2692

Index

Pastoral Council: cf. **Council, *Pastoral***
Pastors:
of the Church:
social communications to have no ill effect on the faithful, 1609
to make use of means of social communications, 1608
to teach faithful about cooperation in use of media, 1608
of Souls:
anointing the sick, 1957
duty to ensure proper preparation for the sacraments, 1654
assistance of the married faithful, 2079–2083
instruction of faithful about the Mass, 1765
instruction to candidates for confirmation, 1752–1753
to dissuade the young from too early marriage, 2107
to ensure the sick are anointed in good time, 1954
to take assiduous care of the sick, 1814
to teach the faithful how to baptise, 1692
Paternity:
of illegitimate child, 1724
Patriarch:
description of, 879
selects place where he will give evidence, 3086
Eastern:
and the College of Cardinals, 735
Patrimony:
alienation of, 2571–2573
of Institutes of Consecrated Life, 1135
Payment:
immoderate payment sought by advocates and procurators prohibited, 2979
Penal Case: cf. **Case, Penal**
Penalties:
Church's right to impose ecclesiastical, 2833
imposition of by trial, 2831
Cessation of:
norms for, 2706–2726
Remission of:
based on purged contempt, 2716–2717
by Apostolic See, 2707
by confessors in urgent cases, 2713–2715

by Ordinaries, 2711–2712
extorted by grave fear, 2719
in case of multiple, 2718
manner of remission, 2720–2722
Ordinaries who can remit, 2708
powers to remit from law or precept, 2706
Penalty:
ignorance or error of, 43
interpretation of law prescribing, 57
Application of:
appeal/recourse against, 2703–2705
binds offender everywhere, 2700
deferment of, 2691
imposed by decree, 2686–2687
imposition on cleric, 2698–2699
imposition procedures, 2686–2689
indeterminate penalty in the law, 2697
judge's discretion in imposition of, 2690
judicial or administrative procedure, ordinary, 2684–2685
moderation of penalties, 2693
non-imposition or change of, 2691
observation of effects of, 2701–2702
perpetual, 2688, 2697
suspension of observance of, 2691
warning to offender, 2694
Cessation of:
execution of, 2726
person bound by a number of, 2718
remission of by those who can dispense, 2706
Obligation to observe:
person who violates obligations imposed by, 2802
Penal law:
completed offence, 2655
diminished, 2648
discretionary, 2634
ferendae and *latae sententiae*, 2631
for conspiracy, 2656
for deliberate violation of law, 2644
infliction of graver penalty by judge, 2652–2653
lapses when law removed, 2630
means of maintenance of ecclesiastical discipline, 2636

requirements for liability to, 2647
temporary cessation of effects of, 2670
threatened by legislator, 2637
uniformity of, 2635
Penalties, expiatory:
description of, 2628
legislator not to establish perpetual, 2638
list of, 2671–2673
suspension of observance of, 2691
Penalty, Medicinal: see also *Ferendae Sententiae* **Penalty**
see also *Latae Sententiae* **Penalty**
or censure, 2627
Penance:
description and norms, 2681–2683
celebration of at shrines, 2446
imposed in remitting a censure, 2717
imposition on penitent, 1921
may be applied by extra judicial decree, 2686–2687
obligation of faithful to do, 2470–2471
one of the Church's sanctions, 2629
role of penitent in the sacrament of, 1933
Days of:
dispensation from, 2462–2463
establishment by Diocesan Bishop, 2461
establishment, transfer, suppression of by Apostolic See, 2461
regulations concerning, 2470–2475
Sacrament of:
description of, 1881
frequent use by seminarians, 522
priest is minister of, 1895
to precede marriage where necessary, 2086
when to precede celebration of eucharist, 1803
Work of:
part of the sanctifying office of the Church, 1646
Penitent:
and false denunciation of confessor, 1922
choice of confessional, 1893
doubt about dispositions, 1920
numbers of and general absolution, 1884–1886
obligation to fulfil penance, 1921
role of, in confession, 1933

Index

sacramental seal, 1923–1924
use of knowledge from confession to detriment of, 1927
Penitentiary: cf. Canon Penitentiary
Penitentiary, Sacred:
  dispensation of occult impediment granted by, 2134
  exercise of orders with irregularity or impediment, 2044–2045
  rescripts of, 137
Pension:
  for removed parish priests, 3395
People of God:
  constituted through baptism, 424–426
  evangelisation, a fundamental duty of, 1553
  united under Bishop in liturgical actions, 1641
Peregrini:
  and exercise of executive power, 299–300
  description of, 202
  dispensation, general, 185
  dispensation of oaths made by, 2414
  dispensation of vows made by, 2406
  laws which do not bind, 37
Periodicals:
  faithful not to write in certain, 1627
Perjury:
  penalty for, 2741
Personnel, Court:
  and obligation to secrecy, 2926–2928
  forbidden to accept gifts, 2929
  punishment for infringement of secrecy, 2930–2932
  to take oath to exercise office faithfully, 2925
Persons:
  Aggregates:
    amalgamation of, 246–248
    approval of statutes required, 237
    collegial and non-collegial, 232
    conditions for becoming juridical, 231
    constituted as, 229
    distinguished from aggregates of things, 232
    exercise of rights by surviving member of, 245
  In general:
    development of human, 1590–1592
    error about, and marriage, 2196
    in the Church, 192–194
  Juridical: General:
    constitution of, 229
    description, general, of, 228
    description of public and private, 233–236
    division of, 249–252
    extinction of, 253–254
    may not be a parish priest, 1030
    moral, 228
    perpetual; suppression and dissolution of, 243–244
    privileges and rights of, 9–12
    religious institutes, provinces, houses, 1258
    religious, responsibility towards debts and obligations, 1269
    representing of, 238
    subject to diocesan levy for seminary, 545–546
  Juridical: and temporal Goods:
    acquiring, retaining, administering, alienating, 2480–2481
    acquisition and retention of sacred objects, 2518–2519
    and alienation, 2571–2574
    and legal proceedings, 2566
    appointment of administrator, 2547
    forbidden to make collections without permission, 2505–2506
    invalid acts of administration, 2553–2554
    levy of tax upon, 2496–2501
    norms in any dealings which jeopardise, 2589
    obligation to celebrate Foundation Masses, 2605–2607
    offerings made to cannot be refused, 2510–2514
    permission required to accept a pious foundation, 2609
    prescription and goods belonging to, 2520
    qualifying conditions and, 2510–2514
    supervision by Ordinary of temporal goods of, 2537–2538
    to have Finance Committee as part of administration, 2548
  Judical Procedures:
    controversy involving Religious, 2883
    pursuit in litigation of rights of, 2830–2831
    represented by Ordinary, 2968
    Rota's right to judge, 2843–2846
    stands in court through lawful representative, 2967
  Moral:
    Catholic Church and Apostolic See, 228
  Physical:
    distinguished from juridical, 228
    privileges and rights of, 9–12
Petition:
  acceptance of, in oral contentious process, 3249
  additional requirements in oral contentious process, 3247–3248
  content of, 2998–3001
  corrected, submitted after rejection, 3004
  oral plea read over to plaintiff, 2997
  presented to lawfully competent judge, 2996
  reasons for rejection of, 3003
  request to amend decree or administrative act by means of, 3373–3375
  time for acceptance or rejection, 3006
  to be accepted or rejected by judge as soon as possible, 3002
  to be produced by plaintiff or promoter, 2995
Pilgrimage:
  and general absolution, 1886
Pilgrims:
  use of shrines by, 2444
Pious Cause: cf. Cause, pious
Places, exempt:
  confirmation in, 1748
Place, sacred:
  blessing of, 2418
  dedication of, 2417
  desecration of, 2423
  description of, 2416
  exercise of ecclesiastical authority in, 2425–2426
  use of dedication or blessing, 2424
  use of, 2421–2422
Plaint of Nullity:
  against decision of judge on competence, 2936
  considered by judge, 3191
  dealt with in oral contentious process, 3195
  judgement not remedied after plaint has been lodged, 3194
  made against irremediably null judgement, 3188
  made against remediably null judgement, 3190

Index

Plaint of Nullity: *(contd)*
  made by parties, defender and promoter, 3193
  made with appeal, 3192
Plaintiff:
  appeal made by, benefits respondent, 3208
  bound to be present in court, 2962
  can bring several exceptions simultaneously, 2986
  case decided against if no moral certainty, 3167
  competence for, 2849
  form of plea, 2998–3001
  joint appeal by several parties, 3209
  non-appearance of and consequences, 3138
  obligation to pay expenses on non-appearance of, 3139
  oral plea read back to one who makes it, 2997
  removal of exceptions by counter-action, 2987
  renunciation of trial by, 3034–3036
  time limits for, 3149–3151
  to receive copy of judgement, 3179–3180
  use of judicial forum of, 2852
  who makes plea before a court, 2960
Plea, Oral:
  see also **Petition**
  permitted in certain cases, 2997
  to be recorded in writing, 2997
Pleadings:
  exchange applies to observations of defender or promoter, 3156–3158
  in writing, 3153
  length of, 3155
  oral discussion allowed, 3159–3160
  printed, 3154
  time allowed for production of, 3152
Point at Issue:
  determination of in oral contentious process, 3251
Ponens:
  appointment and role of, 2887
  commences discussion of judges in case, 3168–3169
  prepares judgement, 3174
  Marriage Procedure:
    decree of commencement of case, 3281
    formulation of doubt, 3279
    nature of formulation, 3280
    notification of summons, 3278
Pontifical Right: cf. **Right, Pontifical**
Possession:
  Action for recovery of:
    competence and action for recovery, 2853
  Of Parish:
    arrangements for taking, 1044
    parish priest put in, 1043
  Canonical:
    by Auxiliary Bishop, 826–828
    by coadjutor Bishop, 826–828
    by Diocesan Bishop, 793–794
    preceded by profession of faith by Bishop, 786–787
    within two months of notification of transfer for Diocesan Bishop, 848
Postponement:
  not to be allowed to prolong litigation, 2944
Postulation:
  description of, 376
  requirements for, 378–385
  reversion to college or group if not admitted, 385
Pouring:
  baptism by, 1679
Poverty: see also **Counsels, Evangelical**
  description of, 1182
Power:
  Administrative:
    controversies determined by Signatura, 2912
    disputes settled by trial, 2832
  Ecclesiastical:
    penalty for abuse of, 2789–2790
    penalty for hindrance of exercise of, 2756
  Executive:
    and the Diocesan Bishop, 289–293
    cessation of, 311
    delegation and sub-delegation of, 302
    enjoyed by Vicar general, 953–954
    exercised by Bishop, 807
    exercised by inferior authority, 305
    interpretation of, 303
    provisions for, 298
    required to issue general executive decrees, 86–87
    subjects of, 299–300
    supplied, 313–314
    suspension of, 304, 312
    to issue singular administrative acts, 93
    to publish instructions, 291–292
  Judicial:
    description of, 297
    exercised by Bishop, 807
    of Diocesan Bishop exercised personally or through others, 2863
    observance of Book VII in exercise of, 939
  Legislative:
    description of, 295–296
    exercised by Bishop, 807
Power of Governance Ordinary: cf. also **Governance:** *Ordinary power of*
  acquisition of, by Roman Pontiff, 697–698
  of Roman Pontiff over universal church, 694–696
  of Roman Pontiff over particular church, 700
  possessed by Diocesan Bishop, 788–789
  possessed by episcopal Vicar, 946
  possessed by Officialis, 2865–2866
  possessed by Vicar general, 945
Prayer:
  part of the sanctifying office of the church, 1646–1647
  Books:
    publication with permission of local Ordinary, 1618
  Eucharistic:
    to be said at Mass only by priest, 1785
  Mental:
    before Blessed Sacrament, 1840
    for clerics, 571
    for religious, 1322–1326
    for seminarians, 522
    People of God and, 2367, 2394
Preaching:
  content of, 1533
  faculty to preach everywhere, 1526
  homily, 1529–1531
  laity may be allowed to preach, 1528
  manner of, 1534
  obligation of chaplain, 1108
  office of, for individual Bishops, 1518
  permission required of Superior to preach to Religious, 1527
  primary task of priests, 1524
  right of Bishops to preach everywhere, 1525

Index

role of Bishop, 801
role of spouses, 2080
Roman Pontiff and College of
  Bishops, 1517
to reach non-believers, 1536
to reach those outside ordinary
  pastoral care, 1536
Precept:
  defines the extent of penalty of
    suspension, 2669
  deliberate violation of involves
    penalty, 2640–2644
  excusing, attenuating, aggravating
    circumstances for crime, 2654
  grants power to remit penalties,
    2706
  issuing an administrative act, 93
  requirements for issue of penal,
    2638
  threatening penalty by means of,
    2638
  violation of, but no liability to
    penalty, 2647
  Paschal:
    fulfilment of, 1810
  Singular:
    cessation of, 124
    description of, 110
Prefect Apostolic:
  in charge of Apostolic Prefecture,
    765–766
  not bound to *ad limina* visits, 819
  refusal of dimissorial letters, 1986
  to appoint Missionary Council,
    989
Prefecture Apostolic:
  definition of, 765–766
  equivalent to diocese, 758–759
  Missionary Council functions as
    College of Consultors, 1004
  sede vacante, 850
Prelate:
  in charge of territorial prelature,
    764
Prelature:
  Personal:
    and delegation of laity, 620
    concept and purpose, 613–616
    incardination into, 548, 618
    relationship between diocese and,
      621
    statutes in seminaries, spiritual
      formation, 617–619
  Territorial:
    definition of, 762
    equivalent to a diocese, 758–759
Preparation:
  for baptism (of parents), 1700
  for marriage by one other than
  parish priest, 2096
  for Mass by priest, 1787
  of children for first Holy
    Communion, 1794–1795
  personal preparation for marriage,
    2079–2083
Presbyterium:
  cooperation with Bishop, 760–761
  preparation of students for, 521
  represented on Council of Priests,
    988
  role of clerical members of secular
    institutes, 1441
Prescription:
  action to extinguish execution of
    penalty by, 2726
  acquisition of temporal goods freed
    from obligations, 2517
  description of, 407–409
  extinction of criminal actions by,
    2724
  for penal action, 2691
  matters unaffected by, 413
  means of acquiring sacred objects,
    2518–2519
  of immovable or precious movable
    goods, 2520
  validity of, 410–412
  when it runs for criminal actions,
    2725
Presence of Christ:
  marked by lamp before tabernacle,
    1847
Presentation:
  consultation for, 339
  exercise of right of, 342–343
  for ecclesiastical office, 321
  judgement of suitability for, 345
  made to competent authority,
    336–337
  no self-presentation, 341
  right of, 336–338
  right to, of parish priest, 1036
  timing of, 344
Pretence:
  penalty for, in administering
    sacraments, 2763–2768
Presumption:
  description of, 3124
  judge not to make one which is not
    stated in the law, 3127
  onus of proof with the law, 3126
  Of Validity:
    doubtful baptism, 2155
    of marriage in general, 2071
Previous Marriage:
  bond of as impediment,
    2148–2149
Priest:
  at particular council has consultative
  vote, 888–889
concern of Bishop for, 799
daily Mass, 570
duty of to foster vocations, 493
Penalties:
  penalty for unlawful exercise of
    office of priest, 2777
  penalty if attempting marriage,
    2803–2805
Procedure:
  incapable of being witness about
    internal forum, 3076
Proper Acts of Public Worship:
  as minister for consecrations
    and dedications, 2359
  as minister of blessings, 2361
  blessing of sacred places,
    churches, 2418
  dedication of sacred places, 2417
Sacraments: Anointing:
  blessing of oil of sick, 1951
  minister of, 1956
  obligation to anoint the sick,
    1957
*Sacraments: Baptism and
  Confirmation:*
  ordinary minister of baptism,
    1690
  power to confirm, 1741–1743
  share in sanctifying office of the
    church, 1637
  use of faculties for confirmation,
    1745
Sacraments: Eucharist:
  any priest taking Viaticum to the
    sick, 1791–1792
  daily celebration of Mass, 1777
  entitled to offer Mass for anyone,
    1771
  eucharistic fast – special
    provisions, 1807
  minister of exposition, 1851
  not to concelebrate with
    non-catholic ministers, 1786
  one daily celebration, 1778
  ordinary minister of communion,
    1788
  part of, at Mass not to be said by
    others, 1785
  permission for celebration of up
    to three Masses on certain days,
    1781
  preparation before Mass, 1787
  presence of faithful at celebration
    of Mass, 1782–1784
  proper vestments for Mass, 1825
  role of, in eucharistic celebration,
    1766
  the only minister of the eucharistic
    sacrifice, 1769

Index

Priest: *(contd)*
  visiting priest allowed to celebrate Mass, 1776
  Sacraments: Marriage:
    celebrant at marriage, duty to inform parish priest or local Ordinary, 2262
    delegation of local Ordinary for, 2237
    dispensing power in danger of death, 2125–2126
    dispensing power *Omnia parata*, 2129–2132
    presence of delegated priest for valid celebration of marriage, 2230–2232
    to notify local Ordinary of dispensation given, 2133
  Sacraments: Penance:
    absolution in danger of death, 1915
    minister of the sacrament of Penance, 1895
    obligation of, to hear confessions in danger of death, 1932
    only suitable priests to receive confessional faculties, 1906
    questions in confessional, 1919
    revocation of faculties, 1910–1913
    role as confessor, 1917–1918
  Teaching Role:
    faculty to preach everywhere, 1526
    homily reserved to priests and deacons, 1529
    importance of office of preaching, 1524
    solicitude in teaching those outside pastoral care 1536
    teaching to reach non-believers, 1536
    to proclaim gospel, 1519

Priest, Assistant:
  appointed by Bishop with consultation, 1083
  appointment and work of, 1080–1081
  area of responsibility, 1080–1081
  common life, 1088
  confessional faculties from law or by concession, 1902
  governs parish during absence of parish priest, 1087
  governs parish during vacancy, 1076
  holidays, 1088
  must be ordained priest, 1082
  offerings of faithful to, 1089
  removal of, 1090
  residence of, 1088
  right and duty to take Viaticum to the sick, 1791–1792
  rights and obligations of, 1084–1086

Priesthood:
  age and maturity required for, 2006
  candidate for undertakes obligation of celibacy, 2019
  candidate to be ordained by proper Bishop, 1980
  dimissorial letters for religious, 1987
  impediment to marriage, 2156–2157
  impediments not dispensed by local Ordinary, 2122–2128
  judgement about qualities of candidate, 1996
  only for a baptised male, 1993–1994
  proper Bishop for the secular clergy, 1984
  refusal of admission to, 2004–2005
  retreat to be made before Ordination, 2021
  Training for:
    length of studies, 496
    outside of seminary - special provisions for, 497–498
    same human and scientific formation, as in other places of education, 495

Priests, Blind:
  use of approved text at Mass and assisted by another, 1827

Priests, shortage of:
  special provisions for pastoral care in case of, 1040

Priests, unable to stand:
  not to celebrate publicly, 1826

Primate:
  description of, 879

Privilege:
  abuse of, 171
  centennial or immemorial possession of, 158
  cessation of, 169
  cessation of real privilege, 162
  description of, 155
  extinction of, 167
  granted by Apostolic See, 9, 12
  granted by rescript, 125, 154
  interpretation, 159
  non-use of, 168
  of the faith enjoys favour of law, 2318
  personal, extinguished with person, 161
  presumed to be perpetual, 160
  renunciation of, 164–165
  revocation of, 163
  under excommunication, no enjoyment of, 2661

Pauline:
  description of and requirements for, 2302–2318

Procedure:
  Administrative:
    issue of penalty by extra-judicial decree, 2686
    norms for Superior using in penal cases, 2689
    obligation to commence, 2684–2685
  Judicial:
    obligation to commence, 2684–2685
    reasons against its use, 2686

Proceedings, Legal:
  permission required for commencement of civil, 2566

Process:
  Documentary:
    norms for, in marriage case, 3296–3299
  For declaration of invalidity of orders:
    intervention of defender of the bond, 3333
    legal effects after two conforming sentences of nullity, 3334
    petition sent to the Apostolic See, 3330
    procedure for case, 3332
  Oral Contentious:
    acceptance of petition and summons, 3249
    appeals tribunal remits back case invalidly tried, 3263
    cases for which process may be used, 3243–3244
    collection of proofs, 3254
    deals with plaints of nullity, 3195
    exceptions and objections, 3253
    further hearings as necessary, 3258
    immediate review and decision of case by judge, 3260
    in first instance, before sole judge, 3246
    judgement notified to parties within fifteen days, 3262
    norms for admission of proofs, 3257
    norms, general, 3264
    norms to govern appeals, 3199

Index

nullity (marriage) cases cannot be dealt with by, 3301
oral discussion of evidence, 3259
postponement of decision for five days, 3261
recording of all evidence by notary etc., 3256
requirements in petition, 3247
Penal:
  accused to have advocate, 3356–3357
  acquittal of accused, 3360
  appeals, 3361–3362
  care for good name, 3343
  dealt with by extra-judicial decree, 3350–3352
  equivalent of auditor, 3344
  involves promotor, 3353–3354
  Ordinary to consider facts and decide next course, 3345
  Ordinary to make investigation into alleged offence, 3342
  other procedures to be observed, 3363
  prohibition against exercising office during process, 3355
  resignation of promoter, 3358
  rights of accused, 3359
  secrecy of acts collected, 3349
  For *Removal of Parish Priests*: see **Parish priest**: *Process, Removal*
  For *Transfer of Parish Priest*: see **Parish priest**: *Process, Transfer*
Processions:
  conduct of by parish priest, 1052
  of Blessed Sacrament, 1852
  regulated by Diocesan Bishop, 1852
Proclamation of Christian Doctrine:
  exposition of doctrine in places of learning, 1523
Procreation:
  and ends of marriage, 2058
Procurator:
  appointed by plaintiff and respondent, 2962
  can be suspended by judge, 2950
  discretion of judge to admit, 2974
  dismissal of, 2976
  effect of cessation in office, 3029
  forbidden to bribe, seek immoderate payments etc., 2979
  forbidden to remove cases for a favourable outcome elsewhere, 2980
  may not perform any act without required special mandate, 2975
  only one, 2971
  permanently salaried by tribunal, 2982

present at interrogation of witness, 3087
prior depositing of mandate before undertaking office, 2974
qualities of, 2973
removal from office by judge, 2978
replacement of, 3029
right of appeal lies with, 2977
suspension for misbehaviour, 2981
several, 2971
to receive copy of judgement, 3179
Profanation:
  of sacred objects, penalty for, 2757
Profession:
  First religious:
    admission to temporary, 1305
    anticipation of, 1291
  Perpetual:
    admission to, 1311
    and exclaustration, 1385–1386
    and request to depart from Institute, 1402–1403
    anticipation of, 1313
    conditions for validity of, 1314
  Religious:
    description of, 1307
  Temporary:
    departure after or during, 1394–1395
    dismissal, 1414
    duration of, 1309, 1312
    extension of, 1312
    new period of after re-entry, 1399–1400
    renewal of or departure from, 1311
    requirement for validity of, 1310
Profession of Faith:
  for members of team ministry, 1077
  for new Bishops, 786–787
  in general, 1630
Professors:
  cooperation between, in ecclesiastical universities and faculties, 1606
  Seminary:
    coordination between, in studies, 505
    different professors for different subjects, 532
    manner of teaching, 534
    participation in rector's responsibilities, 507
    profession of faith, 1630
    qualifications, 531
    removal of, 533
    remuneration of, 544
    responsibilities of, 542

Programme of Priestly Formation:
  adaptation of provisions, 518
  ecclesiastical studies for seminarians, 530
  languages necessary for seminarians, 526
  length of studies for seminarians, 527
  requirement for each country to have, 516
Prohibiting Clause:
  added to decree of nullity or imposed by Ordinary 3292–3293
Prohibition: see also **Prohibiting Clause**
  constituting expiatory penalty, 2671–2673
  disobedience to lawful prohibition of Apostolic See or Superior, 2747–2748
  exercise of ministry pending penal process, 3355
  extent of effect of, 2677
  for abduction, imprisonment, mutilation, wounding, 2821–2822
  for solicitation, 2782–2784
  invalidating clause attached to, 2115
  of marriage by local Ordinary, 2114–2115
  of marriage by Supreme Authority, 2112–2113
  suspension of in danger of death, 2701
Promise:
  by Catholic party in mixed marriage, 2272
Promises, Baptismal:
  renewal in confirmation, 1750
Promotor of justice:
  appeal to higher court, 3196
  appointment and role of, 2889–2890, 2896
  can be defender in a different case, 2896
  cannot be judge in same case in another instance, 2916
  cases which cannot be dealt with by, 2917
  examination of witnesses, 3089
  forbidden to accept gifts etc., 2929
  hearing of objection against, 2918
  in appeal and contentious process, 2889–2890
  intervention of, in hearing of legal objections, 2920
  invalidity of acts without required citation, 2892–2893
  obligation of secrecy, 2926

Index

Promotor of justice: *(contd)*
  qualities of, 2895
  removal of, 2896
  right to be present at interrogation and present submissions, 2894
  to take oath to exercise office properly and faithfully, 2925
  Contentious Trial:
    appeal from judgement to higher court, 3196
    can submit formal plea, 2995
    can propose questions to be asked of party, 3051
    can raise plaint of nullity of judgement, 3193
    consulted before judgement, 3162
    examination of witness, 3089
    renunciation of appeal by, 3207
    right to reply to advocate/parties, 3158
  Marriage Process:
    can challenge validity of marriage, 3274
    separation cases, 3308
    to be present at all evidence sessions, 3282
  Penal Process:
    involved as plaintiff, 3354
    renunciation of case, 3358
    right to appeal, 3362
Promulgation of Law:
  authentic interpretation must be promulgated, 51
  how law comes into effect, 21–22
  manner of promulgation, 23–25
Proof:
  any lawful type admitted, 3042
  by means of documentary evidence, 3058
  by witnesses admitted in all cases, 3069–3070
  collected after joinder of issue, 3045
  collected by others than judge, 3044
  completion of, 3147
  matters not requiring, 3041
  provides basis for moral certainty, 3165
  rejection by judge, 3043
  Onus of:
    rests on one making the allegation, 3041
Property, Immovable:
  laws concerning, 37
Pro-Prefect Apostolic:
  assumption of power, *sede vacante*, 850

giving dimissorial letters, 1985–1986
Propriety, Public, impediment of:
  description of, 2178
Pro-Vicar Apostolic:
  assumption of power, *sede vacante*, 850
  giving dimissorial letters, 1985–1986
Province:
  Ecclesiastical:
    establishment, suppression, alteration of, 868
    formed by groups of particular churches, 866
    has juridical personality, 870
    presided over by Metropolitan, 874
  Religious:
    capacity to acquire, possess, administer, alienate temporal goods, 1258
    description of, 1228
    necessity for and role of Financial Administrator for, 1262
Provision, Canonical:
  deferral of, 327
  for ecclesiastical office, 320
  in case of negligence, 333
  invalid, 324
  invalidated by simony, 325
  made in writing, 334
  manner of making, 321
  prerogative of competent authority, 322
  timing of, 333
  to non-vacant office, 329
Provocation, Unjust:
  and diminution of penalty, 2648
Proxy Marriage:
  description of and requirements for, 2221–2222
  reference of to local Ordinary, 2106
  special documentary process to establish lack of valid mandate, 3296
Psychological Causes:
  inability to assume obligations of marriage, 2189–2192
Psychological Defect: cf. Infirmity
Publishing:
  approval for valid only for first edition, 1623
  of catechisms, writings on catechetical formation, 1619
  of liturgical books and translations, 1617
  of liturgical books by Apostolic See, 1643

of prayer books, 1618
of translations of liturgical books by Bishops' Conferences, 1644
permission or approval of, 1611–1613
Punishment, temporal:
  remission by indulgences, 1940–1941
Pyx:
  to keep consecrated hosts, 1846
  use of for exposition, 1848

Q

Quality:
  deceit concerning quality of person, 2199–2201
  error about quality of person, 2197–2198
Quarrels:
  secrecy in trial so as to avoid, 2928
Quasi-domicile:
  acquisition of, 205–208
  laws binding those with, 34
  forum for one where unknown, 2852
  forum of one without, 2851
  forum of trial in case of inheritance or legacy, 2857
  loss of, 213–214
  of *advena, peregrinus, vagus*, 202
  of members of Religious Institutes, 210
  of minors, 212
  of spouses, 211
  parish of, as place for marriage, 2246
  parish priest and Ordinary of person with, 215
  parochial or diocesan, 208
  trial before tribunal of, 2850
Quasi-parish:
  description of, 1023

R

Radio:
  norms for christian teaching on, 1537
Ratification:
  decree of, by appeal court, 3290
  of case in documentary process, 3299
Reason, use of:
  adult baptism, 1677
  age at which presumed, 196
  anointing those who have reached, 1959
  confirmation, 1750–1751
  ecclesiastical laws bind the baptised with, 31

1048

Index

first Communion for children on
  reaching, 1797–1800
habitual use of and commission
  of crime, 2646
imperfect use of, and diminished
  penalty, 2648
imperfect use of, and judge's
  discretion, 2692
lack of, 201
lack of and liability to penalty,
  2647
lack of, caused by drunkenness,
  diminished penalty, 2648
those lacking it incapable of
  marrying, 2183
those lacking use of in conflict with
  those representing them, 2693
Reconciliation:
ordinary means of, 1882–1883
use of, to avoid judicial disputes,
  3336
Recourse:
against judgements or penalty,
  is suspensive, 2702–2705
difficulty in, 177
following decree of dismissal
  for Religious, 1421
in cases of remission of penalty by
  confessor, 2714–2715
Recourse, Procedures:
by parties against award of expenses
  and damages, 3229
does not suspend execution of
  judgement, 3220
following rejection of petition,
  3005
Against Administrative Decrees:
against decree of parish priest's
  removal, 3396
amendment of decrees or
  administrative act, 3376
appointment of advocate for
  person making, 3384
decrees equivalent to
  administrative acts, 3371
interim suspension of decree or
  act, 3378
petition for amendment of decree
  of administrative act,
  3373–3375
to hierarchical Superior of author
  of decree or act, 3381
Rector:
of Church:
appointment of, 1098
celebration of certain liturgical
  functions by, 1100–1101
description of, 1096–1097
obligations of, 1104
permission required to celebrate

in his church, 1102–1103
removal of, 1105
requires consent of parish priest
  for certain functions, 1099
to be chaplain to a non-parochial
  church, 1114
to keep special Mass offering
  book, 1879
of Seminary:
acts in person of seminary, 503
consultative vote at particular
  council, 888–890
is rector of church attached to
  seminary, 1098
not to hear confessions of
  students, 1930
obedience of students to, 541
of Major Seminary, to be
  summoned to diocesan synod,
  525
profession of faith, 1630
responsibilities of, 542
Records:
of rights of church or Institute to its
  goods, 2559
Reduction:
of obligations because of reduced
  income, 2620–2623
Region, Ecclesiastical:
cooperation and common pastoral
  action by Bishops of, 872
has juridical personality, 871
made up of neighbouring
  ecclesiastical provinces, 871
powers of, 872–873
Register:
of Advocates:
elimination from, by Bishop,
  2979
Baptismal:
details to be entered into,
  1723–1725
marriage to be entered into,
  2265
recording details of confirmation,
  1761
recording Ordination in, 2056
registration of non-consummation
  rescript in, 3325
registration of nullity and
  prohibiting clause in, 3295
special matters to be noted in,
  1061–1062
Confirmation:
details to be entered into and
  location of, 1761
Death:
entry into after burial, 2386
Marriage:
recording dispensations in, 2133

registration of non-consummation
  rescript in, 3325
registration of nullity and
  prohibiting clause in, 3295
registration of secret marriage in
  special, 2288
requirements in registration of
  marriage, 2260–2264
validation, decree of nullity
  and dissolution to be recorded,
  2266–2267
Ordination:
registration in, 2055
Tribunal:
registration of cases received,
  2933
Reinstatement, total:
against unjust judgement,
  3221–3222
judge to give judgement on merits
  of case, 3227
plaint for, against judge's decision
  on competence, 2936
plea for, does not suspend
  execution of judgements, 3226
to be requested from judge who
  gave judgement, 3223–3224
Rejection:
corrected petition formulated after
  its, 3004
of petition reasons for, 3003
of petition, recourse after, 3005
Relationship, impediment of:
description of, 2180
Relationships, Human:
seminary training in, 520
Relator:
appointment and role of, 2887
commences judges' discussion of
  case, 3168–3169
prepares judgement, 3174
Relics:
alienation or transfer of, 2398
sale of sacred, 2398
within a fixed altar, 2452
Religion:
norms for taking part in media
  programmes on, 1628
penalty for stirring up hatred
  against, 2742
teaching of, 1585
virtue of and fulfilment of oath,
  2411
virtue of and fulfilment of vows,
  2400–2401
Religions:
Non-catholic:
penalty for non-catholic baptism
  and upbringing of children,
  2736–2738

1049

Religions: (contd)
  Non-christian:
    and papal legates, 754
Religious:
  completion of formation after profession, 1315–1316
  description of, 1195
  individual religious and financial obligations, 1269–1274
  institute's law defines nature and period of formation, 1316
  no occupations which interfere with formation, 1319
  public witness to be given by, 1199
  spiritual, doctrinal and practical formation to continue, 1320
  Departure:
    after completion of temporary profession, 1394
    cleric to find sponsoring Bishop, 1406
    during period of temporary profession, 1395
    effects of exclaustration, 1405
    exclaustration for cloistered nuns, 1387
    exclusion of further profession, 1396
    imposition of exclaustration, 1388–1390
    insanity of Religious, 1398
    physical or psychological infirmity of, 1397
    re-entry into Institute after lawful departure, 1399–1400
  Disciplinary:
    absence from Religious House, 1331
    enclosure, 1333
    entry into enclosure by Diocesan Bishop, 1336
    making and changing wills, 1337–1340
    monastic enclosure, 1334
    papal enclosure, 1335
    to bear particular witness to gospel, 1520
  Dismissal:
    claims on Institute by dismissed Religious, 1423
    conditions of automatic, 1408
    declaration of automatic, 1409
    effect of decree of dismissal, 1422
    instant expulsion of religious, 1424–1425
    of religious for specific offences, 1410–1411

procedure for case in 696, 1415–1416
procedure of Supreme Moderator and Council, 1418
proceedings in cases of offence, 1412
right to communicate with Supreme Moderator, 1417
Mendicants:
  right to beg, 2505
  rules for begging made by Bishops' Conference, 2506
Obligations:
  annual retreat, 1326
  avoidance of things harmful to vocation or chastity, 1332
  can be banned from diocese by Bishop, 1364
  ceding administration of goods before first profession, 1337–1339
  conferral of ecclesiastical office by Diocesan Bishop and removal, 1369–1370
  contemplation and union with God in prayer, 1322
  daily Mass and communion, 1323
  devotion to BVM and rosary, 1325
  earnings of, belong to Institute, 1341–1343
  loss of capacity to acquire goods, 1346
  not to undertake tasks outside own Institute, 1351
  other special obligation, 1352–1353
  reading scriptures and mental prayer, liturgy of the hours, other exercises of piety, 1324
  subject to own Superiors in exercise of apostolate, 1361
  to approach sacrament of penance, 1327
  to bear particular witness to gospel, 1520
  to be supplied by Institute with all things necessary to fulfil vocation, 1350
  to hold fast to mission and the work proper to Institute, 1358
  to strive for conversion of soul, daily examination of conscience, frequent confession, 1327
  total renunciation of goods through perpetual profession, 1344–1345

to wear religious habit of Institute or clerical dress, 1347–1349
Penalties:
  can be constrained by local Ordinary, 2639
  penalty for attempting marriage, 2806–2808
Procedures:
  and execution of judgement, 3237
Raised to Episcopate:
  on retirement, residence outside Religious house, 1431
  ownership, use and administration of goods, 1430
  remains member of Institute, subject to Roman Pontiff by vow of obedience, 1428–1429
  upkeep and maintenance of retired Religious Bishop, 1431
Religious Institute: cf. **Institute, *Religious***
Remedy, Penal:
  even when not guilty, 2695–2696
  may be applied by extra-judicial decree, 2686
  nature of, 2678–2680
  purpose of, 2629
  record of to be preserved in curial archives, 2680
Removal:
  from office, 398–405
  of parish priest, 3387–3396
Renunciation:
  of trial by guardians, administrators, 3035
  of trial by plaintiff or respondent, 3034
  of trial, has same effect as a batement, 3037
  requirements for valid, 3036
Reproof:
  action taken if no effect, 2684–2685
Republishing:
  of collections of ecclesiastical acts or decrees, 1622
Reputation:
  exemption from testifying in court when danger to, 3072
  secrecy in trial to safeguard, 2927–2928
Requiem Mass:
  those to whom refused, 2393
Rescinding Action: cf. **Actions, rescinding**
Rescript:
  and obreption, 132
  and privilege, dispensation, 154

1050

Index

and subreption, 130
contrary rescripts, 143–144
description of, 125
doubt about validity, 145
errors in, 142
execution of, 129, 147
execution of, by Vicar general or episcopal Vicar, 953–955
expired, 150–151
external forum and, 153
issued *motu proprio*, 97
issuing an administrative act, 93
motivating reasons, 134
no executor, 146
obtained for another, 128
oral favour and internal forum, 153
refusal by Bishop, 138
refusal by Roman Curia, 136–137
refusal by Vicar general or episcopal Vicar, 139–141
taxes on execution of, 2502–2503
use of, 149
who may obtain, 127

Reservation:
of penalties, strictly interpreted, 2707
of penalty to Apostolic See for absolution of accomplice, 2762
of penalty to Apostolic See for consecration of Bishop without pontifical mandate, 2775
of penalty to Apostolic See for scattering sacred species, 2739–2740
of penalty to Apostolic See for striking Roman Pontiff, 2744
of penalty to Apostolic See for violation of the seal of confession, 2785–2786
Of the Blessed Eucharist:
in Religious house or house of piety, 1839
marked by lamp before tabernacle, 1847
person responsible for, 1837
place of, 1835–1836

Residence:
and judicial forum, 2851
judicial forum when residence unknown, 2852
of Bishop in diocese, 813
penalty for violation of, 2819–2820
prohibition of, 2675–2676

Resignation:
and administrators of juridical person, 2567
conditional, of parish priests, 3392

general requirements for, 391–395
of auxiliary Bishops, 841
of coadjutor Bishop, 841
of Diocesan Bishops, 821–823
of papal legates, 757
of parish priests, 1070, 1072–1073
Res Judicata: cf. **Matter**: *Adjudged*

Respondent:
benefits from appeal by plaintiff, 3208
bound to be present in court, 2962
can bring counteraction against plaintiff, 2987
competence in regard to, 2849
duty to respond, 2960–2961
joint appeal by several parties, 3209
legal effects of non-appearance of, 3137
non-appearance of, 3134–3135
notification of case in oral contentious process, 3249
obligation to pay expenses if no appearance, 3139
to receive copy of judgement, 3179–3180
who refuses service of summons regarded as lawfully summoned, 3015

Restraint:
guarantee of repayment of any loss by reason of, 2992
on another's exercise of rights, 2989
when it cannot be decreed, 2991

Retention:
of ecclesiastical office, penalty for unlawful, 2773

Retreat, spiritual:
for religious, 1326
for seminarians, 522
obligation for clerics, 571
parish priests to arrange for parishes, 1535
to be made before any ordination, 2021

Revelation:
basis for Catholic teaching, 530

Reverence:
towards sacraments, 1649

Revocation:
in cases of doubt, 67
of administrative act, 108
of confessional faculties, 1910–1913
of general executory decrees, 90
of instructions, 92
of proxy mandate, 2225

Right, Pontifical:
clerical institutes of and confessional faculties, 1903, 1905
Institute of Consecrated Life of, 1160
Institute of, subject exclusively to Apostolic See, 1167

Rights:
pursuit and vindication of, 2831
reinforced by an action and exception, 2983
restraints of the rights of another can be obtained, 2989
Acquired:
and administrative acts, 94
harmed by administrative act, 97
of public juridical person (amalgamation), 246–248
of public juridical persons (division), 249–252
remain intact, 9–11
Human:
church's right to make judgements about, 1495
Matrimonial:
lack of discretion of judgement concerning, 2188
Patrimonial:
distribution of on extinction, 253–254
division of, 250–252
Restriction of:
by administrative act, 94
interpreted strictly, 57

Rite:
confession to minister of another, 1939
dimissorial letters sent to Bishop of same rite as ordinand, 1990
in marriage ceremony, 2234
proper rite to be followed in administration of the sacraments, 1665
Non-Roman:
appointment of episcopal Vicar for, 946
provision for members of by Bishop, 797
Oriental:
observance of form of marriage for lawfulness only, 2274–2275
subject of may not be ordained without apostolic indult, 1980–1981

Rites: see also *Funerals*
Funeral:
description and purpose of, 2375

1051

Index

Rites: (contd)
  Liturgical:
    Bishops' Conferences can draw up own rite of marriage, 2259
    governed by liturgical laws, 4–6
    to be observed for marriage, 2258
Roman Curia: cf. Curia
Roman Pontiff:
  acquisition of power, 697
  and Cardinals and Bishops, 703
  and Ecumenical Council, 711
  confirming decrees of Ecumenical Councils, 716
  definition of, 695
  granting rescript, 136–137
  joined in full communion with the Bishops, 701
  no recourse against judgement or decree of, 702
  power over particular churches, 700
  resignation of, 699
  sede vacante, 704
  And Election:
    announcement of election by senior Cardinal Deacon, 743
    ordination to Bishop by Cardinal Dean or Sub-Dean, 743
  And Missionary Activity:
    overall direction of coordination for, 1554
  And Religious:
    establishes Institutes of Consecrated Life as of Pontifical Right, 1160–1161
    special obedience of members of Institutes of Consecrated Life to, 1163
  And Sacraments and Sacramentals:
    blessings, 2361
    burial of, in church, 2458
    faculties to hear confession, 1898
    grant of indulgences, 1944
  And Temporal Goods:
    Supreme Administrator and steward of all ecclesiastical goods, 2523–2526
    Supreme Authority in ownership of goods, 2482
  Penalties:
    for physical force against, 2744
  Primacy of:
    any tribunal cases can be referred to Apostolic See, 2861
  Procedures:
    cases a judge cannot review, 2842
    no appeal against judgement of, 3197
  only Pope gives dispensation from a non-consummated union, 3311
  primacy of, 2861
  right to judge, 2840
  supreme judge for whole world, 2905
Rota, Roman:
  cases judged by, 2908–2909
  cases reserved to, 2843
  ordinary court of appeal, 2906–2907
Rotation:
  judges assigned to cases by, 2876

S

Sacrament, Blessed: see also **Eucharist, Blessed**
  exposition of, with pyx or monstrance, 1848
  ministers of exposition, 1851
  no exposition during Mass in same church or oratory, 1849
  prayer before, 1840
  prolonged exposition in churches and oratories, 1850
Sacramental Seal: cf. **Seal of Confession**
Sacramentals:
  celebration of and excommunication, 2659
  celebration of, and interdict, 2663
  description of, 2354
  established, interpreted, suppressed, changed by Apostolic See, 2355
  offerings made on the occasion of the administration of, 2504
  minister of, 2357
  rites for the celebration of, 2356
Sacraments: see also **Initiation:**
  Sacraments of
    celebration of and excommunication, 2659
    celebration of and interdict, 2663
    character sacraments not repeated, 1662
    definition of, 1648
    instruction for seminarians in the celebration of, 536
    offerings on the occasion of the administration of, 2504
    regulation of, by church, 1650
    to whom to be given, 1653
  Administration of:
    according to liturgical books, 1664
    according to rite of celebrant, 1665
    administration to non-catholics, 1655–1661
    by Catholic ministers to the faithful, 1655
    by Catholic ministers to the Orthodox, 1658–1659
    conditional administration of, 1663
    offerings made on the occasion of administration of, 1668
    use of holy oils, 1666
Saints:
  cult of, 2394
  to be canonised or beatified for public veneration, 2395
Salvation:
  baptism necessary for, 1669–1670
Sanatio in Radice: cf. **Validation, retroactive**
Sanctions, Penal:
  church's right to use, 2624–2626
  kinds of, 2627–2629
Scandal, public:
  Church funeral rites and public sinners, 2390–2391
  clerics causing, 2809–2810
  giving occasion for a penal remedy, 2679
  giving rise to penal procedure, 2684–2685
  increasing penalty due to, 2732
  marriage, clerics, religious attempting, 2804
  penalty intended to repair, 2829
  repair of, 2694, 2722
  secrecy in trial to avoid, 2928
  suspension of penalty where there is danger of, 2702
Schism:
  definition of, 1509
  irregularity for orders, 2024
  penalty for, 2728–2731
Schismatic:
  penalty upon, 2728–2731
  refused church funeral, 2391
Sciences, sacred:
  in ecclesiastical universities and faculties, 1601
Schools:
  academic standards of Catholic, 1589
  church's right to establish and direct, 1577
  conducted by Religious Institutes, 1579
  definition of 'Catholic', 1582–1584
  establishment of, by Diocesan Bishop, 1580
  inspection and supervision of Catholic, 1588

Index

parental choice of, 1574
professional and technical, 1581
promotion of by faithful, 1578
role of in Catholic education, 1573
teachers of religion in, 1586
use of textbooks in, 1620
use of the title 'Catholic', 1584

Scripture, Sacred:
instruction in for seminarians, 530
publication of books on and translations of, 1613
use of books on as textbooks, 1620

Seal of Confession:
and interpreter's obligation, 1925
is inviolable, 1923–1924
penalty for violation of, 2785–2786

Secrecy:
and the production of documents in evidence, 3068
obligation of court personnel to, 2926–2928
of judges' conclusions, 3168
punishment of court personnel for infringement of, 2930–2932
to be observed in curial matters, 938

Secretariat General:
of synod, 730

Secular Institute: cf. **Institute:** *Secular*

Security, Social: see also **Fund:** *Social Security*
concern of Bishops on behalf of priests, 799
provided by social security fund, 2529–2530
right of laity employed by Church to, 490

Sede Vacante:
and papal legates, 757
and power of College of Cardinals, 747
appointment of parish priests by Diocesan Administrator, 1039
definition of, 846
nihil innovetur, 862
of Apostolic See, 704
suspension of ecumenical council, 715
suspension of synod of Bishops, 729

See, First:
judged by no one, 2837–2839

Self-Defence:
against aggressor and diminution of penalty, 2648
against aggressor and liability to penalty, 2647

Seminary:
buildings and maintenance of, 544
control of administration of, 540
enjoys juridical personality, 503
exempt from parish governance, 543
need for, 518
observance of Programme of Priestly Formation, 516–517
Rector acts in the person of, 503
Rector, Vice-Rector, Financial Administrator, Professors, 504–505
residence outside of, 497
responsibility of Bishop, 540
rules of, 541
spiritual formation in, 519
statutes of, 507

Inter-Diocesan:
establishment of, 502
needs to have rule, 518
observance of Programme of Priestly Formation, 516–517

Major:
admission of those dismissed from elsewhere, 514
admission requirements and documentation, 510–513
approval of statutes for Apostolic See, 502
diocese to have, 501

Minor:
retention, fostering, and establishment of, 494

Seminary Rector: cf. **Rector:** *of Seminary*

Senate of Priests: cf. **Council:** *Priests'*

Sentences, two conforming:
recourse against, 3219

Separated Brethren:
cooperation with, in publication of scriptures, 1615

Separation of spouses, lawful:
by decree of diocesan Bishop or judgement of judge, 3303
cases which never become adjudged matter, 3218
conciliation to be attempted, 3307
description and requirements of, 2322–2330
effect on domicile or quasi-domicile, 211
norms for competence of court for, 3306
oral contentious process used, 3305
permission for, 3304
promoter of justice involved in, 3308

Sequestration:
guarantee of repayment of any loss by reason of, 2992
of goods allowed for security of a loan, 2990
of goods allowed for upon assets of a debtor, 2990
of goods with appropriate arguments, 2989
when it cannot be decreed, 2991

Servants of God:
special norms for canonisation of, 2836

Sexes:
provision of norms for religious apply to both, 1194

Sexual:
penalty for sexual crime by cleric, 2812–2818

Shrine:
activities carried out in, 2446
approval of statutes of, 2445
description of, 2444
national and international, 2445
privileges of, 2445
votive offerings made at, 2447

Sick: see also **Anointing of the Sick**
no delay in Viaticum for, 1814
no eucharistic fast for, 1808
repetition of anointing for, 1962
to be anointed in good time, 1954
Viaticum for those in danger of death, 1811

Signatura, **Apostolic:**
competence of, 2910–2912
decides conflict of competence, 2860
no appeal against judgement of, 3197

Signs:
expression of matrimonial consent by means of, 2220
sacramentals as, 2354
used in marriage celebration, 2205

Simony:
penalty for, 2769–2771
invalidates provision of office, 325

Sin:
absolution of in danger of death by any priest, 1915
church's right to judge, 2833–2834
use of knowledge through confession, 1927–1929
valid absolution of, 1896

Grave:
confession of, before Mass or holy communion, 1803
no anointing for a person in manifest grave, 1966

1053

Index

Sin: *(contd)*
  obligation to confess, 1934–1935
  obligation to confess annually, 1937
  persistence in manifest grave, 1801
  Venial:
    recommendation to confess, 1936
Sinners:
  manifest, refused church funeral, 2390–2391
Social Communications, means of:
  abuse of, 2742–2743
  instruction in the meaning of christian marriage, 2080
  means of proclaiming christian doctrine, 1523
  role of in religious formation and education, 1585
  to be imbued with human and christian spirit, 1608
  use of by the Church, 1608
  use of to preach gospel, 1494
  Order:
    right of Church to proclaim principles about, 1495
Societies of Apostolic Life: cf. **Apostolic Life, Societies of:**
Society, Civil:
  acknowledgement of freedom of choice of schools for parents, 1574
  assistance for parents from, 1569–1570
  laws for formation of the young, 1576
Solicitation:
  false denunciation of confessor for, 1922
  penalty for solicitation, 2784
Species, Consecrated:
  penalty for scattering, 2740
Spiritual Director: cf. **Director, Spiritual**
Sponsor:
  choice of name for baptism, 1680
  number for baptism, 1716
  proper instruction of, for baptism, 1675–1676
  requirements for, at confirmation, 1757–1759
  requirements in, for baptism, 1720–1721
  role of, at confirmation, 1756
  role of, in baptism, 1714
  same sponsors for confirmation and baptism, 1759

Spouse:
  can challenge validity of own marriage, 3274
  no challenge of validity after death of, 3275
  obligations and right to maintain life, 2322
  pardon of adulterous, 2323–2324
  provision to be made for children by separated, 2328–2329
  re-admission of partner by innocent, 2330
State:
  Authorities:
    and papal legates, 755
  Clerical:
    dismissal from, not in particular law, 2636
Statues:
  veneration by faithful, manner of display, 2396
Status of Persons:
  actions concerning, never extinguished, 2984
  appeal against two conforming sentences on, 3219
  cases concerning, never become adjudged matter, 3218
Statutes:
  description of, 188
  regulation of, 190
  those bound by, 189
Sterility:
  does not invalidate marriage, 2146–2149
Students:
  selection of, for universities and faculties, 1605
  spiritual and pastoral provisions for Catholic and Ecclesiastical Universities, 1599
  teaching of sacred and other sciences to, 1601
  Admission of:
    no vote for Spiritual Director or confessors in the, 509
  Lay:
    lectures in theology for, 1597
  Seminary:
    financial support of, 544
    holidays and special assignments during, 1539
    rector of, not to hear confessions, 1930
    training of, 521
Studies:
  for seminarians, 527–536
  in ecclesiastical universities and faculties approved by Apostolic

  See, 1602
  required for promotion to diaconate, 2011
  Prefect of:
    responsibilities of, 542
Sub-delegation:
  of executive power, 302
Subject Matter:
  competence by reason of, 2853
Submission, Religious:
  of intellect and will, 1511
  of the faithful to the authentic magisterium, 1512
Subreption:
  definition of, 130
Suburbicarian Church:
  and Cardinals, 745
Suffragan See, Bishop of:
  consulted by Metropolitan on Provincial Council, 885–887
  presides over Provincial Council in absence of Metropolitan, 886
  responsibility to appoint Diocesan Administrator, 851, 859
Suicide, attempted:
  giving rise to irregularity for orders, 2027
Summons:
  acts are null if no, 3016
  communicated by post or other secure means, 1313–1314
  delivery assumed to have been made, 1315
  fact, manner of notification of, shown in acts, 1313
  in contentious process, 3249, 3251
  issued within 20 days of petitioner's request, 3006, 3009
  legal effects of lawful, 3017
  occasions when to be communicated to guardian, curator, special curator or other person, 3012
  of witnesses by a decree of judge, 3083
  parties in matrimonial case, 3278
  petition to be attached to, 3011
  respondent's non-appearance, 3134
  to be notified to respondent, 3010
  Prior:
    competence by reason of, 2859
Sundays:
  celebration of sacrament of Orders on, 1974
  number of Masses that may be celebrated on, 1778–1781
  obligation attached to, 2466
  obligation of Bishop to preside at Eucharistic celebrations on, 805

1054

Index

primary day of obligation, 2464
solemn celebration of liturgy by parish priest, 1052
transfer of holydays to, 2465

Superior:
And Apostolate:
consultation with Diocesan Bishop 1363
obligation to visit houses, 1241
to hold fast to mission and work of, proper to their Institute, 1358
And Governance:
authority, 1229
conduct with subjects, 1250
elected according to Constitutions, 1234–1235
manner of fulfilling office, 1219–1222
need for consent or advice of council, 1240
not to hear subject's confessions, 1249
obligation of residence, 1244
obligations regarding debts, 1269–1274
observance of law in conferring office, 1237
of monastic congregation, 1224
period of office, removal and transfer, 1231–1233
provision of suitable confessors, 1247
requirements for appointment or election of, 1230
role of, 1223
subject's freedom concerning confession, 1245–1246
to have own council, 1238–1239
And Sacraments:
commendatory letters of visiting priests, 1776
confessional faculties from the law, 1903
granting faculties for confession, 1905
permission to use confessional faculties, 1904
revocation of habitual confessional faculties, 1910–1913
right and duty to take Viaticum to sick, 1792
to ensure ordinands properly instructed, 2001
to grant confessional faculties, 1901
to oversee fulfilment of Mass obligations, 1878

And Temporal Goods:
offerings made to superior are for the juridical person, 2508–2509
And Universities:
selection of suitable candidates for, 1605
Other Provisions:
dispensation of oaths, 2414
dispensation of vows, 2406
dispensing from holydays of obligation or days of penance, 2462–2463
Procedures:
dealing with disputes, 2832
cases before, 2898
judge in the case of controversies, 2882–2883

Superior, Major:
an Ordinary, 289–293
consultative vote at particular council, 880–890
moderator of an autonomous Religious house is, 1209
And Admission:
can exclude further profession, 1396
Conference of Major Religious Superiors, 1432–1434
instant expulsion of religious, 1424–1425
permission for another residence for novices, 1285
permission of to write on faith and morals, 1629
permission to anticipate first profession, 1291
responsibilities in the admission of candidates, 1277–1281
right to admit candidate to novitiate, 1276
to be advised when Diocesan Bishop has banned Religious from diocese, 1364
And Elections etc:
confirmation of election of, 1236
description of, 1224–1227
requirements for appointment of election, 1230
And Sacraments:
deacon who refuses to be ordained to the priesthood, 2020
granting dimissorial letters for subjects, 1987
judgement about qualities of candidates, 1996
judgement that candidate is beneficial for the Ministry of the church, 1997
notification of ordination to place of baptism, 2056
receives petition for orders from ordinand, 2018
refusal of admission to orders, 2004–2005
refusal of use of confessional faculties, 1901
regulations for deacons' pastoral year, 2012
to be certain of ordinand's qualities, 2002–2003

Support:
for the married, 2079–2083
local Ordinary's responsibility for, 2084
Financial:
faithful to provide for the needs of the Church, 464
provision for the Church and the poor by Religions Institutes, 1275

Supreme Authority:
declares when divine law prohibits or invalidates marriage, 2112–2113
establishes ecclesiastical law impediments to marriage, 2112–2113

Surety:
clerics to avoid acting as, 594

Suspension:
Bishop or priest under cannot assist at marriage, 2235
effects of, 2665–2668
extent of, 2669
for cleric attempting marriage, 2803–2805
for cleric living in concubinage, 2809
for false denunciation of confessor, 2791–2793
for ordination without dimissorials, 2776
for solicitation, 2782–2784
for simony, 2769–2771
for striking a Bishop, 2745
non-declared *latae sententiae* censure, effects, 2702
of effects of penalty in danger of death, 2701

Synod:
Bishops:
cessation of function of, 728–729
composition of secretariat of, 730
cooperation with Roman Pontiff, 703

1055

Index

Synod: *(contd)*
  definition of, 718–720
  extraordinary general assembly, 726
  forms of meeting, 723–724
  function and power of, 721
  ordinary general assembly, 725
  powers of Roman Pontiff over, 722
  profession of faith, 1630
  special assembly, 727
  Diocesan:
    description of, 918–920
    diocesan Bishop communicates decrees to Metropolitan and Bishops' Conference, 932
    diocesan Bishop convenes, 923
    diocesan Bishop presides over, 924
    diocesan Bishop sole legislator at, 931
    free discussion at, 929–930
    non-catholics may be invited, 926
    profession of faith, 1630
    proxy attendance, 927
    suspension or dissolution of, 933–934
    those to be summoned to, 925
    when held, 921

T

Tabernacle:
  construction of, 1843
  key of, 1845
  lamp before, 1847
  location and adornment of, 1844
  only one, in church or oratory, 1843
  pyx or ciborium, 1846
  removal of for security reasons, 1844

Tape Recorder:
  use of in evidence session, 3098

Tax:
  diocesan Bishop's right to levy, 2496–2501
  for acts of executive authority or execution of rescripts, 2502–2504

Teachers:
  appointment and removal of, in Catholic and ecclesiastical universities, 1595
  appointment of religious as, 1586
  approval or removal of religious, 1587
  cooperation between parents and, 1573
  of theology, mandate for, 1598

Of the Faith:
  Bishops, Bishops' Conferences, Particular Councils as, 1512

Teaching:
  by Bishops, 801
  condemned doctrine, penalty for, 2747–2748

Team Ministry:
  conducted by Religious Order, 1030–1031
  description and control of, 1025
  obligations, duties and powers of members, 1078
  qualities required, appointment of, and effects, 1077
  replacement of members, 1079
  residential obligation and *missa pro popula*, 1078

Telegram and Telephone:
  when local Ordinary cannot be reached, 2125

Television:
  preaching on, according to norms of Bishops' Conference, 1537

Temporal Goods: see also **Administration of temporal goods**
  are ecclesiastical goods, 2484–2485
  donated by the faithful, 2493
  harmful administration of, 3383
  immovable, precious movable, and prescription, 2520
  inventory before Administrator takes up duties, 2556–2557
  of private juridical persons regulated by own statutes, 2486–2487
  Roman Pontiff, Supreme Administrator and steward of all, 2523–2526
  Acquisition of:
    by means of prescription, 2517
    by universal church, Apostolic See, Particular churches, juridical Persons, 2480
    church's rights, 2476–2478
  Administration of:
    by Universal Church, Particular Church, Apostolic See, juridical persons, 2480
  Alienation of:
    invalid in canon law but valid in civil law, 2590–2591
    by Universal Church, Particular Church, Apostolic See and juridical persons, 2480
    competent authorities who give permission for, 2575–2580

    for lower than valuation price, 2587
    information required to give permission for, 2588
    manner of requesting permission for, 2581
    permission required for valid, 2571
    proceeds to be invested or prudently spent, 2588
    requirements for, 2583–2585
  Ownership of:
    belongs to juridical person who has acquired them, 2482–2483
    to be safeguarded in civil law, 2559

Territory:
  laws enacted for a particular, 33–34

Testator, intentions of:
  to be observed by heirs, 2596, 2597

Textbooks:
  use of, on religious and moral subjects, 1620

Thanksgiving:
  after Mass, by priest, 1787

Theology:
  Dogmatic:
    lectures in Catholic Universities, 1597
    teachers of in Catholic and ecclesiastical universities and faculties, 1598
    training in for seminarians, 530
    use of textbooks on, 1620

Third Orders:
  concept of, 635–636

Third Party:
  action for damages brought by, 3336–3367
  intervention of, 3140–3143

Threats:
  used in sexual crimes, 2812

Time:
  description of, 415–416
  manner of reckoning, 417–423
  Limits, Canonical:
    appeal to be lodged within, 3198
    for incidental matters in conjunction with appeal, 3210
    description of, 2942
    expiry of, 3194
    expiry of for appeal, 3205
    expiry of in oral contentious process, 3251–3252
    extension and shortening of, 2493
    for claims of total reinstatement, 3223–3224

Index

for exceptions in oral contentious
process, 3250
for execution of judgement in
personal actions, 3240
for raising plaint of nullity,
3189–3190
for recourse against two
conforming sentences, 3219
in recourse procedure, 3374,
3376, 3378 3382
Total Reinstatement: cf.
Reinstatement, total
Trading:
prohibited: penalty for clerics,
2800–2801
Tradition:
Canonical:
canons of Code to be assessed in
the light of, 1720
Sacred:
basis for dogmatic theology, 530
Trafficking:
in Mass offerings, penalty
for, 2778–2779
Transaction, juridical:
exercised by Bishop on behalf of
diocese, 809–811
Transcription:
of documents, 3068
Transfer: see also **Parish Priest:**
Process Transfer
for grave reason, 396
penalty, 2673
remuneration in connection with,
397
Translations:
approval required for, 1623
of books of sacred scriptures,
censorship of, 1614
of liturgical books, 1616
of liturgical texts and review by
Apostolic See, 1643
of works on catechetical formation,
1619
Trial:
abatement of, 3030
acceptance of gifts forbidden on
occasion of, 2929
admission of documentary evidence
at, 3058
before tribunal of domicile or
quasi-domicile, 2850
before tribunal of place where
obligations arise, 2855
initiated by summons, 3027
manner and effect of abatement of,
3031–3032
object of, 2830–2831
place of, in non-penal cases, 2857

place of, in penal case, 2856
place of trial, at tribunal
office, 2947
return of document to owners at
end of, 2957
suspension of, 3028–3029
use of sole judge in, 2877–2878
Criminal:
norms for judges refer also to
Superiors, 2689
Tribunal:
Administrative:
appeal to, 2898
dealing with disputes,
2830–2831
Bishop in charge of:
removal of advocate from
register, 2979
to establish norms for judicial
expenses and legal aid, 3228
Collegiate:
appointment of auditor,
2884–2886
difficult cases entrusted to, 2875
judgements signed by all present,
3176
manner of proceeding of,
2880–2881
recourse to after rejection of
petition, 3005
time limit for issue of judgement
by, 3174
which cases referred to, 2874
Diocesan:
for trial of penal cases, 2856
governed by canons of the Code,
2835
of domicile or quasi-domicile,
2850
of place of domicile or
quasi-domicile of inheritance or
legacy, 2857
of place where administration is
exercised, 2857
right to call for assistance of
other tribunals, 2862
of Appeal:
certified copies of acts sent to,
2955
correct tribunal, 3200
dispute between two tribunals of,
3203
invalid use of oral contentious
process, 3263
recourse to on rejection of
petition, 3005
reference of case of non-
competence to, 2936
Sacred Roman Rota is ordinary,
2908

to act collegially, 2904
to deal with question of right of
appeal urgently, 3201
of Appeal – Marriage Cases:
acts and judgements sent to,
3289
admission of new grounds by,
3291
decides whether to ratify decision
or not, 3290
metropolitan tribunal of, 2898
new marriage permitted after
issue of decree of nullity by,
3293
reference of separation cases to,
3305
of First Instance:
Diocesan Bishop is judge of,
2863
duration of case, 2924
of Second Instance:
duration of case, 2924
establishment by *Signatura*, 2912
establishment of other Second
Instance, 2902
for regional courts, 2899
manner of establishment, 2904
Office:
establishment of, and opening
times, 2947
place for interrogation of
witnesses, 3085
usual location for decision of
cases, 3168–3169
Regional:
appeal court arrangements, 2899
establishment by *Signatura*, 2912
establishment of, 2871
Truth:
oath of truthfulness to be
administered to parties,
3049–3050
obligation to seek, 1496
witness to tell truth to judge
questioning, 3071
Tutelage:
prevents promotor, defender,
auditor or assessor from dealing
with case, 2917
relationship of prevents judge from
hearing a case, 2917

U

Union:
Institutes of Consecrated Life,
1143–1144
Unity:
error about unity of marriage,
2202

Index

Unity: *(contd)*
essential property of marriage, 2063–2064
Sacrament of:
the church, 1641

Universities:
Church's right to establish and govern, 1590
use of adjective 'catholic', 1593
within territory of Bishops' Conference, 1594
Catholic:
appointment and removal of teachers in, 1595
faculty or chair of theology in, 1597
profession of faith by rector of, 1630
rectors of, with consultative vote at particular council, 888–890
theological lectures in, 1597
use of adjective 'catholic', 1593
Ecclesiastical:
approved degrees in, 531
canonical effects of degrees in, 1603
Church's right to have, 1601
Constitution and direction belongs to Apostolic See, 1602
cooperation between faculties and universities, 1606
mandate for teachers of theology, 1598
observance of principles of Catholic doctrine in, 1596
profession of faith by rector of, 1630
rectors of with consultative vote at particular council, 888–890
right of laity to acquire fuller knowledge of sacred sciences in, 483
spiritual and pastoral care of students, 1599
statutes approved by Apostolic See, 1602
teachers, appointment and removal, 1595

University Centres:
provision of in Catholic ecclesiastical universities, 1599

Unlawful exercise:
of office of priest, penalty for, 2777

Upbringing:
of children, as end of marriage, 2058

Urgent Case:
remission of penalties in, 2713–2715

Usurpation:
of ecclesiastical office, penalty for, 2772

V

Vacancy of Parish:
does not occur in team ministry, 1079
governance of parish in interim, 1076

Vacatio Legis:
time specified in law itself or three months, 23–25

Vagi:
bound by universal and particular laws, 37
child of, 203
description of, 202
parish priest or Ordinary of, 215
place of marriage for, 2246
to be referred to local Ordinary to allow marriage, 2098

Validation:
description and requirements of simple, 2332–2343
retroactive, description and requirements of, 2344–2353
to be advised to parish priest for registration, 2266–2267
when all is ready for marriage, 2132

Veneration:
of BVM and the cult of Saints, 2394–2395

Vestments:
proper vestments to be used in celebration of Mass, 1825

Vetitum: cf. Prohibiting Clause

Viaticum:
for those in danger of death, 1811
frequent (daily) reception of, 1813
function of parish priest, 1052
more than once on the same day, 1812
no delay in, for the sick, 1814
obligations of chaplain in connection with, 1108
who may take, to the sick, 1791–1792

Vicar:
Apostolic:
ad limina visit, 819–820
in charge of Apostolic Vicariate, 766
refusal of dimissorial letters, 1986
to appoint Missionary Council, 989
Episcopal:
and impeded See, 843
an Ordinary, 289–290
appointment, role and power of, 946
can be delegated to preside over diocesan synod, 924
cessation of power of, 848, 957
competence of, 953–955
consultative vote at particular council, 888–890
exercise of power until notification of Bishop's death, resignation, transfer or deprivation, 847
exercises executive power, 807
freely appointed and removed by Diocesan Bishop, 947
habitual faculties of, 953–955
not canon Penitentiary nor related to Bishop, 952
profession of faith, 1630
provision of, for different rites, 797
qualities of, 951
replacement of, 947–949
reports to Diocesan Bishop, 956
to be summoned to diocesan synod, 925–926
work of coordinated by Bishop, 940–941
Forane:
appointment by Diocesan Bishop, 1192
consultation with parish priest on appointment of assistant priest, 1083
consulted by Diocesan Bishop on new parish priest, 1038
known also as dean or archpriest, 1091
period of office, 1093
qualities of, 1093
removal of, 1093
rights, duties and obligations of, 1094–1095
summoned to diocesan synod, 925
General:
and impeded See, 843
and profession of faith, 1630
an Ordinary, 290
appointment, role and power of, 944–945
can be delegated to preside over diocesan synod, 924
cessation of power of, 848, 957
competence of, 955
consultative vote of particular council, 888–890

Index

exercise of power until certain
notification of Bishop's death,
resignation, transfer or
deprivation, 847
exercises executive power, 807
freely appointed, and removal by
Diocesan Bishop, 947
habitual faculties of, 955
Moderator of curia, 941
not canon penitentiary nor related
to Bishop, 952
number of, 944
qualities of, 951
replacement of, 950
reports to Diocesan Bishop, 956
restriction of ordinary power,
293
to be summoned to diocesan
synod, 925
work of coordinated by Bishop,
940–941

Vicars for Major Superiors:
are also Major Superiors
equivalently, 1226

Vicariate:
Apostolic:
Council of three missionary
priests, 989
definition of, 765
equivalent to a diocese, 759
Missionary Council has function
of College of Consultors, 1004
sede vacante, 850
Forane:
one priest from each to be
summoned to diocesan synod,
925
part of particular church, 772
ruled by Vicar Forane, 1091

Vice-Officialis:
appointed as necessary, 2867–2868
period of office and removal, 2870
presides over Collegiate Tribunal,
2881
qualities of, 2867

Virgins, Order of:
existence and description of,
1189–1191

Visitation:
conduct of Religious towards
Diocesan Bishop during, 1243
inspection of parish books and
archives, 1064
of diocese by Bishop, 814
of Religious by Bishop, 816
Right of:
not affected by prescription, 413

Vocations:
concern of Bishops for, 800

duty of christian community,
priests and Bishops to foster and
promote, 492
promotion of by Bishop, 803
Late:
promotion and fostering by
Bishops and Priests, 493

Vows:
cessation of, 2404
commutation of, 2407
definition of, 2400
description of public, private,
solemn, simple, personal, real,
mixed, 2402
dispensation of, 2406
invalidated by force, unjust fear
and deceit, 2401
means of professing Evangelical
Counsels, 1121–1124
obligation of, 2403
perpetual or temporary,
1196–1198
public vow of chastity as marriage
impediment, 2120
suspension of, 2405
taken before religious profession,
2408
who may take, 2400

W

Wage:
payment of just, 2662

Warning:
by Ordinary even when no strict
crime committed, 2696
necessity of, before imposition
of censure, 2694

Water:
added to chalice at Mass, 1816
used in baptism, 1678

Week:
definition of, 417

Will:
consent of the will affects of
penalty, 2648
positive act of the will excluding
marriage, 2206–2209

Wine:
holy communion under the species
of, 1821
used in Mass, 1816–1820

Witness:
establishes dedication or blessing of
churches, 2420
marriage in the presence of two,
2247–2250
two required for valid celebration
of marriage, 2231
Giving evidence:

can be recalled for further
examination, 3101
confrontation of, 3087
examination of, 3089
examined at Tribunal Office,
3085
illness or other impediment of,
3085
interrogated not in presence of
parties, 3087
manner of questioning,
3094–3095
oath of truthfulness, 3091
priest not to be witness
concerning internal forum,
3076
source of information established
by judge, 3093
to answer orally and not consult
notes, 3096
to be examined individually,
3088
Obligations:
cannot be judge in case, 2916
notary to record if witness does
not sign acts, 2954
obligation of secrecy, 2928
Production of:
anyone can be, 3073
arrangements when witness
refuses to testify before judge,
3044
judge moderates excessive
number of, 3080
may be excluded at request of
party, 3082
may be questioned at request of
other party, 3077
names and addresses of witnesses
to be submitted to court, 3078
names of witnesses to be
submitted to both parties in
advance, 3081
norms for questioning, 3052
proof by means of, admitted in
all cases, 3069
properly summoned witness to
appear, 3084
questions for, within allowed
time limit, 3079
summons of, by decree of judge,
3083
those exempted from answering
questions, 3072
those incapable of being, 3075
to tell truth to judges
questioning, 3071
Qualified:
evaluation of evidence of, 3107

1059

Index

Witness: *(contd)*
  evidence of experts, 3108–3121
  Various:
    credibility of, 3284
    defender, advocate, promoter present at evidence session, 3282
    norms for evaluation of evidence of, 3103–3106
    norms for reimbursement of expenses, 3228
    presence of parties and advocate at evidence session in oral contentious process, 3255
    refund of expenses, 3102
    value of evidence of, 3105
Woman:
  consent of woman and man makes marriage, 2066–2067
  involvement in marriage covenant, 2057–2058
Word:
  Liturgy of:
    exercise of, by laity, 488
    to be founded on scripture, tradition, liturgy, magisterium and the life of the church, 1522
    use of, to arouse and enlighten the faith, 1640
    when Mass not possible, 2468
Words:
  expression of matrimonial consent in, 2220
  proper form of in administration of the sacraments, 1672
  used in marriage celebration, 2205
  use of, in confirmation, 1729
Worship:
  Divine:
    celebrated in blessed or dedicated church, 2433
    in church, 2425
    in oratory, 2435
    in private chapel, 2441
    oratories or private chapels to be reserved for, 2443
    regulation of by the church, 2479
  Public:
    celebration of and excommunication, 2661
    celebration of and interdict, 2663
    exercised through sacred liturgy, 1633
    in the church, 2427
    offered in the name of the church, 1634
Wounding:
  penalty for, 2821–2822
Writings:
  additional permission to publish required for Religious, 1629
  newspapers, periodicals, pamphlets, 1627
  permission to publish, 1611–1612
  publication of writings on catechetical formation, 1619
  right of ecclesiastical authority to judge writings on faith and morals, 1609

Y

Year:
  canonical definition of, 417
Young:
  dissuasion by pastors to marry too early, 2107